A History of Western Public Law

Bruno Aguilera-Barchet

# A History of Western Public Law

## Between Nation and State

with the collaboration of M.I. Fajardo, Ph. D. Librarian.
University of Granada

Springer

Bruno Aguilera-Barchet
Legal History
Rey Juan Carlos University
Madrid
Spain

Translation from the Spanish language edition: Entre Estado y nación. Sociedad, poder y derecho, de la prehistoria a la integración europea by Bruno Aguilera-Barchet, © Instituto de Estudios Jurídicos Internacionales 2011. All rights reserved.

ISBN 978-3-319-11802-4 ISBN 978-3-319-11803-1 (eBook)
DOI 10.1007/978-3-319-11803-1
Springer Cham Heidelberg New York Dordrecht London

Library of Congress Control Number: 2014959258



Printed on acid-free paper

Springer International Publishing AG Switzerland is part of Springer Science+Business Media (www.springer.com)

*To my mother Anne Barchet Daniel*

Europe has been built up in the form of small nations. In a way, the idea and the sentiment of nationality have been her most characteristic invention. And now she finds herself obliged to exceed herself. This is the outline of the enormous drama to be staged in the coming years. Will she be able to shake off these survivals or will she remain for ever their prisoner? Because it has already happened once before in history that a great civilisation has died through not being able to adopt a substitute for its traditional idea of the state...

José Ortega y Gasset
The Revolt of the Masses (1937)[1]

[1] Ortega y Gasset (1994, 150) "*Europa se ha hecho en forma de pequeñas naciones. En cierto modo, la idea y el sentimiento nacionales han sido su invención más característica. Y ahora se ve obligada a superarse a sí misma. Éste es el esquema del drama enorme que va a representarse en los años venideros. ¿Sabrá libertarse de supervivencias, o quedará prisionera para siempre de ellas? Porque ya ha acaecido una vez en la historia que una gran civilización murió por no poder sustituir su idea tradicional de Estado....*"

# Preface

The state-building process is currently considered as an achievement of history, while nation-state has always been mistaken as a universal way of organizing politics. In fact, our naive and universal vision of history mixed European post-medieval history with history of humanity as a whole. Those who are presently ruled by imported European models are reputed to be "developing" countries as long as they have not perfectly reached the unique and common target. Epistemology is strongly affected by this common sense: the same concept and the same word are currently used, and particularly in Latin and Roman traditions, for coining all the polities around the world and through history. International Law contributed in this oversimplification, as all members of United Nations, all sovereign units in the present world, are commonly designated as states, without any restrictions; at the most, they would exist everywhere in essence, but would only vary according to their level of development, the role of "bad guys" who are at power or even the result of bad luck...

Hypocrisy or dogmatism? In any way, we face here an incredible faking of history! The excellent book of Bruno Aguilera-Barchet precisely shows up the amazing complexity of European state-building history: Roman origins, role of the feudal and post-feudal societies (as it was strongly stressed by the wonderful book of Perry Anderson, *Lineages of the Absolutist State*), and influence of Christian theology. Moreover, Bruno Aguilera-Barchet points out the main historical tensions from where European states were finally shaped: church and politics; absolutism and liberalism; kings and nation; civil society and public space. Reinhart Bendix, Joseph Strayer or Stein Rokkan played here a role of pioneer...

Three major questions are then at stake. First one: how such a complex and specific history can be found back elsewhere for generating the same model of politics? In fact, we are, quite the reverse, encouraged to rebuild our own history, to interpret from our state history all the exceptions—sometimes pathologies—of our own development: excessive fragmentation of European map into small political units, tradition of a dramatic inter-state competition (Hobbes), role of war as state-making process (Tilly)...

Second question: what are the alternative models of ruling? Are they to be found among other histories? Would China or Russia achieve an imperial model which would finally stand differently from Western states? Are African societies presently reinventing tribal or community polities? Alternatively, would it be more relevant to consider, in Africa, Middle East or Far East, a forthcoming political invention which should be compared with the state invention that took place during the European Renaissance? In any case, European state cannot be exported like a plant: "failed states" are first of all failed exportations.

Then we move to the last question. If state dawned in Europe at the end of Middle Age, its own decay or its transformations are obviously conceivable. Those who were born will finally die... Bruno Aguilera-Barchet is right to consider the potential end of nation-states. Presently, their resilience is first imputable to law which does not recognize any alternative international actors. However, this option is at its turn questioned by a slow evolution which is looming through the invention of international soft laws and new regional laws (like European community law). A main question then arises: is nation-state still able to meet all the new challenges stemming from globalization?

Sciences Po Paris
France

Bertrand Badie

# Contents

1 **Introduction** . . . . . . . . . . 1
References . . . . . . . . . . 5

**Part I From the City State to the Roman Empire**

2 **From the Origins to the Polis** . . . . . . . . . . 9
2.1 From Nomadic to Sedentary Society: The Neolithic Revolution . . . . . . . . . . 10
2.2 The First Literate Societies: Power and Social Structure in the Great Ancient Civilization of the Near East . . . . . . . . . . 11
2.2.1 The Civilizations of the Indus Valley . . . . . . . . . . 11
2.2.2 Egypt Under the Pharaohs . . . . . . . . . . 12
2.2.3 Power in Ancient Mesopotamia . . . . . . . . . . 13
2.2.4 Confucius and the Origin of the State in China . . . . 14
2.3 Family and Power in the West . . . . . . . . . . 16
2.3.1 The Indo-Europeans Lay the Linguistic and Social Foundations of Western Culture . . . . . . . . . . 16
2.3.2 Indo-European Family Structure and the Formation of Society in the West: From the Tribe to the City . . . 16
2.4 The Greek Polis as the First Precursor of the State in the West . . . 19
2.4.1 An Initial Stage of Monarchy: The Minoan and Mycenaean Civilizations . . . . . . . . . . 19
2.4.2 From the Homeric Kingdoms to the Appearance of the Polis (800–500 BC) . . . . . . . . . . 20
2.4.3 Synoecism as the Basis of the Polis . . . . . . . . . . 21
2.4.4 The Consolidation of the Polis and Its Aristocratic Model: The Case of Sparta . . . . . . . . . . 22
2.4.5 The People Versus the Aristocrats: The Origin of the "Democratic" System . . . . . . . . . . 24
2.4.6 Athens' Cleisthenes, History's First "Democrat" . . . . 25
2.4.7 Pericles' Athens . . . . . . . . . . 26

2.5 The Drawbacks of the Polis Model . . . . . 26
2.5.1 The Division of Hellas . . . . . 27
2.5.2 Attempts to Improve Upon the Polis Model . . . . . 27
References . . . . . 33

**3 The Roman Political Model: From *Res Publica* to *Imperium*** . . . . . 37
3.1 Rome and the Origins of the Western State . . . . . 38
3.1.1 The Flaw of the Polis Model . . . . . 38
3.1.2 The Roman *Civitas*: An Expanding Polis . . . . . 39
3.2 The Indo-European Origins of Roman Society and the Structural Basis for the Roman *Civitas* . . . . . 40
3.2.1 *Gentilitates*, *Curiae* and *Tribus* . . . . . 41
3.2.2 The Popular Assemblies as the Basis of the Roman Republic . . . . . 42
3.3 An Aristocratic *Polis* . . . . . 43
3.3.1 The Leadership of the Roman Aristocracy . . . . . 43
3.3.2 A Political Constitution Designed to Prevent Dictatorship . . . . . 45
3.4 From Republic to Empire . . . . . 47
3.4.1 An Extraordinary Territorial Expansion . . . . . 47
3.4.2 From Conquest to Stable Dominion . . . . . 47
3.4.3 The Consequences of Rome's Territorial Expansion: The Crisis of the Republican System . . . . . 48
3.5 Augustus and the Singular Reestablishment of the Republican Regime . . . . . 50
3.5.1 The First Citizen . . . . . 50
3.5.2 From Diarchy to Monarchy: The Birth of the Roman Empire . . . . . 52
3.6 The Era of the Dominate, or the Triumph of Imperial Absolutism . . . . . 54
3.6.1 From *Imperator* to *Dominus* . . . . . 54
3.6.2 The Disappearance of the Republican System . . . . . 55
3.7 An *Avant La Lettre* State . . . . . 56
3.8 Roman Citizenship: History's First "Nationality"? . . . . . 57
References . . . . . 61

**4 From Territorial Power to Spiritual Rule: Christianity's Political Dimension** . . . . . 65
4.1 Church and State in the Western Tradition . . . . . 66
4.2 The Origins of Christianity . . . . . 67
4.2.1 It All Started with Judaism . . . . . 67
4.2.2 A Provincial Jew Named Jesus, Aka "Christ" . . . . . 68
4.2.3 Had It Not Been for St. Paul . . . . . 70
4.3 Christianity and the Roman Empire . . . . . 72
4.3.1 A Threat to the Empire? . . . . . 72
4.3.2 From Forbidden Cult to Official State Religion (380 AD) . . . . . 73

4.3.3 The Origins of Catholicism . . . . . . . . . . . . . . . . . . 76
4.3.4 Emperors vs. Bishops: "Caesaropapism" . . . . . . . . . 78
4.4 The Church as a Political Body . . . . . . . . . . . . . . . . . . . . . . 79
4.4.1 The Origin of the Ecclesiastical Profession: Bishops, Deacons and Presbyters . . . . . . . . . . . . . . . 79
4.4.2 The Development of Church Organization: Parishes and Dioceses . . . . . . . . . . . . . . . . . . . . . . 80
4.4.3 Metropolitans and Patriarchs . . . . . . . . . . . . . . . . . . 81
4.4.4 The Councils as Collective Decision-Making Bodies . . . . . . . . . . . . . . . . . . . . . . . . . . . . . . . . . . 81
4.4.5 The Origins of the Papacy as a Moral Authority . . . . 82
References . . . . . . . . . . . . . . . . . . . . . . . . . . . . . . . . . . . . . . . . 85

**Part II The Origins of the European "Nations"**

**5 From the Germanic Tribes to Kingdoms** . . . . . . . . . . . . . . . . . . . 93
5.1 The Invasions . . . . . . . . . . . . . . . . . . . . . . . . . . . . . . . . . . . . 94
5.1.1 The First Germanic Wave: The Visigoths (Late Fourth Century) . . . . . . . . . . . . . . . . . . . . . . . 94
5.1.2 The Second Wave: The Suebi, Vandals and Alani (Early Fifth Century) . . . . . . . . . . . . . . . . . . . 96
5.1.3 The Third Wave: Franks, Burgundians, Alamanni, Angles and Saxons (Mid Fifth Century) . . . . . . . . . . 96
5.1.4 The Last Wave: The Lombards . . . . . . . . . . . . . . . . 97
5.2 The Germanic Kingdoms . . . . . . . . . . . . . . . . . . . . . . . . . . . . 97
5.2.1 Diversity Versus Unity . . . . . . . . . . . . . . . . . . . . . . 97
5.2.2 The Social and Political Transformation of the Germanic Peoples . . . . . . . . . . . . . . . . . . . . . . . . . 98
5.2.3 Roman Monarchy vs. German Royalty . . . . . . . . . . 99
5.2.4 The Gradual Assimilation of the Roman Imperial Tradition . . . . . . . . . . . . . . . . . . . . . . . . . . . . . . . 101
5.2.5 The Structural Weaknesses of the New Kingdoms: Patrimonial Possession, Inheritance and Protofeudalism . . . . . . . . . . . . . . . . . . . . . . . . . . . 102
5.3 The Church and the Preservation of the Roman "State" Tradition . . . . . . . . . . . . . . . . . . . . . . . . . . . . . . . . . . . . . . 103
5.3.1 The Emergence of the Monastic Movement . . . . . . . 103
5.3.2 St. Gregory the Great and the Consolidation of Papal Authority . . . . . . . . . . . . . . . . . . . . . . . . . . . 104
5.3.3 Christianity and the New Germanic Peoples . . . . . . . 105
5.3.4 The Church and the "Romanization" of the Germanic Kingdoms . . . . . . . . . . . . . . . . . . . . . . . . 106
5.4 The Origin of the European "Nations?" . . . . . . . . . . . . . . . . . 108
References . . . . . . . . . . . . . . . . . . . . . . . . . . . . . . . . . . . . . . . . 115

**6 Popes vs. Emperors: The Rise and Fall of Papal Power** . . . . . . . . . 121
6.1 The Transformation of the Papacy: From Spiritual to Temporal Power . . . . . . . . . . . . . . . . . . . . . . . . . . . . . . . . . . . 122
6.1.1 The Popes vs. the Byzantines and Lombards . . . . . . 122
6.1.2 The Alliance with the Frankish Monarchy and the Rise of the Papal States . . . . . . . . . . . . . . . . . . . . . . 123
6.2 Charlemagne and the Resurgence of the Imperial Idea in the West . . . . . . . . . . . . . . . . . . . . . . . . . . . . . . . . . . . . . . . 126
6.2.1 Charlemagne and the End of the Lombardian Kingdom . . . . . . . . . . . . . . . . . . . . . . . . . . . . . . . . . 126
6.2.2 The Appearance of the Kingdom of Italy . . . . . . . . . 126
6.2.3 The Reappearance of the Imperial Idea in the West . . . 127
6.3 From the Carolingian Empire to the Holy Roman Empire . . . . 129
6.3.1 The Frankish Monarchy Dissociates Itself from the Empire . . . . . . . . . . . . . . . . . . . . . . . . . . . . . . . . . 129
6.3.2 The Germanic Revival of the Imperial Idea . . . . . . . 130
6.4 The Era of "Papal Theocracy", or the Peak of Ecclesiasticism . . . 134
6.4.1 Ecclesiastical Decline During the Feudal Period . . . . 134
6.4.2 The Ecclesiastical Resurgence: The Eastern Schism, Cluny and the Gregorian Reform . . . . . . . . . . . . . . . 136
6.4.3 The Papacy's Power Swells . . . . . . . . . . . . . . . . . . 139
6.4.4 The Legal Consequences of the Papal Victory: The Secularization of Non-ecclesiastical Public Authorities . . . . . . . . . . . . . . . . . . . . . . . . . . . . . . 140
6.4.5 Papal Decline and the Fragmentation of Europe . . . . 140
6.5 The Survival of the Imperial Idea . . . . . . . . . . . . . . . . . . . . 142
References . . . . . . . . . . . . . . . . . . . . . . . . . . . . . . . . . . . . . . . . . 147

**7 From Public to Private Power: Europe in the Feudal Age** . . . . . . . 153
7.1 The Origins of Feudalism . . . . . . . . . . . . . . . . . . . . . . . . . . 154
7.1.1 The Administrative Shortcomings of the Carolingian Monarchy . . . . . . . . . . . . . . . . . . . . . . . . . . . . . . . 154
7.1.2 Vassaldom: A Formula for Permanent Control over Local Authorities . . . . . . . . . . . . . . . . . . . . . . . . . . 155
7.1.3 The Limits of the Feudal Relationship: Its Lifelong Character . . . . . . . . . . . . . . . . . . . . . . . . . . . . . . . . 157
7.1.4 The Consuetudinary and Judicial Regulation of Vassal Relations . . . . . . . . . . . . . . . . . . . . . . . . . . . . 157
7.2 The Consolidation of the Feudal System: The Era of "Classic Feudalism" . . . . . . . . . . . . . . . . . . . . . . . . . . . . . . . . . . . . . 158
7.2.1 The Degradation of the System: From Lifelong to Hereditary Benefits . . . . . . . . . . . . . . . . . . . . . . . . . 158
7.2.2 The Transformation of the Feudal Relationship . . . . 160

7.2.3 The Accumulation of Fiefdoms . . . . . . . . . . . . . . . . 160
7.2.4 From Public to Private Rule: The "Feudal Revolution" . . . . . . . . . . . . . . . . . . . . . . . . . . . . . . 161
7.3 The Church as a Bulwark Against the Disintegration of Public Power . . . . . . . . . . . . . . . . . . . . . . . . . . . . . . . . . . 162
7.3.1 The Defense of Royal Authority . . . . . . . . . . . . . . . 162
7.3.2 The Armed Church . . . . . . . . . . . . . . . . . . . . . . . . . 163
7.3.3 Moral vs. Political Commitment . . . . . . . . . . . . . . . 164
7.3.4 The Ecclesiastical Imposition of Peace: The Peace and Truce of God Movement . . . . . . . . . . . . . . . . . 165
7.4 Feudalism and the "Pactist Concept" of Power . . . . . . . . . . . . 167
References . . . . . . . . . . . . . . . . . . . . . . . . . . . . . . . . . . . . . . 170

**Part III The Origins of the "European States"**

**8 From Kings to Monarchs: The Resurgence of Public Power in Late Medieval Europe** . . . . . . . . . . . . . . . . . . . . . . . . . . . . 177
8.1 Late Medieval Monarchy and the Origin of the Western State . . . 178
8.2 From Kings to Monarchs . . . . . . . . . . . . . . . . . . . . . . . . . . . . 178
8.2.1 The Consolidation of the Hereditary Principle as the Basis of Royal Legitimacy . . . . . . . . . . . . . . . . 179
8.2.2 A Territorial Monarchy . . . . . . . . . . . . . . . . . . . . . 182
8.2.3 An Expanding Monarchy . . . . . . . . . . . . . . . . . . . . 183
8.2.4 An Administrative Monarchy . . . . . . . . . . . . . . . . . 183
8.3 The Triumph of Monarchy Over Christian Universalism . . . . . 185
8.4 The Medieval Origins of the "Rule of Law": Pacts as a Legal Restraint on Territorial Monarchy . . . . . . . . . . . . . . . . . 187
8.4.1 The Nobility's Resistance to Losing Its Political Power . . . . . . . . . . . . . . . . . . . . . . . . . . . . . . . . . . 188
8.4.2 Urban Autonomy . . . . . . . . . . . . . . . . . . . . . . . . . . 188
8.5 Towards the Shared Exercise of Power . . . . . . . . . . . . . . . . . 190
8.5.1 The Rise of State Assemblies . . . . . . . . . . . . . . . . . 190
8.5.2 The Origins of the Representative Principle . . . . . . . 192
8.6 A King Subject to the Law . . . . . . . . . . . . . . . . . . . . . . . . . . 197
8.7 Europe's First "Constitutional" Texts? . . . . . . . . . . . . . . . . . . 198
References . . . . . . . . . . . . . . . . . . . . . . . . . . . . . . . . . . . . . . 203

**9 The Apogee of Royal Power: Absolute Monarchy (The Sixteenth and Seventeenth Centuries)** . . . . . . . . . . . . . . . . . . 211
9.1 From Territorial to Absolute Monarchy . . . . . . . . . . . . . . . . . 212
9.1.1 The Modern Age and the Triumph of Royal Absolutism . . . . . . . . . . . . . . . . . . . . . . . . . . . . . . . . 212
9.1.2 From Christian Universalism to Independent Monarchies . . . . . . . . . . . . . . . . . . . . . . . . . . . . . . . 212
9.1.3 Searching for a New Legitimacy: The Prevention of Anarchy as a Justification for Power . . . . . . . . . . 216
9.2 The Abandonment of Medieval Pact-Based Rule . . . . . . . . . . 220

9.2.1 Cities' Loss of Political and Legal Autonomy . . . . . 220
9.2.2 The Subjugation of the Nobility . . . . . . . . . . . . . . . 223
9.2.3 The Decline of the Assemblies of the Estates . . . . . . 224
9.3 The State of the Prince . . . . . . . . . . . . . . . . . . . . . . . . . . 229
9.3.1 The Expansion of Royal Jurisdiction . . . . . . . . . . . . 230
9.3.2 A King Above the Law? . . . . . . . . . . . . . . . . . . . . . 231
9.4 Absolutism Versus Autocracy: The Legal Limits of Royal Absolutism . . . . . . . . . . . . . . . . . . . . . . . . . . . . . . . . . . . . 234
9.4.1 Absolute Kings, Constrained by Divine and Natural Law . . . . . . . . . . . . . . . . . . . . . . . . . . . . . . . . 235
9.4.2 The Limits of "Fundamental Laws" . . . . . . . . . . . . . 236
9.4.3 Respect for Traditional Customs . . . . . . . . . . . . . . . 237
9.4.4 The Relative Autonomy of the *Ancien Regime's* Judges . . . . . . . . . . . . . . . . . . . . . . . . . . . . . . . . 238
9.5 Absolute Monarchy and the Increasing Power of the European States . . . . . . . . . . . . . . . . . . . . . . . . . . . . . . . 240
9.5.1 The Technical Advantages of Absolutism . . . . . . . . 241
9.5.2 The Administrative Expansion of Absolute Monarchies . . . . . . . . . . . . . . . . . . . . . . . . . . . . . . 242
9.5.3 Towards a Europe of "National" Monarchies . . . . . . 244
References . . . . . . . . . . . . . . . . . . . . . . . . . . . . . . . . . . . . . . 249

**10 From the Conservative King to the Reformist Monarch: The Stage of Enlightened Absolutism (Eighteenth Century)** . . . . . . 257
10.1 The Crisis of Classic Absolutism . . . . . . . . . . . . . . . . . . . . 258
10.1.1 A Century of Transformation . . . . . . . . . . . . . . . . . 258
10.1.2 The "Philosophes" and the Kings . . . . . . . . . . . . . . 259
10.1.3 Absolutism vs. Despotism . . . . . . . . . . . . . . . . . . . 260
10.2 A New Legitimacy: From Christian to Secular Monarchs . . . . 260
10.3 Enlightened Reformism or the New Spirit of Absolute Power . . . 264
10.3.1 The State: From Guardian of Order to Protector, Educator and Reformer . . . . . . . . . . . . . . . . . . . . . . 264
10.3.2 The "Depatrimonialization" of the Monarchy and the Transformation of the State . . . . . . . . . . . . . 267
10.4 Enlightened Absolutism and the "Rule of Law" . . . . . . . . . . . 270
10.4.1 The Enlightened Monarchs and the Law . . . . . . . . . 270
10.4.2 Frederick II's *Sonderweg* . . . . . . . . . . . . . . . . . . . . 272
10.4.3 The Rationalization of the Legal System . . . . . . . . . 273
10.5 The Expansion of Enlightened Absolutism in Eighteenth Century Europe: The Great Enlightenment Monarchs . . . . . . . 274
10.5.1 The Austrian and the Prussian Models and Its Reception in Russia . . . . . . . . . . . . . . . . . . . . . . . . . 274
10.5.2 Portugal in the Pombal Era . . . . . . . . . . . . . . . . . . . 276
10.5.3 The Eighteenth Century Revolution in Spain . . . . . . 277
10.5.4 The French and British Exceptions . . . . . . . . . . . . . 279
References . . . . . . . . . . . . . . . . . . . . . . . . . . . . . . . . . . . . . . 281

**11 From Absolute to Limited Monarchy: The British Origins of Parliamentary Government** . . . . 287
11.1 A Peculiar Constitutional History . . . . 288
11.2 The Origins of Assembly-Based Government . . . . 289
11.2.1 From the Germanic Kingdoms to the Feudal Stage . . . 289
11.2.2 The Westminster Parliament Appears . . . . 291
11.2.3 The Political Consolidation of Parliament . . . . 293
11.3 Parliament and the Absolutism of the Tudors . . . . 294
11.4 Dynastic Change and the Triumph of Parliament: The Two English Revolutions of the Seventeenth Century . . . . 296
11.4.1 The Kings of Scotland on the English Throne: The Stuarts . . . . 296
11.4.2 The First English Revolution: Oliver Cromwell and the Only "Republic" in English History . . . . 297
11.4.3 The Appearance of Political Parties . . . . 297
11.4.4 The Second (and Last) English Revolution (1688) . . . 298
11.4.5 The Religious Issue and the Transformation of England's Constitutional Framework . . . . 300
11.5 The Emergence of the United Kingdom and the Consolidation of Parliamentary Preeminence . . . . 301
11.6 The Rise of the Hanover Dynasty and the Formation of the Parliamentary Regime . . . . 302
11.6.1 Robert Walpole and the Linguistic Origins of the Parliamentary Regime . . . . 302
11.6.2 The Consolidation of the "Parliamentary System" . . . 303
11.6.3 The Democratization of the Parliamentary System (1832–1928) . . . . 306
11.6.4 The Consolidation of the Legislative Superiority of the House of Commons: The Parliament Act (1911) . . . . 308
11.6.5 The Legislative Recognition of the Prime Minister (1937) . . . . 308
References . . . . 311

**Part IV The Rise of the Nation-State**

**12 From Monarchy to Representative Government: The American "Revolution"** . . . . 321
12.1 Revolution as a Social Instrument of Political Change . . . . 322
12.1.1 The Example of Prussian Social Inflexibility . . . . 322
12.1.2 The English Case: The Gradual Transformation of a Political Constitution . . . . 323
12.1.3 Rupture as an Instrument of Change: The American and French Revolutions . . . . 324
12.2 From the War of Independence to the American Revolution . . . 325
12.3 The First Europeans in the Americas . . . . 326

12.3.1 The Spanish and the Portuguese . . . . . . . . . . . . . . . 326
12.3.2 French and Dutch Expeditions . . . . . . . . . . . . . . . . 326
12.3.3 The Origins of the English Presence in America . . . 327
12.4 Spanish vs. English Colonization . . . . . . . . . . . . . . . . . . . . 328
12.4.1 The "Centralized" Model of Spanish Colonization . . . 328
12.4.2 The English Model: "Decentralized" Colonization . . . 330
12.5 The Development of English Colonization . . . . . . . . . . . . . . . 331
12.5.1 The First English Colony: Virginia (1607) . . . . . . . . 331
12.5.2 Religious Colonization . . . . . . . . . . . . . . . . . . . . . 333
12.5.3 The Proprietary Colonies . . . . . . . . . . . . . . . . . . . . 336
12.5.4 New Colonies After the Restoration (1660) . . . . . . . 338
12.5.5 Political Variety and Legal Autonomy of the English Colonies in America . . . . . . . . . . . . . . . . . 341
12.6 The Colonists and the British Crown . . . . . . . . . . . . . . . . . . . 343
12.6.1 The Colonial Explosion . . . . . . . . . . . . . . . . . . . . . 343
12.6.2 The First American Intervention of the English Crown: The War Against France . . . . . . . . . . . . . . . 344
12.6.3 The Price of Victory . . . . . . . . . . . . . . . . . . . . . . . 345
12.6.4 The Fiscal Origins of the Rebellion . . . . . . . . . . . . . 345
12.6.5 The First Continental Congress in Philadelphia (1774) . . . . . . . . . . . . . . . . . . . . . . . . . . . . . . . 347
12.7 The War of Independence (1776–1781) . . . . . . . . . . . . . . . . 347
12.7.1 The First Armed Clash: The "Battle" at Lexington (April 19, 1775) . . . . . . . . . . . . . . . . . . . . . . . . . 347
12.7.2 The Second Continental Congress and the Declaration of Independence . . . . . . . . . . . . . . . . . . 348
12.7.3 The Course of the Conflict . . . . . . . . . . . . . . . . . . . 348
12.7.4 The Peace of Versailles and the Recognition of a New Nation: The United States of America . . . . . . . 350
12.8 The West's First Liberal State . . . . . . . . . . . . . . . . . . . . . . . 351
12.8.1 From Locke to Jefferson . . . . . . . . . . . . . . . . . . . . 351
12.8.2 The American Revolution as a Rupture with the Old Order . . . . . . . . . . . . . . . . . . . . . . . . . . . . . . 352
12.8.3 A Precarious "Union": The Articles of Confederation . . . . . . . . . . . . . . . . . . . . . . . . . . . . . 355
References . . . . . . . . . . . . . . . . . . . . . . . . . . . . . . . . . . . . . . 358

**13 From Absolute Monarchy to Democratic Absolutism: The French Revolution** . . . . . . . . . . . . . . . . . . . . . . . . . . . . 371
13.1 A Turning Point in European Constitutional History . . . . . . . . 372
13.2 The Monarchy as the Historical Basis of the French State . . . . 373
13.2.1 From Clovis I to Charlemagne . . . . . . . . . . . . . . . . 374
13.2.2 A Hereditary, Sovereign and Territorial Monarchy . . . 375
13.2.3 The Hundred Years' War and the Bolstering of Monarchical Prestige and Power . . . . . . . . . . . . . . . 376

13.2.4 The Era of Absolutism: Louis XIV's Monarchy as a Landmark Reign . . . 377
13.3 From the *Ancien Régime* to the Revolution . . . 378
13.3.1 Louis XV and the Decline of the French Monarchy . . . 378
13.3.2 Reactionary Forces Prevail in French Society . . . 381
13.4 The French Revolution . . . 384
13.4.1 From the Revolt of the Privileged to the Estates General . . . 384
13.4.2 The Estates General . . . 386
13.4.3 From the Estates General to the Rebellion of the Third Estate (May 5–June 27, 1789) . . . 388
13.4.4 The Rebellion of the Third Estate . . . 389
13.4.5 The Two Revolutions . . . 391
13.4.6 From Monarchy to Republic . . . 392
13.5 What Lasting Effects Did the French Revolution Have? . . . 394
13.5.1 The Appearance of "National Sovereignty" . . . 394
13.5.2 The Origins of "National" Patriotism . . . 394
13.5.3 The Symbols of the French State . . . 395
13.5.4 The Reinforcement of the State . . . 396
13.5.5 The Social Transformation of France . . . 398
13.5.6 The European Dimension of the French Revolution . . . 398
13.6 The Failure of Assembly-Based Government . . . 399
References . . . 405

**14 The Return of the Monarchical Principle (I). The Origins of North American Presidentialism . . . 415**
14.1 The Development of a Republican "Monarchy": The Presidential System . . . 416
14.1.1 The Crisis of Democratic Assembly-Based Governments . . . 416
14.1.2 The Resurgence of Executive Power . . . 416
14.2 Thirteen States, One Nation: From the Articles of Confederation to the Federal Republic . . . 417
14.2.1 The Stage of the Constitutional Debate (1783–1787) . . . 418
14.2.2 The Reopening of a Constitutional Convention . . . 420
14.3 The Origins of the Presidential System . . . 422
14.3.1 The Constitutional Convention Endorses the Principle of a Strong National Government . . . 422
14.3.2 The Placement of Limits on Federal Power: The Strict Application of the Division of Powers and the Establishment of a "Presidential" System . . . 422
14.3.3 A "Great Compromise" for the Legislative Branch (Congress) . . . 423

14.3.4 A President Heading the Executive Branch . . . . . . . 423
14.3.5 The Separation of Powers as the Essence of the Presidential System . . . . . . . . . . . . . . . . . . . . . . . . 424
14.3.6 The Judicial Power as a Constitutional Referee: The Revolutionary Principle of "Judicial Review" as a Safeguard Against the Tyranny of the Majority . . . . 424
14.4 A New Constitution for a New Federal State . . . . . . . . . . . . . 425
14.4.1 Approval and Ratification of the Constitution . . . . . . 425
14.4.2 A New Limit on Federal Power: The Bill of Rights . . . . . . . . . . . . . . . . . . . . . . . . . . . . . . . . . . 426
14.4.3 The Principle of Term Limits . . . . . . . . . . . . . . . . . 427
14.4.4 The Constitution as the New Nation's Birth Certificate . . . . . . . . . . . . . . . . . . . . . . . . . . . . . 427
14.5 Relations Between the States and the Federal Government After 1789 . . . . . . . . . . . . . . . . . . . . . . . . . . . . . . . . . . 427
14.5.1 The Implementation of Judicial Review . . . . . . . . . . 429
14.5.2 From 13 to 50 States . . . . . . . . . . . . . . . . . . . . . . . 430
14.5.3 A Problematic Expansion . . . . . . . . . . . . . . . . . . . . 434
14.5.4 The Protection of Fundamental Rights: The Union vs. the States . . . . . . . . . . . . . . . . . . . . . . 437
References . . . . . . . . . . . . . . . . . . . . . . . . . . . . . . . . . . . . . . . . . 443

**15 The Return of the Monarchical Principle (II). The French State. From Imperial Bonapartism to Republican Presidentialism** . . . . . . 449
15.1 Napoleonic France: From Republic to Monarchy . . . . . . . . . . 450
15.1.1 A Genius Named Napoleon Bonaparte . . . . . . . . . . . 451
15.1.2 The Peculiar "Napoleonic Constitutionalism" . . . . . 452
15.1.3 A Return to the Roman Model? . . . . . . . . . . . . . . . . 454
15.1.4 A New Monarchy for a New Regime . . . . . . . . . . . . 455
15.2 From Assembly-Based Government to Executive Government . . . . . . . . . . . . . . . . . . . . . . . . . . . . . . . . . . . . 456
15.2.1 Napoleon and State Reform . . . . . . . . . . . . . . . . . . 456
15.2.2 The Extreme Centralization of the New Administrative State . . . . . . . . . . . . . . . . . . . . . . . . 457
15.2.3 Judicial Reform and the Creation of Administrative Jurisdiction . . . . . . . . . . . . . . . . . . . . . . . . . . . . . 457
15.3 An Interventionist State . . . . . . . . . . . . . . . . . . . . . . . . . . . . 458
15.3.1 Religious Reform . . . . . . . . . . . . . . . . . . . . . . . . . . 459
15.3.2 Economic Reform . . . . . . . . . . . . . . . . . . . . . . . . . . 459
15.3.3 A Failed Attempt at Social Reform: The "Legion of Honor" . . . . . . . . . . . . . . . . . . . . . . . . . . . . . . 460
15.3.4 Educational Reform: Grammar Schools, Special Schools of Higher Education, and Universities . . . . . 461
15.3.5 Legal Reform and the Unification of Private Law: *Le Code Civil* (March 21, 1804) . . . . . . . . . . . . . . . 463

15.4 The Constitutional History of France After Napoleon: From Monarchy to Republic . . . 465
15.4.1 From Absolutist Restoration to the July Monarchy . . . 465
15.4.2 From the Second Republic to the Second Empire . . . 466
15.4.3 From the Commune to the Third Republic . . . 468
15.4.4 From Petain's "French State" to De Gaulle's Presidential Republic . . . 471
15.4.5 French Semi-presidentialism: A Return of the Napoleonic Model of State? . . . 474
References . . . 479

**16 The Golden Era of Liberalism and the Apogee of the Nation-State . . . 489**
16.1 From Absolutism to Liberalism . . . 491
16.2 The Europe of the Restoration (1815–1848) . . . 493
16.2.1 The Congress of Vienna . . . 493
16.2.2 The Holy Alliance or the Return of Divine Legitimacy . . . 494
16.2.3 Metternich and the Counterrevolutionary Principle of Legitimate Intervention . . . 495
16.2.4 An Exception to the Principle of Nation-State Confrontation: The Metternich System as a Forerunner of European Integration . . . 495
16.2.5 The Impossibility of Restoring Absolutism . . . 496
16.3 The Liberal Alternative: A State with Limited Powers and Controlled by an Economic Elite . . . 497
16.3.1 Legal Limits on State Power: Constitutions and Fundamental Rights . . . 497
16.3.2 The Politicization of the Term "Nation" . . . 499
16.3.3 From Absolute Monarchy to Liberal Oligarchy: The Era of Censitary Suffrage . . . 500
16.4 The Liberal Revolution . . . 502
16.4.1 Moderate Liberalism . . . 503
16.4.2 "Revolutionary Liberalism" . . . 504
16.4.3 Spain, Spearheading the Liberal Revolution: Riego's Revolt (1820) . . . 505
16.4.4 France Comes to Lead the Liberal Revolution (1830) . . . 509
16.5 The Revolution of 1848 as the Key to the Spread of the Liberal State in Europe . . . 511
16.5.1 Another Italian Liberal Revolution . . . 512
16.5.2 The Revolution of 1848 in the German Territories . . . 513
16.5.3 The Austrian Empire and the Revolution . . . 515
16.5.4 Prussia vs. Austria: The Fight for German Supremacy . . . 516
16.5.5 Prussia Becomes a Constitutional Kingdom . . . 518
16.5.6 Relative Calm in Europe by 1850 . . . 519

16.6 The Unification of Italy ... 519
16.6.1 *Il Risorgimento* ... 520
16.6.2 French Support for the Italian Cause ... 521
16.6.3 A Democratic Integration ... 521
16.6.4 Garibaldi and the Annexation of the South ... 521
16.6.5 The Kingdom of Italy Is Founded (March 14, 1861) ... 522
16.6.6 The "Roman Question" ... 522
16.7 German Unification ... 523
16.7.1 Bismarck, Architect of Prussian Hegemony ... 524
16.7.2 The Defeat of Austria and the North German Confederation ... 524
16.7.3 The Franco-Prussian War and the Second Reich ... 525
16.7.4 A Top Down Integration in a Federal and Laic State ... 526
16.8 Imperial Russia as a Final Bastion of Autocracy ... 527
16.8.1 From Enlightened Absolutism to the Consolidation of Autocracy ... 527
16.8.2 Speransky and the First Attempt to Establish the Principle of the Rule of Law in Imperial Russia ... 528
16.8.3 The Revolution of 1905 and the First Russian Constitution (1906) ... 529
16.9 Colonialism and Confrontation: The International Consequences of the Triumph of the Nation-State Model ... 530
16.9.1 The Golden Age of Colonialism ... 530
16.9.2 Nationalism and Confrontation: The Europe of the "Armed Peace" ... 531
16.10 World War I and the Crisis of the Liberal State Model ... 533
16.10.1 The Implosion of the Nation-State System ... 533
16.10.2 The Assassination in Sarajevo and Europe's Suicide ... 533
16.10.3 The Dominos Fall ... 535
16.10.4 An Apocalyptic Conflict ... 535
16.10.5 The Constitutional Consequences of World War I: The End of Liberalism and the Resurgence of State Power ... 536
References ... 541

**17 The Triumph of the State Over the Nation: From Totalitarianism to Interventionism** ... 555
17.1 From Liberalism to Interventionism ... 557
17.2 The Triumph of Big Capitalism and the Transformation of the Western World ... 558
17.2.1 The Inventions That Changed the World ... 558
17.2.2 Demographic Expansion and the Concentration of Urban Populations ... 563

17.3 The Social Consequences of Economic Expansion . . . . . . . . . 564
17.3.1 The Middle Class and the Proletariat . . . . . . . . . . . . 564
17.3.2 The Origins of "the Social Question" . . . . . . . . . . . 565
17.4 The Constitutional Consequences of the Social Question . . . . . 567
17.4.1 From Censitary to Universal Suffrage . . . . . . . . . . . 567
17.4.2 The Questioning of the *Laissez Faire* Principle: The Socialist Approach . . . . . . . . . . . . . . . . . . . . . . 568
17.4.3 The Conservative Approach: Bismarck's *Sozialpolitik* . . . . . . . . . . . . . . . . . . . . . . . . . . . . . . . 571
17.4.4 The Return of the Interventionist State . . . . . . . . . . 573
17.5 The Russian Revolution and the First Triumph of Totalitarianism . . . . . . . . . . . . . . . . . . . . . . . . . . . . 573
17.5.1 Lenin and the Soviet Revolution . . . . . . . . . . . . . . . 574
17.5.2 International Proletarianism vs. the Capitalism of the Liberal Nation-States . . . . . . . . . . . . . . . . . . 574
17.6 The European Oligarchies React by Defending "National Socialism" . . . . . . . . . . . . . . . . . . . . . . . . . . . . . . 576
17.6.1 Perfectly Legal Dictatorships . . . . . . . . . . . . . . . . . 578
17.6.2 An Adapted Legal Theory: From Ihering to Carl Schmitt . . . . . . . . . . . . . . . . . . . . . . . . . . . . . 581
17.6.3 The Expansion of Social/Legal Protection in the Interbellum Period . . . . . . . . . . . . . . . . . . . . . . 583
17.6.4 The Crisis of the Liberal State Model in the U.S.A.: The New Deal . . . . . . . . . . . . . . . . . . . . . . 583
17.6.5 A New Deal for Europe? . . . . . . . . . . . . . . . . . . . . 587
17.7 The Road to War . . . . . . . . . . . . . . . . . . . . . . . . . . . . 592
17.7.1 The Expansion of Totalitarianism: The Confrontation Between Communism and Fascism . . . 592
17.7.2 From the Spanish Civil War to World War II . . . . . . 593
17.8 The Triumph of the Welfare State Model . . . . . . . . . . . . . . . 597
17.8.1 The Welfare State and the Rule of Law . . . . . . . . . . 598
17.8.2 The Spread of the Welfare State After 1945 . . . . . . . 601
17.8.3 The United States Stands Alone: From Roosevelt to Obama . . . . . . . . . . . . . . . . . . . . . . . . . . . . . . 602
17.9 The Transformation of the Totalitarian Model of State: Communism After 1945 . . . . . . . . . . . . . . . . . . . . . . . . . . 603
17.9.1 The Marshall Plan and the Raising of the Iron Curtain . . . . . . . . . . . . . . . . . . . . . . . . . . . . . . . . 604
17.9.2 The Expansion of Communism After 1945 . . . . . . . 605
17.9.3 The Transformation of the Communist Model of State: The Chinese Example . . . . . . . . . . . . . . . . . . 606
17.10 The Contemporary Transformation of the State Model in Western Capitalist Countries: A Return to Oligarchy? . . . . . . . 608
17.10.1 The "Thirty Glorious Years", or the Contemporary Way of Addressing the Social Question . . . . . . . . . . 608

17.10.2 The Neoliberal Way and John Rawls' Theory of Justice . . . 609
17.10.3 Growing Inequality and Its Constitutional Consequences . . . 609
17.10.4 Towards a New Oligarchic Model of the State? . . . 611
17.11 The End of the Nation-State Era and the Beginning of Global Constitutional History? . . . 613
17.11.1 From the League of Nations to the United Nations . . . 613
17.11.2 Governments and Governance: From Authority to Negotiation . . . 615
References . . . 621

**Part V The End of the Nation State?**

**18 The Crisis of the Nation-State in the Era of European Integration . . . 647**
18.1 The Precedents for European Integration . . . 650
18.1.1 The Survival of the Universal Model . . . 650
18.1.2 "Composite Monarchies" as a Prime Example of Unions of States in Europe . . . 652
18.1.3 Assembly-Based Integration: The Singular Case of the Swiss Confederation . . . 657
18.1.4 Westphalia's Peace and the Triumph of the Europe of States . . . 662
18.1.5 Europe Between Imperialism and Coordination: 1789 to 1914 . . . 663
18.2 The Idea of Europe from 1918 to 1939 . . . 664
18.2.1 Europe Lies in Ruins, at the Mercy of the United States and the Soviet Union . . . 664
18.2.2 The Resurgence of Nationalisms and Disunity in Europe . . . 665
18.2.3 Some Attempts at Integration . . . 667
18.3 European Integration During World War II . . . 672
18.3.1 The Franco-British Union (June 1940) . . . 672
18.3.2 Hitlerian Europe . . . 673
18.3.3 The "Integrationist" Idea in Anti-Hitlerian Europe . . . 674
18.4 European Integration During the Post-War Period (1945–1949) . . . 677
18.4.1 Europe in 1945 . . . 677
18.4.2 A First, Unsuccessful Attempt at Integration: The Congress of The Hague (1948), and the Failure to Form a Federal Europe . . . 681
18.5 Step by Step Integration: The Invention of the "Community Method" (1950) . . . 684
18.5.1 The Pioneers: Jean Monnet and Robert Schuman . . . 684
18.5.2 The Schuman Declaration of May 9, 1950 . . . 687

18.6 From the European Coal and Steel Community to the European Economic Community (1951–1957) . . . . . . . . . . . . 689
18.6.1 The 1951 Treaty of Paris and the Creation of the ECSC . . . . . . . . . . . . . . . . . . . . . . . . . . . . . . . . . 689
18.6.2 From the Failure of the EDC to the Treaties of Rome (1951–1957) . . . . . . . . . . . . . . . . . . . . . . . . . . . . . 690
18.7 The Extension of the Community Method to Create a Common European Market, and the Institutionalization of European Integration (1957–1965) . . . . . . . . . . . . . . . . . . . . 691
18.7.1 The Court of Justice of the European Communities and the European Parliament . . . . . . . . . . . . . . . . . . 691
18.7.2 The European Free Trade Association: A British "Tantrum" . . . . . . . . . . . . . . . . . . . . . . . . . . . . . . . . 692
18.7.3 The Merging of Community Executives . . . . . . . . . 692
18.8 A Step Back in the Integration Process: A Return to the Intergovernmental Method (1966–1986) . . . . . . . . . . . . . . . . . 693
18.8.1 The Rejection of Qualified Majority Voting and the Return of Unanimity: The Luxembourg Compromise . . . . . . . . . . . . . . . . . . . . . . . . . . . . 693
18.8.2 On the Path Towards Expansion . . . . . . . . . . . . . . . 693
18.8.3 The Democratization of the Integration Process: An Elective European Parliament . . . . . . . . . . . . . . 694
18.9 Returning to the Community Method: From the Single European Act to the Maastricht Treaty (1986–1992) . . . . . . . . 694
18.9.1 The Schengen Agreement . . . . . . . . . . . . . . . . . . . . 695
18.9.2 The Single European Act . . . . . . . . . . . . . . . . . . . . 695
18.10 Combining the Community and the Intergovernmental Methods: From the Europe of Communities to the European Union (1992–2009) . . . . . . . . . . . . . . . . . . . . . . . . . . . . . . . . 695
18.10.1 The Maastricht Treaty and the Appearance of the Structured Integration Pillar . . . . . . . . . . . . . . . . . . 696
18.10.2 Towards an Economic and Monetary Union: The Euro as a Common Currency . . . . . . . . . . . . . . 697
18.10.3 Many New Members . . . . . . . . . . . . . . . . . . . . . . . 698
18.10.4 The Need to Reorganize the EU: From Amsterdam to Lisbon . . . . . . . . . . . . . . . . . . . . . . . 698
18.11 The EU of the Twenty-First Century . . . . . . . . . . . . . . . . . . . 699
18.11.1 The Lisbon Treaty . . . . . . . . . . . . . . . . . . . . . . . . . 699
18.11.2 A Legally Complex Integration . . . . . . . . . . . . . . . . 700
18.12 A Provisional Conclusion for an Unfinished Process: What Kind of Integration Are Europeans Looking For? . . . . . . 702
References . . . . . . . . . . . . . . . . . . . . . . . . . . . . . . . . . . . . . . . . . 711

**Index** . . . . . . . . . . . . . . . . . . . . . . . . . . . . . . . . . . . . . . . . . . . . 731

# Chapter 1
# Introduction

'In any case, I hate everything that merely instructs me without augmenting or directly invigorating my activity.' These words are from Goethe, and they may stand as a sincere ceterum censeo[1] at the beginning of our meditation on the value of history. For its intention is to show why instruction without invigoration, why knowledge not attended by action, why history as a costly superfluity and luxury, must, to use Goethe's word, be seriously hated by us – hated because we still lack even the things we need and the superfluous is the enemy of the necessary. We need history, certainly, but we need it for reasons different from those for which the idler in the garden of knowledge needs it, even though he may look nobly down on our rough and charmless needs and requirements. We need it, that is to say, for the sake of life and action, not so as to turn comfortably away from life and action, let alone for the purpose of extenuating the self-seeking life and the base and cowardly action. We want to serve history only to the extent that history serves life [. . .][2]—Friedrich Nietzsche (1844–1900)

Nothing in the world can keep man from feeling that he was born to be free. Never, no matter what happens, can he accept servitude, because he thinks.—Simone Weil (1909–1943)

Study the past to predict the future.—Confucius (551–570 BC)

---

[1] But I am of the opinion.

[2] "Übrigens ist mir alles verhaßt, was mich bloß belehrt, ohne meine Tätigkeit zu vermehren oder unmittelbar zu beleben." Dies sind Worte Goethes, mit denen, als mit einem herzhaft ausgedrückten Ceterum censeo, unsere Betrachtung über den Wert und den Unwert der Historie beginnen mag. In derselben soll nämlich dargestellt werden, warum Belehrung ohne Belebung, warum Wissen, bei dem die Tätigkeit erschlafft, warum Historie als kostbarer Erkenntnis-Überfluss und Luxus uns ernstlich, nach Goethes Wort, verhaßt sein muss – deshalb, weil es uns noch am Notwendigsten fehlt, und weil das Überflüssige der Feind des Notwendigen ist. Gewiß, wir brauchen Historie, aber wir brauchen sie anders, als sie der verwöhnte Müßiggänger im Garten des Wissens braucht, mag derselbe auch vornehm auf unsere derben und anmutlosen Bedürfnisse und Nöte herabsehen. Das heißt, wir brauchen sie zum Leben und zur Tat, nicht zur bequemen Abkehr vom Leben und von der Tat, oder gar zur Beschönigung des selbstsüchtigen Lebens und der feigen und schlechten Tat. Nur soweit die Historie dem Leben dient, wollen wir ihr dienen.... (Nietzsche 2007, 57)



B. Aguilera-Barchet, *A History of Western Public Law*,
DOI 10.1007/978-3-319-11803-1_1

The terms "state" and "nation" continue to form part of our vocabulary, despite the fact that the world has changed dramatically since both words came into being. In the global age in which we live, being the citizen of a state is progressively losing its meaning, as we are increasingly becoming citizens of the world, in what Bertand Badie considers a fresh new start as far as History is concerned (Badie 2012, 47).

This seems even truer if we concentrate on the European Union, as it is clear that the expansion of the "Community Acquis" (*Acquis Communautaire*) has seriously and irrevocably reduced national sovereignty, a situation leading some to conclude that the old problems and dynamics of nationalism are increasingly immaterial and outmoded (Geary 2002, 2).

Notions of national identity, however, are far from extinct. As Smith (2004, 1) observes, the belief that the age of nations is behind us and that true units of cultural identity now consist of ones that are small, local and untainted by power, and/or vast and transnational, is not borne out by an examination of political realities. In many ways, the scope and impact of the national state has actually intensified as a result of its involvement in regulation of health and reproduction, mass education, culture, leisure, communications, the media, criminal justice, as well as its more traditional roles in the areas of taxation, legislation and law enforcement. In fact, in what has probably been a backlash against this trend towards supranational integration, many Europeans identify more and more with their "homelands", calling for regional pride, autonomy, and, at times, separation from the state.[3] In Belgium, the Flemish and the French-speaking community (Walloons), have achieved almost total separation; in the United Kingdom, the Scottish National Party pushes for independence; and in Spain, many Basques and Catalonians harbor fiercely regionalist sentiments, calling for a divorce from the Spanish state.[4]

One of the purposes of this work, then, is to clarify the role and relevance both terms, "nation" and "state", have in the world we live in today. As such, and to avoid what Geary (2002, 13) calls the "pseudoscience of ethnic nationalism", my objective is not to provide a series of theoretical disquisitions,[5] but rather, more modestly, to offer an empirical analysis of concrete historical realities that may reveal how our states and nations developed down to the present day.[6] In these

[3] On the contrary, as Geary (2002, 3) points out, nationalism, ethnocentrism and racism—specters long thought exorcised from the European soul—have returned, their powers enhanced by a half-century of dormancy.

[4] Nevertheless, in international athletic competitions, for example, Spaniards still tend to feel a strong identification with their country and its symbols. On July 12, 2010, when Spain defeated Holland in the World Cup final, all Spaniards, including most Basques and Catalonians, coincided in their celebration of the Spanish national team's victory. At that time, Spain's national flag could be seen up and down the streets, waved without reservations, something that had practically not occurred since the death of dictator Francisco Franco (1975). Fortunately, as Geary (2002, 13) points out, if the "pseudoscience" of nationalism has destroyed Europe twice, and may do so yet again, Europe's peoples have always been far more fluid, complex and dynamic than the imaginings of modern nationalists.

[5] For an excellent theoretical approach to this issue, see Hobsbawm (2010).

[6] Strayer (1972, 5–7) convincingly argues that instead of looking for theoretical definitions of the state, we ought to look for signs that show us that a state is coming into existence: a human

pages, readers will not find no ivory tower treatise, for as Nietzsche (2007, 57) observed in his early work *Untimely Meditations*, history is not a luxury, an activity reserved for erudite scholars, but rather a means to spur us to actively engage the era during which we are destined to live.

The history of the different western nation-states, however, one marked by diversity and particularities, but also by shared traits, is not easy to trace. As Gellner (2006, 6) has indicated, nations, like states, are not a universal necessity. Neither nations nor states exist at all times and under all circumstances. The idea of the state arose without a total dependence on the nation, while some nations, conversely, have emerged without the blessings of their respective states.[7] This is especially true of Europe's longest-standing nation-states, which boast centuries of history on their own. When we talk about today's "globalization", it is essential that we have, logically, an international idea of how and why our own particular national trajectories have converged.

One needs, therefore, to appreciate that, as westerners, the bedrock of our culture is the Roman Empire, defined by its audacious aspirations to universalism and coherent codification, later sustained thanks to the Papacy and medieval emperors who harked back to Rome for both inspiration and guidance. The Roman model was destroyed by Germanic invasions in the early fifth century and supplanted by a patchwork of ethnically and tribally based kingdoms across Europe whose diversity contrasted starkly with the Roman universalism which had preceded them. A central empire had given way to a whole set of nations, whose identities took firmer shape, and whose power was consolidated by the territorial monarchies of the late Middle Ages. These nations ultimately evolved into the powerful absolute monarchies of the sixteenth and seventeenth centuries. The nation-state model of political organization proliferated and flourished after the Peace of Westphalia in 1648, reaching its zenith in the second half of the nineteenth century during the golden age of colonialism. During the first half of the twentieth century, national competition and jockeying for power would drag the states of Europe into two massive wars, which left the West utterly dazed and devastated. This era saw the rise of a new western superpower, the United States, whose burgeoning might was due precisely to its successful forging of a "nation of states"—though it had paid a heavy price to establish its indivisibility in the form of its brutal Civil War. All of this helps us to understand why Europe, which found itself in ruins in 1945, had no

community that endures in a certain space over time, and the formation of impersonal, relatively permanent political institutions that survive changes in leadership and other fluctuations. Institutions that allow for a certain degree of specialization in political affairs, increasing the efficiency of the political process and strengthening the group's sense of political identity, indicate that a turning point in state-building has been reached.

[7] It is more debatable, however, whether the normative idea of the nation in its modern sense did not presuppose the prior existence of the state. Nationalists hold that state and nation were destined for each other and that either without the other is incomplete. However, the reality is that before they could become intended for each other, each of them had to emerge, and their emergence was independent and contingent. This is what Geary (2002, 11–12) calls the "rhetoric of ethnic nationalism", that is, the demand for political autonomy for all persons belonging to a particular ethnic group, and the right of that people to govern its historic territory, usually defined in terms of early medieval kingdoms, regardless of who may now live in them.

choice but to unite, even if it was reluctantly. Europeans had no choice if they hoped to survive and continue to play an important role in the world.

A final remark on the mainspring of these pages: my reading of R.C. Van Caenegem's splendid historical introduction to Western constitutional history (Van Caenegem 2003), which I discovered the year it was published, during my time at Harvard Law School. This work made me realize and appreciate how important it is to offer a global view of constitutional and legal history to cultivate an understanding of our legal past. My conviction was reinforced after the implementation of the major European higher education reform measure known as the Bologna Plan (1999), and the drastic reduction that its new curriculum called for as regards class hours in the History of Law.

Detecting the need for an accessible, historical approach to Law for those aiming to undertake legal studies, I began an academic blog for my classes, which not only led to a notable improvement in my students' academic results, but also represented an opportunity for me to learn as well. To my surprise, the blog also happened to receive considerable media attention.[8] This interest gave me the idea of restructuring all these materials to offer the simplest possible global synthesis of the subject, from the very beginnings, all the way through European integration.

The result is intended as nothing more than an aid, an instrument to recover what in the Middle Ages was known as *lectio*, when classes—in Bologna and other European universities of the day—began by reading a text drawn from a book. This, however, was nothing more than the "pre-text" to initiate a debate between teachers and students in an effort to approach the subject in question as one open to discussion. The idea was to avoid offering a static view of science and knowledge, which only leads to their decay.

This undertaking is not devoid of a certain audacity and presumption, which is why, even if every chapter includes extensive bibliographical information for those who might be interested in deeper coverage of specific points, this book might not be considered strictly academic in nature. Rather, the work's style aims to provide first-year students with an accessible body of information, equipping them with concepts and knowledge that may very well prove crucial during their university studies and careers.

In this highly technical and specialized twenty-first century, it is more important than ever for students to possess the firmest grasp possible of their cultural background, Western Civilization, essential for them to be able to analyze and think critically about the world they are living in today. It is therefore, expressly, a work suitable for students and the public alike, an instrument to promote an understanding of and appreciation for our western identity in a global world.

In short, the ultimate aim of this book is to restore in the rising generations a taste and hunger for general culture that is, sadly, disappearing in our societies, drowned out by more "practical" technological and economic concerns. This work seeks to

[8] As evidenced by the over 190,000 visits received in 3 years, not only from Spain but also from around the world, a noteworthy result for an academic blog.

allow them to understand the contemporary meaning of crucial realities such as Law, the State, Government and Politics. Finally, a secondary intention is to spur them to become active and engaged citizens who are culturally literate and aware of their historical backgrounds; informed citizens who, having enjoyed the thrilling experience of rediscovering the roots of our Western Civilization, stand ready to take part in its ongoing development.

## References


Badie, B. (2012). *Quand l'histoire commence*. Paris: CNRS éditions.

Geary, P. J. (2002). *The myth of nations. The medieval origins of Europe*. Princeton: Princeton University Press.

Gellner, E. (2006). *Nations and nationalism*. Malden, MA: Blackwell.

Hobsbawm, E. J. (2010). *Nations and nationalism since 1780: Programme, myth, reality* (2nd ed., 17th printing). Cambridge: Cambridge University Press.

Nietzsche, F. (2007) On the use and Abuse of History for Life. In *Untimely meditations: Thoughts out of season. Parts I and II (Unzeitgemässe Betrachtungen 1874)* (11th printing, pp. 96–133). Cambridge, UK: Cambridge University.

Smith, A. D. (2004). *The antiquity of nations*. Cambridge, UK: Polity.

Strayer, J. R. (1972). *On the medieval origins of the modern state*. Princeton, NJ: Princeton University Press.

Van Caenegem, R. C. (2003). *An historical introduction to western Constitutional law* (1st ed., 1995). Cambridge: Cambridge University Press.

# Part I
# From the City State to the Roman Empire

# Chapter 2
# From the Origins to the Polis

As the long winter ended, the tempo of the clan's life increased to match the pace of life quickening within the rich earth. The cold season enforced not true hibernation, but an alteration in metabolic rates brought about by reduced activities. In winter they were more sluggish, slept more, ate more, causing an insulating layer of subcutaneous fat to develop as protection against the cold. With a rise of temperature, the trend was reversed, making the clan restless and eager to be out and moving.—Jean Marie Auel[1]

## Contents


2.1 From Nomadic to Sedentary Society: The Neolithic Revolution ........ 10
2.2 The First Literate Societies: Power and Social Structure in the Great Ancient Civilization of the Near East ........ 11
2.2.1 The Civilizations of the Indus Valley ........ 11
2.2.2 Egypt Under the Pharaohs ........ 12
2.2.3 Power in Ancient Mesopotamia ........ 13
2.2.4 Confucius and the Origin of the State in China ........ 14
2.3 Family and Power in the West ........ 16
2.3.1 The Indo-Europeans Lay the Linguistic and Social Foundations of Western Culture ........ 16
2.3.2 Indo-European Family Structure and the Formation of Society in the West: From the Tribe to the City ........ 16
2.4 The Greek Polis as the First Precursor of the State in the West ........ 19
2.4.1 An Initial Stage of Monarchy: The Minoan and Mycenaean Civilizations ........ 19
2.4.2 From the Homeric Kingdoms to the Appearance of the Polis (800–500 BC) ........ 20
2.4.3 Synoecism as the Basis of the Polis ........ 21
2.4.4 The Consolidation of the Polis and Its Aristocratic Model: The Case of Sparta ........ 22
2.4.5 The People Versus the Aristocrats: The Origin of the "Democratic" System ........ 24
2.4.6 Athens' Cleisthenes, History's First "Democrat" ........ 25
2.4.7 Pericles' Athens ........ 26


[1] *The Clan of the Cave Bear* (1980). Auel (2011, 196).



B. Aguilera-Barchet, *A History of Western Public Law*,
DOI 10.1007/978-3-319-11803-1_2

2.5 The Drawbacks of the Polis Model .... 26
2.5.1 The Division of Hellas .... 27
2.5.2 Attempts to Improve Upon the Polis Model .... 27
References .... 33

## 2.1 From Nomadic to Sedentary Society: The Neolithic Revolution

The first scholars to study the prehistoric era sought to establish a timeline based exclusively on material evidence of human intelligence, specifically in the form of tools found at archeological sites. Thus was established the first classifications of the ages prior to the appearance of writing: The Stone Age and the Metal Age. The first of these was, in turn, divided into the Paleolithic (meaning "old stone") and the Neolithic ("new stone"), according to the sophistication of the instruments used. The second, meanwhile, was divided according to the metals employed: copper, an easily malleable material; bronze, an alloy in which copper is strengthened with aluminum, a procedure requiring a certain level of metallurgical technique; and iron, which requires a much more complex metallurgical manipulation process.

Over time, however, the progress made in archeological discoveries ended up transforming the initial meanings of the terms "Paleolithic" and "Neolithic". The former came to refer to the age of nomadic man, who essentially lived by hunting, which forced him to constantly move to pursue game, while the latter came to refer to the era following man's discovery of agriculture and his establishment of the first sedentary communities, as he came to fix his residence in specific territories.

When men are nomadic and human groups are small, group organization and leadership tends to be entrusted to the individual who can best assure everyone's survival. However, during past ages these leaders tended to be aided in their tasks by another member of the group: a shaman, witch doctor, druid or high priest, one who, as the wisest, maintained the tribe's cultural traditions and acted as an intermediary between his people and supernatural forces. From the point of view of social cohesion, what kept the group together was, essentially, the drive to survive amidst conditions that were quite hostile and difficult, and life was organized around this function.[2]

It should not be ruled out, however, that in some cases these prehistoric peoples achieved forms of social organization featuring greater cohesion. How else can one explain the erection of megalithic monuments but the existence of a social framework allowing for harmony sufficient to organize the transport of stones of such dimensions? The lack of written documents, however, confines us to the realm of speculation.

What is undeniable is that, at a certain point, man became a sedentary creature who came to settle down in fixed locations. His transformation from a nomad, leading a life based on hunting, to a sedentary lifestyle, rooted in agricultural

[2] As Fagan (2010, xiii) points out, the Cro-Magnon story is a tale of ordinary men and women going about the business of survival in unpredictable, often bitterly cold environments that required them to adapt constantly and opportunistically to short and long term climate changes, a story of endless ingenuity and adaptability.

production and livestock breeding, was such a landmark event in human history that the term "Neolithic Revolution" was coined to refer to it.[3]

The transition from the Paleolithic to the Neolithic came about slowly as a consequence of climatic changes occurring in the wake of the last Ice Age (10000 BC). This is why there is frequent talk of an intermediate Mesolithic Era which, depending on the areas in question, is identified as having occurred between 15 and 8 millennia BC. The Neolithic Revolution, however, did not occur simultaneously all over the world. It first appeared where geographical conditions were most favorable for agricultural development (Bellwood 2005, 19–24). Conversely, it appeared latest where climatic conditions were adverse, which explains why there are still nomadic peoples living in desert areas, such as the African Bushmen of the Kalahari.

## 2.2 The First Literate Societies: Power and Social Structure in the Great Ancient Civilization of the Near East

Our knowledge of the humans who came before us becomes much more precise when the past can be reconstructed using written documents left by our predecessors. Thus, once a group discovers writing, it is said to have entered the historical era.

Writing only appears in societies featuring advanced degrees of civilization. Thus, the oldest written records conserved come from the first great civilizations known, which appeared—in what was no accident—in the most fertile lands of the Middle East, ones generally benefitting from major rivers. Among these regions Sumer is of particular note, arising in the territory lying between the Tigris and Euphrates Rivers ("Mesopotamia" meaning "the land between the rivers"), and that of Egypt, which arose along the Nile. Both civilizations developed between the fourth and third millennia BC. Somewhat later came the Harappan and the Mohenjo-Daro civilizations, which appeared along the Indus and Ganges Rivers, dating from 2800 BC, and the Chinese civilization along the Yangtze, as of the second millennium BC.

### *2.2.1 The Civilizations of the Indus Valley*

Of these great civilizations the one featuring the most highly developed social structure was that which appeared in the Indus Valley, in the twin cities of Harappa and Mohenjo-Daro, from 2500 to 1500 BC. Both succeeded and were based upon a previous civilization whose characteristics are recorded in the religious texts known

[3] For an overview of how the agricultural economy was the crucial first step towards greater social complexity, population growth, and the ensuing emergence of states see Bocquet-Appel (2008).

as the *Vedas*.[4] Factors leading to the social cohesion of both cities included their beliefs in myths and religious ceremonies, leading them to be classified as theocracies. From the point of view of their social development, they were never unified under the leadership of a common political power,[5] although it is possible that they featured some early version of the social classes upon which the current Indian caste system is based.[6]

### 2.2.2 Egypt Under the Pharaohs

The case of Egypt is the most interesting in terms of the history of social structures because of its uniqueness. Unlike the Indus Valley civilization, Ancient Egypt was not urban. The villages which emerged along the shores of the Nile, circa 4000 BC, had not evolved into cities a 1,000 years later, despite their spectacular demographic growth (Smith 1972). This is why it was relatively simple to unify Egypt

[4] The oldest of the four *Vedas* is the *Rig-Veda*, written between 1700 and 1100 BC. The name *Rig-Veda* comes from *rig* (praise) and *veda* (truth). It contains a series of hymns dedicated to the gods and is probably humanity's oldest creation of its kind, having been transmitted orally until approximately the eleventh century AD, when it was recorded in writing. However, the Pyramid Texts—funerary inscriptions that were written on the walls of the early Ancient Egyptian pyramids at Sakkara—are dated back to the fifth and sixth dynasties, approximately the years 2350–2175 B.C.E. These texts are to a large extent a composition, a compilation and joining of earlier texts which must have circulated orally or were written down on papyrus many centuries earlier. Because of extensive internal evidence, it is believed that they were composed much earlier, circa 3000 B.C.E. The Pyramid Texts are, therefore, essentially the oldest sacred texts known (Mercer 1952, viii). Also, Faulkner (2004) with his authoritative English translation, considered the standard today.

[5] The cities were not walled, so it would not seem that they suffered military attacks. Both do have a fortress on a nearby mountain, where the authorities must have resided, probably religious figures. However, there exist no large temples or funerary monuments which would lead one to envision a great power with the ability to mobilize masses (Wright 2010, 242–246)—unlike what would occur with its neighboring "*khmer*" civilization in Angkor, where the kings demonstrated their power through gigantic constructions surrounded by immense pools, though certainly in a much later period (the Temple of Angkor Vat dates from the twelfth century AD).

[6] The origin of the castes (*varna* y and *jati* in Sanskrit, the sacred language of Hinduism and the equivalent of our Latin) may be found in the *Rig-Veda* (approximately 2,000 years BC), the oldest of the Hindu religious texts, in which the four main castes, or *varna*, are described: the *Brahmans* (priests and intellectuals), the *Kshátriyas* (warriors and kings), the *Vaishyas* (merchants), and the *Shudras* (peasants and workers). Each one proceeds from a different part of Brahma's body. The pariahs, or untouchables, are not considered a caste, for they proceed from his waste (since the 1990s they have called themselves *dálits*, or "the oppressed"). In this division, valid to classify the different strata of the Aryan civilization which, coming out of Afghanistan, populated the Indian subcontinent 2,000 years BC, what differentiates one caste from the other is not power or money, but rather something much more related to religion: one's state of purity or impurity. *Varna* means "color" but does not refer to any supposed racial characteristic, but to a system of color-based symbolism which reflects the social hierarchy and the qualities present in each stratum. For a historical explanation of the origins of the caste system see Dumont (1980, 27–28).

under the theocratic power of a pharaoh, who was called upon to assure the economic survival of his people, which depended on the organization of the cultivation system exploiting the Nile's annual flooding. To this end the pharaoh governed through "divinely-inspired decisions" which assured the cohesion of Egyptian society.

The pharaoh based the legitimacy of his wielding of supreme power upon his role as the representative of the Divine. Egypt, thus, was a "theocracy". It is telling that during the era of Egyptian civilization's greatest splendor, that of the New Kingdom (1570–1070 BC), the capital Thebes (present day Luxor) arose around the Karnak Temple Complex, dedicated to the God Amun,[7] located on the shore opposite where the royal necropolis (the Valley of the Kings) was excavated. It was religious belief in the hereafter which made it possible to mobilize tens of thousands of Egyptians during the pharaoh's reign to build the pyramids and the temples, whose dimensions continue to awe the world. Egypt was a society hierarchically structured from the top. There were, in fact, no social classes, only the rulers and the ruled. The male children and male relatives of the pharaoh occupied the highest posts in the bureaucracy and priesthood, while secondary positions were held by less immediate family.

### 2.2.3 Power in Ancient Mesopotamia

The case of the civilizations which appeared in ancient Mesopotamia is different. In this region between the Tigris and Euphrates Rivers, especially apt for agriculture, the urban model was that which determined the social structure—at least in the first stage, called the "dynastic" (2900–2500 BC), when some 20 independent cities (Kish, Wark, Lagash, Ur) coexisted in the southern Mesopotamian area. However, unlike the Indus Valley cities, it appears that the Mesopotamian ones did develop a degree of social structure which could be considered to constitute a precursor of the state, probably because military confrontations between these cities (Pollock 1999, 9) favored the emergence of a military caste led by a strong political power, perhaps a hereditary monarchy. In fact, one of the most important characteristics of these societies is their remarkable and early stratification. At the top there was a ruling class composed of the prince and a few aristocratic families, dominating a much broader strata made up of peasants and artisans served, in turned, by a slave class.[8]

The process forging the "state" accelerated when the dynastic era gave way to the "imperial era", during which the different cities fell under the dominion of a single and very powerful king. This would first occur with the Akkadian Empire of

[7] Egyptian cities grew normally around a temple, Karnak being the most important of the New Empire, when Pharaonic Egypt was at its peak (Routledge 1997).

[8] For an overview of the development of Sumerian society see Crawford (2004, 214–220).

Sargon, circa 2400 BC.[9] Mesopotamia came to be governed by a successive series of monarchs, such as Babylon's Hammurabi, author of one of the first known compilations of laws known, the famous Code bearing his name, promulgated in approximately 1760 BC. Then came the Assyrians, followed by the Neo-Babylonian Nebuchadnezzar, who destroyed Jerusalem and deported the Jewish population to Babylon in 587. The last link in this chain, marked by its centralizing, state-like centralizing traditions was the Persian Empire, which would face off against the Greek *polis*, eventually being conquered by Alexander the Great when the Macedonian king occupied Babylon itself in 331 BC.

### *2.2.4 Confucius and the Origin of the State in China*

Of all the ancient eastern civilizations, that which probably boasted the most advanced degree of state development is that which appeared in China in the especially fertile region found on the Great Bend of the Yellow River. Chinese society began to take on its structure around 2200 BC during the Hsia (or Xia) Dynasty, which lasted until 1766 BC, successively supplanted by the Shang Dynasty (up to 1122 BC) and the Chou (1000–256 BC). In the latter period the pivotal figure of Confucius (551–479) would appear, a contemporary of Pericles and Buddha, who would transform the spiritual and organizational foundations of Chinese society.

Confucius is important when considering political history because of the way he sought to mitigate the negative effects of the spread of feudalism during his era. At the time of his birth China was dominated by powerful rulers at war with one another.[10] To rectify this situation Confucius endorsed the idea of a single empire headed by a sole sovereign. It is interesting to note that Confucius did not base the social structure he envisioned on any divinity. China was not a theocracy, as its religion consisted essentially of the veneration of one's ancestors and a morality according to which rulers were to be accepted by the people because they were

[9] As Postgate (1996, 40) points out, Sargon of Akkad was not only a conqueror famous for his military accomplishments, but also introduced a new level of central intervention in the south. After razing the walls of the principal cities—Uruk, Ur, Lagas and Umma—he installed "sons of Akkad" as governors, accompanied by some kind of administrative cadre and some military support, which in any case displaced the traditional local civilian hierarchy. The Akkadian language was introduced in administrative documents and documents referred to the Akkad king.

[10] Confucius lived between the Spring and Autumn period (722–481 BC) and the Warring States Era (403–221). As Van Norden (2002, 5) points out these periods were characterized by increasingly brutal interstate and intrastate violence and warfare. In this fluid social context there was increased social mobility, as the old nobility quickly fell from power. For the first time in Chinese history there arose a class of educated individuals who were not, from birth, in the employ of any particular nobility. Confucius was one of these scholars.

virtuous, not because they had imposed themselves upon them by military force.[11] According to Confucius, government should be based not on force, but on the encouragement of just and good conduct. From a practical point of view he defended a centralized model of governmental organization, presided over by an emperor who would administer and govern the state through a bureaucratic class. Confucius, however, argued that these bureaucrats should be selected based on merit, and not simply drawn from the hereditary nobility; thus, appeared the famous "mandarins", who obtained their posts only after passing very difficult tests requiring years of study.[12]

Confucius's ideas on government and the state were, for the first time, placed into practice by the Chin Dynasty (223–206 BC), whose emperors were so important that the line would give the country its name today: China. They were the first rulers who managed to impose a strong and centralized government with an organized and permanent imperial army and a new imperial bureaucracy that developed an efficient administration. This achievement, among others, made colossal public works such as the "Great Wall" possible. The Chin was succeeded by the Han Dynasty, which in the first century BC created the first stable and efficient state. Thanks to it, of all the great eastern civilizations, China was the most structured and stable, as the Japanese empire appeared much later.[13]

---

[11] Confucianism is, above all, a doctrine of ethical behavior according to which the good man seeks to perfect himself to properly head his family. A man's highest aspiration should be to take over the reins of government, in which he is to assure equality and the maintenance of peace. This is why he was called the "eternal, model Teacher". For Confucius there existed 6 arts which the best (mandarins) should cultivate: the rites, music, archery, horseback riding, calligraphy and numbers. His teachings were recorded in two types of texts: the "Canonical Books": *Book of Changes* (Divination), *Book of History* (Historical Documents), *Book of Odes* (Poetry and Folklore), *Spring and Autumn Annals* (History), *Book of Rites* (Ritual and Ceremonies), *Book of Ritual* (Etiquette and ceremonial), *Rites of Chou* (Governmental institutions and regulations) and the "Classic Books": *Analects* (Ethics), *The Middle Way* (Metaphysics), *The Great Learning* (Metaphysics and ethics), and *Mencius* or *Meng-tzu* (Politics, ethics).

[12] If aristocracy (*ἀριστοκρατία*, from *ἄριστος*, *aristos*: excellent, and *κράτος*, *kratos*: poder) is "government by the best", meritocracy (from the Latin *mereo*: to deserve, to obtain) is a form of government based on personal capacities. It is commonly associated with the bureaucratic state and the way in which civil servants are selected for their positions through qualifying examinations.

[13] The imperial house of Japan claims to be the oldest continuous hereditary monarchy, as the current emperor, Akihito (born in 1933), is said to descend from the legendary emperor Jimmu, said to have ruled in the seventh century BC. Nevertheless, there is no historical evidence of emperors until the sixth century AD, despite some archeological and ethnographical efforts at reconstruction (Piggott 1997, 3).

## 2.3 Family and Power in the West

Civilization came much later to the West. The first great western culture, that of Greece, peaked in the fifth century BC, many centuries after the great Egyptian or Mesopotamian civilizations did.

However, this relative backwardness would later be made up for by the development of more sophisticated social structures. Whereas in the East power generally preceded from above, and in connection with a divinity (in the cases of Mesopotamia and Egypt) in the West it was structured from below, based on kinship ties. The family is the cornerstone of western culture.

### 2.3.1 *The Indo-Europeans Lay the Linguistic and Social Foundations of Western Culture*

Beginning in the second millennium BC a series of peoples began to appear on the European continent about which little is known, except that they spoke languages which proceeded from a common linguistic branch: what has been called "Proto-Indo-European", a language that is thought to have fragmented into different ones between 3000 and 2000 BC, evolving into Sanskrit, Greek and Latin, among others.

In addition to a shared language, the Indo-Europeans boasted a high degree of social structuring, considerably higher, in any case, than that of the indigenous peoples they encountered as they settled across the European continent.[14] This greater degree of social structuring generally allowed the Indo-Europeans to establish themselves as a superior caste ruling over the indigenous populations of Greece, Rome and the Iberian Peninsula.[15]

### 2.3.2 *Indo-European Family Structure and the Formation of Society in the West: From the Tribe to the City*

Little is known of the Proto-Indo-European societies, and we still rely heavily on the studies of linguists and anthropologists. The classic works by Fustel de Coulanges (2001) and Morgan (2003) are still extremely interesting in spite of the fact that they can only be considered to offer likely, though not certain,

[14] As Anthony (2007, 18) has indicated, more than 100 years ago scholars noticed that the oldest well documented Indo-European languages—Imperial Hittite, Mycenaean Greek, and the most ancient form of Sanskrit, or Old Indic—were spoken by militaristic societies that seemed to appear in the ancient world driving chariots pulled by swift horses, a fact which might explain how Indo-Europeans emigrated and imposed themselves upon preexisting societies.

[15] For a general description of these Proto-Indo-European societies see Fortson (2010, 19–24).

suppositions about past eras about which we can never be sure because of the scarcity of the historical sources available.[16]

#### 2.3.2.1 Family and *Gens*

Today the family is a restricted human group which, essentially, features people linked by blood ties who relate to each other during their lifetimes, that is, progenitors and their progeny (parents–children, grandparents–grandchildren) and their closest collateral relatives (brothers, uncles and cousins). Formerly, however, the family was conceived in a broader sense which transcended the temporal dimension of people's lives. A family was understood to include all those who shared a common ancestor, who they generally venerated. The members of the ancient family were united by something more powerful than birth, affection, or physical strength. This was the religion of the sacred fire, and of dead ancestors, in which the family formed a single body, both in this life and in the next (Fustel de Coulanges 2001, 31). This family structure, in the broad sense, is an essential characteristic of the first societies established and structured by the Indo-Europeans.

The family was understood as a group of people sharing a common predecessor, usually designated in ancient sources by the Latin term *gens* (*genos* in Greek), from which comes the Castilian term *gentilicio*, a synonym of the word *apellido* (last name). Thus, all those bearing the same *gentilicio*, or surname, belonged to the same *gens*.[17]

[16] This is why they are still being published. As Momigliano (2012, 325) affirms, when one talks of the ancient city as a society within which institutions operate and ideas circulate, the first modern historian whose names comes to mind is Fustel de Coulanges. In the view of Moses (2009, 2), Morgan did much more than dream, producing trailblazing scholarly work that captured the spirit of his times, which explains why he is the only American to be cited by some the most revolutionary minds of our age, such as Darwin, Marx and Freud. The value of Morgan's work relies in the fact that he contributed to the paradigm of human origins and the human trajectory on this planet which most educated westerners now take for granted.

[17] Such was the case, for example, with the Roman patrician Scipio Africanus, or Publius Cornelius Scipio Africanus (236–183 BC), so named for his decisive intervention in the second Punic War against Carthage. Publio was the first name (*praenomen*) and Scipio the added name (*agnomen*). The *nomen* Cornelio denoted his belonging to the gens of Cornelia. What the Romans called *nomen*, then, was the name of the ancestor from whom all the descendants and members of the gens claimed to descend. Morgan (2003, 284) cites another example related to the family of Augustus: "Julia, the sister of Caius Julius Caesar, married Marcus Attius Balbus. Her name shows that she belonged to the Julian gens. Her daughter Attia, according to custom, took the gentile name of her father and belonged to the Attian gens. Attia married Gaius Octavius, and became the mother of Augustus the first Roman emperor. The son, as usual, took the gentile name of his father and belonged to the Octavian gens". Upon his adoption by Caesar he became *Gaius Julius Caesar Octavianus*. After becoming emperor he dropped *Octavius* and added *Augustus*.

### 2.3.2.2 The Urban Origins of the State: *Clientela, Phratry, Curia* and *Tribe* as Precursors of the City

In Indo-European society the *gens* formed the basis of society. Thus, isolated individuals who did not belong to any *gens* sought to become part of one to survive. Hence, the old *gens* encompassed not only blood descendants of a common ancestor, but also included people who did not share kinship ties. First, forming a natural part of the gens' main family group were their servants and slaves. Secondly, there were also those who joined the *gens* by virtue of a pact or agreement. This pact, called a "clientela relationship" was of a sacred character and, once sealed, was binding upon the "clients" and their descendants. Through it primitive Indo-European families were reinforced, forming more extensive groups.[18]

Thus, there came a time when a certain number of families joined to form a group called the phratry, from the Greek *phratria*, or the *curia*, from the Latin. Emerging united by their common veneration of an ancestor, the *phratria* and eventually became socially structured groups with their own leaders and assemblies, which deliberated and were able to make decisions binding upon all. It is worth observing that during the era of republican Rome there were still *comitia curiata*, one of the assemblies making up the city of Rome's political structure.

The process by which the gens were grouped did not cease, and several *phratria* or ended up forming tribes, which also had their own rite, with their own leader (*tribuno*), assemblies (*comitia tributa*) and tribunals. Vestiges of this tribe-based organization are still visible in the political and legal institutions of the ancient Greek cities. In Athens, for example, there were ten tribes, which each chose 50 members forming part of the Council of 500. There was also a magistrate for each tribe, and it was within them that citizens were chosen to serve in judicial capacities.

The integration process continued, gathering momentum, with the tribes ultimately grouping into cities when different ones came to live in one place: the *urbe*.[19] Over time cities' social and legal organization became increasingly

[18] In 1877 Morgan (2003, 222), when his *Ancient Society* was first published, described Athenian society as a pyramidal structure: "The social system of the Athenians exhibits the following series: first, the gens, founded upon kin; second, the phratry, a brotherhood of gens derived by segmentation, probably, from an original gens; third, the tribe, composed of several phratries, the members of which spoke the same dialect; and fourth, a people or nation, composed of several tribes united by coalescence into one gentile society, and occupying the same territory".

[19] The terms *civitas* and *urbs*, either of which may be translated as *city*, were not synonymous words among the ancients. A *civitas* was a religious and political association of families and tribes, while an *urbs* was the place of assembly, the dwelling-place, and, above all, the sanctuary of this association. Morgan (2003, 300) explained that the *societas* was founded upon *gens*, while the *civitas* was founded upon territory and property, and that the latter gradually supplanted the former. Service (1975, 4) wrote that "urban" and "civil" can be accurately used to mean that the society was characterized by the presence of cities or large towns and that the inhabitants were citizens of some kind of legal commonwealth [. . .] Conversely, the earlier, simpler stage of society was characterized by the absence of urban agglomerations and formal legal structures and their associated institutionalized governments.

structured. The first "urban" model to develop was the city-state, the Greek polis standing as the quintessential example. In fact, it was then when the word "politics" appeared in the history of western society.

## 2.4 The Greek Polis as the First Precursor of the State in the West

The city-state did not just appear in Greece overnight. Rather, it was the result of a long road, the first steps being taken towards it in the third millennium BC. Tracing the process which led to the formation of the polis is absolutely fascinating.

### *2.4.1 An Initial Stage of Monarchy: The Minoan and Mycenaean Civilizations*

The history of ancient Greece begins circa 2300 BC in the archipelago of the Cyclades. We do not know, however, about these peoples' social and political organization because of the absence of written records.

It was not until the year 2000 BC, in Crete, when the first urban centers such as Knossos, Phaestos and Malia arose around royal palaces. Among these, beginning in 1600 BC that of King Minos is of special note, as it was able to impose itself upon others, leading ancient Cretan civilization to be termed "Minoan". Although the size and opulence of these palaces constitute proof of the existence of a powerful royalty backed by a bureaucracy following the Near Eastern model (i.e. Egypt and Mesopotamia), the absence of precise written sources prevents us from knowing more.

Minoan civilization suddenly disappeared around 1500 BC, perhaps because of the massive volcanic eruption that destroyed the island of Thera (Santorini now) in the Cyclades. The Greeks, nevertheless, would retain a vague memory of the era of the Minoan palaces in their legend of how Daedalus, the architect of Minos, designed a labyrinth in which the king imprisoned a Minotaur, a monster born of Queen Pasife's relations with a bull. Theseus, the son of Athens' king, slayed the Minotaur and emerged from the maze, able to enter and emerge from it thanks to the thread given him by Ariadne. Theseus would eventually inherit the throne of Athens and marry Phaedra, a sister of Ariadne's.

After the disappearance of Minoan civilization, the second stage of political organization we find in Greece arose on the Peloponnesian Peninsula: Mycenaean civilization (1500–1100 BC), which left impressive ruins of fortified palaces located at Mycenae, Tiryns and even the Acropolis of Athens, in addition to lavish royal tombs. Mycenaean society was strongly structured around a king (*wanax*), assisted by a commanding general (*lawagetas*) and numerous officers, officials and scribes, as well as by priests whose influence was considerable. Below this civil service clerical and class surrounding the monarch stood the free people (*demos*), composed of peasants and artisans. Finally there was an underclass of slaves, essentially prisoners of war, though little is known about their situation. Among all these kingdoms that of Mycenae stood out, its prestige inspiring Homer's *Iliad*, in which the Mycenaean king Agamemnon managed to unite the Achaeans to lead a military expedition against the city of Troy (destroyed in the year 1180 BC, according to tradition, though the archeological evidence discovered by Schliemann suggests 1230 BC).[20]

The Mycenaean palaces were destroyed around the year 1200 BC by a new invading force of Indo-European origin: the Dorians. The settlement of the Indo-Europeans in Hellas constitutes a milestone in Greek political and legal history because their high degree of social organization made the emergence of the polis possible.

From the twelfth to the tenth centuries BC Greece went through a kind of dark age from a political point of view, one which saw the Greeks living in small communities which turned to autarchy as a result of the severe depopulation following the collapse of the great monarchies of the archaic period.[21] This trend was aggravated by the start of a major migration to Asia Minor, where the Greeks founded their first colonies during this period.

### *2.4.2 From the Homeric Kingdoms to the Appearance of the Polis (800–500 BC)*

This state of things shifted beginning during the era of Homer (circa eighth century BC) when more structured political communities appeared, which in the historiography are called the "Homeric kingdoms" because they were contemporaneous with the author of *The Iliad* and *The Odyssey*.[22] Said communities were organized under the authority of nobles possessing large amounts of land and livestock. These were the *aristoi* (the best), who imposed their hegemony upon the people (*demos*). Power, however, was formally wielded on their behalf by a king (*basileus*), who

[20] For an overview of the social and political organization in the Aegean Bronze Age: Nakassis et al. (2012).

[21] As Meier (2011, 52) suggests, though we know very little about the early "dark" centuries of Greek history (1200–800) because whatever light archaeological finds can shed on the period is dim and flickering, it seems that the Greeks of this period lived in small, loosely organized units, cultivating pastures and farming, practicing hunting and fishing, and, a bit later, turning to piracy and sea trade.

[22] Mark (2005, 17) uses the term "chiefdom" to describe Greek society during the Homeric period, between the Dark Ages and the early Archaic Period. According to anthropologists, a "chiefdom" is a transitional phase between tribal and state societies, and is roughly defined as a regional, social, and economic organization that is centrally controlled.

usually fulfilled primarily religious functions. It was within this framework that the model of the polis would be forged.[23]

### 2.4.3 *Synoecism as the Basis of the Polis*

The formation of the polis was initially a result of the economic transformation which Greek society underwent as agriculture took precedence over livestock and metallurgy with iron expanded, triggering an increase in trade with the East that allowed the Greeks to move beyond autarchy.

Economic growth led to a phenomenon of concentrated settlement whereby small communities were gradually integrated into larger cities. This was *synoecism*.[24] Thanks to it, the Homeric kingdoms' lack of structure would gradually give way to a model of judicial/public organization in which power resided in three specific social bodies: the popular assembly, bringing together all the citizens; a restricted council, dominated by the landowning aristocracy; and, finally, a group of magistrates[25] who, after gradually shedding their traditional religious role, came to exercise increasingly "political" power.

The Greeks were so aware that synoecism was the basis of their prosperity that Athens' most important festival was its Panathenaea, which celebrated the union of

---

[23] Nevertheless, as Sealey (2003, 22) points out, within the polis early in the Archaic Period public authority was weak and political institutions were rudimentary, as society was agrarian and each community was made up of people of different status: wealthy landowners, small farmers, landless laborers, artisans and, in some places, serfs bound to the land under locally varying conditions. The strong unit was still the family, a powerful group which attracted a range of different dependents, who sought protection or economic help from it, in turn contributing to its strength. A man of modest standing directed his political loyalty not towards other men of the same class but towards his protector. Hence, the divisions in political society were vertical, not horizontal; conflicts were usually not between disparate classes but between groups, each of which was led by a prominent family or a few prominent families and commanded many humbler followers.

[24] The term "synoecism" (from the Greek *συνοικισμός*, *synoikismós*, literally "cohabitation") alludes to a historical process through which a series of isolated populations united to mutually protect each other, forming a city-state. It is the process by which democracy in the ancient Greek world originated and developed. The word itself means "dwelling together" or "to unite together under one capital city". Synœcism stands in contrast to the Greek word *διοικισμος* (*dioikismos*). Synoecism, which led to the creation of the polises in ancient Greece, was a gradual process featuring different modalities, though in the classic Hellenic source it tended to arise from foundational acts carried out by a legendary hero, such as Theseus in the cases of Athens. Also being founded in this way were Rhodes (411–407 BC) and Megalopolis (368–367 BC). According to Valdés Guía (2001, 134) Athenian synoecism started around the ninth century BC with an essentially defensive purpose, but it was closely succeeded by an administrative synoecism. It was, nevertheless, not until the beginning of the seventh century that the process ended with the reforms of Theseus, which led to the institutionalization of the Aeropagus as an assembly where all the nobles of the region of Attica convened.

[25] Though the English term "magistrate" today usually refers to a judge, in this context magistrates were high-ranking government officers with legislative, executive and judicial functions.

all the villages of Attica into the great polis protected by the goddess Pallas Athena—so crucial that it was depicted on the frieze of nothing less than the Parthenon itself, the most emblematic building of Athens' Acropolis, holding the city's treasure.[26]

### 2.4.4 *The Consolidation of the Polis and Its Aristocratic Model: The Case of Sparta*

The story of the Lacedaemonian or Spartan polis began in the ninth century BC, shortly after the Dorian conquest. It was then when the incorporation (synoecism) of four peoples came about, the legendary lawmaker Lykourgos furnishing them with a peculiar form of social organization, one of an oligarchic and military nature in which all citizens stood at the service of the state.[27] Spartan society was strictly divided into three classes. At the top were the Spartans (*Σπαρτιᾶται*, *Spartiâtai*), who attained this status at 20 years of age, and who from the fifth century BC saw themselves as *homoioi* (*peers*, or "equals",), descendants of the conquering Dorians, and the only full-fledged citizens.[28] They were the *políteuma o* civic body of the State. From an early age the Spartans received military training, or *agōgḗ*,[29] and were subjected to a regime of harsh discipline preparing them to live in community (*sissitia*).[30] Each of them lived off of rental income, inheriting the

[26] The integration, or synoecism, of Attica did not come about, however, until the outbreak of the Punic War, which concluded with the defeat of the Persians at Marathon (490), Salamis (480) and Plataea (479). As Valdés Guía (2001, 149) points out, through the Panathenaea the Athenians celebrated at the beginning of the year the victory of the gods over the giants and the restoration of internal order against external dangers. This is why the celebration was originally of a military and naval nature.

[27] Traditionally the "Spartan mirage" relied on the "Lykourgos legend" which held that Sparta was the paradigm of a state owing all its institutions to the legislative enactments of a single lawgiver, and the theory of the mixed constitution contending that the most stable and, hence, ideal form of state was either one which combined ingredients from each of the basic constitutional types (monarchy, aristocracy/oligarchy, democracy) into a harmonious whole, or one in which the different elements functioning as checks and balances (Cartledge 2002, 113).

[28] The conditions for assuming this status included pure Spartan blood, completion of the *agoge* and participation in the *syssitia*, to which they had to contribute. Their economic bases were *the klaroi* (*kleros*), which were worked by helots (Welwei 2010, 537). About the leading military role of the *Spartiates*, see Hodkinson (1993, 146–176).

[29] (*ἀγωγή*; *agōgḗ*). *Agoge* meant education and instruction in general and philosophical literature except in Sparta, where was also the technical term for the comprehensive, centrally organized military education and socialization of its citizens (Cartledge 2002, 151).

[30] In fact, the term *sissitia* or *phiditia* (*τὰ συσσίτια/ta syssítia*), was related to a common meal for men and young people in social or religious groups, where they joined to common mess halls (*syssition*) (Flaubert 1982, 54). From their 20s to their 60s, young men were part of the army, integrating themselves in the denominated "common table" (*syssítia*, *andreîa* or *phidítia*), established by Lykourgos to avoid luxury, favor temperance, and as a way to provide a sense of

usufruct of part of the city's lands, which were public and non-transferable. These lands lay outside the city of Sparta and were not tilled by the usufruct holders, but by the lower social class of helots (*ilotas*).

The Helots (the Greek classical authors considered the term an indication of servitude, and its mean "to be captured, to be made prisoner"), were the descendants of the Achaeans, subjugated after the Dorian occupation. They were dependent peasants without civil rights, although they were able, at times, to serve in the army. Their main task, though, was to work the land of the "equals", to whom they paid to rent which was fixed by law. They were subject to *criptias*, ritual ceremonies which functioned as initiation rites for adolescent Spartans, and during which the helots were indiscriminately massacred. Between the Spartans and the helots was the middle class of *perieques* or *perioikoi*, who engaged in trade or produced crafted goods (Hall 2000), and were often made to serve with the Spartan army. They were free citizens living in cities surrounding the Spartan territory who were admitted into the army, but had no political rights in Sparta, and did not form part of the assembly. Intermediary between the helots and the *perioikoi* were the liberated helots or *neodamōdeis*. There were foreigners (*xenoi*) in Spartan society, too, but these were not as welcome as in other city-states, and those that did live in Sparta were sometimes forcibly expelled by their hosts (Cartwright 2013).

Heading up the state were two kings for life, one from an old Achaean family (the original inhabitants, before the Dorian invasion), and another being a descendant of the latter ethnic group. Power, however, was exercised by a Council of Elders (*gerousia*) composed of 28 members belonging to the aristocracy and, beginning in the mid eighth century BC, an executive panel of five judges, or *ephors* (*vigilants*), elected every year by the Assembly (or *Apella*).[31]

Thanks to this rigid social organization Sparta managed to become the dominant military power in the Peloponnese.[32] This was demonstrated in the famous Persian Wars battle in which the Spartan King Leonidas squared off against the Persians with just 300 "equals" at the Pass of Thermopylae (480 BC).

---

community among the Spartans. Also, promoted education (through the *Agoge*) and common values or norms of conduct. Additionally, the *syssitia* was central to the extraordinary security against foreign invasion provided by the Spartan military, with such security being a crucial public good (Bueno de Mesquita 2005, 269–270). There were approximately 15 men in each *syssition*. Such communal food—in Plutarch's words, a "school of sanity"—gathered around a table the companions, who had to contribute to every month with certain foods and wine (Rivera Sabatés 2007, 263). If whoever was not able to comply with this requirement was immediately expelled from the group and would lose his rights as a citizen, turning from *Spartiátai* to *hypomeiones* (*oí ὑπομείονες/hoi hypomeíones*, literally: the "lesser ones"). They were a group of Spartans—socially stigmatized—with limited political rights, due to several reasons: the lack of contribution to the *syssítia*, the failure to complete the *agōgḗ*, cowardice in battle… (Meier 2011, 537).

[31] For an overview of Spartan political institutions during the classic period see Mossé (2008, 126–136).

[32] That tough training resulted in a professional hoplite army capable of relatively sophisticated battle maneuvers and made them feared throughout Greece, a fact perhaps evidenced by Sparta's notable lack of fortifications for most of its history (Cartwright 2013).

### 2.4.5 *The People Versus the Aristocrats: The Origin of the "Democratic" System*

In ancient Greek politics the aristocrats at first imposed themselves on the common people, made up of peasants and artisans, by controlling the council and the magistracies. The members of the oligarchy, nonetheless, had to govern with some degree of consensus because the people were represented in the assembly. In fact, conflict between these social groups was brewing, as by the late eighth century BC the poet Hesiod had denounced the aristocracy's insolent pride and rapacity.

Several factors led to social crisis. Firstly, the fact that the aristocrats saw themselves forced to raise an army to defend the city (hoplite reform),[33] which led them to appeal to the peasants who had sufficient means to pay for their own military equipment. In return, however, the new soldiers called for the right to participate in public life. Meanwhile, the small rural peasantry, whose economic condition was becoming increasingly more precarious, repeatedly rebelled. Finally, one must also take into account the emergence of money as an instrument of exchange, as it favored social mobility in a polis previously controlled by the landowners.

All of these factors led to a serious social crisis which shook the foundations of the aristocratic model (Meier 2011, 180–195). The early Greek legislators sought to resolve the crisis through the enactment of written rules replacing the old common law. However, the efforts of Solon in Athens and Lycurgus in Sparta did not solve the problem for very long, and violence broke out again, at least until the small farmers, artisans and merchants, oppressed by the nobles, managed to seize power and turn in it over to a tyrant,[34] Peisistratus, who ruled Athens in the second half of the sixth century BC.

Tyranny would spark brutal reactions which decimated the ranks of the nobility or, in the best cases, ended with the aristocrats exiled and their lands confiscated. This process occurred in cities such as Corinth, Sicyon, Megara and, somewhat belatedly, in Athens itself. In all of them the tyrant sought to consolidate his power through a policy of accumulating prestige through the backing and execution of large public works (aqueducts, fountains, public buildings, ornate temples) and the patronage of artists and poets. In some cities tyrannical rule tended to become hereditary. This happened in Sicyon, where Orthagoras' line constituted a genuine dynasty that remained in power for a century; and in Corinth, where that of

[33] A hoplite was a citizen-soldier of the Ancient Greek city-states. Hoplites were primarily armed as spear-men and fought in a phalanx formation. As Echeverría Rey (2008, 252) points out, traditionally the constitution of armies was considered the "founding act" defining a polis, which were originally conceived as communities of citizens whose main function was military defense. The people of the polis could also be artisans, merchants and farmers, but they were essentially soldiers.

[34] In Greek the word "tyrant" generally was applied to rulers who had no hereditary or legal claim to rule in their cities. The rule of a tyrant was not exercised through any office, but was based on an informal and extralegal preeminence in the affairs of the city. It was not necessarily oppressive or unpopular, as some of the early tyrants were remembered for the benefits they had provided, and some seem to have risen up as champions of popular movements (Sealey 2003, 39).

Cypselus ruled for 70 years. It is also the case of Athens, where Pisistratus was succeeded by his children Hippias and Hipparcos.

Little by little, however, the tyrannies disappeared, generally because their policies were directed at solving the very social crises which had favored their establishment. In some cases aristocrats did regain power, as in Corinth, though they would exercise it with greater restraint. In Athens, meanwhile, a new political system appeared: democracy, wherein all citizens participated in public life.

### *2.4.6 Athens' Cleisthenes, History's First "Democrat"*

In Athens the tyrannical regime initially imposed by Pisistratus was abruptly toppled in 510 by the intervention of Sparta. Hipparchus, Pisistratus' son, was killed, which sparked another civil war lasting 2 years until the intervention of Cleisthenes, a figure who also rose to power thanks to pressure exerted by the masses. Cleisthenes did not, however, restore tyranny, but founded a new political system: democracy.

To do this, in the year 508 he managed for the assembly, made up of all the citizens of Athens (*ἐκκλησία*, *ecclesia*) to enact a series of measures promoting social harmony. Among these were: curbing the aristocrats' power; putting an end to the influence exercised by the *phratria* and clans; the institutionalization of the tribes (the entire population was divided into ten territorial tribes, which became the basis of the electoral system); and the cession to the popular assembly of all the power which these family groups held. The essential development was that, after Cleisthenes, power was exercised by all the citizens of Athens, regardless of their social origins,[35] a shift made possible by the establishment of a great number of civic organizations whose members succeeded each other in a short space of time, allowing for rapid rotation. The key body was the Council of 500 (*bulé*), elected annually and consisting of ten 50-member commissions—one per tribe—which rotated in power over the course of the year. The citizens who were to exercise judicial functions were chosen by lot. Also appointed was a magistrate for each tribe.[36]

Finally, Cleisthenes created a specific control mechanism to prevent tyranny: ostracism, through which the Athenian people could vote to exile a person for a period of 10 years in a ceremony during which they wrote his name on shards of

---

[35] As Mossé (2008, 22) points out, the originality of Cleisthenes' reforms lay in their destruction of the former system of organization, based on essentially fictitious family ties, and their replacement by a "geometrical" and geographical organization, doing away with the traditionally aristocratic structures of the city and creating the conditions for genuine political democracy.

[36] As González Ochoa (2004, 28) has observed, the essence of Athenian democracy rested upon the fact that there were no professional politicians, as the Athenians believed that the political knowledge belonged to the community and that governing decisions should be made after being publically discussed.

pottery (*ostraka*). In this way public pressure could remove the power-hungry from political life at any time.

### *2.4.7 Pericles' Athens*

Through the application of ostracism the people expelled the leaders of the different parties, bringing an end to the fighting and allowing the Athenian polis to enjoy an era of political stability between 487 and 461 BC. This paved the way for Athens' greatest era. In 461, the *Areopagus*, the council in which the old aristocracy remained ensconced, was stripped of its remaining prerogatives, and in that same year Pericles would appear on the political scene, to be re-elected as general (*strategos*) continuously for a period of 30 years, a time during which he consolidated democracy by allowing all, even the poorest, access to public office by paying their compensation from public coffers, thereby ending the wealthy's domination of political offices.[37] The three decades of Pericles mark the pinnacle of Athenian classicism, whose quintessential expressions include the most famous monuments on the Acropolis (the *Parthenon*, *Erechtheion*, *Propylaea*) and the tragedies of Aeschylus, Sophocles and Euripides, timeless symbols of Ancient Greece.

## 2.5 The Drawbacks of the Polis Model

The polis as the first model of a "state" society in western history was not, however, a perfect one. In fact, it was saddled by a major geographical disadvantage, as it was only able to govern and administrate the relatively small area of the city.

The Greek polises sometimes united into coalitions, but they never managed to establish an organized model which would make territorial expansion possible. When a population increase rendered the economic survival of its inhabitants impossible, the polis organized expeditions to found colonies elsewhere. This settlement, however, did not form part of the founding polis, but became an independent city-state (Meier 2011, 146–149).

[37] Thucydides (460–395), in his *History of the Peloponnesian War*, wrote that the apogee of Athens relied initially on Themistocles and Pericles. From an institutional perspective, however, Pericles was more decisive, as he remained in politics longer, sustaining the empire which Themistocles had founded militarily. Exiled by the Athenians, Themistocles defected to the Persian king. It was, thus, Pericles who continued his policies of collective expense and collective action, and fulfilled Themistocles' imperial objectives (Foster 2010, 130–131).

### 2.5.1 *The Division of Hellas*

Coalitions of polises were forged, of course, though these were of an *ad hoc* nature. Thus did the Greeks unite against the threat of the Persian invasion (the Persian Wars). After the victory against the Persians, however, each polis went back to defending its own interests.

Athens launched an imperialist policy championed by Themistocles, an ambitious character who would end up being exiled in an official act of ostracism, but not before he managed for Athens to become a military power, heading up a federation bringing together most of the cities on the Cyclades: the Delian League (an island located in the geographical center of the archipelago), a volunteer association of a military nature which became mandatory when the Athenians, after forbidding the allies from leaving the League, transferred the federal treasury from Delos to Athens itself.

Pericles died in 429 BC, but not before delivering his famous Funeral Oration for the first victims of the Peloponnesian Wars (431–404 BC). In this clash between Greeks, two leagues of cities, led by Athens and Sparta squared off. Sparta would ultimately win the war, with Athens surrendering in 404 BC, ephemerally marking the end of democracy upon the provisional restoration of the oligarchic regime (The Tyranny of the Thirty) following Alcibiades' victory.

Athens was subjugated by the Spartans until they, in turn, were defeated at the Battle of Leuctra (371) by the army of the city-state Thebes, led by two great generals (*strategos*): Epaminondas and Pelopidas. The battle featured a decisive role played by the famous "Sacred Band of Thebes" composed of an elite 300 hoplites. It was their strategy upon which Alexander the Great would model his invincible Macedonian phalanx.[38] Although Theban hegemony would last only 10 years (until the death of Epaminondas in 362), Sparta would never again be a major power, after the Romans occupied the city in 146 BC.

### 2.5.2 *Attempts to Improve Upon the Polis Model*

The polises tended towards separation and, though there were some attempts at union, they were symbolic and ephemeral. Among the cooperative efforts were the Olympic Games.[39] Institutionalized in the year 776 BC, they constituted one of the

[38] For an overview of Theban hegemony see Sealey (2003, 423–437).

[39] As Golden (1998, 4) observes, the idea that the Games fostered unity among the Greeks is an old cliché; Lysias, in the early fourth century, already told his audience at Olympia that Heracles founded the festival in the hope of encouraging mutual amity among the Greeks. The reality, of course, is that such amity was forged at the expense of other ties, as the athletic exercises and competition at the Olympics set the Greeks apart from their neighbors, with all non-Greeks (*barbaroi*) excluded.

rare occasions on which all the Greek cities gathered peacefully to compete in athletic events. Initially imbued with a religious dimension, they soon served to augment the prestige and fame of the victors' home cities. In fact, they would become so prestigious that in ancient Greece time came to be measured with reference to the Olympics.[40]

The other attempt to unite all the Greeks appeared in northern Greece, in Macedonia, beginning with the reign of Philip II (359–336 BC), who was able to establish a dynasty, subduing nobles and lesser kings as he created an all-powerful military monarchy. Philip built a modern polis, issued high-quality coins and established an excellent government administration, all leading to an era of splendid artistic and cultural development, including the work of Aristotle. He was, above all, a great military leader who, after dominating northern Greece, occupied Thessaly and the sanctuary at Delphi, and conquered the Greek cities of the south. His feats were met with resistance and rejection by the democratic polises, including Athens, where Demosthenes vehemently repudiated Macedonian policy in his famous *Philippics*. The Macedonians defeated the Athenians at Chaeronea (338 BC) but, intelligently, did not impose a tyranny, but rather respected the Greek principle of civil liberty. Instead of presenting himself as the king of Greece, he invited cities to join together in a Pan-Hellenic league, ruled from Corinth. The league—joined by all the polises but Sparta—was commanded by the king of Macedonia, its objective being to organize a joint expedition against the Persian Empire.[41]

Though Philip was assassinated in 336, his son, Alexander the Great, continued his policy in the most brilliant fashion. Once he had wiped out the Theban

[40] As Spivey (2004, xx) points out, the astonishing fact about Olympia's Pan-Hellenic Games is that not only were they held every 4 years for an uninterrupted span of nearly 1,200 years, but the events remained more or less unaltered during that time. "All things are in flux" said the Greek philosopher Herakleitos, but in terms of what athletes were expected to do Olympia was like an island of stable and established rules of conduct, a sanctuary whose very conservatism preserved its enduring *kudos* (acclaim for exceptional achievement) and renown throughout the Mediterranean.

[41] This was absolutely in the Macedonian political tradition. As Lemprière (2001, 12–13) points out, the Macedonian state consisted of two parts: the elected king, exercising constitutional powers which had evolved over three centuries, and the assembly of men serving or having served in the king's forces (as opposed to the local militia). Alexander did well as he was constantly marching, talking and fighting in the company of his soldiers, and accepted their freedom of speech at the assembly. In return they honored and venerated him both for his own qualities and as the representative of the only family which in their opinion had a right to rule. Macedonia was a free society. Firstly, there was no trace of the slave class on which the Greek city-sates rested. Secondly, there was no hereditary aristocracy, as long before Alexander's father Philip became king the tribal system had been replaced by town-citizenships. In Upper Macedonia there had been separate kingdoms and tribal aristocracies, but Philip had deliberately dismantled the apparatus of kingship and dispersed any local groups by transplanting populations, fusing old and new in his city foundation and creating a unified field army of men drawn from Lower Macedonia and Upper Macedonia alike.

resistance, in the space of 11 years Alexander would occupy the entire Persian Empire, reaching as far as India, thanks to his forging of an extremely effective army. Alexander wished to establish a synthesis of the Greek and Persian worlds; though he founded a dozen Greek cities bearing his name, at the end of his life he sought to become a Near Eastern-style monarch, which sparked resentment among many Greeks. His early death (323 BC) prevented the consolidation of his empire, which fragmented into a series of monarchies led by his generals (the Diadochi),[42] such as that of the Ptolemies in Egypt or the Seleucids in Asia Minor. They all end up being conquered by Rome during the second century BC.

## TIMELINE

### Origin of the Earth

| | |
|---|---|
| 4.6 billion years ago | Formation of the Earth. |
| 2.0 | Earliest plant species. |
| 570 million years ago | First vertebrates. |
| 300 | Reptiles appear. |
| 230 | First mammals. |
| 150 | Birds. |
| 65 | Primates. |
| 4 | First hominids. |

### The Appearance of Man

| | |
|---|---|
| 4 million years ago | First remains of *Australopithecus afarensis.* |
| 2,500,000 | *Australopithecus africanus.* |
| 2,000,000 | *Homo habilis.* |
| 1,000,000 | *Homo erectus.* |
| 500,000 | *Archaic Homo sapiens.* |

[42] The Diadochi (plural of the Latin *Diadochus*, from *Diadokhoi*: successors) were the rival successors of Alexander the Great, and the Wars of the Diadochi broke out after Alexander's death. They started a 40-year clash after Alexander's death and ended carving up his vast empire. Nevertheless, as Waterfield (2011, x) has stressed, the early Hellenistic period was no comedown after the conquests of Alexander, and certainly not a period of decline and disintegration. It is true that Alexander had left things in a mess, with no guaranteed succession, no administration in place suitable for such an enormous empire, and huge untamed areas both bordering and within his territory. And yet, far from disintegration, his successors were able to consolidate, in many ways, the conqueror's gains. Their equal ambitions, however, meant that consolidation inevitably led to the breakup of the Empire and the foundation of lesser empires and kingdoms. In any case, it is clear that Greek culture spread and became dominant all over the Mediterranean thanks to the Diadochi, without whom the spread of Macedonian culture would have been impossible, as there is no civilization without structure.

| | |
|---|---|
| 150,000 | *Homo neanderthalensis* (extinct approx. 32,000 years ago). |
| 125,000 | First remains of *Homo sapiens sapiens*. |
| 30,000 | Cro-Magnon man. |

### Prehistory

| | |
|---|---|
| 20,000 years | First figurative representations. |
| 10,000 | The first races exhibit their features. |
| 9,000–5,000 | Mesolithic. |
| 8,000 | First signs of agriculture. |
| 4,500 | Beginning of the Neolithic. |
| 2,500 | Beginning of the Bronze Age. |
| 1,000 | Beginning of the Iron Age. |

### The Great Near Eastern Civilizations

### Indus Valley

| | |
|---|---|
| 2500–1500 BC | Harappa and Mohenjo-Daro civilizations |
| 1700–1100 | The Rig Veda is written. |
| 563–483 | The life of the Buddha. |
| 1000 AD | The Vedas are recorded. |

### Egypt

| | |
|---|---|
| 3200 BC | The appearance of hieroglyphic writings. |
| 2770–2400 | Old Kingdom |
| 2600 | First Pyramid of Giza. |
| 1785–1570 | Middle Kingdom |
| 1750 | Hittite Invasion. |
| 1570–1070 | New Kingdom (Golden Age) |
| 1550 | The Egyptian Empire extends to the Euphrates. |
| 1390 | The Temple at Luxor's age of splendor. |
| 1372 | Amenhotep IV (1289–1235) undertakes religious reform (Akhenaten). |
| 1298 | Reign of Ramses II (1289–1235); successful campaigns against the Hittites and construction of Abu-Simbel. |
| 1070–332 | Period of decline |
| 700 | Assyrian invasion (until 650 BC). |
| 525 | Beginning of Persian rule (until 340 BC). |
| 332–30 | Hellenistic Egypt |

| | |
|---|---|
| 332 | Alexander the Great conquers Egypt |
| 305 | Ptolemy, one of the Diadochi, becomes the first Hellenistic King of Egypt (Ptolemaic Dynasty). |
| 47 | Beginning of Cleopatra's reign (47–30 BC). |
| 30 | Egypt becomes a Roman province. |

**Mesopotamia**

| | |
|---|---|
| 3100 BC | Appearance of cuneiform writing. |
| 2900–2500 | Rise of the Sumerian cities (dynastic period). |
| 2400 | Akkadian Empire (King Sargon) |
| 2100–600 | Sumer under the domination of the Assyrians, Babylonians and Hittites. |
| 1770 | Code of Hammurabi, King of Babylon. |
| 605–562 | Reign of Nebuchadnezzar in Babylon. |
| 558–528 | Reign of Cyrus the Great of Persia. |
| 529–323 | The Persian Empire reaches its greatest dimensions. |
| 485–465 | Reign of Xerxes I (Thermopylae, 480). |

**China**

| | |
|---|---|
| 3000 BC | Beginning of Neolithic period. |
| 2200–1766 | Hsia Dynasty. |
| 2000 | First pictographic writing. |
| 1700–1122 | Shang Dynasty (major advanced in bronze work techniques). |
| 1000–256 | Chou Dynasty. |
| 605–520 | Life of Lao-Tse, the founder of Taoism. |
| 551–479 | Life of Confucius. |
| 223–206 | Hegemony of the Tsin princes (from whom "China" takes its name). |
| 214 | The Great Wall is finished. |

**Greece**

*Pre-Hellenic Cultures*

| | |
|---|---|
| 3200 BC | Beginnings of Cycladic culture. |
| 2000 | First cities in Crete. |
| 1750–1500 | Height of Minoan civilization. |
| 1580–1400 | Supremacy of Knossos (Minoan) Crete. |
| 1500–1200 | Mycenaean civilization. |

| | |
|---|---|
| 1230 | Conquest and destruction of Troy. |
| 1200 | The Dorian (Indo-Europeans). |

*Hellenic Stage*

| | |
|---|---|
| 776 | Foundation of the Olympic Games. |
| 750 | First Greek colonies outside Greece. |
| 750–675 | Colonization of Sicily Sicilia (Magna Graecia). |
| 650 | Foundation of Byzantium by the Greeks of Megara. |
| 600 | The Phocian Greeks found Massalia (Marseille). |
| 560 | The Greeks reach Egypt (foundation of Naucratis). |
| 535 | The Battle of Alalia (Corsica). |
| *ca.* 720 | Writing of the Homeric poems. |
| *ca.* 690 | Birth of Hesiod. |
| 594 | Solon, Athenian lawgiver. |
| 561 | The Athenian tyrant Pisistratus (also in 556 and 542). |
| 508 | Cleisthenes founds a democratic regime in Athens. |
| 490 | First Medic War (Marathon). |
| 480 | Start of the Second Medic War (Thermopylae). |
| 479 | Greek naval victory over the Persians at Salamis. |
| 461–429 | Government of Pericles (495–429) in Athens. |
| 460–451 | First Peloponnesian War. |
| 457 | Hegemony of Athens in central Greece. |
| 448 | Foundation of the Athenian Empire. |
| 446 | Signing of the Thirty Years' Peace between Athens and Sparta. |
| 431 | Beginning of the Second Peloponnesian War. |
| 429 | Death of Pericles. |
| 405 | Decisive Spartan naval victory at Aigos Potamós. |
| 404 | Surrender of Athens. End of the Peloponnesian Wars. |
| 401 | Anabasis, or The March of the 10,000 (Xenophon). |

*Hellenistic Stage*

| | |
|---|---|
| 399 | Trial and execution of Socrates. |
| 371 | Sparta is defeated by Thebes (Battle of Leuctra). |
| 359–336 | Reign of Philip of Macedon. |
| 338 | All Greece brought under the king of Macedonia. |
| 336–323 | Reign of Alexander the Great. |
| 334 | Annexation of Ionia. |
| 333 | Incorporation of Phoenicia. |
| 332 | Conquest of Syria and Egypt. Founding of Alexandria. |

| | |
|---|---|
| 331 | Alexander the Great enters Babylon (decline of the Persian Empire). |
| 329 | Annexation of Eastern Iran. |
| 327–325 | Macedonian campaign in India. |
| 323 | Alexander the Great dies at age 33. |
| 323–279 | Clashes between the Diadochi (Seleucos, Ptolemy, Antigonus). |
| 149–148 | Rome annexes Greece. |

### The Origins of Carthage

| | |
|---|---|
| 1550 BC | First apogee of Tyre. |
| 1300 | Appearance of the 22-letter alphabet, adopted by the peoples of the Western Mediterranean, replacing cuneiform script. |
| 1100 | Invasion of the Sea Peoples Tyre becomes independent of Egypt. |
| 814 | Founding of Carthage by the Tyrians. |
| 573 | After the capture of Tyre by the Babylonians, Carthage becomes independent. |

## References


Anthony, D. W. (2007). *The horse, the wheel and language: How bronze-age riders from the Eurasian steppes shaped the modern world.* Princeton, NJ: Princeton University Press.

Auel, J. M. (2011). *The clan of the cave bear* (1st ed., 1980). New York: Bantam Books.

Bellwood, P. (2005). *First farmers: The origins of agricultural societies.* Oxford: Blackwell.

Bocquet-Appel, J.-P. (2008). Explaining the neolithic demographic transition. In J.-P. Bocquet-Appel & O. Bar-Yosef (Eds.), *The neolithic demographic transition and its consequences* (pp. 35–56). New York: Springer.

Bueno de Mesquita, B. (2005). The shift for public to private goods in Sparta. In B. Bueno de Mesquita (Ed.), *The logic of political survival* (pp. 173–179). Cambridge, MA: The MIT Press.

Cartledge, P. (2002). *Sparta and Lakonia: A regional history, 1300–362 BC* (2nd ed.). New York: Routledge.

Cartwright, M. (2013). Sparta. In *Ancient history encyclopedia.* Available via World Wide Web. http://www.ancient.eu.com/sparta/. Accessed 30 Sept 2013.

Crawford, H. (2004). *Summer and the Sumerians* (2nd ed.). Cambridge, UK: Cambridge University Press.

Dumont, L. (1980). *Homo Hierarchicus: The caste system and its implications.* Chicago: University of Chicago.

Echeverría Rey, F. (2008). La ciudadanía como participación militar. In *Ciudadanos, campesinos y soldados: El nacimiento de la "pólis" griega y la teoría de la "revolución hoplita"* (pp. 252–258). Madrid: Consejo Superior de Investigaciones Científicas.

Fagan, B. M. (2010). *Cro-Magnon: How the Ice Age gave birth to the first modern humans.* New York: Bloomsbury.

Faulkner, R. O. (2004). *The ancient Egyptian coffin texts* (3 Vols.). Warminster: Aris and Phillips.

Flaubert, G. (1982). *The letters of Gustave Flaubert: 1830–1857.* Cambridge, MA: Harvard University Press.

Fortson, B. W., IV. (2010). *Indo-European language and culture. An introduction* (2nd ed., pp. 19–24). Oxford: Blackwell.
Foster, E. (2010). *Thucydides, Pericles, and Periclean imperialism*. Cambridge, UK: Cambridge University Press.
Fustel de Coulanges, N. D. (2001). *The ancient city: A study on the religion, laws, ands institutions of Greece and Rome*. Kitchener, ON: Batoche Books. (Based on 1st French edition Paris: Hachette 1864.).
Golden, M. (1998). *Sport and society in ancient Greece*. Cambridge, MA: Cambridge University Press.
González Ochoa, C. E. (2004). *La polis. Ensayo sobre el concepto de ciudad en Grecia Antigua*. Mexico, D.F.: Universidad Nacional Autónoma de México.
Hall, J. M. (2000). Sparta, Lakedaimon and the nature of Perioikic dependency. In P. Flensted-Jensen (Ed.), *Further studies in the ancient Greek polis* (pp. 57–72). Stuttgart: Steiner.
Hodkinson, S. (1993). Warfare, wealth and the crisis of Spartiate society. In J. Rich & G. Shipley (Eds.), *War and society in the Greek world* (pp. 146–176). London: Routledge.
Lemprière, N. G. (2001). *A history of Macedonia: 336–167 BC*. Oxford: Oxford University Press.
Mark, S. E. (2005). Society, economics and trade. In *Homeric seafaring* (pp. 17–24). College Station, TX: Texas A&M University Press.
Meier, C. (2011). *A culture of freedom: Ancient Greece and the origins of Europe*. Oxford: Oxford University Press.
Mercer, S. A. B. (Ed.). (1952). *The pyramid texts*. New York: Longmans, Green & Co.
Momigliano, A. (2012). The ancient city of Fustel de Coulanges. In *Essays in ancient and modern historiography* (pp. 325–344). Chicago: The University of Chicago Press.
Morgan, L. H. (2003). *Ancient society*. Tucson, AZ/New York: The University of Arizona Press/ Henry Holt & Co. (Photographic reproduction of the 1878 ed.).
Moses, D. N. (2009). *The promise of progress. The life and work of Lewis Henry Morgan*. Columbia, MO: University of Missouri Press.
Mossé, C. (2008). *Les institutions grecques à l'époque classique* (7th ed.). Paris: Armand Colin.
Nakassis, D., Galaty, M. L., & Parkinson, W. A. (2012). Society and culture. In E. H. Cline (Ed.), *The Oxford handbook of the Bronze Age Aegean* (pp. 239–305). New York: Oxford University Press.
Piggott, J. R. (1997). *The emergence of Japanese kingship*. Stanford, CA: Stanford University Press.
Pollock, S. (1999). *Ancient Mesopotamia: The Eden that never was*. Cambridge, UK: Cambridge University Press.
Postgate, J. N. (1996). *Early Mesopotamia. Society and economy at the dawn of history*. London: Routledge (Reprint).
Rivera Sabatés, V. (2007). Noticias sobre el matrimonio en la antigua Esparta. *Foro, Nueva época*, (6), 257–268.
Routledge, C. (1997). Temple as the center in Ancient Egyptian urbanism. In Walter E. et al. (eds), *Aspects of urbanism in antiquity. From Mesopotamia to Crete*. Sheffield, England: Sheffield Academic Press, pp. 221–235.
Sealey, R. (2003). *A history of the Greek City States 700-338 B.C.* Berkeley: University of California Press.
Service, E. R. (1975). *Origins of the state and civilization. The process of cultural evolution*. New York: Norton Company.
Smith, H. S. (1972). Society and settlement in ancient Egypt. In P. J. Ucko, R. Tringham, & G. W. Dimbleby (Eds.), *Man, settlement and urbanism: Proceedings of a meeting of the research seminar in archaeology and related subjects held at the Institute of Archaeology* (pp. 705–719). London: Duckworth.
Spivey, N. J. (2004). *The ancient Olympics*. Oxford: Oxford University Press.
Valdés Guía, M. (2001). El proceso de sinecismo del Ática: cultos, mitos y rituales en la 'primera polis' de Atenas. *Gerión, 19*, 127–197.

Van Norden, B. W. (2002). Introduction. In B. W. Van Norden (Ed.), *Confucius and the analects: News essays* (pp. 3–38). Oxford: Oxford University Press.
Waterfield, R. (2011). *Dividing the spoils: The war for Alexander the Great's empire*. Oxford: Oxford University Press.
Welwei, K.-W. (2010). The Peloponnesian war and its aftermath. In K. H. Kinzl (Ed.), *A companion to the classical Greek world* (pp. 526–542). Chichester, UK: Wiley.
Wright, R. P. (2010). *The ancient Indus: Urbanism, economy, and society. Case studies in early societies*. Cambridge, MA: Cambridge University Press.

## Further Reading

Anson, E. M., & Alonso Troncoso, V. (2013). *After Alexander: The rime of the Diadochi (323–281 BC)*. London: Oxbow Books.
Anthony, D. W. (1991). The archaeology of Indo-European origins. *Journal of Indo-European Studies, 19*, 193–222.
Barber, R. L. N. (1987). *The Cyclades in the Bronze Age*. Iowa City: University of Iowa Press.
Barnes, G. (2010). *State formation in Japan: Emergence of a 4th-century ruling elite*. London: Routledge.
Bryce, T. (2012). *The Routledge handbook of the peoples and places of ancient Western Asia: The near east from the early Bronze Age to the fall of the Persian Empire*. London: Routledge.
Budge, E. A. W. (2013). *A history of Egypt from the end of the Neolithic Period to the death of Cleopatra VII B.C. 30* (2 Vols.). London: Routledge.
Charpin, D. (2012). *Hammurabi of Babylon*. London: Tauris.
Cheshire, K. (2009). *Alexander the great*. Cambridge, UK: Cambridge University Press.
Code of Hammurabi. (2005). *The complete code of Hammurabi*. München: Lincom Europa.
Cohen, M. N. (1977). *The food crisis in prehistory: Overpopulation and the origins of agriculture*. New Haven and London: Yale University Press.
Coomaraswamy, A. K. (2007). *Los Vedas: ensayos de traducción y exégesis*. Madrid: Sanz & Torres.
De Souza, P. (2003). *The Greek and Persian wars: 499–386 BC*. New York: Routledge.
Demand, N. H. (1990). *Urban relocation in Archaic and classical Greece: Flight and consolidation*. Bristol: Bristol Classical.
Durkheim, É. (2001). *The elementary forms of the religious life*. Oxford: Oxford University Press.
Finlayson, C. (2004). *Neanderthals and modern humans: An ecological and evolutionary perspective*. Cambridge, UK: Cambridge University Press.
Finlayson, C. (2011). *The humans who went extinct: Why Neanderthals died out and we survived*. Oxford: Oxford University Press.
Fortson, B. W., IV. (2010). *Indo-European language and culture. An introduction* (2nd ed., pp. 19–24). Oxford: Blackwell.
Francotte, H. (1967). *La polis grecque: recherches sur la formation et l'organisation des cités, des ligues et des confédérations dans la Grèce ancienne*. New York: Johnson Reprint Corporations.
Glassner, J.-J. (2003). *The invention of cuneiform: Writing in Sumer*. Baltimore, MD: Johns Hopkins University Press.
Grainger, J. D. (2007). *Alexander the great failure: The collapse of the Macedonian empire*. London: Hambledon Continuum.
Herodotus. (2003). *On the war for Greek freedom: Selections from the histories*. Indianapolis: Hackett Pub. Co.
Kirk, G. S. (1964). *The Homeric poems as history*. Cambridge, UK: Cambridge University Press.

Kriwaczek, P. (2012). *Babylon: Mesopotamia and the birth of civilization*. New York: Thomas Dunne Books.
Kumar, Y. (2013). *Indus Valley Civilization and the Vedic period: A historical account*. New Delhi: Swastik Publications.
Leick, G. (2010). *The Babylonian world*. New York: Taylor & Francis.
Levi-Strauss, C. (1971). *Les structures élémentaires de la parenté* (1947) (English version: *The elementary structures of kinship*). Boston: Beacon Press.
Li, J. (1996). *Chinese civilization in the making: 1766–221 BC*. New York: St. Martin's Press.
Loewe, M., & Shaughnessy, E. L. (Eds.). (1999). *The Cambridge history of ancient China: From the origins of civilization to 221 BC*. Cambridge, UK: Cambridge University Press.
Martin, P. (1997). *The Chrysanthemum Throne: A history of the emperors of Japan*. Honolulu: University of Hawaii Press.
Mellars, P. (1996). *The Neanderthal legacy: An archaeological perspective from Western Europe*. Princeton, NJ: Princeton University Press.
Moggi, M. (1976). *Sinecismi interstatali greci. 1. Dalle origini al 338 a C*. Paisa: Marlin.
Morris, I. M. (2004). *Leonidas: Hero of Thermopylae*. New York: Rosen Central.
Nagarajan, K. V. (2011). The code of Hammurabi: An economic interpretation. *International Journal of Business & Social Science, 2*(8), 108–117.
Nooten, B., & Holland, G. (1994). *Rig Veda, a metrically restored text*. Cambridge, MA: Department of Sanskrit and Indian Studies, Harvard University Press.
Possehl, G. L. (2006). *The Indus Civilization: A contemporary perspective* (3rd printing). New Delhi: Vistaar.
Shaughnessy, E. L. (1997). *Before Confucius: Studies in the creation of the Chinese classics*. Albany, NY: State University of New York Press.
Shelmerdine, C. W. (Ed.). (2008). *The Cambridge companion to the Aegean Bronze Age*. Cambridge, MA: Cambridge University Press.
Slingerland, E. (2006). *The essential analects: Selected passages with traditional commentary*. Indianapolis: Hackett.
Stoneman, R. (2008). *Alexander the great: A life in legend*. New Haven, CN: Yale University Press.
Swain, S. (1996). *Hellenism and empire: Language, classicism, and power in the Greek world, AD 50–250*. Oxford: Clarendon.
Thomas, C. G. (2007). *Alexander the great in his world*. Malden, MA: Blackwell.
Tracy, S. V. (2009). *Pericles: A sourcebook and reader*. Berkeley: University of California Press.
van Andel, T., & Runnels, C. (1995). The earliest farmers in Europe. *Antiquity, 69*, 481–500.
van de Mieroop, M. (1999). *Cuneiform texts and the writing of history*. London: Routledge.
van de Mieroop, M. (2007). *King Hammurabi of Babylon: A biography*. Malden, MA: Blackwell.
Warry, J. G. (2005). *Alexander, 334–323 BC: Conquest of the Persian Empire*. Westport, CT: Praeger.
Xenophon, H. (2010). *The landmark Arrian: The campaigns of Alexander = Anabasis Alexandrou*. New York: Pantheon Books.
Xu, Y. (2007). *Confucius: A philosopher for the Ages*. Beijing: China Intercontinental Press.
Young, D. C. (2004). *A brief history of the Olympic Games*. Oxford: Blackwell.

# Chapter 3
# The Roman Political Model: From *Res Publica* to *Imperium*

In the infancy of societies, the leading men in the republic form the constitution; afterwards the constitution forms the leading men in the republic.—Montesquieu.[1]

## Contents


3.1 Rome and the Origins of the Western State ..... 37
3.1.1 The Flaw of the Polis Model ..... 37
3.1.2 The Roman *Civitas*: An Expanding Polis ..... 38
3.2 The Indo-European Origins of Roman Society and the Structural Basis for the Roman *Civitas* ..... 40
3.2.1 *Gentilitates*, *Curiae* and *Tribus* ..... 40
3.2.2 The Popular Assemblies as the Basis of the Roman Republic ..... 41
3.3 An Aristocratic *Polis* ..... 42
3.3.1 The Leadership of the Roman Aristocracy ..... 42
3.3.2 A Political Constitution Designed to Prevent Dictatorship ..... 45
3.4 From Republic to Empire ..... 46
3.4.1 An Extraordinary Territorial Expansion ..... 46
3.4.2 From Conquest to Stable Dominion ..... 46
3.4.3 The Consequences of Rome's Territorial Expansion: The Crisis of the Republican System ..... 48
3.5 Augustus and the Singular Reestablishment of the Republican Regime ..... 49
3.5.1 The First Citizen ..... 49
3.5.2 From Diarchy to Monarchy: The Birth of the Roman Empire ..... 51
3.6 The Era of the Dominate, or the Triumph of Imperial Absolutism ..... 53
3.6.1 From *Imperator* to *Dominus* ..... 54
3.6.2 The Disappearance of the Republican System ..... 54
3.7 An *Avant La Lettre* State ..... 56
3.8 Roman Citizenship: History's First "Nationality"? ..... 57
References ..... 61


[1] *Reflections on the causes of the grandeur and declension of the Romans* (1734) (Montesquieu 2005, 27).



B. Aguilera-Barchet, *A History of Western Public Law*,
DOI 10.1007/978-3-319-11803-1_3

## 3.1 Rome and the Origins of the Western State

Rome is the model and the political and legal touchstone for most Western countries (Wagner 2011). If this is patent in the sphere of private law, it is no less evident in the area of public law. Rome is, in short, the first great state in Western history (Arnason 2011), a manifest source of inspiration for many great intellectuals, including the likes of Montesquieu, Gibbon and Ferrero in their reflections on political society, the leaders of the American Revolution[2] and even for Napoleon,[3] one of the architects of the contemporary Western state.

### *3.1.1 The Flaw of the Polis Model*

If the history of the state and of public law in the West undeniably traces its roots to Rome (Johnston 1997), it is because the Greek polis lacked the institutional capacity to organize and control an extensive territory because of the fact that its system of government and judicial structure were totally ineffective beyond the walls of the city. Thus, when the population swelled and economic resources were insufficient, the surplus of citizens abandoned their polis to found another in a new location so as to avert social conflict (Davies 1993, 24)[4] Greece was a relatively

[2] As Edwards (1999, 9) points out, it is interesting that the American revolutionaries rebelling against British rule, also envisioned themselves as Romans, founders of new republican institutions. George Washington lacked a classical education (unlike many of the leaders of the American Revolution) but claimed his favorite play was Addison's *Cato* (1713)—a story celebrating the self-sacrifice of a Roman republican hero. America's first president, recalled from his rustic retreat, was himself hailed as a new Cincinnatus. The rule of a foreign monarch overturned, the political classes of the 13 states declared they would follow the examples of Brutus, founder of the Roman republic, and Publius Valerius Publicola, another semi-mythical figure crediting with initiating key elements in Rome's constitution. Their new balanced constitution, they claimed, was based on that of ancient Rome as described by Cicero and Polybius. Rome could offer Americans dissatisfied with British rule an alternative model of government sanctioned by centuries of tradition—and associated with the classical education which remained a prime marker of elite status in the American states.

[3] Napoleon built columns commemorating his victories, such as those currently found in the center of the *Place Vendôme* en París, which is an imitation of Trajan's Column in Rome, built triumphal arches (the *Arc de Triomphe du Carrousel* and that at the *Place de l'Étoile*) like the victorious Roman generals did, used Roman judicial terms (e.g. senate, consulate, first consul) reminiscent of the *princeps*, the first citizen of Rome during the times of the Empire under Augustus (Huet 1999). He himself appeared dressed as a Roman emperor, with a laurel leaf, and his troops carried imperial eagles—although these were, along with bees, symbols of the Merovingian monarchy. The roman fashion even extended to women's hairstyles and clothing, with the "Imperial" style evoking Roman ways. Napoleon was born in Corsica in 1769, the year in which Louis XV annexed the island into France, and his rise to fame was a result of his brilliant Italian Campaign (1796–1797). As a good Italian, Napoleon was fascinated by Rome and its history.

[4] Colonization, by now a traditional way out, continued intermittently in the fifth century and after, while the argument that overseas expansion at the expense of Persia was a morally acceptable and socially preferable alternative to revolution was repeatedly formulated by Isokrates in the fourth century.

poor territory, spurring many Greeks to emigrate to found colonies along the coasts of the Mediterranean which, once founded, did not maintain political ties with the Greek polis from which they had proceeded.[5] Rather, they became independent for all intents and purposes and, as a result of the anarchic structure of interstate relations and the fact that international law among the polises was barely existent (Eckstein 2006, 37). Ancient Greece was never to become a great, unified state. This was to precipitate its decline at the close of the fourth century BC, in the wake of Alexander's fleeting empire.[6]

### *3.1.2 The Roman* Civitas*: An Expanding Polis*

The Roman Empire constitutes a towering landmark in the history of public law in the West because it successfully adapted its model of political and judicial organization to the circumstances of its expansion. Unlike the Greek polis, as the Romans conquered territories, they managed to incorporate them in a stable and structured manner (Briscoe 1986) into a powerful constitutional framework, centered around the Roman *civitas*, although this process of integration was gradual and fraught with difficulties.

It was progressive because it was successively based on provincial divisions and the development of an urban network that was the mark of a strong and self-assured imperial power reflecting the willingness of Western peoples to cooperate in the process of their own Romanization (Drinkwater 2002, 351), and which fast spread

[5] As Malkin (1987, 1) points out, during the Archaic and Classical periods (eighth to fourth centuries BC) Greek colonization meant the establishment of independent city-states in relatively distant territories. It is precisely the creation of a new polis which distinguishes this colonization from earlier forms of migration (e.g. the "Ionian migration") on the one hand, and from later colonization during the Hellenistic period, in which the polis lost its political independence and colonization was conducted inside areas already controlled by Hellenistic rulers, on the other.

[6] Before Rome, international politics in the Mediterranean was a "multipolar anarchy" (Eckstein 2006, 1). That is, a world containing a plurality of powerful states, contending with each other for hegemony, within a situation where international law was minimal and, in any case, unenforceable. None of these powerful states ever achieved lasting hegemony around the shores of the great sea: not Persia, not Athens, not Sparta, not Tarentum, not Syracuse, not Carthage. Alexander III the Great, the fearsome king of Macedon, might have established a permanent political entity encompassing the entire Mediterranean, but the conqueror of Asia died prematurely, and the empire he had created almost immediately fell apart. During the chaos that followed Alexander's death, several of his generals founded great territorial states themselves, Macedonian dynasties with worldwide ambitions, each in bitter competition for power with the others: the Ptolemaic regime based in Egypt; the Seleucids based in Syria and Mesopotamia; the Antigonids based in Macedonia. However, despite the brilliance, vigor, and ruthlessness of the founders—and that of some of their successors—none of these monarchies was ever able to establish universal domination. Eventually, however, one state would come to enjoy predominance throughout the Mediterranean world: the Republic of Rome.

throughout the territories dominated by Rome, with newly founded colonies and native cities transformed into *urbes* organized according to Roman models (*municipia*).[7] The integration of the new territories, however, was difficult, because it carried with it a profound shift in the system of government and administration of the Roman state; the crisis which the Roman version of the polis, the Republic, would suffer in the first century BC was a direct consequence of the Romans' spectacular territorial expansion.[8] This was the period of what have been called the "civil wars", lasting for almost 60 years in the first century BC, between the dictatorship under Sulla (86 BC) culminating in Augustus's victory over Mark Anthony at Actium (31 BC).

Augustus is a key figure in Western history for having laid down the foundations of a new form of political organization which continues to inspire and shape our Western societies. Having brought peace to a turbulent time, he is commemorated every summer in August, the month named for him. Despite wielding uncontested authority over Rome, Augustus was clever enough not to abolish the Roman Republic, seeking instead to protect it in his capacity as "first citizen" (*princeps*). However, Augustus would, in fact, end up paving the way for a monarchical regime as the era's rulers would become emperors in the second century, and absolute lords during the age of the Dominate, following the reforms introduced by Diocletian (284–305 AD).

## 3.2 The Indo-European Origins of Roman Society and the Structural Basis for the Roman *Civitas*

The Romans were a people of Indo-European origin (Dumézil 1996), as were the Greeks and a good number of peoples who inhabited modern-day Europe in the pre-Roman era. Thus, from the outset Roman society was structured in the same way as that of other peoples of the same sociolinguistic group, according to a *gentilicium*-based family scheme featuring a pyramidal structure.[9]

---

[7] Unlike the Greek model of colonization, Rome is often seen to have had a uniform view of her relationship to her colonies. As Bispham (2006, 74) has been pointed out, modern interpretations of literary evidence for colonization, both Greek and Roman, have tended to underscore their "statist" activity designed to meet public aims. Roman colonies are seen as having strong ties to the mother city, unlike what happened with Greek colonization. For the differences between *coloniae* and *municipia* see Abott and Johnson (2012, 3–9). For an overview of the history of cities and urban life in the Western provinces of the Roman Empire between 30 BC and 250 AD, see Edmonson (2010, 250–280).

[8] On the debate over whether territorial gain and annexation and consequent provincial stabilization was determined by an empire-wide perspective, or if Roman expansion and the consolidation of political control were related to regional circumstances and opportunities, and, therefore, the result of ad-hoc decision making, see Fulford (1992, 294–305).

[9] For an overview of Indo-European aspects of Roman culture, Cornell (1995, 77–79).

### *3.2.1* Gentilitates, Curiae *and* Tribus

It seems that the family structure based on the *gens*, also constituted the basis of Roman society. The Latin word *gens* referred to a group of families who had, initially, lived in a area, in a given territory, and considered themselves descendants of a common ancestor, therefore, sharing certain religious practices. It is possible that at an early stage, the *gens* was an independent political unit. In fact, some vestiges of this primitive condition still persisted in the early days of the Republic; we know through Titus Livius that in the years 479–477 NC the *gens Fabia*, with the Roman Senate's permission, led a war against the Etruscan city of Veii (Livius 2002, 2.48).[10] It is impossible, however, to know what the *gens*' internal organization was like during this period. Chances are that the *gens* was a loose association of families who chose a common chief, only to deal with emergencies. Whatever their original nature, what is certain is that in the Republican period membership in the *gens* was mainly devoid of legal significance, although there were exceptions. Thus, any person belonging to a *gens* had a right to seize the property of any other member who died without heirs. Membership in a *gens* also entitled one to claim the guardianship of a minor or unfit individual belonging to the same *gens* who did not have relatives.

In Rome, as in other Indo-European societies, it appears that the different *gentes* ended up comprising higher social groups, the best known being the *curiae* and *tribus*.[11] Unfortunately, little is known of these *tribus* of the archaic period, except that they were nothing at all like the local "*tribus*" which would appear later (Taylor 1960). Subsequently, however, in historical times, it is undeniable that said Indo-European structure was reflected in Roman society, specifically in two Republican assemblies: the *comitia curiata* and the *comitia tributa*.

---

[10] [...] the Fabian family addressed the senate; the consul, in the name of the whole, speaking in this manner:—"Conscript fathers, ye know that the Veientian War requires rather an established, than a strong force, on the frontiers: let your care be directed to other wars: commit to the Fabii that against the Veientians. We pledge ourselves, that the majesty of the Roman name shall be safe on that side: that war, as the particular province of our family, we propose to wage at our own private expense. The state shall not be troubled either for men or money to support it".

[11] According to the tradition the legendary founder of the Roman Republic, Servius Tulius (578–535 BC), organized the Roman people into 30 curiae, 10 for each one of the tribes. Each curia was, in turn, made up of 10 *gentilitates*. In this legend the only element that is certainly true is that of the curiae, associations with certain religious functions which also functioned as electoral units when it came time to elect members of the first Roman legislative assemblies. On the reforms of Servius Tullius see Cornell (1995, 173–197).

### 3.2.2 *The Popular Assemblies as the Basis of the Roman Republic*

Ancient peoples did not conceive the idea of delegating the power to pass laws and decide on policy issues to assemblies of elected representatives. Basically, this was because it was unnecessary, as the political and legal system was manageable directly by the citizens gathered in assemblies within the territorial limits of the old city-state. Rome was no exception. Since the beginning of the Republic, the people of Rome exercised their power through assemblies.

The first Roman assemblies were the *comitia*, electoral meetings and acts held on a mandatory basis, on specific days, by order of the magistrate in power (Wolff 1995, 39–42). All adult male citizens could participate in them. The oldest were the *comitia curiata*,[12] although these were not the most important, as they would be followed by the *comitia centuriata*,[13] clearly of military origin, which had more

[12] The *comitia curiata* were the oldest assemblies, made up of the curiae to which originally only the patricians belonged, though the plebeians gained access to them at a relatively early stage. The *comitia curiata* probably existed in the royal period, though it is impossible to determine what their role was at that time. The essential function of the *comitia curiata* was to authorize—or perhaps only to bear witness to—the acts of individual citizens. However, they were also the organizational channel through which the Roman people could choose and accept the decisions of the magistrates, elected or designated by the kings, or by the citizens. Because they could refuse to accept said proclamations, some historians have argued that, in a way, they represented a form of popular participation in the government. Under the Republic they lost their political importance, eclipsed by the succeeding assemblies: the *comitia centuriata*, the *comitia tributa* and the *concilia plebis* (Millar 1989). The progressive fading of the role played by the *comitia curiata* is evident when it is observed that the 30 traditional curiae in the period of the late Republic appeared represented not by said assembly, but by 30 *lictors*. Nevertheless, during the first phase of the Empire these curiae assemblies were charged with the bestowal of *imperium* upon the elected magistrates—though this function would end up being reduced to a mere formality and probably never constituted anything more than a symbolic act of homage and submission to the new military leader.

[13] The organization of the Roman people into *centurias* (centuries) is another of the reform measures attributed to Servio Tulio, though it is most likely that they did not appear until well into the Republican era. The *centuria* was also the basic unit of the Roman army, which was made up of a variable number of legions (from two to six). Each legion was divided into cohorts, maniples and centuries. Each cohort was made up of three maniples and each maniple of two centuries. After the reform carried out by Gaius Marius (157–186 BC), each legion featured ten cohorts and six centuries. The century was composed of 100 men, of which 80 were soldiers and 20 auxiliary personnel. They were led by a foot soldier promoted to centurion. The century was divided, in turn, into *contubernii* (singular, *contubernius*), groups of eight men who shared a tent. However, the century was the fundamental unit, camping, marching and fighting as an autonomous unit in terms of arms and supplies, which afforded the legion greater agility on the move. The rise of the *comitia centuriata* came in response to the idea that the *populus romanus* and its army were one and the same, hence its markedly military nature. Because military service was obligatory in the Roman republic for all citizens fit for active service, without social distinction, with patricians and plebeians sharing the same status in the military sphere, the *comitia centuriata* admitted the plebeians as member of the political community from the outset—which certainly explains why they would end up being the most important plebeian assemblies of the Republican era. The organization of the *comitia centuriata* followed, in general terms, the military organization of the Roman people, though it did not mirror exactly the army itself. The *comitia centuriata* could only be convened by consuls, and their function was to elect the high-ranking magistrates (consuls, praetors and censors) and vote on the laws which the consuls brought before them. The *comitia centuriata* were, therefore, without any doubt the most important plebeian assemblies of the Republican era.

relevant functions. At the end of the Republic appeared the *comitia tributa*,[14] whose essential purview was to appoint the representatives who would ultimately form the most important Roman popular assemblies: the plebeian councils (*concilia plebis*), which undertook intensive legislative work during the Republican period,[15] especially in the field of private law.

Upon this Indo-European basis Rome developed, between the sixth century BC and the first century AD, its own version of the *polis*: the Republic.

## 3.3 An Aristocratic *Polis*

### *3.3.1 The Leadership of the Roman Aristocracy*

The Roman Republic was originally a city-state, akin to the Greek *polis*. It did not opt, though, for the democratic Athenian model, but for an aristocratic one. The great protagonist of Rome's extraordinary success, at least until the Third Punic War (146 BC) was the Roman aristocracy. And not because it produced famous

[14] Also in the era of Servius Tullius, Roman territory was ostensibly divided into local districts called *tribus* (*tribes*). Initially there would be only four, and it is not clear whether they encompassed the city or also its outlying areas. It is most likely that they were confined to the urban perimeter, if we consider that a few years later, after the establishment of the Republic, 17 new tribes were added, this time proceeding exclusively from rural districts. More tribes were gradually added to Rome's territorial organization until, circa 241 BC, there were 31 rural tribes and 4 urban ones, a figure which would end up being final. To be the member of a tribe, it was originally necessary to own property in the tribe's area. Each citizen could only belong to one tribe, even if he owned land in various tribal districts. Over time the strictly territorial criteria dissolved and membership in a given tribe became hereditary. In 312 BC the tribes began to admit citizens without the need for them to satisfy the landowning requirement. However, these new members who did not own land were limited to the four urban tribes, as were free men and those who had been newly granted Roman citizenship, evidencing the fact that this organizational scheme was driven by a political intention to favor the preeminence of the landowners. The plebeian assembly or *comitia tributa* elected the lower-ranking magistrates. It also boasted legislative functions, though these overlapped with those of the *comitia centuriata*. The *comitia tributa* were, above all, the institution before which the magistrates serving beneath the consuls could present laws to garner popular support for them. In any case, the *comitia tributa* were not of great importance. The "tribal" organization itself, however, was key, as within it the members of the plebeian assemblies were elected, and the *concilia plebis* did play an essential legislative role during the Republican era, especially in the area of private law.

[15] As Williamson (2005, 4) points out, for centuries, Romans reached decisions about law relating to the most critical aspects of their society in a public process concluded in the voting assemblies of Rome. The first reported lawmaking occasion came in the first year of the Republic, 509, when First Consul M. Iunius Brutus, in accordance with a Senate decree, carried a measure to exile all members of the Tarquin clan. The last reported occasion of certain date occurred during the reign of emperor Nerva 96–98, when the emperor himself presented a bill assigning land to poor Romans; in between lay roughly 600 years and 750 unevenly reported public laws, proposals or ultimately enacted laws.

figures, but because, as a whole, it managed to maintain, until the middle of the second century BC, both a quiet dignity (*gravitas*), an unusually high ethical standard, great political wisdom, and a boundless tenacity in the face of adversity (Wolff 1995, 26). These factors, along with its selfless patriotism, justified and assured its undisputed leadership.

Rome was never a democracy, either in the Athenian sense or in the current one. The transition from monarchy to republic probably meant no more than the transfer of power from a king for life to some annually elected magistrates (Nicholas 1992, 3–4), a change aimed at assuaging the patricians' fears of tyrannical governments, like that of Tarquinius Superbus.[16] This transformation, however, did not alter the original thrust of Rome's legal-public organization, nor did the plebeian movement which, though allowing this social class access to the conduct of public affairs, and leading to the emergence of institutions aimed at countering the oppression by patrician magistrates, did not alter the essentially aristocratic character of the government.[17] Although in theory the Republican magistracies were open to any citizen, in practice they remained in the hands of a few families, both patrician and plebeian, whose members all had in common their status as landowners and holders of wealth, which permitted them the luxury of being able to dedicate most of their time to public affairs, without compensation. In this way, the patricians' main activity involved their "public careers" (*cursus honorum*), which assured them significant social prestige, thereby practically monopolizing public offices (Lintott 2002, 144–146). Only on rare occasions did a *homus novus* from outside this closed circle manage to reach the highest magistracies. Cicero, belonging to the equestrian order,[18] is undoubtedly the best-known exception.

---

[16] On the departure of the Etruscans and the origins of Roman republic (Cornell 1995, 223–225).

[17] Hölkeskamp (1993, 18–19), believes that the element of popular participation should be viewed in the context of a new understanding of aristocratic structures, resulting from the so-called Struggle of the Orders. This emergence of a new "political class" was shaped by three factors: (1) Rome's conquest of Italy, her territorial expansion, and political and military ascendancy (2) the importance of *imperium* and the magistracies with *imperium* and, correspondingly, the importance of the rules according to which magistrates and commanders were selected, and the standards they had to meet (3) the functional role of the Senate as the institutional centre of the system.

[18] The equestrian class was so named because originally, it was made up of those citizens wealthy enough to fight on horseback who initially did not mix with the old patrician nobility. The Law of the Twelve Tables (450 BC), specifically Table XI, expressly prohibited marriages between patricians and plebeians. Cicero (106–43 BC), who did not belong to the patrician class, considered this law wicked and inhuman, but during his time the law was not applied. As Treggiari (2007, 6), points out, in first century BC society, despite some political and economic conflicts of interest, patricians and *equites* were actually closely intertwined. Not only did their families intermarry but some *equites* were as rich as or richer than members of the senatorial class. There were, however, some differences. For instance, a man whose brother had advanced from the equestrian order to the Senate would still count as a new man if he too attempted to enter the Senate. So would one whose mother was descended from a long line of consuls, but whose father was an *eques* and descended from *equites*.

This lack of democracy was particularly evident in the assemblies. Arising in theory to facilitate the people of Rome's access to public affairs, in reality they were not democratically composed. The popular assemblies elected magistrates and passed laws, but their power was limited and they were organized in such a way that they could be controlled by the wealthy as they voted in blocks, and there was no difference in their value, regardless of how many people each actually represented (Taylor 1990, 1). Political power, then, was concentrated in the hands of the landholding class, which virtually monopolized the seats in the Senate, which is why it came to be also known as the senatorial class.[19]

The people only acquired a measure of political influence during the turbulent years of the civil war which shook Rome in the first century BC, though even then the masses were mere instruments in the hands of demagogues—usually aristocrats—who manipulated them (Lintott 2002, 199–207). In addition, this "revolutionary" period led to the establishment of a new form of monarchical government which seized from the masses their last remnants of power, and gradually undermined the aristocracy while increasing the burgeoning bureaucracy surrounding the emperor.

### 3.3.2 A Political Constitution Designed to Prevent Dictatorship

Although the Roman Republic was never democratic, it *was* designed to prevent power from falling into the hands of just one person. As a remedy against an individual amassing excessive political influence, the Athenians had invented

[19] In Republican Rome, citizens were divided into classes based on their levels of income, in such a way that the wealthy were assured preeminence (Lintott 2002, 49–60). The connection with military organization rested essentially, on the fact that each citizen was required to equip himself with certain military gear which varied in complexity, depending upon what he could afford. The *comitia centuriata* were made up of five classes. The first, that of the wealthiest citizens, was made up of 80 centuries. The second, third and fourth featured 20 centuries each, and the fifth, 30 centuries. There were, in addition, 18 centuries of members of the equestrian class: those well-off enough to be able to fight on horseback, who in the *comitia*, occupied a place above that of the first class; four centuries of artisans and musicians; and a mixed century, featuring all those who did not satisfy the requisites to form part of any of the preceding ones. In total, the *comitia centuriata* were initially composed of 193 centuries. The supremacy of the privileged classes was somewhat undermined when, from 214 to 218 BC, each of the "tribes" was granted a century of "seniors" and "juniors". This raised the number of centuries to 350, and left each one of the classes with the same number of centuries. Despite this the rich continued to be favored, as they retained 18 equestrian centuries. In addition, the traditional landowning class continued to enjoy privileges, as under the new arrangement only 40 of the recently-created centuries corresponded to the city of Rome and, among them, only eight to the first class, with all the rest being assigned to the patrician aristocracy (Wolff 1995, 40–41).

collegial bodies that were replenished annually, along with the procedure of ostracism. The Romans arrived at the same result through an ingenious system of checks and balances between the various powers, which earned them the admiration of the great Greek historian Polybius (200–118 BC),[20] a friend to Scipio Aemilianus, the conqueror of Carthage and the most respected Roman statesman of the second century BC. The institutional system of the Roman Republic did not arise in a conscious and planned-out fashion. The virtually unlimited powers wielded by those who held the highest magistracies (*magistrati*)[21] were curbed by control mechanisms, firstly by the very fact that there were several magistrates, who usually pursued careers serving the state (*Cursus honorum*).[22] Secondly, the magistrate post was held only for 1 year, at least in Rome proper. Thirdly, because each magistracy was dual and each official was able to veto the other. Finally, the magistrates were subject to political control exercised by the Senate, the tribunes of the plebeians, and the people themselves through their assemblies, the latter control being most effective, given that the magistrate himself depended on the votes of the assembly to obtain his office.[23] It was, however, more difficult for the assemblies to control the magistrates, as it was more complicated to convoke these bodies. As a result, they proved less effective than the Senate, a stable assembly composed of the city's dignitaries who would ultimately serve as the collective expression of the Republic and an instrument curtailing political protagonism (Lintott 2002, 86–88).

[20] On Polybius's view of the Roman constitution, see Lintott (2002, 16–26).

[21] The magistrates in the Roman Republic were elected officials. To prevent dictatorship by one single man, there were different magistracies dealing with the most important public functions of the state: consuls were the highest magistracy because they exerted executive power, praetors dealt with judicial matters, plebeian tribunes represented the interest of the plebeians, *aediles* were responsible for maintaining public buildings and overseeing public festivities, and *quaestors* dealt with public finances. They were dual, with two magistrates for every magistracy, with the two able to counteract each other by veto, and the term in office was only one year, with no opportunity for reelection, at least in Rome. They could be nominated in provinces as pro-consuls, pro-praetors, etc., which was the only way of extending the magistrates' time in office (Wolff 1995, 27–38). Former magistrates went on to form part of the Senate, the Roman Republic's most influential collegial body.

[22] Talbert (1984, 522), provides a simplified summary of the *cursus honorum* of the senatorial magistracies, which started with the granting of *latus clavus* from the emperor (for those not already members of the senatorial class), followed successively by Vigintivirate (as *tribunes militum*), quaestorship, tribunate, praetorship and, finally, consulship.

[23] As North (1990, 18) states, politics in Rome was, consequently, a function of the degree and type of competition in progress between oligarchic families, groups and individuals. It is simply a fact that the ruling class accepted the arbitration of popular voting, in certain extremely important circumstances, just as they accepted that the power and success of families and individuals should be limited by the rotation of office, regular succession to commands, and so on.

## 3.4 From Republic to Empire

### *3.4.1 An Extraordinary Territorial Expansion*

Rome's subjugation of Italy, which can be considered to have been achieved in the year 265 BC,[24] and its victory over Carthage, culminating in the wars against Hannibal (219–201 BC), made it one of the greatest powers of all Antiquity. After becoming masters of the western half of the Mediterranean, the Romans headed to the East. In a period of 150 years, Rome came to dominate as far as the Euphrates and the Black Sea, with relative ease, and despite the serious internal crises plaguing the Roman state. In this way, Rome ended up taking over the entire Mediterranean basin—which in ancient times meant the entire world.

### *3.4.2 From Conquest to Stable Dominion*

The Romans were successful at occupying these lands because, besides their military power, they had the ability to divide, weaken and conquer their enemies. In the end, Roman rule was based on an extraordinarily varied and complicated system of alliances and situations of dependence, all revolving around the city-state of Rome. The most singular fact of all, however, was not that Rome was able to conquer so much territory, but that it managed to continue to rule it in a stable manner, creating *provinces* and naming governors,[25] and that they did not hesitate to destroy the indigenous political communities they encountered, whose existence posed a threat to their rule; they did not tolerate alliances or pacts between Rome's allies and subjects, assuring in this way that each one of the communities they annexed had legal relationships only with Rome itself, all other connections being barred. The establishment of a progressive administrative network in the provinces,

[24] On the nature of Roman control in Italy and the dynamics of its rising imperialism see Cornell (1995, 364–368).

[25] The Romans, rapidly organized conquered territories into *provinces* (from "*pro-vincere*", literally "to defeat") to consolidate the control of the new territory by the metropolis, the Roman *civitas*. As Burton (2002, 423) observes, although the number of provinces increased during the Principate, especially in the first century, through imperial expansion and, occasionally, through the division of a single geographically large area in two, provinces remained the basic unit for all administration. The Romans arrived in Spain (Hispania), for instance, in 218 BC, to fight the Carthaginians in the Second Punic War. The conflict ended in 201, and by 197 Rome had already created two provinces in the new territory separated by the Ebro river, with *Hispania Citerior* on the west side and *Hispania Ulterior* on the east. On the organization of the first provinces, see Boatwright et al. (2004, 120–122).

consolidated as time elapsed, the control which the metropolis exerted over Rome's provincial dominions (Ando 2010). This is particularly extraordinary when we consider how relatively few administrators were charged with overseeing the territories integrated into the Roman *civitas*.[26]

The resistance of the conquered populations was also mitigated as another operating principle of Rome's imperial policy was to let its subjects, as far as was possible, maintain their religion and customs, in addition to an autonomous administration. This was in large part because, at least initially, the Roman city-state did not have the resources to develop a large-scale bureaucratic apparatus. Thus, Rome sent out a relatively small number of governors and procurators, who essentially saw to the regular collection of taxes and the maintenance of internal order (Burton 2002, 423). In any case, this attitude contributed decisively to making Roman domination less onerous upon the peoples they conquered, and facilitated the acceptance of Roman ways and culture, a process known as "Romanization".[27]

Rome also consolidated its rule through an intelligent policy of reinforcing the Empire's borders and building a network of strategic roads and fortified posts in Italy, during the first republican era and later, at the time of the Principate, in the Empire's frontier provinces. Thanks to all of these circumstances, Rome city-state was able to become an Empire.[28]

### *3.4.3 The Consequences of Rome's Territorial Expansion: The Crisis of the Republican System*

The Roman state model did not evolve from aristocracy towards democracy, as happened in Athens, but from aristocracy to monarchy. This transformation was the result of a gradual process that began at the time of Julius Caesar (100–44 BC), and did not end until the reform of Diocletian (284–311 AD), when the emperors became absolute monarchs (*dominus*). Triggering this transformation were the civil wars (86–31 BC), whose root cause can be traced to a republican system of government

[26] As Burton (2002, 426) indicates, at the height of Roman empire in the mid-second century there were about 150 elite administrators, belonging to the senatorial class to govern an estimated population of 50–60 million; that is, one for every 350,000–400,000 inhabitants, which is very few compared to China in the twelfth century, for example, where there was an elite administrator for every 15,000 people.

[27] As Bispham (2007, 5) points out, the "Romanization" of Italy was something which came as a reflex to the process of conquest and domination, and the need of local elites and masses to adjust, even without direct prompting, to the new circumstances of Rome's hegemony.

[28] For an overview of this process in a comparative perspective, see Raaflaub (2011, 39–66).

and administration, which was not effectively adapted to accommodate Rome's extraordinary territorial expansion.[29]

The most extraordinary aspect of the process described is that the incorporation of new territories into the Roman orbit, not only led the occupied peoples to accept their integration into the Roman model of civilization, but transformed the Roman political constitution itself (Boatwright et al. 2004, 140–145). This occurred because the republican system, designed to govern and administrate the city of Rome, was inapplicable to the massive series of new territories.[30]

This imbalance meant that, little by little, the protagonists of Roman political life ceased to be the magistrates or the assemblies, or even the Senate. Rather, power was increasingly held by the army, and particularly by the great generals, whose prestige, consideration and wealth, depended upon them incorporating new territories. The price to pay for this new state of things was the outbreak of the "civil wars", which raged from 86 BC, with the dictatorship of Sulla, until 31 BC, when Octavian defeated Mark Antony at Actium.[31]

After Octavian's (later to be named "Augustus") victory, however, the Roman public system of law would never be the same, as Rome's new leader was politically adept enough to tailor the Roman constitution to the needs of its burgeoning borders, without provoking a radical rupture with the republican regime (Flaig 2011, 67–84).

The most interesting aspect of Rome's political and legal configuration was not its theoretical formulation, but how it pragmatically adapted to each time and its situation. Rome was initially a *polis*, featuring institutions characteristic of an Indo-European society, though certainly concretized in a *sui generis* manner by the Republic's regime. Later, because of Rome's massive expansion following its victory over Carthage in 209 BC, the republican model was flexible enough to allow for the integration of the new territories conquered. Republican institutions, however, were conceived primarily to govern the territorial scope of the *civitas*, and not to handle such dramatic territorial expansion. This precipitated the crisis of the republican regime in the first century BC, only resolved when Augustus laid the bases of a large centralized state (Raaflaub 2011, 62–66).

---

[29] During this period (200–133 BC), competition centered on the consuls' access to overseas commands, as Roman power expanded in to the East and West. Following this for some decades, it shifted to rival legislative schemes for reform proposed by tribunes and opposed by the majority in the Senate. During Cicero's most active years, the real conflict was between rival leaders (Sulla, Caesar, Antony, Octavian), too rich and powerful to be contained within the system, and exploiting their popularity with voters to build unrivalled power for themselves. After Cicero's lifetime, the final transformation consisted of the ending of all competition and domination by a single family (North 1990, 19).

[30] For an overview of the impact of expansion on the Roman state and society after the end of the Second Punic War, during the crucial period of 201–167 BC, when the first provinces were incorporated into the metropolis, see Feig Vishnia (1996, 161–175).

[31] On the aftermath of the Civil War and its institutional consequences, see Gruen (1995, 449–497).

## 3.5 Augustus and the Singular Reestablishment of the Republican Regime

### *3.5.1 The First Citizen*

Augustus did not dare to impose a regime excessively based on his personage, given the fate of his adoptive father, Julius Caesar, assassinated in 43 BC. Rather, he formally preserved a republican regime and portrayed himself as its protector[32] to prevent the resumption of civil strife.[33] In this way, he did not officially hold power, acting instead as "first citizen" (*princeps*), though this did not keep him from progressively shoring up his personal power, over the course of the 45 years he headed the state, which was willingly accepted by the People of Rome because his reign marked a long period of peace and stability. It is no coincidence that a month was named after him (August), and that the idea of an imperial cult was born, precisely, during this period.[34]

From the point of view of constitutional history, the regime established by Augustus, which historians have termed a "Principate", led to not so much a change in the republican constitutional scheme,[35] as a radical concentration of political power—something that Augustus achieved through his clever exploitation of the possibilities offered by Roman public law.[36] Thus, although in 23 BC, he relinquished the post as Consul he had held permanently since 27 BC, he retained

[32] On January 13th in the year 27 the Senate assembled to hear a proclamation: Caesar's heir resigned all his powers, transferring sovereignty where it belonged, to the Senate and People of Rome. The senators urged him not to abandon the *res publica*, which he had saved and preserved, and the Imperator was persuaded to accept a special position, involving command over Rome's principal military territories lying to both the West and East, to be held for a period of 10 years. Three days later, on the motion of a senior consul, the high chamber voted various honors to be conferred upon the new "Augustus" (Syme 1989, 2).

[33] "After so much civil war, there were hopes for a return from army service to 'life on the land.' After all the devastation, there was a pride in the special qualities of Italy, potentially such a blessed country [. . .]. In 30/29 BC these themes came together in Virgil's marvelous poem, *The Georgics*. The 'best poem by the best poet' combined praise of Italy and country living with tributes (often playful) to the new 'Caesar.' A virtuoso ending blended Greek myths into a new, entrancing whole. As the poem shows, there was hope and also confidence after so much terror. It was up to the new 'Caesar' to harness them, for they underlie what he was to make into a classicizing age". (Lane Fox 2006, 420).

[34] As Fishwick (2004, 2) notes, it was Virgil (70–19 BC), the author of *The Aeneid*, at the behest of Augustus himself, the national epic of ancient Rome meant to embellish the dark origins of Rome; in the prologue of *Georgics III*, the author describes a sacred place where processions converged, a site for horse races, plays and pugilistic contests: the *palaestra*. This site is reminiscent of the palaces of Hellenistic kings, and foreshadows the monumental complex of Augustus which was under construction at the time, in the southwest sector of the Palatine Hill. (The word "Palace" proceeds precisely from "*Palatine*".). On the deification of Augustus, see Taylor (2002, 224–238).

[35] In fact, Augustus believed that he was restoring the Republic (Boatwright et al. 2004, 291).

[36] For an overview of Augustus's reforms of the Roman constitution, see Campbell (2011, 93–119).

his *imperium*,[37] or scope of power, as a proconsul, which a law in this year granted him for a period of 10 years. Thanks to successive renewals, he ended up retaining the position for life (Ferrary 2009). Moreover, shortly before his death, Augustus granted this *imperium*, by way of adoption, to Tiberius (14–37 AD). This proconsular *imperium* not only implied command of the army and, consequently, control of the imperial provinces, but in so far as it was eventually declared *imperium maius*, it also gave the *princeps* authority over the pro-magistrates (*proconsuls*, *propretores*), who governed the senatorial provinces, whose titles became increasingly nominal.

In Rome itself, Augustus assured his permanent supremacy in a more indirect but no less, effective way. After giving up a position as consul, he received *tribunicia potestas* for life (Wirszubski 2004, 50–51), which granted him the rights and powers of the plebeian tribunes, namely: inviolability, the right to veto, to convene the Senate, and to present bills to said tribunes. As this power was also transferred to Tiberius, it became one of the prerogatives which Roman emperors came to hold permanently.

There was, thus, no ostensible alteration of the traditional constitution. The magistracies were formally maintained, and the only new development was the concentration in the hands of Augustus of powers that no single man had ever held in Rome, and which, for the most part, Augustus exercised until the end of his days. Formally, Augustus was nothing more than the *princeps* (first citizen) but, in practice, his authority extended over every area of government. The popular assemblies were not abolished, but their decisions became mere ratifications of the Emperor's wishes. In fact, they began to meet less and less frequently before disappearing late in the first century AD.

The counterweight, supported by Augustus himself, was the swelling influence of the Senate, which came to share power with the *princeps*, especially in the area of legislation, traditionally the purview of the assemblies—leading some legal historians to describe his regime as a "diarchy".[38] At the beginning of the second century AD, the Roman jurist Gaius mentioned in his "Institutions" that, in his era, no one doubted that the Senate's resolutions (*senatus consulta*) had the force of law.[39]

---

[37] In Roman society *imperium* referred to a formal concept of legal authority. A man with *imperium* ("*imperator*") had, in principle, absolute authority to apply the law within the scope of his magistracy, or pro-magistracy, but could be overruled by a magistrate or pro-magistrate having *imperium maius* (a higher degree of imperium). It is worth noting that terms like *empire* and *imperative*, are derived from the term.

[38] It is interesting that, as Talbert (1984, 174) points out, before Augustus, emperors, prior to their accession, had been senators themselves, or members of the senatorial class, and thus appreciated the traditional feeling that it was a vital part of any senator's role to attend the meetings of this body.

[39] "A Decree of the Senate is what the Senate orders and establishes, and, therefore, it obtains the force of law, although this formerly was disputed". -*Senatus consultum est, quod senatus iubet atque constituit*; *idque legis vicem optinet, quamvis* [*de ea re*] *fuerit quaesitum* (Gaius 1904, 1.2.4).

Over time, however, the Senate too ended up merely doing the emperor's bidding.[40]

### 3.5.2 *From Diarchy to Monarchy: The Birth of the Roman Empire*

Augustus had managed to maintain his personal power over the Roman state, but, upon his death, the problem of his succession arose (Boatwright et al. 2004, 295). As the hereditary principle had never taken hold, successors were theoretically designated through the principle of "adoption",[41] though in reality, the keys were the army and Roman people's fears of a return to the chaos caused by the civil wars, during the last years of the Republic. The growing power of the army was evident in the year 69 AD, when, after the death of Nero, four different generals were proclaimed emperors by their troops in various parts of the Empire. This situation, nevertheless, was resolved by one of them, Vespasian, who managed to restore order and good governance by fostering a climate of peace, which was to last more than a century.

In the long term, the constitutional position of the *princeps* resulted in the transformation of the Roman state into a monarchy. The *comitia* were not abolished, but their functions vanished. Popular legislation was supplanted by Senatorial legislation.[42] During the Republican period the Senate was, technically, never more than an advisory body consulted by magistrates, as since Sulla its acceptance and action were required for the execution of its resolutions. The advice

[40] It is very significant that in the *Institutiones* of Justinian, published in 533, four centuries after those of Gaius, a resolution of the Senate became a law decided and enacted by the upper assembly (*a command and ordinance of the Senate*) because: "*When the Roman people became too large to be easily called together in a body for legislative purposes, it seemed reasonable to turn to the Senate instead*" (*senatus consultum est, quod senatus iubet atque constituit nam cum auctus est populus Romanus in eum modum, ut difficile sit in unum eum convocare legis sanciendae causa, aequum visum est senatum vice*) (Justinian 1993, 1.2.5).

[41] In principle, adoption had to be confirmed by the Senate. As Peachin (2010, 144) points out, though the Senate had little say over the naming of the emperors, it was essential for the emperor, once he had been officially proclaimed, that the Senate ratify his position. The only available method of giving a new ruler the sheen of legitimacy was through a law, passed by one of the popular assemblies, like the one given to Vespasianus (Brunt 1977). The problem was that the last of these assemblies was held in 97 CE.

[42] "A resolution of the Senate is a law decided and enacted by the Senate. When the Roman people became too large to be easily called together in a body for legislative purposes, it seemed reasonable to turn to the Senate instead" (*senatus consultum est, quod senatus iubet atque constituit nam cum auctus est populus Romanus in eum modum, ut difficile sit in unum eum convocare legis sanciendae causa, aequum visum est senatum vice*) (Justinian 1993, 1.2.5).

of the Senate, initially lacked the legal authority which could be bestowed by a popular assembly, but as Rome expanded, assemblies faded and the *senatus consulta* gained legislative force almost by default. However, no measure was ever promulgated formally investing the *senatus consulta* with legal authority (Talbert 1984, 432). The Senate's influence would ultimately dwindle, as supreme control passed to the emperor, even in the city of Rome itself. During the second century the Senate's approval of the legislation which the emperor brought before it would become a mere formality. In fact, during the last stage of the Principate, the *senatus consulta* were foregone conclusions, and their importance was limited to the speeches the Emperor gave to the Senate to formally request them.[43] The consuls and the praetors, although in theory retaining the prerogatives of their offices and their *imperium*, eventually became mere administrative implementers of the emperor's will, as well.[44]

In fact, all these important political changes led to the emergence of the huge administrative apparatus necessary to govern the Empire. It is interesting that most of the emperors of the second century, the apex of the Roman Empire, were themselves of provincial birth (Rostovtzeff 1998, 118).[45] Thus, alongside the traditional magistracies new imperial officials appeared during the time of Hadrian (117–138 AD), most of them from the equestrian class, responsible only to the emperor, and whose function was to administer the Empire based on bureaucratic criteria and according to imperial instructions.[46] These new officers not only increasingly eclipsed the traditional magistracies, but gave rise to the emergence of a new financial administration, which depended upon the imperial treasury (*fiscus Caesaris*). This "set of assets" constituted, in principle, the Emperor's private fortune, making him and his administration effectively unaccountable to the Senate. Over time, however, the *fiscus* ended up being considered the authentic "patrimony of the Empire" because, although the government continued to turn to the old republican Treasury (*aerarium*), this came to be of secondary importance (Jones 1950).

---

[43] Nevertheless, as Talbert (1984, 458–459) indicates, the scarcity of the *senatus consulta* preserved make it impossible to know why it was that one emperor decided to settle a matter by constitution, and another through the Senate, especially because legislative policy varied among individual rulers; for instance, while the Julio-Claudians, Hadrian and Marcus Aurelius usually turned to the Senate, other emperors did not.

[44] "A pronouncement of the emperor also has legislative force because, via the Regal Act relating to his sovereign power, the people conferred on him their whole sovereignty and authority" ("*Sed et quod principi placuit, legis habet vigorem, cum lege regia, quae de imperio eius lata est, populus ei et in eum omne suum imperium et potestatem concessit*") (Justinian 1993, 1.2.6).

[45] Some were citizens from Hispania (Trajan and Hadrian), while some descended from Roman citizens settled in Gaul (Antoninus Pius and Marcus Aurelius).

[46] On the increasing responsibilities of high-ranking equestrians in the Imperial administration, see Mennen (2011, 137–155).

## 3.6 The Era of the Dominate, or the Triumph of Imperial Absolutism

The Roman Empire reached its peak in the second century at a time when its dramatic territorial expansion, made sound government and administration difficult.[47] This explains why, beginning in the late second century, Rome began to suffer a series of economic and social crises (Campbell 2011, 195–215) which, from the standpoint of the history of its political constitution, caused the regime to become increasingly monarchical.[48]

From an institutional standpoint the crisis of the third century was resolved by Diocletian, when he augmented the power of the emperor, making him a "*Dominus*", or absolute ruler (Boatwright et al. 2004, 438–444). This brought about the definitive demise of the republican system and an administrative centralization designed to facilitate the Empire's governance.[49]

### *3.6.1 From* Imperator *to* Dominus

The crisis affecting the Roman Empire beginning in the third century, profoundly transformed its legal organization. The emperor was no longer the Republic's protector and *princeps*, but gradually became the sole repository of power. The Republic finally gave way to absolute monarchy. To avoid the disintegration of the Empire the emperors reacted by securing and bolstering their absolute power, and replacing the old magistracies with a huge bureaucratic network utterly dependent upon the emperor.

The last stage of the Roman Empire, in the historiography, is expressively referred to as the "Dominate", so named because under this regime the last vestiges of the republican constitution disappeared and the figure of the emperor was regarded in a new way, shifting from first citizen (*princeps*) to *dominus*, that is: lord and master, an Eastern-style oriental monarch, rarely appearing in public, despite having a large court. He also took on status as a divine ruler; after the formal endorsement of Christianity, the emperor came to be considered a ruler by the grace of God, and came to be exalted through a series of very strict court ceremonies (Rees 2004, 46–56), inspired by the Near Eastern monarchies and which symbolized the people's total submission to his power. Wearing special clothes and a distinctive crown, all visitors were to express obeisance before him.

---

[47] On why the Roman Empire's borders stopped where they did, see Whittaker (1994, 60–97).

[48] On the factors which influenced the transformation of the Emperorship between 193 and 284, see Mennen (2011, 22–39).

[49] For the background to the Third-Century crisis, Ziolkowski (2011, 113–133).

As a sacred figure, even the most important dignitaries were expected to prostrate themselves in his presence.[50]

### *3.6.2 The Disappearance of the Republican System*

The emperor wielded all power, exercising it through a body of officials beholden to him alone. The Senate, lost even the appearance of legislative power, and became little more than the city council of Rome proper (Jones 1990, 329–333). In the other cities of the Empire, the senates also became aristocratic assemblies which, at best, managed to defend the privileges of their class, but generally had little influence on weighty political matters.

Under the Dominate, there continued to be consuls, praetors, quaestors and senators, in both the old and the new Rome (Constantinople). However, the title of consul had been reduced to but an honor, albeit one of great prestige, often adopted by the emperor himself. The year was still named for the two consuls, one of whom was appointed by the emperor of the West, and the other by the emperor of the East. The praetors and quaestors became, however, officials appointed by the emperor. The central government, in any case, fell under the exclusive purview of the emperor and his bureaucratic apparatus, to the point that the court and central administration travelled with the emperor (Liebeschuetz 2002, 457).[51] In the

[50] From Augustus and until the end of the third century BC, there was a *princeps* in Rome, wielding political power, but with the Julio-Claudian Dynasty and, above all, beginning with Diocletian, the first emperor ruling during the early Dominate, there would be a *dominus* ("*dominus et deus*"), meaning lord or master, which lent this period its name. The terminology allows one to appreciate the change in the conception of the leader vis-à-vis the citizens, who come to be viewed as his subjects. He was no longer a "first among equals", as were the senators, but rather an absolute monarch, elevated to a higher level. As of 282 AD, the emperors no longer requested Senatorial ratification, though they retained their quasi-Republican status. They continued to serve as consuls, if only formally, and still claimed *potestas tribunicia*, at least nominally. In reality, however, they remained in power through the support of the army, and their election was normally arranged by their predecessor. This new phase of the Empire was particularly visible in court ceremonies. Diocletian and, above all, Constantine (Elton 2010), introduced a series of rules and practices, modeled on the Persian Court, in order not only to impress their subjects with their imperial majesty and power (which clearly took on divine undertones), but also for their safety.

[51] The court (*comitatus*) consisted of the officials and attendants of the emperor's household (*sacrum cubiculum*), his advisers (*consistorium*), the confidential shorthand writers (*notarii*), who took down the discussions and decisions of the *consistorium*, and could be sent out to see to their enforcement in the provinces; and, finally, the principal officers of state with their office staff. As for much of the fourth century emperors travelled constantly from crisis area to crisis area, and spent longer periods of time in large cities with easy access to borderland areas, the system proved so intolerably inconvenient that by the end of the century, there was a return to permanent capitals as Constantinople in the East and Ravenna or Milan in the West.

exercise of his governmental tasks the emperor was advised by a council (*consistorium*) composed of senior military, civil and ecclesiastical dignitaries.[52]

Local government was also totally structured. At the top, it was administrated by the *praefecti praetorio*, who governed the "prefectures", which were divided into dioceses, governed by "vicars". In turn, the dioceses were divided into provinces headed up by "presidents" (*praesides*). The old provinces were subdivided into smaller territorial units to increase administrative efficiency. The government of this entire territorial structure was assured by a large body of hierarchically organized officials, responsible for their administration, in general, and particularly for tax collection and judicial functions.[53]

## 3.7 An *Avant La Lettre* State

Even though a number contemporary Romanists have written brilliant works on Roman public law, it is clear that the Romans were never conscious of the fact that they were laying the foundations for a new legal model of power. They did not view the state, as we do today, as an abstract authority imposed on individuals (Genet 1990). They were markedly pragmatic and little given to abstraction. Therefore, they identified that power with something concrete: the set of persons forming Roman society.

Initially, the Roman state encompassed the inhabitants of the city (*civitas*) of Rome, or the *Populus Romanus*, according to the expression enshrined in the texts,

[52] As Harries (1999, 36) points out, during the Dominate imperial law was, in fact, more often negotiated than imposed. Its content was determined by precedent, current policy, the state of information available, and pressures from interests groups with access to the consistory. Although laws were announced and were intended to endure "in perpetuity", in practice, they could be, and were, modified in the light and further representations from those who operated the law or were affected by it.

[53] During the era of the Principate, the "praetorial prefect" (*praefectus praetorio*) had been the chief of the *praetoriani*, the members of the imperial guard, headquartered in Rome itself. Although it had always had considerable political power, it was during the time of Septimius Severus (193–211), when this military official became the head of the ordinary and judicial administration of the city of Rome (Mennen 2011, 159–187). The importance of the charge prompted Diocletian (284–313 AD) to grant the title of *praefectus praetorio* to the heads of the four main administrative districts into which the Empire was divided. In the East, two prefectures were created (which included Egypt, the Asian provinces and Thrace) and that of Illiricum (made up of Macedonia, including Greece, and the lands of the Danube), and in the West, there was the prefecture of Italy (comprised of the Italian peninsula and Africa) and the prefecture of Gaul (with the diocese of Brittany, Hispania and Gaul). As Liebeschuetz (2002, 457) points out, though they had lost their military command, praetorial prefects remained responsible for the feeding and supplying of the army and were the superiors of all provincial governors, with great influence over appointments.

at least until late in the Empire's history. The official documents would also cite, along with the people, the Senate of Rome, an assembly made up of the former magistrates and, in general, the city's most eminent citizens, a fact that made it a very influential body. It is significant that in the official name of Rome the Senate preceded the people and the magistrates acted on behalf of the *Senate and People of Rome* (SPQR = *Senatus Populusque Romanus*).[54]

Even the term *republic*, from *res publica* (of the people) lacked the abstract sense it has today, referring to a model of state standing in opposition to monarchy. Originally, in Rome, the republic designated the affairs (also the patrimony) of the *Populus*, conceived as a group of citizens. Only after Augustus's reforms when, paradoxically, the monarchy reappeared; the term *republic* began to be used at times in its modern sense, i.e. as a synonym of the state, specifically when the writers of the imperial era used the word as opposed to the sovereignty of the emperor.[55]

## 3.8 Roman Citizenship: History's First "Nationality"?

The attempt to govern the conquered territories from the city of Rome eventually shaped the conquered peoples, who ended up undergoing "Romanization", and not just economically and culturally, but also in the legal field. Roman law, undoubtedly one of the pillars of Roman power, began to spread to the new inhabitants as Rome's presence was consolidated.

Initially, they received a limited judicial system providing for *ius latii* (Latin Rights), allowing them to enter into economic and commercial agreements and operations. In 74 AD, Vespasian granted "Latin rights" to all the cities of Hispania (Caballos Rufino 2001, 104–105) but over time, these prerogatives proved insufficient, and concessions of full "citizenship" multiplied. First one became a Roman citizen for having served as a magistrate, later it sufficed to form part of the corresponding urban assembly and, finally, in 212 AD, Emperor Antoninus

---

[54] Lintott (2002, 3) mentions that the authority behind a law was that of the *populus Romanus* or *plebs Romana* voting in an assembly: "Titus Quinctius Crispinus the consul lawfully asked the people, and the people lawfully resolved". Polybius reports that the people had the right to make or rescind any law ("*It has also the absolute power of passing or repealing laws; and, most important of all, it is the people who deliberate on the question of peace or war*".) (Polybius 2012, 6.14.10) and, he implies, no other body. The authority behind a *senatus consultum* under the Republic, was different and less absolute.

[55] As Wirszubski (2004, 122–123) points out, it appears that there were valid reasons to consider Rome under the Augustan Principate a *res publica* in which *libertas* existed. The real change was in the fundamental principle of government, rather than in its form or purpose; whereas the salient feature of Republican government was the distribution of power and a resultant system of checks and balances, the new regime rested on a concentration of power in the hands of the *princeps*.

Caracalla granted Roman citizenship to all inhabitants of the Empire, who thereby became *cives romani*.[56]

To the extent that territorial unification entailed the application of a single law to the inhabitants of the Empire, citizenship could also be considered a kind of *avant la lettre* nationality—a status which politically and legally fostered a sense of belonging to Roman civilization.[57]

## TIMELINE

### The Origins of Rome

753 BC Legend tells of the founding of Rome by Romulus and Remus (*Ab urbe condita*).
509 Servius Tullius establishes the republican regime.
321 The Romans are defeated by the Samnites ("Battle" of the Caudine Forks.)
275 Defeat of Pyrrhus at Beneventum. Rome, after dominating the north and center of the Italian peninsula, controls the south.

### First Extra-Peninsular Expansion (289–264 BC)

264–241 First Punic War.
219–202 Second Punic War.

---

[56] As Treggiari (2007, 4) indicates, citizens had the right to marry other citizens (*conubium*), the right to enter into contracts according to Roman law (*commercium*), the right to appeal against actions by elected officials (*provocation*), and, if male and adult, the vote, the right (in theory) to stand for public office and follow a *cursus honorum*. All the citizens constituted the Roman People (*Populus Romanus*) which, through their different assemblies, were sovereign to pass laws, decide on war or peace, and elect magistrates to annual office. To be recognized as a Roman citizen, it was necessary to be registered in the official census. Dupont (2000, 6) mentions how every 5 years each male Roman citizen had to register for the census, declaring his family, wife, children, slaves and riches. If he failed to do so, his possessions would be confiscated and he himself would be sold into slavery. Throughout the entire Republican era, census registration was the only way that a Roman could ensure that his identity and status as a citizen were recognized. Fathers registered their sons, employers their freedmen. An employer wishing to free one of his slaves needed only to enter him in the census register.

[57] Concerning the question of Roman citizenship, after 212 it effectively spread throughout the whole Roman Empire. As Sherwin-White (1996, 402) points out, the final solution to the "world state problem" depended on the influence which the imperial name came to exercise over the peoples of the Empire—one ultimately based on the *beneficia* which the establishment of the imperial power conferred upon the world. These *beneficia* essentially consisted of the "twofold blessing of the *Pax Augusta* and the imperial administration. In fact if in the western and northern provinces the provincials literally became part of the Roman state, in the Asiatic provinces the situation was different, as the place largely filled in the West by zealous pursuit of the constitutional privileges and titles of the Roman state was taken in the East by an ever-expanding development of the imperial cult, a process that was only slowly followed by the spread of citizenship, as the former municipal categories of the Greeks persisted unchanged for a long time".

| | |
|---|---|
| 197 | Hispania divided into two provinces (*Hispania Ulterior* and *Hispania Citerior*). |
| 197–191 | Rome conquers Cisalpine Gaul. |
| 148 | The annexation of Greece as a Roman province. |
| 146 | The destruction of Carthage (Third Punic War). |
| 133 | Taking of Numancia. End of the Celtiberian-Lusitanian Wars in Hispania. |
| 123–122 | The Romans occupy the Balearic Islands. |
| 105 | After his victory over Jugurtha, King of the Numidians, Rome creates its first province in Africa: Numidia (Algeria and Tunisia) would end up being called *Ifriquiya*, the origin of the word *Africa*. |

**The Collapse of the Republican System (88–31 BC)**

| | |
|---|---|
| 88 | Start of the civil war in Rome (Mario-Sertorius-Caesar against Sulla-Pompey). |
| 86 | Beginning of Sulla's dictatorship. |
| 82 | Sertorius establishes his base at Tingis (Tangier). |
| 80–72 | Sertorian War in Hispania.<br>*80* Landing of Sertorius in Hispania.<br>*77* Pompey in Hispania.<br>*72* Murder of Sertorius. Pompey destroys the Sertorian army. |
| 63 | Catilinarian Conspiracy. Cicero (106–43) manages to reestablish republican law. |
| 60–54 | First Triumvirate: Caesar, Pompey and Crassus. Clear break with the republican order.<br>*58–52* Julius Caesar conquers Transalpine Gaul (Gallic Wars).<br>*54* Death of Crassus. |
| 52 | Pompey is appointed sole consul. |
| 49 | Caesar crosses the Rubicon with his army and occupies Rome. Pompey takes refuge in Greece. |
| 48 | Battle of Pharsalus (Thessaly). Pompey's army is decimated by Caesar. |
| 46 | Caesar fights in Hispania against Pompey's children. |
| 45 | Pompeian troops defeated at Munda. Caesar manages to be named *Imperator* (dictator for life). |
| 44 | Assassination of Julius Caesar in the Senate of Rome on the Ides (15) of March. |
| 43 | The attempt to restore republican legality by killing Caesar fails, as the second triumvirate is established, consisting of Octavius, Mark Antony and Lepidus. |
| 42 | Death of Lepidus. Confrontation between Octavius and Mark Antony. |
| 31 | Naval battle at Actium (Egypt) ends with Mark Antony's suicide. Octavius, ruler of Rome. |

## The Principate (31 BC–96 AD)

| | |
|---|---|
| 29 | Senate confirms Octavius as the ruler of Rome. |
| 27 | Political reform. Official establishment of the Principate (from *princeps* = first) as the Republic's parallel and protective institution. Octavius receives the honorary title of *Augustus* from the Senate. |
| 19 | Virgil's death. Publication of *The Aeneid.* |
| 14 AD | Death of Octavius Caesar Augustus. |

*Julio-Claudian Dynasty*

| | |
|---|---|
| 14–37 | Tiberius. |
| 37–41 | Caligula. |
| 41–54 | Claudius. |
| 54–68 | Nero. |
| | *64* The Burning of Rome. First persecutions of the Christians. |
| | *67* Decapitation of St. Paul. |

*Flavian Dynasty*

| | |
|---|---|
| 68–69 | Galba-Otho-Vitellius-Vespasian. |
| 69–79 | Vespasian. |
| 79 | 24 August. The eruption of Vesuvius (Naples). Destruction of Pompeii, Herculaneum and Stabies. |
| 79–80 | Titus. |
| 80–96 | Domitian. |

## The High Empire (96–191 AD)

| | |
|---|---|
| 96–98 | Nerva. |
| 98–117 | Trajan. The Roman Empire reaches its greatest dimensions. |
| 117–138 | Hadrian. |
| 138–161 | Antoninus Pius. |
| 161–180 | Marcus Aurelius. |
| 180–191 | Commodus. |

## The Crisis (191–284)

| | |
|---|---|
| 191–238 | The Severans. |
| 212 | Caracalla grants Roman citizenship to all inhabitants of the Empire. |
| 238–249 | Military anarchy. |
| 249–283 | The Illyrians. |

### The Decline of the Roman Empire (284–395 AD)

284–293 Diocletian.
293–305 First Tetrarchy (East: Diocletian [Augustus] and Galerius [Caesar]; West: Maximian [Augustus] and Constantius Chlorus [Caesar]).
305–306 Second Tetrarchy (East: Galerius [Augustus] and Maximinus Daia [Caesar]; West: Constantius Chlorus [Augustus] and Severus [Caesar]).
306–337 Rupture of the Tetrarchy system. Clashes between the different aspirants to the imperial throne.
324–337 Constantine I manages to reunite the Empire.
337–340 After the death of Constantine I the Empire is divided among his three sons. The fights for power resume.
361–363 New unification with Julian. Brief pagan reaction against the excesses of Constantius II.
394–395 Theodosius I is the last emperor who manages to reunite the Empire.
395 After the death of Theodosius I the Empire is divided: the Western Empire is inherited by Honorius (395–423) and the Eastern by Arcadius (395–408).

### The End of the Western Empire (395–476 AD)

476 September 4. Romulus Augustulus is deposed by Odoacer, the Germanic chieftain of the Heruli. The end of the Western Empire.

## References

Abott, F. F., & Johnson, A. C. (2012). *Municipal administration in the Roman Empire*. New Orleans: Quid Pro (Reprint of the 1926 edition. Princeton: Princeton University Press).

Ando, C. (2010). The administration of the provinces in Potter. In S. David (Ed.), *A companion to the Roman Empire* (pp. 177–192). Malden, MA: Blackwell.

Arnason, J. P. (2011). The Roman phenomenon: State, empire, and civilization. In J. P. Arnason & K. A. Raaflaub (Eds.), *The Roman Empire in context: Historical and comparative perspectives* (pp. 353–386). Malden, MA: Wiley-Blackwell.

Bispham, E. (2006). *Coloniam deducere*: How Roman was Roman colonization during the middle republic? In G. Bradley & J.-P. Wilson (Eds.), *Greek and Roman colonization: Origins, ideologies and interactions* (pp. 73–160). Swansea, UK: The Classical Press of Wales.

Bispham, E. (2007). *From Asculum to Actium: The municipalization of Italy from the social war to Augustus*. Oxford: Oxford University Press.

Boatwright, M. T., Gargola, D. J., & Talbert, R. J. A. (2004). *The Romans: From village to empire*. Oxford: Oxford University Press.

Briscoe, J. (1986). Greek Polis and Roman Rule. *The Classical Review* (New Series), *36*(2), 267–270.

Brunt, P. A. (1977). Lex de Imperio Vespasiani. *The Journal of Roman Studies, 67*, 95–116.

Burton, G. (2002). Government and the provinces. In J. Wacher (Ed.), *The Roman world* (Vol. I, pp. 423–439). London: Routledge.
Caballos Rufino, A. (2001). Latinidad y Municipalización de Hispania bajo los Flavios. Estatuto y normativa. *Mainake,* (23), 101–120.
Campbell, J. B. (2011). *The Romans and their world.* New Haven, CT: Yale University Press.
Cornell, T. J. (1995). *The beginnings of Rome: Italy and Rome from the Bronze age to the Punic wars (c. 1000–264 BC).* London: Routledge.
Davies, J. K. (1993). *Democracy and classical Greece.* Cambridge, MA: Harvard University Press.
Drinkwater, J. F. (2002). Urbanization in Italy and the Western Empire. In J. Wacher (Ed.), *The Roman world* (Vol. I, pp. 345–386). London: Routledge.
Dumézil, G. (1996). The Indo-European heritage at Rome. In *Archaic Roman Religion* (Vol. 1, pp. 79–82). Baltimore: The Johns Hopkins University Press.
Dupont, F. (2000). *Daily life in Ancient Rome* (6th Reprint). Oxford: Blackwell.
Eckstein, A. M. (2006). *Mediterranean anarchy, interstate war and the rise of Rome.* Berkeley: University of California Press.
Edmonson, J. (2010). Cities and urban life in the western provinces of the Roman Empire 30 BCE–250 CE. In D. S. Potter (Ed.), *A companion to the Roman Empire* (pp. 250–280). Malden, MA: Blackwell.
Edwards, C. (1999). Introduction: Shadows and fragments. In C. Edwards (Ed.), *Roman presences: Receptions of Rome in European culture, 1789–1945* (pp. 1–18). Cambridge, UK: Cambridge University Press.
Elton, H. (2010). The transformation of government under Diocletian and Constantine. In D. S. Potter (Ed.), *A companion to the Roman Empire* (pp. 193–205). Malden, MA: Blackwell.
Feig Vishnia, R. (1996). *State, society and popular leaders in mid-republican Rome 241–167 BC.* London: Routledge.
Ferrary, J. L. (2009). The powers of Augustus. In J. Edmonson (Ed.), *Augustus* (pp. 90–136). Edinburgh: Edinburgh University Press.
Fishwick, D. (2004). *The imperial cult in the Latin West. Studies in the ruler cult of the western provinces of the Roman Empire.* Part 3 (Vol. 3). Leiden: Brill.
Flaig, E. (2011). The transition from republic to principate: Loss of legitimacy, revolution, and acceptance. In J. P. Arnason & K. A. Raaflaub (Eds.), *The Roman Empire in context: Historical and comparative perspectives.* Malden, MA: Wiley-Blackwell.
Fulford, M. (1992). Territorial expansion and the Roman Empire. *World Archeology, 23*(3), 294–305 (Archeology of Empires).
Gaius. (1904). *Gai Institutiones or Institutes of Roman Law by Gaius (160 AD)* (4th ed.). Oxford: Clarendon.
Genet, J. P. (1990). L'Empire romain est-il un État moderne? In N. Coulet & J. P. Genet (Eds.), *L'État moderne: le droit, l'espace et les formes de l'État* (pp. 111–128). Paris: CNRS.
Gruen, E. S. (1995). *The last generation of the Roman Republic* (Reprinted with a new introduction). Berkeley: University of California Press.
Harries, J. (1999). *Law and empire in late antiquity.* Cambridge, UK: Cambridge University Press.
Hölkeskamp, K. J. (1993). Competition and consensus: Roman expansion in Italy and the rise of the "Nobilitas". *Historia: Zeitschrift für Alte Geschichte, 42*(1), 12–39.
Huet, V. (1999). Napoleon I: A new Augustus? In C. Edwards (Ed.), *Roman presences: Receptions of Rome in European culture, 1789–1945* (pp. 53–69). Cambridge, UK: Cambridge University Press.
Johnston, D. (1997). The general influence of Roman institutions of state and public law. In D. L. Carey Mille & R. Zimmermann (Eds.), *The Civilian Tradition and Scots Law: Aberdeen Quincentenary essays* (pp. 87–101). Berlin: Duncker & Humblot.
Jones, A. H. M. (1950). The Aerarium and the Fiscus. *Journal of Roman Studies, 40*(1–2), 22–29.
Jones, A. H. M. (1990). *The later Roman Empire, 284–602: A social, economic and administrative survey* (2nd ed., 2 Vols). Oxford: Basil Blackwell.

Justinian. (1993). *Justinian's institutes*. With the Latin text of Paul Krueger. Ithaca, NY: Cornell University Press.

Lane Fox, R. (2006). *The classical world: An epic history from Homer to Hadrian*. New York: Basic Books.

Liebeschuetz, J. H. W. G. (2002). Government and administration in the late empire. In J. Wacher (Ed.), *The Roman world* (Vol. I, pp. 455–469). London: Routledge.

Lintott, A. W. (2002). *The constitution of the Roman Republic*. Oxford: Clarendon (Reprint).

Livius, T. (2002). *Ab urbe condita: The early history of Rome: Books I–V of the history of Rome from its foundations*. New York: Penguin (Printed English version).

Malkin, I. (1987). *Religion and colonization in Ancient Greece*. Leiden: Brill.

Mennen, I. (2011). *Power and status in the Roman Empire: AD 193–284*. Leiden: Brill.

Millar, F. (1989). Political power in mid-Republican Rome: Curia or Comitium? *The Journal of Roman Studies, 79*, 138–150.

Montesquieu, Charles-Louis de Secondat, Baron de la Brède et de. (2005). *Considérations sur les causes de la grandeur des romains et de leur décadence*. Amsterdam: J. Desbordes, 1734. English version: Farmington Hills, Mich: Thomson Gale, 2005 [Electronic resource], p. 27. Printed version Cambridge: Hackett, 1999.

Nicholas, B. (1992). *An introduction to Roman Law*. Oxford: Clarendon.

North, J. A. (1990). Democratic politics in republican Rome. *Past and Present,* (126), 3–21.

Peachin, M. (2010). Rome the superpower: 96–235 CE. In D. S. Potter (Ed.), *A companion to the Roman Empire* (pp. 126–152). Malden, MA: Blackwell.

Polybius. (2012). *The histories*. Cambridge, MA: Harvard University Press.

Raaflaub, K. A. (2011). From city-state to empire: Rome in comparative perspective. In J. P. Arnason & K. A. Raaflaub (Eds.), *The Roman Empire in context: Historical and comparative perspectives* (pp. 39–66). Malden, MA: Wiley-Blackwell.

Rees, R. (2004). *Diocletian and the tetrarchy*. Edinburgh: Edinburgh University Press.

Rostovtzeff, M. I. (1998). *The social and economic history of the Roman Empire* (2nd ed., rev). Oxford: Oxford University Press.

Sherwin-White, A. N. (1996). *Roman citizenship* (2nd ed., rev). Oxford: Oxford University Press.

Syme, R. (1989). *The Augustan Aristocracy*. Oxford: Oxford University Press.

Talbert, R. J. A. (1984). *The senate of imperial Rome*. Princeton: Princeton University Press.

Taylor, L. R. (1960). *The voting districts of the Roman Republic: The thirty-five urban and rural tribes*. Rome: American Academy in Rome.

Taylor, L. R. (1990). *Roman voting assemblies: From the Hannibalic War to the dictatorship of Caesar* (2nd ed.). Ann Arbor, MI: University of Michigan Press.

Taylor, L. R. (2002). *The divinity of the Roman Emperor*. Atlanta, GA: Scholars Press (Reprint of the 1931 ed.).

Treggiari, S. (2007). *Terentia, Tullia and Publilia: The women of Cicero's family*. New York: Routledge.

Wagner, P. (2011). Roman-European continuities: Conceptual and historical questions. In J. P. Arnason (Coed.), *The Roman Empire in context: Historical and comparative perspectives* (pp. 387–406). Malden, MA: Wiley-Blackwell.

Whittaker, C. R. (1994). *Frontiers of the Roman Empire: A social and economic study*. Baltimore: Johns Hopkins University Press.

Williamson, C. (2005). *The laws of the Roman People: Public law in the expansion and decline of the Roman Republic*. Ann Arbor: University of Michigan Press.

Wirszubski, C. (2004). *Libertas as a political idea at Rome during the late republic and early principate*. Cambridge, UK: Cambridge University Press (Reprint of 1950 ed.).

Wolff, H. J. (1995). The historical and constitutional background of Roman Law. In *Roman law. An historical introduction* (pp. 7–48). London: University of Oklahoma Press.

Ziolkowski, A. (2011). The background to the third-century crisis of the Roman Empire. In J. P. Arnason (Coed.), *The Roman Empire in context: Historical and comparative perspectives*. Malden, MA: Wiley-Blackwell.

## *Further Reading*

Ando, C. (2000). *Imperial ideology and provincial loyalty in the Roman Empire*. Berkeley, Los Angeles, and London: University of California Press.

Bartel, B. (1980). Colonialism and cultural responses: Problems related to Roman provincial analysis. *World Archaeology, 12*(1), 11–26.

Bispham, E. (2007). *From Asculum to Actium: The municipalization of Italy from the social war to Augustus*. Oxford: Oxford University Press.

Brooks, R. O. (Ed.). (2009). *Cicero and modern law*. Burlington, VT: Ashgate.

Corcoran, S. (1996). *The Empire of the Tetrarchs, imperial pronouncements and government AD 284–324*. Oxford: Clarendon.

Edmonson, J. (2009). *Augustus*. Edinburgh: Edinburgh University Press.

Fower, H. I. (2010). *Roman republics*. Princeton, NJ: Princeton University Press.

Gaudemet, J. (1985). *Les Gouvernants à Rome: Essais de droit public romain*. Naples: Jovene.

Gibbon, E. (2000). *Decline and fall of the Roman Empire (1776–1788)*. London: Penguin.

Gwynn, D. M. (Ed.). (2008). *A.H.M. Jones and the later Roman Empire*. Leiden: Brill. (Some contributions originally presented at a seminar held at Oxford in 2004 to commemorate the 40th anniversary of the publication of A.H.M. Jones's Later Roman Empire, 284–602).

Harries, J., & Wood, I. (Eds.). (1993). *The Theodosian Code: Studies in the imperial law of late antiquity*. London: Duckworth.

Hill, H. (1974). *The Roman middle class in the Republican period*. Westport, CT: Greenwood.

Kelley, D. R. (2002). What pleases the prince: Justinian, Napoleon and the lawyers. *History of Political Thought, 23*(2), 288–302.

Lintott, A. W. (2002). *The constitution of the Roman Republic*. Oxford: Clarendon (Reprint).

Mennen, I. (2011). *Power and status in the Roman Empire: AD 193–284*. Leiden: Brill.

Mommsen, T. (2010). *Römisches Staatsrecht*. Cambridge: Cambridge University Press; Reissue edition. From the original Leipzig: Hirzel, 1871–1888. The chronological order of the appearance of the five volumes is as follows: 1 (1871, 18873); 2, 1 (1874, 18873). 2, 2 (1875, 18873). 3, 1 (1887). 3, 2 (1888). Spanish version by Dorado, P. (1999), *Compendio del Derecho Público Romano,* facsimile edition of the Madrid version: Library of Jurisprudence, Philosophy and History, 1893, Pamplona: Marcial Pons. French version (1984) *Le droit public romain*. Translated from the third German edition by Girard, Paul Frédéric and Thorin, Ernest ed. 1892. Reimpression Paris De Boccard.

Montesquieu Charles de Secondat, baron de. (1734). *Reflections on the causes of the grandeur and declension of the Romans*. By the author of the Persian letters. Translated from the French. London: printed for W. Innys and R. Manby; C. Davis; and A. Lyon. Original French, as follows: *Considérations sur les causes de la grandeur des romains et de leur décadence*. Amsterdam: J. Desbordes. There is a reproduction from the original by the Bodleian Library: electronic version, 2006.

Muñiz Coello, J. (2004). *Moral e Imperio (siglos II-I a. C.): la tradición romana sobre el Estado*. Oxford: John and Erica Hedges Ltd.

Reid, J. S. (2006). *The municipalities of the Roman Empire*. Mansfield Centre, CT: Martino Pub.

Rees, R. (2004). *Diocletian and the Tetrarchy*. Edinburgh: Edinburgh University Press.

Rosenstein, N., & Morstein-Marx, R. (Eds.). (2006). *A companion to the Roman Republic*. Oxford: Blackwell.

Syme, R. (1986). *The Augustan aristocracy*. Oxford: Oxford University Press.

Tellegen-Coperus, O. (1993). *Short history of Roman law*. London: Routledge.

Virgil. (1999). *[Complete works of] Virgil*. Cambridge, MA: Harvard University Press.

Williams, S. (2000). *Diocletian and the Roman recovery*. London: Routledge.

# Chapter 4
# From Territorial Power to Spiritual Rule: Christianity's Political Dimension

> Render therefore unto Caesar the things which are Caesar's, and unto God the things which are God's.—Matthew 22:21

## Contents


4.1 Church and State in the Western Tradition ........ 66
4.2 The Origins of Christianity ........ 67
  4.2.1 It All Started with Judaism ........ 67
  4.2.2 A Provincial Jew Named Jesus, Aka "Christ" ........ 68
  4.2.3 Had It Not Been for St. Paul ........ 70
4.3 Christianity and the Roman Empire ........ 72
  4.3.1 A Threat to the Empire? ........ 72
  4.3.2 From Forbidden Cult to Official State Religion (380 AD) ........ 73
  4.3.3 The Origins of Catholicism ........ 76
  4.3.4 Emperors vs. Bishops: "Caesaropapism" ........ 78
4.4 The Church as a Political Body ........ 79
  4.4.1 The Origin of the Ecclesiastical Profession: Bishops, Deacons and Presbyters 79
  4.4.2 The Development of Church Organization: Parishes and Dioceses ........ 80
  4.4.3 Metropolitans and Patriarchs ........ 81
  4.4.4 The Councils as Collective Decision-Making Bodies ........ 81
  4.4.5 The Origins of the Papacy as a Moral Authority ........ 82
References ........ 85




B. Aguilera-Barchet, *A History of Western Public Law*,
DOI 10.1007/978-3-319-11803-1_4

## 4.1 Church and State in the Western Tradition

After examining the effectiveness and utter practicality of the Roman polity,[1] in our journey through the history of the Western state it is time for us to delve into the realm of religion, a turn which shall certainly surprise more than one in this skeptical world in which we live, where man alone is increasingly, as Protagoras used to say, "the measure of all things". However, the contrast between what is happening today and what happened in Antiquity, when the transcendent was considered an essential dimension of human existence, is very much worth looking at. This is no trivial side note we are dealing with here, for religion played an absolutely crucial role in the history of the state, and it is worth understanding why.

Here and now, however, what should be made clear and underscored is that the Church represented an extension and continuation of Roman civilization. It is no coincidence that the head of the Catholic Church, the Pope, resides in the Eternal City. In fact, after the fall of the Western Roman Empire it was the Church which preserved consciousness of the Greek and Roman tradition, cornerstones of our civilization (Larrainzar 2004). The Church is an institution which, despite all its crises and difficulties, has existed continuously for over 2,000 years, a rather unique historical phenomenon. It is, thus, no exaggeration to say that we are Westerners because of our shared Christian legacy; as Lane Fox (2006, 11) points out, the transition from paganism to Christianity is the point at which the ancient world still touches ours directly.

Let us, then, examine some essential aspects of Christian history, which will allow us to understand our political and legal past, for after our Roman heritage, it is Christianity which stands as the second pillar upon which our unique Western civilization rests. The barbarian invasions destroyed Europe's initial unity, but all was not lost. Christianity had already spread widely throughout Continental Western Europe. It was through the apparently tenuous but ultimately enduring bonds forged by the Catholic Church that the broken unity of Roman Europe was reconstructed. This is why, for instance, there would be no point in asking a medieval man about his country or his nationality. He may have been ignorant of his king, but he certainly knew his parson. With Christianity all roads came to lead, yet again, to Rome, as the papacy established itself as the undisputed center of a new, Catholic West (Brown 2003, 4). It needs to be understood that in the West Christianity is not just a religion, but an essential part of our history and culture. Thus, any understanding of the organization of our states and the development of our laws requires us to study it.

[1] When we refer to the polity here we are alluding to what we might call "political constitution", but not in exclusive reference to the written constitution setting down the government's powers and structure, but the comprehensive nexus of factors involved in determining the political composition and functioning of a given state.

## 4.2 The Origins of Christianity

### *4.2.1 It All Started with Judaism*

The origins of Judaism can be traced back to Ancient Egypt, when Amenhotep IV imposed his monotheistic religious reform and became Akhenaten IV (1352–1335 BC).[2] The new cult did not survive its creator, but a century later, it very likely inspired the Jews' famed leader, Moses, who in his younger years had been an Egyptian prince.[3] However, Judaism was not only a religion, as it featured a political and a legal dimension as well, which is why the famed *Torah* contains legal aspects in addition to religious ones. Concretely, its first five books (the Pentateuch), the most important for the Jews, contain rules aimed at allowing early Hebrew society to become the Kingdom of Israel after its flight from Egypt.[4] The best-known law, of course, is that of the Ten Commandments, said to have been bestowed by Yahweh upon Moses on Mount Sinai (Exodus 20:3–17; Deuteronomy 5:7–21), but this is not the only one appearing in the Biblical text.

[2] As Assmann (1998, 23) has observed, it is a paradox that, unlike Moses, Amenhotep IV was a historical figure of paramount significance whose legacy and achievements were, nevertheless, all but obliterated: shortly after his death his name was erased from the lists of kings, his monuments dismantled, his inscriptions and representations destroyed, and almost every trace of his existence expunged. For centuries no one knew of the extraordinary revolution he led. Until his rediscovery in the nineteenth century there was virtually no evidence of Akhenaten or consciousness of his role in history. Moses, on the other hand, is exactly the opposite: though no traces have ever been found of his historical existence, he grew into a historical giant, a towering figure whose shadow was cast upon a range of traditions, affecting legislation, inspiring liberation, and embodying monotheism.

[3] Osman (1999) argues that the Egyptian roots of Christianity were deliberately covered up by the early Church at the time of the burning of the library at Alexandria—roots which are only now being uncovered again by archaeology. Freud (2010) was the first among Western intellectuals to consider the possible connection between Akhenaten's religious reform and the origins of Jewish monotheism. As Freud was a Jew, his book troubled and offended many of his critics (Bernstein 1998, 2), though, as Yerusalmi (1991, 2) points out, reactions to Freud's last major work have ranged from its total acceptance as literal history to outraged condemnation as a malicious attack upon the very foundations of Jewish existence.

[4] *Pentateuch*, from the Greek "Five Boxes" (*pente*: five; *téukhos*: boxes) for the five tubes in which the texts of the first five books (the five parts of the Law) of the Bible were rolled and stored. Attributed to Moses, they constitute the Torah, or Law: Genesis, Exodus, Leviticus, Numbers and Deuteronomy. They are also called the Books of the Law because they contain Yahweh's instructions bestowed upon Moses (Mosaic Law) featuring the famous "Ten Commandments" or "Decalogue" in the Book of Exodus. The Decalogue is not the Bible's only legal text, as in the very same book of Exodus appears the "Covenant Code" (Ex 20: 22–25, 33), and Deuteronomy features the "Second Law" (12–26) the "First Law" having been received by Moses on Mt. Sinai.

Scholars (Wright 2009, 91–120), detect Babylonian influence on the *Book of the Covenant* (Exodus 20:22–25, 33), a code of laws and customs, featuring religious norms (condemning false gods and regulating celebrations and clerical statutes), social norms (regulations of slavery) and penal ones (the death penalty for cases of murder, punishments for beatings or injuries, robbery and rape; indemnification for damages, etc.)[5]

Despite the fact that modern research has concluded that the oldest portion of the Bible, the Pentateuch, was composed by different authors from different periods (Van Seters 2003, 3), the important point for us is that the laws included in the sacred book came to form the basis of Jewish civilization, allowing the Jews to survive as a people for 18 centuries, without a homeland, dispersed throughout the world. In spite of the "Diaspora" the Jewish people were able to maintain their religion and their laws, even without a fixed territory. The Jews constitute a unique illustration in history of how religion can serve as the instrument through which a society is structured and the source of its law.

### *4.2.2 A Provincial Jew Named Jesus, Aka "Christ"*

Jesus Christ was a Jew belonging to 1 of the 12 tribes of Israel, although he did not form part of the intellectual elite, neither a Pharisee nor a specialist in the Torah. Nor did he live in the capital of Jerusalem, but in Galilee, i.e., a provincial area.[6] Nevertheless, possibly after a period spent in the desert surrounding the Dead Sea, in one of the monastic communities—it is speculated that he might have spent time with the Essenes (Broshi 2004)—which studied the Jewish religious tradition,[7]

[5] According to Van Seters (2003, 56–57) this large block of casuistic laws has made obvious the Covenant Code's association with the Code of Hammurabi. The similarity between them, however, goes beyond the similarity of laws to also include their narrative setting, as both Hammurabi and Moses receive laws from God. Both play a mediating role in the reception and transmission of legal codes. Researchers think that this borrowing probably took place during the exile of the Jews in Babylon. Moses is the Jewish Hammurabi, and the Jews had laws that were comparable to those of the Babylonians, and of similar antiquity—a comparison that should have been appealing to the Jewish community within Babylon, strengthening their identity.

[6] Intellectuals began to take an interest in Jesus Christ as a historical figure beginning in 1863 with the publication of Ernest Renan's *Life of Jesus*, a work written because its author believed that Jesus was a figure to be embraced by all sharing a common humanity, and that his glory did not hinge upon him being spared from standard historical analysis. Renan sought to study his life as a historian would the life of any other figure, and believed that he was best honored by the demonstration that all history was incomprehensible without him (Renan 2007, 26). The task was not easy; as Horsley (2010, I-209) points out, Jesus is still more or less confined to the religious sphere and the economic context in which he taught. The political implications of his teachings may be acknowledged but not considered relevant by historians, as for most of them Jesus is still discussed mainly in the religious context of Judaism.

[7] About which we are aware thanks to the extraordinary discovery of the Dead Sea Scrolls between 1946 and 1956 in the Caves of Qumran, which utterly revolutionized our knowledge of the sources

Jesus decided to spread his version of Judaism. To do so he did not address the learned class of the Pharisees, or the reactionary Sadducees, nor, of course, the chief priests of the Temple of Jerusalem, founded by Solomon, guarantors of the strictest orthodoxy. Rather, he addressed the common people, conveying his teachings using parables which could be understood by all.[8]

The teachings of Jesus Christ, whose essence is captured in the Sermon on the Mount, with its well-known Beatitudes (Matthew 5–7) touched many sympathetic followers, among them a group of fishermen from Lake Tiberius. These men formed the core "apostles"—from the Greek *apostolos* meaning "sent one"—or "disciples". Jesus Christ was accepted by them as the Messiah—*Christ* (anointed one) in Greek—and the new David the Jews had awaited after the decline of the Kingdom of Israel. Thus arose "Christianity" as an interpretation of Judaism spreading the teachings of Christ.[9]

Jesus Christ's success, however, worried the Jewish establishment. Thus, after his triumphant entry into Jerusalem (which Christians celebrate on Palm Sunday) the chief priests resolved to accuse him of blasphemy. After the Last Supper, they had him arrested in the olive grove at the Garden of Gethsemane, where he was brought before the Sanhedrin (the highest Jewish religious court). There he was sentenced to death by Hanas and Caiaphas, but the Jewish religious authorities did not have the power to enforce the sentence, and the death penalty had to be carried out by the civil authorities. As at that time Palestine was already occupied by the Romans, Jesus was taken to the nearby praetorian, where Pontius Pilate, then the Governor of Judea,

of Biblical tradition. Jesus Christ probably took from the Essenes the ritual of sharing bread and wine with his disciples, which today constitutes the sacrament of Communion. Nevertheless as Chadwick (1993, 14) points out, even if Quran texts and Greek sources are not in complete harmony, they feature important differences between the Essenes and the early Christians. The Essenes seemed to lie somewhere between the Pythagorean ascetics of the Hellenistic world and the Jews: they kept the Sabbath day, rose before dawn to offer prayer to the rising sun, and embraced esoteric teachings about the properties of roots and stones and the secret names of angels. They devoted much attention to the exegesis of the inner meaning of Scripture, and made predictions regarding the future. In any case, it is practically impossible for either Jews or Christians who are studying their roots, to ignore the Dead Sea Scrolls (Thiede 2001, 9).

[8] Dunn (1999, 3) believes that Jewish Christianity plays a central role in the story of how and when the Jews and Gentiles separated, as it continued to represent Christianity within the Jewish community even after substantial parts of the Church had become Gentile. As long as Jewish Christianity remained a significant presence within the Palestinian Jewish community, we cannot speak of a final rupture. The story of the parting of the ways is, in essence, the story of the triumph of Rabbinism and of the failure of Jewish Christianity to convince a majority of Palestinian Jews of the Gospel's claims.

[9] Chadwick (1993, 9) highlights the continuity between the first Christians and the Jews based on the simple fact that the first Christians were Jews whose faith varied in that they believed that Jesus of Nazareth was the Messiah the Jews had been expecting, and whose coming had been prophesied. They took it for granted that his coming, as such, must be consonant with God's revelation to his people, and did not mark a break either with the old covenant made with Abraham, symbolized by circumcision, or with the Law given to Moses on Mount Sinai. If this momentous event had come to pass it was the action of the same God, Creator of the world, Lord of history, the God of Abraham, Isaac, Jacob, and the Twelve Patriarchs. His new word to his people must be consistent with that spoken in the past by the prophets.

found Jesus innocent. Ceding to the insistence of the Jewish people, however, he "washed his hands" of the affair and allowed them to execute him on a cross.[10]

### 4.2.3 *Had It Not Been for St. Paul*

The death of Jesus Christ would have marked the end of Christianity had it not been for Paul of Tarsus (St. Paul). The disciples, uneducated people without social influence and frightened by the stance of the Jews towards them, fell silent after Christ's death, not daring to spread his teachings. In fact, the Scriptures state that, on the night of his trial, Peter denied being a follower of Jesus three times.

Ironically, it was an enemy of the Christians who would assure the new religion's triumph: Saul of Tarsus, a Pharisee, who in his youth had been one of the most zealous persecutors of the new "sect".[11] However, Saul suddenly converted to Christianity (The Acts of the Apostles, Chapter 9)[12] and, to the dismay of his former allies, decided to spread the teachings of Christ among non-Jews

---

[10] Crucifixion did not form part of Jewish penal law. The four types of death provided for under Hebrew law were stoning, the stake, decapitation and strangling. Invented by the Persians, more than a form of capital punishment death on the cross was used as a form of excruciating torture which, after horrid torment and a slow and painful agony, the victim died. The Romans considered the *crux*, the most effective means of maintaining order and security for deterring slave revolts, for robbers, bandits or rebels (Chapman 2008, 70) and subjugating any and all dangerous individuals, forcing them to yield to their power, though Roman citizens generally did not fear such a penalty. During the Romans' war against the rebel Jews (67–70 AD) crucifixion was regularly used to terrify the insurgents, as reported by the eyewitness Titus Flavius Josephus (37–100). After being whipped the victim was firmly tied to a horizontal board (in Latin: *patibulum*) and taken outside the city, with a tablet hanging from his neck indicating his crime. This tablet was then affixed to the vertical post, which was only slightly taller than a man. Long posts were only used in special cases in which the Romans wished for all to see the victim, was then disrobed, whipped again and raised onto the post. Half way up it there was a small wooden anchor point, which served to prolong his agony and to assure that he was not afforded a swift death. There is little testimony regarding the use of nails in crucifixions. In the case of Jesus we know, from the accounts of the resurrection, that he was nailed to the cross. Death came from exhaustion and suffocation after 3–7 days, and the cadaver was often left on the cross to be devoured by vultures and scavengers. This was not the case with Jesus Christ, who died in a question of hours and whose body was taken down and buried in a tomb, in response to a request approved by Pontius Pilate, made by Joseph of Arimathea, a wealthy man from Jerusalem. On the background and significance of crucifixion in Antiquity and in the New Testament see Samuelsson (2011).

[11] A fact that he recognizes himself in his epistle to the Galatians: "For you have heard of my former way of life in Judaism, that I persecuted the church of God to an extreme and was trying to destroy it; and was advanced in Judaism beyond many of my own age in the nation, being more extremely zealous for our ancestral traditions" (Gal. 1:13–14).

[12] As Ehrman (2008, 99–100) has explained, Acts is a not a repository book of historically factual data but "a collection of stories about the early Christian movement and its chief apostles, especially Peter and Paul. Some of these stories are rooted in historical facts, whereas others represent ways these apostles were remembered by one author (Luke) and the community that passed along the stories over the years before he heard them and wrote some of them down. If we

("Gentiles".)[13] This was crucial because, as, Ehrman (2008, 103) has observed, of the 60 million people living in the Roman Empire of his time, only around 7 % were Jews. To this end Paul organized and paid visits to various communities of Christians, and later sent them letters: the famous Epistles of St. Paul.[14] Coming from a lettered person and a former Pharisee,[15] Paul's writings had an enormous impact. Thanks to the "apostle of the Gentiles" Christianity spread rapidly among non-Jews, the vast majority of the Empire's inhabitants.[16] Had it not been for Paul, Christianity would not have become one of history's major religions.[17]

It is worthy of note that Paul, despite being of Jewish origin and educated as a Pharisee, was quite exceptional in the fact that he was legally a Roman citizen. It was this that bolstered his influence amongst the Gentiles. In fact, when he was arrested as a subversive by the Roman authorities, he appealed to Rome, as was his right, and was, therefore, not crucified like St. Peter, but beheaded by order of Nero in 67 AD.[18]

---

want to know about the historical Paul we have to treat Acts for what it is and not pretend that it records events that you would have been able to capture on your camcorder if you had been there".

[13] For an overview of Paul's relationship with Gentiles after his conversion see Segal (1990, 150–186).

[14] St. Paul's epistles, chronologically, are the first writings of the New Testament, as they predate the Four Gospels. Of the seven letters considered genuine by most scholars (First Thessalonians, Philippians, Philemon, First Corinthians, Galatians, Second Corinthians and Romans) the first addressed to the Thessalonians was written in 50 AD, and the last to the Romans was completed in the year 56, 11 years before his death (Murphy-O'Connor 1996, 114 and 332).

[15] In his epistle to the Philippians Paul affirms his Jewish origins and that he knew the law well and defended it: "If anyone else thinks that he can be confident in his flesh, I have greater reason: I was circumcised on the eight day, of the nation of Israel, and the tribe of Benjamin; a Hebrew born of Hebrews; with respect to the law, a Pharisee, with respect to zeal, a persecutor of the church, with respect to the righteousness that comes through the law" (Phil. 3:4–6).

[16] Christianity offered all the advantages that made Judaism appealing to serious-minded pagans: monotheism, high ethical standards, a close-knit social community, the authority of an ancient Scripture, a rational worship, and it did not carry the liabilities that Judaism did. Christianity offered contact with antiquity through its claim to the fulfillment of Biblical prophecy, but it also offered a satisfaction of the newer religious aspirations: salvation and deliverance through a personal Redeemer (Ferguson 2003, 618).

[17] As Ehrman (2008, 122) points out: "after Jesus himself, Paul was the most important figure in the history of Christianity. It was Paul's missionary work that helped transform the followers of Jesus from a small Jewish sectarian movement in Palestine to a worldwide religion comprising both Jews and Gentiles. It was his theological reflections on the significance of the death and resurrection of Jesus that came to form the heart of the Christian message for all time. And it was his writings that were to play such an enormous role in the canon of the new Christian Scriptures, the New Testament, of whose twenty-seven books, thirteen are attributed to Paul".

[18] The manner of Paul's death, beheading, is understood to imply that he was condemned by a regularly constituted court (Murphy-O'Connor 1996, 371).

## 4.3 Christianity and the Roman Empire

### *4.3.1 A Threat to the Empire?*

The Romans were not very religious, worshipping their ancestors and little else. This situation did not fail to provoke a great spiritual vacuum, already lamented by Cicero (106–43 BC). Many Romans, however, did yearn to infuse their lives with meaning, spurring a large number of them to join certain Near Eastern mystery cults (such as that of Mithras).[19] As Schott (2008, 25) points out, the fact that the Roman Empire facilitated commerce and contact between disparate peoples created a receptive spiritual framework, as philosophers were seeking to bridge cultural gulfs and cultivate an intellectual ecumenism. This receptivity made them amenable to the teachings of Christ, leading to mass conversions.[20]

The new religion, however, posed a political problem, as it elevated God over the civil power of the emperors,[21] making it a threat to the cohesion of a state which had deified its "monarchs", the figure of the emperor providing a religious focus shared by the entire Empire (Rives 2007, 156). As Brent (1999, 126) notes, the key to the problem was that Christian Gentiles were Roman citizens. The Jews, on the other hand, were not, exempt from Greco-Roman religious customs and able to avoid the requirement, whether purely social or legal, to take part in the Imperial Cult.

Beginning with Nero (37–68 AD) the persecutions would begin, yielding the first martyrs.[22] These suppressive efforts would end up backfiring on the emperors, as the example set by the tortured Christians infused the new religion with an aura and a prestige which quickly multiplied its numbers (Fredriksen 2010). In the end the emperors had to give in.

[19] The most popular cults of pagan cult associations throughout the Greco-Roman world were mystery cults such as the one at Eleusis, the Sibyline cult at Rome, the Mithras cult, and the cults of Isis and Serapis. All of these cults had in common that their adherents assembled at set times for feasting, with an opulent meal (Alikin 2010, 23–24).

[20] The Roman army, distributed throughout the Empire, was an essential factor when it came to assuring conversion throughout imperial territory (Shean 2010). It has been estimated that of the Empire's 50 million inhabitants in the late third century some 7 million had converted to Christianity. On the Greco-Roman understanding of Christianity, see Hartog (2010).

[21] This is why gentile Christians faced persecution by the Roman government, unlike the Jews who, at least in theory, were protected under Roman law (Cohick 2010, 70).

[22] Historians do not know precisely how the Roman people felt about Nero's persecution of the Christians. We do know, however, that many educated Romans did not approve. The case of the Roman historian Tacitus (55–120), is interesting, as he recorded that spectators exposed to Nero's execution of Christians understood that they were being eliminated to indulge Nero's savagery, an action not justified by the "public utility" which the ruler claimed warranted the just and well-deserved punishment of Christians (Cook 2010, 111). Tacitus's opinion is even more interesting because he later became a consul, senator and a governor, though he was only 13 years old when Nero died. For a good overview of the conflict between Christians and Roman emperors, see De Palma Digeser (2006).

### 4.3.2 From Forbidden Cult to Official State Religion (380 AD)

"If you cannot beat them, join them". This well-known saying sums up the attitude adopted by the Roman emperors who, beginning with Constantine, relied upon Christianity to strengthen their political positions. The imperial decrees issued in 311 and 313, officially recognizing and tolerating Christianity, merely recognized what was already a fact: the significant expansion of the Christian churches and the considerable social power which the bishops had come to possess.[23] This development was evident in the 313 Edict of Milan itself, through which Constantine and Licinius accepted Christianity, thereby, among other things, ordering the restitution of goods which had been confiscated from the Christians.[24] When we consider as well

[23] Though, as Cameron (2011, 8) mentions, emperors had to face opposition by Roman nobility, which had remained largely pagan. In 357, the Senate of Rome had the first clash with the imperial court when the Altar of Victory was removed from the Senate House by Constantius II, though the hostility of pagan senators to Christianity went all the way back to Constantine.

[24] "*When I, Constantine Augustus, as well as I, Licinius Augustus, fortunately met near Mediolanum (Milan), and were considering everything that pertained to the public welfare and security, we thought, among other things which we saw would be for the good of many, those regulations pertaining to the reverence of the Divinity ought certainly to be made first, so that we might grant to the Christians and others full authority to observe that religion which each preferred; whence any Divinity whatsoever in the seat of the heavens may be propitious and kindly disposed to us and all who are placed under our rule. And thus by this wholesome counsel and most upright provision we thought to arrange that no one whatsoever should be denied the opportunity to give his heart to the observance of the Christian religion, of that religion which he should think best for himself, so that the Supreme Deity, to whose worship we freely yield our hearts) may show in all things His usual favor and benevolence. Therefore, your Worship should know that it has pleased us to remove all conditions whatsoever, which were in the rescripts formerly given to you officially, concerning the Christians and now any one of these who wishes to observe Christian religion may do so freely and openly, without molestation. We thought it fit to commend these things most fully to your care that you may know that we have given to those Christians free and unrestricted opportunity of religious worship. When you see that this has been granted to them by us, your Worship will know that we have also conceded to other religions the right of open and free observance of their worship for the sake of the peace of our times, that each one may have the free opportunity to worship as he pleases; this regulation is made we that we may not seem to detract from any dignity or any religion. Moreover, in the case of the Christians especially we esteemed it best to order that if it happens anyone heretofore has bought from our treasury from anyone whatsoever, those places where they were previously accustomed to assemble, concerning which a certain decree had been made and a letter sent to you officially, the same shall be restored to the Christians without payment or any claim of recompense and without any kind of fraud or deception, Those, moreover, who have obtained the same by gift, are likewise to return them at once to the Christians. Besides, both those who have purchased and those who have secured them by gift, are to appeal to the vicar if they seek any recompense from our bounty, that they may be cared for through our clemency. All this property ought to be delivered at once to the community of the Christians through your intercession, and without delay. And since these Christians are known to have possessed not only those places in which they were accustomed to assemble, but also other property, namely the churches, belonging to them as a corporation and not as individuals, all these things which we have included under the above law, you will order to be restored, without any hesitation or controversy at all, to these Christians, that is to say to the corporations and their conventicles: providing, of course, that the above arrangements be followed so that those who return the same without payment, as we have said, may hope for an indemnity from our bounty. In all these*

the progressive weakening of imperial power, undermined by civil strife, it is not difficult to understand that the emperors were tempted to ally with the Christians to shore up their power. The first to clearly embrace this policy was Constantine (306–307), advised by one of the most important Christian figures of the era: Hosius, Bishop of Cordoba, in the province of Hispania. It should be pointed out that Constantine was successful at unifying the Empire in large measure thanks to the support of the Christian bishops, establishing an alliance between the secular and the religious authorities that would last for a long time.[25]

The ascent of Christianity was consolidated by Constantine's successors Constant (337–350), and Constantius II (337–361). In addition to prohibiting pagan sacrifices, they decreed the closure of the temples and banned outdoor demonstrations of non-Christian worship, sanctioning the violation of these rules with harsh penalties (Noethlichs 2006). These excesses certainly explain the reaction of the Emperor Julian (361–363), who the Christians accused of trying to restore ancient pagan practices, dubbing him the "Apostate"—from the Greek *apostasis* (abandonment). In reality, Julian had only acted to restore the freedom of worship which had been proclaimed in 313, and to allow pagans religious freedom by returning their temples to them.[26]

---

*circumstances you ought to tender your most efficacious intervention to the community of the Christians, that our command may be carried into effect as quickly as possible, whereby, moreover, through our clemency, public order may be secured. Let this be done so that, as we have said above, Divine favor towards us, which, under the most important circumstances we have already experienced, may, for all time, preserve and prosper our successes together with the good of the state. Moreover, in order that the statement of this decree of our good will may come to the notice of all, this rescript, published by your decree, shall be announced everywhere and brought to the knowledge of all, so that the decree of this, our benevolence, cannot be concealed*". Text in Lactantius (1998, Ch. 48, §9–12). According to Gaudemet (1989, 8), between others major scholars, there are two divergents versions of the so-called "Edict of Milan": a Greek version, translated by Eusebius in his *H. E.* X. §4–14, and a Latin copy of the letter (*litterae*) sent to the governor of Nicomedia, preserved in *De M. P.* Ch. 48, §9–12, by Lactantius, providing evidence of parallels between Roman and Greek legal terminology in the fourth century (Inwood and Miller 2007, 159). The discussion between historians whether the "Edict" is merely a confirmation (by Constantine and Licinus during their meeting in Milan, after the former's victory over Maxentius) of the already existing edict of Galerius promulgated in 311, or a letter to the provincial governors instructing how they should treat the Christians, is inconclusive, and irrelevant to our purposes: the political and juridical consequences of his conversion.

[25] From this point of view Emperor Constantine (312–337), became more important for Christianity itself than any pontiff. French Dominican Chenu (Chenu 1961, 59–87) hailed the decree of Vatican II (1962–1965) on Church-state relations as the "end of the Constantinian era", by which they meant the end of 1,700 years of certain patterns of Church-state relationships that traced their origins to the emperor. Even if this assertion may be exaggerated, it indicates how momentous Constantine's endorsement of Christianity was. For an overview of Constantine's conversion and the battle for toleration, see Stephenson (2010, 167–189).

[26] Julian's strategy for dealing with the Christians was threefold (Hoffmann 2004, 32). First, he attempted to isolate Christians from the mainstream of Roman society by limiting their rights and abrogating some benefits to which they were entitled under the law. Secondly, he attempted to circumscribe their influence in a way that does not seem to have occurred to his predecessors: creating a "pagan church" to rival the organization of the Christians, seeking to make Christianity irrelevant in a social sense. Finally, Julian returned to the custom of conservative pagan intellectuals like Celsus and Porphyry, by actively assailing Christian belief in philosophical polemics

However, Julian's early death made the Roman Empire's process of Christianization unstoppable.[27]

After a period of relative reconciliation under Valentinian I and Valens (364–375), Gratian and Valentinian II again stepped up the pressure against paganism in a process that culminated with Theodosius I (379–395), issuing the Edict of Thessalonica (380), decreeing the official status of the Catholic faith:

> We authorize the followers of this law to assume the title of Catholic Christians; but as for the others, since, in our judgment they are foolish madmen, we decree that they shall be branded with the ignominious name of heretics, and shall not presume to give to their conventicles the name of churches. They will suffer in the first place the chastisement of the divine condemnation and in the second the punishment of our authority, which, in accordance with the will of Heaven, we shall decide to inflict.[28]

It was Justinian (527–565), who was responsible for doing away with the last vestiges of paganism. To this end, he had the philosophical school of Athens closed; imposed Christian education upon all families, excluding pagans and heretics from all schools; made baptism mandatory, with anyone not baptized rendered unable to own property; and sanctioned heresy with the death penalty. As Sotomayor stated, in less than a century the panorama had completely changed. During the first centuries being a Christian had been a risk. By the late fourth century the risk consisted of continuing to be a pagan, or at least insisting on exhibiting it. Throughout this period it is not surprising that the number of those officially having converted to Christianity grew at a rapid rate, though profound convictions or faith were not necessarily the main motivations for requesting baptism (Cf. Sotomayor y Muro 1979, I, 178). It is interesting that from a legal point of view, in the Code of Justinian (534 AD), Catholic principles were already associated with the idea of the "common good" (Ando 2006, 130).[29]

Following the Edict of Milan, the various Christian churches were not only recognized but received favorable treatment by the Roman authorities, particularly after 324, when Constantine remained as the sole Roman emperor. The imperial administration then not only restored to them all the property seized during the persecutions, but also subsidized the clergy and promoted the construction of new

---

designed to prove the unoriginality of the faith. Julian wanted to portray Christianity as an apostate form of Judaism which did not remain true to the worthy aspects of a much older religious philosophy.

[27] On the crucial period from the disappearance of Julian to the imperial consolidation of Christian religion, see Chadwick (1993, 160–173).

[28] Text in Pharr (2001, 16.1.2). For an analysis of the Theodosian Decree: Judge (2008, 456–462).

[29] In the edict that authorized its publication, the Code represented the culmination of its author's efforts *ad prima communium rerum sustentationis* ("to provide for the maintenance of the common good"), and in the first section are included laws urging "that no one should dare to argue about (Catholicism) publicly". For an overview of imperial legislation in ecclesiastical and religious matters after 380, see Gaudemet (1992).

basilicas[30] in which Christians could gather. All this made possible the consolidation of the ecclesiastical apparatus which had been developing from the beginning.

### 4.3.3 *The Origins of Catholicism*

Originally, the main interest of the Church during the difficult second and third centuries was to organize its functioning and teachings. The first bishops and presbyters had to preserve the teaching of Christ against deviations, adapt it to the Gentile mind using the best in pagan thought, and face persecution and martyrdom. When conditions started to become more favorable in the course of the fourth century, the main concern of Church leaders was to build a closely-knit organization, which was as uncompromising towards heresy and schism as it was towards the demands of the state (Richardson 1996, 26).

Following the Council of Elvira (early fourth century) records indicate that councils were held with increasing frequency. In these early councils, the bishops not only resolved organizational issues, but began to define the dogmatic features which would eventually come to define official Christian doctrine in an effort to reinforce the unity of the Church. The churches continued to retain their autonomy, but above them the idea of a universal Church was crystallizing, whose members embraced a single body of beliefs (Hanson 1989).

The universality of the Church required, however, choosing the correct interpretation of the Scriptures which, once adopted by all the bishops, were to be maintained as the only valid ones for all churches. Fundamental to the orthodox consensus (Pelikan 1975, 333), was the affirmation of the authority of a tradition believed "everywhere, always, by all" (*Ubique, Semper, Ab Omnibus*).[31] This

[30] Another clear indication of the osmosis existing between the late Roman Empire and the consolidation of Christianity after 313, is illustrated by the evolution of the basilica (from the Greek *basiliké*: "royal") which originally made reference to the chamber in which the king dispensed justice. Beginning with the Roman era, it came to denote a public building generally located in the forum, the main square of all Roman cities. As Bardill (2012, 230), points out, before Constantine, for two and a half centuries Christians had been meeting and worshipping in ordinary houses. However, once persecutions ceased and the Church began to enjoy imperial favor, the number of converts increased and larger places of worship were required worthy of the dignity of the new officially recognized religion. The basilica was particularly appropriate to the Church's purpose, being an official building type of a suitable scale and grandeur. As of the first century the word began to refer to buildings featuring religious functions, and after the promulgation of the Edict of Thessalonica (380), the term "basilica" came to designate a large and important church which had received special privileges from the pope in matters of worship.

[31] As MacMullen (1984, 6) points out, the Church's duty to perfect its converts was carried out in quite a remarkable fashion by schools of instruction, weekly lectures offered authoritatively from pulpits, and other pastoral devices familiar to everyone. They also included tight control over the publication and dissemination of facts and opinions that dealt with Church matters. Secular literature from the pagan past was avoided, the non Christian setting of the Church was ignored in Christian historical accounts, and hostile writings and discarded views were not recopied or

approach entailed condemning views which deviated or diverged from those approved by the councils. Thus emerged the concept of heresy—from the Greek *hairesis* (choice)—to designate all those doctrines rejected by the gatherings of bishops. In this way, a whole series of beliefs were dismissed and condemned, among them those of the Arians, the Pelagians, the Pneumatomachi, the Monothelites, the Nestorians, the Monophysites, the Donatists and the Priscillianists. Thus was constituted a body of interpretations of the Scriptures established as "orthodox"—from the Greek words *orthos* (straight) and *doxa* (opinion).[32]

All this work involving the unification of dogma was also possible because during the fourth century, there appeared a number of remarkable Christian authors and thinkers producing writings of great importance (Young 1989). This second generation of Christian intellectuals came to be called the "Fathers of the Church", to differentiate them from the previous "Apologists".[33] While the latter arose primarily in the West, the Fathers of the Church were more numerous in the Eastern area of the Empire (Greek Patrology), though there were also important Fathers in the Western sphere, as well (Latin Patrology.)[34]

The orthodox interpretation of Scripture led to a progressive universalization of Christianity. Thus, did the Christian churches come to conform a single, coherent and uniform entity: the Catholic Church (from the Greek *katholikós*, meaning

passed on, or were actively suppressed. On the influence of the rhetorical schools on patristic exegesis, see Young (1989).

[32] For an overview of this issue, see Perkins (2010).

[33] The case of St. Augustine of Hippo (354–430), is quite representative. Raised in a Catholic family, as a boy he considered his religion to be True Wisdom. As Brown (2000, 31) points out, the Christ of the popular imagination in the middle of the fourth century, was no suffering savior. There were no crucifixes at that time. Christ was, rather, "the Great Word of God, the Wisdom of God". For a cultivated man of the time, the essence of Christianity consisted in just that Christ had established a monopoly on Wisdom and therefore the clear Christian revelation had trumped and replaced the conflicting opinions of the pagan philosophers. Apologists in the first two centuries of Christianity had done a good job defending the new rising faith from its detractors, which enabled Augustine's generation to develop a more intellectual interpretation of the new religion. On the Apologists movement, see Brent (2009, 209–250).

[34] Among the Eastern Fathers of the fourth century, we can point out St. Athanasius (295–373), the Patriarch of Alexandria who played a major role at the Council of Nicea (325); St. Basil (329–379), Bishop of Caesarea; Gregory of Nazianzus (330–393), who became the Patriarch of Constantinople; St. John Chrysostom (344–407), Bishop of Antioch and Patriarch of Alexandria; and St. Cyril of Alexandria (376–444), another Patriarch of the city, who fought against Nestorianism. Among Western fathers, we can highlight St. Ambrose (340–397), Archbishop of Milan, who had a hand in the conversion of St. Augustine; St. Jerome (345–419), who translated the Old Testament into Latin and corrected the Latin version of the New Testament, texts which would stand for a long time as the official Catholic versions of Holy Scriptures, or the "Vulgate"; and St. Augustine (354–430), Bishop of Hippo Regius, without any doubt the premiere Christian intellectual of his era.

"universal" or "general"; the preposition *katha* meaning "on" or "downwards", while the adjective *holós* means "whole" or "complete".)[35]

### 4.3.4 *Emperors vs. Bishops: "Caesaropapism"*

The recognition of Christianity as the official religion of the Empire would give rise to the problem of relations between the civil and ecclesiastical powers, as the emperors were loath to tolerate the existence of an independent power over a strictly spiritual domain.[36] This was called "Caesaropapism", a term coined by Max Weber who considered a Caesaropapist the "secular ruler that exercises supreme authority in ecclesiastic matters by virtue of his autonomous legitimacy" (Weber 2007, 1158–1204). It may be said that following the Edict of Milan (313), the emperors acted to intervene in the ecclesiastical sphere, even in regards to strictly doctrinal matters, to strengthen their political positions, as they wanted the complete subordination of priests to secular power (Swedberg and Agevall 2005, 22). In this sense, it was a system whereby an absolute monarch had supreme control over the Church within his dominions, and exercised it even in matters (e.g. doctrine), normally reserved for the ecclesiastical authority (Livingstone 2000, 218).

Worthy of note in this regard is the imperial attitude in the case of the Arian controversy: despite the formal condemnation of Arianism at Nicea in 325, the emperors came to favor the Arians, who they considered much more pliant to the pressures of civil authority. It is significant in this regard that at the Synod of Antioch, Constantine himself chose to condemn the "rebel bishops" (Catholics), who remained faithful to the Nicene doctrine, supporting the Arians instead.[37]

---

[35] The terms "catholic" (or "Catholic") have various levels of meaning. Dulles (1987, 185), mentions up to five. To be a Catholic is to share in the universal community, rooted in cosmic nature, that transcends the barriers of time and place, and has its source in God's self-communication. It can also mean "universal", as opposed to local or particular, a "catholic" approach being an all-inclusive one. In a polemical sense, used by some Church fathers, "catholic" meant "true" or "authentic", as opposed to false or heretical. The two last meanings concern the Church: "catholic" may refer the type of Christianity which attaches particular importance to visible continuity in space and time, and visible mediation through social and institutional structures, such as creeds, sacraments, and the historic episcopate. Finally, it is the title of the Church (Roman Catholic) which, organized in the world as a society, is governed by the bishop of Rome, as the successor of Peter, and by the bishops in communion with him.

[36] As Drake (2000, 7–8) notes, for three centuries, the Christian faith had to contend with a government that was, during the best of times, mildly resentful of its existence, and during the worst, ready to launch the most bitter persecutions upon it, unprecedented in their severity and duration. With Constantine, relations between the Church and state not only warmed but became intertwined, leading to the institution of Caesaropapism in the East, and to a less easy alliance in the West, the traces of which lie but thinly beneath the contours of modern Europe.

[37] On the attitude of Constantine at the Council of Nicea, see Chadwick (1993, 125–132).

His successor, Constantius II (337–361), went even further, persecuting the Catholics and even attacking Pope Julius I (337–352).

The imperial attitude triggered, of course, protests by leading Church figures of the day, including an almost centenarian Hosius of Cordoba (257–359). However, the clashes between civil and ecclesiastical power had only just begun. Imperial interventionism would recur with Theodosius I, whom St. Ambrose of Milan (340–397) criticized several times for his conduct in this regard.[38] The result was that Christianity was a religion at first prohibited by the state, then tolerated by it, and ultimately, endorsed and favored by it (Gaudemet 1973), a transformation that would have major consequences in the history of Western public law.

## 4.4 The Church as a Political Body

Official recognition by Rome of Christianity had far-reaching implications for it, as it took on a political dimension which it originally lacked. The church (*ekklesia* in Greek: "assembly") as the meeting of all the faithful, went from being a mere abstraction to a strong and thoroughly structured political and administrative organization, extending territorially throughout the Empire, featuring parishes and patriarchates, overseen by dioceses presided over by bishops, in what amounted to a veritable state within a state, with its own governing bodies, bishops gathered in councils, and its own law determined by council-issued ecclesiastical accords (canons). The emergence of churches called for a class of people devoting all of their time to ministerial activities.

### *4.4.1 The Origin of the Ecclesiastical Profession: Bishops, Deacons and Presbyters*

In the times of the 12 apostles, there existed no other credential qualifying one to spread the teachings of Christ than knowing them. When there were relatively few Christians pastoral activity was a joint effort led by those who best knew Christ's teachings: the "bishops" or "episcopal" authorities—from the Greek *episképtomai* (to inspect).[39]

[38] On the dispute between Theodosius and St. Ambrose during the Easter crisis of 386, see Mclynn (1994, 181–195).

[39] In 1 Timothy 3:1 St. Paul mentions the function of "overseer": *ei tis episcopes oregetai, kalou ergou epithymei* which means: "If someone desires the function of overseer, he wishes for a noble task". The Greek word for "task" is *ergon*, the Latin *opus*. From this passage, Greek and Latin commentators considered an episcopate a task, a "ministry", and not an honorific distinction. Christians were supposed to avoid vainglory and ambition in seeking the episcopate (Rapp 2005, 166).

Bishops were the undisputed leaders of every Christian community. Their mission was to ensure the preservation of the faith, discipline, and the proper execution of liturgical functions, to serve as guarantors of ecclesiastical unity, and to represent their churches in their relationships with fellow congregations.[40] Along with bishops appeared "deacons" (from the Greek *diakonos*, meaning "servant"), the former's trusted associates, initially responsible for the administration of the Church's temporal assets. As consultants and advisors to the deacons came the "presbyters"—from *presbyteros* (the oldest).[41]

The growth of the Christian communities, a consequence of the religion's astonishing spread over the course of the second and third centuries, soon made it necessary for the bishops and their assistants to devote all their time to pastoral work. In this way, the *ordo clericalis* began to establish itself, from which the laity would ultimately be excluded.

### *4.4.2 The Development of Church Organization: Parishes and Dioceses*

The first organized groups of Christian churches appeared just a few years after Christ's death. The assembly of Christians was originally a community of pilgrims and strangers[42]; hence the word "parish" (from *paroikois*: foreigner) to designate

---

[40] Originally, a bishop ruled over a congregation with his council of presbyters, as together they developed a closely-knit organization that was able to withstand the concerted persecutions of the third century. However, it is not clear how bishops acquired powers earlier vested in local bodies of presbyters (Richardson 1996, 20). What we know is that the development was orderly and spread rapidly because of a series of different factors. The obvious expedience of having a single administrative head, the fact that a congregation could only afford to maintain one full-time official, the forcefulness of certain leading figures, and the suitability of having a single celebrant for worship all, doubtless played a role in the rise of the monepiscopate.

[41] In the middle of the third century, the church in Rome featured 46 priests, 7 deacons, 7 subdeacons, 42 acolytes, and a combined total of 52 exorcists, readers and doorkeepers. Three centuries later, under Justinian, the staff attached to the Great Church in the Eastern capital of Constantinople, was fixed at 60 priests, 100 deacons, 40 deaconesses, 90 subdeacons, 110 readers, 25 singers, and 100 doorkeepers. There was also a substantial increase in the number of bishoprics. By the fifth century, all major cities had their own bishop, and additional bishops (*chorepiskopoi*) were assigned to smaller rural settlements. It has been calculated that there were a total of 2,000 bishops in the later Roman Empire (Rapp 2005, 172–173).

[42] As stated in the New Testament itself and, more specifically, in Chapter 11 of the Paul's epistle to the Hebrews, in paragraphs 13–16: "These all died in faith, not having received the promises, but having seen them afar off, and were persuaded of them, and embraced them, and confessed that they were strangers and pilgrims on the earth". (11:13) "For they that say such things declare plainly that they seek a country". (11:14). "And truly, if they had been mindful of that country from whence they came out, they might have had opportunity to have returned". (11:15) "But now they desire a better country, that is, an heavenly: wherefore God is not ashamed to be called their God: for he hath prepared for them a city" (11.16).

the private homes in which the first pastoral meetings were held. In Rome, the meeting places of the faithful were originally presided over by bishops, deacons or presbyters. They were, thus, the first pastors in the Church's history.

Over time, the parishes were grouped together, for administrative purposes, into "ecclesiastical provinces", usually coinciding with the imperial divisions of the same name. In this way, a hierarchically organized territorial structure gradually developed. The first gatherings of Christians presided over by bishops, were initially held in secret (in the catacombs). After Catholicism became the official religion of the Roman Empire, the bishops exercised their functions with authority over larger territories which would, eventually, be referred to as "dioceses"—from the Greek words *dioikeo* (administrate) and *oikos* (home). Traditionally, the diocese was a Roman administrative district, which serves to show how bishops could combine their ecclesiastical role with a secular magistracy. Once a bishop was ordained, he could, nevertheless, aspire to a civic office (Rapp 2005, 205). In fact, it seemed a regular practice in these paleo-Christian times for active ministers of the Church to sometimes attempt to join the secular administration. Dioceses were consolidated before in the Near East (Corinth, Ephesus, Thessalonica, Antioch), where the increased penetration of Eastern religions favored Christianity's rapid spread. In fact, Asia Minor provided the most fertile soil for Christian evangelism, as this region was dotted with Jewish communities, which had already accommodated themselves to Hellenistic thought and life (Hinson 1996, 60).

### 4.4.3 Metropolitans and Patriarchs

The development of the aforementioned territorial structure soon called for a power structure as well. All the bishops of a province recognized a "metropolitan"—from the Greek *meter* (mother) and the *polis* (city). Above the metropolitans, in turn, were the patriarchs, the bishops of especially important cities. The most important decisions, however, were made collectively in assemblies, composed of bishops from different provinces.[43]

### 4.4.4 The Councils as Collective Decision-Making Bodies

The bishops of a province which recognized the authority of a metropolitan began meeting in synods—from the Greek *synodos* (meeting)—to solve the problems of

[43] There were initially three patriarchates, corresponding to the apostolic sees of Rome, Alexandria and Antioch, a situation which would be maintained until the Council of Chalcedon (451), when the patriarchates of Constantinople and Jerusalem were added. The Moorish expansion in the seventh century, would wipe out the patriarchates of Jerusalem, Antioch and Alexandria, leaving only Rome and Constantinople.

their respective communities. At a higher level were the assemblies of all the bishops of several provinces or councils—from the Latin *concilium* (meeting, council). Collective decision-making in the Church on matters of teaching and practice surely commenced in apostolic times, but there is no evidence of consultation and common action among the Christian communities themselves until late in the second century (Hess 2002, 5). And it would not be until the beginning of the fourth century that we have the first written evidence of decisions made by a council: the first of these was held in Hispania, in Iliberis, near modern-day Granada, attended by 19 bishops from all over Spain, who approved 81 rules (Dale 2012). These collegial agreements amongst the bishops became binding on the Christian communities of the different ecclesiastical provinces. Conciliar rules were called ecclesiastical *canons*, which is why Church law came to be known as "canon law".

The official recognition of Christianity led to the practice of holding regular councils of this type. It is highly significant that a year after Constantine became the sole ruler of the Empire, in 325, the first of the "ecumenical"—from the Greek *oikúmene* (world)—councils was held in Nicaea to condemn Arianism. Nicaea marked the first of a series of ecumenical councils which laid down the doctrine of the Church, among which were those at Ephesus (431) and Chalcedon (451).[44]

### *4.4.5 The Origins of the Papacy as a Moral Authority*

In the West, the bishops of the first churches to emerge in the various provinces of the Empire, while maintaining a manifest autonomy, granted almost from the outset a certain degree of moral supremacy to the bishop of Rome,[45] who they began to call the "Pope"—from the Greek *pappas* (father). It is worthwhile to note that the title was formerly given, especially from the third to the fifth century, to any bishop and sometimes to simple priests as an ecclesiastical title expressing affectionate respect. It is still used in the East in reference to the Orthodox patriarch of Alexandria, and to Orthodox priests. Only during the ninth century, was its use restricted to the bishop of Rome, a constraint officially imposed in 1073, by Pope Gregory VII.[46]

[44] On the emergence of canonical legislation from early fourth-century councils, the ecumenical councils and the appearance of the Eastern and Western canonical collections, see Hess (2002, 35–59). On the relationship between the councils and imperial legislation, see Bajo (2006).

[45] Rome and Alexandria ranked first and second among the great cities of the Roman Empire. The Council of Nicea (325), recognized the bishops of those cities as having authority that extended over a considerable region beyond the limits of their own churches (Sullivan 2001, 171). However, over time Rome became the capital of Christendom. On the rise to power of the bishop of Rome in the city's post-curial civic government, see Liebeschuetz (2003, 137–168).

[46] About the pope's spiritual authority, it may be stated at the time of St. Ignatius of Antioch, the bishop of the city who was martyred by Trajan in 117, even Eastern Christian communities

The popes exercised their moral authority through letters called "decretals", in which they settled questions raised by other bishops. These documents will end up soon having legal value, giving the popes the same legislative power that Roman emperors enjoyed during the Dominate.

## TIMELINE

### A. Judaism

### The Origins of Judaism

| | |
|---|---|
| 1800 BC | Arrival of the Israelites to Judea. |
| 1700 | Emigration to Egypt. |
| 1372–1350 | Amenhotep IV (Akhenaton). Religious reform. |
| 1250 | The Israelites flee to Egypt, led by Moses. |
| 1029–974 | David, King of the Hebrews. |

### First Temple: The Writing of the Bible Begins (Old Testament) (13th–10th—Thirteenth Centuries BC)

| | |
|---|---|
| 973–935 | Rule of Solomon. Construction of the Temple. |
| 931 | Scission of Jewish territory into the kingdoms of Israel and Judah. |

*Age of the Prophets (Eighth to Sixth Centuries BC)*

| | |
|---|---|
| 722 | The Kingdom of Israel is conquered by the Assyrians. |
| *586* | Nebuchadnezzar takes Jerusalem. Start of captivity in Babylon. End of the Kingdom of Judah. |

(churches) recognized, to an extent, the supremacy of the Bishop of Rome, who they considered the primary defender of orthodoxy, as the direct successor of St. Peter who, according to tradition, was the first to occupy the Holy See. However, was really Peter the first pope? In reality, the earliest lists of popes do not begin with Peter but a man named Linus, but it should be noted that, as an apostle, Peter was far more important than a bishop or pope. And "it is inconceivable that Peter, an apostle, came to Rome, the capital of the empire, and did not have a determining role in that community. If that is true, then it follows that Peter can, with qualification, but justly, be called the first bishop of Rome. And if he is the first bishop of Rome, then he is the first pope" (O'Malley 2010, 11–12). In any case, Popes came to be commonly referred to themselves as "the vicar of Peter", *vicarius Petri*. Among the cities of the ancient Roman world, Rome was unique in that it was the site of the preaching and death of *two* apostles: Peter and Paul. Rome's double "apostolicity" allowed it to refer to itself as apostolic not only because of Peter's leadership among the disciples of Jesus, but also because the great Paul also came to Rome and died there. The bishopric of Rome became the "Apostolic See", a status consolidated when Christianity became the official religion of the Roman Empire. For an overview of the origins and consolidation of the institution of the papacy see Chadwick (1993, 237–246).

### Second Temple: Beginning of the Talmudic Era—Mishnaic Stage—(Sixth Century BC—First Century AD)

| | |
|---|---|
| 539 | Cyrus the Great destroys Babylon. The Israelites return to Jerusalem. |
| 320 | The diadochus Ptolemy, governor of Egypt, conquers Jerusalem. |
| 167 | Beginning of Hellenistic domination. Persecutions (Antiochus IV). |
| 165 | Revolt of Judah Maccabee. |
| 160 | Start of the reign of the Maccabees. |
| 142 | Judea, an autonomous territory. |
| 63 BC | Pompey conquers Jerusalem. Judea, a Roman province. |
| 74 AD | Conquest of Masada by the Romans. End of the Jewish resistance (Third Temple [74–135]). |

### The Diaspora (135–1948)

| | |
|---|---|
| 135 | After another rebellion by the Jews, the Emperor Hadrian orders the definitive destruction of the Temple of Solomon. Thus begins the Diaspora, to last 1,813 years, until the foundation of the State of Israel in 1948. |

*End of the Talmudic Period*:

| | |
|---|---|
| Fourth century | Palestinian or Jerusalem Talmud |
| Sixth century | Babylonian Talmud ("Babli") |

## B. Christianity

### The Origins (First Century)

| | |
|---|---|
| 7 BC | Birth in Bethlehem (Palestine) of Jesus during the Principate of Augustus (27 BC–14 AD). |
| 26 AD | Crucifixion of Jesus during the Principate of Tiberius (14–37). |
| Circa 33 AD | St. Peter is elected bishop of Rome (according to tradition). |

*Writing of the New Testament* (*Second Half of the First Century*):

| | |
|---|---|
| 54–68 | Emperor Nero. First persecutions of the Christians. |
| | *Circa 64* Martyrdom of St. Peter. |
| | *Circa 66* Death of St. Mark the Evangelist. |
| | *Circa 67* Decapitation of St. Paul. |
| 74 | End of the Jewish era of the Second Temple. |
| Circa 100 | Death of St. John the Evangelist. |
| 135 | Destruction of the Third Temple. Initiation of the Jewish Diaspora. |

### The Spread of Christianity (Second to Third Centuries)

*The Apologists*

| | |
|---|---|
| 165 | Death of St. Justin (born 100). |
| 208 | Death of St. Irenaeus (born 130). |
| 240 | Death of Tertullian (born 160). |
| 258 | Death of St. Cyprian (born 210). |
| 270 | Death of St. Gregory the Wonderworker (born 215). |

*The Last Persecutions*

| | |
|---|---|
| 270–275 | Emperor Aurelian attempts to impose a new official religion. |
| 284–305 | Emperor Diocletian. Last persecution of the Christians. |

### The Official Establishment of Christianity (Fourth Century)

| | |
|---|---|
| 311 | The Edict of Toleration by Galerius recognizes Christianity. |
| 313 | Promulgation of the Edict of Milan by Constantine and Licinius. Possible celebration of the Council of Elvira (old Iliberis, near Granada, Spain). |
| 314 | Council of Arles. |
| 325 | Council of Nicea, First Ecumenical Council. |
| Circa 345 | Birth of St. Jerome (419), translator into Latin of the Old Testament, or Jewish Bible. |
| Circa 354 | Birth of St. Augustine. |
| 361–363 | Julian (the Apostate), emperor. Last attempt to restore the ancient pagan rites. |
| 380 | Edict of Thessalonica through which Theodosius (379–395) decrees the official status of Christianity. |
| 381 | Ecumenical Council of Constantinople. |
| 392 | The Edict of Constantinople prohibits all pagan practices. Christianity is the only religion tolerated. |
| 431 | Ecumenical Council of Ephesus. |
| 451 | Ecumenical Council of Chalcedon. |

## References

Alikin, V. A. (2010). *The earliest history of the Christian gathering: Origin, development, and content of the Christian gathering in the first to third centuries*. Leiden: Brill.

Ando, C. (2006). Religion and Ius publicum. In C. Ando (Coed.), *Religion and law in classical and Christian Rome* (pp. 126–146). Stuttgart: Franz Steiner.

Assmann, J. (1998). *Moses the Egyptian: The memory of Egypt in western monotheism*. Cambridge, MA: Harvard University Press.
Bajo, F. (2006). Concilios y legislación imperial. *Studia historica. Historia antigua*, (24), 131–142.
Bardill, J. (2012). *Constantine, divine emperor of the Christian golden age*. Cambridge, UK: Cambridge University Press.
Bernstein, R. J. (1998). *Freud and the legacy of Moses*. Cambridge, UK: Cambridge University Press.
Brent, A. (1999). *The imperial cult and the development of church order: Concepts and images of authority in paganism and early Christianity before the Age of Cyprian*. Leiden: Brill.
Brent, A. (2009). The apologists and the politics of the trinity: Logos and Ignatius. In *A political history of early Christianity* (pp. 209–250). London: T & T Clark.
Broshi, M. (2004). What Jesus learned from the Essenes: The blessing of poverty, the bane of divorce. *Biblical Archaeology Review, 30*(1), 32–37.
Brown, P. (2000). *Augustine of hippo: A biography* (Revised edition). Berkeley, CA: University of California Press.
Brown, P. (2003). *The rise of western Christendom* (2nd ed.). Oxford, UK: Blackwell.
Cameron, A. (2011). *Last pagans of Rome*. Oxford: Oxford University Press.
Chadwick, H. (1993). *The early church. The story of emergent Christianity from the apostolic age to the dividing of the ways between the Greek Eats and the Latin West* (Revised edition, Vol. 1). London: Penguin.
Chapman, D. W. (2008). *Ancient Jewish and Christian perceptions of crucifixion*. Tübingen: Mohr Siebeck.
Chenu, M. D. (1961). La fin de l'ère constantinienne. In J. P. Dubois-Dumée et al. (Eds.), *Un concile pour notre temps: Journée d'études des informations catholiques internationales* (pp. 59–87). Paris: Cerf.
Cohick, L. H. (2010). Jews and Christians. In D. J. Bingham (Ed.), *The Routledge companion to early Christian thought* (pp. 68–86). New York: Routledge.
Cook, J. G. (2010). *Roman attitudes toward the Christians: From Claudius to Hadrian*. Tübingen: Mohr Siebeck.
Dale, A. W. W. Sir. (2012). *The synod of Elvira and Christian life in the fourth century* (Reprinted from the 1882s edition). Stockbridge, MA: HardPress Publishing.
De Palma Digeser, E. (2006). Religion, law and the Roman polity: The era of the great persecution. In C. Ando & J. Rüpke (Eds.), *Religion and law in classical and Christian Rome* (pp. 68–84). Stuttgart: Franz Steiner.
Drake, H. A. (2000). *Constantine and the bishops: The politics of intolerance*. Baltimore, MD: Johns Hopkins University Press.
Dulles, A. (1987). *The catholicity of the Church*. Oxford: Oxford University Press.
Dunn, J. D. G. (1999). *Jews and Christians: The parting of the ways, A.D. 70 to 135*. Grand Rapids, MI: Eerdmans Publishing.
Ehrman, B. D. (2008). *Peter, Paul and Mary Magdalene: The followers of Jesus in history and legend*. Oxford, UK: Oxford University Press.
Ferguson, E. (2003). *Backgrounds of early Christianity* (3rd ed.). Grand Rapids, MI: William B. Eerdmans Pub.
Fredriksen, P. (2010). Christians in the Roman Empire in the first three centuries CE. In D. S. Potter (Ed.), *A companion to the Roman Empire* (pp. 587–606). Malden, MA: Blackwell.
Freud, S. (2010). *Moses and monotheism: Three essays* (Reprint of 1939 Edition). Eastford, CT: Martino Fine Books.
Gaudemet, J. (1973). De la liberté constantinienne a une Église d'état. *Revue de droit canonique*, (23), 59–76.
Gaudemet, J. (1989). Le cadre historique: De la reconnaissance du christianisme à la religion d'Etat. In G. Le Bras (Ed.), *Histoire du droit et des institutions de l'Eglise en Occident. 3. L'Église dans l'Empire romain: (IVe-Ve siècles)* (pp. 7–14). Paris: Sirey.

Gaudemet, J. (1992). Politique ecclésiastique et législation religieuse après l'édit de Théodose I de 380. In *Droit et société aux derniers siècles de l'empire romain* (pp. 175–196). Napoli: Jovene.
Hanson, R. (1989). The achievement of orthodoxy in the fourth century AD. In R. Williams (Ed.), *Making of orthodoxy: Essays in honor of Henry Chadwick* (pp. 142–156). Cambridge, UK: Cambridge University Press.
Hartog, P. (2010). Greco-Roman understanding of Christianity. In D. J. Bingham (Ed.), *The Routledge companion to early Christian thought* (pp. 51–67). New York: Routledge.
Hess, H. (2002). *The early development of Canon law and the Council of Serdica*. Oxford: Oxford University Press.
Hinson, E. G. (1996). *The early Church: Origins to the dawn of the Middle Ages*. Nashville, TX: Abingdon.
Hoffmann, R. J. (2004). Introduction: Julian the restorer. In *Julian's against the Galileans* (pp. 11–86). Amherst, NY: Prometheus Books.
Horsley, R. A. (2010). Jesus-in-context: A relational approach. In T. Holmén & S. E. Porter (Eds.), *Handbook for the study of the historical Jesus* (Vol. I, pp. 207–240). Leiden: Brill.
Inwood, B., & Miller, F. D. (2007). Law in Roman philosophy. In F. D. Miller & C.-A. Biondi (Eds.), *A history of the philosophy of law from the ancient Greeks to the Scholastics* (pp. 136–165). Dordrecht, Netherlands: Springer.
Judge, E. A. (2008). *The first Christians in the Roman world: Augustan and New Testament essays*. Tübingen: Mohr Siebeck.
Lactantius, L. C. F. (1998). *De mortibus persecutorum = On the deaths of the persecutors*. Armidale, New South Wales: Northern Antiquities Press (First published in the Ante-Nicene Christian Library, Edinburgh, 1867–1872).
Lane Fox, R. (2006). *Pagans and Christians: In the Mediterranean world from the second century to the conversion of Constantine* (Reissued). London: Penguin.
Larrainzar, C. (2004). Las raíces canónicas de la cultura jurídica occidental. *Annaeus: anales de la tradición romanística,* (1), 207–224.
Liebeschuetz, J. H. W. G. (2003). *The decline and fall of the Roman city*. Oxford: Oxford University Press.
Livingstone, E. A. (2000). Caesaropapism. In F. F. L. Cross & E. A. Livingstone (Eds.), *The concise Oxford dictionary of the Christian Church* (p. 264). Oxford: Oxford University Press.
Macmullen, R. (1984). *Christianizing the Roman Empire: AD 100–400*. New Haven, CT: Yale University Press.
Mclynn, N. B. (1994). *Ambrose of Milan: Church and court in a Christian capital*. Berkeley, CA: University of California Press.
Murphy-O'Connor, J. (1996). *Paul: A critical life*. Oxford, UK: Clarendon.
Noethlichs, K. L. (2006). Revolution from the top? "Orthodoxy" and the persecution of heretics in imperial legislation from Constantine to Justinian. In C. Ando & J. Rüpke (Eds.), *Religion and law in classical and Christian Rome* (pp. 115–125). Stuttgart: Franz Steiner.
O'Malley, J. W. S. J. (2010). Peter: Bishop of Rome? In *A history of the popes: From Peter to the present* (pp. 3–12). Lanham, MD: Rowman & Littlefield Publishers Inc.
Osman, A. (1999). *Out of Egypt: The roots of Christianity revealed*. London: Arrow.
Pelikan, J. J. (1975). *The Christian tradition: A history of the development of doctrine*. I. *The emergence of the Catholic tradition (100–600)* (5 Vols.). Chicago: University of Chicago Press.
Perkins, P. (2010). Schism and heresy: Identity, cracks, and canyons in early Christianity. In D. J. Bingham (Ed.), *The Routledge companion to early Christian thought* (pp. 227–240). New York: Routledge.
Pharr, C. (2001). *Theodosian code and novels and the Sirmondian constitutions*. Princeton, NJ: Princeton University Press (Reprint of 1952 edition. A Translation with Commentary, Glossary, and Bibliography.).
Rapp, C. (2005). *Holy bishops in late antiquity: The nature of Christian leadership in an age of transition*. Berkeley, CA: University of California Press.

Renan, E. (2007). *The life of Jesus*. San Diego, CA: The Book Tree.
Richardson, C. C. (1996). Introduction to early Christian literature and its settings. In *Early Christian fathers* (pp. 15–26). New York: Touchstone.
Rives, J. B. (2007). *Religion in the Roman Empire*. Malden, MA: Blackwell.
Samuelsson, G. (2011). *Crucifixion in antiquity: An inquiry into the background and significance of the New Testament terminology of crucifixion*. Tübingen: Mohr Siebeck.
Schott, J. M. (2008). *Christianity, empire, and the making of religion in late antiquity*. Philadelphia, PA: University of Pennsylvania Press.
Segal, A. F. (1990). *Paul, the convert: The apostolate and apostasy of Saul the Pharisee*. New Haven, CT: Yale University Press.
Shean, J. F. (2010). *Soldiering for god: Christianity and the Roman army*. Leiden: Brill.
Sotomayor y Muro, M. (1979). La Iglesia en la España romana y visigoda: (siglos I–VIII). In R. García Villoslada (Ed.), *Historia de la Iglesia en España*. I. (pp. 7–400). Madrid: B.A.C.
Stephenson, P. (2010). *Constantine: Roman emperor, Christian victor*. New York: Overlook Press.
Sullivan, F. (2001). *From apostles to bishops: The development of the episcopacy in the early Church*. New York: Newman Press.
Swedberg, R., & Agevall, O. (2005). *The Max Weber dictionary: Key words and central concepts*. Stanford, CA: Stanford University Press.
Thiede, C. P. (2001). *The Dead Sea scrolls and the Jewish origins of Christianity*. New York: Palgrave.
Van Seters, J. (2003). *A law book for the Diaspora: Revision in the study of the covenant code*. Oxford: Oxford University Press.
Weber, M. (2007). *Economy and society*. Berkeley, CA: University of California Press.
Wright, D. P. (2009). *Inventing god's law: How the covenant code of the bible used and revised the laws of Hammurabi*. New York: Oxford University Press.
Yerusalmi, J. H. (1991). *Freud's Moses: Judaism terminable and interminable*. New Haven, CT: Yale University Press.
Young, F. (1989). The rhetorical schools and their influence on patristic exegesis. In *Making of orthodoxy: Essays in honor of Henry Chadwick* (pp. 182–199). Cambridge, UK: Cambridge University Press.

## Further Reading

Attridge, H. W., et al. (Eds.). (1990). *Of scribes and scrolls: Studies on the Hebrew Bible, intertestamental Judaism, and Christian origins, presented to John Strugnell on the occasion of his sixtieth birthday*. Lanham, MD: University Press of America.
Beilby, J. K., & Eddy, P. R. (Eds.). (2009). *The historical Jesus: Five views*. Downers Grove, IL: IVP Academic.
Bettenson, H., & Maunder, C. (1999). *Documents of the Christian church* (3rd ed.). Oxford: Oxford University Press.
Bowes, K., & Kulikowski, M. (Eds.). (2005). *Hispania in late antiquity: Current perspectives*. Boston, MA: Brill.
Boyd, W. K. (2006). *The ecclesiastical edicts of the Theodosian Code* (2nd print). Clark, NJ: The Lawbook Exchange Ltd.
Brent, A. (2009). *A political history of early Christianity*. London: T & T Clark.
Brown, P. (1992). *Power and persuasion in late antiquity: Towards a Christian Empire*. Madison, WI: University of Wisconsin Press.
Brown, P. (2012). *Through the eye of a needle: Wealth, the fall of Rome, and the making of Christianity in the west, 350–550 AD*. Princeton, NJ: Princeton University Press.

Crossan, J. D. (1993). *The historical Jesus: The life of a Mediterranean Jewish Peasant*. New York: HarperOne.

Cunningham, A. (Ed.). (1982). *The early Church and the state*. Philadelphia: Fortress Press.

Curchin, L. (1991). *Roman Spain: Conquest and assimilation*. London: Routledge.

Elm, S. (2012). *Sons of Hellenism, fathers of the Church: Emperor Julian, Gregory of Nazianzus, and the vision of Rome*. Berkeley: University of California Press.

Esler, P. F. (2004). *The early Christian world*. New York: Routledge.

Finkelstein, I., & Mazar, A. (2007). *The quest for the historical Israel: Debating archaeology and the history of early Israel*. Atlanta, GA: Society of Biblical Literature.

Frend, W. H. C. (2002). *Orthodoxy, paganism, and dissent in the early Christian centuries*. Aldershot: Ashgate.

Gooder, P. (2010). In search of the early 'Church': The New Testament and the development of Christian communities. In G. Mannion & L. S. Mudge (Eds.), *The Routledge companion to the Christian Church* (pp. 9–27). London: Routledge.

Harvey, S. A., & Hunter, D. G. (Eds.). (2008). *The Oxford handbook of early Christian studies*. Oxford: Oxford University Press.

Lenski, N. (Ed.). (2006). *The Cambridge companion to the age of Constantine*. Cambridge: Cambridge University Press.

Lilla, M. (2007). *The stillborn god: Religion, politics, and the modern west*. New York: Vintage.

Lynh, J. H. (2010). *Early Christianity: A brief history*. New York: Oxford University Press.

Matthews, V. H. (2003). *A brief history of ancient Israel*. Louisville, KT: Westminster John Knox Press.

Mitchell, M., & Young, F. M. (Eds.). (2006). *The Cambridge history of Christianity. I. Early Christianity: Origins to Constantine*. Cambridge, UK: Cambridge University Press.

Murdoch, A. (2005). *The last pagan: Julian the Apostate and the death of the ancient world*. Stroud: Sutton Pub.

Norris, R. A. (1980). *The Christological controversy: (Sources of early Christian thought)*. Minneapolis, MN: Fortress Press.

Schweitzer, A. (1998). *The mysticism of Paul the apostle*. Baltimore, MD: Johns Hopkins University Press.

Sessa, K. (2012). *The formation of papal authority in late antique Italy: Roman bishops and the domestic sphere*. New York: Cambridge University Press.

Stanton, G. N., & Stroumsa, G. G. (Eds.). (2008). *Tolerance and intolerance in early Judaism and Christianity* (2nd ed.). Cambridge, UK: Cambridge University Press.

Taylor, L. R. (2002). *The divinity of the Roman emperor* (Reprint of the 1931 edition). Atlanta, GA: Scholars Press.

Van Dam, R. (2007). *The Roman revolution of Constantine*. Cambridge, MA: Cambridge University Press.

Walzer, M. (2012). *In God's shadow: Politics in the Hebrew Bible*. New Haven, CT: Yale University Press.

Wessel, S. (2008). *Leo the great and the spiritual rebuilding of a Universal Rome*. Leiden: Brill.

# Part II
# The Origins of the European "Nations"

# Chapter 5
# From the Germanic Tribes to Kingdoms

In minoribus rebus principes consultant; of maioribus omnes ... (Princes resolve the minor things, the major ones are dealt with at meetings for all ...)—Tacitus (55–120)[1].

## Contents


5.1 The Invasions ... 94
5.1.1 The First Germanic Wave: The Visigoths (Late Fourth Century) ... 94
5.1.2 The Second Wave: The Suebi, Vandals and Alani (Early Fifth Century) ... 96
5.1.3 The Third Wave: Franks, Burgundians, Alamanni, Angles and Saxons (Mid Fifth Century) ... 96
5.1.4 The Last Wave: The Lombards ... 97
5.2 The Germanic Kingdoms ... 97
5.2.1 Diversity Versus Unity ... 97
5.2.2 The Social and Political Transformation of the Germanic Peoples ... 98
5.2.3 Roman Monarchy vs. German Royalty ... 99
5.2.4 The Gradual Assimilation of the Roman Imperial Tradition ... 101
5.2.5 The Structural Weaknesses of the New Kingdoms: Patrimonial Possession, Inheritance and Protofeudalism ... 102
5.3 The Church and the Preservation of the Roman "State" Tradition ... 103
5.3.1 The Emergence of the Monastic Movement ... 103
5.3.2 St. Gregory the Great and the Consolidation of Papal Authority ... 104
5.3.3 Christianity and the New Germanic Peoples ... 105
5.3.4 The Church and the "Romanization" of the Germanic Kingdoms ... 106
5.4 The Origin of the European "Nations?" ... 108
References ... 115


[1] Tacitus 2006, XI.




B. Aguilera-Barchet, *A History of Western Public Law*,
DOI 10.1007/978-3-319-11803-1_5

## 5.1 The Invasions

Along with the rise of Christianity, the other factor which transformed the political constitution of Roman society were invasions by a series of Germanic peoples who, because they lived outside the borders of the Empire, were called "barbarians".[2] These peoples penetrated the Empire beginning in the late fourth century, and in many cases ended up as allies of Rome (*foederati*), defending the Empire's borders. During the fifth century they settled in different areas of the Western Empire, although it was only after 476—when Odoacer deposed Romulus Augustulus—that Visigoths, Ostrogoths, Franks, Burgundians, Alamanni, Angles, and Lobards formed independent kingdoms.[3]

### *5.1.1 The First Germanic Wave: The Visigoths (Late Fourth Century)*

The Goths were the first of the Germanic peoples to come into contact with the Romans. Hailing from the Black Sea, by the end of the third century, they had split into two groups: the Western Goths (Visigoths) and the Eastern Goths (Ostrogoths).[4] Driven by the Huns, the former crossed the border of the Roman Empire, defeating and killing Emperor Valens at the Battle of Adrianople (378). As it was clear that Rome could not contain them, Theodosius I signed a first treaty (*foedus*) with the Visigoths in the year 382, whereby in exchange for their aid in defending the Empire they were granted permission to settle within its boundaries (specifically Lower Moesia, modern-day Bulgaria). After the death of Theodosius and the rupturing of the Roman Empire into Eastern and Western divisions, the Visigoths elected their first leader from among one of their most illustrious lineages, the Balthes: Alaric I (395–410), who aimed to exploit the youth of Honorius (395–423),

---

[2] The word came from the Greek term to designate "all he who was not Greek", and was not the citizen of a *polis*. The Greeks had first used it in reference to the Persians. In the Roman Empire a person not inculcated in Roman culture was considered a barbarian. Thus were the German peoples living outside the Empire's borders referred to as *barbari*. In more modern times the term acquired its meaning of "savage" or "uncivilized" (Mathisen 2006, 1011–1040).

[3] Chrysos (2003, 13–16) sees three phases in the route taken by the individual *gentes* in the process of establishing themselves as *regna*, on or at the periphery of the Roman Empire. In the first phase, during the migration period, barbarians, individually or as a group were recruited into the Roman army. In the second phase, the migrating *gentes* entered the orbit of the Roman Empire, either in accordance with a peace treaty, such as a *foederati*, or subjected to Roman domination, via *dediticii*. Finally, in the third phase, barbarians transformed their *gens* into *regna*, initially within the framework of the Empire, at least until the Western Roman Empire disappeared in 476 AD.

[4] The term "Goth" appears for the first time between AD 16 and 18, but initially it was a general name which replaced "Scythians" and encompassed a diverse range of Germanic and even non-Germanic people. The first recorded division of the Gothic people into the Visigoths and Ostrogoths dates from 291 (Wolfram 1990, 20 and 24).

the first emperor of the West, and invade Italy (Wolfram 1990, 143–145). He was stopped, however, at the Battle of Pollentia (near Asti) in the spring 402, by the regent Stilicho, who chose to negotiate with the Germanic leader, appointing him commander-in-chief (*magister militum*) of the Western Empire. However, it would be necessary for Stilicho to soundly defeat Alaric I at Verona, in 403, before the Visigoths agreed to serve as federated troops (allies) of Rome. This was a decisive step, as the knowledge and experience acquired opened up to individual members of the Visigothic nation a path which, once taken, would lead them to a more or less substantial affiliation and even solidarity with the Roman world (Chrysos 2003, 14).

The relationship between Rome and the Visigoths, however, was stormy. Stilicho was the last Roman general capable of defending the Western Empire. After his death in 408, Alaric I set out to conquer Italy, managing to plunder the city of Rome from August 24–26, 410. He would die just months later, but Roman history was changed forever.[5] The result for the Visigoths was that they became more exposed to—and engaged in—Roman civilization. Ataulf, the new Visigothic leader, married the sister of Emperor Honorius, Galla Placidia, a union through which he sought to make the Visigoths the armed wing of the Western Empire, to defend its borders and maintain internal order.[6] However, Ataulf's murder at the hands of Sigeric and the premature death of Ataulf and Galla Placidia's son, Theodosius, would foil these plans. After the brief reign of Sigeric, who was also assassinated, the Visigoths elected Valia as king, who in 416 signed a new *foedus* with the Emperor Honorius. The accord required the Visigoths to defend the Empire, in return receiving wheat and permission to settle in imperial territory, specifically in Aquitaine (southwestern France). The *foedus* would be renewed 2 years later. Theodoric I (418–451) succeeded and broke with Rome by invading Narbonese Gaul (southeastern France) and creating what was, *de facto*, the first Germanic kingdom on Roman soil.[7] This was the beginning of the Kingdom of Toulouse (Wolfram 1990, 172).[8] The occupation was ultimately accepted by Rome when, after Honorius's death (423), the Roman General Aetius (390–454), on behalf of Emperor Valentinian III, renewed the *foedus* with the Visigothic leader in 425. However, by that time the Goths were heavily Romanized. In the first

[5] For 3 days the Goths sacked Rome, generally sparing the churches, including the Church at the Vatican which housed the tomb of St Peter. They looted, however, everything else, including the great houses of the city. The magnitudes of the treasures seized were on such a scale that the world reeled in shock and horror. "The mother of the world" had been murdered (Kulikowski 2007, 10). On the aftermath of the sacking, see Moorhead (2010, 138–150).

[6] On Ataulf's contribution to the ethnogenesis of the Visigoths, see Wolfram (1990, 164–166).

[7] Wolfram (1997, 106–107), mentions how, in practice, imperial policy had to steer a path between the claims of the Roman–Germanic kings and an attempt to maintain the Roman Imperial administration to the greatest possible extent, while federated kings pressured to have their own armies supplant the Roman military. Where the imperial administration had to allow this to happen, the Roman *res publica* was temporarily or permanently suspended. Germanic *regna* on Roman soil was at this stage simply a fact of life. They would not go away and had to be dealt with.

[8] On the conditions of this settlement which was, in fact, a prelude to an independent Visigoth kingdom, see Sivan (1987, 759–772).

decades of the fifth century they had already lived under the shadow of Rome for a whole century; no longer products and victims of Roman history, they now formed part of it themselves (Kulikowski 2007, 184).

### 5.1.2 The Second Wave: The Suebi, Vandals and Alani (Early Fifth Century)

Neither the Visigoths nor the Romans managed to prevent the Suebi, Vandals and Alani from breaching the Danube border and, after ravaging Gaul, occupying Hispania (409). To expel these people, Rome turned to the Visigoths, whose soldiers were deployed in the years 417 and 418 to vanquish the Vandals, Silingi and Alani. While the Suebi took refuge in Galicia, from whence they would not be expelled until Leovigild did so in the late sixth century, the Hasdingi Vandals migrated to North Africa.[9]

### 5.1.3 The Third Wave: Franks, Burgundians, Alamanni, Angles and Saxons (Mid Fifth Century)

In the first half of the fifth century, the Huns, a people from the steppes of Asia, led by Attila from 434 to 453, began to move westward. Their advance forced a series of Germanic peoples (Angles, Saxons, Franks, Burgundians and Alamanni) to cross the northern border of the Western Empire. Despite some Roman victories, such as that of Aetius against the Burgundians in 436, these Germanic peoples eventually came to permanently settle inside the Empire, on the island of Great Britain (Angles and Saxons), in Gaul (Franks), in the Rhone Valley (Burgundians), and on the right bank of the Rhine (Alamanni). Attila, meanwhile, threatened to devastate the Western Empire, but was checked by Aetius, who succeeded in forming a coalition of Romans, Visigoths, Franks, Burgundians and Saxons who, in 451, defeated the Huns at the Battle of the Catalaunic Fields (Halsall 2009, 242–253). The Visigoth king Theodoric I, was killed in the battle.

---

[9] Even if the occupation of North Africa by the Vandals after 429, was a decisive turning point in the disintegration of the Western Empire, as Liebeschuetz (2003, 57–58 and 83) mentions, the Vandal kingdom did not last because once they settled and become accommodated to Roman society, they soon became as vulnerable to the *gentes* evolving along their borders as the Romans had been to the Vandals. In any case, we know very little about them because the Vandals left practically no records. As we have no documentation of Vandal laws, it is almost impossible to assess what changes to the constitution of the *gens* were linked to the establishment of their North African kingdom.

### *5.1.4 The Last Wave: The Lombards*

After the formal dissolution of the Western Empire, the Italian Peninsula was occupied by the Ostrogoths, led by Theodoric the Great (ruler of Italy from 493 to 526). After his death, his descendants took on the troops of the Emperor Justinian (527–565), in a long and bloody war which allowed them to occupy all of Italy (552). However, this Byzantine domain did not preclude an invasion by another Germanic tribe, the Lombards (or Longobards, so named for the long beards) (Pohl 2002, 21–24), who, commanded by Alboin in the year 568, set foot in northern Italy, this region being subsequently named for them (Lombardy).[10]

## 5.2 The Germanic Kingdoms

The overthrow on September 4, 476, of the last Roman emperor of the West, Romulus Augustulus, by a barbarian chieftain, Odoacer, King of the Heruli, marked the conquest of the Western portion of the former Empire by the Germanic peoples (Pohl 2002, 15–16), who had been settling there since the late fourth century—although officially it was understood as a reunification of the Empire in the person of the Near Eastern Emperor Flavius Zeno. The Franks, Angles and Saxons, Visigoths, Ostrogoths, Burgundians and Lombards, founded in the territories they occupied "kingdoms" independent of the Roman Empire what had ceased to exist.

### *5.2.1 Diversity Versus Unity*

In contrast to the unity of the Imperial Era, the West thereafter broke into a series of "kingdoms", the most important being:

- The **Visigoths**, who between 418 and 507 established themselves in southern France, setting up their capital at Toulouse. In this period reigned Euric (466–484), the most powerful Germanic king within the borders of the old Western Roman Empire. With him ended what Heather (2004, 166–178), has called the "Transformation of the Goths", which began in 376. After being severely defeated by the Franks at Vouillé in 507, the Visigoths migrated to Spain where Leovigild (573–586), fixed the new Visigothic capital at Toledo, which became the West's most well-structured Germanic kingdom until it was wiped out by Islamic occupation in 711. Herwig Wolfram has even called the Spanish

[10] Alboin began his trek in Pannonia in carts, on horses, and on foot, with an army consisting of perhaps 150,000 or more forming an immense migratory column, including women and children, household goods and animals. On the occupation of Italy in what he calls the "Longobard Epilogue", see Wolfram (1997, 285–300).

Kingdom of the Visigoths, the "First Nation of Europe" (Wolfram 1997, 260–278).[11]

- The **Ostrogoths**, headed by Theodoric. After driving out Odoacer in 493, they settled in Italy for 60 years, developing one of the most Romanized Western Germanic kingdoms (Heather 2004, 216–258), until Justinian's reconquest in 552. Three decades later, the **Lombards** arrived in the Italian peninsula, their reign to last for two centuries (568–774).
- The **Vandals** arrived in Spain in the early fourth century, and proceeded to Africa, where they would remain for practically a century (435–534), until the territory was occupied, first by Justinian and then by the Muslims.
- The **Suebi**, also present in Spain since 409, founded an independent kingdom in the northwestern region of the Peninsula that lasted until they were conquered by the Visigoths under King Leovigild in the year 585.
- The **Burgundians**, who established themselves between Geneva and Lyon, retained their kingdom for nearly a century (443–534), until they were conquered by the Franks.
- The **Franks**, forged into a kingdom by Clovis in 481, rapidly expanded throughout Gaul after defeating the Visigoths in 507 and the Burgundians in 534, which enabled them to establish a protectorate over the territories already occupied by the Alamanni and the Bavarians (James 1991, 79–87). After the Muslim occupation of Visigothic Spain, the Frankish realm became the most important of the West's Germanic kingdoms (Becher 2011, 179–198).
- Finally, between 500 and 650, the **Angles** and **Saxons** settled most of southern Great Britain, confining the Britons to the western reaches of Cornwall and Wales (Stenton 2001, 31).

### *5.2.2 The Social and Political Transformation of the Germanic Peoples*

After the disappearance of the Western Roman Empire, the Germanic kings became independent. The establishment of solid political structures in these new Germanic kingdoms, however, was no easy task, because the Germanic tribes traditionally had a model of political organization which might be described as "collective", in the sense that it contrasted sharply with the "monarchical" structure of the Roman Empire. As a result, the kings' power was undercut by their patrimonial conception of their kingdoms, and the considerable power wielded by the chiefs of the clans

[11] This explains why the history of Visigoth Spain is one of the most studied and best known of this period (Collins 2004; Orlandis Rovira 2003; Thompson 1969), as Visigoths were not only the first Germanic people to enter into permanent contact with the Empire, but they developed (up to 711), the most politically and legally structured Germanic kingdom, where by 654 (when the last stage of their national law, the *Liber Iudiciorum*, was promulgated), Roman and Germanic communities had merged.

making up the Germanic peoples. As Noble (2006, xiv) affirms, the old idea that barbarian tribes suddenly toppled Rome and replaced its Empire with their own kingdoms and cultures, has been replaced by the conclusion that, in reality, the Germanic *gentes* adapted to, accommodated and absorbed Rome. It was a bidirectional process: the Germanic tribes conquered Rome, but Rome also "conquered" the Germanic tribes, transforming their culture and infusing it with Roman ideas and institutions.

Originally, the most characteristic feature of the Germanic tribes was that they governed themselves "collectively". The Germanic peoples described by Julius Caesar in his *Bellum Gallicum* (Murray 1983, 42–50), and especially by the Roman historian Tacitus (55–120), were initially, nomadic societies featuring a military structure in which major decisions were made by all the warriors gathered in assemblies.[12] The Germans, at this stage, had no kings but those occasionally elected as leaders to lead the army in war, and who held power only as long as war was being waged.

When these peoples came into contact with the Roman Empire beginning in the late third century, the structures of their polities underwent a profound transformation, as they abandoned their nomadic ways and became sedentary peoples occupying fixed territories (Goffart 2006, 195–216). As a result, they began to gradually abandon their traditionally collective decision-making and to exhibit practices more akin to the Roman model. To begin with, the Germanic warlords gave way to "kings", although the traditional spirit of their assemblies did survive to some extent in the ecclesiastical councils, where the king met with the members of the *aula regia* and the bishops, and the creation of the popular jury as an instrument to resolve legal conflicts.

### *5.2.3 Roman Monarchy vs. German Royalty*

The Germanic peoples had no tradition of politically structured societies. Unlike the Romans, the Germans did not feature "monarchy", that is, the sustained possession of power by one individual. In fact, it should be noted that the Germans did not use the Latin word "rex", of Indo-European origin that designates the leader of a human group, the one person (*monarch*) who exerts the political power, the drafter of the "rules" (*regula*) (Lupoi 2007, 233). Germans had another word for referring to the idea of kingship: *cyning* that derives from the root kun- "kin,

[12] As Murray (1983, 51) points out, the unique status of Tacitus's account is because of the fact that during the century and a half between the accounts of Caesar and those of Tacitus the Germanic group became a familiar and persistent consideration affecting Roman policy, and the Rhine border a common destination for officers and men of the imperial army. For a recent overview of the social organization of the early Germanic tribes, its institutions and warfare, see Todd (2004, 29–46).

family", where the words "king" and "König" comes from, and was equivalent to the Latin term *gens*.[13]

In times of war Germans used to designate a temporary military commander, elected to lead their people or tribe's army during a campaign. Wolfram (1997, 19–20) makes a difference between tribal kingship and military kingship. Though there is very little information in sources about archaic tribal kingship, as they are only dimly visible in old names and tales of abandoned cults, the tribal kings,—*theodcyning*—were charitable "normal" gods, as they had divine ancestors. They were "heros" that assured the "eternal return" of traditional order and maintained a geographically small, stable system of laws and traditions by ensuring fertility and peace. On the contrary, the military kings of the age of migration came always from a good family *ex nobilitate* and his military success was the precondition to be named king.[14]

In any case the Germanic king, thus, was no *dominus* with absolute power over a territory and its inhabitants. He stood at the head of a people who elected him, but after his appointment power still resided in the community. Traditionally the most important decisions were made by the assembly of all the free men (*mallus*). Over time, however, between the assembly of free men and the king, a group of eminent members of the community came to intercede (*nobiles*, *magnates*), the equivalent of the old companions of the emperor (*comes*) comprising the *comitatum* (*Gefolgschaft* in German). They swore allegiance to the king, in return for which they obtained a substantial portion of the spoils from military campaigns. As Halsall (2009, 497) has indicated, the fall of the Empire and the barbarian migrations did not overturn the traditional bases of aristocratic power.

Delving into the realm of concrete examples, in the case of the Visigoths, before establishing themselves in Spain (sixth century), the king was assisted by an assembly

[13] From Proto-Germanic kuninggaz, Old Saxon and Old High German kuning, Middle High German künic, German König. As Lupoi mentions, *cyning* denotes simply someone belonging to a specific family. In the earlier English legal texts, as the laws of Aedelberth of Kent (c. 590–616), the first Anglo-Saxon king to be baptized, appears the word "cyning" suggesting "noble birth", meaning originally one who descended from royal stirp (Lupoi 2007, 232–233). Wolfram explains that Biblical Gothic, one of the most important sources for investigating the Germanic constitution, reflects past influences and cultural contacts. They are Celticisms in the important military and political sphere that appear only in Gothic and no other Germanic language: *thiudans*, the king that the Gospels mention. However, absorbed into the sphere of sacral language, that old word increasingly lost its connection with worldly politics. Biblical Gothic used the Celtic word *reiks* (pronounced *rix*, singular and plural) to describe the kings of this earth and the rulers of nations, and the other East Germanic people adopted this Celtic royal title, as the many personal names with the root word *reiks* reveals (Wolfram 1997, 17).

[14] What we know about the first Germanic leaders comes from Tacitus's description. In its *Germania*, he writes about *reges* that were taken *ex nobilitate* (*Ger.* 7, 9). This phrase does not mean "from among the nobles" but "in virtue of nobility", i.e. out of the noblest stock (Kern 2013, 13). In this way, they differed from certain military leaders that he calls *duces*. *Reges* were named for their *virtus* or prowess in the field. He adds that the authority of the *reges* was not absolute in the way Romans understood it, but rather their *auctoritas* relied on how they could assert their age, birth, military prestige and eloquence before the assembly. Tacitus's idea of the Germanic *rex* is more that of a tribal leader, than a warrior or a priest (Wallace-Hadrill 2000, 2–3).

of elders belonging to the most influential families (*seniores*).[15] In Visigothic Spain, this assembly endured, initially as the *senatus*, until the late sixth century, to be replaced by a new assembly: the *Aula Regia*, also called *Palatium Regis* or *Officium Palatinum*. After Reccared's official conversion to Catholicism (589), the king began gathering more and more frequently at the councils held in the capital, Toledo, with the nobles and bishops, meetings where decisions were made that were of greater importance to the kingdom, as occurred at the Fourth Council of Toledo (633), where Isidore of Seville and his fellow bishops instituted a system for choosing new monarchs, which sought to prevent instability surrounding the succession (Wood 2012, 61). By seventh century, the Germanic elites had mixed with the old Hispano–Roman nobility (García Moreno 2011, 271–282).

Consequently, the power of these Germanic kings, unlike that of the Roman *dominus*, was by no means absolute. First, because they were elected and could be deposed. Secondly, because, in principle, the kings were bound by their traditional law. Such was the case, for instance, with the Frankish kings (James 1991, 162–65). Thirdly, because the vast majority of their subjects were former Roman citizens who had their own institutions and who, generally, were truly led by the only territorial power which had remained intact after the demise of the imperial state: the Church. If the bishops exercised clear influence on the emperors from the fourth century onwards, their power over the new monarchs became even more crucial, as they represented Romans constituting some nine tenths of the kingdom's population.

### 5.2.4 The Gradual Assimilation of the Roman Imperial Tradition

After their settlement in the territory of the extinct Western Roman Empire, a sedentary lifestyle transformed the political practices of the Germanic peoples. Once they had an increasingly territorial state structure, the new "barbarian" leaders assimilated some features of the former Roman state.

First of all, the Germanic peoples, once settled, began to choose kings, which triggered constant conflicts and struggles for the crown between the various clans, led by *notabiles*, which quite often ended with the monarch's murder at the hands of a rival family. Therefore, the kings gradually tried to introduce the hereditary principle as a way to suppress the fighting between clans. This represented a variation from the Roman Empire, in which the hereditary principle of imperial succession never took hold.

If in the field of succession the Germanic kings gradually moved away from the Roman imperial tradition, in the legislative and jurisdictional fields they moved closer to it. They not only began to legislate, but appointed judges. Originally, the law for the Germans had been the custom of each people, clarified by the assembly of warriors when there was a conflict. The same assembly was the entity which

[15] For an overview of Visigoth society in the fourth century, see Thompson (2008, 43–54).

judged cases and issued verdicts. Thus, law was not created *ex novo*. Rather, the unwritten tradition was simply concretized when necessary.

From the time when the Germanic kingdoms emerged, however, monarchs strove to monopolize the legislative function by following the example of the emperors of the Dominate. Submission to the traditional or customary law of each people, inspired by the practices of past Germanic kings, gave way in many cases to monarchs gradually enacting laws. Some of them consolidated this new power to create law with the support of the Church, as happened, for example, at the councils of Toledo in the Visigothic kingdom, which approved the laws proposed by the monarch (King 2006, 23–51).

The kings also tended to monopolize the exercise of judicial functions, whether by themselves or through judges they appointed to act on their behalf. Thus, emerged a relatively bureaucratic administration of justice in which judges were organized hierarchically, with the possibility of appealing decisions of lower courts, following the scheme of Late Roman due process (*cognitio extraordinem*) all the way up to the king himself.

### 5.2.5 The Structural Weaknesses of the New Kingdoms: Patrimonial Possession, Inheritance and Protofeudalism

Despite the progressive assimilation of the concepts and structures of the former Roman state, the Germanic monarchies were politically very unstable, though there were exceptions, of course. Thus, when a charismatic monarch came along, such as the Franks' Clovis (481–511), of the Merovingian dynasty, he was able to forge a great kingdom by way of conquest.

However, these moments of brilliance were most often limited to a single reign. First, because an uncharismatic monarch was seldom respected by his subjects and, above all, by the representatives of the rival clans. Secondly, because when the Roman Empire dissolved the abstract notion of the state and its leadership, conceived as public authority, disappeared along with it. The Germanic kings adopted a patrimonial conception of their kingdoms, envisioned as the property of the reigning family, which caused, among other things, hereditary divisions among the heirs of the deceased monarch.[16] Finally, the need to establish an effective administration of the royal domains demanded that they cede parts of the territory to nobles, who ended up ruling with considerable autonomy. This is what the specialized historiography has termed *protofeudalism*, as it was the first step towards feudal fragmentation, a phenomenon which ultimately took root when royal power faded in the Early Middle Ages.

[16] Geary (1988, 19) cites the example of how, upon the death in 560 of Chlotar I, Clovis's last surviving son, the kingdom was divided once more among his four sons, one of whom died 6 years later, leaving the kingdom in three major portions. This tradition of dividing the kingdom would continue to be the norm well into the ninth century.

## 5.3 The Church and the Preservation of the Roman "State" Tradition

If the acceptance of Christianity and the recognition of the Church radically transformed the Roman Empire beginning in the fourth century, the collapse of the Western Roman Empire in 476, made the various Western churches the only organized power. Beginning in the sixth century, Christianity was further reinforced by the emergence of the monastic movement and the consolidation of papal authority. From the point of view of the history of the western polity it is important to emphasize that the Church, during the stage of the Germanic kingdoms, became the standard-bearer of the Roman imperial tradition.

### *5.3.1 The Emergence of the Monastic Movement*

The first monastic communities in the Near East arose in reaction to the "officialization" of Christianity as a state religion. Thus, faced with a Church integrated into a complex territorial organization and subject to doctrinal unity (orthodoxy) which became universal (Catholic), a number of people decided to abandon the world in pursuit of penance and prayer. These individuals embraced the ideal of the ascetic life, retiring to the desert or any remote location. First they were called *anchorites* (from the Greek *anajorein*: separation), *hermits* (from the Greek *eremos*: desert), or Cenobites (from *koinobion*: common life) and, finally, by the generic name of *monks* (from the Greek *monakhós*: lonely). At the beginning of the sixth century, monastic communities, very numerous in the Near East,[17] were virtually unknown in the West. Having emerged in Egypt in the third century, with the hermits Anthony and Pachomius (Gorg 2011), Christian monasticism took on a coenobitic orientation which initially developed in Ireland, a barely Romanized Celtic territory where many Christians had taken refuge to escape the invasions of the fifth century (Dunn 2008). The Irish monks became, from the outset, an intellectual class dedicated to preserving the Christian tradition by copying the old texts (Harmless 2004). However, in a second phase they undertook a major

[17] Because of the Buddhist monastic tradition. Retiring from the world to meditate is a practice which appeared in the East during the era of Siddhartha Gautama, better known as the Buddha (circa 560–480 BC), an Indian prince who saw his tranquil life of luxury shattered when he was exposed to sickness, misery and death, after which he decided to abandon his home and dedicate his life to asceticism, as the precepts of Brahmanism did not satisfy him. According to tradition, he sat down to meditate under a fig tree, where he remained for 7 years until he was illuminated with the truth, thereby becoming the "Buddha", meaning "enlightened one" in Sanskrit. Thus arose Buddhism, a doctrine which considered *dukkha*, or dissatisfaction, as the essence of life, a consequence of the passions. To overcome one's constant discontent, Buddha prescribed the overcoming of the self and the realization of one's nature through meditation, an instrument through which one may achieve *nirvana* (a Sanskrit Word meaning "the evasion of pain"), a supreme state in which one's ego disappears as he realizes his relationship to all things. For a critical, detailed study on the monastic aspects of Buddhism in ancient India, see Daswani (2006).

proselytizing campaign, which led them to preach the gospel, first in Scotland and later in Europe (Vosges, Switzerland and northern Italy), where they founded new monastic communities (O'Neill 1989, 270–287).

One of these communities was founded in 529 at Monte Cassino, the site of an ancient temple to Apollo, by a monk named Benedict of Nursia (circa 480–547), who was admired and recognized in the region for his rigorous asceticism. Benedict gathered some lay people who wished to abandon the world and lead lives of meditation and prayer together, led by an abbot (from the Aramaic *abba*: father). To govern this monastic community, its founder would develop the famous *Rule* that bears his name (Dunn 2000, 111–137). The success of the Benedictine order was significant, mainly because its rule was less severe than that of the Irish monks and attached great importance to manual labor, mainly the cultivation of the land surrounding the monasteries, which allowed them to become economically self-sufficient. Moreover, the rule complemented the intense manual labor with intellectual work, which included not only reading the Bible, but other texts comprising the cultural heritage of the era (Clark 2011). This was a major event in Western history, as the work of transcription carried out by these monks assured the transmission of ancient culture.

### 5.3.2 St. Gregory the Great and the Consolidation of Papal Authority

The initial foundation of Monte Cassino was soon followed by new monasteries in Rome and Naples. In the Roman capital, the Benedictine Rule was soon discovered by a Roman aristocrat named Gregory, who had held a series of important public offices which had allowed him to occupy, at the age of just 30, the city's most important position: *praefectus urbi*. Gregory, however, was captivated by the Rule of St. Benedict to such a degree that in 575, he retired to devote himself to the monastic life, donating his considerable wealth to the founding of convents. A few years later, he would give up the contemplative life when he was virtually obligated to occupy the papal throne. His 14-year papacy (590–604), would prove an essential chapter in Church history.[18]

Until the time of Gregory I (590–604), it can be said that local churches resisted the introduction of Roman centralism, especially in the Near East, where since the Council of Chalcedon (451), they had patriarchates in Alexandria, Antioch, Jerusalem and Constantinople. However, the fact that Rome was the only Western

[18] At a time when popes tended to be men of no great social standing, Gregory came from an established and wealthy family. As Moorhead (2005, 3) points out, Gregory brought a number of qualities to the papal office: besides his personal and genuine concern for spiritual life and experience in practical administration, both secular and ecclesiastical, Gregory benefited from the self-assurance which came from belonging to a wealthy and established family. This proved important, as Gregory served as pope during a difficult time for Italy, racked by the confrontation between the Byzantine Empire and the Lombards.

patriarchy, gradually led to the Pope becoming the natural head of all the churches. Gregory the Great was the first pope to become the pontiff wielding power over the whole Church, even if this primacy was more a matter of moral authority than of actual administrative power (Fichtenau 1991, 15). The role and work of Gregory the Great marks an essential milestone in the history of the Catholic Church, not only because during his papacy there was a clear strengthening of papal authority, but because Gregory realized that his main task was not the preservation of the gradually decaying Romanism of the provinces, but the recruitment to the Catholic faith of pagan and Arian tribes. This is why he pushed for the evangelization of the Lombards, Anglo-Saxons and Germans, which allowed for Roman Catholicism to become the prevailing religion on the Continent.

From the legal point of view, as well, Gregory's efforts served to shape what was undoubtedly one of the pillars of the Western Church's legal system (Llewellyn 1974, 363–380): his idea of a *societas reipublicae christianae*, a community of all Christians over which the Roman Church exercised its *principatus* unimpeded by considerations of a constitutional nature. As Ullmann (1970, 37–38) points out, this conception of Gregory's was a prophetic vision of medieval Europe, a *societas* made up of the nations and kingdoms outside the imperial but inside a universal, Christian framework.

### 5.3.3 Christianity and the New Germanic Peoples

One of the reasons Germanic kings had problems consolidating their power was that, from the beginning, they had to deal with local churches representing the whole of the predominantly Roman population. This conflict would be resolved in favor of ecclesiastical power after the kings converted to Catholicism. At this juncture, the Church came to support royalty in exchange for the kings' endorsement and defense of this religious organization, profoundly influenced by the Roman political and legal model.

Christianity flourished relatively quickly amongst the Germanic peoples. In fact, those who came into contact with the Empire were quick to convert to Christianity. In this respect the role of the Goth Ulfilas (311–383), is worthy of note; to spread Christianity among his people he translated the Bible into the Gothic dialect, creating the oldest text written in a Germanic language (Wolfram 1990, 75–84).[19]

[19] This was the Gothic Bible, preserved in the *Codex Argenteus*, in which Ulfilas (or Wulfilas, meaning "little wolf" in German) employed a method that was simple, giving a word-to word rendering of the standard fourth-century Greek Bible text in the language of the Goths. Hence, although Ulfilas was proficient in at least three languages, his translation was essentially shaped not by Latin—as was the standard practice during the era—but by Greek. Ulfilas translated everything except the Old Testament's Book of Kings, which he thought would have encouraged the Goths to become even more warlike than they already were (Heather 2006, 78). About the circumstances in which Ulfilas carried out his essential task of transcription, see Penzi (1950, 217–230). In those days the custom was that someone read the Bible to the congregation, so Ulfilas wished his translation and its alphabet to be usable by Gothic clerics who may have known no other language (Marchand 1973, 13).

However, Ulfilas was an adherent of the early Christian school of thought known as Arianism, which denied that Jesus Christ was coeternal with God the Father.[20]

The Arians and pagans in each of the new Germanic kingdoms found themselves openly squaring off with the Catholic bishops, who stood as the natural representatives of the Roman population. The episcopal pressure was so great that beginning in the late fifth century the Germanic kings, one by one, converted to Catholicism.

The first to embrace Catholicism was the Frankish King Clovis, baptized at Reims by the bishop St. Remigius circa 496 (James 1991, 121–123). He was followed by the Burgundian King Sigismund in 516; Rechiar, King of the Suebi in 550, catechized by St. Martin of Dumium (Thompson 1980, 77–92); Authari, King of the Lombards, in 585; and the Visigoth Reccared in 589, whose conversion was brought about by St. Leander.[21]

The successive conversion of the Germanic kings to Catholicism augmented the political influence of the churches, which henceforth made every effort to preserve the Roman idea of political organization of which they were custodians.

### *5.3.4 The Church and the "Romanization" of the Germanic Kingdoms*

The influence of the Church on the government and the legal organization of the new kingdoms was crucial because it served to sustain the Roman model of government. Moreover, it can be said that the Church encouraged its continuation by imposing its political ideology on the Germanic kings who converted to Catholicism.

The clearest and most relevant case is that of Visigothic Spain, where after the conversion of Reccared (589), at the Third Council of Toledo (Orlandis Rovira 2007, 531–538), the Church clearly imposed itself on the civil authority (Nirenberg 2012, 12–20). Of special note in this regard was the role played by the councils of Toledo, mixed assemblies in which the members of the Visigothic nobility served

[20] The Arians taught that God the Father and the Son did not coexist eternally. Rather, they believed that the pre-incarnate Jesus was a divine being created by (and therefore inferior to) God the Father at some point, before which the Son did not exist. Arianism was a doctrine which had been condemned at the first ecumenical council, that of Nicea (325), but one which, without any doubt, was better suited to the simple mentality of the Germanic peoples recently settled in the West, who had little culture and lacked the capacity for advanced abstraction. As Ulfilas was largely responsible for shaping the mass conversion of the Visigoths to Arianism, his doctrine was fought by St. Augustine (Sumruld 1994, 38 and 120–134).

[21] One must take into account that, along with motivations of a religious nature, political considerations influenced the German monarchs, as conversions inevitably entailed local churches' support of the converted kings (Mathisen 1997, 664–697). The most notable case is that of Clovis I (Shanzer 1998, 29–57), whose conversion to Catholicism bolstered his position vis-à-vis the Romans in the province of Gaul, allowing him to successively defeat the Alamanni (496), Burgundians (500), and Visigoths (507), who still subscribed to Arianism.

together with the bishops, and which adopted rules essential to the organization of the kingdom (Stocking 2000). For example, at the Fourth Council of Toledo (633), an elective procedure to designate the king was approved,[22] having the important consequence that the nominee was anointed by the Church, a ceremony that made him a sacred and inviolable individual, with the crucial corollary that, by becoming a Christian king, he was made subject to the Church's authority. It is in this significant sense that Canon 9 of the 16th Council of Toledo (693), regarded kings as "vicars of God". A Christian ruler was thus given a consecrated quality, but this was balanced by the duties which it entailed, including the necessity of royal obedience to bishops (Chaney 1970, 255).

The last Germanic kings to be anointed would be the Franks. It was in 751, at the behest of Pope Zachary, that the Frankish King Pippin, after being elected king "according to the Frankish custom", was duly anointed.[23] As Geary (1988, 220) points out, this rite—which had Gothic, Irish and Anglo-Saxon precedents—was an innovation in the Frankish kingdom, as before Charlemagne's father never before had a king been confirmed in his office by ecclesiastical ritual.

The transformation of the meaning of the royal institution as a result of ecclesiastical influence, reached its peak with St. Isidore of Seville (556–636), probably the leading European intellectual of his time thanks to his *Etymologiae*, in which, among other things, he set forth a "theory of kingship" (Feller 2001, 43). In his view, kings were obligated to conduct themselves uprightly (*Recte igitur faciendo, regis nomen tenetur*) or sacrifice their royal status.[24]

Ecclesiastical influence in the political and legal sphere would be decisive in the West until the Late Middle Ages and, more specifically, until the kings became "monarchs" and sought to shake off ecclesiastical authority over them.

---

[22] Following the original Germanic tradition, the king was not, in reality, elected. Rather, the assembly limited itself to confirming that the candidate possessed all the necessary merits and qualities to exercise his position in the service of Christendom. Anointment turned the kings into "ministers of God".

[23] Anointed a first time in 752 in Soissons by the archbishop of Mainz, Pepin's power was buttressed when Pope Stephen II anointed him a second time in 754, granting him the additional title of *patricius Romanorum* (Patrician of the Romans)—the first recorded crowning of a civil ruler by a pope. As Ullmann (2010, 77) points out, Pepin was anointed to make up for his lack of royal blood justifying his enthronement and legitimize the *coup d'état*.

[24] In this regard, St. Isidore noted that: *Rex eris, si recte facies, si non facies, non eris* (Isidore of Seville 2010, IX, III. 4). For an overview of Isidore and his thought, see Feller (2001, 43–45). As Madden (2007, 22) points out, the importance that the Spanish Church had acquired after the abjuration of Arianism, was due essentially to the fact that the clergy operated the only schools preserving the knowledge of Greco-Roman culture, thereby educating the entire ruling class. Regarding Isidore of Seville and the impact of European ideas on his thinking, see Herren (1980, 243–250).

## 5.4 The Origin of the European "Nations?"

It is significant that most of these different kingdoms adopted the name of the Germanic people which had settled the territory. Over the course of the Middle Ages, these denominations ended up designating either kingdoms or regions. In the early thirteenth century, the kingdom of the Franks would end up becoming the kingdom of France. The Alamanni (Drinkwater 2007), ended up giving their name to what in Spanish is *Alemania*, in Portuguese *Alemanha*, in French *Allemagne* (Germany). England is so named as it was the "land of the Angles". Burgundy, meanwhile, is the region where the Burgundians settled; Bavaria, the land of the Bavarians; and Lombardy, the land of the Lombards. The names of other regions in Europe, however, retained evidence of their Roman heritage, probably because they were settled by multiple peoples: this was true of Spain (originally *Hispania*, *España* in Spanish) settled by the Romans, Byzantines, Suebi and Visigoths before the Muslim takeover in the eighth century; and with Italy (*Italia*), occupied by the Romans, the Ostrogoths, the Byzantines and the Lombards. In both cases, the geographical denominations prevailed. Thanks to this, legal historians in the nineteenth century influenced by the Romantic and Nationalistic Movements, jumped to the conclusion that these peoples formed a "nation" (Smith 2004, 236–257). Therefore, they considered that the territory of the old Western Roman Empire was now occupied by the Visigothic, Ostrogothic, Frankish, Burgundian or Lombardian nations, and that every Germanic nation tended, therefore, to have its own "national" law.[25] As Wormald (2003, 21) points out, the possession of a *lex* came to be a highly significant element in the forging of any acknowledged political unit in the West.

It is true that two communities initially existed in all these kingdoms: the dominant Germanic minority and the remaining population, of Roman origin, as occurred, for instance, in Gaul when the Visigoths arrived (Goffart 1980, 103–126). These two "nations", however, melded into one people over time, as the categories of Roman and non-Roman were not always sharply defined, and the coming to power of the latter may have a less decisive event than formerly thought (Moorhead

[25] This is why there soon appeared "national" legal bodies, compilations of traditional Germanic law of the specific nation. The Visigoths' *Codex Euricianus*, formed before 484, was the first of these "national laws", to be followed by the *Lex Burgundionum* for the Burgundians, the *Lex Salica* and the *Lex Ripuaria* for the Franks, the *Edictum Rothari* for the Lombards, the *Lex Alammannorum* for the Alamanni, and the *Lex Bajuvariorum* for the Bavarians. Every "nation", therefore has its own law. The situation was a little more complicated because the Germanic kings had to legislate for their Roman subjects as well, which explains the promulgation of legal bodies such as the *Lex Romana Visigothorum*—also called *the Breviary of Alaric* (507)—and the *Lex Romana Burgundionum*. During this stage the legal "principle of personality" prevailed, with each nation or group applying its laws to its people, as such, notwithstanding their precise geographical location, the principle stands in contrast to its counterpart, the territorial system, under which the law is applied in a uniform manner throughout a given territory regardless of personal origins and group affiliations. For an overview of this fascinating process of Law and ethnicity, see Halsall (2009, 462–465).

2001, 3). For example, in the case of Visigothic Spain the merging of these two communities had taken place by the middle of the seventh century.[26] Eventually, the Germanic kingdoms tended to become genuine *territorial states* in which Germans and Romans ended up forming a single body of citizens. However, were these Germanic kingdoms really European nations?

This is not clear and, as Geary (2002, 15) has rightly indicated, the real history of the nations which populated Europe in the early Middle Ages begins not in the sixth century, but in the eighteenth, as modern history begins then, and through the nineteenth century, developed as an instrument of European nationalists[27] following the outbreak of the American and French Revolutions, in 1776 and 1789, respectively, when a "nation" came to be understood as a "body of citizens whose collective sovereignty constituted them into a state which was their political expression",[28] as subsequently stated by John Stuart Mill in 1861,[29] and Ernest Renan in 1882.[30] This meaning of the term would persist after the end of the First

---

[26] Which we know about because in the year 654, the Visigoth King Recceswinth promulgated the *Lex Visigothorum*, also known as the *Liber Iudiciorum*, a compilation of national Visigothic laws with "territorial" validity, that is, binding throughout the Kingdom of Toledo upon all the subjects of the Visigothic king, regardless of whether they were of Germanic or Roman origin (King 1980, 131–157). In Ostrogothic Italy, Amory (2003, 82) indicates how during the reign of Theoderic, though society was divided into *barbari* and *Romani*, they all belonged to a single *res publica* and had to observe Roman *iura* and *leges*. The king was the prime supporter of the law that he had inherited, and added to it for the same purposes for which it was formulated. By faithfully observing this Roman-royal law the population ensured the *securitas* of the realm.

[27] Though the history of Europe's nations was a great success, the manipulation and exploitation of nationalist ideology has perverted and distorted the practice of history, contaminating it with the poison of ethnic nationalism, which has seeped deep into popular consciousness. Cleaning up this waste is the most daunting challenge facing historians today (Kumar 2006, 7–21).

[28] This was originally the meaning of the word "nation", as pointed out by Hobsbawm (1994, 18–19).

[29] John Stuart Mill believed that "a portion of mankind" could be said to constitute a nationality if "they are united among themselves by common sympathies which do not exist between them and any others- which make them co-operate with each other more willingly than with other people", and also have the "desire to be under the same government, and desire that it should be government by themselves or a portion of themselves exclusively". National feeling sometimes is dependent upon and shaped by racial identity and notions of descent, language, religion, and common geographical boundaries. Perhaps what most contributes to this feeling is the conviction that a given people shares a common past: "the possession of a national history, and a consequent community of recollections, collective pride and humiliation, pleasure and regret, connected with the same incidents in the past" (Mill 2008, 179–180).

[30] In his famous speech given at the Sorbonne on March 11, 1882, entitled *Qu'est-ce qu'une nation*?. For Renan: "A nation is [...] a large-scale solidarity, constituted by the feeling of the sacrifices that one has made in the past and of those that one is prepared to make in the future. It presupposes a past; it is summarized, however, in the present by a tangible fact, namely, consent, the clearly expressed desire to continue a common life. A nation's existence is, if you will pardon the metaphor, a daily plebiscite, just as an individual's existence is a perpetual affirmation of life" [...] "Man is a slave neither of his race nor his language, nor of his religion, nor of the course of rivers nor of the direction taken by mountain chains. A large aggregate of men, healthy in mind and

World War, when U.S. President Woodrow Wilson argued at Versailles that the new European order should be based on a strict respect for the "principle of nationalities",[31] a posture which gave rise to the appearance of new states and sparked a resurgence of nationalism, leading directly to World War II.[32]

With reference to the Early Middle Ages, it seems unwarranted to employ the term "nation" to refer to the Germanic peoples which ultimately developed independent kingdoms; as Smith (1999, 8) has explained, anything which appears to resemble a nations or nationalism, either in antiquity or the Middle Ages, must be understood as purely incidental and exceptional. It should be noted, however, that in the later Middle Ages the same term "nation" *was* used, but with another meaning: Europe's medieval universities were made up of "nations", a term which designated a group of students from the same region or province who spoke the same language.[33] These "nations" made their appearance in Bologna at

---

warm of heart, creates the kind of moral conscience which we call a nation. So long as this moral consciousness gives proof of its strength by the sacrifices which demand the abdication of the individual to the advantage of the community, it is legitimate and has the right to exist". Nevertheless, Renan believed that "Nations are not something eternal. They had their beginnings and they will end. A European confederation will very probably replace them. However, such is not the law of the century in which we are living. At the present time, the existence of nations is a good thing, a necessity even. Their existence is the guarantee of liberty, which would be lost if the world had only one law and only one master" (Renan 1996, 41–55).

[31] An idea that, paradoxically, Woodrow Wilson shared with Lenin. This is why in the Soviet Union the Communist regime deliberately set out to create ethno-linguistic territorial "national administrative units", i.e. "nations" in the modern sense, where none had previously existed or been considered. As Eric J. Hobsbawm notes: "The idea of Soviet Republics based on the Kazakh, Kirghis, Uzbek, Tajik and Turkmen "nations"" was a theoretical construct of Soviet intellectuals rather than a primordial aspiration of any of those central-Asian peoples" (Hobsbawm 1994, 166).

[32] It was indeed the opinion of George Orwell when in 1945, in the first number of *Polemic: A Magazine of Philosophy, Psychology & Aesthetics*, he wrote: "By "nationalism" I mean first of all the habit of assuming that human beings can be classified like insects and that whole blocks of millions or tens of millions of people can be confidently labeled "good" or "bad". However, secondly -- and this is much more important -- I mean the habit of identifying oneself with a single nation or other unit, placing it beyond good and evil and recognizing no other duty than that of advancing its interests. Nationalism is not to be confused with patriotism. Both words are normally used in so vague a way that any definition is liable to be challenged, but one must draw a distinction between them, since two different and even opposing ideas are involved. By "patriotism" I mean devotion to a particular place and a particular way of life, which one believes to be the best in the world but has no wish to force on other people. Patriotism is of its nature defensive, both militarily and culturally. Nationalism, on the other hand, is inseparable from the desire for power. The abiding purpose of every nationalist is to secure more power and more prestige, not for himself but for the nation or other unit in which he has chosen to sink his own individuality..." Orwell (2007, III, 361).

[33] As Kiber (1948, 3–4) points out, the term "nation" generally had a more limited connotation in the Middle Ages than our modern socio-political or cultural concept of the term. It was frequently employed interchangeably with the word *gens*, or was used to refer to the family, tribe or clan to which an individual belonged. It was also used with reference to the country of one's birth. It is in this sense that it was used in medieval universities. However, place of birth and country of origin was not the only determining factor. The statutes of the German nation at Bologna from 1497 also emphasized the principle of a common language; as the German nation was considered to encompass

the beginning of the thirteenth century, as subdivisions of the *collegia* of foreign law students, and formed for mutual protection and collective security against local authorities (Kiber 1948, 3).[34] It is significant that the term "nation" would also be used to refer to the areas settled by merchants from the same region or kingdom, who did business in Europe's different trading squares; that is, associations of "foreign" merchants whose function was to defend the interests of their "nationals".[35]

In any case it should be noted that the historical meaning of the term "nation" should be considered carefully when wielded by "nationalist" historians in states featuring separatist movements, such as in Quebec (Canada); in Belgium, where the state is on the verge of disappearing because of the irreconcilable division of the Flemish and the Walloons; in Russia's Georgia and Chechnya; and, to a lesser extent, in Spain's Autonomous Communities of Catalonia and the Basque Country, where there exist regional autonomy parties which, to varying degree, endorse

all those scholars with German as their native tongue, regardless of their place of residence. At the Spanish Universities of Salamanca or Lerida there were, essentially, students coming from the Iberian Peninsula, but they were still divided in nations. In the *studium* of Lerida, founded by King James II of Aragon in 1300, among the 12 nations two of them were from Catalonia, as they drew a distinction between Catalonians from the Sea (Barcelona, Tarragona, Mallorca and Tortosa) and Catalonians from the Mountains (Urgel, Vich and Gerona) (Kiber 1948, 157–158).

[34] At the University of Paris "nations" emerged within the faculty of arts. The fact is that the most important medieval European universities were gradually divided into "nations" (*nationes*) made up of students of a particular geographical origin. The number and names of these nations constantly changed over the course of time, following and reflecting changes in the geographical recruitment of students (Gieysztor 2003, 110). The University of Bologna, the oldest of the European medieval universities, featured, for instance, two "nations": the *intramontani*, who came from Italy (from "this side" of the Alps), and the *ultramontani* (from "the other side" of the Alps), Frenchmen, Germans and Spaniards. However, *ultramontani* was also a term used to refer to students coming from a range of different regions. In thirteenth century Cardinal Gil de Albornoz founded the *Real Colegio Mayor de San Clemente de los Españoles* (a student residence facility for Spanish students) for those hailing from Castile. It continues to welcome Spanish students even today. Spanish and Portuguese scholars attended the Sorbonne in the fourteenth and fifteenth centuries (Courtenay 2007, 110–119). In 1661 Cardinal Mazarin created the *Collège des Quatre Nations*, a school to educate, free of charge, 60 nobles hailing from four regions newly integrated into France by virtue of the Treaties of Westphalia (1648), specifically students from the regions of Artois, Alsace, Pinerolo, Roussillon and Sardinia—a measure to integrate the elite of these previously foreign territories into the kingdom of France. Today it is the headquarters of the *Institut de France* in one of the most beautiful Paris buildings along the Seine, across from the Palace of the Louvre.

[35] Over the course of the Late Middle Ages, Europe's most important trading squares frequently featured groups of European merchants which were organized in "nations" that lived in a certain district, with common privileges and their own authorities (consuls) which formed merchant courts to solve commercial disputes without the intervention of the official justice system, as they fell under a special "international" jurisdiction (Benson 2002, 127–150). Today, the term "consul" continues to designate diplomatic authorities who defend their nations' interests abroad. The street layout of many cities continue to reflect this former circumstance. Such is the case with the Genoese in Seville, and the Castilians in Bruges (González Arce 2010, 161–202), a Flemish city in which there is still a street named for the Spanish (*Spanjaardstraat*). The Castilian merchants settled in one of the wealthiest cities in Late Medieval Europe, forging associations not only to promote their national interests, but to provide help to their more helpless members, such as widows and orphans (Casado Alonso 1995, 15–56).

independence. The same dynamic has appeared most recently in Scotland. In these cases, "nationalism" usually becomes a secular form of religion as well as an ideological movement. As such, it is hardly compatible with historical objectivity. As Geary (2002, 6–11) observes, a historian of the Middle Ages who listens to the rhetoric of nationalist leaders, and who reads the scholarship produced by officials or quasi-official historians is immediately struck by how interpretations of the period of the dissolution of the Roman Empire and the barbarian migration have become, once again, the fulcrum of political discourse across much of Europe. The problem is that it is not only nationalistic political leaders who exploit history for political reasons, but reputable scholars are also drawn into polemical uses of the past as well. This is why Geary believes that any historian who has spent much of his career studying this earliest period of ethnic formation and migration, can only look upon the development of politically conscious nationalism and racism with apprehension and disdain, particularly when these ideologies appropriate and pervert history for their justification.[36]

## TIMELINE

### First Wave: The Visigoths (378–382)

378 The Visigoths defeat Emperor Valens at Adrianople.
382 Theodosius signs a first *foedus* with the Visigoths. They may settle in the Empire if they pledge to defend it.

### The Second Wave: The Suebi, Vandals and Alani (406–425)

406 The Suebi, Vandals and Alani cross the Rhine, defeating the federated troops defending the Empire's border.
407 The Romans abandon the British Isles.
410 August 24. Alaric I sacks Rome.
414 Ataulf's marriage to Placidia.
416 Second *foedus* between Rome and the Visigoths, signed this time between Honorius and Valia.
425 Signing of the third *foedus* between Theodoric and Aetius.

---

[36] This "pseudo-history" assumes, first, that the peoples of Europe are distinct, stable and objectively identifiable social and cultural units, distinguished by language, religion, custom and national which are unambiguous and immutable. These peoples supposedly arose either in some impossibly remote moment of prehistory, or the process of ethnogenesis which took place at some moment during the Middle Ages, but then came to a definitive stop. Second, ethnic claims demand the political autonomy of all persons belonging to a particular ethnic group and, at the same time, the right of that people to govern its historic territory, usually defined in terms of early medieval settlements or kingdoms, regardless of who may now live in it. For a scholar discussion on ethnicity and nationalism, Spira (2004, 248–256). For the relationship between racism and nationalism in the case of Basque nationalism, Douglass (2004, 98–106).

### Third Wave: Franks, Burgundians, Alamanni, Angles and Saxons (434–451)

434 Attila (+453) becomes leader of the Huns.
436 Aetius' victory over the Burgundians. Rome, however, cannot prevent the Burgundians from permanently settling in the Rhone Valley, nor keep the Angles and Saxons out of Great Britain, nor the Franks from Gaul.
451 Attila is defeated at the Battle of the Catalonian Fields (Chalons, northern France). The Hun leader fights alongside a series of Germanic tribes paying homage to him (Ostrogoths, Burgundians, Gepids, Heruli and Thuringians, etc.). Fighting against the Huns was Rome's General Flavius Aetius, supported by Rome's Germanic allies (Visigoths, Franks, and Alani).
453 Death of Attila.
454 Assassination of Aetius.
455 Capture of Rome by the Vandals. The emperor takes refuge in Ravenna.
463 The Burgundians settle in the Rhone Valley.

### The Early Germanic Kingdoms: The Visigothic Kingdom of Toulouse and the Frankish Kingdom (451–507)

466 Euric (+484) becomes the King of the Visigoths.
476 Following the overthrow of Romulus Augustulus by Odoacer, King of the Heruli, the Visigothic kingdom of *Tolosa*, having arisen in 416 with Valia, becomes the largest Germanic kingdom in the West.
481 Clovis (+511), of the Merovingian clan, becomes King of the Franks.
486 The Franks, led by Clovis, defeat the Gallo-Romans, led by Afranius, at Soissons.

### The Last Germanic Invasions: The Ostrogoths and Lombards Occupy Italy (493–568)

493 The Ostrogoth Theodoric the Great (+526) creates a powerful Germanic kingdom in Italy.
496 Clovis converts to Catholicism. Soon after he defeats the Alamanni at Tolbiac.
500 The Burgundians are defeated by the Franks.
507 Clovis annihilates the Visigoths at Vouillé (*Campus Vogladensis*) in southern France. Death of the Visigoth King Alaric II.
511 Death of Clovis.
516 The Burgundian King Sigismund converts to Christianity.
526 Death of the Ostrogoth King Theodoric the Great.
550 Rechiar, King of the Suebi, converts to Christianity through the influence of St. Martin of Dumium.
552 Byzantine troops sent by Justinian (527–565) fail to conquer the entire Italian Peninsula after a brutal war.

568 The Lombards, led by King Alboin, invade Italy when pressured by the Avars, soon driving the Byzantines out of northern Italy (Po Valley, which comes to be called "Lombardy").

## The Visigoth Kingdom of Toledo and the Muslim Expansion (573–711)

573 Leovigild (573–586) ascends to the Visigoth throne and is considered the founder of the Kingdom of Toledo, which would last until 711.
585 Authari, King of the Lombards, converts to Catholicism.
589 Reccared I renounces Arianism.
622 Muhammad flees from Mecca and takes refuge in Medina (Hijra).
631 The Byzantines are expelled from the Iberian Peninsula by Suintila.
632 Muhammad dies in Medina.
642 The Muslims manage to conquer Alexandria.
647 The Byzantines are defeated by the Muslims at Sbeitla. However, Emperor Constant II buys the Muslims' withdrawal from North Africa.
655 The Byzantine fleet is defeated by the Muslims at Lycia.
676 After 4 years the Arabs lift their siege of Constantinople. The caliph Ahmed-ben-Moavia signs a 30-year peace.
695 The Muslims conquer Carthage (Tunisia) and manage to permanently drive the Byzantines out of the Maghreb.
709 The Visigoths lose Ceuta to the Moors.
711 The Visigoths' King Roderic is defeated by the Muslims.

## Christianity and the Germanic Peoples (Fifth and Sixth Centuries)

325 Council of Nicaea. Condemnation of Aryanism.
380 The Edict of Thessalonica, issued by Theodosius (379–395), decrees the official nature of Christianity.
383 Death of Ulfilas (born in 311).
392 The Edict of Constantinople prohibits all pagan practices. Christianity is the only religion tolerated.
431 St. Patrick commences the evangelization of Ireland.
496 Baptism of the Frankish king Clovis by St. Remigius.
516 The Burgundian King Sigismund converts to Christianity.
529 Foundation of the first monastery in the West. Monte Cassino (Italy) of the Benedictine Order (St. Benedict of Nursia [480–547]).
550 Rechiar, King of the Suebi, converts to Christianity, thanks to the influence of St. Martin of Dumium.
585 Authari, King of the Lombards, converts to Catholicism.
589 The Visigoth King Reccared I renounces Arianism.
590–604 Pope Gregory the Great significantly bolsters the authority of the Church of Rome over all of Christendom.

## References


Amory, P. (2003). *People and identity in Ostrogothic Italy: 489–554*. Cambridge, MA: Cambridge University Press.

Becher, M. (2011). The Franks: Rome's heirs in the West. In J. P. Arnason (Coed.), *The Roman Empire in context: Historical and comparative perspectives* (pp. 179–198). Malden, MA: Wiley-Blackwell.

Benson, B. L. (2002). Justice without Government: The Merchant Courts of Medieval Europe and their modern counterparts. In D. Beito (Coed.), *The voluntary city: Choice community, and civil society* (pp. 127–150). Ann Arbor, MI: The University of Michigan Press.

Casado Alonso, H. (1995). Las colonias de mercaderes castellanos en Europa (s. XV–XVI). In *Castilla y Europa: Comercio y Mercaderes en los siglos XIV, XV y XVI* (pp. 15–56). Burgos: Diputación Provincial.

Chaney, W. A. (1970). *The cult of kingship in Anglo-Saxon England: The transition from Paganism to Christianity*. Berkeley: University of California Press.

Chrysos, E. (2003). The Empire, the *Gentes* and the regna. In H. -W. Goetz et al., (Coed.), *Regna and Gentes: The relationship between late antique and early medieval peoples and kingdoms in the transformation of the Roman world* (pp. 13–20). Boston: Brill.

Clark, J. G. (2011). *The Benedictines in the Middle Ages*. Woodbridge, UK: Boydell Press.

Collins, R. (2004). *Visigothic Spain, 409–711*. Oxford: Blackwell.

Courtenay, W. J. (2007). Spanish and Portuguese scholars at the University of Paris in the fourteenth and fifteenth centuries. In I. A. Corfis (Coed.), *Medieval Iberia: Changing societies and cultures in contact and transition* (pp. 110–135). Rochester, NY: Tamesis.

Daswani, R. (2006). *Buddhist monasteries and monastic life in ancient India: From the third century BC to the seventh century AD*. New Delhi: Aditya Prakashan.

Douglass, W. A. (2004). Sabino's sin: Racism and the founding of Basque nationalism. In D. Conversi (Ed.), *Ethnonationalism in the contemporary world: Walker Connor and the study of nationalism* (pp. 95–112). London: Routledge.

Drinkwater, J. F. (2007). *The Alamanni and Rome: 213–496*. Oxford: Oxford University Press.

Dunn, M. (2000). *The emergence of monasticism: From the Desert Fathers to the early Middle Ages*. Malden, MA: Blackwell.

Dunn, M. (2008). *The emergence of monasticism: From the Desert Fathers to the early Middle Ages*. Malden, MA: Willey.

Feller, L. (2001). *L'Église et la société en Occident: pouvoir politique et pouvoir religieux du VIIe au XIe siècle*. Paris: Sedes.

Fichtenau, H. (1991). *The Carolingian Empire*. Toronto: University of Toronto Press.

García Moreno, L. A. (2011). Building an ethnic identity for a new Gothic and Roman nobility: Córdoba 615 AD. In D. Shanzer (Ed.), *Romans, barbarians, and the transformation of the Roman world: Cultural interaction and the creation of identity in late antiquity* (pp. 271–282). Burlington, VT: Ashgate.

Geary, P. J. (1988). *Before France and Germany: The creation and transformation of the Merovingian World*. New York: Oxford University Press.

Geary, P. J. (2002). *The myth of Nations. The Medieval origins of Europe*. Princeton: Princeton University Press.

Gieysztor, A. (2003). Management and resources. In *A history of the University in Europe. Universities in the Middle Ages* (Vol. 1, pp. 108–143). Cambridge, UK: Cambridge University Press.

Goffart, W. A. (1980). *Barbarians and Romans: A.D. 418–584: The techniques of accommodation*. Princeton: Princeton University Press.

Goffart, W. A. (2006). The barbarians in late antiquity and how they were accommodated in the West. In T. F. X. Noble (Ed.), *From Roman provinces to medieval kingdoms* (pp. 195–226). London: Routledge.

González Arce, J. D. (2010). La universidad de mercaderes de Burgos y el consulado castellano en Brujas durante el siglo XV. *En la España medieval,* (33), 161–202.
Gorg, P. (2011). *The Desert Fathers: Saint Anthony and the beginnings of monasticism.* San Francisco, CA: Ignatius Press.
Halsall, G. (2009). *Barbarian migrations and the Roman West, 376–568.* Cambridge, UK: Cambridge University Press.
Harmless, W. (2004). *Desert Christians: An introduction to the literature of early monasticism.* Oxford: Oxford University Press.
Heather, P. J. (2004). *The Goths.* Oxford: Wiley-Blackwell.
Heather, P. J. (2006). *The fall of the Roman Empire: A new history of Rome and the Barbarians.* Oxford: Oxford University Press.
Herren, M. (1980). On the earliest Irish acquaintance with Isidore of Seville. In E. James (Ed.), *Visigothic Spain: New approaches* (pp. 243–250). Oxford: Oxford University Press.
Hobsbawm, E. J. (1994). *Nations and nationalism since 1780: Programme, myth, reality* (2nd ed., Reprint). Cambridge, UK: Cambridge University Press.
Isidore of Seville. (2010). *The etymologies* (pp. 199–201). Cambridge, UK: Cambridge University Press.
James, E. (1991). *The Franks: The peoples of Europe.* Oxford: Basil Blackwell.
Kern, F. (2013). *Kingship and law in the Middle Ages: Studies.* Clark, NJ: The Lawbook Exchange, Ltd.
Kiber, P. (1948). *The nations in the mediaeval universities.* Cambridge, MA: Mediaeval Academy of America.
King, P. D. (1980). King Chindasvind and the first territorial law-code of the Visigothic kingdom. In E. James (Ed.), *Visigothic Spain: New approaches* (pp. 131–157). Oxford: Clarendon.
King, P. D. (2006). *Law and society in the Visigothic kingdom.* Cambridge, UK: Cambridge University Press.
Kulikowski, M. (2007). *Rome's Gothic wars: From the third century to Alaric.* Cambridge, UK: Cambridge University Press.
Kumar, K. (2006). Nationalism and the historians. In G. Delanty & K. Kumar (Eds.), *The Sage handbook of nations and nationalism.* London: Sage.
Liebeschuetz, J. H. W. G. (2003). Gens into regnum: The Vandals. In H. -W. Goetz (Coed.), *Regna and Gentes: The relationship between late antique and early medieval peoples and kingdoms in the transformation of the Roman world* (pp. 55–83). Boston: Brill.
Llewellyn, P. (1974). The Roman Church in the seventh century: The legacy of Gregory I. *Journal of Ecclesiastical History, 25*, 363–380.
Lupoi, M. (2007). Public Allegiance: Succession to the throne and heritability of kingdoms. In *The origins of the European legal order* (pp. 232–235). Cambridge, UK: Cambridge University Press.
Madden, M. R. (2007). Doctrines of St. Isidore of Seville which influenced Spanish legal thought. In *Political theory and law in medieval Spain* (2nd print, pp. 19–27). Clark, NJ: Lawbook Exchange.
Marchand, J. W. (1973). *The sounds and phonemes of Wulfila's Gothic.* The Hague: De Gruyter.
Mathisen, R. W. (1997). Barbarian bishops and the churches in "Barbaricis Gentibus": During late antiquity. *Speculum, 72*(3), 664–697.
Mathisen, R. W. (2006). *Peregrini*, *Barbari*, and *Cives Romani*: Concepts of citizenship and the legal identity of Barbarians in the later Roman Empire. *The American Historical Review, 111* (4), 1011–1040.
Mill, J. S. (2008). Of nationality, as connected with representative government. In *Considerations on representative government.* Rockville, MD: Serenity Pub.
Moorhead, J. (2001). *The Roman Empire divided: 400–700.* London: Harlow.
Moorhead, J. (2005). *Gregory the great.* New York: Routledge.
Moorhead, S. (2010). *AD 410: The year that shook Rome.* London: British Museum Press.

Murray, A. C. (1983). *Germanic kingship structure: Studies in law and society in antiquity and the early Middle Ages*. Toronto: Political Institute of Medieval Studies.

Nirenberg, D. (2012). The Visigothic conversion to Catholicism: The third council of Toledo. In O. R. Constable (Ed.), *Medieval Iberia: Readings from Christian, Muslim, and Jewish sources* (2nd ed., pp. 12–20). Philadelphia: University of Pennsylvania Press.

Noble, T. F. X. (Ed.). (2006). *From Roman provinces to Medieval Kingdoms*. London: Routledge.

O'Neill, J. C. (1989). The origins of monasticism. In *The making of orthodoxy: Essays in honour of Henry Chadwick* (pp. 270–287). Cambridge, UK: Cambridge University Press.

Orlandis Rovira, J. (2003). *Historia del reino visigodo español*. Madrid: Rialp.

Orlandis Rovira, J. (2007). El significado del Concilio III de Toledo en la Historia hispánica y universal. *Altar Mayor*, (111), 531–538.

Orwell, G. (2007). Notes on nationalism. In G. Orwell (Ed.), *The collected essays: Journalism and letters of George Orwell* (Vol. 3, pp. 361–379, 4 Vols). Boston, MA: David R. Godine.

Penzi, H. (1950). Orthography and Phonemes in Wulfila's Gothic. *The Journal of English and Germanic Philology, 49*(2), 217–230.

Pohl, W. (2002). Invasions and ethnic identity. In C. La Rocca (Ed.), *Italy in the early Middle Ages* (pp. 11–33). Oxford: Oxford University Press.

Renan, E. (1996). What is a nation? In G. Eley & R. G. Suny (Eds.), *Becoming national: A reader* (pp. 42–56). Oxford: Oxford University Press.

Shanzer, D. (1998). Dating the baptism of Clovis: The bishop of Vienne vs the bishop of tours. *Early Medieval Europe, 7*(1), 29–57.

Sivan, H. S. (1987). On Foederati, Hospitalitas, and the settlement of the Goths in A.D. 418. *American Journal of Philology, 108*(4), 759–772.

Smith, A. D. (1999). *The ethnic origins of nations*. Malden, MA: Blackwell.

Smith, A. D. (2004). *The antiquity of nations*. Cambridge, UK: Polity.

Spira, T. (2004). Ethnicity and nationality: The twin matrices of nationalism. In D. Conversi (Ed.), *Ethnonationalism in the contemporary world: Walker Connor and the study of nationalism*. London: Routledge.

Stenton, F. (2001). *Anglo-Saxon England*. Oxford: Oxford University Press.

Stocking, R. L. (2000). *Bishops, councils, and consensus in the Visigothic Kingdom: 589–633*. Ann Arbor, MI: University of Michigan Press.

Sumruld, W. A. (1994). *Augustine and the Arians: The bishop of Hippo's encounters with Ulfilan Arianism*. Selinsgrove, PA: Susquehanna University Press.

Tacitus, C. (2006). *The Germany and the Agricola of Tacitus: With a revised text, English notes, and maps*. Stockbridge, MA, SC: Hard Press.

Thompson, E. A. (1969). *The Goths in Spain*. Oxford: Clarendon.

Thompson, E. A. (1980). The conversion of the Spanish Suevi to catholicism. In E. James (Ed.), *Visigothic Spain: New approaches* (pp. 77–92). Oxford: Oxford University Press.

Thompson, E. A. (2008). *The Visigoths in the time of Ulfilas* (2nd ed.). London: Duckworth.

Todd, M. (2004). *The early Germans* (2nd ed.). Malden, MA: Blackwell.

Ullmann, W. (1970). *The growth of Papal government in the Middle Ages. A study in the ideological relation of clerical to lay power*. London: Methuen.

Ullmann, W. (2010). *The Carolingian renaissance and the idea of Kingship*. New York: Routledge.

Wallace-Hadrill, J. M. (2000). Germanic kingship and the Romans. In *Early Germanic kingship in England and on the continent* (pp. 1–20). Oxford: Clarendon.

Wolfram, H. (1990). *History of the Goths*. Berkeley: University of California Press.

Wolfram, H. (1997). *The Roman Empire and its Germanic peoples*. Berkeley, CA: University of California Press.

Wood, J. P. (2012). *The politics of identity in Visigothic Spain: Religion and power in the histories of Isidore of Seville*. Leiden: Brill.

Wormald, P. (2003). The Leges barbarorum: Law and ethnicity in the post-Roman west. In H.-W. Goetz et al. (Eds.), *Regna and Gentes: The relationship between late antique and early medieval peoples and kingdoms in the transformation of the Roman world* (pp. 21–53). Boston: Brill.

## *Further Reading*

Barbero, A., & Loring, M. I. (2005). The formation of the Sueve and Visigothics kingdoms. In P. Fouracre (Ed.), *The new Cambridge medieval history* (Vol. 1, pp. 162–192). Cambridge: Cambridge University Press.
Barbero, A., & Loring, M. I. (2005). The Catholic Visigothics Kingdom. In P. Fouracre (Ed.), *The new Cambridge medieval history* (Vol. 1, pp. 346–370). Cambridge: Cambridge University Press.
Barton, S., & Linehan, P. (Eds.). (2008). *Cross, crescent and conversion: Studies on medieval Spain and Christendom in memory of Richard Fletcher*. Boston: Brill.
Breuilly, P. (1994). *Nationalism and the state* (2nd ed.). Manchester: Manchester University Press.
Caesar, J. (2006). *De bello gallico (The Gallic war)*. Cambridge, MA: Harvard University Press (Latin text and parallel English translation on opposite pages. Reprinted from the first published by the Harvard University Press, in 1917).
Caner, D. (2002). *Wandering, begging monks: Spiritual authority and the promotion of monasticism in late antiquity*. Berkeley: University of California Press.
Cantoni, D., & Yuchtman, N. (2012). *Medieval universities, legal institutions, and the commercial revolution*. Cambridge, MA: National Bureau of Economic Research.
Chadwick, H. (1993). *The early Church: The story of emergent Christianity from the apostolic age to the dividing of the ways between the Greek Eats and the Latin West* (Revised edition). London: Penguin.
Cherry, D. (1998). *Frontier and society in Roman North Africa*. Oxford/New York: Clarendon/ Oxford University Press.
Cobban, A. B. (1975). *The medieval universities: Their development and organization*. New York: Harpers & Row.
Conant, J. (2012). *Staying Roman: Conquest and identity in Africa and the Mediterranean, 439–700*. New York: Cambridge University Press.
Cooper, K., & Hillner, J. (Eds.). (2007). *Religion, dynasty, and patronage in early Christian Rome, 300–900*. Cambridge, UK: Cambridge University Press.
Dal Santo, M. (2012). *Debating the saints' cult in the age of Gregory the Great*. Oxford: Oxford University Press.
DeRidder-Symoens, H. (Ed.). (1992). *A history of the university in Europe: Universities in the Middle Ages*. Cambridge, UK: Cambridge University Press.
Escher, K. (2006). *Les Burgondes: Ie-VIe siècle apr. J-C*. Paris: Éditions Errance.
Favrod, J. (2002). *Les Burgondes: Un royaume oublié au coeur de l'Europe*. Lausanne: Presses polytechniques et universitaires romandes.
Ferreiro, A. (Ed.). (1999). *The Visigoths: Studies in culture and society*. Boston: Brill.
Gagnon, A. G., et al. (Eds.). (2011). *Contemporary majority nationalism*. Montreal: McGill-Queen's University Press.
Gargano, I. (2013). *Il libro, la parola e la vita: l'esegesi biblica di Gregorio Magno*. Cinisello Balsamo (Milano): San Paolo.
Gellner, E. (2009). *Nations and nationalism* (2nd ed.). Ithaca: Cornell University Press.
Green, J. D. (2007). St Gregory the great. In *Augustinianism: Studies in the process of spiritual transvaluation* (pp. 33–52). Dudley, MA: Peeters.
Guelke, A. (2010). *The challenges of ethno-nationalism: Case studies in identity politics*. Houndmills: Palgrave Macmillan.
Guichard, R. (1965). *Essai sur l'histoire du peuple burgonde, de Bornholm (Burgundarholm) vers la Bourgogne et les Bourguignons*. Paris: A. et J. Picard et Cie.
Heather, P. J. (1994). *Goths and Romans 332–489*. Oxford: Clarendon.
Hillgarth, J. N. (2010). *The Visigoths in history and legend*. Turnhout: Brepols Publishers.
James, E. (2009). *Europe's barbarians: AD 200–600*. New York: Pearson Longman.
Karolewski, I. P., & Suszycki, A. M. (2011). *The nation and nationalism in Europe: An introduction*. Edinburgh: Edinburgh University Press.

Krebs, C. B. (2011). *A most dangerous book: Tacitus's Germania from the Roman Empire to the Third Reich*. New York: W. W. Norton & Company.

Liebeschuetz, J. H. W. G. (2004). *Barbarians and bishops: Army, Church, and state in the age of Arcadius and Chrysostom*. Oxford: Clarendon Paperbacks.

Liebeschuetz, J. H. W. G. (2006). *Decline and change in late antiquity: Religion, barbarians and their historiography*. Aldershot: Ashgate.

Livermore, H. (2006). Sueves, Visigoths and Romans. In *The twilight of the Goths: The rise and falls of the Kingdom of Toledo, C. 575–711* (pp. 51–65). Bristol: Intellect Books.

Mathisen, R. W. (2012). Clovis, Anastasius, and political status in 508 C.E: The Frankish aftermath of the battle of Vouillé. In R. W. Mathisen & D. Shanzer (Eds.), *The battle of Vouille, 507 CE: Where France began* (pp. 79–110). Boston: Walter de Gruyter.

Mathisen, R. W., & Sivan, H. S. (Eds.). (1996). *Shifting frontiers in late antiquity*. Aldershot: Variorum.

Mcguire, B. P. (2010). *Friendship and community: The monastic experience, 350–1250*. Ithaca, NY: Cornell University Press.

Murray, A. C. (1983). *Germanic kinship structure. Studies in law and society in antiquity and the early Middle Ages*. Turnhout (Belgium): Brepols.

Musset, L. (1979). *The Germanic invasions: The making of Europe AD 400–600*. University Park, PA: The Pennsylvania State University Press.

Noble, T. F. X. (1984). *The Republic of St. Peter: The birth of the Papal State, 680–825*. Philadelphia: University of Pennsylvania Press.

Orlandis Rovira, J. (2000). La doble conversión religiosa de los pueblos germánicos (siglos IV al VIII). *Anuario de historia de la Iglesia, 9*, 69–84.

Ozkiriml, U. (2010). *Theories of nationalism: A critical introduction* (2nd rev. and ext. ed.). Basingstoke: Palgrave Macmillan.

Pedersen, O. (1997). *The first universities: Studium generale and the origins of university education in Europe*. Cambridge, UK: Cambridge University Press.

Richards, J. (1980). *Consul of god: The life and times of Gregory the great*. London/Boston: Routledge & Keatland Paul.

Schutz, H. (2000). *The Germanic realms in pre-Carolingian Central Europe, 400–750*. New York: Peter Lang.

Spencer, P., & Wollman, H. (2002). *Nationalism: A critical introduction*. London: Sage.

Straw, C. E. (1988). *Gregory the great: Perfection in imperfection*. Berkeley, CA: University of California Press.

Thompson, E. A. (1963). The Barbarian Kingdoms in Gaul and Spain. *Nottingham Mediaeval Studies, 7*, 3–33.

Wieacker, F. (1995). *A history of private law in Europe; with particular reference to Germany*. Oxford: Oxford University Press.

# Chapter 6
# Popes vs. Emperors: The Rise and Fall of Papal Power

*Quod a fidelitate iniquorum subiectos potest absolvere* (The Pope may excuse his subjects from their obligations to iniquitous princes)—Gregory VII, *Dictatus Papae*, XXVII, (1075)

## Contents


6.1 The Transformation of the Papacy: From Spiritual to Temporal Power .............. 122
6.1.1 The Popes vs. the Byzantines and Lombards .................................. 122
6.1.2 The Alliance with the Frankish Monarchy and the Rise of the Papal States .. 123
6.2 Charlemagne and the Resurgence of the Imperial Idea in the West .................. 126
6.2.1 Charlemagne and the End of the Lombardian Kingdom ....................... 126
6.2.2 The Appearance of the Kingdom of Italy ....................................... 126
6.2.3 The Reappearance of the Imperial Idea in the West ........................... 127
6.3 From the Carolingian Empire to the Holy Roman Empire ............................ 129
6.3.1 The Frankish Monarchy Dissociates Itself from the Empire .................. 129
6.3.2 The Germanic Revival of the Imperial Idea .................................. 130
6.4 The Era of "Papal Theocracy", or the Peak of Ecclesiasticism ...................... 134
6.4.1 Ecclesiastical Decline During the Feudal Period .............................. 134
6.4.2 The Ecclesiastical Resurgence: The Eastern Schism, Cluny and the Gregorian Reform ........................................................................ 136
6.4.3 The Papacy's Power Swells .................................................... 139
6.4.4 The Legal Consequences of the Papal Victory: The Secularization of Non-ecclesiastical Public Authorities ................................................ 140
6.4.5 Papal Decline and the Fragmentation of Europe .............................. 140
6.5 The Survival of the Imperial Idea ...................................................... 142
References ........................................................................................ 147




B. Aguilera-Barchet, *A History of Western Public Law*,
DOI 10.1007/978-3-319-11803-1_6

## 6.1 The Transformation of the Papacy: From Spiritual to Temporal Power

In the year 476 of the Christian era the Western Roman Empire collapsed, succeeded by a series of independent Germanic kingdoms, as Visigoths, Ostrogoths, Franks, Angles and Saxons, Alemanni, Burgundians and Lombards created their own political units and founded the bases of future European nation-states. In reality things were a bit more complex, as the Germanic kings were subject to the Church, which imposed the political model of Roman universalism upon them. Thus, with authority over the "national" kingdoms were the popes, established as the highest ecclesiastical authority and arbiters of civil authority as well, to such an extent that by the ninth century they were responsible for recovering the imperial title in the western sphere (*pars occidentalis*) of the former Roman Empire.

Since the pontificate of Gregory I (590–604), Rome's successive bishops had become the undisputed heads of the church, thereby initiating a trend towards unification that contrasted sharply with the political disintegration caused by the rise of the various Germanic kingdoms. To consolidate its spiritual preeminence, however, the popes had to fight a tough battle in the Italian Peninsula in the political arena, as they were at the mercy of the Lombard kings in the north and the Byzantine emperor in the south. The confrontation between the two powers, Germanic and imperial, would favor the papacy's *de facto* independence.

### 6.1.1 The Popes vs. the Byzantines and Lombards

Beginning with Emperor Leo III the Isaurian's (717–741), rise to the throne, Byzantium sought to strengthen its presence in Italy. From Ravenna, the imperial capital[1] it had to face the Lombards, the Pope and other local powers. The most effective resistance was put up by Pope Gregory II (715–731), as after the outbreak of the Iconoclastic Crisis[2] he was supported by the vast majority of the Peninsula

---

[1] Ravenna was the late Roman imperial seat, maintained by the Ostrogoths and thereafter by the Byzantine governor (exarch), which explains why the region was called the Exarchate. As Christie (2005, 177) points out, Ravenna and its rulers always had a prickly relationship with Rome and the popes, exacerbated by the prominence attained by its archbishop under Byzantine rule. The rivalry persisted even after Byzantine control was lost in 751 with the ephemeral Lombard takeover. For an overview of Byzantine Italy, see Pohl (2002, 25–26).

[2] The iconoclasts were those who destroyed sacred images in paintings or sculptures (icons, from the Greek *eikon*: image). Proponents of this position believed that images of God and the divine should not be created by man, just as they are not to be crafted in Judaism. In the case of Islam the representation of any animal or creature created by God is also prohibited. As Brubaker and Haldon (2011, 11) points out, what is interesting in the "image struggle" is how the conception of the relationship between the Roman state and God changed during the second half of the seventh century after the collapse of imperial forces against Islam, as Christian ideology identified the interests of Christians with those of the Roman State. For an overview of this tumultuous period of Byzantine history, see Brown (1973, 1–34).

(Feller 2001, 123) and, thus, able to face the Byzantines with some local militias and troops of the Dukes of Spoleto and Benevento in a war which has been termed the *Rivoluzione Italiana* (Salvatorelli 1982, 76).

The Lombards' King Liutprand (712–744) sought to take advantage of the confrontation with the Byzantine Empire to unite the Italian Peninsula under his leadership (Feller 2001, 124). Having conquered the Exarchate and Pentapolis, he managed to lead his army to Rome itself, but failed to conquer it because of the strong resistance offered by Gregory II. Liutprand then chose to ally with the new Byzantine exarch Eutychius, affording him an army of imperial and Lombard soldiers which took Rome (Christie 1998, 102–103). The restoration of imperial authority over Rome, Ravenna and Venice did not prevent Gregory III (731–741), and his successor, Pope Zacharias (741–752), from defending the papacy's ecclesiastical independence. In fact, the latter signed a 20-year truce with Liutprand to deal more effectively with the Byzantine exarch.[3]

### *6.1.2 The Alliance with the Frankish Monarchy and the Rise of the Papal States*

The arrival of Constantine V Copronymus (741–775), an emperor who took no interest in Italy, and the death of Liutprand in 744, created a political framework very favorable to the strengthening of papal power over Italy. To achieve this, the popes sought an alliance with the Frankish kings, the most powerful in the West after the disappearance of the Visigothic Kingdom of Toledo in 711.

#### 6.1.2.1 Pepin the Short and Pope Zacharias

Gregory III tried unsuccessfully to form an alliance with Charles Martel, who had seized power[4] after his victory over the Muslims in 732.[5] In the end, it was Pope Zacharias who managed to reach an agreement with Martel's two sons: Carloman

[3] For an overall view of the history of the papacy from Byzantine–Lombard Italy to the Carolingian Empire, see Azzara (2002, 109–114).

[4] Although Charles Martel exercised power in his capacity as mayor of the palace, the throne was still formally occupied by a Merovingian monarch. Only at the end of his life did he use the titles of Duke and Prince of the Franks (*dux et princeps francorum*) (Nicolle 2008, 24–25). After defeating the Moors near modern-day Poitiers in 732, he was offered the title of Consul by the pope, but he refused. On his relationships with Rome, see Geary (1988, 212–218).

[5] On the military aspects of this decisive battle, see Fouracre (2000, 148–149).

and Pepin the Short,[6] through the mediation of the Archbishop of Mainz, Boniface, a promoter of ecclesiastical reform in the Frankish kingdom. When Pepin became the sole heir it was he who requested papal support to legally legitimize his dynasty.[7] Zacharias was willing, and in 751 authorized Archbishop Boniface to anoint Pepin as the King of the Franks,[8] following a precedent taken from the Spanish Visigothic kings of Toledo (Riché 1993, 68).[9] The "revolution" of 751 was completely successful and no attempts were made to reinstate Childeric III, who died in 753, and whose son was never king (McKitterick 1983, 38).

#### 6.1.2.2 The Popes as the Legitimate Arbiters of Divine Authority

By turning to the Pope to become the King of the Franks, Pepin accepted that it was the pontiff's prerogative, as the highest representative of God on Earth, to legitimize him. Henceforth the popes would play a decisive role in international politics, as they could not only support the legitimate enthronement of kings, but were also able to bar them from the community of believers through "excommunication",

[6] Upon the death of Charles Martel on October 22, 741 at age 55, strife soon erupted within the family (Fouracre 2000, 166), resulting in the fragmentation of the Frankish Kingdom once again. Martel's eldest son, Carloman, was mayor of the palace in Austrasia, Alemannia—or Alamannia—and Thuringia, while his younger brother, Pepin the Short, also spelled Pippin, was appointed mayor in Neustria, Burgundy and Provence. This state of things, however, was temporary, as Pepin soon emerged as the sole, if still only nominal, ruler of the Franks (Nicolle 2008, 85).

[7] As Fouracre (2000, 173) affirms, it was in 749 when the papacy supported Pepin's desire to become king, essentially because he had already the power of one, even if prior to his elevation he had exercised this power as mayor of the palace, as his father Charles Martel had done before him. After becoming king, there was no longer any need for a mayor of the palace, as the post would have been redundant.

[8] In fact, it was the pope who legitimized the overthrow of Childeric III (743–751), the last of the Merovingians. With Pepin the Short a new dynasty rose to the Frankish throne: the Carolingians, named for Charles Martel, Pepin's father, who came to be considered the founder (head) of the new royal family (Costambeys et al. 2011, 51–64). The French Church performed an essential role in the consolidation of the alliance established between the papacy and the Carolingian Dynasty. Nevertheless, the Carolingian propagandists worked so hard to discredit the previous Merovingian kings (Riché 1993, 52) that by the sixteenth century, they were ignominiously dubbed the "do-nothing kings" (*rois fainéants*).

[9] Pepin's counselors did not, in fact, invent the ceremony, but rather took it from a canon law collection known as the *Hispana*, which had been introduced to Gaul by Visigothic refugees who knew that King Wamba had reacted to a rebellion of nobles in 672, by asking the archbishop of Toledo to anoint him to consolidate his legitimacy.

a procedure relieving a king's subjects from the obligation to obey him.[10] By wielding this canonical instrument the popes maintained a powerful political role.

#### 6.1.2.3 Stephen II and the Emergence of the Papal States

After his consecration as the legitimate king of the Franks Pepin intervened militarily in Italy to support Pope Stephen II, who was again threatened by a Lombardian offensive conducted by King Aistulf, who captured Ravenna in 751 and wanted to conquer Rome.[11] Stephen II reacted by visiting Pepin and negotiating an alliance (Feller 2001, 125–127) with him.

The terms of the Franks' intervention were defined in 754 in a treatise called the *Promissio carisiaca*, for having been signed in Quierzy-sur-Oise, then the capital of the new Frankish monarchy. Pepin led two expeditions that allowed him to defeat the Lombards under King Aistulf in 756, and occupy their capital, Pavia. The king of the Lombards was further obliged to restore the Exarchate and Pentapolis to Pope Stephen II (Christie 1998, 105), and the papacy became one of the major Peninsular powers.

The *Promissio carisiaca* had important political consequences: on the one hand it strengthened the French monarchy as the leading Western power and, on the other, it enabled the pope to become a temporal sovereign. The Frankish king pledged to aid the papacy and the Roman people in exchange for Stephen II's anointing of Pepin and his two sons as King(s) of the Franks and "patrician(s) of the Romans", a ritual designed to establish the authority and legitimacy of the new royal family on the throne and to create a dynasty (McKitterick 2011, 72).[12] In return,

---

[10] Excommunication was a canonical statement through which the Pope excluded the ruler from the Church community, carrying with it the serious consequence that his subjects were relieved of their duty to obey a prince who had ceased to be a Christian. Thus, when a king was excommunicated other sovereigns were entitled to seize his kingdom. Consequently, excommunication became a powerful instrument of political pressure wielded by the popes. Ullmann (2009, 302) points out that excommunication must be distinguished from "deposition" as far as kings were concerned. "Excommunication is the effective exclusion of individuals from membership of the *societas christiana*". Deposition was the consequence of excommunication, as once he was outside the Church the king was necessarily deprived of his title to rule. For example, when deposing Henry IV, Gregory VII underscored that he was doing so because only a Catholic within the fold of the Church could ever be a legitimate monarch. In this way the religious sphere intersected with the political sphere, with the most far-reaching consequences.

[11] The pretext for the action was the rise to the Lombardian throne in 751 of Astolfo, who began a military offensive that allowed him to conquer the part of Italy occupied by the Byzantines (the Exarchate) and retake its capital, Ravenna. This done, the Lombard soldiers moved against Rome. The new pope, Stephen II (752–757), requested French assistance to hold off the attack (Christie 1998, 104–105).

[12] Pope Stephen II visited the Frankish kingdom in 753–754 to seek assistance against the Lombards. In January 754, at St. Denis Abbey the pope anointed Pepin, his wife Bertrada, and his two sons Charles (the future Charlemagne), and Carloman. The Pope also confirmed that Pepin and his family were henceforth the only rightful rulers of the Frankish Kingdom.

Pepin recognized the pope as the head of the territorial Duchy of Rome, the Exarchate and Pentapolis, a title that led to the emergence of the "Papal States".[13] At this point the popes, in addition to boasting spiritual supremacy over all Christendom as heads of the Church, became sovereigns of their own states as well.

## 6.2 Charlemagne and the Resurgence of the Imperial Idea in the West

### *6.2.1 Charlemagne and the End of the Lombardian Kingdom*

Charlemagne (768–814), the son of Pepin the Short, defeated the Lombards so resoundingly that, after his victory over Desiderius, he was recognized as King of the Lombards in 774 (Costambeys et al. 2011, 66–67). That same year the Carolingian king reached Rome itself, where he was solemnly received by Pope Adrian I (772–795). In his dual role as King of the Franks and the Lombards, Charlemagne confirmed his father Pepin the Short's donation of the Papal States to the pope, in return for which Adrian I legitimized his dual royal title. The alliance between the Franks and popes was proving very beneficial for both parties.

### *6.2.2 The Appearance of the Kingdom of Italy*

The enthronement of the Frankish dynasty in Lombardy did not mark the end of the Lombardian kingdom, but only its transformation into the Kingdom of Italy (Barbero 2004, 38), whose first ruler was Charlemagne's son, Pepin, crowned in Rome in 781. Central Italy also fell under the influence of Charlemagne, including the Exarchate, Pentapolis, and the Duchies of Rome and Spoleto. The exception was the Duchy of Benevento, whose lords took advantage of the conflict between Charlemagne and the Byzantine Empire to maintain a *de facto* independence. Naples, Sicily and Calabria remained, at least theoretically, under the rule of Byzantium, though in reality their respective dukes were virtually independent.

[13] Pope Paul I (757–767), would still face a serious confrontation with the Lombard King Desiderius and the Archbishop of Ravenna. This came during the pontificate of Paul I and most likely arose because of the curious document known as the *Constitutum Constantini* (Donation of Constantine), an apocryphal text prepared by the Roman clergy featuring an alleged "donation" by Constantine to Pope Sylvester upon whom, in gratitude for his baptism, the emperor had supposedly conferred power and jurisdiction over Rome and the provinces of Italy and the West. In this way, Constantine purportedly transferred the seat of the Western Empire in order not to interfere with the spiritual power of Rome's bishops (Ullmann 2009, 58–66). This was a legal justification for the temporal power of the pontiffs, fabricated by papal jurists. On the origin and fate of the Donation of Constantine in the Early Middle Ages, see Fried (2007, 11–34).

### 6.2.3 *The Reappearance of the Imperial Idea in the West*

Charlemagne's new position in Italy reinforced his alliance with the papacy to the point that when Leo III (795–816), suffered a revolt by the Roman aristocracy, the pontiff accused of adultery and perjury, he took refuge at the Frankish court (799). Once there, the deposed pope convinced Charlemagne to personally head up a military expedition which enabled him to recover the papal throne. A grateful Leo crowned Charlemagne as Emperor of the West in St. Peter's Basilica.

Charlemagne's coronation is considered pivotal in western constitutional history because with it Byzantium lost its imperial monopoly, and the western part of the former Roman Empire recovered the importance it had lost in 476. Hence, the "emperor of the flowery beard" is widely considered one of the founders of Europe (Ullmann 2009, 105).

Despite its importance, we know little about how the coronation happened. Collins (2005, 52) reminds us that Einhard, in his *Vita Karoli* (written around AD 830), states that the king of Italy went to Rome in 800 "to restore the very disturbed state of the Church" and spent most of the winter there. However, he does not give any detail about how Charlemagne came to receive the imperial title. The nature of the proceedings and the rituals involved in this process of emperor-making are not described at all, and even the location and exact date of his elevation are implied rather than stated explicitly. Tradition maintains that Charlemagne was crowned as the new Emperor of the West on Christmas Day. However, this date may be merely symbolic, as it was also Christmas Day on which Clovis had converted to Christianity and been baptized.[14]

#### 6.2.3.1 The Pope vs. the Emperor: The Eminently Christian Nature of the New Western Empire

What we do know, also as indicated by Einhard, is that Charlemagne was not pleased at all with the coronation, to the point that he protested that he would never have entered St. Peter's Basilica in Rome on Christmas Day 800, had he known the symbolically damaging protocol the pontiff was going to employ during his crowning (McKitterick 2011, 26), as he realized that receiving the imperial crown

[14] It seems that the coronation ceremony, following the Byzantine rite, was comprised of three distinct parts: (1) acclamations by the populace and the army; (2) the coronation itself (3) and the reverence, or *prokynesis* of the patriarch before the new emperor. According to the well informed compiler of the Annals of Lorsch (Collins 2005), Leo III decided to invert this order and retain the first place for himself, so he began by setting the crown on Charlemagne's head and then, invited the congregation to acclaim him thrice. The pope then knelt before the new emperor (Riché 1993, 122). Einhard wrote in imitation of the Roman biographer Suetonius (c. 69—after 122), especially his *Life of Augustus*. About the Annals of Lorsch Abbey, see Kaschke (2010), and Wormald (1999).

from Leo III did imply a formal recognition of the pope's supremacy.[15] When Charlemagne wished his son Louis the Pious crowned emperor 13 years later to assure his succession, he organized the ceremony according to an entirely different protocol: the ceremony was held in the Palatine Chapel at Aachen, Louis was acclaimed not by the Romans but by the Franks, and the new emperor did not kneel before the pope, but was crowned by his father, or, according to another chronicler, placed the crown on his own head (Barbero 2004, 94).

Charlemagne was from the beginning, fully aware that the new Empire was not the same as its Roman namesake which had disappeared in 476. In Rome, the emperor's power had been based on the support of the people, the Senate, and the army, while in the case of Charlemagne it depended on papal legitimation. As Maglio (2006, 39) points out, the reappearance of the new Empire was not only the result of military action and the political machinations of the Carolingians, but was largely a project of papal inspiration. The dilemma facing the new Western Empire, therefore, was that it possessed two heads, which would prove to be a source of endless conflict.

#### 6.2.3.2 The Question of Succession and the Precarious Nature of the Carolingian Empire

The new Carolingian Empire was quite fragile, not only because of its formal subjection to the papacy, but because Charlemagne sought to gain formal recognition of his Empire from Byzantium (Fichtenau 1991, 71), and the Franks harbored a patrimonial conception of monarchy. Proof of this is that Charlemagne, 6 years after his coronation, organized his succession through a division of his kingdoms (*divisio regnorum*) among his legitimate children: Charles, Pepin and Louis (McKitterick 2011, 96–102). This distribution did not, however, materialize because when Charlemagne died in 814, he was survived only by Louis, entitled to the entire paternal inheritance.

The new emperor, who for his devoutness was dubbed "Louis the Pious", sought to amend the rule of succession in the interest of unity. In the year 817, he enacted an *ordinatio imperii* (Ganshof 1971, 273–276) through which he ceded the Empire to his eldest son, Lothair, who was crowned King of Italy and, as such, entitled to inherit the imperial throne by virtue of this designation.[16] However, Lothair's two brothers, Charles and Louis, did not accept the change in the rules of succession after

[15] It is highly significant, as Becher (2003, 11) points out, that Leo III decorated the right side of the *triclinium* of the Lateran, the most important of the papal audience chambers, with a mosaic depicting an enthroned St. Peter handing the *pallium* to Pope Leo, and a *vexillium*, a standard, to King Charlemagne, with an inscription beneath that read: "St. Peter gives life to Pope Leo and victory to King Charles".

[16] Lothair was even crowned in 823 as King of Italy in Rome by Pope Paschal I. At this time the monarchy was still not hereditary. As with the Roman emperors and the Germanic kings, the Carolingian emperor would designate the person to succeed him. There was, however, a tendency for him to name one of his sons, generally his eldest. The appointed individual had to be crowned King of Italy, as Italy was the foundation of the Empire, in accordance with the Roman tradition.

their father's death, and fought to overthrow their brother, which they did on June 25, 841, at the Battle of Fontenoy in Puisaye, in the heart of modern-day France.[17]

#### 6.2.3.3 The Treaty of Verdun and the Disintegration of the Carolingian Line

The disputes between the brothers ended up being resolved through the Treaty of Verdun (843), which established the division of the Carolingian Empire into three areas: the western zone (approximately the territory of present-day France), was assigned to Charles; the eastern (Germania) to Louis; and the territories between the two, plus the title of Emperor, to Lothair.[18] The agreement reached at Verdun has even been called the "birth certificate" of modern Europe (Riché 1993, 168).

#### 6.2.3.4 A Virtual Empire

As a result of this division, the title of Emperor no longer denoted a "universal state" and took on a merely symbolic meaning, ceasing to imply effective control over all the territories of Charlemagne's empire.[19] The imperial idea, however, did not disappear in the West.

## 6.3 From the Carolingian Empire to the Holy Roman Empire

### *6.3.1 The Frankish Monarchy Dissociates Itself from the Empire*

The breakup of the Empire led to numerous struggles for the imperial title among Charlemagne's descendants.[20] One of these dynastic conflicts eventually led to the Frankish kingdom's detachment from the Empire. The first step was the dethronement of the Carolingian ruler Charles the Simple, by Hugo the Great in 923, a situation that would definitively establish the authority of the latter's son,

[17] A description of the battle is provided by Angelbert, a Frankish soldier and a poet, who fought on Lothair's side, in his poem *Versus de Bella quae fuit acta Fontaneto = Verses on the Battle that was Fought at Fontenoy*, also known as *The lament on Fontenoy* (Godman 1985, 262–265).

[18] On the genesis and significance of the Treaty of Verdun, see Ganshof (1971, 289–302).

[19] This did not prevent some emperors from bringing all the territories under their rule, as was the case with Charles the Bald, from 875 to 877, who survived his brothers Lothair (+855) and Louis II the German (+875), becoming the last great Carolingian emperor (Riché 1993, 197) before being finally deposed in 887 (MacLean 2003, 191–198).

[20] The best general overview of this crucial period is the work by Goldberg (2006).

Hugh Capet (987–996), by imposing the hereditary principle for succession to the throne (Bautier 1992, 27–37), thereby ensuring a surprising continuity which would last until the rise of the French monarchy in the early thirteenth century.[21] The Franks were resolved to break off from the Empire largely because of the fact that it had become "Germanized", as in 962 the imperial title had gone to a Germanic nobleman: Otto, Duke of Saxony.

## *6.3.2 The Germanic Revival of the Imperial Idea*

German historiography establishes 911 as a chronological milestone to mark the passage from the Frankish to the Germanic Empire. According to tradition, it was in this year that Conrad I was elected the first King of Germany.[22] The authority exercised by the German king was largely theoretical, however, as the Germanic territories were ruled by powerful nobles (usually dukes) whom the king had to subjugate, whether by arms or by means of alliances. The problem was that the *novus rex*, although crowned and publicly acknowledged by all, were in perpetually tenuous positions, as they had to face potential opposition from two camps: their defeated rivals and the members of their clans, and those who had voted for him, but with a view to their own self interest, expecting greater wealth in return, ever willing to rescind their support if they concluded that doing so would benefit them (Reuter 1991, 203). Under these conditions only the strongest kings prevailed, such as Henry I (919–936), Duke of Saxony[23] and, above all, his son Otto I.

### 6.3.2.1 Otto I and the Rise of the Holy Roman Empire of the Germanic Nation

In the year 936, Henry I of Saxony's heir was elected "King of Germany"[24] with the name of Otto I (936–973). The new German king managed to expand the

[21] Philip II Augustus (1180–1223) was the first king to officially receive the title of "King of France", instead of the traditional "King of the Franks". During the crucial eleventh century, the bases of French kingship were set down.

[22] Conrad I was elected at Forchheim in early November 911, by Franks, Saxons, Alemanni and Bavarians. However, what really qualified him as the first German king was that he succeeded in forcing the other great magnates to accept his authority (Reuter 1991, 135).

[23] On the situation of Franconia, Saxony and Bavaria in the late Carolingian Empire, see MacLean (2003, 97–99).

[24] Unlike the Frankish monarchy, which by the close of the tenth century under Hugh Capet (987–996), had consolidated the hereditary principle, the German monarchy was elective, the king being designated by the high nobility (prince-electors). The only condition was that, in principle, the new monarch was supposed to be related to his predecessor—though this was not always respected. The process was not always peaceful, and in some cases there were double elections. On the origins of monarchy in Germany, see Barraclough (1976, 106–123).

boundaries of his kingdom and shore up his authority. In the East, he definitively halted the Hungarians and imposed his protectorate upon the Slavs of Bohemia, while in the West, he annexed modern-day Lorraine and part of today's Belgium to the German kingdom. In just years Otto I managed to become the most powerful ruler in the West, which prompted him to aspire to the Kingdom of Italy which since the time of Charlemagne had been the key to wielding the imperial scepter. To this end he invaded the Italian peninsula and was crowned Emperor in Rome by Pope John XII on February 2, 962 (Bryce 2012, 94–95), thereby seizing a title which had been unclaimed for more than 40 years, becoming the founder of what would ultimately be known in the historiography as the Holy Roman Empire.[25] From this moment forward the man designated as the King of Germany would possess the right to be King of Italy and to be crowned Emperor, though his coronation still lay in the hands of the Pope.

#### 6.3.2.2 Eight and a Half Centuries of History

The imperial coronation of Otto I marked the dawn of a nearly 300-year period known in German historiography as the *Kaiserzeit* ("Time of the Emperors"), the apogee of the Germanic Empire (van Caenegem 1995, 63), to last until the end of the Hohenstaufen Dynasty upon the death of Frederick II in 1250. From that moment forward, the Holy Roman Empire lost its splendor, though this did not keep it from recovering a key role in the history of Europe, as occurred during the era of Charles V (1519–1558), or during the reign of Maria Theresa's husband, Francis I (1745–1765).[26] It would survive until 1806, when it was dissolved by Francis II after his defeat by Napoleon at Austerlitz (Whaley 2011, II, 645–650).

#### 6.3.2.3 The Imperial Territories in 962

In the eleventh century, "Germany" did not exist as a unitary political entity. The term originally denoted a patchwork of peoples (Franks, Saxons, Bavarians and Swabians) dominated by various lords whose only common ground was that

[25] The king of Germany's official title initially was "King of the Franks". Henry IV (1050–1106), added the title "King of the Romans" (*Rex Romanorum*), which began to be given to the elected king, who started to be known as the *römisch-deutscher König* before his coronation as emperor. The epithet "Holy" was added by the Hohenstaufen Emperor Frederick I in 1157, reflecting his ambitions to dominate Italy and the papacy.

[26] Because Maria Theresa (1745–1780), as a woman, could not bear the title, it passed to her son Joseph II (1764–1790).

they were all able to communicate in the *Theotisca lingua*, which featured various dialects.[27] From the moment when Otto I was crowned king all the aforementioned territories came to be referred to as *Teutonicorum regnum*.[28] However, because the King of Germany also had to be the King of Italy to claim the imperial title, and he depended on the Pope to be crowned, he also needed to dominate the Italian Peninsula, which was a source of strife. In fact, Otto I ended up opposing and contesting the authority of John XII, who he deposed after convening a council which appointed Leo VIII as the new Pope (Bryce 2012, 132–133).

#### 6.3.2.4 The New Germanic Empire's Political Weakness

Just like the Empire of Charlemagne after its division at Verdun in 843, the Holy Roman Empire was in reality limited to a largely symbolic role, in this case, the exaltation of the Germanic monarchy, as only German kings could be named emperors. The Germanic Empire only achieved a universal dimension during the reigns of a few emperors of exceptional magnetism and charisma—essentially during the eras of Frederick Barbarossa (1152–1190), and Frederick II (1212–1250), the grandson of the first, both of the Hohenstaufen House of Swabia, for instance. Not even these great rulers, however, managed to establish lasting imperial supremacy over the other princes of Christian Europe. After 1250, the German electors who designated the emperor preferred to appoint unremarkable figures to avoid having to submit to imperial authority (Bryce 2012, 191–192). Thus, great monarchs such as Alfonso X of Castile (1252–1284), or Philip the Fair of France (1285–1314) were never named, while lesser nobles were, such as Rudolf of Habsburg (1273–1291).

The German Holy Roman Empire was an artificial political construct in so far as it was an attempt to recreate a universal state that had disappeared—something that can only be understood from the perspective of medieval man, for whom the era in

[27] The term *Deutsch* first appeared in the eighth century in a small dictionary (a short glossary, or kind of Thesaurus) of Latin-German called "Abrogans" or the *Codex Abrogans* (for the first entry in the glossary, which means "submissive" or "humble" in Latin "humility"), circa 770, and initially referred only to the language spoken in the eastern part of the Frankish Empire. It is an incomparable source of information for over 3,600 Old High German terms. There are some extant manuscripts of *Abrogans*, though the original copy has been lost (Grange 2010, 53). Germany was first referred to as *Deutschland*: "Land of the Germans".

[28] The territory bordered to the north on the sea of that name, Denmark and the Baltic Sea; to the west on the modern-day Netherlands (Belgium and Holland), Lotharingia (present-day Lorraine), and Switzerland; to the east with the dukedoms of Pomerania and Silesia; and the Slavic dukedom of Bohemia to the Oder River, in addition to Poland and Hungary. To the south, it encompassed the Italian territories, specifically all of northern Italy, except for Venice, and south to Lazio. These territories maintained, for the most part, the principle of feudal submission to the king of Germany, with the exception of the Netherlands (the counties of Hainatu, Brabante and Holland) which, thanks to their buoyant economic situation, ended up securing virtual independence, allowing them to initiate a policy of expansion in the North Sea (Bryce 2012, 167–173).

which it was his fate to live was considered a pale reflection of a brilliant, bygone time.[29] Firstly, this was because the kings of Germany could not claim the imperial title without being crowned by the popes. Between their election as kings of Germany and their papal coronation, the German monarchs held the temporary title of "King of the Romans" which was a fallacy, as neither the Roman citizenry nor the Roman state any longer existed, and the emperor was merely the visible head of a whole series of territories which were, in fact, legally and politically independent.[30]

#### 6.3.2.5 The Legal Relevance of the Holy Roman Empire

The fact that the political importance of the medieval emperors was limited, and their title largely symbolic, did not prevent them from playing an undeniably important legal role. Thus, for example, the rediscovery and renewed application of Roman law (Bryce 2012, 159–160), which became the basis of the new European law of the Late Middle Ages, proceeded politically from the idea that the different European kingdoms were ultimately the heirs to the legacy of the Roman emperors. Brian Tierney has defined the century from 1150 to 1250 as the "age of lawyers", not only because of the study of Roman law, beginning with Irnerius at the University of Bologna around 1100, which utterly transformed the art of jurisprudence, as law started being created by scholars (glossators and postglossators or commentators), but also because the study of Roman law provided "a very exalted theory of legislative sovereignty together with a wholly non-papal account of the origins of imperial authority" (Tierney 2004, 97–98).[31] This explains why some of the medieval Germanic emperors' edicts were integrated into the Justinian *Corpus*

[29] "The whole strange contraption can only be understood in the light of the conviction of medieval man that his own epoch was a weak copy of the brilliance of Antiquity. This same sentiment inspired his awe for the great authoritative texts of the past, the Bible, the Church Fathers, Roman law and Aristotle, giants on whose shoulders the medieval dwarfs were sitting" (van Caenegem 1995, 64).

[30] This is why the Holy Roman Empire came in for heavy criticism by the philosophers. Voltaire, for instance, considered that: "This agglomeration which was called and which still calls itself the Holy Roman Empire was neither holy, nor Roman, nor an empire" (*Ce corps qui s'appelait et qui s'appelle encore le saint empire romain n'était en aucune manière ni saint, ni romain, ni empire*) (Voltaire 1835, 121). Nineteenth century scholars presented the First Reich as "a weak state, a failed state, or a non-state, even a 'monstrosity,' thankfully put out of its misery by Napoleon" (Coy et al. 2010, 1).

[31] It is highly significant that the new study of Roman jurisprudence stimulated the canonists to develop their own ecclesiastical law into a system "of comparable scope and subtlety". This was possible because, on the one hand, a monk from Bologna named Gratian had systematized the law of the Church in his *Decretum* (1140), and, on the other hand, the legal norms of the popes, the decretals, were compiled in 1234 by the Spanish confessor of Gregory IX, the Dominican St. Raymond of Penyafort. Jurists educated in European universities could then apply the canon contained in Gratian's *Decretum* (decretists) and the *Decretals of Gregory IX* (decretalists) to real cases.

*iuris*,[32] and there appeared the Tribunal of the Imperial Chamber Court (*Reichskammergericht*), created by the Diet of Worms in 1495, which applied Roman law.[33] There was, in addition, a practical reason for this reverence for the Roman legacy: the Empire was composed of a number of states that had their own political and legal systems, so that the only unifying factor was their reference to the Roman legal tradition, effective as general suppletory law in a good number of the German states all the way down until January 1, 1900, when the German Civil Code, the *Bürgerliches Gesetzbuch* (BGB) went into effect.

This perspective is even more important today, when the concept of the nation-state is in crisis in Europe as a result of the supranational integration trends initiated in 1950. Thus, from this point of view, the attempts of medieval emperors to create a public law common to all the kingdoms of their era seems less utopian, especially since German Unification in 1989 and the collapse of the Soviet Union in 1991. This is why the Holy Roman Empire is increasingly presented in positive terms by current historiography, as it is seen as having provided a durable and dynamic political framework that protected the privileges and liberties of its constituents while coordinating collective action (Coy et al. 2010, 1).

## 6.4 The Era of "Papal Theocracy", or the Peak of Ecclesiasticism

### *6.4.1 Ecclesiastical Decline During the Feudal Period*

The theoretical supremacy of the Church's authority over civil power was evident after the popes' crowning of Charlemagne (800), and Otto I (962). The actual exercise of this power, however, was quite limited during the ninth and tenth centuries, not only because the popes had to deal with powerful monarchs—such as Charlemagne's

[32] As Bellomo (1995, 68–69) points out, although the Holy Roman emperors continued to make laws, very few of them were inserted in the Justinian framework. Some exceptions were the *Constitutio* "Habita" of Frederick I Barbarossa, a few laws on heresy from Frederick II, and the entire text of the *Consuetudines feudorum* (*Libri feudorum*), containing jurisprudential rules of feudal law.

[33] Political fragmentation in medieval Germany had as a consequence that effective government lay in the principalities. As a result of this situation, the Imperial Diet (*Reichstag*) had no power to enforce any acts it passed, and the imperial court of justice (*Reichshofgericht*), known since 1415 as the *Kammergericht*, was rended impotent by the widely granted privilege of exemption from its jurisdiction. It would be necessary to wait until 1495 for the reinforcement of the imperial position from a legal perspective through the creation by Maximilian I of the *Reichskammergericht*, as a refurbished imperial court of justice (Robinson et al. 2000, 188 and 194).

great-grandson Louis II (850–875), who managed to unify the Italian Peninsula[34]—but also because of the fact that papal authority was hampered by the general process of feudalization, clearly at odds with the Church's aspiration to comprehensive authority, directly inherited from Roman universalism (Bryce 2012, 104).

#### 6.4.1.1 "Feudalization" and the Appearance of "Proprietary Churches"

The privatization of political ties and the disintegration of the very notion of public authority caused ecclesiastical apparatuses (ecclesiastical provinces, bishoprics, abbeys) to fall under the dominion of local, secular authorities. This was the era of "proprietary churches" (*ecclesia propria* or *Eigenkirche*), so named because they were controlled by secular lords who, as owners of land and buildings, appointed individuals to clerical positions.[35] The feudalization of ecclesiastical offices greatly contributed to the atomization of public power in the Holy Roman Empire.[36]

#### 6.4.1.2 The German Holy Roman Empire and the "Imperial Church"

The submission of the ecclesiastical authorities to the great secular lords, reached its pinnacle in Germany following the imperial coronation of Otto I during the era of the *Reichskirche* (Imperial Church), characterized by the spreading practice of princes and great feudal lords who were also part of the clergy (bishops or abbots).[37] On the one hand, they were the ecclesiastical heads of their territories (*cura animarum*) and, on the other, their political heads as well, as they governed

[34] After being King of Bavaria (817–843), Louis the German became King of Eastern France until his death in 876. Nevertheless, as Goldberg (2006, 304) points out, during the last years of his reign he focused all his energies on controlling Italy and the western imperial crown, either for himself or for his son, Carloman.

[35] At the local level, owners built churches on their lands for their peasants and administrated earnings and ecclesiastical expenses. Some abbeys were overseen by dynasties of abbots belonging to preeminent families. In the regional sphere, the dukes and kings named bishops who they vested with their offices and with whom they forged feudal ties through the corresponding relationships of vassaldom. For an overview of the "proprietary system", see Tellenbach (1991, 71–72 and 178–179).

[36] Bryce (2012, 127) mentions how, when Otto I founded churches and appointed bishops, he acted partly as suzerain of feudal lands, and partly as protector of the faith, charged with guiding the Church in worldly matters. The emperor's dual position as head of both the Church and state required the two organizations to be exactly parallel. This is why in the eleventh century, a full half of the land and wealth of the HOLY ROMAN EMPIRE and an important part of its military strength was in the hands of churchmen, and ecclesiastical influence over the Diet was predominant.

[37] The *Reichskirche* (Imperial Church) was the sum of all prince-bishoprics and other immediate ecclesiastical foundations (Whaley 2012, 648). For an overview of the relationship between the German emperors and Rome during the Ottonian and Early Salian dynasties, see Blumenthal (1995, 28–40).

and exercised administrative, police, judicial, military and fiscal functions on behalf of the emperor. As Atwood (2001, 8) points out, certain bishoprics became more important as secular offices rather than religious ones. The system had many advantages, not only because the prince-bishops were chosen from among the educated classes of the population, but because, to the extent that these ecclesiastical princes were members of the clergy, they could not marry, which prevented the formation of hereditary dynasties that could tear the empire apart. Thus, the system endured and within the geographical scope of the German Holy Roman Empire there were small states that continued to be ruled by prince-bishops until the French Revolution. Thus, for example, was the case with the bishops of Liege, Strasbourg and Salzburg, to name but a few of the best known, all featuring prince-archbishops who served as heads of state, for life, for over eight centuries.[38]

### 6.4.2 *The Ecclesiastical Resurgence: The Eastern Schism, Cluny and the Gregorian Reform*

In the mid eleventh century the gradual waning of the Roman Church in general,[39] and the papacy, in particular, was exploited by the ambitious patriarch of Constantinople, Michael Cerularius,[40] to separate the Eastern (Orthodox) Church from the authority of Rome in 1054 (the Eastern Schism), in spite of the efforts of Pope Leo IX (Chadwick 2003, 206–218). The incident was a terrible blow, laying bare the debilitated state of the Western Church and the need for it to be reformed. The first efforts at this ecclesiastical renewal were the Cluniac Reforms, a major monastic movement sprouting in the tenth century at France's Cluny Abbey from within the Benedictine Order.[41]

---

[38] As Tellenbach (2000, 57) indicates, there was not one church but a number of churches that were endowed with land and "public" governmental rights which as a last resort became the property of the kingdom, using feudal forms for the transfer of rights and property. All these separate churches theoretically belonged to an "imperial Church", because the kingdom was a kingdom of the Church and the king's office was divinely conferred.

[39] Tellenbach (1991, 163) believes that the Church's eleventh-century crisis could be explained by many factors: ecclesiastical organization had spread far and wide, and monastic religion had taken a strong hold on men and made them more concerned for theirs soul's health, spurring them to greater conscientiousness and making them more concerned for the purity and good order of the Church.

[40] As Runciman (1971, 44) points out, if Cerularius is to be blamed, equal if not greater blame should be laid on his Catholic counterpart, Cardinal Umberto; even if he was a man of some erudition and of genuine piety, he was also hot-tempered and truculent, and he disliked the Greeks.

[41] Cluny was founded on the initiative of William the Pious, Duke of Aquitaine and Count of Auvergne, who asked Abbot Berno of Beaume, famous for his monastic asceticism and rigorous discipline, to establish a new monastery where the Rule of Saint Benedict was to be strictly observed, in an attempt to arrest the decay of monastic customs (Feller 2001, 242–243). It was founded on William's property and its founding charter (909), afforded protection to the new monastic community and its property from intervention and alienation by any secular power, insured independent abbatial elections, and subjected the monastery to the direct protection of the Pope, who owed the community *tuitio* and *defensio*. Thanks to its privileges, Cluny could develop and grow free from interference by either laymen or bishops (Blumenthal 1995, 11).

The new Cluniac spirituality spread throughout Christendom thanks to Hildebrand, a Germanic member of the new order[42] who would become Pope Gregory VII (1073–1085). As pontiff he concentrated his efforts on making the Catholic Church an independent institution completely separate from any civil powers.

What came to be called the Gregorian Reforms were aimed at eradicating a number of practices which had corrupted ecclesiastical life, including clergy who were marrying, a practice widespread among parish priests, though uncommon among bishops and non-existent among monks. Convinced that married priests became too involved in secular issues, Gregory VII decided to restore the celibacy requirement, which became mandatory during the twelfth century, and by the thirteenth, was being strictly observed. There was also a major backlash against "proprietary churches", and a campaign to recover a large number of church lands which had been usurped by secular lords. Also prohibited was simony, the commercialization of spiritual elements through which the kings and prelates sold ecclesiastical offices to the highest bidders. Henceforth, ecclesiastical assemblies were to choose the most suitable candidates.

To ensure the independence of the Church from secular powers, Gregory VII issued a historic decree, the *Dictatus papae* (1075), featuring 27 statements summarizing the new papal ideology (Cowdrey 2004, 496–501). One of these expressly recognized the Pope's status as the head of the Western Christian Empire, which meant that he held the power to exempt his subjects from their obligation to obey iniquitous kings. This was obviously not well received by the princes, let alone the emperors, who resolved to oppose the papal claims with all their might.

#### 6.4.2.1 The Investiture Contest: Henry IV Against Gregory VII

The strongest opponent of Gregory VII's aspirations was the German Emperor Henry IV (1084–1106), with the two squaring off in what was dubbed the "Investiture Contest". The dispute revolved around who should have the right to appoint or "invest" the holders of public ecclesiastical offices: civil or ecclesiastical authorities.[43] The question was problematic because many of the bishops were also

[42] On the relationship between Gregory VII and Cluny, see Tellenbach (1991, 186–192).

[43] As Robinson (1978, 1) points out, the Investiture Contest is a misleading term as it concentrates attention on a single issue—that of lay investiture—when it had a clearly political dimension. On the one side, it was seen as the struggle of Catholic orthodoxy against oppression by a secular power, and on the other, as the assault perpetrated by *sceleratus Hildebrandus* against the liberty of the German nation, defended by King Henry IV.

feudal lords subject to the Empire. Hence, when receiving their offices they had to be appointed not only by the Pope, but also by the emperors.[44]

In 1076, Gregory VII excommunicated Henry IV for ignoring the 1075 *Dictatus Papae*. As Henry was still only King of Germany, the excommunication sparked a revolt among the nobles, which forced Henry to plead for a papal pardon at Cannossa Castle in the winter of 1077. After accepting all of Gregory VII's demands, he was not only pardoned, but crowned emperor. The restoration of his authority, however, did not stop Henry from going on to lead a military expedition against Rome in which he managed to occupy the city (Blumenthal 1995, 113–126). Gregory VII died in exile in 1085, though Henry IV was ultimately defeated by Urban II (1088–1099). The papacy emerged triumphant not just because Urban II was able to retake Rome from imperial forces in 1093, but because, by backing the First Crusade (1096–1099), he was also able to strengthen papal prestige and authority.

#### 6.4.2.2 Balance Between Empire and Papacy: The Concordat of Worms

The question of investitures was ultimately resolved through negotiations leading to the Concordat of Worms (1122), signed by Emperor Henry V and Pope Calixtus II (Tellenbach 1991, 122–124). Based on the theological principle of the distinction between spiritual and temporal investiture, the Concordat established the German kings' waiving of their right to bestow upon bishops and abbots the ring and staff denoting their spiritual authority, which only the pope could do. The kings would be limited to granting them the scepter, which symbolized the feudal concession of temporal goods. The removal of investiture rights from royal hands, was offset by the kings' maintenance of the tribute which new bishops were to render to the king. Yet, as far as the Church was concerned in this crucial period, the popes had fully

[44] In the early medieval era, the "collation" (the concession of benefits and honors which entailed revenue) of ecclesiastical titles, from the bishops to the election of the very pope, was controlled by secular princes. Things began to change during the papacy of Nicholas II (1059–1061, Bishop Gerard of Florence, of Cluniac origins), who reformed the election system for bishops and implemented the current system through which the election of popes lay with cardinals (bishops who had achieved this rank, a kind of noble, honorific title), though the approval of their appointment was submitted to the Roman clergy, and the acclamation of the pontiff was left to the people. The essential shift was that the pope's election was extracted from pressure exerted by the Roman aristocracy and the unilateral actions of emperors. The next step was taken by Gregory VII (1073–1085)—Hildebrand—who in 1075, published a decree on investitures in which he expressly forbade any secular figure from vesting any member of the clergy with ecclesiastical authority (Tellenbach 1991, 113). In addition, to enforce this requirement, as well as others included in what was an entire program of disciplinary reform, he sent a papal representative with full powers to each one of the different Catholic kingdoms as "papal legates". Finally, to maintain direct control over the bishops, he affirmed the pope's right to transfer them to different dioceses, or even dismiss them, along with the principle that any legal decision issued by a bishop could be appealed before the pope.

succeeded in establishing their primacy in relation to councils and bishops (Schatz 1996, 95).[45]

### 6.4.3 *The Papacy's Power Swells*

The conflict between emperors and popes, however, would resurface, violently, yet again with Frederick I (1152–1190), and Frederick II (1215–1250) of the House of Hohenstaufen, although neither emperor was able to challenge a papacy that had been considerably strengthened, especially following the era of Innocent III (1198–1216). The latter pontiff served with considerable effectiveness as the West's spiritual leader,[46] imposing his authority on kings such as Peter II of Aragon, who died at Muret fighting against what Strayer (1971b, 123) calls a "political crusade",[47] and England's King John I, who was first excommunicated and later became a vassal of Rome.[48] Finally, Innocent IV (143–1254), took a further step to defend the system of absolute papal monarchy (Schatz 1996, 94), identifying the Church with the Pope (*papa, qui potest dici ecclesia*). For nearly two centuries, the popes stood as the highest authorities in the West (Ullmann 2003, 131–147), and the Church enjoyed a golden age in the intellectual sphere, largely thanks to the colossal figure of Thomas Aquinas (1224–1274), who managed to reconcile

[45] Because the restoration of the institution of the ecumenical council did not come as a continuation of the ancient councils, but as a derivation from papal synods, and because within two centuries (from 1200 to the end of the fourteenth century), the bishops, instead of being elected, would be appointed by Rome.

[46] As Powell (1994, 5) points out, if Gregory VII was content to be the Vicar of St. Peter, Innocent III considered himself the Vicar of Christ, less than God but greater than man, placed above all peoples and kingdoms, endowed with the fullness of power, judging all but judged by God alone.

[47] For him there was an obvious difference between a crusade against the Saracens—or even the Albigensians—and a crusade against Manfred or Peter of Aragon. Peter II was the first king of Aragon to be crowned. On November 11, 1204, Innocent III crowned him at the Monastery of San Pancrazio Martyr, near Trastevere, bestowing upon the king all the royal insignia: the mantle and tabard, the scepter and orb, the crown and miter, and receiving from Peter an oath. The king swore upon the Gospel that he would always be faithful and obedient to his lord, Pope Innocent, to his Catholic successors, and to the Roman Church, and would keep his kingdom in faithful obedience, defending the Catholic faith and persecuting heretical wickedness (Smith 2004, 43). Peter II was killed at Muret Castle on September 13, 1213, defending the Count Raymond VI of Toulouse, Peter's brother-in-law and vassal, against the papal army commanded by the leader of the Albigensian Crusade, Simon de Montfort.

[48] King John was excommunicated in November 1209. The confrontation with the pope produced a steady exodus of bishops from England. Most of them took refuge in the lands of John's enemy, Philip II Augustus (Moore 2009, 194). John ultimately reconciled with the pope, surrendered his kingdom to the papacy, and promised a large sum of money to the Holy See in May 1231, through the agreement known as the Golden Bull (*Bulla Aurea*). This humiliation and the severe defeat that John suffered at Bouvines (July 27, 1214), against Philip August prompted the English barons to revolt against the king and oblige him to sign the Magna Charta (June 15, 1215).

Aristotelian philosophy with the Biblical tradition, thereby considerably enriching Catholicism's theological foundations, allowing for an effective adaptation of traditional dogmas to the reality of his time.[49]

### 6.4.4 The Legal Consequences of the Papal Victory: The Secularization of Non-ecclesiastical Public Authorities

The conflict between emperors and popes seemed to have culminated with the latter's supremacy, but in the long run this ecclesiastical separation from civil power ended up backfiring on the papacy, as it favored the emancipation of secular powers from pontifical authority. This is what Strayer (1971a, 251) calls the process of "laicization" of society, which started in the thirteenth century. It was not the emperors but rather the kings of the Late Middle Ages who proclaimed their independence from the papacy in the political sphere, basing themselves on the arguments of the Italian jurist and philosopher Marsilius of Padua (1275–1343),[50] who defended the legitimate autonomy of secular power over that of the papacy.[51] This was the very first step in a process which would ultimately culminate in the French Revolution.

### 6.4.5 Papal Decline and the Fragmentation of Europe

The golden age of the papacy, in general terms, extended until the pontificate of Boniface VIII (1294–1303), the pope who confronted Philip IV of France,[52] the first

[49] Nichols (2003, 182) considers urgent a return to the ontological theology of Thomas of Aquinas to perpetuate a sane and adequate metaphysics in the Church, according to the Thomistic principle that "truth follows upon the being of things" (*veritas sequitur esse rerum*). For an overview of Aquinas's ideas on society and government, the nature of law, and the relationship between Church and state, see Tierney (2004, 165–171).

[50] As Canning (2011a, 81) observes, Marsilius was the product of two intellectual millieux: those of Padua and the University of Paris, where he was rector in 1313. At Padua, his professional training was in Medicine, and at Paris, the Faculty of Arts, where he completed his main political work *Defensor Pacis* (1324).

[51] Marsilius not only considers the Roman bishop, the pope, the enemy of peace, but distinguishes between the emperor (*princeps*), and the ruler (*pars principians*), which represents the community of citizens (*Universitas Civium*). The former executes the laws on behalf of the latter, who is the legislator and the supreme judge (Lee 2008, 135–136 and 141).

[52] The origin of the quarrel, as Langlois (1971, 27) mentions, was the bull *Clericis laicos* of February 24, 1296 that forbade, in general terms and under pain of excommunication, all secular princes from demanding or receiving extraordinary subsidies from the clergy, and forbade the clergy from paying such subsidies unless they received authorization to do so from the apostolic see. The problem was that the French kings had become accustomed to counting on the ecclesiastical tax for their war expenses, a tax that had been granted and imposed on the clergy of France by former popes for support of the Crusades.

European monarch to argue that the legitimacy of royal authority did not depend on the papacy, as he held that he was monarch by divine right, duly anointed through the coronation ceremony.[53] After obtaining the authorization of the French Estates General, which he convened for the first time in history in the year 1302, Philip IV (the Fair) sent his troops to seize and imprison the Pope in Anagni (Tierney 2004, 190–191), and managed to relocate the papacy from Rome to Avignon, where it remained under his aegis.

The era of the Avignon Papacy ended with what came to be called the Western Schism, in which Christian Europe beheld with dismay as multiple popes sought to simultaneously assert and exercise their authority, a situation that provoked a process of "constitutional redefinition" (Swanson 1980, 225), intended to reunite the Church.[54] The ensuing 40-year debate resulted in a considerable loss of prestige for the papacy, a profound crisis of papal authority, and an institutional breakdown in the governing structure of the Church (Canning 2011b, 165), that facilitated the outbreak of the Protestant Reformation in the early decades of the sixteenth century.

The religious crisis would, in general terms, have major consequences from the point of view of the history of the European state; by tending to precipitate the fragmentation of Europe, it had the effect of turning kingdoms into essential political units. As Ullmann (1972,189) points out, this happened because: "the tendencies of ecclesiastical thinkers to curtail the pope's powers ran in a direction diametrically opposed to the tendencies which can be observed in the field of secular government. Whilst ecclesiastical scholars and thinkers were endeavoring to change the ancient constitution of the Church by basing her government upon a broader basis, secular scholars and thinkers were doing their best to strengthen the constitutional and legal position of the monarch, until, in the 16th century, there emerged the stark absolutism of the prince". The era of independent states succeeded that of Christian universalism.

---

[53] The king's jurists, basing themselves on Roman canonical law, which they studied at European universities as of the late eleventh century, defended the king of France's independence with the argument that the French kings had been consecrated at Reims since the time of Pepin the Short (who was the first to receive the episcopal anointing, in the year 751). By virtue of this anointment, they argued, French kings ruled by "divine right" and, therefore, did not require legitimization by the pope. The jurists of Phillip IV (Guillaume de Nogaret o Enguerrand de Marigny) sought to erase the idea of Christian universalism and establish monarchs as autonomous sovereigns with full powers to rule. It was based on this theory that the French king sent his troops to Anagni. The conflict with the French monarchy marked the beginning of the end for papal theocracy.

[54] The conflict was resolved at the Council of Constance (1414–1418), which dredged up the old premise that the collegial relationship took precedence over the monarchical conception of ecclesiastical power, according to the opinion of thinkers like William of Ockham and Marsilius of Padua (Padoa Schioppa 2007, 108). For an overview of the conciliar tradition in the Catholic Church see Oakley (2003, 20–40).

The decline of papal power would accelerate in the eighteenth century when enlightened despots renounced their divine legitimization, except for in France, where the principle would survive until the fall of the monarchy upon the outbreak of the French Revolution,[55] although the French Church enjoyed considerable autonomy as a result of the adoption of Gallicanism.[56] After 1789, there would be a tremendous backlash against the Church in France, which peaked in 1793 with the introduction of the revolutionary calendar and the celebration of the Festival of the Supreme Being, presided over by Robespierre (Van Kley 2003, 1081–1104). The separation between the Church and state, however, would not be legislatively affirmed until 1905.

The papal states disappeared after the military occupation of Rome by Italian troops on September 20, 1870, although they would reappear in a different form through the establishment of the Vatican State agreed to in the Lateran Accords (February 11, 1929), signed by Pio IX and Benito Mussolini.[57]

## 6.5 The Survival of the Imperial Idea

The end of Christian universalism would not, however, spell the end of the imperial idea in Europe. The Holy Roman Empire enjoyed another moment of splendor under Charles V (1519–1558), because of the fact that he inherited Spain's immense dominions and possessed the financial means to stand as the premier political arbiter of his time. Mercurino Gattinara, a key advisor to Charles, encouraged him to realize the vision of a universal monarchy, as proposed by Dante in his *De Monarchia* (Yates 1999, 21).[58] His son, Phillip II, despite the fact that he headed the Spanish Empire, then the world's most powerful political entity, was not elected German Emperor and could not aspire to the imperial title. He was, however, honored with the title of "universal monarch". What Germans call the First Reich would endure until 1806 (Wilson 2009, 22–41), when it was abolished by Francis II

[55] As Van Kley (1996, 7) points out, the religious history of eighteenth-century France is entwined with that of constitutional relationship between the parlements and Bourbon absolutism.

[56] Nevertheless, since Phillip IV (the Fair), the French kings maintained a *status quo* vis-à-vis the papacy thanks to the rise of "Gallicanism", a movement through which the king of France, though not recognizing the pope's supremacy in the political sphere, and still affirming that French kings, upon their anointing, received their legitimacy directly from God, did respect the pope's religious authority. The kings endorsed the autonomous organization of the Church of France, free of Roman control. The Gallican doctrine (Gallican Articles), was officially approved by a 1682 Assembly of the French clergy at Louis XIV insistence (Parsons 2004, 277).

[57] The agreement was formally validated by the Plebiscite of March 24, 1929. From a total of 8.63 million, 90 % of the registered electorate, they were only 135,761 "no" votes (Pollard 2005, 59).

[58] For an overview and analysis of Dante's main political work see Fajardo Gómez (2010, 18–19).

in response to pressure by Napoleon,[59] who in 1804, had crowned himself "Emperor of the French" in the pope's presence to avoid the "humiliation" suffered by Charlemagne.[60]

With Napoleon things changed, as the imperial idea no longer relied on tradition but on brute power (Sanmartín 2009, 177–197). In fact, Napoleon created a brand new kind of monarchy. Heir to the French Revolution, formally he did not become the French Emperor but rather the "Emperor of the French" (*Empereur des Français*).[61] After Napoleon's resignation in 1815, the imperial idea would reappear in France between 1852 and 1870, with Napoleon III.[62]

It is interesting to note that although Queen Victoria was formally named "Empress of India", the British Crown was never "constitutionally" an empire. In fact, after the French interlude, the imperial idea resurfaced in Germany. After the Congress of Vienna (1815), the emperor of Austria, once again, headed the confederation of the Germanic states, at least until 1867,[63] when Bismarck brought about the establishment of the North German Confederation, which in 1871, became the Second Reich at the Palace of Versailles, following his crushing defeat of Napoleon III. Wilhelmine Germany would last until 1918, but did not survive Prussia's defeat in the First World War.[64] After the humiliation suffered by Germany

[59] After his crushing victory at Austerlitz (December 2, 1805) Napoleon compelled Francis II to recognize Württemberg, Bavaria and Saxony as sovereign kingdoms. In July 1806 he forced Bavaria, Württemberg, Baden, Hessen-Darmstadt, the Duchy of Berg, and 11 lesser dukes and princes in western Germany to join a newly formulated Confederation of the Rhine. The member states, with Napoleon as their "Protector", had to abandon the Holy Roman Empire and raise an army of 63,000 men. After the loss of these 16 states Francis II abdicated in August 1806, as Holy Roman Emperor. "An empire of a thousand years passed away with him" (Brose 1997, 51).

[60] To denote the independence of imperial power from the papacy, Napoleon symbolically seized the crown from Pio XII and placed it on his head on December 2, 1804. As Doyle (2009, 85) observes, Napoleon often described himself, especially in speaking of his relations with the pope, as a new Charlemagne. The imperial coronation was replete with Carolingian echoes and imitations.

[61] For an analysis of the nature of the Napoleonic monarchy see Forrest (2009, 112–130).

[62] The formal continuity with the first empire was made clear in the *sénatus-consulte* of November 7, 1852, which revised the constitution and stated: "the imperial dignity is reestablished. Louis-Napoleon Bonaparte is Emperor of the French, under the name of Napoleon III", Napoleon II being Napoleon's son, the Duke of Reichstadt (1811–1832), nicknamed the Eaglet (*L'Aiglon*). The proposal was sanctioned by a plebiscite on November 21 with 7,824,000 positive votes, 253,000 against and nearly 2 million abstentions (Price 2001, 43).

[63] It was Emperor Leopold I who precipitated the decline of the Holy Roman Empire by creating the Kingdom of Prussia in 1701, and placing it under Frederick I (1701–1713) of the Hohenzollern Dynasty, until then the Elector of Brandenberg, which he did to secure his support in the War of Spanish Succession (1704–1714). Prussia then, set about engineering its ascendancy, as it would become Germany's premier power under Bismarck (1862–1873).

[64] For a definition of the nature of the Second Reich, considered either as a nation-state, a colonial empire, or a continental empire, see Dickinson (2008, 273–289).

in the Versailles Treaty (1919), from 1933 to 1945, Hitler would later head the Third Reich[65]—which may be considered the last attempt at a European "empire".[66]

## TIMELINE

### Ostrogoths, Byzantines and Lombards

| | |
|---|---|
| 493–526 | Reign of Theodoric the Great. Peak of the Ostrogoths' presence in Italy. |
| 527–565 | Justinian |
| | *552* The Byzantines occupy Italy following a devastating war against the Ostrogoths. |
| 568 | The Lombards, led by Alboin, invade Italy. |
| 572 | The Byzantines lose control of northern Italy (Lombardy), where the Lombards found a kingdom with its capital at Pavia. |
| 590–604 | The Pontificate of Gregory I. |

### The Popes vs. the Byzantine Emperors

| | |
|---|---|
| 653 | Byzantine Emperor Constans II orders the arrest of Pope Martin I, who dies in exile. |
| 681 | Emperor Constantine IV condemns Monothelitism (third council of Constantinople, Sixth Ecumenical) to reconcile with Rome. |
| 695 | An anti-Byzantine rebellion breaks out in Ravenna. |
| 715–731 | Pontificate of Gregory II, who condemns the iconoclasts and confronts Emperor Leo III the Isaurian and all Byzantium. |

[65] The Third Reich was effective as far as the centralization of Germany was concerned, but not in terms of Germanizing Europe. As Clark (2006, 663) indicates, the Law on the Reorganization of the Reich of January 1934, placed regional governments and the new imperial commissars under the direct authority of the Reich's interior ministry. The Prussian ministries were gradually merged with their Reich counterparts (with the exception, for technical reasons, of Finance) and plans were drawn up (though they remained unrealized in 1945), to partition the state into its constituent provinces. "Prussia was still an official designation and a name on the map, indeed it was the only German state not to be formally absorbed into the Reich. However, it ceased *de facto* to exist as a state of any kind". Nevertheless the idea of an imperial Germany endured at the level of propaganda (Umbreit 2008, 8) in the form of phrases like "New Order" and "Greater German Reich".

[66] For many observers, nevertheless, the idea of Germany as the preeminent European nation (*Mitteleuropa*) is gaining ground thanks to European integration. If it was originally based on the union of France and Germany, now the latter is becoming, by virtue of its economic power, the *de facto* leader of the European Union. For an interesting analysis of this crucial question, see Reagin (2004, 273–289).

### The Papacy's Alliance with the Frankish Monarchy

| | |
|---|---|
| 732 | Charles Martel defeats the Muslims at Poitiers and wields *de facto* power in the kingdom of the Franks. |
| 741–752 | The papacy of Zacharias, who signs a truce with the Lombard king Liutprand. |
| 751 | Pope Zacharias authorizes St. Boniface to crown Pepin the Short (Charles Martel's son) as the King of the Franks at Soissons, which means dethroning Childeric III, the last Merovingian king. |
| 754 | *Promissio carisiaca.* Under this treaty Pope Stephen II commits to anointing Pepin the Short as the king of the Franks and "Patrician of the Romans". The Frankish monarch recognizes the Pope's territorial domain over the Duchy of Rome, Exarchate and Pentapolis—the legal/territorial title making possible the emergence of the *Papal States.* |
| 774 | Charlemagne (son of Pepin the Short), King of the Franks since 768, after defeating the Lombard king Desiderius and occupying Pavia, is acknowledged as King of the Lombards. The *Kingdom of Italy* appears. |

### The Empire of Charlemagne

| | |
|---|---|
| 800 | September 24. Charlemagne is crowned emperor by Pope Leo III. |
| 814–840 | After Charlemagne's death he is succeeded by his son Louis the Pious. |
| 841 | June 25. The Battle of Fontenoy in Puisaye. The defeat of Lothair, the eldest son of Louis the Pious, by his brothers Charles and Louis. |
| 843 | Treaty of Verdun. The Empire of Charlemagne is divided. |
| 875 | Charles the Bald is crowned emperor by Pope John VIII in exchange for relinquishing imperial authority over Rome and part of southern Italy, in favor of the papacy. |
| 911 | Conrad I is elected the first king of Germany. |
| 923 | Dethronement of the Carolingian king Charles the Simple by Hugo the Great. |

### Foundation of the German Holy Roman Empire

| | |
|---|---|
| 962 | Otto I, Duke of Saxony, is crowned Emperor. He is the founder of the German Holy Roman Empire (First Reich), which would last until 1806. |
| 987–996 | Hugh Capet succeeds in leaving his throne to his son. Consolidation of the hereditary dynasty in the Kingdom of the Franks and separation from of the Empire. |
| 1054 | July 16. The Eastern Schism. Michael Cerularius and Pope Leo IX excommunicate each other. Separation of the Orthodox and Roman Churches. |

## The Era of Papal Theocracy

| | |
|---|---|
| 1075 | Gregory VII (1073–1085) promulgates the *Dictatus Papae*, 27 statements in which he asserts the pope's supremacy over secular authorities. This document was not published in the German Holy Roman Empire, in the Iberian kingdoms, or in England. |
| 1077 | Henry IV humbles himself before Gregory VII at Canossa. |
| 1083 | Emperor Henry IV conquers Rome. |
| 1093 | Pope Urban II retakes Rome. |
| 1096–1099 | First Crusade. |
| 1122 | Concordat of Worms. End of the Investiture Controversy. |
| 1155–1190 | Reign of Frederick I Barbarossa. |
| 1198–1216 | Papacy of Innocent III, the chief exponent of papal theocracy. |
| 1220–1250 | Reign of Frederick II Hohenstaufen. |
| 1291–1293 | Reign of Rudolph I of Habsburg. |
| 1274 | Death of Thomas Aquinas (b. 1224). |

## The Decline of the Papacy

| | |
|---|---|
| 1303 | September 7. The attack at Anagni. Philip IV of France's troops seize Pope Boniface VII. |
| 1309–1377 | The Avignon Papacy. The popes reside outside Rome, in Avignon. |
| 1378–1417 | The Western Schism. Multiple popes vie for St. Peter's throne. |

## Reformation and Counterreformation

| | |
|---|---|
| 1519 | Charles V is elected Emperor. |
| 1521 | Diet of Worms. Luther explains the principles of the "Reformation" to Charles V. |
| 1527 | May 6. The troops of Charles V, sharply at odds with Clement VII, occupy and sack Rome (*Sacco di Roma*). The popes will never again meddle in civil political affairs. |
| 1529 | Diet of Spires. The Lutheran princes "protest" against Charles V's request for them to submit to the Pope's authority. They come to call themselves "Protestants". |
| 1536 | Henry VIII breaks with Rome when Clement VII refuses to annul his marriage to Catherine of Aragon (Ferdinand and Isabella's daughter). The king declares himself the head of the Church of England. The Anglican Church is born. |
| 1540 | September 27. Pope Paul III accepts the creation of the Society of Jesus, founded by Ignatius of Loyola. The Jesuits become Catholicism's quintessential advocates and defenders. |

| | |
|---|---|
| 1545 | The Council of Trent begins. It would not close until 1563 (Counterreformation). |
| 1555 | Peace of Augsburg. Each German prince may profess the religion he desires, and has the right to impose it upon his subjects (*cuis regio eius religio*). |
| 1572 | August 24. Massacre of Protestants in Paris (St. Bartholomew's Day Massacre). The most dramatic episode of France's Wars of Religion (1562–1598). |
| 1618–1648 | Thirty Years War. At its close Europe is divided into Catholic and Protestant kingdoms. |

### Papacy and Empire: From the French Revolution to the Third Reich

| | |
|---|---|
| 1790 | July 12. Civil constitution of the clergy. The French revolutionaries seek to convert the Catholic priests into government officials of the new French state, prompting a break with Rome. |
| 1793 | October. Publication of the French revolutionary calendar, with no reference to the traditional church calendar (Gregorian). |
| 1794 | June 8. Robespierre celebrates the Festival of the Supreme Being. |
| 1801 | Napoleon signs a Concordat with the Pope and reconciles with French Catholics. |
| 1804 | December 2. Napoleon is crowned Emperor of the French in the presence of Pope Pius VII in the Cathedral of Notre Dame (Paris). |
| 1806 | Napoleon abolishes the German Holy Roman Empire. |
| 1852–1870 | Second French Empire (Napoleon III). |
| 1870 | September 20. Rome becomes the capital of the Kingdom of Italy, after its military occupation. After the demise of the Papal States, dating back to 754, Pope Pius IX describes himself as a prisoner of the Italian State. |
| 1871–1918 | Second German Reich. |
| 1905 | French Law of separation of the Church and the State (*Loi de separation des Églises et de l'État*). |
| 1929 | February 11. Lateran Pacts. Mussolini and Pius XI agree to the founding of the Vatican State. |
| 1933–1945 | Hitler's Third Reich. |

## References

Atwood, C. D. (2001). *Always reforming: A history of Christianity since 1300*. Macon, GA: Mercer University Press.

Azzara, C. (2002). The papacy. In C. La Rocca (Ed.), *Italy in the early Middle Ages* (pp. 102–117). Oxford, UK: Oxford University Press.

Barbero, A. (2004). *Charlemagne: Father of a continent*. Berkeley, CA: University of California Press.

Barraclough, G. (1976). The rise of the German monarchy. In *The crucible of Europe: The ninth and tenth centuries in European history* (pp. 106–122). Berkeley, CA: University of California Press.

Bautier, R. -H. (1992). L'avènement d'Hugues Capet. In *Le roi de France et son royaume autour de l'an mil* (pp. 27–37). Paris: Picard.

Becher, M. (2003). *Charlemagne*. New Haven, CT: Yale University Press.

Bellomo, M. (1995). *The common legal past of Europe, 1000–1800*. Washington, DC: The Catholic University of America Press.

Blumenthal, U.-R. (1995). *The investiture controversy: Church and monarchy from the ninth to the twelfth century*. Totowa, NJ: Barnes and Noble Books.

Brose, E. D. (1997). *German history 1789–1871: From the Holy Roman Empire to the Bismarckian Reich*. Oxford, UK: Berghahn.

Brown, P. (1973). A dark-age crisis: Aspects of the iconoclastic controversy. *English Historical Review, 88*(346), 1–34.

Brubaker, L., & Haldon, J. (2011). *Byzantium in the iconoclast era, c. 680–850: The sources, an annotated survey*. Cambridge, UK: Cambridge University Press.

Bryce, J. (2012). *The Holy Roman Empire* (3rd ed., repr.). Oxford, UK: Oxford University Press.

Canning, J. (2011a). Marsilius of Padua. In *Ideas of power in the late Middle Ages 1296–1417* (pp. 81–106). Cambridge, UK: Cambridge University Press.

Canning, J. (2011b). The power crisis during the Great Schism: (1378–1417). In *Ideas of power in the late Middle Ages 1296–1417* (pp. 165–191). Cambridge: Cambridge University Press.

Chadwick, H. (2003). *East and west: The making of a rift in the Church. From apostolic times until the Council of Florence*. Oxford, UK: Clarendon.

Christie, N. (1998). *The Lombards: The Ancient Longobards*. Oxford: Blackwell.

Christie, N. (2005). Charlemagne and the renewal of Rome. In J. Story (Ed.), *Charlemagne: Empire and society* (pp. 167–182). Manchester: Manchester University Press.

Clark, C. (2006). *Iron kingdom: The rise and downfall of Prussia, 1600–1947*. Cambridge, MA: Belknap Press of Harvard University Press.

Collins, R. (2005). Charlemagne's imperial coronation and the annals of Lorsch. In J. Story (Ed.), *Charlemagne: Empire and society* (pp. 52–70). Manchester, UK: Manchester University Press.

Costambeys, M., Innes, M. MacLean S. (2011). *The Carolingian world*. Cambridge, UK: Cambridge University Press.

Cowdrey, H. E. J. (2004). *Pope Gregory VII: 1073–1085*. Oxford, UK: Clarendon (Reprint).

Coy, J. Ph., Marschke, B., & Sabean D. W. (2010). *The Holy Roman Empire, reconsidered*. New York/Oxford: Berghahn.

Dickinson, E. R. (2008). The German Empire: An empire? *History Workshop Journal, 66*(1), 129–162.

Doyle, W. (2009). The political culture of the Napoleonic Empire. In A. Forrest & P. H. Wilson (Eds.), *The bee and the eagle: Napoleonic France and the end of the Holy Roman Empire, 1806* (pp. 83–93). Basingstoke: Palgrave Macmillan.

Fajardo Gómez, M. I. (2010). La ciencia política: Dante Alighieri. In S. Delgado Fernández (Coord.), *Dando voz a los clásicos: autores y textos clásicos para una historia de las ideas políticas* (pp. 18–19). Granada, Spain: Comares.

Feller, L. (2001). *L'Église et la société en Occident: pouvoir politique et pouvoir religieux du VIIe au XIe siècle*. Paris: Sedes.

Fichtenau, H. (1991). *The Carolingian Empire*. Toronto: University of Toronto Press.

Forrest, A. (2009). Napoleon as a monarch: A political evolution. In A. Forrest & P. H. Wilson (Eds.), *The bee and the eagle: Napoleonic France and the end of the Holy Roman Empire, 1806* (pp. 112–130). Basingstoke: Palgrave Macmillan.

Fouracre, P. (2000). *The age of Charles Martel*. New York: Longman.

Fried, J. (2007). *Donation of constantine and constitutum constantini: The misinterpretation of a fiction and its original meaning*. Berlin: Walter de Gruyter.
Ganshof, F. L. (1971). *The Carolingians and the Frankish monarchy: Studies in Carolingian history*. Ithaca, NY: Cornell University Press.
Geary, P. (1988). *Before France and Germany: The creation and transformation of the Merovingian world*. Oxford, UK: Oxford University Press.
Godman, P. (1985). *Poetry of the Carolingian renaissance*. London: Duckworth.
Goldberg, E. J. (2006). *Struggle for empire: Kingship and conflict under Louis the German, 817–876*. Ithaca, NY: Cornell University Press.
Grange, W. (2010). *Historical dictionary of German literature to 1945*. Plymouth, UK: Scarecrow Press.
Kaschke, S. (2010). Annales Laureshamenses. In G. Dunphy (Ed.), *Encyclopedia of the medieval chronicle* (pp. 69–70). Leiden: Brill.
Langlois, C. V. (1971). The power politics of France. In C. T. Wood (Ed.), *Philip the fair and Boniface VIII: State vs. Papacy* (2nd ed., pp. 26–32). New York: Holt, Rhinehart, and Winston.
Lee, H.-Y. (2008). *Political representation in the later Middle Ages: Marsilius in context*. New York: Peter Lang.
MacLean, S. (2003). *Kingship and politics in the late ninth century: Charles the fat and the end of the Carolingian Empire*. Cambridge, UK: Cambridge University Press.
Maglio, G. (2006). *L'idea costituzionale nel Medioevo: dalla tradizione antica al 'costituzionalismo cristiano'*. Verona: Il segno dei Gabrielli.
McKitterick, R. (1983). *The Frankish Kingdoms under the Carolingians*. London: Longman.
McKitterick, R. (2011). *Charlemagne: The formation of a European identity*. Cambridge, UK: Cambridge University Press.
Moore, J. C. (2009). *Pope Innocent III (1160/61-1216): To root up and to plant*. Notre Dame, IN: University of Notre Dame Press.
Nichols, A. (2003). The aftermath, Thomas in history. In *Discovering Aquinas: An introduction to his life, work and influence* (pp. 129–146). Gran Rapids, MI: Eerdmans.
Nicolle, D. (2008). *Poitiers AD 732: Charles Martel turns the Islamic tide*. Oxford, UK: Osprey.
Oakley, F. (2003). *The Conciliarist tradition: Constitutionalism in the Catholic Church, 1300–1870*. Oxford, UK: Oxford University Press.
Padoa Schioppa, A. (2007). *Storia del diritto in Europa: Dal medioevo all'età contemporanea*. Bologna: Il Mulino.
Parsons, J. (2004). *The Church in the Republic: Gallicanism & political ideology in renaissance France*. Washington, DC: Catholic University of America Press.
Pohl, W. (2002). Invasions and ethnic identity. In C. La Rocca (Ed.), *Italy in the early Middle Ages* (pp. 11–33). Oxford, UK: Oxford University Press.
Pollard, J. F. (2005). *The Vatican and Italian Fascism, 1929–1932: A study in conflict*. Cambridge, UK.: Cambridge University Press.
Powell, J. M. (Ed.). (1994). *Innocent III: Vicar of Christ or Lord of the world?* (2nd expanded ed.). Washington, DC: Catholic University of America Press.
Price, R. (2001). *The French second empire: An anatomy of political power*. Cambridge, MA: Cambridge University Press.
Reagin, N. R. (2004). Recent work on German national identity: Regional? Imperial? Gendered? Imaginary? *Central European History, 37*(2), 273–289.
Reuter, T. (1991). *Germany in the early Middle Ages: 800–1056*. New York: Longman.
Riché, P. (1993). *The Carolingians: A family who forged Europe*. Philadelphia, PA: University of Pennsylvania Press.
Robinson, I. S. (1978). *Authority and resistance in the investiture contest: The polemical literature of the late eleventh century*. Manchester: Manchester University Press.
Robinson, O. F., Fergus, T. D., & Gordon, W. M. (2000). *European legal history*. London: Butterworth.
Runciman, S. (1971). *The Eastern Schism*. Oxford: Clarendon Press.

Salvatorelli, L. (1982). *Sommario della storia d'Italia*. Torino: Einaudi.
Sanmartín, J. J. (2009). La idea imperial en Napoleón: La simbiosis entre modernización política y tradición ideológica. *Res publica: Revista de filosofía política*, (21), 177–197.
Schatz, K. (1996). *Papal primacy: From its origins to the present*. Collegeville, MN: Liturgical Press.
Smith, D. J. (2004). *Innocent III and the crown of Aragon: The limits of papal authority*. Burlington, VT: Ashgate.
Strayer, J. R. (1971a). The laicization of French and English society in the thirteenth century. In *Medieval statecraft and the perspectives of history* (pp. 251–265). Princeton, NJ: Princeton University Press.
Strayer, J. R. (1971b). The political crusades of the thirteenth century. In *Medieval statecraft and the perspectives of history* (pp. 123–158). Princeton, NJ: Princeton University Press.
Swanson, R. N. (1980). The problem of the cardinalate in the Great Schism. In B. Tierney & P. Linehan (Eds.), *Authority and power: Studies on medieval law and government presented to Walter Ullmann on his seventieth birthday* (pp. 225–236). Cambridge: Cambridge University Press.
Tellenbach, G. (1991). *Church, state and Christian society at the time of the investiture contest*. Oxford, UK: Basil Blackwell.
Tellenbach, G. (2000). *The Church in Western Europe from the tenth to the early twelfth century*. Cambridge: Cambridge University Press (Reprint).
Tierney, B. (2004). *The crisis of Church and state: 1050–1300*. Toronto: University of Toronto Press.
Ullmann, W. (1972). *Origins of the Great Schism: A study in fourteenth-century ecclesiastical history*. Hamden, CT: Archon Books.
Ullmann, W. (2003). *A short history of the papacy in the Middle Ages* (2nd ed.). London: Routledge (1972).
Ullmann, W. (2009). *The growth of papal government in the Middle Ages: A study in the ideological relation of clerical to lay power*. New York, NY: Routledge.
Umbreit, H. (2008). Hitler's Europe. In R. Bernhard et al. (Eds.), *Germany and the Second World War* (Vol. V/II, pp. 8–137). Organization and mobilization in the German sphere of power. War administration, economy, and manpower resources 1942–1944/5. Oxford, UK: Oxford University Press.
van Caenegem, R. C. (1995). *An historical introduction to western constitutional law*. Cambridge, MA: Cambridge University Press.
Van Kley, D. K. (1996). *The religious origins of the French revolution: From Calvin to the civil constitution, 1560–1791*. New Haven, CT: Yale University Press.
Van Kley, D. K. (2003). Christianity as casualty and chrysalis of modernity: The problem of dechristianization in the French revolution. *The American Historical Review, 108*(4), 1081–1104.
Voltaire, L. (1835). De l'empereur Charles IV. De la bulle d'or. Du retour du saint-siége de Avignon à Rome. De sainte Catherine de Sienne, etc. In *Essai sur les moeurs et l'esprit des nations* (Vol. II, Chapter 70, pp. 116–123). Paris: Treuttel et Würtz.
Whaley, J. (2012). *Germany and the Holy Roman Empire* (Vol. I: Maximilian I to the peace of Westphalia (1493–1648). Vol. II: The peace of Westphalia to the dissolution of the Reich, 1648–1806). Oxford, UK: Oxford University Press.
Wilson, P. H. (2009). The meaning of empire in Central Europe around 1800. In A. Forrest & P. H. Wilson (Eds.), *The bee and the eagle: Napoleonic France and the end of the Holy Roman Empire, 1806* (pp. 22–41). Basingstoke: Palgrave Macmillan.
Wormald, P. (1999). *Legal culture in the early medieval West*. London: A&C Black.
Yates, F. A. (1999). Charles V and the idea of empire. In *Astraea: The imperial theme in the sixteenth century* (pp. 20–28). New York: Routledge & Kegan Paul.

## *Further Reading*


Alighieri, D. (2013). *The De Monarchia*. Cambridge: Cambridge University Press.

Andersen, P., Vogt, H., & Münster-Swendsen, M. (2007). *Law before Gratian: Law in Western Europe c. 500–1100: Proceedings of the third Carlsberg academy conference on medieval legal history 2006*. Copenhagen: DJØF Pub.

Appold, K. G. (1976). *The crucible of Europe: The ninth and tenth centuries in European history*. Berkeley, CA: University of California Press.

Barnard, L. W. (1974). *The Graeco-Roman and oriental background of the iconoclastic controversy*. Brill: Leiden.

Barraclough, G. (1979). *The Medieval Papacy*. New York: Norton.

Booker, C. M. (2009). *Past convictions: The penance of Louis the Pious and the decline of the Carolingians*. Philadelphia, PA: University of Pennsylvania Press.

Bradbury, J. (2007). *The Capetians: Kings of France, 987–1328*. New York: Hambledon Continuum.

Brown, P. (2003). *The rise of western Christendom: Triumph and diversity, AD 200–1000* (2nd ed.). Oxford: Blackwell.

Brubaker, L., & Haldon, J. (2001). *Byzantium in the Iconoclast Era (ca. 680–850): The sources: An annotated survey*. Aldershot: Ashgate.

Copleston, F. C. (1991). *Aquinas. An introduction to the life and work of the great medieval thinker*. London: Penguin.

Cowdrey, H. E. J. (1970). *Cluniacs and the Gregorian reform*. Oxford: Oxford University Press.

Cowdrey, H. E. J. (2000). *Popes and Church reform in the 11th century*. Aldershot: Ashgate.

De Jong, M. (2011). *The penitential state: Authority and atonement in the age of Louis the Pious, 814–840* (Reissued ed.). Cambridge, UK: Cambridge University Press.

Duffy, E. (2006). Between two empires: 461–1000. In *Saints and sinners: A history of the popes* (2nd ed., pp. 48–108). New Haven, CT: Yale University Press.

Dunbabin, J. (2000). *France in the making: 843–1180* (2nd ed.). Oxford: Oxford University Press.

Dutton, P. E. (2004). *Carolingian civilization: A reader* (2nd ed.). Peterborough, ON: Broadview Press.

Einhard. (2004). *The life of Charlemagne (Vita Karoli Magni)*.Whitefish, MT: Kessinger Publishing.

Evans, R. J. W. (2012). *The Holy Roman Empire, 1495–1806: A European perspective*. Leiden: Brill.

Fischer, F. (1991). *From Kaiserreich to Third Reich: Elements of continuity in German history, 1871–1945*. London: Routledge.

Godman, P., & Collins, R. (Eds.). (1990). *Charlemagne's heir. New perspectives on the reign of Louis the Pious: (814–840)*. Oxford, UK: Clarendon.

Guillot, O. (2002). *Hugues Capet et les premiers capétiens: 987–1180*. Paris: Tallandier.

Gutmann, J. (1977). *The image and the word: Confrontations in Judaism, Christianity and Islam*. Missoula, MT: Scholars Press for the American Academy of Religion.

Hallam, E. M. (2001). *Capetian France: 987–1328* (2nd ed.). Harlow: Longman.

Hallenbeck, J. T. (1982). Pavia and Rome: The Lombard monarchy and the papacy in the eighth century. *Transactions of the American Philosophical Society New Series, 72*(4), 1–186.

Hamilton, B. (2003). *The Christian world of the Middle Ages*. Stroud, Glos: Sutton.

Hartmann, W., & Pennington, K. (Eds.). (2008). *The history of medieval canon law in the classical period, 1140–1234: From Gratian to the Decretals of Pope Gregory IX*. Washington, DC: Catholic University of America Press.

Headley, J. M. (1997). *Church, empire, and world: The quest for universal order, 1520–1640*. Brookfield, VT: Ashgate.

Karlin-Hayter, P. (2002). Iconoclasm. In C. Mango (Ed.), *The Oxford history of Byzantium* (pp. 153–162). Oxford, UK: Oxford University Press.

Lewis, A. W. (1981). *Royal succession in Capetian France: Studies on familial order and the state*. Cambridge, MA: Harvard University Press.

Leyser, K. (1994). *Communications and power in medieval Europe: The Carolingian and Ottonian centuries*. London: Hambledon Press.
Marsilius of Padua. (2005). *Defensor pacis: The defender of peace*. Cambridge, UK: Cambridge University Press.
Mastnak, T. (2002). *Crusading peace: Christendom, the Muslim world, and western political order*. Berkeley, CA: University of California Press.
McKitterick, R. (1979). *The Frankish Church and the Carolingians reforms: 789–895*. London: Royal Historical Society.
Morrison, K. F. (1969). *Tradition and authority in the western Church: 300–1140*. Princeton, NJ: Princeton University Press.
Müller, W. P., & Sommar, M. E. (Eds.). (2006). *Medieval Church law and the origins of the western legal tradition: A tribute to Kenneth Pennington*. Washington, DC: CUA Press.
Mullins, E. (2006). *Cluny: In search of god's lost empire*. New York: BlueBridge.
Noble, T. F. X. (2011). *Images, iconoclasm and the Carolingians*. Philadelphia: University of Pennsylvania Press.
Offer, H. S. (2000). *Church and Crown in the fourteenth century: Studies in European history and political thought*. Aldershot: Ashgate.
Ousterhout, R., & Brubaker, L. (Eds.). (1995). *The sacred image: East and west*. Urbana: University of Illinois Press.
Pentcheva, B. V. (2006). Origins of the civic cult. In *Icons and power: The mother of god in Byzantium* (pp. 11–36). University Park, PA: Pennsylvania State University Press.
Robinson, I. S. (Ed.). (2004). *The papal reform of the eleventh century: Lives of Pope Leo IX and Pope Gregory VII*. Manchester: Manchester University Press.
Sayers, J. (1994). *Innocent III: Leader of Europe, 1198–1216*. London: Longman.
Schutz, H. (2010). *The medieval empire in central Europe: Dynastic continuity in the post-Carolingian Frankish realm, 900–1300*. Newcastle upon Tyne, UK: Cambridge Scholars.
Strayer, J. R. (1980). *The reign of Philip the fair*. Princeton, NJ: Princeton University Press.
Strayer, J. R. (2005). *On the medieval origins of the modern state* (New ed.). Princeton, NJ: Princeton University Press.
Sullivan, R. E. (1989). The Carolingian age: Reflections on its place in the history of the Middle Ages. *Speculum, 64*(2), 267–306.
Theis, L. (1984). *L'avènement d'Hugues Capet, 3 juillet 987*. Paris: Gallimard.
Tierney, B. (1996). *Foundations of the Conciliar theory: The contribution of the medieval canonists from Gratian to the Great Schism*. Leiden: Brill.
Tulard, J. (2004). *Le Sacre de l'empereur Napoléon: Histoire et légende*. Paris: Fayard et Réunion des musées nationaux.
Ullmann, W. (1966). *The relevance of medieval ecclesiastical history: An inaugural lecture*. Cambridge: Cambridge University Press.
Ullman, W. (2010). *The Carolingian renaissance and the idea of kingship*. New York: Routledge.
Valla, L. (2007). *On the donation of Constantine: De falso credita et ementita Constantini donatione declamatio*. Cambridge, MA: Harvard University Press (Parallel text in Latin and English).
Vikan, G. (2003). *Sacred images and sacred power in Byzantium*. Aldershot, UK: Ashgate Variorum.
Wickham, C. (2010). *The inheritance of Rome: A history of Europe from 400 to 1000*. London: Penguin.
Winroth, A. (2000). Gratian and the *Decretum*. In *The making of Gratian's Decretum* (pp. 1–33). Cambridge, UK: Cambridge University Press.

# Chapter 7
# From Public to Private Power: Europe in the Feudal Age

*Si aliquis ex fidelibus nostris, post obitum nostrum (...) seculo renuntiare voluerit et filium vel totem propinquum habuerit, qui rei publicae prodesse valeat, suos honores (...) ei valeat placitare. Et si in alode suo quiete vivere voluerit, nullus ei aliquod impedimentum facere praesumat, neque aliud aliquid ab eo requiratur, nisi solummodo ut ad patriae defensionem pergat.*[1]

If one of our faithful, after our death, wishes to renounce the world for his love of God, leaving a son or a close relative able to serve the Republic [the State], let him be allowed to transmit his estate to whomever he designates. And if he wishes to live placidly on his estate, let no one dare hinder him, and let him not be asked for anything, except to defend his country.—Charles the Bald. Capitulary of Quierzy (877)

## Contents


7.1 The Origins of Feudalism ... 154
- 7.1.1 The Administrative Shortcomings of the Carolingian Monarchy ... 154
- 7.1.2 Vassaldom: A Formula for Permanent Control over Local Authorities ... 155
- 7.1.3 The Limits of the Feudal Relationship: Its Lifelong Character ... 157
- 7.1.4 The Consuetudinary and Judicial Regulation of Vassal Relations ... 157

7.2 The Consolidation of the Feudal System: The Era of "Classic Feudalism" ... 158
- 7.2.1 The Degradation of the System: From Lifelong to Hereditary Benefits ... 158
- 7.2.2 The Transformation of the Feudal Relationship ... 160
- 7.2.3 The Accumulation of Fiefdoms ... 160
- 7.2.4 From Public to Private Rule: The "Feudal Revolution" ... 161

7.3 The Church as a Bulwark Against the Disintegration of Public Power ... 162
- 7.3.1 The Defense of Royal Authority ... 162
- 7.3.2 The Armed Church ... 163
- 7.3.3 Moral vs. Political Commitment ... 164


[1] Bourgeois (1885), 28.



B. Aguilera-Barchet, *A History of Western Public Law*,
DOI 10.1007/978-3-319-11803-1_7

7.3.4 The Ecclesiastical Imposition of Peace: The Peace and Truce of God Movement ... 165
7.4 Feudalism and the "Pactist Concept" of Power ... 167
References ... 170

## 7.1 The Origins of Feudalism

One of the reasons why the Germanic kings wielded less power than the Roman emperors was because the old hierarchical relationship which singled out the emperor as the representative of public authority was replaced, in the case of the Germanic kingdoms, by a series of interpersonal, private accords between the king and his most important subjects: the heads of clans or lineages (*sippe*), which could challenge the crown, as royal succession was based on election rather than hereditary principle. The Germanic kings, thus, struggled to be considered superiors in the way the Roman emperor had been because they had to grapple with the nobles of their kingdoms, to whom they often entrusted territorial government. This important transformation led to a specific form of social organization that historians have called *feudalism*,[2] which, from the perspective of constitutional history, Strayer (2005, 63) has described as a type of government in which political power was considered to be a private prerogative and asset wielded by a whole series of local lords.

### *7.1.1 The Administrative Shortcomings of the Carolingian Monarchy*

If the Germanic kingdoms' existence was precarious, this was in large part because of the disappearance of the Romans' notion of law and public affairs, arising from the fact that the Germanic kings lacked an administrative apparatus of the type

[2] As Ganshof (1996, xv–xvi) indicates, the word "feudalism" (*Feudalismus*, *Lehnswesen*, *fé odalité*), has two essential meanings. In a social and political sense, feudalism is a form of society characterized by the development—carried to an extreme—of the element of personal dependence in society, with a specialized military class occupying the upper echelons of the social scale; an extreme subdivision of rights pertaining to land ownership; a graded system of rights over land, created by this subdivision and generally corresponding to degrees of personal dependence; and, finally, a distribution of political authority amongst a hierarchy of persons exercising in their own interest powers normally attributed to the state and which are often derived from its disintegration or weakness. However, feudalism also has a "legal meaning", as it may be regarded as a body of institutions creating and regulating the obligations of obedience and service (especially military), between a free man (vassal) and his superior (lord), by which the latter undertakes obligations of protection and maintenance with regard to his vassal. The obligation of maintenance usually, entailed the granting to his vassal of a unit of land known as a "fief". These two meanings of the word "feudalism" are not, of course, unrelated to each other, but rather closely intertwined. When we speak of feudal society, the fief—which is related to both meanings—was the most important element in the graded system of rights over land upon which this type of society was based.

afforded by the extensive imperial bureaucracy of the Dominate. As Ganshof (1996, 3) points out, in the Frankish kingdom, the state was largely unable to maintain the peace or secure the safety of its inhabitants because its structure was too primitive, and the officials in its service too few in number and too unreliable for them to successfully carry out basic government functions. Free men who felt insecure, turned to powerful neighbors (*magnates*), who provided them with protection in exchange for some form of service (domestic, economic, military, or all three) through the legal instrument of commendation (*commendatio*). The person commending himself was termed a "vassal" (*vassus*).

The concept of *res publica* existing in the ancient Roman Empire was supplanted in the Germanic kingdoms by a patrimonial conception of royalty. There was, consequently, no official distinction between public and private revenue, which meant that there was no public treasury (the ancient Roman *fiscus*), and the costs of the kingdom's government and administration were covered by the sovereign's private wealth. As Germanic kings did not receive regular taxes, they were forced to depend on the spoils of war[3] and, above all, what their lands produced, with the quality of their administration varying widely (James 1991, 182–191).

Although the royal descendants of Charles Martel initially held an abundance of lands, which were better managed than during Merovingian times, the distances involved and the difficulty of transport made it impossible to establish a centralized system of government and administration. Charlemagne, thus, created the position of the *missi dominici*, royal representatives he charged with the task of monitoring the conduct of local authorities (Barbero 2004, 162–166). This oversight mechanism, however, was inadequate because the *missi* could not be everywhere at all times.[4] Thus, the Frankish kings came up with a way to control those who ruled areas far from the court while ensuring their loyalty: vassaldom.

### 7.1.2 *Vassaldom: A Formula for Permanent Control over Local Authorities*

The vassal relationship was one freely entered into between a lord (*dominus*, *senior*), generally rich and powerful, and a vassal (*vassus*, *homo*), usually a free man of humbler means. The contractual relationship was established for life, and bound the

[3] Early Carolingians gave their soldiers both material and spiritual rewards for their service. Booty was shared, professional soldiers were well paid, and efforts were made to prevent the economic distress of the part-time militia soldiers, who were frequently mobilized for lengthy campaigns, far from home (Bachrach 2001, 245).

[4] As Collins (2010, 306) indicates, Charlemagne made no significant improvements to the governmental apparatus of his greatly expanded kingdom, essentially because he lacked a bureaucratic apparatus, which could not be created overnight. During his reign, central administration remained minimal and consisted of no more than the ruler's immediate entourage. About territorial administration, the restricted nature of existing administration forced the king to oversee his local officials by means of special emissaries (*missi*), dispatched from the court to carry out enquiries and to report back on the functioning of local administration.

parties to respect a set of mutual rights and obligations. The lord was obliged to maintain and protect his vassal, while the latter pledged to serve his lord, particularly by providing him with military defense. The vassal could be maintained by directly providing him with housing, clothing, food, and a share of the spoils, when relevant. However, it became increasingly frequent for vassals to be indirectly maintained as their lords ceded lands to them for the duration of their relationship.[5]

In a society in which agriculture was the prevailing economic activity and the most essential form of wealth, it became expedient to bestow on vassals sufficient land to assure their proper maintenance. If land could not be given in full ownership (*proprietas*), its use was more frequently granted for long periods of "tenement". Via this practice, which the Frankish kings borrowed from the Late Roman Empire, tenants acquired what in Roman Law was considered a right over a thing belonging to another: *ius in re aliena* (Ganshof 1996, 9). During the Carolingian period, land transferred in this way was called *beneficium*,[6] though it would ultimately be known as *feudum*[7]—a term whose historical significance will be obvious to the reader.

Lacking officials to assure sound administration throughout their kingdoms, the Frankish kings devised the practice of ceding to their most eminent subjects, the nobles, the usufruct of lands held by the crown in exchange for their commitment to govern and administrate them on the king's behalf and provide the monarchs with military assistance when summoned to do so (Barbero 2004, 259–260).[8] Their geographical isolation led to most of these nobles ultimately enjoying considerable autonomy, which spurred the kings to require the lords to which they ceded lands to take strictly personal pledges of loyalty and allegiance.[9]

---

[5] On the origins of vassalage and fealty, see Poly and Bournazel (1991, 48–55).

[6] Tenements consisted of fractions (*mansi*) of great estates (*villae*), which were cultivated not by the owners themselves but by *coloni* for their own profit, in return for the payment of certain fixed rents (*census*) and the performance of certain labor duties. When owners had difficulties finding people to work their lands, they could grant tenants very favorable terms: no labor obligations, lower rents, no rent, etc. The favorable conditions according to which these tenements were ceded, explains the term *beneficium* ("benefice" or "benefit"), by which they are described in contemporary texts (Ganshof 1996, 10).

[7] Generally, both terms were synonyms by the end of the eighth century, save for in some regions, including Picardy, Champagne, Lorraine and Paris, where *fevum* was used. The term "fief" was not widely employed until the end of the eleventh century (Poly and Bournazel 1991, 59).

[8] As Strayer (1971, 65) points out, identifying the origins of feudalism is complicated by the fact that there were two feudal levels: the level of the armed retainers, who became feudal knights; and the level of the royal officials, counts, their deputies, and *vassi dominici*, who became rulers of feudal principalities, counties and castellanies.

[9] Anderson (2000, 130–131), believes that feudalism had hybrid origins, having been derived from different practices. Vassalage may have its main roots in either German *comitatus*, or Gallo-Roman *clientela*. The *benefice*, which would form the "fief", could equally be traced both to late Roman ecclesiastical practices and to German tribal land distributions. The "manor" derives from the Gallo-Roman *fundus* or *villa*, with its dependent peasant *coloni*. The communal enclaves of the medieval village are, by contrast, basically a Germanic inheritance of the barbarian peasantry through allodial to dependent tenures. And serfdom itself probably, descends both from the classical statute of the *colonus*, and from the slow degradation of free Germanic peasants by quasi-coercive commendation to clan warriors.

### 7.1.3 The Limits of the Feudal Relationship: Its Lifelong Character

This system of securing men-at-arms by entrusting them with the maintenance of royal lands while granting them the wealth generated by their yields, was widely employed by the Carolingian kings, and to good effect, as in this way they were able to fund the creation of the era's most powerful armies.[10] This practice allowed Charles Martel to defeat the Muslims at Poitiers in 732, and his son Pepin the Short, to intervene in Italy 20 years later on behalf of the papacy, thereby ensuring his legitimate occupation of the French throne thanks to the Church's support.

The Carolingian kings, moreover, tended to name their vassals the holders of the ecclesiastical and civil posts, called for to govern the lands ceded them, thus killing two birds with one stone, simultaneously assuring military service, and sealing royal control over the government and administration of the territory. The practice of vassaldom favored the kings not only because vassals swore allegiance to the monarch, but because the feudal covenant was for life, but not hereditary; upon the vassal's death the king could reassign the fiefdom to someone else.

### 7.1.4 The Consuetudinary and Judicial Regulation of Vassal Relations

As the notion of public power had dissolved, the feudal system was not initially set down in laws, for the king lacked the authority and political power to establish legal precepts. Crowned by bishops, Christian monarchs were primarily considered "righteous kings" (*roi justicier*), whose main mission was to defend the immemorial order created by God—an order at the time defined by tradition and custom. Vassal relationships were part of this ancient order, and this is why time-honored practices defined the legal features of feudal pacts, through the verdicts of feudal courts ruling on conflicts arising between lords and vassals (Ganshof 1996, 158–159).

[10] Many historians consider this military aspect of the feudal relationship the very essence of vassaldom. In fact, the Franks were able to achieve primacy over their contemporary Germanic kingdoms thanks to their highly-effective military structure. According to Bachrach (2001, 243–244), each person who held at least one *manse* (parcel of land), was required to perform military service or provide a substitute when summoned by their lords. The rank and file of large early Carolingian armies was generally composed of part-time militia, who were deployed either in the cities or in the countryside, and of professional soldiers sustained in the military households of lay and ecclesiastical magnates. Great landholders were obligated to send army contingents whose armaments were to be in proportion and consonant with wealth that they possessed. Most professional soldiers were recruited from the ranks of the poor and even the unfree, because small landowners were already required to render military service, when summoned. Nevertheless, military service as a professional soldiers was attractive because it provided potential upward mobility for poor men and their families.

Kings generally, did not enjoy a preeminent position in these tribunals which, as a result of the contractual nature of feudal pacts, were composed of the most important feudal lords, who considered themselves on a level with the king (*Cour des pairs*). In some cases, their judicial decisions were eventually recorded and collected to serve as an example and precedent in the event of future conflicts, leading to the appearance of texts making up "feudal law".[11]

## 7.2 The Consolidation of the Feudal System: The Era of "Classic Feudalism"

### *7.2.1 The Degradation of the System: From Lifelong to Hereditary Benefits*

The fact that the feudal pact was for life, but was not passed down, rendered it intrinsically precarious. Troubled by this, the great vassals sought by every means at their disposal to pressure the king to make fiefdoms hereditary.

A first step was taken in the year 877 when Charles the Bald, at Quierzy-sur-Oise, granted his subjects, via *capitulary*[12] (a law divided into chapters), the privilege of passing their prerogatives down to their heirs in the event that they perished on a military campaign which the king had organized (Dutton 2009, 501–502). This case was an isolated one, but it reflected a trend which would eventually be institutionalized through the force of custom as the Carolingian Empire entered

[11] Texts of feudal law share this origin. Thus, in the Iberian Peninsula, the *Usatges* were composed in the eleventh century of sentences from the tribunal of the Court of Barcelona, and the *Libri feudorum* of those from the feudal tribunals of Lombardy, or the *Sachsenspiegel* (Mirror of the Saxons) of Eike von Repgow, that produced a German version of his own (lost) Latin original. Their purpose was to textualize, and thus to stabilize what up until the thirteenth century had been a long oral tradition of regional jurisprudence. The Sachsenspiegel is divided into two parts, one concerned with laws regarding the management of fiefs, the *Lehnrecht*, and the other with more general laws, the *Landrecht*, or regional law (Dobozy 1999). These examples demonstrate the extent to which the law governing fiefs and *benefices* had become, by the first half of the thirteenth century, a separate branch (Reynolds 1996, 454). On the texts resulting from the compilation of feudal customs, see Robinson et al. (2000, 37–40). It is very interesting to note that, as Pockock (2004, 16) points out, much later feudal law came to be used politically by those who sought to defend threatened privileges or liberties when in the sixteenth and seventeenth centuries there was an increasing tendency to advance royal sovereignty, in the fullest sense of the term. Naturally, they emphasized that their rights were rooted in a law which no king could violate, with many of these national privileges and liberties rooted in feudal custom.

[12] A capitulary was a law divided into paragraphs or chapters (*capitularia*), and represents one of the few examples of written, formal legislation coming out of the Early Middle Ages, a period during which laws were essentially determined by custom. The Capitulary of Quierzy-sur-Oise, issued by the Emperor Charles the Bald (875–877), was an exception to this customary principle in that it worked the other way around, establishing via a legal disposition issued by the political authority the way in which fiefdoms could be transmitted, and altering their status as lifelong pacts.

into decline in the late ninth century.[13] The shift to this process of consolidation, however, was far from smooth.

This is what Taylor (2005, 129) calls *mutation féodale*: a transformation of the public power and social order resulting from the alteration of the vassal's former position in proprietary lordships. The establishment of familial succession in place of royal appointment led to the appearance of autonomous counts who began to consider their fiefdoms fully alienable, which were partitioned among multiple heirs across successive generations. The consequence was the proliferation of castles.[14]

The principle, however, did not take root immediately. In fact, two centuries after the promulgations of the capitulary at Quierzy, the hereditary nature of vassals' prerogatives was still a source of conflict between lords and vassals in Norman England. It was not until the twelfth century that the hereditary principle was firmly established, at which point the bone of contention became the amounts of relief taxes which inheriting vassals were obliged to pay their lords.[15] The obsession with preserving these rights within the family was so great that even women came to be allowed to inherit and transmit them in the absence of male heirs.

---

[13] As Reynolds (1996, 112) points out, if one concentrates on the circumstances in which the 877 Capitulary was promulgated, it does not seem to be a royal surrender to a new principle of inheritance as it only insured that, in the event a vassal died in war, his fief could remain in his family.

[14] It is most significant, for instance, that the word "Catalonia" derives from a reference to feudal lords (literally: land of *castlás*, that is, owners of castles). Catalonia was the only part of the Iberian Peninsula directly dominated by the Carolingians during most of the ninth century (Barcelona was wrested from the Muslims by Louis the Pious in 801). The *féodale* mutation took place after 877, with Wilfred the Hairy, Count of Urgel and of Cerdanya, from 870, and of Barcelona and Gerona from 878. After 877 Wilfred was able to transmit his counties in a *de facto* manner to his heirs, and became the legendary founder of an independent County of Barcelona thanks to the politically-calculated *Gesta comitum Barcinonensium*, a Latin chronicle probably undertaken by a monk at Ripoll shortly after 1162, which fomented and glorified the myth of the first autonomous Count of Barcelona (Taylor 2005, 133). As Bisson (1995, 750) reminds us, during a time when legislation was a rare commodity, the *gesta*, or chronicles written by clerks familiar with royal and princely courts, or even songs celebrating deeds, were nearly as "official" as charters and diplomas. The title "Count of Barcelona" went to the King of Aragon in 1164, when Alfonso II, called the Chaste or the Troubadour, inherited both titles, as the second son and heir of the Count of Barcelona, Ramon Berenguer IV, and his wife, the Queen of Aragon, Petronilla. After the death of Peter of Aragon, the oldest son and first child of the royal couple, Wilfred the Hairy transmitted the County of Barcelona to his heirs, but remained a vassal of the Carolingian king. The counts of Barcelona would be vassals of the kings of France until the Treaty of Corbeil, in 1254. Catalonia, significantly, was the only region of the Iberian Peninsula that became entirely feudal, not only because of Frankish domination, but because the Reconquest in Old Catalunya (*Catalunya Vella*), the northern part of present-day Catalonia, was completed by the ninth century, unlike in the rest of Spain. For an overview of feudal Catalonia and the political transformation of the County of Barcelona, see Bisson (2009, 345–348, 371–377 and 499–514).

[15] Under the feudal contract, the lord was obligated to provide the fief for his vassal, to protect him, and to provide him justice in his court. In return, the lord had the right to demand the services which the fief entailed (military, judicial, administrative), and a right to various sources of revenue known as "feudal incidents". Examples of incidents are "relief", a tax paid when a fief was transferred to an heir, and "scutage", a tax paid in lieu of military service. Arbitrary arrangements were gradually replaced by a system of fixed dues, on occasion limited by custom.

### 7.2.2 *The Transformation of the Feudal Relationship*

When vassals' privileges became hereditary, the original feudalism which had originated during the Carolingian period was transformed, altering both the customs governing the relationships between lord and vassal and the legal nature of the latter's entitlements. Thus, where Carolingian feudal vassaldom was predominantly a personal tie, the prerogatives it entailed later became the essence the feudal relationship, in what Marc Bloch has called the "second feudal age" (Bloch 2004, 69). Whereas before land was *an incidental effect* of becoming a vassal, under classic feudalism one became a vassal precisely and expressly *to obtain* the fiefdoms and privileges which vassaldom promised. This is why in the twelfth century, as Bisson (2009, 40) indicates, there was an explosive proliferation of castles, knights, and princes and bishops.

The consequence was that, in response to competition and economic pressure, aristocratic families preferred a vertical, dynastic structure of succession, seeking to restore the indivisibility of lordship and embrace a new custom of primogeniture. The result was the appearance during the twelfth century, of dynasties indentified with regional power bases and led by a single head, generally a male (Taylor 2005, 130).

### 7.2.3 *The Accumulation of Fiefdoms*

As land ownership came to take precedence over the personal bond in feudal relationships, a struggle began to acquire the greatest possible number of new fiefdoms. In this way, those who were vassals to various kings, earls and archbishops managed to accumulate an abundance of fiefdoms.[16] This land grab led some kings not to hesitate to actually become vassals of their vassals to secure certain fiefdoms, such as strategically-located castles. It goes without saying that when one had sworn loyalty to a number of different lords, a conflict could arise if any number of the latter went to war. A remedy was sought for this situation through the establishment of privileged or preferential vassal ties known as *liege homage* (Bloch 2004, 215).

In the end, the development of the feudal bond resulted in the formation of a particular legal regime applied to feudal lands, whose vassal occupants maintained certain well-established duties (essentially military and judicial) to their lords who, as they owned these lands outright, were beholden to no one.

[16] Bloch (2004, 212) indicates that in the closing years of the thirteenth century, one German baron became the enfeoffed vassal of 20 different lords, and another of 43.

### 7.2.4 From Public to Private Rule: The "Feudal Revolution"

From the point of view of the history of the Western polity, feudalism is a period in which a coherent, centralized public power disappeared, replaced by a vast network of private relationships. This process was accelerated by the diffusion of governmental powers resulting from the Merovingian and Carolingian kings' granting of "immunities" to their vassals, a privilege that released them from the authority of royal officials and their orders concerning taxation and jurisdiction (Robinson 2000, 31–32).

As Reynolds (1996, 20) specifies, what made vassalage so relevant was that at the time when it arose there was simply no idea of impersonal, public obligation; the Germanic tribes did not harbor the Roman notion of *res publica*, and the Merovingian kings perceived and administrated their kingdoms as their own private property.

Strayer (1971, 14) has indicated, that during the feudal era, interests and loyalties were primarily local, limited to the family, the neighborhood and the county. Royal officials tended to become leaders of autonomous local communities rather than agents of central authority. By the tenth century, they were practically independent, but their own authority, in turn, was being eroded by viscounts, castellans, and other leaders of smaller communities. Kings and princes were powerless to maintain control over castles they had built themselves, so they handed them over as fiefs to their vassals, at times even to prevent the raising of new fortresses, which became administrative capitals for surrounding districts and the centers of a whole network of facilities.[17] Soon lords found themselves being defied by their own castellans, who tended to become themselves the heads of their own dynasties. As counties became hereditary and were partitioned the counts' rights as legitimate heirs of the Frankish officials disintegrated, with the upshot that the idea of public office gave way to new conceptions and realities of power informed by feudal concepts (Bloch 2005, 124).

As Ganshof (1996, 60) points out, the feudal bond became a check on the disintegration of the state through a process that has been called the "Feudal Revolution", conventional shorthand for the disappearance of any center capable of controlling localities, and the ascendancy of small-scale forms of organization (Reuter 2010, 72). According to Bisson (1994, 18), this altered the nature and social role of violence, as it was no longer monopolized by a strong authority in the interest of maintaining public order, yielding newer "private" forms of violence, practiced by the masters of castles and those beholden to them. Lordship became predatory, militant, aggressive and unconstructive.

A near-permanent state of war was aggravated by the absence of political and social order. Orders issued in capitals were ineffectual, no longer enforceable in lands lying far from them. The lack of effective authority meant that merchants and traders were perpetually vulnerable to assault and robbery when transporting their goods. Thus, long-distance commerce was frustrated, and the economy regressed towards a model defined by local production and self-sufficiency. Finally,

[17] As Stephenson (2007, 81) observes, for civil and military purposes the county was divided into *châtellenies*, which were entrusted to a *châtelain*, who in all respects acted as the count's deputy, for this reason often being referred to as a *vicomte*.

civilization collapsed "in the sense that the pursuit of inessentials did not enhance life but threatened survival" (Robinson 2000, 27).

The only significant and effective resistance to this state of anarchy and violence was put up by the Church which, as heir to the Roman imperial ideal, endeavored to counteract the disintegration of authority and to restore the notion of power exercised in the common interest.

## 7.3 The Church as a Bulwark Against the Disintegration of Public Power

The consolidation of the hereditary character of vassals' prerogatives, dealt a harsh blow to kings and their power, and to social stability, as it generated an almost continuous state of war between subjects, who jockeyed to increase their wealth and power through the acquisition of fiefdoms by force of arms. When the kings were unable to restore order, the Church stood as the only institution seeking to rectify this feudal anarchy, sustaining some ideas inherited from Roman public law (Reynolds 1996, 20).

### *7.3.1 The Defense of Royal Authority*

In the first place, the bishops did their best to maintain the kings' supremacy over the feudal lords, at least in terms of formal recognition. Thus, in France, for example, the Church refused to consecrate or crown the great lords. According to the accord reached with Pepin the Short in 752, only kings were to be anointed by the Church.[18] In this regard, it is important to mention that another important contribution made by Pope Gregory I, was his interpretation of royal unction, included in the Old Testament, which he viewed as a Divine sanctioning of the

[18] The great nobles, like those of Britain, Aquitaine and Burgundy, pressured the bishops to crown them. The French Church's refusal to do so was essential in preventing them from becoming kings and maintaining the formal supremacy of the King of France. Anointment became the symbol of royal power, a ceremony which consolidated the monarchy's divine status. Moreover, beginning in the fourteenth century, it would serve to justify the independence of the king of France from the pope, as through anointment he received his powers directly from God. As McKitterick (1983, 194) mentions, though the first anointing took place in 751, with Pepin the Short, it was not until the anointment of Charles the Bald in 848, at Orleans that this ceremony became a necessary part of the king-making ritual. In this particular case, the new king tried desperately to secure his position by elevating the monarchy to a sacred office, sanctioned by God. As they did in the Visigothic kingdom in 633 (4th Council of Toledo) the Frankish bishops, led by Hincmar, the Archbishop of Reims and the principal initiator of the new rites (Kershaw 2011, 220–222), stressed that anointing Charles the Bald in 848, constituted him as king. The consequence was that in exchange for his anointing and coronation, the king undertook certain obligations as a ruler: to uphold the Christian faith, the privileges of the Church, the secular laws of the kingdom, and the welfare of his people. A formal oath was incorporated into the coronation to this effect. By virtue of the constitutive character of anointing and coronation, kings became the only legitimate secular authorities.

king's legitimacy. By virtue of unction, Gregory believed that the king held, thus, a ministerial office, and was called upon to serve in accord with his "divine inheritance". His interpretation includes many elements of successive conceptions of kingship, based on what Ullmann (2010, 71) calls the "rebirth of the ruler". In the Iberian Peninsula, meanwhile, to shore up their power, the kings relied upon papal authorization, as was clearly the case in Aragón and Portugal.[19]

The favoring of royal authority was also evident in the privilege the popes assigned the kings of France, who were permitted to create abbeys wherever they wished—even in territories belonging to feudal lords. These abbeys fell under royal patronage, thereby bolstering the kings' preeminence.

Given these conditions, it is not surprising that the kings' chief advisers belonged to the clergy.

### 7.3.2 The Armed Church

With the purpose of restoring order and eradicating the state of permanent warfare, bishops and even parish priests, did not hesitate to organize armed forces (episcopal and parochial militias), to fight the feudal lords.[20] The image of the warrior bishop is a quintessential icon of the medieval era (Reuter 1992, 79).[21] The emergence of

[19] The principle of papal theocracy made the pope the supreme authority legitimating rulers. In this sense Peter II, the Catholic, was the first King of Aragon to be crowned by the pope, namely Innocent III in the Church of San Pancrazio in the presence of a multitude of nobles, judges, advocates, notaries, and cardinals (Smith 2004, 43), following the ceremony used for imperial crowning adapted to the circumstance. This explains, for instance, why the king of Aragon was first anointed by the bishop of Porto before being crowned by the pope himself (Palacios Martin 1975, 25). In the case of Portugal, Pope Alexander III in 1179, through the papal bull *Manifestis Probatum* (Pereira 1979, 125–130), declared the *Comitatus Portucalensis* independent from the Kingdom of León, and recognized Alfonso Enríquez as *rex portugalensium* (Disney 2009, 74–76).

[20] As Messier (2010, xv) states, the Almoravid *jihad* in Spain mirrors a vital chapter of any comprehensive account of the Crusades, as the monastery of Cluny spearheaded a reform movement in Western Christendom, comparable to the reform movement of the Almoravids. The Cluniac movement certainly added fervor to the Crusades in the East, but it affected Spain as well. It is no coincidence that just after the Gregorian Reform (1073–1085), Popes Urban II and Gelasius II and other Christian Church leaders, such as St. Bernard of Clairvaux (1090–1153), urged French knights to carry their crusades to Spain, thereby merging the concepts of pilgrimage, crusade and *Reconquista*.

[21] In Spain, Cardinal Cisneros still played a major political role during the era of the Regencies (1504–1517) after the rule of the Catholic Kings, organizing and participating in numerous military campaigns. It was said that he claimed to revel in the smell of gunpowder. Among other initiatives, Cisneros created an urban militia, *Gente de la Ordenanza*, a forerunner of a modern police force. This armed body was involved in the famous anecdote in which the cardinal, when supposedly asked by a group of nobles where he obtained the power to exercise political authority, allegedly pointed to a group of these officers in the patio and laconically responded: "Those are my powers". In 1506, Cisneros had hoped to obtain plenipotentiary powers from Queen Juana for himself. A document was drawn up to this effect, but remained unsigned. 10 years later, Cisneros was appointed Regent of Castile by Ferdinand the Catholic in his will, in which he stated "said Cardinal might do what we would do or have the authority or obligation to do, until Charles decides on a course of action... trusting in his conscience, religion, rectitude and good will" (Rummel 1999, 76 and 80).

military orders, made up of monk soldiers, was to be an important stabilizing factor, following the example of the Order of the Temple (The Knights Templar), founded to protect the pilgrims traveling to the Holy Land. This example would be of particular importance in Reconquest-era Spain where, after invasion by the Almoravids and Almohads, there appeared different orders (Santiago, Calatrava) which played an essential role in driving the Moors from the south of the Peninsula between the eleventh and thirteenth centuries.[22]

Similarly, the Crusades were another of the Church's contributions which had the effect of quelling the state of constant war in Europe, and restoring order to feudal societies by channeling the lords' aggression and warmongering towards the conquest of Jerusalem and other holy sites.

### *7.3.3 Moral vs. Political Commitment*

The area in which the Church had the greatest influence on reducing feudal anarchy would come in the spiritual realm. Thus, for example, the practice of oath-taking upon the Holy Scriptures was fomented by the Church, compensating for the waning of state authority by establishing believers' personal, formal and overt commitment to God. This commitment, in addition, was legally binding in so far as the Church was authorized to try cases of perjury—not to mention that in some cases, the testimony of several people claiming the accused's innocence in a solemn oath taken upon the Scriptures, known as an act of compurgation, or wager law, was legally admitted and served to exonerate him.[23]

The Church employed its spiritual authority to impose Christian obligations upon the feudal lords, through the creation of a specific ceremony to declare them knights, including a retreat of 48 h during which they were to fast and pray before

[22] This military activity allowed the orders to accumulate significant wealth. The Templars even managed to become important bankers in the West by assuring the transport and safekeeping of money carried between castles. Their wealth was one of the reasons Philip IV of France, in the early fourteenth century, decided to prosecute them, prompting a trial which led to the execution of their last Grand Master, Jacques de Molay, the end of the order, and the expropriation of all its considerable assets. As Barber (2012, 295 and 298) mentions, the explanation of the Order's demise must be sought in the motives of the king of France, and his government rather than in the Order itself. There were obvious financial reasons for the sudden arrest of the Templars in France. As bankers, they possessed considerable liquid wealth and negotiable assets and, as landowners, immovable properties in every region of France, from Normandy to Provence. In Spain, the extraordinary amount of land acquired by the military orders during the Reconquest, spurred the monarchy to create a specific "Council of Orders" to administrate their impressive territorial patrimony.

[23] Compurgation, or "wager of law", was still relatively frequent in the processes of the Spanish Inquisition, created in 1478, and initiating its activities two years later. On the practice of compurgation, see Aguilera-Barchet (1993, 167–171), with specific examples taken from the court records.

receiving the Church's backing. Knights were obligated, moreover, to pledge to defend widows and orphans, and assume the moral commitment which their status entailed. Thanks to this, as Stephenson (2007, 75–76) points out, the strong personal bonds inherent to vassalage made it possible, in some cases, for feudalism to be reconciled with efficient government.

### 7.3.4 The Ecclesiastical Imposition of Peace: The Peace and Truce of God Movement

In this context, we must mention the oaths of peace (*conjuratio*) promoted by ecclesiastical authorities, usually bishops, through which the people of particular places plagued by war were convened and forced to swear that henceforth they would live in peace. This trend would give rise to institutions such as the King's Peace and the Peace and Truce Councils. As Poly and Bournazel (1991, 151) indicate, the Peace and Truce of God movement (*Pax Dei*) began at the end of the tenth century in southern France, the first council of peace held in Charroux in 989, and the second in Narbonne in 990.

In Catalonia, an essentially feudal territory, the Peace and Truce of God movement was very significant. The spread of the feudal system considerably undermined Catalonia's political organization, not only because of the absence of a potent superior power[24] (as the prince was only a *primum inter pares*, or "first among equals") but because the appearance of a multitude of powerful lords sparked constant private wars, in large measure because of the custom of private revenge, typical of the Early Middle Ages. To suppress this climate of permanent confrontation, beginning in the second half of the eleventh century, the counts of Barcelona, in their capacity as "princes", convened Peace and Truce of God Councils (*Tregua Domini* or *Pax Dei*).[25]

The institution arose in the ecclesiastical sphere when councils and synods convened by the provincial churches began to issue "Peace of God" decrees for

---

[24] As Gonzalvo I Bou (1994, xxi) mentions, in Catalonia feudalism appeared rapidly in the first decades of the eleventh century because the weakness of the Count of Barcelona, Berenguer Ramon I (1017–1035), created a power vacuum that soon provoked a climate of violence and extortion.

[25] Traditionally, the rise of *Pax Dei* movement has been seen as a reaction by the Church to the decline of royal and secular power, and to the feudal anarchy spawned by the rise of local powers and lords. In this sense, the Church superseded the king as a guardian of law and order. In fact, as Goetz (1992, 260) points out, *Pax Dei* could not have succeeded without the help of the noblemen, whose presence at the councils was key. This practice developed in southern France, Catalonia (Bisson 1977, 290–311), and Aquitaine (Head 1999, 656–686).

particular regions.[26] In territories declared "at peace", any offenders were excommunicated. The next step was "Truce of God" declarations, which prohibited any acts of violence in certain places or for a certain period of time.

The first evidence we have of such prohibitions dates back to the early decades of the eleventh century (Cowdrey 1970, 47–62). Specifically, in 1027, a synod met in the Pyrenean village of Tuluyas (Tuluges) at which a "Peace and Truce of God" was declared throughout the region of Roussillon (in what is today southeastern France), prohibiting anyone from attacking his enemy between 3:00 in the afternoon[27] on Saturday and the same time on Monday. In the year 1033, the Benedictine Abbot Oliva, Bishop of Vic, proclaimed a "Peace and Truce of God" in his diocese (Gonzalvo I Bou 1994, xxii). From then on such declarations were issued by a growing number of synods and episcopal bodies.[28]

Beginning in the middle of the eleventh century, the "Peace and Truce of God" declarations transcended the ecclesiastical sphere, taken up and employed by the synods of the Prince (Count of Barcelona) and the members of his curia. The first record we have of these assemblies bringing together clergy and laity (Duby 1980, 123–133), dates from 1064, presided over by Ramón Berenguer I and his wife Almodis de la Marche. The most important aspect of these assemblies was that the agreements reached by them became laws, to be enforced by the princes' "constitutions". For instance, at the aforementioned gathering in 1064, a "Constitution of Peace and Truce" was proclaimed, and the prince's involvement resulted in his authority ensuring the implementation of the decrees approved in the territories under his sovereignty. Thus did this type of assembly end up becoming a forum to which the princes turned for imposing order over specific areas of their domains. To enforce the Peace and Truce decrees, the Count of Barcelona appointed a series of public officials in each locality, *paciarii* (*pahers* in Romance), whose mission it was to collaborate with the bishops on the maintenance and implementation of the precepts approved by the Peace and Truce Councils.

The Peace and Truce of God Councils constituted the forerunner of feudal councils in so far as they propagated the practice of having major public decisions

[26] As Poly and Bournazel (1991, 151–152) point out, if the idea of peace was not new, what was really innovative was the fact that bishops took the place of kings in their mission to defend churches and the poor—manifest proof that public tribunals were no longer working satisfactorily. Therefore, "truly ecclesiastical sanctions were coming to the assistance of crumbling laws".

[27] According to an Ancient Greek and Roman custom, the day was, like the night, divided into four parts, each consisting of 3 h. As the last hour of each division gave its name to the respective quarter of the day, the third division (from noon to about 3), was called the None (from the Latin *nona*, or ninth). In the ecclesiastical sphere, it was the last of the minor hours and preceded that of vespers, coinciding with dusk or sundown.

[28] The typical peace and truce declaration included the permanent protection, under penalty of excommunication, of people, clerical goods, and widows and orphans within 30 paces of temples and sacred sites—an area termed *sacraria* or *sagrera*, as was the case with the peace and truce agreed to in Tuluyes in 1027 (Gonzalvo I Bou 1994, 3–5).

approved by the community, presided over by the ecclesiastical or political authority. From this point of view, the idea that kings had to negotiate pacts regarding the most important decisions with their subjects (the "pactist" conception of power), can be traced precisely to the feudal era. From this point of view, as Goetz (1992, 260) indicates, the Peace of God movement should not be seen as a substitute for a supreme power, but an attempt to provide newly ascendant powers with newfound stability, and a social order parallel to that provided by new political and social organizations.

## 7.4 Feudalism and the "Pactist Concept" of Power

In our Western legal tradition, "feudalism" has a pejorative connotation,[29] one in large measure justified because the disintegration of a powerful, central authority and its replacement by a multitude of personal agreements in the West generated a state of constant war and anarchy which, as we have seen, the Church sought to mitigate by imposing its moral authority.

However, given the historical hindsight which we enjoy today, it is clear that the disappearance in the feudal pact of the hierarchical relationship under which subjects were utterly subservient to their sovereigns, and its replacement by legal pacts between lord and vassal, also had the pivotal result that subjects came to occupy a common legal plane, *vis-à-vis* their superiors, who ultimately became *primum inter pares* (firsts among equals). Under feudal pacts, kings entered into contractual relationships of a bilateral and reciprocal nature with their subjects, through which both parties took on obligations and were granted rights (Mitteis 1975, 56). When one steps back and looks at the whole course of Western political history, it is clear that the ultimate political consequences of this development could not be more profound.

If the monarch, as a result of his anointing by the Church, ruled by the grace of God, on whose behalf he exercised his jurisdictional powers (*iurisdictio*), he was also personally linked to nobles with whom he had entered into feudal covenants, that is, through pacted relationships entailing reciprocal rights and obligations. This relationship implied that rulers who breached their obligations could be held accountable for doing so. The next step was the assertion that the king ought to seek his subjects' approval when exercising power. As Anderson (2000, 151–152) points out, in the feudal era the monarch was a suzerain of his vassals, to whom he was bound by reciprocal ties of fealty; he was *not* a supreme sovereign set above his subjects, as he did not have direct political access to the population as a whole.

[29] As Ganshof (1996, xv) points out, this negative image of feudalism goes back to the French Revolution, when it was generally associated, in a categorical and imprecise way, with the abuses of the *Ancien Régime*.

Rather, his jurisdiction over it was filtered through innumerable layers of subinfeudation. The consequence was that royal power always had to be asserted and extended against the spontaneous grain of the feudal polity as a whole, in a constant struggle to establish a "public" authority outside the compact web of private jurisdictions.

Along the same line, Marc Bloch (2005, 172) notes that vassal homage was a genuine bilateral contract in which lords who failed to fulfill their duties, lost their rights—a principle that was inevitably transferred to the political sphere, where the king's leading subjects were, at the same time, his vassals. The idea of such a covenant binding upon rulers was, obviously, to have the most far-reaching and profound repercussions on Western politics and society.

As far as the history of public law is concerned, perhaps the most important aspect to underscore is how the feudal relationship affected political and legal concepts and institutions. As Poly and Bournazel (1991, 210) explain, the renaissance of royal power in the twelfth century, far from opposing feudalization, completed the process by controlling it, bringing in as royal counselors petty knights who had trained for service, having rose from humble origins. These counselors surrounded the crown as the representatives of a new and autonomous social group: seigneurial officers.

The attempts by various kings to emulate the Roman emperors and replace the old Germanic collective social organization with a monarchical model, was stymied by the contractual nature of the feudal relationship established between sovereign and vassal, significantly curbing the former's power. This is what came to be called "pactism,[30]" as it implied that power emanates from an accord or pact reached between a king and his subjects, a principle that would be consolidated by the Commercial Revolution transforming European societies in the Late Middle Ages. As Kosto (2004, 2–3) observes, the general expansion of the European economy in the eleventh and twelfth centuries, brought with it a restructuring of the social order, necessary to allow the ruling classes to transform prosperity into power.

We shall analyze the consequences of this principle in greater detail in the next chapter when we examine the key question of the internal limits placed on the medieval monarchs' authority because, as Petit Dutaillis (Petit-Dutaillis 1995, 1–2) points out, feudalism was not merely a temporary expedient. Rather, for centuries it served as a powerful source of inspiration through its appeal to personal devotion, loyalty and the vassal's spirit of sacrifice. The lords' patronage laid deep and lasting foundations for this form of organization, which replaced a declining state with a "doctrine making the maintenance of civilization dependent on a respect for the mutual obligations which bind lord and vassal, and the observance of the traditional customs of the old and new laws made in the feudal court".

[30] Translator's Note: "Pactism" (*pactismo*) is a Spanish term that refers to the political system in which the king was expected to secure the approval of representatives of his kingdom, as royal power theoretically depended upon a "pact" between them and the monarch. We have "adopted" the Spanish term as there is no English word which entirely transmits this precise idea.

## TIMELINE

### Early Middle Ages (Eighth–Eleventh Centuries)

#### Eighth Century

| | |
|---|---|
| 711 | The Muslims invade the Iberian Peninsula. End of the Visigoth kingdom of Toledo. |
| 722 | Pelayo initiates the Reconquest in Asturias. |
| 732 | Battle of Poitiers. Charles Martel defeats the Muslims. The end of Islamic expansion in Europe. |
| 751 | Pepin the Short is recognized as the legitimate king of the Franks by Pope Zachary. |
| 754 | Creation of the Papal States. |
| 756 | Abderramán I founds the Umayyad Emirate of Córdoba. |
| 771 | After the death of his brother Carloman, Charlemagne becomes the sole king of the Franks. |
| 778 | The rearguard of Charlemagne's army is annihilated at Roncesvalles. |
| 791–842 | Reign of Alfonse II of Asturias, restoring the principles of the Visigoth monarchy in Oviedo. |

#### Ninth Century

| | |
|---|---|
| 800 | Charlemagne is crowned Emperor by Pope Leo III. |
| 801 | The Franks take Barcelona from the Muslims. |
| 814 | Death of Charlemagne. |
| 843 | The Treaty of Verdun. Division of the Carolingian Empire. |
| 877 | The Capitulary of Quierzy establishes hereditary profits for vassals. Important precedent consolidating the process of feudalization. |
| 898 | Death of Wilfred the Hairy, the first autonomous Earl of Barcelona (since 873). |

#### Tenth Century

| | |
|---|---|
| 905 | Sancho I Garcés (+925), the first king of Navarre, takes the throne. |
| 911 | The Treaty of Saint Clair-sur-Epte. The Normans settle in the western part of present-day France (Normandy). |
| 914 | Garcia I moves his capital to León. The Kingdom of León is formed. |
| 923–970 | Fernán González unifies the County of Castile. |
| 929 | Abderramán III creates the Caliphate of Córdoba. |
| 962 | Otto I of Saxony founds the Holy Roman Empire. |
| 987 | Hugh Capet becomes the first king of France, in reaction to the Germanization of Charlemagne's Empire. |

**Eleventh Century**

| | |
|---|---|
| 1031 | End of the Caliphate of Córdoba. Spread of the *taifas*. |
| 1035 | Death of Sancho III Garcés of Navarre. He divides his dominions among his sons. The oldest, García, receives the Kingdom of Navarre. The second, Fernando, becomes Count of Castile. Another illegitimate son, Ramiro I, receives the Kingdom of Aragon. |
| 1037 | Bermudo III of León is defeated and killed at the Battle of Tamarón by the Count of Castile, Ferdinand I, who becomes the King of León and the Count of Castile. |
| 1054 | The Eastern Schism. The Patriarch of Constantinople, Michael Cerularius, repudiates Pope Leo IX. |
| 1063 | Sancho Ramírez (+1094) takes the throne, the first king of Aragon expressly receiving the title. |
| 1065 | After the death of his father, Ferdinand I, Sancho II, his eldest son, becomes the first King of Castile. His second son, Alfonse, becomes Alfonse VI of León. |
| 1066 | Battle of Hastings. The Anglo-Saxon Harold is defeated by the Norman William the Conqueror, who becomes the King of England. |
| 1072 | After the death of his brother, Sancho II, at the siege of Zamora, Alfonse VI becomes the King of Castile and León. |
| 1073–1085 | Papacy of Gregory VII (Gregorian Reform). |
| 1085 | Alfonse VI takes Toledo. |
| 1088 | Foundation of the University of Bologna, the first in Europe. |
| 1090 | The Almoravids move to occupy the Iberian Peninsula. |
| 1093 | Urban II endorses the First Crusade (1096–1099). |
| 1099 | Death of El Cid in Valencia (July 10). The Crusaders take Jerusalem (15th of July). |

## References

Aguilera-Barchet, B. (1993). El procedimiento de la Inquisición española. In J. Pérez Villanueva & B. Escandell Bonet (Eds.), *Historia de la Inquisición en España y América* (Vol. II). Madrid: B.A.C.

Anderson, P. (2000). *Passages from antiquity to feudalism*. London: Verso.

Bachrach, B. S. (2001). *Early Carolingian Warfare. Prelude to empire*. Philadelphia, PA: University of Pennsylvania Press.

Barber, M. (2012). *The new knighthood: A history of the order of the temple*. Cambridge, UK: Cambridge University Press (Reprint).

Barbero, A. (2004). *Charlemagne: Father of a continent*. Berkeley, CA: University of California Press.

Bisson, T. N. (1977). The organized peace in Southern France and Catalonia, ca. 1140–ca. 1233. *The American Historical Review, 82*(2), 290–311.

Bisson, T. N. (1994). The "Feudal Revolution". *Past & Present, 142*, 6–42.

Bisson, T. N. (1995). Medieval Lordship. *Speculum*, (70), 743–759.
Bisson, T. N. (2009). *The crisis of the twelfth century: Power, lordship, and the origins of European government*. Princeton, NJ: Princeton University Press.
Bloch, M. (2004). *Feudal society. Volume I. The growth of ties of dependence*. London: Routledge.
Bloch, M. (2005). *Feudal society. Volume II. Social classes and political organization*. London: Routledge.
Bourgeois, É. (1885). *Le capitulaire de Kiersy-sur-Oise, 877: étude sur l'état et le régime politique de la société carolingienne à la fin du IXe siècle d'après la législation de Charles le Chauve*. Paris: Librairie Hachette.
Collins, R. (2010). *Early medieval Europe: 300–1000* (3rd ed.). Basingstoke, UK: Palgrave Macmillan.
Cowdrey, H. E. J. (1970). The peace and the truce of god in the eleventh century. *Past & Present, 46*, 42–67.
Disney, A. R. (2009). Afonso Henriques and the founding of the kingdom. In *A history of Portugal and the Portuguese Empire: From beginnings to 1807* (Vol. 2, pp. 74–76). Cambridge: Cambridge University Press.
Dobozy, M. (1999). *The Saxon Mirror: A Sachsenspiegel of the fourteenth century*. Philadelphia, PA: University of Pennsylvania Press.
Duby, G. (1980). The laity and the peace of god. In *The age of chivalry* (pp. 123–133). Berkeley: University of California Press.
Dutton, P. (2009). The Capitulary of Quierzy, 877. In *Carolingian civilization: A reader* (2nd ed., pp. 501–502). North York, ON: University of Toronto Press.
Ganshof, F. L. (1996). *Feudalism*. Toronto: University of Toronto Press.
Goetz, H.-W. (1992). Protection of the church, defense of the law and reform: On the purposes and character of the peace of god, 989–1038. In T. Head & R. Landes (Eds.), *The peace of god: Social violence and religious response in France around the year 1000* (pp. 259–279). Ithaca, NY: Cornell University Press.
Gonzalvo I Bou, G. (Ed.). (1994). *Les Constitucions de Pau i Treva de Catalunya (segles XI–XIII)*. Barcelona: Generalitat de Catalunya, Departament de Justícia.
Head, T. (1999). The development of the peace of god in Aquitaine: (970–1005). *Speculum, 74*(3), 656–686.
James, E. (1991). *The franks: The peoples of Europe*. Oxford, UK: Basil Blackwell.
Kershaw, P. J. E. (2011). *Peaceful kings: Peace, power and the early medieval political imagination*. Oxford, UK: Oxford University Press.
Kosto, A. J. (2004). *Making agreements in medieval Catalonia: Power, order, and the written word, 1000–1200*. Cambridge, UK: Cambridge University Press.
McKitterick, R. (1983). *The Frankish kingdoms under the Carolingians*. London: Longman.
Messier, R. A. (2010). *The Almoravids and the meanings of Jihad*. Santa Barbara, CA: ABC-CLIO.
Mitteis, H. (1975). *The state in the Middle Ages: A comparative constitutional history of feudal Europe*. Amsterdam: North-Holland.
Palacios Martin, B. (1975). *La coronación de los reyes de Aragón 1204–1410: Aportación al estudio de las estructuras medievales*. Zaragoza: Universidad de Zaragoza.
Pereira, I. da R. (1979). O Papa Alexandre III e a Bula 'Manifestis Probatum'. In *8.° Centenário do Reconhecimento de Portugal pela Santa Sé (Bula "Manifestis Probatum" 23 de Maio de 1179): Comemoração Académica* (pp. 125–130). Lisboa: Academia Portuguesa da História.
Petit-Dutaillis, C. (1995). *The feudal monarchy in France and England from the tenth to the thirteenth century*. London: Kegan Paul.
Pocock, G. A. (2004). *The ancient constitution and the feudal law: A study of english historical thought in the seventeenth century*. Reissued with a retrospect. Cambridge: Cambridge University Press.
Poly, J. P., & Bournazel, E. (1991). *The feudal transformation, 900–1200*. New York: Holmes and Meier.

Reuter, T. (1992). Episcopi cum sua militia: The prelate as warrior in the early Staufer Era. In T. Reuter (Ed.), *Warriors and Churchmen in the high Middle Ages: Essays presented to Karl Leyser* (pp. 79–94). London: The Hambledon Press.

Reuter, T. (2010). *Medieval polities and modern mentalities*. Cambridge: Cambridge University Press.

Reynolds, S. (1996). *Fiefs and Vassals: The medieval evidence reinterpreted*. Oxford: Oxford University Press.

Robinson, O. F., Fergus, T. D. & Gordon, W. M. (2000) *European legal history: Sources and institutions* (3rd ed.). London: Butterworth.

Rummel, E. (1999). *Jiménez de Cisneros on the threshold of Spain's golden age*. Tempe, AR: Arizona Center for Medieval and Renaissance Studies.

Smith, D. J. (2004). *Innocent III and the crown of Aragon: The limits of papal authority*. Burlington, VT: Ashgate.

Stephenson, C. (2007). Feudalism and the mediaeval state. In *Mediaeval feudalism* (pp. 75–96). New York: Detzer Press.

Strayer, J. R. (1971). The two levels of feudalism. In *Medieval statecraft and the perspectives of history* (pp. 63–76). Princeton, NJ: Princeton University Press.

Strayer, J. R. (2005). *On the medieval origins of the modern state*. Princeton, NJ: Princeton University Press.

Taylor, N. L. (2005). Inheritance of power in the house of Guifred the Hairy; Contemporary perspectives on the formation of a Dinasty. In R. F. Berkhofer et al. (Eds.), *The experience of power in medieval Europe, 950–1350* (pp. 129–152). Aldershot, UK: Ashgate.

Ullmann, W. (2010). *The Carolingian Renaissance and the idea of Kingship*. New York: Routledge.

## *Further Reading*

Abdy, J. T. (2010). *Feudalism: Its rise, progress and consequences: Lectures delivered at Gresham College (1890)*. Reprint. Charleston, SC: Nabu Press.

Airlie, S. (2012). *Power and its problems in Carolingian Europe*. Burlington, VT: Ashgate Variorum.

Aurell i Cardona, J. (2012). *Authoring the past: History, autobiography, and politics in medieval Catalonia*. Chicago, IL: The University of Chicago Press.

Besserman, L. (Ed.). (2006). *Sacred and secular in medieval and early modern cultures: New essays*. Basingstoke, UK: Palgrave Macmillan.

Casanovas, P. (2011). Catalan legal mind and the legal Catalan mind: A brief overview on legal and political principles. *Journal of Catalan Intellectual History, I*(2), 161–177.

Cheyerre, F. L. (2010). 'Feudalism': A memoir and an assessment. In B. S. Tuten & T. L. Bilado (Eds.), *Feud, violence and practice: Essays in medieval studies in honour of Stephen D. White* (pp. 119–134). Burlington, VT: Ashgate.

Coss, P. (2002). From feudalism to bastard feudalism. In N. Fryde, P. Monnet, & O. Oexle (Eds.), *Die Gegenwart des Feudalismus = Présence du féodalisme et présent de la féodalité = The presence of feudalism* (pp. 79–108). Göttingen: Vandenhoeck & Ruprecht.

Curta, F. (Ed.). (2010). *Neglected barbarians: International congress on medieval studies*. Turnhout: Brepols.

Duby, G. (1992). *The early growth of the European economy: Warriors and peasants from the 7th to the 12th century* (6th print). New York: Cornell University Press.

Earenfight, T. (Ed.). (2005). *Queenship and political power in medieval and early modern Spain*. Aldershot: Ashgate.

Evans, G. R. (2007). *The church in the early Middle Ages*. London: I.B. Tauris and Co.

Fernández Viladrich, J. (1983). *Notas en torno a las asambleas condales en la Cataluña de la Alta Edad Media*. Barcelona: P.P.U.

Fouracre, P., & Ganz, D. (Eds.). (2008). *Frankland: The Franks and the world of the early Middle Ages: Essays in honour of Dame Jinty Nelson*. Manchester, UK: Manchester University Press.

Freedman, P. (1994). *Church, law and society in Catalonia, 900–1500*. Aldershot, UK: Variorum.

Garipzanov, I. H. (2008). *Symbolic language of authority in the Carolingian world: (c. 751–877)*. Leiden: Brill.

Guillemain, B. (1960). *The early Middle Ages*. London: Burns & Oates.

Head, T. (2006). Peace and power in France around the year 1000. *Essays in Medieval Studies, 23*, 1–17.

Hen, Y. (2007). *Roman Barbarians: The Royal Court and culture in the early medieval West*. Basingstoke: Palgrave Macmillan.

Herlihy, D. (Ed.). (1998). *The history of feudalism*. Amherst, NY: Humanity Books.

Jordan, W. C. (2003). *Europe in the high Middle Ages*. New York: The Viking Press.

Kagay, D. J. (2007). *War, government, and society in the medieval crown of Aragon*. Aldershot (Hampshire): Ashgate.

Lachaud, F., & Penman, M. (Dirs.) (2008). *Making and breaking the rules: Succession in medieval Europe, c. 1000–c. 1600. Établir et abolir les normes: la succession dans l'Europe médiévale, vers 1000–vers 1600*. Turnhout: Brepols.

Lewis, A. R. (1976). The Dukes in the Regnum Francorum, A.D. 550–751. *Speculum, 51*(3), 381–410.

Leyser, K., & Reuter, T. (1992). *Warriors and Churchmen in the high Middle Ages: Essays presented to Karl Leyser*. London: The Hambledon Press.

McCormick, M. (2002). *Origins of the European economy: Communications and commerce, A.D. 300–900* (2nd print). Cambridge, UK: Cambridge University Press.

Mitterauer, M. (2010). The feudal system and the estates: a special path of feudalism. In *Why Europe?: The medieval origins of its special path* (pp. 99–143). Chicago, IL: University of Chicago Press.

Nelson, J. (1986). *Politics and ritual in early medieval Europe*. London: The Hambledon Press.

O'Callaghan, J. F. (2013). The ascendancy of Islam: 711–1031. In *A history of medieval Spain* (pp. 89–190). Ithaca, NY: Cornell University Press.

O'Callaghan, J. F. (2004). Reconquest. Holy war and crusade. In *Reconquest and crusade in medieval Spain* (pp. 1–22). Philadelphia, PA: University of Pennsylvania Press.

Reynolds, S. (2012). *Medieval law in the Middle Ages without feudalism: Essays in criticism and comparison on the medieval West* (pp. 485–502). Farnham, UK: Ashgate Variorum.

Reynolds, S. (2012). *Feudalism, law and nations: Essays in criticism and comparison on the medieval West*. Farnham, UK: Ashgate Variorum.

Rollason, D. W. (2012). *Early medieval Europe 300–1050: The birth of Western society*. London: Routledge.

Sassier, Y. (Ed.). (2011). *Dieu, le prince et le peuple au Moyen Âge: Vie-XVe siècles*. Paris: Cujas.

Southern, R. (2007). *The making of the Middle Ages* (4th printing). New Haven, CT: Yale University Press.

Strayer, J. R. (1979). *Feudalism*. Huntington, NY: R. E. Krieger.

Vanlandingham, M. (2002). *Transforming the state: King, court and political culture in the realms of Aragon: (1213–1387)*. Leiden: Brill.

Wells, P. (2008). *Barbarians to angels: The Dark Ages reconsidered*. London: W. W. Norton.

# Part III
# The Origins of the "European States"

# Chapter 8
# From Kings to Monarchs: The Resurgence of Public Power in Late Medieval Europe

Let nobody, therefore, suppose that we wish to disrupt or diminish the jurisdiction or power of the illustrious King of the French, just as he does not wish nor should he impede our jurisdiction and power...—Innocent III, Decretal *Novit Ille* issued to the French bishops in 1204[1]

## Contents


8.1 Late Medieval Monarchy and the Origin of the Western State ........ 178
8.2 From Kings to Monarchs ........ 178
8.2.1 The Consolidation of the Hereditary Principle as the Basis of Royal Legitimacy ........ 179
8.2.2 A Territorial Monarchy ........ 182
8.2.3 An Expanding Monarchy ........ 183
8.2.4 An Administrative Monarchy ........ 183
8.3 The Triumph of Monarchy Over Christian Universalism ........ 185
8.4 The Medieval Origins of the "Rule of Law": Pacts as a Legal Restraint on Territorial Monarchy ........ 187
8.4.1 The Nobility's Resistance to Losing Its Political Power ........ 188
8.4.2 Urban Autonomy ........ 188
8.5 Towards the Shared Exercise of Power ........ 190
8.5.1 The Rise of State Assemblies ........ 190
8.5.2 The Origins of the Representative Principle ........ 192
8.6 A King Subject to the Law ........ 197
8.7 Europe's First "Constitutional" Texts? ........ 198
References ........ 203


[1] Literally: "He who knows all and is ignorant of nothing", in Navarro Valls and Palomino (2003, 108–109).



B. Aguilera-Barchet, *A History of Western Public Law*,
DOI 10.1007/978-3-319-11803-1_8

## 8.1 Late Medieval Monarchy and the Origin of the Western State

The considerable surge in economic activity because of the multiplication of trade links (Commercial Revolution),and the rising cultural level coinciding with the emergence of the first European universities (Bologna, La Sorbonne, Oxford and Cambridge, Salamanca), were to transform European society in the Late Middle Ages. The rigid tripartite structure into which feudal society was organized, featuring a landed nobility, peasants, and the clergy, was to fundamentally shift as a result of commercial expansion, the growth of cities, and the emergence of a new social class: the bourgeoisie, which would amass considerable wealth and gradually upset traditional relationships of power.

These important changes would be reflected in the nature of Europe's political and legal organization. Late medieval society would necessarily shed its feudal scheme as bourgeois city dwellers became the natural allies of the kings, in opposition to the traditional privileged classes. As we have seen in the last chapter, as of the late twelfth century, the old *curia regia* (royal court), composed of nobles and bishops, would absorb representatives of this new social class, which would discuss the kingdom's key affairs with the traditional elite and the king.

Moreover, in the final medieval centuries, the confrontation between popes and emperors would enable a set of strong monarchs to assert the independence of their kingdoms from the papacy and the Holy German-Roman Empire, above all, in chronological order, in the kingdoms of Castile, France and England.

In European society, universalism and the feudal model would gradually decline as a series of kings tended to invest all power in their person. In this sense, the Castilian, French and English kings of the Late Middle Ages, had little in common with the German "royalty" which arose after the fall of the Western Roman Empire, because the very nature of the royal institution underwent three major transformations: the "kings" became "monarchs;" their crowns came to be inherited; and kings no longer ruled over a certain "nation" or "people", but rather over entire territories.

## 8.2 From Kings to Monarchs

Kings in the Late Middle Ages were to recover much of the power they had lost in the early medieval period, both externally, by gaining independence from emperors and popes, and internally, where they gained ground against their great vassals, the feudal barons. By becoming the undisputed holders of power, kings evolved into monarchs—a concept much more akin to the imperial Roman conception of political rule. It is no coincidence that European lawyers trained in the late medieval universities turned to citing Roman law texts to justify the kings' political autonomy, in accord with the well-known maxim: *Rex est imperator in regno suo*, which sanctioned the independence of the new monarchs from the Holy Roman Empire and from papal authority.

The political consolidation of the monarchs of the Late Middle Ages (in contrast to the kings of the Early Middle Ages) was possible, firstly, because royal status came to be hierarchically posited, at least in theory, above all feudal bonds. The first to advance this principle was Abbot Suger de Saint Denis (1081–1151), royal adviser to Louis VI and Louis VII, and a historian who described feudal society as a pyramid at whose apex stood the king of France, whose suzerainty prevailed over that of all other lords,[2] as Suger distinguished for the first time, between the crown as a concept and the king as a person (Grant 1998, 178).

Somewhat later, also in France, there appeared the legal term "sovereignty", coined by "legists" of Louis IX (1226–1270), better known as St. Louis. Inspired by the Roman concept of *imperium*, these jurists contended that the King of France prevailed over all lords because he was "sovereign". As Hallam and Everard (2001, 317) affirm, during his reign the king's feudal powers were extended to the fullest extent, as he exercised all the rights of suzerainty, to the point that the extension of traditional royal powers, both ecclesiastical and feudal, began to modify the very nature of royal authority, transforming the king from a suzerain into a sovereign.

### *8.2.1 The Consolidation of the Hereditary Principle as the Basis of Royal Legitimacy*

The late medieval monarchs were able to consolidate their power largely because their legitimacy was not based on an elective procedure of designation, as in the time of the Germanic kingdoms, but on the hereditary principle. This stood in stark contrast to the system employed under the Roman Empire, in which the Emperor appointed his successor by "adoption"—a procedure which frequently sparked struggles for power. By retaining the principle of "elective succession", the

[2] Specifically, in his *Historia Gloriosi regis Ludovici* (Suger 1992), in which he argues that the French king was the suzerain, or "lord of lords" (Lemarignier 1965, 167–176). According to Lewis (1987, 51–52), Suger's articulation of at least an inchoate theory of suzerainty and his conception of kingship makes him an authoritative spokesman for royalist ideas, essential for understanding Capetian ideology in his time. For an overview of Suger's writings, see Grant (1998, 32–49). France is not the only case. In the Iberian Peninsula, the same situation appeared in "Catalonia" as we saw in the previous chapter—the only territory where feudalism fully triumphed in medieval Spain. The Catalonian feudalistic pyramid was described by a thirteenth-century Catalonian jurist, Pere Albert, in his work *Les Commemoracions* (Albert 2002), in which he defended the preeminence of royal law and privileges (Kagay 2007, 693–703). In Catalonia there was no king, *per se*, but the Count of Barcelona appeared at the top of the pyramid, as the first (*princeps*) among all Catalonians (Ferran i Planas 2006, 145–68).

Germanic kings had generated great political instability, as this principle gave rise to warfare between noble clans.[3]

The hereditary principle did not appear overnight because it was not easy to consolidate (Fedou 1977, 52–61). As Jackson (1984, 6–7) has indicated, the transition from elective to hereditary monarchy went through an initial stage in which early Capetians crowned their successors as heirs to the throne to bring about an instantaneous transmission of power upon the king's death. Thus, Philip Augustus was designated as heir to the throne on November 1, 1179, and stood as heir until the death of his father, Louis VII, at which point he became the king, serving until his own death on July 14, 1223.[4] Philip Augustus's son, Louis VIII, *immediately* inherited the throne upon his father's death without even having been formally designated heir. The monarch's power came, then, to stem from his birth as the "legitimate heir" of the deceased king. "The king is dead, long live the king" was the refrain to formally announce the death of the sovereign in France; though the king had died, his successor automatically ensured the monarchy's uninterrupted continuity. The royal institution, thus, came to guarantee the stability of power, averting the chaos and anarchy born of the perpetual state of war between lords which had characterized and marred the feudal era.

To ensure the peaceful nature of succession, this process became subject to a series of specific legal procedures. Thus, in every kingdom there arose rules of succession allowing for the uncontested succession of one ruler by the next which generally came to stand, initially in the medieval period, as the first of the "laws of the realm". In the sixteenth century these precepts came be called "fundamental laws", a set of customary rules to which even the king was bound to respect

[3] It is noteworthy, for example, that historian Gregory of Tours (Riom, near Clermont-Ferrand, 538-Tours, 594) in his *Historia Francorum* spoke of the *morbus gothicus—detestabilis consuetudo*—to explain why so many Gothic kings died violently in disputes over successions (Wolfram 1990, 245). Also, in the principal and, often the only, source for Frankish history after the end of the work of Gregory of Tours in 591: the *Chronicle of Fredegar*, a compilation—38 manuscripts, in 4 books—of events in Frankish Gaul from 584 to around 641, that begins with the last years of the Queen Brunhilde, daughter of the Visigothic king of Spain, Athanagild. The *Chronicle* accuses to the Queen of import the *gothic disease*: she ordered the death of ten kings of the Franks and many churchmen between 570 and 613 year of her execution (Goffart 1963, 206, and Frassetto 2003, 81–83 and 166–167). To prevent clashes over succession, the IV Visigothic Council at Toledo, expressly approved a rule instituting the election of kings: "Let nobody orchestrate the death of kings. Rather, when the king dies, in peace, the nobility of the entire people, along with the bishops, shall designate of common accord the successor to the throne, so that we might preserve a concord of unity, and there be not any division of our country and people born of violence and ambition" (*...nemo meditetur interitus regum, sed defuncto in pace príncipe primatus totius gentis cum sacerdotibus succesorem regni concilio communi constituant, ut dum unitatis concordia a nobis retinetur, nullum patriae gentisque discidium per vim atque ambitium oriatur*). Canon LXXV, IV Council at Toledo (633) (Vives 1963, 218). As Stocking (2000, 152) points out, Canon LXXV did not only establish obedience to the duly elected Visigothic kings, but also expressed the bishop's insistence on the necessity of establishing and maintaining a Christian consensus regarding the inviolability of oaths taken in the name of God, as they were essential to the stability of kingship.

[4] On the crucial succession of Philip Augustus, see Lewis (1981, 64–77).

(Desrayaud 1996, 306), and that became the "constitutional" basis of a monarchy, which, according to medieval French jurists, was subject to rules (*puissance réglée*).

From the moment when royal legitimacy was based on the hereditary principle and was legally stipulated, the monarch became untouchable, as the crown came to transcend political faction. As the monarch did not depend on an election involving compromises between the most powerful figures in his kingdom, his authority being assured by the mere fact that he was in the line of succession, he became *au dessus de la mêlée*, or "above the fray",[5] an arbiter exercising mediating roles between parties in conflict.

When did the order of succession to the Crown begin to be respected? One of the first places was in Spain, specifically in the kingdom of León, where records from the second half of the tenth century evidence respect for hereditary rights in three cases involving minors destined to become kings. The first, dates from 966, during the regency of Ramiro III (966–982), and the second, from 999, when a young Alfonso V rose to the throne; and the third from 1027, after the latter's death.[6]

It is also important to point out that it was in this same period when the word *princeps* first appeared to designate the heir to the throne, denoting that he was the "first" in the order of succession.[7]

---

[5] The essential role as an arbiter played by the king, appears even today in the current Spanish Constitution, dating from 1978, whose Article 56.1 states that: "The King is the head of state, symbol of its unity and permanence; he arbitrates and moderates the regular functioning of the institutions and is charged with the highest representation of the Spanish State in international relations..." To guarantee this role as an intermediary, which allows him to remain above the political fray, the order of succession to the throne continues to be one of the pillars upon which the monarchy's constitutional viability is based. Thus, Article 57.1 of the Spanish Constitution states that "The Spanish Crown is hereditary: (inherited by) the successors of H.M. Juan Carlos I de Borbón, legitimate heir of the historic dynasty (...)".

[6] The monarchy of León was the heir to the Asturian monarchy. García I of León, in the early tenth century, transferred the capital from Oviedo to the city of León as a result of advances made during the Reconquest. Likewise, King Alfonso II of Asturias (759–842), stood as the heir to the legendary Don Pelayo. Alfonso II was the founder of the Kingdom of Asturias, as according to the *Crónica Abeldense* (881), "he instituted in Oviedo, in everything, both in the Church and at the palace, the order which the Goths had had in Toledo" (*Omnemque gotorum ordinem sicuti Toletu fuerat, tam in ecclesia quam palatio in Ovieto cuncta statuit*). That is, he revived the dynastic tradition of the Visigoth kings and came to consider himself a descendent of them. Thus, the kings of Asturias-León were, initially, Christian Spain's only legitimate monarchs. This explains why it was within this first medieval Spanish monarchy of Asturias-León where the principle of hereditary succession was consolidated, as demonstrated by the "regencies" indicated (Aguilera-Barchet 1998, 15–21).

[7] In a document by the Leonese monarch Ramiro III in the year 978, after the names of the king, queen and bishops, appears, *Virmundus, Serenissimus Princeps [confirmat]* (Flórez and Risco 1793, Volume XXXVIII. Trat. LXXVI. Appendix IV, pp. 276–277.) Bermudo was not the son of Ramiro II, but rather his uncle, and would come to occupy the Leonese throne in 984, with the name Bermudo II the Gouty (+999). See text in Flórez and Risco (1793, 276–277). The trend towards the legal designation of a successor was consolidated throughout Europe with the appearance of specific titles granted to crown princes: in the case of England, it was the "Prince of Wales", a title created by Edward I (1272–1307), for the future Edward II; in France Philip VI of Valois (1328–1350), did the same when he created the title "Dauphin of France;" in the Crown of Aragon, Peter IV linked the title "Duke of Gerona" to the crown prince as of 1349; in Castile and León, the title "Prince of Asturias" appeared in 1388 to designate the heir to the throne; and in Navarra, the heir to the throne came to be called the "Prince of Viana", when the title was created in 1423 by Charles III the Noble.

The hereditary principle preserved monarchy. This is why, even today in the twenty-first century, there are still kings in Europe: in Spain, England, the Netherlands, Belgium, Denmark, Sweden and Norway, demonstrating that monarchy is not incompatible with democracy, at least when monarchs reign but do not govern.[8]

### 8.2.2 A Territorial Monarchy

The Late Medieval monarchs not only managed to become "sovereigns", staking their legitimacy upon the hereditary principle, but also exerted their power over whole territories. This situation stood in sharp contrast to what happened during the era of the Germanic kingdoms, when kings represented Germanic groups. The Visigoth and Frankish monarchs were, for example, elected by their respective nations.[9]

In the Late Middle Ages, monarchies came to be defined by the territories over which they ruled. The king's power was exercised over entire regions, a new reality reflected in the royal titles themselves: as of 1190 Philip II Augustus (1179–1223), was referred to in some official documents as King of France ("Rex Franciae") (Guenée 1981, 158), instead of "Rex Francorum" (King of the Franks), as his predecessors had been designated, and in 1205, there appeared the term *regnum Franciae* (Lombard-Jourdan 1989, 317),[10] a crucial terminological transition which for some historians, marks the beginning of the history of the French nation.[11]

The emergence of territory-based monarchies meant that kings had to possess the means to govern and manage all the land under their rule. Unlike what occurred with the kings during the feudal period, in the Late Middle Ages the monarch had at

[8] The expression "The king reigns but does not govern" is not of English but Polish origin. It comes from the doctrine summed up by Chancellor Jan Zamoyski (1542–1605), the first to use the expression *Rex regnat et non gubernat* to describe the peculiar political system of Golden Liberty in which the nobility (*szlachta* in Polish) dominated the king and all the social estates. The king was obliged to respect the citizens' rights, as approved in King Henry's Articles (1573), in accordance with the "pact-based" conception of power discussed in the previous chapter. On the governmental machine, the correlation between *auctoritas* and *potestas*, the articulation between power as government and effective management, and power as a ceremonial and liturgical regality, see Agamben (2011, 71–72 and 84).

[9] Significantly, in 1804, Napoleon declared himself "Emperor of the French" (*Empereur des Français*) instead of "Emperor of France", a distinction intended to convey that he respected Revolutionary principles and had been nominated by the people through a popular plebiscite (Huet 1999, 55).

[10] On the emergence of royal ideology under the reign of Philip Augustus, see Baldwin (1991, 362–366). It is interesting to note that the use of the words "of France" originated with the common people (Lewis 1981, 185), and was only later taken up by the royal chancery for use in formal texts, becoming widespread over the course of the fourteenth century.

[11] On the pivotal debate as to whether the state preceded the nation or the nation preceded the state, see Fedou (1977, 185–192).

his disposal a group of "officials"[12] he was able to pay because he consistently collected taxes. He also possessed a permanent and professional army, which had already appeared in France in the mid fifteenth century under Charles VII (1422–1461)—a factor which proved crucial to ensuring the French House of Valois' triumph in the Hundred Years' War.[13]

### *8.2.3 An Expanding Monarchy*

The burgeoning power of the great medieval European kings led them to attempt to absorb the greatest amounts of territory possible into their domains. This explains, for example, the imperialist approach of England to Wales and Scotland; the Kings of France's progressive assimilation of important feudal territories during the reign of Philip Augustus (1180–1223); and, in Spain, the progressive incorporation at the end of the Middle Ages of territories arising as a result of the Reconquest (Asturias, León, Castile, the County of Barcelona, the Kingdoms of Aragón, Valencia and Mallorca), forming two great political blocks: The Crown of Castile and the Crown of Aragón. In some cases, the kingdoms were unified, as was the case with France and Castile, while in others, the union of realms led to composite monarchies, such as the Crown of Aragon and the British Crown.[14]

### *8.2.4 An Administrative Monarchy*

The territorialization of the monarchy required adaptation to the new circumstances facing royal institutions. Thus, the *curia regis*, the old feudal council that advised

[12] "Officials" because they held "offices", or public posts. Today, the equivalent term would be "civil servants". For an overview of the decisive transition from feudal private service to late medieval public service in European monarchies during the Late Middle Ages, see Fedou (1977, 158–164).

[13] The creation of a permanent army (initially approved in Orleans at the Estates General of September 1439, and consolidated through the creation of the *Compagnies d'ordonnance*—20 *compagnies* of 100 lances each—by the royal order of Louppy-le-Châtel of May 26, 1445), justified by the need to defend the kingdom from English armies (Minois 2005, 495–501), allowed Charles VII to create a set of stable taxes (*taille*, *gabelle*) without any need for the Estates General to renew them annually. This tax system would last until the French Revolution. As Vale (1974, 231) points out, under Charles VII taxation was heavy, and got heavier with each successive war. The contemporary historian Philippe de Commynes (1447–1511), has calculated that by the end of his reign Charles was collecting the equivalent to some 1,800,000 francs a year, while his son Louis XI (1461–1483), was raising 4,700,000 by the time of his death. The result was that the French were among the most heavily taxed people in Renaissance Europe.

[14] For an overview of the late medieval monarchies' territorial integration processes, see Ladero Quesada (1997, 19–68).

and counseled the monarch, was gradually divided into specialized units headed by royally appointed, professional officials who proceeded in accordance with pre-established procedures.[15] As Desrayaud (1996, 346) points out, the end of the Middle Ages was characterized by the emergence of a strongly structured royal administration, resulting from the consolidation of royal power.

The oldest of these bodies was the "Accounts Chamber" or "Comptos "(*Exchequer* in England), which administrated the royal agents' finances. The *curia* was also deprived of its judicial functions, prompting the emergence of *royal tribunals* such as the Court of Common Pleas at Westminster,[16] the French *parlements*,[17] and the Castilian *audiencias* (high courts) and *chancillerías* (chanceries).[18] These institutions fast came to preside over the justice administrations because of the

[15] As Guenée points out (1985, 120–121), in the Early Middle Ages the court was not specialized, as kings received assistance in administrating their lands from vassals, friends and companions, who filled all kinds of roles in temporary and imprecise ways.

[16] As Pollock and Maitland underscore, the new court "was no longer to be a special tribunal, a court for great men, for great causes, for matters that concerned the King; but was to become an ordinary tribunal for the whole realm". It started in 1178, when Henry II chose five men, two clerks and two laymen, "who are not to depart from the king's court, but are to hear all the complaints of the kingdom" (Pollock and Maitland 2010, I, 153–154).

[17] In France, the term *parlement* does not refer to the estate-based assembly (as in England's Parliament), which was known as the Estates General. Rather, France's *parlements* were its high courts of justice in a given region, guarantors of the application of the customs of each. They did not only play a judicial role, however, but also were of significant political importance because they were charged with registering royal edicts—an action without which royal legislation did not go into effect, save in special cases in which a *lit de justice* was resorted to. Thus, the French *parlements* became symbols of opposition to the absolute power of the French kings of the *Ancien Regime*. On the technical mechanism of legislative control exercised by the French parlements, see Saint-Bonnet (2010, 1–6).

[18] The kingdom of Castile had no laws before the reign of Alfonso X the Wise (1252–1284). Rather, local judges—generally laymen with no legal education—decided judicial conflicts based on their sense of equity and free will (*equidad* y *libre albedrío*), and created law through their decisions (case law). Alfonso X changed all this, creating, on the basis of the Roman and canon law traditions studied at European universities, complex legal texts such as the *Fuero Real* (Royal Law), *El Espéculo*, and, best known of all, *Las Partidas*. The Castilians, however did not care for the new law proceeding from the *ius commune* (common law) universities, preferring their traditional customs, and rebelled against the king, who was forced to reestablish traditional legal customs. Though Alfonso X was unable to create new laws, he was successful in extending royal jurisdiction to a series of penal cases, which were to be heard only in royal courts (*casos de corte*), pursuant to an agreement reached between the *Cortes de Zamora* and the Castilian cities in 1274 (Iglesia Ferreiros 1971). He transformed the old *Curia regis* into a royal court (*Tribunal de la Corte*), staffed by royal judges (*alcaldes de corte*). Finally, these royal judges applied the *Fuero Real*, which became the law of the royal courts (Pérez De La Canal 1975). Due to opposition by the Castilian nobility, however, the system of royal courts was only consolidated in the *Cortes de Toro* in 1371, where Henry II of Castile, in an important Act on the Administration of Justice (*Ordenamiento sobre Administración de Justicia*), created the first *audiencia* as an appellate court—so named because the judges were *oidores* (from the verb *oir*, to hear), who heard its cases. If an *audiencia* received a royal seal of justice, issued by the chancellor (*canciller*) it became a *chancillería*. By the end of the fourteenth century, the *Audiencia* ended up forming part of the royal *Chancillería* (Garriga 1994, 101–102).

quality of their work, which guaranteed a more dependable application of the law than that provided by local judges, essentially because these new courts were run by professional lawyers educated at European universities. Thus, emerged a new type of process with more guarantees in which fundamentally oral processes gave way to written, documented procedures. The old local courts from the early medieval period did not entirely disappear, but their powers were reduced and gradually became hierarchically subject to the royal courts via the instrument of appeals.[19] To the extent that kings were considered God's representatives, their essential role was to act as judges. Thus, the late medieval monarchs often turned to the judicial sphere to consolidate their power.

The medieval kings were essentially judges because their function as Christian monarchs was to maintain the order created by God. As custom initially prevailed over the law in the Middle Ages, monarchs such as Henry II of England in the twelfth century, or Alfonso X, the Wise, in Castile in the second half of the thirteenth century, succeeded in consolidating their power by expanding the king's jurisdiction over local judges. As Anderson (2006, 152) has indicated, one of the "constitutional" consequences of feudalism was that secular government itself was characteristically narrowed into a new mold, as it became essentially the exercise of "justice", which under feudalism occupied a functional position, as it became the central modality of political power.

## 8.3 The Triumph of Monarchy Over Christian Universalism

Kings generally endorsed the ideal of political universalism and, as such, were at least theoretically beholden to the pope and the emperor, a restriction which they came to throw off over the course of the Late Middle Ages as kings asserted their autonomy and independence. By 1250, emperors played no significant role in European politics,[20] and the popes had been losing their supremacy ever since the beginning of the fourteenth century when Philip IV, the Fair, of France abducted Boniface VIII, in the aforementioned episode at Anagni. The "captivity of the papacy" at Avignon, the Great Schism and the Protestant Reformation would further serve to severely undercut papal supremacy.

---

[19] This explains the historical origin of common law, as most cases were presented in royal courts, far more reliable than local judges. In any case it made possible the unification of procedures all over England and, since the time of Henry II (1154–1189), the law tended to be common throughout the realm because the king had devised expedients by which trials could be decentralized in an ingenious system of itinerant justice that helped greatly to promote the popularity and effectiveness of the new royal remedies, preserving, at the same time, uniformity in their administration and making it possible for the law built around the new remedies to become a truly national law (Dawson 1968, 1–2). For an overview of this fascinating process, see Baker (1990, 14–43).

[20] For an overview of the decline of Imperial influence was especially evident in France in the late medieval centuries Jones (2007).

The evolution from papal to "pact-based" legitimation is especially evident in the case of the Portuguese monarchy. In 1179, Alfonso I Henriques became King of Portugal via papal concession.[21] However, when his successors to the throne, Alfonso II (1211–1223), and Sancho II (1223–1248), confronted and squared off against the papacy, they were excommunicated and stripped of their rights to legitimately occupy the throne. It was Alfonso III, who managed to overpower the papacy by winning the support of the Portuguese *Cortes* (parliament), which met for the first time in 1254, in Leiría. Henceforth the Portuguese kings' legitimacy rested exclusively on pacts with the social classes. In March of 1385, the Portuguese *Cortes* gathered in Coimbra demonstrated its capacity to instate a new dynasty when it chose as king John I of Portugal rather than John II of Castile who, in theory, held a greater dynastic right by virtue of his marriage to the daughter of former king, Ferdinand I.[22]

Another example will help us to understand this phenomenon. In 1493, Pope Alexander VI, through what are known as the "Alexandrine Bulls" divided the New World between the Spaniards and Portuguese to formalize rights to the conquest of the recently discovered overseas territories.[23] A year later, however, through the bilateral Treaty of Tordesillas (1494), the kings of Portugal and Spain decided the limits of their respective spheres of expansion on their own, disregarding the papacy.[24]

More significant for the history of western law and the western polity, were the "internal" limitations curtailing the power of the late medieval kings, as these would prove to be more lasting and effective.

[21] The relationship between the Portuguese kings and the papacy had been constant since the very inception of the Portuguese kingdom, specifically since Alfonso I Henriques defeated the Moors in Ourique in 1139, a military triumph which led him to drop his title of *comites portugalensium* (*Portuguese Count*), and adopt that of *rex portugalensium* (*King of the Portuguese*). To do so legitimately, however, he had to submit to the pope, declare himself *miles beati Petri et Romani pontificis* (*a soldier of Saint Peter and of the Roman pontiff*), and agree to pay an annual tribute to the Holy See. Pope Lucius II expressly accepted the offer in 1144, but only recognized his title of *Portugalensium dux* (*Portuguese Duke*). It would be Alexander III, who would expressly recognize Alfonso I Henriques as king via a bull dated May 23, 1179 (O'Callaghan 2013, 241).

[22] Though John of Avis was more than interested in receiving the papal blessing as well (Olivera Serrano 2005, 95–96).

[23] After Columbus returned from his first voyage of discovery, the Catholic Kings reached agreements with Pope Alexander VI (born in Valencia) in 1493, calling for a Castilian monopoly on journeys to the newly-discovered lands in the form of 4 legal documents: a papal brief called the *Inter caetera*; the bull *Eximiae devotionis*, of May 3; the bull *Inter caetera* of May 4; and the bull *Dudum siquidem* of September 26. In these documents the pope drew a longitudinal line running around the globe, and forbade anyone from venturing "to the west and south to be distant one hundred leagues from any of the Azores or Cape Verdes" without the express consent of the Catholic Kings, under pain of excommunication. On the Alexandrine Bulls, see Vander Linden (1916, 1–20).

[24] The treaty was created on June 7, 1494; ratified on July 2 by the Crowns of Castile and Aragon; and on September 5 by the King of Portugal, pushing the Papal Line of 1493 to a meridian situated 370 leagues west of the Cape Verde islands, thanks to which Portugal could include among its domains Brazil, discovered by Pedro Alvares Cabral on April 22, 1500. On the Treaty of Tordesillas, see Bown (2012, 155–157).

## 8.4 The Medieval Origins of the "Rule of Law": Pacts as a Legal Restraint on Territorial Monarchy

The great kings of the late medieval era had much more power than the feudal kings of the early medieval period, but less than modern states' heads of government. Firstly because, at least initially, when crowned they had to formally defer to the Church, represented by the papacy. As God's representatives they were not able to create law, but were to limit themselves to protecting the divine order. At most, they were able to "confirm" the law, but never to create it *ex novo*. The monarch in the medieval period was essentially a *roi justicier* (Desrayaud 1996, 237)",[25] meaning the king was a dispenser of justice.

Moreover, within the scope of government, a function assigned to the executive branch today, late medieval kings could not make major decisions alone, but had to have backing from their kingdoms' representatives. In the early Middle Ages, kings only needed to consult the nobles and bishops assembled in the royal court (*curia*). Beginning in the Late Middle Ages, kings were also compelled to consult representatives of the cities. In fact, the most important decisions had to be settled via pacts reached with the representatives of various institutions and social groups (nobility, clergy and urban leaders). In Spanish legal historiography, this monarchical model has been aptly termed "*pactista*" (pact-based) as it is rooted in the principle that the king's decisions must be endorsed by his subjects (Bisson 2003a, b, 141–142). Thus, in this class of monarchy sovereigns were compelled to respect a traditional order and vow to obey its laws, in return for which their subjects took the corresponding oath of allegiance and obedience.[26] This obligation was assigned particular importance in some kingdoms, as in the case of the Crown of Aragon, beginning in 1286 (Palacios Martin 1975, 178).

It is commonplace to envision medieval kings as absolute monarchs. This notion, however, could not be more inaccurate, as in reality they were bound to

[25] French judicial historiography draws an institutional distinction between the era during which the king was, above all, a judge (*roi justicier*) from that during which he began to create law (*roi lé gislateur*). This pivotal change in the king's role came about in different eras: in Castile it occurred in the first half of the fifteenth century, while in France it did not transpire until the reign of King Louis XIV (1643–1715). For an overview of the figure of the king as fountain of justice, and largely, on the relations between justice and royal power, see Menegaldo and Ribémont (2012).

[26] In the previous chapter, we saw how the Church managed to stem the anarchy resulting from the feudal structure of European society during the Early Middle Ages, as oaths taken on the Bible were a judicial instrument used by the Church in to maintain control by appealing to consciences. Perjury was a crime and, above all, a sin sanctioned with eternal damnation. This is why the oath became a legal check on the kings' sovereignty (David 1951). On the medieval origins of the coronation oaths, see Palacios Martin (1975, 133–141); on the meaning of the coronation oaths in France's medieval monarchy, see Jackson (1984, 57–59).

adhere to a whole series of external and internal legal limits which restricted their authority and ability to act.[27]

### 8.4.1 The Nobility's Resistance to Losing Its Political Power

The emergence of the "administrative monarchy" did not spell the end of the feudal order. In fact, the nobility struggled to maintain its political influence. Such was the case, for example, in England when the nobles imposed the Magna Carta (1215) on John Lackland; or when they rebelled against Henry III.[28] Meanwhile, the Peers of France refused to submit to the jurisdiction of the Parlement of Paris, as they aspired to be judged by their peers (*cour des pairs*), as was the practice in the old days of the *curia regis*. In Aragon, Valencia and Catalonia, nobles grouped into *uniones* (unions) and managed to seize upon moments when the king was weak, seriously curbing the powers of Peter III and Alfonso III, in the last third of the thirteenth century. Finally, in Castile the nobility imposed its political hegemony upon the kings in the first two thirds of the fifteenth century, during the reigns of John II and Henry IV. It would not be until the reign of Ferdinand and Isabella (1474–1504), that the monarchy would regain its supremacy.

### 8.4.2 Urban Autonomy

If the Romans' development of their municipal network was one of the instruments which most effectively assured their expansion all over the Mediterranean, in the early Middle Ages, cities virtually disappeared as entities enjoying political and legal autonomy. However, because of the urban renaissance which Europe saw in the eleventh century, cities regained undeniable political importance—particularly those which received privileges consolidating their legal autonomy,[29] as was the

[27] Some legal historians believe that we can even speak of "contractual kingship" (*royauté contractuelle*) in reference to the late medieval monarchs ruling during the eleventh to fifteenth centuries (Desrayaud 1996, 197).

[28] Also, in Scotland, *The Declaration of Arbroath*, a Latin letter that was drafted on the April 6, 1320, is one of the first expressions of the idea of a contractual monarchy and a prototype of contractual kingship in Europe. The document received the seals of several Scottish barons and was sent to Pope John XXII at Avignon in France, attempting to abate papal hostility. See Cowan (2002). About contractual kingship in Catalonia, Earenfight (2010, p. 134).

[29] In some cases, one could speak of "constitutional" texts in the modern sense of the term, as certain municipal privileges were to be respected by monarchs. A clear example is the municipal Charter of St. Omer, granted by Thierry of Alsace, Count of Flanders in 1129. Its Article 25 indicated that the Flemish nobles had sworn that, should the count violate certain municipal privileges, thereby doing harm to the people of the city by transgressing the decisions of its judicial authorities, the city would sever relations until legal order was reestablished (Caenegem 1990, 102–107). On the text of the St. Omer Charter, see Espinas (1947, 43–48).

case in the Iberian Peninsula, Germany, northern Italy and Flanders. In England, the centralism imposed by the monarchy since the days of William the Conqueror in the second half of the eleventh century prevented cities from attaining full political autonomy.

In the Iberian Peninsula, two situations must be distinguished. In its western region, municipal autonomy appeared in borderlands as a result of the Reconquest, when the monarchs or corresponding repopulation authority granted *fueros*—charters grating special political privileges and authorities—to "resettle" the territories taken from the Muslims and assure that they would remain in Christian hands (García de Valdeavellano 1986, 1188–1191). Over time, these cities developed more extensive legal systems retaining these privileges, which afforded them considerable autonomy.[30] In contrast, in the eastern part of the Peninsula the emergence of urban privileges (*costums*) came later, spawned by the rise of a bourgeoisie rebelling against the feudal nobility, which until then had been dominant. This type of municipal rights arose especially in Catalonia, the only territory in Spain in which feudalism fully triumphed[31] (Hughes 2011, 93–125).

Something very different happened in northern Italy, without any doubt the most urbanized area in Europe in the Late Middle Ages, as it featured cities with populations of over 100,000, which were practically independent, having managed to exploit the struggles between popes and emperors. Thus, appeared urban republics with their own autonomous governments and legal systems based on lengthy documents called "statutes" that, in a way, functioned on a local level very much like the constitutions of contemporary states. However, the absence of a strong power generated permanent internal strife between families grappling for control of city governments, and wars with other cities, which in some cases led to the formation of leagues, as cities conducted independent relations with other cities, whether to negotiate agreements over issues such as boundaries or coinage, or to pursue expansion through warfare (Waley and Dean 2010, 8–9). It is, therefore, not surprising that it was in late medieval Italy where a relatively democratic political system arose for the first time in European history. In were cities such as Florence and Siena, where in the fourteenth and fifteenth centuries important decisions were not made unilaterally by municipal magistrates, but rather by assemblies of citizens. This was possible because they were organized into neighborhoods and perfectly structured guilds, which in some cases were headed up by leaders known as *capitani del popolo*.[32]

---

[30] For an overview of this privileged local legal system, which prevailed over royal law in Castile and León until the middle of the fourteenth century, see García Gallo (1956, 388–398).

[31] This is what happened, for instance, in the Catalonian city of Tortosa in the beginning of the thirteenth century (Font Rius 1985, 146–147). For an overview of this transition, specifically with respect to the relationships between cities and the monarchy in Catalonia, and the markedly pact-oriented territory of the Crown of Aragon, see Marongiu (1973, 653–659) and Sabaté I Curull (2000–2002, 255–282). Also, Corteguera (2002, 24–47).

[32] On the political organization of the Italian cities in the medieval period, see Waley and Dean (2010, 141–154).

In Germany, the emperor's power waned while the territorial princes' power grew as they exploited imperial weakness to consolidate the feudal system, initially allowing merchants to form a union to protect their interests and, eventually, permitting cities like Lübeck and Bremen to form urban leagues, which not only protected the interests of German merchants abroad, but become great powers in northern Europe (Dollinger 1970, 62).

In France, the municipal movement's consolidation was inversely proportional to the political strengthening of the monarchy. Though initially the crown's weakness allowed some cities to achieve significant autonomy, as of the late thirteenth century, the strengthening of royal authority served to quash municipal power. In some cases the kings did not hesitate to subjugate rebellious cities by force of arms, as occurred, for example, in the revolt of Etienne Marcel, the leader of Paris's merchants, who was killed in 1358.[33]

In Flanders exceptional urban growth was the result of both great economic prosperity and the weakness of the Germanic Empire, to which the territory was theoretically subject. In the mid fourteenth century, under the leadership of Captain Van Artevelde of Ghent, Ghent, Bruges and Ypres managed to become true city-states (Caenegem 1995, 79). However, the political savvy of the Dukes of Burgundy allowed them to reassert their authority. Only Ghent rebelled, successively, against Philip the Good of Burgundy, Charles V and Philip II, who finally subjugated the city in 1584.

## 8.5 Towards the Shared Exercise of Power

In the previous chapter, we saw how feudalism radically altered relationships of power as kings became bound to their vassals through a contractual relationship, the feudal pact, which placed them on a plane of equality. The most important consequence of this relationship was that, when exercising their power, kings were obligated to seek the support of their subjects, or at least those with the greatest social and political power: the nobles and urban oligarchs. This is what Bisson (2009, 556) calls the "Parliamentary custom of consent".

### *8.5.1 The Rise of State Assemblies*

Though the "parliamentary system" in the strictest sense emerged in eighteenth century England (as we shall see below), it is clear that the principle according to

[33] It is interesting to note that Etienne Marcel was killed not by the royal army but by the citizens of Paris, who were afraid he had gone too far in his rebellion and rejected him. Cazelles (1965, 426). Also, Duby (2000, 276–279) and Le Goff (2006, 56–57).

which the sovereign was expected to make decisions by reaching a consensus with the representatives of his kingdom had already appeared by the Late Middle Ages. To this end assemblies of the estates were constituted, so termed because in them the most important social groups (the estates) convened—usually nobles, clergy and representatives of the cities.[34] The assemblies of the estates received various names in the different European kingdoms. In the Iberian Peninsula, they were called the *Cortes*; in England, Parliament; in France and the Netherlands, the "Estates General;" and in Poland or the Empire, the "Diet" (Desrayaud 1996, 419).[35]

Even if the origin of these medieval assemblies is obscure (Fedou 1977, 197), their precedent may be traced back to the "feudal court", composed of the king's most important vassals—essentially nobles and bishops—who owed him *consilium* (Desrayaud 1996, 185), as the kingdoms emerging from the feudal experience found it essential to secure the support of the propertied classes for many acts of government (Strayer 1965, 72). The principle that kings should consult with their subjects—or at least with the most important (*magnates*)—regarding important political decisions became institutionalized through the *curia regis*, a kind of select assembly presided over by the king and made up of the great landowning nobles and the highest-ranking ecclesiastical authorities, a body of advisers and courtiers who assisted the king and supervised the administration of the realm whose origins may be traced back to the ancient Germanic *aula regia*, or the Anglo-Saxon *witenagemot* (Baker 1990, 20). As part of this forum the great nobles, barons and bishops convened to *parler* (from the French, to speak) with the king—hence the term *parliament*, which in England came to designate the assembly which discussed the most important matters of state with the king.[36]

Following the flourishing of cities in the late medieval period, this restricted body was expanded through the integration of representatives from the burgeoning urban bourgeoisie. The kings would seek to offset the nobility's considerable influence by simply admitting representatives from the cities into the royal *curia*, in accordance with the Roman legal principle that "what concerns all should be

[34] The age of estates was a period spanning from the thirteenth to the eighteenth century, during which monarchies ruled over societies dominated by orders, corps and bodies, corporations, colleges and societies, each with important duties and privileges. German historians have called this form of state *Ständestaat*. This vision of *Ancien Regime* society was clearly expressed by the *avocat du roi* Séguier, in a *lit de justice* (the most solemn session of a French Parlement) held on March 12, 1776, by Louis XVI at the *Parlement de Paris*: "The clergy, the nobility, the highest courts, the lower tribunals, the officers attached to these tribunals, the universities, the academies, the financial and commercial companies, all present, in all parts of the state, living bodies which one can consider as links in a great chain of which the first link is in the hands of Your Majesty, as head and highest administrator of all that makes up the body of the nation" (Myers 1975, 9 and 11).

[35] For a typology of these representative institutions, see Bulst (1996, 44–46).

[36] In this period, English did not exist as a unified language. Henry II of England (1154–1189) spoke essentially French, as a descendent of the French Normans who arrived in England in 1066, and Latin, which was the language of learned people and the only one used for writing official documents.

approved by all" (*quod omnes tangit, ab omnibus approbetur*) (Post 2008, 163–219), taken from the Justinian Code (C. 5, 59, 5, 3) (Ullmann 2009, 21–26).[37]

This marked a revolution. As there were so many city dwellers, not all could attend the meeting with the king, so they elected representatives. Thus did the "representative principle" appear for the first time, constituting a major contribution to western political organization (Post 1973, 92–102). It was not democracy, as the appointments were usually controlled by urban oligarchies, but it was a very important step towards it.

### *8.5.2 The Origins of the Representative Principle*

This crucial initiative of admitting city representatives into the royal *curiae*, was adopted for the first time in European history in Spain, specifically in the Kingdom of León. In 1188, King Alfonso IX summoned the representatives of cities, along with nobles and bishops, convening the first *cortes* in Spanish history (Procter 2010, 105–106). These state assemblies were so termed because they brought together the three *curiae*, or *cortes*,[38] representing the kingdom's most important "estates" or social groups.[39] The example spread to other European kingdoms thereafter. In Spain over the course of the thirteenth century, *cortes* took hold in Castile and the eastern kingdoms of the Crown of Aragon, in Catalonia, Aragon and Valencia.[40]

As shall be further discussed in Chap. 10, representatives from English cities came to form the Parliament of Westminster as of the late thirteenth century, while

[37] What would seem to be the Roman justification of the democratic principle was, in fact, taken out of context, as it does not refer to the organization of the state, but rather to the institution of judicial/private wardship. Its original technical meaning refers to that, for certain acts involving the administration of a minor's property, the consent of all those responsible for his wardship is required. About the misinterpretation of the phrase, see Hall (1972, 125–145); on the origins of the political use of the formula in medieval times, see Gouron (1989, 277–286); and on its development in Spain, see Maravall (1983, 175–190).

[38] Referring to the three courts or royal councils, made up of nobles, prelates and citizens, who met with him to reach decisions on crucial matters facing the kingdom.

[39] On the origins of the first estate-based assemblies in European history, see O'Callaghan (1969, 1503–1537) With reference to the role played by the representatives of the cities in the *Cortes de Castilla-León*, see Salcedo Izu (1980, 223–242).

[40] Specifically, the Catalonian, Aragonese and Valencian *cortes* were consolidated following the decisive episode of the Sicilian Vespers (1282), an anti-French rebellion which allowed Peter III of Aragon to take the island, angering Pope Martin IV, who excommunicated the Aragonese monarch on March 21, 1283 (Runciman 2012, 242–243). This, in turn, spurred France's Philip III to invade Catalonia. The weakened position which the Aragonese suffered made it possible for parties in Catalonia, Aragon and Valencia to force the king to convene their respective *cortes* at certain times of year. Thus, for example, at the *Cortes de Barcelona* in 1283 Peter III was obliged to accept the Catalonians' right to convene the *Cortes del País* and not to legislate without the intervention of Catalonia's estate-based assembly. Aragonians and Valencians immediately followed their example (Bisson 2003a, b, 88 and 98–99).

in France those from the cities made up the Estates General beginning in 1302, when Philip IV the Fair summoned them to ensure his political supremacy over and independence from the authority of Pope Boniface VIII.[41] In this way, little by little, the old royal *curiae* in the different European kingdoms gradually evolved into feudal assemblies, which approved the special outlays requested of them by the monarchs, as well as the most important legislation. This incorporation of the citizenry into the old royal *curiae* was crucial because members of the urban class were appointed or elected and, therefore, served as representatives, by virtue of which they were declared deputies. This constituted another essential advance, as subjects came to exercise control over royal power.[42]

One must keep in mind that among the contingent or "estate" of citizens there were "jurists" who had been educated at European universities (*noblesse de robe*), mostly proceeding from the lesser nobility or the urban bourgeoisie, in the tradition of Roman law, where they studied the texts compiled by Justinian, which served to bolster royal power from a legal point of view (Post 1943, 211–232). The substantial reception of Justinian's law and the unrestricted dominance of the academically-trained jurist appointed by a sovereign (Wieacker 1981, 259) became an effective instrument to rein in the privileged classes which had dominated feudal society.

Medieval assemblies, however, were not democratic, at least not by any modern standard. They generally presented a tripartite structure, ideally featuring late medieval society's three estates: the nobility, the clergy, and a third group, usually composed of representatives of the cities. This structure favored the privileged classes, as the clergy and nobility tended to vote in unison, united against the urban representatives. Nevertheless, the tripartite structure could vary. Some assemblies featured a fourth division through which the peasants had their own set of representatives, or in which the nobles were divided into two distinct feudal bodies, as occurred in Spain in the *Cortes del Reino de Aragón*.[43]

[41] On the origins of the first gatherings of these assemblies during Philip IV's reign, see Bisson (1972, 537–564).

[42] Initially, the cities sent representatives to the *États Généraux*, designated directly by the town council or the mayor. Nevertheless, the situation changed upon the decline of political feudalism, and beginning in 1468 real elections were held, with electors voting to choose their corporative representatives. Henceforth the city representatives elected had an imperative mandate, having to obey the instructions received from their electors (Desrayaud 1996, 425–427). For an overview of medieval parliamentarian practice in England, see Cam (1953, 11–26).

[43] As González Antón (1975, 437–438) points out, initially there was only one estate for nobility. Nevertheless, as the kings of Aragon gained power the Aragonese nobles went to the *cortes* divided into two "arms" (*brazos*): the high nobility belonged to the one made up of the barons (*barones*) and "wealthy men" (*ricoshombres*), while the low nobility joined the group of knights (*caballeros*), nobles (*hidalgos*) and gentlemen (*infanzones*). In this way the Aragonese nobility controlled 50 % of the assembly. As nobles usually voted with the clergy, the representatives of the cities had their political influence reduced to one fourth. More recently VanLandingham (2002, 96–100).

The English Parliament was special, though, as it was composed of only two assemblies: the House of Lords and the House of Commons, which from the outset meant that the privileged classes only controlled half the body. The House of Lords was the prolongation of the old *curia regis*, and in it the great lords and high-ranking prelates continued to meet. The House of Commons was formed during the last third of the thirteenth century when representatives elected by small land-owners and the urban bourgeoisie began to enter Parliament. As a consequence of the outbreak of the Hundred Years War, the kings of England required large sums of money and, to this end, more frequently convened Parliament. Thus, by the mid-fourteenth century the structure of the English Parliament—which came to be permanently headquartered not in London, but in the neighboring city of Westminster—was consolidated with its characteristic bipartite structure and its full political power (Edward 1968, 141–154).

The purviews of these assemblies of the estates were diverse. Initially, their role was to provide the king with money when the Crown's traditional revenue was inadequate—a situation that became increasingly common as the monarchy's regular and non-recurrent expenses grew greater and greater.[44] Constitutionally this was a great advance, as by the end of the thirteenth century the principle that taxation required the assent of the House of the Commons was established, for instance, in the English Parliament, which sparked protest from the nobles (Harris 1975, 66), jealous or their prerogatives. In 1340, Edward III ended up conceding that no taxation should be imposed without the Commons' consent. From a historical standpoint we can say that current budget laws represent the most important legislation that national parliaments approve, despite the fact that in modern, contemporary states tax revenues are constantly being collected anyway.

In return for providing their financial support parliaments tended to lodge specific requests with the king, with whose approval they became law.[45] This was the origin of the legislative function that these assemblies would play as of the late medieval period, a principle that would be defended by the great medieval jurist Bartolus (1313–1357), when he argued that the state was its own prince (*civitas sibi princeps*) and could legislate "as it pleases" (*prous sibi placet*) on any matter affecting the public weal, with the crucial consequence that, according to him, legislative sovereignty relied on a "free people" possessing all law-creating capabilities through its popular assembly (Ullmann 2010, 284). This doctrine explains

[44] For an overview of the role of these representative medieval assemblies in the creation of national taxation systems, see Ertman (1999, 59–73).

[45] In England, between 1310 and 1327, the Commons began to present petitions and fashion them into a series of articles. In the following decade presentations of comprehensive sets of articles became frequent (Harris 1975, 118). By 1348 it was said that laws were made by the king with the assent of the peers and commons, but the need for consent by the House of Commons to all legislation was not established beyond doubt until after 1400, as it remained possible for the House of Lords to introduce variations when assenting to petitions from the Commons. In 1407, Henry IV recognized that the proper legislative procedure was for the Lords and Commons to debate propositions as separate houses, and only when they agreed should the matter be submitted to the king for his approval. Ever since Parliamentary legislation requires separate consent by the king, the Lords and the Commons (Baker 1990, 235). Also, Levy (2009, 199–201).

why, for instance, in Castile, a kingdom that can be considered the oldest consolidated European state, in the first half of the fourteenth century the *Cortes* passed laws (*ordenamientos*)[46] which, beginning in 1348, prevailed over local customary local law.[47]

In some cases, the assemblies of the estates also claimed judicial authorities, as was the case with the English Parliament, which continued to be regarded as a "high court", with the difference relative to other courts being that its acts were not tied to the course of common law; its judgments were not *inter partes*, but bound everyone on the medieval principle that, as all the estates were represented in Parliament, everyone was "privy" to its acts. By the middle of the fourteenth century, however, all the judicial work of Parliament had been assumed by the House of Lords, as Parliament's legislative or deliberative function was distinguished, while it shed any contentious or judicative ones (Baker 1990, 238).

The exercise of these functions afforded the assemblies of the estates an undeniable political significance because of the fact that they discussed major domestic and foreign policy issues with the king. Their political clout, however, varied greatly. In England it became decisive in the Late Middle Ages, especially after the defeat of the English monarchy in the Hundred Years War and the debacle for the nobles following the War of the Roses, as the Westminster Parliament played a decisive role in the civil war between the House of York and the House of Lancaster, which led to the crowning of a new King of England. To explain, in 1327 the English Parliament forced Edward II to abdicate in favor of his son, Edward III, thereby imposing its will and effecting a change of monarch. The War of the Roses, by pitting two powerful rival forces against each other vying for the crown, had the effect of bolstering the power and prestige of the English Parliament, which served as the arbiter ending the conflict and ushering in a new royal dynasty: the Tudors, under King Henry VII.

In France, the Estates General, however, would prove anemic compared to the robust English Parliament. It would not meet regularly, but only when the monarchy found itself in a bind and needed to call upon it. As Strayer (1980, 384) has indicated, the Estates were not convoked by the king with the idea of obtaining formal approval of his initiatives. Rather, these assemblies were "exercises in propaganda, not in constitutionalism". As long as there were enough people from enough regions to ensure that information about the reasons for the royal decision would be disseminated widely, it did not matter which individuals attended or what communities were represented. This is why the French Estates General did not take

[46] The Spanish term *ordenamiento* conveys two important meanings: laws that were organized (*ordenadas*) into chapters, and which were also issued by the king. In Castile, during this period, the word referred to important laws, approved by the king and the *cortes*. These were "*normas pactadas*" (pact-based laws) established through agreement and consensus, not issued unilaterally by the king. *Ordenamientos* were in Castile the ordinary way of legislating in the fourteenth century.

[47] Royal legislation prevailed officially in Castile over local customs ever since the agreement reached by King Alfonso XI in the *Cortes de Alcalá de Henares* in 1348, was incorporated into the *Ordenamiento de Alcalá*, an essential law that became the base of the Castilian legal system and that Otero (1993–1994, 475) considers a "constitutional" change.

part in the legislative process.[48] Thus, throughout the entire *Ancien Regime*, it did not become a regular organ of government. To an extent, this fact would lie at the root of the French Revolution centuries later.

On the Iberian Peninsula, the political importance of the *cortes* varied. In Castile, they only acquired a certain relevance in the fourteenth century. However, during the fifteenth century the *cortes* suffered a clear decline, growing more pronounced in the following two centuries. In contrast, in the kingdoms of the eastern peninsula, until the late Middle Ages forming part of the Crown of Aragon, the *cortes* boasted undeniable political power, largely maintained after their integration into the Spanish Monarchy, until their abolition by Philip V at the beginning of the eighteenth century.[49] *Las Cortes de Navarra*, in contrast, were not very active during medieval times, but would become extraordinarily important after the conquest of the kingdom by Ferdinand the Catholic in 1512, and its integration into the Spanish Catholic Monarchy.

In these eastern Spanish kingdoms, pact-making would be reinforced by another essential institution, the *Diputación del General*, which arose when the *cortes*, upon being dissolved, named permanent delegates representing the kingdom (*el General*) before the king.[50] In the kingdom of Aragon, mention must be made of the

[48] As Timbal and Castaldo (1985, 292–294) point out, initially it was far more difficult for the king of France to impose his legislation than his justice, as he had lost the power to legislate during the feudal period. The king could not alter the political and social order created by God. Rather, he could only maintain it through the exercise of justice, and the only compulsory rules he could issue were privileges given to individuals or communities, but not general prescripts. At the end of the twelfth century, the kings began to legislate again, but until the reign of Saint Louis (1226–1270), they required the assent of their barons to do so. In the fourteenth century the kings' legislative power was reinforced as they could enact laws following the deliberations of a king's council and the involvement of the Estates General was not required to create law. Only the French parlements, as the realm's superior courts of justice, were engaged in the legislative process; to enact and implement laws the parlements had to register or record them, a powerful function which they wielded.

[49] For a comparison of the *cortes* of the Crown of Aragón to that of Castile, see González Antón (1989, 633–676) and Payne (1994, 141–172).

[50] Thus, the government of the Autonomous Community of Catalonia continues today to be called the *Generalitat de Cataluña*. The *Diputación del General* appeared in Catalonia in the mid fourteenth century. Its original function was to control the use of the taxes agreed to with the king and assure that he complied with everything agreed to in the sessions of the *cortes* while these were not in session. Over time, however, the *Generalitat* evolved into the representative body of the people before the king, and soon was able to raise armies and organize fleets for the service of the crown. With the arrival of the new Trastamara Dynasty to the Crown of Aragon, the *Generalitat* assumed a role as a defender of Catalonian liberties. Fernando I, in the *cortes* of 1413, recognized it as a body permanently representing the Principality when the *cortes* were not operating, and their right to enforce the observance of Catalonian laws (O'Callaghan 1975, 591). In 1460, they rebelled against John II, and until a royal victory in 1472, the *Generalitat* basically governed Catalonia. Since 1978 this tradition of pacts has constituted the basis legitimizing Catalonian autonomy, cited by and inspiring the region's separatists. For a recent analysis of this "representative" tradition in eastern Spain, focusing on a critical approach to the exaggerated influence of the legacy of pact-making (*pactismo*) in modern Catalonian separatism, see Hargreaves (2000, 96–112). The *Diputación* as an institution was introduced in Aragón in 1412, and in Valencia in 1419. In the Kingdom of Navarra it was created in the fifteenth century, but did not became a permanent institution until 1501.

particular institution of the *Justicia de Aragón*, which became an essential pillar of Aragon pact-based government, as it boasted a function similar to that of today's constitutional courts).[51]

## 8.6 A King Subject to the Law

From what we have seen it can be most clearly observed that the power of late medieval sovereigns was bound by significant limitations in their submission to the law.

This idea that the kings were obliged to respect the law gained ground after the rediscovery of Roman law, which was once again studied in European universities beginning in the late eleventh century. Significantly, the Englishman Henry Bracton (d. 1268), one of the first jurists to codify common law (Bracton 1997), expressly placed the king *sub Deo et sub lege* (under God and the Law) (Loughlin 2010, 40). Similarly, Accursio, the author of the *Magna Glossa*, and one of the leading scholars of Justinian's *Corpus Juris Civilis*, believed that the emperor was compelled to obey the law, even though there was nobody empowered to judge imperial infractions under the ancient Roman Empire. In this manner, at least theoretically, the idea that the law could limit the king's authority began to take shape, without any doubt setting the stage for what we know as the modern-day "rule of law" (Caenegem 1995, 89).

Strayer (1971, 209) has described one of the most important kings of France, Philip the Fair (1285–1314), as a "constitutional king", as the monarch strove to conform to the traditions of the French monarchy and the practices of the French government, endeavoring to stay within the letter of the law and observe the customs of the kingdom. Moreover, when he had to act outside of established custom he always sought to justify his action and obtain the consent of those affected. This is why the monarch convened the Estates General to explain his policies toward Boniface VIII and the Templars, for example, or sought approval for unusual taxes, reflecting the king's desire to recognize legal limitations.

---

[51] Initially, the *Justicia Mayorde Aragón* was a lord appointed by the Aragonian nobles to defend them in their dealings with the king. Over time it morphed into the institution which guaranteed that the king did not violate laws passed by the *Cortes de Aragón*, which could nullify royal laws conflicting with agreed ("pactist") legislation (García de Valdeavellano 1973, 571). In this way, the *Justicias Mayores* played an essential role in the development of Aragonian law, also featuring a special jurisdiction to which Aragonians who did not wish to be judged under royal jurisdiction could turn, as the sentences (*observancias*) of the tribunal of the *Justicia Mayor* had the same validity as laws approved by the *Cortes*.

## 8.7 Europe's First "Constitutional" Texts?

While Strayer's contention might be somewhat anachronistic if we assign the term "constitutional" its broadest meaning, it is a fair description of the legal positions of medieval kings. The term "constitution" has a range of meanings. Among these, it may refer, in a broad sense, to the way in which states are constituted, established, organized and governed. More narrowly, it may refer to the written document which sets out the fundamental principles governing the exercise of authority. In this sense, "constitutionalism" represents a legal tradition which, as we have seen, dates back to the feudal period, based on the idea that the exercise of political power should be subject to a fundamental pact entered into between rulers and the ruled to protect the latter's rights and define the former's tasks and authorities.

Therefore, although "constitutionalism" tends to be a term used in relation to the era of the liberal state when, based on the premises prevailing in the French Revolution (1789–1799), most European nation-states accepted nineteenth century constitutional texts as their legal bases, in reality the constitutional principle, understood as a legal text circumscribing royal power, is one which appeared in the Late Middle Ages. In fact, it emerged as a reaction to the substantial increase in kings' power and a way to protect subjects and their property from potentially arbitrary actions by the crown.[52]

These documents were solemnly agreed to between the monarch and his subjects, such as the decrees approved under the initiative of Alfonso IX of León at the Cortes of 1188, which has been called the "León Carta Magna" (Arias 1948, 147–149) because in it the king promised the representatives of his kingdom that he would not wage war, declare peace, or make important decisions without the consent of the bishops, nobles and leading men of the cities, whose advice was to inform the king's conduct (Bisson 2009, 531).[53] The Integration of Christian Spain

[52] As Reynolds (2012, XII, 11–12) suggests, there was a common tendency in late medieval Europe to grant liberties to all free men in different kingdoms. The English charters, such as the Magna Carta, certainly contain provisions that protect those outside the nobility, but so do the German charters of 1231–2, Philip IV of France's reform ordinance of 1303, and his son's charters of 1315. The fact that the German charters are now considered constitutions in favor of princes, the 1303 document is called an ordinance, and that the charters of 1315 are said to have been granted to leagues of nobles, say more about the difference between national historiographical traditions than about the documents' contents. All of them, including the Magna Carta, concentrate first on the grievances of important people, but all go on to include others, as kings were supposed to look after the humble as well as the great, and the powerful were supposed to represent and speak up for the humble. For an overview of the constitutional value of medieval law Kern (2012, 149–206).

[53] "In the name of God. When I held a *cortes* at León with the archbishop and the bishops and magnates of my kingdom, and with the citizens chosen from every city, I Alfonso, King of León and Galicia, established and confirmed with an oath that I would preserve for all the inhabitants of my kingdom, whether clergy or laity, the good customs which they enjoy, as established by my predecessors. I promised also that I would not make war or peace or treaties, except with the counsel of the bishops, the nobles and the 'good men' *by whose counsel I ought to rule*". Cited by Wilkinson (1972, 55). The best study on this essential text in Spanish medieval legal history is that by Fernández Catón (1993).

into Europe: The Role of Alfonso VI of León-Castile. In *Santiago, St.-Denis and Saint Peter*, pp. 101–120.

The best known of this class of documents which we might call "protoconstitutional" was the *Magna Carta Libertatum* (Great Charter of Freedoms) or simply the "Magna Carta", a document by which the English nobility, backed by the City of London and the Church in 1215, imposed themselves upon King John of England (John Lackland) for having suffered serious defeats to Philip Augustus of France and to Pope Innocent III, which resulted in major territorial losses.[54] The importance of the Magna Carta lies not so much in its specific content, but rather in the importance it had for the constitutional history of England itself, as it was successively confirmed by the kings of England,[55] and its influence on the American Revolution and the forging of the United States of America (Linebaugh 2008, 119–143). Moreover, as Holt (1985, 289–307) points out, the Magna Carta was a stepping stone in English legal history, as it established the pattern for legislation by statute. It was the first English statute, paving the way for the subsequent development of statute law.

In another "pact-based" monarchy, that of the Crown of Aragon, worthy of mention are the *Privilegios de la Unión* which the Aragonese nobility imposed upon Alfonso III in the *Cortes de Zaragoza* in 1288, taking advantage of the king's political weakness at the time (González Antón 1975, I, 201–214). This was a dynamic which the *unionistas* (nobles integrated into a union which limited the kings power) had begun during the previous reign of Peter III, seizing upon this monarch's excommunication because of the conquest of Sicily, carried out against the wishes of the pope, which had prompted the King of France, Philip III, the Bold, to invade Catalonia (Runciman 2012, 257–258).[56] In general in the Crown of Aragon this *avant la lettre* "constitutionalism" (González Antón 1986, 1017–1041) would eventually become consolidated in the Late Middle Ages as "pactism" in the kingdoms of Aragon, Valencia, Mallorca, Sicily and Naples, and the County of Barcelona (Piña Homs 2007, 333–370)—the latter a "constitutional" regime that preserved its historical constitutions almost intact, despite being integrated into the Spanish Crown after the death of Ferdinand the Catholic (1516).

---

[54] On the "crisis" that led to the Magna Carta, see Bisson (2009, 515–526). Also, McKechnie (2005, 3–47).

[55] In 1225 Henry III confirmed the Magna Carta, though with some substantial changes. This version was confirmed in 1297 by Edward I and became a statute (Linebaugh 2008, 272). According to the English jurist Edward Coke (1552–1634) the Magna Carta was confirmed 32 times. On Coke's interpretation of this crucial constitutional document, see Pocock (2008, 44–45).

[56] Peter III's excommunication for conquering Sicily in 1282 led to Phillip III the Bold's invasion of Catalonia, in an attempt to take it with the pope's blessing. The French occupation was a failure, yet the disorder created was seized upon by Aragonian and Catalonians to rise up and impose severe limitations upon his power, including the obligation to convene the *cortes* at regular intervals. These limitations were placed in writing in the abovementioned 1288 *Privilegios de la Unión*.

Absolute monarchy, of course, which as a political model first appeared in Spain, specifically in Castile, in the late fourteenth century, would tend to curtail the authority of these estate-based assemblies, which were overpowered by sovereigns who could unilaterally modify the legislation passed by the *cortes* (González Alonso 1980, 469–488).[57] An exception, however, came in England, where Parliament was able to curb royal prerogatives as of the mid seventeenth century, and in the Spanish kingdoms under the Crown of Aragon, until the early eighteenth century, when the political organization of these kingdoms was abolished by the Nueva Planta Decrees.[58]

## TIMELINE

### Twelfth Century

| | |
|---|---|
| 1118 | Alfonso I, the Battler, recaptures Zaragoza. |
| 1122 | The Concordat of Worms. The investiture conflict between the popes and emperors is resolved. |
| 1125 | Death of Irnerius (circa 1050), founder of the School of Glossators (The University of Bologna). |
| 1129 | The Order of the Temple, the first Christian military order receives papal recognition. It had been created at the Temple of Jerusalem by the French knight Hughes Payns to protect Christian pilgrims in the Holy Land. |
| 1137 | A personal union is forged between the Kingdom of Aragon and the County of Barcelona (Petronila and Ramón Berenguer IV). |
| 1140 | Gratian completes his *Decretum* (*Concordia discordantium canonum*). |
| 1147 | Alfonso Enriques reconquers Lisbon. |
| 1152–1190 | Reign of Emperor Frederick I Barbarossa. With him the Holy German Roman Empire enjoys ones of its greatest eras. |
| 1154–1189 | Reign of Henry II of England. Creator of the legal system of "Common Law" through the creation of royal courts and important legislative reforms (Constitutions of Clarendon, 1164). |
| 1162 | Alfonso II of Aragon—I of Barcelona—(d. 1196) becomes the King of Aragon, and simultaneously the Count of Barcelona. |

[57] As of the fifteenth century the kings of Castile were empowered to create laws called *pragmáticas*, which had the same validity as legislation approved by the *cortes*. The Castilian monarchs were the first kings in Europe able to unilaterally create legislation (Iglesia Ferreiros 1977, 115–198).

[58] As VanLandingham (2002, 12) points out, the universal medieval obstacles to centralization were in full force in the Crown of Aragon, as the nobles, particularly in Aragon, were powerful and fractious; the towns, especially in Catalonia and Valencia, were rich and well-endowed with privileges; and representative assemblies were more advanced than nearly anywhere else.

| | |
|---|---|
| 1170 | Henry II of England orders the assassination of Thomas Beckett, Archbishop of Canterbury, for opposing royal power. |
| 1185 | The death of Alfonso I Henriques, founder of the Portuguese monarchy. |
| 1187 | Saladin recaptures Jerusalem from the Crusaders. |
| 1188 | Alfonso IX convenes the *cortes* in León. It is the first time in European history that a meeting of the *curiae* is attended by representatives of the bourgeoisie. It is the first assembly of estates. |
| 1198–1216 | Papacy of Innocent III, the Pope attaining the greatest political influence in the history of Christendom. |

**Thirteenth Century**

| | |
|---|---|
| 1208 | Innocent III preaches for a crusade against the Albigenses. |
| 1215–1250 | Reign of Frederick II, the last of the Emperors of the Holy Roman Empire. |
| 1215 | The English nobility imposes the Magna Carta on John Lackland. |
| 1216 | Foundation of the Dominican Order by St. Dominic of Guzmán (1170–1221). Its members would be the first inquisitors. |
| 1218 | Alfonso IX of León founds the University of Salamanca, the first university on the Iberian Peninsula. |
| 1229 | Jaime I, the Conqueror, begins his conquest of Mallorca. |
| 1230 | Fernando III definitively unites the kingdoms of Castile and Aragon. |
| 1234 | The collection of Decretals is promulgated, compiled by Raymond of Peñafort. |
| 1236 | Ferdinand III conquers Cordoba. |
| 1238 | Jaime I, the Conqueror, takes Valencia. |
| 1246 | Ferdinand III of Castile and Leon conquers Seville. |
| 1250 | Accursio completes the Magna Glossa. |
| 1252–1284 | Reign of Alfonso X, the Wise, of Castile. |
| 1264 | For the first time representatives of the cities enter the British Parliament after the victory of Simon de Montfort at Lewes over the royal troops. |
| 1270 | St. Louis of France dies in St. John of Acre (Palestine). End of the Crusades. |
| 1272–1307 | Reign of Edward I of England, who strengthens royal power by relying on the cities as allies against the great nobility. |
| 1276 | July 27. Death of Jaime I, the Conqueror. By creating the Kingdom of Valencia as an autonomous kingdom and integrating it into the Union of Catalonia and Aragon, he founds the Crown of Aragon. Mallorca would be an independent kingdom until 1349. |
| 1279 | The reign of Dionis I of Portugal begins (d. 1357). His long rule represents the zenith of the Portuguese branch of the House of Burgundy. |

| | |
|---|---|
| 1282 | March 31. Anti-French Rebellion of the Sicilian Vespers. This would be the pretext for Pedro III of Aragon's occupation of the island. |
| 1285–1314 | Philip IV (the Fair) of France becomes the first king to directly defy the Pope: Boniface VIII (1294–1303). |

## Fourteenth Century

| | |
|---|---|
| 1302 | First meeting of the French Estates General, convened by Philip IV, who asks for aid to fight against the pope. |
| 1303 | The attack at Anagni. French troops arrest Pope Boniface VIII. |
| 1305–1377 | Transfer of the papal seat from Rome to Avignon (Avignon Captivity). |
| 1328 | Death of the last Capet. The election of the Valois (1328–1498) triggers a dynastic conflict will be the pretext for Edward III of England's initiation of the Hundred Years War. |
| 1339 | Start of the Hundred Years War with the invasion of France by Edward III (1327–1377). |
| 1340 | Battle of Río Salado. The victory of Alfonso XI of Castile definitively blocks the advance of North African Muslims. |
| 1348 | Serious outbreak of the Black Plague in Europe. Adoption of the Ordinance of Alcalá in Castile. |
| 1350 | The House of Commons arises in the Westminster Parliament. |
| 1357 | Bartolo Sassoferrato dies (b. 1313), the leading glossator. |
| 1358 | Death of Etienne Marcel, the leader of the Paris merchants who had rebelled against King Charles V of France, imposing the Great Ordinance on him. |
| 1369 | After defeating and killing his brother, Peter I, in Montiel, Henry II rises to the Castilian throne, founding the new Dynasty of Trastamara. |
| 1385 | 6 April. *Las Cortes de Coimbra* recognize John I as King of Portugal. August 14. Battle of Aljubarrota. John I of Castile fails in his attempt to occupy Portugal. |

## Fifteenth Century

| | |
|---|---|
| 1400 | Baldus de Ubaldis dies (born 1327) one of the most famous glossators. |
| 1412 | Compromise of Caspe. After the death without heirs of Martin I, Ferdinand I of Trastamara is elected the King of the Crown of Aragon. In Castile and Aragon the same dynasty reigns. |
| 1417 | With the election of Martin V the Western Schism comes to a close, initiated after the death of Gregory XI in 1387. |
| 1420 | Treaty of Troyes. King Henry V of England claims almost all of France. |
| 1429 | Joan of Arc takes Orleans, allowing King Charles VII to be named King of France in Reims. |

1431 Joan of Arc dies at the stake.
1453 Capture of Constantinople by the Ottoman Turks. The fall of the Western Empire, created in 395.
1455 In England the War of the Roses (House of York vs. House of Lancaster) begins, a 30-year conflict which will erode the power of the nobility and bolster that of the Parliament.
1460 Death of Henry the Navigator (born 1394), architect of Portugal's maritime expansion.
1461 Death of Charles VII, King of France from 1422. During his reign he manages to drive the English from France and end the Hundred Years War.
1469 Isabella of Castile and Ferdinand, Prince of Aragon, are married in Valladolid, becoming the "Catholic Kings".
1474 Beginning of the reign of Ferdinand and Isabella.
1477 Death of Charles the Bold, the last independent Duke of Burgundy. His disappearance is essential for the unification of France under Louis XI (1461–1483).
1478 The Catholic Kings receive papal permission to create their own tribunal: the Spanish Inquisition.
1479 Beginning of the reign of Ferdinand the Catholic in the Crown of Aragon. The personal union of Castile and Aragon under the Catholic Kings is forged.
1481 Start of the War of Granada. It would last until January 1492.
1485 End of the War of the Roses. Henry VII rises to the English throne, the first monarch of the Tudor Dynasty, inaugurating a century of royal absolutism in England.
1487 Bartholomew Diaz discovers the Cape of Good Hope.
1492 January 2. The Catholic Kings enter Granada. End of the Reconquest.
March 31. In Granada the Catholic Kings sign the decree expelling the Jews from Spain.
October 12. Christopher Columbus discovers America.

## References

Agamben, G. (2011). The kingdom and the government. In *The kingdom and the glory: For a theological genealogy of economy and government* (pp. 68–106). Stanford, CA: Stanford University Press.

Aguilera-Barchet, B. (1998). La figura constitucional del Príncipe de Asturias. In *La figura del Príncipe de Asturias en la Corona de España* (pp. 11–43). Madrid: Dykinson.

Albert, P. (2002). *The customs of Catalonia between Lords and Vassals. A practical guide to castle feudalism in medieval Spain.* Tempe, AR: Arizona Center for Medieval and Renaissance Studies.

Anderson, P. (2006). *Passages from antiquity to feudalism.* London: Verso.

Arias, I. A. (1948). La carta magna leonesa. *Cuadernos de Historia de España,* (9), 147–153.

Baker, J. H. (1990). *An introduction to English legal history* (3rd ed.). London: Butterworths.
Baldwin, J. W. (1991). *The government of Philip Augustus: Foundations of French royal power in the Middle Ages*. Berkeley, CA: University of California Press.
Bisson, T. N. (1972). The general Assemblies of Philip the Fair. *Studia Gratiana, XV*, 537–564.
Bisson, T. N. (2003a). *The medieval crown of Aragon: A short history*. Oxford: Oxford University Press.
Bisson, T. N. (2003b). The general assemblies of Philip the Fair: Their character reconsidered. In *Medieval France and her Pyrenean neighbours: Studies in early institutional history* (pp. 97–122). London: Continuum.
Bisson, T. N. (2009). *The crisis of the twelfth century: Power, lordship, and the origins of European government*. Princeton, NJ: Princeton University Press.
Bown, S. R. (2012). *1494: How a family feud in medieval Spain divided the world in half*. New York: Thomas Dunne Books.
Bulst, N. (1996). Rulers, representative institutions and their members as power elites: Rivals or partners? In W. Reinhard (Ed.), *Power, elites and state building. The origins of the modern state in Europe, 13th–18th centuries* (pp. 41–58). Oxford: Clarendon.
Cam, H. M. (1953). Theory and practice of representation in medieval England. *History, 38*, 11–26.
Cazelles, R. (1965). Etienne Marcel au sein de la haute bourgeoisie d'affaires. *Journal des savants,* (1), 413–427.
Corteguera, L. (2002). *For the common good: Popular politics in Barcelona, 1580–1640*. Ithaca, NY: Cornell University Press.
Cowan, E. J. (2002). *For freedom alone: The declaration of Arbroath, 1320*. East Linton: Tuckwell Press.
David, M. (1951). *Le serment du sacre du IXe au XVe siècle: Contribution à l'étude des limites juridiques de la souveraineté*. Strasbourg: Palais de l'Université.
Dawson, J. P. (1968). The formative period of English case Law. In *The oracles of the law* (pp. 1–6). New York, NY: Legal Classics Library (Reprint).
de Bracton, H. (1997). *De legibus et consuetudinibus Angliae: On the laws and customs of England* (4 vols.). Buffalo, NY: W.S. Hein.
Desrayaud, A. (1996). *Cours d'Histoire du Droit Public: Des invasions barbares jusqu'à la Ré volution*. Saint Maur: Éditions Novelles.
Dollinger, P. (1970). *The German Hansa*. Stanford, CA: Stanford University Press.
Duby, G. (2000). *France in the Middle Ages, 987–1460: From Hugh Capet to Joan of Arc*. Oxford: Wiley-Blackwell.
Earenfight, T. (2010). *The king's other body: Maria of Castile and the crown of Aragon*. Philadelphia, PA: University of Pennsylvania Press.
Edward, J. G. (1968). The plena potestas of English parliamentary representatives. In J. E. A. Jolliffe (Ed.), *Oxford essays in medieval history presented to Herbert Edward Salter* (pp. 141–154). Freeport, NY: Books for Libraries Press.
Ertman, T. (1999). *Birth of the leviathan: Building states and regimes in medieval and early modern Europe*. Cambridge, UK: Cambridge University Press (Reprint).
Espinas, G. (1947). Le privilège de Saint-Omer de 1127. *Revue du Nord,* (29), 43–48.
Fedou, R. (1977). *El Estado en la Edad Media*. Madrid: EDAF Universitaria.
Fernández Catón, J. M. (1993). *La Curia regia de León de 1188 y sus "decreta" y constitución*. León: Centro de estudios e investigación "San Isidoro".
Ferran i Planas, E. (2006). *El jurista Pere Albert i les "Commemoracions"*. Barcelona: Institut d'Estudis Catalans.
Flórez, E., & Risco, M. (1793). Ramiro III. In *España Sagrada: Theatro geographico-historico de la Iglesia de España. Origen, divisiones, y limites de todas sus provincias. Antiguedad, tradaciones, y estado antiguo, y presente de sus sillas, con varias dissertaciones criticas* (pp. 276–277). Madrid: Imprenta de Blas Román, Volume XXXVIII. Trat. LXXVI. Appendix IV.

Font Rius, J. M. (1985). El procès de formació de las Costums de Tortosa. In *Estudis sobre els Drets i institucions locals en la Catalunya medieval* (pp. 141–162). Barcelona: Universitat de Barcelona.

Frassetto, M. (2003). *Encyclopedia of Barbarian Europe: Society in transformation*. Santa Barbara, CA: ABC-CLIO.

García de Valdeavellano, L. (1973). *Curso de Historia de las Instituciones españolas. De los orígenes al final de la Edad Media*. Madrid: Revista de Occidente.

García de Valdeavellano, L. (1986). Fueros municipales. In G. Bleiberg (Dir.), *Diccionario de Historia de España* (pp. 1188–1191). Madrid: Alianza Editorial (Reprint).

García Gallo, A. (1956). Aportación al estudio de los fueros. *Anuario de Historia del Derecho Español,* (26), 388–398.

Garriga, C. (1994). *Las Audiencias y las Chancillerías castellanas. Historia política, régimen jurídico y práctica institucional (1371–1525)*. Madrid: Centro de Estudios Constitucionales.

Goffart, W. (1963). The Fredegar problem reconsidered. *Speculum: A Journal of Medieval Studies, 38*(2), 206–241.

González Alonso, B. (1980). La fórmula 'obedézcase pero no se cumpla' en el Derecho castellano de la Baja Edad Media. *Anuario de Historia del Derecho Español,* (50), 469–488.

González Antón, L. (1975). *Las Uniones aragonesas y las Cortes del Reino: (1283–1301)*. Zaragoza: C.S.I.C.

González Antón, L. (1986). La Corona de Aragón: régimen político y cortes. Entre el mito y la revisión historiográfica. *Anuario de Historia del Derecho,* (56), 1017–1042.

González Antón, L. (1989). Cortes de Aragón y Cortes de Castilla en el Antiguo Régimen. In *Las Cortes de Castilla y León en la Edad Moderna: actas de la segunda etapa del Congreso Científico sobre la historia de las Cortes de Castilla y León...* (pp. 633–676). Valladolid: Cortes de Castilla y León.

Gouron, A. (1989). Aux origines médiévales de la maxime quod omnes tangit. In J. L. Harouel (Dir.), *Histoire du droit social: Mélanges en hommage à Jean lmbert* (pp. 277–286). Paris: Presses universitaires de France.

Grant, L. (1998). *Abbot Suger of St. Denis: Church and state in early twelfth-century France*. Essex, UK: Addison Wesley Longman Limited.

Guenée, B. (1981). *Politique et histoire au moyen âge*. Paris: Publications de la Sorbonne.

Guénée, B. (1985). *States and rulers in later medieval Europe*. Oxford, UK: Basil Blackwell.

Hall, E. (1972). King Henry III and the English reception of the Roman law maxim quod omnes tangit. In J. R. Strayer & D. E. Queller (Eds.), *Post Scripta: Essays on medieval law and the emergence of the European state in honor of Gaines Post* (pp. 125–146). Rome: Librería Ateneo Salesiano.

Hallam, E. M., & Everard, J. (2001). *Capetian France: (987–1328)* (2nd ed.). Harlow, UK: Pearson Education Limited.

Hargreaves, J. (2000). *Freedom for Catalonia?: Catalan nationalism, Spanish Identity and the Barcelona Olympic Games*. Cambridge: Cambridge University Press.

Harris, G. L. (1975). *King, parliament, and public finance in medieval England to 1369*. Oxford, UK: Clarendon.

Holt, J. C. (1985). *Magna Carta and medieval government* (2nd ed.). Cambridge: Cambridge University Press.

Huet, V. (1999). Napoleon I: A new Augustus? In C. Edwards (Ed.), *Roman presences: Receptions of Rome in European culture, 1789–1945* (pp. 53–69). Cambridge: Cambridge University Press.

Hughes, R. (2011). The old city. In *Barcelona* (pp. 55–252). New York: Knopf Doubleday Pu.

Iglesia Ferreiros, A. (1971). Las cortes de Zamora de 1274 y los casos de corte. *Anuario de Historia del Derecho,* (41), 945–971.

Iglesia Ferreiros, A. (1977). Derecho municipal, derecho señorial, derecho regio. *Historia, Instituciones, Documentos,* (4), 115–198.

Jackson, R. A. (1984). *Vive le Roi! A history of the French Coronation from Charles V to Charles X*. Chapel Hill: University of North Carolina Press.

Jones, C. (2007). *Eclipse of Empire?: Perceptions of the Western Empire and its rulers in Late Medieval France*. Turnhout: Brepols.

Kagay, D. J. (2007). The kings right must be preferred to the lord's sovereignty and suzerainty in the treatises of Pere Albert. In *War, government, and society in the medieval crown of Aragon* (pp. 693–703). Aldershot, UK: Ashgate.

Kern, F. (2012). Law and constitution in the Middle Ages. In *Kingship and law in the Middle Ages: Studies* (pp. 149–206). Clark, NJ: The Lawbook Exchange.

Ladero Quesada, M. Á. (1997). Poderes públicos en la Europa medieval: (Principados, Reinos y Coronas). In *XXIII Semana de Estudios Medievales* (pp. 19–68). Pamplona: Gobierno de Navarra.

Le Goff, J. (2006). *Marchands et banquiers du Moyen Âge*. Paris: P.U.F.

Lemarignier, J.-F. (1965). *Le gouvernement royal aux premiers temps capétiens (987–1108)*. Paris: Editions A. et J. Picard.

Levy, J. T. (2009). Not So *Novus* an *Ordo*: Constitutions without social contracts. *Political Theory, 37*(2), 191–217.

Lewis, A. W. (1981). *Royal succession in Capetian France: Studies on familial order and the state*. Cambridge, MA: Harvard University Press.

Lewis, A. W. (1987). Suger's views on kingship. In P. L. Gerson (Ed.), *Abbot Suger and Saint Denis: A symposium* (pp. 49–55, 2nd printing). New York: The Metropolitan Museum of Art.

Linebaugh, P. (2008). *The Magna Carta Manifesto: Liberties and commons for all*. Berkeley: University of California Press.

Lombard-Jourdan, A. (1989). *Montjoie et Saint Denis: le centre de la Gaule aux origines de Paris et Saint Denis*. Paris: Presses du CNRS.

Loughlin, M. (2010). *Foundations of public law*. Oxford: Oxford University Press.

Maravall, J. A. (1983). La corriente democrática medieval en España y la fórmula "quod omnes tangit". In *Estudios de historia del pensamiento español* (pp. 175–190). I, Madrid: Instituto de España.

Marongiu, A. (1973). La cità nelle Corts en el parlamenti catalani del secolo XIV. In E. Sáez Sánchez (Ed.), *La investigación de la Historia hispánica del siglo XIV: Problemas y cuestiones* (pp. 653–659). Barcelona: Instituciò Milá y Fontanals.

McKechnie, W. S. (Ed.). (2005). *Magna Carta: A commentary on the great charter of King John, with an historical introduction* (2nd ed. rev. and in part re-written). Union, NJ: The Lawbook Exchange.

Menegaldo, S., & Ribémont, B. (Eds.). (2012). *Le Roi fontaine de justice: pouvoir justicier et pouvoir royal au Moyen Âge et à la Renaissance*. Paris: Klincksieck.

Minois, G. (2005). *Charles VI: Un roi shakespearien*. Paris: Perrin.

Myers, A. R. (1975). *Parliaments and estates in Europe to 1789*. London: Thames and Hudson.

Navarro Valls, R., & Palomino, R. (2003). *Estado y religión: textos para una reflexión crítica* (2nd ed.). Barcelona: Ariel.

O'Callaghan, J. F. (1969). The beginning of the Cortes of León Castile. *American Historical Review, 74*(5), 1503–1537.

O'Callaghan, J. F. (1975). *A history of medieval Spain*. Ithaca, NY: Cornell University Press.

O'Callaghan, J. F. (2013). *A history of medieval Spain*. Ithaca, NY: Cornell University Press.

Olivera Serrano, C. (2005). *Beatriz de Portugal: la pugna dinástica Avis-Trastámara*. Betanzos: Lugami.

Otero, A. (1994). Las Partidas y el Ordenamiento de Alcalá en el cambio del ordenamiento medieval. *Anuario de Historia del Derecho Español,* (63–64), 451–548.

Palacios Martin, B. (1975). *La coronación de los reyes de Aragón (1204–1410). Aportación al estudio de las estructuras medievales*. Valencia: Anubar.

Payne, S. G. (1994). Castile and Aragón in the late Middle Ages. In *A history of Spain and Portugal* (pp. 141–176). Ann Arbor, MI: University of Michigan Press.

Pérez De La Canal, M. A. (1975). La justicia de la Corte de Castilla durante los siglos XIII al XV. *Historia, Instituciones, Documentos,* (2), 383–481.

Piña Homs, R. (2007). Los Reinos de la Corona de Aragón. In *Obra dispersa: Corona de Aragón y América Hispana* (pp. 333–370). Palma de Mallorca: Universitat de les Illes Balears.

Pocock, J. G. A. (2008). *The ancient constitution and the feudal law. A study of English historical thought in the seventeenth century* (Reissued). Cambridge, UK: Cambridge University Press.

Pollock, F., & Maitland, F. W. (2010). *The history of English law before the time of Edward I* (2nd reimpr. of the 2nd edition). Indianapolis: Liberty Fund.

Post, G. (1943). Roman law and early representation in Spain and Italy, 1150–1250. *Speculum: A Journal of Medieval Studies, 18*(2), 211–232.

Post, G. (1973). Medieval representation: A consequence of the revival of Roman law. In T. N. Bisson (Ed.), *Medieval representative institutions, their origins and nature* (pp. 92–102). Hinsdale, IL: Dryden Press.

Post, G. (2008). A Romano-canonical maxim 'quod omnes tangit', in Bracton and in early Parliaments. In *Studies in medieval legal thought: Public law and the state, 1100–1322* (3rd pr., pp. 163–219). Clark, NJ: The Lawbook Exchange, Ltd.

Procter, E. S. (2010). *Curia and Cortes in Leon and Castile: (1072 1295).* Cambridge: Cambridge University Press.

Reynolds, S. (2012). How different was England? In *The Middle Ages without feudalism. Essays in criticism and comparison on the medieval West* (Part II. States and Nations, XII, pp. 1–16). Farnham, UK: Ashgate.

Runciman, S. (2012). *The Sicilian Vespers: A history of the Mediterranean world in the later thirteenth century* (10th printing). Cambridge, UK: Cambridge University Press.

Sabaté I Curull, F. (2000–2002). Municipio y monarquía en la Cataluña bajomedieval. *Anales de la Universidad de Alicante. Historia Medieval,* (13), 255–282.

Saint-Bonnet, F. (2010). Le contrôle a posteriori: les parlements de l'Ancien Régime et la neutralisation de la loi. *Les Cahiers du Conseil constitutionnel,* (28), 23–27 (Dossier: L'histoire du contrôle de constitutionnalité).

Salcedo Izu, J. (1980). La autonomía municipal según las cortes castellanas en la Baja Edad Media. *Anuario de Historia del Derecho Español,* (50), 223–242.

Stocking, R. (2000). *Bishops, councils, and consensus in the visigothic kingdom: 589–633*. Ann Arbor, MI: The University of Michigan Press.

Strayer, J. R. (1965). *Feudalism.* Princeton, NJ: D. Van Nostrand Company, Inc.

Strayer, J. R. (1971). Philip the fair—A "constitutional" king. In *Medieval statecraft and the perspectives of history* (pp. 195–212). Princeton, NJ: Princeton University Press.

Strayer, J. R. (1980). *The reign of Philip the Fair.* Princeton, NJ: Princeton University Press.

Timbal, P. C., & Castaldo, A. (1985). *Histoire des institutions publiques et des faits sociaux.* Paris: Dalloz.

Ullmann, W. (2009). *Medieval Papalism: The political theories of the medieval Canonist.* New York: Routledge.

Ullmann, W. (2010). *Principles of government and politics in the Middle Ages.* London: Routledge.

Vale, M. G. A. (1974). *Charles the Seventh.* Berkeley, CA: University of California Press.

van Caenegem, R. C. (1990). Galbert of Bruges on serfdom, prosecution of crime, and constitutionalism: (1127–1128). In B. S. Bachrach & D. Nicholas (Eds.), *From law, custom and the social fabric in medieval Europe: Essays in honor of Bryce Lyon* (pp. 89–112). Kalamazoo, MI: Medieval Institute Publications.

van Caenegem, R. C. (1995). *An historical introduction to Western Constitutional Law.* Cambridge, UK: Cambridge University Press.

Vander Linden, H. (1916). Alexander VI and the demarcation of the maritime and colonial domains of Spain and Portugal, 1493–1494. *The American Historical Review, 22*(1), 1–20.

VanLandingham, M. (2002). The King's Law: Royal justice and royal administration. In *Transforming the state: king, court, and political culture in the realms of Aragon: 1213–1387* (pp. 83–100). Leiden: Brill.
Vives, J. (Ed.). (1963). *Concilios visigóticos e hispanorromanos*. Barcelona: Consejo Superior de Investigaciones Científicas.
Waley, D., & Dean, T. (2010). *The Italian City-Republics* (4th ed.). London: Prentice Hall.
Wieacker, F. (1981). The importance of Roman law for western civilization and western legal thought. *Boston College International and Comparative Law Review, 4*(2), 257–281.
Wilkinson, B. (1972). *The creation of medieval parliaments*. New York: Willey.
Wolfram, H. (1990). *History of the Goths*. Berkeley, CA: University of California Press.

## Further Reading

Airlie, S., Pohl, W. Reimitz, H. (2006). *Staat im frühen Mittelalter*. Wien: Verlag der Österreichchischen Akademie der Wissenchaft.
Alfonso Antón, M. I., et al. (Eds.). (2004). *Building legitimacy: Political discourses and forms of legitimacy in Medieval societies*. Leiden: Brill.
Barnwell, P. S., & Mostert, M. (Eds.). (2003). *Political assemblies in the earlier Middle Ages*. Turnhout: Brepols.
Bisson, T. N. (2010). *The crisis of the twelfth century: Power, lordship, and the origins of European government*. Princeton, NJ: Princeton University Press.
Blythe, J. M. (1992). *Ideal government and the mixed constitution in the Middle Ages*. Princeton, NJ: Princeton University Press.
Bonney, R. (2002). Revenues. In R. Bonney (Ed.), *Economic systems and state finance: The origins of the modern state in Europe 13th to 18th centuries* (Reprint, pp. 423–506). Oxford, UK: Clarendon.
Bradbury, J. (2010). *The Capetians: Kings of France, 987–1328*. London: Continuum.
Brown, E. A. R. (1991). *Politics and institutions in Capetian France*. Aldershot: Variorum.
Brown, E. A. R. (1991). *The Monarchy of Capetian France and Royal Ceremonial* (p. 1991). London: Variorum.
Brown, E. A. R., & Famiglietti, R. C. (1993). *The Lit de Justice: Semantics, ceremonial and the Parlement of Paris, 1300–1600*. Sigmaringen: Jan Thorbecke.
Canning, J. (1996). *A history of medieval political thought: 300–1450*. London: Routledge.
Canning, J. (2011). *Ideas of power in the late Middle Ages: 1296–1417*. Cambridge: Cambridge University Press.
Chrimes, S. B. (2013). The nature of parliament. In *English constitutional ideas in the fifteenth century* (Repr., pp. 66–141). Cambridge, UK: Cambridge University Press.
Collins, R. (1985). 'Sicut lex Gothorum continet': Law and charters in ninth- and tenth-century León and Catalonia. *The English Historical Review, 100*(396), 489–512.
Collins, R. (2007). *Die Fredegar-Chronikon*. Hannover: Hahnsche Buchhandlung.
Collins, R. (2010). *Early medieval Spain: Unity in diversity, 400–1000* (3rd ed.). La Vergne, TN: St Martin's Press.
Fawtier, R. (1964). *The Capetian Kings of France: Monarchy and nation (987–1328)*. London: Macmillan.
Febrer Romaguera, M. V. (2004). El parlamentarismo pactista valenciano y su procedimiento foral de reparación de agravis i contrafurs. *Anuario de Estudios Medievales, 34*(2), 667–712.
García Gallo, A. (1980). El pactismo en el Reino de Castilla y su proyección en América. In *El pactismo en la Historia de España* (pp. 143–168). Madrid: Instituto de España.
Gibert, R. (1961). El derecho municipal de León y Castilla. *Anuario de Historia del Derecho Español*, (31), 695–754.

Goffart, W. (2005). *The Narrators of Barbarian history (A.D. 550–800): Jordanes, Gregory of Tours, Bede, And Paul the Deacon*. Princeton, NJ: Princeton University Press.

Hanley, S. (1983). *The Lit de Justice of the Kings of France: Constitutional ideology in legend, ritual, and discourse*. Princeton: Princeton University Press.

Henderson, J. (2007). *The Medieval World of Isidore of Seville: Truth from words*. Cambridge, MA: Cambridge University Press.

Hirschbiegel, J., & Zeilinger, G. (2009). Urban space divided?: The encounter of civic and courtly spheres in late-medieval towns. In A. Classen (Ed.), *Urban space in the Middle Ages and the early modern age* (pp. 481–504). Berlin: Walter de Gruyter.

Jacoby, D. (2014). *Travellers, merchants and settlers in the Eastern Mediterranean, 11th–14th centuries*. London: Ashgate.

Jones, C. (2011). Understanding political conceptions in the later Middle Ages: The French imperial candidatures and the idea of the nation-state. *Viator: Medieval and Renaissance Studies, 42*(2), 83–114.

Jordan, W. C. (2000). *Louis IX and the challenge of the crusade: A study in rulership*. Princeton, NJ: Princeton University Press.

Kantorowicz, E. H. (1997). *The King's two bodies. A study in mediaeval political theology*. Princeton, NJ: Princeton University Press.

Lalinde Abadia, J. (1979). Los Parlamentos y demás instituciones representativas. In *La Corona de Aragón y el Mediterráneo: aspectos y problemas comunes desde Alfonso el Magnánimo a Fernando el Católico (1416–1516): IX Congreso de historia de la Corona de Aragón* (Vol. I, pp. 103–179). Zaragoza: Institución Fernando el Católico.

Lalinde Abadia, J. (1980). El pactismo en los reinos de Aragón y de Valencia. In *El pactismo en la Historia de España* (pp. 111–139). Madrid: Instituto de España.

Le Goff, J. (2009). *Saint Louis*. Notre Dame, IN: University of Notre Dame Press.

Lecuppre, G. (2005). *L'imposture politique au Moyen Âge: la seconde vie des rois*. Paris: Presses Universitaires de France.

Leprai, S. (2008). *I luoghi e le forme del potere nel Medioevo*. Bologna: CLUEB.

Lewis, P. (1968). *Later Medieval France: The polity*. New York: St. Martin's Press.

Linehan, P. (2007). Patronage and indebtedness: Portugal, Castile and the papal court around the year 1300. *Historia, instituciones, documentos,* (34), 147–158.

Marongiu, A. (1968). *Medieval parliaments: A comparative study*. London: Eyre & Spottiswoode.

Marongiu, A. (2005). Il principio della participazione e del consenso, 'Quod omnes tangit ab omnibus approbari debet', nell XIV secolo. In *Dottrine e istituzioni politiche medievali e moderne: raccolta* (pp. 255–279). Milano: Giuffré.

Martínez, H. S. (2010). *Alfonso X, the learned: A biography*. Leiden: Brill.

Menant, F. (2005). *L'Italie des Communes (1100–1350)*. Paris: Belin.

Nelson, J. L. (2011). The limits of power in medieval Europe. In A. MceElligott et al. (Eds.), *Power in history: From medieval Ireland to the post-modern world* (pp. 3–24). Dublin, Ireland: Irish Academic Press.

Nicholas, D. (1996). *Trade, urbanisation and the family: Studies in the history of medieval Flanders*. Aldershot: Variorum.

North, M. (2012). *The expansion of Europe, 1250–1500*. Manchester: Manchester University Press.

O'Callaghan, J. F. (1985). The integration of Christian Spain into Europe: The role of Alfonso VI of León-Castile. In *Santiago, Saint Denis and Saint Peter* (pp. 101–120). New York: Fordham University Press.

O'Callaghan, J. F. (1989). *The cortes of Castile-Léon, 1188–1350*. Philadelphia: University of Pennsylvania Press.

O'Callaghan, J. F. (1993). *The Learned King: The Reign of Alfonso X of Castile*. Philadelphia: University of Pennsylvania Press.

O'Callaghan, J. F. (1998). *Alfonso X, the Cortes, and government in medieval Spain*. Aldershot: Ashgate.

Pallister, A. (1994). *Magna Carta: The heritage of liberty*. Norwalk, CT: The Easton Press (Reprint). Originally published: Oxford: Clarendon Press, 1972.
Post, G. (1967–1968). Bracton on kingship. *Tulane Law Review, 42*(3), 519–554.
Reilly, B. F. (1988). *The kingdom of Leon-Castilla under King Alfonso VI: 1065–1109*. Princeton, NJ: Princeton University Press.
Reilly, B. F. (1993). The passing of medieval Iberia 1248: 1474. In *The Medieval Spains* (pp. 190–194). Cambridge, UK: Cambridge University Press.
Reinhart, W. (Ed.). (1996). *The origins of the modern state in Europe: 13th–18th centuries: Power elites and state building*. Oxford: Oxford University Press.
Renouard, Y. (1969). *Les villes de l'Italie du Xe siècle au début du XIVè siècle*. Paris: Société d'Enseignement Supérieur.
Reynolds, S. (2002). *Kingdoms and communities in Western Europe: 900–1300* (2nd ed., Reprint). Oxford: Clarendon.
Sánchez, G. (1922). Sobre el ordenamiento de Alcalá y sus fuentes. *Revista de Derecho Privado, X* (111), 353–368.
Schulz, F. (1945). Bracton on kingship. *The English Historical Review, 60*(237), 136–176.
Steane, J. (2001). *The archaeology of power: England and Northern Europe. AD 800–1600*. Stroud: Tempus.
Strayer, J. (1980). *The Reign of Philip the Fair*. Princeton: Princeton University Press.
Suger, Abbot of Saint Denis. (1992). *The Deeds of Louis the Fat: Vita Ludovici Grossi Regis*. Washington, DC: Catholic University of America Press.
Tang, F. (2005). "The 'rex fidelissimus': Spanish-French rivalry in the reign of Alfonso XI of Castile (1312–1350)". *Tijdschrift voor rechtsgeschiedenis = Revue d'histoire du droit (The Legal History Review),* (1), 93–109.
Thompson, F. (1967). *The first century of Magna Carta: Why it persisted as a document*. New York: Russell & Russell (Reissued).
Thompson, F. (2008). *Magna Carta: Its role in the making of the English constitution, 1300–1629*. Stroud, Gloucestershire: Sutton Press.
Tracy, J. D. (1997). *The political economy of merchant empires: State power and world trade, 1350–1750*. Cambridge: Cambridge University Press.
Tyerman, C. (2013). Sed nihil fecit? The last Capetians and the recovery of the Holy Land. In *The practices of crusading: Image and action from the eleventh to the sixteenth centuries* (pp. 170–181). London: Ashgate.
van Caenegem R. C. (2009). Galbert of Bruges and "Law is Politics". In J. Rider & A. Murray (Eds.), *Galbert of Bruges and the historiography of Medieval Flanders* (pp. 39–55). Pittsboro, NC: Catholic University of America Press.
von Below, G. (1975). *Der deutsche Staat des Mittelalters: ein Grundriss der deutschen Verfassungsgeschichte*. Leipzig: Quelle & Meyer.
Watts, J. (2009). *The making of polities: Europe, 1300–1500*. Cambridge, UK: Cambridge University Press.
Zimmerman, M. (1988). *L'Occident médiéval: états et pouvoirs (XIe-XVe siècles)*. Paris: La Documentation française.

# Chapter 9
# The Apogee of Royal Power: Absolute Monarchy (The Sixteenth and Seventeenth Centuries)

> And in order to consolidate and reinforce this privilege which I grant you, and so that there might be no doubts regarding its concession, by virtue of my clear understanding and absolute royal power, I desire that nothing hinder or obstruct its partial or total application, whether these be local laws, rights, regulations, statutes, or any other custom or practice which could in any way contravene, limit or preclude what is here asserted.[1]—Henry III of Castile (1390–1406)

## Contents


9.1 From Territorial to Absolute Monarchy ..... 212
- 9.1.1 The Modern Age and the Triumph of Royal Absolutism ..... 212
- 9.1.2 From Christian Universalism to Independent Monarchies ..... 212
- 9.1.3 Searching for a New Legitimacy: The Prevention of Anarchy as a Justification for Power ..... 216

9.2 The Abandonment of Medieval Pact-Based Rule ..... 220
- 9.2.1 Cities' Loss of Political and Legal Autonomy ..... 220
- 9.2.2 The Subjugation of the Nobility ..... 223
- 9.2.3 The Decline of the Assemblies of the Estates ..... 224

9.3 The State of the Prince ..... 229
- 9.3.1 The Expansion of Royal Jurisdiction ..... 230
- 9.3.2 A King Above the Law? ..... 231

9.4 Absolutism Versus Autocracy: The Legal Limits of Royal Absolutism ..... 234
- 9.4.1 Absolute Kings, Constrained by Divine and Natural Law ..... 235
- 9.4.2 The Limits of "Fundamental Laws" ..... 236
- 9.4.3 Respect for Traditional Customs ..... 237
- 9.4.4 The Relative Autonomy of the *Ancien Regime's* Judges ..... 238


[1] In a 1393 Royal Charter. *Y porque esto sea firme y sin alguna duda, a mayor firmeza, de mi cierta ciencia y **poderío Real absoluto**, cualesquier ley o leyes de fueros y derechos y ordenanzas, o estatutos, y qualesquier costumbre o costumbres, estilo o estilos, o otra cosa cualesquier que contra esto que dicho es fuesen o pudiesen ser en manera alguna, por vos contrallar o embargar esta merced que vos Yo fago, en todo o en parte, quiero que non valgan ni vos puedan empecer* Henry III (1830) (González 1830, V, 427).



B. Aguilera-Barchet, *A History of Western Public Law*,
DOI 10.1007/978-3-319-11803-1_9

9.5 Absolute Monarchy and the Increasing Power of the European States ............... 240
9.5.1 The Technical Advantages of Absolutism ..................................... 241
9.5.2 The Administrative Expansion of Absolute Monarchies ....................... 242
9.5.3 Towards a Europe of "National" Monarchies ................................. 244
References ............................................................................... 249

## 9.1 From Territorial to Absolute Monarchy

### *9.1.1 The Modern Age and the Triumph of Royal Absolutism*

For some historians, the Middle Ages came to a close upon the taking of Constantinople by the Ottoman Turks on May 29, 1453. For others, it ended with the discovery of America on October 12, 1492. In any case, the period that follows directly precedes our own times and has traditionally been known as the Early Modern Period,[2] spanning the sixteenth and seventeenth centuries. During this stage, the major development in terms of the history of the state, was the spectacular growth in the power of kings, who consolidated a new model of political organization termed *absolute monarchy*, whose paradigmatic summation came in the famous phrase attributed to Louis XIV: "I am the state" (*L'État c'est moi*), conveying the complete identification of the state with the figure of the king.[3]

The first consequence was that kings did not recognize any authority superior to their power, considering themselves unbeholden to popes and emperors.

### *9.1.2 From Christian Universalism to Independent Monarchies*

Some medieval jurists had already advanced the proposition that in their kingdoms, kings reigned supreme, that they were "emperors" (*Rex in regno suo est imperator*) (Post 1953, 296–320). In fact, after the death of Frederic II Hohenstaufen (1220–1250), emperors would no longer aspire to be the supreme authorities in the West, save perhaps, for the exceptional Charles V (1519–1558). The second step would be independence from the papacy.

---

[2] The early period of modern history is generally identified as following the late Middle Ages. Although the period's chronological boundaries are somewhat imprecise, the timeframe runs from the period after the late stage of the Middle Ages (c. 1500), until the beginning of the Age of Revolutions (c. 1800), and is traditionally identified by historians as beginning with the conquest of Constantinople by the Ottoman Empire in 1453 AD.

[3] The only problem is that the Sun King never said it. The day after Mazarin died, when asked who would handle state affairs henceforth, he limited himself to stating that he himself would take charge, and that he would do so in a manner different from that of the deceased cardinal (Wolf 1968, 145–161). Louis XIV, in fact, was fully conscious of the fact that the king was *not* the State, stating before his death: "I shall go, but the state will always remain" ("*Je m'en vais mais l'État demeurera toujours*") (de Dangeau and de Courcillon 1859, XVI, 128).

Since the late fifth century, the churches had managed to impose their power upon the Germanic kings. Meanwhile, since the time of Charlemagne, the popes had succeeded in establishing themselves as the legitimizers of imperial and royal power across Europe. This "papal theocracy", however, would collapse in the fourteenth century, firstly because Philip the Fair of France dared to defy Pope Boniface VIII, backed by the representatives of the kingdom, gathered in the Estates General, affirming that anyone who was *in regno* and *de regno*, had to accept the king as final and supreme judge (Strayer 1980, 270). Secondly, this collapse was brought about by the Western Schism, which seriously discredited papal authority. Finally, the Lutheran Reformation dealt a definitive blow to imperial power and the pope's former authority.

A landmark moment arrived in western constitutional history when Frederick III of Saxony granted Martin Luther protection at his Castle of Wartburg, despite the fact that Charles V, in the Edict of Worms (May 25, 1521), had declared Luther a fugitive and a heretic, and had prohibited his works. This pivotal event marked the beginning of what MacCulloch (2004, 119–127) has described as an accidental revolution that transformed law and politics based on Luther's theory of the two kingdoms.[4] The ensuing Catholic response (Counter-Reformation), advanced by the foundation of the Company of Jesus, or Jesuits (1547), and the convening of the Council of Trent (1545–1563),[5] only served to split Europe, between 1520 and 1648, into two halves which would square off in a series of bloody civil wars. These

---

[4] According to Luther, God created two kingdoms: the earthly kingdom, which is the realm of creation, of natural and civil life, where people operate primarily based on reason and law; and the heavenly kingdom, the realm of redemption, of spiritual and eternal life, where people operate essentially based on faith and love. Both kingdoms interact as they embrace parallel heavenly and earthly, spiritual and secular forms of righteousness and justice, government and order (Witte 2002, 5).

[5] The fact that Spain became the spearhead of the Counterreformation meant that the Spanish Monarchy, in the religious sphere, was to constitute an oasis of peace amidst all the chaos, though at the price of exhibiting a manifest intolerance towards anything not in strict accord with Catholic orthodoxy. This was achieved through the Inquisition, *La Sagrada Congregación de la Romana y Universal Inquisición* (it would not become the *Santo Oficio* until 1908), established in 1184 by virtue of Pope Lucius III's bull *Ad abolendam*, as an instrument to combat the heresy of Catharism. The Inquisition would give rise to the *Tribunal de la Santa Inquisición y del Santo Oficio*. On November 1, 1478, Pope Sixtus IV issued the bull *Exigit Sinceras Devotionis Affectus*, which instituted the Inquisition for the Crown of Castile, according to which the appointment of inquisitors fell under the exclusive purview of the monarchs. For a long time, the Crown and Inquisition were the only two institutions common to all Spanish territories, and it is true that one of the few areas in which all the Spanish Monarchy's Peninsular territories were of one mind was in that of their religion, which to a great extent explains why there was no significant opposition to royal supremacy until the major crisis of the War of Independence in the nineteenth century. The price Spain paid for its religious unity was great, as it aggravated the isolation of Catholic Spain from the rest of Europe. This traditional vision, however, has been questioned by recent historiography, which has rejected the idea of a dominant, monolithic Spanish Catholic Church, paralyzed by dogmatism during this period, contending that the supposed dichotomy between progressive Erasmianism and regressive Scholasticism described by an earlier generation of scholars, is overly simplistic. In fact, the Spanish Catholic Church during the Counter-Reformation was, according to many, a multifaceted, often disorganized institution with varying and conflicting priorities (Poska 2008, 295).

would include the conflicts which ravaged France in the second half of the sixteenth century,[6] the rebellion of the Netherlands against Phillip II in 1581, and the Thirty Years War (1618–1648), which ended up dividing Europe into two camps: the Protestant north and the Catholic south.[7] The conflict also had momentous consequences in terms of European constitutional history, as it promoted the ascendancy of kingdoms as opposed to the notion of a pan-European political authority, i.e. the Holy Roman Emperor or the pope.[8] After the Peace of Westphalia, Europe fractured into a series of independent states warring with each other to impose their hegemony, a state of affairs which would last all the way down until almost the middle of the twentieth century.[9]

[6] Classic French historiography identifies up to eight religious wars during the period from 1562 to 1593, which culminated with the killing of Protestants in Paris on August 22, 1572 in an event which came to be known as the St. Bartholomew's Day Massacre. The clash between Protestants and Catholics was on the verge of costing France its independence, as defending the League Spain's famed *tercios*, under the command of Alejandro Farnesio, occupied Paris in 1590, and Philip II's daughter, Isabel Clara Eugenia, almost became the Queen of France (Holt 2007, 138–149). With the arrival of Henry IV and the proclamation of the Edict of Nantes (1598), the violence subsided, though French Protestants continued to represent a kind of state within the French state, at least until 1628, when Richelieu took the French Protestant capital, La Rochelle, after a long siege. Later, Louis XIV concluded that the consolidation of the French monarchy required the suppression of religious freedom, prompting him to revoke the Edict of Nantes in 1685, which led to a massive exodus of Huguenots from France, one of its most industrious and productive groups. The Huguenots would emigrate to points throughout the world, including South Africa (Baird 2010). The failure of reform in France had important consequences as far as Public Law is concerned, as it made possible the consolidation of a highly centralized royal administration and the reinforcement of a solid and powerful French state (Ertman 1999, 91–109).

[7] The mass influx of businessmen, bankers and industrialists into England and northern European countries, like Holland and Prussia, would bolster these regions' economic growth and create a special idiosyncrasy in Protestant countries, which differed notably from those states that remained essentially Catholic. The influence of the Reformation on economic expansion was analyzed by Max Weber in his classic work *The Protestant Ethic and the Spirit of Capitalism*, initially published in two articles in 1904 and 1906 (Weber 2003) and later by Richard Henry Tawney in his most famous work *Religion and the Rise of Capitalism*, initially published in 1926 (Tawney 2008).

[8] As Witte (2002, 6 and 12) brings up, the primacy of states was developed from a theoretical point of view by Lutheran jurists such as Philip Melanchton, Johannes Eiserman, and Johann Oldendorp. The most influential of them was the second, who argued that the precise form and function of every Christian commonwealth differs, as each community strikes its own balance between "nature, custom and reason" in the determination of its laws, and has its own, unique interpretation of the Commandments of Scripture and tradition. This perspective broke with the view that God's creation was hierarchically structured, a vast chain if being that emanated from God and descended through various levels and layers of reality, a chain in which each creature found its place and its purpose, and each human society found its natural order and hierarchy. It was simply the nature of things that some people and institutions were higher or lower on this chain of being. Protestant jurists rejected the Catholic approach to society and polity that justified traditional Catholic arguments of the superiority of the pope to the emperor, or of the clergy to the laity, of the spiritual sword to the secular sword, of canon law to civil law, of the Church to the State.

[9] As Croxton (2013, 3) points out, the Peace of Westphalia was the first peace treaty established by sovereign states in pursuit of security though the balance of power, which explains why it has been compared in importance to the founding of the United Nations, which, curiously, also took place

The papacy's loss of influence was also manifest in England, when Henry VIII (1509–1547) nationalized the Anglican Church through the Act of Supremacy in 1534 (Lehmberg 1970, 202–203), after Clement VII refused to recognize the validity of his divorce from Catherine of Aragon and the legitimacy of his subsequent marriage to Anne Boleyn. The rift with the papacy prompted the king to adopt anti-ecclesiastical measures such as the dissolution of monasteries and the confiscation of church lands. This policy was reversed by his eldest daughter Mary Tudor,[10] who via a 1555 law, restored Catholicism, declaring it treason to speak out against the Church of Rome. However, her half-sister and successor Elizabeth I (1558–1606), again defied Rome, imposing in 1559 a new Act of Supremacy (Haig 2012, 239–242), a middle way between Roman Catholicism and the strain of Calvinism, which the Puritans wished to establish in the country.[11]

However, even on the Catholic side, monarchs did not want the popes to intervene in the affairs of their kingdoms. The symbol of this state of things was the "Sack of Rome" in 1527 by Charles V's army, which demonstrated that the popes had lost prestige and the capacity to arbitrate between sovereigns (Flemer 2002). Thereafter, popes retreated into the spiritual realm, and were confined, like the Holy Roman emperors, to be sovereigns within the territorial limits of their own domains, especially following the signing of the Peace of Habsburg in 1555 (*Cuius regio eius religio*), which resulted in the introduction, even in the Catholic states, of the doctrine of the ecclesiastical supremacy of sovereigns (regalism), which entailed a whole series of limitations when it came to applying ecclesiastical law and prerogatives within each kingdom. For example, the establishment of the "placet" (the Spanish *pase regio*) for the application of ecclesiastical rules (Vázquez García Peñuela and Morales Payán 2005, 15–35), was an attempt to resolve conflicts between royal and church power and disputes over the authority to appoint bishops, which leading to the signing of the first concordats between the monarchies and the Holy See. All this did not prevent the rise of movements calling for the establishment of autonomous national churches independents of the pope, though without breaking with Rome. The most representative case of this is that of French Gallicanism (Harouel et al. 2007, 382–386).[12] It is significant that in 1610,

on October 24. Westphalia was, in fact, far more important, as the United Nations Charter has been in effect for less than a century, while the Peace of Westphalia endured for well over 350. Scholars have only recently begun to suggest that we are moving into a "post-Westphalia" international system.

[10] By virtue of his union with his first wife, Catherine of Aragon (1485–1536), the youngest daughter of the Spanish Catholic Kings. For an overview of this Roman Catholic interlude, see Haig (2012, 219–234).

[11] Beginning with his rule, however, the Catholics were gradually marginalized for obeying the pope, who Henry VIII and the burgeoning English gentry considered a chief of state who wished to meddle in their internal affairs. For an overview of how the Crown and the Anglican Church dealt with Catholics and Puritans, see Dickens (1993, 362–377).

[12] As Holt (2007, 9) observes, Gallicanism was rooted in the sacred nature of French kingship, which entailed a special relationship between the French monarch and God. As the General Assembly of the Clergy declared in 1625, French kings were not only ordained by God, but

the Parlement of Paris ordered the burning of the works of the Spanish Jesuit Juan de Mariana (1536–1624), who they considered intellectually responsible for Ravaillac's killing of Henry IV.[13]

The fact that the kings were no longer under the authority of the pope also meant that the power of absolute monarchs' could not any more be justified by the fact that they were the rulers of traditionally ordered societies created and ordained by God. The problem, then, was that a new legitimization of royal power was needed.

### 9.1.3 Searching for a New Legitimacy: The Prevention of Anarchy as a Justification for Power

In the Middle Ages, kings were able to assert their authority over feudal powers because there appeared jurists and political thinkers who justified this imposition, invoking legal validations. The old Roman law contained in Justinian's *Corpus Iuris Civilis* was revived and applied to a whole range of customary, feudal, statutory, imperial and canon law issues (Robinson et al. 2000, 109), facilitated by academic interpretations produced by Glossators and Commentators (*mos italicus*), Decretists and Decretalists, with the pope ever considered the supreme authority.[14] As this new scholar-produced (rather than politically imposed) law was studied in universities all over Europe, and featured a common language (Latin) and a common legal culture (Calasso 1954, 453–454), it was considered *Ius commune*, a new body of law more original in the methods and reasonings underlying it than in its core principles (Reynolds 2012, VII, 497), which were eminently traditional and Christian.

---

"they themselves were gods". This is why, though the popes recognized other monarchs for their services, such as Ferdinand and Isabella, who were dubbed the "Catholic Kings", and Henry VIII, termed the "defender of the faith", French kings had earned the much older and more grander title of "most Christian king" (*Rex christianissimus*).

[13] Henry IV was killed by a Catholic fanatic, François Ravaillac, in Paris May 14, 1610. It is not unlikely that the assassin of the House of Bourbon's first monarch was financed by Catholic Spain. In any case, it was justified by the Spanish Jesuit Juan de Mariana who in his treatise *De rege et regis institutione* (1599), considered it lawful to overthrow a tyrant, and defended papal supremacy, in accordance with the doctrine of the pope's "indirect power", which maintained that the pontiff could intervene politically in France should the king's behavior place the souls of French Catholics in danger. In the Wars of Religion, the members of the Catholic Party (The League), headed by Henry of Guise, accepted the Spanish Jesuits' doctrine and were steadfast allies of the Spanish Monarchy. The book of Mariana was declared subversive by the magistrates of the Parlement of Paris (as most of the French jurists were fervent Gallicanists), condemned, and publicly burned (Nelson 2005, 159–170). With another two works, written by members of the Society. This fact potentially placed the Society of Jesus squarely back at the centre of the debate over regicide in France (Nelson 2005, 158).

[14] As Bellomo (1995, 158) affirms, the paradigm of the legal culture during this period, the supreme model, was the universal legal system represented by the Holy Roman Empire and the Church, headed by the emperor and the pope.

The justification of royal power, then, was based on Roman legal texts appearing in the Justinian compilation. Principles such as *Rex in regno suo est imperator* and *princeps legibus solutus est* were taken and interpreted by medieval jurists precisely to buttress royal authority.[15] The jurists (*légistes*) of Philip IV of France, such as Guillaume de Nogaret (1260–1313),[16] turned to Canon Law to defend the proposition that the consecration of the king made him a monarch by divine right, thereby justifying his supreme authority over his kingdom—an argument used to thwart the pope's claims to authority. The political leadership of the papacy collapsed and the dream of a united, Christian West vanished, with the consequence that political decisions henceforth fell into the hands of secular authorities, with whom the Church was not to interfere (Strayer 1980, 389).

The next key development was that the *Ius commune*, based on the Roman canonical legal tradition, lost its *ratio scripta* status,[17] a trend which began in the Renaissance, with movements such as Legal Humanism (*mos gallicus*). Demonstrating the historicity and the relativity of the *Corpus iuris* destroyed the absolute authority which it had hitherto enjoyed. If Roman law was no more than the product of a given society from a given period, there was no reason why its authority should be applicable to others period, or be superior to current laws (van Caenegem 1994, 56). Therefore, the legitimacy of power had to rely on Natural Law, which fueled the new argument that the absolute power of kings was simply the only way to prevent chaos and maintain social order.

Everything started during the Renaissance, in an Italy torn between supporters of the pope and the emperor, with the Guelphs and Ghibellines in constant conflict,[18] generating a permanent state of chaos. From this anarchy arose a multitude of

[15] It is interesting to note, as Canning (2011, 149) points out, that Baldus de Ubaldis (1327–1400), the great Italian commentator, also applied the language of sovereignty found in Roman and Canon law not only to kings and *signori* but also to city republics, which he considered to be equivalent to small empires, entitled to their own rulers (*civitas sibi princeps*).

[16] Guillaume de Nogaret, one of the main advisors to Philip the Fair, for instance, had studied Law at the University of Montpellier, where, after receiving a doctorate, in 1287 he became a member of its Faculty of Law, before becoming a judge. By 1299 he sat in the Parlement of Paris and on the King's Council. Nogaret took charge of the propaganda war against Boniface VIII and led the attack on the pope at Anagni (September 7, 1303). For an overview of this key figure under Philip IV's reign, see Strayer (1980, 52–55).

[17] As Padoa-Schioppa (2007, 98) points out, the Glossators were convinced that every legal case could be resolved by referring to the texts of the Justinian compilation. Francesco di Accursio (1188–1260), the author of the *Glossa magna* (Great Gloss), who labored from 1220 to 1250 organizing more than 96,000 annotations to the *Corpus Iuris*, believed that it included everything: "*Omnia in corpora iuris inveniuntur*". Carpintero (1977, 177) points out that glossators and commentators were convinced that "*civilis scientia est vera philosophia*", and did not require any contributions from other sciences, as it was complete in itself.

[18] Weary of all this conflict, the ever-ingenious Italians came up with the idea of hiring the services of a professional ruler: the *podestá*, normally a stranger who was not involved in the city's strife. He was contracted for a time, his contract only extended if he managed to subdue rival clans and establish law and order. There are many cases recorded of a *podestá* becoming involved in a civil dispute and being thrown out of office before his term had expired (Waley and Dean 2013, 44).

political units whose existence was founded on their brute power, provoking, as Burckhardt (2010, 2) points out, the rise of a new phenomenon in history: the state as an outcome of reflection and calculation, "the state as a work of art". It was amidst these circumstances that Niccolo Machiavelli (1469–1527) lived. In his landmark work *The Prince* (1513), he offered rulers a series of formulas and pieces of advice to maintain, at any price, the power which guarantees social order. The "prince" no longer justified his power on the premise that he was the legitimate representative of God on Earth, or by tracing his authority back to the Roman emperors, but rather exclusively on his capacity for political survival.[19]

> With the actions of all men, but especially those of princes, against whom there is no higher authority to which to appeal, their ends are simply considered. The prince, therefore, must dedicate himself to overcoming difficulties and preserving his state. If he is successful in this, the means he employs will always be considered honorable, and be praised everywhere: the masses always focus on appearances, and are seduced by results. Now the world is almost entirely made up of the masses, and the small number of insightful minds in it do not announce what they can see until the countless hordes who see nothing no longer know what to think.[20]

There thus began a secularization of the justification of political power which received its first theoretical formulation by jurist Jean Bodin (1529–1596), who lived in a France plagued by the long and bloody French Wars of Religion.[21] This situation naturally, made him a firm supporter of strong and undisputed authority. Bodin presented his arguments in *The Six Books of the Commonwealth*, published in 1576, advancing the idea of *sovereignty*,[22] which he understood as absolute power, which takes precedence over everything and everyone else:

> Sovereignty is that absolute and perpetual power vested in a commonwealth which in Latin is termed *majestas* (...) Sovereignty is not limited, in power, responsibility, or in time (...)

---

[19] Burckhardt (2010, 5) praised the Italian despot: "With his thirst for fame and his passion for monumental works, it was talent, not high birth, which he needed. In the company of the poet and the scholar he felt himself in a new position, almost, indeed, in possession of a new legitimacy". As Skinner (2008, 4–5) observes, in Florence in 1498, when a 29 year old Machiavelli was recruited as the Republic's second chancellor there was a well established method of recruitment for its major offices which, in addition to requiring diplomatic skills, also called for aspiring officials to have a solid humanist education, as they believed that this type of training offered the best preparation for political life.

[20] "In the actions of all men, and most of all of Princes, where there is no tribunal to which we can appeal, we look to results. Wherefore if a Prince succeeds in establishing and maintaining his authority, the means will always be judged honorable and be approved by every one" (di Machiavelli 2010, p. 133).

[21] Bodin's work *Les six livres de la Républiqu*e was published, significantly, in 1576, 4 years after the Saint Bartholomew's Day Massacre (1572). As Franklin (2009, VII) points out, one consequence of the Massacre was the polarization of French constitutional ideas. On one side, appeared a radicalized version of the French constitutional tradition, backed by Huguenots to justify their resistance to royal power, and on the other side, stood the theory of royal absolutism, systematically advanced by Bodin.

[22] Though, as we know, the word "sovereignty" itself had been coined in the second half of the thirteenth century by the jurists of Saint Louis of France (Louis IX).

> it is necessary for sovereigns not to be subject to anyone else's power so that they may (...) impose law upon their subjects and rescind or amend useless laws (...). The term needs careful definition, because although it is the distinguishing mark of a commonwealth, and an understanding of its nature fundamental to any treatment of politics, no jurist or political philosopher has in fact attempted to define it...[23]

Bodin, however, affirmed more than he actually explained the expedience of an absolute respect for sovereign power. Thomas Hobbes (1588–1679), went one step further.[24] After enduring the English Civil War, from which Cromwell emerged victorious, Hobbes offered a justification for absolute submission to state power in his most famous work *The Leviathan*, the first edition being published in 1651 in an England profoundly affected by the beheading of Charles I (January 30, 1649).[25] Hobbes was reacting against the anarchy of the civil war he had witnessed. Thus, after writing that "where there is no common power, there is no law; where there is no law, there is no justice", he went on to state that:

> The only way to erect such a common power, as may be able to defend them from the invasion of foreigners, and the injuries of one another, and thereby to secure them in such sort as that by their own industry and by the fruits of the earth they may nourish themselves and live contentedly, is to confer all their power and strength upon one man, or upon one assembly of men, that may reduce all their wills, by plurality of voices, unto one will. Which is as much as to say: to appoint one man, or assembly of men, to bear their person; and every one to own and acknowledge himself to be author of whatsoever he that so beareth their person shall act, or cause to be acted, in those things which concern the common peace and safety; and therein to submit their wills, every one to his will, and their judgments to his judgment. This is more than consent, or concord; it is a real unity of them all in one and the same person, made by covenant of every man with every man, in such manner as if every man should say to every man: *I authorise and give up my right of governing myself to this man, or to this assembly of men, on this condition*; *that thou give up, thy right to him, and authorise all his actions in like manner*. This done, the multitude so united in one person is called a COMMONWEALTH; in Latin, CIVITAS. This is the generation of that great LEVIATHAN, or rather, to speak more reverently, of that mortal god to which we owe, under the immortal God, our peace and defence.[26]

Despite their different approaches, Machiavelli, Bodin and Hobbes all came to the same conclusion: the state should be placed in the hands of a single person, a monarch

---

[23] Bodin (2009, 24–25). For an overview of the defenders of the kings' absolute sovereignty in the French political tradition, see Harouel et al. (2007, 422–426).

[24] For a comparative study of the work of Jean Bodin and that of Hobbes: King (1999).

[25] *Leviathan, or the Matter, Form, and Power of a Commonwealth, Ecclesiastical and Civil* was firstly published in English "for Andrew Crooke at the Green Dragon in St. Paul's Churchyard" in 1651. The work spread throughout Europe once published in Latin (1668). It was published in Dutch in 1678 and in German in 1794.

[26] Hobbes (2007, 118). The Leviathan is a great sea creature created by God, appearing in the Old Testament (Genesis 1:21) and also mentioned in Psalm 74 (13–14), Job 41 and Isaiah 27:1. The term alludes to any giant aquatic creature, and in the Bible tends to be associated with Satan. In modern Hebrew, the term (*lewyatan*) refers simply to a whale.

whose power ought not to be contested in any way.[27] This figure, the *prince*, became the great protagonist of a new era in European constitutional history. As Anderson (2013, 15) points out, the rise of the absolutist state marked the demise of the feudal conception of law and power, as the centralized monarchies of France, England and Spain represented decisive ruptures with the old pyramidal medieval social structure, with its three estates and liege systems.

Although in some kingdoms royal absolutism appeared early, such as in Castile, where the kings imposed their supremacy as of the late fourteenth century,[28] the era of classic absolutism (*Hochabsolutismus*) would span the sixteenth and seventeenth centuries, even if in some countries, such as France, it would last until the second half of the eighteenth. This period of the history of Western Public Law is also known in German historiography as the *Fürstenstaat*, literally the "State of the Prince", because all branches of the state—executive, legislative and judicial—relied upon the monarch and exercised their powers in his name.

## 9.2 The Abandonment of Medieval Pact-Based Rule

The independence of the kings from external authorities, such as the emperors and popes, was, however, not enough. Royal preeminence was also sought over every internal obstacle which had curbed monarchs' power in the Late Middle Ages. Specifically favoring the growth of the kings' power, aggravating the crisis of the medieval polity, and serving to consolidate the modern state were the following factors: cities' loss of autonomy, the subjugation of the nobility, and, finally, the decline of Europe's estate-based assemblies.

### *9.2.1 Cities' Loss of Political and Legal Autonomy*

The principle of urban autonomy, favored by the emergence of great politically and legally autonomous cities in the Late Middle Ages, entered into crisis in the Modern Age, in large part because the most independent cities which had managed to stand up

[27] Crossman (1969, 60) points out that the connection between Machiavelli and Hobbes is their "realism", as they portray man stripped of all theological trappings as a being moved by purely worldly interests. From this point of view Machiavelli differs deeply from the idealized vision that Dante offers of man, as differ the artistic approaches between Michelangelo and the sculptor of the western façade of Chartres: "one sees through the flesh to the anatomy of muscle and bone, the other expresses in human form the supernatural essence of the spirit. Strictly one is no more realistic than the other, but each sees a different reality and calls it man. Each has a different philosophy of life, and in the *Leviathan* the anatomical outlook of the Renaissance is developed into a full-fledged political system".

[28] See the opening text of this chapter and footnote number 1.

to royal power came under military siege by monarchs. Such was the case in Ghent and Florence, whose respective rebellions were put down by Charles V; the Castilian cities, which fought the king in the War of the Communities; and the German cities, which were also militarily vanquished by the king-emperor in the early sixteenth century. It must be said that royal intervention encountered scant resistance from the masses, as the governments of the cities lay in the hands of local oligarchies which perpetuated their power by purchasing key offices from the monarchs,' who needed the revenue obtained from their sale.[29]

Inevitably, this situation sapped municipal autonomy, which was soon also restricted by the appointment of royal officials charged with overseeing those who held local offices. Thus, for example, in Castile, beginning in 1348, along with the municipal officials (*regidores*) there arose the figure of the *corregidor*: the royal agent who would end up controlling city life during the Modern Age up to the era of Liberal revolutions (González Alonso 1970).[30] In the legal sphere this diminished municipal autonomy was evident at the legislative level, where there was a "petrification" of anachronistic and obsolete municipal legal terms from the medieval period, which gave royal legislators ample leeway to adapt local legal ordinances to the times, especially after the defeat of the Comuneros Revolt at Villalar (1521). Therefore, in the Spanish monarchy, as of the reign of Comuneros Revolt (1621–1665), municipal ordinances had to receive royal approval before entering into effect.[31] To all this, one must add the progressive submission of municipal law to royal law,[32] and that of local tribunals to

[29] The "patrimonialization" of public offices was a common practice in Europe during the *Ancien Régime*, as of the end of the fifteenth century. Though there were some attempts to prohibit this practice every form of graft spread across Europe, whether legal or clandestine, with a peak being reached during the era of the Thirty Years War. Following the return of peace in 1648 some successful efforts were undertaken to limit the privatization of public authority. While the practice of selling public offices survived into the eighteenth century it no longer played a dominant role, either in the state's finances or in society (Descimon 1996, 111). It was, however, very common for a time in Spain (Tomás y Valiente 1980), and also in France, where in 1522, Francis I actually legalized it as an ordinary procedure of the Royal Treasury (Desrayaud 1996, 460). During the reign of Louis XV, the sale of offices was abolished via dispositions promulgated in 1764 and 1765, and an elective system for the determination of local offices was reintroduced. Both dispositions, however, were revoked in 1771.

[30] In principle the *corregidor* was named to control the local authorities (*regidores*) but this check on the power of the local oligarchies did not always work because, as Thompson (1993, 92) points out, there were many cases of collusion between the *corregidor* and the *regidores*, as evidenced by widespread complaints about their graft and their failure to root out malfeasance.

[31] The confirmation of local ordinances was one of the functions assigned to the *Consejo Real de Castilla* (Royal Council of Castile) (Hernández 1995, 19).

[32] In Castile, the supremacy of royal law over traditional municipal privileges (*fueros*) was asserted by the famous set of laws approved by the *Cortes of Alcalá de Henares* in 1348, the *Ordenamiento de Alcalá*, which sanctioned the preeminence of the *Ordenamiento* itself over local custom (XXVIII, 1). See one of the first printed editions by Jordán de Asso and Manuel y Rodríguez (1774, 69–73). Alfonso XI's *Ordinances* of Medina del Campo 1328, Villarreal 1346, and Segovia 1347 were not enacted in the *cortes*, contrary to common opinion. Even so, the *Ordinance* of Medina del Campo was incorporated into the *cuadernos* of the *cortes* of Madrid 1329 and the *Ordinances* of Villarreal and Segovia into the *Ordinance of Alcalá* 1348, that established an order of precedence among the different legal

those of the monarchy since 1348. All of these factors led to a progressive derogation of cities' legal autonomy, as old municipal laws had become virtual relics by the end of the Old Regime.

Cities' political decline was also evident in Italy, where powerful families gradually took over the governance of urban republics like Florence, Siena and Milan. The divisions between cities, meanwhile, opened the door to foreign invasions, from France as of the time of Charles VIII and Louis XII, and Spain, since the era of the Catholic Kings, thanks to the victories of the *Gran Capitán* (Gonzalo Fernández de Córdoba)[33] over the French in southern Italy.[34] During the sixteenth and seventeenth centuries, most of Italy—essentially Milan, Sicily and Naples—was incorporated under the Spanish Crown which, in accordance with the model of the compound Catholic Monarchy, respected traditional public institutions.[35] The king did appoint the governors, however, and Philip II created a Council of Italy at the royal court (*corte regia*). As a result, powerful city-states entered into decline, such as the Republic of Venice—though it was still powerful enough to fight victoriously with Spain against the Ottoman fleet at the Battle of Lepanto (1571).[36]

In the United Provinces, the rebellion against the king of Spain (1566), sparked a war won by the cities, which had achieved considerable political autonomy thanks to their commercial prosperity. These would evolve into maritime republics governed by a bourgeois oligarchy of merchants, which enjoyed its greatest degree of prosperity in the seventeenth century, though ultimately this did not prevent the consolidation of hereditary monarchy and the rise to power of the House of Orange-Nassau.[37]

---

systems in the realm, giving first place to the *Ordenamiento* itself, followed by the *fueros* of the towns and of the nobility, and then by the *Siete Partidas*. The ordinances and constitutions of the *cortes* of the several kingdoms, also contributed to the general body of laws (O'Callaghan 2013, 451).

[33] Gonzalo Fernández de Córdoba was one of the founders of modern warfare. As a field commander he, like Napoleon three centuries later, aimed not just to defeat, but to obliterate the enemy's army, systematically pursuing them after victories. Córdoba helped found the first modern standing army and the nearly invincible Spanish infantry, which would dominate European battlefields for most of the sixteenth and seventeenth centuries.

[34] In fact, the Franco-Spanish rivalry dated back to the sinking of imperial ambitions in Italy after the disappearance of the Hohenstaufen Dynasty and the election of the Rudolph of Habsburg in 1273. Then began a struggle for Sicily and Naples between France's House of Anjou, an ally of the pope's, and the Crown of Aragon which, after the revolt known as the Sicilian Vespers (1282), would seize the opportunity to occupy the island thanks to the impetus of Peter III of Aragon. Naples would not be conquered by the Aragonian crown until the reign of Alfonso V the Noble in the mid fifteenth century.

[35] As Waley (1963, 98) points out, for 150 years of Spanish domination (1559–1713), Spain's policy was based on the principle of minimum interference, which explains why even in the provinces under the king's direct rule it was not unpopular.

[36] On the decay of the Most Serene Republic (*Republica Serenissima*) in the sixteenth century, see Lane (1973, 240–249). For an overview of the survival and transformation of the European city-states between 1450 and 1600, see Scott (2012, 193–213).

[37] As Koenigsberger (2001, 315) indicates, the House of Nassau could not help but become involved in disputes over political power within the republic of the United Provinces, as had

In France, the cities fell under royal control during the reign of Louis XIV with the increase in the number of "Intendants" during the Colbert Era (Mousnier 1984, 519), which became an extremely effective instrument of centralization (Desrayaud 1996, 632). In 1683, an edict set down the detailed mechanisms through which the monarchy would exercise its control over the cities. All this said, it was not so much the case that the monarchs abolished the cities' traditional prerogatives as that they progressively fell into disuse.[38]

### 9.2.2 *The Subjugation of the Nobility*

The nobility, which during the Middle Ages had shared political power with the monarchy, was finally overpowered by the absolute kings, with the result that the nobility, at least a section of it, generally ended up cooperating with the monarchs, to the point that, as Zmora (2001, 6) observes, absolutism essentially rested upon a renewed covenant between the monarchy and the nobility, though in every kingdom this relationship took featured different characteristics.

In France, it is worth noting the attitude of Louis XIII's prime minister, Cardinal Richelieu, who waged a relentless struggle against the kingdom's most powerful figures, determined to impose the king's supremacy. The nobles did not truly lose their influence, however, until they were vanquished after the revolt known as the Fronde (1648–1653), during the reign of Louis XIV, thanks to the determined actions of Mazarin and the Queen Mother and Regent, Anne of Austria. Louis XIV finally, tamed the nobility by creating a vast court through which he distributed spoils and pensions to all the great French nobles, who settled near Versailles in an effort to curry favor with the Crown and secure royal pensions in what Desrayaud (1996, 515) calls the "domestication" of the French nobility. This approach was a costly but effective remedy. The nobles, close to and dependent upon the king, were in no position to rise up against him. It is also significant that most of the great servants of the French state in the seventeenth century, hailed from the gentry or bourgeoisie.[39]

In Spain the great nobles, after having had their way in Castile during the first two thirds of the fifteenth century (during the reigns of John II and Henry IV), were subdued by the Catholic Kings (1474–1504), who systematically relied upon jurists from the gentry and bourgeoisie to construct a modern state, at least in Castile, part

been the case in the former princely regimes, to settle the conflicts that arose among the different provinces and their main cities, and between the central government and the representative assembly.

[38] Some of these privileges, however, have been maintained. The Queen of England, for example, may not enter the city of London without its Mayor's consent.

[39] The most representative case is that of Jean Baptiste Colbert (1619–1683), who was born into a rich bourgeois family (Bourgeon 1986), and worked first as a banker and a notary before entering the service of Louis XIV in 1661.

of a trend that would be continued by Charles I and Phillip II in the sixteenth century. Beginning in the seventeenth century, the great nobles would become servants of the state, filling the most important territorial positions, as *validos* ("favorites"), viceroys and governors, though in general royal authority would never be challenged again (Carrasco Martínez 2000).

In England, after the anarchy sown by the War of the Roses (1455–1485), a struggle between rival nobles to determine who would control the throne of England, the people readily accepted the authoritarian rule of the Tudors as the best way to restore law and order (Bernard 1992). The result was that the old military nobility never again recovered the leverage it once held with the Crown, while the bourgeoisie was not yet strong enough to limit royal prerogative through Parliament, unlike what would ultimately happen in the second half of the seventeenth century under the Stuarts, as a consequence of two English revolutions.[40]

### 9.2.3 *The Decline of the Assemblies of the Estates*

Among the institutions which had decisively limited the power of the late medieval monarchs were, as we know, the assemblies of the estates, which reached agreements with the monarch regarding everything, from the fundamental laws of the kingdom to the finances needed by the monarchy. During the absolutist era, the general trend was for these types of bodies to be brought under royal authority—with the notable exception of England, which we shall examine separately, where Parliamentary power surged dramatically in the second half of the seventeenth century.

#### 9.2.3.1 The English Parliament

The English Parliament, which at the close of the Middle Ages had managed to impose significant restrictions on royal prerogative, during the era of the Tudors almost completely abandoned its judicial functions, and became essentially a legislative body. This political acquiescence was a result of the overwhelming charisma of Henry VIII and his daughter Elisabeth I. Henry VIII openly supported the creation of a mercantile and financial class, which soon ended up joining the gentry, and which became a firm defender of royal authority. Isabel I, meanwhile, was able to impose a kind of "state of emergency" because England was at war with

[40] During the II Civil War and its subsequent Interregnum, the high English nobility suffered a sharp but temporary decline. On the other hand, the status of the gentry as a social group improved considerably during the same period. It is interesting that the number of knights rose sharply during the Stuart Era: there were about 600 at the time of Elisabeth's death, and James I created over 900 in only his first 4 months in England. This distribution of honors was aimed at curbing the social ascendancy of the high nobility (Fritze and Robinson 1996, 497).

the all-powerful universal monarchy of Philip II, at least until the defeat of the Spanish Armada (1588), after which the "new regime of national independence had come to stay ... from now on patriotism would always be on the side of the new commercial and landowning class against any king who tried to thwart it, as the balance of power was already swinging away from the central government towards the bourgeoisie" (Crossman 1969, 50).

This new situation resulted in a strengthening of the monarchy over Parliament during the Tudor Era, to such an extent that, as van Caenegem (1995, 105) points out, Elisabeth I managed to impose upon Parliament the distinction (of dubious constitutionality) between affairs of common interest (*commonwealth matters*), which could be freely debated in the House of Commons, and *matters of state*, which could only be addressed by Parliament with the monarch's consent.[41]

It is true that the most important laws still took the form of Acts of Parliament because, in principle, they represented legislation that had been agreed upon by the king and Parliament, even though the latter was constantly being pressured and even coerced by the king, and not only in religious matters, such as divorce and the king's subsequent marriage, but also concerning strictly civil affairs. In fact, during the reign of Henry VIII, Parliament passed significant reform legislation on important aspects of private law: wills, debts, limitation of prescription, the protection of lessees, wrongful dispossession, joint tenancies' and marriage (Elton 1979, 17). The vast majority of these laws, however, were conceived and advanced by the monarch. As Baker (1990, 237) explains, this was largely because of the fact that legislation during the Tudor era was no longer the government's vague reply to vaguely worded complaints, but rather the deliberate adoption of specific proposals embodied in specific texts, in part because Parliament was extending its sphere of activity, but also because, in addition to the laws agreed to with Parliament, Henry VIII did not hesitate to enact a whole series of ordinances without consulting Parliament. All of these lower-level legislative ordinances acquired status as ordinary law upon validation by an Act of Parliament (Statute of Proclamations) in 1539 (Adair 1917),[42] which is why Elton (1974, 260) speaks of the existence of the Rule of Law in sixteenth-century England.

Parliament's relative weakness under the Tudor regime was due in part to the monarchy's financial solvency. Henry VII was so thrifty that his regime was almost able to rely solely upon the revenues it drew from the Crown's lands, which spared him from having to convene Parliament to petition it for funds. By confiscating the assets of the regular clergy when he broke up with Rome, his sales of large expanses of royal property, and the initiating of lucrative colonial ventures,[43] Henry VIII and

[41] She did have the precedent of her father, who in 1532, had prohibited the members of the Westminster Parliament from discussing the question of his divorce.

[42] Thanks to this, during King Henry VIII's reign, 677 statutes were approved, occupying almost as much space as all the legislation produced since the Magna Carta until then (Baker 1990, 237).

[43] Among other reasons, thanks to the granting of letters of marque by Elisabeth I to figures such as Francis Drake (1540–1596), who managed to attack numerous Spanish galleons and wrest major amounts of wealth from attacks on Spain's overseas possessions.

Elisabeth I assured that the Crown held enough assets to avoid appealing to Parliament for money. Most important of all was that during their reigns there came about what Crossman (1969, 54) very aptly describes as a middle class revolution, a phenomenon which reached England two centuries earlier than France, and made possible the consolidation of a wealthy class of entrepreneurs that would end up controlling Parliament in the following century.[44]

Notwithstanding the foregoing, it is indisputable that the Westminster Parliament continued to exist, and did play an important role during the Tudor period. The kings never intended to dispense with the Parliament, and formally respected the traditional legal procedures, even though the monarch was able to impose his will without difficulty. It should be noted, however, that there were cases in Parliament of groups which organized in opposition to royal policy. Under the reign of Mary Tudor, when the rejection of the Edwardian Reformation was debated, 80 of the 359 members of the House of Commons voted against the Crown. And when it came to debating the issue of returning the *décima* tax to the Papacy,[45] the royal proposition was approved by a vote of only 193 to 126 (van Caenegem 1995, 107). Also worth mentioning were the legislative initiatives being advanced by cities, companies and even some individuals. Even though only a small number of these proposals actually resulted in the passing of legislation, the very existence of these practices demonstrates the vitality of the institution.[46]

#### 9.2.3.2 The French Estates General

The Estates General in France was less effectual than the English Parliament, as the king convened it very sporadically in the Modern Age, only when he found himself in a critical situation (van Caenegem 1995, 100).

The first was convoked in 1302, because Philip IV needed the support of his kingdom to oppose the papacy. Charles VII (1422–1461), had to convene the body to win the Hundred Years War, although he seized the opportunity to establish a set of permanent taxes which, for the most part, would endure until 1789. His son Louis XI also convened the Estates, in 1468, to put down a rebellion among the nobles. However, the entity did not meet again until 1483, in Tours. In the wake of the king's death, it was called to issue a statement condemning the late monarch's authoritarian methods and to endorse the principle that the king could not levy taxes

[44] "The Tudor epoch was essentially a period of action and of expansion. Men were so busy making the new state that they had no time to speculate about it. Neither Henry nor Elisabeth explicitly claimed Divine Right for their sovereignty or explicitly demanded passive obedience. They ruled as secular autocrats on the model of Machiavelli, and they were prudent enough to placate their supporters and often submit to their wishes" (Crossman 1969, 51).

[45] As its name indicates, the *décima* was a tax consisting of paying 10 % of production, generally agricultural, to the Church.

[46] On the Parliament's sovereignty and its relationship to royal supremacy during the Tudor era, see Elton (1999, 236–240).

without their consent. However, when the monarchical principle and royal power was secured, the kings ceased to convene the Estates General: neither Louis XII (1498–1515), nor Francis I (1515–1547) nor Henry II (1547–1559), ever did so. They were convoked once again, even with some frequency, by the last Valois kings in the second half of the sixteenth century, but this was a direct consequence of the turbulent Wars of Religion (1562–1598), a period during which the French kingdom was immersed in a permanent state of civil war. Beginning with the reign of the first Bourbon, Henry IV, the king's power was strengthened and the Estates General lost their importance once again. Convoked in 1614 by the widow of the first French Bourbon and the regent of Louis XIII, Marie de Medici, it would not be convened again until 1789.[47]

The Estates General were "put into dormancy" (Desrayaud 1996, 506) because Richelieu, prime minister from 1630 to 1642, was of the opinion that the Estates General were incompatible with royal sovereignty. Richelieu also acted to abolish the Provincial Estates,[48] which were convened by the king when he needed subsidies and could not convene the Estates General (Sueur 1989, 273).[49]

#### 9.2.3.3 The Spanish Monarchy and the *Cortes* of the Iberian Kingdoms

In the Iberian Peninsula, the *Cortes* in Castile could not counteract the crown's burgeoning authority and entered into a clear decline following the reign of Isabella and Ferdinand. The number of towns represented dropped from 49 in 1391, to 17 by 1480 (O'Callaghan 2013, 585). Their political influence virtually disappeared after the defeat at Villalar (1523), ending the rebellion of the Castilian cities (War of the Communities), against Charles V. The fatal blow, nevertheless, came in 1538, when Castilian prelates and nobles who had traditionally attended them, though irregularly, ceased to do so at all, which undercut the representativeness of the Castilian

[47] For an overview of the formation and development of the Estates General from 1302 to 1614, see Harouel et al. (2007, 392–397).

[48] In addition to the Estates General there were the Assemblies of Notables which, as they did not convene the representatives of the cities, were more easily manipulated than the former, and which only acquired a certain importance at the end of the Old Regime, after 1787. Also a factor were the Provincial Estates, though these assemblies almost disappeared in the geographical area stretching from the Seine to the Loire, even prior to Richelieu's death. In other areas of France, they continued to enjoy some importance, specifically the Provincial Estates of Brittany, Languedoc and Burgundy, and those from smaller regions, such as Artois, the French region of Flanders. These assemblies were essentially gatherings of representatives drawn from the local oligarchies, and their essential charge was to negotiate the taxes levied by the authorities in Paris, as well as to secure advantages from the monarchy's government (van Caenegem 1995, 100). Neither were these other estate-based assemblies successful in terms of limiting the power of France's monarchs. On this interesting aspect of France's Old Regime, see Swann (2012, 93–110).

[49] Louis XIV continued his policy and at the beginning of the eighteenth century they were only four Provincial Estates left in France: Britanny, Burgundy, Languedoc and Provence (Jones 1995, 35).

assembly of the estates. Clear evidence of this was the consolidation of unilateral royal legislation outside the purview of the *Cortes* and its dictates, with the issuance of what were known as *pragmáticas*. The case was that the *Cortes* was unable to pressure the kings based on the body's capacity to generate revenue, as the Spanish monarchs were receiving massive quantities of gold and silver from their American colonies. Thus, it is hardly surprising that henceforth the *Cortes* in Castile and León played an increasingly formal, token role, with the kings convening them essentially to add greater solemnity to the announcement of certain decisions and acts which they had proposed. Another of their primary functions involved the royal succession; it was the *Cortes* which heard the oath taken by the crown prince, a necessary step for him to become king.[50]

The weakness of the *Cortes* in Castile did not mean, however, that the Castilians did not resist the absolute authority of the king. The lack of a powerful central administration led the monarchy to delegate to local powers essential aspects, such as military recruitment and the collection of taxes. It should also be noted that tax revenues in Castile depended essentially on the peculiar *servicio de millones*, which charged local authorities with collecting special taxes. The Crown had no organizational system capable of obtaining what the king required, its effective financial administration relying upon the assent of a complex network of private individuals and public corporations, each with particular interests and conditions (MacKay 2006, 9).[51]

In contrast, the *Cortes* formally preserved their authority and political relevance in the eastern kingdoms of the old Crown of Aragon (Aragon, Catalonia and Valencia), in which the structure of pact-based rule was relatively solid during the sixteenth and seventeenth centuries, and where there were still three separate assemblies. There existed, however, a progressive submission on the part of the Catalonian, Valencian and Aragonian *Cortes* to the crown, as demonstrated by, for example, the practice of the Aragonian, Valencian and Catalan representatives meeting together in one locality (generally Monzón), because the kings didn't have time to convene them separately. In addition, the manner of convoking the *cortes* and the procedure according to which its sessions were conducted were simplified in such a way as to favor royal power over the course of the sixteenth and seventeenth centuries. Nevertheless, the *cortes* still decided important matters. For instance, the *Cortes de Catalunya* reorganized the Catalonian legal system,[52] the

---

[50] Such was the case with the *Cortes de Toledo* of 1480, which resolved the problem of territorial usurpations by the nobles, or the *Cortes de Toro* of 1505, which made possible the approval of the era's most complete private, Castilian stipulation of statutory law. Henceforth the monarchs would convene the Castilian *Cortes* above all to recognize the heir to the throne.

[51] In 1660, for instance, the Council of Finance (*Consejo de Hacienda*) was considering a dossier of information from dozens of towns in Castile, Galicia and Extremadura, submitted in support of demands for fiscal remission (Stradling 2002, 296).

[52] In 1599, the *Cortes de Barcelona*, presided over by Philip III established the legal rank (*orden de prelación*) of the different orders of Catalonian legislation (Tomás y Valiente 2004, 279).

*Cortes de Aragón* tried to adopt measures against the economic crisis,[53] and the *Cortes de Valencia* were active defending the Valencian legal system.[54]

*Cortes* were also quite active in Portugal between 1580 and 1640, when the kingdom became part of the Catholic Monarchy (Bouza Álvarez 1987). *Las Cortes del Reino de Navarra*, became extremely active once the kingdom was absorbed into the Catholic Monarchy by military occupation in 1512 (Arvizu y Galarraga 1989), and would go on to become the most powerful and lasting *cortes* in Spain, continuing to exist until the nineteenth century.

#### 9.2.3.4 The Case of the German Assemblies

In Germany, most of the parliaments maintained their authorities during the sixteenth century, later losing their political influence during the seventeenth, relegated to serving as mere administrative bodies that executed the princes' decisions.[55]

## 9.3 The State of the Prince

In absolute monarchy, the king becomes the sole repository of power. As such, all state functions are placed in his hands, not only judicial functions (which he already held in medieval times), but also legislative ones. Unlike what happened in the monarchies of the Late Middle Ages, the absolute monarchs could make decisions and pass laws without necessarily consulting the assemblies of the estates. This marked an important development, as in the Middle Ages the king could not alter the order established by God through creation, but only maintain and protect it. Ultimately, the absolute kings established themselves as governors and developed a centralized administration with a very dense network of royal agents, paid for by an efficient tax system that, among other things, enabled them to maintain powerful armies and bring about a "military revolution" (Downing 1993, 10) that consolidated Europe's system of modern states.[56] As Zmora (2001, 9) points out, the modern state was built upon the pillars of war and taxation.

---

[53] Especially in the last third of the seventeenth century, during the reign of Charles II (Aguilera-Barchet 2007, 37–47).

[54] Concretely, by opposing royal laws that went against the rules approved by the *cortes* (*contrafueros*) (Guía Marín 1984, 97–103).

[55] On the decline of the Landtag, see Myers (1975, 105–110).

[56] The "military revolution" refers to the process whereby small, decentralized, self-equipped feudal powers were dominated by increasingly large, centrally financed and supplied armies wielding ever more sophisticated and expensive weaponry (Parker 1976, 195–214). This led to an exponential growth of public expenses and the consolidation of huge bureaucratic apparatuses

### 9.3.1 The Expansion of Royal Jurisdiction

The absolute king inherited from his medieval forerunners status as the *supreme judicial authority*. Relevant in this regard is the case of France in which, although the courts and parlements generally exercised their functions without interference by the king, their decisions theoretically could always be overridden by the *Conseil du Roi* (Hamscher 1987) by virtue of the principle of "retained jurisdiction" (*justice retenue*), according to which the king continued to stand as the supreme judge, a status which he never transferred to the magistrates (Lebigre 1995, 48). Moreover, the king could forgo regular court proceedings and imprison certain individuals unilaterally through the use of *lettres de cachet*, which required no justification.[57]

In England, along with the traditional courts there appeared the *prerogative courts*: special tribunals created by the Crown to deal with offenses considered particularly antisocial, or to prosecute especially recalcitrant individuals. One of these bodies was what was called the Star Chamber (*Camera stellata*),[58] which became a court under the presidency of Cardinal Wolsey, and was not bound by general common law procedure, therefore generally imposing stricter sentences. Under the Tudors, the King's Privy Council, the supreme governmental body, and the state's security services went so far as to employ torture, resorting to the rack to secure confessions in criminal cases with political implications. The legal channel through which to handle political process were bills of attainder.[59] Used with some frequency since the War of the Roses in the middle of the fifteenth century, the practice peaked in the sixteenth, particularly during the reign of Henry VIII, who employed this legal instrument to have his political enemies executed, as was the case with Thomas More, Anne Boleyn, and Thomas Cromwell, who all ended up on the scaffold. These bills were also used by Elisabeth I and the Stuarts and, more rarely, in the eighteenth century. This special process suspended all guarantees, as

---

reinforcing the power of the state. On the relationship between war and the rise of the state, see Tilly (2002).

[57] The *lettres de cachet* became one of the symbols of arbitrary criminal law under France's absolute monarchy, and were already criticized by one of its main revolutionary leaders, Le Comte de Mirabeau (1749–1791) on the eve of the French Revolution in a book published in Hamburg in 1782, but written in 1778 (de Mirabeau 1782).

[58] The "Star Chamber" was so called because the body's sessions were held at the Palace of Westminster in a room with gilded stars on the ceiling. The Star Chamber offered the government an effective forum for prosecuting sedition and ecclesiastical offences when juries might not cooperate. The association of the Star Chamber with unpopular prosecutions and vindictive punishments led to its abolition in 1641 (Baker 1990, 136–137).

[59] From the French word a*tteindre* (to attain, hit, reach or affect). According to Black's Legal Dictionary an "attainder" under common law involved the suspension of civil rights and capacities whenever a person who had committed treason or felony received a sentence of death for his crime. The effect of "attainder" upon such a felon was, in general terms, that all his assets were forfeited (Black 2009, 160). Bills of attainder were legislative acts, regardless of their form, that applied either to named individuals or to easily ascertainable members of a group in such a way as to inflict punishment on them without a judicial trial (Ibidem, 146 and 188).

individuals could be condemned for treason based on nothing more than a simple accusation, even if uncorroborated by witnesses. The accused were not even assured access to a minimally competent defense.[60]

In the Spain of the Catholic Monarchy, one of the few instruments of the Castilian model through which the kings asserted their power over the former Crown of Aragon, involved the creation of *audiencias* (courts) and *chancillerias* (chanceries); in 1493, the High Court of Catalonia was created, and in 1506 that of Valencia, both established at King Ferdinand's behest. Philip II would later found the Royal Court of Mallorca in 1571. The Spanish Monarchy also employed another powerful instrument: the Tribunal of the Holy Office of the Inquisition, created by a papal bull in 1478, in response to a request by the Catholic Kings. The Tribunal became the only royal court authorized to everywhere with full territorial jurisdiction, and was not abolished until 1834.[61]

### 9.3.2 A King Above the Law?

If the expansion of the kings' judicial authority was relatively easy, it was far more difficult for the medieval monarchs to exercise legislative powers (Desrayaud 1996, 399). Thus, the essential development bolstering absolutism was that the sovereign laid claim to the authority to create laws. Previously kings had only been able to conserve traditional customs; they could confirm them and, above all, protect them by exercising their roles essentially as judges, a function afforded them as representatives of God on Earth. Unlike their medieval predecessors, however, absolute monarchs came to stand above the law (*legibus solutus*), and were able to actually devise it, which is precisely why they were regarded as *absolute monarchs*. In this way, they had fully recovered the legislative function which had been a prerogative

[60] A bill of attainder, as a legislative act directed against a designated person, pronouncing him guilty of an alleged crime (usually treason), without a trial or conviction according to the recognized rules of procedure, was employed in criminal sentences whose sole justification was for reasons of state and political expediency. The most serious abuse of attainders involved their use against prisoners who were, in principle, within the jurisdiction of the common law courts and, therefore, could have been lawfully tried (Plucknett 1956, 205). This procedure was used for the first time in 1321 against Hugh Despenser the Younger, Earl of Gloucester, and his father, the Duke of Winchester, Hugh Despenser the Elder. Both, paradoxically, were condemned by the barons and feudal lords for supporting the king. The last bill of attainder was issued in 1798, against the leader of Irish rebels Lord Edward Fitzgerald (1774–1798). Bills of attainder are expressly prohibited by the United States Constitution: "No bill of attainder or *ex post facto* law shall be passed" (Article 1, Section 9, 3rd Clause).

[61] Through the original bull of November 1, 1478, Pope Sixtus IV enabled Isabella and Fernando to name three royal inquisitors, but only in the Crown of Castile. In the Crown of Aragon, the medieval Inquisition, depending upon Rome, was still active until the Catholic Kings received papal authorization to extend the royal (or New) Inquisition to their eastern kingdoms (Contreras and Dedieu 1993, 5) in 1481.

of the Roman emperors. In the Early Modern Period the old medieval *roi justicier* would become a *roi législateur* (Olivier-Martin 1997, 197–199).

The aspect in which the absolute monarchies of the Modern Age most clearly differed from their late medieval precursors lay in their capacity to openly "create" law, as they were no longer limited to merely upholding traditional customs. The king was, then, no longer just a judge. Rather, he now stood above the law (*princeps legibus solutus est*)[62] and to actually create it (Esmein 2004, 201–214).

It would be in Castile where, without any doubt, kings first exercised this legislative function. The first Castilian legislation was the product of negotiations, as the king approved laws with the *Cortes* through what were called *ordenamientos de leyes* (legal ordinances), agreements which took precedence over local customs since 1348.[63] Beginning in the first decades of the fifteenth century the legislative power of Castilian kings was so well established that even the *Cortes* recognized that the king's right to create law.[64] The Castilian monarchs, in fact, began to introduce laws without the need for the *Cortes*' approval, as they were able to

[62] The problem in the medieval period was that the texts included in the Justinian Corpus Iuris were contradictory. On the one hand in the Digest Ulpian states that *princeps legibus solutus est* (D. I. IV, 31), and in the Institutes *Quod principi placuit legis habet vigorem* (Inst. I, II, 6) but on the other an imperial constitutions states the contrary: "It is a word worthy of the majesty of the ruler that the Prince professes himself bound to the Law: so much does our authority depend upon the authority of the Law. And truly, greater than the imperium is the submission of the principate to the laws" ("*Digna vox maiestate regnantis legibus alligatum se principem profiteri*; *adeo de auctoritate iuris nostra pendet auctoritas. Et re vera maius imperio est submittere legisbus principatum*" C.1.14.4). As Kantorowicz (1997, 105–106) points out the medieval lawyers could not possibly fail to notice the antinomy prevailing between the maxims *princeps legibus solutus* and *princeps legibus alligatus*, and this explains why the emperor Frederic II emphasized that he was *legibus solutus*, but at the same time, he acknowledged that he was bound to Reason which commands all kings ("*Sed quamquam solute imperialis a quibuscumque legibus sit maiestas, sic tamen in totum non est exempta iudicio rationis, que iuris est mater*").

[63] This is the famous first law of Title 28, passed by the *Cortes de Alcalá de Henares* convened by Alfonso XI, that include the first express legal official recognition of royal legislative power (Otero Varela 1993–1994, 507–508) and his full triumph over traditional custom. According to the legal ordinance of 1348, conflicts were to be decided by first applying the terms set down in said "legal disposition", with law proceeding from local customs only to be turned to as a secondary recourse. Over time the disposition came to be interpreted in a more comprehensive manner, as kings concluded that all law created by the crown, with or without the *Cortes*' approval, was to be applied, by default.

[64] It is significant that in 1445, the *Cortes de Olmedo*, held in the presence of John II of Castile, declared that the law was subject to the king, who could not be judged by men "because he does not have his power from men, but from God, whose place he holds in secular affairs". Divine law "expressly commands and forbids anyone to dare to touch the king and prince as one who is anointed by God, or even to comment or say anything evil about him, or even to think it in spirit; rather, he should be held as God's vicar... no one should dare to oppose him, because those who resist the king evidently wish to resist the ordinance of God" (O'Callaghan 2013, 580).

promulgate *pragmáticas*, edicts which were as valid and effectual as laws approved through pacts with said body.[65]

This tendency for kings to monopolize the power to legislate, became widespread in Europe during the sixteenth century. Even the English Parliament, which in the Late Middle Ages was Europe's most powerful assembly of the estates, exhibited a surprising degree of deference to monarchs, such as Henry VIII (1491–1547), and his daughter Isabel I (1558–1603), with both chambers accepting, without protest, the laws which said sovereigns submitted to them.[66]

In France, however, paradoxically, the kings were slow to adopt a role as legislators. It would not be until Louis XIV (1643–1715), that the monarchy began to introduce reform through legislation, prevailing over the jealously-guarded power of traditional customs which had been respected by his predecessors. In this he was helped by Colbert, who flattered the Sun King with the title of "the new Justinian" and called for the codification of royal laws, which was to represent the major achievement of the king's reign (Birn 2005, 121).[67]

---

[65] The power of the Castilian kings by the end of the Middle Ages was so great that their *pragmáticas*, could nullify laws approved by the *Cortes*, and the representatives of the Castilian cities accepted not only the legislative power of the kings, but also the supremacy of royal laws over all other Castilian prescripts (González Alonso 1980, 476).

[66] Thus, for example, when it approved the law declaring Henry VIII's marriage to Catherine of Aragon null and void, or in 1536, when another law of Parliament, imposed by the monarch, also voided his second marriage, to Anne Boleyn. The law also stipulated that any person who deemed the marriage valid would be condemned for treason. As Baker (1990, 564) points out, Henry VIII did not introduce a novel approach to divorce, as what he had really done was to interpret the canonical rules to his own advantage. From this perspective, the statutes he passed concerning his marriages were merely confirmations of his interpretation of the universal law of the Church. The problem was that his divorces had bastardized two future queens of England: Mary, the daughter of Catherine of Aragon, and Elisabeth, the daughter of Anne Boleyn. Each of them upon their accession, restored her legitimacy via an act of Parliament, and in doing so demonstrated more respect for the sovereign power of parliament than their father.

[67] It is interesting to note that the task was immense as from north to south contradictory, Germanic and Roman legal traditions divided France. Clerical courts ruled for the laity on matters of domestic life, such as marriage contracts, while regions and corporations had their own law. More than 80 different civil laws existed, and procedure varied from place to place. Colbert convened a commission of experts that was able to draw up some "Great Ordinances" (*Grandes Ordonnances*) in the royal French tradition. In 1669, he devised one to protect forest lands for eventual use in primary industries, such as shipbuilding, though it was based on Francis I's 1516 *Grande Ordonnance des Eaux et Forêts*. In 1673, there appeared a commercial ordinance, the *Code Savary* for Jacques Savary (1622–1690), its main author. A maritime ordinance appeared in 1680, and another for colonies and slaves in 1685, called the *Code Noir*. Nevertheless, in civil and criminal law, Colbert's commission never managed to do more than establish uniform procedures, and arbitrary and brutal punishments were left untouched.

## 9.4 Absolutism Versus Autocracy: The Legal Limits of Royal Absolutism

The liberal tradition strongly condemns absolutism in all its manifestations. The negative aspects of absolutist autocracy may jar observers today who are accustomed to living under regimes which are at least, formally bound to respect the rule of law. The main contemporary dictionaries consider as synonyms of the word *absolute*, with regards to its political meaning, the words *arbitrary*, *autarchic*, *autocratic*, *despotic*, *tyrannical*, *tyrannous and totalitarian.*[68]

Obviously, there were cases of arbitrary arrests ordered by French monarchs via *lettres de cachet*, which condemned whomever the king designated to the Bastille without due process, such as in the ominous Calas Affair (1763), which was publically denounced by Voltaire,[69] who was sent to the Bastille on several occasions.[70] A number of prominent prisoners died in a dungeon, such as the former ex minister Nicolas Fouquet,[71] not to mention the arbitrary processes and executions carried out, such as those of the ex *controleur général des finances* Jacques de Beaune, Baron of Semblançay, during the reign of Francis I (Knecht 2005, 195–198).

In the Spain of Philip II, we can cite the emergence of special courts such as the *Tribunal de Tumultos*, organized in 1567 by the Duke of Alba in the Netherlands, which put to death the counts of Horn and Egmont, among others; the shocking murder of Juan de Escobedo (1578), ordered by the king for reasons of state (Pérez de Tudela y Bueso 2003, 221–229); the dubious guarantees in criminal proceedings handled by bailiffs and clerks; and the indiscriminate use of torture, censured by Cervantes in the Quixote.[72]

In England, we have already mentioned the "special" proceedings of the Star Chamber, the bills of attainder, the actions of Henry VIII to divorce his first wife,

---

[68] In the Merriam-Webster Dictionary of Synonyms, the word *absolute* is considered a synonym of the terms: *autocratic*, *arbitrary*, *despotic*, *tyrannical*, *tyrannous* (1984, 5). The authors of the Pocket Oxford American Dictionary and Thesaurus (2010, 3), add the word *dictatorial*.

[69] Calas died of torture on the wheel, despite being innocent. In 1763, Voltaire, in his *Treatise on Tolerance* (Voltaire 2000, 107–136), denounced that the Huguenot Calas was a victim of Christian religious fanaticism. The sentence was annulled in 1764, and another court exonerated the unfortunate Calas posthumously in 1765.

[70] Thus, in the end he moved to Switzerland, just a short distance from the French border in Ferney, to keep from being bothered again by the monarchy for his opinions.

[71] Louis XIV's Minister of Finance was jailed for life via a simple royal order, without any trial, after being accused of embezzlement—probably for having raised suspicions over the origins of the fortune of a king who he had hitherto faithfully served. The enmity between Fouquet and Colbert, the Sun King's powerful minister, was the key to the former's arrest (Drazin 2008, 234).

[72] Don Quixote I, 22_ "Regarding the liberty that Don Quixote gave to many unfortunate men who, against their wills, were taken where they did not wish to go" (de Cervantes 2003, 163–172). On the abuses in the use of torture in criminal procedure under *Ancien Regime* Spain, see Alonso (1982, 250 and 290–302) and Tomás y Valiente (2000, 15–36). For an overall view of criminal law during the era of absolutism, see Tomás y Valiente (1992).

and his execution of multiple, succeeding wives, including Anne Boleyn and Catherine Howard, reinforce this same idea of autocratic despotism. Defying the king's will constituted a crime of high treason, punishable by death. Thus, former chancellor Sir Thomas More's refusal to accept the king's religious policy led him to the scaffold in 1535, even though he had been one of the monarch's most trusted men.[73]

However, when one examines the reality of the absolute monarchies of the sixteenth and seventeenth centuries more closely, it is surprising the degree to which the monarch's power was actually checked by a series of forces and mechanisms, in states that were, in the end, not, in fact, absolute (Harouel et al. 2007, 454).

A common impression is that the absolute monarchs could do whatever they wished, beholden to nobody and needing nothing. Yet things were hardly this simple. Although the absolute monarchs of the era did have more power than their Late Medieval predecessors, their autocracy was subject to a series of restrictions which mitigated the absolutism of their regimes, including: the limits imposed by natural and divine laws, fundamental laws, the monarchy's financial struggles, obstacles to territorial unification, and the relative autonomy of judges.[74]

### 9.4.1 Absolute Kings, Constrained by Divine and Natural Law

The Christian kings during the Absolutist Era continued to subscribe to the idea of divine right as the base of their legitimacy. Not only were the kings of France anointed, but were called the "most Christian king" (*Roi très chrétien*), while as of 1494, the king of Spain was "His Catholic Majesty". They were, therefore, at least subject to Catholic principles, as their legitimacy was based upon the laws of God and nature. Thus, for example, Philip II, before ordering the killing of John of Austria's secretary, Juan de Escobedo, first sought out the opinion of a board of theologians. In the case of the king of France, subjects were actually authorized to disobey monarchs who acted in ways contrary to the teachings of the Church and the Christian religion. In this way, the role of royal confessors was essential, as in many cases, it should be noted, the king's chief advisers were clergy.

In addition to divine laws, the kings were to respect the limits of natural laws established by principles such as marriage and the freedom to move about freely.

[73] For a general overview of the history of English criminal procedure, see Baker (1990, 550–591). On the criminal law during the Tudor Era: Bellamy (1984).

[74] As Bernard (1979, 1) observes, absolutism did not preclude the rule of law. A ruler may himself be above the law, and even have the power to make law without reference to any other agency, but the manner in which he administered existing law could still be determined by fixed and generally recognized rules. It might not be illegal for an absolute ruler to ignore these rules, strictly speaking, but it was certainly an affront to tradition. Even the notorious *lettres de cachet* in France represented no more than a minor and very occasional exception to this rule.

They were bound to respect as well certain elements of private law, such as a respect for their subjects' property and freedom—a principle which in France was called *honnête liberté des français* (Desrayaud 1996, 546) and explains why the subjects of the French kings considered themselves to be collectively free (Olivier-Martin 1988, 308–309).

### *9.4.2 The Limits of "Fundamental Laws"*

Although in theory the absolute monarchs could create law, they still had to adjust their actions to respect and maintain their kingdoms' traditional order. In this regard, in 1574 the French Protestant lawyer Theodore de Bèze coined a term when he referred to the "fundamental laws of the kingdom".[75] This term referred to an indefinite set of norms and customs which had gradually come to shape monarchies' actions over time,[76] governing aspects such as succession to the throne, the Catholic character of the monarchy, and the inalienability of the prerogatives constituting royal authority.[77]

Given this state of affairs, royal jurists drew a distinction between "ordinary laws" (*lois ordinaires*), which expressed the king's will, and which he himself could abolish, and "fundamental laws", which transcended him. The legal consequence of this was that if the monarch established a law contrary to a fundamental principle of the monarchy, it came to be considered arbitrary and, though it had to be obeyed during his reign, it could be repealed after his death. For instance, the young Louis XVI's repeal of the severe measures taken against the parlements at the end of the reign of Louis XV (Maupeou Reform), was based on this principle, aimed at restoring the basic laws of the kingdom (Harouel et al. 2007, 581–582). Ultimately, however, it is true that it was the king himself who decided when legislation represented a fundamental law.

---

[75] In his treaty *Du Droit des Magistrats sur leurs sujets* (García Pérez 2008, 49–50). On the political thought of Théodore de Bèze, see Kingdon (1992, 96–108).

[76] For an overview of the meaning of the term "Fundamental Laws", García Pérez (2008, 49–62) and Thompson (1986, 1103–1128).

[77] In France, the following were accepted as fundamental laws: the hereditary nature of the Crown (based on the principles of primogeniture and masculinity); the continuity of the Crown; and the inviolability of the *dominio regio*, that is, the set of properties which belonged to the monarchy. Debated, on the other hand, was whether the provinces' traditional privileges were fundamental laws of the kingdom. Local jurists maintained that they were, while those on the king's council argued that they were not (Harouel et al. 2007, 297–299).

### 9.4.3 Respect for Traditional Customs

Another check on kings' absolute power was the respect that they were expected to exhibit for traditional customary law. While this was not the case in Castile, where kings by the Late Middle Ages could unilaterally abrogate the old ways, it was the case in France, where in the sphere of private law the parlements were the guarantors of respect for the different *coûtumes*—even when they clashed with the monarchy.

To this must be added kings' respect for their kingdoms' territorial distribution, inherited from the medieval period. France was divided into three provinces determined by when and under what circumstances, they had been brought under the French Crown: *pays d'élection*, *pays d'états* and the territories known as *pays conquis*. The first of these enjoyed the largest apparatus of self-government, while the latter were more directly linked to the government in Paris. Moreover, in the second half of the eighteenth century, among the different territories there was a whole series of variations in customs barriers and traditional law—prompting Voltaire to observe that one travelling through France changed laws as often as he did horses.[78]

Under the Spanish monarchy, the respect for traditional law (the privileges of the kingdom) was also the order of the day in the eastern kingdoms formerly forming part of the Crown of Aragon (the kingdoms of Aragon, Valencia, Mallorca and the Principality of Catalonia), with them conserving almost all of the privileges which had been secured by their medieval *cortes*. Interestingly, their private law was even respected by Philip V when he abolished their traditional constitution through the *Nueva Planta* Decrees.[79] Thus, in the sixteenth and seventeenth centuries, though the kings of Spain were the West's most powerful, on paper, in practice they occupied a very different constitutional position in each and every one of their kingdoms. In fact, they were only absolute monarchs in Castile,[80] which explains why whenever possible, the Spanish monarchs brought the territories they conquered or occupied, such as Navarre and the Americas, under the Castilian Crown, where their power was not constrained by all the impediments upon it in places such

[78] "Outre ces quarante mille lois, dont on cite toujours quelqu'une au hasard, nous avons cinq cent quarante coutumes différentes, en comptant les petites villes et même quelques bourgs, qui dérogent aux usages de la juridiction principale; de sorte qu'un homme qui court la poste, en France, change de lois plus souvent qu'il ne change de chevaux" (Voltaire 1836, 430). On the respect the Kings owed French customary law, see Harouel et al. (2007, 406–409).

[79] Except the Kingdom of Valencia, which completely lost its private law under the Decree of 1707, Aragon, Mallorca and Catalonia retained their traditional law under the Decrees of 1711, 1715 and 1716 (Escudero López 2003, 642–644).

[80] With the notorious exception of the Basque Provinces, incorporated under the Castilian Crown in 1200 (Guipuzcoa), 1332 (Alava) and 1379 (Vizcaya), preserving their peculiar legal regimes until 1876. On the origins of the regulatory system of the three Basque Provinces, see Tomás y Valiente (2004, 249–261).

as Aragon, Catalonia, Valencia, the Netherlands, Italy, Sicily, Naples, Milan, Franche-Comte, Luxembourg and, after 1580, Portugal.

In England, the kings administrated their kingdom directly but held a different legal position in those territories which had been brought under the Crown later in history (Wales, Scotland and Ireland) to form the United Kingdom, territories which largely retained their own legal peculiarities (Baker 1990, 36–40).[81]

### *9.4.4 The Relative Autonomy of the* Ancien Regime's *Judges*

Absolute monarchies' freedom of action was also checked by the autonomy of judges, who in many areas became the guarantors of traditional privileges and freedoms. A good example is that of France's parlements. These bodies were the highest courts of each province, being made up of jurists who had studied at the most prestigious universities and belonged to the leading families, who bought their "offices" and enjoyed social prestige. The most important of these was the Parlement of Paris, the oldest of them all, founded in the mid thirteenth century.[82] However, the parlement was not simply a judicial court, as it also had political functions (Rogister 2002, 10) as well. In addition to constituting the highest courts in their areas of territorial jurisdiction, since the late Middle Ages, they also acquired the authority to register or transcribe new royal orders—a step without which said mandates were not considered officially published and, therefore, did not enter into force. Registration was not a mere formality. The Parisian parlement even had the right to express criticisms (*remontrances*) of the king's proposals before registering any law. If the king did not address and resolve these complaints, the parlement would return them to the government, which could consider the objections received and revise the text, or order the registration of the law by virtue of royal authority by holding what was known as a *lit de justice*[83]; although the parlement had the right to review royal laws, it could not actually refuse to register them (Desrayaud 1996, 511).

[81] It is interesting that in the case of Scottish Law, the merger of the crowns of Scotland and England in 1603 did not lead to a merger of laws, even though James I wished to see one country with a "uniformity in laws". The reason was that English lawyers, led by Edward Coke, were fearful of "Roman infiltration". When full political union took place in 1707, there was no question that Scottish law should be preserved, subject to any future alterations by the Parliament of Great Britain (Baker 1990, 40).

[82] In 1301, Philip the Fair made it a permanent court in Paris, based in the Royal Palace (Rogister 2002, 2). The provincial parlements were created subsequently to take one part of the Parlement of Paris's work, as it was unable to assume all of it.

[83] A ceremony in which the king personally visited the parlement or summoned it to Versailles, accompanied by the "princes of the blood" and the great officers of the crown to announce its intentions. It was a legal fiction designed to give the impression that the monarch was consulting the parlement, when in fact he was imposing his will (Swann 1995, 2–3).

Thanks to this law of "admonishment", the parlements, especially that of Paris, played an important political role in France under the *Ancien Regime*, especially since the sporadic convocation of the Estates General meant that the parlements came to function as the kingdoms' permanent bulwarks against royal autocracy. They were, as the magistrate D'Aguesseau (1668–1751) said, "the last shout of dying liberty" (*le dernier cri de la liberté mourante*).[84] Thus, it was the parlements which acted against the monarchy in rebellions such as that of The Fronde under Louis XIV (Hamscher 1983), which explains why in 1673, the Sun King introduced the new *caveat* that these criticisms of royal orders could only be presented a posteriori, after they had been registered (Hurt 2002).[85] Nevertheless, under the reign of Philip of Orleans (1715–1723), the right to *remontrance* was reestablished and the parlements would operate once again as the main bodies opposing the monarchy[86]—at least until 1771, when Louis XV ordered Chancellor Maupeou to arrest the defiant members of the Parlement of Paris, and replace them with others more pliant to the Crown's wishes (Harouel et al. 2007, 579–581). Louis XVI's decision to abolish this reform measure would prove to be rash, for the members of the parlements did not defend democratic principles as much as they did the status of the privileged class, as judges were not selected for their ability or legal knowledge, but rather bought or inherited their legal offices.[87] It is no coincidence that the French Revolution of 1789 began with the "revolt of the privileged".

Under the Spanish Monarchy, in the "pact-based" territories the judges safeguarded the kingdoms' traditional privileges from possible royal encroachment.

---

[84] In contrast, Colbert stated that "the noises of parlements are out of season" (*les bruits des parlements ne sont plus de saison*"). See Desrayaud (1996, 515). On the figure of the chancellor Henri François d'Aguesseau, Storez (1996). "*Un ministre, respectable d'ailleurs, mais assez jaloux de l'autorité du Roi, et peut-être de la sienne, pour regarder la moindre résistance comme une révolte, voulut, suivant ce qu'on a dit de Louis XI, mettre totalement "le Roi hors de page", et rompre jusqu'à ces foibles liens qui pouvoient encore embarrasser plutôt qu'arrêter l'autorité du Roi. C'est ce qui fut exécuté par la déclaration du 24 février 1673, par laquelle les parlements furent réduits à ne pouvoir faire éclater leur zèle par leurs remontrances qu'après avoir prouvé leur soumission par l'enregistrement pur et simple des lois qui leur seroient adressé es. Il seroit inutile de parler ici des célèbres remontrances que le parlement de Paris fit en cette occasion* ***et qui furent regardées comme le dernier cri de la liberté mourante****. En effet, depuis cette déclaration, les remontrances furent non seulement différées, mais par là-même abolies. On n'en trouve plus aucun exemple jusqu'à la mort du feu Roi; et pendant le reste de son règne, c'est-à-dire pendant quarante-deux ans, l'enregistrement de tous les édits et de toutes les déclarations est devenu tellement de style que les conseillers ne prenoient pas même la peine d'opiner sur ce sujet*" D'Aguesseau (1819, pp. 14–15).

[85] Which effectively made the *remontrance* useless. When Louis XIV died in 1715, registering a royal edict had become a mere formality (Desrayaud 1996, 515).

[86] In September, the Regent Philip of Orleans rescinded the 1673 declaration because he needed the support of the Parlement to defy Louis XIV (Rogister 2002, 10).

[87] As Swann (1995, 8) points out, the Parlement of Paris was never made up of a closed caste, as of the 590 families represented in it between 1715 and 1771, no fewer than 228 were present for the first time. It was the permanent corporate existence of the Parlement of Paris which enabled it to preserve its strong *esprit de corps*.

The most famous case was that of the jurisdiction of the *Justicia Mayor de Aragón* (Chief Justice Ministry of Aragon) an institution initially imposed by noble marriages, which ended up defending the traditional legal system of Aragon, which the *Justicia* adapted to the times through *observancias*: sentences which were the "direct expression of Aragon's fundamental laws" (Morales Arrizabalaga 2007, 62) and functioned as precedents. This is why they were compiled in collections to be used by Aragonian lawyers and judges (Martínez Díez 1975). It is significant that Philip II himself was unable to imprison Antonio Pérez after he had crossed over into Aragon and placed himself under the jurisdiction of the *Justicia Mayor*,[88] thereby removing him from the scope of royal authority. Out of financial necessity the Spanish monarchy was forced to sell offices, with judgeships being passed down from fathers to sons. The monarchy, however, always retained a certain degree of control over the justice system, at least in Castile, as there existed no institution like the French parlements.

In the England of Henry VIII, the traditional royal tribunals which applied the kingdom's common law continued to enjoy a considerable degree of autonomy, and the same procedural rules as always. However, it should be noted that the authoritarianism of the Tudors and Stuarts did not alter a state of affairs in which Common Law remained the cornerstone of the English legal system, taking precedence over statutes, *ius commune* law, and the special tribunals, which all occupied positions peripheral to it.[89]

## 9.5 Absolute Monarchy and the Increasing Power of the European States

Despite the legal mechanisms restraining the absolute kings' power, they were still powerful enough to transform their kingdoms into great states. They did so internally through the expansion and rationalization of their administrations. At the same time, they sought to expand the scope of their authority externally, a trend which led to a continuous grappling for hegemony among the different European kingdoms.

---

[88] Hence, Philip II tried to accuse his former Secretary Antonio Pérez of heresy. Pérez escaped from royal justice and sought refuge in Aragon under the protection of the special jurisdiction of the *Justicia Mayor*. Those accused of heresy, however, were not protected by the *Justicia*, and had to be remitted to the Royal Inquisitorial Tribunal—the only court under the Spanish monarchy with universal jurisdiction (Martínez Navas 1991, 147). In the end, Pérez managed to escape, finding refuge in France and England.

[89] Baker (1990, 241) mentions the case of Thomas Bonham vs. College of Physicians (1610), in which the court established the principle that common law could prevail over acts of Parliament: "for when an act of Parliament is against common right and reason, or repugnant, or impossible to be performed, the common law will control it and adjudge such act to be void". This was a bold assertion that had some influence on the establishment of legislative judicial review in the U.S.

### 9.5.1 The Technical Advantages of Absolutism

If the absolute kings were all despots and tyrants, it is hard to explain why the absolutist model became widespread throughout Europe and, above all, why it lasted for several centuries. The explanation for the entrenchment and consolidation of absolute monarchy is partly to be found precisely, in the fact that, generally, the absolute kings headed strong governments which managed to maintain domestic order and ensure expansion abroad. This is why Louis XIV, the paragon of absolutism, became the model to be emulated across Europe, essentially because France during his reign was the Continent's most powerful state. Thus did the last Stuart kings in England in the second third of the seventeenth century, seek to follow the legal and political model imposed by the Sun King.

From the point of view of the history of the modern state, it is also indisputable that absolute monarchy became the tool which broke the power of those groups which had hitherto constantly threatened government stability through their infighting and struggling vying for power: the nobles, local oligarchies, cities and religious sects (Wallerstein 2011, 132–163). The people perceived a king wielding overwhelming power as the only force capable of bringing all these privileged classes to heel, dissolving estate-based society and assuring the implementation of the principle that all subjects were equal before their king. The French Calvinist Pierre Bayle (1647–1706), in his *Historical and Critical Dictionary* (1695–1697), wrote that "the only way of preventing civil war in France is the absolute power of the sovereign, vigorously sustained and armed with all necessary force so that is duly feared".[90]

It is telling and significant that the establishment of regimes of absolute monarchy was invariably preceded by situations of anarchy. In Castile, royal authority was overwhelmingly buttressed by the Catholic Monarchs after half a century of long wars between factions of Castilian nobles, which had taken a considerable toll on the kingdom. The strengthening of royal authority was consolidated by Charles I as a result of the "Rebellion of the Communities".[91] Similarly, in France, Henry IV, the first Bourbon, rose to the throne after the ordeal of the Wars of Religion. The strengthening of royal authority was relentlessly continued by Cardinal Richelieu (the chief minister of Henry's son, Louis XIII) who took on the nobility and the Protestants to create a powerful monarchy. The absolutism of Louis XIV was a reaction against the fear and humiliation that the young king suffered during the regency as a result of the Fronde Rebellion, backed by the Parliament and the

[90] "Le seul et le vrai moyen d'éviter en France les guerres civiles est la puissance absolue du souverain, soutenue avec vigueur, et armée de toutes les forces nécessaires à la faire craindre" (Bayle 1820, 441).

[91] The cities of Castile, represented in their *cortes*, rebelled against Charles I, who they accused of being dominated by foreign advisers. After being defeated in 1523, leaders Juan Bravo, Padilla and Maldonado were executed, marking the end of Castilian autonomy and the definitive establishment of the preeminence of royal power.

nobles. The absolutism of the Tudors in England was accepted because it brought an end to the dark chapter of civil strife and anarchy among the nobility spawned by the War of the Roses. Henry VIII was also a popular king because he was able to tame the nobility and even the Church, as he nationalized the secular clergy, dissolved the monasteries and expropriated ecclesiastical holdings.[92]

Most astonishing of all, as Sevillia (2003, 135) points out, is that when we read memoirs, personal diaries, and private letters from the sixteenth and seventeenth centuries we realize that absolutism, as a concept, was not widely contested. A concrete measure of the king's might be unpopular, or his ministers criticized, but the monarch's supreme authority and functions went largely unquestioned. Perhaps this was because, as Anderson (2013, 18) points out, the absolute monarchs were able to pacify the nobles by convincing and reassuring them that their policies would not favor the nascent bourgeoisie in such a way that the traditional elite's position would be threatened. In the same line Dessert (2000, 8) argues that Louis XIV's absolute monarchy was not an autocratic regime, but a centralized and unifying system under which monarchical authority tended to dominate all the dissenting groups and bodies that aspired to play a political role, administrating the country through commissioners named by the king and entirely committed to his authority.[93]

It also should be considered that public opinion throughout Europe began to shift as people realized that royal, absolute governments were more orderly and efficient than the ones which had preceded them under feudalism, especially when absolute monarchs were instilled with the mercantilist ideas of the Modern Age, which endorsed the protection of national economies and favored a conception of the economy better suited to the times, promoting national prosperity.

### *9.5.2 The Administrative Expansion of Absolute Monarchies*

Finally, we must identify as one of the major factors giving rise to the absolutist model of the state, the growing complexity of the government and its administration,

[92] Henry VIII committed atrocities, such as his order to torture and kill 18 Carthusians of the London Charterhouse between 1535 and 1537, simply because they refused to endorse his divorce from Catherine of Aragon, and to back him when he broke with Rome. The monks' approval was important for Henry VIII because the Carthusians enjoyed great prestige in English public opinion. Their opposition to the king's will infuriated Henry VIII to the point that he moved to annihilate them (Gasquet 2006, 202–243).

[93] Rowlands (2002, 2), however, dissents and rejects the traditional depiction of Louis XIV's personal rule as the expression of an authoritarian, bureaucratic and centralizing regime, arguing that the success of Louis XIV's reign owed much to a conscious royal effort to be far more sensitive to the interests and aspirations of the social elite. On the same line, see Beik (2005, 194–224).

which justified the professionalization of governmental tasks and consolidated what Ertman calls the triumph of "Patrimonial Absolutism" (1999, 90).

The absolute ruler personally wielded executive power, as he was able to decide all questions of domestic and international policy, including declarations of war and signings of peace. Consequently, the task of governing became so complex and constraining that kings usually appointed men to the most important administrative offices, and could even delegate the government to trusted individuals. Such was the case with a number of powerful chief ministers during the era, who effectively served as *de facto* rulers: Cardinal Richelieu (1585–1642)[94] and Cardinal Mazarin (1602–1661) in France; Cardinal Thomas Wolsey (1471–1530), and Chancellors Thomas More (1478–1535) and Thomas Cromwell (1485) in England, under Henry VIII. Spain's Catholic Monarchy featured influential royal secretaries such as Francisco de los Cobos (1477–1547), who served under Charles I, and Mateo Vázquez and Antonio Perez under Philip II. Beginning with the reign of Philip III (1598–1621), there appeared the figure of the *valido*, responsible for handling all matters of government in the name of the king,[95] the first of these officials being the Duke of Lerma. The most famous of these *validos* was the Count Duke of Olivares, who effectively governed the Catholic Monarchy during the first phase of Philip IV's reign, beginning in 1621, and during the Portuguese and Catalonian rebellions of 1640.

The exception was Louis XIV, who after Mazarin's death in 1661, personally governed France for more than half a century, though assisted by able ministers and advisory bodies such as the "High Board" (*Conseil d'en haut*),[96] whose members were freely appointed by the monarch, their function being to counsel the king, who made final decisions (Harouel et al. 2007, 342–348). Also noteworthy was the case of England, with its Privy Council (Dicey 2009) under Elizabeth I, chaired successively by William Cecil (1520–1598), and his son Robert Cecil (1563–1612). Under the Spanish Catholic monarchy, affairs of state were handled by different councils, both territorial (Castile, Aragon, Italy, Flanders and America) and specialized (the Councils of State, Treasury and Orders)—all entities created since the era of the Catholic Kings, and consolidated under Charles I and Philip II.[97]

---

[94] On Richelieu's death, Pope Urban III famously said: "If there is a God, Cardinal Richelieu will have much to answer for. If not, he has done very well" (Ohanian 2009, 45).

[95] A *valido* is the person who has access to the monarch and enjoys his friendship and trust, therefore controlling certain areas of the government and its power (Escudero López 2004, 18).

[96] The famous *Conseil des Affaires* which ended up as the *Conseil d'en haut*, the predecessor of the subsequent *Conseil d'État*, a restricted council made up, depending upon the case, of 3–6 members.

[97] At the end of the sixteenth century, the Spanish Catholic Monarchy came to depend on 13 different councils: State, War, the Inquisition, Military Orders, Taxation, Castile, Las Indias (the Americas), Aragon, Navarre, Italy, Portugal, Flanders, and the Chamber of Castile. As Valero Torrijos (2002, 102) observes, despite the heterogeneous nature of these institutions, they shared a certain systematic character, with similar organizing and political principles. Some councils occupied subordinate positions to others, they were all bodies answering to the monarch, they were established at the Court, their functions were political, and their members were able to sit on

As Strayer (1970, 103) notes, the principle of collegiality was a practical solution that allowed the monarch to use experienced, professional councilors freely without delegating too much power to any one of them.

The substantial growth of royal administration and the ensuing consolidation of the state as an institution, proved that the triumph of absolute monarchy was not, however, so much the product of jurists' theoretical constructions as it was the result of significant economic and political transformations experienced by European kingdoms in general after 1500, which demanded a significant bolstering of royal power. As Mulgan (1998, 1) observes, the rising administrative costs of the new monarchies spurred each government to make its financial machinery more effective and to better administrate its resources. The final aim was to augment the wealth of the state through "mercantilism", a protectionist approach by which monarchies sought to bolster their national economies, favoring their industries and establishing a favorable balance of trade, exporting more than importing and monopolizing as many trades as possible. This vision of the economy and national power, encouraged Europe's kings to compete and even clash in a sort of protonational competition; some authors think that the absolute monarchies might be fairly called "national monarchies".

### *9.5.3 Towards a Europe of "National" Monarchies*

However, can we speak of "national" sentiments before the rising of the nation-state at the end of the eighteenth century? It is true that, as Strayer (1970, 109) points out, nationalism is such a vague term that it is not easy to say when it evolved, or how it differs from mere xenophobia, its relationship to old local and regional loyalties, or what its connections are to religious, cultural and linguistic differences. Despite this, it is clearly possible to affirm that in the seventeenth century, there arose signs of what might be called nationalism in the long-established kingdoms of England, France, and Spain, and that it tended to strengthen those states.[98]

As Anderson (2013, 38–39) explains, the royal states during the absolutist period did not disdain to foment patriotic sentiments amongst their subjects during the political and military conflicts which constantly brought the various monarchies of Western Europe into conflict with one another. In his view, we cannot speak of proto-nationalism, as in Tudor England, Bourbon France and Habsburg Spain these feelings did not emanate from a loyal people who felt invested in, and identified with, their land and its institutions. In fact, in his view these "national passions" under absolutism, though they may have appeared to be significant, were in reality

multiple councils at the same time, which assured an indispensable interrelationship between the different parts of this complex government apparatus.

[98] On the formation of the national idea in Spain before the French Revolution, from Roman times to the early eighteenth century, see Aguilera-Barchet (2008, 132–148).

highly contingent and volatile, as power and political legitimacy were of a dynastic nature, constantly vulnerable to manipulation by grandees and sovereigns.

Regardless of the abovementioned debate, it is quite clear that after the Peace of Westphalia (1648), the idea of a universal Christian empire was replaced by an international order based on the struggle between different secular "national monarchies" that would struggle to impose their hegemony through successive wars during the next three centuries.

## TIMELINE

### Fifteenth Century

| | |
|---|---|
| 1494–1497 | First Italian War between France and Spain. |
| 1496 | With the conquest of the island of Tenerife, the occupation of the Canary Islands initiated by the Crown of Castile in 1477 comes to an end. |
| 1497 | Conquest of Melilla by the Castilian knight Salvador de Estopiñán. |
| 1498–1504 | Second Italian War. |
| 1498 | April. Portugal's Vasco de Gama reaches India. |

### Sixteenth Century

| | |
|---|---|
| 1500 | April. Portugal's Pedro Alvares Cabral discovers Brazil. |
| 1502 | On his third voyage, begun in 1501, Amerigo Vespucci (1454–1512) realizes that he has discovered a new continent, which is named for him: *America*. |
| 1504 | December 26. Isabel the Catholic dies. |
| 1506 | May 19. Christopher Columbus dies in Valladolid. |
| 1512 | Conquest of the Kingdom of Navarre (territory located south of the Pyrenees) by Ferdinand the Catholic. |
| 1513 | Niccolo Machiavelli (1469–1527) publishes *The Prince*. |
| 1515 | Francis I becomes the King of France (serving until 1547). |
| 1516 | Charles I, King of Spain (Serving until 1556). |
| 1519 | June 28. Charles I is elected Emperor of the Holy Roman Empire. November 8. Hernán Cortés enters Tenochtitlán (Mexico). |
| 1520–1521 | War of the Communities (April 23, 1521). Spain. The *comuneros* are defeated at Villalar). |
| 1521 | April. Martin Luther defends the Protestant Reformation before Charles V at the Diet of Worms. |
| 1522 | September 6. Juan Sebastián Elcano completes the first circumnavigation of the world. |
| 1525 | February 24. The Battle of Pavia. Charles V captures Francis I of France. |

| | |
|---|---|
| 1527 | Sack of Rome. Charles V's troops, at war with Pope Clement VII, pillage Rome. |
| 1530 | Charles V is crowned Emperor in Bologna by Clement VII. |
| 1532 | Francisco Pizarro conquers Peru. |
| 1534 | After his marriage to Anne Boleyn (1533) Henry VIII of England (1509–1547) severs the Church of England from Rome (Act of Supremacy). |
| 1535 | October. Jacques Cartier founds Quebec in Canada. The beginning of the French colonization of North America. |
| 1540 | The papacy authorizes the founding of the Society of Jesus (Jesuits), created by Ignacio de Loyola. |
| 1542 | Charles I promulgates the "New Laws". Inspired by Bartolomé de las Casas, they are an instrument to protect indigenous peoples in the Americas from abuse by Spanish colonists. |
| 1545 | The Council of Trent begins (ending in 1563). |
| 1547 | Francis I of France dies, succeeded by Henry II, who marries Catherine de Medici. |
| 1553 | Mary Tudor is Queen of England (until 1558). Catholicism gains ground. She marries the future Philip II of Spain on July 25, 1554. |
| 1555 | The Peace of Augsburg. The conflict with the Protestants ends in a stalemate (*cuius regio e ius religio*). |
| 1556 | Charles V abdicates, leaving to his son Philip II all his domains, except those of the Empire. He will continue to hold the imperial title until his death. |
| 1557 | August 10. The Battle of St. Quentin. Momentous Spanish victory on the Feast Day of St. Lawrence. |
| 1558 | September 21. Charles V dies at Yuste. |
| | November 17. Mary Tudor dies in London. Isabel I rises to the throne (1558–1603). |
| 1559 | April 2. The Treaty of Cateau Cambressis. The beginning of Spanish hegemony. |
| | July 10. Death of Henry II of France. Beginning of the regency of Catherine of Medici. |
| 1561 | July. Madrid becomes the capital of the Spanish monarchy. |
| 1563 | The Council of Trent comes to a close (begun in 1545). |
| 1566 | July. Revolt of the Sea Beggars in the Netherlands. The Calvinists attack Catholic churches. |
| 1567 | August 28. The Duke of Alba reaches Brussels at the head of an army. |
| 1568 | June 5. Execution of the Counts of Egmont and Horn. |
| | The anti-Spanish rebellion in the Netherlands spreads. |
| 1571 | October 7. The Battle of Lepanto. |
| 1572 | August 24. The St. Bartholomew's Day Massacre. Killing of Protestants in Paris. |

1576 Jean Bodin (1529–1596) publishes *The Six Books of the Republic.*

1579 Union of Utrecht. Splitting of the Netherlands: The northern, Protestant provinces (Holland) separate from the Catholic provinces in the south.

1580 June. The Duke of Alba invades Portugal at the head of Philip II's troops.

1581 April 15. The Portuguese *Cortes* recognize Philip II as King of Portugal. In exchange the monarch agrees to respect the traditional jurisdiction and privileges of the Portuguese kingdom. On July 27 Philip II arrives in Lisbon, remaining in the Portuguese capital until February 11, 1583.

1588 Failure of Spain's invasion of England (the Invincible Armada).

1589 After converting to Catholicism ("Paris is worth a mass") Henry IV becomes the first king of the House of Bourbon (King of France, until 1610).

1590 Philip II's Secretary, Antonio Pérez Aragón, flees.

1591 Spanish troops under the command of Alejandro Farnesio occupy Paris in support of the Catholic party (until 1595).

1592 *Las Cortes de Tarazona*. Philip II puts an end to the Aragonian revolt, suppressing the lifelong appointment of the Chief Justice of Aragon.

1598 April 13. Henry IV signs the Edict of Nantes. Protestantism is tolerated in France. The "Wars of Religion" which had plagued France (1562–1598) ended.
September 13. Philip II of Spain dies.

### Seventeenth Century

1601 Philip III of Spain (1598–1621) moves the capital of the monarchy to Valladolid.

1603 March 24. Death of Elizabeth I of England.

1605 Publication of the first part of *Don Quixote* by Miguel de Cervantes.

1606 Madrid is once again the capital of the Catholic Monarchy.

1607 The English found their first settlement in North America: *Jamestown* (John Smith and Pocahontas) in Virginia.

1609 April 9. Felipe III, under pressure from the Duke of Lerma, signs the Twelve Years Truce with the United Provinces of the Netherlands. On the same day the decree is issued expelling the *moriscos* (Moors) from the Iberian Peninsula. The effective expulsion would remain in effect until 1614.

1610 Assassination of Henry IV of France. Louis XIII (1610–1643) takes the throne. The regency of his mother, Marie de Medici, lasts until 1614.

1616 April 23. Miguel de Cervantes dies in Madrid. On the same day William Shakespeare dies in Stratford upon Avon (England) (May 3 on the Gregorian calendar).

1618 Defenestration of Prague. The Thirty Years War begins.
1620 November 11. The *Mayflower* reaches the coast of North America (Cape Cod, Massachusetts). On November 21 the occupants of the boat sign the *Mayflower Compact*, a landmark document and harbinger of self-rule in the American colonies.
1621 March 31. Philip II of Spain dies. Philip IV (1621–1665) rises to the throne. The Count Duke of Olivares takes charge of the government (until 1643).
1624 Cardinal Richelieu becomes Chief Minister to Louis XIII.
1625 Charles I, King of England (until 1649).
1626 Philip IV (1621–1665) proclaims the "Union of Arms", a plan advanced by the Count Duke of Olivares to create a common army composed of troops hailing from all across Spain's territories in the service of the Spanish Monarchy.
1628 Richelieu takes La Rochelle. The Protestants are politically subdued by the king of France.
1630 November 10. Richelieu becomes Louis XIII's all-powerful chief minister.
1631 Grotius publishes his work *De iure belli ac pacis.*
1640 Catalonian and Portuguese revolts against Philip IV.
1642 December 4. Cardinal de Richelieu dies in Paris.
1643 May 14. Death of Louis XIII. Regency of Anne of Austria and Mazarin (until 1661).
May 19. Major Spanish defeat at Rocroi.
1645 August 28. Death of the Dutch jurist Hugo Grotius (born in Delft, 1583).
1648 January 30. Execution of Charles I of England, the first time a monarch is publicly beheaded in Europe. Oliver Cromwell is the ruler of England until his death (1658).
August 26. The Fronde Rebellion begins against the Regent Anne of Austria and Mazarin.
October 24. Treaties of Westphalia. The Thirty Years War ends. Spain recognizes the independence of the United Provinces (Northern Netherlands). Triumph of the "Europe of nations" over imperial universalism.
1650 February 11. Death of French philosopher René Descartes.
1651 Thomas Hobbes (1588–1679) publishes *The Leviathan.*
1653 End of the Fronde Rebellion (begun in 1658) with the victory of Mazarin and Anne of Austria.
1656 Velázquez (1599–1660) paints *Las Meninas.*
1658 September 3. Death of Oliver Cromwell.
1659 November 7. Signing of the Treaty of the Pyrenees between France and Spain. End of Spanish hegemony. The "French Century" begins.
1660 May 30. The Stuarts regain the throne in England, with Charles II (until 1685).
1661 March 9. Death of Mazarin. Start of the personal rule of Louis XIV (until 1715).

1665 Philip IV of Spain dies, succeeded by Charles II (1665–1700). The regency begins, lasting until 1676.
1673 February 17. Death of French playwright Molière.
1682 May. Louis XIV moves to the Palace of Versailles.
1685 February 6. After the death of Charles II of England, he is succeeded on the throne by James II (1685–1688).
March 21. Birth of Johann Sebastian Bach (1685–1750).
October 18. Louis XIV revokes the Edict of Nantes.
1688 The Glorious Revolution in England.
1689 The English Parliament passes the Bill of Rights. King William III (of Orange, 1689–1702), marries the daughter of James II, Mary II (1689–1694).
1695 April 13. Death of French poet Jean de La Fontaine.
1700 November 1. Death of Charles II.
November 12. Acceptance by Louis XIV of his grandson Philip of Anjou's inheritance of the Spanish Crown; Philip becomes Philip V of Spain.

## References


Adair, E. R. (1917). The statute of proclamations. *The English Historical Review, 32*(125), 34–46.

Aguesseau, H. -F. D.' (1819). Fragmens sur l'origine et l'usage des Remontrances. In *Oeuvres complètes du chancelier d'Aguesseau* (Vol. X, pp. 4–31). Paris: Fantin et Cie.

Aguilera-Barchet, B. (2007). La creación legislativa en Aragón durante el reinado de Carlos II. In M. Á. González de San Segundo (Eds.), *El Doctor Juan Luis López, primer marqués del Risco (1644–1703)* (pp. 23–63). Zaragoza: Gobierno de Aragón.

Aguilera-Barchet, B. (2008). Las raíces jurídicas del Estado español contemporáneo: la Guerra de la Independencia y el afianzamiento del sentimiento nacional. Notas para un ensayo de historia constitucional europea comparada. In E. Álvarez Conde & J. M. Vera Santos (Eds.), *Estudios sobre la Constitución de Bayona* (pp. 85–207). Madrid: La Ley.

Alonso, M. P. (1982). *El proceso penal en Castilla (siglos XIII–XVIII)*. Salamanca: Universidad de Salamanca.

Anderson, P. (2013). *Lineages of the absolutist state*. London: Verso.

Arvizu y Galarraga, F. (1989). Las Cortes de Navarra en la Edad Moderna: estudio desde la perspectiva de la Corona. In *Cortes de Castilla y León en la Edad Moderna: Actas de la IIª etapa del Congreso Científico de Historia de las Cortes de Castilla y León* (pp. 593–632). Valladolid: Cortes de Castilla y León.

Baird, H. M. (2010). *The Huguenots and the revocation of the edict of Nantes* (2 Vols). Piscataway: Gorgias Press.

Baker, J. H. (1990). *An introduction to English legal history* (3rd ed.). London: Butterworths.

Bayle, P. (1820). *Dictionnaire Historique et Critique* (Vol. IX, pp. 438–471). Word/Paris: Louis XIII/Desoer.

Beik, W. (2005). The absolutism of Louis XIV as social collaboration. *Past & Present, 188*(1), 195–224.

Bellamy, J. G. (1984). *Criminal law and society in late medieval and Tudor England*. New York: St. Martin's Press.

Bellomo, M. (1995). *The common legal past of Europe, 1000–1800*. Washington, DC: The Catholic University of America Press.

Bernard, G. W. (1992). The Tudor nobility in perspective. In G. W. Bernard (Ed.), *The Tudor nobility* (pp. 1–48). Manchester: Manchester University Press.
Bernard, P. P. (1979). *The limits of enlightenment: Joseph II and the law*. Chicago, IL: University of Illinois Press.
Birn, R. (2005). *Crisis, absolutism, revolution: Europe and the world 1648–1789* (3rd ed.). Toronto: Broadview Press.
Black, H. C. (2009). *Black's law dictionary* (9th ed.). St. Paul, MN: West.
Bodin, J. (2009). Concerning sovereignty. In *Six books of the commonwealth* (Book I, Chapter VIII, pp. 24–36). Lexington, KY: Seven Treasures Publications.
Bourgeon, J.-L. (1986). *Les Colbert avant Colbert: Destin d'une famille marchande* (2nd ed.). Paris: Presses Universitaires de France.
Bouza Álvarez, F. J. (1987). *Portugal en la monarquía hispánica (1580–1640): Felipe II, las Cortes de Tomar y la génesis del Portugal católico*. Madrid: Universidad Complutense.
Burckhardt, J. (2010). *The civilization of the Renaissance in Italy*. New York: Dover Publications.
Calasso, F. (1954). *Medioevo del Diritto. I. Le fonti*. Giuffré: Milano.
Canning, J. (2011). The treatment of power in juristic thought. In *Ideas of power in the late Middle Ages 1296–1417* (pp. 133–164). Cambridge, UK: Cambridge University Press.
Carpintero, F. (1977). Mos italicus, mos gallicus y el Humanismo racionalista: Una contribución a la historia de la metodología jurídica. *Ius Commune, VI*(6), 108–171.
Carrasco Martínez, A. (2000). *Sangre, honor y privilegio: La nobleza española bajo los Austrias*. Barcelona: Ariel.
Contreras, J., & Dedieu, J. P. (1993). Estructuras geográficas del Santo Oficio en España. In J. Pérez Villanueva & B. Escandell Bonet (Eds.), *Historia de la Inquisición en España y Amé rica*. Volume II. *Las estructuras del Santo Oficio* (pp. 48–62). Madrid: Biblioteca de Autores Cristianos.
Crossman, R. H. S. (1969). *Government and the governed. A history of political ideas and political practice* (5th ed.). London: Chatto and Windus.
Croxton, D. (2013). *Westphalia the last Christian peace*. New York: Palgrave Macmillan.
Dangeau, P. de, & Courcillon, M. de (1859). *Aout de 1715 in* Journal du Marquis de Dangeau. *Volume XVI (1715–1716)* (pp. 117–136). Paris: Firmin Didot frères, fils et Compagnie libraires.
de Cervantes, M. (2003). *Don Quixote*. New York: HarperCollins.
Descimon, R. (1996). Power elites and the prince: The state as enterprise. In W. Reinhard (Ed.), *Power elites and state building* (pp. 101–122). New York: Oxford University Press.
Desrayaud, A. (1996). *Cours d'Histoire du Droit Public: (des Invasions barbares jusqu'à la Ré volution)*. Saint Maur: Editions Novelles.
Dessert, D. (2000). *Louis XIV prend le pouvoir. Naissance d'un mythe? 1661*. Paris: Ed. Complexe.
di Machiavelli, N. (2010). *The Prince: On the art of power*. Chichester, UK: Capstone Pub (Manuscript, circa 1513. 1st ed: *Il Príncipe*. Roma: Antonio Blado nel 1532).
Dicey, A. V. (2009). *The Privy Council*. Charleston: BiblioBazaar (Reprint of the 1860 edition: Oxford: T. and G. Shrimpton.).
Dickens, A. G. (1993). *The English reformation* (2nd ed.). University Park, PA: Pennsylvania State University Press.
Downing, B. M. (1993). *The military revolution and political change. Origins of democracy and autocracy in early modern Europe*. Princeton, NJ: Princeton University Press.
Drazin, C. (2008). *The man who outshone the Sun King: The rise and fall of Nicolas Fouquet*. Philadelphia, PA: Da Capo Press.
Elton, G. R. (1974). The rule of law in sixteenth-century England. In *Studies in Tudor and Stuart politics and government* (Vol. II, pp. 260–284). Cambridge, UK: Cambridge University Press.
Elton, G. R. (1979). *English law in the sixteenth century: Reform in an age of change*. London: Selden Society.

Elton, G. R. (1999). *The Tudor constitution: Documents and commentary* (2nd ed., reprint). Cambridge, UK: Cambridge University Press.

Ertman, T. (1999). *Birth of the leviathan: Building states and regimes in medieval and early modern Europe* (Reprint). Cambridge, UK: Cambridge University Press.

Escudero López, J. A. (2003). *Curso de Historia del Derecho. Fuentes e Institutciones Político-Administrativas* (3rd ed.). Madrid: Solana e Hijos.

Escudero López, J. A. (2004). Primeros, validos y primeros ministros en la monarquía española del antiguo régimen. In J. A. Escudero López (Ed.), *Los Validos* (pp. 15–33). Madrid: Dykinson.

Esmein, A. (2004). La maxime *Princeps legibus solutus est* dans l'ancien droit public français. In P. Vinogradoff (Ed.), *Essays in legal history* (pp. 201–214). London/Clark, NJ: Oxford University Press/The Lawbook Exchange (1913).

Flemer, P. (2002). Clement VII and the crisis of the sack of Rome. In W. J. Connell (Ed.), *Society and individual in renaissance Florence* (pp. 409–434). Berkeley: University of California Press.

Franklin, J. H. (2009). *Jean Bodin and the rise of absolutist theory*. Cambridge: Cambridge University Press.

Fritze, R. H., & Robison, W. B. (Eds.). (1996). *Historical dictionary of Stuart England: 1603–1689*. Westport, CT: Greenwood.

García Pérez, R. D. (2008). *Antes Leyes que Reyes: Cultura jurídica y constitución política en la Edad Moderna (Navarra 1512–1808)*. Milano: Giuffré.

Gasquet, F. A. (2006). *Henry VIII and the English Monasteries*. Stockbridge, MA: Hardbooks (Volume I. Reprint of the Sixth edition of 1902. London: Elibron Classics) (2012).

González, T. (1830). *Colección de privilegios, franquezas, exenciones y fueros, concedidos a varios pueblos y corporaciones de la Corona de Castilla* (6 vols., Vol. V, Document No CXXXVIII (138), fol. 424–428). Madrid: Imprenta Real.

González Alonso, B. (1970). *El corregidor castellano: (1348–1808)*. Madrid: Instituto de Estudios Administrativos.

González Alonso, B. (1980). La fórmula obedézcase pero no se cumpla en el Derecho castellano de la Baja Edad Media. *Anuario de Historia del Derecho Español,* (50), 469–488.

Guía Marín, L. (1984). Estudio preliminar. In *Cortes del reinado de Felipe IV. II. Cortes valencianas de 1645* (pp. 1–192). Valencia: Universidad de Valencia.

Haig, C. (2012). *English reformations. Religion, politics and society under the Tudors* (Repr.). Oxford: Oxford University Press.

Hamscher, A. (1987). *The Conseil Privé and the Parlements in the age of Louis XIV: A study in French absolutism*. Philadelphia, PA: The American Philosophical Society.

Hamscher, A. N. (1983). *The Parlement of Paris after the Fronde: 1653–1673*. Pittsburgh, PA: University of Pittsburgh Press.

Harouel, J.L., Barbey, J., Bournazel, E., & Thibaut-Payen, J. (2007). *Histoire des institutions de l'é poque franque à la Révolution* (11th ed.). Paris: Presses universitaires de France.

Henry III, King of Castile. (1830). Privilegio de villazgo, jurisdicción y otras franquezas, otorgado al Concejo de Ladrada el 14 de octubre de 1393. In T. González (Ed.), *Colección de privilegios, franquezas, exenciones y fueros, concedidos a varios pueblos y corporaciones de la Corona de Castilla* (6 Vols, Vol. V, Document No CXXXVIII (138), fol. 424–428). Madrid: Imprenta Real.

Hernández, M. (1995). *A la sombra de la corona: poder local y oligarquía urbana, Madrid 1606–1808*. Madrid: Siglo XXI.

Hobbes, T. (2007). *Leviathan, or the matter, form, and power of a commonwealth, ecclesiastical and civil*. Radford, VA: Wilder Publications.

Holt, M. P. (2007). *The French wars of religion: (1562–1629)* (2nd reprint). Cambridge, UK: Cambridge University Press.

Hurt, J. J. (2002). *Louis XIV and the Parlements: The assertion of royal authority*. Manchester: Manchester University Press.

Jones, P. M. (1995). *Reform and revolution in France: The politics of transition, 1774–1791*. Cambridge, UK: Cambridge University Press.

Jordán de Asso, I., & de Manuel y Rodríguez, M. (1774). *El Ordenamiento de leyes que D. Alfonso XI hizo en las Cortes de Alcalá de Henares el año de mil trescientos y quarenta y ocho*. Madrid: Joaquin de Ibarra.

Kantorowicz, E. H. (1997). *The King's two bodies: A study in medieval political theology*. Princeton: Princeton University Press.

King, P. T. (1999). *The ideology of order: A comparative analysis of Jean Bodin and Thomas Hobbes*. London: Frank Cass.

Kingdon, R. M. (1992). The first expression of Theodore Beza's political ideas. In R. C. Gamble (Ed.), *Calvinism in Switzerland, Germany, and Hungary* (pp. 96–108). New York: Garland.

Knecht, R. J. (2005). The fall of Semblançay: (January–August 1527). In *Francis I* (Re-issued edition). Cambridge, UK: Cambridge University Press.

Koenigsberger, H. G. (2001). *Monarchies, states generals and parliaments: The Netherlands in the fifteenth and sixteenth centuries*. Cambridge, UK: Cambridge University Press.

Lane, F. C. (1973). *Venice, a maritime republic*. Baltimore: The Johns Hopkins University Press.

Lebigre, A. (1995). *La Justice du Roi: La vie judiciaire dans l'ancienne France*. Paris: Editions Complexe.

Lehmberg, S. E. (1970). *The reformation parliament: 1529–1536*. Cambridge, UK: Cambridge University Press.

MacCulloch, D. (2004). *The reformation. A history*. New York: Viking Penguin.

Mackay, R. (2006). *The limits of royal authority: Resistance and obedience in seventeenth-century Castile*. Cambridge, UK: Cambridge University Press.

Martínez Díez, G. (1975). *Dos colecciones de Observancias de Aragón* (pp. 543–594). XLV: Anuario de Historia del Derecho Español.

Martínez Navas, I. (1991). Proceso inquisitorial de Antonio Pérez. *Revista de la Inquisición,* (1), 141–200.

*Merriam-Webster dictionary of synonyms: A dictionary of discriminated synonyms with antonyms and analogous and contrasted words*. (1984). Springfield, MA: Merriam-Webster, Incorporated.

Mirabeau, H. G de R., comte de (1782). *Des lettres de cachet et des prisons d'État*. Hamburg: [S.n.].

Morales Arrizabalaga, J. (2007). *Fueros y Libertades del Reino de Aragón: De su formación medieval a la crisis preconstitucional (1076–1800)*. Zaragoza: Rolde.

Mousnier, R. E. (1984). *The institutions of France under the absolute monarchy 1598–1789*. Volume II: *The organs of state and society*. Chicago, IL: The University of Chicago Press.

Mulgan, C. (1998). *Renaissance monarchies, 1469–1558*. New York: Cambridge University Press.

Myers, A. R. (1975). *Parliaments and estates in Europe to 1789*. London: Thames and Hudson.

Nelson, E. (2005). *The Jesuits and the monarchy: Catholic reform and political authority in France (1590–1615)*. Burlington, VT: Ashgate.

O'Callaghan, J. F. (2013). *A history of medieval Spain*. Ithaca, NY: Cornell University Press.

Ohanian, H. C. (2009). *Einstein's mistakes: The human failings of genius*. New York: Norton.

Olivier-Martin, F. (1988). *L'absolutisme Français*. Paris: Éditions Loysel.

Olivier-Martin, F. (1997). *Les lois du roi*. Paris: Libraire Générale de Droit et Jurisprudence.

Otero Varela, A. (1993–1994). Las Partidas y el Ordenamiento de Alcalá en el cambio del ordenamiento medieval. *Anuario de Historia del Derecho Español, 63*, 451–548.

Padoa-Schioppa, A. (2007). *Storia del diritto in Europa: Dal Medioevo all'età contemporanea*. Bologna: Il Mulino.

Parker, G. (1976). The "Military Revolution" 1550–1669 – a myth? *Journal of Modern History, 48*(2), 195–214.

Pérez de Tudela y Bueso, J. (2003). Antonio Pérez. In F. Ruiz Martín (Ed.), *La monarquía de Felipe II* (pp. 199–268). Madrid: Real Academia de la Historia.

Plucknett, T. F. T. (1956). *A concise history of the common law* (5th ed.). Boston: Little, Brown and Company.

*Pocket Oxford American dictionary and thesaurus.* (2010). Oxford: Oxford University Press.

Poska, A. (2008). Spain. In D. M. Whitford (Ed.), *Reformation and early modern Europe: A guide to research* (pp. 290–308). Kirksville, MO: Truman State University Press.

Post, G. (1953). Two notes on nationalism in the Middle Ages. In *Traditio: Studies in ancient and medieval history, thought, and religion* (Vol. IX, pp. 281–320).

Reynolds, S. (2012). Medieval law. In *The Middle Ages without feudalism. Essays in criticism and comparison on the medieval west* (Part I Feudalism, VII, pp. 485–502). Farnham UK: Ashgate Publishing.

Robinson, O. F., Fergus, T. D., & Gordon, W. M. (2000). *European legal history. Sources and institutions* (3rd ed.). London: Butterworths.

Rogister, J. (2002). *Louis XV and the Parlement of Paris: 1737–1755.* Cambridge, UK: Cambridge University Press.

Rowlands, G. (2002). *The dynastic state and the army under Louis XIV: Royal service and private interest, 1661–1701.* Cambridge, UK: Cambridge University Press.

Scott, T. (2012). *The city-state in Europe: 1000–1600.* Oxford: Oxford University Press.

Sevillia, J. (2003). *Historiquement correct: Pour en finir avec le passé unique.* Paris: Perrin.

Skinner, Q. (2008). *Machiavelli: A very short introduction.* Oxford: Oxford University Press.

Storez, I. (1996). *Le chancelier Henri François d'Aguesseau (1688–1751). Monarchiste et libéral.* Paris: Publisud.

Stradling, R. A. (2002). *Philip IV and the government of Spain: 1621–1665.* Cambridge, UK: Cambridge University Press.

Strayer, J. R. (1970). *On the medieval origins of the modern state.* Princeton, NJ: Princeton University Press.

Strayer, J. R. (1980). *The reign of Philip the fair.* Princeton, NJ: Princeton University Press.

Sueur, P. (1989). *Histoire du droit public français: Affirmation et crise de l'État sous l'ancien Ré gime.* Paris: Presses Universitaires de France.

Swann, J. (1995). *Politics and the Parlement of Paris under Louis XV: 1754–1774.* Cambridge, UK: Cambridge University Press.

Swann, J. (2012). Parlements and provincial estates. In W. Doyle (Ed.), *The Oxford handbook of the Ancien Régime* (pp. 93–110). Oxford, UK: Oxford University Press.

Tawney, R. H. (2008). *Religion and the rise of capitalism.* New Brunswick, NJ: Transaction Publisher.

Thompson, I. A. A. (1993). *Crown and Cortes: Government, institutions and representation in early-modern Castile.* Aldershot: Variorum.

Thompson, M. P. (1986). The history of fundamental law in political thought from the French wars of religion to the American Revolution. *The American Historical Review, 91*(5), 1103–1128.

Tilly, C. (2002). War making and state making as organized crime. In P. B. Evans et al. (Eds.), *Bringing the state back in* (pp. 169–191). Cambridge, UK: Cambridge University Press.

Tomás y Valiente, F. (1980). Venta de oficios públicos en Castilla durante los siglos XVII y XVIII. In *Gobierno e Instituciones en la España del Antiguo Régimen* (pp. 151–177). Madrid: Alianza Editorial.

Tomás y Valiente, F. (1992). *El derecho penal de la monarquía absoluta: (siglos XVI, XVII y XVIII)* (2nd ed.). Madrid: Tecnos.

Tomás y Valiente, F. (2000). *La tortura judicial en España.* Madrid: Crítica.

Tomás y Valiente, F. (2004). *Manual de Historia del Derecho Español.* Madrid: Tecnos.

Valero Torrijos, J. (2002). *Los órganos colegiados: Análisis histórico de la colegialidad en la organización pública española y régimen jurídico-administrativo vigente.* Madrid: Instituto Nacional de Administración Pública.

van Caenegem, R. C. (1994). *An historical introduction to private law.* Cambridge: Cambridge University Press.

van Caenegem, R. C. (1995). *An historical introduction to western constitutional law*. Cambridge, UK: Cambridge University Press.
Vázquez García Peñuela, J. M., & Morales Payán, M. A. (2005). *El pase regio. Esplendor y decadencia de una regalía* (pp. 57–155). Almería: Universidad de Almería.
Voltaire. (1836). Précis du siècle de Louis XV. In *Oeuvres complètes de Voltaire* (Vol. IV, pp. 310–434). Paris: Chez Furne.
Voltaire. (2000). *Treatise on tolerance*. Cambridge, UK: Cambridge University Press.
Waley, D. P. (1963). *A short history of Italy, from classical times to the present day*. Cambridge, UK: Cambridge University Press.
Waley, D. P., & Dean, T. (2013). *The Italian city republics* (4th ed.). New York: Routledge.
Wallerstein, I. (2011). The absolute monarchy and Statism. In *The modern world-system* I: *Capitalist agriculture and the origins of the European world-economy in the sixteenth century* (pp. 132–162). Berkeley, CA: University of California Press.
Weber, M. (2003). *The protestant ethic and the spirit of capitalism*. Mineola, NY: Dover Publications.
Witte, J. (2002). *Law and Protestantism: The legal teachings of the Lutheran reformation*. Cambridge: Cambridge University Press.
Wolf, J. B. (1968). *Louis XIV*. New York: Norton & Company.
Zmora, H. (2001). *Monarchy, aristocracy and the state in Europe: 1300–1800*. New York: Routledge.

## *Further Reading*

Ash, R. G., & Birke, A. M. (1991). *Princes, patronage, and the nobility: The court at the beginning of the Modern Age, c. 1450–1650*. Oxford: Oxford University Press.
Aubert, G., & Chaline, O. (Eds.). (2012). *Les Parlements de Louis XIV. Opposition, coopération, autonomisation?* In *Annales de Bretagne et des Pays de l'Ouest* (nr. 119-2), pp. 207–209
Beik, W. (2000). *Louis XIV and absolutism: A brief study with documents*. Boston, MA: Bedford.
Belloc, H. (1938). *Monarchy: A study of Louis XIV*. London: Cassel.
Bergin, J. (2004). *Crown, Church and episcopate under Louis XIV*. New Haven, CT: Yale University Press.
Blanchard, J.-V. (2011). *Eminence: Cardinal Richelieu and the rise of France*. New York: Walker & Company.
Burke, V. L. (1996). *The clash of civilizations: War-making and state formation in Europe*. Oxford: Polity.
Campbell, P. R. (1993). *Louis XIV: 1661–1715*. London: Longman.
Campbell, P. R. (2012). Absolute monarchy. In W. Doyle (Ed.), *The Oxford handbook of the Ancien Régime* (pp. 11–38). Oxford, UK: Oxford University Press.
Caplan, J. (1999). *In the King's wake: Post-absolutist culture in France*. Chicago, IL: University of Chicago Press.
Collins, J. B. (1988). *Fiscal limits of absolutism: Direct taxation in early seventeenth-century France*. Berkeley, CA: University of California Press.
Contamine, P., & Gnet, N. (2003). *War and competition between states* (1st ed., reprint). Oxford: Clarendon.
Church, W. F. (Ed.). (1980). *The impact of absolutism in France: National experience under Richelieu, Mazarin, and Louis XIV*. New York: Wiley.
Duffy, E. (1994). *The stripping of the altars: Traditional religion in England c. 1400-c. 1580*. New Haven, CT: Yale University Press.
Elton, G. R. (2006). *England under the Tudors* (3rd ed., reprint). London: Routledge.
Ergang, R. R. (1971). *Emergence of national state*. New York: Van Nostrand Reinhold.

Evans, R. J. W. (2002). *Crown, Church and estates: Central European politics in the sixteenth and seventeenth centuries* (10th print). Basingstoke: Macmillan Press.
Friedland, P. (2012). *Seeing justice done: The age of spectacular capital punishment in France*. Oxford, UK: Oxford University Press.
Garrisson, J. (1991). *Guerre civile et compromis (1559–1598)*. Paris: Seuil.
Gouron, A., & Rigaudière, A. (1988). *Renaissance du pouvoir législatif et genèse de l'État*. Montpellier: Société d'Histoire du Droit et des Institutions des anciens pays de droit écrit.
Graves, M. A. R. (2001). *The parliaments of early modern Europe*. New York: Longman.
Guía Marín, L. (2007). The brac reial or royal estate of Valencia and Sardinia at the time of Philip IV. *Parliaments, Estates and Representation,* (27), 159–173.
Hatton, R. (Ed.). (1976). *Louis XIV and absolutism*. London: Macmillan.
Henshall, N. (2001). *The myth of absolutism. Change and continuity in early modern European monarchy* (4th reimp). London: Longman.
Johnson, L. R. (2011). *Central Europe: Enemies, neighbors, friends*. New York: Oxford University Press.
Kelly, H. A., et al. (Eds.). (2011). *Thomas More's trial by jury: A procedural and legal review with a collection of documents*. Woodbridge: Boydell.
Kimmel, M. S. (1988). *Absolutism and its discontents: State and society in seventeenth-century France and England*. New Brunswick, NJ: Transaction Books.
Klaits, J. (1996). *Printed propaganda under Louis XIV: Absolute monarchy and public opinion*. Ann Arbor, MI: U.M.I (orig. ed. Princeton, NJ: Princeton University Press, 1976).
Knafla, L. A. (2003). *Crime, punishment, and reform in Europe*. Westport: Greenwood.
Koenigsberger, H. G. (1976). *Dominium regale or Dominium politicum et regale: Monarchies and parliaments in early modern Europe*. London: King's College.
Konnert, M. W. (2008). *Early modern Europe: The age of Religious War, 1559–1715*. Toronto: University of Toronto Press.
Loades, D. (2011). *Henry VIII*. Amberley: Stroud.
Lublinskaya, A. D. (2008). *French absolutism: The crucial phase, 1620–1629*. Cambridge: Cambridge University Press.
Lynn, J. A. (2005). States in conflict: 1661–1763. In G. Parker (Ed.), *The Cambridge history of warfare* (pp. 167–188). Cambridge, MA: Cambridge University Press.
Major, J. R. (1997). *From Renaissance monarchy to absolute monarchy: French kings, nobles, & estates*. Baltimore, MA: Johns Hopkins University Press.
Mcilwain, C. H. (1987). *Constitutionalism: Ancient and modern* (Rev ed.). Ithaca: Cornell University Press.
Mettam, R. (1988). *Power and faction in Louis XIV's France*. New York: Blackwell.
Miller, J. (Ed.). (1993). *Absolutism in seventeenth century Europe* (Reprint). New York: Palgrave Macmillan.
Mousnier, R. (1982). *La monarchie absolue en Europe: du Ve siècle à nos jours*. Paris: Presses Universitaires de France.
Munck, T. (2005). *Seventeenth-century Europe: State, conflict and social order in Europe 1598–1700* (2nd ed.). London: Palgrave Macmillan.
Olivier-Martin, F. (1988). *Les parlements contre l'absolutisme traditionnel au XVIIIe siècle*. Paris: Editions Loysel.
Parker, D. (1990). *The making of French absolutism*. London: Edward Arnold.
Parker, G. (1997). *The general crisis of the seventeenth century* (2nd ed.). London: Routledge.
Parker, G. (2001). *Europe in crisis: 1598–1648* (2nd ed.). Malden, MA: Blackwell.
Parker, G. (2002). *Empire, war and faith in early modern Europe*. London: Penguin.
Petiet, R. (2010). *Du pouvoir législatif en France: depuis l'avènement de Philippe le Bel jusqu'en 1789*. Charleston, SC: BiblioBazaar (Reprint of the 1891 edition).
Porter, B. D. (1994). *War and the rise of the state: The military foundations of modern politics*. New York: Free Press.

Russell, C. S. R. (1982). Wars, and estates in England, France, and Spain, c. 1580 – c. 1640. *Legislative Studies Quarterly*, (7–2), 205–220.
Shennan, J. H. (1998). *The parlement of Paris*. Stroud: Sutton Publishing.
Smith, D. L. (1992). *Louis XIV*. Cambridge: Cambridge University Press.
Smith, J. M. (1996). *The culture of merit: Nobility, royal service, and the making of absolute monarchy in France, 1600–1789*. Ann Arbor, MI: University of Michigan Press.
Soulé, C. (1968). *Les États Généraux de France (1302–1789). Étude historique, comparative et doctrinale*. Heule: UGA.
Sturdy, D. J. (2002). *Fractured Europe: 1600–1721*. Oxford: Wiley-Blackwell.
Sturdy, D. J. (2004). *Richelieu and Mazarin: A study in statesmanship*. Basingstoke, UK: Palgrave Macmillan.
Tilly, C. (Ed.). (1975). *The formation of national states in Western Europe*. Princeton, NJ: Princeton University Press.
Tremlett, G. (2010). *Catherine of Aragon: Henry's Spanish queen: A biography*. London: Faber.
Wilkinson, R. (2007). *Louis XIV*. London: Routledge.
Wilson, P. H. (2000). *Absolutism in central Europe*. New York: Routledge.
Witte, J. J. (2008). *The reformation of rights: Law, religion and human rights in early modern Calvinism*. Cambridge: Cambridge University Press.
Wolf, J. B. (1983). *The emergence of great powers, 1685–1715*. Westport, Conn: Greenwood.

# Chapter 10
# From the Conservative King to the Reformist Monarch: The Stage of Enlightened Absolutism (Eighteenth Century)

"The sovereign is attached by indissoluble ties to the body of the state; hence it follows that he, by repercussion, is sensible of all the ills which afflict his subjects; and the people, in like manner, suffer from the misfortunes which affect their sovereign. There is but one general good, which is that of the state. [. . .] the sovereign represents the state; he and his people form but one body, which can only be happy as far as united by concord. The prince is to the nation he governs what the head is to the man; it is his duty to see, think, and act for the whole community that he may procure it every advantage of which it is capable".—Frederick II, King of Prussia. Essay on the Forms of Government and the Duties of Rulers. (1781).[1]

## Contents


10.1 The Crisis of Classic Absolutism ..... 258
10.1.1 A Century of Transformation ..... 258
10.1.2 The "Philosophes" and the Kings ..... 259
10.1.3 Absolutism vs. Despotism ..... 260
10.2 A New Legitimacy: From Christian to Secular Monarchs ..... 260
10.3 Enlightened Reformism or the New Spirit of Absolute Power ..... 264
10.3.1 The State: From Guardian of Order to Protector, Educator and Reformer . . 264
10.3.2 The "Depatrimonialization" of the Monarchy and the Transformation of the State ..... 267
10.4 Enlightened Absolutism and the "Rule of Law" ..... 270
10.4.1 The Enlightened Monarchs and the Law ..... 270
10.4.2 Frederick II's *Sonderweg* ..... 272
10.4.3 The Rationalization of the Legal System ..... 273


[1] Frederick II (1789, 14–15).



B. Aguilera-Barchet, *A History of Western Public Law*,
DOI 10.1007/978-3-319-11803-1_10

10.5 The Expansion of Enlightened Absolutism in Eighteenth Century Europe: The Great Enlightenment Monarchs ... 274
10.5.1 The Austrian and the Prussian Models and Its Reception in Russia ... 274
10.5.2 Portugal in the Pombal Era ... 276
10.5.3 The Eighteenth Century Revolution in Spain ... 277
10.5.4 The French and British Exceptions ... 279
References ... 281

## 10.1 The Crisis of Classic Absolutism

As we know, absolute monarchy took hold in the sixteenth and seventeenth centuries because it was a more effective system of government than feudal monarchy and, above all, because the unchallenged authority of the king was the best bulwark against chaos.

### *10.1.1 A Century of Transformation*

The major economic changes (*Industrial Revolution*), which began to transform Europe in the eighteenth century, however, gave rise to the emergence of a new cultural framework which necessarily affected the European kingdoms' political adaptations to the new times. The seventeenth century in Europe was an era of pivotal scientific breakthroughs thanks to thinkers such as Leibniz, Newton and Descartes. It is no wonder, then, that the latter's best-known work received the title *Discourse on the Method of Rightly Conducting One's Reason and of Seeking Truth in the Sciences* (1637),[2] one vividly reflecting the seventeenth and eighteenth century's euphoric embrace of rationalism and the era's growing conviction that men could improve their lives and achieve full happiness through scientific development. This was the proposition defended by the philosophes (friends of wisdom), and the men who embraced the *Encyclopedia*, the proponents of the movement

[2] A method based on the four following principles: "*The first was never to accept anything for true which I did not clearly know to be such; that is to say, carefully to avoid precipitancy and prejudice, and to comprise nothing more in my judgment than what was presented to my mind so clearly and distinctly as to exclude all ground of doubt. The second, to divide each of the difficulties under examination into as many parts as possible, and as might be necessary for its adequate solution. The third, to conduct my thoughts in such order that, by commencing with objects the simplest and easiest to know, I might ascend by little and little, and, as it were, step by step, to the knowledge of the more complex; assigning in thought a certain order even to those objects which in their own nature do not stand in a relation of antecedence and sequence. And the last, in every case to make enumerations so complete, and reviews so general that I might be assured that nothing was omitted*" (Descartes 1998, II, 10).

known as the Enlightenment (*Lumières* in French, *Aufklärung* in German, *Ilustración* in Spanish and *Illuminismo* in Italian).[3]

### 10.1.2 The "Philosophes" and the Kings

It is only to be expected, therefore, that philosophers such as Voltaire, Diderot, D'Alembert, Montesquieu and Rousseau were highly critical of the established order, particularly the Church and, of course, absolute monarchy. The *philosophes* did not, in fact, object to the absoluteness of the monarch's authority as much as they did to the way in which he wielded it. In line with their Enlightenment ideas, they believed that the king's function was not only to maintain order but to bring progress to his people. The king, then, was no longer envisioned as an agent merely expected to defend an established order, in accordance with the old medieval idea of the "justice-dispensing king". Rather, the era's leading lights viewed monarchs as "reformist" agents who ought to free their kingdoms and peoples from obscurantism. In this sense it is significant that Voltaire was a strong advocate of "enlightened despotism" through which the *souverains civilisateurs* (Gorbatov 2006, 62) dedicated their governments' actions to achieving the greatest level of well-being for their subjects.[4]

The *philosophes* proved able to convince and win over the ruling monarchs to their way of thought. In the Habsburg monarchy, after 1748, for instance, Maria Theresa and her son Joseph II, believed very firmly that expanded state power should be used to address all society's ills. At the same time, this idea was ratified by most Austrian legal thinkers, who concluded that the dangers posed by feudal, decentralized justice were far more pernicious than those which could be expected from absolute monarchs, essentially because an enlightened despot, far from an arbitrary tyrant, exercised his power in the interest of the state, a sufficient guarantee that it would be exercised also in the interest of all his subjects (Bernard 1979, 3).

[3] As Cassirer (2009, 6–7) points out, in seventeenth-century Europe thinkers strove to attain philosophical knowledge through proof and rigorous inference, beginning with fundamental certainties, upon which they lay down additional, solid propositions, in this way constructing an indivisible, static structure of interrelated knowledge from which no part could be extracted. In the eighteenth century, on the other hand, this kind of deduction was abandoned in favor of an approach rooted in another concept of truth and philosophy, its aim to extend the boundaries of both and make them more elastic and vital, as it constructed its ideal according to the model and pattern of contemporary natural science. About the term *Enlightenment* and its meanings, see also, Lough (1985) and Schmidt (2003).

[4] As Williams (2003, xv) indicates, Voltaire made a crucial distinction between absolute and arbitrary power, as he believed that the absolutism of the monarch was legitimized not by divine right, but by his submission to the rule of law and by acting within the confines of reason and justice.

### 10.1.3 *Absolutism vs. Despotism*

Today the term "despot" is decidedly pejorative, but in the middle of the eighteenth century it was not saddled with this negative connotation.[5] It is extremely telling that one as cultured and intelligent as Diderot imagined the ideal ruler, the "philosopher king",[6] to be "a despot", and he best suited to govern wisely (Strugnell 1973, 93–98).[7] In this sense, the case was quite similar to that of the term "tyrant", which is today one of the worst epithets one can use to label a political leader, while in classical Greece it was simply a form of government which, in many cases, preceded and made possible the consolidation of democracy, as was the case, for example, in Athens under Peisistratus. After the French Revolution, however, the term "despot" came to acquire its negative connotation (Anderson 2000). Thus, in the late nineteenth and twentieth centuries, historians began to speak of "enlightened absolutism" as a more appropriate description of eighteenth-century political practice than "enlightened despotism" (Beales 2005, 55), a term they found misleading and pejorative (Szabo 1994, 5).

## 10.2 A New Legitimacy: From Christian to Secular Monarchs

A fundamental and defining aspect, in which Enlightenment monarchs differed from their predecessors, was that they did not justify their exercise of power on religious grounds.[8] As these sovereigns did not base their authority upon any divine

[5] On the relationship between the terms "despot", "despotism", "absolute monarchy", and "absolutism", see Beales (2005, 43–53).

[6] As Beales (2005, 34) points out, in Diderot's articles of the *Encyclopédie*, such as "Autorité politique" and "Despotisme", discussion resolves around the need to limit royal power. However, in "Philosopher" a "philosopher king" is simply assumed, without arguments or regret, to be in a position to grant or deny his people's happiness. Lough (1968, 424–462) states that Diderot's aforementioned article which appeared in the first volume of the *Encyclopédie*, come close to cause the cancellation of the work, because Diderot wrote that "*all power that comes from God is a limited power*". This doctrine, which is one way of interpreting Romans xiii.1, struck the believers in divine right monarchy as positively seditious (Wilson 1970, 412). See also Goyard-Fabre (1984).

[7] As Mason and Wokler (2005, vii) observe, besides the articles he wrote for the *Encyclopédie* and his contributions to the *Histoire des Deux Indes* (1772)—a book condemned by the Paris Parlement in 1780—Diderot's most important political writings were his *Supplément au Voyage de Bougainville* (1772) and the *Observations sur le Nakaz* (1773–1774). For an analysis of Diderot's political views, see Wilson (1967) and Lough (1985).

[8] The new approach to the religious dimension was one of the most distinctive features of the Enlightenment. Yet, as Grell and Porter (2000, 1–2) explain, religion did not merely remain present throughout eighteenth century Europe, but was central to the Enlightenment agenda itself. It is true that some philosophes were atheists, the prime example being Voltaire, the author of the *Traité de la Tolérance* (1763), who attacked not just Catholicism but also the natural religion and

right to rule, in this sense they were not "Christian rulers",[9] a fact which allowed them to establish their independence from the papacy. Even during the era of absolutism, however, this also represented an objective, external limitation on the king's power.[10]

The exception came in France, where the monarchy never accepted the main theories of enlightened absolutism (Outram 2007, 34). Louis XIV, for example, was profoundly Catholic, and though he supported Gallicanism, his Christian principles limited his actions as a ruler. His confessors, among them the famous Father Lachaise, constantly reminded him of his obligations as a Catholic monarch. Throughout France's *Ancien Regime*, the monarchs continued to regularly summon the "General Assembly of the Clergy", which had a permanent representative, the "general agent of the clergy", at Versailles. Finally, once a week the king met with the "Council of Conscience", to deal with all those matters in which the king could have problems of conscience arising from his role as a Christian monarch.[11]

In contrast, in the states in which the guiding principles were those of enlightened absolutism, the king was not considered to be chosen by God, nor to be his representative, nor to base his power on a Divine concession awarded him after the ceremony of anointing, coronation or consecration. Significant in this regard was that Joseph II of Austria refused to be crowned King of Hungary and Bohemia in accordance with a traditional liturgy; an enlightened king, in his view, did not rule by the grace of God (Agnew 2004, 92). Rather, his power was based on a new source of legitimacy: that provided by his education, which was, in turn, a consequence of his illustrious origins. As the king had been trained from childhood for his office, he was the one most apt to achieve those objectives of government which justified the existence of the state's apparatus, including the monarchy itself. Thus, in principle, did the ruler stand above interests and prejudices, thanks to a preparation which enabled him to extract himself from pressure groups and exercise an arbitral role permitting him to resolve conflicts. In his *Essay on Forms of Government*, Frederick the Great wrote that a prince "is but a man, like the least of his subjects", and that "if he be the first general, the first minister of the realm, it is not that he should remain the shadow of authority, but that he should fulfill the duties of such titles", as "he is only the first servant of the state, who is obliged to act with

optimism of the rationalists. Most enlightened thinkers, however, did not seek to abolish religion, but rather to eliminate bigotry and superstition, and develop a conception of God that would be fully compatible with Reason, Nature, Science, Morality and civic duties.

[9] Monod (1999, 45) highlights that this crucial transformation had begun with the Humanist scholars of the Renaissance, who placed a new emphasis on the worldly achievements of sovereigns. Henceforth the quasi-divinity of the crown could manifest itself through a variety of secular endeavors, from patronage of the arts to military science. In this sense they might be compared to pagan rulers like Alexander the Great or the Roman emperors.

[10] For a general overview of the new approach to religion amongst Europe's enlightened monarchies, see Schaich (2007).

[11] It is extremely significant that within a week of Mazarin's death, Louis XIV resurrected the *Conseil de Conscience* and reconstituted its membership, as its first meeting took place on March 18, 1661 (Bergin 2004, 158).

probity and prudence and to remain as totally disinterested as if he were each moment liable to render an account of his administration to his fellow citizens" (Frederick II 1789, 29).

Upon shedding his sacred aura, the king was unshackled from religious fetters. Enlightenment principles no longer depended on a particular creed, or dogmas interpreted by an ecclesiastical apparatus, but only on the monarch's personal conscience. In this sense, the power of the enlightened kings was more "absolute" because they were not subject to particular religious creeds. This explains in large measure why in a country like England, where the Church depended directly on the king, Parliament resorted to approving a Bill of Rights in 1689, to place objective limits on royal powers.[12]

The advent of the kings' new secular legitimacy, divorced from the divine right theory which had prevailed during the Middle Ages, precipitated a manifest process of general secularization which further weakened the role which the Church had played hitherto, advancing the secularization of the state. In fact, the most illustrious representatives of enlightened absolutism endorsed secular policies and did not hesitate, for example, to abolish the Society of Jesus (The Jesuits) and expel it, a measure applied in Portugal in 1759, in France in 1764 and in Spain in 1767.[13] The order would be ultimately abolished by Pope Clement XIV on July 21, 1773, in his bull *Dominus ac Redemptor*, which disbanded the Society of Jesus (Riccards 2012, 229). The principle of the separation between Church and State emerged, and processes were implemented to liquidate Church property (disentailment) to improve public finances.

Joseph II of Austria stands as a clear embodiment of a monarch illustrating the precepts of enlightened absolutism (Szabo 2011, 111–138). The emperor was a practicing Catholic, yet this did not prevent him from seeking to strip the monarchy of any vestige of religion. Politically, he sought to turn the Austrian Church into a national entity subject to the emperor ("Josephism") (Dickson 1993, 89–114). To do this, he did not hesitate to undertake a whole series of radical reforms, suppressing processions and pilgrimages, and depriving monasteries and religious orders of their educational functions. Joseph II founded state schools (a policy which had already been adopted during his mother's life), to counter the educational monopoly the Jesuits had held in Austria since the Thirty Years War (1618–

[12] In fact, the rejection of submission to the pope's authority was expressly included in the 1689 Bill of Rights: "*I* [. . .] *do swear, that I do from my heart abhor, detest, and abjure as impious and heretical, that damnable doctrine and position, that princes excommunicated or deprived by the pope or any authority of the see of Rome, may be deposed or murdered by their subjects, or any other whatsoever. And I do declare that no foreign prince, person, prelate, state, or potentate, hath, or ought to have any jurisdiction, power, superiority, preeminence, or authority, ecclesiastical or spiritual, within this realm*" (Williams 1970, 30).

[13] By the reign of Philip V, Spain's Bourbons were fiercely opposed to excessive papal power. This idea was called either "Regalism" or "Jansenism" because of its concern with jurisdiction, authority, and power, on the one hand, and encouraging change, outward and inward, among both laymen and clergy, on the other (Paquette 2008, 70).

1648), and secularized the universities (Outram 2007, 39). As of 1783, the government took over the education of the clergy itself, which came to be taught at state seminaries, with lessons consonant with the new Enlightenment ideas. Charity hospitals, another area which had until then been essentially ecclesiastical, was entrusted to the state. Joseph II even forbade church burials for public health reasons. The emperor also introduced civil marriage, and even divorce, breaking the exclusive authority which the Church had held hitherto over these matters. Finally, by virtue of the Patent of Tolerance (1781), he authorized the practice of religions other than Catholicism in the territories of the Austrian Empire (Vocelka 2000, 201–202).[14]

Frederick II of Prussia, meanwhile, broke sharply with divine right monarchy, creating a religiously neutral state, which permitted the practice of all religions without preference shown to any one of them.[15] The king, himself, confirmed this principle by stating that in his kingdom everyone was saved in his own way as "each man believes that which appears to him to be the truth" and "the sovereign has no right to interfere in the belief of the subject" (Frederick II 1789, 28). In this regard, it is worthy of note that Frederick II's religious tolerance prompted him to welcome the Jesuits into his kingdom at a time when they had been expelled from most Catholic states because of their submission to the papacy. However, Frederick II was, above all, extremely pragmatic. Although he considered himself to be a philosopher king, Frederick II of Prussia only put philosophical principles into practice when he considered them compatible with the interests of the Prussian state. The clearest evidence of this was the Edict on Religion he issued on July 9, 1788, which forbade evangelical ministers from teaching anything not contained in their official books, proclaimed the necessity of protecting the Christian religion against the "enlighteners" (*Aufklärer*), and placed educational establishments under the supervision of orthodox clergy.[16]

[14] For an overall view of Joseph's II religious policy, see Wangermann (2007).

[15] Hubatsch (1975, 211) points out that Frederick's maxim that all religions were equally worthy of toleration, so long as they tolerated one another, can be explained because the king was a freethinker, a deist, a Freemason, and a somewhat metaphysically superficial *philosophe*, who sought, above all, rational solutions. Having said that, his personal rejection of Christian beliefs did not have an impact on his public life, as he took very seriously his role as the *summus episcopus* of the Lutheran Church in Prussia, to the point that he denied everyone, even the king, the right to mock religion publicly, despite the fact that he did so in private. Religion under Frederick's reign, held a protected place in the structure of the Prussian state.

[16] As Sauter (2009, 103) points out, the Edict of 1788 came in response to the inability of traditional elites to maintain control over "their public". It was, therefore, necessary to discipline the populace through state power. In any case, the result was that on the eve of the French Revolution the fusion of enlightened philosophy and public order was coming to an end.

## 10.3 Enlightened Reformism or the New Spirit of Absolute Power

Enlightened absolutism was, in principle a variety of "classical absolutism" or *Hochabsolutismus*. Enlightened despots would continue to govern without requiring their subjects' consent or seeking their engagement in public affairs. There was, however, a substantial difference between enlightened absolutism and its forerunner, as the former pursued a state which would no longer limit itself to functioning as a mere guarantor of order. Unlike classical absolutist monarchs, whose essential mission was to prevent chaos, enlightened sovereigns were expected to do everything possible to foster progress in their subjects' interest.[17] Thus, they made major efforts to do away with age-old prejudices, and construct a new society, according to Enlightenment ideals (Ingrao 1986).

### *10.3.1 The State: From Guardian of Order to Protector, Educator and Reformer*

Enlightened absolutism represented public power's complete embrace of eighteenth-century ideas. It was based on the principle then in vogue that the state rests upon a contract between the ruler and his people for the advancement of their general welfare and security, an objective which subjects could not (yet) achieve by themselves, as they lacked the knowledge necessary to advance in the right direction. The prince, in contrast, was fully qualified to do so, having been educated expressly from birth for this purpose. Thus, for Enlightenment monarchs, the state, while continuing to play its traditional role as a guardian of order, was also committed to protecting and educating its people[18] to achieve the highest possible

---

[17] Beales (1987, 4) mentions how Joseph II of Austria (1741–1790), from the moment he became involved in affairs of state, was aware that the monarchy required drastic reform, which he was very much willing to undertake, as expressed in a letter he wrote to his brother Leopold, Grand Duke of Tuscany, in 1768: "Love of country, the welfare of Monarchy, that is genuinely... the only passion I feel, and I would undertake anything for its sake. I am so committed to it that, if I cannot satisfy myself that its condition is good and that the arrangements we are making are beneficial, my mind cannot be at peace nor my body in good health".

[18] In 1765, Diderot, in the Foreword to Volume VIII of the *Encyclopedia*, hoped that general education would make such rapid progress that in 20 years it would be impossible to find a line in the *Encyclopedia* that was not common knowledge. He wrote that "It is for the world's rulers to hasten this happy revolution, for they have the power to spread or to restrict the sphere of enlightenment. Happy will be the time when they have all understood that security consists in ruling over educated men!" (Diderot 1969, 50).

level of development and to promote the reforms needed to ensure social progress.[19]

The state took on an educational role, for example, in Austria, where Maria Theresa founded an academy, Vienna's *Theresianum*, designed to train public servants for the Austrian state and to inculcate in them a spirit of public service.[20] The general educational system was overhauled, with the creation of primary schools and the transformation of universities, which shifted from religious into state institutions. Maria Theresa's son, Joseph II, took the same line, in 1774, promulgating his *Allgemeine Schulordnung* (*General School Ordinance*) which introduced into Austria the principle of compulsory education for children between 6 and 12 years of age (Melton 2002, 212–224). In the field of higher education universities lost their medieval status as independent entities—generally with ecclesiastical origins—and became public institutions, administrated by the state.

Frederick II of Prussia, meanwhile, in an effort to promote the welfare of his people, adopted a very ambitious educational policy, especially at the elementary school level through the *General-Landschul-Reglement* of 1763.[21] When he acceded to the throne, primary education was in the hands of volunteers, who taught mainly during the winter months when they did not have to work the land. Frederick the Great brought stability and rigor to the system by creating public schools that contributed very effectively to raising Prussians' educational level (MacDonogh 2001, 348–349). This educational ideal would be endorsed by Wilhelm von Humboldt (1767–1835), who introduced essential reforms of schools and universities during his brief period as head of the Prussian section for Education and Instruction in 1809–1810 (Philips 2011, 15). In 1810, he created the University that still bears his name in Berlin, and whose core philosophy was to give students broad, intellectual education rather than solely utilitarian training.

In Portugal, the expulsion of the Jesuits (1759), left the country virtually bereft of teachers at the secondary and university levels, which spurred the Marques de

[19] The initiative was essential, as literacy rates were extremely low in eighteenth-century Europe. As Melton (2002, 10) indicates, only 10 % of adult peasants in East Prussia could sign their names around the mid eighteenth century, although some 1,500 parish schools existed in the countryside. In Austria, Jesuit missionaries travelling through the village of Zell in the province of Carinthia in 1760, reported that only 4 of the 650 inhabitants could read. In the 1787 census in the Upper Styria parishes the representatives of the peasant communes (*Gemeinde*) were rarely able to sign their names to census reports.

[20] The *Theresianum* was founded in 1745, upon the initiative of Maria Theresa as an institution to train the sons of the nobility for service in the upper echelons of the state bureaucracy, maintaining its reputation as the monarchy's most prestigious school until 1918 (Godsey 1999, 47).

[21] The 1763 *Reglement* required that children attend school from their 5th to their 13th or 14th year. The very poor had their fees paid from parish funds and fines were imposed for truancy. At his time, Frederick the Great was credited for initiating a uniform system of compulsory schooling that drew the admiration of foreign observers. Yet, as Philips (2011, 16) observes, he cannot be credited with a wholly enlightened perspective on the need to provide universal elementary education; in a 1779 order he expressed to his minister for ecclesiastical affairs, Karl Abraham von Zedlitz, his view that for the peasantry a little reading and writing would suffice, as too much learning might drive them to the cities to become clerks. For a general overview of the *General-Landschul-Reglement*, see Melton (2002, 173–179).

Pombal to support the development of a state-sponsored system of secondary education headed by a Director of Studies. He also transformed higher education through the creation of a "Junta for the Provision of Learning" and reformed the University of Coimbra. The Pombaline educational reform had the clear utilitarian purpose of providing a new learned class to staff the state and the Church (Maxwell 1994, 101–102).

In Spain, the exodus of the Jesuits (1767), spurred reformers to modify educational institutions, which hitherto had been some of the kingdom's most reactionary forces. Enlightened figures such as Jovellanos and Cabarrús viewed education as a national problem, and believed that the transformation of schools, universities, and particularly *colegios mayores*[22] would transform the monarchy and the kingdom. Concerning higher education, they wanted universities to be better incorporated into society to satisfy its economic and cultural requirements, and reflect the greatest achievements of modern science and research. New, advanced schools were opened by the crown, with ministerial encouragement at the secondary level in Madrid and the main cities, and attempts were made to support affordable and even free primary education.[23]

The principle of the state's educational role would extend into the nineteenth century in France, after the Revolution. Napoleon (1799–1815), despite establishing a new monarchy, in accordance with revolutionary principles, in 1806 implemented the "university" in France, understood as a state institution designed to educate citizens of the new French society, from primary school up to the university level.[24] In addition, in the last third of the nineteenth century, Jules

[22] Spain's *colegios mayores* were university divisions similar to the colleges at Britain's Oxford and Cambridge. Each one was made up of students belonging, in general, to the social elite, and constituted a powerful political lobby. Charles III's regime sought to suppress them, in addition to the Jesuits, as factions which put up resistance to royal power.

[23] As Noel points out (1994, 135–136), the reformers wanted the schools and universities taken out of the hands of the religious orders, whose teaching they considered deficient and backwards. At the university level they sought the elimination of the influence of the *colegios mayores*, which educational reform figures like Pérez Bayer and Roda believed to be totally antagonistic to the public good. In 1771, there began a drastic reform of the *colegios* that was every effective in reducing their influence over university teaching. In 1798, Charles IV banned them outright. Professorial resistance and the lack of funding frustrated university reform, yet by 1780, medical and scientific curricula had been largely brought up to date and, generally speaking, the reformist movement did foster a new spirit of curiosity and philosophical daring while fueling the debate about new ideas, the nature of education, and the role of university. A noteworthy initiative was the reorganization of Madrid's Seminary of the Nobility to teach its members scientific and technical subjects to prepare them to lead Spanish society more effectively.

[24] The law of May 10, 1806, founding the *Imperial* University, or University of France, defined it as a "body charged exclusively with public teaching and education in the whole empire, having as its primary function to direct political and moral opinions". Hence, its director was placed directly under the emperor's orders. Under his watch were the academies, which ruled over the different geographical areas, each directed by rectors who oversaw inspectors who, in turn, supervised school principals. At the university level the only departments existing at the outset were those of Law and Medicine, which had existed as special schools before 1806. The departments of Letters

Ferry founded republican schools to foment public, secular and free education for the entire French population as a way of conveying republican principles and values (Harrigan 2001, 52–83). In this same sphere it is significant that the 1815 Constitution of the United Kingdom of the Netherlands expressly indicated the state's role as an educator. In fact, throughout his reign King William I (1815–1840) supported the educational system in the Netherlands, from primary school to the university.[25]

### 10.3.2 The "Depatrimonialization" of the Monarchy and the Transformation of the State

An important consequence of the secularization of the monarchy was a resounding rejection of the traditional patrimonial concept of the royal institution. Since the time of the Romans, and even during the era of Visigoth Spain, a distinction had developed between the emperor or king's personal patrimony (*fiscus*), and that belonging to the empire or kingdom. Subsequently, however, as a result of the expansion of feudalism there was a *de facto* privatization of European kingdoms, to the point where kings actually inherited and divided the realm among their descendants. In the Modern Age, even though the state was still identified and associated with the figure of the sovereign, his assets, or patrimony, gradually came to be considered as the property of the state.[26]

Under Enlightenment principles the monarch, then, became the administrator of the crown's property, but did not actually *own* it, nor could he do with it whatever he deemed fit. This process, however, would not be complete until well into the nineteenth century.[27]

---

and of Sciences had a very limited number of professors, remaining a simple extension of the *lycé es* (Bergeron 1990, 34–35). The *Imperial* University obtained in 1808 by several decrees, the monopoly of higher education. For a classical overview, see Aulard (1911). Also, Savoie (2004, 39–55) and Brambilla (2009, 97–119).

[25] William I's efforts met strong resistance in the Catholic, French-speaking South. The king had tried to unify the education system under the state and to build a national Catholic Church, but both reforms did not work in the southern provinces because of, on the one hand, the opposition of the Roman Catholic Church, and on the other, the disappointment of the Liberals, many of them belonging to the French-speaking upper middle class, who were very disappointed with the king's promotion of the Dutch language, the use of which he mandated in the schools (Robbers 2007, 90).

[26] Beginning with Charles I in Spain, for example, the monarchs passed the royal painting collection down in their wills, an example followed by the Spanish kings until 1827, when Ferdinand VII established the Museo del Prado, which absorbed the royal art collections. On this fascinating chapter of Spanish legal history see Monsalve Escriña (2004, 45–66).

[27] In Spain this would not come about until the reign of Isabel II, who made major contributions to the state from her private holdings, which she consolidated via the "Royal Patrimony Demarcation Law" of 1865, harshly criticized by Emilio Castelar (1832–1899) in two newspaper articles—"Of whom it is the Royal Patrimony?" and "The Cheat"—published on February 21 and 25 of 1865 (Castelar 1870, 193–203 and 205–213), in which he ridiculed royal donations. Emilio Castelar's thesis was that all the queen's assets were, *per se*, public. The articles were censured, but

This "depatrimonialization" of the monarchy led to a professionalization of state administration, a field in which the enlightened monarchs undertook major reform efforts to enhance public administration and make it more efficient. In this area the work of Maria Theresa of Austria (1740–1780) is notable[28]; to ensure her kingdom's unity she established a centralized administration while respecting the particularities of each of its territories to keep from stirring up resentment,[29] as she did not inherit a country, but rather a princely house holding disputed sway over many lands and many peoples (Crankshaw 1970, 6). In this task she was ably assisted by Chancellor Haugwitz, the former administrator of Silesia, who in 1749 began to reorganize the State Chancellery, and by Gottfried van Swieten, who introduced reform in the areas of education and health. In 1753, Haugwitz would be replaced by Chancellor Kaunitz.[30]

Maria Theresa's son, Joseph II, went even further, suspending the feudal assemblies of medieval origin in the empire's different territories, deeming such meetings a waste of time and inefficient from a governmental point of view. Instead, the emperor divided his state into 13 districts, each organized, in turn, into "circles" (*Kreise*) headed by "captains". The aim was to dissolve traditionally regional dynamics and standardize territorial administration. In pursuit of this objective, he also abolished what was left of municipal autonomy, with local authorities coming to be designated by the government.[31]

nevertheless they were distributed by Madrid in the form of pamphlets. Castelar was stripped of his position as a tenured professor (*catedrático*) of Critical and Philosophical Spanish History at the University of Madrid, a position he had held since 1857. Government's repression pushed students and professors to revolt in what was known as the Night of San Daniel or the Night of the Slaughter house (Smith 2009, 451). Castelar ended up becoming president of the First Spanish Republic in 1873. On the legal history of the shift from royal patrimony to national patrimony, see Díez Moreno (1989, 129–130) and Clarke (2013, 288).

[28] As Yonan (2011, 3) states, Maria Theresa's reign was enormously successful because during it the empire "underwent a series of administrative reforms, political consolidations, and cultural developments that not only laid the groundwork for the development of multiple modern European states, but also enabled Austria to claim for itself a golden age comparable to the Elisabethan or Catherinian ones". What is more significant is that under her rule "the Habsburg Empire enjoyed significant international political influence" because "her policies instigated internal reorganizations of education, medicine, and civic administration" that "revitalized territories far beyond Austria's modern borders, ranging from Belgium to Ukraine, and from Tuscany to Poland".

[29] According to Szabo (1994, 36–37), even if ministries did not exist in eighteenth-century Austria the monarch remained the ultimate executive and legislative authority. Ministers, called Court Chancellors (*Hofkanzler*) were simply heads of specific departments of the central government's administrative machinery. There were many Court Chancellors responsible for a variety of executive departments, all with different regional jurisdictions: Austria, Bohemia, Hungary, Transylvania and the Holy Roman Empire, all of which were unified in 1742, with the creation of a Court Chancellery that was soon called the Chancellery of State (*Staatskanzlei*), headed by a *Staatskanzler*, a charge that required a comprehensive view of the dynasty's net patrimony.

[30] On the Haugwitz Revolution and the Kaunitz Reform, see Szabo (1994, 73–98).

[31] For an overview of this administrative transformation of the Austrian Empire, see Dickson (1995, 323–367).

The key to these reforms was that enlightened monarchs entrusted royal administration to professional civil servants. Thus, for example, to impose his enlightened policies and implement his reforms, Joseph II employed a veritable army of officials. These were mainly lawyers, appointed directly by the emperor based on merit, to positions which they then occupied for life, allowing them to devote themselves fully to their tasks. In Austria, state offices were not purchasable, unlike in Spain or France, where the standard practice was the "sale of offices" through which monarchs obtained substantial revenues, a practice already examined in the previous chapter. The downside, however, was that these positions were transmitted from father to son, creating a hereditary caste of officials in which merit and capacity were not requisites. Neither did Austria employ a system of "patronage" (very close to Spain's *caciquismo* in the late nineteenth century), one which had become firmly entrenched in England under the Tudor monarchy and consolidated under the Stuarts.[32]

This contingent of civil servants in the Austrian state proved extremely effective, especially in areas such as tax collection, which could be obtained directly and not through the unfair and inefficient system of ad-hoc tax-collectors, who operated for profit as commissioned agents of the state rather than permanent civil servants. The administration of the state improved markedly and royal reform was implemented more effectively.[33]

Concerning Prussia, though Frederick II harbored great admiration for his father's administrative achievements, he did his best to improve the efficiency of the highest administrative body of his kingdom, the General Directory, through his order of May 20, 1748, which completely reorganized it. At the territorial level he also developed the War and Domains Chambers, the executive authorities in the provinces which provided precious information about the actual situation in different parts of the kingdom. He sought to streamline their functioning through the creation of *Kammerdeputationen* and the redistribution of the *Kreise*. Meanwhile, to form a body of excellent civil servants he decreed examinations and practical training for them. Finally, he did not rely entirely on a centralized approach to

[32] As Peck (1993, 4) explains, early Stuart England was governed by a personal monarchy which ruled through a patrimonial bureaucracy organized within a hierarchical society structured by patron-client relationships. Officials received fees paid by those who used their services, annuities, pensions granted by the crown, and informal payments in addition to the traditional fees charged by royal officials. There was, generally, no great social distance between patrons—often belonging to the nobility or gentry—and their clients, who also belonged to these same groups, or the merchant class.

[33] Unlike what happened in modern Spain, where there existed a peculiar system of tax collection carried out through the *Servicio de Millones*, by which cities were in charge of collecting taxes through the use of private collectors, who gave an established portion to the king. On this peculiar aspect of public finances, and the Spanish kings of the House of Austria, see Andrés Ucendo (1999, 33–47) and Ruiz Rodriguez (1992, 1073–1088). For an overview of the state of public finances during Ancien Regime Spain, see Thompson (2002, 140–180).

administration, but rather, in an effort to favor reconstruction,[34] standardized the office of the *Landrat* throughout the Prussian provinces, against the wishes of his central administrators, who wished to get rid of the Provincial Estates and country deputies. Frederick continued to keep those institutions alive, as he saw in them a useful counterweight to his own bureaucracy (Hubatsch 1975, 151–168).

## 10.4 Enlightened Absolutism and the "Rule of Law"

When we think about absolute monarchs today, we have a tendency to envision them as dictators who did whatever they wished in their realms, with no respect at all for legality. Such a view is very far from reality, as Absolutism, in fact, did not preclude the rule of law (Bernard 1979, 1).

### *10.4.1 The Enlightened Monarchs and the Law*

It is true that the absolute rulers stood, at least theoretically, above the law, which they could create unilaterally. They could not, however, do whatever they wanted about preexisting law, as they were bound to observe fixed and widely recognized rules concerning the manner in which they were expected to rule. To ignore these was not, strictly speaking, illegal, but it was certainly an affront to tradition. This is why the expansion of royal power that Enlightened reformism required was not necessarily incompatible with respect for the law.

In fact, the monarchs themselves did not hesitate to establish limits to prevent the sovereign from undertaking arbitrary actions. A clear example is that of Maria Theresa, who in 1749, as part of an overall reorganization of the Habsburg state administration, created a high court of appeal: the *Oberste Justizstelle*. This measure was intended not merely to centralize the appeals procedure in criminal cases, but also to establish the firm principle that judges appointed by the sovereign and serving for life would be independent from the general administration.[35]

Concerning the Prussian state, the expansion of absolutism was even clearer. Frederick II was able to consolidate his power from the beginning because Prussia was only a recently-created kingdom (founded in 1701), whose kings were not

[34] As Hubatsch (1975, 148) explains, Prussia had lost 400,000 inhabitants during the Seven Years War, more than 10 % of the total population in 1756, and almost 20 % of the estimated population in 1740. Given Prussia's circumstances, and the low density of the population, this was an enormous loss.

[35] See Bernard (1979, 6). As Kuzmics and Axtmann (2007, 87) indicate, through the 1749 reform, the Austrian and Bohemian chancelleries were abolished and the newly established supreme judicial authority, the *Oberste Justizstelle*, was responsible for settling legal controversies of both the Austrian and Bohemian Crowns. The result was that the constitutional division between the two states was, in effect, institutionally removed and a new, centrally led "core state" was created.

obligated by any agreements to consult any feudal assembly whatsoever about governmental affairs.[36] This situation allowed Prussian kings to enjoy ample fiscal resources without having to negotiate with feudal representatives from throughout the realm.[37] This was a uniquely favorable situation compared to what was generally the rule in Latin Christendom, where rulers had widely accepted that few taxes could be imposed without the consent of the assemblies of states.[38] Moreover, the King of Prussia freely appointed and dismissed his ministers, who reported only to him while he, in turn, was answerable only to God (Johnson 1975). Despite all this, Frederick the Great was no arbitrary ruler. His efforts to improve the law accounted for the greater part of his administrative activity, and he firmly believed that the monarch's primary function was not to create law, but to protect and support it (Hubatsch 1975, 211).

Frederick II exercised his autocratic power in accord with the political ideals of the Enlightenment (*Aufklärung*),[39] which explains why he enjoyed a rare popularity, unequaled by any other European state of his time (Beck 1997, 34). Thanks to his Enlightenment-based education he believed that he was the agent most qualified to know what his people needed. In fact, in 1739, a year before his accession to the throne, the king himself authored a critique of Machiavelli's work (*Anti-Machiavel: Essay on the Criticism of Machiavelli*) which was extensively revised by Voltaire, who the king welcomed on more than one occasion to his palace of Sans-Souci.[40]

---

[36] The Estates in Brandenburg had been powerful in the fifteenth century, but the decay of towns and the rising influence of the landed nobility had enabled the Great Electors to collect taxes without their consent. By the end of the seventeenth century the financial control formerly exercised by them in Brandenburg had fallen into complete disuse (Myers 1975, 107).

[37] This situation enabled him to forge the Prussian State from the ground up. Frederick II believed that "No government can exist without taxation, which is equally necessary to the republic and to the monarchy. The sovereign who labors in the public cause must be paid by the public; the judge the same, that he may have no need to prevaricate. The soldier must be supported that he may commit no violence, for want of having whereon to subsist. In like manner, it is necessary that those persons who are employed in collecting the finances should receive such salaries as may not lay them under any temptation to rob the public. [...]" People are obliged to pay ("This money must all be necessarily levied on the people") and the only limit is that taxation should not be oppressive ("the grand art consists in levying so as not to oppress"); should be "equally and not arbitrarily laid;" and "should be proportionate to the income of the persons paying;" as he viewed it as an "unpardonable fault in finance if ill-imposed taxes should disgust the husbandman with his labors". This is why "having performed his duties, it is afterwards necessary (that) he and his family should live in a certain degree of ease". Frederick II (1789, 21–22).

[38] As Myers (1975, 29) underscores, this went against the German saying "*Landtage sind Geldtage*" ("representative assemblies are financial assemblies".) The power of the King of Prussia was, therefore, overwhelming, as the power structure not only of the English Parliament, but most of the *Ancien Regime*'s representative assemblies, was built upon the "rock of financial control".

[39] For an overview of Enlightened precedents about the state and the "rule of law", see Tamahana (2004, 39–41).

[40] In a 1739 letter addressed to Frederick, Crown Prince of Prussia, Voltaire urged him to "destroy the odious policies which have turned crime into virtue. The word "politics" originally referred to the citizens, but today, thanks to our perversity, it refers to their deception. Restore to it, my lord, its true meaning. Make men know and love virtue". (*A Frédéric, prince héritier de Prusse... J'ose*

Much later Frederick II would write his *Essay on the Forms of Government and the Duties of Sovereigns*, which he published in 1781 in French. In this work he argued that the prince is to society as the head is to the body, seeing, thinking and acting for the whole community to benefit it (Frederick II 1789, 15).

### *10.4.2 Frederick II's* Sonderweg

It is no wonder, then, that Frederick II made an important contribution to the European public legal tradition, developing in Germany an *avant la lettre* idea of the "rule of law".[41] Specifically, he supported the concept of the *Rechtsstaat* (state of law) as opposed to the *Obrigkeitstaat* (the authoritarian state) (Van Van Caenegem 2003, 136), as he maintained that the king served in a capacity of service to the state, rejecting the old patrimonial conception of the monarchy. In his

*exhorter toujours votre grand génie à honorer Virgile dans Nisus et dans Euryalus, et à confondre Machiavel. C'est à vous à faire l'éloge de l'amitié; c'est à vous de détruire l'infâme politique qui é rige le crime en vertu. Le mot politique signifie, dans son origine primitive, citoyen, et aujourd'hui, grâce à notre perversité, il signifie trompeur de citoyens. Rendez-lui, monseigneur, sa vraie signification. Faites connaître, faites aimer la vertu aux hommes...*) (Voltaire 1846, 322). In 1740, Frederick became King of Prussia, and a new epoch in the relations between the two men began. The next 10 years were, on both sides, years of growing disillusionment. Voltaire very soon discovered that his phrase about "un prince philosophe qui rendra les hommes heureux" was indeed a phrase and nothing more. His *prince philosophe* started out on a career of conquest, plunged all Europe into war, and turned Prussia into a great military power. Frederick, it appeared, was at once a far more important and a far more dangerous phenomenon than Voltaire had suspected. On the other hand, the matured mind of the King was not slow to perceive that the enthusiasm of the Prince needed a good deal of qualification. This change of view was, indeed, remarkably rapid. Nothing is more striking than the alteration of the tone in Frederick's correspondence during the few months which followed his accession: the voice of the raw and inexperienced youth is heard no more, and its place is taken—at once and for ever—by the self-contained caustic utterance of an embittered man of the world (Strachey 2006, 140–141). Voltaire continued however to regard Frederick as a true enlightened monarch, as he promoted tolerance, had abolished torture, reformed the legal system, and developed education, industry and commerce, prompting him to accept the king's 1749 offer to host him at his court at Potsdam. The French philosopher arrived at Frederick's court in 1750 and remained there for 3 years, leaving in 1753 after their relationship deteriorated; although Frederick appreciated Voltaire's genius, he could not abide his personality (Gorbatov 2006, 59–60). In Voltaire's "posthumous" *Memoires pour servir à la vie de M. de Voltaire écrits par lui-même*, the philosopher includes a malicious description of Frederick the Great, partial, and biased, especially in relating the King's alleged homosexuality. On the personal side, Voltaire never forgave Frederick II for ordering his incarceration at Frankfurt and for holding him and his niece prisoners for 5 weeks in the late spring and early summer of 1753. Recent biographers agree that this incident had an effect on Voltaire as profound as the thrashing he had received some 30 years earlier from le chevalier de Rohan. Langille (2007, 49–58). See also Pomeau (1995, 737–748), and Hellegouarc'h (2011, 7–68). Frederick II had also a difficult relationship with Kant, who also had a critical opinion of the monarch (Kant 1991, 61–92).

[41] On the historical background of the *Rechtsstaat* in the German legal tradition, see Gozzi (2007, 237–259), Smith (1985, 253–280) and Ripstein (2009, 114–123).

aforementioned *Essay on the Forms of Government*, Frederick II held that citizens granted preeminence to one of their equals (their king) with an exclusive view to the services which they expected of him. Nevertheless, he believed in equality before the law[42] and argued that princes, sovereigns and kings were not entrusted with the highest authority to bask in impunity, depravity and luxury.[43] Rather, for Frederick II the monarch was subject to the law and obligated to respect it. Hence, from this point of view he was not an "absolute" monarch in the original sense of the term of someone who was above the law (*legibus solutus*).[44] At the same time Frederick II rejected falling into the excesses of legislative dictatorship like the one that which the French Revolution would spawn, therefore advocating a "middle path" (*Sonderweg*) between autocratic monarchy and radical, Jacobin republicanism, holding that in no case should the assemblies' power exceed that of the sovereign.[45]

This preeminence of what today we would call the Executive left a very strong mark on Prussia. Hence, after the Revolution of 1848, though Prussia became a constitutional regime (in 1850), it did not become a parliamentary one. The monarchical model of the state became more pronounced upon the proclamation of the II Reich in 1871. Thus, in cases of conflict with the legislature the monarch could rule via ordinance—something which Bismarck often, in fact, did when he headed up the Prussian Empire (1862–1890) according to the idea that *Recht* (law) had become a formal attribute of the state (Crosby 2008, 7). Prussia would not subscribe to a "parliamentary system" until as late as the Weimar Republic (1919–1933).

### *10.4.3 The Rationalization of the Legal System*

Finally, the speed at which the rule of law spread was facilitated by the fact that enlightened monarchs sought to streamline and unify their realms' legal systems. It is important to remember that in the eighteenth century monarchies ruled over

[42] As he showed in an order addressed to Baron Von Zedlitz on November 7, 1777, in which he expressed his displeasure upon learning that poor people involved in lawsuits in Berlin were being harshly treated, a practice that he had strictly forbidden. He informed the recipient: "[...] that in my eyes a poor peasant is as worthy as the most distinguished count and the richest nobleman, and the law exists for high and low alike" (Lentin 1985, 111).

[43]
> Princes and monarchs ... are not invested with supreme authority that they may with impunity riot in debauchery and voluptuousness. They are not raised by their fellow citizens in order that their pride may pompously display itself, and contemptuously insult simplicity of manners, poverty and wretchedness. Government is not entrusted to them that they may be surrounded by a crowd of useless people whose idleness engenders every vice (Frederick II 1789, 12).

[44]
> Let it be carefully remembered that the preservation of the laws was the sole reason which induced men to allow, and to elect, a superior; because this is the true origin of sovereign power. The magistrate, thus appointed, was the first servant of the state (Frederick II 1789, 8).

[45] As Clark (2007, xxiv–xxv) points out, the Prussian state staked its legitimacy on its role as a vehicle of historical progress and a model of a particular kind of modernity, in contrast and opposition to the revolutionary challenge coming out of France.

patchworks of territories that possessed traditional laws and institutions that were usually left partly or wholly intact when they were incorporated into larger states. This explains why in a single kingdom there coexisted a great variety of different laws and jurisdictions, a phenomenon that was an eternal source of confusion and expense (Gagliardo 1968, 51). Enlightened monarchs did their best to unify and simplify the body of laws and judicial systems in their realms. To do so, they decided that old customs and books of authority had to be replaced by new law, freely conceived by modern man, based on reason and fee of obscurantism. The enlightened legal system was to be clear and certain, comprehensible to the people, whom it was meant to serve. The result was the first national Enlightenment-era codes, based on natural law and conceived of as a body of basic principles from which positive law ought to be directly derived, the best example being the Prussian *Allgemeine Landrecht* of 1794 (Van Caenegem 1994, 123–124).

## 10.5 The Expansion of Enlightened Absolutism in Eighteenth Century Europe: The Great Enlightenment Monarchs

Enlightened absolutism prevailed in many European monarchies. Although the prime examples of this new conception of the monarchy's function arose in Austria and Prussia—and, therefore, in Italy, as the Peninsula was ceded to the Austrian empire by virtue of the Peace of Utrecht in 1713,[46] its principles were also applied in Russia, Spain and Portugal.

### *10.5.1 The Austrian and the Prussian Models and Its Reception in Russia*

Enlightened absolutism was not, however, just an abstract model, but rather one applied by specific monarchs who would become, a posteriori, the paradigms of

[46] Philip V of Spain, remarried to the Italian princess Elisabeth Farnese, reconquered Naples and Sicily. Because of the Treaty of Utrecht, however, he did not dare to incorporate them directly into the Spanish Monarchy, therefore creating the independent Kingdom of the Two Sicilies in 1734. His first king was his oldest son from his second marriage, Charles (V of Naples and VII of Sicily), the future Charles III of Spain, who would excel as a leader, his kingdom becoming one of the leading paradigms of the Enlightenment in Europe (Calabria 1990). As Imbruglia (2007, 2–3) observes, the Kingdom of Naples shows us what it meant in the eighteenth century to construct and modernize a state during the Age of Enlightenment: "...it was not just a question of making the institutions efficient, starting from the military ... it was necessary to give a new vitality to civil society and form the ethos of a new citizenship". The new Kingdom would end as a revolutionary republic in June 1799. For an overall view of Italian Enlightenment, see Venturi (1990), Tarello (2000) and Anderson (1994, 55–74).

Enlightenment-era kings. These would include the aforementioned Germanic monarchs Maria Theresa and Joseph II of Austria, Frederick II of Prussia, and Catherine II of Russia (who was also of German origin).[47] Catherine II managed to establish a stable regime and serve as a worthy successor to Peter the Great (1682–1725). In addition to pursuing an ambitious foreign policy, essentially aimed at expanding Russia's borders, mainly at the expense of Poland and Turkey, Catherine "the Great" was infused with French culture, regularly corresponding with the leading French philosophes (Whittaker 2003). This explains her religious tolerance, which led her to offer asylum in Russia to the Jesuits after the suppression of the order in 1773, and her tolerant stance towards Muslims (Fisher 1968, 542–539), one surely driven as well, by her desire to counter the influence of the Orthodox clergy, who she ended up bringing to heel by confiscating their property (de Madariaga 2002, 21–22). Domestically, Catherine II's great push involved the colonization of southeastern Russia, a task she entrusted to Orlov and Potemkine, who went about seeing to the repopulation of a vast territory that remained virtually uninhabited, despite the fertility of its soil, to this end building roads, towns and cities, and encouraging its settlement by German peasants.[48] In addition to all this she was a great reformer, through the Legislative Commission, convened in 1767 (Alexander 1989, 112–120) which, following the guidelines of the statement of legal principles known as *Nakaz*, (Butler and Tomsinov 2010), authored by Catherine herself,[49] carried out major reforms of government, legal proceedings, courts and territorial organization, especially at the municipal level.[50] When Catherine II died in 1796,

---

[47] As De Madariaga (2002, 1) points out, it is a paradox that Catherine II, who reigned over Russia from 1762 to 1796, had no claim whatsoever to the Russian throne. Peter III was married to Catherine, a German princess born in what is today Szczecin, Poland in 1729. Peter had married her when he was Duke of Holstein (a title he held since 1739). The tsar intended to repudiate her when Catherine took advantage of her husband's unpopularity to orchestrate a plot against him. Able to win over the support of the Imperial Guard, Catherine managed to overthrow her husband and be proclaimed empress, taking the title Catherine II. Days later (July 9, 1762), Peter died under suspicious circumstances after a 6-month reign.

[48] Streeter (2007, 139) considers the Empress's most obvious success her extension of Russia's border to the south, achieving her historic objective of gaining access to the Black Sea, a policy that she pursued with determination and vision, even surpassing the efforts of Peter the Great.

[49] As Beales (2005, 39) points out, this extraordinary document was not originally composed with a legislative commission in mind, but largely consisted of selections Catherine had produced, drawing upon the writings of philosophes. Of its 655 clauses it has been calculated that 294 derived wholly or in large measure from works like Montesquieu's *De l'esprit des lois* (1748), 108 from Beccaria's *Crimes and Punishments* (1764), 35 from Baron Bielfeld's *Institutions politiques* (1760), 24 from J.H.G von Justi's textbook *Die Grundfeste zu der Macht und Glückseeligkeit der Staaten* (*The Basis of Power and Happiness of States*;1760–61), 20 from the *Encyclopédie*, and even a few from Adam Smith's lectures at Glasgow.

[50] As Madariaga (1994, 291–292) points out, the Nakaz and the Legislative Commission have been widely misunderstood, as the "Instruction" has been viewed as a Code of Laws, or even a "constitution" which was never promulgated, and the Commission as a Parliament which failed. There were precedents in previous reigns, but they had been small *ad hoc* consultations with deputies from the nobility and the towns alone. What made Catherine's initiative so significant was that only 5 years after her *coup d'état*, she felt confident enough to embark upon the kind of large-scale consultation suggested by Diderot in his *Encyclopédie*'s article "Représentants", calling together representatives

even though most of the population still lived in destitution or slavery, Russia had significantly expanded its territory, the Russian upper classes were more cultured, the government more reliable, and its administration more effective.[51]

Enlightened absolutism triumphed also on the Iberian Peninsula, in the kingdoms of Portugal and Spain.

## *10.5.2 Portugal in the Pombal Era*

In Portugal, the reign of Joseph I (1750–1777) is noteworthy, thanks to his powerful minister Sebastião José de Carvalho e Mello (1699–1782), better known by his title of Marquis of Pombal, granted to him by the king. Of humble origins, when he came to head the government, Pombal forcefully applied in Portugal the political philosophy of enlightened despotism which he had absorbed in London and Vienna. With energy, vigor and determination he set about reforming the Portuguese state and its economic and social life, though this would spark violent resistance by Portugal's most privileged bodies, as their interests were in jeopardy. The growing opposition to his policies led Pombal to exercise a genuine dictatorship (Cheke 1969) and to employ repression as an instrument of government, including the death penalty, in what Maxwell (1994, 75) has defined as the paradox of Enlightenment and Despotism.[52]

from all the realm's free estates, government bodies, and non-Russian people to examine the chaotic state of Russian law and to draft a new code. The result was that over 500 deputies were elected, each bringing with him an "instruction" from his electors setting out local grievances. Such a public consultation would not be carried out again until the meeting of the first Duma in 1906.

[51] Despite her contradictions and inconsistencies, her hubris and obstinacy, Catherine the Great did an extraordinary deal for Russia. She expanded its borders, but, more importantly, she established a new framework of relationships between the government and the governed, as through the legislative commission, she lay down the foundations for a genuine national debate. By multiplying the instruments dedicated to overseeing the functioning of public institutions, she made it possible for her reform efforts to more deeply penetrate into Russian society. She placed the courts at the service of the people, transforming the view of an overwhelmingly uneducated population of their justice system. Not only did she promote the expansion of private initiative, but also Literature and the Arts while decisively contributing to the formation of a governing class in Russia (Madariaga 1987, 627). Catherine did for Russia what Louis XIV did for France before becoming a prisoner of Versailles.

[52] A good example is how Pombal reacted to the revolt that took place in Oporto on February 23, 1757. The court tried 478 people and condemned 442 (375 men and 50 women and young boys), considering the riot an act of lese-majesty. On October 14 of the same year 13 men and 1 woman were hanged, their quartered limbs placed on spikes for 15 days. Ten women and forty-nine men were exiled to Africa and Portuguese India, and the remaining prisoners were flogged, sent to the galleys, or imprisoned. Most of them had all their goods confiscated (Maxwell 1995, 71). This why some historians have a critical vision of the minister. Storrs (2003, 323), states that "it is difficult to regard him as truly enlightened, particularly in view of his intolerance of opposition and his harsh treatment of his critics", and for Israel (2006, 526) Pombal was not in any meaningful sense "enlightened.", as he considers that Pombal's Enlightenment "was primarily a mechanism for enhancing autocracy at the expense of individual liberty, and especially an apparatus for crushing".

As a thorough adherent to Enlightenment political ideas, Pombal aggressively imposed secularism, the most relevant sign of this commitment being his expulsion of the Jesuits, which took place from 1758 to 1759. The Jesuits' opposition to his radical political and social reforms, and the problem of what to do about the largely autonomous Jesuit missions in Paraguay, rose after Spain's transfer of part of its territory to Portugal, spurred Joseph I's all-powerful minister to convince the king to issue a decree eradicating these missions in the American colonies. Shortly thereafter Pombal took advantage of an attempted regicide in which the Society was unfairly implicated to order the expropriation the Jesuits' property and to expel them from Portugal on January 19, 1759, a measure carried out with unrelenting ferocity through the laws of September 3, 1759 and the expelling of the Papal Nuncio on June 14, 1760 (Maxwell 1995, 101).

### *10.5.3 The Eighteenth Century Revolution in Spain*

Spain was a country ripe for the full application of enlightened absolutism thanks to the abolition of the public legal institutions of the former states of the Crown of Aragon, by Philip V. The imposition of Castilian absolutism in Valencia, Aragon, Mallorca and Cataluña after the promulgation of the "Nueva Planta Decrees", made possible a renovation of Spanish royal power which stands in contrast to the prostration of the Catholic Monarchy during final stage of the Spanish Habsburg monarchy. This shift came about because, among other things, for the first time the Spanish king's subjects had access to all the monarchy's different political and administrative positions throughout the realm's different territories, which meant that the monopoly held by local oligarchies had been broken, with new people permitted to occupy key posts, in many cases based on their merit and capacities.[53]

The peak of enlightened despotism in Spain would coincide with the reigns of Philip V's children, Ferdinand VI (1746–1759), and Charles III (1759–1788),[54]

[53] This was a direct consequence of the Nueva Planta Decrees, which from the start lifted restrictions on "foreigners". Under the terms of these historic decrees, Valencians, Aragonians, Mallorcans and Catalonians were to be authorized to work in Castile and do business with the American colonies, which had previously been prohibited. Castilians, meanwhile, were to be eligible for posts in the former kingdoms of the Crown of Aragon. The Nueva Planta Decrees sought to replace traditional requirements of birth with new standards based on merit and ability, thereby obtaining "for my most faithful subjects, the Castilians, offices and work in Aragon and Valencia, in the same way that the Aragonians and Valencians are to enjoy (the same rights) in Castile, without any discrimination". Decree of 29 June, 1707, calling for the "Derogation of the laws of Aragon and Valencia and their submission to the laws and government of Castile" New Collection III, 3, 1 (1992, II, 13). Only the Old Kingdom of Navarre and the Basque Provinces were able to preserve their own laws and public institutions, as they had remained faithful to Philip of Anjou throughout the War of the Spanish Succession. In fact, they would not lose these privileges until the nineteenth century, as a result of their defeat in the Carlist Wars (1833–1876).

[54] Though from different mothers: Ferdinand VI was the son of Philip V's first wife, María Luisa Gabriela de Saboya, and Charles II was the fruit of the king's second marriage, to Isabel de Farnesio.

though the latter had an advantage over his brother, as prior to governing in Spain he had extensive experience, having served as king in Naples and Sicily for 25 years (1734–1759) (Petrie 1971). The reformism of the early Spanish Bourbons was so effective that it triggered what has been called "the 18th-century Revolution" (Herr 1980), which radically transformed Spain.[55]

Enlightened Spanish economists came to embrace the liberalization of the domestic economy, defending the elimination of deep-seated obstacles to agrarian growth, including restrictions on the domestic grain trade, the end of highly disruptive transhumance practices protected by the traditional privileges enjoyed by the powerful stockbreeders lobby known as La Mesta, and a moratorium on the further acquisition of property by the Church (Paquette 2008, 65). The abolition of internal customs, the liberalization of trade with the American colonies, and major fiscal and administrative reforms allowed the monarchy to multiply its revenues,[56] which facilitated the creation of a permanent army and navy, indispensable to defend the country's overseas territories and allow Spain to regain its status as a great international power.

Also noteworthy was the extensive reform of Spain's governmental structure, with the development of a powerful central government featuring new institutions, such as secretariats, ministries and the Council of Ministers, the Junta Central Suprema[57] and the reinforcement of the Royal Council of Castile as the monarchy's highest advisory body, the imposition of administrative centralization thanks to the creation of the office of the *intendente* (intendant), and a territorial reorganization of the state at the provincial and local levels. All of this was made possible by the Bourbons' appointments of capable government ministers, first foreigners, such as Orry, under the reign of Philip V, and Esquilache under Charles III, with Spanish ministers soon to follow, such as José Patiño, the Marquis of Ensenada, and the Count of Floridablanca. The crucial state reform initiatives undertaken by the Spanish Bourbons between the reign of Philip V and Charles III, nurtured a feeling of "Spanishness" among the Crown's subjects, evidenced by the establishment of

[55] As a result of political and economical stability the Spanish population rose from 9.3 to 11.5 million between 1749 and 1797, representing almost 20 % in half a century (Paquette 2008, 63).

[56] As Paquette (2008, 66) points out, by the end of the reign of Charles III, the link between state power, population, and commercial development had been well established. In a royal decree of 1782, the reformist spirit of the Spanish monarchy was clear, as it declared that the "protection of commerce and industry is the cause which most influences the power, wealth and prosperity of a state".

[57] Centralization in Spain was also carried at the government level by the creation of the Junta Central Suprema, established in 1787, with five Secretariats: State (Estado), Treasury (Hacienda), the Americas (Indias), Grace and Justice (Gracia y Justicia) and Navy and War (Marina y Guerra) jointly advised the king. The power of the Secretariats increased steadily at the expense of the traditional Councils inherited from the Austrian period (1517–1700) towards the end of the reign of Charles III (Paquette 2008, 96).

the Spanish *Cortes*[58] and the emergence of two of the symbols of the Spanish state still existing today: the flag and the national anthem.[59]

All of this put Spain and its monarchy back on the European map after the crisis of the seventeenth century. In 1721, Montesquieu would describe how Spain had become once again one of the great European monarchies: "The most powerful states of Europe are those belonging to the emperor, and to the kings of France, Spain and England. Italy, and a large part of Germany, are divided into an infinite number of small states ruled by princes who are, in reality, the martyrs to sovereignty" (Montesquieu 2008, 136).

It is true that in many cases, reform went further than the people could bear and ended up failing, such as virtually all those measures imposed by Joseph II in Austria. In Portugal, part of the reform introduced during the reign of Joseph I failed because of the Portuguese nation's indifference and even hostility to it. Under Pombal, Portugal's intellectual class would split (as in Spain) into two camps: traditionalists and encyclopedists. In Spain, Charles III had to deal with the Esquilache Riots (1766), instigated by the privileged classes, who frowned upon the king's reform measures. In the end, however, Charles demonstrated a great ability to implement his policies in a very effective manner, though one more pragmatic than systematic (Bottineau 1993, 295).

### *10.5.4 The French and British Exceptions*

Paradoxically, where enlightened absolutism had the least practical impact was in France, despite the fact that most of the leading philosophes were from there. The French monarchy during the reigns of Louis XV (1715–1774) and Louis XVI continued to embrace divine right theory, with the kings adhering to the schemes of government characteristic of classical absolutism, albeit with some exceptions—such as when Louis XVI abolished torture and slavery, granted legal status to Protestants in 1787, and the following year appointed a commission to study the question of the Jews in France (Gagliardo 1968, 47). This fact surely goes a long way to explaining the violent reaction of the French Revolution, which broke out in a kingdom ruled by a monarchy which had insisted upon conserving the old order and had rejected reform.

Nor did enlightened absolutism triumph in England, but for totally different reasons: since the "revolutions" of the seventeenth century, the principle of autocratic monarchy had been rejected, and by the eighteenth century, the English polity

[58] On December 4, 1724, Philip V assembled in Madrid what can be considered the first "Spanish" *Cortes*, as for the first time after the abolition of the *Cortes* of Aragon, Valencia and Catalonia the representatives of Castile sat together with those from Aragon, Valencia and Catalonia. After the premature death of his son, Louis I, the king convened again this assembly to designate his second son, the future Fernando VI, his heir to the throne.

[59] For an overall view of eighteenth-century reformism in Spain, see Paquette (2008).

had already evolved into a model of government in which “royal prerogative” was kept in check by Parliament. The key entity transformed by reform and the adaptation of the government to new times in Britain was not the crown but, as we shall see, Parliament.

## TIMELINE

1701 Rise of the Kingdom of Prussia (capital at Berlin). Frederick of Hohenzollern, son of the Great Elector (of Brandenburg) Frederick William (1640–1688) receives from the Emperor of Austria, Leopold I, the title of “King of Prussia” for his support of the Archduke Charles of Austria in the War of the Spanish Succession.

1711 The Archduke Charles of Austria, aspirant to the throne as a rival to Philip V, is elected as Emperor Charles VI (1711–1740). His election precipitates the end of the war and the signing of the Peace of Utrecht.

1713 Frederick William I rises to the throne of Prussia (1713–1740), the “Sergeant King” who forges Prussia into Europe’s premiere military power. He is the father of Frederick the Great.

1715 September 1. Death of Louis XIV (king from 1643, personal reign from 1661).

1723 End of the Regency of Louis XV of France (born in 1710).

1725 Death of Tsar Peter I the Great (1682–1725), founder of St. Petersburg, after converting Russia into a great European power.

1740 Frederick II the Great of Prussia (1740–1796) and Maria Theresa of Austria (1740–1780) ascend to the throne.

1746 Ferdinand VI assumes the Spanish throne (1746–1759).

1750 Joseph I takes the throne in Portugal (1750–1777), leaving the government in the hands of the Marquis of Pombal, Sebastião José de Carvalho e Melo (1699–1782). This would be Portugal’s last era of splendor.

1755 Death of Charles Louis de Secondat, better known as Montesquieu (born in 1689).

1756 Birth in Salzburg (Austria) of Wolfgang Amadeus Mozart (1756–1791).

1759 Charles III (1759–1788) rises to the Spanish throne after having been king of Naples and Sicily (bearing the title of Charles VII) between 1734 and 1759.

1762 The Russian throne is occupied by a German princess married to Tsar Peter III, who she overthrows after organizing a conspiracy against him. Catherine II (1762–1796), better known as the Catherine the Great, along with Peter I, would serve as the leading paladins of enlightened absolutism in Russia.
1774 Death of Louis XV of France after a reign of 59 years. He is succeeded by Louis XVI.

1778 May 30. Death of François Marie Arouet, better known as Voltaire (born in 1694). On July 2 of the same year Jean Jacques Rousseau dies.

1780 Joseph II becomes Emperor of Austria (1780–1790). Unlike his mother, he adopts a policy of aggressive reform which ultimately fails, rejected by the majority of his subjects.
1784 Death of Denis Diderot, one of the leading French encyclopedists.
1786 Death of Frederick II of Prussia.
1788 Death of Charles III of Spain.
1790 Death of Joseph II of Austria.
1796 Death of Catherine II of Russia.

## References

Agnew, H. L. (2004). *The Czechs and the lands of the Bohemian crown*. Stanford, CA: Hoover Institution Press.

Alexander, J. T. (1989). *Catherine the Great: Life and legend*. New York: Oxford University Press.

Anderson, M. S. (1994). The Italian reformers. In H. M. Scott (Ed.), *Enlightened absolutism: Reform and reformers in later eighteenth-century Europe* (Repr.). London: Macmillan.

Anderson, M. S. (2000). Monarchs and despots: Tensions within the state. In *Europe in the eighteenth century* (pp. 160–209). Harlow, UK: Pearson education.

Aulard, A. (1911). *Napoléon Ier et le monopole universitaire: Origine et fonctionnement de l'Université*. Paris: Armand Colin.

Beales, D. E. D. (1987). *Joseph II: In the shadow of Maria Theresa, 1741–1780*. Cambridge, UK: Cambridge University Press.

Beales, D. E. D. (2005). *Enlightenment and reform in eighteenth-century Europe*. London: I.B. Tauris.

Beck, H. (1997). *The origins of the authoritarian welfare state in Prussia. Conservatives, bureaucracy and the social question, 1815–70*. Ann Arbor, MI: The University of Michigan Press.

Bergeron, L. (1990). *France under Napoleon*. Princeton, NJ: Princeton University Press.

Bergin, J. (2004). *Crown, church and episcopate under Louis XIV*. New Haven, CT: Yale University Press.

Bernard, P. P. (1979). *The limits of enlightenment: Joseph II and the law*. Chicago, IL: University of Illinois Press.

Bottineau, Y. (1993). *Les Bourbons d'Espagne*. Paris: Fayard.

Brambilla, E. (2009). Lycées et Université impériale. *Rives méditerranéennes*, (32–33), 97–119.

Butler, W. E., & Tomsinov, V. A. (2010). *The Nakaz of Catherine the Great: Collected texts*. Clark, NJ: Lawbook Exchange, Ltd.

Calabria, A. (1990). *Good government in Spanish Naples*. New York: P. Lang.

Cassirer, E. (2009). *The philosophy of the enlightenment*. Princeton, NJ: Princeton University Press.

Castelar, E. (1870). ¿De quién es el patrimonio español? and El rasgo. In *Cuestiones políticas y sociales* (pp. 193–203 and 205–213). V.I. Madrid: A. de San Martín.

Cheke, M. (1969). *Dictator of Portugal: A life of the Marquês of Pombal, 1699–1782*. Freeport, NY: Books for Libraries Press.

Clark, C. (2007). *Iron kingdom: Rise and downfall of Prussia, 1600–1947*. London: Penguin.

Clarke, H. B. (2013). The last years of Isabel's reign (1863–1868). In *Modern Spain: 1815–1898* (pp. 281–307). Cambridge: Cambridge University Press. (Facsimile reprint. Originally published: Cambridge: University Press, 1906.)

Crankshaw, E. (1970). *Maria Theresa*. New York: Viking Press.

Crosby, M. B. (2008). *The making of a German constitution: A slow revolution*. New York: Berg.

de Madariaga, I. (1987). *La Russie au temps de la Grande Catherine*. Paris: Fayard.

de Madariaga, I. (1994). *Catalina la Grande. La rusa europea*. Madrid: Espasa Calpe.

de Madariaga, I. (2002). *Catherine the Great: A short history*. New Haven, CT: Yale University Press.

Descartes, R. (1998). *Discourse on method* (3rd ed.). Indianapolis, IN: Hackett Publishing Company Inc.

Dickson, P. G. M. (1993). Joseph II's reshaping of the Austrian Church. *The Historical Journal, 36* (1), 89–114.

Dickson, P. G. M. (1995). Monarchy and bureaucracy in late 18th-century Austria. *English Historical Review, 110*(436), 323–371.

Diderot, D. (1969). Foreword to Volume VIII. In J. L. R. d'Alembert & D. Diderot (Eds.), *Denis Diderot's the encyclopedia: Selections* (pp. 49–51). Indianapolis, IN: Bobbs-Merrill. (Originally published as: Avertissement in d'Alembert, Jean Le Rond and Diderot, Denis (1765) *Encyclopédie ou Dictionnaire raisonné des sciences, des arts et des métiers*, Paris: Briasson et al., V. VIII, pp. I–II.)

Diez Moreno, F. (1989). La consideración jurídico-constitucional del patrimonio nacional. *Boletín de la ANABAD, 39*(1), 127–136.

Fisher, A. W. (1968). Enlightened despotism and Islam under Catherine II. *Slavic Review, 27*(4), 542–553.

Frederick II, King of Prussia. (1789). An essay on forms of government, and on the duties of sovereigns. In *Political, philosophical and satirical miscellanies* (Vol. V, pp. 5–33). London: G. G. J. and J. Robinson.

Gagliardo, J. G. (1968). *Enlightened despotism*. London: Routledge and Kegan Paul.

Godsey, W. D., Jr. (1999). *Aristocratic redoubt: The Austro-Hungarian foreign office on the eve of the First World War*. West Lafayette, IN: Purdue University Press.

Gorbatov, I. (2006). *Catherine the Great and the French philosophers of the enlightenment*. Bethesda, MD: Academica Press.

Goyard-Fabre, S. (1984). Les Idées Politiques de Diderot au Temps de l'Encyclopédie. *Revue Internationale de Philosophie,* (148–149), 91–119.

Gozzi, G. (2007). Rechtsstaat and individual rights in German constitutional history. In P. Costa & Z. Danilo (Eds.), *The rule of law: History, theory and criticism* (pp. 237–259). Dordrecht: Springer.

Grell, O. P., & Porter, R. (2000). Toleration in enlightenment Europe. In O. P. Grell & R. Porter (Eds.), *Toleration in enlightenment Europe* (pp. 1–22). Cambridge, UK: Cambridge University Press.

Harrigan, P. J. (2001). Church, state, and education in France from the Falloux to the Ferry laws: A reassessment. *Canadian Journal of History/Annales Canadiennes d'Histoire, 36*(1), 51–83.

Hellegouarc'h, J. (Ed.). (2011). Introduction in Voltaire. In *Memoires pour servir a la vie de M. de Voltaire ecrits par lui-meme* (pp. 7–68). Paris: Honoré Champion.

Herr, R. (1980). *The eighteenth-century revolution in Spain* (2nd ed.). Princeton, NJ: Princeton University Press.

Hubatsch, W. (1975). *Frederick the Great of Prussia: Absolutism and administration*. London: Thames and Hudson.

Imbruglia, G. (Ed.). (2007). *Naples in the eighteenth century: The birth and death of a nation state*. Cambridge, UK: Cambridge University Press.

Ingrao, C. (1986). The problem of enlightened absolutism and the German states. *Journal of Modern History, 58*, 161–180.

Israel, J. (2006). Enlightenment! Which enlightenment? *Journal of the History of Ideas, 67*(3), 523–545.

Johnson, H. C. (1975). *Frederick the Great and his officials*. New Haven, CT: Yale University Press.

Kant, I. (1991). On the common saying: That may be correct in theory, but it is of no use in practice. In M. J. Gregor (Ed.), *Political writings* (pp. 61–92). Cambridge, UK: Cambridge University Press.

Kuzmics, H., & Axtmann, R. (2007). *Authority, state and national character. The civilizing process in Austria and England, 1700–1900*. Aldershot: Ashgate.

Langille, E. M. (2007). Voltaire's satire on Frederick the Great: Candide, His Posthumous Memoires, Scarmendado, and Les Questions Sur l'Encyclopedie. *Romance Notes, 48*(1), 49–58.

Lentin, A. (Ed.). (1985). *Enlightened absolutism (1760–1790): A documentary sourcebook*. Newcastle: Avero.

Lough, J. (1968). The article *Autorité Politique*. In *Essays on the Encyclopédie of Diderot and D'Alembert* (pp. 424–462). Oxford: Oxford University Press.

Lough, J. (1985). Reflections on enlightenment and Lumières. *British Journal for Eighteenth-Century Studies, 8*(1), 1–15.

MacDonogh, G. (2001). *Frederick the Great: A life in deed and letters*. New York: St. Martin's Press.

Mason, J. H., & Wokler, R. (Eds.). (2005). *Diderot political writings*. Cambridge, UK: Cambridge University Press.

Maxwell, K. (1994). Pombal the paradox of enlightenment and despotism. In H. M. Scott (Ed.), *Enlightened absolutism. Reform and reformers in later eighteenth-century Europe* (Repr., pp. 75–118). London: Macmillan.

Maxwell, K. (1995). *Pombal: Paradox of the enlightenment*. Cambridge, UK: Cambridge University Press.

Melton, J. v. H. (2002). *Absolutism and the eighteenth-century: Origins of compulsory schooling in Prussia and Austria*. Cambridge, UK: Cambridge University Press.

Monod, P. K. (1999). *The power of kings: Monarchy and religion in Europe, 1589–1715*. New Haven, CT: Yale University Press.

Monsalve Escriña, A. (2004). *Historia jurídica del Museo del Prado: (1819–1869)*. Madrid: Universidad Complutense de Madrid.

Montesquieu, Charles Louis de Secondat, Baron of. (2008). Letter 103, Usbek to Ibben, at Smyrna. In *Persian letters*. Oxford, UK: Oxford University Press.

Myers, A. R. (1975). *Parliaments and estates in Europe to 1789*. London: Thames and Hudson.

Noel, C. C. (1994). Charles III of Spain. In H. M. Scott (Ed.), *Enlightened absolutism: Reform and reformers in later eighteenth-century Europe* (Repr., pp. 119–143). London: Macmillan.

Outram, D. (2007). *The enlightenment* (3rd ed.). Cambridge, UK: Cambridge University Press.

Paquette, G. B. (2008). *Enlightenment, governance and reform in Spain and its empire: 1759–1808*. Basingstoke, UK: Palgrave Macmillan.

Peck, L. L. (1993). *Court patronage and corruption in early Stuart England*. London: Routledge.

Petrie, C. A. (1971). *King Charles III of Spain: An enlightened despot*. London: Constable.

Philips, D. (2011). *The German example: English interest in educational provision in Germany since 1800*. London: Continuum International.

Pomeau, R. (1995). *Voltaire en son temps*. Paris: Fayard.

Riccards, M. P. (2012). *Faith and leadership: The papacy and the Roman Catholic Church*. Plymouth, UK: Lexington Books.

Ripstein, A. (2009). *Force and freedom: Kant's legal and political philosophy*. Cambridge, MA: Harvard University Press.

Robbers, G. (Ed.). (2007). *Encyclopedia of world constitutions*. New York: Infobase publishing.

Ruiz Rodríguez, J. I. (1992). Estructura y recaudación del servicio de Millones: (1590–1691). *Hispania: Revista española de historia, 52*(182), 1073–1088.

Sauter, M. J. (2009). *Visions of the enlightenment: The edict on religion of 1788 and the politics of the public sphere in eighteenth-century Prussia*. Leiden: Brill.

Savoie, P. (2004). Construire un système d'instruction publique: de la création des lycées au monopole renforcé (1802–1814). In J.-O. Boudon (Ed.), *Napoléon et les lycées: Enseignement et société en Europe au début du XIXe siècle* (pp. 39–45). Paris: Nouveau Monde Éditions.

Schaich, M. (2007). *Monarchy and religion: The transformation of royal culture in eighteenth-century Europe*. Oxford: Oxford University Press.

Schmidt, J. C. (2003). Inventing the enlightenment: Anti-Jacobins, British Hegelians, and *the Oxford English Dictionary*. *Journal of the History of Ideas, 64*(3), 421–443.

Smith, A. A. (1985). Kant's political philosophy: Rechtsstaat or council democracy. *The Review of Politics, 47*(2), 253–280.

Smith, A. (2009). *Historical dictionary of Spain* (2nd ed.). Lanham, MD: Scarecrow Press.

Storrs, C. (2003). Pombal in Kors. In A. Charles (Ed.), *Encyclopedia of the enlightenment* (Vol. 3, p. 323). Oxford: Oxford University Press.

Strachey, L. (2006). Voltaire and Frederick the Great. In *Books and characters: French and English* (pp. 137–166). Charleston, SC: Bibliobazaar.

Streeter, M. (2007). *Catherine the Great*. London: Haus Publishing.

Strugnell, A. (1973). A coherent absolutism. In *Diderot's politics. A study of the evolution of Diderot's political thought after the encyclopédie* (pp. 93–117). The Hague: Martinus Nijhoff.

Szabo, F. A. J. (1994). *Kaunitz and enlightened absolutism 1753–1780*. Cambridge, UK: Cambridge University Press.

Szabo, F. A. J. (2011). Changing perspectives on the revolutionary emperor: Joseph II. Biographies since 1790. *The Journal of Modern History, 83*(1), 111–138.

Tamahana, B. Z. (2004). *On the rule of law: History, politics, theory*. Cambridge, UK: Cambridge University Press.

Thompson, I. A. A. (2002). Castile: Polity, fiscality and fiscal crisis "and" Castile: Absolutisms, constitutionalism and liberty. In P. T. Hoffman & K. Norberg (Eds.), *Fiscal crisis, liberty and representative government: 1450–1789* (pp. 140–180, and 181–225). Stanford, CA: Stanford University Press.

Andrés Ucendo, J. I. (1999). *El servicio de millones durante el siglo XVII*. Bilbao: Universidad del País Vasco.

Van Caenegem, R. C. (1994). *An historical introduction to private law*. Cambridge, UK: Cambridge University Press.

Van Caenegem, R. C. (2003). *An historical introduction to western constitutional law*. Cambridge, UK: Cambridge University Press.

Venturi, F. (1990). *The first crisis = Settecento riformatore*. Princeton, NJ: Princeton University Press.

Vocelka, K. (2000). Enlightenment in the Habsburg monarchy: A history of a belated and short-lived phenomenon. In O. P. Grell & R. Porter (Eds.), *Toleration in enlightenment Europe* (pp. 196–211). Cambridge: Cambridge University Press.

Voltaire, P. (1846). Lettre de Voltaire à Frédéric, Cirey, avril 1739. In *Oeuvres de Frédéric le Grand* (Vol. XXI, p. 322). Berlin: Imprimerie Royale Decker.

Wangermann, E. (2007). Reform Catholicism and political radicalism in the Austrian enlightenment. In R. Porter & M. Teich (Eds.), *The enlightenment in national context* (pp. 127–140). Cambridge: Cambridge University Press.

Whittaker, C. (2003). *Russian monarchy: Eighteenth-century rulers and writers in political dialogue*. DeKalb: Northern Illinois University Press.

Williams, E. N. (1970). *The eighteenth-century constitution: 1688–1815 (documents and commentary)*. New York: Cambridge University Press.

Williams, D. (2003). Introduction. In *Voltaire political writings* (pp. XIII–XXXIV). Cambridge, UK: Cambridge University Press.

Wilson, A. M. (1967). The development and scope of Diderot's political thought. In *Studies on Voltaire and the eighteenth century* (Vol. 27, pp. 1871–1900). Oxford: Voltaire Foundation.

Wilson, A. M. (1970). Essays on the "Encyclopedie" of Diderot and D'Alembert (a review). *Eighteenth-Century Studies, 3*(3), 411–412.
Yonan, M. (2011). *Empress Maria Theresa and the politics of Habsburg Imperial Art*. University Park, PA: Pennsylvania State University Press.

## Further Reading

Arendt, H. (1992). *Lectures on Kant's political philosophy*. Chicago: The University of Chicago Press.
Beales, D. E. D. (2009). *Joseph II against the world: 1780–1790*. Cambridge, UK: Cambridge University Press.
Behrens, C. B. A. (1985). *Society, government and the enlightenment: The experiences of eighteenth-century France and Prussia*. London: Harper & Row.
Bhat, G. (2007). Recovering the historical Rechtsstaat. *Review of Central & East European Law, 32*(1), 65–97.
Blanning, T. (2008). *The pursuit of glory: The five revolutions that made modern Europe, 1648–1815*. London: Penguin.
Blanning, T. C. W. (2013). *Joseph II*. New York: Routledge.
Broadie, A. (2003). *The Cambridge companion to the Scottish enlightenment*. Cambridge, UK: Cambridge University Ptess.
Byrne, J. M. (1997). *Religion and the enlightenment: From Descartes to Kant*. Louisville, KY: Westminster John Knox Press.
Crocker, L. (1984). Diderot as a political philosopher. *Revue Internationale de Philosophie*, (148'149), 120–139.
d'Alembert, J. L. R., & Diderot, D. (Eds.). (2003). *Encyclopedia of Diderot & d'Alembert*. Ann Arbor, MI: University of Michigan Library. (Originally published as: d'Alembert, J. L. R., & Diderot, D. (Eds.). (1765). *Encyclopédie ou Dictionnaire raisonné des sciences, des arts et des métiers*. Paris: Briasson et al.)
Dickson, P. G. M. (1985). *Finance and government under Maria Theresia: 1740–1780*. Oxford: Clarendon Press.
Ferguson, R. A. (1997). *The American enlightenment: 1750–1820*. Cambridge, MA: Harvard University Press.
Gay, P. (1996). *The enlightenment: An interpretation. The science of freedom* (repr., 2nd ed.). New York: W. W. Norton.
Gershoy, L. (1983). *From despotism to revolution, 1763–1789* (Repr.). Westport, CT: Greenwood Press.
Hampson, N. (2004). The enlightenment. In E. Cameron (Ed.), *Early modern Europe: An Oxford history* (pp. 265–297). Oxford, UK: Oxford University Press.
Hargreaves-Mawdsley, W. N. (1979). *Eighteenth-century Spain, 1700–1788: A political, diplomatic and institutional history*. London: Rowman and Littlefield.
Hayton, D. W., & Bergin, J. (2010). *The eighteenth-century composite state: Representative institutions in Ireland and Europe, 1689–1800*. Basingstoke, UK: Palgrave Macmillan.
Hespanha, A. M. (1992). *Poder e Instituições na Europa do Antigo Regime*. Lisboa: Cosmos.
Israel, J. (2011). *A revolution of the mind: Radical enlightenment and the intellectual origins of modern democracy*. Princeton, NJ: Princeton University Press.
Jacob, M. (2006). *The radical enlightenment: Pantheists, freemasons, and republicans* (2nd rev. ed.). Lafayette, LA: Cornerstone Book.
Krieger, L. (1975). *An essay on the theory of enlightened despotism*. Chicago: The University of Chicago Press.

Krüger, P., & Schroeder, P. W. (2003). *The transformation of European politics, 1763–1848*. Oxford: Clarendon Press.

Lefebvre, G. (1969). Enlightened despotism. In H. Lubasz (Ed.), *The development of the modern state* (pp. 48–64). London: Macmillan.

Lynch, J. (1989). *Bourbon Spain: 1700–1808*. Oxford: Basil Blackwell.

McKay, R. (2007). *The limits of royal authority: Resistance and obedience in seventeenth-century Castile*. Cambridge: Cambridge University Press.

Melton, J. V. H. (2001). *The rise of the public in enlightenment Europe*. Cambridge, UK: Cambridge University Press.

Merrick, J. (1990). *The desacralization of the French monarchy in the eighteenth century*. Baton Rouge, LA: Louisiana State University Press.

Mittenzwei, I. (1970). Über das Problem des aufgeklärten Absolutismus. *Zeitschrift fur Geschichtswissenschaft*, (18), paragraphs 1162–1172.

Padover, S. K. (1967). *The revolutionary emperor, Joseph the Second, 1741–1790*. Hamden, CT: Archon Books.

Paquette, G. B. (2013). *Imperial Portugal in the age of Atlantic revolutions: The Luso-Brazilian World, c. 1770–1850*. Cambridge, UK: Cambridge University Press.

Porter, R. (2000). *The creation of the modern world: The untold story of the British enlightenment*. New York: W. W. Norton and Company.

Proust, J. (1995). *Diderot et l'Encyclopédie*. Paris: Albin Michel.

Rasmussen, D. C. (2013). *The pragmatic enlightenment*. Cambridge, UK: Cambridge University Press.

Reill, P. H. (2008). *Rethinking the enlightenment: Nature and culture in the high and late enlightenment*. Amsterdam: Holland University Press.

Robertson, R., & Timms, E. (1995). *Austrian enlightenment and its aftermath* (New ed.). Edinburgh: Edinburgh University Press.

Roche, D. (1998). *France in the enlightenment*. Cambridge, MA: Harvard University Press.

Schmidt, J. (2004). *What is enlightenment?: Eighteenth-century answers and twentieth-century questions*. Berkeley, CA: University of California Press.

Sorkin, D. (2011). *The religious enlightenment: Protestants, Jews, and Catholics from London to Vienna*. Princeton, NJ: Princeton University Press.

Szabo, F. A., Szántay, A., & Tóth, I. G. (Eds.). (2005). *Politics and culture in the age of Joseph II*. Budapest: Institute of History, Hungarian Academy of Sciences.

Szabo, F. A. J. (2008). *The Seven Years War in Europe: 1756–1763*. London: Longman.

Tarello, G. (2000). *Storia della cultura giuridica moderna*. Bologna: Il Mulino.

Trénard, L. (1979). L'absolutisme éclairé: le cas français. *Annales Historiques de la Révolution Française*, (51), 627–646.

Valsecchi, F. (1990). *Il riformismo borbonico in Italia*. Roma: Bonacci.

Venturi, F. (1972). *Italy and the enlightenment: Studies in a cosmopolitan century*. New York: New York University Press.

Venturi, F. (1976). Church and reform in enlightenment Italy: The sixties of the eighteenth century. *The Journal of Modern History, 48*(2), 215–232.

Voltaire, P. (2000). *Treatise on tolerance*. Cambridge, UK: Cambridge University Press.

Williams, E. N. (1999). *The Ancien regime in Europe: Government and society in the major states 1648–1789*. London: Pimlico.

# Chapter 11
# From Absolute to Limited Monarchy: The British Origins of Parliamentary Government

[Man]. . . is capable of rectifying his mistakes by discussion and experience. Not by experience alone. There must be discussion to show how experience is to be interpreted.—John Stuart Mill (1806–1873). *On Liberty* (1859)[1]

## Contents


11.1 A Peculiar Constitutional History ..... 288
11.2 The Origins of Assembly-Based Government ..... 289
11.2.1 From the Germanic Kingdoms to the Feudal Stage ..... 289
11.2.2 The Westminster Parliament Appears ..... 291
11.2.3 The Political Consolidation of Parliament ..... 293
11.3 Parliament and the Absolutism of the Tudors ..... 294
11.4 Dynastic Change and the Triumph of Parliament: The Two English Revolutions of the Seventeenth Century ..... 296
11.4.1 The Kings of Scotland on the English Throne: The Stuarts ..... 296
11.4.2 The First English Revolution: Oliver Cromwell and the Only "Republic" in English History ..... 297
11.4.3 The Appearance of Political Parties ..... 297
11.4.4 The Second (and Last) English Revolution (1688) ..... 298
11.4.5 The Religious Issue and the Transformation of England's Constitutional Framework ..... 300
11.5 The Emergence of the United Kingdom and the Consolidation of Parliamentary Preeminence ..... 301
11.6 The Rise of the Hanover Dynasty and the Formation of the Parliamentary Regime . 302
11.6.1 Robert Walpole and the Linguistic Origins of the Parliamentary Regime ... 302
11.6.2 The Consolidation of the "Parliamentary System" ..... 303
11.6.3 The Democratization of the Parliamentary System (1832–1928) ..... 306
11.6.4 The Consolidation of the Legislative Superiority of the House of Commons: The Parliament Act (1911) ..... 308
11.6.5 The Legislative Recognition of the Prime Minister (1937) ..... 308
References ..... 311


[1] Mill (2012, 38–39).



B. Aguilera-Barchet, *A History of Western Public Law*,
DOI 10.1007/978-3-319-11803-1_11

## 11.1 A Peculiar Constitutional History

England and the United Kingdom (which, in addition to England, includes Wales, Scotland and Northern Ireland), boast one of the most peculiar and interesting "constitutional" histories of all the western countries. At the center of these histories stand two specific institutions: the Crown and Parliament.

"Fog in Channel, Continent Cut Off". With this phrase the English sum up a disposition, a special spirit that differs profoundly from the rest of Europe. Firstly, for geographical reasons, as it is located on the island of Great Britain, invaded in 1066 by the Norman King William the Conqueror. After defeating King Harold II at the Battle of Hastings, William rose to the British throne.[2] The Normans, as their name indicates, were men from the north (Norsemen) who in the ninth century had navigated Europe's largest rivers, attacking the towns located along them, aided by ships which benefitted from their minimal draft. Among these towns was Paris, which was sacked several times. In 911, the Frankish king Charles the Simple, weary of their raids, made a pact with the Norman leader Rollo at Cheptel sur Epte through, which in exchange for peace, he turned the city of Rouen over to him, along with the provinces as far west as Brittany (Crouch 2007, 4). Settled on France's northwestern coast, the Normans invaded the island of Great Britain in 1066 (incidentally, the last time the island would be successfully invaded: Philip II's Armada, Napoleon and Hitler would all fail to match this feat).

The history of English public law is one of the West's most interesting. Many "Continental" legal scholars contend that the UK has no constitution, but in this they err. While it does not have, of course, a written constitution (Jenkins 2003), the British enjoy Europe's oldest series of political customs and habits, a body of customs and usages called the "conventions" of the Constitution (Chrimes 1970,

[2] To commemorate and justify his violent seizure of power, William commissioned the embroidering of the marvelous "Bayeux Tapestry", today found in the French locality of Bayeux (Normandy). The cloth measures 70 m and narrates the tale of how the Conqueror had become the legitimate King of England and how Harold suffered a defeat which was made inevitable by his turpitude, for his perjury and ingratitude to Williams, as well as the magnitude and decisiveness of the Norman achievement (Cowdrey 2005, 9). The work was displayed in the cathedral so that the subjects of the new English king could understand why William had rightfully taken the English throne. One must remember that during this era only a select few—priests and members of the clergy—knew how to read. In fact, the illiterate faithful were taught the Gospel through the sculptures on columns in Romanesque cloisters and churches, such as in Silos (Burgos, Spain). Following the same principle, the legitimacy of a throne was demonstrated through the illustrations appearing on a tapestry which, almost 1,000 years later, remains remarkably intact. On the political connotations of this masterpiece of medieval iconography see Ashe (2007, 35–49), Werckmeister (1976, 535–595) and Wissolik (1979, 69–97).

7), a legacy which makes their political system extremely stable.[3] And the most imitated. The British were the principal architects of Parliamentary government, in which the executive is elected—and controlled—by the legislature (Wintertorn 1976, 591–617). This model of representative government has prevailed in many western countries, beginning with most European democracies, and has become a reference in western constitutional history (Irvine of Lairg 2003, 227–250).

We have already seen how classical absolutism evolved towards an "enlightened" approach, adapting in response to the circumstances of eighteenth-century Europe. The absolute monarchs strove to be more effective, but while respecting the sacred principle that government should be exercised by one person. Their reformist policies surely transformed the realities of their kingdoms, but they also emphasized the authoritarianism of the king, thereby exacerbating his isolation from his subjects. The rigidity and intransigence of the absolutist regimes was gradually overcome in England as the principle of the British Parliament's control of the monarchy was reestablished in the seventeenth century. Thus did British "constitutional" practice progressively move towards "assembly-based government" during the eighteenth century, developing into a "parliamentary system" in the nineteenth century.[4]

## 11.2 The Origins of Assembly-Based Government

### *11.2.1 From the Germanic Kingdoms to the Feudal Stage*

Rome had "popular" assemblies during the Republican period, but they were almost always controlled by the wealthy, and gradually lost their influence and power following the triumph of the imperial monarchy because of the process initiated by Augustus and the establishment of the Principate. In contrast, we have already seen how originally, during their stage as nomads, the Germanic peoples made their most important decisions through assemblies of warriors (*mallus*), the origin in Anglo-Saxon England of councils known as the *witan* and *moots*, held from the eighth to

[3] The classic approaches to British constitutional History are *The English Constitution*, by Walter Bagehot (1826–1877), first published in 1867 (Bagehot 2009), and the *Lectures Introductory to the Study of Law of the Constitution*, by Albert Venn Dicey (1835–1922); first edition in 1885 (Dicey 2013). For a recent critical approach to these two basic books, see McLean (2012) and Griffith (2001, 42–67).

[4] About this point, the distinction that Dicey (2013, 15–16 and 18) draws between "constitutional historians" and "legal constitutionalists" is noteworthy; whereas the former are mainly dedicated to ascertaining the steps by which a constitution has grown to be what it is, and are ("sometimes excessively") deeply concerned with the question of "origins", the latter essentially concentrate on identifying the constitution's rules in current times. In his view, constitutional historians should carefully avoid "formalism and antiquarianism" to keep from misleading students in their search for constitutional law.

the eleventh centuries.[5] In Anglo-Saxon England, for instance, the law forbade men from seeking the king's justice unless they had failed to have their case heard in the local "hundred courts,[6]" made up of rich and poor men alike (Pollock and Maitland 2010, 42). The principle of collective justice, however, would endure down to our days in institutions such as the jury (Stanley 2000, 136–145).[7]

It should be noted that after the various Germanic peoples settled in a particular territory and organized into kingdoms, their popular assemblies tended to become restricted, composed solely of "notables" acting as royal advisers—*aula regia* in Visigothic Spain or *witenagemot* (Gneist 2005, 101–103) in Anglo-Saxon England. The "aristocratic" assembly took on special importance during the feudal stage, evolving into the *curia regis*. Made up of bishops and the most influential noblemen, it was the body of advisers and courtiers who assisted the king and supervised the administration of the realm, the ancestor of the king's privy council, which later splintered into Parliament and the Privy Council (Baker 1990, 20). The *curia* became the centerpiece of royal administration in England during the twelfth century, and gradually evolved, as in the rest of Europe, into an assembly of estates (Gneist 2005, 260–263),[8] though featuring the peculiarity that the medieval English assembly of "estates", the Parliament, would play a more important legal and political role than in other European kingdoms.

[5] As Pollock and Maitland (2010, 40) indicate, the most general Anglo-Saxon term for an assembly empowered to do justice is *gemót*, a word that denotes the authority of all types of courts, from the king and his *witan* downwards. Yet, as Oleson (1955, 62) points out, the *witan* were made up of respected counselors who always regarded themselves as a body reporting to the king, not as a separate or independent corporate assembly. The *wita* was the assembly the king consulted, and the *witenagemot* the occasion on which this consultation took place.

[6] A hundred was a body of justice and government in medieval England. Each hundred had a court that met once a month, usually outside, at a well-publicized time and place. Both criminal matters and private disputes were heard by it. Initially all residents of the hundred were expected to attend the hundred court, but over time attendance was reduced to the tenants of specific lands. Regular attendants acted as judges, except when the sheriff filled the role on his biannual visits. Eventually private lords took control of the hundred courts.

[7] As Masschaele (2009, 86) points out, the extraordinary range of responsibilities assigned to jurors under the different forms of medieval juries is striking, which included not just trial juries, but also presentment and assize juries as well. Jury service was a significant and demanding practice, as royal judges and administrators continued to develop new procedures making use of jury verdicts over the course of the thirteenth and fourteenth centuries. They rarely reduced the scope of earlier ones, as new areas of responsibility were added to those already existing.

[8] As Wilkinson (1972, 4) highlights, in developing parliamentary institutions men grappled to reconcile conflicting principles in what was a pan-European response to solve common problems throughout Christendom by finding and building upon common ground. From this point of view Europe's parliaments were more than merely instruments to defend special privileges, but rather the supreme medieval instrument for preserving liberty, and a forum for cooperation, reconciliation, and conflict resolution. For a recent study on the complex sources of the period see Aurell (2007).

## 11.2.2 *The Westminster Parliament Appears*

### 11.2.2.1 From the Assize of Clarendon to the Magna Carta

Following the Norman invasion England was ruled by a series of authoritarian kings, such as William I himself, and his descendant Henry II Plantagenet, who in 1166 had the *curia regia* approve the historic legislative text known as the Assize of Clarendon,[9] which limited the purview of feudal jurisdictions and laid down the foundation for the expansion of royal justice (Caenegem 1988, 40–42). It became the first step towards the unification of legal practice throughout the kingdom (common law).[10] His son John I—a brother of Richard the Lionhearted—ruined all that his father had achieved. His reign was so disastrous for England that he was called "John Lackland" because the French king, Philip Augustus, wrested from him all his domains in France. This, coupled with his voracious fiscal policy, so enraged the nobles that they forced the king to accept the *Magna Carta* in 1215, a document limiting the king's power (and granting them more, of course).[11]

There after the English kings began to consult the most eminent members of the nobility before making the most important decisions for the kingdom. In fact, these

[9] Because it was approved by an assembly (*assize*) (from the French *assis*, the past participle of *asseoir*: to sit down) or *curia*, made up of the nobles and bishops, with the king ("Here begins the Assize of Clarendon, made by King Henry II, with the assent of archbishops, bishops, abbots, earls, and barons of all England".) The word *assize* also referred to a 16-man jury created in 1066 for the bringing of criminal charges against the accused ("King Henry has ordained, on the advice of all his barons, to preserve the peace and maintain the several hundreds by twelve of the most lawful men of the hundred, and by four of the most lawful men of each *vill* (township), upon oath that they will tell the truth, as to whether in their hundred or in their *vill* there is any man who is accused or said to be a robber, or a murderer, or anyone who has been a harborer of robbers or murderers or thieves since the lord king was king".) The word *assize*, therefore, referred as well to the procedures for indictment, the court sessions themselves, and ultimately ended up designating an itinerant justice tribunal (*assize circuits*). The term could also refer to the legislation approved by this type of assembly, royal decrees (*writs*), and was widely used in reference to legislation in general (Janin 2004, 76). In medieval France it referred to the provincial sessions held by the Parlement of Paris. Even today in France the criminal tribunal issuing verdicts continues to be called the *cour d'assises*. For the original Latin version of the text of the Assize of Clarendon, see Stubbs (1960, 170–173). For the English version, see Henderson (2004, 16–20).

[10] On the essential contribution of Henry II and his descendants to English constitutional and legal history, see Biancalana (1988, 433–536) and Brand (2007, −215–241).

[11] The limitation imposed by barons on the king was especially obvious in Clause 61 of the Magna Carta: "*. . . we have granted all these concessions, desirous that they should enjoy them in complete and firm endurance forever, we give and grant to them the underwritten security, namely, that the barons choose five and twenty barons of the kingdom, whomsoever they will, who shall be bound with all their might, to observe and hold, and cause to be observed, the peace and liberties we have granted and confirmed to them by this our present Charter . . .*" (Holt 2003, 471).

nobles began to meet with the king in the city of Westminster—at that time separated from London—to discuss affairs of state. (The term *Parliament*[12] would evolve from the French verb *parler*,[13] meaning "to talk".) These meetings of the king with his nobles constituted the origins of the English Parliament (Maddicott 2012).

#### 11.2.2.2 From the Council of Nobles to the Assembly of Estates

In 1258, an English nobleman named Simon de Montfort, Earl of Leicester and a brother of King Henry III, weary of the monarch's weakness and misrule, rebelled against him, and imposed upon the monarch the "Provisions of Oxford", a document which left power in the hands of a restricted council of nobles and was considered, until 1264, the law of the land by the barons (Valente 2005, 40). At the Battle of Lewes in 1264 (Sadler 2008, 55–70) Monfort defeated Henry III and imposed upon him the presence in Parliament of representatives from every county and the most important cities, in addition to its nobles and bishops (Maddicott 2001, 284–289). The citizens' representation at Westminster was consolidated by Edward I (1272–1307), who as of 1295 relied upon knights and town representatives to counter the influence of the nobility, and to finance his military campaigns.[14]

[12] As Lyon (1980, 413) observes, towards the end of the twelfth century the *curia regis* was divided into the great council—called the *magnum concilium* (Gneist 2005, 414–423)—and the small council, simply called the *concilium*. The word *colloquium* was initially used to describe the sessions of both councils, and during the thirteenth century the great council's meetings began to be referred to as *parliamentum*, a term used for the first time in a record of the king's bench to describe a meeting of this royal court of law. It is also mentioned in the Provisions of Oxford (1258), and after 1275, appeared often in official records.

[13] It should not be forgotten that Henry II, the king who laid the basis for common law, had been raised in France and, despite reigning as the King of England, never spoke a word of English. Quite the paradox, though it should be noted that during this period, English had not been established and defined as Great Britain's common language. What has been termed Old English was a hodgepodge of dialects from the different realms of Anglo-Saxon Great Britain, though just one, western Saxon, would become predominant. English originated from the dialects spoken by the Anglo-Frisians and Saxons, brought to England by Germanic tribes. The *lingua franca* after the Roman conquest—during the era the people spoke Celtic dialects—was Latin. One of the Germanic tribes was the Anglos, which gave rise to the term *Engla land* and, ultimately, *England*, the land of the Anglos: "...for some time after the conquest the English language seems to have a fair chance of holding its own legal affairs. In the first place, the combat between English and French, if it must begin sooner or later, can for a while be postponed or concealed, for there is a third and powerful rival in the field. Latin becomes the written language of the law" (Pollock and Maitland 2010, 82). On the relations between Henry II and the French continent, see Bachrach (1984, 111–130) and Everard (2006, 123–145).

[14] As we know, knights and town representatives had previously joined the Parliament thanks to Simon of Monfort. However, the Commons' presence in the Parliament was ephemeral, and its role was merely to assent to what the barons and bishops had already decided. Under Edward I the presence of knights and borough representatives became permanent, and for the first time they received *plena potestas* from their communities, as their assent to Parliamentary decisions was required. As Morris (2008, 121) explains, 800 representatives of knights from the shires, burgesses

This explains as well why he was extremely active legislating, to the point that Frederick W. Maitland considered him the "English Justinian" (Maitland and Montague 2005, 2).[15]

### *11.2.3 The Political Consolidation of Parliament*

In 1307, the successor to the energetic Edward was his son, Edward II who, unlike his father, was an utter disaster, so inept that in 1327 Parliament forced him to abdicate in favor of his son Edward III (Raban 2000, 149–151). This was the first time that Parliament succeeded in such a decisive political intervention, but it would not be the last.[16]

Edward III reigned for 50 years and proved to be one of England's finest kings. It should be noted, however, that he was responsible for involving his kingdom in the Hundred Years War in 1346, after his resounding victory at the Battle of Crecy (Ormrod 2011, 277–284). The ensuing conflict would be a long one and take a heavy toll on the English monarchy, forcing its kings to summon Parliament often to ask for money. Over the course of its gatherings the current bicameral structure of the English Parliament developed, with one body made up of nobles (House of Lords), and another composed of the representatives of the cities (House of Commons).[17] This was a unique structure as compared to the assemblies of estates in the various European kingdoms,[18] as in England the underprivileged classes, the

and towns met, with the usual turnout of earls, barons, bishops and abbots, to constitute not only the largest body imaginable, but also the largest parliament assembled in England in the Middle Ages.

[15] For an overview and analysis of Edward I's statutes, see Plucknett (1970).

[16] On January 13, 1327, Queen Isabella of France's closest advisor (and, incidentally, lover), Roger Mortimer announced in Parliament that it had been agreed among the lords that Edward (II) should be deposed and replaced by his son. The queen's Episcopal supporters gave then a series of sermon-like speeches on Biblical texts and proverbs designed to justify and popularize the rebel's cause. Bishop Orleton preached on the text "A foolish king shall ruin his people" (Ecclesiastes 10:16) and his audience reportedly cried out "We do not wish him to reign over us any longer". Archbishop Reynolds then read out a series of articles composed the previous evening at a meeting of the magnates and prelates, accusing the king of weakness and incompetence, receiving evil counsel, losing his possessions and rights in Scotland, Ireland and France; and abandoning the realm. Reynolds concluded by declaring that the magnates, clergy and people had provided their unanimous consent for the overthrow of Edward II, and expressed their desire that his eldest son, Lord Edward, take the crown. Immediately there was a threefold shout of *fiat* "Let it be done" (Ormrod 2011, 51).

[17] As Harriss (1975, 118) points out, it was after 1334, that knights and burgesses acted in common to approve taxes and determine the procedure for the redressing of grievances.

[18] Originally the English Parliament featured the same three-estate structure. As Lyon (1980, 537–538) observes, a typical Parliament under Edward I consisted of one estate comprised of the spiritual and secular barons and knights, another of the representatives of the lower clergy, and a third one of the representatives of the counties and boroughs. See Maitland and Fisher (2001, 75–90). The first development contributing to the formation of the two-house Parliament was the

commoners, enjoyed 50 % of Parliamentary representation, rather than the one third they wielded in Spain's *Cortes*, or France's Estates General, where the other two thirds were controlled by the privileged classes: the clergy and the nobility. By the final years of Henry III's reign the Commons would play a decisive political role in English politics (Harris 2006, 437–443).

The growing power of Parliament was evident in 1399, when the two chambers acted to remove Richard II and usher in a new dynasty, the House of Lancaster, installing Henry IV on the throne (Dodd 2007, 324–325). The new king would reinitiate hostilities with France (prolonging the 100 Years War), which would reinforce Parliament's political importance, as the monarchs once again required large sums of money to finance their military campaigns. Parliament's power was further bolstered by the fact that England eventually lost the lengthy conflict, which left the crown's prestige badly tarnished.[19] The defeat also led to the outbreak of a bloody civil war: the War of the Roses (1455–1485), in which the houses of Lancaster and York grappled for the throne. In the end it was Parliament which served as the arbitrator designating a new dynasty: the Tudors.[20]

## 11.3 Parliament and the Absolutism of the Tudors

The War of the Roses, in addition to plunging the kingdom into anarchy, decimated the nobility, making it possible for the new king, Henry VII (1485–1507), to restore royal authority (Hicks 2003, 90–91), which would ultimately be shored up by his son, Henry VIII, who reigned until 1547, and his granddaughter, Elizabeth I (1558–1603). These three Tudor monarchs were able to reassert royal prerogative and prevail against Parliamentary power, which certainly did not disappear, but was held in check during this period, during which there were long intervals without a session (Maitland and Fisher 2001, 248–251).[21]

withdrawal of the representatives of the lower clergy, a process that began in 1295. After 1332 we find no more references to them. During the first half of the fourteenth century, the great prelates and barons formed the House of Lords, while the knights ended their association with the barons and coalesced with the burgesses to form the House of Commons. Though the House of Lords did not receive this name until the reign of Henry VIII.

[19] For an overview of the consolidation of the constitutional role of the English Parliament in the crucial period from 1360 to 1461, see Harris (2006, 66–73).

[20] It is true, as MacCaffrey (2008, 130) observes, that the decades between the accession of the House of York and the convocation of the Reformation Parliament were marked by diminished Parliamentary activity and less frequent meetings. Nevertheless, it would be a mistake to consider this a period of Parliamentary decline as, in fact, this situation reflected the relative contentment of the Parliamentary classes with the government's conduct, stronger royal leadership, a decline in conflict between factions, as well as a reduction of fiscal pressure. Parliament strove not to reduce royal power, but to assure that the monarch was more effective in the execution of his duties.

[21] Henry VII, enthroned by the Tudor Dynasty, was the last English king to win his crown on the field of battle, by defeating (along with the army of the House of Lancaster, to which he was related), the House of York. By marrying Elizabeth of York, he united the two factions. Thus, the Tudor's coat of

It must be said that, despite their authoritarian tendencies, the Tudors demonstrated undeniable political skill. Specifically, they astutely favored a bourgeoisie which had become richer by acquiring many of the assets of the nobles who had perished in the War of the Roses, and others expropriated from the religious orders, abolished by Henry VIII after his divorce from Catherine of Aragon and his break with Rome (Law of Supremacy, 1534). Thanks to these events, England grew from a country of herders and farmers into an industrial and mercantile power. Thus emerged a powerful class of merchants who rubbed shoulders and eventually merged with the old landed nobility, giving rise to a new ruling class in England: the gentry.[22]

With such a wide and solid social background, Henry VIII firmly consolidated his authority over the "Reformation Parliament" (Lehmberg 2009),[23] creating a strong government and an efficient administration in what Geoffrey Rudolph Elton called the "Tudor Revolution".[24] As Crossman (1969, 51) points out, the Tudor era was essentially one of action and of expansion; men were so busy forging the new state that they had little time to speculate about it. Therefore, neither Henry nor Elisabeth explicitly claimed Divine Right for their sovereignty, nor did they explicitly demand passive obedience. Rather, they ruled as secular autocrats, in a way that Machiavelli himself would have endorsed, and were prudent enough to often placate their supporters and submit to their wishes.[25]

---

arms came to feature two roses: one white and one red, alluding to the hitherto warring houses of York and Lancaster, respectively. Ever since this crest has been one of the symbols of the English monarchy and the country. The War of the Roses, a drawn-out civil conflict, left few insurgent nobles alive, which allowed the first Tudor monarch to rule amidst relative calm. On the relations between the first Tudor and the Westminster Parliament, see Cavill (2009).

[22] On the late medieval origins of the English gentry, see Harriss (2006, 136–148). On its political evolution during the Tudor period, see Elton (1969) and Bradshaw (1979, 455–476).

[23] Also Elton (1979) and Coby (2006).

[24] To justify Tudor authoritarianism, Dr. Elton (1969, 1) argued that there were periods when the needs of "good government" prevailed over the demands of "free government", and that in this regard the Tudor Age was exemplary, as it was a time when men were ready to be governed, and when order and peace seemed more important than principles and rights. In view of the importance of Dr. G. R. Elton's reinterpretation of early Tudor history, the Editorial Board of *Past and Present* invited a historian of Elizabethan England, Dr. Penry Williams, and a fifteenth-century specialist, Dr. G.L. Harriss, to consider it from their respective standpoints. See Williams (1963, 3–8) on the perspectives of Dr. Elton (1964, 24–69) and Dr. Harriss (1965, 87–96). For an overview of recent approaches to the question, see Coleman and Starkey (1986) and Harris (2011, 1355–1385).

[25] Elisabeth I, the daughter of Henry VIII and his second wife, Anne Boleyn, was even more authoritarian than her father. She did not hesitate to suspend laws passed by Parliament and to frequently employ the Star Chamber to judge her enemies. She also governed without Parliament, through a private council made up of men enjoying her total trust. Nevertheless, the Westminster representatives, members of the gentry, accepted this state of things, not just because the bourgeoisie in the House of Commons continued to grow considerably richer, but because the queen managed to defeat the powerful Spanish monarchy (when Phillip II's Invincible Armada was destroyed in 1588), making England a major European power for the first time, which increased the popularity and prestige of the Crown. On the relationship between Elisabeth I and the English Parliament, see Dean (2002, 63–97), Graves (2014, 17–65), Lee (2007, 22–37), Williams (2006, 124–159).

## 11.4 Dynastic Change and the Triumph of Parliament: The Two English Revolutions of the Seventeenth Century

### *11.4.1 The Kings of Scotland on the English Throne: The Stuarts*

Elisabeth I died without leaving an heir.[26] Thus, after her death, a Scottish dynasty came to occupy the English throne: the Stuarts, descendants of Queen Mary, who Elizabeth I had ordered beheaded. The arrival to the English throne of the kings of Scotland, in the person of James VI of Scotland and I of England (1603–1625), allowed the two kingdoms to be united.

The new kings of England and Scotland sought to wield the same authority as their predecessors, but the Stuarts lacked the Tudors' charisma. James I, although writing several books on the divine right of kings, such as *The True Law of Free Monarchies* and the *Basilokon Doron* (literally "royal gift"), a kind of guide for princes,[27] was relatively moderate and did not square off against Parliament.[28]

---

[26] Because Elizabeth I never married she was called the "Virgin Queen". In her honor the first English colony in North America, founded in 1607, was dubbed "Virginia". For an overview of the constitutional transition from the Tudors to the Stuarts, see Guy (2000).

[27] James I also had to deal with the fact that Scotland was Presbyterian, squarely opposing the principle of Anglicanism, leading the monarch to write a whole series of books to demonstrate that kings' power came from God and stood above the Church, specifically in his work *The True Law of Free Monarchies; or, The Reciprocal and Mutual Duty Betwixt a Free King and His Natural Subjects* (1598). Written while he was only King of Scotland, in it he sought to advance his idea that the monarchy was based on the divine right of kings, and to reject the contract theory in vogue in Presbyterian Scotland, as evidenced in, for example, George Buchanan's *De Jure Regni apud Scotos*, published in 1579. In *Basilikon Doron, Or His Majesties Instructions to His Dearest Sonne, Henry the Prince* (Βασιλικὸν Δῶρον in the Greek language means royal gift) a treatise on government, published in 1599, in the form of advice for his son on kingship. The subjects covered ranged from international relations and civic administration to religion and philosophy. The views expressed in the book are somewhat ambiguous, as Doelman observes. The king criticized not only the Presbyterians, but the Catholics as well. He particularly singled out Spanish Jesuits, with James I stating that Jesuits were "nothing but Puritan-papists", who defended the supremacy of Papal power over that of kings and justified Papal intervention in the affairs of kingdoms when kings placed the souls of their subjects in danger. In fact, composed of three short books, James I had no intention to publish *Basilicon Doron* for the public. He bound his printer, Robert Waldegrave, to secrecy, and ordered an edition of only seven copies for his own private use. The first part (*Of a King's Christian Duty Towards God. The First Book*) contains the king's duties to God. In it, he urges Prince Henry to love God, first because He has made him a man, "and next, for that he made you a little God, to sit on his Throne, and rule over other men". The second work (*Of a King's Duty in His Office. The Second Book*), deals with his political function as a monarch, and the third (*Of a King's Behaviour in Indifferent Things. The Third Book*), defines how the king ought to conduct himself in his private life. For an analysis of this work, see Doelman (1994, 1–9). For published versions of both works: James I (2010) and Fischling and Fortier (1996). As King of England, James I wrote two additional political works: *An Apology for the Oath of Allegiance* (1608) and *A Premonition to All Most Mighty Monarchies* (1609).

[28] Partly because of the Gunpowder Plot: on November 5, 1605, a group of Catholic fanatics led by Guy Fawkes tried to blow up Parliament while it was in session and presided over by the king.

### 11.4.2 The First English Revolution: Oliver Cromwell and the Only "Republic" in English History

James I's successor, however, Charles I (1625–1649), would soon collide head on with Parliament as a result of the initiative of Sir Edward Coke and his *Petition of Right*, of 1628 (Ryan 2005, 9–16). Besides having an authoritarian disposition—which he revealed by dissolving both Houses in 1629 and governing alone for 11 years—he was married to a Catholic princess: Henrietta Maria of France, Louis XIII's sister. As most members of the House of Commons defended the independence of the Church of England, declared by Henry VIII and consolidated by Elizabeth I, civil war soon broke out.[29] The conflict was won by the Parliamentary leader Oliver Cromwell (1649–1658) who, in addition to supporting the king's beheading for treason (along with 59 other deputies), established a "republic" over which he declared himself "Lord Protector" (Seel 1999, 73–90). In reality what he established was a dictatorship which, following his death, his son could not sustain. Thus, weary of Cromwellian tyranny (Woolrych 2003, 61–89), the English chose to restore the Stuarts to the throne in the person of Charles II (1660–1685).

### 11.4.3 The Appearance of Political Parties

Parliament soon clashed with the new king, not only because they believed him to be unduly lenient with Catholics, but because he forged an alliance with Louis XIV, the personification of absolutism in Europe at the time. Parliament reacted by unilaterally adopting two very important laws: the first forbade Catholics from serving as Parliamentary representatives or holding public through the Test Act of 1673 (Harris 2006, 74–75), while the second declared arbitrary arrests to be illegal (*Habeas corpus*, 1679).[30]

Parliament's belligerence also had another momentous consequence in British constitutional history, as it favored the formation of two political groups in the House of Commons: the Tories (conservatives) and Whigs (liberals). The former were Anglicans loyal to the king, and the latter, were essentially members of the bourgeoisie who opposed the Stuarts. This organization of representatives into

---

The plot was discovered and its conspirators arrested and executed. Ever since on November 5, the British celebrate "Bonfire Night" or "Guy Fawkes Day".

[29] What is called by British historians "The English Civil War" saw the supporters of Parliament (Roundheads) and the supporters of King Charles I (Cavaliers) square off. The English Civil War was actually comprised of three different conflicts: 1642–1646, 1648–1649, and, after the execution of Charles I (January 30, 1649), the war started again in 1649, finally concluding with the victory of pro-Parliament forces at the Battle of Worcester on September 3, 1651. On the political and constitutional consequences of the English Civil War, see Kennedy (2000).

[30] On the juridical/constitutional value of this important document, see Nutting (1963, 527–543) and Sharpe (2008, 1–17).

ideologically homogeneous groups greatly facilitated the formation of majorities, enabling Parliament thereafter to pressure the king much more effectively.[31] Thus, for the first time in the constitutional sphere there appeared political parties which, beginning with the French Revolution, would become one of the decisive instruments in the government of the contemporary state.[32]

### *11.4.4 The Second (and Last) English Revolution (1688)*

Charles II was succeeded by his brother James II (1685–1688). Although the new king was a devout Catholic,[33] he was tolerated by the Parliament because he had two daughters married to Protestant princes: Mary to William of Orange, Stadtholder of Holland; and Anna to the King of Denmark. James II, however, was widowed and married a Catholic Italian princess who bore him a son. Faced with the threat of a Catholic dynasty occupying the throne, a number of Tory representatives allied with the Whig majority in 1688, with Parliament then asking William of Orange,[34] the husband of the king's eldest daughter, to occupy the English throne (Nenner 2003, 83–94).

When William sailed for England, James, rather than confronting him, chose to flee. As the throne was left vacant, the Parliament assembled without being

[31] The first party divisions had originated in the 1680s, in disputes over religion and the succession to the throne, but it was only after 1694, when William III reluctantly agreed to the holding of elections every 3 years (Triennial Act), that the development of party politics triggered an unprecedented level of party-based competition and confrontation in Parliament. This trend yielded a new form of political and Parliamentary life, ushering in a new age of modern politics (Seaward 2009, 127).

[32] A system that Albert Venn Dicey (1835–1922), viewed with great skepticism, as he believed that the essential vice of party government was that it was 'government by and for a party, and not by and for the nation' (Plant of Highfield 2009, 3).

[33] As Pincus (2009, 6) observes, James II sought to forge a modern Catholic polity, as he was deeply influenced by the successful political model of his cousin, Louis XIV of France. The British king and his supporters wished to develop a centralized bureaucratic state, with a professional standing army and a world-class navy, and they insisted on the king's absolute sovereignty. Wanting Catholic subjects, James II did what he could to Catholicize his Protestant country through the dissemination of pro-Catholic literature, the proliferation of Catholic schools and colleges, and the opening of Catholic churches. He was not willing, however, to submit to Papal authority, but rather sought an independent Church following the Gallican model of Louis XIV's France. James II's opponents, on the other hand, believed that only a modernized English state could compete in contemporary Europe, and they looked to the Dutch Republic rather than to the French monarchy for political inspiration, as they held that England would be more powerful if it encouraged wider and greater political participation rather than embracing absolutism.

[34] On the circumstances in which William of Orange acceded to the throne of England, see Troost (2005, 215–237).

summoned by the king in a "Convention",[35] a sort of "constituent assembly"[36] formed to transfer the Crown from James II to William III and his wife Mary, imposed upon the two a Declaration of Rights (Maitland and Fisher 2001, 281–288). This essential constitutional document, later reenacted in statutory form[37] as the Bill of Rights in 1689, was a stipulation of liberties that had been partially recognized in the Carta Magna and subsequent laws.[38] This second English revolution, dubbed the "Glorious Revolution", was shorter and less spectacular than Cromwell's, but much more pivotal.[39]

---

[35] Blackstone held that, in principle, only the king could convene a Parliament, an exception being if the throne was vacant, something that only occurred, in his view, on two occasions. The first one was in 1660, when there was a first convention-parliament which restored King Charles II. On this occasion "[...] the lords by their own authority and the Commons in pursuance of writs issued in the name of the keepers of the liberty of England by authority of Parliament", one that "sat till the twenty-ninth of December, full seven months after the restoration". The second occasion was during the 1688 revolution. "[...] at a time of the revolution, AD 1688, the lords and commons by their own authority, and upon the summons of the Prince of Orange (afterwards King William) met in a *convention* and therein disposed of the crown and kingdom. But it must be remembered that this assembling was upon a like principle of necessity [...] upon an apprehension that king James II had abdicated the government, and that the throne was thereby vacant [...] And in such a case as the palpable vacancy of a throne, it follows *ex necessitate rei*, that the form of the royal writs must be laid aside, otherwise no Parliament can ever meet again [...]. And upon this and no other principle did the convention of 1688 assemble. The vacancy of the throne was precedent to its meeting without any royal summons, not a consequence of it. They did not assemble without a writ, and then make the throne vacant, but the throne being previously vacant, because of the king's abdication, they assembled without a writ, as they had to do if they were to assemble at all. Had the throne been occupied their meeting would not have been justified. Yet, as it was really empty, such a meeting became absolutely necessary" (Blackstone 1979, I, 147–148).

[36] The Convention-parliament of 1688–1689, was an important constitutional precedent, as it would inspire the American Constitutional Convention of 1787, and the French Convention (1792–1795). On the Convention Parliament, see Minor (1933). On the convention-parliament of 1660, see Wittmayer Helms (1963).

[37] Blackstone mentions that after the first convention-parliament that sat until December 29, 1660, "a full seven months after the Restoration", the first thing that Charles II did was to pass an act validating all the laws and decisions taken by the convention-parliament, as it was an assembly that had been summoned without a royal writ and was, therefore, irregular according to the English constitutional tradition: "And the first thing done after the king's return, was to pass an act declaring this to be a good parliament, notwithstanding the defect of the king's writ" (Blackstone 1979, I, 151). The same thing happened with the convention-parliament of 1688. On February 23, 1689, the King William III dissolved the Convention and summoned a new Parliament that legalized its acts through the "Crown and Parliament Recognition Act". Another law, the "Act Declaring the Rights and Liberties of the Subject and Settling the Succession of the Crown", better known as the Bill of Rights, was approved on December 16, 1689, by the Westminster Parliament, which had been convened by a royal writ of William III.

[38] For a general overview of the "Glorious Revolution", see Vallance (2006). For its constitutional consequences, see the classic study by Western (1972).

[39] The Bill of Rights came about as a reaction against repeated violations of traditional English privileges and laws committed by the late Stuart kings. However, unlike the Declaration of the Rights of Man and the Citizen, approved by the French National Assembly in 1789, the English Bill of Rights did not aspire to uphold universal values. Rather, it was only to be applied to the English. For an analysis of this cornerstone of the British Constitution, see Schwoerer (1981).

### 11.4.5 The Religious Issue and the Transformation of England's Constitutional Framework

One last point is essential to understand the political transformation England underwent during the reigns of the Tudors and Stuarts: the religious question. We know that the consolidation of the major European monarchies came at the expense of the papacy, as kings asserted their power and rejected the principle of Christian universalism, which had previously made the popes the supreme political authorities. In England, Henry VIII's break with the Church, motivated by his divorce from Catherine of Aragon and marriage to Anne Boleyn, led to the clergy's submission to the monarchy and the king's establishment as the head of the English (Anglican) Church in what is called the "Reformation Statutes" (Bernard 2007, 68). This policy would be sustained by his daughter, Elizabeth I, who undid the work done by her predecessor to the throne, her half-sister Mary Tudor.[40]

The consolidation of a state religion was not easy, however, as the kings had to fight against Papist Catholics, many of whom took refuge in Ireland, and Protestant extremists, principally Puritans, Baptists and Presbyterians. In this sense, the Cromwellian Revolution triumphed largely because Charles I was married, as we know, to a Catholic princess, and James II had to flee England, in large measure because he was Catholic (Clifton 1971, 23–55). In fact, his daughters Mary and Anne sat on the English throne because they were married to Protestant princes. Parliament not only came to prevent the Catholics from serving as kings of England, through the Act of Settlement (1701),[41] but also banned them from holding any public office in the kingdom, a prohibition not lifted until well into the nineteenth century.[42]

Concerning non-Anglican Protestants, in principle they were also excluded from political activity—at least until Parliament passed and William and Mary approved the Bill of Rights in 1689. The Bill of Rights, however, only applied to dissident Protestant sects; Catholics and Jews did not benefit from the protection offered by this civil rights law.[43]

---

[40] Mary Tudor, the daughter of Henry VIII and Catherine of Aragon, the granddaughter of the Catholic Kings, and second wife of Philip II of Spain, reestablished a vigorously Catholic regime, including reconciliation with Rome (Edwards 2011, 224–225), though her short rule kept "Popery" from being consolidated. Her sentencing of hundreds of Protestants to be burned at the stake made her quite unpopular and earned her the moniker "Bloody Mary". For a good biography see Loades (1991), and for an approach, focusing on the constitutional changes effected during her reign, see Prescott (2003).

[41] On the constitutional significance and legacy of the Act of Settlement, see Tarkow (1943, 537–563).

[42] Especially Catholic Irish, who did not even have the right to own horses. Anti-Catholicism remained extremely strong in England through the end of the eighteenth century (Fitzpatrick 1990, 339–372 and Philp 1985, 35–46).

[43] Unlike the French Declaration, which had "universal value", the English Bill of Rights (1689) only applied to Protestant English citizens, an interesting observation made by Émile Boutmy (1835–1906) in his critique (Boutmy 1902, 415–443) of a book written by George Jellinek (1851–1911) on the

## 11.5 The Emergence of the United Kingdom and the Consolidation of Parliamentary Preeminence

When Mary and William died without leaving heirs, the throne passed to James II's other daughter, Anne (1702–1714), who was also a Protestant. During her reign the union between England and Scotland was fortified, giving rise to the United Kingdom with the "Acts of Union".[44] It was at this point when the Union Jack flag appeared, representing the union of the kingdoms of England and Scotland.[45]

From the standpoint of public law the momentous development in British constitutional history was that Anne I (1702–1707), accepted the legislative preeminence of the Parliament of Westminster. Following the custom established by her sister and predecessor, Mary II, she never opposed a law passed by both houses, thereby establishing a precedent and custom which has since been respected by all the kings of England—even though it has never been placed in writing. She did not, however, accept the principle of Parliamentary government. As Gregg (2001, 403) points out, Queen Anne was fully conscious of the fact that she was a constitutional monarch and, therefore, never attempted to challenge the supremacy of Parliament or of statute law. At the same time, she jealously guarded the prerogatives of the Crown and interpreted the constitution as she saw fit. This is why she personally attended Cabinet meetings (Somerset 2012, 216) and always refused to concede that majorities in both houses of Parliament gave either a party an inherent right to dominate the executive councils of government. All this would change, however, under Anne's successors: the Hanover dynasty.

---

*Declaration of the Rights of Man and the Citizen* (Jellinek 1901). For the response of Jellinek to Boutmy's critique see Jellinek (1902). For a recent overview of the controversy, see Baker (1994, 154–155) and Klippel (1995, 79–94). On the universality of the French declaration, see Letteron (2001, 146–164).

[44] Since England and Scotland were two separate states with the same monarch, but with two different parliaments. After a series of contentious political negotiations (Riley 1969, 498–527) the Treaty of Union was signed on July 22, 1706 and legally consolidated through two Acts of Parliament. The Parliament of England approved the Union in 1706, and the Parliament of Scotland in 1707. The Treaty was finally ratified on January 16, 1707 (Macinnes 2007, 313–325).

[45] On the new flag Wales was represented by the red cross of Saint George, symbolizing England and Wales, as this last territory had been incorporated by Henry VIII through the "Laws in Wales Acts", approved between 1535 and 1542. After 1707, the blue field with the white saltire of Saint Andrew's cross, representing Scotland, was included. After the incorporation of Ireland into the British Union in 1801, the Union Jack included, in addition, the red saltire of Saint Patrick's flag, which remained even after Irish independence (1919–1922), representing Northern Ireland. On the origins and historical vicissitudes of the British flag, see Perrin (2012, 54–73).

## 11.6 The Rise of the Hanover Dynasty and the Formation of the Parliamentary Regime

Queen Anne I, like her sister Mary I, also died without heirs, making her closest relative, the Elector of Hanover, another Protestant prince, the king: George I of England (1714–1727). The change of dynasty was because of the aforementioned 1701 Act of Settlement, which forbade a Catholic from becoming His Gracious Majesty. George I was succeeded by George II (1727–1760) and George III (1760–1820). This dynastical change would have crucial consequences for British constitutional history.

### *11.6.1 Robert Walpole and the Linguistic Origins of the Parliamentary Regime*

When they ascended to the British throne, neither George I nor George II spoke English, which prevented them from presiding over meetings with their ministers. The result was that for 46 years English monarchs did not attend the deliberations of their governments, leaving this task to their ministers. Thus arose the custom of one of the ministers informing the kings (in French or Latin) about affairs discussed at the ministerial cabinet's meetings and, reciprocally, conveying to his colleagues the sovereign's point of view (Maitland and Fisher 2001, 394–400).

This state of things was facilitated by the circumstance that for over 20 years (between 1721 and 1742), this role of intermediary was played by Sir Robert Walpole, Earl of Oxford (1676–1745), then the leader of the Whig party. Such longevity in office proved to be crucial, as it ended up ingraining Walpole's character and political ideas into English political practice. With a naturally authoritarian disposition, he gradually managed to have the king remove all those ministers who did not share his ideas, thereby coming to head up a homogeneous cabinet. As he presided over the government, he became the "Prime Minister".[46]

[46] As Pearce (2008, 1–2) points out, it is essentially by convention that Robert Walpole is considered the first Prime Minister of Great Britain, as before him the figures of Sir Sidney Godolphin (1645–1712), who was the King's most important minister in the 1680s, and James Stanhope, First Minister between 1717 and 1721, played important roles in English politics too. Yet what made Walpole so special was that in 1727, he was able to survive the death of the approving George I and the accession of the hostile George II, thanks to the good offices of the latter's wife, Queen Caroline. Walpole can be called the first Prime Minister because "he combined an exceptionally good span of office, happily never again equaled, with a delight in parliamentary management, conducted with exceptional success through good sense and lucid argument". He was also able to survive such a long time because he employed bribery and corruption on an industrial scale, consolidating the patronage system that would be dismantled in the Reform Act of 1832 - a system that "if not his creation, (was) his life work of perfection and augmentation". Nevertheless, despite all this, he kept the country solvent, out of foreign wars and, quite simply, held the reign of power during his time.

Walpole believed that ministers ought to enjoy not only the king's confidence but also—and this was profoundly novel—that of the Parliament. Thus, when most of the Westminster representatives reproached him for his policy of peace with France, he resigned, even though he enjoyed George II's confidence (Pearce 2008, 418). Thus did Parliamentary government arise by way of "constitutional tradition" in what can be called the power shift from Monarch to Prime Minister (Wicks 2006, 59–62).

### *11.6.2 The Consolidation of the "Parliamentary System"*

#### 11.6.2.1 The Case of William Pitt the Elder and the Emergence of "Public Opinion"

Walpole's resignation proved pivotal to the consolidation of the parliamentary system, as thereafter kings considered the opinion of Parliament's two chambers about government affairs. Not only that of the representatives in Parliament, but also "public opinion", which would begin to acquire political clout as a result of the diffusion of England's first newspapers (Harris 1993).[47] This, for instance, was the case in 1757, when British public opinion, after a war in which England had been resoundingly defeated by France, in an outburst of patriotic fervor, forced George II to appoint the Whig leader William Pitt "the Elder", also known as Lord Chatham (1708–1778), as Prime Minister (Black 1990, 172–173).[48]

#### 11.6.2.2 George III Seeks to Tame Parliament

With the arrival to the throne of George III (1760-1820), the Crown's attitude towards Parliament radically changed. The new king was of an authoritarian bent, and immediately locked horns with William Pitt, who the monarch forced to resign in 1761 (Watson 2001, 74). One must keep in mind that, unlike his predecessors, George III had been born in England and spoke English perfectly. Thus, he strove to

---

[47] The interest in newspapers was a consequence of what James V. H. Melton calls the "reading revolution". As a result of the spread of literacy there was a dramatic explosion of print culture: books, newspapers and periodicals, including broadsheets, handbills and political cartoons (Melton 2001, 86). For an overview of the different newspapers published during this period, see Black (2011, 1–17). On the political impact of the press in eighteenth-century England, see Barker (2003). For a resume about the impact of printing on Western society and thought during Enlightenment, see Fajardo (2012, 14–17).

[48] As Melton (2001, 31) points out, Britain's engagement in almost constant warfare between 1739 and 1782 meant that for most British subjects the press was their chief source of information on military and diplomatic affairs. This is the reason why the press became a "self-appointed fourth estate", usurping the traditional role of the House of Commons as the appropriate arena for canvassing and articulating the opinions of the nation.

rule by himself and to impose his royal will upon his ministers.[49] Initially, however, he was unable to do so in his dealings with the Westminster Parliament, and had to readmit Pitt as Prime Minister between 1766 and 1768 (Thomas 2002, 180–196). After devoting himself to unabashedly buying off electors and representatives, George III ended up achieving a docile Parliament over which he was able to place Lord North as Prime Minister.[50] This attempt to fully restore royal prerogative, however, would fail for two reasons: the Wilkes Affair and the War of Independence against the American colonies (1776–1783).

#### 11.6.2.3 The Wilkes Affair and the Consolidation of Public Opinion as a Political Force (1770)

The Wilkes Affair marked the emergence of public opinion as a political force in England. John Wilkes (1727–1797) was a member of the House of Commons who began to attack the king's policies in his newspaper *The North Briton* (Melton 2001, 31). George III reacted by ordering his arrest. British public opinion, however, found the king's response unfair, a violation of Parliamentary immunity and the freedom of the press. In 1768, Wilkes was reelected as a representative but, by order of the King, Parliament invalidated his election. Elected again, his appointment was again overruled by the Houses. This time, however, the public was incensed and there appeared a large number of pamphlets vehemently reproaching the king and the House of Commons for their disrespect for the rights of voters to freely choose a candidate.[51] The pressure was effective. As a result of it, Parliament adopted a law allowing the press to publish the contents of its sessions.[52]

---

[49] On George III's relations with English politicians during the early years of his reign, see Thomas (2002) and Namier (1988).

[50] As Whiteley (1996, 78) observes, the king was concerned with respecting his constitutional duty and wished to find a prime minister who Parliament would consider acceptable. Knowing that, Grafton's departure was imminent, he very much wanted a minister acceptable to himself as well. He did not want Grenville, Rockingham, Chatham or any other factional leader, and this is why he pushed for the nomination of his friend, Lord North. After Grafton's resignation, North had to face the House of Commons, where the opposition had just presented a censure motion against the government on the pretext of the Wilkes affair, but North did well; following the debate he emerged with a majority of 40 votes, confirming his position as prime minister. The North administration took hold and remained in power for the next 12 years (Ibidem 80–81). For an overall view of Lord North's early years and political career, see Watson (2001, 147–172).

[51] For an overview of the Wilkes affair, see Watson (2001, 131–138). On the constitutional transcendence of the Wilkes Case, see the classic work by Rudé (1962). Other noteworthy works are those by Cash (2006) and Thomas (1996).

[52] This resulted in the founding of several major newspapers, most notably London's *The Times*, the press thereby becoming part of English political life as a tool shaping public opinion (Dean 2006, 631–649).

#### 11.6.2.4 The Independence of the American Colonies and the End of Absolutism in England (1783)

George III's authority, quite undermined by the Wilkes Affair, was further weakened when the English colonies in North America achieved independence from the British Crown after a rebellion which began in 1776 (McConville 2006). Public opinion blamed the monarch for defeat in a conflict which had been brought about by the king's intransigence, as he had refused to make any concessions to the American colonists (Thomas 1985, 16–31). Thus, when in 1782, George III was forced to recognize the independence of the 13 colonies, the general discontent forced him to accept as prime minister one of the leaders of the opposition, who dared to form his government without consulting the monarch regarding its composition.[53]

#### 11.6.2.5 King George's Madness and Its Constitutional Implications

To make matters worse, at the end of his reign George III went insane. Exhibiting the first symptoms of madness in 1788, he was definitively deranged by 1811.[54] This situation provoked a constitutional crisis in 1788, in which the question arose as to whether the heir to the throne, the Prince of Wales, could unilaterally declare himself regent, or if it was Parliament's prerogative to appoint one (Derry 1963, 67–119). In 1811, the Parliamentary option prevailed and the Prince of Wales, the future George IV, was invited by Parliament to exercise the regency by virtue of a law that was not sanctioned by the king—who was incapacitated—but by a commission named by the Parliament.[55] This would prove to be a crucial precedent.

[53] On January 16, 1784, the Commons, by a vote of 205 to 184, endorsed the following motion: "[...] that in the present situation of his Majesty's dominions, it is peculiarly necessary there should be an administration which has the confidence of this House and of the public; and that the appointments of his Majesty's present ministers were accompanied by circumstances new and extraordinary, and such as do not conciliate or engage the confidence of this House; the continuance of the present ministers in trusts of the highest importance and responsibility is contrary to constitutional principles and injurious to the interests of His Majesty and his people". Text cited in Black (2006, 260).

[54] On the medical causes of George III's madness, see Rushton (2008, 35–47). For a contemporary commentary of the royal illness see the pages of Mary Wollstonecraft, better known as Mary Shelley (1797–1851), Wollstonecraft (2010, especially 55–60). On the impact which the king's disorder had on English public opinion see Rovang (2006, 23–44) and Kaufman (1998, 17–25).

[55] The circumstances were critical, as the United Kingdom was waging a difficult war against Napoleon; hence, again the debate was raised in Parliament about regency (David 1999, 101–115). The Regency Bill was finally passed on February 6, 1811, and the prince was sworn in as regent at a Privy Council held at his residence at Carlton House (Smith 1999, 138–141).

#### 11.6.2.6 Victoria: The Queen Who Did Not Govern

Beginning with the reign of Victoria I (1837–1901), the English monarchy ceased to assert a political role and began to limit itself to functions of institutional representation. In fact, the exercise of royal prerogative ever since has been defined by the constitutional precept that "the king reigns but does not govern" (Arnstein 1990, 178–194). The long Victorian period allowed for the normalization of the alternation between the two major parties, thanks in large part to the liberal Gladstone and the conservative Disraeli, the era's political giants, especially after the election reform of 1867, which helped to establish a tradition of political debate (Matthew 1979, 615–643). In large part, this explains why the Victorian Age marked the zenith of British power and prestige.

### *11.6.3 The Democratization of the Parliamentary System (1832–1928)*

While the Parliamentary system established since the first half of the eighteenth century did curtail royal prerogative, it did not turn the British political system into a democratic regime *per se*. In fact, until the essential Lord Grey's electoral reform of 1832, Parliament was controlled by a very small oligarchy: the gentry.[56] Only thereafter was the electoral map reorganized, with the elimination of 143 "rotten" or "pocket" boroughs: areas that had elected representatives ever since the Middle Ages even though they were practically devoid of any population. Rotten boroughs had survived because they made it possible to control elections through patronage, the purchasing of votes and electoral fraud. Moreover, the reform created electoral districts with their corresponding parliamentary representatives in the new industrial cities such as Manchester and Liverpool, which until then had no MPs in Westminster (Wicks 2006, 76–81).[57] The "democratization" of the English electoral system took shape by expanding the system of censitary suffrage, requiring increasing incomes for one to vote or be elected through the successive reforms of 1867, 1873 and 1884 (Smith 2004, 156–173.)[58]

---

[56] On the lack of electoral representation in the Parliament prior to the Reform Act of 1832, see Hill (1985), O'Gorman (1989) and Philips (1982). On the social pressure exerted by the middle class to secure Parliamentary representation, see Warham (1995). For an overview of England in the years prior to electoral reform, see Evans (2008).

[57] On the crucial Electoral Law of 1832, see Brock (1993), Evans (1983) and Pearce (2004).

[58] The 1867 reform was an initiative of the Conservative Prime minister, Benjamin Disraeli, who "dished the Whigs" by improving the distribution of seats and extending the franchise, bringing a million new voters, who nearly doubled the size of the electorate. This brought in the "respectable" artisan class of the towns, and urban workers who were not householders, while rural workers were still generally excluded. The number of voters again increased thanks to the 1873 and 1884 reforms. This last one, an initiative of the Liberal Prime Minister William Ewart Gladstone, increased the electorate by nearly a further 70 %, bringing it to over four and a quarter million.

The British parliamentary system would not be fully democratized until after the First World War, when the requirement of being a property owner, or at least a lessee in one's own name, was lifted to vote. Then, the only requisite was to meet certain age requirements: 21 for males and 30 for women. Though unfair, this nevertheless marked a great victory for women, as it came after more than half a century of struggle for women's suffrage (Kent 2005, 191–228)[59] in a movement that started with the Parliamentary debates that led to the approval of the Second Reform Act of 1867 (Bolt 2000, 34),[60] and required the brave determination of courageous women like Emmeline Pankhurst (1858–1928)[61] to succeed. British women finally achieved voting equality in 1928, when the age at which they could vote was made the same as that of men (van Wingerden 2002, 172–180).[62]

---

A Redistribution Act of the following year changed drastically the distribution of seats and the delimitation of constituencies, making them less like the ancient organic communities and more like arithmetical divisions of population (Chrimes 1970, 128–129).

[59] As Bolt (2000, 34) points out, Queen Victoria provided British feminists with scant support. Though she privately lamented the burden of frequent pregnancies, she was known to regard women's rights agitation as a "mad, wicked folly". Her position infuriated the American suffragist Elizabeth Cady Stanton, who at meetings with British activists stated that the queen had "never done anything to merit the approbation of the advocates of suffrage for women" (Stanton 2002, 354).

[60] On May 20, 1867, John Stuart Mill proposed amending the recently-approved bill to enfranchise women by replacing the word "man" with "person", but some MPs described his initiative as a "pleasant interlude [. . .] interposed to the grave and somewhat somber discussions on the subject of Reform" (van Wingerden 2002, 11).

[61] Though she was educated by her parents to be a wife and mother, Pankhurts went to France and was accepted at the prestigious *École Normale Supérieure*, the country's leading institution for the study of Philosophy, Literature and Classical Studies, where figures such as Jean Paul Sartre and Raymond Aron studied. At the age of 20, she married Richard Pankhurst, a barrister who was 24 years her senior and supported women's right to vote. Emmeline had five children, but this did not stop her from being actively involved in the Suffragist movement. In 1898, after her husband's death, Emmeline founded the Women's Social and Political Union because she believed that winning the vote for women required "deeds and not words". Pankhurst, her daughters and other WSPU activists were sent on several occasions to jail, where they conducted hunger strikes. Upon the outbreak of World War I, Emmeline decided to halt her militant activism for suffrage and support the British government in its war effort, urging women to help with industrial production while the men were fighting on the front. The consequence of this attitude was the Representation of the People Act (February 6, 1918), which granted women over the age of 30 the vote. In her later years, Emmeline Pankhurst joined the Conservative Party, as she was concerned by the threat of Bolshevism. She died at the age of 69, 2 weeks before the approval of the Equal Franchise Act on July 2, 1928 (Bartley 2002, 39). For more on Pankhurst, see her autobiography (Pankhurst 1979) and the work by Purvis (2002).

[62] For an overview of the struggle by British women to win the right to vote, see van Wingerden (2002).

### *11.6.4 The Consolidation of the Legislative Superiority of the House of Commons: The Parliament Act (1911)*

Another important step towards the democratization of the British Parliamentary regime was the approval of the Parliament Act on August 18, 1911, a consequence of the constitutional crisis provoked by the rejection of the Budget Law in November 1909 by the Conservative-dominated House of Lords. After two ensuing general elections (January and December 1910), the Liberal Government of Herbert Henry Asquith approved a Bill that deprived the House of Lords of its ability to reject funding bills, and replaced their veto power over other public bills, with a power to delay them for up to 2 years.[63] The result of the 1909–1911 conflict between the two Houses, left the House of Commons in a dominant position within Parliament, which meant that the legislative authority of Parliament came to be based on the electorate's political support, as holding a majority of seats in the Commons became the source of true political power (Bradley and Ewing 2007, 54).

### *11.6.5 The Legislative Recognition of the Prime Minister (1937)*

The figure of the "prime minister", and even of the Cabinet itself, however, retained an unofficial status for much longer, as it would not be until 1937 that a law officially created the position: the Ministers of the Crown Act (1937), which also assigned the office remuneration (Brazier 1997, 90).

**TIMELINE**

**Roman Period**

| | |
|---|---|
| 43–409 AD | Roman occupation of Great Britain. |

**Anglo-Saxon Period**

| | |
|---|---|
| 577 | Battle of Dyrham. Decisive victory of Angles and Saxons. Beginning of Anglo-Saxon rule. England is divided into several kingdoms (Heptarchy). |
| 590–616 | Reign of Aethelbert, King of Kent (c. 600 Aethelbert Code). |
| 871–899 | Reign of Alfred the Great, first king of the Anglo-Saxons. |

[63] The Parliament Act was passed by the House of Lords by a 131–114 votes. It also reduced the maximum duration of a Parliamentary term from 7 to 5 years (Wicks 2006, 83–108).

1017–1035 Reign of Cnut II the Great, king of England, Denmark and Norway.
1042–1066 Reign of Edward the Confessor, the last Anglo-Saxon king.

**Late Middle Ages**

1066 Battle of Hastings. End of the Anglo-Saxon period, beginning of the Norman period.
1086 Completion of the "Domesday Book" ordered by William I the Conqueror (1066–1087).
1154–1189 Reign of Henry II Plantagenet. Expansion of Royal justice.
1166 Assize of Clarendon
1170 Assassination of Thomas Becket, Archbishop of Canterbury.
1180 Henry II appoints Ranulf of Glanville Chief Justiciar of England. Author of the first treatise on English Law (*Tractatus de legibus et consuetudinibus regni Angliae*), he was decisive in consolidating Henry II's judicial reforms, which led to the establishment of a "Common Law" for the realm.
1215 John I Lackland is forced by nobles to sign the *Magna Carta Libertatum*.
1259 "Provisions of Oxford". An in-law of the weak and unpopular Henry III (1217–1272) rebels against the king and imposes a council of 15 nobles, assigned all powers.
1264 Simon de Montfort defeats Henry III at Lewes and summons a Parliament in which, together with two nobles per county, for the first time sit two representatives of the bourgeoisie for each city.
1272 Beginning of the reign of Edward I (1272–1307), who renders the presence of the bourgeoisie in the Westminster Parliament permanent.
1327 Parliament demands the abdication of Edward II in favor of his son Edward III (1327–1377).
1346 Overwhelming English victory over the French at Crecy. Start of the Hundred Years War. Growing financial requirements imposed by the war force Edward III to convoke Parliament often, which features two chambers: the House of Commons and the House of Lords.
1399 The English Parliament removes Henry II and grants the throne to Henry IV, which marks the first reign of the Lancaster Dynasty.
1455 The War of the Roses begins (1455–1485).

**Sixteenth Century**

1507 Beginning of the reign of Henry VIII (1507–1547).
1534 Henry VIII breaks with Rome (Act of Supremacy).
1558 Beginning of the reign of Elizabeth I of England (1558–1603).

**Seventeenth Century**

1649 Execution of Charles I. Oliver Cromwell comes to power (1649–1658). In 1653 he dissolves Parliament and declares himself "Lord Protector of the Republic".

1660 Restoration of the Stuarts on the English throne in the person of Charles II (1660 1685). Under his reign Parliament unilaterally adopts a law preventing Catholics from holding public office (Bill of Test, 1673) and prohibiting illegal arrests (*Habeas corpus*, 1679).

1688 Second English Revolution ("Glorious Revolution"). King James II's flight from England (crowned in 1685). His daughter Mary's husband, William of Orange, takes the throne as William III (1688–1702).

1689 Parliament approves a Bill of Rights.

**Eighteenth Century**

1701 Parliament approves a law preventing Catholics from reigning in England (Establishment Act, 1701).

1707 Queen Anne (1702–1714) sanctions the law creating the United Kingdom (Union Act), made up of England, Wales and Scotland.

1714 George I (1714–1727) takes the throne as the first king of the Hanover Dynasty.

1721 Robert Walpole begins his period of government (1721–1742). He will serve as the United Kingdom's *de facto* prime minister, the first in its history. He lays the foundations of a "parliamentary system" that will be built on tradition and custom.

1757 George II (1727–1760) appoints William Pitt the Elder as prime minister, forced by public opinion.

1783 England's defeat in the War of Independence against the American colonies forces George III (1760–1820) to accept the head of the opposition as his prime minister.

**Nineteenth Century**

1801 Integration of Ireland into the UK.

1815 King George III goes definitively insane.
Parliament is the power which designates the Prince of Wales as regent, making it clear that this is not a right which he possesses through dynastic inheritance.

1832 Major English electoral reform. The first step towards the "democratization" of the parliamentary system. "Censitary suffrage" would be expanded with reform introduced in 1867 and 1882.

| | |
|---|---|
| 1837 | Victoria rises to the throne I (1837–1901). During her reign the alternation between the two major parties takes root, and the principle that the king "reigns but does not govern" is accepted. |

**Twentieth Century**

| | |
|---|---|
| 1900 | Foundation of the Labour Party. |
| 1911 | Parliament Act: consolidation of the Legislative superiority of the House of Commons. |
| 1918 | After the end of First World War "universal suffrage" is granted in England. |
| 1919–1921 | Irish War of independence. |
| 1922 | Independence of the Irish Republic. Northern Ireland (Ulster) remains in the UK. |
| 1928 | Women achieve the same voting rights as men. |
| 1937 | The position of prime minister is placed into law for the first time (Ministers of the Crown Act). |
| 1998 | The UK Parliament approves the Scotland Act, which establishes a Scottish Parliament. |

**Twenty-First Century**

| | |
|---|---|
| 2012 | The UK Parliament approves amendments devolving further powers to Scotland. |

# References


Arnstein, W. L. (1990). Queen Victoria opens parliament: The disinvention of tradition. *Historical Research, 63*(151), 178–194.

Ashe, L. (2007). The Bayeux Tapestry: Performative texts. In *Fiction and history in England 1066–1200* (pp. 35–49). Cambridge, UK: Cambridge University Press.

Aurell, M. (2007). *The Plantagenet Empire 1154–1224*. Harlow, UK: Pearson.

Bachrach, B. S. (1984). Henry II and the Angevin tradition of family hostility. *Albion: A Quarterly Journal Concerned with British Studies, 16*(2), 111–130.

Bagehot, W. (2009). *The English Constitution* (2nd ed., London: Hapman and Hall, 1873). Oxford: Oxford University Press.

Baker, J. H. (1990). *An introduction to English legal history* (3rd ed.). London: Butterworths.

Baker, K. M. (1994). The idea of a Declaration of Rights. In D. Van Kley (Ed.), *The French idea of freedom: The old regime and the Declaration of Rights of 1789* (pp. 154–199). Stanford, CA: Stanford University Press.

Barker, A. (2003). *Newspapers, politics, and public opinion in late eighteenth-century England* (Reprinted). Oxford: Clarendon.

Bartley, P. (2002). *Emmeline Pankhurst*. London: Routledge.

Bernard, G. W. (2007). *The King's reformation: Henry VIII and the remaking of English Church.* New Haven, CT: Yale University Press.

Biancalana, J. (1988). For want of justice: Legal reforms of Henry II. *Columbia Law Review, 88* (3), 433–536.

Black, J. (1990). *British politics and society from Walpole to Pitt, 1742–1789.* Basingstoke, UK: Palgrave Macmillan.

Black, J. (2006). *George III: America's last king.* New Haven, CT: Yale University Press.

Black, J. (2011). *The English press in the eighteenth century* (Reprint). London: Routledge.

Blackstone, W. (1979). *Commentaries on the laws of England* (4 Vols) (A Facsimile of the First Edition of 1765–1769). Chicago, IL: The University of Chicago Press.

Bolt, C. (2000). The ideas of British Suffragism. In S. S. Holton & J. Purvis (Eds.), *Votes for women* (pp. 34–56). London: Routledge.

Boutmy, É. (1902). La Déclaration des droits de l'homme et du citoyen et M. Jellinek. *Annales des sciences politiques, 17*, 415–443.

Bradley, A. W., & Ewing, K. D. (2007). *Constitutional and administrative law* (14th ed.). Harlow, UK: Pearson Education Limited.

Bradshaw, B. (1979). The Tudor commonwealth: Reform and revision. *The Historical Journal, 22* (2), 455–476.

Brand, P. (2007). Henry II and the creation of the English common law. In C. Harper-Bill & N. Vincent (Eds.), *Henry II: New interpretations* (pp. 215–241). Woodbridge, UK: Boydell Press.

Brazier, R. (1997). *Ministers of the crown.* Oxford: Oxford University Press.

Brock, M. (1993). *The Great Reform Act.* Aldershot, UK: Gregg Revivals.

Caenegem, R. C. (1988). *The birth of the English common law* (2nd ed.). Cambridge, UK: Cambridge University Press.

Cash, A. H. (2006). *John Wilkes: The scandalous father of civil liberty.* New Haven, CT: Yale University Press.

Cavill, P. (2009). *The English parliaments of Henry VII: 1485–1504.* Oxford: Oxford University Press.

Chrimes, S. B. (1970). *English constitutional history* (4th ed., Reprinted). Oxford: Oxford University Press.

Clifton, R. (1971). The popular fear of catholics during the English Revolution. *Past and Present, 52*, 23–55.

Coby, P. (2006). *Henry VIII and the reformation parliament.* New York: Pearson Longman.

Coleman, C., & Starkey, D. (Eds.). (1986). *Revolution reassessed: Revisions in the history of Tudor government & administration.* Oxford: Oxford University Press.

Cowdrey, H. E. J. (2005). King Harold II and the Bayeux Tapestry: A critical introduction. In G. R. Owen-Crocker (Ed.), *King Harold II and the Bayeux Tapestry* (pp. 1–15). Woodbridge, UK: The Boydell Press.

Crossman, R. H. S. (1969). *Government and the governed: A history of political ideas and political practice.* London: Chatto and Windus.

Crouch, D. (2007). *The Normans: The history of a Dinasty.* London: Hambledon Continuum.

David, S. (1999). *Prince of pleasure: The Prince of Wales and the making of the regency.* New York, NY: Grove.

Dean, A. C. (2006). Court culture and political news in London's eighteenth-century newspapers. *English Literary History, 73*(3), 631–649.

Dean, D. M. (2002). *Law-making and society in late Elizabethan England: The parliament of England, 1584–1601.* Cambridge, UK: Cambridge University Press.

Derry, J. W. (1963). *The regency crisis and the Whigs: 1788–1789.* Cambridge, UK: Cambridge University Press.

Dicey, A. V. (2013). *The law of the constitution.* Oxford: Oxford University Press. (Based on the first edition (1885) of Dicey's *Lectures Introductory to the Study of Law of the Constitution.* London: Macmillan and Co. Since its third edition (1889) it was called simply *Introduction to the Study of the Law of the Constitution*)

Dodd, G. (2007). *Justice and grace: Private petitioning and the English parliament in the late Middle Ages*. Oxford, UK: Oxford University Press.
Doelman, J. (1994). A king of Thine own heart: The English reception of King James VI and I's Basilikon Doron. *Seventeenth Century, 9*(1), 1–9.
Edwards, J. (2011). *Mary I: England's Catholic queen*. New Haven, CT: Yale University Press.
Elton, G. R. (1964). The Tudor revolution: A reply. *Past & Present, 29*, 26–49.
Elton, G. R. (1969). *The body of the whole realm: Parliament and representation in medieval and Tudor England*. Charlottesville, VA: University Press of Virginia.
Elton, G. R. (1979). *English law in the sixteenth century: Reform in an age of change*. London: Seldon Society.
Evans, E. J. (1983). *The Great Reform Act of 1832*. London: Methuen and Co.
Evans, E. J. (2008). *Britain before the Reform Act: 1815–1832* (2nd ed.). New York: Pearson Longman.
Everard, J. A. (2006). *Brittany and the Angevins: Province and empire 1158–1203* (4th ed.). Cambridge, UK: Cambridge University Press.
Fajardo, M. I. (2012). *In tanta Luce Seculi: Una reflexión sobre el pensamiento penal y el Derecho del Occidente ilustrado*. Granada, Spain: University of Granada [Faculty of Law (Ph. Thesis)].
Fischling, D., & Fortier, M. (Eds.). (1996). *The true law of free monarchies and Basilikon Doron*. Toronto: Centre for Reformation and Renaissance Studies.
Fitzpatrick, M. (1990). Heretical religion and radical political ideas in late eighteenth-century England. In E. Hellmuth (Ed.), *The transformation of political culture: England and Germany in the late eighteenth century* (pp. 339–372). Oxford, UK: Oxford University Press.
Gneist, R. (2005). *The history of the English constitution*. Whitefish, MT: Kessinger Publishing.
Graves, M. A. R. (2014). *Elizabethan parliaments: 1559–1601* (2nd ed., rev.). London: Routledge.
Gregg, E. (2001). *Queen Anne* (New ed.). New Haven, CT: Yale University Press.
Griffith, J. A. G. (2001). The common law and the political constitution. *Law Quarterly Review, 117*, 42–67.
Guy, J. (2000). *Politics, law and counsel in Tudor and early Stuart England*. Aldershot, UK: Ashgate.
Harris, I. (2011). Some origins of a Tudor revolution. *English Historical Review, CXXVI*(523), 1355–1385.
Harris, R. (1993). *A patriot press: National politics and the London press in the 1740s*. Oxford: Oxford University Press.
Harris, T. (2006). *Restoration: Charles II and his kingdoms*. London: Penguin.
Harriss, G. L. (1965). A revolution in Tudor history? *Past and Present, 31*, 87–96.
Harriss, G. L. (1975). *King, parliament and public finance in medieval England to 1369*. Oxford: Clarendon.
Harriss, G. L. (2006). *Shaping the nation: England 1360–1461* (Reprint). Oxford: Oxford University Press.
Henderson, E. F. (Ed.). (2004). *Select historical documents of the Middle Ages* (Reprint from the 1912 edition). Honolulu, HI: University Press of the Pacific.
Hicks, M. (2003). *The wars of the roses: 1455–1485*. Oxford: Oxprey.
Hill, B. W. (1985). *British parliamentary parties, 1742–1832: From the fall of Walpole to the first Reform Act*. London: Allen & Unwin.
Holt, J. C. (2003). *Magna Carta* (Reprint). Cambridge, UK: Cambridge University Press.
Irvine of Lairg, A. A. M. I. B. (2003). Sovereignty in comparative perspective: Constitutionalism in Britain and America. In *Human rights, constitutional law and the development of the English legal system: Selected essays* (pp. 227–250). Portland, OR: Hart.
James I, King of England. (2010). *The political works of James I*. Whitefish, MT: Kessinger Publishing. (Reprinted from the edition of 1616, with an introduction by Charles Howard McIlwain.)
Janin, H. (2004). *Medieval justice: Cases and laws in France, England and Germany, 500–1500*. Jefferson, NC: McFarland and Company.
Jellinek, G. (1901). *The Declaration of the Rights of man and the citizen: A contribution to modern constitutional history*. New York: Henry Holt.

Jellinek, G. (1902). La Déclaration des droits de l'homme et du citoyen: Réponse de M. Jellinek à M. Boutmy. *Revue du Droit Public et de la Science Politique en France et à l'étranger, 18*, 385–400. (1995, reedition in *Revue française d'Histoire des Idées Rolitiques, 1*, 167–178.)
Jenkins, C. D. (2003). From unwritten to written: Transformation in the British common-law constitution. *Vanderbilt Journal of Transnational Law, 36*, 863–960.
Kaufman, R. (1998). The madness of George III, by Mary Wollstonecraft. *Studies in Romanticism, 37*(1), 17–25.
Kennedy, D. E. (2000). *The English Revolution: 1642–1649*. London: Macmillan.
Kent, S. K. (2005). *Sex and Suffrage in Britain: 1860–1914*. London: Routledge.
Klippel, D. (1995). La polémique entre Jellinek et Boutmy: une controverse scientifique ou un conflit de nationalismes? *Revue française d'histoire des idées politiques, 1*, 79–94.
Lee, S. J. (2007). *The reign of Elizabeth I: 1558–1603: (Questions and analysis in history)*. London: Routledge.
Lehmberg, S. E. (2009). *The reformation parliament 1529–1536*. Cambridge, UK: Cambridge University Press.
Letteron, R. (2001). L'universalité des droits de l'homme: apparences et réalités L'idéologie des droits de l'homme en France et aux Etats-Unis. *Annuaire Français de Relations Internationales, 2*, 145–164.
Loades, D. M. (1991). *The reign of Mary Tudor. Politics, government and religion in England, 1553–58* (2nd ed.). London: Longman.
Lyon, B. D. (1980). *A constitutional and legal history of medieval England* (2nd ed.). New York: Norton.
MacCaffrey, W. T. (2008). Parliament: The Elizabethan experience. In D. J. Guth & J. McKenna (Eds.), *Tudor rule and revolution: Essays for G R Elton from his American friends* (pp. 127–148). Cambridge, UK: Cambridge University Press.
Macinnes, A. I. (2007). *Union and empire: The making of the United Kingdom in 1707*. Cambridge, UK: Cambridge University Press.
Maddicott, J. R. (2001). *Simon de Monfort* (Reprinted). Cambridge, UK: Cambridge University Press.
Maddicott, J. R. (2012). *The origins of the English parliament: 924–1327*. Oxford, UK: Oxford University Press.
Maitland, F. W., & Fisher, H. A. L. (2001). *The constitutional history of England: A course of lectures delivered*. Union, NJ: The Lawbook Exchange. (Originally published: Cambridge: Cambridge University Press, 1908.)
Maitland, F. W., & Montague, F. C. (2005). *A sketch of English legal history*. New York: Elibron Classics. (Facsimile of the 1915 edition: New York: G.P. Putnam's Sons.)
Masschaele, J. (2009). *Jury, state, and society in medieval England*. New York, NY: Palgrave Macmillan.
Matthew, H. C. G. (1979). Disraeli Gladstone and the politics of mid-Victorian budgets. *The Historical Journal, 22*(3), 615–643.
McConville, B. (2006). *The king's three faces: The rise & fall of royal America, 1688–1776*. Williamsburg, VA: The University of North Carolina Press.
McLean, I. (2012). *What's wrong with the British constitution*. Oxford: Oxford University Press.
Melton, J. V. H. (2001). *The rise of the public in enlightenment Europe*. Cambridge, UK: Cambridge University Press.
Mill, J. S. (2012). *On liberty*. Toronto: Dover. (Unabridged, unaltered republication of the 1859 2nd standard edition: London: John W. Parker & Son.)
Minor, R. H. (1933). *The convention parliament, 1689–1690*. Athens, GA: University of Georgia.
Morris, M. (2008). *A great and terrible king: Edward I and the forging of Britain* (Updated ed.). London: Hutchinson.
Namier, L. Sir (1988). *The structure of politics at the accession of George III* (2nd ed.). Hampshire, UK: Macmillan Press.

Nenner, H. (2003). Pretense and pragmatism: The response to uncertainty in the succession crisis of 1689. In L. G. Schwoerer (Ed.), *The revolution of 1688–89: Changing perspectives* (pp. 83–94). Cambridge, UK: Cambridge University Press.
Nutting, H. A. (1963). The most Wholesome law – The Habeas Corpus Act of 1679. *The American Historical Review, 65*(3), 527–543.
O'Gorman, F. (1989). *Voters, patrons, and parties: The unreformed electoral system of Hanoverian England, 1734–1832*. Oxford: Clarendon.
Oleson, T. J. (1955). *The Witenagemot in the reign of Edward the confessor: A study in the constitutional history of eleventh-century England*. Toronto: University of Toronto Press.
Ormrod, W. M. (2011). *Edward III*. New Haven, CT: Yale University Press.
Pankhurst, E. (1979). *My own story*. London: Virago Ltd.
Pearce, E. (2004). *Reform!: The fight for the 1832 Reform Act*. London: Pimlico.
Pearce, E. (2008). *The great man: Sir Robert Walpole: Scoundrel, genius and Britain's first prime minister*. London: Pimlico.
Perrin, W. G. (2012). *British flags: Their early history and their development at sea: With an account of the origin of the flag as a national device* (Reprint). Cambridge, UK: Cambridge University Press.
Philp, M. (1985). Rational religion and political radicalism in the 1790s. *Enlightenment and Dissent, 4*, 35–46.
Philips, J. A. (1982). *Electoral behaviour in unreformed England: Plumpers, splitters and straights*. Princeton, NJ: Princeton University Press.
Pincus, S. (2009). *1688: The First Modern Revolution*. New Haven, CT: Yale University Press.
Plant of Highfield, Raymond, Baron. (2009). Foreword. In A. V. Dicey (Ed.), *General characteristics of English constitutionalism: Six unpublished lectures* (pp. 9–35). Oxford: Peter Lang.
Plucknett, T. F. T. (1970). *Legislation of Edward I*. Oxford: Clarendon.
Pollock, F., & Maitland, F. W. (2010). *The history of English law before the time of Edward I* (2nd ed., 2 Vols). Indianapolis: Liberty Fund.
Prescott, H. F. M. (2003). *Mary Tudor: The Spanish Tudor* (Repr.). London: Phoenix.
Purvis, J. (2002). *Emmeline Pankhurst: A biography*. London: Routledge.
Raban, S. (2000). *England under Edward I and Edward II: 1259–1327*. Oxford: Blackwell.
Riley, P. J. W. (1969). The union of 1707 as an episode in English politics. *The English Historical Review, 84*(332), 498–527.
Rovang, D. (2006). When reason reigns: Madness, passion and sovereignty in late 18th-century England. *History of Psychiatry, 17*(1), 23–44.
Rudé, G. (1962). *Wilkes and liberty: A social study of 1763 to 1774*. Oxford: Clarendon.
Rushton, A. R. (2008). *Royal Maladies: Inherited diseases in the ruling houses of Europe*. Victoria, BC, Canada: Trafford publishing.
Ryan, K. (2005). Lex et ratio: Coke, the rule of law, and executive power. *Vermont bar Journal & Law Digest, 31*(1), 9–16.
Sadler, J. (2008). *The second Barons' war: Simon de Montfort and the battles of Lewes and Evesham*. Barnsley: Pen & Sword Military.
Schwoerer, L. G. (1981). *The Declaration of Rights, 1689*. Baltimore, MD: Johns Hopkins University Press.
Seaward, P. (2009). The house of commons 1660–1707. In C. Jones (Ed.), *A short history of parliament* (pp. 126–147). Woodbridge, UK: Boydell Press.
Seel, G. E. (1999). *The English wars and republic: 1637–1660*. London: Routledge.
Sharpe, R. J. (2008). Historical aspects of Habeas Corpus. In *The law of Habeas corpus* (3rd ed., pp. 1–16). Oxford: Oxford University Press.
Smith, E. A. (1999). *George IV*. New Haven, CT: Yale University Press.
Smith, M. S. (2004). Parliamentary reform and the electorate. In C. Williams (Ed.), *A companion to 19th-century Britain* (pp. 156–173). Oxford: Blackwell.
Somerset, A. (2012). *Queen Anne: The politics of passion*. London: Harper Press.

Stanley, E. G. (2000). *Imagining the Anglo-Saxon past: The search for Anglo-Saxon paganism and Anglo-Saxon trial by jury*. Cambridge, UK: D.S. Brewer.

Stanton, E. C. (2002). *Eighty years and more: Reminiscences, 1815–1897*. Auckland: Humanity Books.

Stubbs, W. (Ed.). (1960). *Select charters and other illustrations of English constitutional history from the earliest times to the reign of Edward the first* (9th ed.). Oxford: Clarendon.

Tarkow, N. (1943). The significance of the act of settlement in the evolution of English democracy. *Political Science Quarterly, 58*(4), 537–561.

Thomas, P. D. G. (1985). George III and the American Revolution. *History, 70*(228), 16–31.

Thomas, P. D. G. (1996). *John Wilkes: A friend to liberty*. Oxford, UK: Clarendon.

Thomas, P. D. G. (2002). *George III: King and politicians, 1760–1770*. Manchester, UK: Manchester University Press.

Troost, W. (2005). *William III, the stadholder king: A political biography*. Aldershot, UK: Ashgate.

Valente, C. (2005). The provisions of Oxford: Assessing/assigning authority in time of unrest. In R. F. Berkhofer, et al. (Eds.), *The experience of power in medieval Europe: 950–1350* (pp. 25–42). Aldershot, UK: Ashgate.

Vallance, E. (2006). *The glorious revolution: 1688 – Britain's fight for liberty*. London: Abacus.

van Wingerden, S. A. (2002). *The women's suffrage movement in Britain: 1866–1928*. New York: Palgrave Macmillan.

Warham, D. (1995). *Imagining the middle class: The political representation of class in Britain, c. 1780–1840*. Cambridge, UK: Cambridge University Press.

Watson, J. S. (2001). *The reign of George III: 1760–1815* (Reprint). Oxford, UK: Oxford University Press.

Werckmeister, O. K. (1976). The political ideology of the Bayeux Tapestry: Estratto dagli Studi Medievali. *Studi Medievali* (3rd series), *17*(2), 535–595.

Western, J. R. (1972). *Monarchy and revolution: The English state in the 1680s*. London: Blandford.

Whiteley, P. (1996). *Lord North: The prime minister who lost America*. London: The Hambledon Press.

Wicks, E. (2006). *The evolution of a constitution: Eight key moments in British constitutional history*. Portland, OR: Hart.

Wilkinson, B. (1972). *The creation of medieval parliaments*. New York: Wiley.

Williams, P. (1963). A revolution in Tudor history?: Dr. Elton's interpretation of the age. *Past & Present, 25*, 3–8.

Williams, P. (2006). *The later Tudors: England, 1547–1603* (Repr.). Oxford, UK: Clarendon.

Wintertorn, G. (1976). The British Grundnorm: Parliamentary supremacy reexamined. *Law Quarterly Review, 92*, 591–617.

Wissolik, R. D. (1979). The Saxon statement: Code in the Bayeux Tapestry. *Annuale Mediaevale, 19*, 69–97.

Wittmayer Helms, M. E. (1963). *The convention parliament of 1660*. Bryn Mawr, PA: Bryn Mawr College.

Wollstonecraft, M. (2010). *A vindication of the rights of men in a letter to the right honourable Edmund Burke; Occasioned by his reflections on the revolution in France*. Cambridge, UK: Cambridge University Press. (Facsimile edition of 1790: London: Joseph Johnson.)

Woolrych, A. (2003). The Cromwellian protectorate: A military dictatorship? In D. L. Smith (Ed.), *Cromwell and the interregnum* (pp. 61–90). Oxford, UK: Blackwell.

## *Further Reading*


Black, J. (1992). *Pitt the elder*. Cambridge, UK: Cambridge University Press.

Black, J. (2001). *Walpole in power*. Stroud: Sutton Publishing.

Bloch, H. (2006). *A needle in the right hand of god: The Norman conquest of 1066 and the making and meaning of the Bayeux Tapestry*. New York: Random House.

Boyer, A. D. (2003). *Sir Edward Coke and the Elizabethan Age*. Stanford, CA: Stanford University Press.

Bracton, Henry of. (1922). *On the laws and customs of England* (Facsimilar ed. from *De Legibus et Consuetudinibus Angliae*). New Haven, CT: Yale University Press.

Brown, K., & MacDonald, A. R. (Eds.). (2010). *Parliament in context: 1235–1707*. Edinburgh: Edinburgh University Press.

Burt, C. (2012). *Edward I and the governance of England: 1272–1307*. Cambridge, UK: Cambridge University Press.

Cannon, J. (1973). *Parliamentary reform 1640–1832*. New York: Cambridge University Press.

Churchill, W. S., Sir. (2011). Pitt the elder. In *A history of the English-speaking peoples* (pp. 436–445). New York: Skyhorse Pub.

Conancher, J. B. (1971). *The emergence of British parliamentary democracy in the nineteenth century*. New York: Wiley.

Crafton, J. M. (2007). *The political artistry of the Bayeux tapestry: A visual epic of Norman imperial ambitions*. Lewiston, NY: Mellen.

Craigie, J. (Ed.). (1944–1950). *The Basilicon Doron of King James VI* (3 Vols). Edinburgh: William Blackwood.

de Glanvill, R. (1993). *The treatise on the laws and customs of the realm of England commonly called Glanv* (Facsimilar ed. From: *Tractatus de legibus et consuetudinibus regni Angliae*). Oxford: Oxford University Press.

Dichfield, G. M. (2002). *George III: An essay in monarchy*. Basingstoke, UK: Palgrave.

Dickinson, H. T. (1973). *Walpole and the Whig supremacy*. London: English Universities Press.

Eisenstein, E. L. (2005). *The printing revolution in early modern Europe* (2nd ed.). Cambridge, UK: Cambridge University Press.

Elton, G. R. (1974). *The Tudor revolution in government: Administrative changes in the reign of Henry VIII*. Cambridge: Cambridge University Press.

Elton, G. R. (1986). *The parliament of England, 1559–1581*. Cambridge, UK: Cambridge University Press.

Elton, G. R. (1999). *The Tudor constitution: Documents and commentary* (2nd ed.). Cambridge, UK: Cambridge University Press.

Gentle, I. J. (2007). *The English revolution and the wars of the three kingdoms: 1638–1652*. Harlow, UK: Pearson/Longman.

Gillingham, J. (2001). *The Angevin empire*. Oxford, UK: Oxford University Press.

Gneist, R. (1889). *History of the English parliament, its growth and development through a thousand years: 800 to 1887* (4th ed.). London: W. Clowes.

Gneist, R., & Keane, A. H. (2012). *The student's history of the English parliament*. Holmes Beach, FL: Gaunt. (Originally published: New English ed., rewritten, with a complete index by A.H. Keane. New York: G.P. Putnam's Sons, 1887.)

Haakonssen, K. (2006). *Enlightenment and religion: Rational dissent in eighteenth-century Britain*. Cambridge, UK: Cambridge University Press.

Hanham, H. J. (1978). *Elections and party management: Politics in the time of Disraeli and Gladstone*. Hassocks, Sussex: Harvester Press.

Hoppen, K. T. (2000). *The mid-Victorian generation: 1846–1886*. New York: Oxford University Press.

Keay, A. (2008). *The magnificent monarch: Charles II and the ceremonies of power*. London: Hambledon Continuum.

Kelly, D. (2004). Revisiting the rights of man: Georg Jellinek on rights and the state. *Law and History Review, 22*(3), 493–529.
King, A. (2007). *The British constitution.* Oxford: Oxford University Press.
Lakin, S. (2008). Debunking the idea of parliamentary sovereignty: The controlling factor of legality in the British constitution. *Oxford Journal of Legal Studies, 28*(4), 709–734.
Lawrence, J., & Taylor, M. (Eds.). (1997). *Party, state, and society: Electoral behaviour in Britain since 1820.* Aldershot, UK: Scolar Press.
Lehmberg, S. E. (2008). *The later parliaments of Henry VIII, 1536–1547.* Cambridge, UK: Cambridge University Press.
Low, S. (1904). *The governance of England.* London: T. Fisher.
Mandler, P. (1990). *Aristocratic government in the age of reform: Whigs and liberals, 1830–1852.* Oxford: Clarendon.
McAuslan, P., & McEldowney, J. F. (1985). *Law, legitimacy, and the constitution: Essays marking the centenary of Dicey's law of the constitution.* London: Sweet & Maxwell.
Mitchell, J. (2008). *The organization of opinion: Open voting in England 1832–1868.* New York: Palgrave Macmillan.
Montague, F. C. (2011). *The elements of English constitutional history: From the earliest times to the present day.* Holmes Beach, Fla: Gaunt, Inc. (Reprinted. Originally published: New York: Longmans, Green and Co., 1894.)
O'Shauhnessy, A. J. (2004). 'If others Will Not Be Active, I Must Drive': George III and the American Revolution. *Early American Studies: An Interdisciplinary Journal, 2*(1), 1–46.
Parry, J. P. (1996). *The rise and fall of Liberal government in Victorian Britain.* New Haven, CT: Yale University Press.
Pearce, E. (2011). *Pitt the elder: Man of war.* London: Pimlico.
Prestwich, M. (1992). *War, politics and finance under Edward I.* Aldershot, UK: Gregg Revivals.
Reitan, E. A. (Ed.). (1964). *George III, Tyrant or constitutional monarch?* Boston, DC: Health and Company.
Rollison, D. (2010). *A commonwealth of the people: Popular politics and England's long social revolution, 1066–1649.* Cambridge, UK: Cambridge University Press.
Sandoz, E. (Ed.). (2008). *The roots of liberty: Magna Carta, ancient constitution, and the Anglo-American tradition of rule of law.* Indianapolis, IN: Liberty Fund.
Smith, G. (1990). *A constitutional and legal history of England.* New York: Dorset Press.
Stubbs, W. (1874). *The constitutional history of England, in its origin and development.* Oxford: Clarendon.
Trevelyan, G. (2004). *George the third and Charles Fox: The concluding part of the American Revolution* (Reprint). Whitefish, MT: Kessinger Publishing.
Turner, M. J. (2000). *The age of unease: Government and reform in Britain, 1782–1832.* Stroud, UK: Sutton.
Ward, I. (2004). *The English constitution: Myths and realities.* Oxford: Hart.
Warren, W. L. (1997). *King John.* New Haven, CT: Yale University Press.
Warren, W. L. (2000). *Henry II.* New Haven, CT: Yale University Press.

# Part IV
# The Rise of the Nation-State

# Chapter 12
# From Monarchy to Representative Government: The American "Revolution"

> A wise and frugal Government, which shall restrain men from injuring one another, shall leave them otherwise free to regulate their own pursuits of industry and improvement, and shall not take from the mouth of labor the bread it has earned. This is the sum of good government, and this is necessary to close the circle of our felicities.—Thomas Jefferson (1743–1826)[1]
>
> In America the principle of the sovereignty of the people is not either barren or concealed, as it is with some other nations; it is recognized by the customs and proclaimed by the laws; it spreads freely, and arrives without impediment at its most remote consequences. If there be a country in the world where the doctrine of the sovereignty of the people can be fairly appreciated, where it can be studied in its application to the affairs of society, and where its dangers and its advantages may be foreseen, that country is assuredly America.—Alexis de Tocqueville (1805–1859)[2]

## Contents


12.1 Revolution as a Social Instrument of Political Change ........ 322
 12.1.1 The Example of Prussian Social Inflexibility ........ 322
 12.1.2 The English Case: The Gradual Transformation of a Political Constitution ........ 323
 12.1.3 Rupture as an Instrument of Change: The American and French Revolutions ........ 324
12.2 From the War of Independence to the American Revolution ........ 325
12.3 The First Europeans in the Americas ........ 326
 12.3.1 The Spanish and the Portuguese ........ 326
 12.3.2 French and Dutch Expeditions ........ 326
 12.3.3 The Origins of the English Presence in America ........ 327
12.4 Spanish vs. English Colonization ........ 328
 12.4.1 The "Centralized" Model of Spanish Colonization ........ 328
 12.4.2 The English Model: "Decentralized" Colonization ........ 330


[1] From his First Inaugural Address, on March 4, 1801. (Jefferson 1854, 1) Text also in Browne (2003, 71).

[2] From *Democracy in America I* (1835). (Tocqueville 2010, 43).


B. Aguilera-Barchet, *A History of Western Public Law*,
DOI 10.1007/978-3-319-11803-1_12

12.5 The Development of English Colonization ... 331
12.5.1 The First English Colony: Virginia (1607) ... 331
12.5.2 Religious Colonization ... 333
12.5.3 The Proprietary Colonies ... 336
12.5.4 New Colonies After the Restoration (1660) ... 338
12.5.5 Political Variety and Legal Autonomy of the English Colonies in America ... 341
12.6 The Colonists and the British Crown ... 343
12.6.1 The Colonial Explosion ... 343
12.6.2 The First American Intervention of the English Crown: The War Against France ... 344
12.6.3 The Price of Victory ... 345
12.6.4 The Fiscal Origins of the Rebellion ... 345
12.6.5 The First Continental Congress in Philadelphia (1774) ... 347
12.7 The War of Independence (1776–1781) ... 347
12.7.1 The First Armed Clash: The "Battle" at Lexington (April 19, 1775) ... 347
12.7.2 The Second Continental Congress and the Declaration of Independence ... 348
12.7.3 The Course of the Conflict ... 348
12.7.4 The Peace of Versailles and the Recognition of a New Nation: The United States of America ... 350
12.8 The West's First Liberal State ... 351
12.8.1 From Locke to Jefferson ... 351
12.8.2 The American Revolution as a Rupture with the Old Order ... 352
12.8.3 A Precarious "Union": The Articles of Confederation ... 355
References ... 358

## 12.1 Revolution as a Social Instrument of Political Change

The Europe of absolute monarchy, whether in its classical or enlightened versions, could not prevent the disadvantaged classes (initially the bourgeoisie, and, century later, the proletariat) from seeking to take on the privileged classes dominant under the old order and to transform the economic, social and political structure of their states in their favor.

### *12.1.1 The Example of Prussian Social Inflexibility*

It is significant that even a monarch as enlightened and capable as Frederick the Great of Prussia did virtually nothing to forge a more egalitarian society. As we know, Frederick clearly applied the principles of the *Aufklärung* (Enlightenment), promoted education for the people, abolished torture, streamlined the administration of justice, and put his jurists to work drafting an organized code of laws.

In the social sphere, however, he was a staunch defender of the existing order. In Prussia, in Eastern Germany (Brandenburg) and in the *Ostelbien* (lands lying to the east of the River Elbe) only the nobles and great landowners, known as *Junkers* (from the German *juncherre*, meaning "young gentleman", or "son of a landowner") were able to serve the state in public offices and positions.[3] The burghers of the towns were engaged in industry or were merchants, while the peasants worked the lands of nobles, who stood as the authorities controlling the justice and administrative system.

Under this system, no one had the right to transcend the class or social group into which he was born. The son of a nobleman was forbidden from being a merchant, and that of a merchant could not work as a peasant. The alliance between the monarchy and the Prussian aristocracy would ultimately prove disastrous for the German state, as it significantly delayed the fall of the autocratic regime and slowed its move towards the kind of liberal regime which prevailed in Europe after 1848. In fact, the parliamentary system would not appear in Germany until the Weimar Republic (1919–1933), whose constitution, significantly, still upheld the principle of the supremacy of the executive, inherited from the Prussian Constitution of 1850, specifically, in its famous Article 48, which allowed the government to seize full power "when overall security and the maintenance of order in the German Reich were in danger". The article would be invoked frequently after 1930 by Chancellor Heinrich Brüning. In fact, Adolf Hitler would employ it to legitimize the establishment of his dictatorship after 1933.[4]

### 12.1.2 *The English Case: The Gradual Transformation of a Political Constitution*

The case of the UK, and, specifically England, stands in stark contrast to that of Prussia. As we know, the process of English social transformation began in the sixteenth century when the Tudors unconditionally supported the enrichment and

---

[3] On the origins of the Prussian ruling class, see Carsten (1947, 145–168). For a general overview of the Prussian social structure, see Clark (2006, 145–182) and Hagen (2003). For a sociological approach, see Weber (2008, 163–168).

[4] "In the event that the public order and security are seriously disturbed or endangered, the Reich President may take the measures necessary for their restoration, intervening, if necessary, with the aid of the armed forces. For this purpose he may temporarily abrogate, wholly or in part, the fundamental principles laid down in Articles 114 [personal liberty], 115 [inviolability of dwelling], 117 [secrecy of postal, telephonic, and telegraphic communications], 118 [freedom of expression], 123 [freedom of assembly], 124 [freedom to form associations], and 153 [inviolability of property]". ("*Der Reichspräsident kann, wenn im Deutschen Reiche die öffentliche Sicherheit und Ordnung erheblich gestört oder gefährdet wird, die zur Wiederherstellung der öffentlichen Sicherheit und Ordnung nötigen Maßnahmen treffen, erforderlichenfalls mit Hilfe der bewaffneten Macht einschreiten. Zu diesem Zwecke darf er vorübergehend die in den Artikeln 114, 115, 117, 118, 123, 124 und 153 festgesetzten Grundrechte ganz oder zum Teil außer Kraft setzen*"). Second paragraph of Article 48 of the 1919 Weimar Constitution (Steinweis and Rachlin 2013, 191).

rise of a merchant and financial class which ended up merging with the old nobility, thereby yielding the new English governing class, the gentry, 200 years earlier than the development of any comparable group in France. The truly significant aspect from the point of view of constitutional history is that ever since then the representatives of this new "aristocracy" began to exercise, through Parliament, a decisive influence on the kingdom's policies. This is why, with the exception of the two English revolutions of the seventeenth century, there was no drastic regime change in England, but rather a gradual adaptation to new circumstances. The participation of English society in the government of the kingdom, as we saw in the last chapter, was decisively bolstered through the progressive expansion of the franchise between 1832 and 1928. The gentry proved flexible enough to gradually expand its social base—though this did not keep the U.K. from featuring a highly pronounced class structure into the early twentieth century.[5] The English elite continued to be educated at select institutions such as the "public schools" of Harrow and Eton, and the universities of Oxford and Cambridge.[6]

### *12.1.3 Rupture as an Instrument of Change: The American and French Revolutions*

The transformation of political and legal systems to adapt them to social realities was much less peaceful in other western states, where one cannot speak of "evolution" but rather "revolution". Violent conflict would break out in Britain's American colonies in 1776, in France in 1789, and revolutionary movements would shake Europe in 1820, 1830, 1848, 1868–1870, and as late as 1905, when Russia's *Ancien Regime* was finally toppled. In each of these cases there came a break with the established order in a relatively short period of time as a result of armed actions of a revolutionary nature, with monarchies overthrown by bodies of representatives aspiring to speak for the people. These groups appealed to the theory of the social contract and, through the establishment of representative

[5] Class tension and resentment is an underlying theme in the novels of the Bronte sisters Charlotte (1816–1855) and Emily (1820–1849) (Foster 2012, 71–109). Especially, Charlotte's *Jane Eyre* and Emily's *Wuthering Heights*, both published in 1847 (Shuttleworth 2004). For an overview of the origins of the English landed ruling class, see Rosenheim (1998). Another element of British political idiosyncrasy is what Kuzmics and Axtmann (2007, 221–232) call their "proud detachment", as portrayed by Jane Austen in her novel *Pride and Prejudice*, first published in 1813. For an overview of British society between 1780 and 1880, see Perkin (2002, 17–62). Also, Garrard (2002) and Price (1999).

[6] In fact, in Great Britain the accent which one acquires during his early upbringing and education determines, to a large extent, the course of his life, as suggested by Bernard Shaw in *Pygmalion* (1916). In this regard, Steinbach (2012, 141–145) and Tyerman (2000, 1) point out that the importance of public schools in English political and social history may not be admirable or admired, but it is inescapable. For an overview of the history of the English educational system, see O'Day (1982) and Stephens (1998). On the history of British Universities and the making of the English elites, see Anderson (2006), Pietsch (2013) and Soffer (1994).

assemblies, sought to wipe away the preceding system and create, *ex novo*, new regimes in which legislative power was the state's supreme or only instrument.

We shall examine two specific examples crucial to western constitutional history: the American Revolution and the French Revolution, pivotal precedents which serve to explain most of the nineteenth century's political struggles for reform and revolution. The two broke out for different reasons, but both led to revolutionary assemblies drafting social pacts recorded in written constitutions. The people, represented by these assemblies, created nations which claimed the power (sovereignty) to decide the type of political regime which they would adopt. The idea was to sweep away the old order (*Ancién Régime*) and usher in a new one.

In this chapter we focus on the American Revolution, which came first because, among other things, it was much easier to build a new society in a "New World" than in an old Europe marked by deeply rooted, ancestral social and political traditions.

## 12.2 From the War of Independence to the American Revolution

The most powerful contemporary western nation, the United States of America, arose as consequence of a revolt against a European state: the United Kingdom of Great Britain. This "rebellion" was actually a "revolution" in so far as subjects of His Gracious Majesty agreed to separate, voluntarily and unilaterally, from British sovereignty to found a new nation, and monarchy was thrown off in favor of republicanism.[7] This aspect was clearly stated in the final paragraph of the Declaration of Independence of July 4, 1776:

> We, therefore, the Representatives of the United States of America, in General Congress Assembled, appealing to the Supreme Judge of the world for the rectitude of our intentions, do, in the Name, and by Authority of the good People of these Colonies, solemnly publish and declare, that these United Colonies are and of Right ought to be Free and Independent States; that they are Absolved from all Allegiance to the British Crown, and that all political connection between them and the State of Great Britain, is and ought to be totally dissolved, and that as Free and Independent States, they have full Power to levy War, conclude Peace, contract Alliances, establish Commerce, and to do all other Acts and Things which Independent States may of right do.[8]

In the case of the colonies which emancipated themselves from the sovereignty of the British Crown, the monarchical regime was replaced by 13 united "republics", sharing as a common body an assembly called "Congress" by virtue of an

[7] As Wood (1993, 95) indicates, the late eighteenth century in the Atlantic world has been called "the age of the democratic revolution" but it might better be called "the age of the republican revolution", as it was republicanism and republican principles that ultimately destroyed monarchical society.

[8] For the text of the Declaration, see Armitage (2007, 165–171). On the circumstances in which the Declaration was written, see Maier (1998). For a thorough analysis of the text, see Grimes (1976, 1–19). On its ideological framework, see the classic study by Becker (1922).

initial constitutional text known as the Articles of Confederation, approved in 1777 by the representatives of the former colonies, now states.

To understand the events of the American "Revolution", one must examine the history of English colonization and its peculiarities in the light of other European efforts at settlement in the Americas. We shall compare it, above all, with the case of Spanish colonization, the oldest and most long-standing.

## 12.3 The First Europeans in the Americas

### *12.3.1 The Spanish and the Portuguese*

When the first English settlers came to America in 1607, the Spanish had been settling the New World for more than a century already. Theoretically, what the Spanish called *Las Indias* (because Columbus was convinced that he had reached Asia) was a territory exclusively reserved for the subjects of the Spanish crown,[9] and not to all of them, as the general rule was that only Castilians had the right to travel to *Las Indias*.

The reality was, however, that the Spanish and Portuguese were only present in Central and South America, save for some expeditions launched by the Catholic Monarchy in the sixteenth century, to explore what is today the southern United States. Among these was that of Francisco Vázquez de Coronado (1540–1542), who crossed what is modern-day Arizona, New Mexico, Kansas and Oklahoma.[10] North America, however, remained a largely virgin territory until French, Dutch and English explorers and settlers came to this geographic area.

### *12.3.2 French and Dutch Expeditions*

In the sixteenth century the French, as a result of initiatives backed by King Francis I, began to explore North America, with Giovanni da Verrazano conducting expeditions to Newfoundland and on to New York Bay, and Jacques Cartier reaching modern-day French Canada (Quebec and Montreal) (Love 2006, 70). During the seventeenth century, French settlement in America advanced significantly thanks to the efforts of Samuel de Champlain (1567–1635), who, after establishing the colony

[9] In accordance with a papal order (the Alexandrine Bulls of 1493), and an agreement reached between Isabella and Ferdinand, the kings of Castile and Aragon; and John II of Portugal, in the Treaty of Tordesillas (1494), the monarchs of the two kingdoms divided up the world for its conquest and colonization. The Portuguese were granted the right to settle Brazil, a territory discovered by the Portuguese explorer Pedro Alvares Cabral in 1500. On the Treaty of Tordesillas, see Bown (2012, 134–161).

[10] On the Coronado expedition, see Flint and Flint (2011), and Hoig (2013). For an overview of the Spanish frontier in North America, see Weber (2009).

of Acadia, founded the city of Quebec in 1608 (Fischer 2008, 227–253), and crossed North America on its major rivers, travelling down the Mississippi, reaching its mouth in the Gulf of Mexico, and taking possession of a territory which later came to be called "Louisiana" in honor of France's King Louis XIV.[11]

The Dutch began their operations in the Americas with attacks beginning in 1624 on Portuguese possessions in Brazil, which allowed them to occupy San Salvador de Bahia (1625), and Pernambuco (1630). As a result, they managed to settle in the territory of present-day Dutch Guiana (Surinam) and the island of Curacao in the Antilles. In North America, the first Dutch expedition was headed by Peter Stuyvesant, who in 1624 founded Fort Orange on the present site of Albany, now the capital of the State of New York (Goodfriend 2005).

In 1626, Peter Minuit bought the island of Manhattan from the Indians on behalf of the Dutch West India Company and founded the city of New Amsterdam (today New York) at the mouth of the river discovered by English navigator Henry Hudson in 1609.[12] The city would remain in Dutch hands until 1667, when it was conquered by the English, redubbed "New York" in honor of the Stuart Charles II's brother, the Duke of York, owner of the entire area, ceded to him by his brother the king.[13]

### 12.3.3 *The Origins of the English Presence in America*

The British first reached North America when John and Sebastian Cabot, father and son, respectively, made two trips in 1497 and 1498, during which they discovered the coast of Labrador and, probably, what is today the Hudson River. However, as the Bristol ship owners who had financed their travels concluded that the lands they discovered lacked commercial value, the Cabots eventually entered the service of the Spanish crown.[14]

---

[11] Though discovered by Champlain, it was the explorer René Robert Cavelier (1643–1687), who named it "Louisiana" in honor of the Sun King, after claiming the entire Mississippi River basin for France. For an overview of Champlain's explorations, see Gervais (2004, 180–190). On the French colonization of North America, see Marchand (2009).

[12] According to tradition, Minuit bought the island of Manhattan from the natives on May 24, 1626, for goods worth the pittance of 60 Dutch guilders, leading some to consider the transaction almost the greatest bargain in History—only surpassed by Thomas Jefferson's purchase of the Louisiana Territory from France in 1803. About the governor Minuit and the Dutch colonization of what would become New York, see McNeese (2009, 63–72).

[13] The Duke of York would become the King of England as James II (1685–1688). For the history of the Dutch colony, see Jacobs (2009).

[14] Of Italian origin, John Cabot and his entire family moved to England around 1490. He was 46 when, after residing for a time in Bristol, he set sail on his famous voyage across the Atlantic, on March 5, 1496, Henry VII having conceded his request to prepare the expedition "upon their own proper costs and charges to seek out, discover, and find whatsoever isles, countries, regions or provinces of the heathen and infidels, whatsoever they be, and in what part of the world soever they be, which before this time have been unknown to all Christians" (Harrisse 1896, 38 and 47). On the lives and accomplishments of John Cabot and his son Sebastian, see Ober (2011).

## 12.4 Spanish vs. English Colonization

### *12.4.1 The "Centralized" Model of Spanish Colonization*

In 1600, there were no permanent settlements of English colonists in America, while the Spanish had been present in the New World for more than a century, having established a solid foothold in the Americas by the early sixteenth century (Lockhart and Schwartz 1999, 61–85) in large part because the Spanish Crown had followed from the beginning a centralized and interventionist model of colonization.[15] Each expedition was organized by the crown and each territory discovered was owned by the king and governed and administrated by his officers (McAlister 1989, 96–99). The economic exploitation of *Las Indias* was also monopolized by the state through a public institution: the *Casa de Contratación* (House of Trade) established in Seville, the point of departure and arrival for all the expeditions to the American colonies (Elliott 1987, 61–62).[16]

By virtue of this centralized model of colonization, the Spanish managed to tightly control their American dominions for more than three centuries (Mahoney 2010, 36–43). The strict monopoly exercised by the monarchy over the American colonies was apparent in their territorial organization, perfectly structured into viceroyalties, which were divided into *audiencias* (Dougnac Rodríguez 2004, 539–586), each made up, in turn, of various "provinces" or "governments". The highest authorities were representatives of the king. At the top were the viceroys, followed in rank by the captains general and governors. These one-person offices were often controlled by a collegial body: the *audiencias*, to which only Castilian Spaniards were admitted and originally functioned as courts of justice. In the Americas, they often exercised governmental and oversight functions over the individual bodies (Garriga 1994, 418–428).[17] In addition, the viceroys and governors were supervised by "visitors" or even "special envoys", as was the case with Pedro de Lagasca, who was sent to Peru in 1546, to subdue the rebellion led by Gonzalo Pizarro. The monarchy also controlled its colonial officials and authorities in the Americas, a posteriori through *juicios de residencia*, judicial procedures to which they were subject upon their return to Spain at which their service was

[15] Following the model initially developed by the Portuguese in their exploration of the African coast during the early decades of the fifteenth century, and the voyages of Henry the Navigator (McAlister 1989, 46–51). On the origin of Portuguese expansion, see Newitt (2005, 1–34). On the organization of Portuguese colonization, see Russell-Wood (2007, 161–196).

[16] On the first organization of the *Casa de Contratación*, see Brown (2006, 1, 179–180) and Fisher (1997, 22 and 47–48). In 1717, the *Casa de Contratación* was transferred to Cádiz, though the crown continued to maintain stringent control over all seafaring to the Americas, at least until the liberalizing measures introduced by Charles III from 1765 to 1788, after which one could sail freely to Spain's colonies from virtually any port in Spain.

[17] For an overview of how the original Castilian jurisdictional institution became an instrument of government and control in Spanish America, see Garriga (2004, 711–794).

assessed and, at times, severely punished, as occurred in the cases of Columbus, Cortés and Pedro de Alvarado (Vallejo García-Hevia 2008, 72).

Spanish colonists were able to participate, to some extent, in government through their *cabildos*—the name given in the Indies to the traditional Castilian town governments (Tapia 1966). However, as happened in the city, the *cabildos* eventually fell into the hands of local oligarchies. In some cases, though relatively rare, Spanish colonials gathered in assemblies or congresses (Sanz Camañes 2004, 131). Sometimes government was entrusted to a commercial company, as occurred in Venezuela.[18] Also worthy of note was the peculiarity of mission territories (e.g. Paraguay) for which a special administrative arrangement was created, the *reducción*, administrated by religious orders (essentially Jesuits), under which the Indians enjoyed a certain degree of autonomy (Ganson 2003, 87–136). This system began to fade in the eighteenth century as a result of the greater centralization imposed by the Bourbons and their suppression of the Society of Jesus (Jaenike 2008).[19]

In general, we can say that the colonization of Spanish America was strictly subject to the king's absolute authority, with the Indies, in fact, legally forming part of the Crown of Castile (Brading 1998, 213–227). This centralism would be reinforced during the Bourbon era of enlightened despotism as a result of the reform of the *audiencias* and the introduction of "intendants"—officials who embodied all the executive and interventionists ambitions of the Bourbon state (Brading 1987, 127–128).

[18] Welser Brothers, the company of Bartholomew Welser, which was based in Augsburg and was dedicated to commerce, banking, mining products (essentially silver and copper), trading in spices from the West Indies, textiles, insurance and shipmaking. The firm had factories in Ulm, Mainz, Frankfurt, Cologne, Nuremberg, Leipzig, Milan, Genoa, Venice, Rome, Lyon, Danzig, Antwerp, Salzburg, Vienna, Lisbon and Seville, among other cities. After 1526, it expanded its trade with the New World, particularly in Santo Domingo. Two years later the company was empowered by Charles V, in a *capítulación* issued on March 27, 1528, to explore, conquer and populate the province of Venezuela (Avellán de Tamayo 1999, 35).

[19] As Bost (2002, 150) explains, Jesuits founded the Indian settlements which came to be called *reducciones*, not only as a way of indoctrinating the Indians, but also in an effort to educate them, improve their economic and social status, and protect them from Brazilian and Spanish slave traders. The "reductions" spread rapidly, to the point that in the seventeenth century there were more than 180 of these settlements in South America. As the system completely protected the Indians from colonists, in search of their cheap labor, it was strongly opposed by settlers, other factions within the Church, and civil authorities. The Jesuits were expelled from the reductions by the Portuguese and Spanish army according Cushner (2006, 112–113) when they were banished from Portugal and Spain in 1767, before the definitive suppression of the Society of Jesus came through a papal brief, *Dominus Ac Redemptor*, issued by Clement XIV in 1773. On the Jesuit reductions in South America, see Caraman (1990).

### *12.4.2 The English Model: "Decentralized" Colonization*

Despite having defeated Philip II's Armada in 1588, England, in 1600, was a relatively small state compared to the vast Spanish Empire, which from 1580 to 1640, also boasted the Kingdom of Portugal and colonies in the Americas, Africa and Asia. The English and Dutch warships were able to attack isolated Spanish vessels—which is why they sought safety in the Indies by sailing in fleets—and could strike isolated locations along the coast, but they were no match for Spanish power in a full-blown conflict in the region. It was mainly for this reason that British and Dutch colonial expansion was approached in a way different from that of the Spanish crown,[20] with small expeditions organized which sought to settle locations far from places occupied by the Spanish. Hence, the English expeditions tended to target North America.

Another element affecting England's Atlantic expansion was the fact that, as we already have seen, during the era of the Tudors—essentially the sixteenth century—a prosperous and powerful bourgeoisie arose which altered England's social and economic structure, transforming the country from a land of farmers and herders into a powerful industrial and mercantile force. Thus, from the start, English colonization was conceived of more as a commercial undertaking than as a colonization of a public nature, intended to provide new land and resources for the crown. It was, therefore, private initiative (albeit duly approved by the Crown) which spearheaded English settlement in America. This would have important consequences from a political standpoint, as from the outset the English colonies enjoyed high degrees of self-government. In fact, when in the last third of the eighteenth century, the British Crown sought to exert greater control over its colonists, they were so accustomed to their prerogatives and freedoms that they responded by rebelling against his Gracious Majesty.

When James I (1603–1625), inherited the British throne his country had been at war with the Spanish monarchy for 50 years. The beginnings of the first Stuart's reign coincided, in Spain, with the period of government under the Duke of Lerma, Philip III's (1598–1621) chief advisor, who endorsed a policy of peace with Holland and England. However, it was the new English king who in June of 1603, began to call for peace negotiations. On August 28, 1604, talks began, and diplomatic relations were restored between the two kingdoms in 1606 (Feros 2006, 197). After signing the peace with Spain, the English monarchy could for the first time turn to pondering a long-term settlement policy in North America.

[20] For a comparative overview of the Spanish vs. the British Crown's approach to the colonization of the Americas, see Elliot (2006, 117–151).

## 12.5 The Development of English Colonization

### *12.5.1 The First English Colony: Virginia (1607)*

The peace created a favorable scenario for merchants and investors. The very same year that peace was signed with Spain, a group of English merchants asked James I for permission to explore the territory of Virginia, officially established in 1585 by Sir Walter Raleigh on Roanoke Island, off the coast of present-day North Carolina, but it was abandoned.[21] The British would not successfully settle the area until 1607. The first lasting—though struggling and suffering—settlement came at Jamestown, named in honor of the king who authorized the arrival of the first colonists.

#### 12.5.1.1 Royal Authorization, but Private Initiative

When James I granted them permission to settle the area the expedition's backers were two trading companies, one controlled by investors in London and another by a group from Plymouth and Bristol.[22] The London and Plymouth companies were created by James I in 1606, for the purpose of establishing the first permanent English settlements in North America, one to colonize southern Virginia, and the other to settle the northern Virginia.[23]

The London Company was the first to organize an expedition to the New World, consisting of 3 boats and 144 people under the command of Captain John Smith,[24]

[21] The "Lost Colony" of Roanoke had vanished when, after a long delay because of the Spanish War, the English returned to the island in 1590. The fate of the settlers has never been determined. England largely forgot its interest in American settlements for 20 years as the leading figures who had backed such ventures died, like Secretary Walshingham, in 1589 and Richard Hakluyt, in 1591 (Kupperman 2007, 138). On the tragic history of Roanoke also see Loker (2006) and Stick (1993).

[22] As Craven (1957, 5–6) points out, commercial interests prevailed over religious motivations. If at the beginning of the first charter the colonists sought to propagate the Christian religion "to such people, as yet live in darkness and miserable ignorance of the true knowledge and worship of God", it is quite telling and significant that they only included one minister in the expedition, and that 10 years passed before they started a school for the Indians. The conversion and education of Indians was, evidently, not a priority.

[23] The Plymouth Company and London Company fused to form what was called the Virginia Company, but the initiative was a commercial failure and the Company was dissolved in 1624 by the decision of a London's King's Bench court. For an overview of the decay and dissolution of the Virginia Company, see Craven (1932).

[24] The ships were the 120-ton *Susan Constant*, carrying 54 passengers and a crew of 17; the *Godspeed*, with 39 passengers and 13 crew; and the *Discovery*, with 12 passengers and a crew of 9. The voyage would take 5 months, leaving London on December 20, 1606, passing through the Canary Islands from February 17–21, sailing through the Caribbean between March 24 and April 10, and reaching the coast of present-day Virginia on April 26, near Chesapeake Bay (Hoobler 2006, 78–81).

whose relations with the local Indians, the *Powhatan* confederation, were key to the survival of Jamestown (Price 2003, 47–48).[25]

#### 12.5.1.2 A Royal Colony, but an Autonomous One

On 12 March 1612, the Virginia Company received its Third Charter, which included royal authorization to administrate its own affairs in Virginia (Bemiss 1993, 76–94). This concession of self-government allowed the investors to appoint a governor, who was granted powers sufficient to rule the colony. In 1619, an assembly of colonists termed the House of Burgesses (Vile 2010, 1) was convened, composed of delegates from each district. This was the first English representative body in America (Rabushka 2008, 138). The House began meeting in Jamestown to advise the governor. While its resolutions were not binding upon the owners of the Company, it proved a model representative assembly for those English colonies which would later be established in North America.[26]

[25] The first building at Jamestown was the fort, completed by the middle of June 1607. It featured a triangular shape with a bulwark at each corner shaped like a half moon, equipped with four or five pieces of artillery. The fort enclosed about 1 acre, with the main gate facing south and overlooking the river. Inside the fort was a church and storehouse. The living quarters were built of perishable materials and located within the walls of the fort along streets and around an open yard. For the first few years this fort essentially *was* Jamestown (Hatch Jr 2009, 4). For a balanced and complete accounting of the early years of the Jamestown colony to date, see Gleach (2000). Custalow and Daniel (2007) state that based on Native oral tradition, Pocahontas, the daughter of the paramount Chief Powhatan Wahunsenaca, was a reflection of her Powhatan culture, not an exception, as promoted by the English, many Euro-American scholars, and popular myth. Pocahontas was indeed a symbol of peace, but she was not the peacemaker many Euro-American narratives and myths indicate. The peacemaker attributes, which have been ascribed to Pocahontas, were actually an extension from Chief Powhatan Wahunsenaca and the Powhatan culture, which Pocahontas became a symbol of. For Captain Smith's own version, see Kupperman (1988, 63–73).

[26] On July 30, 1619, two burgesses from each of the 11 settlements met with the governor and councilors in a unicameral body, the General Assembly. It remained in session only 5 days, but followed parliamentary procedure. The elected body was confirmed by "An Ordinance and Constitution from the Treasurer and Company in England Calling for a Council and Assembly in Virginia, July 24, 1621". Two further assemblies met in 1621 and 1624, before Virginia became a royal colony. Subsequent assemblies convening in 1629, 1630 and 1632, imposed local taxation. Charles I acknowledged the General Assembly of Virginia as the colonists' representative in negotiations with tobacco agents when he established a monopoly for the import of Virginian tobacco into England (Rabushka 138). For the text of the 1621 "Ordinance and Constitution", see Bemiss (1993, 126–128).

### 12.5.2 Religious Colonization

The fact that the English Crown was sanctioning settlements in America drew the attention of a group of religious dissidents later known as the Pilgrims,[27] a group interested in emigrating to escape persecution by the official Church of England. The Pilgrims were more radical than Cromwell's Puritans who sought to "purify" the Anglican Church by purging it of any Catholic vestiges, establishing simpler services, and rejecting the mediation of priests (pastors). While the Puritans stopped short of calling for a break with the Church presided over by the king, the Pilgrims called for total rupture, as they felt that the Church of England was beyond redemption, too corrupt to be saved. In fact, they opposed the very idea that the church ought to be organized hierarchically, as in their view each congregation should be able to administrate its own affairs without the mediation of a church hierarchy. As they outright rejected the authority of the official Church, they had no choice but to emigrate.

To escape from Anglicanism in 1608, as a first step, they took refuge in Leiden (Netherlands). However, after 10 years living in the Protestant Netherlands (United Provinces), they feared that their children would end up shedding their British traditions. Thus, the group of Puritan Separatists which would come to be known as the Pilgrims resolved to emigrate to the New World to create a new society in which they could freely practice their religion. As they had no money to organize the expedition, they adopted the model employed to colonize Virginia, establishing a trading company, backed by a number of investors who demanded half the profits. The Pilgrims were eventually joined by other emigrants. In September of 1620, a group of 100 people, of which only 35 were Pilgrims (Johnson 2006, 11–17), set sail from Plymouth in a ship called the *Mayflower*. Glad to be rid of these religious dissenters, James I authorized their departure for Virginia, and agreed not to disturb them as long as they caused no problems.[28]

#### 12.5.2.1 The *Mayflower Compact*: The First American Constitution?

If the *Mayflower* had actually reached Virginia, its voyage would never have gone down in history as it did. After a very rough journey, the vessel ended up much

---

[27] The term "pilgrims" was first used by one of the members of the expedition, William Bradford, in an account of his recollections and observations, written in the form of two books recording the colony's experiences and travails. When he writes of the group's departure in 1620 he uses the expression "they knew that they were pilgrims", taken from the Epistle to the Hebrews, 11:13–14, which refers to those who, like Abraham, died with faith, though without having achieved their aims, only seeing the Promised Land from afar: "confessing themselves strangers and pilgrims on the Earth". The term did not become widespread until the late eighteenth century (Sargent 1993, 18–41).

[28] As Philbrick (2006, 5) points out, to spurn the Church of England was an illegal act in Jacobean Era.

farther north than its intended destination, landing at Cape Cod (in present-day Massachusetts), its passengers and crew weary of enduring storms (Bunker 2010, 53–54).

The good news was that the land where they had arrived was far outside the jurisdiction of the London Company operating in Virginia. Thus, the contingent of Pilgrims on board the Mayflower, concluding that circumstances warranted their disavowal of royal authority, before leaving the ship acted to draft a contract to be signed by all the passengers.

In this document, the *Mayflower Compact*, all its signatories agreed, on November 11, 1620, "to covenant and combine ourselves together into a civil Body Politic, for our better Ordering and Preservation and furtherance of the ends aforesaid; and by virtue hereof to enact, constitute, and frame such just and equal laws, ordinances, acts, constitutions and offices, from time to time, as shall be thought most meet and convenient for the general good of the Colony, unto which we promise all due submission and obedience". All of this was done in the name of God and as loyal subjects of the King of England, "our sovereign lord".[29] In any case, many U.S. constitutional scholars consider this unique "contract" the first instance of American constitutionalism.[30]

#### 12.5.2.2 Thanksgiving Day

In November of the following year, 1621, the Pilgrims, after surviving a dreadful first year fraught with calamities,[31] celebrated the first Thanksgiving Day in American history (Hilton 2005, 170). This tradition is still observed on the fourth Thursday of November, and certainly represents America's most cherished holiday unique to the American nation (Hodgson 2006).[32]

---

[29] "Do by these Presents, solemnly and mutually, in the Presence of God and one another, covenant and combine ourselves together into a civil Body Politic, for our better Ordering and Preservation, and Furtherance of the Ends aforesaid: And by Virtue hereof do enact, constitute, and frame, such just and equal Laws, Ordinances, Acts, Constitutions, and Officers, from time to time, as shall be thought most meet and convenient for the general Good of the Colony; unto which we promise all due Submission and Obedience". For the original transcription, see Bradford (2006, 441–443).

[30] In 1802, John Quincy Adams, the sixth U.S. President, opined that the Mayflower Compact represented the premier historical example of an original covenant in which the citizens of a community consented to live under particular rules (Breslin 2009, 156).

[31] As Philbrick (2006, 5) points out, the conditions of the English settlements in North America were extremely precarious. Jamestown, the only settlement that did not fail, could hardly be considered a success; in its first year 70 of its 108 settlers died, and the following winter was known as the "starving time", when 440 of 500 settlers were buried in the space of 6 months. And then it got even worse: between 1619 and 1622, the Virginia Company sent close to 3,600 settlers to the colony, and over this 3-year period 3,000 would die.

[32] For an overview of the development of the legends behind this major American holiday between 1780 and 1880, see Baker (2009, 62–77).

#### 12.5.2.3 The Great Migration

James I died in 1625, succeeded by Charles I (1625–1649), who was far less tolerant than his father with the Puritans. As a result of the new monarch's policies, as of 1630, Englishmen began to abandon their country *en masse* to settle in America on expeditions financed through the establishment of trading companies. In the fall of 1630, one of them, the Massachusetts Bay Company, founded the city of Boston. Over the next 10 years, there occurred what in American historiography has been called the Great Puritan Migration: by 1640 more than 13,000 Puritans had settled in Massachusetts (Anderson 1991, 15). These emigrants followed the model of self-government established by the Pilgrims on the *Mayflower* in 1620, with each adult male involved in his group's decisions.[33] According to the 1629 Massachusetts Bay Company original charter, the colonists were permitted to choose a governor and appoint an advisory council, as well as elect representatives to a local assembly, called the General Court (Bremer 2003, 159–160)[34]—a practice owing much to the character of Jonathan Winthrop, the leader of the Massachusetts community.[35]

#### 12.5.2.4 Harvard's First Students

As the Puritans believed it essential that all citizens should be able to read the Bible, from the very start, they began to take a great interest in creating a high level educational system. Thus, Harvard College was founded in 1636,[36] and in 1647, the General Court passed a law declaring basic public education obligatory.[37]

[33] In 1649, the original Plymouth colony, initially settled in 1620, came under Massachusetts Bay control.

[34] "*That yearely once in the yeare, for ever hereafter, namely, the last Wednesday in Easter Tearme, yearely, the Governor, Deputy-Governor, and Assistants of the saide Company and all other officers of the saide Company shalbe in the Generall Court or Assembly to be held for that Day or Tyme, newly chosen for the Yeare ensueing by such greater parte of the said Company* [...]" From the *Records of the governor and company of the Massachusetts bay in New England. Printed by order of the legislature...* (Wakelyn 2006, I, 88). After the Glorious Revolution a second charter was bestowed in 1691 by William and Mary offering a larger measure of self government. From then on in March and May the people of the Massachusetts Bay Colony gathered in their town halls to vote for local and provincial officials (Schutz 1997, ix).

[35] As Bremer (2003, 208) explains, Winthrop had learned how to seek consensus through compromises that respected the views of all, and believed that order was best achieved through persuasion and securing consent rather than the wielding of power and enforcement of discipline. Thus, he favored leading by example rather than by setting down laws whenever possible.

[36] The first educational institution was, however, the Boston Latin School. Founded in that city in 1635, it has become the oldest free, public, non-endowed secondary school continuously existing in the United States (Holmes 1970).

[37] In 1636, the Great and General Court of the Governor and Company of the Massachusetts Bay in New England approved an outlay of 400 pounds for the establishment of a "schoale or colledge" later to be called "Harvard" in honor of its first benefactor, the young English minister John Harvard (1607–1638), who upon his death left his library and half his estate to the institution (Morrison 1995, 103–108), established in 1637, in "Newetone", which was renamed "Cambridge"

This strong interest for education was considered by Edmond Burke (1729–1797) one of the most powerful causes of the "fierce spirit of liberty" that prevailed in the English colonies (Burke 1854, 467–468).

#### 12.5.2.5 The Puritan Inquisition

The success of the Massachusetts Bay Company prompted the establishment of new colonies, such as Rhode Island, founded by a series of dissident Puritans lead by the Reverend Roger Williams, Samuel Gorton, and Anne Hutchinson, who had been banished from Massachusetts. All of them felt oppressed by the religious fundamentalism that prevailed in said colony, which was witness to a number of shameful episodes, including the Salem Witch Trials (1692–1693).[38] Rhode Island received its charter from the Westminster Parliament in 1644, later confirmed by Charles II after the Restoration (Jones 2006, 174–175).

During the seventeenth century, the number of English colonists in America also rose considerably because of the introduction of a third foundational model: the "proprietary colony".

### *12.5.3 The Proprietary Colonies*

In addition to royal colonies, like Virginia, and religious ones, like Massachusetts, in Colonial America there appeared the third modality of proprietary colonies created by the king through the concession of a territory to a person or family charged with financing and organizing colonization.[39]

---

in 1638. Harvard College received its first Corporate Charter in 1650 (Monaghan 2005, 59–60). Harvard is the oldest institution of higher education in the United States. For an overview of the origins of education in the American colonies, see Horwitz (2012, 107–143).

[38] For a legal historian, the Salem trials offer excellent insights and information on the constitutional organization of this religious colony at the end of the seventeenth century. For a good overview of the interventions of the magistrates, judges and ministers during this tragic episode, see Hoffer (1997, 54–81).

[39] As Roper and Van Ruymbeke (2007, 2) note, colonial proprietary ventures took various forms, and received their respective rights to engage in "imperial" activity in a range of ways. In some cases, they were chartered companies charged with maintaining a national interest, as they engaged in commerce and colonization. In other cases, individuals or non-incorporated groups received charters from central governments that granted them powers to recruit settlers, exercise governmental functions in colonies, and own land overseas. Other times they controlled local and provincial government by virtue of designations by royal or other overarching authorities. Whatever their different names and forms, all these versions replicated the social and governmental links between central authorities and their localities, as they served as imperial points of contact corresponding to justices of the peace, provincial estates, and other institutions proceeding from the Old World. For an overview of the nature of the government of this type of colonies, see Osgood (1904–1907) and Burrell (2011, 76–83).

#### 12.5.3.1 An Autonomous Catholic Colony: Maryland

The first colony of this type was Maryland,[40] which was granted to Lord Baltimore, who would lend his name to the colony's first city and the present capital of the state. In 1629, George Calvert, First Lord Baltimore—an English politician, MP, and Secretary of State under King James I—asked King Charles I for a charter to establish the Province of Maryland, intended, among other things, as a haven for English Catholics in the New World. In 1632, Charles I granted its proprietor 7 million acres (some 3 million hectares) in the area. Baltimore died the same year he received the proprietorship, but his children, Cecil and Leonard, inherited their father's rights to the overseas territory. The two brothers were determined to realize their father's vision of a new colony which would serve as a haven for England's Catholic nobility, which had been persecuted during the era of the Tudors. Thus, while Cecil remained in London to curry royal favor and obtain financial support for the project, Leonard led the first expedition, which landed on American shores on March 3, 1634 (Menard and Carr 1982).

A private colony, Maryland enjoyed a considerable degree of legal autonomy. Under the terms of the royal grant issued, the Calverts were almost independent in their American dominion. They could issue laws, organize their own court system, appoint officials, and freely distribute land. They did not, however, establish a feudal system because, in practice, to attract settlers, the Calverts had to grant them a degree of autonomy similar to that in the other English colonies, as otherwise immigrants would have headed elsewhere. Thus, the settlers of Maryland also enjoyed a great degree of legal and political autonomy. The Calverts did use the powers granted them by their royal charter to adopt the Toleration Act in 1649, the year King Charles I of England was decapitated. This measure guaranteed religious liberty through Maryland to "anyone who believed in Jesus Christ".[41]

---

[40] The name recorded in the charter was phrased "Terra Mariae, anglice, Maryland". Maryland officially received this name in honor of the Queen Henrietta Maria, Charles I's wife, though in reality it was in homage to the Virgin Mary, paid by the Catholic family of George Calvert, its lord proprietor. Maryland soon became one of the few regions in the English Empire where Catholics held the highest positions of political authority. See Baylin (2012, 117–161).

[41] "*And whereas the inforceing of the conscience in matters of Religion hath frequently fallen out to be of dangerous Consequence in those commonwealthes where it hath been practised, And for the more quiett and peaceable governement of this Province, and the better to preserve mutuall Love and amity amongst the Inhabitants thereof, Be it Therefore also by the Lord Proprietary with the advise and consent of this Assembly Ordeyned and enacted (except as in this present Act is before Declared and sett forth) that noe person or persons whatsoever within this Province, or the Islands, Ports, Harbors, Creekes, or havens thereunto belonging professing to beleive in Jesus Christ, shall from henceforth bee any waies troubled, Molested or discountenanced for or in respect of his or her religion nor in the free exercise thereof within this Province or the Islands thereunto belonging nor any way compelled to the beleife or exercise of any other Religion against his or her consent* [...]". Maryland Toleration Act; September 21, 1649 (Maclear 1995, 45–47). Also, Browne (1883, 244–247). Maryland thus became the first English colony in which the principle of religious tolerance took root. As the Calverts knew that they would not be able to impose Catholicism as the Puritans had done with their faith in Boston, they opted for a position of

#### 12.5.3.2 The Founding of New Hampshire and Maine

New Hampshire and Maine were other proprietary colonies, at least originally, the former at first the private property of Captain John Mason, which he sold to the Crown. Maine had belonged to Sir Ferdinando Gorges, who sought to establish a feudal regime there before selling it to Massachusetts (Esbeck 2004, 1530–1537).[42]

### *12.5.4 New Colonies After the Restoration (1660)*

During the English Civil War and under Cromwell's rule, new English colonies were not founded in America. After 1660, however, and the restoration of the Stuarts, with Charles II, a new wave of migration departed from England for the New World. In fact, this was the period during which most of the English colonies were founded.[43] The model preferred by the new monarch was the granting of proprietary colonies to allies who had supported him in exile during the Cromwellian Protectorate.

In 1662, the colony of Connecticut broke away from Massachusetts after obtaining a royal charter that consolidated the Fundamental Orders adopted by Connecticut's colonial council in 1639 (Kemp 2010, 37–41). A year later, Charles II granted new colonial proprietorships to Lord Ashley, Earl of Shaftesbury, and Sir John Colleton to exploit the lands between southern Virginia and Spanish Florida. Thus arose in 1663, a new colony dubbed "Carolina" in honor of the English King (from the Latin word for Charles, *Carolus*).

---

tolerance and a society in which, unlike the case in England, Catholicism could be publicly practiced (Patrick and Long 1999, 3–15).

[42] Though he has been called the Father of English Colonization in North America, Ferdinando Gorges (1565–1647) never actually set foot there. Rather, he invested his money sponsoring an expedition in 1605, to explore the coast of the present day state of Maine. In 1607, he was a shareholder of the Plymouth Company, which explored Virginia. In 1622 the Plymouth Council for New England granted Gorges and John Mason a land patent for the Province of Maine. In 1629, they divided the province and Mason received the Province of New Hampshire. It was Ferdinando Gorges's son, Robert Gorges, who actually became Governor General of New England from 1623 to 1624, but he did not last because of his seigneurial ideas about settlement and governance of the colonial lands. Ferdinando Gorges died in 1647, and the Province of Maine was inherited by his eldest son, John. In 1677, a grandson of Ferdinando Gorges, named after his grandfather, sold Maine to Massachusetts. The former remained part of the latter until obtaining statehood in 1820 (Preston 1953).

[43] Earle (2003, 34) highlights the remarkable continuity between Cromwell's ambitious expansion plan for American colonization (Western design) and the colonial policy of Charles II, who managed to reinforce the Commonwealth's policies on overseas trade and colonization.

#### 12.5.4.1 Growing Political and Legal Autonomy

Carolina was a private colony, and its charter granted the colonists settling in it extensive legal, political and administrative autonomy. This was consolidated thanks to its base of laws and help from the philosopher John Locke, then Lord Ashley's secretary, and one of the promoters of Carolina's colonization. Locke assisted in authoring a set of "Fundamental Constitutions" which in general terms followed the model previously established in Virginia and Maryland, and according to which the settlers, in addition to owning their lands, enjoyed great political and legal autonomy.[44] Significant settlement of Carolina began in 1670, when Charlestown (named in honor of King Charles) was founded as the colony's first city.[45] In 1729, the owners of the colony sold it to the crown and King George II split the territory into two provinces: South Carolina and North Carolina.

The proprietary colony model was also used to create New Jersey (1664), Pennsylvania (1681) and Georgia (1733), the latter being the first not-for-profit American colony; its promoters were a group of philanthropists in London, led by James Oglethorpe,[46] determined to give a second chance to "honest people" who had been imprisoned for debt in England. Thus, in 1732 they obtained from George

---

[44] The *Fundamental Constitutions* are usually attributed to John Locke, in collaboration with his patron Anthony Ashley-Cooper, first Earl of Shaftesbury, a leading lord proprietor with a long-standing interest in colonial affairs (Haley 2008). Looking for a career, in 1667, Locke moved into Shaftesbury's home at Exeter House in London, to serve as Lord Ashley's personal physician, and resumed his medical studies under the tutelage of Thomas Sydenham, who had a major impact on his ideas about natural philosophy. The *Fundamental Constitutions* were drafted initially in 1669 during the period of Locke's secretaryship to the Lords Proprietors of Carolina. See Armitage (2004, 602–627). The *Fundamental Constitutions*, however, were not entirely democratic, as they assumed the existence of slavery and defended slaveholders' absolute authority over their chattel. They also erected the first hereditary nobility on North American soil, which may explain why they did not enjoy wide support among early settlers in the south of the province, who preferred a more flexible royal charter as a basis for government. As a result, they were never ratified by the assembly, and were all but forgotten by 1700. However, some of their provisions, such as the guarantee of religious freedom and the modest property requirement for suffrage, helped to determine the political cultures of the Carolinas. On the *Fundamental Constitutions of Carolina* see Hsueh (2002, 425–446) and Milton (1990, 111–133).

[45] Carolina received a first Charter in 1663, and a second in 1665, replaced the same year by the "Concessions and Agreements of the Lords Proprietors of the Province of Carolina", in turn replaced by the "Fundamental Constitutions of Carolina", adopted in March 1669 by the eight lords proprietor of the Province of Carolina, which included most of the land between modern Virginia and Florida.

[46] James Edward Oglethorpe (1696–1785) had served for 5 years in Parliament on 42 different committees dealing with the poor. As a result of this service he became concerned with the situation of debtors, and sat on a committee which studied relief measures for them. Over the years he assisted the poor of Gloucester, youths under the age of 16 who worked as boatmen on the Thames, and shipwrecked sailors. In 1728, he published an unsigned pamphlet called *The Sailors Advocate*, an attack on the common British practice of forcibly recruiting men for the Royal Navy through the use of press gangs (Russell 2006, 5).

II a charter allowing them to create and administrate the new colony "without benefit for themselves" for a period of 21 years.[47]

#### 12.5.4.2 The War Against Holland and the Origins of New York, New Jersey and Delaware (1664–1667)

In 1664, King Charles II of England ordered attacks upon Dutch possessions in North America. In March of that year, prior to the outbreak of war, the English monarch bestowed his brother, the Duke of York (the future James II), with the largest territorial grant ever issued by a British sovereign, encompassing not only the current state of New York, but the entire region between the Connecticut and Delaware rivers. The concession gave the Duke of York immense powers over his American dominions. He did not need the people's consent to enact laws and regulations, he could organize the government as he saw fit, and dispose of his lands however he wished. In fact, the first thing he did was to cede a significant portion of his dominions to two friends: Sir George Carteret and Lord Berkeley, the governor of Virginia's brother. Both thereby became proprietors of what would become New Jersey, a territory which began to be settled in 1665. The need to attract settlers spurred the proprietors to make generous concessions concerning the property terms and the political and legal autonomy to be enjoyed by those establishing themselves in the new colony.[48]

The war with Holland was short and the British were victorious. The conflict ended with the signing of the Westminster Treaty (1667), through which the United Provinces ceded to Britain the territories corresponding to the present-day states of

[47] In 1730, Oglethorpe and a set of philanthropists created a group called the "Trustees for the Establishment of the Colony of Georgia in America", which applied for a charter to settle a charitable colony on land south of the Savannah River. The charter was conceded by George II in April of 1732, setting the colony's borders between the Savannah and Altamaha rivers, westward from their headwaters to the Pacific, and establishing it as a separate province by the name of Georgia. The trusteeship was to last 21 years, after which the Crown would determine the future governance of the colony. The charter established a Common Council of 15 trustees authorized to pass laws and carry out general functions of government, but the Crown and the Privy Council retained the right to veto its legislation. The charter excluded the forming of a legislative assembly, and the free exercise of Catholicism was forbidden (Rabushka 2008, 63).

[48] On the basis of the 1664, concessions, the New Jersey proprietors established six towns. One of them was Newark, founded by dissident Puritan clergy from New Haven, who were dissatisfied with the colony's annexation to Connecticut in 1665. The town was named in honor of Reverend Abraham Pierson after the place he was ordained in England, Newark-on-Trent, in Lincoln County. Abraham's son, a Harvard's graduate, was the founder and first President of Congregational College at New Haven, Connecticut, 1701–1707, later Yale University. The government of the new colony was quite democratic, as each town was authorized to send two representatives to a provincial assembly, and town matters were to be decided by a majority of the local freemen. The first New Jersey assembly convened in May 1668. In 1702, the owners ceded ownership to the Crown and the Royal Province of New Jersey was created (Rabushka 2008, 222 and 349).

New York, Delaware and New Jersey. The city of New Amsterdam became, of course, New York.[49]

#### 12.5.4.3 The Singular Case of Pennsylvania (1681)

Of all the English colonies in North America, the only one that was most truly the work of one man was Pennsylvania. The colony's proprietor, William Penn (*Pennsylvania* meaning "Penn's forest") personally took charge of bringing colonists from Europe, and established a legal system based on the principle of religious freedom, which today constitutes one of the cornerstones of the United States' constitutional system. In 1681, William Penn received from the Duke of York the property for the colony that bears the former's name, and the corresponding charter granted by King Charles II (Soderlund 1983, 39–50). A year later, he personally began to organize the colony, committed to the premise that it would welcome any and all, regardless of their religious beliefs. Symbolically, Penn founded the city of Philadelphia (meaning the "city of brotherly love") prior to setting down the conditions governing the colony in a series of charters which would come to constitute the new colony's constitutional framework.[50]

### *12.5.5 Political Variety and Legal Autonomy of the English Colonies in America*

Based upon the three colonial models examined, 13 colonies were founded between 1607 (the founding of the first colony, Virginia) and 1733 (Georgia, the last), and

[49] The Treaty of Peace and Alliance between the United Netherlands and Great Britain was concluded at Breda on July 21, 1667, and ratified by the Estates General of the United Netherlands on July 28, 1667, and by Charles II on the following August 8. For the text of the treaty and a commentary on it, see Davenport and Paullin (2004, 119–131).

[50] In 1681, was written a document called *Some Account of the Province of Pennsylvania* in which Penn set down the type of settlers he desired, and gave instructions for the journey. *Some Account* was soon translated into German, French and Dutch, and was widely distributed throughout Europe. In 1681, Penn had already written down a first draft of the *Frame of Government*, approved in London on May 5, 1682 (Soderlund 1983, 118–133). A second *Frame of Government* would be approved in the Pennsylvania General Assembly, lasting from March 10 to April 4, 1683 (Soderlund 1983, 265–276). In 1699, William Penn returned to Pennsylvania in what would be his final stay. In 1701, he promulgated a "Charter of Privileges" under which Penn was authorized to name the governor and his advisory council, but legislative power was assigned to an assembly made up of four representatives from each county. Under the terms of the document, the territory of Delaware was allowed to have its own assembly, though it continued to fall under the authority of Pennsylvania's governor. This Charter of Privileges, to remain in force until 1776, sufficed to guarantee the colony's autonomy until it became a state in 1783, and stands as a landmark of religious liberty in American constitutional history (Hutson 2003, 133). For the text of the First Article of the Charter, see Patrick and Long (1999, 22–23).

gradually settled. Despite the diversity of colonial regimes it may be said that the English developed a uniform, basic model of colonial rule in America, though the idea of creating a uniform system of administration in the colonies, bringing all in line with a common type, and rendering them more dependent on the Crown, developed very slowly (Andrews 2004, 37–38). Regardless of whether the colony had been created directly via a royal grant or by the initiative of its settlers, English political and legal institutions were strongly embraced in each American colony. This pattern included the introduction of common law, the concept of private property, the election of an assembly of representatives to discuss common issues, and the development of local administrative systems. The government in London limited itself to retaining the right to veto any action considered contrary to the interests of the Crown in the colonies, and to controlling foreign policy.[51]

Each colony had its own governor, appointed by the king in the royal colonies, and by the proprietors of the private colonies. In the religious colonies, meanwhile, they were elected by the settlers themselves. The governor applied the laws of the colony and appointed intermediate-level officials, summoned and dissolved the assemblies, and took the lead proposing legislation. In principle, the governors could veto laws approved by the assembly, but they did not tend to do so, as they depended financially—even for their own salaries—on the taxes which the assemblies approved.[52] It was the king who generally appointed the top officials and judges, though in the private colonies it was the proprietors who appointed the magistrates. In the religious colonies, jury trials became standard practice, through which the resolution of cases was entrusted to common citizens.

In every colony there was a legislative assembly, their creation and practices modeled on the Parliament of Westminster. Thus, the bicameral structure prevailed, with one chamber more oriented towards the elite, and one more democratic. The latter chamber was elected by the colonists and wielded legislative and financial powers, including the approval of taxes. The franchise requirements varied, though in general all white male adults could vote. In the royal colonies, the members of the upper chambers, the senates, were appointed by the king and their function was to advise the governor. Although theoretically the lower chambers (assemblies) had limited powers, in practice it was these which ended up dominating colonial government.

---

[51] This loose control over the colonies was especially pronounced in New England, where colonists were quite content to effectively ignore those possessing legal authority over them. The few royalists who lived in the colony exercised no influence on the government and were powerless to alter the convictions of the majority (Andrews 2004, 41).

[52] As Andrews (2004, 37) points out, London's attitude towards colonial legislation was vague and ill-defined: though in principle no colony was allowed to make laws contrary to those of England, initially no colony was required to transmit its acts to England for acceptance or rejection. The first such case came with Penn's charter, (1681) after which colonies were, in principle, obliged to report their laws to London within 5 years after their passage. A similar clause was inserted in the Massachusetts charter of 1691, but this colony refused to acknowledge the right of English authorities to invalidate its laws, even when they were contrary to those of England.

Finally, it is important to underscore that each colony had its own "constitutional system" based on the political instrument through which it had been founded—that is, the type of charter or sanction which the colony had received. In most cases there were other rules and regulations stipulated in the royal charters laying down the basic legal framework which was to govern colonial life.[53] In some cases, these regulations took the form of genuine constitutional documents, as in the case of the "Fundamental Constitutions" drafted by John Locke for Carolina, or the "Charter of Privileges" issued in 1701 by William Penn to his colony in Pennsylvania.

Because each colony had been founded for different reasons and under different circumstances, the government in London was slow to consider the king's possessions in the New World as an integrated whole. It is extremely significant that during the first half of the seventeenth century, the English government made scarcely any attempt to control the colonies through a system of agents, as they were only sent when required (Andrews 2004, 36).[54] In fact, the colonies maintained their autonomy until 1754, when the English clashed with their French counterparts settled in modern-day Canada. In the war between these countries, the colonists would receive the unconditional support of the British monarchy, which hitherto had acted as a mere umpire (Hoffmann 2013). For the first time, Britain was forced to directly intervene in territories which, though theoretically subject to it since the seventeenth century, had previously enjoyed considerable autonomy.

## 12.6 The Colonists and the British Crown

At the beginning of the eighteenth century, the English Crown wielded a dubious level of real control over its colonies in North America, among other things because the English kings were too distracted by the political events that shook England between the mid seventeenth century and the arrival of the Hanover Dynasty in 1714.

### *12.6.1 The Colonial Explosion*

Following the Peace of Utrecht (1713), there began, nevertheless, a long period of peace that favored colonial expansion, with the number of English colonists in America rapidly increasing. Where in 1670 there were around 85,000 colonists, by

[53] This is why, for instance, the charter corporations always denied the validity of the acts of Parliament in America unless re-enacted by their own assemblies (Andrews 2004, 37).

[54] On July 4, 1660, the Crown created a Council Committee for Foreign Plantations, which continued to act until 1675, before it was replaced by a council composed of 24 members henceforth known the Lords of Trade. For an overview of the English administration of the colonies during the period of 1660–1689, see Andrews (2004, 22–40).

1713 there were 360,000. The settlements had quadrupled in size by the mid eighteenth century because of massive immigration, not only English, but also Scottish, Irish and German. As a result of these shifts the English kings became more involved in colonial politics: Georgia was founded by the crown in 1733, while a number of colonial proprietors ended up selling their domains to the crown, thereby bolstering royal influence in North America.[55] It would be the full engagement of the British Crown in the affairs of its American colonies which set the stage for war between the British and French colonists in 1754.

### *12.6.2 The First American Intervention of the English Crown: The War Against France*

In the early eighteenth century, the French monarchy had major colonial interests in North America, located in what is today eastern Canada. The growing number of English colonists settling in the New World, sparked increasing tensions with French settlers vying for the fur market, the exploitation of the southern coast of Hudson Bay, and the fishing monopoly in Terranova and Acadia. War loomed for some time on the horizon before finally breaking out in 1754, when a detachment of Virginia militia commanded by a young officer named George Washington attacked a French post. Though the conflict would drag on for 7 years (1754–1760) the two sides were very uneven. William Pitt the Elder, the most important minister in the British cabinet between 1757 and 1761, sent 30,000 troops to occupy Canada and the Ohio Valley.[56] Louis XV, on the other hand, throughout the conflict sent very few reinforcements to its American colonies. Canada was of little interest at the time to the government of his Christian Majesty and to French public opinion, as the war the country was waging in Europe against Frederick II of Prussia was considered more important. Despite being abandoned by their king, the French colonists went on the offensive, led by an extraordinary leader: Louis-Joseph de Montcalm-Gozon, a.k.a. the Marquis of Montcalm, who initially managed to inflict several defeats upon the English. The overwhelming numerical superiority which the British enjoyed, however, supported by their American colonists, would prove decisive. In 1759, the British seized the city of Quebec at the pivotal Battle of the

[55] As Pannu (2005, 105) indicates, after the signing of the Utrecht Treaty for the British government the issue of overseas trade would come to overshadow affairs in Europe—a new priority that opened a new chapter in English politics, initially to be written by William Pitt the Elder.

[56] Pitt's effort was even more extraordinary when one considers that after the peace of Aix-la-Chapelle (1748), England had an army of only 18,000 thousand men, including the garrisons at Menorca and Gibraltar, and six or seven companies in the American colonies. The Royal Navy, meanwhile, had less than 17,000 sailors (Parkman 2008, 16).

Plains of Abraham, in which both General Montcalm and his English adversary, General Wolfe, perished. The following year, Montreal also fell.[57]

Through the Treaty of Paris in 1763 Louis XV had to cede almost all of France's territories in America to England. As Spain had allied with Louis XV in the conflict with England, after the French defeat it was forced to cede the Floridas to the British crown. In compensation, the King of France ceded the city of New Orleans and the part of Louisiana west of the Mississippi to Spain—a massive territory constituting approximately one third of the present-day United States.[58]

### *12.6.3 The Price of Victory*

England had historically allowed its colonists almost complete autonomy, but this would change in the wake of the war against France, which had forced Britain to make considerable outlays to cover the costs of the war effort. The crown decided to make its investment worthwhile by implementing an interventionist policy for the first time in America. This effort, however, came some 150 years late, as the colonists had become accustomed to a virtually autonomous government. George III largely ignored this fact, as he was determined to restore royal authority in his domains, and insisted that the American colonists were indebted to the crown for the war it had won against France. Beginning in 1763, then, Britain's institutional presence began to increase in North America, paving what Dale (2004, 78–85) calls "the road to Revolution".

### *12.6.4 The Fiscal Origins of the Rebellion*

#### 12.6.4.1 The Tax Revolt

The need to quell an Indian rebellion gave the British government the perfect excuse to maintain a small standing army in the 13 colonies for the first time.

---

[57] For an overview of the Seven Years War (or "French and Indian War") see Borneman (2007) and Flower (2006).

[58] The "Spanish interregnum" lasted from 1763 to 1800, when Napoleon recovered the territory from Spain via the Treaty of San Ildefonso (October 1, 1800), though this was not made public until 2 years later. Napoleon sold the territory (828,000 square miles, or 2,140,000 km$^2$) to the US government in 1803, for 15 million dollars (233 million USD, or less than 42 cents per acre) (Fleming 2003). During the American Revolutionary War, the Spanish governor of Louisiana, Bernardo Gálvez (1776–1785), negotiated directly with Thomas Jefferson, supporting the rebels from the very outset. Spain blocked the Port of New Orleans so that British vessels could not use the Mississippi river, and facilitated transport for the Americans throughout the territory, providing them with arms and ammunition (de Reparaz 1993). On the capital figure of Gálvez, see Caughey (1998).

In addition, to better control the governors of the various colonial territories, George III decided that they were to be paid directly by the Crown instead of being compensated by the different colonial assemblies, as had been the previous practice.

This obviously, augmented the cost of maintaining the colonies for the Crown, which sought to pass the expense on to the colonists. To achieve this it first severely repressed smuggling to increase revenue from customs duties. Next, the Westminster Parliament voted to levy a series of indirect taxes, collected via the Stamp Act, the first direct tax (as opposed to tariffs on imported goods) levied by the British after more than 150 years of North American settlement (McCraw 2012, 21) upon the colonists,[59] who responded by rejecting the new taxes, arguing that as British subjects, and according to the constitutional principles of the United Kingdom, they were not obligated to pay any tax which they had not approved. As the American colonists had no representatives in the British Parliament, they asserted, this body had no right to impose taxes on them (White 2012, 61–85).

#### 12.6.4.2 Incidents in Boston (1770–1773)

The unrest created by the "tax dispute" would spark specific incidents which, when exaggerated by the press, exacerbated tensions between London and the colonists. In 1770, there occurred what colonial agitators termed the "Boston Massacre", an incident in which four protestors were killed by British soldiers who had been harassed in the street. In 1773, the "Boston Tea Party" took place when a group of colonists, disguised as Indians, threw some 340 chests of tea overboard from a British ship which had just docked in Boston Harbor in an act protesting the king's plan to monopolize this key product and place a tax upon it.

The incident so infuriated George III that he ordered the closing of Boston Harbor until the people had defrayed the cost of the lost tea. Through the Coercive Acts (Forman 2012, 197), or "Intolerable Acts", as colonial critics called them, the king ordered the dispatch of additional troops to the city, authorized the quartering of soldiers in colonials' homes, and moved to levy additional taxes on articles like lead, paint, paper and glass. In this way, the Boston Tea Party spurred the crown to endorse a series of measures which would ignite fierce resistance and generate wider popular support for revolt against Britain.

[59] The Stamp Tax applied to a wide range of documents, such as newspapers, pamphlets, land grants, attorney's licenses, legal certificates, and even playing cards (Morgan 1995). After the intense uproar following the passage of the Stamp Act in most of the 13 colonies, and by the English merchants who exported goods to America, the British Parliament repealed the Stamp Act in 1766. Yet the British Crown still needed money to finance its American colonial policy, so new taxes followed: the Townshend Act of 1767, which taxed paper, glass, paint, lead and other items, and finally the Tea Act of 1773, which would trigger the Boston Tea Party (McCraw 2012, 22).

### *12.6.5 The First Continental Congress in Philadelphia (1774)*

The colonists of Massachusetts requested assistance from the other 12 colonies. Thus emerged the revolutionary idea of holding an assembly of the 13 colonies to propose a common position in their dealings with England. This body, termed a "congress", gathered in Philadelphia in 1774, and was attended by delegates from all the colonies except Georgia.[60]

The congress issued a "Declaration" which, among other things, affirmed that no subject of the King of England was bound to pay taxes to which he had not consented. It was simultaneously decided that the settlers ought to amass weapons to be able to undertake an armed uprising should this prove necessary. In April 1775, when Britain's General Gage, commanding the British troops stationed in Boston, found out that weapons were being stockpiled in Concord, he resolved to confiscate them. On the night of April 18, 700 British soldiers began marching towards the city. The colonists, however, were forewarned by the celebrated feat of silversmith Paul Revere, who that evening rode from Boston to Lexington (Miller 2010, 188–198) to alert his fellow patriots that the British were coming, allowing the two leaders of the rebellion, John Hancock and Samuel Adams, to muster the militia (minute men).

## 12.7 The War of Independence (1776–1781)

### *12.7.1 The First Armed Clash: The "Battle" at Lexington (April 19, 1775)*

After spending all night awake, 77 militia commanded by Captain Parker formed on the green, awaiting the arrival of the English soldiers. The British troops arrived in Lexington by 5 o'clock. In an initial skirmish, the British killed eight militiamen and drove the rest to Concord, where they were joined by allies who had been watching the maneuvers of the English army from the nearby hills. Entering Concord, the British found no weapons, and proceeded to set fire to the village, which incensed the minute men, who descended from the hills to fight the British

---

[60] As Forman (2012, 198) points out, it was Massachusetts, the province most aggrieved by the Parliamentary acts, that determined the time and the place for this First Continental Congress, which began in Philadelphia on September 1, 1774. This was not, however, the first time colonists had convened a congress, as they had already met in New York City in 1765, for two and a half weeks (between October 7 and 25) in what was called the Stamp Act Congress. As Jillson and Wilson (1994, 41) explain, however, the members of the first Continental Congress never imagined that they and their successors would continue to convene over the course of the next 15 years.

troops. The battle lasted several hours and ended with the defeat of the "redcoats", who retreated to Boston, hounded all the way back by groups of militia. The British lost 250 men in what went down in history as the first battle of the War of Independence (Fischer 1995, 227).

### 12.7.2 *The Second Continental Congress and the Declaration of Independence*

The armed conflict at Lexington triggered the final split between London and the colonies. George III resolved to subjugate the settlers by force of arms, while the rebels, in a Second Continental Congress in Philadelphia, assumed sovereign authority (Ellis 2013, 101–102). This same Congress ordered the formation of an army, whose command was entrusted to George Washington, as we know a Virginia landowner who had military experience as a veteran of the French–Indian War (Maier 1991, 244). In early 1776, the Virginia colonists joined the uprising.

The rebels' situation was extremely precarious. In the first place, most of the colonists were still reluctant to break with the British Crown. Secondly, the leaders of the insurrection were aware that they could not triumph against the English without foreign aid. Thus, they intended to appeal to France and Spain, the two powers which had been humiliated in the Peace of Paris of 1763. Considering it essential to formalize their break with Britain, on July 4, 1776, the members of the Second Continental Congress approved the Declaration of Independence, a document drafted by Thomas Jefferson (Armitage 2007, 157–164).

### 12.7.3 *The Course of the Conflict*

#### 12.7.3.1 The Phase of British Victories (1776–1777)

During the initial months of the war, the British were victorious, in part thanks to the well-trained German mercenaries they employed. The colonial army, meanwhile, lacked professional soldiers and was in disarray.[61] The 13 colonies were very jealous of their own authorities, and considerably reluctant to recognize the authority of a central government, even during wartime. To make matters worse, among the colonists there were a number of "Loyalists"—essentially large landowners and

[61] As Spring (2010, 7) points out, the rebels sought to counter the superiority of the British Army through the strategy of "forward defense", as Washington and his subordinates endeavored to avoid general engagements. The problem with this defensive strategy was that the British, especially when they were supported by the Royal Navy, proved very capable of encircling exposed rebel positions, as happened with the near destruction of the rebel army on Long Island in August of 1776.

merchants—who still did not wish to break with Britain. The rebel troops lacked weapons and shrank from fighting far from their homes. Thus, once they served the stints to which they had committed, they would abandon the front.[62] Finally, the rebels had few good officers and no great general to lead them. Washington himself has been called a mediocre military tactician—though his tenacity, dedication and determination went a long way to making up for his technical shortcomings (Ellis 2013, 25–28).[63]

#### 12.7.3.2 Saratoga

It is, therefore, understandable that the British enjoyed the initial military advantage, quickly able to occupy New York and Philadelphia. They were, however, fighting in a country they did not know, devoid of roads and, at times, even paths (which made provisioning difficult) and blanketed with immense forests which made it easy to ambush the enemy. In fact, this is precisely what happened at Saratoga, on October 17, 1777, where the colonists were able to tend a trap for English General John Burgoyne, who was coming from Canada with reinforcements. Despite their superior numbers and arms, the English were forced to surrender and the rebels scored their first victory of the war (Ferling 2007, 239–241). More important than the military value of victory itself, Saratoga would prove a turning point because it convinced the governments of France and Spain that the colonists were, in fact, capable of defeating the British (Dull 1985, 50–56). Louis XVI and Charles III would soon declare war against George III (Graebner et al. 2011, 41–61 and 63–84).

Foreign intervention would dramatically turn the tide in the war. The French government, in line with a proposal by Foreign Minister Vergennes (Hoffman and Albert 1981), began providing the rebels with equipment and weapons. After

[62] As a striking example, in November of 1776, while the American Army was retreating in New Jersey, they received no assistance from the local militia, nor did civilians provide substantial assistance to the Continental Army. Militiamen did not turn out or remain with their unit when were mustered, and the bulk of residents, many of whom had supported independence, hid their food and valuables as the American Army approached, fearing that the desperate and undisciplined soldiers would plunder or confiscate their property. This attitude contrasted with that of Tory Loyalists, who assisted the British as guides and intelligence gatherers, and carried out reprisals for the attacks they had endured. An armed band of Loyalist even kidnapped Richard Stockton, one of the signers of the Declaration of Independence, and tried to persuade him to recant his support for the Revolution (Ferling 2007, 164–165).

[63] From a military point of view the role played by General Henry Knox was far more decisive. On this relatively unknown figure, see Drew (2012) and Puls (2008). On the participation of George Washington in the War, see Leckie (2008) and Phelps (2001, 165–197). For an overall examination of George Washington as an American revolutionary leader, see Chadwick (2004).

signing a 1778 treaty of alliance with Benjamin Franklin, the rebels' representative in Paris, the French sent General Lafayette to fight with them.[64]

In 1779, Spain joined the alliance in the hope of recovering the two Floridas, Gibraltar and Menorca.[65] The war dragged on for 5 more years. The decisive battle would come in the south, where a French army led by General Rochambeau helped the colonists, led by Colonel Alexander Hamilton, to corner a British army at Yorktown (in southeastern Virginia). The siege continued until the British General Charles Cornwallis was finally forced to surrender on October 17, 1781 (Ferling 2007, 523–539). Despite the decisive defeat, the British took 2 years to sign the peace.

### 12.7.4 *The Peace of Versailles and the Recognition of a New Nation: The United States of America*

In the peace signed at Versailles on September 3, 1783, the 13 colonies officially broke with the British Empire and became a newly independent nation: the United States of America.[66]

In terms of its territory, the new nation stretched west to the Mississippi River on a line beginning at the western tip of Lake Superior and continued down to the south, to what was then part of the Spanish Empire. This wide strip of land is currently made up of the eight states of West Virginia, Ohio, Kentucky, Tennessee, Indiana, Illinois, Michigan and Wisconsin. To the south, the United States bordered on Spanish possessions. Since 1765, much of these formed part of the vast Louisiana territory ceded by France, to which Spain added the two Floridas in 1783, ceded to it by England. Thus, the King of Spain theoretically, held the entire southern coast of the Gulf of Mexico, and two thirds of the territory making up the modern-day United Sates—though most of this land had not actually been settled by the Spanish.[67]

---

[64] For an overview of French intervention on behalf of the rebels, see Chartrand (2004) and Dull (1976).

[65] On Spain's participation in the American War of Independence, see Chávez (2011, 163–176).

[66] Though the Treaty was signed at the Palace of Versailles, in American historiography it has been referred to as the "Treaty of Paris" to prevent confusion with the 1919 treaty which put an end to World War I. On the negotiation of the Treaty, see Kaplan (1983, 431–442) and Meacham (2012, 216–230). For an assessment of the Treaty from the European perspective, see Stockley (2001). For the text of the Treaty signed on September 3, 1783, see Kemp (2010, 143–147).

[67] As Barnes (2003, 93–96) points out, though Britain's defeat restored Spain's North American colonies, with East and West Florida ceded to Spain, the northern boundaries of their territory were never clearly defined, which led Spain, during the first years of the new American republic's life, to claim land north all the way to the Ohio River. Another contentious issue left unresolved by the peace treaty was that of navigation rights on the Mississippi River. Both of these pending questions were ultimately settled by the Treaty of Madrid, signed between Spain and the fledgling US in 1795. In any case, Madrid's Court was strongly motivated to prevent any further expansion of the American republic. The government of Charles III, with the Count of Floridablanca as the monarch's chief minister, feared American expansionism because Spain's colonies in North America, though sparsely populated and weakly defended, were important as a territorial barrier to protect its more valuable colony of Mexico.

## 12.8 The West's First Liberal State

### *12.8.1 From Locke to Jefferson*

The former British colonies' tradition of self-government justified the consolidation of a constitutional regime in which governmental power was severely limited, in accordance with the natural law and social contract theories propounded by John Locke, whose ideas were embraced by the leaders of the American Revolution, including Thomas Jefferson (1743–1826), the author of the Declaration of Independence and the nation's third president, from 1801 to 1809.[68]

John Locke (1632–1704) was not just a thinker and a theorist, but one willing to put his ideas into practice, as he demonstrated by drafting, as mentioned above, the "Fundamental Constitutions" (1669) for the colony of Carolina. For Locke civil society was based on a contract[69] whose purpose was to improve the shortcomings of the state of nature.[70] The "community" (commonwealth)[71] resulting from said

[68] As Arneil (1998, 187) points out, though the degree to which Jefferson was influenced by John Locke is a matter of debate among American historians, particularly the influence of his *Two Treatises of Government* on the composition of the Declaration of Independence, it is clear that Jefferson thought most highly of John Locke; in a 1789 letter he considered Locke, Bacon and Newton to be "the greatest men that ever lived without any exception", (Jefferson 1958, 561) and in another one from 1811 he repeats that they "were my trinity of the three greatest men the world has ever produced" (Jefferson 2006, 304–308).

[69] Men being, as has been said, by nature, all free, equal, and independent, no one can be put out of this estate, and subjected to the political power of another, without his own consent. The only way whereby any one divests himself of his natural liberty, and puts on the bonds of civil society, is by agreeing with other men to join and unite into a community for their comfortable, safe, and peaceable living one amongst another, in a secure enjoyment of their properties, and a greater security against any, that are not of it . . . whosoever, therefore, out of a state of nature unite into a community, must be understood to give up all the power, necessary to the ends for which they unite into society, to the majority of the community, unless they expressly agreed in any number greater than the majority. And this is done by barely agreeing to unite into one political society, which is all the compact that is, or needs be, between the individuals, that enter into, or make up a commonwealth. From *The Second Treatise of Government*, VIII, 95 and 99 (Locke 2012, 44–45).

[70] . . . it is evident, that absolute monarchy, which by some men is counted the only government in the world, is indeed inconsistent with civil society, and so can be no form of civil-government at all: for the end of civil society, being to avoid, and remedy those inconveniencies of the state of nature, which necessarily follow from every man's being judge in his own case, by setting up a known authority, to which every one of that society may appeal upon any injury received, or controversy that may arise, and which every one of the society ought to obey. . . *The Second Treatise of Government*, VII, 90 (Locke 2012, 40).

[71] By commonwealth, I must be understood all along to mean, not a democracy, or any form of government, but any independent community, which the Latines signified by the word *civitas*, to which the word which best answers in our language, is commonwealth, and most properly expresses such a society of men, which community or city in English does not. . . *The Second Treatise of Government*, X, 133 (Locke 2012, 60).

pact had the essential function of guaranteeing the exercise of men's basic (natural) rights, such as liberty, equality, life and property.[72]

American colonists from the beginning embraced private enterprise and had a profound respect for private property.[73] By adopting and formulating this conception (Jensen 1943, 356–379) the new United States, arising as a nation in 1783, became the prototype of the liberal state which would eventually spread throughout Europe in the nineteenth century,[74] a model of state based on constitutional limitations curtailing government's actions in the pursuit of law and order and a rejection of absolutism. In no way was the state to intervene in matters of an economic, social or political nature.[75]

### 12.8.2 *The American Revolution as a Rupture with the Old Order*

While European historians tend to view the colonists' war against England mainly as a struggle for independence, American historians emphasize its "revolutionary" nature (Bonwick 1986, 355–373). The colonists, in their view, not only rebelled against their king but, by virtue of the Declaration of Independence of 1776, created

[72] For an analysis of John Locke's political thought and its influence on Western Public Law, see Loughlin (2010, 383–387).

[73] This conception had important social consequences. As Johnson (1973, 7) points out, the Founding fathers defended a "democracy of property owners". It is significant that John Adams, the second president of the United States, believed that civil society had to find a mean between tyrannical despotism and democratic anarchy. The consequence was that "a society, to be stable, must be based on property" because ownership of things always "breeds responsibility".

[74] For an overview of the American patriots' political ideas, see Baylin (1992) and McDonald (1995).

[75] Beard (2004, 31–51), in his classic economic interpretation of the US Constitution, concluded that the dire economic conditions which the new country suffered after the Revolutionary War, gave rise to the constitutional pact, following a struggle between the interests of the Federalists—mainly bankers, merchants and businessmen—and the Anti-Federalists—essentially small landowners and planters. As the former won the debate, the Union born was an essentially liberal state. For a recent interpretation of this interesting question, see McGuire (2003, 16–48). For an overview of the economic thought that led to the constitutional framing of the new country, see McDonald (2008) and Johnson (1973, 262–312).

a new state inspired by Enlightenment principles[76] and based on a social contract endorsed by the delegates of the states gathered in a series of congresses (Tate 1965, 375–391, and Adams 2001, 122–125).

#### 12.8.2.1 Congresses, Constitutions and Declarations of Rights

The very idea of a congress or a convention, as a meeting called to discuss issues of common interest, was in itself already profoundly novel (Wood 1998, 306–309). In the case of the United States, this assembly was fundamental because each colony featured its own system of government. In fact, the congress was the essential instrument of the process which would ultimately give rise to the new United States of America. The 13 colonies, having become independent states, followed the procedure of convening in a constituent assembly in which representatives of the fledgling states created and approved the texts for state constitutions. The English, as we have seen, had constitutional texts, such as the Magna Carta and the Bill of Rights of 1689, but they never adopted a comprehensive legislative text governing the state's functions. Therefore, by employing written constitutions the 13 new American states marked a new era in the history of western public law. Though the framers of these first constitutions talked about continuity and the need to preserve familiar governmental structures during a time of political unrest, they were committed to state governments (Kruman 1997, 4) based on the new model. Through constituent assemblies the states drafted their own constitutions setting down their organization and governmental principles (Greene 2011, 94–95).[77]

It must be observed that each state's constitutional process was very much affected by the precedent of each colonial charter, enabling each new state to

[76] As Outram (2007, 134) explains, the American Revolution has often been viewed as the context in which Enlightenment ideas and violent regime change, can best be seen in conjunction. It is clear that Americans wished to create a *novus ordo saeculorum* in the New World, though the extent to which the American colonists were inspired by purely Enlightenment ideals in their struggle against British rule is debatable. In fact, the ideologies which fueled the conflict were several, including Puritanism and republicanism, the latter inspired by classical models and Renaissance civic humanists.

[77] As Kruman (1997, 157) explains, it was the British Parliament's assertion of boundless legislative power that convinced the authors of the American constitution that the danger of arbitrary government lay not only in the judiciary, but also in the legislature. They believed that the Westminster Parliament had become tyrannical, as it refused to alter its policies in the face of colonial resistance. It was the fear of this kind of tyranny which led Americans to deny the legislature the authority to draft constitutions. Rather, with one exception, they relied upon provincial congresses and constitutional conventions to draft them. Unlike legislatures, these were transitory bodies made up of members with no permanent interest in the framing of government, which rendered them more apt to draft constitutions. Delegates to the congresses and conventions also assumed the need for the popular approval of the constitutions produced; virtually all of the constituent assemblies convoked new elections to elect new political bodies once the constitution was approved and ratified. This understanding forged the beginnings of a new constitutional tradition that was a genuine creation of a distinctive American polity.

draw up a constitution quickly by closely following the traditions of self-government they had observed during the colonial era (Wood 1998, 134). All of them featured an elected assembly, a governor and a court system. Generally, the power of the governor and the judges was strictly limited, while the legislative assembly was the most powerful body, as the institution directly advocating for the citizens' interests.[78]

The constitutions, in addition, also generally ended up including bills of rights which protected civil liberties against the powers of the new states. The first of these was George Mason's Virginia Declaration of 1776, which had a major impact on all subsequent bills of rights,[79] preceding both the Declaration of the Rights of Man and of the Citizen, approved by the French constituent assembly in 1789, and the US federal Bill of Rights of 1791 (McClellan 2000). It should be emphasized that the amendments contained in the latter, have constitutional status, making them inviolable by the government. The same, however, cannot be said of the French Declaration of 1789, which had merely declarative value.[80]

#### 12.8.2.2 The First Viable Western Republics of the Contemporary Era, Under the Representative Assembly System

In general the governments of the new United States incorporated many of the best aspects of the British constitutional system, including a respect for judicial precedent and the rejection of excessive power, principles which would prove crucial to the American legal system. The essential difference was that they did *not* recognize, of course, the authority of the British monarch, and they formed themselves into republics (Wood 1998, 91–92), a model of state in which the representative assembly took precedence over the governor and his executive power. This democratic tradition led directly to the framing of the first constitutions, which reflected the revolutionary principle that *the people* were America's new "sovereign" (Fritz 2008, 1).

[78] As Adams (2001, 5) points out, the American Revolution differed from the French because it was carried out by a large number of already organized and nearly autonomous political entities: the towns, counties, colonial assemblies, and provincial congresses. For an overview of this original aspect of the United States' constitutional tradition see Dinan (2006) and Fritz (2004, 1327–1369).

[79] The Virginia Declaration of Rights, drafted by George Mason in May of 1776, and amended by Thomas Ludwell Lee and the Virginia Convention, was a clear source of inspiration for Thomas Jefferson when he drafted the Declaration of Independence 1 month later. Despite his key role in the struggle for independence, Mason was for a long time overlooked. On his role in the Revolution, see Broadwater (2006) and Miller (1975). On his constitutional contribution, see Cohen (1988) and Miller (2001). On Mason's contribution to the Declarations of Rights, see Billings (1992, 335–369) Hawkes (1996, 5328–5338), and Polin and Polin (2006, 179–260).

[80] For a comparative legal approach to both Declarations of Rights, see Baker (1994, 154–196).

### 12.8.3 *A Precarious "Union": The Articles of Confederation*

What is certainly confusing about the early structure of the United States of America is that it actually featured two overlapping constitutional processes: one involved each former colony's conversion into an independent state, with its own constitution, bill of rights and government institutions, while the other dealt with the 13 colonies' joint adoption of a union to more effectively and powerfully confront the British crown.[81]

#### 12.8.3.1 The "Continental Congresses"

From the very outset, beginning in 1774, the American rebels began to organize their revolt against England through a series of Continental Congresses, meetings at which representatives from each colony discussed their disputes with the English crown. These "congresses" were not, however, mere gatherings of representatives from the colonies, but genuine constituent assemblies whose objective was to create a new constitutional order (Adams 2001, 25–46). In fact, at the First Continental Congress in Philadelphia in 1774, the colonies adopted a Declaration of Rights affirming every Englishman's right not to pay taxes to which he had not consented, and called for the amassing of weapons in armories to prepare for an armed insurrection. The Second Continental Congress (1775–1776), also meeting in Philadelphia, went a step further, with the Congress no longer a mere meeting of representatives, but rather a sovereign authority[82] which, among other things, authorized it to muster an army. It was this second body which on July 4, 1776, issued the celebrated Declaration of Independence, which began by referring, in large letters, to "The unanimous Declaration of the thirteen United States of America" and went on to state that "these United Colonies are, and of right ought to be, Free and Independent States". After the constitutional phase, however, "Congress" became institutionalized, first as a government body, and ultimately as the "national" legislature (Bernstein 1999, 76–108).

#### 12.8.3.2 The Articles of Confederation: A "Constitution of Constitutions"?

After the War of Independence broke out all of the former colonies, now states, met in a new congress—the third—to approve, in November of 1777, a joint constitutional accord called the Articles of Confederation, which granted a certain degree of

[81] The process was further complicated by the fact that the Continental Congress advised the states on constitution-making (Wood 1998, 130–132).

[82] On the transformation of the Second Continental Congress into a constituent power, see Adams (2001, 81–82).

authority, though limited, to a national Congress (Ellis 2013, 90–100). The Articles of Confederation did not actually go into effect until 1781, after a long, 4-year ratification procedure.[83] The national Congress was henceforth established as the nation's sole collective body authorized to make sovereign decisions binding upon all the states.[84]

This instrument of union, though granting very limited powers to the national government,[85] was fruitful to the extent that under Articles of Confederation system, the insurgents fought the Revolutionary War, which concluded with victory over England, leading to the emergence of a new nation through the Treaty of Paris in 1783.

#### 12.8.3.3 The Weakness of the "Union" and the Crisis of the Democratic Republic

When the war had ended in 1783, despite the fact that legally the former English colonies had become 13 independent states, they decided to retain their ties and recognition of Congressional authority. However, the tenuous institutional ties that bound them together and the lack of a strong executive troubled the ruling classes, who believed it essential that both be reinforced. Thus began a debate which would lead to the drafting of what we know today as the United States Constitution (1787–1789), which called for a federal government featuring broader powers for Congress and a more powerful Executive, to replace the Articles of Confederation regime.[86] As we will see in Chap. 13, the different states did not disappear, but fell

---

[83] The first state to ratify was Virginia, on December 16, 1777, and the last was Maryland, on February 22, 1781. The Articles of Confederation government, the precursor to America's current constitutional framework, would last for 8 years (Jensen 1976, 238).

[84] "Each state retains its sovereignty, freedom, and independence, and every power, jurisdiction, and right, which is not by this Confederation expressly delegated to the United States, in Congress assembled". (Article II). Just as with the Second Continental Congress, the new Congress could do only what the states let it do, which, according to the terms set down in other articles, was not very much (Feinberg 2002, 27).

[85] As Jensen explains (1976, 243), while the Articles of Confederation placed few restraints upon the states, some limits were drawn. No state could receive or send diplomatic representatives, enter into alliances, or sign treaties without the consent of the Congress. Neither could two or more states enter into a confederation without Congressional approval. No state could levy imposts or duties which might interfere with the terms of treaties endorsed by Congress. No treaty made by Congress could interfere with the right of a state to subject foreigners to the same imposts and duties as were levied on its own citizens. The states were not to keep vessels of war in peacetime unless Congress deemed it to be necessary for purposes of defense. Neither could a state maintain troops unless Congress considered them necessary to garrison forts. States were forbidden to declare war without the consent of Congress, except where a sudden invasion would permit of no delay. None of these restraints, however, were a serious check upon the states' sovereignty.

[86] For an overview of the decline of the Articles of Confederation government, see Rakove (2002, 225–45).

under the authority of a robust national government granted authorities and purviews previously assigned to the states.

## TIMELINE

### Fifteenth Century

1492 October 12. Columbus discovers America.
1494 Treaty of Tordesillas between Castile and Portugal.

### Sixteenth Century

1500 Portugal's Cabral discovers Brazil.
1502 Nicolas de Ovando becomes the first governor of La Española (modern-day Dominican Republic and Haiti).
1513 Basque sailor Núñez de Balboa discovers the South Sea (Pacific Ocean).
1519 Hernán Cortés takes the Aztec capital of Tenochtitlan (Mexico).
1522 After 8 months and 10 days of sailing Juan Sebastian Elcano completes the first circumnavigation of the Earth.
1524 Giovanni Verrazano's first trip to North America, on behalf of France's Francis I. He discovers New York Bay.
1533 Francisco Pizarro occupies the Incan capital of Cuzco.
1534 First voyage of Jacques Cartier to Canada. He founds Quebec in 1536.
1540 Francisco Vázquez de Coronado begins his first expedition through the south of the modern-day United States. His journey would last for 2 years.
1584 Sir Walter Raleigh discovers Virginia.

### Seventeenth Century

1607 The first English settlers reach Virginia (John Smith and Pocahontas).
1609 English navigator Henry Hudson discovers the river that still bears his name.
1620 The Mayflower "pilgrims" land at Cape Cod. (On November 11 they sign the "Mayflower Compact".) The first English religious colony is founded at Plymouth. Over time it would evolve into the colony and state of Massachusetts.
1626 Dutchman Peter Minuit buys Manhattan Island from the Indians and founds New Amsterdam.
1630 Boston is founded.
1634 The founding of Maryland, the first "proprietary colony".
1682 William Penn, proprietor of Pennsylvania, founds Philadelphia. In 1701 he grants the colony a "Bill of Rights".

### Eighteenth Century

1733 The founding of Georgia, the last of England's 13 colonies in America.
1754 War breaks out between France and England in North America.
1763 The Peace of Paris is signed. France loses its colonies in North America, which are occupied by England. Under the "Law of Quebec" (1774) the English allow the French colonists to conserve their language, religion and law.
1773 December 16. "Boston Tea Party".
1774 September 5–October 26. The First Continental Congress meets in Philadelphia.
1775 April 19. The first armed clash takes place between colonial militia and English regulars. On May 10 the meetings of the Second Continental Congress begin.
1776 July 4. The Declaration of Independence.
1777 October 17. First victory of the rebels at Saratoga. In November the members of the Second Continental Congress approve the Articles of Confederation.
1778 The government of Louis XIV signs a treat of Alliance with the rebels, represented by Benjamin Franklin.
1781 Surrender of England's General Cornwallis at Yorktown.
1783 September 3. The Peace of Versailles.
1787 September 17. Approval of the federal Constitution by the Continental Congress. (Ratification pending by the states).

## References

Adams, W. P. (2001). *The first American constitutions: Republican ideology and the making of the state constitutions in the revolutionary era* (Expanded ed.). Lanham, MD: Rowman & Littlefield.

Anderson, R. D. (2006). *British universities: Past and present*. London: Hambledon.

Anderson, V. D. J. (1991). *New England's generation: The great migration and the formation of society and culture in the seventeenth century*. Cambridge, UK: Cambridge University Press.

Andrews, C. M. (2004). *Colonial self government: 1652 to 1689*. Whitefish, MT: Kessinger Publishing. (Reprint of the 1904 original edition, New York: Harper and Brothers.)

Armitage, D. (2004). John Locke, Carolina, and the two treatises of government. *Political Theory, 32*(5), 602–627.

Armitage, D. (2007). Thomas Jefferson's "Original Rough Draft" of the declaration of independence. In *The declaration of independence: A global history* (pp. 157–164). Cambridge, MA: Harvard University Press.

Arneil, B. (1998). *John Locke and America: The defence of English colonialism*. Oxford, UK: Clarendon.

Avellán de Tamayo, N. (1999). Los primeros alemanes que llegaron a la provincia de Venezuela en el siglo XVI y algunos de sus descendientes. In J. Á. Rodríguez (Ed.), *Alemanes en las regiones equinocciales* (pp. 35–57). Caracas: Alfadil Ediciones.

Baker, J. W. (2009). *Thanksgiving: The biography of an American holiday*. Lebanon, NH: University of New Hampshire Press.

Baker, K. M. (1994). The idea of a declaration of rights. In D. Van Kley (Ed.), *The French idea of freedom: Origins of the declaration of the rights of man and of the citizen*. Stanford, CA: Stanford University Press.

Barnes, C. (2003). *Native American power in the United States: 1783–1795*. Cranbury, NJ: Associated University Press.

Baylin, B. (1992). *The ideological origins of the American Revolution* (Enlarged ed.). Harvard, MA: Harvard University Press.

Baylin, B. (2012). Terra-Maria. In *The Barbarous years: The peopling of British North America: The conflict of civilizations, 1600–1675* (pp. 117–161). New York: Knopf.

Beard, C. A. (2004). *An economic interpretation of the constitution of the United States*. Mineola, NY: Dover Publications (Reprint of the 1913 edition New York: Macmillan).

Becker, C. L. (1922). *The declaration of independence: A study in the history of political ideas*. New York: Harcourt, Brace, and Co.

Bemiss, S. M. (1993). *Three charters of the Virginia Company of London. With seven related documents: 1606–1621*. Baltimore, MD: Clearfield.

Bernstein, R. B. (1999). Parliamentary principles, American realities: The Continental and Confederation Congresses, 1774–1789. In K. R. Bowling & D. R. Kennon (Eds.), *Inventing congress: Origins & establishment of the first Federal Congress* (pp. 76–108). Athens, OH: Ohio University Press.

Billings, W. M. (1992). 'That All Men Are Born Equally Free and Independent': Virginians and the origins of the Bill of Rights. In P. Conley & J. P. Kaminski (Eds.), *The Bill of Rights and the states: The colonial and revolutionary origins of American liberties* (pp. 335–369). Madison, WI: Madison House.

Bonwick, C. C. (1986). The American Revolution as a social movement revisited. *Journal of American Studies, 20*(3), 355–373.

Borneman, W. R. (2007). *The French and Indian War: Deciding the fate of North America*. New York: Harper Perennial.

Bost, D. H. (2002). Historians of the colonial period: 1620–1700. In R. González Echevarria & E. Pupo-Walker (Eds.), *The Cambridge history of Latin American literature* (Vol. 1, pp. 143–190). Cambridge, UK: Cambridge University Press.

Bown, S. R. (2012). *1494: How a family feud in medieval Spain divided the world in half*. New York: Thomas Dunne Books.

Bradford, W. (2006). *Of Plymouth plantation, 1620–1647*. New York, NY: A. Knopf. (Reprint from the edition of 1856: Boston, MA: Little Brown.)

Brading, D. A. (1987). Bourbon Spain and its American empire. In L. Bethell (Ed.), *Colonial Spanish America* (pp. 112–314). Cambridge, UK: Cambridge University Press.

Brading, D. A. (1998). *The First America: The Spanish Monarchy, Creole Patriots, and the Liberal State, 1492–1867*. Cambridge, MA: Cambridge University Press.

Bremer, F. J. (2003). *John Winthrop. America's forgotten founding father*. Oxford: Oxford University Press.

Breslin, B. (2009). *From words to worlds: Exploring constitutional functionality*. Baltimore, MD: The Johns Hopkins University Press.

Broadwater, J. (2006). *George Mason, forgotten founder*. Chapel Hill, NC: University of North Carolina Press.

Brown, K. W. (2006). Casa de Contratación. In J. M. Francis (Ed.), *Iberia and the Americas: Culture, politics, and history* (Vol. I, p. 179, 3 Vols). Santa Barbara, CA: ABC-CLIO.

Browne, W. H. (Ed.). (1883). Maryland Toleration Act, April 21, 1649. In *Archives of Maryland* (Vol. I, pp. 244–247). Baltimore, MD: Maryland Historical Society.

Browne, S. H. (2003). *Jefferson's call for nationhood: The first inaugural address*. College Station, TX: Texas A&M University Press.
Bunker, N. (2010). *Making haste from Babylon: The Mayflower Pilgrims and their world: A new history*. New York: Knopf.
Burke, E. (1854). Speech on moving his resolutions for conciliation with the colonies (March 22, 1775). In *The works of the right honourable Edmund Burke* (Vol. I, pp. 450–512). London: H. G. Bohn.
Burrell, T. H. (2011). A story of privileges and immunities: From medieval concept to the colonies and United States Constitution. *Campbell Law Review, 34*(1), 7–124.
Caraman, P. (1990). *The lost paradise: The Jesuit Republic in South America*. New York: Dorset Press.
Carsten, F. L. (1947). The origin of the Junkers. *English Historical Review*, (62), 145–178.
Caughey, J. W. (1998). *Bernardo de Gálvez in Louisiana 1776–1783*. Gretna, CA: Pelican Publishing Company.
Chadwick, B. (2004). *George Washington's War: The forging of a Revolutionary leader and the American presidency*. Naperville, IL: Source Books Inc.
Chartrand, R. (2004). *The French army in the American War of independence*. Wellingborough, UK: Oshprey Publishing.
Chávez, T. E. (2011). Spanish policy and strategy. In D. J. Stoker et al. (Eds.), *Strategy in the American War of independence: A global approach* (pp. 163–175). London: Routledge.
Clark, C. (2006). Powers in the land. In *Iron Kingdom: The rise and downfall of Prussia, 1600–1947* (pp. 145–182). Harvard, MA: Harvard University Press.
Cohen, M. B. (Ed.). (1988). *Federalism: The legacy of George Mason*. Fairfax, VA: George Mason University Press.
Craven, W. F. (1932). *Dissolution of the Virginia Company: The failure of a colonial experiment*. New York: Oxford University Press.
Craven, W. F. (1957). *The Virginia Company of London: 1606–1624*. Clearfield, UT: Genealogical Publishing Company.
Cushner, N. P. (2006). *Why have you come here? The Jesuits and the first evangelization of native America*. Oxford, UK: Oxford University Press.
Custalow (Little Bear), L., & Daniel (Silver Star), A. L. (2007). *The true story of Pocahontas: The other side of history*. Golden, CO: Fulcrum Pub.
Dale, R. J. (2004). *The fall of New France: How the French lost a North American Empire, 1754–1763*. Toronto: James Lorimer and Company, Ltd.
Davenport, F. G., & Paullin, C. O. (2004). *European Treaties bearing on the history of the United States and its dependencies*. Washington, DC: Carnegie Institution of Washington.
de Reparaz, C. (1993). *I alone: Bernardo de Gálvez and the taking of Pensacola in 1781: A Spanish contribution to the independence of the United States*. Madrid: Cultura Hispánica.
Dinan, J. J. (2006). *The American state constitutional tradition*. Lawrence, KS: University Press of Kansas.
Dougnac Rodríguez, A. (2004). Las Audiencias Indianas y su trasplante desde la metrópoli. In F. Barrios Pintado (Ed.), *El Gobierno de un mundo. Virreinatos y audiencias en la América Hispana* (pp. 539–586). Cuenca: Ediciones de la Universidad de Castilla-La Mancha.
Drew, B. A. (2012). *Henry Knox and the Revolutionary War trail in western Massachusetts*. Jefferson, NC: McFarland & Co.
Dull, J. R. (1976). *The French Navy and American independence: A study of arms and diplomacy, 1774–1787*. Princeton, NJ: Princeton University Press.
Dull, J. R. (1985). *A diplomatic history of the American Revolution*. New Haven, CT: Yale University Press.
Earle, C. (2003). *A geographical history of crisis and recovery*. Oxford, UK: Rowman & Littlefield.
Elliott, J. H. (1987). Spain and America before 1700. In L. Bethell (Ed.), *Colonial Spanish America* (pp. 59–11). Cambridge, UK: Cambridge University Press.

Elliott, J. H. (2006). *Empires of the Atlantic world: Britain and Spain in America, 1492–1830*. New Haven, CT: Yale University Press.

Ellis, J. J. (2013). *Revolutionary summer: The birth of American independence*. New York: Knopf.

Esbeck, C. H. (2004). Dissent and disestablishment: The Church-State settlement in the early American Republic. *Brigham Young University Law Review*, (4), 1385–1592.

Feinberg, B. S. (2002). *The articles of confederation: The first constitution of the United States*. Brookfield, CT: Twenty First Century Books.

Ferling, J. (2007). *Almost a miracle: The American victory in the war of independence*. Oxford: Oxford University Press.

Feros, A. (2006). *Kingship and Favoritism in the Spain of Philip III: 1598–1621*. Cambridge, UK: Cambridge University Press.

Fischer, D. H. (1995). *Paul Revere's Ride*. New York: Oxford University Press.

Fischer, D. H. (2008). *Champlain's Dream*. New York: Simon and Schuster.

Fisher, J. R. (1997). *The economic aspects of Spanish imperialism in America, 1492–1810*. Liverpool: Liverpool University Press.

Fleming, T. (2003). *The Louisiana Purchase*. Hoboken, NJ: Wiley.

Flint, R., & Flint, S. C. (2011). *The latest word from 1540: People, places, and portrayals of the Coronado Expedition*. Albuquerque, NM: University of New Mexico Press.

Flower, W. M. (2006). *Empires at war: The French and Indian War and the struggle for North America, 1754–1763*. New York: Walker & Co.

Forman, S. (2012). *Dr. Joseph Warren: The Boston tea party, Bunker Hill, and the birth of American liberty*. Gretna, LA: Pelican.

Foster, S. (2012). Charlote Brönte: A vision of individuality. In *Victorian women's fiction: Marriage, freedom, and the individual* (Reprint, pp. 71–109). London: Routledge.

Fritz, C. G. (2004). Fallacies of American constitutionalism. *Rutgers Law Journal, 35*(4), 1327–1369.

Fritz, C. G. (2008). *American sovereigns: The People and America's constitutional tradition before the Civil War*. Cambridge, UK: Cambridge University Press.

Ganson, B. (2003). *The Guaraní under Spanish Rule*. Stanford, CA: Stanford University Press.

Garrard, J. (2002). *Democratisation in Britain: Elites, civil society, and reform since 1800*. New York: Palgrave.

Garriga, C. (2004). Las Audiencias: la justicia y el gobierno de las Indias. In F. Barrios Pintado (coord.), *El Gobierno de un mundo: Virreinatos y audiencias en la América Hispana* (pp. 711–794). Cuenca: Ediciones de la Universidad de Castilla-La Mancha.

Garriga, C. (1994). *La Audiencia y las chancillerías castellanas (1371–1525)*. Madrid: Centro de Estudios Constitucionales.

Gervais, G. (2004). Champlain and Ontario: (1603–35). In R. Litalien & D. Vaugeois (Eds.), *Champlain: The birth of French America* (pp. 180–190). Montréal: McGill-Queen's University Press.

Gleach, F. W. (2000). *Powhatan's world and colonial Virginia: A conflict of cultures*. Lincoln, NE: University of Nebraska Press.

Goodfriend, J. D. (2005). *Revisiting New Netherland: Perspectives on early Dutch America*. Boston, MS: Brill.

Graebner, N. A., Burns, R. D., & Siracusa, J. M. (2011). *Foreign affairs and the founding fathers: From confederation to constitution, 1776–1787*. Santa Barbara, CA: ABC-CLIO.

Greene, J. P. (2011). *The constitutional origins of the American Revolution*. Cambridge, MA: Cambridge University Press.

Grimes, A. P. (1976). Conservative revolution and liberal rhetoric: The declaration of independence. *Journal of Politics, 38*(3), 1–19.

Hagen, W. W. (2003). *Ordinary Prussians-Brandenburg Junkers and Villagers, 1500–1840*. Cambridge, UK: Cambridge University Press.

Haley, K. H. D. (2008). *The first earl of Shaftesbury* (Reprint). Michigan, MI: University of Michigan Press.

Harrisse, H. (1896). *John Cabot, the discoverer of North America, and Sebastian, his son: A chapter of the maritime history of England under the Tudors, 1496–1557*. London: Benjamin Franklin Stevens.

Hatch, C. E., Jr. (2009). *The first seventeen years: Virginia, 1607–1624* (Reprinted). Baltimore, MD: Clearfield Co.

Hawkes, R. T. (1996). An uncommon American hero: George Mason and the Bill of Rights. *Northern Neck of Virginia Historical Magazine, 46*(1), 5328–5338.

Hilton, C. (2005). *Mayflower: The voyage that changed the world*. Stroud, UK: Sutton.

Hodgson, G. (2006). *A great and godly adventure: The Pilgrims and the myth of the first thanksgiving*. New York: Public Affairs.

Hoffer, P. C. (1997). *The Salem witchcraft cases: A legal history*. Lawrence, KS: University Press of Kansas.

Hoffman, R., & Albert, P. J. (1981). *Diplomacy and revolution: The Franco-American alliance of 1778*. Charlottesville, VA: University of Virginia Press.

Hoffmann, E. C. (2013). To compel acquiescence: Or, how federalism replaced empire with umpire, 1648–1789. In *American Umpire* (pp. 21–51). Cambridge, MA: Harvard University Press.

Hoig, S. (2013). *Came men on horses: The conquistador expeditions of Francisco Vázquez de Coronado and Don Juan de Oñate*. Boulder: University Press of Colorado.

Holmes, P. (1970). *A tercentenary history of the Boston Public Latin School: 1635–1935*. Westport, CT: Greenwood.

Hoobler, D. T. (2006). *Captain John Smith: Jamestown and the Birth of the American Dream*. Hoboken, NJ: Wiley.

Horwitz, P. (2012). Where ideas begin: Universities and Schools. In *First amendment institutions* (pp. 107–143). Harvard, MA: Harvard University Press.

Hsueh, V. (2002). Giving orders: Theory and practice in the fundamental constitutions of Carolina. *Journal of the History of Ideas, 63*(3), 425–446. (Also in Hsueh, V. (2010). *Hybrid constitutions: Challenging legacies of law, privilege, and culture in colonial America* (pp. 55–82). Durham, NC: Duke University Press.)

Hutson, J. (2003). *Forgotten features of the founding: The recovery of religious themes in the early American Republic*. Lanham, MD: Lexington Books.

Jacobs, J. (2009). *The Colony of New Netherland. A Dutch settlement in seventeenth-century America* (2nd ed.). Ithaca, NY: Cornell University Press.

Jaenike, W. F. (2008). *Black robes in Paraguay: The success of the Guaraní missions hastened the abolition of the Jesuits*. Minneapolis, MN: Kirk House.

Jefferson, T. (1854). First inaugural address, on 4 March 1801. In *The writings of Thomas Jefferson: Being his autobiography, correspondence, reports, messages, addresses, and other writings, official and private. Published by the order of the Joint Committee of Congress on the Library, from the original manuscripts, deposited in the Department of State* (Vol. VIII, p. 1). New York: J. C. Riker.

Jefferson, T. (1958). Letters to John Trumbull, Paris January, 18, 1789 and February 15, 1789. In J. P. Boyd (Ed.), *The papers of Thomas Jefferson: 8 October 1788–26 March 1789* (Vol. XIV, pp. 467, 468 and 561). Princeton, NJ: Princeton University Press.

Jefferson, T. (2006). Letter to Dr. Benjamin Rush, Monticello, January 16, 1811. In J. J. Looney (Ed.), *The papers of Thomas Jefferson: 12 August 1810 to 17 June 1811. Retirement series* (Vol. III, pp. 304–308). Princeton, NJ: Princeton University Press.

Jensen, M. (1943). The idea of a national government during the American Revolution. *Political Science Quarterly, 58*(3), 356–379.

Jensen, M. (1976). *The articles of confederation: An interpretation of the social-constitutional history of the American Revolution, 1774–1781*. Madison, WI: The University of Wisconsin Press.

Jillson, C. C., & Wilson, R. K. (1994). *Congressional dynamics: Structure, coordination and choice in the first American Congress, 1774–1789*. Stanford, CA: Stanford University Press.

Johnson, C. H. (2006). *The mayflower and her passengers*. Bloomington, IN: Xlibris Corporation.

Johnson, E. A. J. (1973). *The foundations of American economic freedom: Government and enterprise in the age of Washington*. Minneapolis, MN: University of Minnesota Press.

Jones, C. (2006). *The history and future of Narragansett Bay*. Boca Raton, FL: Universal Publishers.

Kaplan, L. S. (1983). The treaty of Paris, 1783: A historiographical challenge. *International History Review, 5*(3), 431–442.

Kemp, R. L. (Ed.). (2010). *Documents of American democracy: A collection of essential works*. Jefferson, NC: McFarland and Company.

Kruman, M. W. (1997). *Between authority and liberty: State constitution making in revolutionary America*. Chapel Hill, NC: University of North Carolina Press.

Kupperman, K. O. (Ed.). (1988). *Captain John Smith: A select edition of his writings*. Chapel Hill, NC: University of North Carolina Press.

Kupperman, K. O. (2007). *Roanoke: The abandoned colony* (2nd ed.). Lanham, UK: Rowman & Littlefield.

Kuzmics, H., & Axtmann, R. (2007). *Authority, state and national character: The civilizing process in Austria and England, 1700–1900*. Aldershot, UK: Ashgate.

Leckie, R. (2008). *George Washington's War: The Saga of the American Revolution*. New York: Paws Prints.

Locke, J. (2012). *The second treatise of government and a letter concerning toleration*. Mineola, NY: Courier Dover Publications.

Lockhart, J., & Schwartz, S. B. (1999). *Early Latin America: A history of colonial Spanish America and Brazil*. Cambridge, UK: Cambridge University Press.

Loker, A. (2006). *Walter Ralegh's Virginia: Roanoke Island and the lost colony*. Williamsburg, VA: Solitude Press.

Loughlin, M. (2010). *Foundations of public law*. Oxford: Oxford University Press.

Love, R. S. (2006). *Maritime exploration in the age of discovery, 1415–1800*. Westport, CT: Greenwood.

Maclear, J. F. (Ed.). (1995). *Church and state in the Modern Age: A documentary history*. Oxford: Oxford University Press.

Mahoney, J. (2010). *Colonialism and postcolonial development: Spanish America in comparative perspective*. Cambridge, UK: Cambridge University Press.

Maier, P. (1991). *From resistance to revolution: Colonial radicals and the development of American opposition to Britain, 1765–1776*. New York: W.W. Norton.

Maier, P. (1998). *American scripture: Making the declaration of independence*. New York: Knopf.

Marchand, P. (2009). *Ghost Empire: How the French almost conquered North America*. Westport, CT: McClelland & Stewart.

McAlister, L. N. (1989). *Spain and Portugal in the New World: 1492–1700*. Minneapolis, MN: University of Minnesota Press.

McClellan, J. (2000). America's first constitutions and declarations of rights: The first state constitutions, 1776–1783. In *Liberty, order, and justice: An introduction to the constitutional principles of American Government* (3rd ed., pp. 89–240). Indianapolis, IN: Liberty Fund.

McCraw, T. K. (2012). *The founders and finance how Hamilton, Gallatin, and other immigrants forged a new economy*. Harvard, MA: Harvard University Press.

McDonald, F. (1995). *Novus Ordo Seclorum: The intellectual origins of the constitution*. Lawrence, KS: University Press of Kansas.

McDonald, F. (2008). *We the people: The economic origins of the constitution* (4th printing). New Brunswick, NJ: Transaction Publishers.

McGuire, R. A. (2003). *To form a more perfect Union: A new economic interpretation of the United States constitution*. Oxford: Oxford University Press.

McNeese, T. (2009). Peter Minuit takes charge. In *New Amsterdam* (pp. 63–72). New York: Infobase Publishing.

Meacham, J. (2012). *Thomas Jefferson: The art of power*. New York: Random House.

Menard, R. R., & Carr, L. G. (1982). The Lords Baltimore and the colonization of Maryland. In D. B. Quinn (Ed.), *Early Maryland in a wider world* (pp. 167–215). Detroit, MI: Wayne State University Press.
Miller, H. H. (1975). *George Mason: Gentleman revolutionary*. Chapel Hill, NC: University of North Carolina Press.
Miller, H. H. (2001). *George Mason, Constitutionalist* (Reprint). Cambridge, MA: Harvard University Press.
Miller, J. J. (2010). *The revolutionary Paul Revere*. Nashville, TN: Thomas Nelson.
Milton, J. R. (1990). John Locke and the fundamental constitutions of Carolina. *Locke Newsletter*, *21*, 111–133. (Reprinted in Dunn, J., & Harris, I. (Eds.). (1997). *Locke* (Vol. 2, pp. 463–485). Cheltenham: Edward Elgar.)
Monaghan, E. J. (2005). *Learning to read and write in colonial America*. Boston, MA: University of Massachusetts Press.
Morgan, H. M. (1995). *The Stamp Act crisis: Prologue to revolution*. Chapel Hill, NC: University of North Carolina Press.
Morrison, S. E. (1995). *The founding of Harvard College*. Cambridge, MA: Harvard University Press.
Newitt, M. D. D. (2005). *A history of Portuguese overseas expansion, 1400–1668*. London: Routledge.
O'Day, R. (1982). *Education and society, 1500–1800: The social foundations of education in early modern Britain*. London: Longman.
Ober, F. A. (2011). *John and Sebastian Cabot* (Reprinted ed.). El Paso, TX: Ulan Press.
Osgood, H. L. (1904–1907). *The American colonies in the seventeenth century* (3 Vols). New York: The Macmillan company. (Also The proprietary province as a form of Colonial Government. *The American Historical Review*, *2*(4), 644–664; *3*(1), 31–55 and *3*(2), 244–265.)
Outram, D. (2007). *The enlightenment* (Third Printing). Cambridge, UK: Cambridge University Press.
Pannu, M. S. (2005). *Partners of British Rule*. Mumbai: Allied Publishers Private.
Parkman, F. (2008). *Montcalm and Wolfe: The French and Indian War*. Stilwel, KS: Dirigeads.
Patrick, J. J., & Long, G. P. (Eds.). (1999). *Constitutional debates on freedom of religion: A documentary history*. Westport, CT: Greenwood.
Perkin, H. (2002). *The origins of modern English society: 1780–1880* (2nd ed.). London: Routledge.
Phelps, G. A. (2001). The republican general. In D. Higginbotham (Ed.), *George Washington reconsidered* (pp. 165–197). Charlottesville, VA: The University Press of Virginia.
Philbrick, N. (2006). *Mayflower: A story of courage, community, and war*. New York: Viking.
Pietsch, T. (2013). *Empire of scholars: Universities, networks and the British academic world, 1850–1939*. Manchester, UK: Manchester University Press.
Polin, R., & Polin, C. (2006). *Foundations of American political thought*. Oxford: Peter Lang.
Preston, R. A. (1953). *Gorges of Plymouth Fort: A life of Sir Ferdinando Gorges, Captain of Plymouth Fort, Governor of New England, and Lord of the Province of Maine*. Toronto: University of Toronto Press.
Price, D. A. (2003). *Love and Hate in Jamestown: John Smith, Pocahontas, and the start of a new nation*. New York: Random House.
Price, R. (1999). *British society, 1680–1880: Dynamism, containment, and change*. Cambridge, UK: Cambridge University Press.
Puls, M. (2008). *Henry Knox: Visionary general of the American Revolution*. New York: Palgrave Macmillan.
Rabushka, A. (2008). *Taxation in Colonial America*. Princeton, NJ: Princeton University Press.
Rakove, J. N. (2002). The collapse of the articles of confederation. In J. Barlow et al. (Eds.), *The American founding: Essays on the formation of the constitution* (pp. 225–245). Westport CN: Greenwood Press.

Roper, L. H., & Van Ruymbeke, B. (2007). Introduction. In L. H. Roper & B. Van Ruymbeke (Eds.), *Constructing early modern empires: Proprietary ventures in the Atlantic world, 1500–1750* (pp. 1–20). Leiden: Brill NV.

Rosenheim, J. M. (1998). *The emergence of a ruling order: English landed society, 1650–1750*. London: Longman.

Russell, D. L. (2006). *Oglethorpe and Colonial Georgia: A history, 1733–1783*. Jefferson, NC: McFarland and Company.

Russell-Wood, A. J. R. (2007). Patterns of settlement in the Portuguese Empire, 1400–1800. In F. Bethencourt & D. R. Curto (Eds.), *Portuguese oceanic expansion: 1400–1800* (pp. 161–196). Cambridge, UK: Cambridge University Press.

Sanz Camañes, P. (2004). *Las ciudades en la América hispana: siglos XV al XVIII*. Madrid: Silex ediciones.

Sargent, M. L. (1993). Strangers on the earth: William Bradford, the Epistle to the Hebrews, and the Plymouth 'Pilgrims'. *Fides et Historia*, (24), 8–41.

Schutz, J. A. (1997). *Legislators of the Massachusetts General Court: 1691–1780. A biographical dictionary*. Austin, TX: Thomson-Shore.

Shuttleworth, S. (2004). *Charlotte Brönte and Victorian psychology*. Cambridge, UK: Cambridge University Press.

Soderlund, J. R. (Ed.). (1983). *William Penn and the founding of Pennsylvania, 1680–1684: A documentary history*. Philadelphia: University of Pennsylvania Press.

Soffer, R. N. (1994). *Discipline and power: The University, history, and the making of an English elite, 1870–1930*. Stanford, CA: Stanford University Press.

Spring, M. H. (2010). *With zeal and with bayonets only: The British army on campaign in North America, 1775–1783*. Norman, OK: University of Oklahoma Press.

Steinbach, S. L. (2012). *Understanding the Victorians: Politics, culture and society in nineteenth-century Britain*. New York: Routledge.

Steinweis, A. E., & Rachlin, R. D. (Eds.). (2013). *The law in Nazi Germany: Ideology, opportunism, and the perversion of justice*. New York: Berghahn Books.

Stephens, W. B. (1998). *Education in Britain: 1750–1914*. Basingstoke: Macmillan.

Stick, D. (1993). *Roanoke Island: The beginnings of English America*. Chapel Hill: University of North Carolina Press.

Stockley, A. (2001). *Britain and France at the birth of America: The European powers and the peace negotiations of 1782–1783*. Exeter: University of Exeter Press.

Tapia, F. X. (1966). *El cabildo abierto colonial: un estudio de la naturaleza y desarrollo del cabildo abierto durante los tres siglos de la administración colonial española en América*. Madrid: Ediciones Cultura Hispánica.

Tate, T. W. (1965). The social contract in America, 1774–1787: Revolutionary theory as a conservative instrument. *The William and Mary Quarterly, Third Series, 22*(3), 375–391.

Tocqueville, A. (2010). *Democracy in America*. New York: New American Library. (Translation of *De la démocratie en Amérique*. (1848). Paris: Pagnerre.)

Tyerman, C. (2000). *A history of Harrow school: 1324–1991*. Oxford: Oxford University Press.

Vallejo García-Hevia, J. M. (2008). *Juicio a un conquistador: Pedro de Alvarado*. Madrid: Marcial Pons.

Vile, J. R. (2010). *A companion to the United States constitution and its amendments* (5th ed.). Santa Barbara, CA: Greenwood.

Wakelyn, J. L. (2006). *America's founding charters: Primary documents of colonial and revolutionary era governance*. Westport, CT: Greenwood.

Weber, D. J. (2009). *The Spanish frontier in North America*. New Haven, CT: Yale University Press.

Weber, M. (2008). National character and the junkers. In S. Kalber (Ed.), *Max Weber: Readings and commentary on modernity* (pp. 163–168). Oxford: Wiley.

White, G. E. (2012). The political economy of the original constitution. *Harvard Journal of Law & Public Policy, 35*(1), 61–85.

Wood, G. (1998). *The creation of the American Republic: 1776–1787*. Chapel Hill, NC: University of North Carolina Press.
Wood, G. S. (1993). *The radicalism of the American Revolution: How a revolution transformed a monarchical society into a democratic one unlike any that had ever existed*. New York: Vintage Books.

## Further Reading

Abrams, A. U. (1999). *The Pilgrims and Pocahontas: Rival myths of American origin*. Boulder, CO: Westview.
Ackerman, B., & Katyal, N. (1995). Our unconventional founding. *The University of Chicago Law Review, 62*(2), 475–573.
Axtell, J. (1995). *Rise and fall of the Powhatan Empire: Indians in seventeenth-century* Virginia. Williamsburg, VA: Colonial Williamsburg Foundation.
Baylin, B. (2011). The structure of colonial politics. In *The origins of American politics* (pp. 59–160). New York: Random House.
Bederman, D. J. (2008). *The classical foundations of the American Constitution: Prevailing wisdom*. Cambridge: Cambridge University Press.
Belz, H. (1998). *A living constitution or fundamental law? American constitutionalism in historical perspective*. Oxford: Rowman & Littlefield.
Bemis, S. M. (2009). *The diplomacy of the American Revolution* (Reprint). LaVergne, TN: Hesperides Press.
Bernstein, R., & Rice, K. S. (1987). *Are we to be a nation? The making of the constitution*. Cambridge, MA: Harvard University Press.
Bessette, J. M. (1997). *The mild voice of reason: Deliberative democracy and American national government*. Chicago, IL: University of Chicago Press.
Bolton, H. E., & Marshall, T. M. (2005). *The colonization of North America: 1492 to 1783*. Whitefish, MT: Kessinger Publishing. (Reprint from the original edition. New York: The Macmillan Company 1920.)
Carlisle, R. P., & Golson, J. G. (Eds.). (2007). *Colonial America from settlement to the revolution*. Santa Barbara, CA: ABC-CLIO.
Clemens, P. G. E. (2008). *The Colonial era*. Oxford: Blackwell.
Cogliano, F. D. (2009). *Revolutionary America, 1763–1815: A political history*. London: Routledge.
Conway, S. (1995). *The war of American independence, 1775–1783*. London: E. Arnold.
Dickinson, H. T. (2008). *British pamphlets on the American Revolution, 1763–1785*. London: Pickering & Chatto.
Draper, T. A. (1996). *Struggle for power: The American Revolution*. Boston: Little Brown.
Dworkin, R. (2005). *Freedom's law: The moral reading of the American Constitution* (Reprint ed.). Cambridge, MA: Harvard University Press.
Egnal, M. (2010). *A mighty empire: The origins of the American Revolution*. Ithaca, NY: Cornell University Press.
Fortescue, J. W., Sir. (2010). *The war of independence: The British army in North America 1775–1783*. London: Greenhill Books (2001). (Reprint from the edition first published in 1903 and revised in 1911.)
Fritz, C. G., & Baum, M. L. (2000). American constitution-making: The neglected state constitutional sources. *Hastings Constitutional Law Quarterly, 27*(2), 199–242.
Gammon, C. L. (2012). *The story of the first continental congress*. Savannah, GA: Union Camp Press.

Gerber, S. D. (1996). *To secure these rights: The declaration of independence and constitutional interpretation.* New York: The New York University Press.
Gerber, S. D. (2011). *A distinct judicial power: The origins of an independent judiciary, 1606–1787.* Oxford: Oxford University Press.
Gerstenberger, H. (2009). *Impersonal power: History and theory of the bourgeois state.* Chicago: Haymarket Books.
Gordon-Reed, A. (2009). Thomas Jefferson. In *The Hemingses of Monticello: An American Family* (Reprinted ed., pp. 91–112). New York: W. W. Norton.
Hibbert, C. (2002). *Redcoats and rebels: The American Revolution through British eyes.* New York: W. W. Norton.
Hoffert, R. W. (1992). *A politics of tensions: The articles of confederation and American political ideas.* Niwot, CO: University Press of Colorado.
Horn, J., et al. (Eds.). (2002). *The revolution of 1800: Democracy, race, and the new republic.* Charlottesville, VA: University of Virginia Press.
Jacobs, J. (2005). *New Netherland: A Dutch colony in seventeenth-century America.* Leiden: Brill.
Jensen, M., & Becker, R. A. (Eds.). (1976). *The documentary history of the first Federal elections: 1788–1790.* Madison, WS: University of Wisconsin Press.
Jensen, M. (1981). *The new nation: A history of the United States during the confederation, 1781–1789.* Boston, MA: Northeastern University Press.
Jensen, M. (2004). *The founding of a nation: A history of the American Revolution 1763–1776.* Indianapolis, IN: Hacket Publishing.
Jillson, C. (2009). *American government: Political change and institutional development* (5th ed.). New York: Routledge.
Johnson, G. R. (1991). *The will of the people: The legacy of George Mason.* Fairfax, VA: George Mason University Press.
Kamen, H. (2003). *Spain's road to empire: The making of a world power, 1492–1763.* London: Penguin.
Kaplan, L. (1980). *Colonies into nation: American diplomacy, 1763–1801.* New York: Macmillan.
Klaist, J., & Hazel, M. J. (Eds.). (1991). *Liberty/liberté: The American and French experiences.* Washington, DC: Woodrow Wilson Center Press.
Kramer, L. (2004). *The people themselves: Popular constitutionalism and judicial review.* Oxford: Oxford University Press.
Lepore, J. (2012). *The story of America: Essays on origins.* Princeton, NJ: Princeton University Press.
Levinson, S. (2012). *Constitutional faith.* Princeton, NJ: Princeton University Press.
Martello, R. (2000). Paul Revere's last ride: The road to rolling Copper. *Journal of the Early Republic, 20*(2), 219–239.
McDonald, F. (1997). *E Pluribus Unum: The formation of the American Republic, 1776–1790* (2nd ed., 5th repr.). Indianapolis, IN: Liberty Fund.
McMichael, F. A. (2008). *Atlantic loyalties: Americans in Spanish West Florida, 1785–1810.* Athens, GA: University of Georgia Press.
Middlekauff, R. (2005). *The Glorious cause: The American Revolution, 1763–1789* (Revised ed.). Oxford: Oxford University Press.
Morgan, E. S. (2013). *The birth of the Republic, 1763–89* (4th ed.). Chicago, IL: University of Chicago Press.
Morgan, E. S., & Oats, L. (2008). Accounting for the Stamp Act crisis. *Accounting Historians Journal, 35*(2), 101–143.
Morgan, T. (1993). *Wilderness at dawn. The settling of the North American continent.* New York: Simon and Schuster.
Morris, R. B. (1970). *The peacemakers: The great powers and American independence.* New York: Harper and Row.
Morris, R. B. (1987). *The forging of the Union, 1781–1789.* New York: Harper and Row.
Mulder, P. N. (2007). *Colonial America and the early republic.* Burlington, VT: Ashgate.

Nash, G. B. (2006). *The unknown American Revolution: The unruly birth of democracy and the struggle to create America*. London: Jonathan Cape.

Panetta, R. G. (2009). *Dutch New York: The roots of Hudson valley culture*. New York: Fordham University Press.

Philbrick, N. (2013). *Bunker Hill: A city, a siege, a revolution*. New York: Viking.

Pickett, M. F., & Pickett, D. W. (2011). *The European struggle to settle North America: Colonizing attempts by England, France and Spain, 1521–1608*. North Carolina: McFarland.

Purcell, E. A. (2008). *Originalism, federalism, and the American constitutional enterprise: A historical inquiry*. New Haven, CT: Yale University Press.

Rakove, J. N. (1982). *The beginnings of national politics: An interpretive history of the continental congress*. Baltimore, MD: John Hopkins University Press.

Rakove, J. N. (1996). *Original meanings: Politics and ideas in the making of the constitution*. New York: Knopf.

Raphael, R. (2012). *A people's history of the American Revolution: How common people shaped the fight for independence*. New York: The New Press.

Richter, D. K. (2003). *Facing East from Indian country: A native history of early America*. Cambridge, MS: Harvard University Press.

Roper, L. H. (2009). *The English Empire in America, 1602–1658: Beyond Jamestown*. London: Pickering and Chatto.

Rowland, K. (2004). *Mason. The life of George Mason, 1725–1792: Including his speeches, public papers, and correspondence*. Farmington Hills, MI: Thomson Gale. (Reproduction of original edition. New York: G.P. Putnam's Sons, 1892.)

Rutland, R. A. (Ed.). (1970). *Mason's papers: The Papers of George Mason, 1725–1792* (3 Vols). Chapel Hill, NC: University of North Carolina Press.

Rutland, R. A. (2009). *George Mason: Reluctant statesman* (13th printing). Baton Rouge, LA: Louisiana State University Press.

Schlesinger, A. M. (1935). The colonial newspapers and the Stamp Act. *The New England Quarterly*, *8*(1), 63–83.

Shannon, T. J., & Gellmann, D. N. (2013). *American odysseys: A history of colonial North America*. Oxford: Oxford University Press.

Smith, J. (1988). To the most high and vertuous Princesse Queene Anne of Great Brittanie (letter, 1617). In K. O. Kupperman (Ed.), *Captain John Smith: A select edition of his writings* (pp. 67–71). Chapel Hill, NC: University of North Carolina Press.

Taylor, A. (2013). *Colonial America: A very short introduction*. Oxford: Oxford University Press.

Thomas, P. D. G. (1975). *British politics and the Stamp Act crisis: The first phase of the American Revolution, 1763–1767*. Oxford: Clarendon.

Townsend, C. (2004). *Pocahontas and the Powhatan dilemma*. New York: Hill and Wang.

Triber, J. E. (1998). *A true republican: The life of Paul Revere*. Amherst, MA: University of Massachusetts Press.

Truxillo, C. A. (2001). *By the sword and the cross: The historical evolution of the Catholic world monarchy in Spain and the New World, 1492–1825*. Westport, CT: Greenwood.

Urofsky, M. I., & Finkelman, P. (2001–2002). *A march of liberty: A constitutional history of the United States*. Oxford: Oxford University Press.

Wilentz, S. (2006). *The rise of American democracy: Jefferson to Lincoln*. New York: W. W. Norton.

Wilson, T. D. (2012). *The Oglethorpe plan: Enlightenment design in Savannah and beyond*. Charlottesville, VA: University of Virginia Press.

Wood, G. S. (1992). Democracy and the American Revolution. In J. Dunn (Ed.), *Democracy: The unfinished journey, 508 BC to AD 1993* (pp. 91–106). Oxford: Oxford University Press.

Wood, G. S. (2010). Founding amateurs? *The New York Times Upfront*, *143*, A25.

Wood, G. S. (2010). *The articles of confederation and the constitution: A lecture*. El Paso, TX: The University of Texas Press.

Wood, W. J. (2003). *Battles of the Revolutionary War, 1775–1781*. Chapel Hill, NC: Da Capo Press.

Woodard, C. (2011). *American nations: A history of the eleven rival regional cultures of North America*. New York: Viking.

Woolley, B. (2007). *A savage kingdom: Virginia and the founding of English America*. London: Harper Press.

Woolley, B. (2007). *Savage kingdom: The true story of Jamestown, 1607, and the settlement of America*. New York: HarperCollins Pub.

# Chapter 13
# From Absolute Monarchy to Democratic Absolutism: The French Revolution

Because you are a great gentleman, you believe yourself a great genius! ... Nobility, fortune, a rank, charges, it all turns one so arrogant! What you have done for (to deserve) so many things? You made the effort upon your birth, and nothing else. In every other way you are quite an ordinary man; whereas I, by God, lost in the anonymous mass, have had to draw upon greater wisdom and wiles just to survive than those necessary to govern the entire Spanish Empire in the last hundred years.—Pierre-Augustin de Beaumarchais (1732–1799)[1]

Whoever makes peaceful revolution impossible, makes violent revolution inevitable.—John Fitzgerald Kennedy (1917–1963)[2]

All revolutions fail that do not become part of customs and ideas.[3]—François René de Chateaubriand (1768–1848)

## Contents


13.1 A Turning Point in European Constitutional History .................................. 372
13.2 The Monarchy as the Historical Basis of the French State ............................ 373
13.2.1 From Clovis I to Charlemagne ................................................ 374
13.2.2 A Hereditary, Sovereign and Territorial Monarchy .......................... 375
13.2.3 The Hundred Years' War and the Bolstering of Monarchical Prestige and Power .................................................................... 376
13.2.4 The Era of Absolutism: Louis XIV's Monarchy as a Landmark Reign ...... 377


[1] *Parce que vous êtes un grand seigneur, vous vous croyez un grand génie!... Noblesse, fortune, un rang, des places, tout cela rend si fier! Qu'avez-vous fait pour tant de biens? Vous vous êtes donné la peine de naître, et rien de plus. Du reste, homme assez ordinaire; tandis que moi, morbleu! perdu dans la foule obscure, il m'a fallu déployer plus de science et de calculs pour subsister seulement, qu'on n'en a mis depuis cent ans à gouverner toutes les Espagnes* de Beaumarchais (2008, 192).

[2] Taken from a speech given by John Fitzgerald Kennedy in the White House on the occasion of the first anniversary of the Alliance for Progress during a reception for the diplomatic corps of the Latin American Republics. March 13, 1962 Kennedy (1962, 223).

[3] *Toute révolution qui n'est pas accomplie dans les moeurs et dans les idées échoue.* Chateaubriand (1845, 81).

 
B. Aguilera-Barchet, *A History of Western Public Law*,
DOI 10.1007/978-3-319-11803-1_13

13.3 From the *Ancien Régime* to the Revolution .... 378
13.3.1 Louis XV and the Decline of the French Monarchy .... 378
13.3.2 Reactionary Forces Prevail in French Society .... 381
13.4 The French Revolution .... 384
13.4.1 From the Revolt of the Privileged to the Estates General .... 384
13.4.2 The Estates General .... 386
13.4.3 From the Estates General to the Rebellion of the Third Estate (May 5–June 27, 1789) .... 388
13.4.4 The Rebellion of the Third Estate .... 389
13.4.5 The Two Revolutions .... 391
13.4.6 From Monarchy to Republic .... 392
13.5 What Lasting Effects Did the French Revolution Have? .... 394
13.5.1 The Appearance of "National Sovereignty" .... 394
13.5.2 The Origins of "National" Patriotism .... 394
13.5.3 The Symbols of the French State .... 395
13.5.4 The Reinforcement of the State .... 396
13.5.5 The Social Transformation of France .... 398
13.5.6 The European Dimension of the French Revolution .... 398
13.6 The Failure of Assembly-Based Government .... 399
References .... 405

## 13.1 A Turning Point in European Constitutional History

If there is an event that traditionally marks the transition to modern times in the history of the West, is without a doubt the French Revolution, to such an extent that it is a common convention in European culture to consider 1789 the foremost turning point in the continent's history.[4]

The French Revolution was not, of course, the first bourgeois revolution, as 13 years before it the American Revolution had begun. It had, however, a much greater impact on western public opinion[5] because of the simple fact that it did not occur far off in the New World, but in Old Europe, and, what is more, in one of its premier states: France, a kingdom that had been the Continent's leading power in the seventeenth century during the reign of Louis XIV, and which in the eighteenth,

[4] This is due essentially, as Furet (2001, 17) points out, to the fact that historians of the French Revolution remained locked into the line of discourse that the French Revolution had founded a new society and marked the beginning of history; whether they belonged to the Right or Left, were royalists or republicans, conservatives or Jacobins—with the notable exception of the very lucid conservative political thinker Alexis de Tocqueville, who in his masterpiece *L'Ancien Régime et la Revolution* (1856) suggested that this radical break reflected no more than the illusion of change. For an analysis of the importance of the French Revolution from a contemporary perspective, see Popkin (2002, 801–821), Spang (2003, 119–147) and Soboul (2006, 17–32).

[5] For an overview of the image that Europeans had of the American Revolution, see Palmer (1959, I, 237–281).

was still Europe's greatest cultural juggernaut. All the great enlightened sovereigns spoke French, as it was considered the language of culture, while the philosophers wrote in French and Paris was the capital of Enlightenment (Roche 1998, 659–661). France was, in short, the model to be followed.

The truly impressive thing is that the French colossus, with one of Europe's most powerful and well-established monarchies, crumbled to the ground like a house of cards in a question of just weeks,[6] along the way shaking the foundations of the European monarchies, who continued to uphold the traditional order of estate-based society. The French Revolution quickly transcended its status as an internal affair to become a process of change aimed at taking on and overturning the social, political and legal order of all of Europe. When in the spring of 1792, France's revolutionaries declared war on Austria and Prussia, the conflict acquired a European dimension. When Louis XVI was executed (January 21, 1793), the other European monarchies, including Spain, declared war upon the French Convention. From this point forward, all Europe would ally to save the Old Order.

While the American Revolution was contained in North America, the French Revolution and its momentous Napoleonic spillover, in contrast, definitively transformed the very nature of European politics. In the brief space of 25 years, between 1789 and 1815, the bases of western public law were irreversibly altered.

## 13.2 The Monarchy as the Historical Basis of the French State

France would not have become one of the great European states if it had not had a great monarchy. As we have already seen in previous chapters, it was France's early kings who shaped what is even today the world's most centralized and

[6] This was, to a great extent, a consequence of the fact that the French governing class did not believe in the traditional values of Christian monarchy. For example, Luis XVI's minister the Archbishop of Toulouse, Loménie de Brienne, openly proclaimed his atheism in the salons of Paris. Talleyrand, former bishop of Autun, when celebrating mass at the Celebration of the Federation (July 14, 1790, in the first anniversary of the taking of the Bastille), warned Lafayette, that was behind "above all, don't make me laugh" ("*Ah ça! je vous en prie, ne me faites pas rire*"). It is also significant that Louis XV changed the way in which the kings of France touched the sick to demonstrate their healing power (*toucher des écrouelles*). Traditionally, when touching the sick, the monarch would say "the king touches you, God cures you" (*Le roi te touche, Dieu te guérit*), whereas under Louis XV the phrase became "the king touches you, may God cure you" (*Le roi te touche, que Dieu te guérisse*). What was once affirmation of faith had become an expression of desire (Le Gall 2007, 129, n. 4). The king touching scrofula sufferers was a regular practice until the last days of Louis XIV (by Pentecost in 1698 the king had touched 3,000 invalids and, some days before his death, as late as Pentecost in 1715, 1,700). Louis XV, meanwhile, touched 2,000 scrofulous sufferers the day after his *sacre*, but when he suffered an interdiction in 1738 his thaumaturgic powers were suspended. The practice was taken up again by Louis XVI, who touched 2,400 invalids at his accession in 1774 (Sabatier 2007, 262). Also Bloch (1989).

homogeneous state. Since then, France has demonstrated an impressive institutional continuity, which explains, in part, it is still today one of Europe's most singular and powerful countries. Let us reexamine some of the most notable features of this remarkable history.

### 13.2.1 From Clovis I to Charlemagne

When we look all the way back to the era of the Germanic invasions, just a short time after the fall of the Western Roman Empire, the Merovingian King Clovis I (481–511), already stands out as a notable historical figure. After the collapse of the Visigoth kingdom of Tolosa, when Clovis defeated Alaric II in 507 at Vouillé, in just a few years he would become the most powerful Germanic leader of his time.

However, Clovis would also write the first institutional chapter in the history of the French monarchy, thanks to his being baptized by St. Remigius (Shanzer 1998, 29–57).[7] During the sixth and seventh centuries, Clovis' descendants were so disastrous that they would go down in history as the "do-nothing kings" (*rois fainéants*). At the beginning of the eighth century, however, one of the court's high-ranking officials, Charles Martel, brought prestige back to the Frankish kings after scoring a decisive victory near Poitiers in the year 732, against Muslim invaders who had hitherto seemed unstoppable.

Charles Martel was remembered and celebrated as the savior of Christianity, while his son Pepin the Short (751–768), capitalized upon his father's name to overthrow Childeric III, the last of the Merovingian sovereigns. Accessing the throne of the "Carolingian" kings (the term proceeding from the Latinized name of Charles Martel: Carolus) was possible because Pepin was savvy enough to forge an alliance with the papacy, which ever since Gregory I (590–604), had established itself as the maximum religious authority in what was essentially an entirely Catholic Christendom. Pepin the Short was anointed as the legitimate king of the Franks with papal authorization, in exchange for which his troops intervened militarily in Italy to defend the papacy against its enemies. After him his successors, all the way down until 1830, were made legitimate sovereigns by means of the ceremony of anointment. The idea, then, that France's kings ruled by divine right was deeply rooted in its history. Thus, it was no great surprise that France should become the Church's "eldest daughter" (*Fille ainée de l' Église*) and the king of France its "very Christian Majesty" (*Sa Majesté Très Chrétienne*).[8]

---

[7] For a modern perspective on this legendary figure, see Daly (1994, 619–664).

[8] The origin of the title is disputed. Some trace it back to the baptism of Clodoveo. Most believe that it took root during the final year of the reign of Charles V (1364–1380). The Church, however, frequently used the title to refer to Pepin the Short, Charlemagne, and Philip II Augustus (Valois 1896, 314–327). See also de Pange (1985) and Tallon (2004, 111–125). On how the title became one of the pillars of French royal absolutism, see Krynen (1989, 79–96).

The alliance between the papacy and the Frankish kings would reach its zenith with the coronation on December 24, 800 of Pepin the Short's son, Charlemagne, as the new Emperor of the West. This empire, however, would prove fleeting, as it was shattered in year 843, when Charlemagne's three grandsons split his empire up at Verdun. The imperial title thus drifted from the Frankish Dynasty, in the year 962, falling into the hands of a German nobleman, Otto I, Duke of Saxony, founder of the (Sacred German) Holy Roman Empire.

## *13.2.2 A Hereditary, Sovereign and Territorial Monarchy*

### 13.2.2.1 The Establishment of the Hereditary Principle

The "Germanization" of the medieval Christian Empire led to the breaking off of the Frankish kingdom under Hugh Capet (987–996), the first king who managed to bestow his throne upon his descendants via inheritance in what was an essential step in the institutional consolidation of the monarchy.[9]

### 13.2.2.2 Sovereignty vs. Feudal Bonds

Hugh Capet's descendants, however, saw their power undercut by the profound "feudalization" of Frankish society, at least until Abbot Suger (1080–1151), championed the idea that the king occupied the apex of the feudal pyramid.[10] The

[9] Hugh Capet was elected by an assembly of magnates at Senlis in late May 987, as king of the West Franks. He was "utterly insignificant" but he succeeded in his main aim: to survive and to leave the throne to his son, Robert, who was slated to be king from the age of nine and succeeded his father when he was 24. This way of arranging the succession was the idea of Hugh Capet, and would become a common practice ensuring the transformation of the Capetian monarchy from an elective into a hereditary one (Bradbury 2007, 72 and 82).

[10] Louis VI elevated the king's position to new heights by advancing the doctrine that the king, as the supreme power, was to pay homage and fealty to none. Hence, Louis VI declined to pay homage to the Vexin, a vassal county of St. Denis, on the grounds that the king was superior in rank to any suzerain, lay or ecclesiastical. This act was extremely significant as an assertion of the king's preeminence. He was his own peer, as none on the soil of France was his suzerain. "*Vilcassini siquidem, quod est inter Isaram et Ettam, nobilem comitatum, quem perhibent immunitates ecelesiæ proprium beati Dyonisii feodum, quem etiam rex Francorum Ludovicus Philippi, accelerans contra imperatorem romanum insurgentem in regnum Francorum, in pleno capitulo beati Dyonisii professus est se ab eo habere et jure signiferi, si rex non esset, hominium ei debere* [. . .]. Translation: "The Vexin, between the Oise and the Epte, is, according to the immunities of the church, a fief belonging to St. Denis. When the king of France, Louis, [son of] Philip, was hurrying to counter the invasion of the realm by the roman emperor, he recognized in the plenary chapter of St. Denis that he held it from the saint and, if he hadn't been king, would have done homage for it and its standard [the oriflamme]". Suger, Abbot of St. Denis (1992, 128–130). Also, Latin text in Gasparri (1996, 54). English translation by Panofsky (1979, 232).

next step would be taken by the jurists of France's Louis IX in the thirteenth century, when they developed the concept of royal "sovereignty", which posited that the king stood above and beyond any vassal ties.

#### 13.2.2.3 "France" Appears

Hugh Capet and his descendants bore the title "King of the Franks" until Philip II Augustus (1179–1223), the seventh king of the Capet Dynasty, replaced this title with that of "King of France". No longer was the king to rule over a specific people, but rather a territory and all its inhabitants, a crucial initial step in the development of the identification between monarch and kingdom.

#### 13.2.2.4 *Rex Est Imperator in Regno Suo*

The kings of France, however, would still need to gain their independence from the papacy, a feat achieved by Philip IV the Fair (1285–1314), who successfully secured a series of powers in his confrontation with Pope Boniface VIII. To achieve this, the king had to summon representatives of his kingdom, convoking the first assembly of the estates in French history: the Estates General of 1302. With the political support of the three estates (nobility, clergy and the third state, the citizens) and the technical-legal counsel of the jurists, the king of France became an emperor in his kingdom. By basing his authority upon the ceremony of "anointment" he, at the same time, reaffirmed before the Pope the principle of his divine right and the implication that his legitimacy proceeded directly from God and did not require papal intervention.

### *13.2.3 The Hundred Years' War and the Bolstering of Monarchical Prestige and Power*

The prestige and power of the French kings was considerably eroded as a result of the Hundred Years War. There were periods over the course of this interminable conflict when most French territory was actually held by the king of England, specifically during two the darkest and most dramatic reigns of Philip VI (1328–1350) and Charles VI, the Mad (1380–1422).

The failed military efforts of the French nobility were buoyed by the appearance of Joan of Arc (1412–1431), who, in a surprising development, received the control of an army and managed to take Orleans, allowing Charles VII to be crowned at

Reims.[11] This monarch, who until then the English had contemptuously dubbed the "King of Bourges", initiated a remarkable comeback in which, in just a few years, he scored a definitive military victory against England in this protracted clash.

The end of the One Hundred Years' War had important constitutional consequences for the kings of both England and France. In the former the defeat would finally allow Parliament to trump regal prerogative, while in France the effect was the opposite, the kings seeing their institutional prestige augmented by the victory. In fact, the power of the king of France was consolidated in the mid fifteenth century by the crucial reform measures introduced by Charles VII (1422–1461), such as the establishment of permanent taxes[12] that allowed him, among other things, to maintain a stable professional army at the service of the monarchy for the first time.

### *13.2.4 The Era of Absolutism: Louis XIV's Monarchy as a Landmark Reign*

The kings of France managed to forge one of Europe's most powerful states during the Modern Age thanks to monarchs like Louis XI (1461–1483) and Francis I (1515–1547), of the House of Valois. After the grim period marked by the Wars of Religion (1562–1598), the monarchy grew more stable and strong with the first monarch of the House of Bourbon, Henry IV (1589–1610), who would be succeeded by charismatic kings such as Louis XIII (1610–1643)—especially during the period in which the government was in the hands of Cardinal Richelieu (1630–1642)—and, above all, Louis XIV (1643–1715). The latter's prolonged reign (72 years, with Louis personally ruling for 54 of them, beginning in 1661) marks without any doubt the zenith of French prestige and power in the Europe of the *Ancien Regime*.

During the reign of Louis XIV, France superseded Spain as the premier European power upon the signing of the Treaty of the Pyrenees (1659). This historic pact, coming 2 years before the king was even of legal age, established France as Europe's hegemonic power. Louis XIV would go on to exercise his powers an absolute monarch, assisted by strong advisors whose counsel he heeded, though all final decisions rested with him. In addition, his plans were generally well executed

[11] About Joan of Arc, and the role that she played in the consolidation of French monarchy, see Barker (2012, 95–173) and Duby (1993, 288–297).

[12] In France Charles VII succeeded in introducing significant military and financial reforms which bolstered the power of the French monarchy. On November 2, 1439, when the Estates General opened at Orléans, Charles VII convinced the body to pass a law that enabled the king to establish permanent taxes without its consent, essentially involving the direct *taille* (land tax) and an indirect one, the *gabelle*, a tax on salt. Both were approved to maintain a permanent army, and were accepted because of the need to fund the war effort against England. These taxes would form the basis of the French fiscal system until 1789 (Allmand 2001, 102–110). Also Garillot (1947).

because he almost invariably managed to surround himself with very competent aides (Swann 2001, 139–168).

Under Louis XIV, as we know, for the first time, the French monarchy combined the old medieval conception of the king-judge (*roi justicier*) with the idea that the sovereign ought also be a legislator to reform the traditional order (*roi législateur*) (Gouron 1991, 101–114). To achieve this, he called upon excellent ministers, including the notable Jean Baptiste Colbert, who became the main figure shaping the French state between 1661 and his death in 1683. As Minister of Finance, he not only reconstructed the government and reformed the royal tax administration, but also promoted commerce and imposed an economic doctrine in which the state gave direction to and nurtured economic activity. His policies, thus, served to shore up French prestige and influence throughout Europe, allowing the country to enjoy its *grand siècle* in the eighteenth century—a crucial development from the point of view of constitutional history, as the French monarchy provided the model which most European sovereigns would come to emulate.

## 13.3 From the *Ancien Régime* to the Revolution

### *13.3.1 Louis XV and the Decline of the French Monarchy*

Louis XIV's power was clearly on the wane during the final years of his reign, which had undeniably entered into crisis during the War of the Spanish Succession (1701–1713). In the end, however, through the negotiations carried out at the Peace of Utrecht, the "Sun King" managed to reach a favorable settlement for his kingdom which allowed him to conclude his reign still widely held to be a great king. Just the opposite would happen to his successor, Louis XV.

#### 13.3.1.1 Louis XV: From "Beloved" to Loathed

Louis XV was the Sun King's great-grandson, taking the throne at the age of five, and remaining on it for a reign spanning 59 years (1715–1774). Unlike his great-grandfather, however, the new king took no interested in affairs of state. When reading accounts of his time on the throne one has the impression that France was adrift, as the quality of its government depended entirely upon the minister to whom the reins of power had been entrusted. France's policies were erratic, causing Europe's most powerful kingdom to falter and enter into a spiral of rapid decay.[13]

[13] As Swann stresses (1995, 45–47), in 1744 he had been acclaimed as Louis *le bien aimé* by a grateful people after his recovery from a serious illness while on campaign at Metz. In the following year he would obtain the most celebrated military victory of his reign at Fontenoy. By his fortieth birthday, in 1750, he seemed poised for a long and glorious reign, but in 1774 he would

Among other setbacks, the French monarchy lost virtually all of its colonial possessions in North America (Canada) and India to England, while Louis XV also failed to score any significant victories in the endless wars France was waging against England, Prussia and the Austrian Empire. The nation which capitalized most upon French decline was England, which over the course of the eighteenth century rose to supersede France as Europe's primary power. Worst of all for France was that at the end of Louis XV's reign, its political decline triggered a serious economic crisis which decimated the king's prestige in the eyes of his people. So ultimately maligned was the monarch that when he died had to be buried at night in a clandestine ceremony.

#### 13.3.1.2 Louis XVI: An Intelligent and Educated King, but One Poorly Prepared for Politics

When Louis XVI's reign began, France was suffering a serious economic crisis and the state was still bogged down by the sluggishness characterizing the *Ancien Regime*. Consequently, it was incapable of confronting the changes and transformations spawned by new economic realities and the ideas and trends ushered in by the Enlightenment.[14]

---

die unlamented. Part of this was because of the king's own personal conduct. By behaving like one of his *libertine* courtiers he made the mistake of thinking that a king of France was entitled to a private life. One of his biggest errors was to make Madame du Barry his official mistress in 1769. In any case, these debaucheries appeared to confirm widespread rumors that the king failed to take his responsibilities seriously, though it was the weakness of his government rather than any moral failings which did most to undermine his reputation. Historians had long considered Louis XV to be a lazy, incapable monarch, lacking a conscientious attitude towards his governmental duties. However, this is an interpretation that is no longer tenable. Louis XV was, in fact, one of the most talented men to ever sit upon the French throne. He was handsome, intelligent, a skilled geographer and a cultivated patron of the arts. Louis followed the pattern of his great-grandfather, the mighty Louis XIV and his reign. Just as during his early years, Louis XIV had been tutored by a cardinal, Mazarin, Louis XV was guided by Fleury. Upon the latter's death, in 1743, following the precedent of 1661, the 33-year-old monarch declared his intention to rule alone. Despite later criticisms of his conduct, the king maintained a strict personal routine, holding meetings of the *Conseil d'En haut* every Wednesday and Sunday, and convening the *Conseil des Dépêches* on either Friday or Saturday. It is beyond doubt that he took an active and important part in the proceedings, and his correspondence reveals an informed and critical spirit. Witnesses such as the secretary of state for foreign affairs, the duc d'Aiguillon, noted that at meetings of the council it was frequently the king who produced the most sensible policy or clear analysis. The tragedy of Louis XV was that he lacked the confidence, or perhaps arrogance, necessary to follow his own instincts to rule alone. Another important factor of disarray was that the king designated his ministers individually. Holding their position as a result of his favor, they did not act as a team or respect any concept of collective responsibility. The ensuing rivalries and quarrels were damaging to the government, as the king was unable to steer affairs in a firm and consistent direction. On the evolution of French public opinion concerning Louis XIV and Louis XV, see Engels (2003, 96–126).

[14] For an overview of the crisis France was going through at the beginning of Louis XVI's reign, see Cullen (1993, 635–657).

Louis XVI (May 10, 1774–October 10, 1789) was intelligent, cultured and a man of goodwill who earnestly endeavored to govern to promote his subjects' best interests. He was, however, a terrible politician. He was weak of will and utterly lacked experience, which was no fault of his own, for he simply had not been educated to reign, since he initially was not the crown prince, having been preceded in the line of succession by his father Louis of France (1729–1765), and his older brother Louis Joseph Xavier de Bourbon (1751–1761). Defying all expectations, their premature deaths placed him upon the throne in spite of himself. There is an anecdote that when he was told that his grandfather had died and he had become the new king of France ("The king is dead! Long live the king!") he replied, desperate: "It seems that the whole universe is going to fall upon me! My God! What a burden has beset me, at my age (he was 20) I have not been taught anything!"[15]

Louis XVI was fully conscious of the fact that it was necessary to undertake major reform measures, and actually made efforts to address the situation. During the first years of his reign, he strove to rouse France from its lethargy. The new king, with the best of intentions, successively placed the government in the hands of reformist ministers such as Turgot, Necker, Calonne and Loménie de Brienne (Vardi 2012, 241–242). In fact, the monarch was able to introduce some reform by abolishing in 1781 and 1788 torture in criminal procedure (Johnson 2013, 20), suppressing feudal servitude on royal lands in 1779 (Kropotkin 2009, 20), and eliminating the personal tax levied on the Jews of Alsace in 1784 (Johnson 1998, 306). In 1787 he also promulgated an edict of tolerance to protect Protestants and those who did not profess the Catholic religion (Zagorin 2003, 299), although his most important reform effort was his attempt to introduce an egalitarian direct tax.[16]

---

[15] *Il me semble que l'univers va tomber sur moi*! *Dieu*! *Quel fardeau j'ai là, à mon âge et on ne m'a rien appris* (Aubry 1952, 11). Also telling was the phrase carelessly penned by his wife, Marie Antoinette, Joseph II of Austria's sister, when she referred to her husband as a "poor man" (*Le pauvre homme*) (Zweig 2012, 85). Another two anecdotes that say much about the king's personality occurred on July 14, 1789. When the Duke of Liancourt informed the king that the people had taken the Bastille Louis XVI asked him: "Is it a revolt?" to which the courtesan replied: "No, Sire, it is a revolution" (Zimmermann 2011, 294). It has been often stated that in his journal entry on July 14, 1789, the king would wrote simply: "nothing" (*rien*). Yet, as Johnson (2013, 71) points out, those commentators who have ridiculed Louis XVI for his journal entry, have overlooked the fact that it was only a hunting journal in which the king listed what game had been killed that day, and not a place where he usually recorded what else was happening in his life.

[16] In response to Turgot's suggestion, Louis XVI, along with a general tax-policy review, endeavored to replace the traditional *corvée* with a monetary tax applicable to all classes. The measure, however, encountered immediate resistance from the Parlement of Paris, the Church, and the provincial estates, precipitating the reformist minister's resignation (Elson Roessler and Miklos 2003, 43).

All of this impetus for innovation, however, would be met by opposition amongst the privileged classes who, clinging to the estate-based structure inherited from the Middle Ages, did all they could to foil the king's policies.[17]

## *13.3.2 Reactionary Forces Prevail in French Society*

Unlike what happened in England, where as of the sixteenth century the bourgeoisie, both merchant and industrial, came to form part of the country's powerful gentry, sharing power with the old nobility, in France, the old military nobility, along with the clergy, would fight tooth and nail to retain their ancient, anachronistic privileges.[18] This reaction meant that the bourgeoisie, or "Third Estate", failed to exert influence on the kingdom's government. Firstly, this was because of the ineffectiveness of the French Estates-General, which should have been the institutional channel through which the estate, representing the immense majority of the king of France's subjects, was to participate in the government. Secondly, the only institution in *Ancien Regime* France that could offer significant opposition to the monarchy, the parlements, did not promote the general welfare, but rather defended the established order and sought to protect their own privileges.

### 13.3.2.1 The Ineffectiveness of the Estates-General

As we already know, in France the Estates-General had never been well established as an estate-based assembly because it did not meet regularly. The kings of France only resorted to convoking the Estates during periods of crisis (a confrontation with the pope, the Hundred Years War, Wars of Religion), giving the body an *ad hoc* character. Moreover, we already saw in Chap. 8 how the Estates General were rendered dormant by Richelieu (1630–1642), as he was of the opinion that they were not compatible with royal sovereignty, which spurred him to begin abolishing the Provincial States as well. One fact suffices to indicate the situation in this regard: when Louis XVI summoned the Estates-General to Versailles in May of

[17] As Chaussinand-Nogaret (1995, 13) points out, the ideological grounds for this "right to resist" came from the fact that in the eyes of the French nobility, Louis XIV had broken the "noble contract", a sort of tacit aristocratic social pact established with the official elites ever since the origins of the monarchy. In doing so, the privileged classes held that the king had divorced government from its social foundations and, therefore, considered it their duty to resist an intolerably despotic power they believed had violated the pact that gave the crown its legitimacy.

[18] As Smith (1996, 228) points out, the army continued to be the target of heavy criticism during the reign of Louis XVI, despite the fact that his Minister of War, Saint-Germain, began the gradual elimination of venality. There remained the widespread perception that the system of appointments and promotions favored the wealthiest members of the French nobility, who enjoyed great influence at court. On the situation of the French high clergy on the eve of the French Revolution, see McManners (2007) and Aston (1992).

1789, it had not met since 1614. The kings, then, had governed France without consulting the kingdom's representatives for over 165 years.

This situation had been possible, to a great extent, because the kings did not require the Estates-General's financial support. As of the mid fifteenth century they had been levying permanent taxes assuring them regular revenues.[19] The result was that the Estates-General did not play in France a role moderating royal authority by any means, as occurred with the Parliament in England, or the *cortes* of the kingdoms of the Crown of Aragon in Spain. In fact, they never managed to check or control the king.

#### 13.3.2.2 The Singular Opposition of the "Parlements"

The function of curtailing royal authority which might have lay with the Estates General in the France of the *Ancien Regime* fell upon another institution: the "parlements", which were not estate-based assemblies, but rather high courts of Justice. The most important of them was the Parlement of Paris, but there were regional parlements as well. These bodies were very important because at the close of the eighteenth century the French king, institutionally, continued to be more of a supreme judge than a reformer.

The clout of the parlements essentially stemmed from the fact that they were the guarantors of the application of the old local customs, which in France still constituted, even in the last third of the eighteenth century, the essential nucleus of private law. Thus to legislate in this area, they had to have the approval of a set of parlements which had the right "to register" (formally record) royal laws, a step without which they could not be applied. The members of the parlements developed the practice (Daubresse 2005, 28) of taking advantage of this privilege to present "complaints" (*droit of rémontrance*) to the king, whenever the monarch requested the registration of a law, making its registration (and enactment) contingent upon the satisfaction of their pleas. This right turned the parlements into the only bodies capable of institutional opposition to the monarchy in France under the *Ancien Regime*.

The parlements eventually became renegade institutions, backing a military revolt against the king in the War of the Fronde (1648–1653), during the regency of Louis XIV. The ensuing chaos led the king to resolve to rule in an authoritarian manner once he was old enough to assume the throne.[20]

[19] Davis (1995, 287–288) observes that in the two successive meetings of the Estates General, summoned by the regency government at Orléans and Pontoise in 1560 and 1561 (the first meetings since 1484), in an effort to maintain peace and obtain financial support, the only point on which all the delegates agreed was not to grant new taxes.

[20] The requirements applying to the registration procedure and the issuing of *remontrances* were set down in a royal ordinance of 1667, and the royal declaration of 1673, in which Louis XIV severely pared back the right to present grievances; the king arranged it so that complaints could only be presented *after* royal laws had been registered (Hurt 2002, 114). This restriction was imprudently abolished by the regent Philippe of Orleans in 1715, when Louis XV was still too young to rule.

The problem was that the parlements did not use their power to promote the general welfare, but rather to defend the established order and protect their own privileges. They did not function, by any means, as an institutional channel transmitting the people's concerns to the king. The members of the parlements were jurists (Fitzsimmons 1987, 1–32). Educated at schools of law, they purchased their posts as judges, prosecutors, barristers, solicitors and notaries, charges which they passed down to their sons, paying the crown the corresponding tax. This system turned the legal class from which they proceeded into a closed social group, a kind of caste ("Nobles of the Robe"), predominantly concerned with defending their privileged positions (Stone 1986, 75–124).

Louis XV, weary of the parlements' constant hindrances and hampering, chose to subjugate them by means of force through the reform measures advanced by his Chancellor, René Nicolas Charles Augustin de Maupeou, in 1771. In response to the systematic resistance which the Parlement of Paris put up the chancellor dismissed the defiant body and prohibited judicial offices from being purchased or inherited (Baker 1992, 1–16). With one stroke of the legislative pen, the judges lost their traditional prerogatives and were reduced to simple civil servants. In this way, the monarchy took a major step towards the forging of a new France in which the privileged classes were to be required to serve the general interest (Echeverria 1985).

Louis XVI, undeniably with the best of intentions, though in an utterly imprudent step, abolished Maupeou's reforms, which had made it possible to control the institution that had most effectively stymied royal authority in France.[21] This had serious consequences, as it was the members of the Parlement of Paris, those who most staunchly opposed the reform efforts which the king endorsed, and who led the ideological debate (Baker 1978, 279–303), who initiated the first act of the French Revolution in what came to be called, significantly, the Revolt of the Nobles.[22]

---

[21] As Hardman (1994, 32–3) points out, the problem lay in the fact that Louis believed it was a travesty of justice that the exiled *parlementaires* had not been given financial compensation for the loss of offices, which were regarded as incorporeal property. On this basis, the new Chancellor Maurepas tried to convince the king to dismiss Maupeou and reestablish the old parlement, which the king ultimately did. Maurepas was aided by the fact that Maupeou did not bother to defend his work before the king, and that French public opinion was favorable to the parlements' reputation for defending French legal tradition.

[22] As Goldstone (2011, 222) explains, the Crown and leading political thinkers had sought to improve the kingdom's financial situation through a continuous stream of proposals for reform aimed at reorganizing government administration and finances. All of them, however, were stymied by the resistance of the elites, particularly the Parisian and provincial parlements, which did not appreciate their plight. The leading elites concentrated in Paris saw a thriving urban economy all around them, which they believed reflected a richer France. They were not in touch with the reality in the countryside, blind to the fact that population growth had crowded many peasants into plots too small to feed their families, and that increased landlessness and falling real wages had lowered the incomes of about one-third of the population. Everyone was aware of inflation, but did not attribute it to a rising population, but rather to the evils of speculation. Also, Sonenscher (2009, 1–21).

## 13.4 The French Revolution

### *13.4.1 From the Revolt of the Privileged to the Estates General*

#### 13.4.1.1 The *Révolte Des Privilégiés*

Louis XVI's successive ministers were aware that to resolve the economic crisis, it was essential that they thoroughly reform the French tax system, which had been passed down intact since the fifteenth century. The old nobility, however, the clergy, and the members of the parlements (Nobles of the Robe) insisted that the status quo tax code (which granted them major advantages) could not be modified without convoking the Estates General (Goldstone 2011, 67).

Technically, the privileged classes were right. However, given the desperate plight faced by most of the French during the last third of the eighteenth century, they were playing with fire—especially considering the dangerous precedent set by the American Revolution (which, paradoxically, had been made possible to a great extent by the support France's Louis XVI had lent the rebels). The oligarchy recklessly and stubbornly opposed the fiscal reform proposed by the king (Sonenscher 1997, 64–103) in a movement which historians have called the "Revolt of the Privileged".

Resurrecting a mechanism as complex as the Estates General after 165 years of inactivity, was an undertaking fraught with risks. Thus, Louis XVI, who was much more conscious of the situation than the members of the parlements, fiercely opposed what they requested. An acrimonious and fruitless exchange thus began during which the tone of the parlements' protests became increasingly insolent. Unfortunately for the king, the parlements' attitude began to win over public opinion (Lucas 2006, 33–50), and the people began to organize protests against the monarchy. There came a point at which even the army expressed its willingness to collaborate with the Nobles of the Robe to stem the increasing anarchy, worsened by the general malaise born of the economic crisis.

#### 13.4.1.2 The Provincial Estates of Vizille and the Prelude to the Revolution (June 1788)

As we already know, the Provincial States had almost disappeared by 1700, because Richelieu and Louis XIV tried to abolish them all. Thus, most provinces had forfeited all right to administrative independence by the eighteenth century, with the exception of four regions: Languedoc, Brittany, Burgundy and Provence. When Louis XVI took the throne, one of his reforming minister's priorities was to establish an institutional way by which the country could share power with the king (Jones 1995, 139). Calonne (1783–1786), in an attempt to reinstate the nobility's political power, summoned an Assembly of Notables to approve some reform measures, including a universal land tax, and in 1787, Loménie de Brienne had the idea of revitalizing these Provincial States to provide the stimulus that would lead to repairing the worn-out fabric of absolute monarchy (Jones 1995, 139). [23]

The political crisis came to a head when Louis XVI, poorly advised by his Justice Minister, Guillaume-Chrétien de Lamoignon de Malesherbes, decided to abolish the parlements' right to enact royal legislation. The announcement was ill timed and only ended up fueling the conflict and tensions, exacerbating the rebellion of an entire region, Dauphiné (Dauphiny) where the people, rallied by the Parlement of Grenoble, decided in June of 1788, to unilaterally organize (without the governor's convocation on behalf of the king, as was the legal practice) a meeting of the three estates in the Palace of Vizille. This constituted a clear challenge to the king's authority, as Dauphiné's old provincial estates had been eliminated in the first half of the seventeenth century by Richelieu. [24]

In addition, the meeting in Vizille ended up taking on a revolutionary tone, as the voting was not conducted in accord with tradition, with each estate meeting separately and voting in blocks, with internal, majority polling determining each of the three's votes. Rather, all the representatives met in one chamber, with each man voting individually. This approach gave a clear advantage to the "Third Estate", which had the same number of representatives as the nobles and clergy combined. Finally, the representatives of the three estates decided to jointly demand that the king urgently convoke the Estates General. To force him to accede to their demand they called for the French people to refuse to pay any taxes until the monarch had consented (Chianéa 1988, 33–49).[25]

[23] In fact, in November of 1787, the government had hoped to establish assemblies in 26 regions, the *généralités* of the *pays d'élection*. The measure, however, was not fully enacted because the parlements of Besançon and Bordeaux refused to sanction the edict, and difficulties arose as well in the Dauphiné. Many assemblies were summoned nevertheless, but the plenary meetings did not last for more than a month, and they were all over by Christmas (Jones 1995, 142–143).

[24] As Jones (1995, 149–153) points out, the Parlement of Grenoble had called for the restoration of the province's Estates several times in the 1760s and 1770s, but never secured the approval of the royal intendants. Grenoble's parlement tried again in 1788, as its members saw a propitious moment to propose constitutional reform, as Necker had just unveiled plans to set up a Provincial Administration in the Berry. Throughout the winter of 1787–1788, the numerous supporters of pro-assembly reform in Grenoble continued their efforts to find a compromise, but by the middle of the summer of 1788, Brienne understood that his plans for reforming the *pays d'élections* were jeopardized by Lamoignon's authoritarian initiative. In the end, French public opinion forced Lamoignon's dismissal, and Louis XVI had restored the parlements by September of 1788. The first thing that the Grenoble parliaments did was to take up debate on how to reconstruct the ancient representation of the province. Rivalries between towns and power conflicts between the upper and lower clergy, and between the traditional and more recent nobles, delayed the issue, but finally the Estates of the Dauphiné were duly summoned to meet—after a lapse of 160 years—on December 1, 1788.

[25] For a general look at the political situation of the non-privileged classes in Old Regime France, see Gordon (1994).

## *13.4.2 The Estates General*

### 13.4.2.1 The Convocation

In August of 1788, in light of the state's virtual bankruptcy and the government's manifest inability to restore order, the king yielded. After calling for the Estates General to convene on May 1, 1789, he replaced Loménie de Brienne as his Finance Minister with the more popular Jacques Necker.

### 13.4.2.2 The Patriots vs. the Privileged

The king's decision did not pacify everyone. Though nearly all agreed that absolute monarchy had to be overturned, there was no unanimity about just how to do this. On the one hand the privileged wanted to restore an oligarchical regime in which they wielded authority. The bourgeoisie and the middle-class, meanwhile, whose representatives began to be called "patriots", aspired to play a new role in the regime in line with their actual social importance, both quantitative and qualitative.

The result was that during the months preceding the meeting of the Estates General, a great debate was held on the way in which this event should be organized and administrated. The privileged wanted the meeting to proceed in accordance with the model of its last summoning, which went all the way back to 1614 and the regency of Louis XIII's mother, Marie de Médicis.[26] At previous meetings of the Estates General, the three classes (nobility, clergy and the Third Estate) had met separately and had voted by estate, each class assigned one vote. However, the "patriots" argued that the model should be followed employed at the provincial estates held in Dauphiné 1 year prior. There, at the Palace of Vizille, every man's vote was counted individually.

The debate soon spread to all France thanks to the publication of innumerable pamphlets in which both sides presented their arguments (Margerison 1998). Of all of these one of them soon stood out: "What is the Third Estate?" written by a priest, Abbé Sieyès.[27] The work would prove pivotal not only for its content, but because it made clear that the "patriots" enjoyed the support of the low clergy, and even of some members of the nobility, such as the Marquis of Lafayette, the hero of the American war; the Count of Mirabeau, one of France's finest orators who, because of his unconventional lifestyle—gambling debts, scandalous love affairs, quarrels

[26] The body had been so sorely abandoned that it was actually necessary to look up in the archives how to hold this type of meeting, yielding a revival of the rigid ceremony dating from 1614 (Caiani 2012, 40). On the Estates General of 1614, see Hayden (2008). On the preparation of the 1789 Estates General, see Hardman (1994, 137–144).

[27] Emmanuel Joseph Sieyès had published his political pamphlet in January 1789 defending the abolition of voting by estates and the abolition of privileged orders (Sieyès, Emmanuel-Joseph 2003, 92–162) and also Baker (1989a, 195–205). On Sieyès, see Sewel (1994).

(Zorgbibe 2008)—had been marginalized by the members of his estate; and even Talleyrand, a great nobleman who lost his title because of a lifelong infirmity.[28]

#### 13.4.2.3 The Defeat of the Privileged

The debate seemed to come to a head in December of 1788, when Necker managed to convince Louis XVI to make a series of concessions,[29] among them to double the number of representatives assigned to the Third Estate. To do so he employed the argument that it could be dangerous for the monarchy to stand squarely against majority public opinion. This measure constituted a clear defeat for the privileged classes inasmuch as it opened the door to the patriots playing an effective and decisive role in the Estates General.

#### 13.4.2.4 All of France Mobilizes: The Election of Representatives and "Books of Grievances"

The meeting of the first Estates General since 1614 sparked great excitement and expectation, with all of France mobilizing to prepare for the event. In the first months of 1789, the representatives of the three estates began to meet everywhere, especially those from the Third Estate, to elect representatives and draft "books of grievances" (*cahiers of doléances*) to be presented to the king on behalf of those they represented. The meeting was to commence in Versailles in early May 1789.

The representatives of all three estates agreed unanimously in their attribution of the nation's ills to the king's arbitrary power, and considered it indispensable that it be "confined to its just limits". All coincided in advocating that the meeting of the Estates General ought to serve to draft a constitution clearly setting down "the rights of the king and of the nation", as well as a supreme law serving to guarantee "individual freedom", reduce the powers of the intendants, and establish regular meetings of the provincial estates throughout the kingdom (Shapiro 1998, 257–258).

[28] In France, the high aristocracy's infants were cared for by wet nurses. When just a baby Talleyrand's nurse placed him on a dresser, off of which he fell and broke his leg. The nurse did not realize the severity of his injury, the fracture was never properly mended, and Talleyrand was left a cripple for life. Despite being the eldest child, his condition prevented him from inheriting the paternal title, one of France's most important. Rather, he was relegated to the clergy. Because of his deplorable childhood (Orieux 1974, 14) Talleyrand never shed his bitterness towards his social class for this injustice, his resentment spurring him to become one of the leaders of the Revolution. See also Cooper (2001) and Lawday (2007).

[29] Such as recognizing the principle of all citizens' equality concerning taxes, a commitment to periodically vote on a budget that would detail public expenses, and the monarchy's guaranteeing of certain individual liberties. Necker had presented all these ideas to Louis XVI in a Memorial of the Princes in December of 1788 (Harris 1986, 378).

They were, however, far from being in agreement in regards to a whole series of other questions. For example, the representatives of the nobility and the third state, unlike those from the clergy, generally favored lifting censorship and guaranteeing the freedom of the press. The representatives of the Third Estate, meanwhile, clashed with the nobles and the clergy by defending the principle of equality, while the nobles and clergy only agreed to renounce their fiscal privileges if it did not mean giving up the feudal rights, both honorary and financial, which they enjoyed vis-à-vis the peasants (Markoff 1998, 298–300).

### *13.4.3 From the Estates General to the Rebellion of the Third Estate (May 5–June 27, 1789)*

#### 13.4.3.1 The Great Disappointment

All the high hopes which the representatives had harbored for the Estates General were shattered at the opening ceremony held on May 5, 1789, at which neither Louis XVI nor Necker made any reference whatsoever to the possibility of writing up a constitution, leading the representatives to conclude that the monarch was unwilling to give up his divine right to rule and would not allow constitutional limits to be placed upon his authority.

#### 13.4.3.2 From Voting by Estate to One Man, One Vote

To bend the will of the sovereign and his minister it was necessary for the three estates to unite and act in unison. This would prove to be very difficult, as was evident the following day (May 6), when the nobility and the clergy refused to accede to the patriots' proposal that the traditional ceremony confirming the powers given to each representative and the legality of their election be held in one chamber, in the presence of the representatives of the three classes. One must keep in mind that traditionally in France, the Estates-General featured a tripartite structure, unlike the British Parliament. That is, in the French body each estate voted as a block, leaving the Third Estate at the mercy of the privileged classes.

The nobles were determined to defend the perpetuation of the traditional practice in which the three classes deliberated separately and voted in blocks as estates.[30] The clergy was less adamant on this point, with some of its members clearly in favor of accepting the Third Estate's proposal.[31] Their flexibility led to what would be a prolonged debate on the issue. As discussions dragged on for more than a

[30] On this essential moment of the French revolution see Tackett (2006, 131–164). For a general examination of the dismantlement of the nobility's privileges, see Mackrell (1973).

[31] On the origins of this attitude amongst the French clergy, see Van Kley (2001, 263–299).

month without any agreement being reached, the "patriots", encouraged by Abbé Sieyes, decided to act unilaterally to secure what they had proposed.

## 13.4.4 *The Rebellion of the Third Estate*

### 13.4.4.1 The "National Assembly" Emerges (June 17)

On June 17, 1789, Sieyès declared that the members of the Third Estate were the true representatives of the nation and not simply a sectional interest, and that, as the nobility claimed prerogatives above the nation, they were not capable of being part of it (Mulholland 2012, 35). The Third Estate concluded that, as they represented 96 % of the nation (Boroumand 1990, 322–3), they alone sufficed to constitute the National Assembly and claim total sovereignty concerning fiscal affairs.[32] This act had immediate consequences because once the clergy heard of this development they unanimously voted to join the Third Estate, leaving the nobles isolated.[33]

### 13.4.4.2 The Tennis Court Oath (June 20)

The attitude of the Third Estate infuriated Louis XVI, who summoned a new session of the Estates General for the sole and express purpose of voiding that agreed to on June 17. To prevent such spontaneous meetings in the future, the monarch also ordered the closing of the chamber in which the sessions had hitherto been held. On the following day the representatives of the Third Estate found the door locked. Rather than abandoning Versailles, however, they chose to occupy a neighboring *jeu de paume* (a predecessor of tennis) court (Baker 2006, 68–69). Once gathered all those present (except one), presided over by the astronomer Jean-Sylvain Bailly, took an oath in response to a suggestion by Jean Joseph Mounier, not to separate until a constitution had been approved for the kingdom.[34]

Determined to ignore the unilateral actions of the Third Estate's representatives, on June 23, the king presided over a new session of the Estates General in which,

---

[32] It is interesting to note that, as Mulholland (2012, 34) observes, the Third Estate's representatives were not synonymous with the commercial bourgeoisie: 43 % of its members elected to the Estates General were holders of government offices, one quarter were lawyers, and only 13 % were engaged in trade, industry and banking. Yet, the Third Estate as a whole did voice bourgeois concerns and aspirations.

[33] For an overview of the formation of the National Assembly and how it worked until the approval of the 1791 constitution, see Tackett (1996).

[34] After declaring itself the representative body of the sovereign nation, the members of the constituted National Assembly insisted that they had been called upon to draft a new constitution for the realm, regenerate the public order, and maintain the true principles of monarchy. Thus, they swore to remain assembled "until the constitution of the realm is established and consolidated on a firm foundation" (Richet 1989, 479).

after announcing some reform measures, he decreed that the June 17 resolution was nullified, and expressed his commitment to fully maintaining "the traditional distinction of the state's three classes". When the monarch ordered the representatives to depart, however, only those from the clergy and the nobility obeyed him, as those from the Third Estate refused to abandon the chamber. Its spokesman, Bailly, spat at the Marquis of Dreux Brezé: "It seems to me that the Nation when assembled cannot be given orders". The Count of Mirabeau, the only nobleman who had crossed over to the Third Estate, then pronounced -according the most popular version, his famous phrase: "Go tell your lord that we are here by the will of the people and we will not leave except by force of bayonets.[35]

#### 13.4.4.3 The Constituent Assembly Is Formed (June 27)

The unflinching stand taken by the representatives of the Third Estate bent Louis XVI's will. On June 27, he agreed to yield and ordered the representatives of the nobility and the clergy to unite with the representatives of the people to form a single assembly in which all individual votes would be counted. The king's decision was "revolutionary" as it marked the end of the system employed by the Estates General ever since 1302, when it had arisen from a thoroughly feudal society. As this was a development which the representatives wished to make perfectly clear, on that very day they established themselves as a Constituent Assembly and began to discuss the task of drafting a constitution.

The Constituent Assembly held its sessions between June 27, 1789 and September 30, 1791. This period spanning 2 years and 3 months was, without any doubt, the most crucial of the entire Revolutionary era, as during it were adopted the legislative measures[36] which most contributed to altering France and, with it, the entire western constitutional tradition, forever. The Declaration of the Rights of Man and of the Citizen was approved on August 26, 1789.[37] From the point of view

[35] The exact sentence was: "we will not leave except by force of bayonets" (Ballard 2011, 351).

[36] For an overview of the legislative work of the National Assembly during this period, see Lemay and Patrick (1996).

[37] The Declaration's text was included as a preamble to the 1791 and 1793 constitutions. In 1795, the Declaration of Rights included some duties as well. Concerning the transcendence of the Declaration, as Van Kley (1994, 6) points out, although it is true that the Magna Carta, the Petition of Rights, and the Bill of Rights in England, the American Declaration of Independence, and various state's declarations and bills of rights, all preceded the French Declaration by a decade or more, in the Anglo-Saxon constitutional tradition the notion of human rights still had no universal value. Not even the American states' declarations of rights broke with the premise that the rights in question were peculiarly *English* ones. The French deputies were very conscious of the fact that they were going further than the American example in these respects; as one of the deputies of the National Assembly of 1789 stated, they sought not to receive lessons from others, but rather "to give them" to the rest of the world, as they did not proclaim the rights of Frenchmen only, but those "for all times and all nations". Their lofty aim, then, was not only to protect individual rights from the government, but also to build a foundation for a new kind of government.

of public order, the years of the Constituent Assembly and those of the Legislative Assembly (1791–1792) were relatively calm (at least compared to the following period, from 1792 to 1794) as, despite the popular rebellions of July 14 and October 6, 1789 the Constituent Assembly managed to maintain public order.

### *13.4.5 The Two Revolutions*

Compared to the American Revolution, the French Revolution was absolutely chaotic. Firstly, this was because of the irresolute king, who constantly vacillated and changed his positions. First, he declared himself to be in favor of the revolutionaries, only to later embrace absolutism. His unpredictable announcements were almost invariably ill-timed, which only served to exacerbate the resentments they caused. Secondly, because along with the "bourgeois revolution" of June 1789, that of the "patriots" of the Third Estate, there arose another revolutionary movement led by "popular" elements: the *sans culottes*.[38] The Revolution's social dimension would be transformed by three decisive events taking place on July 14 and October 6, 1789, and August 10, 1792.[39]

This "new revolution" began on July 14, 1789 with the Storming of the Bastille, the state prison which constituted a symbol of royal tyranny, for in it were confined political prisoners. When it was overrun by the people, however, it was virtually empty, though this did not keep its attackers from beheading its defenders and flaunting their heads, nailed on pikes, throughout Paris. As time went by the event would be idealized until it became a "National Act of Faith", becoming in the French consciousness a genuine collective event carried out by *la Nation* (Lüsebrink and Reichardt 1997, 212 and 243).

The people took action again on the following 6th of October, when a group of Parisian women forced the royal family to flee from Versailles to Paris, leaving it at the mercy of the mobs. Finally, on August 10, 1792, wild crowds invaded the Tuileries Palace and took the royal family prisoner after massacring the Swiss guard

---

[38] So dubbed because they did not wear the short trousers (*culottes*) which extended to right below the knee that were the attire typical of the nobility and the high bourgeoisie. On the growth of Parisian popular radicalism, Rose (1983, 6–22). About the part that the *sans culottes* played in the French Revolution, see Sonenscher (2008) and the classic study by Soboul (1972).

[39] The best coverage of this social aspect of the French revolution is still that contained in the classic study by Lefebvre (2005), in which the author distinguishes between the Aristocratic Revolution (7–38), the Bourgeois Revolution (39–92), the Popular Revolution (93–127) and the Peasant Revolution (129–152). Furet (2003) features a different chronological approach, as he distinguishes between "The Revolution of 1789: 1787–1791" (41–100), The Jacobin Republic "1791–1794" (101–149) the Thermidorian Republic "1794–1799" (151–209) and, of course, he considers the Napoleonic era the last period of the Revolution (211–265).

protecting it.[40] This brutal assault on the royal palace marked the beginning of the revolution's most radical phase, the "Terror", during which the revolutionaries decided to abolish monarchy and call for new elections to choose a second constituent assembly: the Convention in what has been called the "Second Revolution" (Whaley 1993, 205–224).

### 13.4.6 From Monarchy to Republic

The confluence of the two revolutions, the bourgeois movement and that driven by the common people, makes the chronology of the "French Revolution" extremely confusing. There were two stages with two different regimes: the first was that of the constitutional monarchy which, in turn, featured two bodies: the Constituent Assembly (1789–1791) and the Legislative Assembly, that ended with the insurrection of August 10, 1792 (Mitchell 1988). The second stage was that of the First Republic, which began when the king was jailed, tried and guillotined. This second stage was, in turn, also composed of two parts. During the first of these the Constituent Assembly returned, dubbed the "Convention", lasting from September of 1792 until 1795, followed by a phase known as the "Directory" (1795–1799), during which the Republic was once again controlled by a bourgeois oligarchy.

The fear sown by the violence of the mobs dissuaded most from participating in the elections, which gave rise to the Convention. Since most citizens were frightened only the most ardent and extreme revolutionaries ended up voting, yielding a set of representatives more radical than the people (Lucas 1994, 57–79). In addition, this came at a time when two thirds of France was occupied by Prussian and Austrian armies, and only the most radical citizens turned out to vote. The second Constituent Assembly, thus, represented a minority of the French people. Nonetheless, following a fierce confrontation between political factions (Patrick 1972), the Convention would impose a dictatorship by seizing upon the state of emergency declared because of the war France had been fighting against Austria and Prussia as of April 1792.

[40] The event was the result of the confrontation between the Girondins and the most radical faction of French revolutionaries, the Montagnards, who represented the people (*sans culottes*), and were headed, among other leaders, by Robespierre, the "Incorruptible". As Slavin (1986, 3–4) points out, the Girondins never resolved the conflict between the power of the state and that of individual liberty, as they favored the latter yet extolled legality, rejecting the principle of insurrection. When they attacked Robespierre for acting illegally, he answered them with his revolutionary logic that "All these things were illegal, as illegal as the Revolution, as the overthrow of the throne and of the Bastille, as illegal as liberty itself. You cannot have a revolution without a revolution". Robespierre (2007b, IX, 88–89) Another of the Montagnards' leaders, Saint Just, argued that government was a necessary evil and than one can never govern without guilt. On the dispute between the Girondins and the Montagnards, see Higonnet (1985, 513–544). For an overview of the political faction of the Girondins, see Kates (1985).

Radicalism prevailed between September of 1792 and July of 1794 (Bouloiseau 1983). This was the era of sweeping and ambitious attacks against Christianity, with the civil constitution of the clergy, the revolutionary calendar, the worship of the Supreme Being (Tallet 1991, 1–28),[41] the mass executions of the Terror, and the dictatorship of the Committee of Public Safety.[42] In reality, the second Constitution of Revolutionary France, that of 1793, was not at all representative of French society at the time, which explains why the Revolution degenerated into civil war during the Terror (Andress 2005) with the uprising of the royalists in Vendée and the harsh repression of the Republican army, in what it became a "total war",[43] leading to the ultimate failure of revolutionary radicalism.

For all these reasons, from 1789 to 1799, France was sunk in chaos, seeing a Constituent Assembly, followed by a constitutional monarchy, a republic, a radical dictatorship and, finally, a bourgeois republic simultaneously threatened by right-wing "realists" (monarchists) and left-wing Jacobins. Three formal constitutions were adopted, in 1791, 1793 and 1795, none of which endured. They either proved unviable, as was the case with that from 1791; were suspended because of a state of emergency, as occurred in 1793; or the regime needed the support of the army to stay in power, and suffered a series of annual *coup d'états*. Such was the case with the 1795 constitution and the "Directory", attacked on the left by radical republican Jacobins, and on the right by those in favor of a return to monarchy as the new regime suffered from a crisis of republican legitimacy (Brown 2006, 23–46).[44]

[41] On the process of de-Christianization, see Vovelle (1991) and Aston (2000).

[42] For an overview of the actions of the Committee of Public Safety during the Terror, see Palmer (2005).

[43] As Bell (2007, 183–134) points out, the War in Vendée was not a genocide but was a tragedy of unspeakable dimensions, a ghastly crime as well as an indelible stain on the Revolution, which became a "total war" of extermination, with all lines between combatants and noncombatants being erased. A member of the sans-culotte movement, and radical political journalist, "Gracchus" Babeuf (2008) coined the term "populicidal" (*populicide*) when he described the nature of the repression in Vendée.

[44] Or simply because there were elections every year in which the government was systematically voted out, and the military had to correct the results of the elections, which were always unfavorable for the regime. By 1798, Parisians no longer even wondered if there would be a *coup d'état*, which they took for granted, but which general would lead it. As Lyons (2008, 227) points out, the government of the Directory tried to steer a neutral course between the two extremes of Jacobinism and Royalism. For instance, on 18 Fructidor of the Year V (September 4, 1797), it had drawn on the support of the Left, while on 22 Floréal of the Year VI (May 11, 1798), the right wing had rallied against Jacobinism. Under the threat of military defeat and economic difficulty these props were no longer available to the republican center, and political division polarized again, as the military and economic crisis not only triggered a resurgence of Jacobinism, but also heralded a renewal of royalist counter-revolutionary activity.

## 13.5 What Lasting Effects Did the French Revolution Have?

At first glance it would seem that the chaos which broke out during the revolutionary decade (1789–1799), did not have a lasting impact on French institutions, as monarchy was ultimately reinstated. First there was a new monarchy, that of Napoleon, between 1804 and 1814, followed by the old monarchy, restored by a brother of Louis XVI, Louis XVIII (1814–1830). A closer look, however, reveals that the Revolution did, in fact, introduce essential changes, not just in France, but throughout Europe, by precipitating the end of the *Ancien Regime*.

### *13.5.1 The Appearance of "National Sovereignty"*

The first momentous effect of the French Revolution was that it transformed the very meaning of sovereignty, as the right to legitimately exercise power was wrested from the king and given to the nation. In the case of Britain's Parliamentary system this transformation was the result, as we know, of a progressive transfer of royal prerogatives and powers to the Parliament. In France, this shift was sudden and violent. With the Tennis Court Oath the idea was imposed in France, overnight, that sovereignty was not held by the monarch, but rather the people, whose representatives exercised power via the National Assembly.[45] While this principle had already been adopted by the United States in 1776, the latter was but a small, nascent and untried state far from Old Europe. France, in contrast was the oldest and most prestigious monarchy on the entire Continent, a country whose social organization and public law had remained virtually intact since the Middle Ages. Thus, the French Revolution had a greater impact in the Old World.

### *13.5.2 The Origins of "National" Patriotism*

Another important consequence of the French Revolution was the reemergence of the former meaning of the "nation", now understood to refer to all the citizens of France. This essential shift was marked by the crucial Celebration of the Federation (*Fête de la Fédération*), held for the first time on July 14, 1790. The event was repeated every year on the same date, with delegations from all over France meeting in Paris to celebrate their "national" brotherhood. This union of all the French in a single and indivisible nation was reflected in the thorough centralization

[45] Though there was debate between those like Sieyès, who invited the Third Estate to proclaim itself a "National Assembly", and the position of those like Mirabeau, who invited its members to convene as an "Assembly of Representatives of the People". Boroumand (1990, 311).

imposed by the Jacobins, who abolished the traditional provinces and established a set of departments which continue to constitute the basis for the territorial organization of the French state. Thus, it was the origin of French "nationalism", an ideological movement aimed at attaining and maintaining autonomy, unity and identity on behalf of a population, an active movement inspired by an ideology and symbolism of the nation rather than simply a shared sentiment or consciousness (Smith 2009, 61).

### 13.5.3 The Symbols of the French State

Another lasting legacy of the French Revolution involves the symbols of the French state: the flag, the national day, and the national anthem, all of revolutionary origin.[46] The French flag is a compromise reflecting both the country's revolutionary and royal heritage: its red and blue are the colors of revolutionary Paris, while its white alludes to the color of the old royal flag. Even today, July 14 is the French National Day that commemorates the first "Celebration of the Federation", on July 14, 1790 (and not the Storming of the Bastille, contrary to common belief).[47] On a night of patriotic fervor, Rouget de l'Isle penned the lyrics to the French national anthem, "La Marseillaise", so named because the delegation from Marseille entered revolutionary Paris singing it in July of 1792.[48]

---

[46] As Leith (1998, 9–10) observes, the use of all these symbols was initially intended as an exercise of propaganda in what he considers the totalitarian aspect of the Revolution, a specter that can clearly be seen in the text of the following prospectus of the *Feuille du salut public*, the mouthpiece of the Committee of Public Safety: "*We will show this Fatherland to the citizens ceaselessly, in his laws, in his games, in his home, in his loves, in his festivities. We will never leave him to himself alone. We will by this continual coercion awaken ardent love for the Fatherland. We will direct his inclination toward this single passion. It is in this way that the Frenchman will acquire a national physiognomy; it is in this way that, by identifying him so to speak with the happiness in his country, we will bring about this vitally necessary transformation of the monarchical spirit into a republican spirit*".

[47] The change was introduced in a bill presented to the Chamber of Deputies on May 21, 1880, by Benjamin Raspail, backed by sixty-four representatives. With strong support in the Parliament, it was officially introduced on July 6. The date was, thus, transformed from an opposition symbol to an emblem of the state, from a subversive commemoration to a national holiday, as the violent character of the storming of the Bastille was glossed over by the ideal image of the national celebration of its first anniversary (Lüsebrink and Reichardt 1997, 229).

[48] Its words are infused with the revolutionary zeal of those days: *Allons enfants de la Patrie/Le jour de gloire est arrivé !/Contre nous de la tyrannie/L'étendard sanglant est levé! (bis)/Entendez-vous dans nos campagnes,/Mugir ces féroces soldats?/Ils viennent jusque dans nos bras,/Égorger vos fils, vos compagnes REFRAIN: Aux armes citoyens!/Formez vos bataillons/Marchons! Marchons/qu'un sang impur/abreuve nos sillons!/Que veut cette horde d'esclaves,/De traîtres, de rois conjurés?/Pour qui ces ignobles entraves,/Ces fers dès longtemps préparés? (bis)/Français! pour nous, ah! quel outrage!/ Quels transports il doit exciter!/C'est nous qu'on ose méditer/De rendre à l'antique esclavage* (Arise, children of the fatherland/The day of glory has arrived/Against us tyranny's/Bloody standard is raised/Listen the sound in the fields/The howling of these fearsome

### 13.5.4 The Reinforcement of the State

From the political and legal point of view, the most important aspect of the French Revolution is that, as an earthquake which shook the very foundations of the French polity, it allowed for a total reconfiguration of its traditional structure. The Revolution paved the way for a series of bases underpinning a very powerful state as the political power arising from the Constituent Assembly was fully dissociated from historic ties to the *Ancien Regime*. Thus, for example, one of the first measures the French revolutionaries took was to eliminate the parlements which had so effectively impeded the monarchy from taking action. Also abolished were the "fundamental laws" which, by force of custom, had gradually laid down the foundations of the French state under the *Ancien Régime*.

In reality, as Tocqueville lucidly observed, more than a true rupture what took place was a reinforcement of the state, extremely clear in the pivotal aspect of the "Administrative Centralization" that in his opinion France owed not to the Revolution, but to the Old Regime,[49] though the body exercising power was no longer the monarch, but an assembly representing France as a sovereign nation. In fact what really happened was that an absolute monarchy gave way to a regime of assembly-based or democratic absolutism, which culminated during the most radical phase of the Revolution: the first stage of the Convention, spanning from August 10, 1792 (the attack on the Tuileries Palace) and July 27, 1784 (the Thermidorian Reaction). Paradoxically, the new regime was far more authoritarian than the old one, as during this stage the government was not in the hands of an elected assembly, but rather in those of two revolutionary committees: that of Public Safety and that of General Security, which imposed an iron-fisted dictatorship.[50]

---

soldiers/They are coming into our midst/To cut the throats of your sons and wives! REFRAIN: To arms, citizens!/Form your battalions!/March, march/Let impure blood/Water our furrows. What do they want, this horde of slaves?/Of traitors and conspiratorial kings/For whom these vile chains/ These long-prepared irons?/Frenchmen, for us, ah!/What an outrage! What methods must be taken?/It is we they dare plan/To return to the old slavery!) On how the Marseillaise was transformed from a *chant de guerre* into a national anthem, see Mason (1996, 93–103) and Michelet (1899, 470–473).

[49] "I once heard an orator, in the days when we had political assemblies, call administrative centralization 'that noble conquest of the Revolution which Europe envies.' I am willing to admit that centralization was a noble conquest, and that Europe envies us its possession; but I deny that it was a conquest of the Revolution. It was, on the contrary, a feature of the Old Regime [...]" (de Tocqueville 2013, 50). *L'Ancien régime et la Révolution.* This work, one of the most insightful analyses of the French Revolution, was translated into English and published the same year as the first French edition.

[50] Both dictatorial bodies operated based on an eminently practical approach in its recommendations, stating that the important thing was not to watch over everybody—which was physically impossible—but to make them *believe* that they were constantly being watched. Its two main instruments were the "Law of Suspects", a decree passed by the National Convention on September 17, 1793, and the "Revolutionary Tribunal", created via a decree of October 20, 1793 (Brissaud 2001, 565–566). Both laws featured only two possible outcomes when suspects

All of this, however, was utterly justified according to figures such as Maximilien Robespierre (1758–1794), one of the Revolution's most radical leaders, whose thinking illustrates that of the revolutionaries who endorsed the idea that absolute power exercised in the name of national sovereignty constituted the incorruptible "theory of the revolutionary government:"

> The theory of revolutionary government is as new as the Revolution that has spawned it. It is not necessary to look for it in the books of political writers, who have not seen this revolution at all, nor in the laws of the tyrants who, content to abuse their power, take little care to secure its legitimacy; this word is for the aristocracy nothing more than a question of terror; for tyrants, a scandal; for many people, an enigma. The principle of constitutional government is to conserve the Republic; that of the revolutionary government is to found it. Constitutional government mainly deals with civil freedom, while revolutionary government deals with public freedom. Under a constitutional regime it is sufficient to protect individuals from the abuses of public power; under the revolutionary regime, public power is forced to defend itself against all the factions attacking it. A revolutionary government owes its good citizens all its national protection; to the enemies of the people it owes nothing but death.[51]

The Thermidorian Reaction, although it began with the inevitable execution of the radical revolutionary leaders, immediately tempered the Revolution's tone. Firstly, because it limited the power of the Assembly by establishing two chambers, rather than just one, as had been the case since June of 1789. In addition, from a sociological point of view, the bourgeoisie recovered power at the expense of the *sans culottes*, with the advantage that it was equipped with the constitutional

---

were apprehended: suspension of the prosecution (*nolle prosequi*) or death. In addition, the "revolutionary process" did not guarantee defendants even the most basic rights. There was not even a requirement that the defendant even be present (as a result of Danton, who vehemently defended himself against public prosecutor Fouquier-Tinville). Neither was any physical proof necessary, "moral proof" sufficing to convict the accused. Under these conditions the procedures boiled down to mere interrogations of the defendants and the confirmation of their identities. The wave of repression carried out under this legislation led to between 16,000 and 40,000 executions and the arrest of some 800,000 suspects. For an overview of what happened during this ominous period called the "Great Terror", see Gough (2010, 67–72). On revolutionary violence as a political tool, see Gueniffey (2003) and Robespierre's vindication of revolutionary terror (2007c). For a statistical study of the victims of the Terror, see Greer (1966) and Louie (1964).

[51] Taken from his *Report on the principles of Revolutionary Government*, a speech delivered at the National Convention on December 25, 1793 (*Rapport sur les principes du gouvernement ré volutionnaire, fait au nom du Comité de salut public par Maximilien Robespierre*; *imprimé par ordre de la Convention*; *le 5 nivôse de l'an second*) in Robespierre (2007a, X, 274). In a speech on February 5, 1794, Robespierre reaffirmed the distinction saying that in "calm waters" democratic government must be trusting towards the people and severe towards itself, guided by virtue as its fundamental principle. However, when the "tempest rages" and the revolutionary government is at war, this principle no longer applies because "if the mainspring of popular government in peacetime is virtue, amid revolution it is at the same time virtue and terror: virtue, without which terror is impotent" and as "terror is nothing but prompt, severe, inflexible justice; it is therefore an emanation of virtue". If terror is the mainspring of despotic Government, "the government of the revolution is the despotism of liberty against tyranny". Quoted also by Reemtsma (2012, 172). On Robespierre's revolutionary convictions, see Jordan (1989, 149–164). For an overall view of Robespierre's government at its height, see Scurr (2006, 288–325).

instruments that would allow it to construct a powerful bourgeois state. To do this, however, Napoleon would still have to construct what de Malafosse (1975, 25) called the "masses of granite of the imperial era", upon which the contemporary French state still rests.

### 13.5.5 The Social Transformation of France

Another of the factors which saw decisive change as a result of the Revolution was France's social structure. In 1789, 80 % of the French were peasants who, practically overnight, became the owners of their lands,[52] triggering a "democratization" of the means of production and turning these new proprietors into the firmest defenders of the Revolution (Cobban 1999, 81–90). This circumstance would push the formal adoption of the male universal suffrage in 1792 (Crook 1996, 79–101) although the principle would not be consolidated until 1848.

### 13.5.6 The European Dimension of the French Revolution

There is still an essential aspect of the French Revolution which must be discussed: its foreign repercussions, as the war which began in 1792 would not only serve to consolidate the ideals of the Revolution, but to extend them all over Europe. Revolutionary France first defended itself from its invaders before going on to become an imperial power, seeking, in the words of Danton—January 31, 1793—its "natural borders" (Richet 1989, 754–762). Military service was implemented and revolutionary armies swelled as France morphed from an invaded nation to an invading empire (Rothenberg 1988, 771–793). The Revolution ultimately gave rise to out-and-out imperialism.[53]

Paradoxically, nevertheless, it is in this last regard in which the French Revolution was, perhaps, most effective. The declaration of war, which originally had been a desperate ploy to save the Revolution, ended up serving as the catalyst uniting all the French under the banner of national patriotism.[54] Moreover, through the war the

[52] On how the Revolution turned France into a republic of property-owners, see Jones (2000, 161–166).

[53] On this crucial aspect of the French Revolution, see Bertaud (1988) and Blanning (1996).

[54] As Forrest (2009, 19) suggests, it had a lot to do with the *levée en masse* decreed on August 23, 1793, as for the first time military service was regarded as an essential aspect of citizenship, incumbent upon all equally, without distinction based on income or property ownership. For the first time the law recognized only one single form of citizenship. Not only were the young men of military age who had to serve in the armies to do their patriotic duty, but the rest of the population as well, as they were assigned a variety of support roles in the country's war effort: women through nursing or by sewing clothes for the warriors, children by making linen for use in hospitals, and old men by preaching the values of the Revolution in public places and exhorting the young to action. In reality, the whole nation was mobilized in defense of its territory, its rights and its people. The idea was powerful, as it appealed to the heart as well as to the head, and would be central to the legend of the revolutionary armies during the nineteenth century.

principles of the French Revolution would be spread all over Europe (Rudé 2000, 155–172). Hence, the absolutist powers, whose monarchs initially rubbed their hands at France's weakness, were ultimately horrified to see the revolutionary spirit leak into their kingdoms. This was only the first blow against the foundations of Europe's Old Order, as the building would crumble to the ground over the course of the nineteenth century.[55]

## 13.6 The Failure of Assembly-Based Government

In the French Revolution, as in the American, assembly-based, legislative government triumphed over monarchical power. This was clear in France on October 10, 1789, when the National Assembly imposed upon Louis XVI a new title: "Louis by the grace of God and, by the constitutional law of the state, King of the French".[56] He was, then, no longer the king by divine right, but because the Constituent Assembly had so named him in the constitutional pact. From a legal point of view it should be noted that he ceased to be an absolute monarch via a decree issued by the Constituent Legislature.

The regime of constitutional monarchy never took firm hold because the Assembly stripped the king of virtually all his powers, except for a limited veto right. The irresolute Louis XVI, after first seeking to ingratiate himself with the new regime, later opted to flee France and join his fellow *emigrées*, though he was frustrated in his attempt, recognized and detained at Varennes, just 30 miles from his destination, the royalist stronghold of Montmedy, on the night of June 20, 1791. The "Flight to Varennes" marked the beginning of the end for the French monarchy. The Constituent Assembly finished writing up the first French Constitution (1791)

[55] As Schroeder (1996, 71–2) highlights, the Revolution posed a challenge to the whole legal and conceptual basis of international politics, as instead of international claims and transactions being argued and fought out on the basis of treaties and legal rights, "popular will" was now to be the decisive factor. The first concrete international disputes provoked by the Revolution came between France and various estates of the German Empire, in the Alsace-Lorraine, over which France claimed exclusive power and rights on the basis of popular sovereignty. The territory was ultimately incorporated into New Revolutionary France. It was also the case of the French enclaves of Avignon and the Venaissin, historically belonging to the Papal State, which were also incorporated into France on the basis of popular sovereignty.

[56] On October 12, 1789, the Constituent Assembly decreed that Louis XVI was "king of the French" (*roi des Français*), and beginning on November 6 the decrees from the Assembly were promulgated in the name of *Louis, par la grâce de Dieu, et par la loi constitutionnelle de l'état, Roi des François*. The new title was not added to the royal seal until February 19, 1790 (Pinoteau 2004, 907).

unilaterally, without consulting with the king.[57] The utter exclusion of the monarch and his loss of all credibility led to a constitution in which power was assigned to the Assembly, with no counterbalance provided by a strong executive. Louis's failed escape attempt also sparked a wave of violent anti-monarchical sentiment among the most radical elements comprising the Mountain (*La Montagne*), who would end up prevailing after the declaration of war (April of 1792), and through the bloody revolution of August 10, 1792, when a mob invaded the Tuileries Palace. The royal family was jailed, the monarchy was abolished, and five months later Louis XVI ascended the scaffold after being sentenced to death by a political process and tribunal.[58]

The "Terror" would come to a stop on July 27, 1794 (*9 Termidor de l'An II*), the end of the popular revolution, when Robespierre and his companions were guillotined, and the *sans culottes* were overpowered. As a result, in what was called the Thermidorian Reaction the bourgeois oligarchy was able to regain control of the Revolution (Lyons 1975, 123–146).[59]

The change of regime from the Radical to the Bourgeois republic (Rudé 2000, 122) made it possible to close the second Constituent Assembly (the Convention), after the drafting of a new Constitution in 1795 (*Constitution de l'An III*)[60] which,

---

[57] As Fitzsimmons (1994, 254) observes, the crisis of Louis' departure marked a watershed in the history of the Constituent Assembly, as it revealed how indissoluble the partnership between the National Assembly and the French nation had become, forcing the nation to make an absolutely unprecedented choice between the monarch and the Assembly; it decisively embraced the latter.

[58] Louis XVI's trial started on December 10, 1792, and the king was condemned to suffer the death penalty of January 17, 1793. The Convention then initiated an exhausting and fierce debate over whether the execution had to be carried out immediately or not. At 2.00 A.M. on Sunday, January 20, 1793, a roll call vote decided against adjournment by a vote of 380–346. On the motion of Cambacerès, the Convention adopted four articles fixing the king's fate in the following terms: *I. The National Convention declares Louis Capet, last king of the French, guilty of conspiracy against the liberty of the nation and of attacks against the general security of the state. II. The National Convention decrees that Louis Capet will suffer the death penalty. III. The National Convention declares null the act of Louis Capet, carried to the bar by his counsels, called "the appeal to the nation of the judgment against him rendered by the Convention" and prohibits any person whatsoever to reintroduce this appeal, under pain of being pursued and punished as guilty of attacking the general security of the republic. IV. The Provisional Executive Council will notify during the day, will present itself to Louis Capet, and will take the measures of security necessary to insure the execution within 24 hours... and to render an account of everything to the National Convention immediately after it will have been done.* The session ended at 3 A.M. (Jordan 2004, 198–199). The king was publicly beheaded the following day, Monday, January 21, 1793, at 10:22 A.M. For a transcription of the trial speeches, see Walzer (1992), with an interesting introduction (pp. 1–92). For an interpretation of the meaning and consequences of Louis XVI's execution, see Dunn (1994).

[59] On the crucial development of the Thermidorian Reaction, see Baczko (1994).

[60] The new constitutional text was voted by the National Convention on August 22, 1795, and ratified in early September by a popular referendum in which less than a million French citizens participated. As Craiutu (2012, 136) points out, the new constitution reflected the moderates' desire to come to terms with the complex legacy of the Terror by building a system of ordered liberty. The problem was that it tried to stabilize republican institutions in a highly volatile political context.

first of all, overturned the principle of the unicameral legislature which had been fiercely maintained since 1789. There was no one-man Executive (but rather a five-man Directory) and there were two legislative chambers: the Council of the Five Hundred and the Council of the Elders, with 250 members. There was no bicameralism, however, in the sense that the two chambers represented the same population. Legislative power was split in two, as the Thermidorians feared the Convention's potential for assembly-based absolutism. As a result, the first chamber was to propose laws, while the second approved them (Lyons 2008, 18–19). Restrictions on the electorate were imposed through the reestablishment of a system of strict and indirect census suffrage; as opposed to the Constitution of 1793, which had established universal and direct masculine suffrage, under that of 1795 only the rich could vote and be voted for (meaning those who had become rich from the sale of ecclesiastical assets, as the nobles had either been guillotined or had fled France).[61]

Did the Constitution of 1795 establish a liberal state like that in America or the one that would end up emerging in England? One might be led to think so, as its preamble included a 22-article preamble called the "Declaration of the Rights and Duties of Man and the Citizen".[62] In reality, however, the bourgeois government which arose from the Thermidorian Reaction was unable to win the French people's support for the principles of the new regime. One faction, the "realists", wished to return to the monarchical regime (Godechot 1971), while another wished to return to radical republicanism (the Jacobins) (Woloch 1970). Caught between the two camps, the Directory had no choice but to turn to the military time and time again to preserve order (Lucas 1977, 231–260). When Napoleon seized power through a *coup d'état* in 1799, the French people, weary of 10 years of chaos, largely approved.

[61] This is what Livesey (2001, 48) calls "Commercial Republicanism" as opposed to the revolutionary "Modern Republicanism" born on September 22, 1792, whose 1793 Constitution established the principle of universal male suffrage. The constitution, however, was never applied, as during the Terror the French Republic existed under a dictatorship.

[62] The title of the Declaration differed from the 1789 version that was simply called "Declaration of the Rights of Man and of the Citizen". As Baker (1994, 182) explains, in 1789 the demand for a declaration of duties was strong enough to produce a roll-call vote, but not to convince a majority of deputies, as the motion was defeated by 570 to 433. As was the case in 1789, in the 1795 constitution the declaration of rights was really included as a preamble to the constitutional text, a formal detail that in principle enforced its constitutional value. Necker, one of the last ministers of Louis XVI, had a poor opinion of the 1795 constitution in this aspect, as he thought it jeopardized individual liberty and rights. He criticized the fact that the legislative power had the right to curtail civil liberties, such as freedom of the press, and the right to travel, and could send individuals into exile if any suspicion arose that their action might threaten the security of the state. Moreover, the insufficient protection of individuals against encroachment upon their rights was demonstrated by the fact that there was no independent public magistracy empowered to hear the complaints of citizens wronged by unconstitutional acts—a dangerous situation, as citizens were subject to decisions made by administrators removable at the will of the government or the legislative power, against which they had no recourse (Craiutu 2012, 143–144).

It is important to point out that in both the United States and in France, attempts to establish governments with strong legislative branches and weak executive ones would fail. In America, chaos and confusion would break out in the form of Shay's Rebellion, which prompted the "federal debate" that led to the drafting and ratification of the Constitution of 1787, establishing a more solid Union under the rule of a powerful Executive, headed by a President. In France, under the Directory, the system was too artificial and could not sustain itself. The French were really not accustomed to the dynamics and the give and take of parliamentary government, at least until the Restoration of 1815. Democratic, assembly-based government would be attempted again in France in 1830 and in 1848, but would not succeed until the III Republic, in 1875. The French monarchical tradition would reappear with Napoleon Bonaparte, a former supporter of Robespierre's who had actually been on the verge of being guillotined. Napoleon suddenly became a key figure on the French political scene after saving the Directory through his military actions immediately after the approval of the September 1795 Constitution, on October 5 (*13 Vendimiaire de l'An III*) (1958, 191–202). Four years later, he took power, and in 1804 reestablished monarchy in France.

## TIMELINE

### From Louis XIV to Louis XVI

| | |
|---|---|
| 1643 | Louis XIV reigns (1643–1715). |
| 1661 | Louis XIV comes of age, authorized to rule. |
| 1715 | Louis XV reigns (1715–1774). |
| 1723 | Louis XV comes of legal age, authorized to rule. |
| 1754–1761 | The Seven Years War. |
| 1763 | The Peace of Paris. France loses its colonies in America and India. |
| 1771 | Maupeou reforms the parlements. Offices may no longer be purchased or inherited. |
| 1774 | Beginning of the reign of Louis XVI (1774–1789). |
| 1774–1776 | Ministry of Turgot. |
| 1776–1781 | Ministry of Necker. |
| 1778 | France allies with the North American rebels. |
| 1783 | Peace of Versailles. Independence of the United States of America. |
| 1783–1787 | Ministry of Calonne. |
| 1787–1788 | Ministry of Loménie de Brienne. |

### The Origins of the Revolution (June of 1788–October of 1789)

1788 Rebellion of the Nobility. The king clashes with the Parlement of Paris.
June. Rebellion in Dauphine. The provincial estates of Vizille.
August. Necker's return. Convocation of the Estates General.
1789 May 5. Opening of the Estates General.
June 17. The Third Estate is transformed into a National Assembly.
June 20. Tennis Court Oath.
June 27. The Constituent Assembly is established.
July 14. The Storming of the Bastille. First popular revolution.
July 17. The tricolor flag is adopted.
August 4. The abolition of privileges.
August 26. Declaration of the Rights of Man and of the Citizen.
October 6. The people of Paris force the royal family to flee from Versailles to Paris. The Constituent Assembly also moves. Second popular revolution.

### The Stage of the Constitutional Monarchy (October 10, 1789–August 10, 1792)

1789 October 10. The Constituent Assembly grants the king a new title: "Louis, by the grace of God and, by constitutional law, King of the French".
2 November. Expropriation of ecclesiastical assets.
December. The club of the Jacobins is formed. First revolutionary political party (Mirabeau).
1790 January. The creation of popular societies, the Revolution's most radical political parties (Cordeliers Club: Danton, Marat).
July 12. Civil constitution of the clergy.
July 14. Celebration of the Federation. Origin of the French nation.
1791 June 20–21. The Flight to Varennes. The king's attempt to flee France is foiled.
July 17. The National Guard fires on a crowd calling for the abolition of the monarchy.
September 3. Approval of the first French Constitution.
September 30. The end of the Constituent Assembly.
October 1. Opening of the Legislative Assembly.
1792 April 20. The Legislative Assembly declares war on Austria.
July 14. Writing of "La Marseillaise". (French national anthem) Third Celebration of the Federation.
August 1. The Brunswick Manifesto.
August 10. Third popular insurrection. The mob overruns the Tuileries Palace. The king and his family are jailed.

**The Establishment of the First French Republic: The Stage of the Convention (September of 1792–October of 1795)**

1792 September 1–2. First killings. The start of the Terror.
September 2–6. Elections to the Convention.
September 20. First military victory of revolutionary France at Valmy.
September 22. Abolition of the monarchy and proclamation of the "republic".
6 November. Dumouriez defeats the Austrians at Jemmapes.
19 November. Decree through which the Convention announces its intention "to carry brotherhood and aid to all those peoples who wish to recover their freedom". France exports the Revolution. The beginnings of "revolutionary imperialism".

1793 January 21. The execution of Louis XVI.
February. The first coalition of European monarchies against revolutionary France is formed.
March. Monarchical revolt in Vendée (Western France). A bloody civil war breaks out between monarchists and republicans.
April. Creation of the Committee of Public Safety. Restoration of the dictatorship by the most radical revolutionaries (Montagnards). Arrest and execution of the Girondins.
June 24. New French Constitution (*Constitution de l' An II*). Universal masculine suffrage is established. It will be a "virtual" text, its application suspended by the state of emergency declared.
September 5. The *sans culottes* seize power and implement a regime of terror.
September 22. The Convention decrees a massive raising of troops (unmarried men ages 18–25), the first step towards the enactment of compulsory military service, implemented in 1798. In 1 year the revolutionary army grows from 200,000 to 800,000 men.
October 10. A "revolutionary government" is installed. The Revolution's most radical phase begins.
October 16. Execution of Marie Antoinette.
24 November. Implantation of a revolutionary calendar (*Fabré d' Églantine*) as a measure of "de-Christianization".

1794 January. Robespierre seizes power (which he maintains until July).
June 8 (*20 Prarial de l'An II*). Celebration in honor of the "Supreme Being". Peak of Robespierre's power.
July 27 (*9 Termidor*, *An II*). The Thermidorian Reaction. Moderates and centrists arrest and execute Robespierre and other "terrorists". End of the Terror and the beginning of the last phase of the Convention (Thermidorian Convention, July 27, 1794–October 26, 1795).
August 22. Third French Constitution (*L' An III*).

1795 October 5 (*13 Vendimiaire, An IV*). General Bonaparte represses a pro-monarchy rebellion against the Convention, opening fire against the demonstrators in the streets of Paris. His actions earn him favor with the government.
October 26. End of the Convention.

**The Second Stage of the First French Republic: The Directory (October of 1795–November of 1799)**

1796 April. The Conspiracy of Equals (Babeuf).
March 27. Napoleon takes control of the Army of Italy. Napoleon undertakes a victorious 1.5-year military campaign against Austria that ends with the Peace of Campo-Formio (October 7, 1797). His victory makes Napoleon extremely popular.
1797 September 4. The government overpowers the monarchists by force of arms.
1798 May 4. New government, a *coup d'etat* against the extremist republicans (Jacobins).
July 1. Napoleon disembarks in Alexandria. Beginning of his Egyptian campaign.
August 1–2. The English destroy the French fleet at Aboukir Bay.
September 5. The Jourdan Law enacts obligatory military service for unmarried men ages 20–25.
1799 August 23. Napoleon abandons Egypt after ceding control to General Jean Baptiste Kléber.
October 8. Napoleon disembarks in France.

# References


Allmand, C. (2001). *The hundred years war. England and France at War c. 1300–c. 1450*. Cambridge, UK: Cambridge University Press.

Andress, D. (2005). *The terror: Civil war in the French Revolution*. London: Little Brown.

Aston, N. (1992). *The end of an Elite. The French Bishops and the coming of the French Revolution: 1786–90*. Oxford: Clarendon.

Aston, N. (2000). *Religion and revolution in France, 1780–1804*. Washington, DC: Catholic University of America Press.

Aubry, O. (1952). *La Révolution française*. Paris: Flammarion.

Babeuf, G. (2008). *La guerre de la Vendée et le système de dépopulation*. Paris: Cerf (Originally published in 1795, under the title: *Le système de dépopulation ou La vie et les crimes de Carrier*. Paris: Franklin).

Baczko, B. (1994). *Ending the terror: The French Revolution after Robespierre*. Cambridge, UK: Cambridge University Press.

Baker, K. M. (1978). French political thought at the accession of Louis XVI. *The Journal of Modern History, 50*, 279–303.

Baker, K. M. (1989a). Sieyès and the creation of French Revolutionary discourse. In L. Valtz Mannucci (Ed.), *The languages of revolution* (pp. 195–205). Milano: Istituto De Studi Storici.

Baker, K. M. (1992). Introduction: The Maupeou revolution. The transformation of French politics at the end of the old regime. *Historical Reflections (reflexions historiques), 18*(2), 1–16.

Baker, K. M. (1994). The idea of a declaration of rights. In D. Van Kley (Ed.), *The French idea of freedom: The old regime and the declaration of rights of 1789* (pp. 154–199). Stanford, CA: Stanford University Press.

Baker, K. M. (2006). Constitution. In *The French Revolution. Recent debates and new controversies* (2nd ed., pp. 68–84). London: Routledge.

Ballard, R. (2011). *A new dictionary of the French Revolution*. London: Tauris.

Barker, J. R. V. (2012). Jehanne d'Arc. In *Conquest: the English kingdom of France, 1417–1450* (pp. 95–174). Cambridge, MA: Harvard University Press.

Bell, D. A. (2007). *The first total war: Napoleon's Europe and the birth of modern warfare*. London: Bloomsbury.

Bertaud, J. P. (1988). *The army of the French Revolution: From citizen-soldiers to instrument of power*. Princeton, NJ: Princeton University Press.

Blanning, T. C. W. (1996). *The French Revolutionary wars: 1787–1802*. New York: Edward Arnold.

Bloch, M. (1989). *The royal touch*. New York: Dorset Press.

Boroumand, L. (1990). La nation contre le peuple: Le débat sur la vérification commune des mandats aux États généraux de 1789. *Revue française de science politique, 40*(3), 302–338.

Bouloiseau, M. (1983). *The Jacobin republic: 1792–1794*. Cambridge, UK: Cambridge University Press.

Bradbury, J. (2007). *The Capetians, Kings of France*. London: Continuum Books.

Brissaud, J. (2001). *A history of French public law*. Washington, DC: Beard Books (Reprint of 1915 edition Boston: Little Brown and Company).

Brown, H. G. (2006). *Ending the French Revolution: Violence, justice and repression, from the terror to Napoleon*. Charlottesville: University of Virginia Press.

Caiani, A. A. (2012). *Louis XVI and the French Revolution, 1789–1792*. Cambridge: Cambridge University Press.

Chateaubriand, F. -R. vicomte de (1845). Louis X: de 1314 a 1316. In *Analyse raisonnée de l'histoire de France et fragments depuis Philippe VI Jusqu'a la Bataille de Poitiers, suivis de l'analyse raisonnée de l'histoire de France depuis Jean II, jusqu'a Louis XVI* (pp. 78–81). Paris: Firmin Didot Frères.

Chaussinand-Nogaret, G. (1995). *The French nobility in the eighteenth century: From feudalism to enlightenment*. Cambridge, UK: Cambridge University Press.

Chianéa, G. (1988). Institutions dauphinoises, pré-révolution et identité provinciale. In V. Chomel (Ed.), *Les débuts de la Révolution française en Dauphiné: 1788–1791* (pp. 33–49). Grenoble: Presses Universitaires de Grenoble.

Cobban, A. (1999). *The social interpretation of the French Revolution*. Cambridge, UK: Cambridge University Press.

Cooper, D. (2001). *Talleyrand*. London: Grove Press.

Craiutu, A. (2012). *A virtue for courageous minds: Moderation in French political thought, 1748–1830*. Princeton, NJ: Princeton University Press.

Crook, M. (1996). *Elections in the French Revolution: An apprenticeship in democracy, 1789–99*. Cambridge, MA: Cambridge University Press.

Cullen, L. M. (1993). History, economic crises, and revolution: Understanding eighteenth-century France. *The Economic History Review, 46*(4), 635–657.

Daly, W. M. (1994). Clovis: How Barbaric, How Pagan? *Speculum, 69*(3), 619–664.

Daubresse, S. (2005). *Le parlement de Paris, ou, La voix de la raison (1559–1589)*. Genève: Droz.

Davis, R. W. (Ed.). (1995). *The origins of modern freedom in the west*. Stanford, CA: Stanford University Press.
de Beaumarchais, P. A. C. (2008). The follies of a day or the marriage of Figaro: Monologue, Act V, Scene 3. In *The Figaro trilogy: The barber of Seville, The marriage of Figaro and The guilty mother* (pp. 190–216). Oxford: Oxford University Press.
de Malafosse, J. (1975). *Histoire des institutions et des régimes politiques de la Révolution à la IVème République*. Paris: Montchrestien.
de Pange, J. (1985). *Le Roi très chrétien: Essai sur la nature du pouvoir royal en France* (2nd ed.). Paris: Arma Artis.
de Tocqueville, A. (2013). *The old regime and the French Revolution* (Reprint.). New York: Anchor Books (From the original ed., 1856).
Duby, G. (1993). The Maid of Orléans. In *Moyen Age 987–1460. English France in the Middle Ages 987–1460: from Hugh Capet to Joan of Arc* (pp. 288–297). Oxford: Blackwell.
Dunn, S. (1994). *The deaths of Louis XVI: Regicide and the French political imagination*. Princeton, NJ: Princeton University Press.
Echeverria, D. (1985). *The Maupeou Revolution: A study in the history of Libertarianism. France 1700–1774*. Baton Rouge, LA: Louisiana State University Press.
Elson Roessler, S., & Miklos, R. (2003). *Europe 1715–1919: From enlightenment to world war*. Oxford: Rowman & Littlefield.
Engels, J. I. (2003). Dénigrer, Espérer, Assumer La Réalité: Le Roi de France perçu par ses Sujets, 1680–1750. *Revue D'histoire Moderne et Contemporaine, 50*(3), 96–126.
Fitzsimmons, M. P. (1987). *The Parisian order of barristers and the French Revolution*. Cambridge, MA: Harvard University Press.
Fitzsimmons, M. P. (1994). *The remaking of France: The national assembly and the constitution of 1791*. Cambridge, UK: Cambridge University Press.
Forrest, A. (2009). *The legacy of the French Revolutionary Wars. The Nation-in-arms in French Republican Memory*. Cambridge, UK: Cambridge University Press.
Furet, F. (2001). *Interpreting the French Revolution*. Cambridge, UK: Cambridge University Press.
Furet, F. (2003). *The French Revolution, 1770–1814*. Malden, MA: Blackwell.
Garillot, J. (1947). *Les États généraux de 1439: étude de la coutume constitutionnelle au XVe siècle*. Nancy: Imprimerie de l'Est républicain.
Gasparri, F. (1996). *Suger. Oeuvres. I*. Paris: Les Belles Lettres.
Godechot, J. (1971). *The Counterrevolution: Doctrine and action, 1789–1804*. Princeton, NJ: Princeton University Press.
Goldstone, J. A. (2011). The social origins of the French Revolution revisited. In T. Kaiser & D. Van Kley (Eds.), *From Deficit to Deluge: The origins of the French Revolution* (pp. 67–110). Stanford, CA: Stanford University Press.
Gordon, D. (1994). *Citizens without Sovereignty: Equality and sociability in French thought, 1670–1789*. Princeton, NJ: Princeton University Press.
Gough, H. (2010). *The terror in the French Revolution* (2nd ed.). London: Palgrave Macmillan.
Gouron, A. (1991). La double naissance de l'État législateur. In *Théologie et droit dans la science politique de l'État moderne. Actes de la table ronde de Rome* (pp. 101–114). Rome: École française de Rome.
Greer, D. (1966). *The incidence of terror during the French Revolution: A statistical interpretation* (Reprint). Cambridge, MA: Harvard University Press.
Gueniffey, P. (2003). *La politique de la terreur: Essai sur la violence révolutionnaire, 1789–1794*. Paris: Gallimard.
Hardman, J. (1994). *Louis XVI: The silent king and the estates*. New Haven, CT: Yale University Press.
Harris, R. D. (1986). *Necker and the revolution of 1789*. Lanham, MD: University Press of America.

Hayden, J. M. (2008). *France and the estates general of 1614*. Cambridge, MA: Cambridge University Press.
Higonnet, P. (1985). The social and cultural antecedents of revolutionary discontinuity: Montagnards and Girondins. *English Historical Review, 100*(396), 513–546.
Hurt, J. J. (2002). *Louis XIV and the Parlements: The assertion of royal authority*. Manchester, UK: Manchester University Press.
Johnson, A. (2013). *Louis XVI and the French Revolution*. Jefferson, NC: McFarland and Company.
Johnson, P. (1998). *A history of the Jews*. New York: Harper and Row.
Jones, P. M. (1995). *Reform and revolution in France: The politics of transition, 1774–1791*. Cambridge, UK: Cambridge University Press.
Jones, P. M. (2000). *The peasantry in the French Revolution*. Cambridge, UK: Cambridge University Press.
Jordan, D. P. (1989). *The revolutionary career of Maximilien Robespierre*. Chicago, IL: University of Chicago Press.
Jordan, D. P. (2004). *The King's Trial: Louis XVI vs. the French Revolution*. Berkeley, CA: University of California Press.
Kates, G. (1985). *The Cercle Social, the Girondins and the French Revolution*. Princeton, NJ: Princeton University Press.
Kennedy, J. F. (1962). [Speech] Address on the first anniversary of the alliance for progress. In *Public papers of the Presidents of the United States* (pp. 220–224) 86. Washington, DC: United States Government Printing Office.
Kropotkin, P. (2009). *The great French Revolution: 1789–1793*. New York: Cosimo Books.
Krynen, J. (1989). "Rex Christianissimus": A medieval theme at the roots of French absolutism. *History and Anthropology, 4*(1), 79–96.
Lawday, D. (2007). *Napoleon's Master: A life of Prince Talleyrand*. New York: Thomas Dunne Books.
Le Gall, J. M. (2007). *Le mythe de Saint Denis: Entre renaissance et révolution*. Paris: Champ Vallon.
Lefebvre, G. (2005). *The coming of the French Revolution*. Princeton, NJ: Princeton University Press.
Leith, J. A. (1998). The terror: Adding the cultural dimension. In I. Germani & R. Swayles (Eds.), *Symbols, myths and images of the French Revolution* (pp. 3–16). Regina, SK: University of Regina Publications.
Lemay, E. H., & Patrick, A. (1996). *Revolutionaries at work: The constituent assembly, 1789–1791*. Oxford: Voltaire Foundation.
Livesey, J. (2001). *Making democracy in the French Revolution*. Cambridge, MA: Harvard University Press.
Louie, R. (1964). The incidence of the terror: A critique of a statistical interpretation. *French Historical Studies, 3*(3), 379–389.
Lucas, C. (1977). The first directory and the rule of law. *French Historical Studies, 10*(2), 231–260.
Lucas, C. (1994). Revolutionary violence, the people and the terror. In K. M. Baker (Ed.), *The terror: The French Revolution and the creation of modern political culture* (Vol. 4, pp. 57–80). Bingley, UK: Emerald.
Lucas, C. (2006). Nobles, bourgeois, and the origins of the French Revolution. In G. Kates (Ed.), *The French Revolution: Recent debates and new controversies* (2nd ed., pp. 33–50). London: Routledge.
Lüsebrink, H.-J., & Reichardt, R. (1997). *The Bastille: A history of a symbol of despotism and freedom*. Durham, NC: Duke University Press.
Lyons, M. (1975). The 9 Thermidor: Motives and effects. *European Studies Review, 5*(2), 123–146.
Lyons, M. (2008). *France under the directory*. Cambridge, UK: Cambridge University Press.

Mackrell, J. Q. C. (1973). *The attack on Feudalism in eighteenth-century France*. London: Routledge & Kegan Paul.

Margerison, K. (1998). *Pamphlets and public opinion: The Campaign for a union of orders in the early French Revolution*. West Lafayette, IN: Purdue University Press.

Markoff, J. (1998). Allies and opponents: Nobility and third estate in the spring of 1789. In G. Shapiro et al. (Eds.), *Revolutionary demands. A content analysis of the Cahiers de Dolé ances of 1789* (pp. 296–321). Stanford, CA: Stanford University Press.

Mason, L. (1996). *Singing the French Revolution: Popular culture and politics, 1787–99*. Ithaca, NY: Cornell University Press.

McManners, J. (2007). *Church and society in eighteenth-century France*. Oxford: Oxford University Press.

Michelet, J. (1899). La Marseillaise, chant de fraternité et d'héroïsme. In *La Révolution française; La Constituante et la Législative* (pp. 470–473). Paris: Calmann-Lévy.

Mitchell, C. J. (1988). *The French legislative assembly of 1791*. Leiden: E.J. Brill.

Mulholland, M. (2012). *Bourgeois liberty and the politics of fear: From absolutism to neo conservatism*. Oxford: Oxford University Press.

Orieux, J. (1974). *Talleyrand: The art of survival*. New York: Alfred. A. Knopf.

Palmer, R. R. (1959). *The age of the democratic revolution: A political history of Europe and America, 1760–1800* (2 Vols.). Princeton, NJ: Princeton University Press.

Palmer, R. R. (2005). *Twelve who ruled: The year of the terror in the French Revolution*. Princeton, NJ: Princeton University Press.

Panofsky, E. (1979). *Abbot Suger on the Abbey Church of St. Denis and its treasures* (2nd ed.). Princeton, NJ: Princeton University Press.

Patrick, A. (1972). *The men of the First French Republic: Political alignments in the National Convention of 1792*. Baltimore, MD: Johns Hopkins University Press.

Pinoteau, H. B. (2004). Les armes de Navarre au nord des Pyrénées et quelques considérations annexes. In *Anales de la Real Academia Matritense de Heráldica y Genealogía: Homenaje a Don Faustino Menéndez Pidal* (Vol. VIII, No. 2, pp. 889–916).

Popkin, J. (2002). Not over after all: The French Revolution's third century. *The Journal of Modern History, 74*, 801–821.

Reemtsma, J. P. (2012). *Trust and violence: An essay on a modern relationship*. Princeton, NJ: Princeton University Press.

Richet, D. (1989). Natural borders. In F. Furet & M. Ozouf (Eds.), *A critical dictionary of the French Revolution* (pp. 754–770). Cambridge, MA: The Bellknap Press of the Harvard University Press.

Robespierre, M. (2007a). Discours: 27 juillet 1793–27 juillet 1794. In *Œuvres de Màximilien Robespierre* (Vol. 10). Paris: Société des études robespierristes.

Robespierre, M. (2007b). Séance du 5 novembre, 1792: Reponse de Màximilien Robespierre a l'accusation de J.B. Louvet. Discours: Septembre 1792–27 juillet 1793. In *Œuvres de Maximilien Robespierre* (Vol. 9, pp. 88–89). Paris: Société des études robespierristes.

Robespierre, M. (2007c). *Virtue and terror*. London: Verso.

Roche, D. (1998). *France in the enlightenment*. Cambridge, MA: Harvard University Press.

Rose, R. B. (1983). *The making of the Sans-Culottes: Democratic ideas and institutions in Paris, 1789–1792*. Manchester, UK: Manchester University Press.

Rothenberg, G. E. (1988). The origins, causes, and extension of the wars of the French Revolution and Napoleon. *Journal of Interdisciplinary History, 18*(4), 771–793.

Rudé, G. (2000). *Revolutionary Europe: 1783–1815* (2nd ed.). Oxford: Blackwell.

Sabatier, G. (2007). Religious rituals and the Kings of France in the Eighteenth century. In M. Schaigh (Ed.), *Monarchy and religion. The transformation of royal culture in eighteenth-century Europe* (pp. 249–282). Oxford: Oxford University Press.

Schroeder, P. W. (1996). *The transformation of European politics: 1763–1848*. Oxford: Oxford University Press.

Scurr, R. (2006). *Fatal purity: Robespierre and the French Revolution*. London: Chatto.

Sewel, W. J. (1994). *A Rhetoric of Bourgeois Revolution: The Abbé Siéyès and 'What is the Third Estate?'*. Durham, NC: Duke University Press.
Shanzer, D. (1998). Dating the baptism of Clovis: The bishop of Vienne vs. The bishop of tours. *Early Medieval Europe, 7*(1), 29–57.
Shapiro, G. (1998). What were the grievances of France in 1789?: The most common demands in *the Cahiers de Doléances*. In G. Shapiro et al. (Eds.), *Revolutionary demands: A content analysis of the Cahiers de Doléances of 1789* (pp. 253–279). Stanford, CA: Stanford University Press.
Sieyès, E. J. C. (2003). What is the Third Estate?. *Political writings: including the debate between Sieyès and Tom Paine in 1791* (pp. 92–162). Indianapolis, IN: Hackett Pub. Co.
Slavin, M. (1986). *The making of an insurrection. Parisian sections and the Gironde*. Cambridge, MA: Harvard University Press.
Smith, A. D. (2009). *Ethno-symbolism and nationalism: A cultural approach*. New York: Routledge.
Smith, J. M. (1996). *The culture of merit: Nobility, royal service and the making of absolute monarchy in France, 1600–1789*. Ann Arbor, MI: The University of Michigan Press.
Soboul, A. (1972). *The sans-culottes: The popular movement and revolutionary government, 1793–1794*. Garden City, NY: Anchor Books.
Soboul, A. (2006). The French Revolution in the history of the contemporary world. In G. Kates (Ed.), *The French Revolution: Recent debates and new controversies* (2nd ed., pp. 17–32). New York: Routledge.
Sonenscher, M. (1997). The nation's debt and the birth of the modern republic: The French fiscal deficit and the politics of the revolution of 1789. (Part I). *History of Political Thought, 18*(1), 64–103.
Sonenscher, M. (2008). *Sans-culottes: An eighteenth-century emblem in the French Revolution.* Princeton, NJ: Princeton University Press.
Sonenscher, M. (2009). Introduction. In *Before the Deluge: Public debt, inequality, and the intellectual origins of the French Revolution* (pp. 1–21). Princeton, NJ: Princeton University Press.
Spang, R. L. (2003). Paradigms and paranoia: How modern is the French Revolution? *The American Historical Review, 108*(1), 119–147.
Stone, B. (1986). *The French Parlements and the crisis of the old regime*. Chapel Hill, NC: North Carolina University Press.
Suger, Abbot of Saint Denis. (1992). *The deeds of Louis the Fat/Vita Ludovici Grossi Regis.* Washington, DC: Catholic University of America Press.
Swann, J. (1995). *Politics and the Parlement of Paris under Louis XV: 1754–1774*. Cambridge, UK: Cambridge University Press.
Swann, J. (2001). The state and political culture. In W. Doyle (Ed.), *Old regime France* (pp. 139–168). Oxford: Oxford University Press.
Tackett, T. (1996). *Becoming a revolutionary: The deputies of the French national assembly and the emergence of a revolutionary culture, 1789–91*. Princeton, NJ: Princeton University Press.
Tackett, T. (2006). Nobles and Third Estate in the revolutionary dynamic of the National Assembly, 1789–90. In G. Kates (Ed.), *The French Revolution: Recent debates and new controversies* (pp. 131–164). London: Routledge.
Tallet, F. (1991). Dechristianizing France: The Year II and the revolutionary experience. In F. Tallet & N. Atkin (Eds.), *Religion, society and politics in France since 1789* (pp. 1–28). London: Hambledon.
Tallon, A. (2004). Le clergé de France et l'obéissance due au roi très chrétien sous les règnes de François Ier et de Henri II. *Nouvelle Revue du XVIe Siècle, 22*(1), 111–126.
Valois, N. (1896). Le Roi très chrétien. In A. Baudrillart (Ed.), *La France chrétienne dans l'histoire* (pp. 314–327). Paris: Firmin Didot.

Van Kley, D. (1994). Introduction. In D. Van Kley (Ed.), *The French idea of freedom: The old regime and the declaration of rights of 1789* (pp. 5–22). Stanford, CA: Stanford University Press.

Van Kley, D. (2001). Church, state, and the ideological origins of the French Revolution: The debate over the General Assembly of the Gallican clergy in 1765. In R. Schechter (Ed.), *The French Revolutions* (pp. 263–300). Oxford: Blackwell.

Vardi, L. (2012). *The physiocrats and the world of the enlightenment*. Cambridge, UK: Cambridge University Press.

Vovelle, M. (1991). *The revolution against the Church: From reason to the supreme being*. Cambridge, UK: Polity.

Walzer, M. (1992). *Regicide and revolution: speeches at the trial of Louis XVI*. New York: Columbia University Press.

Whaley, L. A. (1993). Political factions and the Second Revolution: The insurrection of 10 August 1792. *French History, 7*(2), 205–224.

Woloch, I. (1970). *Jacobin legacy: The democratic movement under the directory*. Princeton, NJ: Princeton University Press.

Zagorin, P. (2003). *How the idea of religious toleration came to the West*. Princeton, NJ: Princeton University Press.

Zimmermann, E. (2011). *Political violence, crises and revolutions theories and research*. New York: Routledge.

Zorgbibe, C. (2008). *Mirabeau*. Paris: Fallois.

Zweig, S. (2012). *Marie Antoinette: The portrait of an average woman*. New York: Atrium Press.

## *Further Reading*

Andress, D. (1999). *French society in revolution*. Manchester: Manchester University Press.

Andress, D. (2000). *Massacre at the Champ de Mars: Popular dissent and political culture in the French Revolution*. Woodbridge: Boydell Press.

Andress, D. (2004). *The French Revolution and the people*. London: Hambledon.

Andress, D. (2009). *1789: The threshold of the modern age*. New York: Farrar, Straus and Giroux.

Aston, N. (2004). *The French Revolution, 1789–1804: Liberty, authority and the search for stability*. Basingstoke: Palgrave Macmillan.

Baker, K. M. (1989b). Constitution. In F. Furet & M. Ozouf (Eds.), *A critical dictionary of the French Revolution* (pp. 479–493). Cambridge, MA: The Bellknap Press of the Harvard University Press.

Baker, K. M. (1990). *The old regime and the French Revolution*. Chicago: University of Chicago Press.

Baker, K. M. (1994). *Inventing the French Revolution. Essays on French political culture in the eighteenth century* (Reprint). Cambridge: Cambridge University Press.

Behrens, C. B. A. (1989). *The Ancien Régime*. New York: Thames & Hudson.

Bienvenu, R. (Ed.). (1968). *The ninth of Thermidor: The fall of Robespierre*. New York: Oxford University Press.

Blanning, T. C. W. (1998). *The French Revolution: Class war or culture clash?* (2nd ed.). New York: St. Martin's Press.

Boureau, A., & Ingerflom, C. S. (Eds.). (1992). *La royauté sacrée dans le monde chrétien: Actes du Colloque de Royaumont*. Paris: Éditions de L'École Des Hautes Études en Sciences.

Campbell, P. R. (1996). *Power and politics in old regime France: 1720–1745*. New York: Routledge.

Censer, J. R. (2003). Amalgamating the social in the French Revolution. *Journal of Social History, 37*(1), 145–150.

Censer, J. R., & Hunt, L. (2004). *Liberty, equality, fraternity: Exploring the French Revolution* (3rd. printing). The University Park, PA: Pennsylvania State University Press.

Chartier, R. (2004). *The Cultural origins of the French Revolution* (6th printing). Durham, NC: Duke University Press.

Chateaubriand, F. -R., vicomte de. (2010). *Memoirs of Chateaubriand.* Charleston, SC: Nabu Press.

Cobban, A. A. (1991). *History of modern France. 1. Old regime and revolution, 1715–1799.* Baltimore: Penguin.

Danton, G. J. (1920). Discour 134: Sur les rèunions dans la Belgique-D'aprés la *Logotachigraphe.* Convention, jeudi 31 janvier 1793. In *Discours civiques* (pp. 267–272). Paris: Bibliotheque Charpentier.

Doyle, W. (1999). *Origins of the French Revolution* (3rd ed.). Oxford: Oxford University Press.

Doyle, W. (Ed.). (2001). *Old regime France: 1648–1788.* Oxford: Oxford University Press.

Doyle, W. (2003). *The Oxford history of the French Revolution* (2nd ed.). Oxford: Oxford University Press.

Doyle, W. (2009). *Aristocracy and its enemies in the age of revolution.* Oxford: Oxford University Press.

Edelstein, D. (2009). *The terror of natural right: Republicanism, the cult of nature, and the French Revolution.* Chicago, IL: University of Chicago Press.

Egret, J. (1977). *The French Pre-Revolution: 1787–1788.* Chicago: University of Chicago Press.

Fielding, M., & Morcombe, M. (2001). *France in revolution.* Sydney: McGraw Hill.

Forrest, A. (1981). *The French Revolution and the poor.* Oxford: Basil Blackwell.

Forrest, A. (1995). *The French Revolution.* Oxford: Blackwell.

Furet, F., & Ozouf, M. (1989). *A critical dictionary of the French Revolution.* Cambridge, MA: Harvard University Press.

Griffith, P. (1998). *The art of war of revolutionary France 1789–1802.* London: Greenhill Books.

Hagemann, K., et al. (Eds.). (2009). *Soldiers, citizens and civilians: War, culture and society, 1750–1850.* New York: Palgrave Macmillan.

Hampson, N. (1974). *The life and opinions of Maximilien Robespierre.* London: Duckworth.

Hippler, T. (2008). *Citizens, soldiers and national armies: Military service in France and Germany, 1789–1830.* New York: Routledge.

Hunt, L. A. (2004). *Politics, culture and class in the French Revolution.* Berkeley, CA: University of California Press.

Jones, C. (2002). *The great nation: France from Louis XV to Napoleon.* New York: Columbia University Press.

Kaiser, T., & Van Kley, D. (2011). *From deficit to deluge: The origins of the French Revolution.* Stanford, CA: Stanford University Press.

Kennedy, M. L. (1988). *The Jacobin Clubs in the French Revolution: The middle years.* Princeton, NJ: Princeton University Press.

Kwass, M. (2000). *Privilege and the politics of taxation in Eighteenth-century France: Liberté, Égalité, Fiscalité.* Cambridge: Cambridge University Press.

Le Goff, J., & Rémond, R. (Eds.). (2001). *Histoire de la France religieuse, 3. Du roi très chrétien à la laïcité républicaine: XVIIIe-XIXe siècle.* Paris: Éd. du Seuil.

Le Roy Ladurie, E. (1996). *The Ancien Régime: A History of France 1610–1774.* Oxford: Blackwell.

Lewis, G. (1993). *The French Revolution: Rethinking the debate.* London: Routledge.

Luttrell, B. (2000). *Mirabeau.* Carbondale, IL: Southern Illinois University Press.

Lyons, M. (1981). Recent interpretations of the French Directory. *The Australian Journal of Politics and History, 27*(1), 40–47.

McPhee, P. (2012). *Robespierre: A revolutionary life.* New Haven, CT: Yale University Press.

Mirabeau, Honoré-Gabriel de Riquetti, Comte de. (1835). *Memoirs of Mirabeau: Biographical, literary, and political* (4 Vols.). London: E. Churton.

Mitchell, H. (1958). Vendémiaire: A reevaluation. *The Journal of Modern History, 30*(3), 191–202.
Neely, S. (2008). *A concise history of the French Revolution*. Lanham, MD: Rowman & Littlefield.
Price, M. (2004). *The road from Versailles: Louis XVI, Marie Antoinette and the Fall of the French Monarchy*. New York: St. Martin's Griffin Ed.
Rapport, M. (2012). Revolution. In W. Doyle (Ed.), *The Oxford handbook of the Ancien Régime* (pp. 467–488). Oxford: Oxford University Press.
Russell, P. (2005). *Lights of Madness: In Search of Joan of Arc*. Savannah, GA: Frederic C. Beil.
Soboul, A. (1988). *Understanding the French Revolution*. New York: International Publishers.
Stone, B. (1981). *The Parlement of Paris: 1774–89*. Chapel Hill, NC: North Carolina University Press.
Stone, B. (1994). *The genesis of the French Revolution: A global-historical interpretation*. Cambridge, UK: Cambridge University Press.
Sutherland, D. M. G. (2003). *The French Revolution and empire: A quest for a civic order*. Malden, MA: Blackwell.
Sydenham, M. J. (1973). *The first French Republic, 1792–1804*. London: Batsford.
Talleyrand-Périgord, Charles Maurice de, prince de Bénévent. (1892). *Memoirs of the Prince de Talleyrand* (5 Vols.). London: G. P. Putnam's and Son.
Thompson, J. W. (1895). *The development of the French monarchy under Louis VI Le Gros: 1108–1137: A dissertation*. Chicago, IL: University of Chicago Press.
Vignery, R. (1965). *The French Revolution and the schools: Educational policies of the mountain, 1792–1794*. Madison, WI: University of Wisconsin Press.
Vovelle, M. (1989). *The fall of the French Monarchy: 1787–1792*. Cambridge, UK: Cambridge University Press.
Woloch, I. (1995). *New regime: Transformations of the French Civic Order, 1789–1820. The new regime*. New York: Norton & Company.
Woronoff, D. (1984). *The Thermidorian regime and the directory, 1794–1799*. Cambridge, UK: Cambridge University Press.

# Chapter 14
# The Return of the Monarchical Principle (I). The Origins of North American Presidentialism

The care of human life and happiness and not their destruction is the first and only legitimate object of good government—Thomas Jefferson (1743–1826)[1]

Why has government been instituted at all? Because the passions of men will not conform to the dictates of reason and justice, without constraint.—Alexander Hamilton, (1757–1804)[2]

The unity of Government, which constitutes you one people, is also now dear to you. It is justly so; for it is a main pillar in the edifice of your real independence, the support of your tranquility at home, your peace abroad; of your safety; of your prosperity; of that very Liberty, which you so highly prize.—George Washington (1732–1799)[3]

## Contents


14.1 The Development of a Republican "Monarchy": The Presidential System .......... 416
14.1.1 The Crisis of Democratic Assembly-Based Governments .......... 416
14.1.2 The Resurgence of Executive Power .......... 416
14.2 Thirteen States, One Nation: From the Articles of Confederation to the Federal Republic .......... 417
14.2.1 The Stage of the Constitutional Debate (1783 1787) .......... 418
14.2.2 The Reopening of a Constitutional Convention .......... 420
14.3 The Origins of the Presidential System .......... 422
14.3.1 The Constitutional Convention Endorses the Principle of a Strong National Government .......... 422
14.3.2 The Placement of Limits on Federal Power: The Strict Application of the Division of Powers and the Establishment of a "Presidential" System .......... 422
14.3.3 A "Great Compromise" for the Legislative Branch (Congress) .......... 423


[1] Thomas Jefferson to the Republicans of Washington County, Maryland, March 31, 1809. Jefferson (2004, 98–99).

[2] "The Insufficiency of the Present Confederation to Preserve the Union: To the People of the State of New York", *The Federalist*. No 15, December 1, 1787 Hamilton (2011, 107).

[3] *Farewell Address*. September 19, 1796. Coffman (2012, 70).




B. Aguilera-Barchet, *A History of Western Public Law*,
DOI 10.1007/978-3-319-11803-1_14

14.3.4 A President Heading the Executive Branch .......... 423
14.3.5 The Separation of Powers as the Essence of the Presidential System .......... 424
14.3.6 The Judicial Power as a Constitutional Referee: The Revolutionary Principle of "Judicial Review" as a Safeguard Against the Tyranny of the Majority .......... 424
14.4 A New Constitution for a New Federal State .......... 425
14.4.1 Approval and Ratification of the Constitution .......... 425
14.4.2 A New Limit on Federal Power: The Bill of Rights .......... 426
14.4.3 The Principle of Term Limits .......... 427
14.4.4 The Constitution as the New Nation's Birth Certificate .......... 427
14.5 Relations Between the States and the Federal Government After 1789 .......... 427
14.5.1 The Implementation of Judicial Review .......... 429
14.5.2 From 13 to 50 States .......... 430
14.5.3 A Problematic Expansion .......... 434
14.5.4 The Protection of Fundamental Rights: The Union vs. the States .......... 437
References .......... 443

## 14.1 The Development of a Republican "Monarchy": The Presidential System

### *14.1.1 The Crisis of Democratic Assembly-Based Governments*

The American and French placed power in the hands of democratic legislatures: the Congress, in the case of the United States of America, and the National Assembly in France. Both regimes, however, generated a situation of political instability that degenerated into chaos, especially in the case of France. Thus, after a more or less brief stage—4 years in the case of the United States and 10 in that of France—governments in which the legislative branch held virtually all power gave way to others featuring a one-man executive wielding greater power and heading up the government. We will see in this chapter how the Americans developed a system of government which combined the republican form of state with a strong executive power via a system which would prove to be very different from what Napoleon established in France towards the same end—something which we will examine in next chapter.

### *14.1.2 The Resurgence of Executive Power*

In the case of the United States, this solution was reached by consensus through a Constitutional Convention yielding a new founding document: that ratified in 1789, which fortified the union of the states through the creation of a federal bond between them. Thus arose a "super state" assuming a number of the powers which had previously lain with each one of the 13 states. The major new development was that, in addition to the legislative branch (Congress) there appeared a powerful Executive in the form of a president with wide powers, elected every 4 years, a feature for which the new system was named: "presidential". In a way this development represented a return to monarchy (by concentrating power in one man's hands), following Bolingbroke's idea of a "Patriot King",[4] albeit in this case with an elected leader who governed a republic for a limited period of time.[5]

## 14.2 Thirteen States, One Nation: From the Articles of Confederation to the Federal Republic

The victory of the American revolutionaries over England (with key support provided by France and Spain), spawned a new nation made up of all the former colonies which had fought against England, but 1 divided into 13 states, each with its own constitution, government, and institutions. Nevertheless, conscious of the fact that their union had been decisive in their victory against the British crown, the new states from the outset created a joint assembly, a national Congress in which the representatives of all the states met to discuss issues of shared concern and, when appropriate, to approve measures binding upon all of them. This was the first constitutional government of the United States: the "Articles of Confederation". The nation's initial constitutional framework, however, did not include any viable

[4] Henry St. John, first Viscount of Bolingbroke (1678–1751) was a Tory leader who, in 1738, advanced the idea of a "Patriot King" (Bolingbroke et al. 2010), explicitly to replace traditional divine right with legitimacy arising from a public spirit, or patriotism (Mansfield 2013, 83). The works of Bolingbroke were widely read by John Adams, Thomas Jefferson and James Madison, who hoped for patriotic leadership that would remain closely bound within strict republican limits (Gregg 1997, 37). On the influence of Bolingbroke's ideas on American constitutionalism, see Colbourn (1998, 185–193).

[5] As Gregg (1997, 3–4) points out, however, the idea of the president as the direct representative of the American people was not accepted all at once. Washington believed, as he highlighted in his "Farewell Address" of September 19, 1796, that the president was only one of the powers of the Union, as the Constitution had divided political power into different depositories, including the presidency, thereby rendering "each the Guardian of the Public Weal". Thomas Jefferson took a further step, the first who claimed to represent a distinctly national constituency or national interest, as in his view the legislature did not "command a view of the whole ground". As Bailey (2010, 6) states, Jefferson's victory in the 1800 election transformed the constitutional presidency into a democratic one. Yet it would not be until the presidency of Andrew Jackson that the country's leader was determined by electors in the Electoral College chosen not by the state legislatures, but by the people. Jackson was fully aware of this, as he was the first to say publicly in a message to the Senate that "The president is the direct representative of the American people... [as he is] elected by the people and responsible to them" (Jackson 1835, 269).

institutional mechanism to implement and enforce decisions made by the Congress, a flaw which ultimately rendered the "union" almost inoperative.

This fact was not overlooked by America's elite, which clearly perceived that, unless united, the nation would not be able to compete with its European counterparts. Of particular concern was England, which continued to have a firm hold on Canada, and Spain, which after the 1783 treaty still maintained an immense and solid empire in the Americas, including territory which covered a third of the present-day United States of America.

## *14.2.1 The Stage of the Constitutional Debate (1783–1787)*

### 14.2.1.1 The Impotence of the Articles of Confederation

Under the Articles of Confederation system, designed in 1777, the "national Government" was little more than a league of states who met intermittently in congresses when circumstances so required. The states were essentially all-powerful, as the second clause of the Articles of Confederation made it crystal clear that "each state shall retain its sovereignty, its freedom, and its independence, as well as each power, jurisdiction and right which has not been specifically delegated by this Confederation to the United States, gathered in Congress". In addition, the financial maintenance of the national Congress depended on the monies granted it by the governments of the different states, at their discretion. Most of the states were not inclined to augment central power, as they were wary of the establishment of a stronger and more authoritative national government.

A certain sector of American public opinion, however, was in favor of strengthening the union and endowing it with a more powerful national government.[6] Industrialists and merchants, for example, wanted a government capable of establishing tariffs that would protect the 13 states' market and productive system, and argued that it was necessary to enact uniform laws governing commerce throughout the new nation. In addition, those interested in acquiring new property in the west thought that their land would be safer under a strong federal government. Finally, also in favor of a tighter union were those who sought a more uniform national financial system, specifically bankers and creditors who feared that the states would begin to indiscriminately issue their own money, thereby devaluing their assets. The foremost champion of the establishment of a strong central government was Alexander Hamilton (1755–1804), a New York lawyer and former Revolutionary War officer, who believed that republicanism would not

[6] LaCroix (2010, 11–29) sees the antecedents of federal thought in four cases, two of which pertain to theory—the seventeenth-century Anglo-American constitutional debates and Continental European political philosophy—and two to practice—North America's experiments with colonial union, and the Scottish and Irish examples, when the "composite monarchy" of England was transformed into the "multiple kingdom" of Great Britain.

endure and America could not survive as nation if the states were not united by a strong central government under which the states would assume a subordinate position (Murray 2007, 57).

The clash between the two camps grew more and more intense in what came to be known as the Federalist and Anti-Federalist debates. The controversy took shape in a series of pamphlets written in favor of and against the federal union.[7] The most important documents endorsing a fortified union formed part of a series called *The Federalist Papers*, penned by Alexander Hamilton, James Madison and John Jay.[8]

#### 14.2.1.2 Shay's Rebellion (1786) Buoys the Federalist Movement

The fears of those favoring federalism were not unfounded, as the War of Independence had sunk the United States into a serious economic crisis, its most evident result being a chronic cash shortage. Some states sought to remedy this by issuing paper notes, which creditors were reluctant to accept as valid currency. In 1786, this attitude prompted the State of Rhode Island to pass legislation forcing creditors to accept its currency at its face value, which was lower and lower than its actual market value, sowing widespread discontent among the people of the state.

In that same year of 1786, western Massachusetts witnessed an armed uprising of farmers determined to abolish the courts which had ordered the execution of the mortgages on their properties. This pivotal revolt came to be known as Shay's Rebellion.

Daniel Shay was a veteran of the Revolutionary War who had lost his farm when it was impossible for him to pay off his mortgage debt of 12 dollars. Desperate, Shay mustered a group of farmers who were facing the same situation and formed an armed band[9] that on August 29, 1786, headed for the Supreme Court of the State of Massachusetts, located in Springfield. Shay and his men managed to paralyze the sessions of the court, but when they attacked the arsenal at Springfield on February 3, 1787, they were defeated by an army recruited by the State of Massachusetts and financed by the farmers' creditors. Shay and his men took refuge in Vermont (Richards 2002, 159–162).

[7] Perhaps the leading anti-Federalist was George Mason (1725–1792), a firm defender of states' rights (Leffler 1987, 285–292). On the anti-Federalist movement, see Storing (2008) and Main (2004).

[8] This practical publication tied to a particular occasion was, nevertheless, considered by Thomas Jefferson to be the best commentary on the principles of government ever written (Epstein 2008, 1). For an understanding of the Federalist position in this crucial debate which led to the conception of the new federal system in 1787, see Wills (2001).

[9] As Szatmary (1980, 64) explains, Shaysites had military experience on the battlefield as militiamen or soldiers, some even as commanders: Daniel Shays, Luke Day, Agrippa Wells, Adam Wheeler, Luke Drury, Reuben Dickinson, Oliver Parker and Seth Murray had been captains in the Revolutionary War, and recruited soldiers for the patriot forces.

Shay's Rebellion itself did not have dramatic consequences (Brown 1983, 598–615). However, it was decisive in swaying the Federal/Anti-Federal debate in favor of those advocating a stronger union.[10] Among them was George Washington who, when hearing of the uprising, openly told his friends that in his opinion the Articles of Confederation government was driving the country towards anarchy.[11] Washington was outraged by the fact that the State of Massachusetts, though it had the authority to muster an army to quell the uprising, lacked the financial resources to do so, and that its efforts to convoke a national Congress to obtain the necessary funds from the other states had been fruitless. Thus, had it not been for the private initiative of those who financed the army that defeated Shay, the rebellion would not have been put down. To prevent this kind of situation, Washington began to publicly argue that if the United States was to survive, it had no choice but to establish a strong federal government.

The Federalists ended up winning over public opinion, thanks in part to the newspaper coverage[12] of Shay's Rebellion and other similar incidents. Thus, in the 13 states more and more Americans came out in favor of reinforcing their union to more capably defend shared interests and prevent chaos, which could became widespread and wreak havoc with the new states' financial systems.[13]

The problem was that there existed no unanimity when it came to how to reach this objective, as under the terms of the Articles of Confederation the unanimous consent of all the states was required to undertake their revision.

## *14.2.2 The Reopening of a Constitutional Convention*

### 14.2.2.1 A Frustrated Attempt: The Annapolis Convention (September 1786)

The first step towards constitutional reform took place in March of 1785 when representatives of the States of Virginia and Maryland met at George Washington's

[10] As Gross (2009, 112) points out, the insurrection served in the end to briefly prompt moves for a stronger national government and then was forgotten, though from time to time it is recalled as an illustration of the endemic disorder during America's "Critical Period" and as justification for the Federalist miracle at Philadelphia in the summer of 1787. On the constitutional consequences of the revolt, see Feer (1969, 388–410).

[11] On Washington's reaction to Shay's Rebellion, see Richards (2002, 129–131).

[12] Szatmary (1980, 63) points out that widely circulated and read newspapers provided an important mode of communication within rural New England during the uprising. The geographer Jedediah Morse noted in 1789 that no less than 30,000 newspapers were printed in New England every week, and circulated in almost every town and village in the country.

[13] Spectacles such as a group of Rhode Island debtors who chased their creditors, waving handfuls of the paper money they meant to pay them with, fueled the public's concerns about disorder. Rhode Island had been traditionally the most inflationary of the colonies, with the result that Newport, which had been a flourishing center for West Indian imports into Western Massachusetts, lost its trade to Boston and languished (Rothbard 2002, 55).

home to seek to resolve a dispute sparked by a navigation improvement project for the Potomac River (Dunn 2007, 93). At the end of the meeting an agreement was reached to convene a congress of all the states to discuss the possibility of jointly addressing affairs affecting commerce.

In January of 1786 Virginia's General Assembly sent the other states a formal call for a congress to be held in Annapolis (Maryland) in September of that year. During the summer of 1786 several proposals for the revision of the Articles of Confederation were debated, like that drafted by the Massachusetts General Court. None of them, however, were sent to all the states. In the end the meeting at Annapolis took place in September of 1786, although it was disappointing for those who had hoped to reform the Articles of Confederation, as delegates from only five states attended, a number insufficient to propose changes to the states' common constitutional system (Mcferran 2005, 149–153).

#### 14.2.2.2 The Constitutional Convention of Philadelphia (May–September of 1787)

In spite of the failure of the Annapolis meeting the movement in favor of reforming the Articles of Confederation did not lose steam. The main proponent of reform was George Washington himself, who forcefully argued that the Congress must be granted powers sufficient for it to adopt and enforce national policies. Alexander Hamilton went even further, striving to convince the representatives of the 13 states that only drastic centralization could keep the new nation from falling apart. Hamilton proposed that a new convention be held in the city of Philadelphia to discuss constitutional reform, calling for the delegates attending this new body to be empowered to negotiate a sweeping plan of reform remedying the shortcomings of the Articles of Confederation.[14] Hamilton's plan was approved by the Congress and all the states, with the exception of Rhode Island (Bowen 2010, 13), sent delegates to the Philadelphia Convention.[15]

[14] Hamilton drafted an address calling upon the 13 states to send delegates to a new convention which would meet in Philadelphia on the second Monday of May 1787 to discuss not only commercial problems but also all matters necessary "to render the constitution of the Federal Government adequate to the exigencies of the Union". Hamilton's address became the clarion call for the Constitutional Convention of 1787 (Morton 2006, 131).

[15] As Zimmerman (2008, 18) points out, 74 delegates were selected by the states, but 19 of them either did not accept the appointments or failed to attend the Convention. Fourteen of the remaining fifty-five delegates departed Philadelphia before the convention concluded its work. The backgrounds of the delegates ranged widely, though 33 were lawyers. Twenty-eight delegates had been members of the Continental Congress or the Congress of the Confederation, and other delegates had helped to draft the constitutions of their respective states. The most notable delegates were George Washington, Benjamin Franklin, James Madison and Alexander Hamilton. There were also some conspicuous absences, such as Thomas Jefferson, who was in France on a diplomatic assignment; John Hancock, Samuel Adams, Thomas Paine, John Marshall, who later became Chief Justice of the U.S. Supreme Court; and Patrick Henry, who declined to be a delegate from Virginia.

## 14.3 The Origins of the Presidential System

### *14.3.1 The Constitutional Convention Endorses the Principle of a Strong National Government*

The Convention began its sessions on May 29, 1787. George Washington was unanimously elected its president,[16] and the delegates immediately got down to work. The first issue discussed was the powers to be assigned the new national government. There was soon agreement that the central government should have the authority to levy taxes, regulate commerce between the states, and handle the country's foreign policy. The states, then, lost the right to print their own currency, to sign international treaties, and to establish import or export tariffs. It was also agreed that the new central power would be empowered to maintain an army and a navy.[17]

### *14.3.2 The Placement of Limits on Federal Power: The Strict Application of the Division of Powers and the Establishment of a "Presidential" System*

Though the majority clearly wished to bolster the power of the Congress, there were still widespread fears that doing so would mean a substantial reduction in the sovereignty of the states. Thus, defining and restricting the powers which would be assigned to the federal government became an essential issue for many delegates. Firstly, it was agreed that a district division of powers ought to be established. Inspired by the ideas of Montesquieu, Virginia representative James Madison proposed the creation of three independent branches: Legislative, Executive and Judicial.[18]

[16] On the circumstances of George Washington's election, see Bowen (2010, 27–29).

[17] For an overview of the Philadelphia Convention, see Collier and Collier (2007).

[18] James Madison was a crucial figure in designing the federal model of the U.S. Constitution. For an overview of his political ideas, see Banning (1998). On the Anti-Federalists' objections to Madison's project, see Robertson (2005, 225–243).

### 14.3.3 A "Great Compromise" for the Legislative Branch (Congress)

For the forming of the legislature Madison and the delegates from Virginia proposed that representation be proportional to each state's population. This proposal was dubbed the "Virginia Plan".[19] This approach, however, meant that the smallest states would be completed dominated by the largest ones. To prevent this, the delegates from New Jersey proposed that each state have the same number of Congressional representatives, regardless of population (Bowen 2010, 104–108). In the end a compromise was reached (the Great Compromise), a solution worthy of Solomon: a bicameral legislature consisting of a House of Representatives to which each state would send delegates based on population, in such a way that the larger states would have more representatives; and a Senate in which all the states would have two senators (Wirls 2003). Both chambers would comprise the U.S. Congress.

### 14.3.4 A President Heading the Executive Branch

The other novel innovation was the creation of a powerful Executive: the president of the United States,[20] who was assigned considerable power as a way of preventing a tyrannical concentration of power in the Legislative branch (Epstein 2008, 194). While the president's term was limited to 4 years, he could be reelected.[21] Here again there arose the need to mollify those who wished the president to be elected by the people and also respond to those who were concerned with each individual state having an impact on the election, even those with smaller populations (Gregg 1997, 34). The result was a *sui generis* system: instead of a single presidential election there would be 13 simultaneous ones. The people of each state would

[19] The Virginia Plan drafted by James Madison and read to the delegates by Edmund Randolph, featuring proportional representation, was initially preferred to William Paterson's alternative, called the New Jersey Plan, by the delegates of seven states to three in a vote on June 19 (Collier and Collier 2007, 114).

[20] As McDonald (1994, 12) explains, the model available to the creators of the American presidency was that of the crown of England, which had evolved towards a limited monarchy both stable and consistent with ordered liberty. In fact, most members of the Constitutional Convention admired the "mixed" English system. Even Alexander Hamilton stated that the English model was "the only good one".

[21] "*The executive Power shall be vested in a President of the United States of America. He shall hold his Office during the term of four years*". Article 2, First Section. The presidency was perhaps the most important and characteristic institution of the federal government, as for the first time in western constitutional history there appeared a republic with a strong executive. This is why the members of the Philadelphia Convention created a new constitutional model: the "presidential system", in which, as opposed to the "parliamentary system", of British origin, the Executive was elected not by the parliament or a legislative assembly, but directly by the people (Belenky 2012, 9–30).

choose electors (equal in number to the sum of their representatives in the House and Senate) who would actually vote for the president. They were not free to vote for whomever they wished, however, as all of a state's electors were required to vote for the candidate who had obtained the greatest number of votes in their state (Deskins et al. 2010, 2–3).

This system became even more complex after the formation of political parties, as these came up with a process of "primaries", elections through which they nominated their candidate for the presidential election. The first political party in the history of the young nation was the Federalist Party of the United States, founded by Alexander Hamilton (1755–1804), who presided over it until his death (Murray 2007, 235).

### 14.3.5 The Separation of Powers as the Essence of the Presidential System

Both the Congress (Legislative branch), composed of the House of Representatives and the Senate, and the president (Executive branch) were chosen by the people and enjoyed the legitimacy granted them by the ballot box. As such, they were beholden to the people's will, and had to cooperate to make decisions that reflected it. Curiously, this system in which both the Legislative and Executive branches played key roles and checked each other according to James Madison's conception of the Republican government (Ferejohn 2005, 126–155), came to be called a "presidential system" because it stood in contrast and as an alternative to the Parliamentary system in England, in which the Executive, the "prime minister", was determined by the party in control of the legislature. Another important difference between the two nations and systems was that in England the prime minister governed, while the state was represented by the king (the crown). In the American system the president of the United States was simultaneously the head of the state and the president of the government.

### 14.3.6 The Judicial Power as a Constitutional Referee: The Revolutionary Principle of "Judicial Review" as a Safeguard Against the Tyranny of the Majority

In addition to the Legislature (Congress) and the Executive (president) the Founding Fathers created a third power: the Judiciary, represented by a Federal Supreme Court made up of nine judges, nominated by the president and confirmed by the Congress. This judicial institution would ultimately turn out to be absolutely vital, as its main function became that of interpreting the federal Constitution—a role which proved pivotal given that the Constitution of 1787 contained only seven articles.[22] As a product of consensus, the Constitution was a minimalist document. Thus, whole areas of the institutional framework of the new federal system were yet to be defined,[23] such as the dual system of state and federal courts of justice (Abraham 1998, 151).

The Supreme Court's function as the supreme interpreter of the federal Constitution took root only over time. In fact, it was asserted 14 years later through the famous ruling of Justice John Marshall, at that time the Chief Justice of the Supreme Court, as part of the decision handed down in the Marbury vs. Madison case (February 24, 1803). This historic verdict proved decisive in the construction of the federal regime, as for the first time the Supreme Court established the principle that the judiciary could determine whether laws were Constitutional (the principle of judicial review). The system of the "separation of powers" turned the Judicial branch into the "referee" determining the constitutionality of the government's actions.[24]

## 14.4 A New Constitution for a New Federal State

### *14.4.1 Approval and Ratification of the Constitution*

Four months after the first meeting of the Constitutional Congress, on September 17, 1787, the delegates had completed the final draft of what would ultimately be the Constitution of the United States of America.

---

[22] As Feeley and Rubin (2000, 1) indicate, courts perform three interrelated but distinguishable functions: they determine facts, they interpret authoritative legal texts, and they make new public policy. The first two functions are familiar but the third is fraught with controversy, considered blasphemy by some, as in our western constitutional tradition courts are not supposed to act as policymakers, though in fact they do. Policymaking by judges involves a process by which officials exercise power on the basis of their judgment that their actions will produce desirable results, according to Ronald Dworkin's definition (Dworkin 2013, 179). Such a system would have been anathema to the French revolutionaries, who envisioned law as the "expression of the general will", and not something to be decided by a set of judges who were not elected and, consequently, unfit to speak for the people.

[23] As Hansford and Spriggs (2006, 3) point out, the legal reasoning set forth in a Supreme Court decision has more far-reaching consequences than the concrete ruling that settles the case in question, as it alters existing legal policy and helps to structure the outcomes of future disputes.

[24] This is why the Supreme Court of the United States was, for instance, the entity which ultimately proclaimed George Bush's victory in the year 2000, when he won his first term. Bush won the election despite the fact that he had fewer votes than Al Gore (47.9 % as opposed to 48.4 %) after the Supreme Court's justices interpreted which votes were to be counted in the State of Florida. As a result, the countable votes gave the victory to Bush in that state, where he took all its electors. On the constitutional role of the U.S. Supreme Court, see Casey (1974, 385–420) and Rosen (2006). The political importance of the Supreme Court has enabled Abraham (2008) to provide an interesting overall view of its political evolution from the perspective of the successive appointments of its justices. On the legislative role of the U.S. Supreme Court, see Spaeth and Segal (2001).

The final document contained only seven articles, a result of its authors' deliberate intention to create a very flexible instrument, destined to last over time in spite of the changes, challenges, and ups and downs which would inevitably occur in the relations between the states and the new federal government. Articles 1, 2 and 3 dealt with the Legislative, Executive and Judicial branches, respectively. Article 4 regulated relations between the states. Article 5 covered constitutional reform, and Article 6 included a series of miscellaneous stipulations, like those relative to the signing and ratification of treaties with other nations, or the requirements to hold public office. The conciseness of the federal Constitution has been, without any doubt, the key to its success and its longevity. Today it continues to be the oldest functioning constitution in the western world.

The last article of the Constitution, no. 7, stated that the document would take effect upon ratification by at least nine states.[25] On September 28, 1787, the Constitution was submitted to the states for ratification. On June 21, 1788, New Hampshire became that ninth state (Maier 2010, 313) and the U.S. Constitution went into effect on March 4, 1789 (Schwartz 2013, 333). Across the Atlantic, 2 months later the Estates General was convened in France, setting in motion a process that would trigger the French Revolution.

### 14.4.2 A New Limit on Federal Power: The Bill of Rights

Virginia and New York ratified the federal Constitution just a few weeks after New Hampshire, but North Carolina and Rhode Island were still hesitant to sign it. To overcome their reluctance, James Madison suggested the possibility of introducing a set of changes that would be incorporated into the Constitution. The House of Representatives and the Senate ultimately approved 12 amendments that were to be appended to the Constitution rather than incorporated into the original document. The 12 amendments were sent to the states for ratification, but only 10 were ratified (Hickok 1991, 5). Their final ratification by Congress took place on December 15, 1791, by which time the last of the 13 states, Rhode Island, had endorsed them (May 29, 1790). These ten amendments to the U.S. Constitution would go down in history as the "Bill of Rights".

The procedure that made possible the adoption of amendments represented an instrument through which the founding document could be adapted to address new circumstances. Over time, a series of legal and governmental questions have been resolved through the incorporation of new amendments, yielding the 27 today.[26]

---

[25] On the ratification process, see Maier (2010).

[26] The last one, No. 27, approved on July 5, 1992, postpones any salary increases which Congress votes for itself until after the next election: *No law varying the compensation for the services of the Senators and Representatives shall take effect until an election of Representatives shall have intervened.* On the process of adapting the American Constitution to the times via the instrument of amendments, see Bernstein and Agel (1993), and Kyvig (1996). For the Constitutional texts, see Beeman (2010) and Ginsberg and Ackerman (2011).

### *14.4.3 The Principle of Term Limits*

On March 4, 1789, the federal Constitution took effect, and on April 30, George Washington was elected the first president of the fledgling United States, going on to be reelected in 1793. At the close of his second term, however, he refused to stand for re-election (McDonald 1988, 177–186). Since then nearly every president followed his example and only stood for re-election once, the notable exception being Franklin Delano Roosevelt, elected for the first time in 1932 and reelected in 1936, 1940 and 1944—though his fourth term was cut short by his death on April 12, 1945. To prevent this from happening again, the 22nd Amendment to the Constitution was added (ratified on February 27, 1951), limiting presidents to only two terms in office: "No person shall be elected to the office of the President more than twice" (McDonald 1994, 166–171).

### *14.4.4 The Constitution as the New Nation's Birth Certificate*

With the ratification of the Constitution in 1789 the United States saw the culmination of a revolutionary process which had begun 11 years prior. Since 1783 there had been 13 states with 13 constitutions directly inspired by their respective colonial charters. In contrast, the federal government was something totally new, created *ex novo*, arising directly from the Constitution, a pact which has survived through the years, unscathed and in good health, though altered and refined through a series of amendments and Supreme Court decisions. It was the first new nation in the sense that it broke sharply with traditional sources of legitimacy (Lipset 2003, 11). The U.S. Constitution stands above any and all subsequent legislation, and judges can raise the question of a law's constitutionality. It is largely for this reason that the United States of America continues to maintain the very same Constitution which established the new nation, a document representing a shining example of legal and constitutional longevity.

## 14.5 Relations Between the States and the Federal Government After 1789

The ratification of the federal Constitution and the election of George Washington did not bring an end to the debate between the Federalists and Anti-Federalists—that is, proponents of a powerful central government and those who wished to see the states retain the greatest possible levels and scope of power, respectively.[27] Despite the ratification of the nation's new Constitution the Anti-Federalists did not give up, and did all they could to defend the power and autonomy of the states in the face of federal power. As a consequence of their efforts, the unique characteristics of the different states were taken into account and respected not only in the system for the election of the president of the United States, but also in the formula for the composition of the two chambers of the Congress.

Federalism, however, continued to gain ground, expanding in three areas. Firstly, thanks to the establishment of the principle of judicial review, which authorized the Supreme Court of the United States to determine the "constitutionality" of a law. In this way, the Judicial power was designated as the guarantor and arbiter of Constitutional orthodoxy, standing above the powers engaged in the political fray: the Legislative and Executive. Secondly, the federal government was bolstered by the incorporation of new states into the union, which, from 1791 to 1959, went from 13 to 50. The union's expansion process was no easy task, and would even trigger a devastating Civil War, when America's southern slave states sought to secede from the Union, to protect their "states rights" (principally their slaveholding rights), from what they viewed as federal encroachment. The victory of the North (Union) definitively established the supremacy of federal power.[28] Finally, the national government acquired more power vis-à-vis the states, as the restrictive interpretation of the Bill of Rights was discarded. Initially it was the states' view that the fundamental rights and liberties included in the first ten amendments to the U.S. Constitution protected citizens from the federal government, but not from each state government, which could legislate within its jurisdiction without taking them into account. In the wake of the Northern victory in the Civil War, the scope of protection of the essential rights set down in the Constitution came to encompass the states as well. That is, the states, as powers subordinate to the federal government, were compelled to respect all the same rights which the latter was required to.

[27] As McDonald (2002, 4–5) stresses, the Constitution gave general government broad powers within a limited sphere, thereby institutionalizing a system of divided sovereignty that gave rise to the doctrine of states' rights. States' righters, such as John Taylor of Caroline and John Randolph of Roanoke insisted that their doctrine was necessary to prevent the concentration of power in a Leviathan-like central government, as power concentrated in some remote center was the very definition of tyranny. On the opposite side ardent Federalists, such as John Quincy Adams and Nicholas Biddle, argued that vigorous action at the national level was vital if the nation was to fulfill its promise and its destiny, attaining wealth and stature among the family of nations.

[28] Ironically, in Spain there has been recent talk of a "federal" system as a solution to the country's separatist movements, by which the country's regional governments would be granted more power and independence, when in the American context "federalism" refers to precisely the opposite: the clear and unequivocal supremacy of the national government in Washington over the states.

### 14.5.1 *The Implementation of Judicial Review*

Originally, during the crucial years from 1776 to 1787, in every state the general assumption tended to prevail that state legislatures were the sole judges of their own constitutional powers, and very few Americans believed that any state court had the authority to declare a law invalid on the grounds that it violated the U.S. Constitution (Nevins 1991, 168). At the Constitutional Convention in Philadelphia (1787–1789), however, there was a clear reaction to this uncontested supremacy of the state legislatures. In isolated cases, some state courts had asserted the right to deem a statute unconstitutional,[29] but Madison did not wish to directly assign such power to the Judiciary, proposing the establishment of a Federal Council of Revision with the authority to nullify both state and federal bills as a way of countering the factious majorities in state legislatures. However, as Madison failed to win support for this Council at the Constitutional Convention, he would ultimately accept the Supreme Court as the institution of the federal government best suited to determine what laws were and were not constitutional (Hall et al. 2005, 601).

Upon the election of the Anti-Federalist Thomas Jefferson (1801–1809) as President of the United States, the federal government could have been weakened, as Jefferson was an avowed proponent of devolving power to the states in what he called the "Revolution of 1800", featuring the Federalists' defeat (McDonald 1995, 2). His intentions, however, were frustrated by the U.S. Supreme Court, as Chief Justice John Marshal (1801–1835) was a firm Federalist, who ably managed to invest the high court with a powerful and pivotal role within the system of American government.[30]

The turning point came with the famous Marbury vs. Madison case (1803), which established the principle of judicial review, according to which the Supreme Court could declare any law unconstitutional and suspend its enforcement.[31] Thanks to this a political victory in congressional or presidential elections was

[29] The first partial assertion, as Nevins (1991, 170) explains, occurred in New Jersey in 1780. Prior to 1787, there were very few state courts that applied the principle, inevitably encountering opposition in the state legislature. Nevertheless, there was already "a steady and powerful development towards the establishment of the right".

[30] John Marshall (1755–1835), was the leader of the Federalist Party in Virginia and was elected to the House of Representatives from 1799 to 1800, before becoming John Adam's Secretary of State from 1800 to 1801. After the Federalists' defeat in the presidential election of 1800 he was appointed by John Adams before Jefferson took office. Marshall was confirmed by the Senate on January 27, 1801, and took office on the following February 4. He was the fourth Chief Justice of the United States and would be the longest-serving in the U.S. Supreme Court's history. John Adams said publicly "My gift of John Marshall to the people of the United States was the proudest act of my life" (Abraham 2008, 66) and later, wrote to Marshall: "There is no act of my life that look back upon with more pleasure, than the short time I spent with you. And it is the pride of my life that I have given to this nation a Judge equal to a Coke, a Hale, a Holt, or a Mansfield". Marshall (2000, 197). For a classical biography of Chief Marshall, see Beveridge (2013).

[31] On the origins of the Marbury vs. Madison decision, see Newmyer (2001, 157–175). On John Marshall's interpretation of the Constitution, see Wolfe (1994, 39–72).

not sufficient to change the principles upon which the federal union rested, as the Supreme Court guaranteed that the government's laws and measures were always in accord with the Constitution. Placing the founding document "on a pedestal", above the political melee, represented a great victory for the Federalists.[32]

### 14.5.2 *From 13 to 50 States*

When the original 13 states ratified the U.S. Constitution in 1791, the constitutional history of the United States had only just begun. As the years passed, new states were added to the union as the nation surged westward. This process began immediately, with the 1791 incorporation of the states of Vermont and Kentucky, and ended with the 1959 integration of Alaska and Hawaii. The process of the expansion of the United States of America is a fascinating phase of its constitutional history about which many are ignorant, but without studying this crucial aspect the consolidation of the Union and the presidential system cannot be understood.[33]

#### 14.5.2.1 The Legal Principles Governing Westward Expansion: The Ownership of Western Land

Even before the War of Independence was over, representatives from 7 of the 13 states had expressed their intention to annex virgin lands to the west when Britain finally surrendered its claim to them, expansionist plans which were blocked when the other six, which did not have western borders, considered it unfair for their fellow states to be able to expand when they were not.[34] Thus, an agreement was reached by which the expansion of the United States was to fall under the purview of the Congress, already the nation's supreme legislative body according the Articles of Confederation regime (Lawson and Seidman 2004, 73–74),

[32] As Kahn (2002, 10) argues, the transcendence of Marbury lies in the fact that the verdict sought to suppress a politics of revolution through the rule of law. The Court's claim on this case did not reflect a fact, but an aspiration, a judicial response to Jefferson's successful electoral campaign and its promise to effect a new revolution.

[33] And the process is not still finished, as Puerto Rico remains in an interim "territorial" phase, because there is still insufficient popular support among Puerto Ricans in favor of requesting U.S. statehood. For a literary and most interesting overview of the fascinating process of territorial expansion and statemaking, see Morgan (1996).

[34] The issue of western lands had divided the 13 states since the Revolution. Some states had included claims to western lands in their colonial charters, while others, such as Maryland and New Jersey, had made none. The problem was that in some cases these claims conflicted, as was the case with the northern region of the Ohio River, which Virginia claimed in its entirety, and Connecticut and Massachusetts in part. The representatives from states lacking rights to western lands argued that all of them should be ceded to the Confederation, as the trans-Appalachian territory had been won in the war against England by all (Ayers et al. 2009, 184).

establishing the principle that in the western lands distinct states should be formed, to join the Union with "the same rights of sovereignty, freedom and independence as the other states".[35] The states which had once aspired to expand their borders ended up ceding their rights to Congress over a period of two decades; the first to do so was New York in early 1780, forcing Virginia and the others. The last state to cede its claims to Western lands was Georgia, which only did it in 1802.[36]

Congress was, therefore, charged with developing the procedure according to which new territories would be incorporated into the nation. This was no small task, as it called for maintaining the balance which had made the emergence of the federal union possible. The first attempt at legislation governing the expansion process, the Land Ordinance of 1784, would prove, however, a failure.

#### 14.5.2.2 The Land Ordinance of 1784

The first attempt to regulate America's territorial expansion process was the Land Ordinance of 1784 (April 23). Drafted by Thomas Jefferson, it was intended to become the first law governing the territories lying west of the existing states (Berkhofer 1988, 267–298). Passed under the Articles of Confederation government, the law ended up failing because it called for the formation of new states in the west according to a schedule that was considered too hurried by the most influential members of the ruling elite, who believed that a plan to survey and sell the western lands should be undertaken to secure badly needed funds, and that measures should be taken to defend the widely dispersed westerners from threats by Indians or other white settlers (Johnson 2009, 7). Moreover, Congress feared that a rapid increase in the number of states might send the new nation spinning into anarchy.

---

[35] Finally, on September 6, 1780, the Continental Congress passed a resolution stating "that the unappropriated lands that may be ceded or relinquished to the United States by any particular states... shall be disposed of for the common benefit of the United States, and be settled and formed into distinct republican states, which shall become members of the Federal Union, and shall have the same rights of sovereignty, freedom and independence, as the other states" (Patrick 1995, 110).

[36] With the New York cession Virginia found itself in the awkward position of being in opposition not only with the northern states, but with neighboring Maryland which, because of this question, did not wish to ratify the Articles of Confederation. On January 2, 1781, the Virginia General Assembly finally passed an act that ceded all lands northwest of the Ohio River, though with a number of restrictions and continuing claims on the territory that would later become Kentucky. Two months later, Maryland signed the Articles of Confederation (Johnson 2009, 7).

#### 14.5.2.3 The Legal Regulation of the Sale of New Lands: The Land Ordinance of May 20, 1785

To avoid these problems, the Congress decided to restrict itself to regulating only the economic aspect of the measurement and sale of the new lands. To this end the Land Ordinance of 1785 (May 20), established the model for American territorial expansion, based on basic units of 6 square miles (about 9,600 $m^2$, slightly less than a hectare),[37] a new and revolutionary system of measuring and bounding the land (Hine and Faragher 2007, 42). Following the adoption of the Land Ordinance of 1785 Congress created a corps of geographers, who set about surveying western lands that very same year. The process went on for 161 years and only ended when there was no more land left to survey, in 1946, under the presidency of Harry Truman, after the end of World War II (Cazier 1976, 214).

This territorial division would prove essential, as it facilitated the United States' evolution into a nation of small and medium-sized landowners.[38] This, in turn, paved the way for the abandonment of censitary suffrage systems (under which affairs were dominated by great landowners, such as Washington and Jefferson), and the adoption of more democratic models based on universal suffrage, which definitively triumphed after the end of the Civil war (1865)—at least for men, as American women would not be granted the vote until after World War I (Keyssar 2009).

The addition of a large number of new landowners to the body politic made the election of 1828 a watershed in American politics, marking the first featuring mass participation, i.e. not controlled by members of the traditional, privileged gentry. The winner was Andrew Jackson, the victor in the first election featuring much of the phenomena that would characterize more modern electioneering: mudslinging,

[37] According to the 1785 Land Ordinance, the basic building blocks of the survey were to be "lots" and "townships". Each individual lot was to comprise an area of 1 square mile, and each township included a six-mile-by-six-mile area, or 36 lots. Land was to be sold either by township or by individual lot (Carleton 2002, 14). On the 1785 Land Ordinance, see Kemp (2010, 148–153).

[38] Though this was not so clear in the beginning because of the system used to turn western lands over to private ownership. Jefferson advised giving away the land "in small quantities to actual settlers", but his opinion was not shared by his fellow members of the Continental Congress, who instead decided to auction off the surveyed lands in portions no smaller than 640 acres, and at a price no less than one dollar per acre—well beyond the means of most farmers. Congress's main aim was not to spread equal opportunities to western settlers, but rather to generate a source of revenue for the national government. The result was that eastern elites' enjoyed greater access to western lands (Hine and Faragher 2007, 42). As an exception, the 1785 ordinance did reserve the revenue of one section in each township for the maintenance of public schools (Carleton 2002, 14–15). Congress would not undertake a more socially-oriented land policy until Lincoln's Homestead Act of 1862.

rallies, pandering, the grassroots mobilization of voters, leaflets, etc. Jackson was sworn in as the seventh President of the United States (1829–1837).[39]

#### 14.5.2.4 The Public Status of the New Lands: The Northwest Ordinance (July 13, 1787)

Once the process of land parceling and sale had been undertaken by Congress it remained to establish the new lands' public legal status, as the 1784 Land Ordinance had failed to pass. The representatives of the states were in agreement that none of the 13 founding states should be allowed to annex additional territory. Thus, it was necessary to determine how the new territories would be brought into the union as new states.

Based on this understanding a landmark law in the development of the United States was drafted: the Northwest Ordinance of 1787, a pivotal piece of legislation[40] that predates even the Federal Constitution of 1787; the Ordinance was approved on July 13, 1787, while the Constitution was not completed until September 17, and was not ratified until June 21, 1788, entering into force on March 4, 1789. Hence, the Northwest Ordinance is widely considered a "constitutional" text (Duffey 1995, 929–968).

The Ordinance of 1787 was a logical extension of the Land Ordinance of 1785 (Hyman 2008, 18–34), designed to regulate the type of governments to be established in the new territories on the land which had been surveyed and sold. To prevent the excessive haste which the 1784 Ordinance had been criticized for fomenting, the 1787 act introduced the principle (Sections 3–12)[41] that the new states, prior to achieving statehood, would be required to first pass through a provisional status as "territories", during which they were to satisfy a series of conditions (Onuf 1990, 255). Once organized the territories were to petition

---

[39] As Remini (1998, 5–6) points out, the profound economic and social changes that America experienced during the two first decades of the nineteenth century, gave rise to an intense desire for equality; not absolute equality but rather equality of opportunity, based on the belief that no one should have special privileges that worked to the disadvantage of others. This spirit affected politics deeply and brought essential transformations, such as the expansion of the suffrage and the elimination of voting restrictions, the appearance of professional politicians who contributed to the creation of mass political parties (such as the Democratic Party, created by Jackson and his followers) and the organization of national conventions that led to the democratization of American political institutions. This is why American historians often speak of "Jacksonian democracy" in positive terms (Ellis 1987), despite the fact that Jackson had his dark sides as a supporter of slavery and a leader who ordered the forced relocation and resettlement of Indians.

[40] The U.S. Senator from Massachusetts Daniel Webster (1782–1852), who later became Secretary of State, wrote these famous words on the Northwest Ordinance: "We are accustomed to praise lawgivers of antiquity; we help to perpetuate the fame of Solon and Lycurgus; but I doubt whether one single law of any lawgiver, ancient or modern, has produced the effects of more distinct, marked, and lasting character than the Ordinance of '87'" (Webster 1848, 369).

[41] For the text of the Northwest Ordinance, see Onuf (1990, 260–265).

Congress for entry as new American states, a status which would place them on equal footing with all the others.

The historic measure was termed the Northwest Ordinance because, in principle, it only applied to a particular territorial area stretching west of the Ohio River, where, over time, there appeared five new states: Ohio (1803), Indiana (1816), Illinois (1818), Michigan (1832) and Wisconsin (1848), which respectively became states number 17, 19, 21, 26 and 30 of the Union (Anastaplo 2006, 25, 122).

It is true that some new states were incorporated outside of this regulatory framework. Such was the case with Vermont and Kentucky, which in 1791 were directly added as states 14 and 15. However, by 1796 the Northwest Ordinance of 1787 was being applied outside the Northwest Territory to incorporate the state of Tennessee. Since then the addition of new states into the federal union would generally be carried out according to the NWO model. In fact, 31 of the 50 states that today make up the United States joined the Union under the terms of said legislation.[42]

### *14.5.3 A Problematic Expansion*

The process for the integration of new states into the federal union was, however, lengthy and complex, and not devoid of problems. Among other things, it was one of the triggers of the American Civil War (1861–1865), which nearly destroyed the American union. Thus, it may be said that had it not been for the NWO the United States never would have become one of the most powerful nations in the world. It behooves us, then, to examine, if only by way of an overview, the essential stages of the process by which the union expanded.[43] These were as follows:

(1) Firstly, mention must be made of the creation of five states (Ohio, Indiana, Michigan, Illinois and Wisconsin) in the "Northwest Territory", which the United States obtained from England after the signing of the Peace of Versailles in 1783. The integration of this territory was the initial aim pursued by the Northwest Ordinance, enacted in July of 1787.
(2) The second step was taken when the principles and the procedure established in the Ordinance of 1787, were applied for the first time to an area not initially covered by said legislation, which was theoretically only intended for the settlement of the northwest. This precedent was set in the so-called "Southwest Territory", which became the State of Tennessee in 1796, after the express application of the terms set forth in the Northwest Ordinance.
(3) The third wave of state institution involved the territories that the Union had purchased from the Spanish Crown in 1795, 1797, 1813 and 1819 in the

[42] For an overview of this fascinating statehood process, see Onuf (1987).

[43] This overall view has been essentially extracted from the work by Morgan (1996).

southeast, a region which saw the formation of the states of Mississippi, Alabama and Florida, also pursuant to the procedure laid down in the 1787 legislation.

(4) A fourth stage began in 1803, when Napoleon Bonaparte sold the Louisiana Territory (Louisiana Purchase) to the United States, an expanse covering some 823,000 square miles of new land. In addition to doubling the nation's territory, for the first time the United States stretched to the Pacific Ocean (Lawson and Seidman 2004, 17–85).[44] In this immense territory, there would emerge nine full states and parts of five others, beginning with the State of Louisiana itself, which joined the union as the 18th state in 1812, by following, again, the procedure laid down in the Northwest Ordinance.

(5) By 1819, the union was already composed of 22 states, half of which permitted slavery, and half of which prohibited it. In addition to its human rights ramifications, this point of divergence also entailed significant economic factors, as the slave states' economies were based on huge plantations cultivated by slaves, while the free states' economies were characterized by free farmers along with humble to more prosperous landowners, and workers engaged in mining and industry. Therefore, while in the former the principle of censitary suffrage prevailed, whereby only citizens with certain levels of income could vote in elections, in the free states universal suffrage was implemented virtually from the outset. The country, then, featured two different, almost opposite models of the state. This key variance (economic, social and political) would have dramatic consequences.

As long as a balance was maintained between the number of slave and free states, federal institutions reflected that balance, especially in the Senate, where each state was (and still is today) represented by two senators. In 1819, however, Missouri aspired to enter the union as a slave state, which would have upset this delicate balance. To resolve the ensuing crisis in 1820, the slave and free states came to an agreement: Missouri would be permitted to join as a slave state, Maine would join as a free state, and slavery would be banned in all future territories north of the 36° 30′ latitude line. It was also agreed that slavery would be prohibited north of said line (Wilentz 2004, 375–401). What came to be known as the "Missouri Compromise" was respected until 1845, and made possible the subsequent incorporation into the union of another six states:

[44] The Louisiana Purchase was the foundational act of territorial expansion. Lawson and Seidman state that acquisition of territory is constitutionally warranted as an exercise of the treaty power, considered as a means of implementing a textually enumerated power, such as the admission of new states. In other words, territorial acquisition is not an incident of sovereignty that all governments possess, as many lawmakers argued at the time. Indeed, according to the mentioned authors, the argument from sovereignty "fundamentally misunderstands the Constitution and the very concept of a limited government". "The distinctive genius of the American Constitution", they add, "is the idea, clearly codified in the Tenth Amendment, that every exercise of national power must be traceable to an explicit or implicit grant of power in the document" (Lawson and Seidman 2004, 22; Belz 2005, 601–607). Also, Williams et al. (2005). For an analysis of the formation and current state of the American empire, see Nugent (2008).

three slave (Missouri, Arkansas and Florida), and three free (Maine, Michigan and Iowa).[45]

(6) The situation shifted on December 29, 1845, when the State of Texas joined the union via annexation rather than the application of the procedure adopted in 1787. Texas had actually been an independent republic since 1836 and its annexation, in addition to triggering war with Mexico (1846–1848), led to the collapse of the Missouri Compromise, as Texas entered the union as a slave state without its incorporation being balanced out by the addition of another free one.[46]

(7) In 1846, the U.S. bought from the United Kingdom of Great Britain what was known as the Oregon Territory, the New Northwest, or the Far Northwest, where three states would be founded: Oregon, Washington and Idaho, which joined the union following the assimilation procedure called for under the Northwest Ordinance of 1787.

(8) In 1848, the Mexican–American War ended, with the Americans victorious. Via the Treaty of Guadalupe Hidalgo, signed following the Mexicans' defeat, the United States acquired vast western territories which would come to form the states of California, Nevada, Utah, New Mexico, Arizona, and half of the State of Colorado today. This territory was expanded in 1853, when Vice-President Gadsden purchased from Mexico part of what is today the State of New Mexico (Gadsden Purchase).[47] After the war with Mexico, the American government was able to turn its energies to restoring the balance provided by the Missouri Compromise—one which had been broken by the annexation of Texas. In May of 1848, Wisconsin joined the union as a free state, which brought the number of free and slave states to 15 each, thereby leveling the number of free and slave state senators at 30 each.

(9) When California joined the union on September 9, 1850, as a free state, it was already clear that parity between the free and slave states was in peril, as the latter's capacity for expansion was practically non-existent given the aforementioned ban on further slave states north of the 36°-30′ parallel. In 1850, it was agreed that the doctrine of popular sovereignty would be respected, according to which each new territory would be able to determine the legality of slavery within its borders by a vote (Waugh 2003). In accordance with this system, California was incorporated as a free state, but its integration upset the balance in Congress, as the scales were tipped in the free camp's favor (Morgan 1996, 173–175).

(10) The "Compromise of 1850" was complemented by the Kansas–Nebraska Act, signed in 1854 by President Pierce, which rescinded the provision of the Missouri Compromise that had precluded the creation of slave states north

[45] As Forbes (2009, 5) points out, the Missouri controversy ripped off the façade of national consensus from American public life by revealing how powerful anti-slavery sentiment was in the northern states, and exposing the hold that it had acquired over the process of national decision making. It was a "flash of lightning that illuminated the realities of sectional power in the U.S., igniting a fire that smoldered for a generation".

[46] This is why, as Lawson and Seidman (2004, 91) point out, the absorption of Texas generated more constitutional objections than did the incorporation of any other state during the nation's first century.

[47] On the boundary disputes arising from the original 1848 Treaty, including the Gadsden Treaty of 1853, see Del Castillo (1992, 55–61).

of the 36°-30′ parallel. Henceforth states' decisions to join the union as either free or slave states hinged on exclusively upon a "democratic" decision put to their (white male) inhabitants, which unleashed a frenetic rush to settle new territories. When it became clear that Nebraska would be a free state, Missouri slavery supporters did everything they could to keep anti-slavery settlers out of Kansas. The confrontation between the two sides, allowed a free Minnesota to achieve statehood in 1858. However, the civil war in Kansas (for which the territory came to be dubbed "Bleeding Kansas") would prove to be indicative of a deep divide between the states, one which would result in a Civil War between the nation's northern (free) and southern (slave) states (Ponce 2011, 5).

(11) The election of Abraham Lincoln as President of the United States in 1860, prompted the state of South Carolina to secede from the union. The separatist movement spread quickly and in February 1861, delegates from seven states met in Montgomery (Alabama) to found a new union: the Confederate States of America. Jefferson Davis was elected its first President, and Alexander H. Stephens its Vice President. A month later the Confederacy had a new constitution. Lincoln took advantage of the outbreak of the Civil War (War of Secession), between the Union and the Confederacy to facilitate the creation of new free states—a task expedited by the vast majority he held in Congress after all the South's representatives and senators had abandoned their positions. In 1861, Kansas became the 34th state and Nevada became a U.S. Territory. In 1863, West Virginia became the 35th state, without going through the territorial phase provided for under the terms of the 1787 NWO. One year later, Nevada became the 36th state after a territorial stage of only 3 years (Morgan 1996, 218–223 and 230–231).

(12) West Virginia was the last state to join without complying with the terms of the Northwest Ordinance. After the end of the Civil War, the victory of federal forces made it possible for future territories to be brought in as states according to the 1787 NWO system, including the incorporation of Nebraska (1867), Colorado (1876), North Dakota, South Dakota, Washington, Montana (1889), Idaho and Wyoming (1890). In the twentieth century, they would be followed by Oklahoma (1907), New Mexico, Arizona (1912) and, finally, Alaska and Hawaii (1959).

By 1959, the process by which the United States had added states to the union was over. In addition to the original 13 colonies, 31 of the 37 new States had followed the legal process laid down in the Northwest Ordinance of 1787. Only six had been integrated into the Union in a different fashion: Vermont, Kentucky, Maine, Texas, California and West Virginia (Morgan 1996, 509–514).

### *14.5.4 The Protection of Fundamental Rights: The Union vs. the States*

Another area in which the Anti-Federalists put up a fight had to do with defining the scope of application of the Bill of Rights. Most Anti-Federalists held that the historic set of amendments represented restrictions only applicable to the federal government, and did not view it as extending to legislation passed by *state* governments. It should be understood that while the ratification of the Bill of Rights granted the citizens of each state ample protection from federal power, from a legal point of view this protection of fundamental rights was interpreted in a narrow and restricted manner; forming part of the federal Constitution, it was viewed as applicable only to the federal government. Curiously, in this way the states retained a great deal of power, even if this was in detriment to their own citizens' freedoms and liberties.

#### 14.5.4.1 The Restrictive Interpretation of the Bill of Rights

The fact that the legal protections provided for by the Bill of Rights were limited to blocking actions by the federal government[48] meant that Americans' individual rights were totally vulnerable, from a legal perspective, as the governments of the 13 states were not compelled to respect these protections (Currie 2005, 279). It is noteworthy in this regard that slavery continued to be legal in a number of states because the first ten amendments to the Constitution did not protect individual rights under the constitutions and governments of the 13 states, as was made clear in the Supreme Court's infamous Dred Scott Decision (1857), in which the high court not only ruled that African Americans had no right to U.S. citizenship, but that Congress had no authority to prohibit slavery in federal territories.[49] This situation

[48] I would like to thank Professor Sergio Pareja of the University of New Mexico School of Law for his input on this topic. As a Guest Professor serving at the Instituto de Estudios Jurídicos Internationales at the Universidad Rey Juan Carlos in Madrid, he pointed out to me this essential aspect of the debate between the Federalists and Anti-Federalists which, contrary to widespread belief, did not end with the ratification of the federal Constitution. In fact, the nation's conservative party (Republican) continues to be in favor of granting more power to the states, while the more liberal Democratic Party endorses most powers being assigned to the federal government. Most of what appears in this section is taken from his article (Pareja 2013).

[49] Dred Scott v. Sandford, 60 U.S. 393 (1857). The Supreme Court, with Chief Justice Roger B. Taney residing, first stated that African Americans were not citizens and that, consequently, they could not sue in federal court. Secondly, the court found that the federal government had no power to regulate slavery in any territory acquired by the Union after the creation of the United States. The majority opinion met with the opposition of justices Justice and Mclean, who argued, among other things, that there was no Constitutional basis for the contention that blacks could not be citizens. This marked the first time since Marbury vs. Madison that the Supreme Court ruled that an act of Congress was unconstitutional. For an overview of the Scott Case, see Stampp (1990, 68–109). Concerning constitutional issues related to the slavery problem, see Russell (1966, 466–486). In these context, Elizabeth Cady Stanton and Lucretia Mott, two American activists in the movement to abolish slavery called together the first conference to address Women's rights and issues in Seneca Falls, New York, in 1848. Part of the reason for doing so had been that Mott had been refused permission to speak at the world anti-slavery convention in London, even though she had been an official delegate. Applying the analysis of human freedom developed in the Abolitionist movement, Stanton and others began the public career of modern feminist analysis. The Declaration of the Seneca Falls Convention, using the model of the US Declaration of Independence, forthrightly demanded that the rights of women as right-bearing individuals be acknowledged and respected by society. It was signed by 68 women and 32 men—and many of them were Quakers (Wellman 2004).

would be utterly overturned, however, as a result of the landmark event of the American Civil War (1861–1865).[50]

#### 14.5.4.2 The War of Secession and the Consolidation of the American Union

The Civil War was not only an extremely bloody conflict, but also a decisive stage in the constitutional history of the United States (Bestor 1988, 219–234). From a legal point of view, it marked one more clash in a series of confrontations between the states and the federal government, dating all the way back to 1787. Firstly because, as we have seen, the war broke out when the number of free states surpassed the number of slave states, upsetting the delicate balance hitherto maintained in the Senate, a disturbing development for the slave states which prompted them to declare their secession from the Union. Secondly, because President Lincoln was conscious of the fact that, from a legal point of view, the Civil War represented a struggle to preserve the federal Union, saving it from an attempt by the southern states to return to the confederate model which the United States had adopted from 1783 to 1787.[51]

Thus, when the war ended the victorious states of the North forced those in the South to add three amendments to the Constitution: Amendments 13, 14 and 15, which came to be termed the "Civil War Amendments" (McDonald 2002, 193–222),[52] in what has been called the "Second American Revolution" (McPherson 1990).

The 13th Amendment abolished slavery and involuntary servitude, except in those cases when it was imposed as a criminal punishment. The 14th Amendment defined the concept of citizenship to include all those born in the United States, who were to be protected by all constitutional guarantees, with clauses providing for privileges and immunities, due process and equal protection. Finally, the 15th Amendment prohibited the denial of voting rights to any citizen based on race or color, or as a result of his previous enslavement (Farber 2003, 144–175).

Ultimately said amendments sought to extend the protection of individual rights to possible encroachment by any of the nation's 50 states. This expansion, however, did not come about until 1897, when the Supreme Court issued a decision which constituted what in American law schools is known as the "incorporation" of the Bill of Rights via the 14th Amendment.[53] In its ruling the high court stated that the

[50] For an overview of the Constitutional debate in the U.S. during the decades prior to the Civil War, see Fritz (2008).

[51] In fact, it is significant that after the Civil War the "United States" began to be used in the singular rather than the plural generally employed hitherto (McPherson 2003, 859).

[52] They are also, significantly, called the "Reconstruction Amendments" (Kommers et al. 2004, 116).

[53] Chicago, Burlington and Quincy Railroad vs. City of Chicago, 166 U.S. 226 March 1, 1897. In this case, the U.S. Supreme Court, for the first time, incorporated an amendment of the Bill of Rights and applied it to a state or local government; the Bill of Rights had previously been considered to apply only to the federal government.

Bill of Rights ought to be valid and extend to the authority exercised by state governments. Specifically, the Supreme Court employed the legal argument that the due process clause, according to which each state was obligated to respect a citizen's rights, expressly encompassed those set forth in the Bill of Rights of the U.S. Constitution. This marked a watershed victory for advocates of federal authority, as the power of state governments was considerably undercut.

Despite this momentous victory for defenders of federal supremacy, even today some Americans believe that the issues at stake in the War of Secession have yet to be resolved, as fierce debate still rages regarding the different powers and authorities which the states and federal government should wield concerning individual rights. Following the election of the Republican Party's Ronald Reagan (1981–1989), the federal government initiated a sweeping policy of "deregulation" which called for the progressive lifting of federal controls on economic activity, a course of action which Republican detractors allege not only exacerbated the gap between the rich and poor, but also set in motion the process leading to the dire financial crisis which began in September of 2008. Even more recently the Supreme Court made headlines and stirred up fierce controversy when it declared the medical coverage legislation endorsed by President Barack Obama to be constitutional, ruling that the imposition of the obligation to acquire health insurance is justified and endorsed by the tax-levying power which the Constitution assigns to the U.S. Congress.[54]

## TIMELINE

### The Confederal Stage

1776 Declaration of Independence.
1777 Approval of the Articles of Confederation.
1783 Recognition of the United States of America as a nation (Peace of Versailles).
1785 May 20. Land Ordinance.
1786 August 29. Beginning of Shay's Rebellion (through January 1787).
September 11–14. Failure of the Annapolis Convention.

[54] The Supreme Court of the United States, in the case *National Federation of Independent Business v. Sebelius*, 132 U.S. 2566 (2012), declared that Congress had the power to enact most provisions of the Patient Protection and Affordable Care Act (ACA) and the Health Care and Education Reconciliation Act (HCERA). The vote of Chief Justice John G. Roberts Jr. (paradoxically appointed by the Republican President George W. Bush on September 29, 2005), was decisive, as he wrote that the individual mandate to buy health insurance is a constitutional exercise of Congress's taxing power. This was a landmark decision which significantly increased the power of the federal government over that of the states. On this point, see Hoff (2013, 5–20).

## The Origins of the Federal Union

1787 February 21. The Congress calls for a Constitutional Convention in Philadelphia.
May 25. First meeting.
July 13. The Northwest Ordinance.
September 17. Ratification of the federal Constitution.
December 7. Delaware is the first state to ratify the Constitution (30 votes in favor, 0 against).
December 11. Pennsylvania ratifies, 46 to 23.
December 18. New Jersey ratifies, 38 to 0.

1788 January 2. Georgia ratifies, 26 to 0.
January 9. Connecticut ratifies, 128 to 40.
February 6. Massachusetts ratifies, 187 to 168.
April 26. Maryland ratifies, 63 to 11.
May 23. South Carolina ratifies, 149 to 73.
June 21. New Hampshire is the ninth state to ratify, 57 to 47. The U.S. Constitution officially goes into effect.
June 25. Virginia ratifies, 89 to 79.
July 26. The State of New York ratifies, 30 to 27.

1789 January 10. The election of George Washington as the first President of the United States.
March 4. The Constitution goes into effect.
April 30. George Washington is sworn in as president.
November 21. North Carolina ratifies, 194 to 77.

1790 May 29. Rhode Island is the last state to ratify the Constitution.

1791 Vermont and Kentucky become the 14th and 15th states.
December 15. The Congress ratifies the Bill of Rights and the first ten amendments to the Constitution take effect.

1793 Re-election of George Washington.

## The Consolidation of the Federal State

1796 Tennessee becomes the first state outside the northwest region to join the union according to the terms of the NWO and its procedures.

1797 End of Washington's second term. He refuses to stand for election again.

1801 Election of Anti-Federalist Thomas Jefferson as President.

1803 February 24. Sentence in the Marbury vs. Madison case. Federalist John Marshall, Chief Justice of the Supreme Court from 1801 to 1835, frustrates Jefferson's efforts to reduce the power of the federal government. Thanks to Marshall the Supreme Court of the United States becomes a powerful and pivotal instrument: established as the interpreter of the Constitution, its sentences are to shape the form, development and purviews of the federal government.

April 30. The United States buys Louisiana from Napoleon (*Louisiana Purchase*).

1820 Missouri Compromise.

1845 Annexation of the State of Texas (an independent republic since 1836) to the union. The balance is upset in favor of the slave states.

1848 February 2. The Treaty of Guadalupe Hidalgo allowed the United States to incorporate a massive amount of territory across the American west (what makes up the modern-day states of California, Nevada, Utah, New Mexico, Arizona and Colorado).

May. Wisconsin joins as a free State. Recovery of the balance between the free and slave states (15–15).

1850 August 13. California joins the nation.

September. A commitment to the incorporation of new states as slave or free, to be determined by a vote.

1854 May 30. The Kansas–Nebraska Act legalizes the founding of slave states north of the 36°30′ parallel.

1857 March 6. The Supreme Court of the United States rules that African Americans are not citizens (Dred Scott v. Sandford, 60 U.S. 393).

## Civil War and Its Aftermath

1860 November. (11) The election of Abraham Lincoln as President of the United States prompts the State of South Carolina to secede from the union.

1861 February 9. Jefferson Davis is elected President of the Confederate States of America.

March 4. Abraham Lincoln takes office as President.

April 12. A Confederate assault on the garrison at Fort Sumter is the first act of the American Civil War.

1864 April 8. Adoption by the Senate of the 13th Amendment, which outlaws slavery and involuntary servitude, except as punishment for a crime.

1865 April 9. The end of the Civil War.

April 14. President Abraham Lincoln is assassination.

1868 July 9. Adoption of the 14th Amendment, which contains a broad definition of citizenship and establishes that African Americans are indeed citizens of the United States.

1870 February 3. Ratification of the 15th Amendment, which prohibits the governments of the states from denying a citizen the right to vote based on race, color or a previous condition of servitude.

1897 March 1. In the case "Chicago, Burlington & Quincy Railroad Co. v. City of Chicago" (166 U.S. 226), for the first time the US Supreme Court invokes the Bill of Rights to curtail the authority of a state government.

1946 End of the land surveying process initiated under the Land Ordinance of 1785.

1959 Alaska and Hawaii join the U.S. as states 49 and 50.
1951 Ratification of the 22nd Amendment, which limits presidents to two terms.
2012 June 28. The U.S. Supreme Court declares it constitutional for the federal government to require citizens to purchase health insurance, ruling that it is licensed to do so pursuant to the Congress's taxation authority under the U.S. Constitution. (National Federation of Independent Business v. Sebelius.) 132 U.S. 2566.

## References


Abraham, H. J. (1998). *The judicial process: An introductory analysis of the courts of the United States, England and France*. New York: Oxford University Press.

Abraham, H. J. (2008). *Justices, presidents and senators: A history of the U.S. supreme court. Appointments from Washington to Bush II* (5th ed.). Lanham, MD: Rowman & Littlefield.

Anastaplo, G. (2006). The articles of confederation: The Northwest Ordinance (1787). In *Reflections on constitutional law* (pp. 21–26). Lexington, KY: University Press of Kentucky.

Ayers, E. L., Gould, L. L., Oshinsky, D. M., & Soderlund, J. R. (2009). *American passages: A history of the United States* (4th ed.). Boston: Wadsworth.

Bailey, J. D. (2010). *Thomas Jefferson and executive power*. Cambridge, MA: Cambridge University Press.

Banning, L. (1998). *The sacred fire of liberty: James Madison and the founding of the federal republic*. Ithaca, NY: Cornell University Press.

Beeman, R. R. (2010). *The Penguin guide to the United States constitution: A fully annotated declaration of independence, U.S. constitution and amendments, and selections from the federalist papers*. London: Penguin.

Belenky, A. S. (2012). *Understanding the fundamentals of the U.S. presidential election system*. Heidelberg: Springer.

Belz, H. (2005). Review: The constitution of empire: Territorial expansion and American legal history. *The Independent Review, 9*(4), 601–607.

Berkhofer, R. F. (1988). American versus Indians: The Northwest Ordinance, territory making, and native Americans. *Indiana Magazine of History, 84*(1), 90–108.

Bernstein, R. B., & Agel, J. (1993). *Amending America: If we love the constitution so much, why do we keep trying to change it?* Lawrence, KA: University Press of Kansas.

Bestor, A. (1988). The American Civil War as a constitutional crisis. In L. M. Friedman & H. N. Scheiber (Eds.), *American law and the constitutional order: Historical perspectives* (pp. 219–234). Cambridge, MA: Harvard University Press.

Beveridge, A. J. (2013). *The life of John Marshall*. New York: Cosimo.

Bolingbroke, Henry St John, Viscount. (2010). *The idea of a Patriot King: With respect to the constitution of Great Britain. By a person of quality*. Charleston, SC: BiblioBazaar.

Bowen, C. (2010). *Miracle at Philadelphia: The story of the Constitutional Convention, May to September, 1787* (Reprint). New York: Little, Brown.

Brown, R. D. (1983). Shays' rebellion and its aftermath: A view from Springfield, Massachusetts, 1787. *William and Mary Quarterly, 40*(4), 598–615.

Carleton, D. (2002). *Student's guide to landmark congressional laws on education*. Westport, CT: Greenwood.

Casey, G. (1974). The Supreme Court and myth: An empirical investigation. *Law & Society Review, 8*(3), 385–420.

Cazier, L. (1976). *Surveys and surveyors of the public domain: 1785–1975*. Washington, DC: U.S. Department of the Interior. Bureau of Land Management.

Coffman, S. (Ed.). (2012). *Words of the founding fathers: Selected quotations of Franklin, Washington, Adams, Jefferson, Madison and Hamilton, with sources*. Jefferson, NC: McFarland Publishing.

Colbourn, T. H. (1998). *The lamp of experience: Whig history and the intellectual origins of the American Revolution* (2nd Ed., reimp.). Indianapolis, IN: Liberty Fund.

Collier, C., & Collier, J. L. (2007). *Decision in Philadelphia: The Constitutional Convention of 1787*. New York: Random House.

Currie, D. P. (2005). *The constitution in Congress: Democrats and Whigs, 1829–1861*. Chicago, IL: University of Chicago Press.

Del Castillo, R. G. (1992). *The treaty of Guadalupe Hidalgo: A legacy of conflict*. Norman, OK: University of Oklahoma Press.

Deskins Jr., D. R., Walton, Jr., H., & Puckett, S. C. (2010). *Presidential elections, 1789–2008: County, state and national mapping of election data*. Ann Arbor, MI: The University of Michigan Press.

Duffey, D. P. (1995). The Northwest Ordinance as a constitutional document. *Columbia Law Review, 95*(4), 929–968.

Dunn, S. (2007). *Dominion of memories: Jefferson, Madison, and the decline of Virginia*. New York: Basic Books.

Dworkin, R. (2013). *Taking rights seriously*. London: Bloomsbury Academics.

Ellis, R. E. (1987). *The union at risk: Jacksonian democracy, states' rights, and the nullification crisis*. Oxford: Oxford University Press.

Epstein, D. F. (2008). *The political theory of the Federalist* (Reprint). Chicago, IL: University of Chicago Press.

Farber, D. (2003). *Lincoln's constitution*. Chicago, IL: University of Chicago Press.

Feeley, M. M., & Rubin, E. L. (2000). *Judicial policy making and the modern state: How the courts reformed America's prisons*. Cambridge, UK: Cambridge University Press.

Feer, R. (1969). Shays' rebellion and the constitution: A study in causation. *The New England Quarterly, 42*(3), 388–410.

Ferejohn, J. (2005). Madisonian separation of powers. In S. Kernell (Ed.), *James Madison: The theory and practice of republican government* (pp. 126–155). Stanford, CA: Stanford University Press.

Forbes, R. P. (2009). *The Missouri compromise and its aftermath: Slavery and the meaning of America*. Chapel Hill, NC: University of North Carolina Press.

Fritz, C. G. (2008). *American sovereigns: The people and America's constitutional tradition before the Civil War*. Cambridge, UK: Cambridge University Press.

Ginsberg, B., & Ackerman, E. (2011). *A guide to the United States constitution*. London: W.W. Norton & Co.

Gregg, G. L. (1997). *The presidential republic: Executive representation and deliberative democracy*. London: Rowman & Littlefield.

Gross, R. A. (2009). A Yankee Rebellion? The regulators, New England, and the new nation. *New England Quarterly, 82*(1), 112–135.

Hall, K. L., Ely, J. W., & Grossman, J. B. (Eds.). (2005). *The Oxford Companyon to the Supreme Court of the United States*. Oxford: Oxford University Press.

Hamilton, A. (2011). *The federalist papers*. Auckland, NZ: The Floating Press.

Hansford, T., & Spriggs, J. (2006). *The politics of precedent on the U.S. Supreme Court*. Princeton, NJ: Princeton University Press.

Hickok, E. W., Jr. (1991). *The Bill of Rights: Original meaning and current understanding*. Charlottesville, VA: University of Virginia Press.

Hine, R. V., & Faragher, J. M. (2007). *Frontiers: A short history of American West*. New Haven, CT: Yale University Press.

Hoff, J. S. (2013). Obamacare: Chief justice Roberts's political dodge. *The Independent Review, 18*(1), 5–20.

Hyman, H. M. (2008). *American singularity: The 1787 Northwest Ordinance, the 1862 Homestead and Morrill Acts, and the 1944 G.I.* Bill Athens, GA: University of Georgia Press.

Jackson, A. (1835). Message to the Senate protesting [against] censure resolution April 15, 1834. In *Annual messages, veto messages, protest, & c. of Andrew Jackson, president of the United States* (pp. 249–272). Baltimore, MD: Edward J. Coale & Co.

Jefferson, T. (2004). To the republicans of Washington County, Maryland, 31 March, 1809. In J. J. Looney (Ed.), *The papers of Thomas Jefferson: 4 March 1809 to 15 November 1809. Retirement series* (Vol. I, pp. 98–99). Princeton, NJ: Princeton University Press.

Johnson, D. W. (2009). *The laws that shaped America: Fifteen acts of Congress and their lasting impact*. New York: Routledge.

Kahn, P. W. (2002). *The reign of law: Marbury V. Madison and the construction of America*. New Haven, CT: Yale University Press.

Kemp, R. L. (Ed.). (2010). *Documents of American democracy: A collection of essential works*. Jefferson, NC: McFarland and Company.

Keyssar, A. (2009). *The right to vote: The contested history of democracy in the United States*. New York, NY: Basic Books.

Kommers, D. P., Finn, J. E., & Jacobsohn, G. J. (Eds.) (2004). *American constitutional law: Liberty, community, and the Bill of Rights* (Vol. 2). Oxford: Rowman & Littlefield.

Kyvig, D. (1996). *Explicit & Authentic Acts: Amending the U.S. Constitution, 1776–1995*. Lawrence, KS: University Press of Kansas.

LaCroix, A. L. (2010). *The ideological origins of American federalism*. Cambridge, MA: Harvard University Press.

Lawson, G., & Seidman, G. (2004). *The constitution of Empire: Territorial expansion and American legal history*. New Haven, CT: Yale University Press.

Leffler, R. (1987). The case of George Mason's objections to the constitution. *Manuscripts, 39*(4), 285–292.

Lipset, S. M. (2003). *The first new nation: The United States in historical and comparative perspective*. New Brunswick, NJ: Transaction Publishers.

Maier, P. (2010). *Ratification: The people debate the constitution, 1787–1788*. New York: Simon & Schuster.

Main, J. T. (2004). *The anti-federalists: Critics of the constitution, 1781–1788*. Chapel Hill, NC: The University of North Carolina Press.

Mansfield, H. C. (2013). *Statesmanship and party government: A study of Burke and Bolingbroke*. Chicago, IL: The University of Chicago Press.

Marshall, J. (2000). Letter from John Adams to John Marshall, August 17, 1825. In *Correspondence, papers, and selected judicial opinions, January 1824–March 1827: The papers of John Marshall* (Vol. X, p. 197). Chapel Hill, NC: University of North Carolina Press.

McDonald, F. (1988). *The presidency of George Washington* (3rd print). Lawrence, KS: University Press of Kansas.

McDonald, F. (1994). *The American presidency: An intellectual history*. Lawrence, KS: University Press of Kansas.

McDonald, F. (1995). *The presidency of Thomas Jefferson* (8th print). Lawrence, KS: University Press of Kansas.

McDonald, F. (2002). *States' rights and the union: Imperium in Imperio, 1776–1876*. Kansas, KS: University of Kansas Press.

McFerran, W. L. (2005). *Birth of the republic: The origins of the United States*. Gretna, LA: Pelican.

McPherson, J. M. (1990). *Abraham Lincoln and the second American Revolution*. New York: Oxford University Press.

McPherson, J. M. (2003). *Battle cry of freedom: The Civil War era*. Oxford: Oxford University Press.

Morgan, T. (1996). *A shovel of stars: The making of the American West 1800 to the present*. New York: Touchstone.

Morton, J. C. (2006). *Shapers of the great debate at the Constitutional Convention of 1787*. Westport, CT: Greenwood.

Murray, J. A. (2007). *Alexander Hamilton: America's forgotten founder*. New York: Algora Publishers.

Nevins, A. (1991). *The American states during and after the revolution: 1775–1789*. Temecula, CA: Reprint Services Corporation (Reprint of the 1924 ed., New York: Macmillan Company).
Newmyer, R. K. (2001). *John Marshall and the Heroic Age of the Supreme Court*. Baton Rouge, LA: Louisiana State University Press.
Nugent, W. T. K. (2008). *Habits of empire: A history of American expansion*. New York: Knopf.
Onuf, P. (1990). The Northwest Ordinance, 1787. In S. L. Schechter (Ed.), *Roots of the republic: American founding documents interpreted* (pp. 249–265). Oxford: Rowman & Littlefield.
Onuf, P. S. (1987). *Statehood and union: A history of the Northwest Ordinance*. Bloomington, IN: Indiana University Press.
Pareja, S. (2013). The crisis from a comparative law perspective: Resistance to regulation in the United States. *Revista General de Derecho Público Comparado*, (12), 1–21.
Patrick, J. J. (Ed.). (1995). *Founding the republic: A documentary history*. Westport, CT: Greenwood.
Ponce, P. T. (2011). *Kansas's War: The Civil War in documents*. Athens, OH: Ohio University Press.
Remini, R. V. (1998). *Andrew Jackson and the course of American democracy: 1833–1845*. Baltimore, MD: John Hopkins University Press.
Richards, L. L. (2002). *Shays's Rebellion: The American Revolution's final battle*. Philadelphia, PA: University of Pennsylvania Press.
Robertson, D. B. (2005). Madison's opponents and constitutional design. *American Political Science Review, 99*(2), 225–243.
Rosen, J. (2006). *The most democratic branch: How the courts serve America*. New York: Oxford University Press.
Rothbard, M. N. (2002). *A history of money and banking in the United States: The colonial era to World War II*. Auburn, AL: Ludwig von Mises Institute.
Russell, R. R. (1966). Constitutional doctrines with regard to slavery in territories. *The Journal of Southern History, 32*(4), 466–486.
Schwartz, B. (2013). *American constitutional law*. Cambridge, UK: Cambridge University Press.
Spaeth, H. J., & Segal, J. A. (2001). *Majority rule or minority will: Adherence to precedent on the U.S. Supreme Court*. Cambridge, UK: Cambridge University Press.
Stampp, K. M. (1990). *America in 1857: A nation on the brink*. New York: Oxford University Press.
Storing, H. J. (2008). *What the anti-federalists were for: The political thought of the opponents of the constitution*. Chicago, IL: University of Chicago Press.
Szatmary, D. P. (1980). *Shays's Rebellion: The making of an Agrarian insurrection*. Amherst, MA: University of Massachusetts Press.
Waugh, J. C. (2003). *On the brink of Civil War: The compromise of 1850 and how it changed the course of American history*. London: Rowman & Littlefield.
Webster, D. (1848). Speech in the Senate on the resolution of Mr. Foote respecting the sale & c., of public lands, January 1830. In *Speeches and forensic arguments* (8th ed., Vol. I, pp. 358–373). Boston, MA: Tappan, Whittemore and Mason.
Wellman, J. (2004). *The road to Seneca Falls: Elizabeth Cady Stanton and the first woman's rights convention*. Urbana, IL: University of Illinois Press.
Wilentz, S. (2004). Jeffersonian democracy and the origins of political antislavery in the United States: The Missouri crisis revisited. *Journal of the Historical Society, 4*(3), 375–401.
Williams, P. G., Bolton, S. C., & Whayne, J. M. (Eds.). (2005). *A whole country in commotion: The Louisiana purchase and the American Southwest*. Fayetteville, AK: University of Arkansas Press.
Wills, G. (2001). *Explaining America: The federalist*. New York: Penguin.
Wirls, D. (2003). Madison's dilemma: Revisiting the relationship between the Senate and the 'Great Compromise' at the Constitutional Convention. In S. Kernell (Ed.), *James Madison: The theory and practice of republican government* (pp. 156–183). Palo Alto, CA: Stanford University Press.

Wolfe, C. (1994). *The rise of modern judicial review: From constitutional interpretation to judge-made law*. Lanham, MD: Rowman & Littlefield.
Zimmerman, J. F. (2008). *Contemporary American federalism: The growth of national power* (2nd ed.). Albany, NY: State University of New York Press.

## Further Reading

Berkin, C. (2002). *A brilliant solution: Inventing the American Constitution*. Orlando, FL: Harcourt.
Bernstein, R. B., & Rice, K. S. (1987). *Are we to be a nation? The making of the constitution*. Cambridge, MA: Harvard University Press.
Billias, G. (2009). *American Constitutionalism heard round the world, 1776–1989: A global perspective*. New York: New York University Press.
Breyer, S. (2005). *Active liberty: Interpreting our democratic constitution*. New York: Oxford University Press.
Brown, R. H. (2000). *Redeeming the republic: Federalists, taxation, and the origins of the constitution*. Baltimore, MD: Johns Hopkins University Press.
Burnett, E. C. (1941). *The Continental Congress: A definitive history of the Continental Congress from its inception in 1774 to March 1789*. New York: Macmillan.
Cayton, R. L. (1987). The Northwest Ordinance from the perspective of the frontier. In R. M. Taylor (Ed.), *The Northwest Ordinance 1787: A bicentennial handbook* (pp. 1–23). Indianapolis, IN: Indiana Historical Society.
Collier, C. (2003). *All politics is local: Family, friends, and provincial interests in the creation of the constitution*. Lebanon, NH: University Press of New England.
Corwin, E. S. (2008). *The constitution and what it means today* (14th ed.). Princeton, NJ: Princeton University Press.
Cox, G. W., & McCubbins, M. D. (2007). *Legislative leviathan: Party government in the House* (2nd ed.). Cambridge, UK: Cambridge University Press.
de la Teja, J. F., & Frank, R. (Eds.). (2005). *Choice, persuasion, and coercion: Social control on Spain's North American frontiers*. Albuquerque, NM: University of New Mexico Press.
Donald, D. H., Baker, J. H., & Holt, M. F. (2001). *The Civil War and reconstruction*. New York: Oxford University Press.
Finckelman, P. (1988). The Northwest Ordinance: A constitution for an empire of liberty. In A. R. L. Cayton (Ed.), *Pathways to the old northwest: An observance of the bicentennial of the Northwest Ordinance* (pp. 269–305). Indianapolis, IN: Indiana Historical Society.
Finckelman, P. (2010). *Race and the constitution: From the Philadelphia convention to the age of segregation*. Washington, DC: American Historical Association.
Guelzo, A. C. (2012). *Fateful lightning: A new history of the Civil War and reconstruction*. New York: Oxford University Press.
Harris, W. C. (2005). *E pluribus unum: Nineteenth-century American literature and the constitutional paradox*. Iowa City, IA: University of Iowa Press.
Heideking, J. (Eds.). (2012). The constitution before the judgment seat: The prehistory and ratification of the American Constitution, 1787–1791. Charlottesville, VA: University of Virginia Press.
Hendrickson, D. C. (2006). *Peace pact: The lost world of the American founding*. Kansas: University Press of Kansas.
Holton, W. (2008). *Unruly Americans and the origins of the constitution*. New York: Farrar, Straus and Giroux.

Kaminsky, J. P., Saladino, G. J., Leffler, R. Schoenleber, C. H., & Hogan, M. A. (Eds.). (2009). *The documentary history of the ratification of the constitution*. Charlottesville, VA: University of Virginia Press.

Main, T. J. (Ed.). (2013). *Is the American Constitution obsolete?* Durham, NC: Carolina Academic Press.

McDonald, F. (1992). *We the people: The economic origins of the constitution*. Chicago, IL: University of Chicago Press.

McDonald, F. (1995). *Alexander Hamilton: A biography*. Norwalk, CT: Easton Press.

McDonald, F. (1995). *Novus Ordo Seclorum: The intellectual origins of the constitution*. Lawrence, KS: University Press of Kansas.

McDonald, F. (1997). *E pluribus unum: The formation of the American Republic (1776–1790)* (2nd ed., 5th reprint). Indianapolis, IN: Liberty Press.

McFerran, W. L. (2009). *The principles of constitutional government: Political sovereignty*. Gretna, LA: Pelican.

McGuire, R. A. (2003). *To form a more perfect union: A new economic interpretation of the United States Constitution*. New York: Oxford University Press.

McPherson, J. M. (2010). *Ordeal by fire: The Civil War and reconstruction*. New York: McGraw-Hill.

Meacham, J. (2008). *American lion: Andrew Jackson in the White House*. New York: Random House.

Meltzer, M. (1990). *The bill of rights: How we got it and what it means*. New York: Crowell.

Morgan, T. (1993). *Wilderness at dawn: The settling of the North American continent*. New York: Simon & Schuster.

Morris, R. B. (1987). *The forging of the union: 1781–1789*. New York: Harper & Row.

Nelson, W. E. (2000). *Marbury Vs. Madison: The origins and legacy of judicial review*. Lexington, KY: University Press of Kentucky.

Poole, K., & Rosenthal, H. (1997). *Congress: A political-economic history of roll call voting*. Oxford: Oxford University Press.

Quirk, W. J. (2008). *Courts and Congress: America's unwritten constitution*. Edison, NJ: Transaction Publishers.

Robertson, D. B. (2013). *The original compromise: What the constitution's framers were really thinking*. Oxford: Oxford University Press.

Storing, H. J. (Ed.). (2007). *The complete anti-federalist* (3 Vols). Chicago, IL: University of Chicago Press.

Unger, H. G. (2009). *The last founding father: James Monroe and a Nation's call to greatness*. Philadelphia, PA: First Da Capo.

Urofsky, M., & Finkelman, P. (2002). *A March of liberty: A constitutional history of the United States* (2 Vols). New York: Oxford University Press.

Vidal, C. (Ed.). (2014). *Louisiana: Crossroads of the Atlantic world*. Philadelphia, PA: University of Pennsylvania Press.

Warren, J. P. (1905). The confederation and Shays' Rebellion. *The American Historical Review, 11*(1), 42–67.

Whittington, K. E. (2007). *Political foundations of judicial supremacy: The presidency, the Supreme Court, and constitutional leadership in U.S. history*. Princeton, NJ: Princeton University Press.

Williams, F. D. (Ed.). (2012). *The Northwest Ordinance: Essays on its formulation, provisions, and legacy*. East Lansing, MI: Michigan State University Press.

Wood, G. S. (1998). *The creation of the American Republic: 1776–1787*. Chapel Hill, NC: University of North Carolina Press.

Zinn, H. (2003). A kind of revolution. In *A people's history of the United States: 1492-present* (pp. 77–102). Harlow, UK: Pearson.

# Chapter 15
# The Return of the Monarchical Principle (II). The French State. From Imperial Bonapartism to Republican Presidentialism

Yes. Imagination governs the world.[1]

Men are more easily governed through their vices than through their virtues.[2]—Napoleon Bonaparte (1769–1821)

Revolutions are temporary disturbances in the life of states... Order always ends up by reclaiming its own; states do not die like individuals, they transform themselves. It is the task of statesmanship...to guide this transformation and to supervise its direction[3]—Clemens Wenzell von Metternich (1773–1859)

The function of the state consists of simultaneously assuring the triumph of order over anarchy and reforming what is no longer in accord with the exigencies of the time.[4]—Charles de Gaulle (1890–1970)

## Contents


15.1 Napoleonic France: From Republic to Monarchy ........ 450
15.1.1 A Genius Named Napoleon Bonaparte ........ 451
15.1.2 The Peculiar "Napoleonic Constitutionalism" ........ 452
15.1.3 A Return to the Roman Model? ........ 454
15.1.4 A New Monarchy for a New Regime ........ 455
15.2 From Assembly-Based Government to Executive Government ........ 456
15.2.1 Napoleon and State Reform ........ 456
15.2.2 The Extreme Centralization of the New Administrative State ........ 457
15.2.3 Judicial Reform and the Creation of Administrative Jurisdiction ........ 457


[1] *Oui, l'imagination gouverne le monde* (Napoléon I 1916, 13).

[2] *On gouverne mieux les hommes par leurs vices que par leurs vertus.* (Napoléon I 1863, 258).

[3] *Les révolutions sont des perturbations momentanées dans la vie des États... L'ordre finit toujours par reprendre ses droits; les États ne meurent pas comme les individus, ils se transforment; la tâche des pouvoirs protecteurs est donc de diriger la transformation et de veiller à ce qu'elle suive la véritable voie.* Metternich (1883, 8, 485).

[4] *La fonction de l'État consiste à la fois à assurer le succès de l'ordre sur l'anarchie et à réformer ce qui n'est plus conforme aux exigences de l'époque.* (De Gaulle 2003, I, 565). In addition to his gifts as a political thinker and an excellent writer, De Gaulle was also capable of typically French sarcasm, with phrases such as: "The French are capable of anything, even the best", and "How do you expect me to lead a country that has more than 300 types of cheese?" (De Gaulle 2003, II, 235).



B. Aguilera-Barchet, *A History of Western Public Law*,
DOI 10.1007/978-3-319-11803-1_15

15.3 An Interventionist State ..... 458
15.3.1 Religious Reform ..... 459
15.3.2 Economic Reform ..... 459
15.3.3 A Failed Attempt at Social Reform: The "Legion of Honor" ..... 460
15.3.4 Educational Reform: Grammar Schools, Special Schools of Higher Education, and Universities ..... 461
15.3.5 Legal Reform and the Unification of Private Law: *Le Code Civil* (March 21, 1804) ..... 463
15.4 The Constitutional History of France After Napoleon: From Monarchy to Republic 465
15.4.1 From Absolutist Restoration to the July Monarchy ..... 465
15.4.2 From the Second Republic to the Second Empire ..... 466
15.4.3 From the Commune to the Third Republic ..... 468
15.4.4 From Petain's "French State" to De Gaulle's Presidential Republic ..... 471
15.4.5 French Semi-presidentialism: A Return of the Napoleonic Model of State? 474
References ..... 479

## 15.1 Napoleonic France: From Republic to Monarchy

In France the revolutionary chaos also gave way to order. However, the ways in which a strong executive power triumphed and its whole meaning were very entirely different from the case of the United States of America and its constitutional history. In France, the reemergence of a strong state was not the result of consensus expressed through a constitutional convention, but rather the result of the persistence and energy of one man with a spectacular capacity for organization: Napoleon Bonaparte (1769–1821).[5]

In the French case, the reaction against republican assembly-based government came not by consensus but by force of arms and the *coup d'état* carried out by Napoleon on November 9, 1799 (*18 Brumaire de l' An VIII*). The Constitution was no longer written by a constitutional assembly, but was a technical prescript ratified "a posteriori" by a plebiscite, that is, a consultation in which a specific proposal was put to a vote so that the citizens could express their acceptance or rejection of it, in what we today would call a "referendum". In addition, in France, unlike in the United States, a regime change ended up coming about as the republic was

[5] Napoleon, as a historical figure, continues to spark passionate debates in France, such as that of the classic academic argument over whether Bonaparte was the last enlightened despot or the first modern dictator. Recently there has appeared a third interpretation viewing him as the prototype of the modern "manager", leading a team that he encourages, setting goals for it and rousing it to action. Not only did he successfully lead more than 50 military campaigns, but also hundreds of development and rebuilding efforts throughout Europe, including financial reform and the construction of infrastructure elements such as roads, bridges, marinas and museums. He succeeded by implementing sound principles and techniques, applicable to the management of the most modern empire, as sound today as they were then—though without e-mail, telephones or computers, of course (Manas 2006, xiii–xiv).

abandoned and a new regime, created *ex novo*, was established, one not based on the old divine right principle of kingship, but a new monarchy made possible by and created in the wake of the "clean slate" spawned by the Revolution. This new regime reflected Napoleon's conception of legitimacy, based on a purported transfer of sovereignty from a hereditary monarch to a publicly acclaimed emperor acting on behalf of the people, enjoying their confidence, and entirely dedicated to promoting their general welfare (Bergeron 1990, 5).

### 15.1.1 A Genius Named Napoleon Bonaparte

The story of Napoleon is, from every point of view, positively extraordinary. First of all, he was not even of French origin, as his native Corsica was annexed by France in the year of his birth (1769). The island's absorption was a fateful stroke of good fortune for Bonaparte; though his family was not wealthy, young Napoleon was able to study thanks to a royal scholarship for which he was entitled thanks to his father's belonging to the low nobility.[6]

As an artillery officer, Bonaparte was swept up in the tide of history and the events of the Revolution. He would score his first great military success when he retook the Port of Toulon from the English in an audacious maneuver. Ideologically Napoleon was an adherent of Robespierre, which initially bolstered his career.[7] After the Thermidorian Reaction (July 1794), however, his political sympathies landed him in jail and almost cost him his head. And yet, not only did Bonaparte survive the political purge, but his talent as an artillery officer allowed him to save the Directory government from an attempted royalist *coup d'état* in October of 1795. His actions earned him a promotion to the rank of general at the age of just 26, as he became one of the key military figures in the new government as second in command of the Army of the Interior (Dwyer 2008, 177).

However, Bonaparte was also a savvy politician (Hicks 2012, 70–814), who knew how to play his cards and strategically position himself in the new regime.

[6] In total, Louis XVI's government incorporated the members of 78 Corsican families into the French nobility with the intention of currying support for the Crown and dissuading them from any pro-Genoan loyalties. As Englund (2004, 15) point out, if Charles Marie Bonaparte, Napoleon's father, had not been allowed to add the yearned-for "particle" to his family name, signing his name "de Bonaparte", Joseph and Napoleon would have been barred from French "gentlemen's" schools, and could not have aspired to any other form of social promotion.

[7] Napoleon recorded his political progressive republican thoughts in writing for the first time in July 1793, in a pamphlet called *The Supper at Beaucaire* (*Le souper de Beaucaire*), which was read by Augustin Robespierre, Maximilien's brother, who was so impressed that he convinced "The Incorruptible" to advance the career of the young artillery captain named Bonaparte. Robespierre appointed him as commanding officer of the army that took back Toulon's harbor from a British fleet from September to December 1793. Thanks to this success he was promoted, on December 22, 1793, to the rank of Brigadier General, at the age of just 24 (Englund 2004, 63–65).

He rose to stardom after a brilliant campaign (1796–1797), which wrested all of Italy from the Austrians, despite his being far outnumbered (Boycott-Brown 2001). The Directory, wary of the young general's surging popularity, urged to him to pursue a campaign in Egypt (1798). When the English destroyed the French fleet at Abukir Bay, however, Napoleon managed to return to France just in time to intervene. His timing was serendipitous, as he conspired to seize power just when his country was ripe for a strongman to lead it.[8]

When reaching power in November of 1799, Bonaparte found a country that was bankrupt, its people fed up and disillusioned by 10 years of political chaos. Thus, the *coup d'état* of November 9, 1799 was met with relative calm and indifference by the French people, who were willing to accept any government strong enough to stabilize the ailing country (Englund 2004, 166). The new situation was ripe for exploitation by Napoleon. In a question of weeks he had employed his ambition, pragmatism and capacity for hard work to establish his authority via the drafting of a new constitution and the reorganization of the state (Jordan 2012, 95–111).[9]

### 15.1.2 The Peculiar "Napoleonic Constitutionalism"

When Napoleon rose to power, originally forming part of a triumvirate alongside Roger Ducos and Emmanuel Joseph Sieyès, his first initiative was to push for a new constitution.[10] This one, however, would not be the fruit of any new constitutional convention. Napoleon entrusted its drafting to Daunou (Jainchill 2008, 238), a moderate, totally Anti-Jacobin republican, who wrote it in 11 days, and the new document was promulgated on Christmas Day, 1799, just seven weeks after Bonaparte's rise to power. It is important to emphasize that the new constitution actually took effect before it was ratified on February 7, 1800 by a plebiscite in which it received more than three million votes in favor, with only 1,600 against. The 1799 Constitution was essentially a technical legal text, a matter of form aimed

[8] As Dwyer (2008, 469) mentions, not only did Bonaparte arrive in France just when the conspirators happened to be looking for a general, but when he set foot on French soil public opinion and the political elite already associated his name with a coup against the Directory, the groundwork already having been carefully laid by his family and friends.

[9] It is interesting to note, however, that Napoleon was not highly considered by some of his contemporaries. Concretely Thomas Jefferson, as it appears in the following letter: "Instead of the parricide treason of Bonaparte, in perverting the means confided to him as a republican magistrate, to the subversion of that republic and erection of a military despotism for himself and his family, had he used it honestly for the establishment and support of a free government in his own country, France would now have been in freedom and rest; and her example operating in a contrary direction, every nation in Europe would have had a government over which the will of the people would have had some control. His atrocious egotism has checked the salutary progress of principle, and deluged it with rivers of blood which are not yet run out" (Jefferson 1907a, b, 363–365 and 387–393).

[10] Bonaparte went ahead with his *coup d'état* because the Council of the Five Hundred, one of the Directory's legislative assemblies, refused to revise the 1795 Constitution. On the drafting of the first Napoleonic constitution, see Connelly (2000, 201–203).

at providing France with a strong executive authority. It was neither democratic nor representative because, although it theoretically restored universal suffrage, it also eliminated elections, as citizens did not vote but rather presented lists of candidates (*notables*), who could form part of the state's different bodies. In short, it was a "legitimized dictatorship" (Bluche 1980, 24).

The most important institution in the new Constitution of the Year VIII was its executive branch.[11] Practically nonexistent in the period from 1789–1799, it was now vested in one person: the first consul. The Constitution directly named three consuls (along with Napoleon: Jacques-Régis de Cambacérès, a former member of the Convention; and Charles François Lebrun, a moderate monarchist) for a period of 10 years. The three were indefinitely eligible for reelection by the Senate. In reality it was Napoleon who governed, as the other two consuls limited themselves to giving their opinions. In fact, Bonaparte wielded a remarkable amount of power, as not only could he could name and dismiss ministers and officers, accountable to nobody, but also had extraordinary legislative power; in accordance with article 44 of the constitution the executive—called "the government" in the text—proposed the laws and enacted "the regulations necessary to assure their execution". The result was that, for the first time since the Revolution, the executive had an extraordinarily expansive "regulatory power" (Jainchill 2008, 239).

The legislative branch, in contrast, was even weaker than it had been under the Directory. Instead of two there were three chambers: the Senate (in reality an assembly of notables), whose role was to designate the consuls and the main officials in the new regime, the Tribunate, and the Legislative Body (*Corps Législatif*). The legislative assemblies were not democratically elected and the scope of their authority was severely limited. The function of the Tribunate was to discuss bills, and that of the Legislative Body to endorse or reject the proposed legislation it received from the Tribunate. These chambers, nevertheless, had neither legislative initiative nor the power to draft and pass laws. The final proposal of laws lay with the first consul, and their drafting with a high consultative organ created by him: the Council of State (*Conseil d'État*).[12]

[11] It is significant that Napoleon wrote to Talleyrand in 1797—in a confidential letter—that the executive "ought to be considered the true representative of the nation". ("... *Le pouvoir du gouvernement, dans toute la latitude que le lui donne, devrait être considéré comme le vrai repré sentant de la nation, lequel devrait gouverner en conséquence de la charte constitutionnelle et des lois organiques*"). Text of the letter in Napoleon (1819, 177–181). His insistence on creating a strong executive power was bolstered by a growing sentiment among France's political elites, especially Roederer and Talleyrand, that only a strong executive could end the ongoing cycle of political crises. (Jainchill 2008, 238).

[12] As Conner (2004, 31) points out, in the Constitution of the Year VIII, legislative power was only shared on paper. In practice it was completely controlled by the first consul, because it was he, with the assistance of his Council of State, who drafted legislation that was sent to the Tribunate, a body of 100 members at least 25 years of age, where the drafts of the laws were discussed and recommendations were made for their adoption or rejection. The drafts were then forwarded to the Legislative Body, composed of 300 members at least 30 years of age, that voted on the bill without debating the proposal, as orators sent from the Tribunate cited the pros and cons of the draft legislation. After the bill was voted upon by the Legislative Body, the first consul promulgated the law. Legislation began and ended with the First Consul.

### 15.1.3 A Return to the Roman Model?

Conscious of the fact that he was not installing a representative government legitimized by elections, Napoleon looked to history, and far back, prior to the French monarchy, for a model justifying his regime, and was inspired by institutions taken, at least formally, from the Roman political tradition. Power was vested in magistrates, consuls, and an assembly of nobles referred to, tellingly, as the Senate.

In reality, power in the new model of the Napoleonic State rested in the hands of the first consul. Despite appearances, the Roman model had not been copied exactly. There were not two consuls with equal powers like there were in the Roman Republic, but rather three, and only one wielded real power. In theory, the consuls were named by the Senate, but in the French case the consuls were named directly in the constitution itself. The first consul saw his power reinforced even further by the fact that he presided over the new state's key assembly: the Senate. In this regard it was clear that Napoleon was indeed inspired by the model of the Roman Principate (Englund 2004, 214–215). The Senate was an aristocratic assembly that, in addition to choosing its own members from lists of notables, also chose the members of the legislative assemblies, the Tribunate, the Legislative Body, and the three consuls. Moreover, it was authorized to annul acts contrary to the Constitution. The Senate, however, was not an independent institution. Bonaparte's involvement in the election of the first Senate was decisive in assuring his control of an assembly that, theoretically, was to function as the state's most powerful body.[13]

To govern Napoleon relied upon a restricted technical entity: the State Council. Paradoxically, this institution had actually been salvaged from the *Ancien Régime*, as it was the equivalent of the old King's Council, which during the era of absolute monarchy wrote up bills, was authorized to interpret laws, and wielded supreme jurisdiction in administrative affairs. The revival of the State Council is perhaps the most tangible proof that the First Consul had intended from the outset to reestablish monarchy as France's new form of government.[14]

---

[13] The Senate included 80 members, aged 40 or more. Initially Sieyès and Ducos, the other two consuls that ruled theoretically with Bonaparte, named 29 senators, and these selected the rest. In principle members of the Senate were appointed for life. The Senate was given the authority to issue decrees (*senatus consulta*) that bypassed the Legislature. As it was more pliant to Napoleon's will, the First Consul used this legislative mechanism to circumvent any parliamentary opposition (Emsley 2003, 13–14).

[14] We should not forget that before making decisions, Louis XIV always listened to the opinions of the members of his councils, especially the highest (*Conseil du haut*). It is interesting to note that, in the same line, Napoleon was able to choose his own councilors for the new State Council (*Conseil d'État*), whose members he carefully chose based on their relevant expertise. The role of Napoleon's State Council, according to Article 52 of the 1799 Constitution, was to "draft proposals for laws, administrative regulations and resolve difficulties in administrative matters". In this way, the Council played a decisive role in the legislative process (Emsley 2003, 14).

### 15.1.4 A New Monarchy for a New Regime

Napoleon, as an heir to the Revolution, categorically rejected the restoration of traditional absolute monarchy. From the very beginning, however, he found monarchical power the most expedient for the establishment of order and the development of a strong state. Thus, he proceeded to lay foundations which would allow him to institute a new form of monarchy,[15] which he carried out in three phases; during the first stage, as we know, he seized control of the executive branch (through the 1799 Constitution), which would be followed up by constitutional reform in 1802 and 1804.

The first step towards the "monarchization" of the regime came on August 2, 1802 when, by means of another plebiscite, the French voted in favor of naming Napoleon sole Consul for Life. Two days later (August 4, 1802), a new Constitution entered into effect by means of a Senate decree (*senatus-consulte*), which was not put to a plebiscite.[16]

The regime's transformation came to a head with the third "Napoleonic Constitution", that of May 18, 1804 (*28 Floréal, An XII*), in which Napoleon directly established a new monarchy, the new constitution's first article stating that "the government of the Republic is entrusted to an emperor, who takes the title of 'Emperor of the French'" (P. Smith 2005, 36). Its second article directly designated Napoleon as said *Empereur des Français*. This third constitution was written up, like that of 1802, by the Senate and at Napoleon's request, although it was legitimized a posteriori, via plebiscite on November 6, 1804.[17]

[15] This is why he was called the "*roi de la révolution*". As a figure, Napoleon has been highly controversial. Some consider him a dictator, while others view him as the savior of France and the man who liberated Europe from the shackles of the *Ancien Régime*. For an overview of these opposing assessments of Bonapartism, see Geyl (1982) and Tulard (1984).

[16] Napoleon initially refused to accept a proposal by Cambacerès and Talleyrand to name him Consul for Life, following the example of Augustus, who in 37 BC refused to rule as a triumvir for the second time without the consent of the people, before backing a progressive restoration of power to the Senate and people that would allow him to constitute the Principate. Following Augustus's example, Bonaparte wished to reassure the mass of citizens that the legitimacy of the French Republic was not contested and that it was still in operation. Just as Octavian had done, Napoleon sought the legitimization of his power. The State Council, therefore, organized a consultation asking the French people if Napoleon Bonaparte ought to be Consul for Life (*N.B. sera-t-il consul à vie*?). The vote was overwhelmingly in his favor (3,568,855 of the 3,577,299 who took part) and the results were proclaimed on 10 Thermidor of the Year X (July 29, 1802) by a *senatus-consulte* that stated: "The French people names and the Senate proclaims Napoleon Bonaparte 'First Consul for Life.'" In this formulation it was to recognize the familiar "Senatus Populusque Romanus" (SPQR) formula of the Roman Republic (Huet 2007, 55).

[17] As Schmitt (2008, 134) points out, the practice of plebiscites was already present in the Constitution of the Year VIII (art. 95), though before its acceptance through public consultation the 1799 Napoleonic document was already considered legally valid as a constitution. The plebiscite was again used in the *senatus-consult* of the Year XII as a way of legitimizing Napoleon's hereditary empire. Similarly, in 1815, during the Hundred Days, there was another plebiscite on the *Acte additionnel aux constitutions de l'Empire*".

In this third phase, Napoleon abandoned the republican model of government—in effect since September 22, 1792—and replaced it with the implementation of a new regime formally designated an "empire", but which for all intents and purposes was a monarchy, albeit a new kind of one that did not rely upon the *Ancien Régime* model and which purported to derive its legitimacy from the French people and the Revolution.[18]

## 15.2 From Assembly-Based Government to Executive Government

### *15.2.1 Napoleon and State Reform*

The manner in which Napoleon consolidated the French state was very unlike what occurred in the United States of America; where the latter was based firmly upon a founding constitution, Bonaparte turned out constitutions after the fact to legitimize and legalize the succession of regimes over which he ruled.

One of the most momentous consequences of the French Revolution was that, by destroying the entire institutional order of the *Ancien Régime*, it wiped out all the limits which had been placed on absolute monarchy, passed down by the traditions of the French polity. Thus, in the end the revolutionary process served to accentuate the power of the state in France. This progression reached its peak with Napoleon, who not only placed all the state's bodies and divisions under his power, but also created an administrative apparatus so solid that even today it continues to serve as the framework for the French government. Napoleon created what could be called an administrative state, a stable and permanent organization able to withstand the constant tides of change, as those in power enjoyed a series of privileges that afforded them stability by isolating and sparing them from the vicissitudes of politics. This principle would have an impact throughout Europe, as Napoleonic imperialism transformed the *Ancien Régime* systems in most of the countries he occupied, forcing them to abandon their absolute monarchies.[19]

---

[18] When consulted on the possibility of creating a new empire, the State Council objected to the principle of hereditary rule, but the Senate approved a motion from Napoleon to this effect, and drafted a new constitution between May 16 and 18 entrusting the "government of the Republic" to a hereditary emperor who was to receive a compensation for his civil list in the amount of 25 million francs, in addition to the revenues from Imperial lands, to be distinguished from his personal estate. He was also assigned a free hand in the establishment of an imperial court and in the regulation of the royal family's affairs. The main problem was defining the rules for succession, as Bonaparte had no sons. The future Napoleon II was born in 1811. According to the Roman imperial tradition, Bonaparte was granted the right to designate his own successor by adopting an heir (Lefebvre 2011, 156).

[19] On this very important aspect of how Napoleon consolidated his conquests through administrative integration, see Woolf (2003, 83–132). Napoleon's reforms would have, for instance, a major effect on the German states by reducing its number and reorganizing them, while had also a great impact in the Italian Peninsula and even in the Spanish monarchy. For an overview of how the French Revolution and Napoleon contributed to the fall of Europe's Old Order in Italy, Germany and Spain, see Aguilera-Barchet (2008, 115–132 and 166–207).

### 15.2.2 *The Extreme Centralization of the New Administrative State*

The suspension of elections and the consolidation of the central government's absolute power impinged upon the process of "administrative reform"[20] that Bonaparte implemented in February of 1800. Unlike the administrative regime established by the Constituent Assembly, according to which civil servants were elected (which afforded them great autonomy), Bonaparte ordered that public servants be appointed by the government and remain totally answerable to it. In each department, a prefect and several general advisors were named, the districts became *arrondissements* ("rounded offs") and subprefects, with *arrondissement* ministers placed at the head of each. In every municipality (*commune*), there was a mayor (*maire*) and several "municipal councilors". Thanks to Bonaparte, the administration of the state was structured in a perfectly hierarchical pyramid, which made possible a degree of centralization far greater than that under the *Ancien Réegime*, as in the era of absolute monarchy the intendants had to take into consideration the opinions and functions of the privileged bodies (the Parlements, provincial estates, Justice and Tax officials). In this way, France became a country under administrative tutelage (Bergeron 1990, 23).

### 15.2.3 *Judicial Reform and the Creation of Administrative Jurisdiction*

Also very important was the judicial reform Bonaparte introduced in March of 1800, which profoundly modified the regime previously enacted by the Constituent Assembly. Under the new system, judges were not elected but rather appointed by the first consul, as were state attorneys ("government commissioners" who performed the same function as the old "revolutionary prosecutors"). The two differed because the judges, once named, were irremovable, whereas the state attorneys could be dismissed. In addition, Bonaparte created 29 Courts of Appeal.[21]

---

[20] Napoleon was aware that in the aftermath of the Revolution, it would be impossible to dismiss all appeals to popular sovereignty and to ignore popular opinion. Once the framework of his government system was established, organized and running smoothly, however, Napoleon argued that it was logical for the legislature to give way to greater executive government by an elaborate administration (Emsley 2003, 14).

[21] The new system of government also reserved for the state the right to promote judges and select presiding justices (Bergeron 1990, 89).

The most important reform of the judiciary was the creation a special jurisdiction for Napoleon's civil servants. This was the origin of the "Administrative jurisdiction", with its special courts and prefecture councils, and whose sentences could be appealed before the very State Council. This internal and privileged jurisdictional channel kept the French state's civil servants from going before ordinary judges, as most of them came from the *Ancien Régime* judicial system. Thus, the new regime had its own, new judges who followed a specific procedure, making it possible to create a specific body of laws through jurisprudence, yielding the *Droit administratif*, which featured and observed its very own logic within the rule of law system (Lorente 2012, 296). As a result, even today France can continue to be administrated without a central government to oversee it, as the state administration continues to be quite effectively divorced and shielded from the effects of political change and turmoil.[22] This was, without any doubt, Napoleon's greatest contribution to public contemporary law, his "longest-lasting legacy" (Woolf 1992, 95), as the efficacy of the "administrative state" model would lead to its adoption by many European nations.[23]

## 15.3 An Interventionist State

Unlike what happened in the United States, where the Constitution of 1787 adopted a series of mechanisms aimed at impeding the federal government from acquiring excessive power (the separation of powers and their independence, the Bill of Rights, the limitation of the duration and number of presidential terms, the frequency of legislative elections) in France the Revolution, by obliterating the institutions of the Old Regime, gave rise to an all-powerful state. In this Napoleon's actions reflected the sentiments shared by most "republicans of order" of his era, for whom the dual threats posed by counterrevolution and democracy required a strengthening of the state, considered as the depository and guardian of the Revolution (Bergeron 1990, 5). This is why, from Napoleon's perspective, the state had a role to play in regulating all areas of society and people's lives.

---

[22] As Lorente (2012, 296) points out, the essence of Napoleonic administrative jurisdiction lay not so much in the appropriation of judicial affairs by the new regime, which took place during the first years of the Revolution, as in the shielding of bureaucrats as individuals from standard justice, a principle already included in Article 75 of the constitution of the Year VIII.

[23] Under this model, the executive chain descends without interruption from the minister to the administrated, and transmits the law and the government's orders to every level and area of the social order. Napoleon achieved this, augmenting the size of government ministries—notably the Ministry of the Interior, the Ministry of Police and the Ministry of War—and restructuring provincial and local government similarly, along strictly hierarchical lines, through a system of prefectures established in France's provincial departments, which were given a key role in the new centralized administrative state (Laven and Riall 2000, 2).

### *15.3.1 Religious Reform*

Firstly, Napoleon intervened in the religious sphere. Through the Concordat of 1801, he was able to regain favor among French Catholics and control the French Catholic Church, in the purest Gallican tradition, not only because the government named the bishops who, in turn, named the priests, with both required to swear allegiance to the regime, but because the Church of France, which lacked assets, came to depend on state subsidies. The Concordat was fiercely opposed by intellectuals educated in the school of the "philosophes;" by the country's civil servants, including some members of the State Council; and, above all, by the army. In order not to alienate anti-Catholic factions, Napoleon also acted to legalize Protestant worship (for Lutherans and Calvinists) at the same time he tightened the state's grip on the Catholic clergy. To this end in 1802, he published a decree regulating religious worship: the Organic Articles, of clearly Gallican inspiration, which defended the autonomy of the French Church vis-à-vis Rome.[24] The audacious terms of Napoleon's religious policy reached their peak with the publication in 1806 of the Imperial Catechism, which placed civic obligations on a par with religious ones, as if the emperor was seated at the right hand of God.[25]

### *15.3.2 Economic Reform*

When discussing Napoleon's interventionist agenda mention must also be made of the measures that he took to stabilize the French economy and pull the nation out of bankruptcy. He first reestablished the state's tax collecting role and burnished its prestige in this regard through the creation of a General Fiscal Administration, the appointment of "fiscal controllers", and the creation of another body of civil servants also named by the central power: "receivers" and "collectors", whose efforts led to significant improvements in the efficiency of the system, assuring the government a constant source of revenue through tax collection (Bergeron 1990, 37–51).

To stabilize the economy Bonaparte created the Bank of France (February of 1800), an authority charged with administrating the government's monetary policies. The measure was so effective that in 1803, the first consul ordered that it was to enjoy a monopoly on the emission of bank-issued checks made out to

[24] For an overview of Napoleon's religious policy, see Englund (2004, 180–85). It is interesting to point out that Napoleon did not favor a monopoly by Christianity, and accepted other religions under his new state—provided that their institutions were legally organized within the framework of the state, as was the case with the French Jews and their Sanhedrin council (Schwarzfuchs 1979).

[25] Bergeron (1990, 36). At the same time, the celebration of Saint-Napoleon's Day, on August 15 —the date of his birth—supplanted the celebration of the Assumption of the Virgin Mary, which had been a royal and national holy day since "the vow of Louis XIII".

beneficiaries, which could be presented in exchange for cash at any time. As of 1806, the administration of the Bank of France was totally controlled by the government (Conner 2004, 80–82).

France's solid tax base and financial stability made it possible for Napoleon to promulgate, on March 28, 1803 (*7 Germinal Year XI*), a measure which had been devised by the Thermidorian Convention: the creation of a silver currency that came to be called the *franc germinal*, which would remain stable for more than a century, until the outbreak of World War I.[26] Thanks to all these measures Napoleon was able, after decades of massive public deficits, to balance the 1802 budget.

After shoring up his personal power, in 1802 being named Consul for Life, Napoleon was able to take additional steps to lay down the social foundations of his new state. These policies included the attempt to create a new privileged social class recognized and sustained by the state; educational reform to train the top officials serving the new regime; and laying down the underpinnings of a new legal system, its first phase being the approval of the Civil Code.

### 15.3.3 A Failed Attempt at Social Reform: The "Legion of Honor"

In May of 1802, the first consul created the Legion of Honor. Napoleon's intention was to institute an "intermediate body" between the common people and the government, a kind of "patrician class" made up of leading figures selected by the government.[27] The patently "monarchical" character of the institution,

---

[26] Monetary policy had played an essential role in the French Revolution. Louis XVI had been forced to convene the Estates General to address France's serious debts. The Convention government sought to avoid bankruptcy by creating *assignats*, paper money, but it issued so much that soon it was completely devalued, to the point that by the end of the Directory, *assignats* were eliminated. To halt the monetary chaos in April of 1795, the Directory established the *franc* as the national currency, and even stipulated its metallic composition, as the government did not want another disastrous experience like that suffered with the *assignat*. Monetary disorder, however, persisted as there was a shortage of currency, to the point that the old *livre* and even foreign coins continued to circulate. When Napoleon came to power he refused to issue paper money (Bergeron 1990, 42). Instead, on March 28, 1803, he created the *franc de germinal* via a decree that established the content, size and weight of the new gold, silver and copper coins. Later decrees ordered the withdrawal of old money from circulation. Thanks to this monetary reform for the first France possessed a reliable currency. It would become one of the strongest in Europe, lasting for the next 125 years (Grab 2001, 174–175).

[27] The reform program also included an undeniably democratizing component, as hitherto a personal fortune had been legally required for one to hold public office. Through the "Legion of Honor", Napoleon sought to introduce a meritocratic component so that outstanding people without economic resources could hold public office. Thus, it is ironic this reform measure failed because of opposition by indignant republicans and enthusiasts of the Revolution. Nevertheless, after 1804 Napoleon would create a new nobility for the Empire (Woloch 2001, 70–72).

however, rankled the State Council and the assemblies so badly that Napoleon was compelled to abandon the initiative (Bessiere 2008, 12–13). The Legion of Honor would never come to constitute a new noble class. After the proclamation of the Empire, however, it did end up evolving into the state's most prestigious award (*la "legion d'honneur"*), a distinction which it retains even today.

### *15.3.4 Educational Reform: Grammar Schools, Special Schools of Higher Education, and Universities*

If Napoleon was not able to impose—initially—the idea of a new elite between the common people and the state, he did manage to undertake a vital and historic reform of the French educational system, aimed at turning out future generations of well-educated Frenchmen which, according to the Napoleonic ideal, the new state required. It is significant that when presenting his plans for education reform before the Tribunate, Bonaparte explained that the institution in question was not only to be morally instructive one, but to feature a political mission as well: its objective was to unite with the government both the rising and the declining generations, to link parents to the government through their children, and children through their parents, thus establishing a kind of public paternity.[28]

With this intention, by virtue of the decree of 11 Floréal, Year X (May 1, 1802), the Central Schools created by the Revolution were replaced by *lycées*, institutions in which Napoleon wished for educational effectiveness to prevail over all other considerations to train the nation's elite.[29] A return to the principles of Classical

[28] On the transformation of the French educational system through Napoleonic reform, see Barnard (2009, 216–21) and Durant and Durant (2001, 65–69).

[29] As Lefebvre (2011, 133–134) observes, the decree of 11 Floréal, drafted by Fourcroy, left municipalities in charge of the elementary schools (*écoles populaires*), just as under the *Ancien Ré gime*, as Bonaparte believed, like Voltaire, that educating the masses was politically and socially inadvisable. Thus, the education of the elite was left to the secondary schools: the *lycées*. These institutions were patterned on the *Prytanée*, traditionally known as the Collège Louis le Grand, the only such school preserved by the Revolution, restructured by Interior Minister Lucien Bonaparte in 1800. Every court of appeals district was to have a state-supported *lycée*. In the Year XII (1804), the state began to appoint teachers and create 6,400 scholarships for the *lycées*, of which 2,400 were awarded to the sons of military officers and government officials, the rest being set aside for the best pupils. The *lycées* continued to be privately administrated secondary schools, but they were overseen and authorized by the government. See also Boudon (2004).

Antiquity (Neoclassicism),[30] already having gained momentum during the time of Louis XIV, was one of the cultural pillars upon which Napoleonic reform was based (Bergeron 1990, 34). This return, of course, was duly tailored to the era. Students in the *lycées* were organized in a military fashion (Vaughan and Archer 2010, 185) and studied the same curriculum taught at Jesuit schools, which Napoleon considered the most effective.[31] In fact, the administrators and professors of the *lycées* formed a kind of secular congregation totally and zealously dedicated to the education of the young people placed in their charge by the state, to the point that they were prohibited from marrying and were required to remain celibate.[32]

Napoleon's educational reform would be rounded out during the imperial stage, in 1808, when he organized the French university as a centralized institution dependent on the state, and established a government monopoly over all levels of education. [33]

[30] Napoleon's compulsion to seek out classical justifications to legitimize his institutions is noteworthy, as he would argue that Aristotle was educated in a school such as his Lyceum, just as Plato taught at an Academy. About how consideration of Louis XIV's legacy is crucial to understanding the evolution of Napoleon's fascination with imperial Rome, his manipulation of the populist rhetoric of Republican France (and Rome) and how he moved from being a general fighting for the Revolutionary cause to become the absolute ruler of a new empire and appropriated Rome's triumphal architecture and its associated symbolism to relocate Rome in his own times, see Rowell (2012). As minister of the interior, Lucien Bonaparte arranged with the connivance of his brother, in November 1800 for the drafting and distribution of a pamphlet under the title of "A Parallel among Caesar, Cromwell, Monck and Bonaparte" that drew explicit parallels between Bonaparte and Caesar. Napoleon considered himself explicitly as "Charlemagne": "Tell them that I have my eyes open; that I'm only as deceived as I want to be; that I am Charlemagne, the sword of the Church, their Emperor; and that I should be treated as such"., wrote Napoleon to Cardinal Fesch in February 1806, (Napoleon 1861, 40). The Emperor of the French considered himself the suzerain of Rome with the right to have the papal fiefs at his disposal. He was son to warn Pius VII, "Your Holiness is sovereign in Rome but I am its Emperor". Letter to Pius VII, February 13, 1806 (Napoleon 1861, 38–40).

[31] This is why Napoleon affirmed: "I want a corporation, not of Jesuits whose sovereign is in Rome, but of Jesuits who have no ambition but to be useful, with no interests but those of the state". The professors and administrators of the *lycées* had to form a coherent and well organized civil militia, replicating the hierarchy of military ranks and following a similar pattern of promotion. The decree of March 17, 1808 explicitly stated that no one was to reach a superior rank without having passed through the one preceding. This system enabled teachers to dream about glorious careers. The military structure of the *lycée* reflected the military atmosphere pervading much of French life at the time (Lombardo 2001, 613).

[32] Napoleon believed that marriage, a family, or any type of private life would weaken an educational system requiring complete dedication by its teachers. In a decree issued on March 17, 1808, he established a rule of celibacy during the first years of one's career, that applied not only to schoolteachers, but also to principals, headmasters, and *censeurs*, who were charged with maintaining discipline. To enforce this rule women would were not admitted into the *collèges* or *lycées* (secondary schools) (Lombardo 2001, 614).

[33] The law of May 10, 1806 founding the University of France defined the institution as "a body charged exclusively with public teaching and education in the whole Empire", having as its function "to direct political and moral opinions" (Bergeron 1990, 34).

The first consul also radically transformed the Special Higher Education Schools (*Grandes Écoles*) with the same intention of assigning priority to usefulness and educational effectiveness, which in some cases led to their militarization, as occurred, for example, at the Polytechnic School, whose graduates even today wear uniforms and are ranked as "officers" of the French Army. Napoleon's educational reforms were one of the pillars of his reformist agenda. Ever since France's governing class has continued to study at the schools and elite institutions which he created.[34]

In 1808, the Order of Academic Palms was also founded to recognize outstanding university students and professors (Klinge 2004, 159).

### *15.3.5 Legal Reform and the Unification of Private Law:* **Le Code Civil** *(March 21, 1804)*

When the Revolution began, France lacked a unified system of law. Reference has already been made to Voltaire's famous observation in his *Dictionnaire philosophique* (1764) that one travelling across the France of his time saw the laws shift every time he had to change horses.[35] Thus, in 1789 the architects of the new constitution viewed legal reform as one of the most urgent tasks facing the government, which was determined to do away with the legal disarray inherited from the *Ancien Régime* by means of a single code of laws to be valid throughout France. This undertaking, however, involved great technical difficulties which prevented the successive revolutionary assemblies (the Constituent and Legislative Assemblies, the Convention, the Directory) from carrying out the proposed reform, despite repeated attempts to do so.

The challenge was to integrate and unify the multiple extant legal bodies, which included the *Ancien Régime's* various systems of customary law from northern France, the traditional written-law system based on the Roman model in place in the south, and, finally, the mass of legislation passed helter-skelter by the National Assembly, the National Convention, and the directorial legislatures (Woloch 2001, 75). This monumental task required a titanic effort by Napoleon, who personally helped to draft and advance the new code, benefitting from the inestimable aid of Jean Jacques Régis de Cambacerès (Chatel de Brancion 2009), the author of several of the preceding plans, as well as other notorious jurists, such as Tronchet,

---

[34] As Brint (2006, 52) stresses, Napoleon established the principle of the *grandes écoles* as an instrument to train leaders for the civil service. Today there are more than 200 of these establishments, designed to train students in specific fields, such as Engineering, Business, and Public Administration. They still attract top students. Admission to the most selective *grandes écoles*, is even more important in French society than the Ivy League colleges are in American society.

[35] Il y a, dit-on, cent quarante-quatre coutumes en France qui ont force de loi; ces lois sont presque toutes différentes. Un homme qui voyage dans ce pays change de loi presque autant de fois qu'il change de chevaux de poste. Voltaire (2009, 282).

Portalis,[36] Préameneu, Maleville and Treilhard (Reich 2004, 455). Thanks to them and Napoleon's utmost commitment to the project, the Civil Code was approved on March 21, 1804. To win support for it the first consul had to exert all of his authority and bring to bear all his influence in the legislative chambers (Jordan 2012, 105–107), where opponents of the regime had grown strong.[37] Napoleon ultimately considered passage of his Civil Code his greatest achievement (Lyons 1994, 94).

From the point of view of its content, the Civil Code was a product of the spirit of "national reconciliation" which had informed the first consul's political actions.[38] In fact, the authors of the French Civil Code drew upon the entire western legal tradition: Roman law, common law, royal legislation and, of course, revolutionary legislation (Arnaud 1969). The result was a Code that was more pragmatic but less liberal than the Convention's previous drafts, mainly because Bonaparte imposed the principles of "social conservation" and of "authority". Thus, the Code of 1804 not only firmly guaranteed the right to property in its article 544, as the "right to enjoy and dispose of things in the most absolute manner provided that one does not make a use of them that is prohibited by laws (*lois*) or regulations (*réglements*)" (Gordley 2013, 224)—including provisions which protected the ownership of "national assets" expropriated from the Church, legalizing a *de facto* situation (Léwy 1998, 169)—but also reestablished the institution of the traditional family in which the father's authority prevailed over his wife and children.[39] The authors of the legislation, at the same time, did not fail to incorporate a good number of revolutionary legislative reforms, such as those upholding individual freedom, equality between citizens, secularism, divorce, the egalitarian distribution of inheritances between children, and the abolition of feudal practices. Its mixed and

[36] Jean Marie Étienne Portalis (1746–1806) wrote the famous preliminary discourse (*Discours Préliminaire*, 1801) of the Civil Code, a superb introduction replete with learned references, both philosophical and legal, and informed by the clarity of a great intellect (Jordan 2012, 105). For the text in French, see Portalis (2004, 10–70).

[37] ... but forget not that the laws are nothing without force (Napoleon 1846, 188).

[38] Schwartz (1998, viii) points out that the dominant characteristic of the Code is its spirit of moderation. Though it was the product of the French Revolution, its provisions were anything but revolutionary, but neither was it a reactionary document seeking to undo the work of 1789, as the French Civil Code sought to preserve the egalitarian ideal while renouncing the radical and violent measures of the Terror.

[39] As Rheinstein (1998, 140) highlights, nearly all the groups that had stood between the individual and the nation under the *Ancien Régime* were either destroyed (the manors, guilds, and provinces) or subdued, like the Church, or the municipalities, transformed into divisions of the national government. The only exception was the family, which remained the basic unit of society, as Napoleon considered it the cradle of the nation's future generations. The individual citizen was part of one indivisible nation, but was born and lived within a family, the only social group existing under the *Ancien Régime* that was preserved after the Revolution.

balanced character ensured the success of the Civil Code, which became the sole body of private law in force in France, superseding all that preceding it.[40]

## 15.4 The Constitutional History of France After Napoleon: From Monarchy to Republic

After the "100 Days" following his defeat at Waterloo, Napoleon finally fell from power (June 18, 1815), for good. In the wake of his downfall, France would repeatedly swing back and forth between monarchism and republicanism.

### *15.4.1 From Absolutist Restoration to the July Monarchy*

Initially Louis XVIII brought back absolute, divine right monarchy (1814–1824), although with the important addition of the "Charter" (*La Charte*), a constitution "granted" in 1814[41] which, paradoxically, allowed for the establishment of a parliamentary regime in France (Alexander 2000, 29–48), theoretically under the absolute monarchy.[42] This disappeared when Charles X was toppled by the Revolution of July 1830 (Pinkney 1973), a popular movement (Newman 1974, 26–59) which ushered in a constitutional monarchy with Louis Philippe I on the throne and Guizot as its most representative minister. The 1830 Revolution, however, did not

---

[40] In reality, however, it began to be effectively applied under the July Monarchy (1830–1848) of Louis Philippe I. Until then, the inertia and complacency of the *Ancien Régime's* old judges led to the application of traditional custom, partly because of successive purges initiated during the Restoration and consolidated under the July Monarchy (van Caenegem 2009, 140).

[41] As Hudson (1973, 31) indicates, the success of the Charter can be explained because, as Chateaubriand observed, it was not a foreign importation but the embodiment of the country's old Christian institutions: "The Charter is not an exotic plant, a fortuitous accident of the moment; it is the result of our present customs; it is a peace treaty signed by the parties which have divided the French People (*La charte n'est donc point une plante exotique, un accident fortuit du moment: c'est le résultat de nos moeurs présents; c'est un traité de paix signé entre les deux partis qui ont divisé les Français: traité ou chacun des deux abandonne quelque chose de ses prétentions, pour concourir à la gloire de la patrie*) (Chateaubriand 2010, 44).

[42] The paradox is even greater when one considers that the respecting of the parliamentary majority endorsed at the ballot box was imposed by the "ultras", who were opposed to Louis XVIII's moderation, and insisted that the king appoint as the head of the government the leader of the party which had won the elections. In this regard it is worth noting the evolution in the thinking of Victor Hugo (1802–1885), according to André Gide the greatest French poet of all time. Initially not only he composed an "ode" to mark the coronation of King Charles X, but was named "Peerage of France" by the July monarchy. After Napoleon III's *coup d'état* he rejected the new regime and went into exile. One must remember that the Romantics were considered "ultras" because of their support for traditional institutions, as opposed to revolutionary rationalism (Weber 1966, 73).

mark a radical constitutional break with the previous regime,[43] as the new constitution retained most of the features of the 1814 Charter (Alexander 2003, 295). Moreover, the new regime was a conservative one, dominated by doctrinaire liberals such as Benjamin Constant (1767–1830), who became the most influential political force in France (Pilbeam 1982, 351–366). This is why, for instance, the government sought to check the power of the legislature's lower house[44] by maintaining the Chamber of Peers (*La Chambre des Pairs*), a French version of the British House of Lords.[45]

## 15.4.2 From the Second Republic to the Second Empire

The "July Monarchy", meanwhile, disappeared as a result of the revolution of February 1848 (Rudé 2005, 164–179), a movement that spread from Paris all over Europe and led to the establishment of the Second French Republic. This revolution was the first in French history to be driven by what today we might call "socialist" aspirations for greater social justice and equality, as the new regime at

[43] As Alexander (2003, 3) points out, though the Charter's provisions for a parliament represented a grafting of British institutions onto the French polity, other elements were distinctly French. The Restoration preserved much of the legacy of the 1789 Revolution, including the Napoleonic Codes, which maintained legal equality, and the proclamation of some essential liberties: freedom from arbitrary arrest, freedom of expression, the inviolability of property ownership, and even freedom of religious opinion, although Catholicism became the religion of the state. The Charter also preserved the highly centralized structure of the state resulting from the preservation of the Napoleonic government apparatus. This extremely centralized governmental system explains why the 1830 Revolution spread so rapidly through the provinces after its success in Paris (Pilbeam 1983, 831–844).

[44] The Revolution had brought with it the principle of unicameralism, as legislative power was vested exclusively in the *Assemblée Nationale* and the other powers were subject to the Assembly, elected by the "nation". After the Thermidorian Reaction (July 1794), the wealthy bourgeoisie once again controlled the situation, and the result was the conservative Constitution of 1795. One of its most significant reforms was the creation of a second chamber to prevent dictatorship by a single assembly. This was the *Conseil des Anciens*, elected by only 30,000 "great electors", essentially *notables* from the provinces, representing rural France—far more conservative than Paris and the rest of the French cities. While the first Council of 500 (*Conseil des Cinq-Cents*) drafted the laws, the *Conseil des Anciens* approved them. Under Napoleon the upper chamber was called the Senate and its members were directly appointed by Napoleon himself. It wielded more power than the lower assemblies (the Tribunat and Legislative Body), as it guaranteed respect for the constitution and its application through its special *senatus-consultes*, the state's most important instruments. In fact, it was so powerful that in 1814 it announced Napoleon's deposition. The Restoration maintained the principle of the high chamber, but imported the British model of the House of Lords. For an overview of the evolution of the Senate in contemporary French constitutional history, see Fiorentino (2008).

[45] The archbishops, bishops and peers created by Charles X, however, were excluded from the new Chamber of Peers, and via a law passed on December 29, 1831, hereditary peerage was abolished (Fortescue 2005, 27).

first aspired to usher in a "social republic" headed up by revolutionaries like Armand Barbès (1809–1870), who that believed that political reform was the only means to social reform (Mészáros 2000, 43). This explains why for the first time social rights were recognized as fundamental liberties in the new constitution, despite the fierce opposition offered by Alexis de Tocqueville in his famous speech on the Right to Work on September 12, 1848 (Tocqueville and de Beaumont 1968, 179–187).[46]

Concerning the form of government, the 1848 French constitution marked a return to a unicameral assembly-based system, and the consolidation of male universal suffrage. The Second Republic sought to avoid the flaws of the First Republic, particularly its lack of a strong executive power, which had paved the way for Napoleon's regime. Thus, following the example of the American Republic,[47] the members of the National Constituent Assembly decided that the new republic was to have an elected president. The constitution was approved on November 4, 1848, and on the following December 10, Prince Louis Napoleon, a nephew of Napoleon I, became the first president of a French republic elected by universal suffrage,[48] as the candidate supported by the conservative bourgeoisie.[49]

The new French republic proved fleeting. After being elected president, Louis Napoleon did not hesitate to launch a coup and establish a Second Empire,[50] a "restoration" of the Bonaparte monarchy that would last nearly two decades. The new regime constitutionally marked a return to the Napoleonic, monarchic model of the state, with a very strong Executive and a weakened Legislative power. In the January 1852 constitution Napoleon III created a Legislative Corps, elected by universal male suffrage, and a Senate, entirely controlled by the emperor, who had free rein to appoint all of its members, a second chamber that acted as a forceful

[46] On the framing of the Second Republic's constitution, see Coutant (2009), Luchaire (1998) and Rolland (2000). American constitutionalism exerted some influence on the Constitution of 1848 largely through the efforts of Tocqueville (Billias 2009, 179–183).

[47] On the important influence of American constitutionalism on France's Second Republic, see Curtis (2013) and Fritz (2000).

[48] The deputies of the Constituent Assembly thought that a direct presidential election would rally the population to the Republic (Fortescue 2005, 123). Napoleon obtained 74.2 % of the votes, with more than five million votes, in contrast to the other five candidates: Cavaignac (1.5 million), Ledru-Rollin (400,000), Raspail (37,000), Lamartine (18,000) and Changarnier.

[49] On the social dimension of Napoleon's coup, see the classic essay published in 1852 by Karl Marx: *The Eighteenth Brumaire of Louis Bonaparte*. One of the clearest examples of Marxist historical analysis applied to contemporary events, starts with Marx's most famous quote: "*Hegel remarks somewhere that all great world-historic facts and personages appear, so to speak, twice. He forgot to add: the first time as tragedy, the second time as farce*" (Marx 2005, 1).

[50] Through a *senatus consultum* on November 7, 1852, Louis Napoleon assumed the imperial title as Napoleon III. Following Napoleon's I practice, he submitted his nomination to the French people via plebiscite on November 21/22, which he won by a huge margin. On December 2, the new emperor issued a decree referring to the earlier *senatus consultum* and proclaiming the Empire (Plessis 1989, 1).

brake.[51] The legislature was further restricted by a decree that limited its power to accept or reject proposals produced by the Council of State, whose members were also appointed by the president (van Caenegem 2003, 208–209).

The Second Empire regime, nevertheless, saw an evolution from despotism towards greater democracy. From 1852 to 1860 France operated under a dictatorship in what historians call the Authoritarian Empire (Price 2001, 25). Beginning in 1860, Napoleon III began to liberalize his regime (Corley 1974), to the point that in May 1870 the opposition forced him to organize a plebiscite, which was, ironically, overwhelmingly won by the government, with the emperor garnering 7,538,000 votes of support versus 1,572,000 negative votes and 1,900,000 abstentions (Zeldin 1963 153–167). It is interesting to note that the emperor considered the plebiscite as an alternative to liberal parliamentary institutions, as he believed it to be the best instrument for the verification of the popular will. Consequently, he did his best to extend the use of this type of consultations (Woodward 1963, 50).[52]

### *15.4.3 From the Commune to the Third Republic*

The Second French Empire would come crashing down, however, upon France's defeat in the war waged against Bismarck's Prussia.[53] Three days after Napoleon's III surrender at Sedan, Léon Gambetta proclaimed the Third Republic in Paris on September 4, 1870. Followed a provisional government named Government of National Defense and presided over by General Trochu (Wawro 2003, 231–234). This ruled during the Siege of Paris (September 1870–January 1871). After France's surrender national elections were held. The New National Assembly, as

[51] The reintroduction of the Senate was an outright return to the model of the first French Empire, under which Napoleon sought to emulate Augustus, turning the Senate into the key body implementing his legislation, as the *senate-consultes* became the imperial regime's primary legislative instruments. From the outset Napoleon III reserved the right to directly appoint the senators he deemed fit. The new chamber was made up of the highest representatives of the state (ministers, high-ranking civil servants, magistrates and academics) along with members of the financial and industrial oligarchy (bankers and leading businesspeople), joined by some former members of the legislature under the Restoration and the July Monarchy. The Senate was a docile chamber until the Second Empire regime embraced a more Parliament-based model. When in 1861 the emperor proposed the sending of troops to support the Pope against King Victor Manuel of Italy's attempt to occupy Rome, the action was approved by a vote of 79 to 61. At this point the Senate began to rebel against the regime. In April of 1871, the Senate officially became the second legislative chamber, to which the ministers were accountable. On the role of the senates in contemporary constitutional history, see Patterson and Mughan (1999, 9–16).

[52] Hence, Napoleon III is a most controversial figure. His regime was called an "extravaganza" (in the sense of a kind of farce) (Baguley 2000) and the emperor himself everything from an enlightened statesman to a proto-fascist (Gooch 1966).

[53] On the origins of the war, see Wetzel (2001).

a "depository of the sovereign authority", in its session of February 19, 1871, elected the conservative Adolphe Thiers as provisional "head of the executive power of the Republic", until the new French institutions were created, under the supervision of the National Assembly.[54] One month later provisional government authority was contested by Paris's City Council, (*Commune*), which proceeded to launch the first socialist revolution in Western history. The Paris Commune (also called the Fourth French Revolution), aspired to extend its authority throughout France, but lasted just 3 months before being brutally crushed by the French National Guard, sent from Versailles where the provisional government was established.[55]

For 5 years uncertainty would reign, as the National Assembly was split between republicans and monarchists. In the end republicanism would prevail, by a single vote (the Wallon Amendment, on January 30, 1875).[56] Thus arose the Third French Republic (1875–1940), notable for its lack of a formal Constitution, as it was based on three "constitutional laws".[57] This would be the most long-lasting French

[54] L'Assemblée nationale, dépositaire de l'autorité souveraine, Considérant qu'il importe, en attendant qu'il soit statué sur les institutions de la France, de pourvoir immédiatement aux nécessités du gouvernement et à la conduite des négociations, Décrète: Mr. Thiers est nommé chef du pouvoir exécutif de la République française. Il exercera ses fonctions sous l'autorité de l'Assemblée nationale avec le concours des ministres qu'il aura choisis et qu'il présidera. From Annales de l'Assemblée Nationale (1871, 5).

[55] Besides its internal political consequences in France, the Paris Commune had an important impact on the socialist movement, as it convinced Karl Marx to exclude Mikhail Bakunin from the Socialist International at The Hague Congress of 1872. While revolutionary anarchists remained allies of Bakunin, many Marxists became social democrats seeking to introduce socialism through regular elections in which mass parties participated for the first time. On the ideas of Bakunin and the Paris Commune, see Bakunin (1871). On The Hague Congress, see Morgan (2008, 217–228). On the aftermath of the Paris Commune, see Starr (2006).

[56] After almost five years of discussions over the regime that was to replace the Second Empire of Napoleon III, republicanism won out over the monarchy thanks to the motion of a single representative, M. Henri Wallon, who proposed the following text for approval: "*The President of the Republic shall be elected by an absolute majority of votes in the Senate and the Chamber of Deputies, convened as the National Assembly. He is to be elected for seven years and may stand for reelection*". This article, known as the "Wallon Amendment", was adopted by a vote of 353 to 352 in January 1875, thereby definitively establishing a republican government France (Everdell 2000, 234).

[57] The Wallon Amendment was followed by three "constitutional laws": one governing the Senate (February 24, 1875), another one governing the public powers (February 25, 1875) and a last one regarding the relations between public powers (July 16, 1875). The monarchical majority in the National Assembly, though divided between *orleanistes* and *legitimists* (the latter rejecting the tricolored flag and seeking to preserve the old white flag of Henry IV), refused to solemnly establish the Third Republic via a constitutional text (Malafosse 1975, 150–151).

regime, even down to the present day, as despite the turmoil of the Dreyfus Affair,[58] it would endure for 65 years.

The new Republic, consolidated by Jules Ferry (Fortescue 2013, 36–48), was unquestionably a secular, democratic, assembly-based regime, with a strong legislature and a weak executive branch. The constitutional laws of 1875 also considerably limited the power of the president of the Republic, who was elected indirectly by the two chambers—the Chamber of Deputies of Representatives (*Chambre des deputés*) and the Senate, which together formed the National Assembly. Each of the presidential acts was to be endorsed by a minister, and the government was to enjoy the confidence of both chambers. The only thing the president of the Republic could do was dissolve the Chamber of Deputies, though for this he required the Senate's approval. This is what de Malafosse (1975, 156) called the "erasure" of the Executive.

Another peculiarity of the new republican regime was that, as an assembly-based regime, it featured a Senate to counterbalance the political power of the Chamber of Deputies, which was elected by universal suffrage. The Senate, theoretically, was to be a conservative chamber, not only because one had to be 40 years of age to be a senator, but because its members were essentially elected by the representatives of rural France, in the main traditionalists. Even more important was what W.H.C. Smith (2005, 377) calls "absolute bicameralism": for the first time the Senate under the Third Republic had the same powers as the directly-elected lower chamber.[59]

Despite the fact that Third French Republic was an assembly-based regime, the state survived thanks to the solid administrative structure established by Napoleon. It is interesting to note that, despite featuring a government with a weak executive, the French Republic won the war of 1914–1918 against the

[58] The Dreyfus Affair was one of the most crucial episodes affecting the Third Republic from a constitutional perspective. It all began with a false accusation: a French officer of Jewish origin and hailing from the Alsace region (a territory occupied by the Prussians after the disastrous 1870 Franco-Prussian War), was wrongly accused of sharing military secrets with Prussian intelligence. The affair split French public opinion in two and almost provoked a civil war between progressives (*Dreyfusards*, those who defended Dreyfus as innocent) and conservatives (*anti-Dreyfusards*, who considered him a traitor). The victory of Dreyfus's supporters demonstrated the independence of the French Supreme Court from the government, and it was also seen as a triumph for the rule of law in the French constitutional system. The victory, however, was difficult and hard-fought, with the issue dragging on for twelve years, from 1894 to 1906. For an overview of this amazing chapter in French constitutional history and its aftermath in the III Republic, see Fortescue (2013, 50–79). About how the *Dreyfus affair* traces the political commitment of French intellectuals, see Drake (2005, 8–34)

[59] Of the 300 senators 225 were elected for nine years by a restricted electoral college made up of the deputies, the elected representatives of the departments (*conseillers généraux*) and a delegate for each one of the 42,000 French city councils. These were joined by 75 permanent senators designated by the legislative chambers. In addition to sharing half of the legislative competencies and policies of the Chamber of Deputies, the Senate of the Third Republic retained the judicial authorities of the Chamber of Peers from the Restoration and the July Monarchy, entrusted with judging the crime of high treason committed by the President of the Republic or his ministers, as well as actions against the security of the state.

authoritarian Prussian monarchy, thanks in large measure to the impetus and leadership of Georges Clemenceau.[60]

### 15.4.4 From Petain's "French State" to De Gaulle's Presidential Republic

The Third Republic fell when Nazi troops invaded France in May of 1940. After the partitioning of France under the Armistice signed on June 22, the two chambers, the Senate and Chamber of Deputies, convened as the National Assembly and decided to liquidate the Third Republic. Of the 666 members of Parliament present on July 10, 1940, only 80 voted against granting full powers to Marshal Petain to reform the constitution (Shirer 1994, 942–944). Thus arose a new French state (*l'État français*), authoritarian and autocratic (de Malafosse 1975, 313),[61] governed from Vichy, marking the start to one of the most maligned and regretted chapters in French history.[62] Petain's regime was not, however, the only government of France, as on June 18, 1940, General Charles De Gaulle, exiled in London, issued his "call to honour" (Vinen 2007, 30) in which he exhorted the French not to accept their defeat and form a government for a free France.

Petain's regime collapsed when Hitler was defeated in 1944, and De Gaulle, who had been promoting a Provisional Consultative Assembly (*Assemblée consultative provisoire*) since September of 1943, began to issue decrees to establish a new French government and regime.[63]

---

[60] Clemenceau was a man of leftist leanings with deeply anti-military views, as expressed in memorable quips of his such as: "military justice is to justice what military music is to music" (often attributed to him, probably on the Dreyfus trial), meaning that war is too serious to be left to the military. Nevertheless, he succeeded in overcoming political divisions and imposing the "Sacred Union" (*l'Union sacrée*) until the end the war. Churchill described the Clemenceau of this period "like a wild animal pacing to and fro behind bars growling and glaring; and all around him was an assembly which would have done anything to avoid putting him there, but, having put him there, felt they must obey" (Churchill 2012, 229–244). See quote also in Terraine (2003, 24–25). On his relationships with the legislature in the last months of the War, see Watson (2009, 38–42).

[61] Petain became chief of the "French State" and the official motto of the new quasi-monarchical regime became "Work, Family, Fatherland" instead of the traditional "Liberty, Equality, Fraternity". The first official act of the marshal was to adjourn the Parliament "until the restoration of order". There were no more elections, even at the municipal level, with every officeholder being appointed by the government. With the courageous exception of the United Kingdom, the entire world recognized Petain's state. The United States even sent him an ambassador (Goubert 2003, 295).

[62] On what contemporary historiography calls the "Vichy Syndrome", see Gordon (1995, 495–518) and Rousso (2006).

[63] The *ordonnance* of April 21, 1944 that reorganized the powers of the state based its legitimacy on the National Assembly vote of July 10, 1940 to declare the 1875 constitution abrogated. On May 21, 1944, the provisional government endorsed the gradual replacement of the Provisional Consultative Assembly of 1943 with an elected assembly. Finally, through the *ordonnance* of August 9, 1944, republican legality in continental France was reestablished, and the Vichy regime was declared null and void (de Malafosse 1975, 335–336). On the thorny issue of the Vichy regime's legitimacy, see Million (2006).

However, the head of liberated France would end up stepping down, as he did not agree with the re-establishment of an assembly-based government similar to that of the Third Republic, the formula proposed by the majority of the politicians elaborating the new constitutional framework.[64] The new republic's charter was a full-fledged constitution, as opposed to the three constitutional laws upon which the Third Republic had rested. It even included in its preamble a concrete reference to the fundamental rights recognized in the 1789 Declaration of the Rights of Man, enriched by new social and economic rights "particularly necessary to our times". Democracy was fully established in France, as the 1946 constitution was the first one to recognize the right of French women to vote (article 4).[65]

The 1946 document marked another return to the parliamentary model, with a strong lower house and a weak executive. Under the new regime, the Senate disappeared and the upper house, called The Republic's Council (*Conseil de la République*), was so irrelevant that in practice it was a unicameral regime.[66]

[64] By the beginning of January the Constituent Assembly had already prepared what was going to be the Constitutional Draft of April 19, 1946, in which it was established a unicameral Assembly which elected the president of the Republic and its prime minister; the former had no real power, and the latter needed to have his government approved by the all-powerful National Assembly. Hence, De Gaulle resigned from the presidency on January 20, 1946. On May 5, the French people rejected the proposed Constitution in a referendum. De Gaulle delivered an important speech in Bayeux on the following June 16 in which he publically announced his constitutional ideas (Flood 2002, 195–198). He wanted a bicameral legislature and an executive power nominated by the president of the Republic and not by the legislature (Mahoney 2000, 111–128). However, De Gaulle lacked political support. The Constituent Assembly of 1945 was dominated by communists and socialists, and the main right-wing party, the *Mouvement Républicain Populaire* (*MRP*), to which all of Pétain's former supporters belonged, was staunchly opposed to him. Thus, De Gaulle created his own party on April 17, 1947: the *Rassemblement du Peuple Français, RPF* ("Gathering of the French People"), which never received enough votes to place De Gaulle in power under the Fourth Republic. The RPF was dissolved in 1955 (Vinen 2002, 216–233).

[65] Women had voted in the United Kingdom since 1918, though they were "equal" to men only as of 1928. In the US voting rights for women were fully recognized by the 19th Amendment, ratified on August 18, 1920. ("The right of citizens of the United States to vote shall not be denied or abridged by the United States or by any State on account of sex".) Spanish women voted for the first time in 1933, and French women in the local elections of April 29, 1945. It was a decree (*ordonnance*) by General De Gaulle on April 21, 1944 that established that "women may vote and be elected under the same terms as men" (articles 1 and 17). (Cavallaro 2003, 10). The 1946 Constitution of the Fourth Republic recognized this principle for the first time in French constitutional history: *Sont électeurs, dans les conditions déterminées par la loi, tous les nationaux et ressortissants français majeurs des deux sexes, jouissant de leurs droits civils et politiques.* (Electors are, under the conditions determined by the law, all French nationals and of-age residents, of both sexes, who enjoy their civil and political rights.)

[66] Stalwart support for legislative sovereignty, which went back to the Jacobin ideas of 1793 and the original constitution proposed in April 1946, was ultimately watered down in the definitive October Constitution, in which presidential powers were reinforced and a second chamber was instituted, though with very limited powers. A weak Constitutional Committee was also established to review the constitutionality of statutes. The new constitution was flawed, however, and underwent a process of revisions in the 1950s aimed at protecting the power of the cabinet and the president when there were major shifts in the Parliament (Thornhill 2013, 329).

The Fourth Republic (1946–1958), would prove to be an era of ephemeral governments, such as that of Pierre Mendès France, one of the most emblematic politicians of period and one of the regime's few real statesmen (Hanley et al. 2005, 27). Mendès became President of the Council of Ministers on June 18, 1954, going on to serve for only seven and a half months (Werth 1957, 168–177).[67] This was the order of the day for the different governments under France's short-lived Fourth Republic.

The crisis in Algeria, a territory integrated into the French State since its conquest in the mid-nineteenth century, which groups of Muslims were struggling to make an independent country, precipitated De Gaulle's return to power in 1958. The new leader began by initiating a process for the drafting of a new constitution, which would result in the adoption of the one still in effect in France today: that of the Fifth Republic.[68] The Gaullist regime was, of course, republican, but unlike the previous one it was markedly presidential, as the Constitution of 1958 conferred major powers upon the president (Lascombe 2010, 30–31), at the expense of the legislature. Under the new system the Senate recovered a significant institutional role,[69] while the executive became the primary legislative power.[70]

---

[67] He definitively resigned on February 23, 1955.

[68] As a result of the failure of the first Algiers Putsch (May 13, 1958), the right-wing partisans of French Algeria succeeded in preventing the formation of a government under Pierre Pflimlin. On May 29, President René Coty called upon De Gaulle to become the president of the Council. De Gaulle accepted upon the condition that he receive special powers for six months, and that the new government proceed with the enactment of a new constitution creating a strong presidency. De Gaulle's cabinet was approved by the National Assembly by 329 votes to 224, and he was granted the power to govern by ordinances for a 6-month period. The new constitutional draft was written by Michel Debré, and reflected the ideas De Gaulle had expressed in his Bayeux Speech of June 16, 1946. The Left opposed the plan. François Mitterrand even denounced De Gaulle's policy as a "permanent *coup d'état*" (Mitterrand 2010), though he later, paradoxically, became the longest-standing president of the Fifth Republic (1981–1995). On 28 September 1958, 79.2 % of the French voted in favor of the new Constitution in the corresponding referendum. The constitution entered into force on October 4 and the Fifth Republic was born (Schain 2011, 83–92). For an overview of the history of the France's Fifth Republic, see Chevallier et al. (2012).

[69] The President of the Senate is the second highest-ranking official in the French state after the President of the Republic. He names three of the nine members of the Constitutional Court (*Conseil Constitutional*), which plays the same role as the US Supreme Court. The French Constitution entrusts the Senate with the representation of the nation's regions and municipalities, participates in the legislative procedure, and the constitution cannot be modified without its consent. The Senate held a conservative majority for 53 years until the 2011 elections in which the Left gained control, seating 177 senators for the first time in the history of the Fifth Republic. For an overview of the current legislative role of the French Senate, see Tsebelis and Money (1995, 101–129).

[70] Firstly, because the constitution recognizes issues which are covered by regulations (administrative decrees), in accordance with Article 34 of the Constitution of 1958, which specifies the areas which may be regulated by law. The legislative power may not act in or encroach upon those areas where regulations apply and prevail. On the other hand, most laws are the result of initiatives promoted by the government, which may even force their approval, the government thus undertaking responsibility thereto, such that the rejection of a law may entail the removal of a government (Article 49.3 of the Constitution). Finally, the government may promulgate laws known as "ordinances" (*ordonnances*) which, despite emanating from the executive power, enter into effect immediately, requiring Parliamentary ratification to be made permanent. The truth is that most of the laws approved by the Fifth Republic are essentially the work of the executive branch and not of a "tamed legislature" (Lascombe 2010, 107).

Presidential power was consolidated after De Gaulle miraculously survived an assassination attempt in the Paris suburb of Petit Clamart on August 22, 1962.[71] As a result of this, fearing that if he disappeared the French Republic could become a Parliamentary regime again, he asked the French people to modify the 1958 Constitution by introducing the direct election of the President via universal suffrage. In the referendum held on October 28, 1962, he won a resounding personal victory against the political parties, as the French people accepted the principle that the President of the Republic ought to receive direct legitimacy from a direct election (Bernstein 1993, 71–82). Since then, the French have elected their President by universal and direct vote and not, as was traditionally done, indirectly via designation by both chambers of the legislature.

### 15.4.5 *French Semi-presidentialism: A Return of the Napoleonic Model of State?*

After the reform of 1962, France's constitutional regime (still in place today) found itself somewhere between Bonapartist republicanism and American presidentialism (Cambadelis 1987). Under it when presidents enjoy majority support in the National Assembly the regime becomes "presidential", as it is the president who holds and exercises power, while when the legislature is controlled by an opposition party, the "parliamentary" system prevails, as executive power is actually wielded by the prime minister. This system, dubbed "cohabitation", (Bell 2000, 31) has prompted some constitutionalists to brand the French regime "semi-presidential" (Marrani 2013, 11–14).

That said, it is necessary to emphasize that the president of the French Republic, provided that he enjoys a political majority in the National Assembly, holds greater constitutional powers than the President of the United States. His term lasts 5 years (formerly seven), and he may be re-elected several times, with the caveat that he may not serve more than two consecutive terms, this last limitation approved in 2008 after being advanced by Nicolas Sarkozy,[72] even though no previous president ever did serve more than two terms in a row under the current constitution.

[71] Surprisingly, De Gaulle emerged unharmed after his car was strafed with machine-gun fire by members of the Secret Army Organisation (OAS), who favored the maintenance of Algeria within the French state, as opposed to De Gaulle, who considered independence to be inevitable. As a result of the attempt, De Gaulle realized that when he was gone the French government could regress back to an assembly-based regime (Bell 2000, 53). Thus, to permanently reinforce the power of the president of the Republic, he resolved to alter the constitution so that he would be directly elected at the polls.

[72] Article 3 of Constitutional Law No. 2008–724 of July 23, 2008, on the "modernization of the institutions of the Fifth Republic" bars presidents of the French Republic from serving for more than two consecutive terms. It does not prevent, however, theoretically, a President from serving a third term after leaving power for an interim period.

Mitterrand (1981 and 1988) and Chirac (1995 and 2002) are the only ones to have been elected twice and served out their second terms.[73]

The power of the president of the Republic has been mitigated, however, by the introduction by President Sarkozy of the *question prioritaire de constitutionalité* (priority preliminary ruling on the issue of constitutionality), a constitutional reform measure passed on July 23, 2008, which strengthens the role of the Constitutional Council and introduces the principle of "judicial review"[74] for the first time in French history.

## TIMELINE

### The Napoleonic Stage (1799–1815)

1769 August 15. Birth of Napoleon Bonaparte in Ajaccio (Corsica).
1785 Napoleon graduates as a 2nd Lieutenant of Artillery.
1792 Bonaparte is promoted to captain.
1793 December 22. Napoleon is promoted to brigadier general because of his decisive action in the taking of Toulon from the British.
1794 July. Napoleon is arrested for his Jacobin ideas and his ties to Robespierre.
1795 October 5. Napoleon saves the Government of the Convention by quelling a monarchist uprising. As a result, he is promoted to division general (*général Vendémiaire*) and is assigned command of the Army of the Interior.
1796 March 8. Napoleon marries Joséphine de Beauharnais.
March 27. Napoleon takes control of the Army of Italy.
1797 November 16. End of the Italian Campaign. His victories make Napoleon France's most popular military figure.
1798 July 21. Battle of the Pyramids (Egyptian Campaign).
August 2. The French war fleet is annihilated at Aboukir Bay by Admiral Nelson.
1799 October 9. After a 47-day voyage in which he manages to evade English warships, Napoleon reaches France.
November 9. Napoleon seizes power through a *coup d'état*.
December 25. The Year VII Constitution (1799) enters into force.
1802 August 2. French electors approve of Napoleon becoming Sole Consul, for life. Two days later the Constitution of the Year X is approved (August 4, 1802).

[73] For an overview of this recent period, see Gaffney (2012, 138–167, for Mitterrand's mandates, and 168–178 for Chirac's).

[74] The *question prioritaire de constitutionalité* was enacted via the abovementioned constitutional law of July 23, 2008, which modifies Articles 61.1 and 61.2 of the French Constitution. For an overview of the institutional role of the Constitutional Council in protecting the French Constitution prior to 2008, see Stone (1992). For an analysis of Sarkozy's constitutional reform, see Camby et al. (2011) and Magnon et al. (2012).

1804 May 18. (*28 Floréal, An XII*). The Senate approves a new constitution under which the government of the Republic is handed over to Napoleon as "Emperor of the French". The Constitution is ratified by plebiscite on November 6, 1804.

1805 October 21. Defeat at Trafalgar.
December 2. Battle of Austerlitz. This victory marks the zenith of Napoleon's military glory.

1812 June. Napoleon invades Russia in command of 700,000 men.
December. Napoleon withdraws from Russia in defeat.

1814 March 31. Marshals force Napoleon to abdicate.
April 3. The Senate removes Napoleon from office.
June 4. Louis XVIII grants the French a *charte*.

1815 March 1. Napoleon disembarks in France.
March 20. The flight of Louis XVIII. Napoleon at the Tuileries Palace.
April 22. Additional Act to the constitutions of the Empire.
June 18. Napoleon is defeated at Waterloo.
June 22. Napoleon's second abdication.
October 14. Napoleon reaches St. Helena on the English warship *Northumberland*.

## The Restoration (1815–1830)

1815 August 14 and 22. Legislative elections. The legislature strongly supports Louis XVIII (*Chambre introuvable*).

1821 May 5. Napoleon dies on St. Helena.

1824 September 16. Death of Louis XVIII. He is succeeded by his brother Charles X (1824–1830).

## The July Monarchy (1830–1848)

1830 July 27, 28, and 29. "July Revolution". Fall of Charles X.
August 9. Louis Philippe, Duke of Orléans, rises to the throne. Absolute monarchy gives way to constitutional monarchy ("July Monarchy"). The Chamber of Deputies thoroughly revises the *Charte* of 1815.

## The Second Republic (1848–1852)

1848 February 22. The people of Paris rise up against Louis Philippe, Duke of Orléans. Barricades.
February 25. Restoration of universal male suffrage.
November 4. Adoption of the Constitution of the Second Republic.

### The Second Empire (1852–1870)

1852 December 2. Louis Napoleon Bonaparte proclaims the Second Empire.
1870 September 1. Napoleon III is taken prisoner by the Prussians at Sedan. The Second Empire comes to an end.
September 4. Proclamation of the Third Republic in Paris.

### The Third Republic (1870–1940)

1871 March 18–May 28. Paris Commune insurrection. The first "proletarian" revolution in Western history.
1875 January 30. The Wallon Amendment.
February 24. The National Assembly passes a law on the Organization of the Senate. This is the first "constitutional law".
February 25. Adoption of the "second constitutional law" on the organization of public powers.
July 16. Third and last constitutional law on the relationships between the public powers. The three constitutional laws underpin the "Constitution of the Third French Republic".
1905 Church and State Separation Law (*Loi de séparation des Églises et de l'État*).

### World War II

1940 June 17. Pétain accepts French surrender to Germany.
June 18. De Gaulle from London calls French people to resist the German occupation.
July 10. The French National Assembly and the Senate grant full powers to General Petain to promulgate a new Constitution of the French State. End of the Third Republic.
1943 September 17. De Gaulle creates a Provisional Consultative Assembly in exile.
1944 April 21. De Gaulle issues an *ordonnance* amounting to a provisional constitution organizing public powers in liberated France.
June 3. Creation of the Provisional Government of the Republic, headed by De Gaulle. June 6. D-Day. Normandy Landing (Operation Overlord).
June 14. De Gaulle delivers a speech in Bayeux, the first city liberated by the Allies.
August 9. Through an *ordonnance* republican legality in France is reestablished and the Vichy regime is declared null and void.
August 25. Surrender of the German garrison occupying Paris.
1945 October 21. Elections to choose a Constitutional Assembly. The same elections approve, via referendum, a provisional "constitutional law".

### The Fourth Republic

1946 January 20. De Gaulle resigns as head of the Provisional Government out of disagreement with the terms of the new constitution.
May 5. The April 19, 1946 draft of the constitution is rejected by the French in a referendum.
June 2. A new Constituent Assembly is elected.
June 16, 1946. De Gaulle delivers a speech at Bayeux articulating his constitutional ideas for a republic with a strong executive.
October 13. The constitution of the Fifth French Republic is approved in a referendum.
October 27. The Constitution enters into force.

### The Fifth Republic

| | |
|---|---|
| 1958 | May 29. The President of the Republic, René Coty, asks Charles de Gaulle to form a government. The National Assembly confirms De Gaulle as the head of the government on June 1.<br>June 3. The National Assembly approves a new constitutional law.<br>September 28. The new Constitution is approved in a referendum by 79.25 % of the votes.<br>October 4. The Constitution is promulgated.<br>November. De Gaulle wins the legislative elections in a landslide.<br>December. De Gaulle is elected President of the Republic with 78 % of the votes cast by 80,000 "great electors" (indirect suffrage). |
| 1962 | August 22. Assassination attempt on De Gaulle in Petit Clamart.<br>September. General De Gaulle proposes amending the Constitution to allow the President of the Republic to be elected by a direct vote.<br>October. In a referendum 62.25 % approve the modification of the Constitution. |
| 1965 | December 19. General de Gaulle is elected in a second round of voting with 55.20 % of the votes. President of the Republic. The first French presidential election by direct vote. |
| 1969 | April 27. De Gaulle loses a referendum on territorial reform (52.41 % of votes against). He resigns the next day.<br>June 15. Georges Pompidou, President. |
| 1970 | November 9. Death of Charles de Gaulle. |
| 1974 | April 2. Death of Georges Pompidou.<br>May 19. Valéry Giscard d'Estaing, President. |
| 1981 | May 10. François Mitterrand is elected President of the Republic. (51.76 %). The Fifth Republic's first leftist president. |
| 1986–1988 | First "cohabitation". Jacques Chirac, Prime Minister. |
| 1988 | May 8. Mitterrand is re-elected President of the Republic (54.02 %). |
| 1993–1995 | Second cohabitation. Édouard Balladur, Prime Minister. |

| | |
|---|---|
| 1995 | May 7. Jacques Chirac is elected President of the Republic. Re-elected in 2002. |
| 1996 | January 8. François Mitterrand dies of cancer. |
| 1997–2002 | Third cohabitation. Socialist Lionel Jospin, Prime Minister. Conservative President Jacques Chirac. |
| 2002 | Jacques Chirac is reelected, but for the first time the presidential term is of 5 years (*quinquennat*, approved in the 2000 referendum). |
| 2007 | May 6. Nicolas Sarkozy is elected the sixth president of the Fifth Republic (53.06 %). |
| 2008 | July 23. A reform measure introduces the principle of "judicial review" into the French constitutional system. |
| 2012 | May 6. Socialist leader François Hollande becomes the seventh president of the Fifth Republic (51.64 %). |

## References


Aguilera-Barchet, B. (2008). Las raíces jurídicas del Estado español contemporáneo: La Guerra de la Independencia y el afianzamiento del sentimiento nacional. Notas para un ensayo de historia constitucional europea comparada. In *Estudios sobre la Constitución de Bayona* (pp. 85–207). Madrid: La Ley.

Alexander, R. (2000). 'No, Minister': French restoration rejection of authoritarianism. In D. Laven & L. Riall (Eds.), *Problems of government in restoration Europe: Napoleon's legacy* (pp. 29–47). Oxford: Berg.

Alexander, R. (2003). *Re-writing the French revolutionary tradition: Liberal opposition and the fall of the Bourbon monarchy*. Cambridge, UK: Cambridge University Press.

Arnaud, A. J. (1969). *Les origines doctrinales du Code civil français*. Paris: Librairie Générale de Droit et de Jurisprudence.

Baguley, D. (2000). *Napoleon III and his regime: An extravaganza*. Baton Rouge, LA: Louisiana State University Press.

Bakunin, M. A. (1871). *The Paris commune and the idea of the state*. New York: Alfred A. Knopf.

Barnard, H. C. (2009). *Education and the French Revolution*. Cambridge, UK: Cambridge University Press.

Bell, D. S. (2000). *Presidential power in fifth Republic France*. Oxford: Berg.

Bergeron, L. (1990). *France under Napoleon* (8th printing). Princeton, NJ: Princeton University Press.

Bernstein, S. (1993). *The Republic of De Gaulle: 1958–1969*. Cambridge, UK: Cambridge University Press.

Bessiere, A. (2008). *Il était une fois la Légion d'honneur: De la croix des braves au ruban rouge*. Paris: L'Harmattan.

Billias, G. A. (2009). *European revolutions of 1848: France in American Constitutionalism heard round the world, 1776–1989: A global perspective* (pp. 179–183). New York: New York University Press.

Bluche F. (1980). La dictature légitimée. *Le Bonapartisme: aux origines de la droite autoritaire (1800–1850)* (pp. 24–35). Paris: Nouvelles Éditions Latines.

Boudon, J.-O. (Ed.). (2004). *Napoléon et les lycées: Enseignement et société en Europe au début du XXe siècle*. Paris: Nouveau Monde Éd.

Boycott-Brown, M. (2001). *The road to Rivoli: Napoleon's first campaign*. Herndon, VA: Cassell & Co.

Brint, S. G. (2006). *Schools and societies* (2nd ed.). Stanford, CA: Stanford University Press.

Cambadelis, J. C. (1987). *Bonapartisme et neocorporatisme sous la Ve République*. Lille, FR: Atelier National de Reproduction des Thèses.

Camby, J. P., Fraisseix P., & Gicquel J. (2011). *La révision de 2008: une nouvelle constitution?* Paris: Lextenso Editions.

Cavallaro, D. (2003). *French feminist theory*. London: Continuum.

Chevallier, J.-J., Carcassonne, G., & Duhamel, O. (2014). *Histoire de la cinquième république: 1958–2012*. Paris: Dalloz.

Churchill, Wiston, Sir (2012) *Clemenceau in great contemporaries* (pp. 229–244). Wilmington, DE: Intercollegiate Studies Institute.

Connelly, O. (2000). *The French Revolution and Napoleonic Era* (3rd ed.). Fort Worth, TX: Harcourt.

Conner, S. P. (2004). *The age of Napoleon*. Westport, CT: Greenwood Press.

Corley, T. A. B. (1974). *Democratic despot: A life of Napoleon III* (Reprint.). Westport, CT: Greenwood Press.

Coutant, A. (2009). *1848: Quand la République combattait la démocratie*. Paris: Mare et Martin.

Curtis, E. N. (2013). *The French assembly of 1848 and American Constitutional Doctrines*. Independence, KY: Gale. (Repr. of the 1917 ed. New York: Columbia University Press).

Chatel de Brancion, L. (2009). *Cambacérès: Maître d'œuvre de Napoléon* (2e éd.). Paris: Perrin.

De Gaulle, P. (2003). *De Gaulle, mon père: entretiens avec Michel Tauriac* (2 Vols.). Paris: Plon.

de Malafosse, J. (1975). *Histoire des institutions et des régimes politiques de la Révolution à la IVe République*. Paris: Montchrestien.

Drake, D. (2005). The Dreyfus affair and the emergence of the French public intellectual. In *French intellectuals and politics from the Dreyfus affair to the occupation* (pp. 8–34). New York: Palgrave Macmillan.

Durant, W., Durant, A. (2001). A revolution in education. In R. Obstfeld & L. Obstfeld (Eds.), *Napoleon Bonaparte* (pp. 65–69). San Diego, CA: Greenhaven Press.

Dwyer, P. (2008). *Napoleon: The path to power, 1769–1799*. New Haven, CT: Yale University Press.

Emsley, C. (2003). *Napoleon*. New York: Routledge.

Englund, S. (2004). *Napoleon: A political life*. New York: Scribner.

Everdell, W. R. (2000). Léon Gambetta and the Troisième: The parliamentary republic. In *The end of kings: A history of republics and republicans* (pp. 219–245). Chicago, IL: University of Chicago Press.

Fiorentino, K. (2008). *La seconde Chambre en France dans l'histoire des institutions et des idées politiques: (1789–1940)*. Paris: Dalloz.

Flood, C. G. (2002). Case studies in Mythopoeic narrative (1): De Gaulle's "Bayeux Constitution". In *Political myth: A theoretical introduction* (pp. 195–234). Oxon, UK: Routledge.

Fortescue, W. (2005). *France and 1848: The end of monarchy*. New York: Taylor and Francis.

Fortescue, W. (2013). *The third republic in France: 1870–1940. Conflicts and continuities.*. London: Routledge.

France. Assemblée Nationale (1871). From 12 february to 11 March. In *Annales de l'Assemblée Nationale*. Paris: Imprimerie et librairie du Journal Officiel.

Fritz, G. (2000). *La question de l'influence américaine dans La Constitution de 1848*. Dijon, FR: Éditions Universitaires de Bourgogne.

Gaffney, J. (2012). *Political leadership in France: From Charles de Gaulle to Nicolas Sarkozy*. Hampshire, UK: Palgrave Macmillan.

Geyl, P. (1982). *Napoleon. For and against*. Harmondsworth: Penguin (Reprint of 1948 edition: New Haven, CT: Yale University Press).

Gooch, B. D. (1966). *Napoleon III,-Man of destiny: Enlightened statesman or proto-fascist?* New York: Holt, Rinehart & Winston.

Gordley, J. (2013). *The Jurists: A critical history*. Oxford: Oxford University Press.

Gordon, B. M. (1995). The 'Vichy Syndrome' problem in history. *Iin French Historical Studies, 19*(2), 495–518.

Goubert, P. (2003). *The course of French history*. New York: Taylor and Francis.

Grab, A. (2001). State, society and tax policy in Napoleonic Europe. In P. G. Dwyer (Ed.), *Napoleon and Europe* (pp. 169–186). Harlow, UK: Pearson Education.

Hanley, D. L., Kerr, P., & Waites, N. H. (2005). *Contemporary France: Politics and society since 1945*. New York: Taylor and Francis.

Hicks, P. (2012). Napoleon as a politician. In M. Broers et al. (Eds.), *The Napoleonic empire and the New European political culture: War, culture and society, 1750–1850* (pp. 70–81). New York: Palgrave Macmillan.

Hudson, N. E. (1973). *Ultra-royalism and the French Restoration*. Cambridge, UK: Cambridge University Press, New York: Octagon Books. (Reprint of the 1936 ed.).

Huet, V. (2007). Napoleon I: A new Augustus? In C. Edwards (Ed.), *Roman presences: Receptions of Rome in European culture, 1789–1945* (pp. 53–69). Cambridge, UK: Cambridge University Press.

Jainchill, A. J. S. (2008). *Reimagining politics after the terror: The Republican origins of French liberalism*. Ithaca, NY: Cornell University Press.

Jefferson, T. (1907a). Letter to William Bentley. Monticello, December 28, 1815. In *The writings of Thomas Jefferson* (Vol. XIV, pp. 363–365). Washington, DC: Bergh.

Jefferson, T. (1907b). Letter to Benjamin Austin, Esq. Monticello, January 9, 1816. In *The writings of Thomas Jefferson* (Vol. XIV. pp. 387–393). Washington, DC: Bergh.

Jordan, D. P. (2012). *Napoleon and the revolution*. London: Palgrave Macmillan.

Klinge, M. (2004). Teachers. In W. Rüegg (Ed.), *A history of the university in Europe* (Universities in the nineteenth and early twentieth centuries (1800–1945), Vol. III, pp. 123–162). Cambridge: Cambridge University Press.

Lascombe, M. (2010). *Le droit constitutionnel de la Ve République* (11th ed.). Paris: L'Harmattan.

Laven, D., & Riall, L. (2000). Restoration government and the legacy of Napoleon. In D. Laven & L. Riall (Eds.), *Problems of government in restoration Europe: Napoleon's legacy* (pp. 1–28). Oxford: Berg.

Lefebvre, G. (2011). *Napoleon*. New York: Taylor and Francis.

Léwy, C. (1998). The code and property. In B. Schwartz (Ed.), *The code Napoleon and the common-law* (pp. 162–176). Clark, NJ: The Lawbook Exchange.

Lombardo, P. (2001). 1808, 17 March: Discipline and Melancholy. In D. Hollier (Ed.), *A new history of French Literature* (3rd ed., pp. 613–616). Cambridge, MA: Harvard University Press.

Lorente, M. (2012). The new Spanish councils. In M. Broers et al. (Eds.), *The Napoleonic empire and the new European political culture: War, culture and society, 1750–1850* (pp. 293–301). New York: Palgrave Macmillan.

Luchaire, F. (1998). *Naissance d'une constitution: 1848*. Paris: Fayard.

Lyons, M. (1994). *Napoleon Bonaparte and the legacy of the French Revolution*. London: Palgrave Macmillan.

Magnon, X. et al. (Eds.), (2012). *Pouvoir exécutif et Parlement: de nouveaux équilibres?: l'impact de la révision constitutionnelle du 23 juillet 2008 sur le rééquilibrage des institutions*. Aix en Provence: Presses universitaires d'Aix-Marseille.

Mahoney, D. J. (2000). *De Gaulle: Statesmanship, grandeur, and modern democracy*. New Brunswick, NJ: Transaction Publishers.

Manas, J. (2006). *Napoleon on project management: Timeless lessons in planning, execution and leadership*. Nashville, TN: Thomas Nelson.

Marrani, D. (2013). *Dynamics in the French constitution: Decoding French republican ideas*. Oxon, UK: Routledge.

Marx, K. (2005). *The Eighteenth brumaire of Louis Bonaparte*. New York: Mondial.

Mészáros, I. (2000). The legacy of 1848 and the Dilemmas of democratic revolutions. In D. Moggach & P. L. Browne (Eds.), *The social question and the Democratic Revolution: Marx and the legacy of 1848* (pp. 43–48). Otawa: University of Otawa Press.

Metternich, C.W.L., Fürst von (1883). Fingerzeige für den Minister des... Nr. 1949–1950. In *Aus Metternich's Nachgelassenen Papieren* (Vol. 8, pp. 462–472). Wien: Wilhelm Braumüller.

Million, C. (2006). L'application des règles dites "lois" de Vichy dans la zone rattachée: la souveraineté en question. In B. Durand et al. (Eds.), *Le droit sous Vichy* (pp. 253–284). Frankfurt am Main: Klostermann.

Mitterrand, F. (2010). *Le Coup d'État permanent*. Reéd. Paris: Les Belles Lettres.

Morgan, R. P. (2008). *The German social democrats and the first international: 1864–1872*. Cambridge, UK: Cambridge University Press.

Napoleon I. Emperor of the French (1819). Quartier général, Passariano, 3è jour complémentaire an V [21 septembre 1797] A Talleyrand, ministre des relations extérieures. In *Correspondance inédite officielle et confidentielle* (Vol. 6, pp. 177–181). Paris: Panckoucke.

Napoleon I. Emperor of the French (1846). To the citizen president of the Cispadane Republic. Milan, 12 Nivose, year 5 [January 1, 1797]. In *The Bonaparte letters and despatches, secret, confidential, and official from the originals in his private cabinet* (pp. 187–188). London: Saunders and Otley.

Napoleon I. Emperor of the French (1861). Lettre de l'empereur a S.S. Le Pape, 13 février 1806 (N° 9805). In *Correspondance de Napoléon Ier* (Vol. XII, pp. 38–40). Paris: H. Plon, J. Dumaine.

Napoleon I. Emperor of the French. (1861). Lettre de l'empereur au cardinal Fesch, 13 février 1806 (N° 9806). In *Correspondance de Napoléon Ier* (Vol. XII, p. 40). Paris: H. Plon, J. Dumaine.

Napoleon I. Emperor of the French (1863). Pensèe 190. In *Maximes de guerre et pensées de Napoléon Ier* (5e éd., revue et aug., p. 258). Paris: J. Dumaine.

Napoleon I. Emperor of the French (1916). *Napoleon in his own words*. Chicago, AC: McClurg & Co.

Newman, E. L. (1974). The blouse and the frock coat: The alliance of the common people of Paris with the liberal leadership and the middle class during the last years of the Bourbon restoration. *The Journal of Modern History, 46*(1), 26–59.

Patterson, S. C., & Mughan, A. (1999). Senates and the theory of Bicameralism. In S. C. Patterson & A. Mughan (Eds.), *Senates: Bicameralism in the contemporary world* (pp. 1–31). Columbus, OH: Ohio State University Press.

Pilbeam, P. (1982). The growth of liberalism and the crisis of the Bourbon restoration, 1827–1830. *The Historical Journal, 25*(2), 351–366.

Pilbeam, P. (1983). The 'Three Glorious Days': The revolution of 1830 in provincial France. *The Historical Journal, 26*(4), 831–844.

Pinkney, D. H. (1973). *The French Revolution of 1830*. Princeton, NJ: Princeton University Press.

Plessis, A. (1989). *The rise and fall of the second empire: 1852–1871*. Cambridge, UK: Cambridge University Press.

Portalis, J. M. É. (2004). Discours préliminaire du premier projet de Code civil. In *Motifs et discours prononcés lors de la publication du code civil* (pp. 10–70). Bordeaux: Éditions Confluences.

Price, R. (2001). *The French second empire: An anatomy of political power*. Cambridge: Cambridge University Press.

Reich, E. (2004). The code civil: 1804. In *Select documents illustrating mediaeval and modern history* (pp. 455–476). New York: Kessinger Publishing.

Rheinstein, M. (1998). The code and the family. In B. Schwartz (Ed.), *The code Napoleon and the common-law world* (pp. 139–161). Union, NJ: The Lawbook Exchange, Ltd.

Rolland, P. (2000). De l'art du préambule: le precedent de 1848. In J. Bart et al. (Eds.), *La Constitution du 4 novembre 1848: l'ambition d'une république démocratique* (pp. 148–186). Dijon, FR: EUD.

Rousso, H. (2006). *The Vichy Syndrome: History and memory in France since 1944* (2nd ed.). Cambridge, MA: Harvard University Press.

Rowell, D. (2012). *Paris: The 'New Rome' of Napoleon I*. London: Bloomsbury Pub.

Rudé, G. (2005). The French revolution of 1848. In *The crowd in history: A study of popular disturbances in France and England, 1730–1848* (2nd ed., pp. 164–178). London: Interlink.

Schain, M. (2011). The fifth republic. In E. Berenson et al. (Eds.), *The French Republic: History, values, debates* (pp. 83–92). Ithaca, NY: Cornell University Press.

Schmitt, C. (2008). *Constitutional theory*. Durham, NC: Duke University Press (Translation of the 1928 German edition *Verfassungslehre*, Munich: Ducker and Humblot).

Schwartz, B. (1998). Preface. In B. Schwartz (Ed.), *The code Napoleon and the common-law world* (pp. VII–X). Union, NJ: The Lawbook Exchange, Ltd.

Schwarzfuchs, S. (1979). *Napoleon, The Jews and the Sanhedrin*. Boston, MA: Routledge and Kegan Paul.

Shirer, W. L. (1994). *The collapse of the third republic: An inquiry into the Fall of France in 1940*. New York: Da Capo Press.

Smith, P. (2005). *A history of the French Senate* (Vol. 1). The third republic, 1870–1940. New York: Edwin Mellen Press.

Smith, W. H. C. (2005). *The Bonapartes: The history of a Dinasty*. London: Palgrave Macmillan.

Starr, P. (2006). *Commemorating trauma: The Paris commune and its cultural aftermath*. New York: Fordham University Press.

Stone, A. (1992). *The birth of judicial politics in France: The constitutional council in comparative perspective*. Oxford: Oxford University Press.

Terraine, J. (2003). *To win a war: 1918 The year of victory*. London: Cassel Military Paperbacks.

Thornhill, C. (2013). *A sociology of constitutions: Constitutions and state legitimacy in historical-sociological perspective*. Cambridge, UK: Cambridge University Press.

Tocqueville, A., & de Beaumont, G. (1968). *Tocqueville and Beaumont on social reform*. New York: Harper and Row.

Tsebelis, G., & Money, J. (1995). Bicameral negotiations: The Navette system in France. *British Journal of Political Science, 25*(1), 105–129.

Tulard, J. (1984). *Napoleon: The myth of the saviour*. London: Weidenfeld and Nicolson.

van Caenegem, R. C. (2003). *An historical introduction to western constitutional law*. Cambridge, UK: Cambridge University Press.

van Caenegem, R. C. (2009). *Judges, legislators and professors: Chapters in European legal history*. Cambridge, UK: Cambridge University Press.

Vaughan, M., & Archer, M. S. (2010). *Social conflict and educational change in England and France: 1789–1848*. Cambridge, UK: Cambridge University Press.

vicomte de Chateaubriand, F. R. (2010). *Réflexions politiques sur quelques écrits du jour sur les intérêts de tous les Français*. Charleston, SC: BiblioBazaar. (Exact reproduction of the 1814 edition: Paris: Le Normant).

Vinen, R. (2002). *Bourgeois politics in France: 1945–1951*. Cambridge, UK: Cambridge University Press.

Vinen, R. (2007). 'More than its Fair Share of History': Europe and its recent past. In M. Demossier (Ed.), *The European puzzle: The political structuring of cultural identities at a time of transition* (pp. 29–48). Oxford: Berghahn Books.

Voltaire (2009). Dictionnaire Philosophique. In T. Besterman (Ed.), *The complete works of Voltaire* (Vol. 40). Geneva: Institut et Musée Voltaire.

Watson, D. R. (2009). *Georges Clemenceau: France*. London: Haus Publishing Ltd.

Wawro, G. (2003). *The Franco-Prussian war: The German conquest of France in 1870–1871*. Cambridge, UK: Cambridge University Press.

Weber, E. (1966). France. In H. Rogger & E. Weber (Eds.), *The European right: A historical profile* (pp. 71–127). Berkeley, CA: University of California Press.

Werth, A. (1957). *Lost statesman: The strange history of Pierre Mendès France and the great conflict over French North Africa*. London: Barrie.

Wetzel, D. (2001). *A duel of giants: Bismarck, Napoleon III, and the origins of the Franco-Prussian War*. Madison, WI: University of Wisconsin Press.
Woloch, I. (2001). The Napoleonic Regime and French society. In P. G. Dwyer (Ed.), *Napoleon and Europe* (pp. 60–78). Harlow: Pearson Education Limited.
Woodward, E. L. (1963). *War and peace in Europe: 1815/1870, and other essays*. London: Thomas Nelson.
Woolf, S. J. (1992). The construction of a European world-view in the Revolutionary-Napoleonic period. *Past and Present, 137*(1), 72–101.
Woolf, S. J. (2003). *Napoleon's integration of Europe*. London: Routledge.
Zeldin, T. (1963). *Émile Ollivier and the liberal Empire of Napoleon III*. Oxford: Clarendon Press.

## Further Reading

Abbott, J. S. (2006). *The life of Napoleon Bonaparte*. Teddington, UK: The Echo Library.
Agulhon, M. (2002). *1848 ou l'apprentissage de la République: 1848–1852*. Paris: Seuil.
Andress, D. (2012). *The savage storm: Britain on the brink in the age of Napoleon*. London: Little, Brown.
Alexander, R. S. (2002). *Bonapartism and revolutionary tradition in France: The Fédérés of 1815*. Cambridge, UK: Cambridge University Press.
Aron, R. (2004). *De Gaulle, Israel and the Jews*. New Brunswick, NJ: Transaction Publishers.
Asprey, R. (2002). *The reign of Napoleon Bonaparte*. New York: Basic Books.
Aston, N. (1988). Orleanism, 1780–1830. *History Today, 38*(10), 41–47.
Bayly, C. A. (1998). The first age of global imperialism, c. 1760–1830. *The Journal of Imperial and Commonwealth History, 26*(2), 28–47.
Begley, L. (2009). *Why the Dreyfus affair matters*. New Haven, CT: Yale University Press.
Beik, P. (1965). *Louis Philippe and the July monarchy*. New York: Van Nostrand.
Bernard, P., & Dubief, H. (1988). *The decline of the Third Republic, 1914–1938*. Cambridge, UK: Cambridge University Press.
Black, J. (2009). *The war of 1812 in the age of Napoleon*. Norman, OK: University of Oklahoma Press.
Boudon, J.-O. (2002). *Les élites religieuses à l'époque de Napoléon: Dictionnaire des évêques et vicaires généraux du Premier Empire*. Paris: Nouveau Monde.
Broers, M. G. (2012). The Napoleonic regimes. In W. Doyle (Ed.), *The Oxford handbook of the Ancien Régime* (pp. 489–505). Oxford: Oxford University Press.
Broers, M., et al. (Eds.). (2012). *The Napoleonic Empire and the New European political culture: (Wars, culture and society, 1750–1850)*. New York: Palgrave Macmillan.
Brogan, D. W. (1966). *The development of modern France: (1870–1939)*. London: Hamish Hamilton.
Burrin, P. (1998). *France under the Germans: Collaboration and compromise*. New York: W. W. Norton.
Bury, J. P. T. (2003). *France: 1814–1940* (6th ed.). London: Routledge.
Cahm, E. (1996). *The Dreyfus affair in French society and politics*. London: Longman.
Chandler, D. G. (2002). *Napoleon*. Barnsley, UK: Pen and Sword.
Chandler, D. G. (2002). *The campaigns of Napoleon: The mind and method of history's greatest soldier*. London/New York: Folio Society/Scribner.
Charpentier, J. (1935). *Napoléon et les hommes de lettres de son temps*. Paris: Mercure de France.
Chevallier, J.-J. (2009). *Histoire des institutions et des régimes politiques de la France de 1789 à 1958*. Paris: Dalloz.
Clemenceau, G. (1929). *In the evening of my thought*. New York: Houghton Mifflin.

Collingham, H. A. C. (1988). *The July monarchy: A political history of France, 1830–1848*. London: Longman.
Comte de Las Cases, E. A. D. (1823). *Mémorial de Sainte Hélène: Journal of the private life and conversations of the Emperor Napoleon at Saint Helena* (Vol. 4). Lexington, KY: Printed by T. Smith.
Coutant, A. (2011). De la valeur d'un texte introductif: la Constitution française de 1848 et son Préambule. *Revue Française de Droit Constitutionnel, 88*(4), 681–707.
Crawley, A. (1969). *De Gaulle*. London: The Literary Guild.
Crozier, B. (1990). *De Gaulle: The first complete biography*. London: Collins.
de Balzac, H. (Ed.). (2011). *Napoléon (suivi de Maximes et pensées de Napoléon)*. Paris: Ed. Payot et Rivages.
De Gaulle, C. (2000). *Mémoires*. Paris: Gallimard.
De la Motte, J., & Przyblyski, J. M. (1999). *Making the new: Modernity & the mass press in nineteenth-century France*. Amherst, MA: University of Massachusetts Press.
de Stoeckl, A. (1957). *King of the French: A portrait of Louis Philippe, 1773–1850*. New York: G.P. Putnam & Sons.
Dippel, H. (Ed.). (2010). *Constitutions of the world from the late 18th century to the middle of the 19th century: sources on the rise of modern constitutionalism*. Europe, Berlin: Walter de Gruyter.
Dreyfus, A. (2013). *Five years of my life: 1894–1899. The diary of Captain Alfred Dreyfus*. Stockbridge, MA: Hardpress Ltd.
Durant, W., & Durant, A. (1992). *The age of Napoleon: A history of European civilization from 1789 to 1815*. Norwalk, CT: Easton Press.
Dwyer, P. (2013). *Citizen Emperor: Napoleon in power*. New Haven, CT: Yale University Press.
Dwyer, P. G. (Ed.). (2001). *Napoleon and Europe*. Harlow, UK: Pearson Education Limited.
Edwards, S. (1971). *The Paris commune, 1871*. London: Eyre & Spottiswoode.
Ellis, G. (1991). *The Napoleonic Empire*. London: Macmillan Press.
Fauvet, J. (1971). *La IVème République*. Paris: Fayard.
Ferguson, N. (2007). *The war of the world: Twentieth-century conflict and the descent of the west*. London: Penguin.
Fiebeger, G. J. (2010). *The campaigns of Napoleon Bonaparte of 1796–1797 Against Austria and Sardinia in Italy*. East Yorkshire, UK: Leonaur Ltd.
Fisher, T., & Fremont-Barnes, G. (2004). *The Napoleonic wars: The rise and fall of an empire*. Oxford: Osprey Publishing Ltd.
France (1876). *Constitution de la IIIe République. Lois constitutionnelles de 1875*. Paris: Imprimerie et librairie du Journal Officiel.
France (1876). *Recueil des lois constitutionnelles et organiques votées par l'Assemblée Nationale*. Paris: Sagnier.
Friedrich, C. J. (1967). *The impact of American constitutionalism abroad*. Boston, MA: Boston University Press.
Gildea, R. (1996). *France since 1945*. Oxford: Oxford University Press.
Giraud, H-C. (2004). *Réplique a l'Amiral de Gaulle*. Paris: Editions du Rocher.
Gunn, J. A. W. (2009). *When the French tried to be British: Party, opposition and the quest for civil disagreement. 1814–1848*. Kingston, Ontario: McGill-Queen's University Press.
Halls, W. D. (1995). *Politics, society and Christianity in Vichy France*. Oxford: Berg.
Hewlett, N. (1998). *Modern French politics: Analyzing conflict and consensus since 1945*. Cambridge: Polity Press.
Howarth, T. E. B. (1975). *Citizen-king: The life of Louis Philippe, King of the French*. London: White Lion Publisher.
Hutton, P. H. (Ed.). (1986). *Historical dictionary of the Third French Republic, 1870–1940*. New York: Greenwood Press.
Isenberg, I. (1967). *France under De Gaulle*. New York: H. W. Wilson.
Jackson, J. (2003). *France: The dark years, 1940–1944*. Oxford: Oxford University Press.

Johnson, P. (2002). *Napoleon: A life*. New York: Viking.

Julliard, J. (1981). *La IVe République*. Paris: Le Livre de Poche.

Kedward, H. R. (1985). *Occupied France: Collaboration and resistance*. Oxford: Blackwell.

Kedward, H. R. (2005). *La vie en bleu: France and the French since 1900*. London: Allen Lane.

Kooreman, M. (1999). *The expectation of Justice: France, 1944–1946*. Durham, NC: Duke University Press.

Laniol, V., et al. (Eds.). (2014). *Deux passions françaises. Pierre Mendès France et Charles de Gaulle*. Paris: CNRS.

Larkin, M. (1997). *France since the popular front: Government and people 1936–1996*. Oxford: Clarendon Press.

Ledwidge, B. (1982). *De Gaulle*. London: Weidenfeld and Nicolson.

Lissagaray, P. O. (2007). *History of the Paris commune of 1871*. St. Petersburg, Florida: Red and Black Publishers.

Lyons, M. (1994). *Napoleon Bonaparte and the Legacy of the French Revolution*. Basingstoke, UK/New York: Macmillan/St. Martin's Press.

Lyons, M. (2000). Napoleon and the revolutionary potential of Bonapartism. *Modern & Contemporary France, 8*(4), 507–10.

Madsen, M. R., & Thornhill, C. (Eds.). (2014). *Law and the formation of modern Europe: Perspectives from the historical sociology of law*. Cambridge, UK: Cambridge University Press.

Magraw, R. (1983). *France 1815–1914: The Bourgeois century*. Oxford: Fontana.

Magraw, R. (1992). *A history of the French working class* (2 Vols.). Oxford: Blackwell.

Magraw, R. (2002). *France, 1800–1915. A social history*. Basingstoke, London: Longman.

Mangold, P. (2006). *The almost impossible ally: Harold Macmillan and Charles de Gaulle*. London: I. B. Tauris.

Mayeur, J.-M., & Rebirioux, M. (1988). *The third republic from its origins to the great war, 1871–1915*. Cambridge, UK: Cambridge University Press.

McLynn, F. (1997). *Napoleon: A biography*. New York: Arcade Publishing Inc.

McMillan, J. F. (1992). *Twentieth-century France: Politics and society 1898–1991*. London: E. Arnold.

Napoleon I, Emperor of the French (2008). *Aphorisms and thoughts*. Richmond, UK: Oneworld Classics.

Napoleon I. Emperor of the French. (2009). *Napoléon par Napoléon: Pensées, maximes et citations*. Paris: Le Cherche Midi.

Nord, P. (2010). *France's new deal: From the thirties to the postwar era*. Princeton, NJ: Princeton University Press.

Nuenlist, C., et al. (Eds.). (2010). *Globalizing de Gaulle: International perspectives on French foreign policies, 1958–1969*. Lanham, MD: Lexington Books.

Paul, R. P. (2012). *The scandal that tore France in two: The Dreyfus affair*. New York: Bloomsbury Press.

Paxton, R. O. (2001). *Vichy France: Old guard and new order, 1940–1944*. New York: Columbia University Press.

Petrey, S. (2005). *In the court of the Pear king: French culture and the rise of realism*. Ithaca, N.Y.: Cornell University Press.

Pilbeam, P. (1989). The economic crisis of 1827–1832 and the 1830 Revolution in provincial France. *The Historical Journal, 32*(2), 319–338.

Pinkney, D. H. (1961). A new look at the French Revolution of 1830. *Review of Politics, 23*(4), 490–506.

Popkin, J. D. (2002). *Press, revolution, and social identities in France: 1830–1835*. University Park, PA: Pennsylvania State University Press.

Rader, D. L. (1973). *The journalists and the July revolution in France: The role of the political press in the overthrow of the Bourbon restoration 1827–1830*. The Hague: Martinus Nijhoff.

Raymond, G. (2008). *Historical dictionary of France* (2nd ed.). Lanham, MD: Scarecrow Press.

Reyn, S. (2010). *Atlantis lost: The American experience with De Gaulle, 1958–1969*. Amsterdam: Amsterdam University Press.
Rioux, J. P. (1982). *La France de la Quatrième République* (2 Vols.). Paris: Seuil.
Robert, T. (1999). *The Paris commune: 1871*. London: Longman.
Rudé, G. (2000). *Revolutionary Europe, 1783–1815* (2nd ed.). Oxford: Blackwell.
Sebbane, J. (2009). *Pierre Mendès France et la question du Proche-Orient: 1940–1982*. Paris: L'Harmattan.
Shafer, D. A. (2005). *The Paris commune*. London: Palgrave.
Schom, A. (1997). *Napoleon Bonaparte*. New York: Harper Collins.
Schroeder, P. W. (1996). *The transformation of European politics: 1763–1848*. Oxford: Oxford University Press.
Stovall, T. (2002). *France since the second world war*. Harlow, UK: Longman.
Tombs, R. (1996). *France: 1814–1915*. London: Longman.
Trinkle, D. A. (2002). *The Napoleonic press: The public sphere and oppositionary journalism*. Lewiston, NY: E. Mellen Press.
von Beyme, K. (1987). *America as a model: The impact of American democracy in the world*. New York: St. Martin's Press.
Werth, A. (1967). *De Gaulle: A political biography*. Harmondsworth, UK: Penguin.
Williams, C. (2005). *Pétain*. London: Little Brown.
Winock, M. (1995). *La Fièvre hexagonale: Les grandes crises politiques de 1871 à 1968*. Paris: Seuil.
Woloch, I. (2002). *Napoleon and his collaborators: The making of a dictatorship*. New York: W. W. Norton.
Woolf, S. J. (1991). *Napoleon's integration of Europe*. London: Routledge.
Zeldin, T. (1958). *The political system of Napoleon III*. New York: Saint Martin's Press.
Zola, E. (1998). *The Dreyfus affair: "J'accuse" and other writings*. New Haven, CT: Yale University Press.

# Chapter 16
# The Golden Era of Liberalism and the Apogee of the Nation-State

For me the word "freedom" has not the value of a starting-point, but rather that of an actual point of arrival. The word "order" denotes the starting-point. Only on the concept of order can that of freedom rest. Without the foundation of order, the call for freedom is nothing more than the striving of some party after an envisaged end. In its actual use, the call inevitably expresses itself as tyranny. Whilst I have at all times and in all situations ever been a man of order, my striving was addressed to true and not deceptive freedom. In my eyes, tyranny of any kind has only the value of absolute nonsense. As a means to an end, I mark it as the most vapid that time and circumstance is able to place at the disposal of rulers.[1]—Clemens Wenzell von Metternich (1773–1859)

Gentlemen, one must not fall prey to anachronism; it is the most dangerous thing, when it comes to governing. There was a time, without any doubt glorious, in which the conquest of social and political rights was the nation's prevailing concern. That was achieved and now there are others to achieve. You wish to continue advancing, to achieve things that your parents did not. You're right. Set aside for the moment the winning of political rights. Now it is time to exercise them. Establish your government, consolidate your institutions, educate yourselves, prosper, improve the moral and material condition of France.[2]—François Guizot (1787–1874)

---

[1] Taken from "My Political Testament", a handwritten and dateless manuscript by Metternich, in separate compositions on loose sheets, drafted from 1849 to 1855. Metternich's collected works were published by his son, Richard Clemens Lothar, Fürst von Metternich-Winneburg (1829–1895). See Metternich (1883, 636–637).

[2] Messieurs, il ne faut pas faire d'anachronisme; ce qu'il y a de plus dangereux en fait de gouvernement, ce sont les anachronismes. Il y a eu un temps, temps glorieux parmi tous, où la conquête des droits sociaux et politiques a été la grande affaire de la nation. Cette affaire-là est faite, la conquête est accomplie; passons à d'autres. Vous voulez avancer à votre tour, vous voulez faire des choses que n'aient pas faites vos pères. Vous avez raison; ne poursuivez donc plus, pour le moment, la conquête des droits politiques À présent, usez de ces droits: Fondez votre gouvernement, affermissez vos institutions, éclairez-vous, enrichissez-vous, améliorez la condition morale et matérielle de notre France.... Guizot (1864, IV, 68).



B. Aguilera-Barchet, *A History of Western Public Law*,
DOI 10.1007/978-3-319-11803-1_16

The greatest concern of a good government should be to gradually accustom its citizens to do without it.[3]—Alexis de Tocqueville (1805–1859)

The indirect powers… seized the legislative arm of parliament and the law state and thought they had placed the Leviathan in a harness. Their ascendancy was facilitated by a constitutional system that enshrined a catalogue of individual rights. The "private" sphere was, thus, withdrawn from the state and handed over to the "free", that is, uncontrolled and invisible forces of society.[4]—Carl Schmitt (1888–1985)

By 'nationalism' I mean, first of all, the habit of assuming that human beings can be classified like insects and that whole blocks of millions or tens of millions of people can be confidently labeled 'good' or 'bad.' But secondly - and this is much more important -- I mean the habit of identifying oneself with a single nation or other unit, placing it beyond good and evil and recognizing no other duty than that of advancing its interests. Nationalism is not to be confused with patriotism. Both words are normally used in so vague a way that any definition is liable to be challenged, but one must draw a distinction between them, since two different and even opposing ideas are involved. By 'patriotism' I mean devotion to a particular place and a particular way of life, which one believes to be the best in the world but has no wish to force on other people. Patriotism is of its nature defensive, both militarily and culturally. Nationalism, on the other hand, is inseparable from the desire for power. The abiding purpose of every nationalist is to secure more power and more prestige, not for himself but for the nation or other unit in which he has chosen to sink his own individuality…[5]—George Orwell (1903–1950)

## Contents

16.1 From Absolutism to Liberalism .... 491
16.2 The Europe of the Restoration (1815–1848) .... 493
16.2.1 The Congress of Vienna .... 493
16.2.2 The Holy Alliance or the Return of Divine Legitimacy .... 494
16.2.3 Metternich and the Counterrevolutionary Principle of Legitimate Intervention .... 495
16.2.4 An Exception to the Principle of Nation-State Confrontation: The Metternich System as a Forerunner of European Integration .... 495
16.2.5 The Impossibility of Restoring Absolutism .... 496
16.3 The Liberal Alternative: A State with Limited Powers and Controlled by an Economic Elite .... 497
16.3.1 Legal Limits on State Power: Constitutions and Fundamental Rights .... 497
16.3.2 The Politicization of the Term "Nation" .... 499
16.3.3 From Absolute Monarchy to Liberal Oligarchy: The Era of Censitary Suffrage .... 500
16.4 The Liberal Revolution .... 502
16.4.1 Moderate Liberalism .... 503
16.4.2 "Revolutionary Liberalism" .... 504
16.4.3 Spain, Spearheading the Liberal Revolution: Riego's Revolt (1820) .... 505
16.4.4 France Comes to Lead the Liberal Revolution (1830) .... 509
16.5 The Revolution of 1848 as the Key to the Spread of the Liberal State in Europe .... 511

[3] Le plus grand soin d'un bon gouvernement devrait être d'habituer peu à peu les peuples à se passer de lui. (de Tocqueville 1991, I, 66).

[4] Schmitt (2008, 73).

[5] Orwell (2007, III, 361).

16.5.1 Another Italian Liberal Revolution .......... 512
16.5.2 The Revolution of 1848 in the German Territories .......... 513
16.5.3 The Austrian Empire and the Revolution .......... 515
16.5.4 Prussia vs. Austria: The Fight for German Supremacy .......... 516
16.5.5 Prussia Becomes a Constitutional Kingdom .......... 518
16.5.6 Relative Calm in Europe by 1850 .......... 519
16.6 The Unification of Italy .......... 519
16.6.1 *Il Risorgimento* .......... 520
16.6.2 French Support for the Italian Cause .......... 521
16.6.3 A Democratic Integration .......... 521
16.6.4 Garibaldi and the Annexation of the South .......... 521
16.6.5 The Kingdom of Italy Is Founded (March 14, 1861) .......... 522
16.6.6 The "Roman Question" .......... 522
16.7 German Unification .......... 523
16.7.1 Bismarck, Architect of Prussian Hegemony .......... 524
16.7.2 The Defeat of Austria and the North German Confederation .......... 524
16.7.3 The Franco-Prussian War and the Second Reich .......... 525
16.7.4 A Top Down Integration in a Federal and Laic State .......... 526
16.8 Imperial Russia as a Final Bastion of Autocracy .......... 527
16.8.1 From Enlightened Absolutism to the Consolidation of Autocracy .......... 527
16.8.2 Speransky and the First Attempt to Establish the Principle of the Rule of Law in Imperial Russia .......... 528
16.8.3 The Revolution of 1905 and the First Russian Constitution (1906) .......... 529
16.9 Colonialism and Confrontation: The International Consequences of the Triumph of the Nation-State Model .......... 530
16.9.1 The Golden Age of Colonialism .......... 530
16.9.2 Nationalism and Confrontation: The Europe of the "Armed Peace" .......... 531
16.10 World War I and the Crisis of the Liberal State Model .......... 533
16.10.1 The Implosion of the Nation-State System .......... 533
16.10.2 The Assassination in Sarajevo and Europe's Suicide .......... 533
16.10.3 The Dominos Fall .......... 535
16.10.4 An Apocalyptic Conflict .......... 535
16.10.5 The Constitutional Consequences of World War I: The End of Liberalism and the Resurgence of State Power .......... 536
References .......... 541

## 16.1 From Absolutism to Liberalism

Under absolute monarchy, the state became the great protagonist of western constitutional history, as the uncontested power of the king proved extremely effective at consolidating a set of very powerful states in Europe. First, by establishing a solid order during the period of Classic Absolutism, and completely transforming this order through the reforms of Enlightened Absolutism.

Absolute control of the state by the king, however, crumbled in the wake of the American and French Revolutions, replaced by the ascendant power of assemblies aspiring to control the state in the name of the people. This system, however, proved ineffectual when not furnished with a strong executive power. Hence, a system with dominant assemblies gave way in the United States to a presidential regime featuring a strong executive, while in France power was concentrated in the hands of Napoleon, who effectively ruled as a monarch, and ultimately a presidential republic was established.

Following the collapse of the Napoleonic Empire, absolute monarchy was restored in the rest of Europe during the first half of the nineteenth century, though with some exceptions. In the UK, the model of a monarchy with a powerful Parliamentary counterbalance (parliamentary system) was clearly consolidated after the British defeat in the American War of Independence and the insanity of George III, the last British king who sought to wield uncontested monarchical power. In the rest of Europe, the constitutional model according to which the state was controlled by the assembly on behalf of the nation became an alternative to the restoration of absolute monarchy, and was a formula pursued by successive liberal revolutions in 1820, 1830 and, finally, 1848. In reality, the new ruling parliamentary assemblies did not represent the common people of these nations, but rather their ruling classes: the English "gentry" or its equivalent in the different European nation-states. These oligarchies ultimately ended up controlling the state through censitary suffrage, which granted political rights exclusively to property owners, industrialists, bankers and businessmen. State policy henceforth centered on promoting and amassing national wealth by favoring the interests and aims of the economic elite, who were spared aggressive intervention by the public authorities; this was the essence of the "liberal model".

This liberal regime was, in any case, extremely effective and the different European nation-states became extremely wealthy through expansive colonial policies, with the result that almost the whole world was controlled by the European nation-states by 1900. Besides the fact that this model generated pronounced and dreadful social differences—an issue that we will address in the next chapter—the major drawback and danger inherent to this model was that the nation-states were engaged in a state of perpetual competition as they struggled to impose their hegemony on their rivals. The trend which had produced a series of wars, dating back to 1648, was taken to new levels by France in its revolutionary wars, during which mass conscription dramatically increased the number of soldiers fighting for the nation, and ultimately left huge numbers of dead soldiers, from nations all across Europe, on the battlefields of the Napoleonic wars. After Napoleon's defeat and the reorganization of Europe through the Congress of Vienna, the nation-states struggled to forge and maintain a *status quo* through the Metternich System, which endured until being strained by the revolutions of 1848. The struggle for hegemony flared up again and reached a new peak when Prussia's Bismarck successively defeated Austria and France. The rise of Prussia as a world power triggered the growing tensions of the "armed peace", which prompted the formation of a series of defensive alliances between European nation-states. This network would constitute a tinderbox that exploded in the form of World War I, which marked the demise of the liberal model of the state and spawned a profound crisis in western history.

## 16.2 The Europe of the Restoration (1815–1848)

Napoleon's defeat at Waterloo (June 18, 1815) marked the dawn of a period during which the European monarchies did all they could to restore absolutism, that is, the order which had prevailed prior to the outbreak of the French Revolution, thereby giving rise to what is known as the "Restoration". To achieve this aim, the powers which had vanquished Napoleon convened a general congress in Vienna which, in addition to politically reorganizing Europe, established a concerted system of armed interventions designed to abort any revolutionary outbreak endangering the restoration of the traditional order (Zamoyski 2007).

### *16.2.1 The Congress of Vienna*

The representatives of the states that had won the war over Napoleon: the United Kingdom, Austria, Prussia and Russia (later joined by France under Louis XVIII, represented by the very adept Talleyrand),[6] hosted by Austrian Chancellor Clemens von Metternich, convened in Vienna, for almost 7 months to reorganize Europe's political order, which since 1792 had seen important transformations introduced by French imperialism, first revolutionary and later Napoleonic.

Although the term "congress" was used to designate these meetings, as in the United States of America, in Europe its meaning was substantially different, where the states were represented by sovereigns rather than delegates elected by the citizens.[7]

The outcome of the lengthy Congress of Vienna (November 1814–June 1815), was that the representatives of the victorious powers, the "Big Four" (King 2008, 44–52), restructured Europe, redefining borders and restoring to the throne most of the absolute monarchs who had been toppled by Napoleon, in what was called Metternich's Europe (Walker 1968). Still pending was the implementation of the mechanisms necessary to prevent new "revolutionary" outbreaks which could upset the reinstated order.

---

[6] Thanks to the support of the British delegate, Castlereagh, and of Metternich himself, Talleyrand played an essential role at the Congress, to the point that, thanks to him, defeated France became one of the leading European powers. In contrast stood Spain, a state that had played an important part in the victory over Napoleon, yet was not recognized as a major European power, in large part because it was represented by a feckless delegate: Pedro Gomez Labrador, considered "the most tiresome of all the plenipotentiaries" (Nicolson 2000, 132 and 146). The consequence was that at this decisive gathering Spain lost a historic opportunity to maintain its role as an important European power.

[7] On the origins of the European Congress system, see Hinsley (2004, 153–185).

### *16.2.2 The Holy Alliance or the Return of Divine Legitimacy*

The first step in this direction was taken by establishing the "Holy Alliance" (Jarrett 2013, 173–177), an initiative of Tsar Alexander I Russia, who considered himself Europe's savior since his victory over Napoleon in 1812. Beyond its mystical aspects, the Holy Alliance represented an attempt to rescue and affirm the legitimacy of the *Ancien Régime* and to eradicate the principles upon which the bourgeois revolution was based: that it is the citizens rather than the monarch who constitute a "nation", it falls upon the people to create the constitutional framework governing the actions of the state, and that it is the nation which should govern, through its duly elected representatives. This constitutional model, termed the "nation-state", clashed head-on with the traditional model of absolute monarchy. Thus, it was necessary to consolidate what had been agreed to in Vienna with a new ideology justifying a political system in which sovereignty, that is, the power of the state, was wrested from the nation and placed back in the hands of sovereigns.

On September 14, 1815, 3 months after the close of the Congress of Vienna, the Tsar of Russia, the King of Prussia and the Emperor of Austria joined in a "Holy Alliance". This unique pact was based, as its name suggests, on the Christian religion professed by the three monarchs. In this way, it marked a resurfacing of the age-old principle that the established order had been determined by God, and that men could not alter it without endangering peace and justice:

> In the name of the Most Holy and Indivisible Trinity: Their Majesties the Emperor of Austria, the King of Prussia, and the Emperor of Russia, having, in consequence of the great events which have marked the course of the three last years in Europe, and especially of the blessings which it has pleased Divine Providence to shower down upon those States which place their confidence and their hope on it alone, acquired the intimate conviction of the necessity of settling the rules to be observed by the Powers, in their reciprocal relations, upon the sublime truths which the Holy Religion of our Saviour teaches. They solemnly declare that the present Act has no other object than to publish, in the face of the whole world, their fixed resolution, both in the administration of their respective States and in their political relations with every other Government, to take for their sole guide the precepts of that Holy Religion, namely, the precepts of justice, Christian Charity, and Peace, which, far from being applicable only to private concerns, must have an immediate influence on the councils of princes, and guide all their steps, as being the only means of consolidating human institutions and remedying their imperfections.

To maintain this divine order, the signees agreed to provide each other aid and mutual support in the event anyone should attempt to alter it. The tone of the first article of the Holy Alliance is quite indicative of the spirit infusing the agreement:

> Conformably to the words of the Holy Scriptures, which command all men to consider each other as brethren, the three contracting Monarchs will remain united by the bonds of a true and indissoluble fraternity, and, considering each other as fellow-countrymen, they will, on all occasions and in all places, lend each other aid and assistance; and, regarding themselves towards their subjects and armies as fathers of families, they will lead them, in the same spirit of fraternity with which they are animated, to protect Religion, Peace, and justice.[8]

[8] From the Holy Alliance Treaty, September 26, 1816. Text excerpted from Aspinall et al. (2000, 949–950).

### 16.2.3 Metternich and the Counterrevolutionary Principle of Legitimate Intervention

Ironically, it was the pragmatic Metternich, the promoter of the Congress of Vienna, initially harboring a cynical disdain for the Holy Alliance (Ingle 1976, 14), who ultimately managed to most fully exploit its possibilities. Months after its establishment he realized the great utility of legitimizing the principle that the signatory powers could intervene to abort any revolutionary outbreaks. It was thus agreed that if a state broke Europe's established order, morally or materially, it was the duty and the right of other rulers to reestablish the stability which had been disturbed. Thus, this provision set the stage for concerted efforts by the powers to maintain the Old Regime.

### 16.2.4 An Exception to the Principle of Nation-State Confrontation: The Metternich System as a Forerunner of European Integration

At Metternich's initiative, on November 20, 1815 the four victorious powers which had defeated Napoleon—England, Austria, Russia and Prussia—signed a Grand Alliance in France to maintain a "protectorate" over the country which would legitimize the occupation of French territory (Jarrett 2013, 183–186). In response to a proposal by the British Foreign Secretary, Lord Castlereagh, a clause (the sixth) was introduced in the pact according to which the signing powers pledged to meet regularly to discuss issues of common interest and to ensure the preservation of order and peace (Bew 2012, 409–418).

The Quadruple Alliance was forged to prevent any revolutionary movement from surfacing in France. Thus, when the monarchy under Louis XVIII seemed to be well established, the allies, meeting in Aachen in 1818, agreed to withdraw their troops from France, which was admitted into the Alliance. In an additional secret protocol Metternich succeeded in adding to the principle of legitimate intervention to prevent revolutionary disorders a call for regular "congresses" by which the powers were to examine the situation in Europe and make decisions, depending upon circumstances, regarding the adoption of appropriate measures to address them (Schroeder 1992, 683–706). The fear of revolution was the guiding principle of all monarchies after 1815 and not only of the Austria of Metternich (Sked 2008).

In the years that followed Napoleon's fall, through 1823, the European powers acted jointly and in concert, though not to maintain a common economic policy, but to preserve the order established at the Congress of Vienna (Sked 1979, 98–121),[9]

[9] Sofka (1998, 133) defines the Metternich System as a Hobbesian universe of relations in which each state aggressively pursued its own interests, with little regard for others beyond simple prudence. Ideally its system of "counterweights" would work best if relative parity was achieved. About Metternich's theory of European Order see Sofka (2011a, b, 33–80).

an action they had been forced to take to counter liberals from all over Europe anxious to promote the nation-state; this came to be called the "Metternich System", which can be considered a kind of early attempt at European integration (Alison 2013).[10]

### 16.2.5 The Impossibility of Restoring Absolutism

The French Revolution and its Napoleonic aftermath ultimately failed to transform Europe, as after 1815 the entire Continent, save for England, reverted to absolute monarchy. Nevertheless, this reestablishment of the Old Order was, in reality, not as absolute as it might seem at first. In France, Louis XVIII laid down the foundations for a parliamentary regime with the 1814 *Charte*. Although this was a unilateral concession, it is certainly telling that this astute monarch realized that a return to the outright, unrestrained monarchy of the era preceding the events of 1789 was simply not viable, as the privileged classes of the *Ancien Régime*, the nobility and clergy, had been supplanted by the ascendant bourgeoisie of businessmen and bankers. Since the Thermidorian Reaction, the most eminent members of the former "Third Estate" had become (from 1794) the dominant social power in France.

Thus, Louis XVIII accepted that, following the model already firmly established in the United Kingdom, monarchies in the post-Napoleonic era were destined to function more as arbiters and intercessors, leaving political action in the hands of representative assemblies (parliaments). By no means was power to be given to the masses, as democracy based on universal suffrage was still unthinkable at this point. However, through censitary and indirect suffrage, the high bourgeoisie was able to monopolize representation of the "nation" in parliaments, thereby controlling states.

This said, the liberal bourgeoisie faced a tough task, having to tenaciously fight to impose its new model of the state, with waves of revolutionary struggle in 1820, 1830, and, above all, 1848, to spread the new order in countries with traditional monarchies, such as France and Spain, and in the new states spawned by the liberal revolution in Belgium, Italy and Prussia. The result was that, one by one, all the European states adopted constitutions and representative assemblies. Even tsarist Russia implemented a parliamentary system following the Revolution of 1905.

The consequence was that over the course of the nineteenth century, a new model of state came to prevail throughout the Continent in which power was clearly delimitated by written constitutions generally guaranteeing citizens' fundamental rights and liberties—hence the term which came to describe these regimes: *liberal*. In them, government institutions' scopes of power and authority were to be defined

[10] On the transformation of the European balance of power as a result of the Vienna Congress, see Schneid (2011) and Schroeder (1996).

and limited, while the nation, through its elected representatives, set the course of public policy.[11]

## 16.3 The Liberal Alternative: A State with Limited Powers and Controlled by an Economic Elite

The social classes wielding political power during the revolutionary period were unwilling to accept any return to the situation which had prevailed under the *Ancien Régime*. Despite the efforts being made by leaders to restore the traditional order of the absolute monarchy, economic power in the western states no longer rested in the hands of the old aristocratic and privileged classes, who had been superseded as the ruling classes by a new bourgeois financial and industrial oligarchy. This new elite would not settle for just economic hegemony, but would also strive to obtain political power to secure governments serving their interests. Hence, they endeavored to exclude the lower classes from the political arena (Wallerstein 2011, 24),[12] and did their utmost to prevent the restoration of monarchical authority and to impose a new regime in which the liberty of individuals (understood as the powerful individuals now atop the social pyramid), would be spared from state interference and control.

### *16.3.1 Legal Limits on State Power: Constitutions and Fundamental Rights*

The instigators of the political revolutions of the nineteenth century (1820, 1830, 1848), sought to limit monarchical power, at the very least by placing legal or customary checks upon it. The restraint of power through the application of legal mechanisms was nothing new. As we have seen, in the Middle Ages there arose texts curbing the king's power, such as England's *Magna Carta* in 1215, or the *privilegios* of the kingdoms under the Crown of Aragon. We have also seen how even during the apogee of absolute monarchy, kings were bound to respect

[11] This is what Vanberg (2001, 42) calls *Ordo-liberalism*, opposed to the *laissez-faire liberalism*, as the defenders of the latter did not appreciate the essential and positive role that government has to play in creating and maintaining an appropriate framework of rules and institutions that allow market competition to flourish, and did not realize that an orderly free market is also a cultural phenomenon dependent upon constitutional order, requiring careful "cultivation" for its maintenance and proper functioning.

[12] For an overall examination of this process, see Simpson (1996).

unwritten rules such as "fundamental laws". Under the *Ancien Régime* power was restrained, to varying degrees, by law through fundamental, unwritten rules, which in some instances continue to form today the basis of constitutional order, as is still the case in the United Kingdom.

Legal restrictions on power, however, took on a new dimension after the American and French revolutions, as they advanced the idea rooted in Natural Law of a social contract between government and the people that legitimized state power, a principle reflected in the adoption and ratification of written constitutions (King 2013, 75–77). The drafting of these foundational documents was the result of processes expressly undertaken to this end, with France drawing up documents in 1791, 1793, 1795, 1830, 1848 and 1875; the United States in 1787; and Spain in 1808 (Statute of Bayonne), 1812, 1837, 1845, 1869 and 1876.

There were also cases in which constitutions were granted by the state whereby monarchs accepted and placed limitations on their own power. Such was the dynamic when France's Louis XVIII issued a *charte* in 1814,[13] Regent María Cristina of Spain signed a Royal Statute in 1834 (Villarroya 1985, 11–15), Frederick William IV endorsed a Prussian Constitution in 1850,[14] and Tsar Nicholas II, the Russian constitution of 1906.[15]

In addition to these two constitutional patterns there was the Napoleonic model of a constitution drafted by the executive power and submitted to a plebiscite (as in the case of the French constitutions of 1799, 1802 and 1804)[16]

Aside from the limits set down by the constitution, in some states there appeared formal declarations of fundamental rights drafted and promulgated so that those in

[13] As Price (2007, 61) points out, Louis XVIII wished for the Charter to appear to be a fundamental law of the kingdom, when in reality it was issued by royal authority. It was approved through the two chambers' tacit acceptance, as they endorsed it without any discussion, preliminary vote, or even a subsequent vote expressing or confirming their acceptance of it.

[14] The constitution was imposed by Frederick William IV, supplanting the more democratic 1848 Prussian Constitution. The Landtag could not force the king to remove a minister, but its approval was required for all bills, including the budget presented to it by the monarch (Caldwell 1997, 17).

[15] The 1906 Fundamental Laws were the result of the 1905 Revolution, as Nicholas II sought to buy off constitutionalist opposition to deal with the revolutionaries, though he meant to water down the concession. He was able to veto legislation, dissolve the Duma, and even change the electoral system by restricting the franchise (Lee 2006, 28).

[16] Contemporary constitutional law tends to combine the constitutional process with the subsequent adoption of constitutions by referendum. Thus, for example, the current Spanish Constitution of 1978 was drafted by a body termed the *Cortes*, formed by elections held on June 15, 1977. After its approval by both chambers, on December 6, 1978 it was submitted to a referendum to receive direct legitimation by the electorate before being endorsed by the king. The Constitution of the 1931 Republic was only approved by the constitutional *Cortes*, which Manuel Azaña designated as qualified to draft the document without calling for new elections—as he feared that he would lose them and the reformist program he had undertaken would be sunk. Franco's fundamental laws were, as a general rule, drafted by the government, but then formally submitted to a referendum since 1945.

power would be compelled to respect them. Some of these texts were included in constitutions and actually represent legally binding documents, such as the 1791 U.S. Bill of Rights (the first ten amendments to the federal constitution), in which case, legal recourse may be pursued when they are violated. Others, however, even if they were meant to be universal, were not legally binding, but rather mere intellectual manifestos, such as the Declaration of the Rights of Man and of the Citizen, advanced during the French Revolution in 1789.

### *16.3.2 The Politicization of the Term "Nation"*

Another important feature of the new model of state that the liberals fought for was the idea that political power must be legitimized by the "nation".

As we have seen, some contemporary historians, prompted by nationalistic enthusiasm, maintain that the term "nation" actually dates far back in European history, at least for European nations such as France, England and Germany, which trace their names back to the Germanic peoples—or "nations"—that settled on the Continent after the fall of the Western Roman Empire. In fact it was much later, during the Middle Ages and even into the modern era, that the term "nation" was used to designate a people united by their linguistic affinity or geographic proximity. Thus, for example, the kingdom of the Franks was transformed under Philip II into the kingdom of "France", and its inhabitants came to be called "French". It was not, however, until the last third of the eighteenth century when the term acquired a manifest political meaning, in the contexts of the American and French revolutions, whose leaders, acting to form, devise and uphold the principles of their respective "nations", claimed that national sovereignty lay with the citizens, not with the monarch, as Machiavelli, and above all, Bodin had contended.

It was not until the triumph of the Romantic ideal, however, that, as a reaction to the Enlightenment, liberals defended the idea of "nationality", just as the twentieth century would spawn "nationalism".[17] Thus, peoples' right to politically and legally organize themselves in accordance with the precepts of Enlightenment revolutions was followed by the flourishing of national sentiments within European groups united by their linguistic, cultural and historic ties. This is what Smith (2009, 61) considers the forming of the "core doctrine" of ideological nationalism.[18]

[17] On the origins of "nationalism", see Perry (2008, 597–620).

[18] This "core doctrine" holds that: (1) humanity is divided into nations, each with its own character, history and destiny. (2) The nation is the sole source of political power. (3) Loyalty to the nation takes precedence over other loyalties. (4) To be free, human beings must belong to a nation. (5) Nations require maximum autonomy and self expression. (6) Global peace and justice can only be built on the basis of a plurality of free nations.

As a result of this movement, European historians began to search for the origins of their peoples' national identities, with scholars such as the brothers Grimm[19] that besides gathering and publishing traditional legends and tales encouraged the work of these early "germanists" (Ziolkowski 1992, 108). This trend impacted the legal organization of nations, thanks to the rise of the German Historical School of law, advanced by jurist Friedrich Carl von Savigny (1779–1861), who rejected the adoption of Napoleonic legal codes, arguing that jurists ought to discover and apply, through historical research, the nation's own, unique law, which was to be rooted in the spirit of the people (*Volksgeist*) (Reimann 1990, 851–858).[20] Thus did linguists, historians and jurists forerun politicians by conceiving of and envisioning a Europe of nationalities, which in some cases contributed to the formation of new states, while causing the disintegration of others, as with the Austro-Hungarian and Ottoman empires. In the late nineteenth and early twentieth centuries, regionalist sentiments intensified in Spain—principally in Catalonia and the Basque Country (Conversi 1997)—as well as in Ireland. In both cases this development led to separatist movements, successful in the latter case, an ongoing struggle in the former (Hall 1993, 1–28).

### 16.3.3 From Absolute Monarchy to Liberal Oligarchy: The Era of Censitary Suffrage

The seizure of power by the wealthy bourgeoisie was achieved by imposing representative, parliamentary-based regimes which replaced (as in the case of the French Republic) or at least restricted royal prerogative. In theory, legitimate power lay in the "nation", that is, the citizens as a whole. Though having embraced some democratic and egalitarian notions and values, it ought to be noted that most of the

---

[19] Jacob Grimm (1785–1863) and Wilhelm Grimm (1786–1859), best known today for their story collections, were linguists and lexicographers educated at the University of Marburg, who centered their efforts on recovering and amassing traditional German folklore, legends and mythology. Scholars such as the brothers Grimm, that studied under the eminent Savigny himself focused their attention in the study of the Middle-High-German language and literature, nevertheless they also received the impulse for a profounder knowledge of jurisprudence. The essay of Jacob "On the Poetry of the Law" (*Über die Poesie des Rechts*) not only show the inextricable links between poetry and law in medieval German thought, but that many of the old poetics texts revolved centrally around legal questions and that these cases could be interpreted only in the context of pre-Reception German Law. The other important work of Jacob Grimm on this field, "On the Antiquities of German Jurisprudence" (*The Deutsche Rechtsalterthümer*) dedicated to Savigny, in which he collected the legal antiquities of the Germanic past—not the laws themselves, but legal practices and beliefs—is still indispensable (Ziolkowski 2003, 7–8). Even Michelet, composed, years after, a book on the legal antiquities of his own country (*Sur les Origines du Droit français*), in which he incorporated a portion of Grimm's work translated by himself. About the life and works of the brothers, see Zipes (2002).

[20] On the pivotal figure of Savigny's Volksgeist theory, see Beiser (2011, 214–252), Gale (1982) and Kantorowicz (1937)

liberal states in nineteenth-century Europe featured constitutional systems dominated by a wealthy, liberal bourgeoisie.

In fact, these regimes only represented the affluent, as delegates were elected through a system of censitary suffrage under which citizens were required to have a certain level of income or property to vote,[21] and even higher levels to stand for office—a practice which ensured that representative assemblies were controlled by the new oligarchic ruling classes.[22] In this way, the financial and commercial bourgeoisie managed to control the state apparatus, enforcing its rules and policies.[23] This meant that the new public power restricted itself to maintaining order, leaving everything else in the hands of the new ruling class, especially economic policy.[24] It was the "liberal" principle of *laissez faire* which developed a specific

---

[21] As Keyssar (2009, 2) notes, at the beginning of its history the United States was not really a democratic nation at all, as relatively few of its inhabitants were even able to participate in elections. Only a small fraction of the American population cast ballots in the elections that made George Washington and John Adams presidents; African Americans, Native Americans, women, and even white males who did not own land were all excluded from voting. The most striking fact, from our contemporary perspective, is the fact that during the era the word "democracy" was actually pejorative, as it evoked images of disorder, government by the unfit, and even mob rule. In nineteenth century Spain, Antonio Cánovas del Castillo (1828–1897), responsible for the consolidation of the parliamentarian regime in Spain, a prime minister, and the most important conservative politician of his time, was staunchly opposed to universal suffrage, and publicly endorsed the principle of censitary suffrage in 1889. See his speech in the *Ateneo de Madrid* in November of 1889, Cánovas del Castillo (2000, I, 181–215). Previously, he had espoused the same ideas in a speech at the same institution on November 25, 1871 (Cánovas del Castillo 2000, 69–82) and even in the Spanish Parliament (*Cortes*) in another speech delivered on February 8, 1888 (Cánovas del Castillo 2006, 404–425).

[22] In some cases, suffrage was also indirect. For example, the 1812 Constitution of Cádiz provided for an electoral system in which citizens with a required income level voted for electors who, in turn, elected representatives. Of course, at each of these three levels, the censitary requirements were progressively greater. For an overview of this philosophy, common to most European parliamentary systems in the nineteenth century, see Kahan (2003).

[23] As far as The United Kingdom is concerned, the Reform Act of 1832 swelled the number of electors from 400,000 to 650,000 (Bernstein and Milza 1996, 134). This greatly undermined the aristocracy's monopoly on power, but did not destroy it, as it was the result of an alliance forged between the middle-classes and the Whig aristocracy. Nevertheless, it would not be until the Representation of the People Act of 1867 that 1,000,000 new voters were made eligible, as "respectable" artisans and other small householders, who formed the majority of the English working class, secured the vote. The rural county laborers were not enfranchised until Gladstone's Act of 1884 (Smith 1987, 456), which increased the electorate by nearly 70 %, bringing it up to more than 4,250,000 citizens (Chrimes 1970, 129). In France the 1848 Revolution and the establishment of male suffrage boosted the number of the enfranchised from 240,000 under the July Monarchy to almost 9.5 million (Huard 2002, 60).

[24] For an overview of the enlightened origins of nineteenth century economic liberalism see the classic book by Laski (2005, 139–201). As Smith (1987, 442) mentions, in England in the decades following the 1832 Reform Act, there was a shift in political control from the landed aristocratic classes to commercial and industrial ones. In 1832 land accounted for 66 % of the economic interests represented in the House of Commons, but by 1865 it accounted for only 44 %, while the portion represented by industrial and commercial interests had risen to 56 %. However, land owners and members of the industrial and commercial classes would unite and form a common front against the demands of working class movements.

constitutional model that allowed the new European nation-states to achieve impressive levels of economic development.[25]

Under the model of the liberal state, at least initially, the middle class wielded barely any clout, and the poor were effectively non-existent in political terms. It was, thus, the high bourgeoisie (gentry) who controlled the nation-states, via censitary, indirect and weighted electoral systems, which assured their ascendency. Even in those cases in which universal male suffrage theoretically existed, the representative system was designed to exclude the middle classes and the most disadvantaged citizens. Such was the case, for example, with the Prussian Constitution of 1850.[26]

The wealthy bourgeoisie's political stranglehold on power in the liberal state, however, would be threatened by the momentous social changes which the liberal revolution had triggered in Europe, leading, on the one hand, to the growth of a significant middle class which clamored for political representation; and, on the other, to the advent of a new social group: the "proletariat", the poorest and most numerous portion of society. The European nation-states' extraordinary economic expansion over the course of the nineteenth century would be jeopardized by the unfair distribution of wealth within them, which bred festering social tensions.

This "social question" would precipitate a crisis of the liberal state model and bring about the resurgence of strong public power—already portended by the model of state conceived by Bismarck for the Second Reich, called upon to play a decisive role to restore social balance. These changes were the direct consequence of the mounting conflicts which pitted European nation-states against each other during the era of colonialism and brought on World War I, a turning point in Western constitutional history. We shall analyze these essential constitutional changes in the next chapter.

## 16.4 The Liberal Revolution

Over the course of the nineteenth century, one by one all the European countries would become "nation-states", according to the aforementioned new liberal model, with the exception of tsarist Russia, where the autocratic model of absolute monarchy would endure until the Revolution of 1905. This process of political transformation and its important economic and social consequences, is what has been called the "Liberal Revolution" (Wallerstein 2011, 66).

[25] On how the new economic conditions ideologically transformed the bases of the liberal constitutional model, see Ikenberry (2011, 33–156) and von Mises (2012, 18–58).

[26] The Prussian Constitution of 1850 featured a curious system of indirect suffrage by which the citizens chose electors who voted for the parliamentary representatives. For the designation of the electors in each district the citizens were divided into three electoral colleges, each of which represented a third of the total taxes paid in the district. In the first third there were few voters, as it was composed of only the wealthiest. The second had more voters, as it included the middle class, and the third was the largest of all, as it included the modest masses. Together, however, the first two groups were able to outnumber the third, thereby assuring the hegemony of the bourgeoisie and the elite classes (Hamerow 1983, 306).

Of course, this phenomenon unfolded in a different way in each different country. In England, for example, although the monarchical principle was respected, the liberal model clearly triumphed, as the parliamentary regime was firmly entrenched, with the monarch reigning but not ruling. In other countries Liberalism's triumph was more tempered because, despite the appearance of representative assemblies, the government remained in the hands of the king. Such was the case in Spain, with its system in which the *Cortes* shared sovereignty with the king, and in Prussia, where government was entirely entrusted to the monarch, with the representative assembly limited to legislative and budgetary functions. Finally, in other states the triumph of the liberal regime marked a definitive rejection of monarchy, as in France, which in 1875 definitively shifted to a republic featuring a powerful representative assembly and a weak executive—though the system functioned thanks to the existence of the all-powerful administrative state established by Napoleon.

The lack of a single approach when it came to carrying out the bourgeois revolution was because of the fact that European liberals were divided into two camps: those who tried to move gradually towards the limitation of monarchical power, from within the system (doctrinaire or moderate liberalism) and another, more extremist class whose members sought a radical break with the *Ancien Régime* and monarchy itself (Revolutionary Liberalism).

### *16.4.1 Moderate Liberalism*

The liberal state model was vigorously advanced in England because of the consolidation of a parliamentary system which effectively limited royal prerogative. However, it was in France during the era of the Restoration, however, where liberal thinkers, without endorsing the extremism of the revolutionaries, advocated a model of the state under which power was limited, as citizens were afforded greater freedom and capacity for initiative.

These liberals, who viewed the monarchy as compatible with the establishment of a constitutional regime, were called "doctrinaires" (Craiutu 2003), and in France were led by Pierre Paul Royer-Collard (1763–1845). The most eminent of these political thinkers, however, was Benjamin Constant (1767–1830), who in a famous speech in 1819, openly called for individual liberty vis-à-vis the state and the establishment of a regime characterized by civil and political freedom and based on adequate education.[27] In response to the influence exercised by these moderate

[27] The work of legislator is not complete when he has simply brought peace to the people. Even when the people are satisfied, there is much left to do. Institutions must achieve the moral education of the citizens. By respecting their individual rights, securing their independence, refraining from troubling their work, they must nevertheless consecrate their influence over public affairs, call them to contribute by their votes to the exercise of power, grant them a right of control and supervision by expressing their opinions, and by forming them through practice for these elevated functions, give them both the desire and the right to discharge these (Constant 2012, 81).

liberals, the French King Louis XVIII, despite not having renounced the principle of absolute, divine right monarchy, in 1814 granted a *Charte* which, among other things, instituted the election of a legislative assembly. Although government formally remained the king's exclusive purview, the "parliamentary system" has triumphed ever since, although voting would be censitary until 1848.[28]

The "constitutional" principle embraced by France since 1814, also affected the German territories, despite the fact that after the Congress of Vienna, most of the German sovereigns had restored absolute monarchy. Thus, for example, the Grand Duke of Saxe-Weimar, following the example of Louis XVIII, also granted his subjects a "constitution", an action applauded by the *Burschenschaft*, an association of university professors and students which had begun to spread liberal principles in Germany under the slogan of "freedom, honor and homeland" (Boime 2004, 179). The initiative had an undeniable impact, as the rulers of Bavaria, Baden and Württemberg soon granted constitutions in their respective states (1818–1819) as well.[29]

These decisions, however, perturbed Metternich, who convened the German princes in Carlsbad (Bohemia) and managed for the *Burschenschaft* to be abolished (Spevack 1997, 88). He was unable, however, to persuade the southern German states to eliminate their constitutional regimes, which set an important precedent in the Germanic-speaking territories.

### *16.4.2 "Revolutionary Liberalism"*

Going further than the doctrinaire liberals, there continued to be radical revolutionaries in Europe who called for the re-establishment of Jacobin principles, arguing that sovereignty lay not with the king but in the nation, and that nations, through their representatives, should adopt constitutions setting down national principles and regulating the functioning of the state.

These reformers, dedicated to establishing the nation-state at all costs, were persecuted by the Restoration monarchs' police,[30] as they struggled to spread their ideas by way of revolutionary activities. The best known of these were the Masonic Lodges which emerged in the eighteenth century, and saw spectacular growth in the nineteenth.[31] Not to be overlooked are Italy's *Carbonari*; Germany's *Tugendbund*,

[28] For an overall view of the doctrinaires' ideology, Craiutu (2004, 39–59).

[29] And not only in Germany, as liberalism also prevailed in the Netherlands (te Velde 2008, 65–79).

[30] For an analysis of police repression of liberal uprisings, see Emerson (1968).

[31] As Martínez Esquivel estates, quoting Rich and Harland-Jacobs, England was established as the centre of International Freemasonry, that played a significant role in the education of the elite, functioning as an ideological vehicle of Modernity that contributed substantially to consolidate England as a global hegemonic power (Martínez Esquivel 2012, 6). In the other side of the Atlantic is the influence of Freemasonry upon American political culture, and the intellectual contribution of "heroic revolutionary Americans" who were at the same time masons (as Franklin, Dickinson, the Adamses, the Randolphs, Hancock, Chief Justice Marshall, or Washington). These Revolutionary generation left an indelible mark upon post-Revolutionary society, too (Pearson 2002, 471–488).

born of the patriotic uprising against Napoleonic rule; and the Society of Prosperity, founded in Russia in 1816, by liberal groups within the army. In Spain the Freemasons, who began their activities under the reign of Ferdinand VI and became well entrenched under Charles IV, were already well organized into secret societies during the reign of Ferdinand VII. The ultimate aim of revolutionary liberals, however, was to seize power through a military coup, generally organized by Masonic lodges (Hamnett 1984, 222–237), a practice which initially spread in Spain after the end of the Peninsular War and which came to be termed a *pronunciamiento*.[32] Spain will become initially the reference for revolutionary rivals thanks to the Riego's uprising.

### *16.4.3 Spain, Spearheading the Liberal Revolution: Riego's Revolt (1820)*

In 1814, General Elío, Captain General of Valencia, had defied the Spanish National assembly, the *Cortes* (Parliament), and placed his troops at the service of Ferdinand VII, who openly restored absolutism in May of that year. Following this precedent, 6 years later a revolt by Spanish liberals was led by Major Rafael del Riego, a prominent Mason, who in early 1820 managed to orchestrate a rebellion at Cabezas de San Juan (Seville) by the troops that Ferdinand VII intended to send to America to subjugate pro-independence rebels (Stites 2014, 28–121). Fernando VII ended up capitulating and restored the 1812 constitution, not so much due to the force of the revolt as the weakness of his own government (Payne 1967, 19).

[32] As Payne (1967, 14–15) points out, the term *pronunciamiento* was first used by Major Rafael de Riego in a speech to his troops on January 3, 1820 before he led them in rebellion. A "pronouncement" could consist simply of strong statements, encouragements, or threats by powerful generals who wanted to influence the government's policy, or could involve some form of force, through a revolt by a section of the Army. It could also take the form of a revolt by a barracks (*cuartelazo*) in which insurgent forces would simply hole up and wait for events to unfold. The classic *coup d'état* was the least frequent form of the *pronunciamiento*. Payne (2011, 244) also states that, in a nonfunctional liberal system, this kind of revolt, in its several forms, moderated access to power. Though most army officers were not strong liberals, the effect of military intervention was to move the political system in a more and more liberal direction, climaxing in the disastrous sexennium of 1868–1874. This was a sobering experience and marked the end of successful pronunciamientos on behalf of greater liberalization. The two successful interventions of 1874 each moved the situation in a more conservative direction, the second restoring the Bourbons and marking the beginning of the more stable system directed by Antonio Cánovas del Castillo.

For an overall view of military interventions in Spanish politics during the nineteenth century, see Boyd (1979) and Jensen (2007, 15–37).

#### 16.4.3.1 Revolution Extends to Italy

The triumph of the "Spanish Revolution" had important repercussions. Firstly, it prevented the deployment of reinforcements to Spanish America, thereby ensuring the rebels' victory there. Most important was that Riego inspired European radical liberals to undertake the same defiance of their absolute monarchs (Mirkine-Guetzevitch 1938, 211–215). Three months after Riego's success, a liberal revolution broke out in the Kingdom of the Two Sicilies when troops occupying Naples also revolted (Stites 2014, 121–185).

It should be noted that for the first time, Italy had extricated itself from the structures of the *Ancien Régime* as a result of a campaign which allowed Napoleon to wrest almost all of Italy from Austria (1796–1797). This shift led to the formation of the first independent Italian republics: in Lombardy, the Cisalpine Republic (which, in 1804, came be called the Kingdom of Italy); in Genoa, the Ligurian Republic; and in Naples, the Parthenopean Republic. Following Napoleon's fall, the ensuing Congress of Vienna reinstalled the respective sovereigns of the different Italian states (Meriggi 2000, 49–64). Thus, in 1815, Italy continued to be nothing more than, as Metternich termed it, a "geographical expression" (Clark 2006, 1). Nevertheless, as we have seen, patriotic and nationalist sentiment had not subsided, as the movement of 1820 would make clear.

#### 16.4.3.2 Revolts in Greece and Russia

In 1822, the Greeks rose up against the Ottoman Empire, and in December of 1825, taking advantage of the death of Alexander I and the accession to the throne of Nicholas I, a group of progressive Russian officials managed to lead a rebellion backed by 3,000 soldiers against the tsar in what was called the Decembrist Uprising (Taylor 2003, 42–46).

#### 16.4.3.3 Metternich Reacts: Congresses and Interventions in Italy and Spain

These revolutionary outbreaks troubled the leaders of the European powers, who were quick to set the machinery of the Metternich system into motion. Representatives of the rulers of Austria, Prussia, Russia, England and France met at the Congresses of Troppau (1820), and Laibach (1821). Despite the formal protest by Britain's Foreign Minister, Lord Castlereagh, Metternich ultimately convinced the delegates to accept his proposal for foreign intervention in Italy, to put an end to the revolutionary upheaval there.

Intervention was entrusted to Austria, the power which had occupied the greater part of Italy, since the Peace of Utrecht (1713). In March of 1821, an Austrian army entered Naples, defeated the liberal troops, and restored absolutism there. That same army then moved on to the Piedmont, where another military uprising had broken out, and put it down as well. The occupation was followed by a relentless crackdown on any form of rebellion or dissent.

After the subjugation of Italy the powers met again in 1822, this time in Verona, where the conservative powers agreed to send a French army to Spain to "liberate" Fernando VII from his submission to the *Cortes*. In Verona, however, the unity of the alliance began to crumble. The tsar wished to intervene both in the Iberian Peninsula and in Spanish America, while England, where the liberal Canning had replaced the conservative Robert Jenkinson, supported intervention only in Spain—in reality because the government of his Gracious Majesty believed that the independence of Spain's overseas territories favored Britain's colonial interests.

In the end, thanks to the pressure exerted on the representatives by writer François René de Chateaubriand, then France's Foreign Minister, it was agreed to intervene in Spain. In April of 1823, the Duke of Angoulême crossed the Spanish border under the command of "The 100,000 Sons of St. Louis". The campaign was a military cakewalk and, after taking Cádiz, where the *Cortes* had once again sought refuge, the French expedition did away with the "Liberal Triennium" (Jarrett 2013, 338–343). The intervention in Spain was the last military operation inspired by the Metternich System and unanimously backed by its powers, as Britain's withholding of support prevented the restoration of the *Ancien Régime* in Spanish America and in Greece.

#### 16.4.3.4 The Metternich System Falters: The Independence of Spanish America

Britain's opposition prevented the powers from getting involved in Spanish America to suppress the uprisings which had begun in 1808, after the outbreak of the Peninsular War. The rebellions initially took the Spanish by surprise, and the authorities quickly lost control of all their territories in the Americas, except for Peru. However, after the restoration of Ferdinand VII in 1814, Spain was able to recover the control it held in America before 1808, with the exception of Argentina (McFarlane 2014, 111–144).

Spain's hold on the new continent, however, would soon weaken, as the rebels received support from the English (who dispatched military commanders they no longer needed on the Continent after the end of the Napoleonic wars) and from the Americans (who sent weapons).[33] The turning point, however, came, as has been mentioned, with the rebellion led by Colonel Rafael de Riego (a member of the same Masonic Lodge as Colonel San Martín), who in 1820, prevented Spanish reinforcements from reaching the country's American colonies. The refusal of the

---

[33] As McFarlane (2014, 359) points out, most of the sailors and almost all the officers of the first Chilean navy that began attacking Spanish ships in 1817, were British or American, recruited by agents in England and the United States.

powers gathered at Verona to intervene in Spanish America was pivotal, ending more than 300 years of Spanish rule over its overseas territories.

In 1821, Iturbide proclaimed the independence of Mexico (Iguala Plan). In Argentina, San Martín formed a small army with which he crossed the Andes and was able to dominate Chile and Peru between 1817 and 1821, while Simón Bolívar occupied Colombia, Venezuela and Ecuador. Finally, in 1824 Bolívar's subordinate, General Sucre, defeated the last regular Spanish army at Ayacucho (Peru). At that point Spain, which had just sold Florida to the United States, only maintained an overseas presence in Cuba and the Philippines. Bolivar envisioned bringing the new states together into a "federal union", modeled on the United States. To this end in 1826, he convened delegates from all the new Spanish American countries, and also from the U.S. The Congress of Panama was a failure, however, and Spanish America ended up fracturing into 15 independent republics.[34] The sole "kingdom" remaining in the Americas was Brazil, where in 1822, Emperor Don Pedro, a son of the Portuguese king, had been proclaimed a constitutional emperor.[35]

The English, who had supported the revolt in the hopes of taking advantage of the Spanish Empire's demise, saw their hopes dashed when in 1823, U.S. President James Monroe declared his determination to prevent any European intervention in the Americas (Gleijeses 1992, 481–605), though this did not stop Napoleon III from seeking to conquer Mexico (1862–1867), seizing upon the outbreak of the American Civil War to do so (Hanna and Hanna 1971). This enterprise, however, led to a complete debacle, with the execution of Emperor Maximilian I in Querétaro on June 19, 1867.

#### 16.4.3.5 The Independence of Greece: A Fatal Blow to the Metternich System

Having suffered a severe setback from the emancipation of Spanish America, the Metternich System was finally dealt a definitive blow when the Greeks revolted against the Ottoman Empire in 1822. The Turks managed to regain control of Greece in 1827, despite the separatist sympathies harbored by European intellectuals, such as Lord Byron (1788–1824). However, the Greeks ultimately won their independence, in the end thanks to Russia: in 1825, Tsar Alexander I died and Nicholas I rose to the Russian throne. Determined to augment Russia's influence in the Mediterranean, the new tsar declared war on Ottoman Turkey (Crawley 2014, 43–62). The Russians went on to win their campaign and in the ensuing Treaty of

[34] For an overview of the process by which Spanish America won its independence, see Kinsbruner (2000, 43–107).

[35] On the remarkable figure of Don Pedro, see Barman (1999). For an overview of the independence process in the area, see Adelman (2006).

Andrinopolis (1829) the Ottoman Empire recognized, among other concessions, Greece's independence.[36]

## 16.4.4 *France Comes to Lead the Liberal Revolution (1830)*

The model of the liberal revolution based on a military uprising, inspired by the coup led by Colonel Riego, was succeeded by another approach: the "popular revolution" through which in July of 1830, the people of Paris took to the streets to overthrow the absolutist Charles X and impose a constituent assembly, from which emerged a new regime: the constitutional monarchy of Louis Philippe of Orléans, also known as the "July Monarchy" (Pilbeam 2002, 37–40).

Its triumph triggered a new revolutionary wave across Europe. The rebellions in Italy, the German territories and Poland, however, would fail, as the reactionary powers, essentially Austria and Russia, were fierce in their stamping out of subversive activities. Liberalism, however, prevailed in the Netherlands, Spain, Portugal and Switzerland. It also had major repercussions in England, where it inspired historic electoral reform in 1832.

### 16.4.4.1 The Birth of the Belgian State

The powers gathered at the Congress of Vienna agreed that the United Provinces of the North (Protestant), and the lands to the south (Catholic), would be unified into one single State: the United Kingdom of the Netherlands. Beginning in 1815, however, the Catholics of the southern provinces entered into perpetual conflict with King William I (1815–1840). Seizing upon the triumph of parliamentary monarchy in France, in 1830 the southern provinces rebelled and created a new state: the Kingdom of Belgium (van Berlo 2005, 43–45). In 1831, the corresponding constitutional assembly approved a liberal constitution "installing" a parliamentary monarchy under King Leopold I (1831–1865). Two legislative chambers were also created, whose members were elected by a very restricted censitary suffrage system which guaranteed that the government would remain in the hands of the high bourgeoisie.[37] The Catholic Church was separated from the State, but received all its traditional privileges. Belgium established itself as a nation-state because its two major parties, liberal and Catholic, which only diverged on the issue of public education, forged a ruling coalition until 1847 (Goldstein 2010, 177), after which they would grapple for power.

[36] On the international dimension of Greek independence, see Dakin (1973, 142–173). For an overall view see Brewer (2011).

[37] For an overview of how the Belgian gentry controlled the new constitutional regime, see de Dijn (2002, 227–245).

### 16.4.4.2 The Triumph of the Liberals in Spain and Portugal

Liberalism also triumphed in Spain and Portugal, although this had less to do with the French Revolution of 1830, than it did with two civil wars.

In Spain, the death of Fernando VII (1833), who left no male heir, sparked the dynastic conflict known as the "Carlist Wars". When the absolutists endorsed the dynastic rights advanced by Carlos María Isidro,[38] a brother of the deceased king to place her daughter Isabella II on the throne, regent María Cristina had no choice but to ally with the liberals. After an attempt to grant a royal charter (the Estatuto Real of 1834), a rebellious group of Royal Guard sergeants, in 1836, in what was called the Mutiny at La Granja, forced the restoration of the 1812 Constitution. At the end, the Constitution of 1837 was ultimately approved, clearly inspired by the Belgian Constitution of 1831,[39] definitively consolidating the constitutional principle in Spain. With the rise of the conservatives to power in 1843, however, the principle of the constitutional state would be replaced by a Napoleon-inspired administrative state (Esdaile 2000, 65–82), a system which would endure all the way down to 1923, with the constitutions of Narváez in 1845 and Cánovas in 1876 (save for the "Revolutionary Sexennial" from 1868 to 1874).[40]

In Portugal, the support of traditionalist forces for a separate candidate, the second son of João VI, D. Miguel, crystallized more rapidly, as Portuguese *miguelismo* emerged a couple years before Spanish *carlismo* (Payne 1994, 513–558). After 1834, the political struggle pitted moderates, defenders of the Constitution of 1824, against "Septembrists", or progressives, supporters of the Constitution of 1822. The latter group managed to seize power thanks to a September 1836 coup, although they were removed in 1842 by the Count of Tomar, who established a much more authoritarian regime than that introduced by Narváez in Spain, which led his political opponents to ally and triggered several dramatic overthrow attempts, such as the Oporto Revolt (1846). Tomar was eventually forced to step down, although he would return to power from 1849 to 1851.[41]

---

[38] Carlos María Isidro disputed the right of women to occupy the Spanish throne, pointing to the Salic Law principle imported from the French dynastic tradition by the first Spanish Bourbon, Philip V. The partisans of Isabella II's rights argued that, historically, before the arrival of the Bourbons, women were indeed able to reign in Spain. Thus, Ferdinand VII, to guarantee the dynastic rights of his daughter, abolished the Salic Law on March 31, 1830 via a royal decree, the Pragmatic Sanction, in which he restored the old law of succession of Las Partidas (Wilson F. G. 2004, 25). This was never accepted by his brother, Carlos María Isidro. The conflict was referred to as the "dynastic question".

[39] Regarding the influence of the Belgian Constitution of 1831 on the Spanish constitutional text of 1837, that in turn appears to have been directly influenced by the Cadíz Constitution, see Elkins (2010, 969–999), Marichal (1977, 191–195) and Pérez Ayala (2002).

[40] For an overall view of Spanish constitutional history from 1833 to 1868 for English readers, see the classic by Carr (2003, 155–304).

[41] On this crucial period of contemporary Portuguese history, see Birmingham (2003, 99–130).

#### 16.4.4.3 England and the Electoral Reform Act of 1832

Finally, mention must be made of England, where there was no revolution but a major law introducing electoral reform, approved by Parliament on June 4, 1832, thanks to the endorsement and leadership of Lord Grey.[42] The Electoral Reform Act introduced a sweeping redistribution of electoral districts. Through it 165 rotten boroughs were eliminated, while new industrial cities such as Manchester and Glasgow acquired Parliamentary representation for the first time, while the income requirement to vote was also lowered. This expansion of the right to vote essentially favored the urban bourgeoisie, altering the English political landscape in just a question of years. Although universal suffrage would not be introduced until after the First World War, the Electoral Reform Act of 1832 was a decisive step towards the democratization of Britain's parliamentary regime.[43]

## 16.5 The Revolution of 1848 as the Key to the Spread of the Liberal State in Europe

With the exception of the aforementioned countries, in the wake of the Revolution of 1830, the reactionary absolutism which had characterized the *Ancien Régime* became the prevailing trend in Europe once again. Such was the case in Austria, Russia, the various German states, and the different Italian kingdoms, all territories in which the Metternich doctrine was firmly applied.

The situation remained more or less stable until a series of revolutions broke out in Italy, France, the German states and Austria. As we know, in France the February Revolution ushered in the short-lived Second Republic, which would disappear 3 years later as a result of the *coup d'état* led by Louis Napoleon, who established the Second Empire. In Spain, this new wave of liberal revolutions was stifled when General Narváez, who headed up the government, managed for Parliament to temporarily grant him full powers.[44] Narváez acted effectively, thereby staving off a liberal revolution in Spain for 20 years, which would finally come about under General Prim in 1868. The 1848 revolution would have, nevertheless, more decisive consequences in Italy, Austria and Prussia.[45]

---

[42] On the fight for electoral reform, see Pearce (2004).

[43] These were non-existent municipal districts in which the MP was directly elected by the landowner in power. On British elections before Lord Grey's reform, see Evans (2008). For an overview and analysis of the Electoral Law of 1832, see Brock (1993) and Evans (1994). For a re-creation of that tempestuous 2-year period in Britain's history, in Fraser (2013).

[44] By virtue of the law of the Spanish *Cortes* of March 13, 1848, in what was called the "Constitutional Dictatorship" (Peña González 2006, 158).

[45] For a narrative of the revolutionary wave of 1848 and its roots and consequences, see Rapport (2014).

## 16.5.1 *Another Italian Liberal Revolution*

### 16.5.1.1 Revolution Breaks Out in Sicily

Italy had revolted against Austrian absolutism in 1820 and 1830, but in every case the liberal rebellions were crushed by Austrian armies.[46] Revolution broke out again in 1848, and this time took hold in one of the Italian states: the Kingdom of Piedmont-Sardinia (Broers 2000, 151–166).

While the most important revolutionary movement took place in France in February, the first revolutionary act of 1848 would come in Italy, on January 12, in Palermo (Sicily), where rebels forced King Ferdinand II (1830–1859) to grant a constitution. This liberal success gave a prompt boost to the revolt, especially after the outbreak of the February Revolution in Paris, which spurred various Italian monarchs to promulgate constitutions in their kingdoms, such as the Grand Duke of Tuscany, King Charles Albert of Sardinia, and even Pope Pius IX. The rebellion also spread to the regions occupied by Austria: Lombardy and Veneto, where "patriots" revolted in March upon hearing the news that Metternich had fled from Vienna. After a bloody 5-day battle, the Austrians were driven from Milan. Revolution also triumphed in the duchies of Parma and Modena, whose dukes opted to abandon their states as well.

### 16.5.1.2 The Advent of "National Wars": Royal Defeat and Republican Triumph

The Italian revolution gave way to a national war when Lombardy, Veneto, and the duchies of Parma and Modena, joined with the Kingdom of Sardinia-Piedmont under the leadership of King Charles Albert, who henceforth adopted the tricolor flag as a symbol of "Italian unity".

Charles Albert, however, was defeated by an Austrian army commanded by General Radetzky at Custoza (July 1848), allowing Austria to regain control over northern Italy. When the monarchy failed to ensure Italian unity and independence, the most extreme liberals, led by Giuseppe Mazzini, proclaimed a republic in Rome (Hearder 2006, 113–128) and in Florence, forcing the pope to flee and take refuge in Gaeta, where he was welcomed by the King of the two Sicilies.[47] After the triumph of republican liberalism the Piedmontese, the Romans and the Florentines forced Charles Albert to break the armistice signed with the Austrians (March 20, 1849). Three days later, however, the Italian army was again thrashed by Radetzky at Novara (Sked 2011, 154).

---

[46] For an overview of the unification movement in Italy from 1796 to 1848, see Wells (2012, 15–42).

[47] On the opposite approaches to Italian unification taken by Mazzini and Cavour, see Gooch (2002, 20–26).

#### 16.5.1.3 Italy Subjugated

Charles Albert abdicated in favor of his son Victor Emmanuel II. The Austrians agreed to sign a new cease-fire in exchange for their occupation of part of the Piedmont, with Radetzky's troops taking Parma, Modena, Tuscany, and the northern Papal states. Rome, meanwhile, was occupied by a French expeditionary force which, after defeating Garibaldi and abolishing the Roman Republic, allowed the Pope to return to his states. Venice soon fell. The Italian patriots' military defeat led to the reestablishment of an absolutist regime and the harsh repression of the liberals, but not without the important consequence that, as a result of the revolts, the King of Piedmont-Sardinia became a compelling symbol of national unity.

#### 16.5.1.4 The Piedmont Exception

The only Italian territory in which liberal principles survived was in the Piedmont, where Victor Emmanuel II refused to abolish the constitution granted by his father: the Albertine Statute (Ghisalberti 2006, 35). Hence, Italian patriots took refuge in Turin, which became the "capital" of liberal Italy. Victor Emmanuel, however, realized that Italians alone could not overcome Austrian power, prompting him to seek aid from Napoleon III, at the initiative of his first minister the Count of Cavour.

### *16.5.2 The Revolution of 1848 in the German Territories*

The 1848 revolution also had a major impact on Austria and Prussia, two of the leading European powers since 1816. As both kingdoms aspired to lead the "German nation", it is important to examine the origins of German nationalism to understand what happened in both states in 1848.

#### 16.5.2.1 The French Origins of the German "Nation": Napoleon and Prussia

German unity proceeded from nationalist sentiment reflecting, as occurred in Spain, a backlash against the Napoleonic invasion (Aguilera-Barchet 2008, 123–132). Napoleon had restructured the German territories on two occasions: in 1803 at Regensburg, he substantially reduced the number of German states.[48] After his

[48] The "Final Recess of February 1803" (*Reichsdeputationshauptschluss*) was a resolution passed on February 25, 1803 by the Imperial Diet (*Reichstag*) of the Holy Roman Empire in accordance with that agreed to in the Treaty of Luneville of 1801. It established a complete reorganization of the states included in the German Empire, which led to the absorption of smaller states by the bigger ones, resulting in a substantial reduction in the total number of German states. This process is known as "mediatization", as small states transferred their sovereignty to their larger neighbors. The Final Recess of the *Reichsdeputation*, unanimously ratified by the Imperial Diet, was the last significant law enacted by the Empire before it disappeared in 1806. On the decisive role Napoleon played in the whole process of German territorial organization, see Schneid (2005, 53–77).

victory at Austerlitz (December 1805), the Emperor of the French created the Confederation of the Rhine (*Rheinbund*),[49] which replaced the old Holy German-Roman Empire, dating back to the year 962.[50] Prussia attempted to counter the French threat (Simms 2002, 291–295), but Napoleon's victories over Frederick William III (1797–1840), led to the dismemberment of the Empire on August 6, 1806, carried out through a set of agreements between Napoleon and Tsar Alexander I through the Treaties of Tilsitt (1807).

The reduction of the Kingdom of Prussia to half its former size was a humiliating blow, engendering a wave of nationalist fervor (Breuilly 2009, 256–284). This was initially seized upon by the aristocrats Stein and Hardenberg, who championed an elite-led movement for Prussian regeneration.[51] This "Prussian protonationalism" would be consolidated thanks to the military reform of General Scharnhorst and the influence of eminent intellectuals like Johann Gottlieb Fichte (1762–1814), and Alexander von Humboldt (1769–1859), founder of the University of Berlin, the leaders of a movement of enlightened nationalism that transformed Prussian political culture (Levinger 2002).

This "nationalist" feeling was decisive in making Prussia one of the forces which would ultimately vanquish Napoleon in 1813, as Prussia rose to become a leading European power during the Restoration period (Simms 2000, 97–114).

#### 16.5.2.2 Austria Heads up the "Germanic Confederation"

The Congress of Vienna (1815) replaced the Napoleonic "Confederation of the Rhine" with a Germanic Confederation (*Deutscher Bund*) of 39 states, once again under an Emperor of Austria, which represented a reversion to the structure of the Holy German-Roman Empire, abolished in 1806 (John 2000, 83–96). As such, it was a weak union in which the states maintained their total independence, only meeting sporadically in assemblies (diets) that represented the sovereigns of their respective states, and not their inhabitants.[52]

---

[49] The Confederation of the Rhine (*Rheinbund*, *Confédération du Rhin*) was created by Napoleon after his victory at Austerlitz, the "Treaty of the Confederation of the Rhine" being signed on July 12, 1806 by 16 founding states, with Napoleon as its protector. As the Austrian emperor dissolved the Holy Roman Empire on August 6, 1806 more states joined the Confederation, which featured 36 in 1808, with Prussia and Austria remaining outside. The latter states would form the Fourth Coalition, but were again defeated by Napoleon (1806–1807). A good introduction to this extremely complex process is provided by Rowe (2001, 204–223).

[50] The Holy Roman Empire was not abolished by Napoleon, but by the Emperor Francis II, as he did not want the Emperor of the French to become the head of the First Reich as well (Koch 1984, 1–9). For an overview of this crucial process, see Wilson (2009).

[51] For an interesting interpretation of the rise of German nationalism, see Dorpalen (1969, 485–516).

[52] For an overall look at the last century of Habsburg rule in Austria, see Sked (2001).

#### 16.5.2.3 The *Zollverein* or the Prussian Way Towards German Integration

The Kingdom of Prussia reacted to this state of things in 1818 by undertaking a momentous initiative: the establishment of a customs union (*Zollverein*).[53] Thanks to it the interior customs services between the states controlled by the Hohenzollern disappeared, while the tariffs paid by those not belonging to the Zollverein increased. With its initiative, Prussia managed to favor commerce within the scope of the "union", bringing about a considerable increase in economic activity. The success of this tariff policy was so great that all the German states ended up forming part of this free economic space which may, without any doubt, be considered a precursor of the current process of European integration. By 1834, all the states of the Germanic Confederation had been incorporated into the Zollverein.[54]

The balance between Austria and Prussia, however, would be broken by the 1848 revolution and a group of intellectuals who hoped to bring about a strong, unified Germany, accompanied by political reforms in the individual German states (Pogge von Strandmann 2002, 107).[55]

### *16.5.3 The Austrian Empire and the Revolution*

#### 16.5.3.1 The Fall of Metternich

Immediately after news spread of the triumph of the revolution in Paris, rebellion broke out in Budapest (Hungary), and Prague (Bohemia). On March 13 the revolutionaries, headed by university students (Robertson 1980, 206–236), took over Vienna, forcing Metternich to flee.[56] Overwhelmed, the Austrian government accepted all the rebels' demands and pledged to convene a constitutional assembly.

---

[53] For an overview of the previous customs policy among the German states, see Billinger (1991). On the British reaction to the creation of the *Zollverein*, see Davis (1997) and Olegario (2013, 60–87).

[54] For an analysis of the interaction between politics and economics in Germany during this period, see Hamerow (1966, 219–237).

[55] For an overview of the 1848 Revolution in the Germanic states, see Dipper and Speck (1998), and Hahn (2001).

[56] Metternich survived by escaping Vienna with his third wife, Countess Melanie, hidden in a washerwoman's carriage. They boarded another carriage outside the city and drove to a train, going on to take refuge in Holland, London and Brussels (Rapport 2014, 64). Metternich returned to Vienna in 1851, but never actively participated in politics again, though Emperor Franz Joseph occasionally sought his counsel. He died in 1859 at the age of 86. On Metternich's personality and actions, see Sked (2008)

#### 16.5.3.2 A Military Backlash and the Crushing of the Rebels

The army, however, remained loyal to the monarchy. Austrian troops counterattacked, first prevailing in Bohemia (June 1848). Four months later they occupied Vienna (October 31). The government soon fell into the hands of the Prince of Schwarzenberg, who suggested to Emperor Ferdinand I of Austria that he abdicate in favor of his nephew, the young Franz Joseph (1848–1916), who dissolved the constitutional assembly and promulgated a constitution which was ultimately suspended (March 1849).

To subjugate the Hungarians, Austria had to ally with Russia, with the Austro-Russian Coalition quelling a rebellion in August of 1848, through a harsh campaign of repression. Hungary lost the broad autonomy it had enjoyed before, and was divided into provinces ruled by Austrian officials who did not even know the Hungarian language (Magyar), and only spoke German.[57]

The 1848 revolution had failed in the Austrian Empire, but not in the other German territories. It had a particularly decisive impact on one of them: Prussia, whose sovereign aspired to secure independence from Austria.

### 16.5.4 *Prussia vs. Austria: The Fight for German Supremacy*

In 1848, the German-speaking population lived in a multitude of states still formally ruled over by the Emperor of Austria. However, as the revolution initially spread to Vienna that year, King Frederick William IV of Prussia (1840–1861) moved to supplant the Austrian Emperor and establish himself as the new champion of all the German-speaking peoples (Pan-Germanism), thereby seeking an integration of all Germans "from the top down".[58]

There soon emerged, however, other, more grassroots attempts to unite the German peoples. Circumstances were favorable to the restructuring of the German states, as the revolutionary triumphs scored across Europe in 1848, advanced the idea of a German nation. In fact, throughout the German territories nationalist agitation had begun in 1847. Just after the triumph of the revolution in France, a group of German patriots in Heidelberg managed to convoke an assembly (diet), composed of members of the various assemblies of the German states (including the Austrian Empire). This body resolved to convene a constitutional parliament, to be elected by universal suffrage amongst all the citizens forming part of the Germanic confederation, including all the German states not forming part of the Austrian Empire (Rapport 2009, 59).

---

[57] For an overview of status of Hungary in the Austrian empire after 1849, see Evans (2006, 245–265).

[58] Nevertheless, the struggle with Austria for Germany had already begun, prior even to the Napoleonic invasion (Kagan 2006, 2–3). For an overview of the period of Prussian history leading up to 1848, see Dwyer (2000).

#### 16.5.4.1 The Political Consequences of the Berlin Rebellion

Prussia was soon enveloped in a revolutionary whirlwind. On March 18, 1848 revolution broke out in Berlin. In response to the turmoil, King Frederick William IV (1840–1861), agreed to convene a National Assembly to be elected by universal suffrage. The resulting parliament, a revolutionary successor to the old German Confederation, a loose body of 39 German states formed at the Congress of Vienna and dominated by Austria (Thackeray 2004, 5), was constituted in May of 1848 in Frankfurt, as a constitutional assembly charged with drafting a Prussian constitution.[59]

#### 16.5.4.2 Testing the "Bottom Up" Approach to German Integration: The Frankfurt Parliament

The Parliament thus chosen was constituted on May 18, 1848 and established a provisional federal government led by a liberal Austrian archduke.[60] It also drafted a "Constitution for Germany", which became a federal state presided over by an emperor. The former states endured, but above them a government was created consisting of an emperor (Kaiser) and an elected parliament. The federal government was assigned powers over some areas of joint concern (diplomacy, army, customs duties) while other authorities were retained by the different states. Finally, the Frankfurt Parliament discussed whether the federal state should include Austria to form a *Großdeutsche Lösung* or Austria should be excluded, thereby creating a *Kleindeutsche Lösung*,[61] the latter option being that which prevailed. In March of 1849, the Austrian representatives abandoned the Frankfurt Parliament (Merkl 1993, 32).

The Frankfurt Parliament, however, failed to achieve its objectives because Frederick William IV, upon learning that revolution had been suppressed in Austria–Hungary, rejected the crown offered him by the representatives, as this would have meant being appointed by an elected assembly and renouncing his dynastic legitimacy. Neither would he accept the constitution adopted by the members of the parliament, which led to its dissolution (Thackeray 2004, 17). German integration "from the bottom up" had failed.

[59] It was, moreover, a "parliament of scholars", as 90 % of the representatives were educated (Kidner et al. 2014, 658).

[60] On the history of the ephemeral Frankfurt Parliament, see Eyck (1968). Concerning the influence of the parliament in the debate over national German identity, see Vick (2002). For the participation of liberals in Prussian politics during this period, see Kahan (1991). On the democratic movement in Germany after the events of 1848 see Sperber (1991).

[61] Literally, the "Small German Solution", as opposed to the "Great German Solution".

#### 16.5.4.3 From the Erfurt Union to the Punctation of Olmütz: Austria's Victory Over Prussia

Despite having rejected the federal constitution proposed by the Frankfurt Parliament, Frederick William did not give up on the unification of all Germans, but rather acted to carry out an integration spearheaded by the Prussian monarchy. Firstly, he moved to head up a German Union consisting of the Austrian Empire and a new "German Empire".

The King of Prussia's proposal, however, was only accepted by small states. Thus arose a limited union which elected a parliament that would meet in Erfurt, and adopt a constitution presented by the King of Prussia (April 1850). This restricted union failed to take shape, however, because of the firm opposition of Austria, which once again enjoyed a position of strength, after having subjugated its rebels. The Austrian government, supported by Tsar Nicholas I, sent an ultimatum to the King of Prussia, and Frederick William ended up accepting all of Austria's conditions in the Punctation of Olmütz, or *Olmützer Punktation*, of November 1850 (Winkler 2007, 112–113). Thus was the restricted union (*Erfurt Union*) dissolved, with the Austrian Empire once again ruling over the German states. In short, the situation reverted to that existing prior to 1848.[62]

### 16.5.5 *Prussia Becomes a Constitutional Kingdom*

Frederick William IV not only rejected the Crown offered by the Frankfurt Parliament, but also the constitution adopted by it.[63] He did not, however, simply restore absolutism, but rather established another constitution (January, 1850), unilaterally endorsed by him. What the king wished to make clear was that the establishment of a constitutional regime was the prerogative of the king and not that of the "nation" (Kolkey 1995, 82–83). In this regard he was successful, as the constitutional system instituted by Frederick William IV would remain in force in Prussia until 1918.

The new Prussian Constitution created a bicameral legislature with two chambers: an upper house (*Herrenhaus*), made up of members of the landowning nobility (*junkers*[64]), appointed by the king; and a lower house of representatives (*Landtag*)

[62] For an overview of Prussian foreign relations before Bismarck, see Young (2006, 1–32).

[63] Frederick William IV was not a democrat and Prussia under his rule had a powerful police system, controlled by the monarch. On this essential aspect of Prussian constitutional practice, see Lüdtke (2009).

[64] A term that in German originally meant "young lord" (*jung Herr*). Bismarck was a "Junker", as he held an estate in Schönhausen, Pomerania, in what is today the *Bundesland* (federated state) of Saxony-Anhalt.

chosen by universal, indirect and weighted suffrage. This legislature, however, was hardly democratic, as it favored the representation of the wealthy. Thus, the middle class was not yet able to exercise real political influence, and Prussian society maintained its rigid class divisions.[65]

The Prussian Constitution of 1850 also failed to establish a parliamentary regime. In theory, the chambers of the legislature voted on the laws, but the king could legislate via *ordonnances*, executive orders, when the legislature was not in session. The parliament also approved taxes, provided that they were new, as all traditional ones were maintained until rescinded by law. The appointment of ministers was the exclusive purview of the king, who could also dismiss them freely. In summary, in Prussia the monarchy retained sovereignty.[66]

### *16.5.6 Relative Calm in Europe by 1850*

By the end of 1850, it seemed that the revolutionary earthquakes which had shaken Europe 2 years earlier had been in vain. The nationalist movements had failed, and the liberals had only obtained tangible results in the form of two constitutional texts: the Albertine Statute of 1848, which continued to be the constitution of the Kingdom of Piedmont-Sardinia; and the Prussian Constitution of 1850. Austria had managed to regain hegemony in Italy and Germany and to consolidate its brand of strict imperial centralism.

This tranquility, however, was misleading, as within 20 years the Austrian Empire would suffer the loss of Italy (which became an independent, unified state) and be defeated by the Kingdom of Prussia, which finally became the core and primary force driving the German integration process. The Austro-Hungarian Empire, nevertheless, would remain a great power until the end of the First World War.

## 16.6 The Unification of Italy

Austria's victory in 1850 did not prevent Italian and German patriots from carrying on with their struggle to found their own nation-states. The Italians would ultimately prevail thanks to the efforts of Victor Emmanuel II's first minister, Camillo

[65] For an overall examination of Prussian society in the nineteenth century, see Blackbourn (1986) and Hagen (2007, 593–645).

[66] As Congleton (2011, 469) points out, the 1850 Prussian constitution was formally a law adopted by the sovereign, who could also revoke it, a situation that enhanced the kings position towards the Landtag, as deputies feared that if they pressed the king too hard on reform he would simply revoke the constitution. For an academic analysis of the Prussian Constitutional model, see Böckenförde (1991, 47–70 and 87–114) and Crosby (2008, 131–166).

Benso, better known as the Count of Cavour. Italian unification constitutes the paradigm of the consolidation of the nation-state principle in the second half of the nineteenth century in Europe.

### *16.6.1* Il Risorgimento

As we have seen, on March 4, 1848 the King of Piedmont-Sardinia, Charles Albert, promulgated a liberal constitution which, in his honor, came to be called the Albertine Statute.[67] This constitutional text, despite the revolution's failure, persisted as a symbol of a free Italy, as it was not abolished, despite the Austrian reoccupation. After being defeated by the Austrians, Charles Albert abdicated and ceded the throne to his son, Victor Emmanuel II, who, was wise enough to appoint as his first minister Camillo Benso, Count of Cavour (1810–1861), a patriot determined to bring about a united Italy.[68] This period during which the Italians managed to integrate and form a single nation-state is known as *Il Risorgimento* (The Resurgence), because it aimed to transform Italy into one of the great European powers.[69]

---

[67] The *Statuto fondamentale* designation constituted a legitimizing historical reference to the "municipal statutes" of the Italian cities, such as Milan, Florence and Siena, which during the medieval era had maintained *de facto*, independence from the Germanic Empire, becoming commercial republics, although in the long run they would transform into monarchies led by powerful families such as the House of Medici in Florence, and the House of Sforza in Milan. Even though Charles Alberto sought in his constitution to set down the bases for "a fundamental statute to establish an accomplished parliamentary government in our states", in fact he wanted to create a sort of limited monarchy in which the Crown would not be a pure formal element but the holder of executive power, actively participating as an executive and judicial power (Ghisalberti 2006, 35–36). The parliamentary model of the Albertine Statute reflected the conception of a representative monarchy in the British style of the moderate liberals, like Constant or Guizot. It created a two-chamber parliament, in which the members of the lower chamber were elected with a franchise requirement on the basis of a property qualification (Beales and Biagini 2002, 93).

[68] Cavour harbored, moreover, a different vision of the regime from the one expressed originally by Cesare Balbo (1789–1853), the author of *Della monarchia rappresentativa en Italia* (1857), whose ideas were decisive in the framing of the Albertine Statute. If Balbo wanted the monarch to play an essential role in the system, Cavour placed the parliament at the center of the new regime (Ghisalberti 2006, 68).

[69] As Riall (1994, 1) mentions, the term *Risorgimento*, literally translated, means "resurgence" and refers to a common, idealized past as well as to a less than perfect present, in accordance with Mazzini's ideal of heroic alternatives against the everyday realities of the Restoration. For a thorough and actualized narrative of the Restoration and the Risorgimento as well, see Patriarca and Riall (2012) and Riall (2009).

### 16.6.2 French Support for the Italian Cause

Cavour came to power in 1852, and spent 7 years at the head of the Piedmontese Government, during which time he converted the Kingdom of Sardinia into a strong state, and secured support from France to oust Austria from Italy through an alliance with Napoleon III (Blumberg 1990, 17). By virtue of the Plombières Agreement of 1858, the French received Nice and Savoy in exchange for providing the Piedmontese with military assistance to free Italy from Austrian occupation. Once signed, Cavour provoked Vienna into declaring war on Victor Emmanuel II. The ensuing conflict was brief (May–July 1859), as two bloody battles (Magenta and Solferino) led to the Austrians' defeat.[70]

### 16.6.3 A Democratic Integration

Despite the fact that France had signed a truce with Austria (Armistice of Villafranca), the army of the Italian patriots continued military operations, annexing the Kingdom of Sardinia and central Italy after the Piedmontese army's occupation of Tuscany, Modena, Parma, and part of the Papal States. The conquest of these territories was legally formalized through the convocation of the corresponding constitutional assemblies which, once elected, approved their incorporation into the Sardinian Kingdom (August–September 1859). The procedure was concluded by a referendum in which the people were asked whether they accepted their integration into the new Italian Kingdom (Ghisalberti 2006, 97–100). One should bear in mind that the new state was based on the constitutional regime of Piedmont-Sardinia, which since 1848, had been grounded on the Albertine Statute, based on the principle of national sovereignty. In this way "Italian unity" was legitimized by the free consent of its people (the "Italian nation").

### 16.6.4 Garibaldi and the Annexation of the South

The next step was the annexation of the south, carried out by Garibaldi and his army of "red shirts". Taking advantage of an insurrection against Ferdinand II of the Two Sicilies, Garibaldi landed in Sicily (May 11, 1860), in command of 1,000 volunteers. After conquering Sicily, the *camicie rosse* proceeded to the mainland, where they took the Kingdom of Naples before moving on to the Papal States. To prevent

[70] On the political consequences of the war against Austria, see Brooks (2009, 87–90), Schneid (2012) and Turnbull (1985). On the social and cultural consequences of which referred to in Italy as the "Second War for Independence", see Marwil (2010).

the Kingdom of the two Sicilies and the Papal States from becoming independent republics, as was Garibaldi's aspiration, in September of 1860, Cavour ordered Victor Emmanuel II's troops to cross the Papal States and enter Naples.[71] As a result, the people of the former King of the Two Sicilies approved their annexation into the Kingdom of Sardinia via successive referendums, and by overwhelming majorities.

### 16.6.5 The Kingdom of Italy Is Founded (March 14, 1861)

By way of successive additions the small Kingdom of Piedmont-Sardinia, which in July of 1859 had a population of just 5 million, 2 years later boasted over 22 million. The next constitutional step was to convene an Italian Parliament. Meeting in Turin, this body proclaimed Victor Emmanuel II King of Italy "by the grace of God and the will of the nation" (March 17, 1861),[72] with the new Italian State promptly adopting its tricolor flag.

Three months later (June 1861), Cavour died, but not before he had realized his objective of Italian unification. As Venice and Rome were still yet to be integrated, Florence served as the capital of Italy (1864).

### 16.6.6 The "Roman Question"

Venice would be incorporated into the Kingdom of Italy in October of 1866 via plebiscite,[73] but Rome was still a holdout, posing a difficult situation as the Pope was simultaneously the spiritual head of the Catholic Church and the political head of the Papal States, making governments and Catholic sovereigns, including Victor Emmanuel II himself, reticent to occupy his territory.[74] It was Garibaldi, supported

[71] On the conflict between Garibaldi and Cavour, see Mack Smith (1985). For new insights on Garibaldi's life and political role, see Riall (2008).

[72] The law had only one article. It was approved by the Senate on February 26 with only two votes against. On March 14, the text was unanimously approved by the lower house, and officially promulgated on March 17, 1861. Victor Emmanuel II assumed for himself and his successors the title of King of Italy ("*Vittorio Emanuele II assume per sé e per i suoi succesori il titolo di re d'Italia... per grazia di Dio e volontà della nazione*") (Ghisalberti 2006, 101).

[73] In July 1866, after being defeated at Königgrätz by Prussian troops (July 1866), Francis Joseph of Austria ceded Veneto to Napoleon III who, in turn, handed it to King Victor Emmanuel II.

[74] For an overview of the position of the Church regarding the *laissez faire* model of the state, see Gould (2002, 115–132). On the conflict between Italian liberals and the Holy See, read McIntire (2008, 114–139) and Hasler (1981, 105–128).

by Italian public opinion, who dared to do so, his volunteers attacking Rome in October of 1867, where they were met with resistance from French soldiers of the Second Empire in Mentana (November 3, 1867). Garibaldi was defeated. On this occasion, Napoleon III, rather than supporting the cause of Italian unification, chose to defend the Pope, as he happened to be married to Spaniard Eugenia de Montijo, a fervent Roman Catholic.

It would not be until the Franco-Prussian War when, after a defeat at Sedan, French soldiers withdrew from the Eternal City. On September 20, 1870, Italian troops finally entered Rome. The annexation was consolidated through an ensuing plebiscite, and the city became the capital of Italy.

In an effort to assuage the concerns of European Catholics,[75] the Italian Parliament then proceeded, via the "Law of Guarantees" (May 1871), to recognize the Pope's spiritual independence.[76] Nevertheless, Pius IX (1846–1878), refusing to accept the loss of the Papal States, rejected subsidies from the Italian State and deeming himself to be a kind of prisoner.[77] The Roman question was not fully resolved for another 60 years, when on February 11, 1929, after difficult negotiations (Pollard 2005, 42–46), Mussolini signed accords with the Papacy in Lateran creating today's Vatican State (Lateran Accords, or Lateran Pacts) (Kertzer 2014).

## 16.7 German Unification

As we have seen, after the outbreak of the revolution in Vienna in 1848 the King of Prussia, Frederick William IV, sought to supplant the Emperor of Austria and to head up the Germanic Confederation himself. Austria's military might, however, forced him to yield to the Austrian leader and sign the Punctation of Olmütz in 1850.

[75] Through these agreements the Pope retained the prerogatives of a sovereign, maintained the Vatican and Lateran palaces, and received a pension from the Italian government. He was also assured of the absolute freedom of the conclaves, and the Italian state relinquished control of the clergy, a function that lay with the Pope.

[76] As Lyttleton (1997, 235) points out, even if the Law of Guarantees gave the Pope the rights of a sovereign and full diplomatic status to the Vatican, it did not recognize the full independence of the papal state because it did not have the force of a treaty. Rather, it was an internal law of the Italian state and, as such, could be revised or repealed. Pius IX could not accept anything less than full territorial sovereignty, and, therefore, declared that there could be no compromise between Christ and the Devil. He denounced Italian unity as an unnatural and fictitious pretence and declared that "it was not expedient" (*non expedit*) to vote in parliamentary elections. Though the ban on voting was widely ignored, it made the formation of a Catholic party in the Italian parliament impossible. The full text of the Law of Guarantees appears in Appendix I of Pollard (2005, 195–197).

[77] On the Pope's opposition to the occupation of the Papal States, see Burns (1990, 1123–1152).

### 16.7.1 Bismarck, Architect of Prussian Hegemony

Frederick William IV died in 1861 without having managed for Prussia to lead the process towards German "national" integration.[78] His brother William I (1861–1888), however, would succeed at this task, as in September 1862, he was shrewd enough to appoint Otto von Bismarck to head his government, who would go down in history as the "Iron Chancellor" (*Eiserner Kanzler*) for having forged his nation into Europe's leading power.

Bismarck rose to power at a time when the government was at loggerheads with the parliament, whose deputies refused to approve the taxes the government needed to supply the Prussian army. The new head of the Prussian government did not hesitate to promulgate a series of decrees allowing him to secure the money necessary to bolster Prussian military power (Darmstaedter 2008, 195–218).

### 16.7.2 The Defeat of Austria and the North German Confederation

In just 4 years, Bismarck managed to build up a Prussian army strong enough to defeat Austria at the Battle of Königgrätz-Sadowa (July 1866). As a result of this, the Iron Chancellor dissolved the German Confederation and created in its place the North German Confederacy (*Norddeutscher Bund*), led by Prussia and made up of the 21 states north of the Main River, with Austria excluded from the new confederation.[79]

The new North German Confederation was personally structured by Bismarck himself[80] as a federal government assuming some of the powers of its 21 member states. It was presided over by the King of Prussia and its chancellor: Bismarck. It featured two assemblies: the *Reichstag*, which represented the German people and was elected by universal suffrage,[81]; and the *Bundesrat*, the heir to the former Diet, which represented the governments of the different states. The federal government

[78] In fact, shortly after the Punctation of Olmütz, Frederick William IV began to suffer mental problems. Following a stroke in 1857, his brother (and successor, as he had no heirs) began to reign as William I, in 1858.

[79] On the foundation of the North German Confederacy, see Darmstaedter (2008, 312–334).

[80] Bismarck personally drafted the constitution in 5 h on a September afternoon in 1866. This Constitution of the North German Confederacy suffered very minor amendments by the *Reichstag*, and in 1871 would become the Constitution of the German Empire (Second Reich). For a comprehensive vision of the Bismarck myth, see Gerwarth (2005).

[81] The Confederation was "weighted" in such a manner that it favored the ruling classes and effectively marginalized the middle class (Anderson 1993, 1448–1474), which enjoyed limited political influence in Germany until the Weimar Constitution of 1919. On this essential aspect of German society during the Imperial Period, see Blackbourn (1977, 409–433), Anderson (2000) and Sperber (1997).

had sovereign jurisdiction over all diplomatic affairs, economic policy and military matters. The Confederation also wielded full powers over the army, formed by soldiers and funded with money from all the states, but organized based on the Prussian model and under the direct command of the King of Prussia.[82]

### *16.7.3 The Franco-Prussian War and the Second Reich*

By this point, Prussia had become a formidable economic and military power, which allowed Bismarck, after taking control of the entire set of German states, to set his sights on German hegemony in Europe, an objective he was able achieve by provoking Napoleon III to declare war on William I, in the curious affair of the Ems Telegram.[83] After Prussia's crushing victory at the Battle of Sedan on September 1, 1870 (Wawro 2003, 211–229), the southern German states joined the Confederation of Northern Germany, giving rise to a new political entity: the German Empire (*Deutsches Reich*).[84] On January 18, 1871, after Prussian troops conquered

[82] For an overview of the new state created by Bismarck from a constitutional point of view, see Abrams (2006, 9–25) and Williamson (2011, 28–31).

[83] In the summer of 1870, Napoleon III protested when Prussian Minister-President Otto von Bismarck proposed King William's nephew Leopold von Hohenzollern for the Spanish throne for replacing Isabella II, dethroned after the 1868 Revolution, just as French kings had opposed Hapsburg encirclement in previous centuries. Bismarck pressed the case to weaken France, mistakenly anticipating that Napoleon III would stop short of war. The incident should have ended when Leopold withdrew his candidacy. However, French Foreign Minister Antoine Gramont pushed William to pledge never to propose a Hohenzollern for the Spanish throne again, a demand that trod too heavily on royal prerogative. On July 13, 1870, the king refused Gramont's request in an encounter at Ems with French ambassador Vincent Benedetti. Knowledge of the king's refusal reached the French public only after Bismarck had doctored the telegram relating the incident to make it appear more provocative. The French press, which Gramont had already primed for war, went into a bellicose frenzy over the news. The French cabinet likely decided in secret that evening to mobilize for war rather than accept a diplomatic defeat, and the Legislative Corps voted war credits on July 16. Whether they viewed the war to be madness, as Piton did, or the correct response to a dangerously aggressive power, the majority of French people reacted to mobilization with surprise and acceptance. According to historian Stéphane Audoin-Rouzeau, this moment played a significant role in the gradual development of French national identity. Despite the dynastic origins of the conflict, by the time fighting commenced at the end of July, public opinion on both sides considered the war to be a clash between nations. With the battlefields so close to home, writes historian Michael Howard, "every individual felt himself involved in a mighty communal endeavour". However, Piton, as a *honnête homme* and good Frenchman, wrote Napoleon III to demand that the emperor spare the country from the ravages of war. Chrastil (2010, 1–17). See also Badsey (2003, 26–54), and (Darmstaedter 2008, 359–362).

[84] German historians also call the Second Reich, between the Holy Roman Empire (First Reich) and Hitler's empire (Third Reich), the *Kaiserlich Deutsches Reich* or simply *Kaiserreich*. As Darmstaedter (2008, 14) points out, it responded to the spirit of an 'imperial German consciousness' (*kaiserlich deutsche Gesinnung*). On the common threads and differences between the Second Empire, the Weimar Republic, and the Third Reich, see Baranowski (2011).

Paris, William I was proclaimed German Emperor (Kaiser) at the Palace of Versailles (Williamson 2011, 175). Germany's Second Reich would last until the abdication of William II in 1918.

### 16.7.4 A Top Down Integration in a Federal and Laic State

While the "Italian nation" became unified through a democratic movement from the bottom up, which took shape from the outset through the adoption of a parliamentary regime, in the case of the "German nation" integration into a single state came about in the opposite way, from the top down, advanced by the princes of the various Germanic states, led first by the Emperor of Austria and later by the King of Prussia, who in 1871 became the German Emperor. In this case integration was legitimized through diplomatic agreements between sovereigns rather than a popular vote.

By 1871 German unity had been achieved, although the organization of this union of states was not decided by the respective peoples concerned, but by their 21 sovereigns, led by the King of Prussia. Unlike Italian unity, which was achieved bottom-up, from the people, German unification came about according to a top-down model, with Bismarck at the top (Cohen 2010, 36). That is, it was the work of the rulers and not something brought about by a popular vote.[85] Bismarck endeavored to consolidate the state structure of the German Empire by all means at his disposal, especially its essential pillar: the Kingdom of Prussia. This is why he never accepted the imperial government depending upon a majority in the Reichstag, insisting that it be freely appointed by the Kaiser, unilaterally. Thus, parliamentary government was not consolidated in the German Empire, as its emperor continued to unilaterally control the government.[86] Another important difference, largely a consequence of the above, was that, unlike in Italy where a unitary state was created, the German Empire continued to be a federation.[87] In fact,

[85] On how Bismarck spearheaded the process leading to German unification, see Hargreaves (1991).

[86] Liberalism still existed, but had to take refuge at the local level, as pointed out by Palmowski (1999). The only Kaiser who was relatively amenable to a liberal approach was Frederick III but, serving as Emperor from March to June 1888, he did not have time to change his position's traditionally authoritarian approach, as he only reigned for 99 days. On this interesting figure, see Müller (2011, 63–104). For the economic consequences of the Franco-Prussian war, see Dedinger (2012, 1029–1054). A political analysis of the French Second Empire in Price (2007).

[87] Bismarck wished, by all means possible, to avoid giving the southern states the impression that north Germany had merely become a "Greater Prussia". This was no easy task, as the majority of the Prussian parliament considered the independent existence of the small states to be non-viable. Nevertheless, Bismarck held that "in the name of the Federal constitution we have guaranteed the existence of these small states... and, therefore, their existence is possible" (Darmstaedter 2008, 337).

the integration of the German nation into a single state would not come about until after World War I and the foundation of the Weimar Republic (1919–1933).[88]

Bismarck's imperial conception was much more than a mere political or administrative idea, as proven by his radical opposition to the Church (Blackbourn 1988, 57–78), or *Kulturkampf*, a frontal assault in which the Iron Chancellor essentially declared on the Roman Catholic Church (Dwyer 2001, 174), as he desired to establish a powerful secular state completely independent of any spiritual or religious organization.[89]

## 16.8 Imperial Russia as a Final Bastion of Autocracy

The last state where the liberal revolution would end up toppling absolute monarchy would be Russia, which would not become a nation-state until the 1905 Revolution.

### *16.8.1 From Enlightened Absolutism to the Consolidation of Autocracy*

Russia became an empire under Peter the Great (1682–1725) and Catherine the Great (1762–1796), but, from a constitutional perspective, it was an absolute monarchy. Even though these two monarchs accepted the principle of enlightened reform, at the beginning of the nineteenth century, Russia was still an autocracy (Pipes 2005, 13–21). While the Napoleonic wars brought the ideas of the French Revolution, they did not introduce changes into the Russian constitution during the reign of Alexander I (1801–1825).[90] After his death, some Russian army officers

---

[88] For an overview of the complicated process of German unification, see Fulbrook (2004, 122–130). For a description of how the North German Confederacy worked in practice, see Darmstaedler (2008, 335–363).

[89] From 1871 to 1875, Bismarck obtained from the *Reichstag* a series of measures (known as the *Maigesetze*, or May Laws) essentially aimed against the Catholic Church, which gradually lost its privileges in German states, such as the right to teach at public schools, inspect its own schools, and freely administrate its assets (Bennette 2012, 15–75). This was the *Kulturkampf* (fight for culture) through which Bismarck wished to consolidate German national identity (Anderson 1986, 82–116) within the Protestant tradition to which he belonged (Smith 1995). Bismarck's religious policy spurred the imperial German government to disband monastic orders, particularly the Society of Jesus. The state assumed the right to name priests, as well as disciplinary authority, previously assigned to bishops. Civil marriage became mandatory prior to religious marriage. The Ecclesiastical resistance to this set of measures landed a number of priests in jail, while many bishops who objected to Bismarck's anti-religious policies were deposed (Gross 2008). This interesting chapter in Bismarck's history has been examined with great interest by many historians. Worthy of note are Lill (1981, 26–45) and Ross (1998). On the consequences of *Kulturkampf* in German universities, see Zwicker (2011).

[90] For an overview of the transformation of the Russian ruling class under Peter the Great and Alexander I, see Hosking (1991).

sought to liberalize the regime through the abovementioned Decembrist Uprising of 1825, following the liberal revolutionary model, pioneered in Spain by Coronel Riego in 1820. The revolt failed and Tsar Nicholas I (1825–1855) reestablished autocracy, becoming the defender of absolutism throughout Europe, dubbed the "gendarme of Europe" by liberals as he brutally suppressed any liberal stirrings, not only in Russia, but also in Poland and Hungary.[91]

At the end of the nineteenth century, the last absolutist regime standing in Europe was Russia, headed by its Tsar, Alexander II (1855–1881), who had failed to liberalize the country, his life cut short by a terrorist's bomb on March 13, 1881, the same day that he had granted a constitution (Radzinsky 2005, 417). The assassination led his successor, Alexander III (1881–1894), to reimpose autocracy.[92]

### *16.8.2 Speransky and the First Attempt to Establish the Principle of the Rule of Law in Imperial Russia*

Despite the brutal reestablishment of absolutist autocracy there were some attempts to introduce the principle of the "rule of law" in Russia, essentially thanks to the initiative of one man: jurist Mikhail Speransky (1772–1839).[93] In 1802 he argued in his work "On the Fundamental Laws of the State" that the monarchy's powers needed to be limited by society. Though it was not truly democracy which Speranski advocated, as he wished for the tsar to share his power with a powerful nobility (Smith-Peter 2006, 2236–2237), he believed that the spirit of the times called for a constitutional monarchy kept in check by public opinion, with a legislative body, the State Duma, to assist in this process (Christian 1976, 192–213). These views, which Speransky put into writing in 1809 in a memorandum (Leontovitsch 2012, 48), earned him many high-ranking enemies which, combined with his social isolation and somewhat difficult personality, led to his exile in March of 1812. He was not allowed to return to St. Petersburg until 1821.[94] During his expulsion he was influenced by the German Historical School of Law, based on the principle that each nation developed according to its own essence, embodied in its unique historical and legal institutions and practices (Beiser 2011, 231). The Historical School's approach provided a foundation for Speransky's codification of

[91] On the struggle between liberals and conservatives in Imperial Russia, see Martin (1997) and Raeff (1959, 218–230). For the Russian history and culture in the age of Catherine II see Kussber (2009, 57–88).

[92] On the reformist policy of Alexander II, see Mosse (1992).

[93] For an overview of Speransky's life and works, see Raeff (1990).

[94] On the liberal influence on Speranski's thought, see Gooding (1986). Lieven (2009) provides an essential reference of this time.

Russian law, based on organizing and publishing the laws and edicts issued since the prior codification carried out in 1649.

Although some "Decembrist" officers stated that Speransky had influenced them, he not only denied this but was one of the organizers of the trial against the rebels, and called for harsh penalties for them. His attitude persuaded Nicholas I to allow him to head up the effort to codify Russia's laws. This was the origin of the 45 volumes of the *Complete Collection of the Laws of the Russian Empire*, issued in 1830, followed up by the 15-volume *Digest of the Laws*, containing laws currently in effect, published between 1832 and 1839. While the *Complete Collection of Laws* contained the texts of nearly all laws and edicts issued from 1649 to 1825, the *Digest* organized laws currently in effect by topic. This was, then, a *bona fide* legal code. This codification was one of the main accomplishments of Nicholas's reign, and Speransky was the man behind it.[95]

### *16.8.3 The Revolution of 1905 and the First Russian Constitution (1906)*

Significant political change in Russia would not come about until Nicholas II (1894–1917). After losing the Russo-Japanese War (1904–1905), the tsar had to grapple with the Revolution of 1905, which forced him to accept the establishment of a constitutional monarchy and a parliamentary system.[96] After signing a manifesto granting civil liberties and universal male suffrage (October 1905), on April 23, 1906 Nicholas II enacted the "Russian Fundamental Law",[97] a sweeping revision of Speranski's code which, among other aspects, contained regulations stipulating how the tsar was to exercise his prerogatives. This legislation is considered the first Russian constitution, and in 1906 for the first time, the tsar shared his power with an elected parliament composed of two houses: the upper chamber, the State Council, and the lower, the Duma.[98]

[95] For an overview of Speranski's codification, see Whisenhunt (2001). After the codification was complete Speransky traveled abroad, acted as a member of the State Council, and lectured to the *tsarevich*, the future Alexander II, on law. For a historical and contemporary development of the Russian constitutionalism, see Medushevskii (2006). On the development of the rule of law principle in Russia, see Wortman (1976).

[96] On the Revolution of 1905, see Verner (1990). On the opposition to the Revolution, see Rendle (2010).

[97] On the manifesto of October 17, 1905 and the Constitution of April 23, 1906, see Leontovitsch (2012, 269–282).

[98] The tsar, however, was unwilling to give up his power. On February 20, 1906, Nicolas II signed the documents enacting into law the proposals leading to the Constitution, adding one word to the description of his "supreme authority". The sentence became "supreme *autocratic* authority" a stark reminder to the country that he did not believe he had yielded any of his prerogatives (Ascher 2004, 125). For an overview of the intervention of the conservatives in the 1905 Revolution and in the framing of the constitutional regime, see Rawson (1995) and Westwood (2002).

Liberal Russians faced an uphill struggle because of tsarist opposition to the parliamentary system and the fact that they were not powerful enough in the Duma.[99] In any case the regime was short-lived, however, as the outbreak of World War I triggered two revolutions (that of February and October) in 1917, which simultaneously obliterated monarchy and liberalism in Russia.[100]

## 16.9 Colonialism and Confrontation: The International Consequences of the Triumph of the Nation-State Model

After Italian and German unification and the 1905 Russian revolution, throughout Europe regimes would come to prevail under which a bourgeois, commercial, industrial and financial oligarchy held power. As a result, these groups advanced policies transforming their states into major economic powers adopting plans to colonize different regions around the world. The model of the liberal state which prevailed in most European countries in the nineteenth century embraced the expansion of "national capitalism", an approach based on each nation-state seeking to promote its own economic development in open competition with others, and struggling to acquire more markets by way of colonial expansion. Thus, the last third of the nineteenth century became a golden age of colonialism. This model, fused with the principle of nationalism, would give rise to considerable tensions at the international level (Bridge and Bullen 2005).

### *16.9.1 The Golden Age of Colonialism*

It was during this period that the Europeans explored and colonized much of Africa, a virgin continent with huge potential, especially because of its abundance of raw materials. Western powers also managed to colonize much of Asia, where states boasting centuries of history (such as China), were successively conquered by European nations in a series of armed conflicts. In China, these included the

[99] The failure of the "Constitutional experiment" was clear from the beginning, considering the great difficulties that the ephemeral First Duma faced, only lasting from April 27 to July 9, 1906. It was an assembly that reflected in its composition the voters' yearning for an end to the revolutionary turmoil, rapid improvements in their condition, and their deep hatred of the tsarist regime (Galai 2012, 196). For an overview of this short but interesting period see Seton-Watson (2004, 628–648).

[100] Essentially because Nicholas II never fully engaged in the parliamentary game, and between 1906 and 1917 Russia remained an essentially authoritarian monarchy (Daly 2004, 16–52). For an overview of Russian parliamentary life from 1906 to the First World War, see Korros (2002). The 1906 Constitution was abolished by Alexander Kerensky on September 15, 1917. For an overview of the Russian Revolution from its origins in the famine crisis of 1891 until its end with the collapse of the Soviet regime, see Figes (2014).

Opium Wars (1839–1842 and 1856–1860) and the Boxer Rebellion (1899–1901).[101] Similarly, the Boer War (1899–1902), allowed England to occupy South Africa, hitherto controlled by the Boers, descendants of Dutch settlers. Western influence in Japan also led to the transformation of the country during the Meiji Era (1868–1912).[102]

### *16.9.2 Nationalism and Confrontation: The Europe of the "Armed Peace"*

By the end of nineteenth century, Europe's nation-states controlled the world but were disunited. The triumph of the principle of nationalism had created powerful countries, but had weakened mechanisms for cooperation and accord between them. In fact, the colonial, overtly imperialist policies advanced by the European ruling classes in each nation soon generated significant international tensions.

The consolidation of nation-states weakened the European political model of stability through coalition which Metternich had striven to maintain from 1815 to 1848, replacing it with a dynamic in which powerful nations squared off against and competed with each other (Holsti 1991, 138–173). The triumph of the nation-state in Italy and Germany, for example, precipitated successive wars, as Italian unity was not achieved without bloody clashes between French-Sardinian and Austrian troops. The battles of Magenta and Solferino (1859), were particularly grim, not so much in terms of those killed in combat, but because of the fact that the medical services were so deficient that most men died as a result of preventable infections and treatable wounds.[103] This appalling situation would inspire Swiss businessman and philanthropist Henri Dunant (1828–1910), to found the Red Cross.[104] Three

[101] Both conflicts are currently considered by Chinese historians, a "National Humiliation" (Standen 2013, 155)

[102] It is significant that during this period Japanese elites sent their youth to study at the best European Universities. On their presence at Cambridge University, see Koyama (2009).

[103] Such appalling numbers were typical of nineteenth-century wars. For example, casualties in the U.S. Civil War came to 1,094,453 dead or wounded: 642,427 for the Union, and 428,000 for the Confederates. However, most of these victims died of infections and disease rather than falling in battle. Roughly three in five Union casualties, and two in three Confederate, died of disease or infections resulting from their wounds. Kingseed (2004, 91) mentions the case of the state of Iowa, where half of the men of military age filled 46 regiments in the Union Army. Between 1861 and 1865, 12,553 Iowans died: 3,540 on the battlefield, 515 in prison camps, and 8,498 from disease.

[104] Dunant was an eyewitness to the carnage which ensued from the Battle of Solferino, and was so horrified that he resolved to create a corps of volunteers to attend to wounded soldiers. This was the origin of the Red Cross (February 17, 1863), whose emblem is the Swiss flag, but with the colors reversed. A year later, Dunant's recommendations led to the signing of the Geneva Conventions, a series of international agreements governing the treatment of prisoners and the war-wounded. The 1864 Geneva Convention would be expanded in 1949, at the end of World War II. Dunant recorded his experiences in his book *A Memory of Solferino* (*Un souvenir de Solferino*) published in 1862, in which he described the horrors of the pain and suffering born of the battle (Dunant 2009). Also, Brooks (2009). On the founding of the Red Cross, see Reinalda (2009, 51–54).

years later, German nationalism, embodied and advanced by Bismarck, waged war to defeat Austria (1866) and, 4 years later, France (1870). Prussia's triumph over Austria and France led to the 1871 founding of the Second Reich, and the generation of serious resentment in France because of Prussia's seizure of the Alsace and Lorraine[105] regions. The Russians, meanwhile, after defeating Napoleon, also managed to gradually overpower the Ottoman Empire, thereby becoming another great colonial power (Geyer 1987, 186–219).[106]

All these wars, however, were nothing more than the beginning of an escalation which would end up taking on global dimensions in the first half of the twentieth century. The root cause of the international tension that arose between the European states during the last third of the nineteenth century, was that Italy and Prussia, the new European nation-states unified in the last third of the century, undertook the process of colonial expansion relatively late, a dynamic hitherto dominated by the British Empire and France, which in 1830 launched an ambitious colonial program.[107] Even the U.S. got involved as well, expanding the Union by overthrowing the Kingdom of Hawaii in 1893, annexing the islands in 1898 (Vowell 2012),[108] and waging war on Spain over Cuba and the Philippines in the same year (Hendrickson 2003), thereby spreading American influence in these areas.[109]

Italy, forged into a nation-state before Germany, moved to exploit territories in Africa: Somalia, Ethiopia, Abyssinia and Tripolitania (Libya). Prussia, however, barely managed to occupy Namibia. This meager achievement was all the more frustrating because the German Empire had become a major industrial power in need of raw materials and new markets. As a result, William II (1888–1918) launched an aggressive expansionist policy which collided head-on with the colonial interests of England and France. It was Bismarck's aspiration for central Europe (*Mitteleuropa*)[110] to overpower the English Empire through expansion to

[105] Prussia, of course, never forgot the repeated humiliations they had suffered at the hand of Napoleon when he occupied Berlin. In 1871, the Second Reich was proclaimed at Versailles in the Hall of Mirrors (dating back to Louis XIV), which would later be chosen by the French, very deliberately, for the signing of the Peace of Versailles in 1919, through which France made every effort to take revenge upon and humiliate Germany. Said treaty would, in turn, fan German resentment under Hitler, who seized upon his country's thirst for revenge to instigate World War II. For an overview on the diplomatic and military brinkmanship that preceded the inevitable outbreak of the First World War, see Massie (2013).

[106] Also, Barkey (2008, 264–296) and Quataert (2005, 54–74).

[107] Holland and Portugal had kept substantial parts of their colonial lands, while Spain had lost most of its by 1824 (Battle of Ayacucho), prompting it to launch a colonial war later in the century under the government of General O'Donnell, occupying a limited extension of northern Morocco in 1859–1860.

[108] Also Osborne (1981).

[109] For an overview of American Imperialism, see Kaplan (2005). Also, Smith (2013) and Thomas (2011).

[110] The idea was initially championed by the conservative German thinker Friedrich Naumann (1860–1919), who described a domain marked out for German economic and cultural hegemony (Sträth 2006, 7). For an overview of the development of the idea, see Naumann himself (1916) and Meyer (1955).

the east (*Ostraum*), to the detriment of Russia (Katzenstein 1997, 9). The upshot was widespread rearmament and the constitution of defensive alliances aimed at regulating colonial expansion, such as that signed between France and Russia in 1892, or that between England and France in 1904 (*Entente cordiale*), a union which the United States would ultimately end up joining (Williamson 2000, 11).

In response to these alliances, William II's German Empire signed others with the Austro-Hungarian and Ottoman empires, which ratcheted up tensions, creating an international situation which historians have come to call the "Armed Peace" referring particularly to the crucial period from 1895 to 1911 (Bridge and Bullen 2005, 251–302).[111] Trade disputes and economic conflicts ended up degenerating into a cataclysmic conflict which would spread throughout the world: World War I (1914–1918).[112]

## 16.10 World War I and the Crisis of the Liberal State Model

### *16.10.1 The Implosion of the Nation-State System*

The creation of sets of alliances (Central Powers vs. the "Triple Entente"), ultimately unleashed an apocalyptic war which would last four and a half years and, in short, change everything. The Great War not only brought an end to the hegemony that Europe had enjoyed throughout most of the globe, but undermined confidence in the liberal state model, highlighted the need for greater international cooperation to prevent global war, and shattered the western world's optimistic confidence in the inevitability of human progress offered by the technological, scientific and economic breakthroughs made during the preceding century.

### *16.10.2 The Assassination in Sarajevo and Europe's Suicide*

The spark which produced the conflagration was a terrorist attack which took the life of the heir to the Austro-Hungarian Empire, Franz Ferdinand, and his wife,

[111] As Stevenson (2006, 75) indicates, on the eve of the First World War the six Great Powers of Britain, France, Germany, Austria–Hungary, Italy and Russia accounted for some three quarters of global defense spending. On this crucial period, see Blom (2010).

[112] On the German attitude during the "Armed Peace" period, see Ferguson (1992) and Wilson P. (2004). For a more detailed description of the causes of this apocalyptic conflict, see Henning (2003). On the causes of the conflict from the perspective of the peace negotiations in Versailles in 1919, see Mombauer (2002, 22–32).

Sophie Chotek, in Sarajevo on June 28, 1914 (Smith 2009). It is not only intriguing, but essential for an understanding of twentieth century history, to note how this particular event was capable of igniting a firestorm which consumed all the western nations, as it demonstrates how the logic of the liberal nation-states' relationships generated international tensions which ultimately proved not only unsustainable, but catastrophic.

The Austro-Hungarian Empire was not, in reality, a nation-state, as it encompassed a multitude of nationalities struggling for their autonomy, along the lines of Belgium, Italy and Germany. It was its two most powerful nations, Germany and Hungary, which dominated the others; the Germans imposed their will on the Czechs, Poles, Slovenes, Ruthenians and Italians, while the Hungarians held sway over the Slovaks, Romanians, Serbs, and Croats. However, the nationalist agitation that triggered liberal movements and revolutions throughout Europe in a series of uprisings defying the Metternich System would generate hope among all these peoples, who aspired to form their own independent nation-states.

The Austro-Hungarian Empire had no intention of tolerating these aspirations to sovereignty, and fully employed its police, secret services and army to maintain the status quo. To resist them a series of secret nationalist societies arose which sought to hurl defiance at the Empire through the assassination of political figures. Such was the situation when Franz Ferdinand, the heir to Francis Joseph of Austria, paid an official visit to Sarajevo in 1914. There, on June 28, Gavrilo Princip, a member of the Young Bosnia nationalist group, shot the heir to Austro-Hungarian Empire and his wife at close range (Mulligan 2010, 208).

In a Europe divided into two blocks, the attack threatened to upset the fragile balance which had hitherto been maintained. Then started the July crisis (Mulligan 2010, 208–226). On July 23, Francis Joseph's government sent an ultimatum to the Serbian government, holding it responsible for the assassination. All the conditions contained therein were accepted, except for two: the participation of Austro-Hungarian official agents in the investigation of the shooting, and the banning of Pan-Serbian propaganda. On July 25, after receiving support from William II of Prussia, at that time the head of the German Empire, Francis Joseph's government severed relations with Serbia, a small country, but one allied with Russia by means of a defensive treaty. The next day, on July 26, Tsar Nicholas II ordered the "premobilization" of the Russian army, which did not dissuade Austria–Hungary from declaring war on Serbia 2 days later. All of Europe held its breath for 5 harrowing days, wondering if the conflict would spread.[113]

[113] For an overview of these prewar tensions in European public opinion, see Clark (2013). An account of the lives and assassination of the Archduke and his wife, with a wide variety of unpublished sources in King and Woolmans (2013).

### 16.10.3 The Dominos Fall

On July 29, Russia ordered partial mobilization. Germany acted to mediate, but its initiative was rejected by St. Petersburg. London then informed Berlin that if Germany were to declare war on Russia, England would be forced to join the conflict.

On July 30, Germany rejected a Russian and a second English proposal to limit the geographical scope of the war. On that day, Russia unilaterally ordered, without consulting France, mobilization against Austria–Hungary and the German Empire.

On July 31, Berlin sent an ultimatum to St. Petersburg, urging the Russians to demobilize. Russia did not respond, and Germany called general mobilization. On the same day France undertook preparations to mobilize its army.

On August 1, William II declared war on Nicholas II, 2 days later on France. The following day a German army invaded Belgium, despite the fact that it had been a neutral state since 1839. The violation of Belgian neutrality dragged England into the war. It was August 4, 1914 and there was no going back (MacMeekin 2013, 373).

### 16.10.4 An Apocalyptic Conflict

In the end, 32 countries ended up fighting in the Great War, 28 of them on the "Allied" side, which included France, the United States, Serbia, Belgium, Canada, Portugal, Japan, the United Kingdom and the Russian Empire. The Allies squared off against the "Central Powers", a coalition composed of the Austro-Hungarian, German and Ottoman empires, ultimately joined by Bulgaria. Finally, Italy began the war on the side of the Central Powers, but ended up changing sides.

The result was a war of extermination in which 65 million soldiers fought, 10 million soldiers died, 19 million were wounded, and 35 million were maimed, in addition to the more than 14 million civilians (10 million in Russia alone), who died as a result of the conflict.[114]

In France 10 % of the male population perished in the Great War, which led to serious demographic stagnation. The republican principle of compulsory military service (conscription) would make the 1914 war the most lethally in the history of French democracy, with 900 men killed daily on average during the 1,556 days that the conflict lasted (Riaud 2008, 137). This explains why even the smallest French

[114] Russia lost 2 million, Germany 1.7 million, Austria–Hungary and France 1.4 million each, and the British Empire 1 million. The U.S. lost over 300,000 men (Homsher 2006, 287–288). On the vital role that medicine played in the war, see van Bergen (2009) and Harris (2010).

towns still have monuments to the *poilus*[115] killed in the conflict—impressive testaments to the devastating impact of one of the greatest tragedies in human history.

### *16.10.5 The Constitutional Consequences of World War I: The End of Liberalism and the Resurgence of State Power*

From the point of view of the history of public law, Word War I is crucial because it overturned the liberal model rooted in a limited state. The colossal effort required by this "total" war demanded general mobilization, both military and civilian. Women played a particularly important civilian role, as the men were fighting on the front (Braybon 2000, 149–162). Thus, in the wake of the Great War, women began to win the vote in a number of western countries.[116] For four and a half years, the efforts of entire nations had centered upon the war, which meant that states acquired new scopes and degrees of power they would never fully relinquish after the conflict.[117]

A far-reaching consequence of the massive and devastating war effort undertaken by the powers which fought in World War I, was the bolstering of state power. The need to concentrate all resources and energies to fight a "total" and ongoing conflict, in addition to bankrupting Europe, necessitated major state intervention in all areas of citizens' lives, especially in the economic sphere—industrial and financial restructuring to sustain the war effort—and in the social—e.g. mandated rationing as a result of shortages, and the seizure of the materials necessary to fight the war (Turner 2000). All these interventionist measures abated after the war, but no country reverted entirely to the liberal system in place in 1914 (Luebbert 1991, 194–198). During the Great War, the states involved would develop the mechanisms of power that would lay the foundations for twentieth-century totalitarianism, as we shall see in the next chapter.

---

[115] Literally, "hairy", as French soldiers in the trenches did not shave.

[116] It was no coincidence that it was after the Great War when women won the right to vote in most Western nations. The first countries granting the vote to women were New Zealand (1893), and South Australia (1895), both then self-governing British colonies. After the Federation of Australia (1901), women obtained the right to vote in 1902—except for aboriginal women, who were not permitted to so until 1962. In Europe, the first country to grant voting rights to women was the Grand Duchy of Finland (1907), then part of the Russian Empire, followed by Norway in 1913. During the World War I Denmark granted the right vote to women, in 1915, and after the War women could vote in 1918 in Germany, Czechoslovakia and Poland. In 1919, female suffrage was granted in the Netherlands, Austria and Sweden. In England it was progressively introduced between 1918 and 1928, when all restrictions were lifted. Women were not allowed to vote until much later in Spain (1931), France (1944), Italy (1946), Belgium (1948), San Marino (1957), Switzerland (1971), Portugal (1974) and Liechtenstein (1984).

[117] For an analysis of what caused the warring nations to develop powerful states and abandon the principles of the liberal model, see Nicholls (2000, 60–89).

## TIMELINE

### The Foundations of the Restoration

1814 April 6. Napoleon abdicates.
May 4. Ferdinand VII reestablishes absolute monarchy in Spain
June 4. Louis XVIII grants *Le Charte*.
October 1. First meeting of the Congress of Vienna.
1815 June 9. Last session of the Congress of Vienna.
June 18. Battle of Waterloo.
July 18. Napoleon definitively exiled.
September 14. Russia, Prussia and Austria sign the Holy Alliance.
1818 October 1–November 15. Congress of Aix-la-Chapelle. France joins the Holy Alliance.

### Revolution and Counter-Revolution Between 1820 and 1830

1820 January 1. Colonel Riego's Revolt at Cabezas de San Juan.
March 8. Ferdinand VII endorses the Constitution of Cádiz.
1821 May 5. Napoleon dies on St. Helena.
1822 November 22. Congress of Verona.
1823 April 7. Entry into Spain of the Hundred Thousand Sons of St. Louis.
August 31. The French take the Fort of Trocadero (Cádiz).
September 30. Surrender at Cádiz. End of the Liberal Triennium.
November 7. Hanging of Riego.
1824 April 19. Lord Byron dies in Mesolonghi fighting for the independence of Greece.
December 9. Battle of Ayacucho. End of Spanish presence in the Americas. Spain's only remaining colonies are Cuba and the Philippines.
1825 December 26. The Decembrist Revolt in St. Petersburg.
1826 June 22–July 15. Congress of Panama. Simón Bolívar fails in his attempt to form a federation comprised of the recently-founded Latin American states.
1829 September 14. The Ottoman Empire recognizes Greek independence (Treaty of Adrianople).

### The July Monarchy as a Model (1830–1848)

1830 March 29. Ferdinand VII abolishes the Salic Law (Pragmatic Sanction). Elizabeth II is born on October 10.
July 27, 28, 29. Revolution in Paris. Fall of Charles X. August. The United Kingdom of the Netherlands' southern provinces fight to secede. Belgium is born.
November 29. The Polish revolt against Russian occupation.
1831 February 7. Adoption of the Belgian Constitution.

1832 June 7. Lord Grey's Electoral Reform Law in England.
December 26. Poland is incorporated into Russia via the Organic Statute and subjected to an autocratic, Orthodox and pro-Russian regime.
1833 September 29. **Spain**. The death of Fernando VII. Regency of María Cristina (1833–1840).
1834 April 10. Enactment of the Royal Statute, a constitution given unilaterally by the Spanish Regent Maria Cristina following the model of the French *Charte* of 1814.
1836 August 12. La Granja Uprising.
1837 June 17. The liberals enact a new Constitution.
1839 March. China. Beginning of the First Opium War (until 1842). British occupation.
August 31. Convention of Vergara (Maroto and Espartero). End of the First Carlist War in Spain.
1840 October 12. The beginning of Espartero's Regency. The progressive liberals seize power in Madrid.
1843 November 10. England. Elizabeth II is declared of age.
1845 May 23. Narváez promulgates a new constitution in Spain.

## The Revolution of 1848 and Its Consequences

1848 January 12. Revolution breaks out in Palermo (Sicily).
February 22–25. Revolution breaks out in Paris.
March 4. Charles Albert of Savoy promulgates a constitution (Albertine Statute).
March 13. Revolution breaks out in Vienna. Metternich flees.
March 18. Revolution breaks out in Berlin.
May 18. The Frankfurt Parliament is constituted.
October. A rebellion is quelled in Vienna.
December 2. Ferdinand I of Austria abdicates in favor of Francis Joseph.
1849 February 9. Promulgation of the Republic in Rome (Mazzini).
March 24. Charles Albert of Savoy hands the throne to his son, Victor Emmanuel II.
March 27. The Frankfurt Parliament proclaims the German Empire's first constitution.
April 3. Frederick IV of Prussia refuses to be appointed king by the Frankfurt Parliament.
May 31. Dissolution of the Frankfurt Parliament.
1850 January 31. Frederick William IV grants a new constitution for the Kingdom of Prussia, which would remain in force until 1918.
March 20–April 29. Failure of the first attempt at a German federation, led by Prussia (Erfurt Union).
November 29. Frederick IV of Prussia yields to Francis Joseph of Austria (Punctation of Olmütz).

## Italian Unification

1852 Camillo Benso (Count of Cavour) becomes Víctor Manuel II's prime minister.
1853 October. The French, Ottoman and British empires and the Kingdom of Sardinia declare war on the Russian Empire; the "Crimean war" lasts until February of 1856.
1856 Beginning of the Second Opium War (until 1860). France and the UK control China.
1858 August. Cavour meets with Napoleon III at Plombières. Franco-Sardinian Alliance.
September. The Spanish and French begin the occupation of Cochinchina (modern-day southern Vietnam), the campaign concluding in 1862. The Spanish pull out but the French remain, with their "Indochina" enduring until 1954.
1859 May–July. Austria is defeated by Franco-Sardinian forces in Magenta and Solferino.
August–September. Tuscany, Parma, Modena and part of the Papal States are incorporated into the Kingdom of Piedmont-Sardinia.
1860 May 11. Garibaldi lands at Marsala (Sicily), leading of force of 1,000 "redshirts".
September. Victor Emmanuel II's troops occupy Naples.
1861 January 2. William I of Prussia succeeds Frederick William IV.
March 14. Proclamation of the Kingdom of Italy (tricolor flag).
June 6. Cavour dies (at age 50).

## German Unification

1862 September 23. Bismarck heads the Council of Ministers.
1866 July 3. The Austrians are defeated by the Prussians at Königgrätz (Sadowa). End of the Seven Weeks' War.
1868 September 19. Glorious Revolution in Spain. Dethronement of Queen Isabella II.
1870 July 13. The Ems Dispatch.
July 19. The beginning of the Franco-Prussian War.
September 2. French defeat at the Battle of Sedan. Napoleon III is taken prisoner.
September 19. Beginning of the siege of Paris by the Prussians.
1871 January 18. William I is proclaimed the kaiser of the German Empire in the Palace of Versailles (Hall of Mirrors). The Germans take revenge for the humiliations inflicted on them by Louis XIV and Napoleon.
January 28. End of the siege of Paris.
March 18–May 28. Paris Commune.
1873 Proclamation of the First Spanish Republic.
1874 December. Alfonso XII is proclaimed King of Spain in Sagunto by General Martínez Campos.

## The Armed Peace

| | |
|---|---|
| 1880–1881 | First Boer War. A second would follow, fought from 1899 to 1902. |
| 1882 | Bismarck forges the Triple Alliance with Austria and Italy. |
| 1885 | November 25. Death of Alfonso XII. The Regency begins in Spain. |
| 1888 | March 9. Death of William I, who is succeeded by his son, Frederick III, who dies of cancer on June 16. William II, age 29, becomes Kaiser upon his father's death. |
| 1890 | March 20. Bismarck resigns. |
| 1892 | August 17. Franco-Russian Alliance. Ratified in 1893 and in 1894 by Russia and by France. |
| 1893 | U.S. marines land in Hawaii and overthrow the Queen Lili'uokalani. |
| 1898 | February 15. The explosion of the U.S. battleship *Maine* in Havana triggers the Spanish–American War. |
| | July. Annexation of Hawaii, which becomes a United States territory 2 years later. |
| | December 10. Peace of Paris. Spain loses Cuba and the Philippines. |
| 1899 | The government of Cuba is handed over to the United States. Fall. Beginning of the Boxer Rebellion in China (Ends in September 1901). |
| 1901 | The Philippines comes under U.S. rule. |
| 1902 | May 17. The Spanish King Alfonso XIII comes of age. |
| 1904 | February 8. Beginning of the Russo-Japanese War. |
| | April 8. Non-aggression and colonial expansion pact signed between France and England (*Entente cordiale*). |
| 1905 | January 22. Bloody Sunday. Beginning of the first Russian Revolution. |
| | September 5. End of the Russo-Japanese War. |
| | October. Nicholas II of Russia agrees to grant civil liberties, including universal male suffrage and the principle of representative government (October Manifesto). |
| 1906 | April 23. Nicholas II endorses the first Russian constitution. |
| 1912 | The Titanic sinks. 1,517 passengers perish. |

## World War I

| | |
|---|---|
| 1914 | June 28. Assassination of the Archduke Ferdinand in Sarajevo. |
| | August 4. The German Army crosses the Belgian border. |
| | August 17–September 2. Battle of Tannenberg (Eastern front). |
| | September 5–12. Battle of the Marne. French counteroffensive. End of mobile warfare and the beginning of Trench warfare. |
| 1915 | April 1. Beginning of air warfare. French pilot Roland Garros is the first pilot to down an enemy plane with a machine gun firing through propeller blades. |

April 22. Germans employ gas warfare at the Second Battle of Ypres.
April 25. Beginning of the Battle of Gallipoli (Dardanelles). After 8 months the British withdraw, defeated, having suffered over 250,000 casualties, the same number as the Turkish soldiers.

1916 February 21. Beginning of a heavy German offensive in Verdun. The battle would last until December (300,000 soldiers killed: 156,000 French and 143,000 Germans, with no territorial gains).
July 1–November 18. Battle of the Somme: over one million casualties, between the dead and injured. Over 600,000 French and British and 500,000 Germans.

1917 April 6. The United States declares war on Germany.
April 16–May 9. Nivelle Offensive. Within a week 100,000 French soldiers die.
May 3. Beginning of French mutinies.
May 15. Pétain replaces Nivelle. Large-scale attacks are suspended.
June 25. The first American troops arrive on French soil. They would not enter the trenches, however, until October.

1918 March 3. Treaty of Brest Litovsk. Russia withdraws from the war.
April 3. French Marshall Foch is named Supreme General of the Allied forces.
August 8. Beginning of the last Allied offensive (Hundred Days' Offensive).
November 11. Signature of the Armistice (Compiègne).

# References


Abrams, L. (2006). *Bismarck and the German Empire, 1871–1918* (2nd ed.). London: Routledge.

Adelman, J. (2006). *Sovereignty and revolution in the Iberian Atlantic*. Princeton, NJ: Princeton University Press.

Aguilera-Barchet, B. (2008). Las raíces jurídicas del Estado español contemporáneo: La Guerra de la Independencia y el afianzamiento del sentimiento nacional. Notas para un ensayo de historia constitucional europea comparada. In *Estudios sobre la Constitución de Bayona* (pp. 85–207). Madrid: La Ley.

Alison, P. W. (2013). *The confederation of Europe: A study of the European alliance, 1813–1823, as an experiment in the International Organization of Peace*. Stockbridge, MA: Hard Press.

Anderson, M. L. (1986). The Kulturkampf and the course of German history. *Central European History, 19*(1), 82–116.

Anderson, M. L. (1993). Voter, Junker, Landrat, Priest: The old authorities and the new franchise in imperial Germany, 1871–1914. *American Historical Review, 98*(5), 1448–1474.

Anderson, M. L. (2000). *Practicing democracy: Elections and political culture in imperial Germany*. Princeton, NJ: Princeton University Press.

Ascher, A. (2004). *The revolution of 1905: A short history*. Stanford, CA: Stanford University Press.

Aspinall, A., et al. (Eds.). (2000). *English historical documents: 1783–1832*. London: Routledge.

Badsey, S. (2003). *Outbreak: The Ems Telegram in The Franco-Prussian War: 1870–1871* (pp. 26–54). Osceola, WI: Osprey.

Balbo, C. C. (1857). *Della monarchia rappresentativa in Italia: Saggi politici*. Firenze: Le Monnier.

Baranowski, S. (2011). From imperial consolidation to global ambitions: Imperial Germany, 1871–1914. In *Nazi Empire: German colonialism and imperialism from Bismarck to Hitler* (pp. 9–66). Cambridge, UK: Cambridge University Press.

Barkey, K. (2008). On the road out of empire: Ottoman's struggle from empire to nation-state. In *Empire of difference: The Ottomans in comparative perspective* (pp. 264–296). Leiden: Brill.

Barman, R. J. (1999). *Citizen Emperor: Pedro II and the making of Brazil, 1825–1891*. Stanford, CA: Stanford University Press.

Beales, D., & Biagini, E. F. (2002). *The Risorgimento and the unification of Italy* (2nd ed.). Harlow, UK: Pearson Education Limited.

Beiser, F. C. (2011). Savigny and the historical School of Law. In *The German historicist tradition* (pp. 214–252). Oxford: Oxford University Press.

Bennette, R. A. (2012). *Fighting for the soul of Germany: The Catholic struggle for inclusion after unification*. Cambridge, MA: Harvard University Press.

Bernstein, S., & Milza, P. (1996). *Histoire du XIXe siècle*. Paris: Hatier.

Bew, J. (2012). *Castlereagh: A life*. Oxford: Oxford University Press.

Billinger, R. D. (1991). *Metternich and the German question: States' rights and federal duties, 1820–1834*. Newark, DE: University of Delaware Press.

Birmingham, D. (2003). *A concise history of Portugal* (2nd ed.). Cambridge: Cambridge University Press.

Blackbourn, D. (1977). The Mittelstand in German society and politics: 1871–1914. *Social History,* (4), 409–433.

Blackbourn, D. (1986). The discreet charm of the Bourgeoisie: Reappraising German history in the nineteenth century. In D. Blackbourn & G. Eley (Eds.), *The peculiarities of German history: Bourgeois society and politics in nineteenth-century Germany* (pp. 159–292). New York: Oxford University Press.

Blackbourn, D. (1988). Progress and party: Liberalism, Catholicism and the state in imperial Germany. *History Workshop Journal,* (26), 57–78.

Blom, P. (2010). *The Vertigo years: Europe, 1900–1914*. New York: Basic Books.

Blumberg, A. (1990). *A carefully planned accident: The Italian war of 1859*. London: Associated University Presses.

Böckenförde, E. -W. (1991). *The German type of constitutional monarchy in state, society and liberty: Studies in political theory and constitutional law* (pp. 47–70 and 87–114). New York: Berg.

Boime, A. (2004). *Art in an age of counterrevolution: 1815–1848*. Chicago, IL: The University of Chicago Press.

Boyd, C. (1979). *Praetorian politics in liberal Spain*. Chapel Hill, NC: The University of North Carolina Press.

Braybon, G. (2000). Women, war and work. In H. Strachan (Ed.), *The Oxford illustrated history of the First World War* (pp. 149–162). Oxford: Oxford University Press.

Breuilly, J. (2009). The response to Napoleon and German Nationalism. In A. Forrest & P. H. Wilson (Eds.), *The bee and the eagle: Napoleonic France and the end of the Holy Roman Empire, 1806* (pp. 256–284). Basingstoke: Palgrave Macmillan.

Brewer, D. (2011). *The Greek War of independence: The struggle for freedom from the Ottoman Oppression and the birth of the modern Greek nation*. New York: Overlook Press.

Bridge, F. R., & Bullen, R. J. (2005). Unstable equilibrium: 1895–1911. In *The great powers and the European states system: 1814–1914* (2nd ed., pp. 251–336). Harlow, UK: Pearson Longman.

Brock, M. (1993). *The Great Reform Act*. Aldershot, UK: Gregg Revivals.

Broers, M. (2000). The restoration in Piedmont-Sardinia, 1814–1848: Variations on reaction. In D. Laven & L. Riall (Eds.), *Problems of government in restoration Europe: Napoleon's legacy* (pp. 151–166). Oxford: Berg.

Brooks, R. (2009). *Solferino, 1859: The battle that won Italy its independence*. Oxford: Osprey.

Burns, G. (1990). The politics of ideology: The Papal struggle with liberalism. *American Journal of Sociology, 95*(5), 1123–1152.

Caldwell, P. C. (1997). *Popular sovereignty and the crisis of German constitutional law. The theory and practice of Weimar constitutionalism*. Durham, NC: Duke University Press.

Cánovas del Castillo, A. (1981) (2000). *Obras Completas. Discursos en el Ateneo* (Vol. 1). Madrid: Fundación Cánovas del Castillo.

Cánovas del Castillo, A. (2006). *Discursos parlamentarios*. Madrid: Congreso de los Diputados.

Carr, R. (2003). *Spain: 1808–1975* (2nd ed.). Oxford: Clarendon.

Chrastil, R. (2010). Introduction. In *Organizing for war: France, 1870–1914* (pp. 1–17). Baton Rouge, LA: Louisiana State University Press.

Chrimes, S. B. (1970). *English constitutional history*. Oxford: Oxford University Press.

Christian, D. B. (1976). The political ideals of Michael Speransky. *The Slavonic and East European Review, 14*(2), 192–213.

Clark, C. (2006). *Iron Kingdom: The rise and downfall of Prussia, 1600–1947*. Cambridge, MA: Belknap Press of Harvard University Press.

Clark, C. (2013). *The sleepwalkers: How Europe went to war in 1914*. New York: Harper.

Cohen, Y. (2010). *The Germans: Absent nationality and the holocaust*. Eastbourne, UK: Sussex Academic Press.

Congleton, R. D. (2011). *Constitutional reform, liberalism and the rise of western democracy*. Cambridge, UK: Cambridge University Press.

Constant, B. (2012). Speech on "The Liberty of the Ancients and the Moderns", 1819. In R. Leroux & D. M. Hart (Eds.), *French liberalism in the 19th century: An anthology* (pp. 68–81). Oxon, UK: Routledge.

Conversi, D. (1997). *The Basques, the Catalans and Spain: Alternative routes to nationalist mobilisation*. Reno, NV: University of Nevada Press.

Craiutu, A. (2003). *Liberalism under siege: The political thought of the French doctrinaires*. Lanham, MD: Lexington Books, Rowman & Littlefield.

Craiutu, A. (2004). The method of French doctrinaires. *History of European Ideas, 30*(1), 39–59.

Crawley, C. W. (2014). *The question of Greek independence: A study of British policy in the Near East, 1821–1833*. Cambridge, UK: Cambridge University Press. (Reprint of the 1930 edition).

Crosby, M. B. (2008). *The making of a German constitution*. Oxford: Berg.

Dakin, D. (1973). *The Greek struggle for independence: 1821–1833*. Berkeley, CA: University of California Press.

Daly, J. W. (2004). Policing the constitutional order in 1906. In *The watchful state: Security police and opposition in Russia, 1906–1917* (pp. 16–52). DeKalb, IL: Northern Illinois University Press.

Darmstaedter, F. (2008). *Bismarck and the creation of the second Reich*. New Brunswick, NJ: Transaction Publishers.

Davis, J. R. (1997). *Britain and the German Zollverein: 1848–1866*. New York: St. Martin's Press.

de Dijn, A. (2002). A pragmatic conservatism: Montesquieu and the framing of the Belgian constitution: (1830–1831). *History of European Ideas, 28*(4), 227–245.

de Tocqueville, A. (1991). *Œuvres*. 1. Paris: Gallimard.

Dedinger, B. (2012). The Franco-German trade puzzle: An analysis of the economic consequences of the Franco-Prussian war. *Economic History Review, 65*(3), 1029–1054.

Dipper, C., & Speck, U. (1998). *1848: Revolution in Deutschland*. Frankfurt am Main: Insel.

Dorpalen, A. (1969). The German struggle against Napoleon: The East German view. *Journal of Modern History, 41*(4), 485–516.

Dunant, H. (2009). *The origin of the Red Cross: Un Souvenir de Solferino*. Whitefish, MT: Kessinger Publishing.

Dwyer, P. G. (2000). *The rise of Prussia: 1700–1830*. New York: Longman.

Dwyer, P. G. (2001). *Modern Prussian history: 1830–1947*. New York: Longman.

Elkins, Z. (2010). Diffusion and the constitutionalization of Europe. *Comparative Political Studies, 43*(8), 969–999.

Emerson, D. E. (1968). *Metternich and the political police: Security and subversion in the Habsburg Monarchy (1815–1830)*. The Hague: Martinus Nijhoff.

Esdaile, C. (2000). Enlightened absolutism versus theocracy in the Spanish restoration: 1814–1850. In D. Laven & L. Riall (Eds.), *Napoleon's legacy: Problems of government in restoration Europe* (pp. 65–82). Oxford: Berg.

Evans, E. J. (1994). *The Great Reform Act of 1832* (2nd ed.). London: Methuen and Co.

Evans, E. J. (2008). *Britain before the Reform Act: 1815–1832* (2nd ed.). New York: Pearson Longman.

Evans, R. J. W. (2006). *Austria, Hungary, and the Habsburgs: Central Europe C. 1683–1867*. Oxford: Oxford University Press.

Eyck, F. (1968). *The Frankfurt Parliament: 1848–1849*. London: Macmillan.

Ferguson, N. (1992). Germany and the origins of the First World War: New perspectives. *The Historical Journal, 35*(3), 725–752.

Figes, O. (2014). *Revolutionary Russia, 1891–1991: A history*. New York: Metropolitan Books.

Fraser, A. (2013). *Perilous question: Reform or revolution? Britain on the brink, 1832*. New York: Public Affairs.

Fulbrook, M. (2004). The unification of Germany. In *A concise history of Germany* (pp. 122–130). Cambridge, MA: Cambridge University Press.

Galai, S. (2012). Kadet domination of the First Duma and its limits. In J. D. Smele & A. Heywood (Eds.), *The Russian revolution of 1905: Centenary perspectives* (pp. 196–217). London: Routledge.

Gale, S. G. (1982). A very German legal science: Savigny and the historical school. *Stanford Journal of International Law, 18*, 123–146.

Gerwarth, R. (2005). *The Bismarck myth: Weimar Germany and the legacy of the Iron Chancellor*. Oxford: Oxford University Press.

Geyer, D. (1987). *Russian imperialism: The interaction of domestic and foreign policy, 1860–1914*. New Haven, CT: Yale University Press.

Ghisalberti, C. (2006). *Storia costituzionale d'Italia : 1848–1948* (5ª ed.). Roma: Laterza.

Gleijeses, P. (1992). The limits of sympathy: The United States and the independence of Spanish America. *Journal of Latin American Studies, 24*(3), 481–505.

Goldstein, R. J. (2010). *Political repression in 19th century Europe*. Oxon, UK: Routledge.

Gooch, J. (2002). What kind of Italy?: Mazzini and Cavour, 1849–1859. In *The unification of Italy* (pp. 21–37). London: Methuen (Reprint).

Gooding, J. (1986). The liberalism of Michael Speransky. *The Slavonic and East European Review, 64*(3), 401–424.

Gould, A. (2002). *Origins of liberal dominance: State, church, and party in nineteenth-century Europe*. Michigan, MI: University of Michigan Press.

Gross, M. B. (2008). Kulturkampf, unification and the war against Catholicism. In *The war against Catholicism: Liberalism and the anti-Catholic imagination in nineteenth-century Germany* (pp. 240–291). Ann Arbor, MI: University of Michigan Press.

Guizot, F. (1864). Discussion d'un crédit supplémentaire de fonds secrets demandé pour l'exercice de 1843. In *Histoire parlementaire de France: recueil complet des discours prononcés dans les Chambres de 1819 à 1848* (Vol. 4, pp. 64–146). Paris: Michel Lévy frères.

Hagen, W. (2007). *Ordinary Prussians: Brandenburg Junkers and Villagers, 1500–1840*. Cambridge, UK: Cambridge University Press.

Hahn, H. J. (2001). *The 1848 revolutions in German-speaking Europe*. Harlow: Longman.

Hall, J. A. (1993). Nationalisms: Classified and explained. *Daedalus, 122*(3), 1–28.

Hamerow, T. S. (1966). *The economics of reaction in restoration, revolution, reaction: Economics and politics in Germany, 1815–1871* (pp. 219–237). Princeton, NJ: Princeton University Press.

Hamerow, T. S. (1983). *The birth of a new Europe: State and society in the nineteenth century*. Chapell Hill, NC: University of North Carolina Press.
Hamnett, B. R. (1984). Liberal politics and Spanish Freemasonry: 1814–1820. *History, 69*(226), 222–237.
Hanna, A. J., & Hanna, K. A. (1971). *Napoleon III and Mexico: American triumph over monarchy*. Chapell Hill, NC: University of North Carolina Press.
Hargreaves, D. (1991). *Bismarck and German unification*. Basingstoke, UK: Macmillan.
Harris, M. (2010). *The medical war: British Military Medicine in the First World War*. Oxford: Oxford University Press.
Hasler, A. B. (1981). *How the Pope became infallible: Pius IX and the politics of persuasion*. Garden City, NY: Doubleday.
Hearder, H. (2006). The making of the Roman Republic: 1848–1849. In P. H. Wilson (Ed.), *1848: The year of revolutions* (pp. 113–128). Farnham, UK: Ashgate.
Hendrickson, K. E. (2003). *The Spanish-American war*. Westport, CT: Greenwood.
Henning, R. (2003). *The origins of the First World War* (3rd revised ed.). London: Routledge.
Hinsley, F. H. (2004). *Power and the pursuit of peace: Theory and practice in the history of relations between states*. Cambridge, UK: Cambridge University Press.
Holsti, K. J. (1991). *Conflict and consent in peace and war: Armed conflicts and international order, 1648–1989*. Cambridge, MS: Cambridge University Press.
Hosking, G. (1991). *Absolutism and ruling class: The formation of the Russian political order, 1700–1825*. Oxford: Oxford University Press.
Huard, R. (2002). Les pratiques électorales en France en 1848. In J. -L. Mayaud (Dir.), *1848: Actes du colloque international du cent cinquantenaire, tenu à l'Assemblée nationale à Paris, les 23–25 février 1998* (pp. 59–77). Paris: Creaphis editions.
Ikenberry, G. J. (2011). Theoretical foundations. In *Liberal leviathan: The origins, crisis, and transformation of the American world order* (pp. 33–156). Princeton, NJ: Princeton University Press.
Ingle, H. N. (1976). *Nesselrode and the Russian Rapprochement with Britain: 1836–1844*. Berkeley, CA: University of California Press.
Jarrett, M. (2013). *The Congress of Vienna and its legacy: War and great power diplomacy after Napoleon*. London: Tauris.
Jensen, G. (2007). The Spanish Army at war: Counterinsurgency at home and abroad. In W. H. Bowen (Ed.), *A military history of modern Spain: From the Napoleonic era to the international war on terror* (pp. 15–37). Westport, CT: Greenwood.
John, M. (2000). The Napoleonic legacy and problems of restoration in Central Europe: The German confederation. In D. Laven & L. Riall (Eds.), *Problems of government in restoration Europe: Napoleon's legacy* (pp. 83–96). Oxford: Berg.
Kagan, F. W. (2006). *The end of the old order: Napoleon and Europe*. Cambridge, MA: Da Capo.
Kahan, A. S. (1991). Liberalism and Realpolitik in Prussia, 1830–1852: The case of David Hansemann. *German History, 9*(3), 280–307.
Kahan, A. S. (2003). *Liberalism in nineteenth-century Europe: The political culture of limited suffrage*. New York: Palgrave Macmillan.
Kantorowicz, H. (1937). Savigny and the historical school of law. *The Law Quarterly Review*, (53), 326–343.
Kaplan, A. (2005). *The anarchy of empire in the making of U.S. culture*. Cambridge, MA: Harvard University Press.
Katzenstein, P. J. (1997). Germany and Mitteleuropa: An introduction. In P. J. Katzenstein (Ed.), *Mitteleuropa: Between Europe and Germany* (pp. 1–38). Providence, RI: Berghahn Books.
Kertzer, D. I. (2014). *The Pope and Mussolini: The secret history of Pius XI and the rise of Fascism in Europe*. New York: Random House.
Keyssar, A. (2009). *The right to vote: The contested history of democracy in the United States*. New York, NY: Basic Books.

Kidner, F., et al. (Eds.). (2014). *Making Europe: The story of the west* (2nd ed.). Boston, MA: Wadsworth.
King, D. (2008). *Vienna, 1814: How the conquerors of Napoleon made love, war, and peace at the congress of Vienna*. New York: Three Rivers Press.
King, J. (2013). Constitutions as mission statements. In D. J. Galligan & M. Versteeg (Eds.), *Social and political foundations of constitutions* (pp. 73–102). Cambridge, UK: Cambridge University Press.
King, G., & Woolmans, S. (2013). *The assassination of the Archduke: Sarajevo 1914 and the murder that changed the world*. London: Macmillan.
Kingseed, C. C. (2004). *The American civil war*. Westport, CT: Greenwood.
Kinsbruner, J. (2000). *Independence in Spanish America: Civil wars, revolutions, and underdevelopment*. Albuquerque, NM: The University of New Mexico Press.
Koch, H. W. (1984). The dissolution of the Holy Roman Empire. In *A constitutional history of Germany in the nineteenth and twentieth centuries* (pp. 1–9). London: Longman
Kolkey, J. M. (1995). *Germany on the March: A reinterpretation of war and domestic politics over the past two centuries*. Lanham, MD: University Press of America.
Korros, A. (2002). *A reluctant parliament: Stolypin, nationalism, and the politics of the Russian Imperial State Council, 1906–1911*. Oxford: Rowman & Littlefield.
Koyama, N. (2009). *Japanese students at Cambridge University in the Meiji Era, 1868–1912: Pioneers for the modernization of Japan*. Morrisville, NC: Lulu Press.
Kusber, J. (2009). The challenge of unification and resistance: Governance, education, and the problems of empire in the age of Catherine II. In I. Gerasimov et al. (Eds.), *Empire speaks out: Languages of rationalization and self-description in the Russian Empire* (pp. 57–88). Leiden: Brill.
Laski, H. J. (2005). *The rise of European liberalism*. Delhi: Aakar Books (Reprint of the 1936 first edition).
Lee, S. J. (2006). *Russia and the USSR, 1855–1991: Autocracy and dictatorship*. Oxon, UK: Routledge.
Leontovitsch, V. (2012). *The history of liberalism in Russia*. Pittsburgh, PA: University of Pittsburgh Press.
Levinger, M. B. (2002). *Enlightened nationalism: The transformation of Prussian political culture, 1806–1848*. Oxford: Oxford University Press.
Lieven, D. (2009). *Russia against Napoleon: The battle for Europe, 1807 to 1814*. London: Penguin.
Lill, R. (1981). The Kulturkampf in Prussia and in the German Empire until 1878. In H. Jedin et al. (Eds.), *History of the Church* (pp. 26–45). 9. London: Crossroad.
Lüdtke, A. (2009). *Police and state in Prussia: 1815–1850*. Cambridge, UK: Cambridge University Press.
Luebbert, G. M. (1991). *Liberalism, fascism, or social democracy: Social classes and the political origins of regimes in interwar Europe*. Oxford: Oxford University Press.
Lyttleton, A. (1997). Politics and society: 1870–1915. In G. Holmes (Ed.), *The Oxford illustrated history of Italy* (pp. 235–263). Oxford: Oxford University Press.
Mack Smith, D. (1985). *Cavour and Garibaldi, 1860: A study in political conflict*. Cambridge, UK: Cambridge University Press.
MacMeekin, S. (2013). *July 1914: Countdown to war*. New York: Basic Books.
Marichal, C. (1977). *Spain, 1834–1844: A new society*. London: Tamesis Books.
Martin, A. (1997). *Romantics, reformers, reactionaries: Russian conservative thought and politics in the reign of Alexander I*. DeKalb, IL: Northern Illinois University Press.
Martínez Esquivel, R. (2012). Modernity and freemasonry in 19th century Central America. In D. Toner (Ed.), *Liberalism and religion: Secularisation and the public sphere in the Americas* (pp. 1–26). London: Institute of Latin American Studies.
Marwil, J. (2010). *Visiting modern war in Risorgimento Italy*. New York: Palgrave.

Massie, R. K. (2013). *Dreadnought: Britain, Germany and the coming of the great war*. New York: Random House.
McFarlane, A. (2014). *War and independence in Spanish America*. New York: Routledge.
McIntire, C. T. (2008). Liberals and the revolution in the Romagna. In *England against the Papacy 1858–1861: Tories, liberals, and the overthrow of Papal Temporal Power during the Italian Risorgimento* (pp. 114–139). Cambridge, UK: Cambridge University Press.
Medushevskii, A. N. (2006). *Russian constitutionalism: Historical and contemporary development*. London: Routledge.
Meriggi, M. (2000). State and society in post-Napoleonic Italy. In D. Laven & L. Riall (Eds.), *Problems of government in restoration Europe: Napoleon's legacy* (pp. 49–64). Oxford: Berg.
Merkl, P. H. (1993). *German unification in the European context*. University Park, PA: The Pennsylvania State University.
Metternich, C. W. L., Fürst von (1883). Epilog: Mein Politisches Testament. In *Aus Metternich's Nachgelassenen Papieren* (pp. 633–642). 7. Wien: Wilhelm Braumüller.
Metternich, C. W. L., Fürst von (2004). *Metternich: The autobiography, 1773–1816*. Welwyn, Garden City: Ravenhall Books.
Meyer, H. C. (1955). *Mitteleuropa in German thought and action: 1815–1945*. The Hague: Martinus Nijhoff.
Mirkine-Guetzevitch, B. (1938). La constitution espagnole de 1812 et les débuts du libéralisme européen: Esquisse d'histoire constitutionnelle comparée. In *Introduction à l'étude du droit comparé: Recueil d'Études en l'honneur d'Edouard Lambert* (pp. 211–219). II. Paris: Librairie Générale de Droit et de Jurisprudence.
Mombauer, A. (2002). *The origins of the First World War: Controversies and consensus*. Edinburg: Pearson Education Ltd.
Mosse, W. E. (1992). *Alexander II and the modernization of Russia* (2nd ed.). London: I.B. Tauris.
Müller, F. L. (2011). *Our Fritz: Emperor Frederick III and the political culture of imperial Germany*. Cambridge, MA: Harvard University Press.
Mulligan, W. (2010). *The origins of the First World War*. Cambridge, UK: Cambridge University Press.
Naumann, F. (1916). *Central Europe = Mittel-Europa*. New York: A. Knopf.
Nicholls, A. J. (2000). Neoliberalism and its enemies: National socialism and social democracy. In *Freedom with responsibility: The social market economy in Germany, 1918–1963* (pp. 60–89). Oxford: Oxford University Press.
Nicolson, H. (2000). *The Congress of Vienna: A study in allied unity, 1812–1822*. New York: Grove.
Olegario, R. (2013). Credit information, institutions, and international trade: The UK, US, and Germany, 1850–1930. In C. Dejung & N. P. Petersson (Eds.), *The foundations of worldwide economic integration: Power, institutions, and global markets, 1850–1930* (pp. 60–86). Cambridge, UK: Cambridge University Press.
Orwell, G. (2007). Notes on nationalism (1945). In *The collected essays: Journalism and letters of George Orwell* (pp. 361–379). 3. Boston, MA: David R. Godine.
Osborne, T. J. (1981). *"Empire Can't Wait": American opposition to Hawaiian annexation, 1893–1898*. Kent, OH: Kent State University Press.
Palmowski, J. (1999). The politics of the 'Unpolitical German': Liberalism in German local government, 1860–1880. *Historical Journal, 42*(3), 675–704.
Patriarca, S., & Riall, L. (2012). *The Risorgimento revisited: Nationalism and culture in nineteenth-century Italy*. New York: Palgrave Macmillan.
Payne, S. G. (1967). *Politics and the military in modern Spain*. Stanford, CA: Stanford University Press.
Payne, S. G. (1994). Portugal under the nineteenth-century constitutional monarchy. In *A history of Spain and Portugal* (pp. 513–558). 2. Ann Arbor, MI: University of Michigan Press.
Payne, S. G. (2011). *Spain: A unique history*. Madison, WI: University of Wisconsin Press.
Pearce, E. (2004). *Reform: The fight for the 1832 Reform Act*. London: Pimlico.

Pearson, F. L. (2002). The revolutionary generation, 1763–1823: American freemasons. In R. W. Weisberger & W. McLeod (Eds.), *Freemasonry on both sides of the Atlantic: Essays concerning the craft in the British Isles, Europe, the United States, and Mexico* (pp. 471–488). Boulder, CO: East European Monographs.

Peña González, J. (2006). *Historia política del constitucionalismo español*. Madrid: Dykinson.

Pérez Ayala, A. (2002). El constitucionalismo del sexenio en el contexto constitucional europeo de mediados del siglo XIX : referencia específica al influjo del modelo belga. *Revista de derecho politico,* (55–56), 241–294.

Perry, M. (2008). The surge of nationalism: From liberal to extreme nationalism. In M. Perry et al. (Eds.), *Western civilization: Ideas, politics, and society* (9th ed., pp. 597–620). Florence, KY: Cengage Learning.

Pilbeam, P. (2002). Upheaval and continuity: 1814–1880. The outbreak of revolution in 1830. In M. Crook (Ed.), *Revolutionary France: 1788–1880* (pp. 36–61). Oxford: Oxford University Press.

Pipes, R. (2005). *Russian conservatism and its critics: A study in political culture*. New Haven, CT: Yale University Press.

Pogge von Strandmann, H. (2002). The German revolutions of 1848–1850 and the Sonderweg of Mecklenburg. In R. J. W. Evans & H. Pogge von Strandmann (Eds.), *The revolutions in Europe 1848–1849: From reform to reaction* (pp. 99–134). Oxford: Oxford University Press.

Pollard, J. F. (2005). *The Vatican and Italian Fascism, 1929–1932: A study in conflict*. Cambridge, UK: Cambridge University Press.

Price, M. (2007). *The Perilous Crown: France between revolutions*. London: Macmillan.

Quataert, D. (2005). The nineteenth century. In *The Ottoman Empire: 1700–1922* (2nd ed., pp. 54–74). Cambridge, UK: Cambridge University Press.

Radzinsky, E. (2005). *Alexander II: The Last Great Tsar*. New York: Free Press.

Raeff, M. (1959). Some reflections on Russian liberalism. *Russian Review, 18*(3), 218–230.

Raeff, M. (1990). *Michael Speransky: Statesman of imperial Russia, 1772–1839*. Westport, CT: Hyperion Press (Reprint).

Rapport, M. (2014). *1848: Year of revolution*. New York: Basic Books.

Rawson, D. C. (1995). *Russian rightists and the revolution of 1905*. Cambridge, UK: Cambridge University Press.

Reimann, M. (1990). Nineteenth-century German legal science. *Boston College Law Review, 31*(4), 837–897.

Reinalda, B. (2009). *Routledge history of international organizations: From 1815 to the present day*. Oxon, UK: Routledge.

Rendle, M. (2010). *Defenders of the motherland: The Tsarist Elite in revolutionary Russia*. Oxford: Oxford University Press.

Riall, L. (1994). *The Italian Risorgimento: State, society and national unification*. London: Routledge.

Riall, L. (2008). *Garibaldi: Invention of a hero*. New Haven, CT: Yale University Press.

Riall, L. (2009). *Risorgimento: The history of Italy from Napoleon to nation-state*. New York: Palgrave Macmillan.

Riaud, X. (2008). *Première Guerre mondiale et stomatologie: des praticiens d'exception*. Paris: L'Harmattan.

Robertson, P. S. (1980). *Revolutions of 1848: A social history* (2nd ed.). Princeton, NJ: Princeton University Press.

Ross, R. (1998). *The failure of Bismarck's Kulturkampf: Catholicism and state power in imperial Germany, 1871–1887*. Washington, DC: Catholic University of America Press.

Rowe, M. (2001). Napoleon and state formation in Central Europe. In P. G. Dwyer (Ed.), *Napoleon and Europe* (pp. 204–224). Edinburgh: Pearson Education.

Schmitt, C. (2008). *The Leviathan in the state theory of Thomas Hobbes: Meaning and failure of a political symbol*. Chicago, IL: University of Chicago Press.

Schneid, F. C. (2005). *Napoleon's conquest of Europe: The war of the third coalition*. Westport, CT: Praeger.

Schneid, F. C. (2011). *European politics: 1815–1848*. Burlington, VT: Ashgate.

Schneid, F. C. (2012). *The Second War of Italian unification: 1859–1861*. Oxford: Osprey.

Schroeder, P. W. (1992). Did the Vienna Settlement Rest on a balance of power? *The American Historical Review, 97*(3), 683–706.

Schroeder, P. W. (1996). *The transformation of European politics: 1763–1848*. Oxford: Clarendon.

Seton-Watson, H. (2004). *The Russian Empire: 1801–1917*. Oxford: Oxford University Press (Reprint).

Simms, B. (2000). Napoleon and Germany: A legacy in foreign policy. In D. Laven & L. Riall (Eds.), *Problems of government in restoration Europe: Napoleon's legacy* (pp. 97–114). Oxford: Berg.

Simms, B. (2002). *The impact of Napoleon: Prussian high politics, foreign policy and the crisis of the executive, 1797–1806*. Cambridge: Cambridge University Press.

Simpson, J. (1996). *Liberalism and the discipline of power: The conservative interlude and the liberal restoration* (2nd ed.). Toronto, ON: University of Toronto Press.

Sked, A. (1979). The Metternich system: 1815–1848. In A. Sked (Ed.), *Europe's balance of power, 1815–1848* (pp. 98–121). London: Macmillan.

Sked, A. (2001). *The decline and fall of the Habsburg Empire: 1815–1918*. London, UK: Longman.

Sked, A. (2008). *Metternich and Austria: An evaluation*. New York: Palgrave Macmillan.

Sked, A. (2011). *Radetzky: Imperial victor and military genius*. London: Tauris.

Smith, G. (1987). *A constitutional and legal history of England*. Littleton, CO: Rothman (Reprint).

Smith, H. W. (1995). The Kulturkampf and German national identity. In *German nationalism and religious conflict: Culture, ideology, politics, 1870–1914* (pp. 19–49). Princeton, NJ: Princeton University Press

Smith, D. J. (2009). *One morning in Sarajevo: 28 June 1914*. London: Phoenix (Reprint).

Smith, P. (2013). *Time no longer: Americans after the American century*. New Haven, CT: Yale University Press.

Smith-Peter, S. (2006). Speransky, Mikhail (1772–1839): Russian politician. In J. Merriman (Ed.), *Europe: 1789 to 1914: Encyclopedia of the age of industry and empire* (pp. 2236–2237). 4. New York, NY: Charles Scribners & Sons.

Sofka, J. R. (1998). Metternich's theory of European order: A political agenda for perpetual peace. *The Review of Politics, 60*(1), 115–149.

Sofka, J. R. (2011a). A review of Metternich's theory of European order. In *Metternich, Jefferson and the enlightenment: Statecraft and political theory in the early nineteenth century* (pp. 55–58). Madrid: Consejo Superior de Investigaciones Científicas.

Sofka, J. R. (2011b). Metternich and the international system (1): Federalism, equilibrium, and the "Conference System" and (2): The workings of the conference system and the collapse of the European Confederation, 1815–1822 in *Metternich, Jefferson and the Enlightenment: Statecraft and Political Theory in the Early Nineteenth Century*. Madrid: Consejo Superior de Investigaciones Científicas, pp. 33–54 and 59–80.

Sperber, J. (1991). *Rhineland radicals: The democratic movement and the revolution of 1848–1849*. Princeton, NJ: Princeton University Press.

Sperber, J. (1997). *The Kaiser's voters: Electors and elections in imperial Germany*. Cambridge, MA: Cambridge University Press.

Spevack, E. (1997). *Charles Follen's search for nationality and freedom: Germany and America, 1796–1840*. Cambridge, MA: Harvard University.

Standen, N. (2013). *Desmytifying China: New understandings of Chinese history*. Lanham, MD: Rowman & Littlefield.

Stevenson, D. (2006). Strategic and military planning, 1871–1914. In T. C. Imlay & M. D. Toft (Eds.), *The fog of peace and war planning: Military and strategic planning under uncertainty* (pp. 75–99). Oxon, UK: Routledge.

Stites, R. (2014). *The Four Horsemen: Riding to liberty in post-Napoleonic Europe*. Oxford: Oxford University Press.

Sträth, B. (2006). Insiders and outsiders: Broders in nineteenth-century Europe. In S. Berger (Ed.), *A companion to nineteenth-century Europe: 1789–1914* (pp. 3–10). Malden, MA: Blackwell.

Taylor, B. D. (2003). *Politics and the Russian Army: Civil-military relations, 1689–2000*. Cambridge, UK: Cambridge University Press.

te Velde, H. (2008). The organization of liberty. Dutch liberalism as a case of the history of European constitutional liberalism. *European Journal of Political Theory, 7*(1), 65–79.

Thackeray, F. W. (2004). *Events that changed Germany*. Westport, CT: Greenwood.

Thomas, E. (2011). *The war lovers: Roosevelt, Lodge, Hearst, and the rush to empire, 1898*. New York: Back Bay Books.

Turnbull, P. (1985). *Solferino: The birth of a nation*. London: Hale.

Turner, J. A. (2000). The challenge to liberalism: The politics of the home fronts. In H. Strachan (Ed.), *The Oxford illustrated history of the First World War* (pp. 163–178). Oxford: Oxford University Press.

van Bergen, L. (2009). *Before my helpless sight: Suffering, dying and military medicine on the Western Front, 1914–1918*. Burlington, VT: Ashgate.

van Berlo, M. (2005). 1830–1831: The revolution and the foundation of the Monarchy. In B. Barnard (Ed.), *How can one not be interested in Belgian history: War, language and consensus in Belgium since 1830* (3rd ed., pp. 43–45). Gent: Academia Press.

Vanberg, V. J. (2001). *The constitution of markets: Essays in political economy*. London: Routledge.

Verner, A. M. (1990). *The crisis of Russian autocracy: Nicholas II and the 1905 revolution*. Princeton, NJ: Princeton University Press.

Vick, B. E. (2002). *Defining Germany: The 1848 Frankfurt Parliamentarians and national identity*. Cambridge, MA: Harvard University Press.

Villarroya, J. T. (1985). *El Estatuto real de 1834 y la Constitución de 1837*. Madrid: Fundación Santa María.

von Mises, L. (2012). The foundations of liberal policy. In *Liberalism: in the classical tradition* (pp. 18–59). New York: Important Books.

Vowell, S. (2012). *Unfamiliar fishes*. New York: Riverhead (Reprinted).

Walker, M. (1968). *Metternich's Europe, 1813–1848*. New York: Harper and Row.

Wallerstein, I. M. (2011). *The modern world-system IV: Centrist liberalism triumphant: 1789–1914*. Berkeley, CA: University of California Press.

Wawro, G. (2003). *The Franco-Prussian war: The German conquest of France in 1870–1871*. Cambridge, UK: Cambridge University Press.

Wells, M. (2012). *Unification and consolidation of Germany and Italy 1815–1890*. Cambridge: Cambridge University Press.

Westwood, J. N. (2002). *Endurance and endeavour: Russian history, 1812–1992* (5th ed.). Oxford: Oxford University Press.

Whisenhunt, W. B. (2001). *In search of legality: Mikhail M. Speranski and the codification of Russian law*. Boulder, CO: University of Michigan Press.

Williamson, D. G. (2011). *Bismarck and Germany: 1862–1890* (3rd ed.). Harlow, UK: Longman.

Williamson, S. R. (2000). The origins of the war. In H. Strachan (Ed.), *The Oxford illustrated history of the First World War* (pp. 9–25). Oxford: Oxford University Press.

Wilson, F. G. (2004). Juan Donoso Cortés: A diagnosis of crisis. In H. Lee Cheek et al. (Eds.), *Political thought in national Spain: Order and legitimacy* (pp. 23–42). New Brunswick, NJ: Transaction Publishers.

Wilson, P. (2004). Imperial and European politics. In *From Reich to revolution: German history 1558–1806 (European history in perspective)* (pp. 305–342). London: Palgrave & Macmillan.

Wilson, P. (2009). *The bee and the eagle: Napoleonic France and the end of the Holy Roman Empire, 1806*. New York: Palgrave.

Winkler, H. A. (2007). *Germany: The long road west. 1789–1933*. 1. Oxford: Oxford University Press.

Wortman, R. S. (1976). *The development of a Russian legal consciousness*. Chicago, IL: The University of Chicago Press.

Young, W. H. (2006). Rise of Prussia to 1862. In *German diplomatic relations: 1871–1945: The Wilhelmstsrasse and the formulation of foreign policy* (pp. 1–31). Lincoln, NE: Universe.

Zamoyski, A. (2007). *Rites of peace: The fall of Napoleon and the Congress of Vienna*. London: Harper Press.

Ziolkowski, T. (1992). The law text of society and the history of legal study in Germany. In *German romanticism and its institutions* (pp. 64–79). Princeton, NJ: Princeton University Press.

Ziolkowski, T. (2003). The evolution of law. In *The mirror of justice: Literary reflections of legal crises* (pp. 6–13). Princeton, NJ: Princeton University Press.

Zipes, J. (2002). *The Brothers Grimm: From enchanted forests to the modern world* (2nd ed.). New York: Palgrave Macmillan.

Zwicker, L. F. (2011). *Dueling students: Conflict, masculinity, and politics in German universities, 1890–1914*. Ann Arbor, MI: University of Michigan Press.

## Further Reading

Ackerman, B. (1994). *The future of liberal revolution*. New Haven, CT: Yale University Press.

Alexander, R. S. (2012). *Europe's uncertain path, 1814–1914: State formation and civil society*. Malden, MA: Wiley.

Anderson, M. S. (2003). *The ascendancy of Europe: 1815–1914*. London: Pearson Education.

Arblaster, A. (1986). *The rise and decline of western liberalism*. London: Basil & Blackwell (Reprint).

Arnold, J., & Wiener, R. (Eds.). (2009). *The encyclopedia of the Spanish-American and Philippine-American wars: A political, social, and military history*. Santa Barbara, CA: ABC-CLIO.

Aston, N. (2002). *Christianity and revolutionary Europe: 1750–1830*. Cambridge, UK: Cambridge University Press.

Barnes, M. (2011). *The Spanish-American war and Philippine insurrection. 1898–1902: An annotated bibliography*. New York: Routledge.

Barclay, D. E. (1995). *Frederick William IV and the Prussian Monarchy: 1840–1861*. Oxford: Clarendon.

Bayly, C. A., & Biagini, E. F. (2008). *Giuseppe Mazzini and the globalisation of democratic nationalism: 1830–1920*. Oxford: Oxford University Press.

Blanning, T. C. W. (2011). *The Romantic revolution: A history*. New York: Random House.

Blackbourn, D. (1986). The politics of demagogy in imperial Germany. *Past and Present,* (113), 152–184.

Blumberg, A. (1991). *A carefully planned accident: The Italian war of 1859*. London: Associated University Presses.

Brewer, D. (2001). *The flame of freedom: The Greek War of Independence, 1821–1833*. London: J. Murray.

Bushkovitch, P. (2011). *A concise history of Russia*. Cambridge, UK: Cambridge University Press.

Burgess, M. (2013). Opening Pandora's Box: Process and Paradox in the Federalism of Political Identity. In A. Lopez Basaguren & L. Escajedo San-Epifanio (Eds.), *The ways of federalism in*

*western countries and the horizon of territorial autonomy in Spain* (pp. 3–14). 1. Berlin: Springer.
Clemente, S. E. (1992). *For King and Kaiser!: The making of the Prussian Army Officer, 1860–1914*. New York: Greenwood.
Collingham, H. A. C., & Alexander, R. S. (1988). *The July Monarchy: A political history of France, 1830–1848*. London: Longman.
Congleton, R. D. (2011). *Perfecting parliament: Constitutional reform, liberalism, and the rise of western democracy*. Cambridge, MA: Cambridge University Press.
Constant, B. (1988). Principles of politics applicable to all representative governments. In B. Fontana (Ed.), *Constant: Political writings* (pp. 169–307). Cambridge, UK: Cambridge University Press.
Cullinane, M. P. (2012). *Liberty and American anti-imperialism: 1898–1909*. New York: Palgrave Macmillan.
de Tocqueville, A. (2012). *The old regime and the revolution*. Mineola, NY: Dover Publications.
de Vooght, D. (2011). Introduction: The *raison d'être* of monarchies in the western world after 1789. In *The king invites: Performing power at a courtly dining table (Belgium, 1831–1909)* (pp. 15–23). New York: Peter Lang.
Dudden, A. P. (2004). *American empire in the Pacific: From trade to strategic balance, 1700–1922*. Burlington, VT: Ashgate/Variorum.
Dynneson, T. L. (2001). Civism and the rise of the republican nation-state. In *Civism: Cultivating citizenship in European history* (pp. 175–190). New York: Peter Lang.
Frevert, U. (2004). *A nation in barracks: Modern Germany, military conscription and civil society*. New York: Berg.
Fishman, J. (1988). *Diplomacy and revolution: The London conference of 1830 and the Belgian revolt*. Amsterdam: CHEV.
Gannett, R. T. (2003). *Tocqueville unveiled: The historian and his sources for the old regime and the revolution*. Chicago, IL: University of Chicago Press.
Goemans, H. E. (2000). *War and punishment: The causes of war termination and the First World War*. Princeton, NJ: Princeton University Press.
Gooch, B. (1963). *Belgium and the February revolution*. The Hague: Martinus Nijhoff.
Gould, A. (1999). *Origins of liberal dominance*. Ann Arbor: University of Michigan Press.
Gray, J. (1995). *Liberalism*. Minneapolis: University of Minnesota Press.
Grimm, J., & Grimm, W. (2012). *The annotated Brothers Grimm*. New York: W.W. Norton & Co.
Hammarlund, P. A. (2005). The decline of the state: The empirical claim. In *Liberal internationalism and the decline of the state: The thought of Richard Cobden, David Mitrany, and Kenichi Ohmae* (pp. 28–51). Basingstoke: Palgrave Macmillan.
Harland-Jacobs, J. (1999). Hands across the sea: The Masonic Network British Imperialism, and the North Atlantic World. *Geographical Review, 89*(2), 237–253.
Harland-Jacobs, J. (2003). All in the family: Freemasonry and the British Empire in the mid-nineteen century. *Journal of British Studies, 42*(4), 448–482.
Hearder, H. (1994). *Cavour*. New York: Longman.
Heirbaut, D. (2001). A Belgian legal tradition after Belgian independence in 1830? In H. Bocken & W. De Bondt (Eds.), *Introduction to Belgian law* (pp. 9–18). The Hague: Kluwer Law International.
Herr, R. (1962). *Tocqueville and the old regime*. Princeton, NJ: Princeton University Press.
Herrmann, D. G. (1996). *The arming of Europe and the making of the First World War*. Princeton, NJ: Princeton University Press.
Homsher, D. C. (2006). *American battlefields of World War I, Chateau Thierry - Then and now*. San Mateo, CA: Battleground Productions.
Jacob, M. C. (2006). *The radical enlightenment: Pantheists, freemasons and republicans: Early modern Europe Today* (2nd revised ed.). Boston: Cornerstone.
Jacobson, A. J., & Schlink, B. (Eds.). (2000). *Weimar: a jurisprudence of crisis*. Berkeley, CA: University of California Press.
Jane, J. C. (1910). *From Metternich to Bismarck: A textbook of European history, 1815–1878*. London: Clarendon.

Johnston, L. (2011). *Politics: An introduction to the modern democratic state*. Toronto: University of Toronto Press.

Jones, G. S., & Claeys, G. (Eds.). (2011). *The Cambridge history of nineteenth-century political thought*. Cambridge: Cambridge University Press.

Judson, P. M. (1996). *Exclusive revolutionaries: Liberal politics, social experience, and national identity in the Austrian Empire, 1848–1914*. Ann Arbor, MI: University of Michigan Press.

Jung, M. -H. (Ed.). (2014). *The rising tide of color: Race, state violence, and radical movements across the Pacific*. Seattle: University of Washington Press.

Kamenetsky, C. (1992). *The brothers Grimm and their critics: Folktales and the quest for meaning*. Athens: Ohio University Press.

Kahan, A. S. (1992). *Aristocratic liberalism: The social and political thought of Jacob Burckhardt, John Stuart Mill and Alexis de Tocqueville*. Oxford: Oxford University Press.

Kissinger, H. (2000). *A world restored: Metternich, Castlereagh and the problems of peace, 1812–1822*. London: Phoenix.

Koerner, K. (1985). *Liberalism and its critics*. Oxford: Taylor & Francis.

Langellier, J. P. (2002). *Uncle Sam's little wars: The Spanish-American war, Philippine insurrection, and Boxer Rebellion, 1898–1902*. London: Greenhill.

Lee, S. J. (2008). Metternich and the Austrian Empire 1815–1848. In *Aspects of European history 1789–1980* (pp. 30–35). Oxon, UK: Routledge.

Le Bris, D. (2012). Wars, inflation and stock market returns in France: 1870–1945. *Financial History Review, 19*(3), 337–361.

Liang, H. H. (1992). *The rise of modern police and the European state system from Metternich to the Second World War*. Cambridge, UK: Cambridge University Press.

Lili'uokalani. Queen of Hawaii. (2007). *Hawaii's story by Hawaii's queen, Liliuokalani*. Whitefish, MT: Kessinger Publishing.

Linz, J. J. (2000). *Totalitarian and authoritarian regimes*. Boulder, CO: Lynne Rienner.

Long, G. (2004). *Relativism and the foundations of liberalism*. Exeter, UK: Imprint Academic.

LoPatin-Lummis, N. (1999). *Political unions, popular politics and the great Reform Act of 1832*. Basingstoke: Macmillan.

Manent, P. (1996). *An intellectual history of liberalism*. Princeton, NJ: Princeton University Press.

Maris, C. W., & Jacobs, F. (2011). Nineteenth century. In *Law, order and freedom: A historical introduction to legal philosophy* (pp. 195–259). Heidelberg: Springer.

McCormick, J. P. (1999). *Carl Schmitt's critique of liberalism: Against politics as technology*. Cambridge, UK: Cambridge University Press.

Merriman, J., & Winter, J. (Eds.). (2006). *Europe 1789–1914: Encyclopedia of the age of industry and empire*. Detroit, MI: Scriber Library of Modern Europe.

Mill, J. S. (2013). *On Liberty: A translation into modern English*. Manchester, UK: Industrial Systems Research.

Miller, B. M. (2011). *From liberation to conquest: The visual and popular cultures of the Spanish-American war of 1898*. Boston, MA: University of Massachusetts Press.

Milne, A. (1975). *Metternich*. London: University of London Press.

Morelli, F., et al. (Eds.). (2009). *Les empires atlantiques: Des lumières au libéralisme (1763–1865)*. Rennes, France: Presses Universitaires de Rennes.

Morrogh, M. M. (2002). *The unification of Italy* (2nd ed.). Basingstoke: Palgrave Macmillan.

Moss, W. (2002). *Russia in the age of Alexander II, Tolstoy and Dostoievsky*. London: Anthem Press.

Mugnaini, M. (1994). Cult of the nation, religion of liberty or reason of state?: Spain in Italian Foreign Policy (1846–1868). In J. G. Beramendi et al. (Eds.), *Nationalism in Europe: Past and present* (pp. 665–676). 1. Santiago de Compostela: Universidad de Santiago.

Paul, E. F., et al. (Eds.). (2007). *Liberalism: Old and new*. New York: Cambridge University Press.

Pearce, R., & Stiles, A. (2006). *The unification of Italy: 1815–1870* (3rd ed.). London: Hodder Murray.

Pilbeam, P. (1994). *The 1830 revolution in France*. London: Macmillan.

Pitts, J. (2005). *A turn to empire: The rise of imperial liberalism in Britain and France*. Princeton, NJ: Princeton University Press.
Price, R. (2001). *The French Second Empire: An anatomy of political power*. Cambridge, UK: Cambridge University Press.
Price, R. (2004). *People and politics in France: 1848–1870*. Cambridge, UK: Cambridge University Press.
Przeworski, A. (2009). Conquered or granted? A history of Suffrage extensions. *British Journal of Political Science, 39*, 291–321.
Riall, L. (2013). *Under the volcano: Empire and revolution in a Sicilian town*. Oxford: Oxford University Press.
Rieber, A. J. (Ed.). (1966). *The politics of autocracy: Letters of Alexander II to Prince A.I. Barjatinskij 1857–1864*. Paris: Mouton.
Russia. (1839–1873). *Polnoe sobranie zakonov Rossiiskoi Imperii = Complete collection of the laws of the Russian empire* (4 vols). Petrograd: Gostipografiia.
Ryan, A. (2002). *The making of modern liberalism*. Princeton, NJ: Princeton University Press.
Saldin, R. P. (2011). *War, the American state, and politics since 1898*. Cambridge, MA: Cambridge University Press.
Schmidt-Nowara, C. (2004). La 'España Ultramarina': Colonialism and nation-building in nineteenth-century Spain. *European History Quarterly, 34*(2), 191–214.
Skinner, Q. (2012). *Liberty before liberalism*. Cambridge, UK: Cambridge University Press.
Smith, G. B., & Sharlet, R. A. (Eds.). (2008). *Russia and its constitution: Promise and political reality*. Leiden: Martinus Nijhoff.
Snyder, J. (1991). *Myths of empire: Domestic politics and international ambition*. Ithaca, NY: Cornell University Press.
Song, R. (2006). *Christianity and liberal society*. Oxford: Oxford University Press.
Stürmer, M. (2007). *The German Empire: A short history*. New York: Modern Library (Reprint).
Tezcan, B. (2012). *The Second Ottoman Empire: Political and social transformation in the early modern world*. Cambridge, UK: Cambridge University Press.
Thompson, D. (1976). *John Stuart Mill and representative government*. Princeton: Princeton University Press.
Valente, M. (2004). *Diplomazia pontificia e Kulturkampf: la Santa Sede e la Prussia tra Pio IX e Bismarck, 1862–1878*. Roma: Studium.
van den Bossche, G. M. H. (1998). Historians as advisers to revolution? Imagining the Belgian nation. *History of European Ideas, 24*(3), 213–238.
Wallerstein, I. M. (2011). The liberal state and class conflict: 1830–1875. In *Centrist liberalism triumphant, 1789–1914* (pp. 77–142). Berkeley, CA: University of California Press.
Weisberger, W. M. L., & Morris, S. B. (Eds.). (2002). *Freemasonry on both sides of the Atlantic: Essays concerning the craft in the British Isles, Europe, the United States, and Mexico*. Boulder, CO: East European Monographs.
Welch, C. B. (Ed.). (2006). *The Cambridge companion to Tocqueville*. Cambridge, UK: Cambridge University Press.
Wetzel, D. (2012). *A duel of nations: Germany, France, and the diplomacy of the war of 1870–1871*. Madison, WI: University of Wisconsin Press.
Winks, R. W., & Neuberger, J. (2005). *Europe and the making of modernity: 1815–1914*. Oxford: Oxford University Press.
Witte, E. (2009). Breakthrough of a liberal constitutional state: 1830–1848. In *Political history of Belgium: From 1830 onwards* (pp. 19–59). Brussels: Asp.
Wolfe, A. (2009). *The future of liberalism*. New York: Random House, Inc.
Zamoyski, A. (2009). *Poland: A history*. London: Harper Press.

# Chapter 17
# The Triumph of the State Over the Nation: From Totalitarianism to Interventionism

The first man, who, after enclosing a piece of ground, took it into his head to say, 'This is mine,' and found people simple enough to believe him, was the true founder of civil society.[1]—Jean Jacques Rousseau (1712–1778)

No, gentlemen, democracy and socialism are not linked to each other. They are not only different but contradictory things. What if by chance, democracy were to consist of a government more interfering, more detailed, more restrictive than all others, the only difference being that it would be elected by the people and would act in the name of the people? In that case, what would you have done, if not have given to tyranny an aura of legitimacy that it did not previously possess and to have secured for it the strength and omnipotence that it lacked? Democracy extends the sphere of individual independence, socialism restricts it. Democracy gives the greatest possible value to every man, socialism turns every man into an agent, an instrument, a number. Democracy and socialism are linked by only one word, equality; but note the difference: democracy wants equality in liberty, and socialism wants equality through constraint and servitude.—Alexis de Tocqueville. (1805–1859)[2]

Arise ye workers from your slumbers
Arise ye prisoners of want
For reason in revolt now thunders
And at last ends the age of cant.
Away with all your superstitions
Servile masses arise, arise
We'll change henceforth the old tradition
And spurn the dust to win the prize.
So comrades, come rally
And the last fight let us face
The International unites the human race.—Eugene Pottier (1816–1887).[3]

---

[1] From Discourse on the Origin and Basis of Inequality Among Men (1754). Rousseau (2009, 63).

[2] Speech made before the Constituent Assembly during the discussion of the new constitution on the right to work. Session of September 12, 1848. Tocqueville (2009, 400).

[3] *The International* (1871). Text in Smaldone (2014, 139). Written by Eugene Pottier, a transport worker (Smaldone 2014, 139), and colleague of Paul Lafargue's (a son-in-law of Marx) at the newspaper *The Socialist*, and active in the foundation of the French Workers Party. He was also a member of the First International. In June 1871, in Paris, he composed *The International* after the repression of the Bloody Week, dedicating it to Gustave Lefrancais, a comrade from the



B. Aguilera-Barchet, *A History of Western Public Law*,
DOI 10.1007/978-3-319-11803-1_17

Fascism establishes the real equality of individuals before the nation. The difference is in the scale of responsibilities ...[] the object of the regime in the economic field is to ensure higher social justice for the whole Italian people...[]What does higher social justice mean? It means work guaranteed, fair wages, decent homes; it means the possibility of continuous evolution and improvement ...[] it means that the workers must enter more and more intimately into the productive process and share its necessary discipline...[] As the past century was the century of capitalist power, the twentieth century is the century of the power and glory of labor—Benito Mussolini (1883–1945)[4]

The indirect powers... seized the legislative arm of parliament and the law state and thought they had placed the Leviathan in a harness. Their ascendancy was facilitated by a constitutional system that enshrined a catalogue of individual rights. The "private" sphere was, thus, withdrawn from the state and handed over to the "free", that is, uncontrolled and invisible forces of society.—Carl Schmitt (1888–1985)[5]

## Contents


17.1 From Liberalism to Interventionism ... 557
17.2 The Triumph of Big Capitalism and the Transformation of the Western World .... 558
17.2.1 The Inventions That Changed the World ... 558
17.2.2 Demographic Expansion and the Concentration of Urban Populations .... 563
17.3 The Social Consequences of Economic Expansion ... 564
17.3.1 The Middle Class and the Proletariat ... 564
17.3.2 The Origins of "the Social Question" ... 565
17.4 The Constitutional Consequences of the Social Question ... 567
17.4.1 From Censitary to Universal Suffrage ... 567
17.4.2 The Questioning of the *Laissez Faire* Principle: The Socialist Approach .. 568
17.4.3 The Conservative Approach: Bismarck's *Sozialpolitik* ... 571
17.4.4 The Return of the Interventionist State ... 573
17.5 The Russian Revolution and the First Triumph of Totalitarianism ... 573
17.5.1 Lenin and the Soviet Revolution ... 574
17.5.2 International Proletarianism vs. the Capitalism of the Liberal Nation-States .. 574
17.6 The European Oligarchies React by Defending "National Socialism" ... 576
17.6.1 Perfectly Legal Dictatorships ... 578
17.6.2 An Adapted Legal Theory: From Ihering to Carl Schmitt ... 581
17.6.3 The Expansion of Social/Legal Protection in the Interbellum Period ...... 583
17.6.4 The Crisis of the Liberal State Model in the U.S.A.: The New Deal ....... 583
17.6.5 A New Deal for Europe? ... 587
17.7 The Road to War ... 592
17.7.1 The Expansion of Totalitarianism: The Confrontation Between Communism and Fascism ... 592
17.7.2 From the Spanish Civil War to World War II ... 593
17.8 The Triumph of the Welfare State Model ... 597
17.8.1 The Welfare State and the Rule of Law ... 598


barricades, including the poem in one of his books: *Revolutionary Songs*. Almost 20 years later, G. Delory, one of the organizers of *La Lyre des Travailleurs*—workers choirs—approached Degeyter, one of its members and a composer, entrusting him with Pottier's words, describing the kind of song he was after and asking him to put the text to music. The hymn was ready by 1888 (Ferro 1996). On the story of the life and work of Pottier, see Gluckstein (2008).

[4] From On the Corporate State. Mussolini (1935, 39–40).

[5] From *The Leviathan in the State Theory of Thomas Hobbes*. Schmitt (2008, 73).

17.8.2 The Spread of the Welfare State After 1945 .... 601
17.8.3 The United States Stands Alone: From Roosevelt to Obama .... 602
17.9 The Transformation of the Totalitarian Model of State: Communism After 1945 .. 603
17.9.1 The Marshall Plan and the Raising of the Iron Curtain .... 604
17.9.2 The Expansion of Communism After 1945 .... 605
17.9.3 The Transformation of the Communist Model of State: The Chinese Example .... 606
17.10 The Contemporary Transformation of the State Model in Western Capitalist Countries: A Return to Oligarchy? .... 608
17.10.1 The "Thirty Glorious Years", or the Contemporary Way of Addressing the Social Question .... 608
17.10.2 The Neoliberal Way and John Rawls' Theory of Justice .... 609
17.10.3 Growing Inequality and Its Constitutional Consequences .... 609
17.10.4 Towards a New Oligarchic Model of the State? .... 611
17.11 The End of the Nation-State Era and the Beginning of Global Constitutional History? .... 613
17.11.1 From the League of Nations to the United Nations .... 613
17.11.2 Governments and Governance: From Authority to Negotiation .... 615
References .... 621

## 17.1 From Liberalism to Interventionism

Over the course of the nineteenth century, a constitutional model of the state took hold in the western world in which power (sovereignty) was posited not only in the king, as was the case under the preceding model of absolute monarchy, but in the nation, conceived of and envisioned as the entire citizenry. Under this new order, the organization of the state and the relationship between the people and the governing powers was based on and governed by an agreed-upon text, a constitution, whose approval established the legal framework according to which all power was to be exercised. State power was, in addition, to be limited by declarations stipulating the citizens' fundamental rights, which were not to be violated by the law or the government.

It is true, however, that while in theory the state was controlled by the nation—meaning the whole body of citizens—through its parliamentary representatives, this national representation was not entirely democratic. As explained earlier, power remained in the hands of a new ruling oligarchy, essentially made up of the industrial and financial bourgeoisie, which had supplanted the traditionally privileged classes that had prevailed under the *Ancien Régime*. This new ruling class controlled European parliaments in large measure by virtue of censitary suffrage systems, which required a certain level of wealth for one to vote and enjoy political representation. The more constitutions curtailed states' capacities to intervene in the economic and social spheres, the more absolute was the hegemony of the new elite.

It must be said, nevertheless, that the policies pursued by the ruling classes that now controlled the legislative, executive and judiciary powers, thanks to their commitment to *laissez-faire* policies, did bring about, in most liberal European states, an era of unprecedented economic prosperity and expansion,[6] with

[6] For an overview of this process in the United Kingdom, see Evans (2001, 47–55). During the period between 1660 and 1800, the English patent system evolved from an instrument of royal

spectacular demographic growth because of higher standards of living, and breakthroughs in nutrition, health, hygiene and medical science. As a result, Europe moved from a focus on the individual to a "mass culture", which prompted a radical transformation in Europe's social structure. This shift led to major alterations in the West's legal and constitutional systems, upon which we shall focus in this chapter.

## 17.2 The Triumph of Big Capitalism and the Transformation of the Western World

If after 1850 one can speak of the triumph of "Big Capitalism", it is because Europe enjoyed exponential economic growth because of the dramatic expansion of production and trade volumes, rendered possible by scientific progress and, more specifically, the appearance of new technical developments that radically altered the conditions of everyday life in western societies.

### *17.2.1 The Inventions That Changed the World*

The Industrial Revolution which started in the middle of the eighteenth century (Pollard 2002, 12–20), with discoveries such as the steam engine,[7] which utterly transformed industry and transport, was complemented, intensified and accelerated by what has been called the Technical Revolution, or Second Industrial Revolution (Boyns and Edwards 2013, 167–203), which began about one century later[8]

---

patronage into one of commercial competition among the inventors and manufacturers of the Industrial Revolution. For an analysis of the legal and political framework within which patenting took place and its relationship with technical change, see MacLeod (2002)

[7] The steam engine, thanks to improvements introduced by the Scot James Watt (1736–1819), to the prototypes created by the French scientist Denis Papin in 1707, and the English mechanic Thomas Newcomen in 1711, spread throughout Europe (France went from having 5,000 in 1850 to more than 100,000 in 1900), revolutionizing transport and industry. This, in turn, led to an exponential increase in the mining of coal, especially coke, of which 90 million tons were extracted in 1850, skyrocketing up to over 1.2 billion tons by 1913. The steam engine allowed for the development of railways, which revolutionized transportation in the western world beginning in the mid-nineteenth century. The railroads completely changed not only transport, but also the entire economy, as their construction required massive investments and huge workforces. On the remarkable lives and achievements of these men, see Thurston (2011, 79–143)

[8] For an overall view of this "revolution" see Atkenson and Kehoe (2007, 64–88), and Caron (2013).

(we shall restrict the use of the term "technological" to what is happening in our own era)[9] and brought about more change in every way than the world had experienced in the previous two millennia (Trebilcock 1981, 1–20). From the perspective of constitutional history, this "Technical Revolution" was a key force behind the spectacular strengthening of European nation-states and their power in the nineteenth century.[10]

[9] The last third of the twentieth century would witness a "technological revolution", which has radically transformed the way we do nearly everything: work, learn, communicate, do business, shop, acquire information, etc. It started with the New Digital revolution brought about by the advent of widely available computer technology. In 1976, Steve Jobs (1955–2011) commercialized the Apple personal computer, which led to a dramatic expansion in PC ownership during the 1980s, the leading company driving and benefiting from this sea change being Microsoft, captained by Bill Gates, who became an icon of his era and the shift it had seen. Computer and software firms based in Silicon Valley (California) turned out a whole series of technologies that, at a breakneck pace, changed world. In 2003, Jobs created the *iPod*, in 2007 the *iPhone*, and in 2010, he commercialized the *iPad*, the first widely purchased tablet computer. On the transformation wrought by the information revolution, with the proliferation of mobile phones and the revolutionary impact of the Internet, see the insightful book by Dans (2010).

[10] The Technical Revolution was also driven by military conflicts such as the Franco-Prussian War of 1870 and, particularly, the two world wars of the first half of the twentieth century. The Great War of 1914–1918 had the effect of promoting exponential improvements in many of these technologies. To illustrate, after the outbreak of World War I the French Cavalry paraded through the streets of Paris in July 1914, dressed in the Napoleonic style, a century after the first French Empire. After the war—on Bastille Day, July 14, 1919—the horses and *cuirassiers* who had paraded down the Champs-Élysées just 5 years earlier had been replaced by tanks (the Renault FT 17, which had proven decisive in the final phase of the war, as it was capable of breaching enemy trenches). In this short time, the war had also precipitated major improvements, mainly in weapons (tanks, machine guns, aviation) and medical treatments. For an overview of how technology became a decisive issue in the War (Travers 1992, 145–174). An interpretation of the causal relationship between technology, warfare and the contemporary social milieu in Boot (2006). Nuclear energy is one of the clearest examples of a technology that brings about progress and risks beyond generational borders. According to World Health Organization (2013, 7), the earthquake and tsunami in Japan on March 11, 2011 led to releases of radioactive material into the environment from the Tokyo Electric Power Company's Fukushima Daiichi nuclear power plant. A major release of radioactivity to the environment is always of concern, owing to potential acute and long-term health effects. Evidence from historic events confirms that any major uncontrolled release of radiation should be cause for immediate response and scientific assessment of potential health effects.

The list of inventions—such as the light bulb, phonograph,[11] photographs[12] and the cinema,[13] the telegraph, telephone, radio and, later,

[11] Both devices were the work of genius Thomas Alva Edison (1847–1931), who patented more than 1,000 inventions (Adair 1997), among them the phonograph (1878), which allowed for recorded sounds to be played back for the first time, and the light bulb (1879). By the turn of the century, this latter invention allowed cities to light their streets all night, significantly improving public safety. On the process of invention through the Menlo Park notes, discussing the full range of experiments, including the testing of a host of materials, the development of such crucial tools as the world's best vacuum pump, and the construction of the first large-scale electrical generators and power distribution systems, see Friedel and Israel (2010). Edison and his associates—one of them the Austro-Hungarian Nikola Tesla set about improving Edison's line of dynamos, developed ideas that led to more than four hundred patents and made major contributions to telegraphy, telephony, and the duplication of texts. In the process, Edison demonstrated how to combine technological innovation and business strategy at his Menlo Park (New Jersey) laboratory during the 6 years between 1876 and 1882 that transformed American life. Afterward, research and development became essential corporate activities (Pretzer 2002). On the amazing life of Nikola Tesla as a scientist and as a public figure, his inventions and controversies with Edison, see O'Neill (2012).

[12] In the field of images, the first photograph had been taken by France's Nicéphore Niépce (1765–1833) in 1826. His countryman Louis Daguerre (1787–1851) commercialized the process for the obtaining of photographs, or daguerreotypes, in 1839. However, maybe, Henry Fox Talbot's 1835 calotype should be listed as the first preservation of a camera image. About their genius, and rivalry in the quest to produce the world's first photograph, and the couple of contentious decades during which early photographers fought over patents and their merits, see Watson and Rappaport (2014). Photography would be popularized by Georges Eastman (1854–1932) who in 1888 created the Kodak machine, which dramatically simplified the process of taking pictures; his motto was "you press the button and we do the rest" (Brayer 2012, 59–72). History's first small, portable camera soon hit the market: the *Brownie* (Brayer 2012, 204–205). In 1899, Eastman unveiled the Celluloid film for his Kodak still camera, an idea he had replicated from inventor Hannibal Goodwin, whose inventions made him a multimillionaire, not only shared profits with his employees, but donated huge sums to charity. For these 'eureka' first moments, see Gustavson (2012, 2–23)

[13] Soon after would appear the figure of the cinematographer (from *kinema*, meaning movement and *graphein*, meaning record or register). It was only one of a series of simultaneous artistic and technological breakthroughs that began to culminate at the end of the nineteenth century. Thomas Edison is often credited with inventing the first motion picture camera in 1891 with the Kinetoscope; his ideas are a culmination of many theories and advances toward the construction of a camera-like device that captured motion beginning in the seventeenth century, with the magic lantern. On December 28, 1895 at the "Salon indien" of the Grand Café on the Boulevard des Capucines in Paris (Popple and Kember 2004, 23–44), history's first film screening took place thanks to the invention developed by the brothers Auguste and Louis Lumière. Their father, Antoine, saw an example of Edison and Dikcnson's peep-show Kinetoscope in Paris during one of his travels and encouraged his sons to devise an apparatus that would take and project moving pictures, stating "You can do better. Try to get the image out of the box". Within a few months, they had produced a successful prototype of the Cinematographe, which were not only a camera but also a printer and projector as well (Gaudreault et al. 2012, 13–118). The first film to be projected for an audience was "Workers Leaving the Lumiere Factory", which lasted six and a half minutes (Lanzoni 2002, 29–30). The seventh art had been born [The first six are: (1) Architecture (2) Dance (3) Sculpture (4) Music (5) Painting (6) Literature]. Curiously, Photography entered as the eighth art, after film. Incidentally, the poster promoting the film, featuring history's first definition of a cinematographer, is priceless: "This device, invented by Mr. Auguste and Mr. Louis Lumière, makes it possible to pick up, through a series of instant tests, all the

television[14]—is truly impressive and allows us to fathom the extent to which the lives of westerners changed forever. We have to bear in mind that it was also during this period that electricity[15] was first produced and

movements which occur in front of the lens during a certain time period, and to reproduce those movements, projecting their images on a screen, life-size, before a room full of people" (Chapman 2003, 53–62). For a brief history of the nature of film, considering its role and impact on society as well as its future in the digital age, see Wood (2012).

[14] Another important breakthrough occurred in the field of telecommunications thanks to American Samuel Morse's invention of the electric telegraph, though the first telegraph line (measuring 1,000 m) was installed by Gauss and Weber in Göttingen (Germany). The next great advance was made by Scotland's Alexander Graham Bell, son of a speech therapist and a deaf mother, teacher—among others—of Hellen Keller and married with a deaf woman, Bell possessed of superbly acute hearing, and developed an early interest in sound. His understanding of how sound waves might relate to electrical waves enabled him to invent the "talking telegraph". The first telephone patent was awarded in 1876. Many of his innovations were far ahead of their time (Gray 2011). Beauchamp (2014) examines the legal battles that raged over Bell's telephone patent, and shows how the telephone was as much a creation of American law as of scientific innovation. However, according to Shulman (2009), that researched and scrutinized Bell's journals, he furtively—and illegally—copied key aspects of the electrical engineer Elisha Gray's design and submitted his patent the very same day from his competitor, – became the most lucrative in history, giving his company, American Telephone & Telegraph, a monopoly on this must-have piece of technology.

Radiophonics and the wireless transmission of sound by waves led to the emergence of the radio, thanks to the Anglo-Italian Guglielmo Marconi, in 1896 (Toscano 2012). The first radio broadcast took place on Christmas Eve, 1906 in Massachusetts (USA). The content of the broadcast was the song "Silent Night", played on the violin, and a reading of a passage from the Bible (Adams 2012, 99–101). Television would not appear until after World War II and not become widely available until the 1950s. Although the earliest television designs dated back to the late nineteenth century, the very first broadcasts were between 1925 and 1930, conducted by the BBC and CBS. Morse was also a noted American artist and a controversial political figure in New York. For an account not only of Morse's role but also the events and individuals surrounding the development of his telegraph system, see Silverman (2008). A view on history of the development and rapid growth of the first electronic network, the telegraph, in Standage (2009).

[15] Electricity was first discovered thanks to the electromagnetic theory formulated by England's James Clerk Maxwell (1831–1879) and confirmed by Germany's Heinrich Hertz (1857–1894). Their discoveries were built upon by Dutch Lorentz, who demonstrated the existence of electrons in 1892. After the discoveries of Michael Faraday (1791–1867) in electromagnetics (Russell 2000, 58–68), electricity began to impact the economy with the invention of a machine capable of producing direct current when Belgium's Zénobe Gramme presented his Gramme Dynamo in 1869. In 1870, Frenchmen Aristide Berges perfected the process for the hydraulic generation of electricity, or what he called white coal. In 1883, his countryman Marcel Deprez, finally solved the problem of conveying electricity by cable (Nye 1986, 86). His discovery led to the sight of high-voltage lines transforming Europe's countryside at the turn of the century, as dams and hydro-electric plants provided thousands of households and industries with light, fundamentally altering everyday life. See also Winston (2002)

developed,[16] while the combustion engine made possible the emergence of cars and aircraft.[17]

Extraordinary progress was also made in medical science, which benefitted from advances made by scientists in the fields of Chemistry and Biology, including, for instance, a water filter devised by Charles Chamberland that prevented the contraction of many diseases, dramatic progress in asepsis and antisepsis (the keys to the prevention of hospital infections), the emergence of vaccines (Louis Pasteur, Edward Jenner), and progress in surgical techniques, revolutionized by the emergence of anesthesia[18] in the United States.

[16] No less revolutionary was the thermodynamic research conducted circa 1860, by Belgium's Jean J. Lenoir, who harnessed the expansive force of gases resulting from combustion inside a cylinder. Thus arose the internal combustion engine, initially powered by gasoline, a highly flammable fuel discovered in 1857, through the distillation of petroleum. The application of this new invention to industry and transport was made possible by German inventor Nikolaus August Otto who, based on Lenoir's work, built the first four-stroke gasoline engine in 1876 (Sánchez Ron 2010, 224). The French engineer Fernando Forest, meanwhile, invented the spark plug in 1880, and in 1885, Karl Benz would begin to install gasoline engines in the first automobile prototypes.

[17] The first automobile factories would appear in France: Panhard and Levassor in 1889 and Peugeot in 1891. The popularization of the automobile, however, was the work of American Henry Ford, who in the first decade of the twentieth century refined the idea of the assembly line, which made it possible to slash automobile manufacturing costs and increase productivity. Thus, in a very short time the price of a car dropped from $850 down to just $360. The first low-cost car was the famous Model T, with its four-cylinder, 20-hp engine and a maximum speed of 44 mph (Duncan 2011). Thanks to Ford, between 1908 and 1927 the use of the car became widespread in the United States. In Spain, the first car factory was a Hispano-Suiza plant built in Barcelona in 1904. In Europe the automobile, however, would remain a luxury item until Hitler promoted the construction of the first "car of the people" (*Volkswagen*) (Taylor 2004, 15–52). As a result of this, automotive expansion oil became one of the planet's most precious natural resources. Internal combustion engines also transformed the shipping industry and made possible the emergence of a revolutionary mode of transportation: aircraft. At the close of the century, America's Wright brothers began to pursue their plans to construct a heavier-than-air aircraft. The first gliders would not appear until 1899, and it would not be until 1903 that there appeared the first aircraft propelled by their own means. The first powered flight was made on December 17, 1903, lasting 12 s and the plane, launched by a catapult, reached an altitude of 37 m and a speed of 30 mph. By 1905, the Wright brothers' invention had managed to fly 39 km in 40 min, and by 1908, their aircraft could take off without a catapult (Goldstone 2014). The first aircraft to fly in front of an audience was that of Brazilian Alberto Santos Dumont, in 1906, in Paris (Hoffman 2003, 251–277), and the first commercial flight cargo in history took place on November 7, 1910, between Dayton and Columbus (cities in Ohio), lasting one hour and two minutes. A Wright Company's airplane that flies carrying 10 bolts of silk to the Morehouse-Martens Company The aircraft travelled 62 miles and set a speed record, travelling at a little over 60 mph (Corn 2002). In January 1914, the St. Petersburg-Tampa Airboat Line became the world's first regularly scheduled airline service (Bilstein 2001, 3–40). For an overview on the historical context and the economic, political, social and cultural impact of aviation, see Millbrooke (2006)

[18] On the development and the social and ethical issues of vaccination, not simply a medical matter, but a divisive political issue, with outcomes strongly influenced by competing partisan interests, see Plotkin (2011). The American dentist Crawford E. Long performed the first operation with ether as the anesthetic agent in 1842 (Boland 2009), and there is no doubt that William T.G. Morton, assisting surgeon John Collin Warren, some four years later, gave the first public

### 17.2.2 *Demographic Expansion and the Concentration of Urban Populations*

Thanks to medical advances and increases in the standard of living, Europe experienced dramatic exponential demographic expansion, the population of the Continent tripling between 1840 and 1914. In this regard Germany is worthy of special note, in 1880 recording the astronomical figure of 37.5 births per 1,000 people.[19] The problem was that this population increase essentially affected urban areas.

The technical breakthroughs made in Europe at the end of the eighteenth century directly affected the means of production. As a result of mechanization, greater quantities of goods were produced, of better quality, and at a lower cost. The tradeoff was that machines completed the tasks formerly performed by men, leaving many farmers in rural areas without work, who were forced to move to cities to find jobs in the factories that began to sprout up around urban areas (Hohenberg and Lees 1996, 179–214).[20]

As a result, cities grew uncontrollably. In England, undoubtedly the world's most economically developed country in the nineteenth century, the urban population shot from a quarter of the population in 1831 to two-thirds in 1870. To varying degrees, urbanization affected all of Europe in the same period. In 1814, the number of cities with populations of more than 50,000 was 46 (the largest at the time being London, which had not yet reached one million). In 1914—only 100 years later—there were 179 cities with populations of over 100,000 inhabitants, three of which (London, Paris and Berlin) exceeded two million. In the United States, urban growth was even more spectacular. The most illustrative case is that of Chicago,

demonstration of the anesthetic effects of ether in Boston on October 16, 1846, by removing a tumor from a patient's neck without him feeling any pain (Schlich 2004, 75; Elkin 2009, v). In 1850, the Austrian von Scherzer brought a sufficient quantum of coca leaves to Europe to permit the isolation of cocaine. As suggested by his friend Sigmund Freud, descriptions of the properties of the coca prompted the Austrian Koller to perform in 1884 the first clinical operation under local anesthesia, by administration of cocaine on the eye. The use of cocaine for local and regional anesthesia rapidly spread throughout Europe and America. Its toxic effects were soon identified resulting in many deaths among both patients and addicted medical staff. Medical use has been largely restricted to producing local anesthesia. Even in this area, the dangers of cocaine led to the early development of safer drugs. One of its first non-medical uses was military. In 1883, Theodor Aschenbrandt administered cocaine to members of the Bavarian army. It was found that the drug enhanced their endurance on maneuver. His positive findings were published in a German medical journal, which brought the effects of this wonder drug to a wider medical audience, including Sigmund Freud (Vijayan 2010). See also, Freud (2011) and Markel (2012). For an overview of medical progress during this period, see Cooter (2011, 100–116).

[19] An impressive figure when one considers that in the year 2012, Germany registered 8.4 newborns per 1,000 people and Spain, 3.5 (in 2009, was a 9.7), while even India posted only about 21 (20.24/1,000).

[20] On the urban consequences of this industrial transformation in the evolution of London between 1870 and 1914, see Forgan (2010, 75–133).

which went from being a mere town in 1830, to a city of 100,000 in 1850, to a metropolis of three million people in 1914.[21]

## 17.3 The Social Consequences of Economic Expansion

### *17.3.1 The Middle Class and the Proletariat*

The wealth amassed by the western nation-states in the second half of the nineteenth century, thanks to the Technical Revolution, the consolidation of the liberal model of state, and the fact that European states controlled virtually the entire globe by way of colonial imperialism, brought essential social and political changes. The first one was that below the wealthy oligarchy was a growing middle class (Butler 1997, 14–34) enjoying gradual improvements in its standard of living and, accordingly, pressing for greater political representation through the introduction of more democratic electoral procedures. This was the thrust of the successive electoral reforms that extended censitary suffrage to a larger group of people, adopted in England in 1832, 1867, 1872 and 1884, and in France between 1814 and 1848 (Crossick and Haupt 2004, 133–165).

Just when the middle class was gaining access to political representation, however, the social order was once again shaken up and blurred as a consequence of the momentous economic transformations spawned by the triumph of Big Capitalism (Wahrman 2003, 411). While the "free" person, i.e. one not subject to any feudal servitude and living off the fruits of his own labor, was a social type which appeared in the Renaissance and spread throughout Europe in the seventeenth century, by the mid-nineteenth century the "working class" was a result of the abovementioned transformations that had led to increasingly uneven distributions of wealth. Enormous fortunes stood in stark contrast to masses of people wallowing in the most absolute poverty. Beneath the middle class arose a new European social stratum: the proletariat (from the Latin *proles*, meaning "offspring"), thus called because its members had no assets but their own children.[22] The proletariat was also referred to as "the Fourth Estate" to differentiate it from the former tripartite estate system under the *Ancien Régime*: the two privileged classes (clergy and nobility) and the Third Estate, made up of the common people. From the point of view of constitutional history, the proletariat burst onto the political

[21] For Weber and other contemporary social scientists "big cities" were those with 100,000 or more inhabitants (Weber 2012). See also Lees and Lees (2007, 129–168) and Beall and Fox (2009, 34–66). For an overview of this process of urban growth during that period, Wrigley (2004, 268–289). On the topic of *gentrification*, see Lees et al. (2013); the 1964 classic study of Glass, specially xiii–xlii, and Slater (2013, 571–585)

[22] Tilly (1997, 293) describes the proletariat as those who worked for wages, using means of production over which they had little or no control. On the origin of the proletariat in Europe, De Vries (2006, 237–238) and Mikkelsen (1996, 8–10).

scene in the mid-nineteenth century, aiming to achieve the political influence necessary to alter a constitutional system in Europe (Neale 1972, 15–40)[23] which had relegated workers to a life of misery. This is what came to be known as "the social question" (Moggach 2000, 21).

### *17.3.2 The Origins of "the Social Question"*

The Industrial Revolution rapidly and dramatically transformed the agricultural society of the Old Regime. With less and less work in the countryside, the cities were flooded with people, where conditions were often dire. The glut of labor available allowed factory owners to impose draconian conditions on their employees. Working hours were endless, there were no mandated rest periods, and workers could barely survive on their wages.

These "labor" difficulties spurred many Europeans to emigrate, primarily to the United States. Between 1580 and 1815 (235 years), three million Europeans had emigrated to America. From 1815 to 1860 (45 years) five million Europeans emigrated to the U.S. alone, and between 1860 and 1927 (67 years) the figure reached 27 million.[24] Major waves of European emigration also headed for South America, particularly Italians and Spaniards leaving for Argentina, and Portuguese

[23] For an overview of the forging of working class consciousness, see Katznelson (1986, 3–44). A political theorist Robert Filmer, in his *Observations upon Aristotle's Politiques, touching Forms of Government*: *Together with Directions for Obedience to Governors in Dangerous and Doubtful times* (1652, 26) wrote about the "poorer sort, or *proletarian* rabble". Derived from the Latin *proletarius*, as we mentioned, the word has had a range of meanings, none of them particularly complimentary. In its original Latin it was a legal term for those who had no property to pay tax on. Adapted to the French *proletaire* it was generalised to a description of common, lower class people. The derogatory meaning prevailed in English until the 1840s. It was the *Communist Manifesto* written in German by Marx and Engels, published in London in 1848 and translated into English 2 years later that catapulted the word into the mainstream. From this time onward the proletarian wage slaves came into their own as a social group with members who wore the label as a badge of honour, and when a popular uprising changed the course of Russian history in 1917 it was clear that this underclass had found its place, and its influence. "Proletarians of all countries unite" became a familiar twentieth century rallying cry, adopted as the motto of the Soviet Union and appearing on early Soviet banknotes and coins. The proletarian has surfaced repeatedly in popular culture, and the description of "*proles*" in George Orwell's *1984*, offers a disturbing warning to future generations. Orwell's society is made up of three classes, with the *proles* at the bottom of the pile. Rejected by their betters, fit only to work and breed, they are kept happy and docile by a steady stream of lotteries, meaningless songs and pornography. Some people might say that sounds a little too familiar for comfort (Orwell 2013). On the nature of class consciousness, and all that prevents its growth, see Reich (2013, 275–358). Published under the pseudonym of Ernst Parell, from exile in Denmark in June of 1934, as a pamphlet, *What is Class Consciousness*? criticizes also the politics of the Communist Party, which had been overwhelmed by Hitler's National Socialism in 1933.

[24] For a general examination of this process, see Haines and Steckel (2000, 305–370). Also, Klein (2012, 107–144)

leaving for Brazil (Moch 2003, 147–157). Millions of Europeans also settled in Australia (West and Murphy 2010, 9). The conditions, which these immigrants encountered, were often precarious. Nevertheless, the New World's unstoppable growth offered many more opportunities than the "Old World", where society was much more structured and opportunities for social mobility much more restricted.

Nevertheless, while many left, even more stayed on the Continent, and this generated an increasingly unsustainable situation for the growing mass of people crowded into its cities, many unemployed, or with jobs that confined them to perpetual poverty.

The abominable conditions to which these proletarian masses were subjected during the second half of the nineteenth century in Europe are expressly described in the following text by Vicens Vives, one of the most lucid Spanish historians of the twentieth century:

> ... the masses and social proletariat were soon melded, as capitalism's evolution tended to concentrate wealth in the hands of a small core of people while an increasing number of had to live off their work, whether in large factories or in the commercial institutions of Big Capitalism. Thus, the proletariat came to be made up not only of former workers and craftsmen, but of the new masses of peasants who flocked to the cities to labor in factories and workshops.
>
> Large industrial companies, which amassed enormous amounts of capital, had thrived thanks to economic liberalism. Liberal economists called for the absence of any intervention in corporate production and labor policies. The enrichment of the nation seemed to ratify the validity of their doctrines, but it should not be overlooked that this wealth ended up in the hands of a relatively small economic elite. To increase their revenues early and mid 19th-century industrialists did not hesitate to subject their workers to the harshest of labor conditions. Although these conditions varied greatly between the different nations, broadly speaking workers toiled for 13 to 14 hours a day, under unhealthy conditions, and for wages which barely allowed them to survive given the cost of living. With unrestrained access to cheap labor, companies even turned to employing children and women, upon whom the long hours and grueling work took a heavy toll (...) There were no social welfare laws providing workers with any protection in the event they were disabled, or any security once they were too old to work any longer.
>
> But even more disturbing was the worker's new spiritual condition and his relationship to his trade and employers. Traditionally apprentices and workers labored alongside master craftsmen to learn the different trades, with the latter group inculcating a love for the craft and a dedication to fine work in the former. Between employer and worker and master and apprentice there existed ties of friendship and solidarity. The "rationalization" of industry shattered these ties. As the Industrial Revolution progressed work became an activity which allowed one to survive - and in many cases just barely. Filling immense factories, employees performed specialized tasks and formed part of assembly lines under the supervision of other wage earners like themselves. Workers began to view their companies as hostile entities for which they had no affection and where they had to struggle (by force, if necessary) to receive higher wages, a reduction in working hours, or compensation during old age or in the event of accidents. (...).
>
> The glaring inequalities between employers and their employees were the first factor giving rise to a collective awareness among them regarding the shared interests it behooved them to defend. (...) Opposition to the working conditions of the day crystallized in a broad social movement, whose manifestations ranged from constructive to destructive, from peaceful to violent. The most relevant and consequential aspect of the workers movement was the collective dimension it adopted, in both the social and political

> spheres. Through this collectivism the masses, for the first time, took history into their own hands and became its protagonists.[25]

The emergence of organized labor movements began to transform European economics and society, soon impacting its politics and constitutions, as the surging pressure exerted by the proletariat called into question the principles of the liberal state which, according to its critics, had allowed for deplorable degrees of human exploitation.

## 17.4 The Constitutional Consequences of the Social Question

### *17.4.1 From Censitary to Universal Suffrage*

The first consequence of these drastic social changes was an expansion in the number of people authorized to vote in elections.

In the mid nineteenth century, the European nation-states' swelling wealth allowed the middle class to achieve a degree of political influence, as it was incorporated into the electoral base when censitary and indirect suffrage was abandoned, giving way to universal (male) suffrage.[26] In the United States, the transition to universal suffrage was a consequence of the incorporation of new, non-slave states into the union populated by many small property owners, a process that would be consolidated after the end of the Civil War in 1865. In Europe, the expansion of suffrage came about in some countries progressively, as it happened in England between 1832 and 1918, and in others abruptly, as it was the case in France in 1848, though it would be consolidated after 1875; in Prussia, in 1850, at least formally; and in Spain, first between 1868 and 1875, and then on a permanent basis after 1890.[27] These were clear signs that European politics was undergoing a historic shift.[28] Women suffrage, as we have seen in the previous chapter, would not appear until the twentieth century.

---

[25] Vicens Vives (1988, II, 387–388).

[26] For an overall view of how the middle class gained political representation and became constitutionally essential in the western states, see Wahrman (2003, 169–183) and Pilbeam (2008, 88–89).

[27] It is striking that even an enlightened and qualified statesman like Cánovas del Castillo, the heart and soul of Spain's First Restoration, vigorously defended censitary suffrage, which was restored after the Revolutionary Sexennium through the Constitution of 1876, before Sagasta definitively abolished it, signing universal male suffrage into law on June 26, 1890. Cánovas considered liberalism and democracy incompatible. In his second speech at the Ateneo de Madrid on November 25, 1871 he affirmed that "Universal suffrage and property are antithetical and will not live together too long". The speech was published in the Official Journal (*Gaceta de Madrid*, December 9, 1871, 827–830). Also in Vidal Manzanares (2009, 166).

[28] This opposition between the censitary and the principle of direct and universal suffrage would be one of the major issues of constitutional European history, from 1848 to the aftermath of World War I. For an overall examination of the process, see Noiret (1990).

Universal suffrage, despite being initially limited to men, swung open the doors to masses of workers who had become "class conscious" in the wake of the publication, on February 21, 1848, of Karl Marx (1818–1883) and Friedrich Engels' (1820–1895) *Communist Manifesto* (*Manifest der Kommunistischen Partei*) a powerful proclamation of communist principles, which ended in the following manner:

> The Communists disdain to conceal their views and intentions. They openly declare that their ends can only be attained by the forcible overthrow of all existing social conditions. Let the ruling classes tremble at the prospect of a communist revolution. The proletariat has nothing to lose but its chains. They have a world to win. Working men of all countries, unite![29]

## *17.4.2 The Questioning of the* Laissez Faire *Principle: The Socialist Approach*

Galvanized by Marxism, the working class struggled to replace the *laissez faire* state with another model, one which endorsed the exercise of political power to prevent the exploitation of man by man, thereby threatening one of the basic individual rights on which the liberal state was based: the right to property.[30]

### 17.4.2.1 From Romantic Socialism to Scientific Socialism

In 1754, Rousseau, in his *Discourse on the Origin and Basis of Inequality Among Men*, had already described private property as the root of social inequality (Viroli 2002, 73). France's François-Noël Babeuf (1760–1797) would seek to apply these ideas as the first to seek to extend the revolution to the social level (Conspiracy of the Equals) before being executed by the Directorate (Rose 1978).

At the theoretical level it was the French Romantic Socialists, such as the Count of Saint-Simon (1760–1825) and Charles Fourier (1772–1837), who laid the foundations for economic authoritarianism by advocating the abolition of inheritances and state acquisition of the "means of production", as a means by which to achieve

[29] Marx and Engels were the perfect team. Marx, a German of Jewish origin, was the theorist, the thinker, while Engels belonged to the affluent Prussian bourgeoisie, his family owning textile mills, producing wine, and forming part of a religious and conservative class. Engels ended up administrating his parents' business and, thanks his family's wealth, was able to financially maintain the author of *Das Kapital* throughout his life. Marx became a legend. There was a time, beginning in the mid-19th century and through the end of the 20th century, when one could hardly be an intellectual without being a Marxist. French political scientist Raymond Aron (1905–1983) was among the few who dared to denounce this situation in his work *The Opium of the Intellectuals* (1955) particularly in his identification of Marxism as a new secular religion (Aron 2009, 265–294). A classic synthesis and exposition on Marx's ideas in Berlin (2013). On Engels, see Hunt (2010)

[30] On the clash between Liberalism and Socialism, see Blainey (2008, 31–44), Lukacs (2013, 78–89) and de Bertier de Sauvigny (1970, 147–166).

social justice, to be based on the principle of "from each according to his ability, to each according to his needs". The movement grew more radical with Pierre Proudhon (1809–1865), Louis Blanc (1811–1882)[31] and, above all, Marx himself.

#### 17.4.2.2 The Revolutionary Approach

Socialism represented a full-on attack against the premises of the liberal state, as it advanced the idea that the defense of the disadvantaged should constitute one of the government's essential aims, a principle openly criticized by liberals, who feared its social consequences and dreaded a return to an all-powerful and authoritarian state.

In France the Revolution of 1848 clearly constituted an uprising of the masses (Geary 1984, 25–89) as opposed to the quintessentially bourgeois Revolution of 1830 (Pilbeam 2006, 168–180).[32] In fact, the first article of the Constitution of the Second French Republic (1848–1851) defined the new regime as a "social republic" and introduced universal (male) suffrage, definitively adopted in France, displacing censitary electoral systems.[33]

It is worth pointing out that in the mid nineteenth century France was, along with the United States, the only western country with a large number of small landowners, in the former as a result of the Revolution of 1789, in the latter as a

[31] The famous Henri de Saint Simon's followers watchword "from each according to his capacity, to each capacity according to its works" (*À chacun selon ses capacités, à chaque capacité selon ses œuvres*) Enfantin and Bazard (1829, 11) was transformed by socialist Louis Blanc (Madrid 1811—Cannes 1882) in his works: "From each according to his means, to each according to his needs *to each according to his capacity, to each capacity according to its works*;" ("*De chacun selon ses moyens a chacun selon ses besoins à chacun selon ses besoins, de chacun selon ses facultés*"), in Blanc (1982, 94). He claimed that it was "*a wise and equitable principle in appearance, but in reality unjust and subversive*" (Blanc 1844, 555). The two authors, though even more the latter, were precursors of the French Revolution of 1848, the first European political movement featuring popular demands by the masses for economic justice. On Blanc, see Loubère (2012). The inspiration for this creed was drawn from two lines in the *Book of Acts* in the Christian Bible: *All that believed were together, and had all things in common*; *And sold their possessions and goods, and parted them to all men, as every man had need* (*Acts* 2:44–45). An extensive, milestone commentary upon socialism and Henri Saint-Simon in Durkheim (2010). About the concept of social justice and its theoretical trajectory and controversies, see Jackson (2005, 356–373). On the French origins of Socialism, see Hanagan (1992) and Rancière (2012). On Babeuf as a political thinker, and a major precursor of the modern revolutionary socialist tradition, see Birchall (1997). An overview about the principles of Distributive Justice and its theorists, i.e. from Babeuf to Rawls, in Fleischacker (2009, 80–124). The historical development of the Welfare State and how the localized "British model" of welfare support persisted alongside the "nationalization" of provision (social insurance, health care, education), in Harris (2002, 409–438).

[32] It is significant that the French Revolution of 1848, and Marx and Engels' *Communist Manifesto* came about almost simultaneously. For an academic analysis of radicalism of the 1848 revolutions, see Gould (1995, 32–64) and Mommsen (2011, 416–420).

[33] Specifically, the first article stated that "sovereignty resides in the universality of French citizens". Suffrage was granted to all males over 21 years of age, voting was secret and direct, and voters had to choose from lists of candidates for each *département* (Jennings 2011, 90).

consequence of the staggering abundance of land available. Thus, in these nations citizens were more sensitive to the dire conditions suffered by workers in the wake of the Industrial Revolution, and convinced by their social realities that this was not an inevitable state of affairs.[34] In fact, the French Constitution of 1848 recognized as one of the state's primary functions that of providing citizens with work, an objective it pursued through the creation of "National Workshops" (*ateliers nationaux*). This policy, without any doubt, marked a precedent in the construction of what would come to be called the "welfare state".[35]

Liberals, however, put up strong resistance to these kinds of developments. It is noteworthy that on September 12, 1848, the very lucid liberal thinker Alexis de Tocqueville (1805–1859) rose to address the French Second Republic's Constitutional Assembly to deliver a "speech against the right to work" in which he rejected a series of social rights which he viewed as utterly incompatible with the individual rights which the liberal state ought to ensure. In his view, accepting these postulates meant opening the door to the return of political authoritarianism.[36]

Following Marx and Engels' *Communist Manifesto* Socialism took on a decidedly political tint and became an international movement overtly aimed at toppling the liberal state. To achieve this Marxist Socialism espoused class struggle, i.e. the proletariat as a united, international class violently overthrowing the exploitative class: the bourgeoisie. For this purpose, the International Workingmen's

---

[34] For an overview of the social consequences of the 1848 Revolution in Europe, see Sperber (2005, 5–55).

[35] As Sewell (1997, 246) points out, through the spring of 1848 the National Workshops, which were seen as a first step towards a state-backed system of producers' associations, were the essential source of income for tens of thousands of workers who had been left jobless by the economic crisis. Most of the employment provided consisted of rudimentary digging and leveling on public works, but their political significance was essential; designating the workshops as "national" implied that they were a fundamental institution of the republic, like the National Assembly or the National Guard.

[36] In its latest formulation, the Commission limits itself to imposing on society the duty to come to the aid, be it by work or by assistance strictly speaking, of all hardships to the extent of its resources. In saying this, the Commission undoubtedly wanted to impose on the state a more extensive and more sacred duty than that which has been imposed until now; but it did not want to create something absolutely new; it wanted to expand, consecrate, and regularize public charity; it did not want to generate anything other than public charity. The amendment, in contrast, does something different, and does much more. The amendment, with the meaning given to it in speeches and, above all, by recent actions, the amendment, which grants to each individual the general, absolute and irresistible right to work, this amendment leads necessarily to one of the following consequences. Either the state will undertake to provide work to all unemployed workers who come forward, thus being drawn little by little into the industrial process; or, as it is the industrial contractor that operates everywhere, the only one which cannot refuse to provide work and the one which usually imposes the least work, it is invincibly led to become the principal, and soon, as it were, the only industrial entrepreneur. Once this point has been reached, taxation is no longer the means of funding the machinery of government but the principal means of supporting industry. By thus accumulating in its hands all individual capital, the state finally becomes the sole owner of everything. Well, this is communism. (Tocqueville 2009, 394–395).

Association (IWA) was founded in London in 1864, also known as the First International (Freymond and Molnár 1966, 3–35).

#### 17.4.2.3 Social Democracy and Mass Parties Emerge

During this stage, "scientific" Socialism was clearly revolutionary in nature, as it called for an armed uprising against the liberal established order, seeking the institution of a totalitarian regime: the dictatorship of the proletariat, as the first stage of a process leading to the creation of a state devoid of social classes. The failure of the Paris Commune (March–May 1871), however, would lead Marx to renounce violence, and at the 1872 Hague Congress, radical anarchists led by Bakunin (1814–1876) were actually expelled from the IWA (Nomad 1966, 68). Henceforth the socialist movement's aim became to control the liberal state by legal means through the corresponding electoral processes. This was Social Democracy, a political movement which arose when supporters of Marx and La Salle met at Gotha in 1875 (Manuel 1997, 208).

This explains why it was at this time when the first mass parties were founded: in 1875 the German Socialist Workers' Party,[37] the Spanish Socialist Workers' Party in 1879 (Gillespie 1989), in 1892 the Italian Socialist Party,[38] the English Labour Party in 1900 (Worley 2009, 3), the Russian Socialist-Revolutionary Party in 1901 (Hildermeier 2000, 42–50), and in 1905 the French Section of the Workers' International (SFIO), the forerunner of the current French Socialist Party.[39]

### *17.4.3 The Conservative Approach: Bismarck's* Sozialpolitik

It is certainly a paradox that the social rights of workers would begin to receive effective protection from a conservative government such as that in Imperial Prussia, a development that started because Bismarck, despite the fact that he

---

[37] As Weichlein (2011, 296) explains, democratic suffrage accelerated the development of the German party system, whose roots dated back to the 1848 Revolution. Traditionally there was a binary party system based on the opposition between order and revolution, but after the introduction of universal suffrage, this was transformed into a four-party system consisting of Liberalism, Conservatism, Political Catholicism, and Socialism. In 1869 the German socialists, led by August Bebel and Wilhelm Liebknecht, had founded the Social Democratic Workers' Party (*Sozialdemokratische Arbeiterpartei*), which in 1875 became the Socialist Workers' Party of Germany (*Sozialistische Arbeiterpartei Deutschlands*).

[38] In August of 1892 at the Congress of Italian Workers, held in Genoa, the Socialists separated from the Anarchists. In 1893, the former founded the Socialist Party of Italian Workers (*Partito socialista dei lavoratori italiani*) in Reggio Emilia (Salvatorelli 1999, 483).

[39] On December 25, 1920, at its 18th Congress in Tours, the SFIO split, giving rise to the French Section of the Communist International (SFIC) the antecedent of what would become the French Communist Party (Saint-Pierre 2006, 44–45). The current Socialist Party was created in 1969 (Alfortville Congress), although it only became France's major leftist party only under Mitterrand and after the Epinay Congress (1971).

belonged to the Prussian aristocracy, was astute enough to realize the need to reduce the pressure exerted by the socialist movement, spurring him to adopt a policy of worker protection which may be considered a precursor of the "welfare state".

After the establishment of the Second Reich in 1871, and despite his resounding victories over France and Austria, the all-powerful Bismarck faced strong internal opposition from the bourgeois parties in the *Reichstag*. It was then when to buttress his political position, he opted to win over and ally himself with the working class by endorsing the state's adoption of policies favoring its welfare (Roth 1984, 59–84). In a speech before the *Reichstag* on November 17, 1881, Emperor William I recognized that it was incumbent upon the state to promote the well-being of all its citizens, especially the most vulnerable and needy, through the appropriate institutions and using those resources at society's disposal. At this point Bismarck's government adopted what would come to be termed "social policy" (*Sozialstaat*), which took the form of a series of legislative measures passed between 1883 and 1889.[40] This set of laws would be incorporated into the Social Insurance Code of 1911, and enabled the Weimar Republic to expressly recognize the right to social welfare protection.[41]

The social protection model backed by Bismarck would be adopted in the United Kingdom from 1906 to 1911, thanks to Lloyd George and his advisors W.H. Beveridge and Winston Churchill, who urged the government to take a step forward and break with the outmoded tradition of social assistance provided exclusively in the form of the "poor laws". It should be noted that 20 years later the British government would take a further step to reinforce social protection by assuring state funding for the system, as under Bismarck's model it was only sustained financially by employers and workers.[42]

[40] The series of social welfare laws began with the 1883 legislation, when he endorsed passage of workers' health insurance for those employees with the lowest wages and, a year later, occupational accident insurance. This insurance would be expanded to salaried workers and even farmers in 1885 and 1886. Employees paid in two thirds of contributions, and employers the rest. In 1884, the law imposing occupational accident insurance was introduced, placing the onus entirely upon employers and guaranteeing two thirds of one's pay in the event of disability. In 1889, also thanks to the initiative of the Iron Chancellor, the German Empire would approve Europe's first system of pensions and disability benefits, a law featuring retirement and disability insurance, their cost being shared by employers and employees. The insurance was obligatory, but was not paid for by taxes, but rather through the contributions of companies and workers. Bismarck's *Sozialstaat* de Bismarck did not constitute a welfare state, per se. For an overview of German Social policy in these years, see Seligman and Mclean (2000, 35–38). Also, Torp (2011, 336–358)

[41] For an analysis of the nature of Bismarck's social policies and their consequences see Eley (1976, 71–86) and Wuthnow (2009, 377–408).

[42] This policy would give rise to the approval of different laws. In 1906 one bill governing unemployment and a minimum wage; in 1908 the *Old Age Pension Act* in 1911 the *National Insurance Act* and in 1912 a law introducing sickness insurance (*Sickness Benefits Act*) (Stolleis 2014, 29–82). For an overview of the extension of social protection in the UK before World War I, see Pugh (2012, 119–178).

### *17.4.4 The Return of the Interventionist State*

In general, however, Europe's governments would remain relatively reluctant to protect the least fortunate classes so long as their liberal states were enjoying considerable economic growth, fruit of their colonial expansion. This would abruptly change, however, with the catastrophic turning point of World War I, a "collective suicide" committed by Europe's all-powerful nation-states which would lead, among many other things, to the success of the Russian "Soviet Revolution" in 1917. These developments in Europe would give rise to a new constitutional model, reflected, on the other side of the Atlantic, in the Mexican Constitution of 1917, which featured references not only to "individual rights" but "social rights" as well (Meade 2010, 169–170).[43] World War I and the Russian Revolution would prompt western governments to generally embrace this recognition of the need for the state to take an active role in mitigating economic inequality and social injustice.

## 17.5 The Russian Revolution and the First Triumph of Totalitarianism

The principle of state intervention to reshape society made huge strides, especially after 1902, when Lenin's ideas prevailed at the Second Congress of Russia's Social Democratic Labor Party, at which he advocated revolutionary radicalism and the triumph of the proletariat by violent means. At this point there appeared "Bolsheviks" ("members of the majority") and "Mensheviks" ("members of the minority"), led by Julius Martov, who advocated a "social-democratic" approach to change, more in keeping with Marxist orthodoxy since 1872.[44]

[43] The "Political Constitution of the United Mexican States" was the work of Venustiano Carranza (1860–1920). Among the "individual guarantees" in its Section 1 was the right to strike and the organization of workers in trade unions, establishing a maximum 8-h workday and the right to decent and socially useful work, principles reinforced in its Section 6, which addressed "Work and Social Security". Although quite modified, the 1917 Constitution remains in force. For an analysis of the social nature of the Constitution, see Andrew and Cleven (1921, 474–487) and Niemeyer (1991). For a history of constitutional rights and their judicial interpretation by Mexico's Supreme Court from the Restored Republic to the Maximato, see James (2014). An overview of Mexico's political evolution since it became independent from Spain in 1821, and its current constitutional arrangements, principles and structures in Serna de la Garza (2013).

[44] For an overview of the preparation, development and consequences of the Second Congress, see Getzler (2003, 63–95).

### 17.5.1 Lenin and the Soviet Revolution

Vladimir Illich Ulianov (1870–1924), a lawyer and intellectual (alias "Lenin" as all Russian revolutionaries used pseudonyms to evade the tsar's police) dissented from Marx in his belief that the road of social democracy, as proposed by the author of *Das Kapital* to transform the social order, was too circuitous. Instead, he advocated a more expeditious route: violent revolution led by a select group of professional revolutionaries. Among this cadre Lenin included Iósiv Dzugashvili (1878–1953), better known by his revolutionary nickname, Stalin, or "man of steel", who was of humble origins and, in contrast to Lenin, not an intellectual but a man of action.[45]

Lenin's strategy led to victory in nothing less than three revolutions: that of 1905 and the February and October Revolutions of 1917 (Haimsom 2005). The first did away with autocracy, the second with monarchy, and the third with private property. These revolutions can be called "soviet" in that they replaced the traditional political and social order of the Russian monarchy with a collectivist regime led by soviets—groups of workers and soldiers designed in 1905 by León Trotsky, the pseudonym of Lev Davidovich Bronstein (1879–1940), one of the Russian Revolution's most radical and effective leaders.[46]

### 17.5.2 International Proletarianism vs. the Capitalism of the Liberal Nation-States

World War I Germany's high staff actually contributed decisively to the October Russian Revolution by making the decision to allow Lenin and all the leading Russian revolutionaries, who had taken refuge in Switzerland, to travel to

---

[45] Stalin was not actually Russian, but Georgian. His mother had been born a servant, and her son was able to learn to read and write only because his mother came to work for a priest. Young Joseph was enrolled in a church school and theological seminary, as his mother was determined for him to become a priest. He never did, but the dogmatic education he received at the seminary he attended molded his mind and predisposed him for his subsequent indoctrination in the Marxist thesis. Dzugashvili caught Lenin's attention when, in command of a group of Bolsheviks in the Caucasus, he was engaged in robbing banks and trains. As Bullock (1993, 52) points out, Lenin considered Stalin not a policymaker or an intellectual but a man who could be given a job and trusted to get on with it; rough, still inexperienced, but with a willingness to learn and an instinct for power. Paradoxically, Stalin was not even present for the great October Revolution of 1917, as he was away from St. Petersburg. As a result, Lenin and Trotsky rose to prominence at Stalin's expense, something for which Stalin would never forgive the latter. When Trotsky later exiled himself to Mexico, Stalin ordered his execution by a secret Soviet agent, of Spanish origin, named Ramón Mercader. A researched, comprehensive portrait of Stalin in Service (2008). On Trotsky, see Swain (2014). An essential reading on Lenin at the London Congress of the RSDLP in 1907, in Gorky (2004). On Lenin's life and political career, see the standard biography by Service (2008).

[46] On the essential role played by Trotsky in the Russian Revolution, see Rees (2006, 147–149) and Trotsky, himself (2014) (En este volumen están refundidas las obras de Trotsky sobre la Revolución de Octubre).

St. Petersburg in a special train, via Helsinki (Pearson 1991).[47] Since the outbreak of the war, the Germans had been forced to fight on two fronts, and wished to overthrow the tsar to be spared fighting the Russians in the east. The German plan seemed to work at first, as after the triumph of the Soviet Revolution Lenin signed the Brest-Litovsk Treaty (March 3, 1918), in which the new Bolshevik Russian regime (Hardach 1981, 233–234) not only pledged to cease hostilities against Germany, but also suffered significant territorial losses.

The German generals did not take into account that Lenin considered the World War I a struggle between capitalists and that, consequently, he was convinced that German workers would not fight against their Russian comrades, but against the German oligarchies that had enslaved them. The Germans perceived the danger posed by the triumph of the Soviet Revolution too late and, as a result, ended up seeking an armistice to end World War I, signed on November 11, 1918.[48] Just months later the Third International, or *Kommintern* (of International Communism) met, with the precise objective of fomenting proletarian revolution throughout the world.[49]

In fact, in the year 1919 a wave of revolutionary processes swept through Europe, starting in recently defeated Germany, where in January of 1919 the Spartacist Uprising (January Strike) broke out, headed by Karl Liebknecht and

---

[47] The German generals' intention was to destabilize the Russian government in an effort to avoid an eastern front, enabling them to concentrate all their military efforts in the west. Despite the Germans' military superiority on the western front, they were still unable to prevail because of the entrance into the war of the United States, drawn into the conflict in large part by the Germans' repeated U-boat attacks on American ships.

[48] It is important to mention that when the Germans signed the armistice ending World War I on November 11, 1918 the Allies had yet to conquered one inch of their territory. The Germans had realized the growing magnitude of the Soviet revolutionary movement, which threatened to spread throughout Europe, starting with Germany. As Eltscher (2013, 31) points out, an important factor favoring the acceptance of the Nazi state was the fear of the "Bolshevik menace", nowhere more evident than in post-World War I Germany, as evidenced by the short-lived Communist uprising of 1919 known as the Spartacist Rebellion, which appeared to confirm the danger posed by political Marxism.

[49] In fact, it was the creation of the *Kommintern* that, as we have already mentioned, divided Socialists all over Europe, as some wished to join the new Communist International while others did not. As a result, in 1920 a number of communist parties arose which were, in fact, splinter groups of formerly socialist bodies—such as in France, at the Tours Congress (December 25–30, 1920), where the French Socialist Party, the SFIO, was split in two, and the French Section of the International Socialist gave rise to the French Section of the International Communist. In Spain, the split came at the III Congress of the Spanish Socialist Workers Party (PSOE), celebrated on April 13, 1921, which gave rise to the foundation of the Spanish Communist Party (PCE) in 1922. The *Comintern*—Third International, also called Communist International, byname Comintern, association of national communist parties founded in 1919, functioned chiefly as an organ of Soviet control over the international communist movement, and cooperated narrowly with Soviet intelligence. On the history of this Association and its significant role in the Stalinist ruling system during the years 1933 to 1943, as well as its relationship with the Popular Front in Europe—especially France, and its implications in the civil wars in Spain and China, and World War II, see Firsov et al. (2014).

Rosa Luxemburg (December 1918–January 1919), violently put down by the government of the Weimar Republic, under the leadership of the socialist Friedrich Ebert (Henig 2006, 8–12).

## 17.6 The European Oligarchies React by Defending "National Socialism"

The Soviet Revolution dealt a great blow to the ruling classes of the western states, which did not hesitate to organize and to back parties appealing to the masses of workers, with platforms of aggressive social reform in a desperate attempt to prevent the triumph of Bolshevism. This was the "Third Way" (Gentile 2005, 59), a compromise between the old parliamentary system and the communist revolution.

This "language of class anxiety" (Maier 2011, 22–38) would lead to the rise of Benito Mussolini (1922–1943) in Italy and Adolf Hitler (1933–1945) in Germany, both populist leaders who ended up imposing fascist dictatorships which actually did make surprisingly significant progress in the area of labor and economic reform.[50]

After coming to power in 1922 by way of a *coup d'état* (The March on Rome), Mussolini strengthened the executive, reorganized the government administration and created public bodies to bolster the economy through massive investment in public works and industrial consortia. As a result, Italy overcame its economic crisis and enjoyed an era of great prosperity that made the fascist regime, at least initially, extremely popular.[51]

[50] On the origins of Fascist movements, see Paxton (2007, 24–54). It is significant that Italy and Germany were Europe's two most recent nation-states.

[51] For an overview of fascist economic and social policies, see Pollard (2005, 77–90). On popular acceptance of the regime, see Duggan (2013, 113–147). Hitler, literally, "bought" his people's consent: while Jews and citizens of occupied lands suffered crippling taxation, mass looting, enslavement, and destruction, most Germans enjoyed an improved standard of living. Buoyed by millions of packages soldiers sent from the front, Germans also benefited from the systematic plunder of conquered territory and the transfer of Jewish possessions into their homes and pockets. Any qualms were swept away by waves of government handouts, tax breaks, and preferential legislation. According to Herz, and the reports by several members of the Frankfurt group for the OSS (see footnote 58) Germany's military setbacks had provoked a decline of German "morale" that opened the way for a transition of political power "quietly, while hostilities were still in progress, and well in advance of the so-called revolution". Still, Nazi totalitarianism presented a qualitatively different scenario: society had been "completely pulverized into its individual atoms which are then organized and manipulated from the top-down", "well-trained" to "want . . . 'peace, bread, and security', not politics" and to recognize "private sorrows, food, shelter, safety for themselves and their children" as its only priorities in a repressive context where "fear and distrust prevents them from articulating even these private sorrows". Apathy, fatigue, and distrust were therefore the fundamental characteristics of the German people, who, though wounded by the setbacks of war, had not been fundamentally transformed (Neumann et al. 2013, 1–24).

In Germany, the authoritarian constitutional tradition stemming back to the 1850 Prussian Constitution, was significantly reinforced by Bismarck's imperial conceptions during the Wihelmine period (Eley 1996). Germany's defeat in World War I, the Spartacist Revolt and the Versailles *Diktat*, rampant inflation, which took off in 1923, and the fallout of the Great Depression after 1929 provided fertile ground for a totalitarian model of the state in Germany.[52] All these circumstances explain why Hitler, after failing to pull off his own coup (Beer Hall Putsch, Munich, 1923), rose to power 10 years later via election in 1933, and quickly imposed a fierce dictatorship. Hitler's regime enjoyed public support because he, like Mussolini in Italy, also launched a policy of state economic intervention which alleviated the massive inflationary crisis that had plagued the country. As a result, in just 3 years the German economy became the world's second strongest, topped only by the United States.[53]

Both Mussolini and Hitler, embraced a state model according to which the government actively intervened in the economy and adopted the measures necessary to prevent social injustice, but on a strictly "national" scale, soundly rejecting any notions of international solidarity, as forwarded by Lenin. It is highly significant that the party with which Hitler came to power was called the National Socialist German Workers Party (*Nationalsozialistische Deutsche Arbeiterpartei*, NSDAP), a political organization founded in 1920, months after the failure of the Spartacist Uprising and the foundation of the *Kommintern*.[54]

Hitler, however, sought not only to take over the German state, but to redefine the very idea of the "nation", propounding a racist concept (McDonough 2003, 60) according to which the German people (*Deutsches Volk*) needed to be purified to

[52] On the radicalization of right-wing movements in Germany since Bismarck, see Frankel (2005, 68–86) and Gerwarth (2005, 118–145).

[53] Progress came thanks to a vast program whose most prominent and spectacular measures were the construction of motorways (*Autobahn*) throughout all Germany (Taylor 2010, 24–62). Hitler hired Ferdinand Porsche, who was known as one of Germany's most successful automobile engineers from his work on military vehicles during World War I, to design and build his Strength Through Joy car. The Strength Through Joy movement was a Nazi enterprise that organized worker recreation programs, sponsoring sports and vacations. However, according Schilperoord, Josef Ganz, a Jewish engineer and journalist, created in May 1931, a revolutionary small car: the *Maikäfer* (German for May Beetle). Seven years later, Hitler introduced the *Volkswagen*. He not only 'took' the concept of Ganz's family car, he even used the same nickname—Ganz was hunted by the Nazis even beyond Germany's borders and narrowly escaped assassination (Schilperoord 2012). The raising of prestigious structures, such as the stadium that would house the 1936 Olympics in Berlin, constituted the greatest moments of glory for Hitler's regime. Hitler also created a Social Security system. On the Nazi "welfare state", see Aly (2008). In just a few years, Germany was transformed into a first-rate economic power, especially when Hitler charged Albert Speer with German rearmament. Hitler's regime actually decreased inflation from 26.3 % in 1933 to 14.9 % in 1934, 11.6 % in 1935, 8.3 % in 1936, 24.6 in 1937, 2.1 in 1938 and 0.4 % in 1939; over 25 points in 6 years. The index of industrial production, meanwhile, doubled, rising from 66 in 1932 to 135 in 1939 (Overy 2001, 35) For an overview and evaluation of Hitler's economic achievements, see Silverman (1998, 219–246). Also, Tooze (2008) and Wiesen (2010). On Todt and Speer, the Hitler's engineers, see Taylor (2010).

[54] On the rise of the NSDAP, see Fulbrook (2009, 42–50).

contain only pure Aryan blood (Mosse 1989, 43–58). This warped notion of the nation (Stolleis 1998, 64–86) led to the extermination of entire ethnic groups (genocide), including the Jews and gypsies, as part of the Nazis' "Final Solution" (*Endlösung*), along with the elimination of persons with physical and mental defects to improve the race through eugenic engineering (Browning 2004, 374–423).

### *17.6.1 Perfectly Legal Dictatorships*

In this general overview, we do not have enough space to present a detailed analysis of totalitarian regimes and their institutions. We can make the general observation, however, that dictators, whether communist or fascist, have invariably sought to adorn their autocratic regimes with the trappings of legality.

Thus, for example, in Italy, Mussolini never repealed the country's constitutional regime, nor did he dethrone the king. Rather, he merely "suspended" the Albertine Statute. In fact, Mussolini never even formally became the head of state. During the fascist *ventenio,* Italy remained a monarchy. This did not, however, prevent the fascists from carrying out a gradual legal assault on the state, which would ultimately allow them to control the government as Italy's sole party, beginning with electoral reform through the Acerbo Law (1923), which rewarded the party winning the elections—even if by a narrow margin—two-thirds of the seats in the national legislature (Ghisalberti 2012, 347–348).[55]

In the case of Nazi Germany, one must remember that Hitler came to power legitimately by winning national elections and forming a coalition with Germany's conservative parties, headed by Vice-Chancellor Franz Von Papen, in a government led by the Nazi leader on January 30, 1933. Following the dissolution of the Reichstag and the call for new elections, Hitler, in response to the Reichstag fire of February 27, 1933, imposed the "Decree for the Protection of the German People and the State" (*Verordnung des Reichspräsidenten zum Schutz von Volk und Staat*), issued by President Hindenburg (Kershaw 2000, 439), which restricted public liberties a week before the elections to the *Reichstag*. This was the beginning of what Alan Bullock calls the "Revolution after power" (Bullock 2005, 137–171), a movement that was consolidated when the new assembly elected on March 5, granted Hitler full powers through the Enabling Act of March 24, 1933.[56] The fascist dictatorship was actually established in a legal manner, within the

[55] Worthy of note is the end of the fascist *ventenio* by a vote of censure from the fascist Grand Council, which aimed to drive Mussolini from power, allows the king to abdicate, and bring about a return to the legality of the Albertine Statute. This initiative failed in 1947 because of the holding of a republican-monarchical referendum that led to creation of the current Italian Republic (Ghisalberti 2012, 380–382).

[56] The official name of the Enabling Act was "Law to Remedy the Distress of People and Reich" (*Gesetz zur Behebung der Not von Volk und Reich*) by the Reichstag and the Reichsrat, and signed by President Hindeburg on March 23, 1933 (Kershaw 2000, 467).

constitutional framework of the Weimar Republic,[57] preserving the façade of the "civil *Rechtsstaat*" (Stolleis 1998, 7) but forcing most German constitutionalists to emigrate.[58] The same situation arose, as we saw in Chap. 14, in France in the spring of 1940, when the National Assembly and Senate voted to invest Marshal Pétain with full powers so that the aging soldier could reform the Constitution and create a new authoritarian state, thereby liquidating the Third Republic.

As for Soviet Russia, the October Revolution generated a very curious totalitarian state featuring successive constitutions (1918, 1924, 1936, 1977) containing a peculiar version of public law, including provisions such as an election rule whereby only the workers were allowed to vote (appearing in Lenin's first constitution), which deprived all other social groups, from the middle class up, of political representation—a kind of censitary suffrage turned on its head to favor the workers rather than the elite. After Lenin's death in 1924, Stalin, from his post as General Secretary of the Communist Party, managed to gain power by, over a 10-year period, killing off all his revolutionary comrades from the first stage—including Kamenev, Zinoviev and Trotsky, among others—through a set of kangaroo courts

[57] For an overview of the debate over the validity of the Weimar Constitution after the Enabling Act and on the Constitutional Legal Theory (*Staatsrechtslehre*) under National Socialism, see Stolleis (1998, 87–101). A historical study on German conceptions of constitutional law in Murkens (2013). About German political and constitutional development from early nineteenth century, see Crosby (2008).

[58] After the "legal" establishment of autocracy, most constitutional theorists were faced with the question of how to respond to these developments. Only a few of them opted for National-Socialism, as was the case with Otto Koellreutter. As what Carl Schmitt called the "the civil constitutional State" (*bürgerlicher Rechtsstaat*) no longer existed, most of them, decided to emigrate. Kelsen and Heller, a democrat and Social Democrat of Jewish descent, left Germany shortly. Heller died in Madrid and Kelsen, reported by one of this own students, escaped to Geneva. Erich Kaufmann did not emigrate until 1938, while Gerhard Leibholz and Hans Nwaiasky left the same year (Stolleis 1998, 96). A leading group of scholars was integrated by the members of The Frankfurt School or The Institute for Social Research (Institute für Sozialforschung) in Frankfurt am Main. The Institute was formed in 1923 by Carl Grünberg as an adjunct of the University of Frankfurt; it was the first Marxist-oriented research centre affiliated with a major German university. Max Horkheimer took over as director in 1930 and recruited many talented theorists, including T.W. Adorno, Erich Fromm, Herbert Marcuse, and Walter Benjamin, but they went into exile in the early 1930s too. Passionately supported and equally attacked, the School has had an enormous impact on philosophy as well as social and political theory in the United States and around the world. On the exodus of legal scholars from Nazi Germany, their political ideas and legal framework, see Beatson and Zimmermann (2007). On the foundations of the Frankfurt School and its theories, see Abromeit (2011) and Tarr (2011). Also, because war makes for strange bedfellows, some thinkers of the group, exiled in USA, as Marcuse and Kirchheimer, were recruited and worked with the U.S. Office of Strategic Services (OSS)—a precursor to the CIA, on the security task of providing advice about the Nazis. Although Frankfurters were ultimately disappointed by the Nuremberg trials and by what one member of the team, Herz, later bitterly described as "the fiasco of denazification" (Herz 1948, 569–594), both of which they deemed insufficiently far-reaching, their OSS reports nevertheless provided much of the theoretical basis for the U.S. approach to postwar justice in Germany (Scheuerman 2013, 171–176). The OSS reports and analysis on Nazi regime by Marcuse, Neumann and Kirchheimer—all of them Jewish, in Neumann et al. (2013).

known as the "Moscow Trials" (1936–1938), in an effort to acquire total power and stigmatize any real or suspected opposition (Pringle 2006, 167–168). From this moment until his death (1953), Stalin went on to impose an iron dictatorship over a monolithic state based on relentless police repression, terror and massive propaganda.[59]

This, however, did not prevent him from approving his own constitution in 1936. Stalin's fundamental law was peculiar, as it underwent constant changes, governing aspects which would normally be dealt with by ordinary laws, or even regulations (Duverger 1973, 422–424). In fact, Soviet constitutions were not lasting and stable foundational texts, but rather legislative hodgepodges undergoing constant change-, including the Brezhnev Constitution of 1977, which officially gave up on the "dictatorship of the proletariat" and inaugurated the era of "Developed Socialism" (Daniels 1993, 313–315). All these attempts at constitutional texts established a legal framework suitable for a regime in which the important thing was not the government, nor the legislatures, nor the courts, but the power of the sole party (Communist Party of the Soviet Union), which constituted the core of the state. This is why one only came to form part of the Party after a long and careful selection process for which it was necessary to spend several years as a candidate before joining the new dominant class (nomenklatura).[60]

All of these classes of totalitarian states certainly merit a more detailed study, as they are extremely germane and valuable towards an understanding of the extent to which law in these regimes did not serve as a limiting force, but rather a legitimizing instrument of power, something necessary after the collapse of the *Ancien Ré gime* and the disappearance of tradition as the legitimate justification of power. Above all, they illustrate how each new autocratic regime ended up creating its own legitimacy and legal framework. From the constitutional history perspective, the most interesting fact is that specific aspects of these totalitarian regimes still form part of our democratic states in the twenty-first century. Without going any further, one can cite the power structure prevailing in our current mass parties, whose leadership is determined by conventions at which cadres of elites are elected

[59] Stalin's purges and totalitarianism would nevertheless be condemned even by the Soviet Union's Communist Party at its 20th Congress (1956), led by Nikita Khrushchev (Daniels 1993, 254–257). On the mass repression and political violence in the era of Stalinist Terror, see Harris (2013). For an analysis of Stalin's model of state, see Branderberger (2002, 77–94) and Straus (1997, 1–10).

[60] According to the Oxford Dictionary—from Latin *nomenclatura* meaning a list of names—the system whereby influential posts in government and industry were filled by Party appointees. Orthodox Trotskyism uses the term *caste* rather than *class*, because they considered the Soviet Union as a degenerated workers' state, not a new class society. The Communist Party of the Soviet Union (CPSU) grew considerably during the existence of the USSR. In 1917, it had 240,000 members, which grew to a million by 1926. In 1933, when Hitler took power the figure had risen to 3.5 million, and swelled to 5.7 by 1945. In 1971, the Party boasted almost 14 million members. Entering it was not easy and a quite long process, as one had to be endorsed by at least three members with a minimum of 3 years of seniority. Those admitted faced a 5-year interim period before acquiring full membership. For an overview of the CPSU's organization and functions during the existence of the Soviet Union, see Duverger (1973, 430–432).

which end up enforcing party discipline, particularly when it comes to drawing up electoral lists. These practices have led specialists in public law to expressively designate our contemporary political party leaders the "New Princes", who have turned our democracies into "Partocracies" (Rubio Carracedo 1995, 72–77). Massification comes at a price.[61]

### *17.6.2 An Adapted Legal Theory: From Ihering to Carl Schmitt*

The consolidation of the nation-state in the nineteenth century also decisively transformed jurisprudence, furnishing law with a political dimension and meaning, as it gradually evolved into an instrument of the state. The herald of this trend was Rudolf von Ihering (1818–1892), significantly, a contemporary of Marx (1818–1883). Over the course of his life, von Ihering shifted from embracing a strictly dogmatic conception of the Jurisprudence of Concepts (*Begriffsjurisprudenz*) towards a more realistic and pragmatic understanding of law (Luhman 2004, 344).[62] In his work *The Struggle for Law* (*Kampf ums Recht*), published in 1872 (von Ihering 1997), he bases his view of the law on the relationships between it and power. His approach culminated in his masterpiece *Law as a Means to an End* (*Der Zweck im Recht*), published between 1877 and 1883, in which he posits law not as an absolute value but as the mere product of a relationship established between parties with clashing interests. The regulatory system, then, reflects a conflict of interest, and it is the juror's duty to ascertain in each instance the interest which ought to be served (von Ihering 1999). This is the basis of what has been called the "Jurisprudence of Interests" (*Interessenjurisprudenz*) (Bomhoff 2013, 17). The following step was for the state to use the law to defend the politically dominant interest.

The association of positive law with state law reached its zenith when Hitler came to power, in the form of the *Rechtserneuerungsbewegung* (Reformist Legal Movement), whose primary exponent was Carl Schmitt (Stolleis 2004, 169–173). When it comes to understanding totalitarian legal systems, it is worth looking at the criticism offered by Carl Schmitt of the liberal model of the state, in which he justified the establishment of an all-powerful regime, imposed upon the citizenry based on social considerations which he ultimately extended to all areas.[63]

---

[61] For an analysis of political parties' transformation from elite political groups into mass organizations, see Kirchheimer (1999, 177–182). A classical guideline on parties and party systems in Sartori (2009)

[62] von Ihering (1964, 347) criticized the misconceptions of our modern jurisprudence which, ignoring the practical ultimate purpose and the conditions of the applicability of law, see in it only an object for a testing a self-serving, logical reasoning which finds its attraction and purpose in itself.

[63] In a letter to Rudolf Smend, dated October 17, 1927, he affirmed that the aim of what today can be considered his magnum opus, *Constitutional Theory* (*Verfassungslehre*), published a year later, was to "remove the death mask from liberalism" (*dem Liberalismus die Totenmaske abzunehmen.* Schmitt 2012, 64–65). He held that European states were still half stuck in the nineteenth century, though the future anti-liberal constitutional model was yet to be clearly defined. To clarify it

The scholarly approach to law of Carl Schmitt (1914–1985), sought to provide theoretical underpinnings for the German National Socialist State before he ended up falling out with Hitler. However, Schmitt's conception of the state went much further. One would expect Schmitt's ideas to have been utterly discredited and forgotten after the collapse of Nazism. In fact, however, his works are still being republished and widely read, a telling indication of the extent to which they contain a lucid analysis of the harsh reality of the mass-based states prevailing in the first decades of the twentieth century.[64]

According to Schmitt, the limits imposed by the liberal model of the state had led to the development of intermediary bodies that completely overpowered and subverted the state, which was reduced to obeying their mandates and, therefore, failed to fulfill its primordial function of protecting civil society.

Schmitt was opposed to the rule of law because the legal system that limited state power was controlled and determined by the indirect and private "powers of society", uncontrolled and unseen, who cared only about their own interests instead of defending the common good.

> As *magnus homo*, or a sovereign person of the state similar to God, the Leviathan was destroyed from the inside in the 17th century... but its work, the state, survived it with an army and a police force, an administrative and judicial apparatus, and an effective and specialized bureaucracy. The state increasingly has come to resemble a mechanism and a machine, and the development of the concept of law has gone hand in hand with this evolution (...) the law has become a technical means of taming the Leviathan ("placing a hook in the Leviathan's nose".). The state itself metamorphoses into a positivist legal system.[65]

---

Schmitt wanted, in contrast to Kelsen, for the president of the Reich to become the "guardian of the constitution", prompting him to work closely with Papen and Schleicher on the final efforts to shore up the presidential dictatorship (Stolleis 2004, 171). A regard on one of the most prominent variation of the law-rule in Frankenberg (2014, 51–96)

[64] Schmitt remains the most controversial, and perhaps the most puzzling figure, at least to British and American academics. His essential works have been translated into English and there are quite recent editions of his *Constitutional Theory* (2008, Durham: Duke University Press); *The Concept of the Political* (2007, Expanded ed. Chicago: University Of Chicago Press); *Legality and Legitimacy* (2007, 3rd print. Durham: Duke University Press); *Political Theology: Four Chapters on the Concept of Sovereignty* (2006, Chicago: University Of Chicago Press); *Political Theology II: The Myth of the Closure of any Political Theology* (2006 Chicago: University Of Chicago Press) and *The Crisis of Parliamentary Democracy* (1988, Cambridge, Mass.: MIT Press). The most important keys to the author's thought including its contextualization in a much larger political and historical context, in Kennedy (2004). On his life and work, Mehring (2014). Carl Schmitt's thought is of special interest from a Spanish perspective, as it had a particular impact on Franco's long-lasting dictatorship. As Manuel García Pelayo (2011, 489–494) has indicated, it was undoubtedly in Franco's regime (1939–1975) where Schmitt's work was most warmly received and widely disseminated. Schmitt's relationship with Spain was certainly strengthened by the marriage of his only daughter, Ánima Schmitt, to the Spanish professor of Legal History Alfonso Otero Varela. For an overview of Schmitt's influence in Spain see also López García (1996, 139–168) and Sosa Wagner (2008).

[65] Schmitt (2008, 65).

This situation, in Schmitt's opinion, called for the reestablishment of a direct link between the individual and the state, instead of one mediated via a so-called "representative assembly", whose laws corrupted this relationship.

### *17.6.3 The Expansion of Social/Legal Protection in the Interbellum Period*

The liberal state model suffered a great blow in Europe as a result of World War I, but in the United States its spirit was not only intact but even reinforced, as the country flourished, establishing itself as the world's most powerful nation after 1918. Yet, in America, which continued to embrace free markets and limited government in the wake of the Great War, the principle of the need for public intervention in economic matters was soon to be accepted, not as a consequence of war, as was the case in Europe, but in response to the devastation wrought by the Great Depression, which shook the nation's faith in *laissez faire* and the liberal model which it had hitherto embraced with few reservations.

### *17.6.4 The Crisis of the Liberal State Model in the U.S.A.: The New Deal*

#### 17.6.4.1 The United States After World War I

Until 1918, the United States had been just one more power within the set of western nations, in a world controlled, as we have seen, by the European nation-states. The Great War, however, would alter this situation forever. A single statistic is sufficient to illustrate the transformation: in 1914, the United States owed the various European states some 3 billion dollars. The trade balance was, thus, heavily tilted in the Continent's favor. By 1918, the European states owed the U.S. federal government no less than 14 billion dollars—almost five times more.[66]

Whereas Europe had been ruined and destroyed during this period, the United States enjoyed an era of burgeoning prosperity. With immense natural wealth, a huge domestic market, the absence of customs barriers, and new techniques that made possible better and cheaper production (like scientific management, or "Taylorism", and assembly lines), the United States became a society marked by mass production and consumption (Chambers 2000, 61–63). This transformation enabled

[66] For an overall view of the transformation of the U.S. economy during World War I, see Rockoff (2005, 310–342) Also, Ott (2011).

the country to become the world's premier economic power.[67] In 1925, the U.S. provided the global economy with more than half its iron, coal, steel, copper, oil and cotton, despite a population accounting for less than 5 % of the world. Thanks to this wealth the U.S. government was able to grant massive loans to a Europe ravaged by war, such those via the Dawes Plan (1924), followed by the Young Plan (1930), for the settlement of German war reparations and national recovery (Murphree 2005, 269–272).

The two terms of President Calvin Coolidge (August 2, 1923–March 4, 1929), were a time of great economic prosperity, the so-called "Roaring 20s", an era of tycoons like the most famous of them all, John Davidson Rockefeller (1839–1937), who amassed huge fortunes and built genuine empires in just a few years (Morris 2005). The private sector's resources dramatically surpassed those of the public sector, a situation consolidated by America's still relatively pristine liberal state model. This spectacular prosperity led people to speculate on the stock exchange without initial capital, using borrowed money to invest on Wall Street, trusting that its constantly rising dividends would enable them to repay their loans and turn a profit. For many years this practice actually worked.[68] Alongside the "real economy", however, a speculation-driven bubble gradually swelled, considerably distorting the appearance of prosperity. At the end of the first decade of the twenty-first century, this situation has become eerily familiar to western economies.

#### 17.6.4.2 The Great Depression

When Coolidge completed his second term, the American presidency remained in Republican hands, as he was succeeded by Herbert Clark Hoover (1929–1933). Within just months of Hoover's election, the U.S. financial system collapsed. From Wednesday, October 23 to Tuesday, October 29 (Black Tuesday), the New York

[67] Between 1925 and 1929, the number of manufacturing establishments increased from 183,900 to 206,700 and the value of their output rose from 60.8 to 68 billion USD. The Federal Reserve index of industrial production averaged 67 in 1921, 110 in July of 1928, and reached 126 in June of 1929. In 1926, the U.S. car industry produced 4,301,000 automobiles. Three years later production had increased by over a million, to 5,358,000—an extraordinary figure if we take into account that 24 years later, in the boom year of 1953, the figure was only slightly higher: 5,700,000 (Galbraith 2009, 2).

[68] At the end of May 1924, according to the *New York Times*, the average price of the top twenty-five industrial stocks was 106. By the end of the year, it had risen to 134, and by December 1925, it had gained nearly another 50 points, reaching 181. The year 1926 was a difficult year, when it dropped to 143. In 1927, there was a major recovery, and by the end of that year, the *Times* industrial reached 245, with a net gain of 69 points in 12 months. The true speculative orgy, however, began in 1928, marked by great volatility. In June of that year, over five million shares were traded on the average day (Galbraith 2009, 7–9 and 11–15).

Stock Exchange plummeted. By the time, the market stabilized in mid November stocks had lost half their value. Fifty billion dollars had disappeared into thin air.[69]

The Wall Street collapse was, in fact, only the symbol and most vivid illustration of a wider crisis. In reality, the entire American economic system unraveled in what came to be called the "Great Depression".[70] The worst part of this crisis was that, because all the western countries depended on America's prosperity, the economic earthquake in the U.S. sent out shock waves that destroyed banks and factories all around the world, leaving millions unemployed. Tariffs were raised and a monetary crisis ensued. On September 21, 1931, the Bank of England abolished the gold standard (Kindleberger 2013, 157), triggering the collapse of the pound sterling, hitherto the world's benchmark currency, which dragged down the currencies of many other countries with it.

This was the first serious *global* financial crisis (Boyce 2012), and it had dramatic social consequences. The middle class was devastated[71] which, among other things, allowed Hitler to win the German elections in 1933, by promoting

---

[69] For an overview of the macroeconomics of the Great Depression, see Bernanke (2000, 5–38). A historical, authoritative analysis on the inflationary boom of the period 1921–1929 (Rothbard 2008, 85–181).

[70] The situation was poignantly portrayed by John Steinbeck in *The Grapes of Wrath*. A compassionate narrative dealing with the great social questions of its era (Bloom 2007, 5), the novel was published in 1939, earned Steinbeck a Pulitzer Prize. It inspired an opera, and John Ford to shoot the film 1 year later that launched Henry Fonda to fame. We have also moving graphic testimonies thanks to great photographers as Dorothea Lange and Walker Evans. The latter, working with writer like James Agee, turned out the book *Let Us Now Praise Famous Men*: *Three Tenant Families*—(1941) which described the lives of poor cotton-growing sharecroppers (Agee and Evans 2000). The work was commissioned by the federal government and played a major role in winning public support for the substantial legislative changes ushered in by the New Deal. The title is taken from a paragraph in an ancient Hebrew text: "Let us now praise famous men, and our fathers that begat us" (*Ecclesiasticus* 44:1). Agee was also the scriptwriter behind *The African Queen* and *The Night of the Hunter*. He posthumously won a Pulitzer. A thematic review on the American social, legal, and political order in those dark years reflected in the John Ford's film, in Frolik (2006, 35–50). A collection of essays on the book of James Agee and Walker Evans in Blinder (2010).

[71] The Great Depression was seriously exacerbated in Germany by the heavy burden of reparation payments imposed on Germany by the Treaty of Versailles, which essentially held Germany responsible for World War I. To meet these payments the German government printed large quantities of money, which led to hyperinflation in 1923 and 1924, wiping out the savings and investments of the German middle class. The 1929 Crisis had, therefore, devastating consequences and was even more acute in Germany than in the United States. In 1931, the German banking system collapsed. The unemployment rate, which stood at 1.5 % in 1922, shot up to 9.6 in 1923, and crept to 13.5 the following year. In 1926, it reached 18 % and 23 % in 1931, peaking in 1932 at 30.1 %. In 1933, the year that Hitler took over power, it was still at 26 %. The Gross Domestic Product, meanwhile, dropped from 79.3 in 1929 to 48.4 between 1929 and 1932 (Overy 2001, 35 and 41). For an overview of the German Slump, see James (1986) and Taylor (2014). On the shared elements in Fascism, Nazism, and the New Deal, see Schivelbusch (2007).

himself as a populist leader,[72] who would put an end to the abuses committed by the capitalists who had plunged the world into chaos, and do so without falling into the hands of Bolshevik revolutionaries.[73] After Communist totalitarianism, Italian Fascism and Germany's "national socialism" became compelling alternatives to the liberal state, whose very survival was called into question. The 1929 Great Depression would have important constitutional consequences in the U.S.[74]

#### 17.6.4.3 Roosevelt's New Deal

The liberal model of the state did not disappear, but it did have to be adapted to address new circumstances, even in the United States of America, the world's most liberal regime. This was the task which befell the nation's 32nd president, Franklin Delano Roosevelt (FDR), the longest-serving in the country's history, as he was in the White House from March 4, 1933 until April 12, 1945. Elected four times, he died in office, cutting short his final term.[75]

FDR, a Democrat, triumphed in the election of 1933 with a platform whose central tenet was protection for the common man from the ravages of the Great Depression. To this end he proposed a "New Deal" based on the premise the state should intervene to stimulate the economy and, in general, to alleviate the situation of the needy.[76] This program was carried out in two phases. Immediately after taking office, Roosevelt began to take steps to revive the U.S. economy in the short term ("The 100 Days".). In 1935 a second, more ambitious, longer-term phase began. The New Deal included federal aid to farmers, public assistance to the homeless, and established the nation's first social welfare system (Social Security Act, August 14, 1935), agricultural protection legislation (Agricultural Adjustment Act, May 12, 1933) and an ambitious initiative known as the National Recovery Administration (NRA), a government body created via the National Industrial Recovery Act of June 16, 1933, a bill encapsulating the very essence of the New

[72] It is quite significant that Point No. 16 of the Nazi Party's Platform demanded: "the creation of a healthy middle class and its conservation, the immediate communalization of the great warehouses and their being leased at low cost to small firms, and the utmost consideration for all small firms in their contracts with the state, county or municipality" (Yeadon and Hawkins 2008, 429). On the relationship between the German middle classes and National Socialism, see Childers (2014, 318–337). A history on the social base of Nazism, its origins and development in Kirk (2014).

[73] As Kahan (2010, 188) points out, for Hitler both the bourgeoisie and the Marxists were materialists who rejected spiritual, national and racial values. This is why his struggle was directed at fighting their materialism in the name of those values.

[74] On the constitutional history of the U.S. during this period, see Skowronek (2003, 173–284).

[75] Until Roosevelt, American presidents had respected the "constitutional custom" established by George Washington of standing for re-election only once. The dramatic circumstances of the Great Depression and the outbreak of World War II, however, led Roosevelt to run four times, as the two-term limit was only a tradition, nowhere stipulated in the Constitution. After his death, Congress did legislate the limit via the 22nd amendment to the Constitution.

[76] For an overview of the origin and consequences of the New Deal, see Fleck (2011, 311–335).

Deal (Beaudrau 2005, 97–120). Its aim was to regulate economic affairs, including work hours, minimum wages and guaranteed prices. The federal government strove to bolster the economy through a bold policy of public works, including the creation of a government agency for the exploitation of the Tennessee River (Tennessee Valley Authority Act, May 18, 1933), featuring major investments to improve its navigability, control floods and generate electricity. Also undertaken was the construction the Hoover and the Colorado River Dam, on the border between the states of Arizona and Nevada, which took 5 years to build (1931–1936) and whose workers founded the nucleus of what is today the city of Las Vegas. Thanks to the New Deal what American constitutionalists call the Administrative State went from a question of words to actual deeds (Rohr 1986, 111).[77]

### *17.6.5 A New Deal for Europe?*

Amidst the aftermath of the First World War, the liberal model would not be reestablished in Europe. In fact, to prevent the spread of Soviet-style revolution the oligarchies of the European states did not hesitate to launch serious social reform to match the promises of Soviet Russia, where in 1918 the platform of the Bolshevik Party called for full employment through the creation of a sweeping Social Security system. Thanks to Nikolai Aleksandrovich in 1925, the Soviet Union introduced the first national system of free medicine, made possible by the "nationalization" of the country's doctors.[78] In the same line, the Stalinist constitution of 1936 stated that citizens had the right to a public health system funded entirely by the state. The Soviet system guaranteed every citizen employment, and favored an increase in birthrates through the assignment of public housing, with larger homes for larger families (Majnoni d'Intignano 1993, 30).

In western Europe states with non-democratic governments actually made greater progress in the area of protection for workers and the socially disadvantaged than did parliamentary democracies, with the clear exception of democratic

---

[77] On the birth and meaning of the Administrative State, see Pestritto (2007, 1–16).

[78] On the official assessment by the State of the Public Health Service immediately after the October Revolution, see Semashko (1990, 130–132). The Soviet regime developed a system of governance of public services that combined targets with an element of terror (Bevan and Hood 2006, 517–538). According to Barr and Field (1996, 307–312) under Stalin, the health system adopted more of a scientific approach to care, its function being to maintain the working capacity of the labor force. Health care was defined as a right of citizenship and became a public service provided by the state, with all health personnel being state employees. The system was highly centralized, bureaucratized, and standardized. Services were free to patients, provided in state-owned facilities, and financed by the state budget and payments from industrial enterprises. Professional associations of physicians were eliminated. As part of the overall scarcity of consumer goods and services that developed in the Soviet economy, there also developed an elaborate system of stratification in the availability and quality of health care services. The best care was reserved for those of the highest occupation or political rank.

England, where the welfare state saw considerable advances during the post-war period when the principles of the Beveridge Plan of 1942 (Rosanvalllon 1992, 147–148) were implemented.

The case of France, meanwhile, is paradigmatic: the Left triumphed in the elections of 1937, with its Popular Front victorious, but the measures adopted in favor of the poor were limited. The most important achievement of André Léon Blum's government were the social benefits it secured for French workers, including a reduction in work hours to 40 per week, guarantees of paid vacation time (15 days per year),[79] and respect for trade union representation and social negotiation through collective bargaining agreements. Moreover, employment immediately became one of the main priorities of the "French State" created by the two legislative chambers by virtue of an act passed on July 10, 1940, which did away with the Third Republic and granted Marshall Petain full powers to draft a new constitution. The French national motto, *Liberté, Egalité, Fraternité* (Freedom, Equality, Brotherhood), was even replaced by *Travail, Famille, Patrie* (Work, Family, Fatherland).[80]

There was also considerable progress made in the area of social protection under the dictatorships established in Italy, Spain, and, above all, Germany. In Italy, Mussolini's fascist government not only bolstered the economy through major public works, such as the Mediterranean Highway and the excavation of the Roman Forum, but also founded major public companies and entities to reorganize production in key industries. At the same time Italy rearmed, launching imperialists campaigns in Libya and Ethiopia and intervening decisively in the Spanish Civil War. Mussolini's regime acted to provide workers with legal protection through the Labor Charter of April 21, 1927,[81] reinforced by the Law on Corporations of February 5, 1934, the creation of a mandatory "worker's card" for salaried employees, and the implementation of the idea of vertical unions in which the

---

[79] This measure was rounded out by a 40 % reduction in railway prices. In the summer of 1936, some 600,000 French workers were able take a vacation. The following year the number soared to 1,800,000. On the Popular Front's social policies, see Jackson (1998, 159–187) and Nord (2010, 17–24).

[80] The text approved by the Congress stated: "*The National Assembly gives full powers to the government of the Republic, under the authority and the signature of Marshall Pétain, to the effect of promulgating by one or several acts a new Constitution for the French state. This Constitution must guarantee the rights of labour, of family and of the fatherland. It will be ratified by the nation and applied by the Assemblies which it has created*". On Petain's constitutional project, see Wright (1970, 24–29). Also, Lemkin (2008, 171–184 and 405–411), Weisberg (2013) and in his political biography by Atkin (2014, especially 179–185).

[81] The authors of the Labour Charter were Giuseppe Bottai, Edmondo Rossoni and Minister of Justice Alfredo Rocco, who had developed the theory of corporativism. Mussolini himself played a minor role in the drafting of the Charter (Neville 2004, 80). On the intellectual debate under Mussolini's dictatorship, see Gregor (2005).

principle of class struggle was replaced by that of corporate promotion. This was the "Corporate State" (Blinkhorn 2006, 39–43).

In Spain, the tepid social protection efforts initiated from 1883 to 1903 by the Social Reforms Commission (de la Calle 1989) led to passage of the Work Accidents Law (*Ley de protección de los trabajadores accidentados*) of 1900, which established Spain's first social insurance system. Though the scope of this legislation was limited, after this point the pace of reform accelerated, with the foundation of the Institute of Social Reform (*Instituto de Reformas Sociales*) in 1905, the National Institute of Social Welfare (*Instituto Nacional de Previsión*) in 1908, and in 1919 the first insurance for retired workers (*Retiro Obrero*), and the law establishing maternity insurance in 1923.[82] Social protection increased considerably under Primo de Rivera's dictatorship because of the regime's commitment to social worker protection and social welfare. Worthy of note is an initiative by Eduardo Aunós,[83]who issued the relatively revolutionary approval of the principle of mixed negotiation commissions consisting of both workers and employers to resolve labor conflicts; the socialist leader Francisco Largo Caballero was appointed in December of 1925 as councilor of state[84]; and a Work Code was approved in 1926.

During the Second Republic (1931–1936), political instability and the outbreak of the Civil War explain the meager progress made towards the consolidation of a social welfare system, save for the creation of a National Savings Bank (*Caja Nacional*) against "forced unemployment" in 1931,[85] in contrast to the New State created by Franco on October 1, 1936,[86] which made social welfare a top priority of the regime from the very outset (Aguilera-Barchet 2012, 671–672). In 1938, in the midst of the civil war, Franco's government promulgated the *Fuero del Trabajo* (Labor Charter), the first of its "Fundamental Laws", which may be considered the

[82] On this first set of social protection laws, see Soto Carmona (2003, 12, 201, 242 and 243).

[83] The key figure behind Spain's social welfare policies during Primo de Rivera's regime, was Eduardo Aunós (1894–1967), a former member of *La Lliga*, Catalonia's conservative party, and a former secretary to Francesc Cambó, its leader. Much influenced by the thinking of the right-wing French theorist Charles Maurras (González Cuevas 1998, 345), Aunós was designated by Primo de Rivera to undertake codification of Spain's labor laws and to implement a very broad series of social measures (Martín 1992, 458–465). He subscribed to an ideology totally opposed to liberal parliamentarism, which he hoped to replace with a corporatist state, as he stated in some of his works. Aunós endorsed the implementation of a corporate state in Spain (Aunós 1928).

[84] A conflict arose between Largo Caballero and other Socialist leaders, such as Fernando de los Ríos and Indalecio Prieto, who opposed Socialist collaboration with the dictatorial government. Both abandoned their leadership positions, though remaining active Socialist supporters (Tamames 2008, 162).

[85] By government decree on May 25, 1931, enacted via the corresponding Regulation on September 30.

[86] In a long investiture speech delivered in Burgos on October 1, 1936, on the occasion of the creation of the New State, Franco stressed that there should be an absolute guarantee of work to prevent it from being subjected to capitalism, and to prevent workers from organizing into social blocks adopting a "combative and bitter" attitude.

foundation upon which Spain's Social Security system was built.[87] The second of Franco's Fundamental Laws, the *Fuero de los Españoles* (1945), in essence a declaration of fundamental freedoms, featured an extensive enumeration of social rights. In this regard Franco was clearly inspired by the ideas of the Spanish fascist party, *La Falange*, and its former leader José Antonio Primo de Rivera, whose legacy Franco sought to adopt (or co-opt, according his detractors) for his regime and party: the "National Movement". This aspiration spurred Franco to create the *Sindicatos del Movimiento* (Movement Unions)[88] and a specific jurisdiction for the defense of employees' interests: the *Magistratura de Trabajo* (Work Magistracy), still in place today.[89] May 1st was declared Labor Day in Spain (*Fiesta del Trabajo*), a celebration over which Franco personally presided every year.[90] A decisive stage in the history of Spanish social welfare provisions began during the long period when José Antonio Girón de Velasco served as Minister of Work, creating Illness Insurance (1942) and an Obligatory Old Age and Invalidity Insurance (1947). It would not be until 1963, however, when a universal Social Security system was created, based on a publically managed, unitary and integrated social protection model funded by mandatory contributions imposed by the state on employees and employers.[91]

During the era of Primo de Rivera Spain's Portugal saw an army takeover in 1926, with Portugal's military class placing university professor Coimbra Oliveira Salazar in power. After serving as Tax Minister in 1928 Salazar was later appointed by the military as President of the Council of Ministers, which 1 year later allowed him to promulgate a corporatist constitution inspired by the Church's social doctrines, specifically the *Rerum Novarum* encyclicals issued by Leo XIII (1891) and

[87] On March 9, 1938, at the psychologically crucial moment of the taking of Teruel, the *caudillo* called for the promulgation of the *Fuero del Trabajo*, a compendium of principles "against liberal capitalism and Marxist materialism" through which he sought to subordinate the economy to policy, a law which "addresses the social sphere with the intention of placing wealth at the service of the Spanish people, subordinating economics to (the regime's) policy". In this first pillar of the Francoist constitution work, thus, became one of the primary pillars of the "national revolution", to be protected "with the force of law". The state, meanwhile, pledged to expand protection for the elderly, disabled, sick and the unemployed.

[88] The Francoist unions were created by decree on April 21, 1938, to "realize the political ideals of our National Syndicalistic Revolution in the area of the economy". They were "vertical" unions, which defended a given profession, including employers and employees in the same organization—a new union concept in opposition to "horizontal", class-based unions.

[89] The work magistracies were created by decree on May 13, 1938, and consolidated via an organic law on October 17, 1940, which established the functions of the new tribunal as the only institution authorized to settle employment-related disputes.

[90] For an overall evaluation of Franco's work-related policies, see Ruiz Resa (2008).

[91] The 1963 Basic Law was enacted by virtue of the Social Security Law of 1966, in effect as of January 1, 1967.

the *Quadragesimo Anno* of Pio XI (1931).[92] With a similar objective Salazar would promulgate a "National Work Statute" in 1933 (Lewis 2002, 135).

An authoritarian and corporatist model of the state designed to achieve social welfare objectives also prevailed in Austria, drawing upon the works of Othmar Spann (Johnston 1983, 311–313) and imposed by Engelbert Dollfuss and Arthur Schuschnigg, until Hitler unilaterally proceeded to annex the country (*Anschluss*) on March 12, 1938 (Steininger 2008, 72–114).

With regards to Germany, it is noteworthy that the social welfare initiatives undertaken by Bismarck, far from being abandoned by Hitler, were actually expanded (Stolleis 2013, 133–148) with measures such as the launching of massive public works to stimulate the economy (12,000 km of highways), the rebuilding of the armament industry, and the creation of a model based on the mass consumption of goods previously available only to the most affluent. This effort included a law for the reduction of forced unemployment which succeeded in slashing the number of Germans out of work from six million to two million in just 3 years;[93] the creation of a Social Security system, and legislation to prevent layoffs and child labor. Other social welfare measures adopted by Hitler's regime included the granting of low-interest loans to engaged couples, major tax reductions for large families, and the construction of affordable housing for one or more families, to be built on the largest possible parcels of land. The social policies of Hitler's government led to the construction of over 677,000 buildings in Germany between 1933 and 1938, and more than 1,458,000 subsidized homes for those of humbler means. This housing policy was complemented by rent control policies which did not allow prices to exceed 20 % of renter income. The sadistic brutality, military belligerence and the crimes against humanity committed by the Nazi dictatorship, however, would overshadow and led people to overlook these surprisingly significant advances in social welfare, which allowed Hitler to convert Germany from a country in shambles in 1933, when he took power, into the world's second strongest economy in just 3 years.[94]

[92] Salazar´s constitution recognized the existence of an *Estado Novo* (New State) which was to be national, authoritarian, corporatist and Christian, as the only way of reestablishing the spiritual values of efficacy, authority, order and hierarchy, while classifying liberalism as a false democracy which reduced men to the lowest common denominator, and had degraded the national consciousness (Sapega 2008, 11).

[93] In 6 years (1933–1939) the new regime brought down the unemployment from 26 % to 0.4 % (Overy 2001, 35).

[94] For an overview of the formation of the welfare state in Germany during Hitler's dictatorship, see Mason and Broadwin (1997, 109–150), On the social system developed by The Nazis see Grunberger (2013).

## 17.7 The Road to War

### *17.7.1 The Expansion of Totalitarianism: The Confrontation Between Communism and Fascism*

From the point of view of constitutional history the triumph of totalitarianism in Russia, Italy and Germany ushered in an era characterized by brutal repression through the development of state security forces that crushed any attempts at dissent. Stalin, Hitler and Mussolini all killed or confined in concentration camps those who opposed their regimes. This system of terror was, however, "justified" by spectacular economic growth and concealed by propaganda touting the regimes' achievements. Thus, liberal parliamentary government spiraled into crisis as attempted military coups and revolutionary uprisings spread, in both cases aimed at overthrowing the constitutional order to impose dictatorships which promised to more effectively solve the social and economic crisis plaguing the era.[95]

The same happened in Asia with Japan, a nation state that had emerged in 1853 from two and a half centuries of self-imposed peaceful isolation, but within a few decades, the country's leaders embarked on a policy of aggressive territorial expansion. During the last half of the nineteenth century, the Western imperialist powers of England, France, and Germany established the model for acquisition of colonies in Asia and for the partition of China into spheres of influence. Near the end of the century, about the same time, Japan began to capture colonial territory, the United States and Russia also initiated their imperialistic expansion in Asia. Imperialism can be defined as direct or indirect domination of an industrialized country over a colonial territory or another country. Japan forcefully acquired three major foreign territories between 1894 and 1910: Taiwan in 1895 after the Sino-Japanese War of 1894–1895; Korea as a protectorate in 1905 after the Russo-Japanese War of 1904–1905, then as a colony when unilaterally annexed by Japan in 1910; and the Kwantung Leased Territories in 1905 in southern Manchuria when Japan succeeded to Russia's leases after the Russo-Japanese War. When Emperor Hirohito ascended to the throne in 1926, Japan was enveloped in a struggle between liberals and leftists on one side, and ultraconservatives on the other, and becomes a semi-democratic regime, according to Takenaka, that had broken down in 1932. Then, an authoritarian regime in which the military projected strong influences was established, and brought Japan to the Second World War (Takenaka 2014, 1).

In line with this trend, in Spain on September 13, 1923 General Primo de Rivera imposed a dictatorship suspending the Constitution of 1876, less than a year after the March on Rome (October 27–29, 1922) which had placed Mussolini in power.

---

[95] Fascism was even present in the United Kingdom, where its partisans fiercely opposed the members of the Labour Party (Thurlow 2005, 27–45) in response to the worldwide economic crisis (Steiner 2007, 635–705). On the British Nazi groups see also Barnes and Barnes (2010). A guide to the essential features of interwar British fascism in Linehan (2000)

His dictatorship lasted until January of 1930, precipitating the fall of the Spanish Monarchy on April 14, 1931.

The Second Republic introduced universal suffrage for the first time in Spanish constitutional history, as the 1931 Constitution gave women the right to vote. However, the triumph of Spain's right wing parties in the general elections of November 1933 was never accepted by the Left. From October 5–9, 1934, as a reaction to the Right's victory in said elections the previous year, PSOE Secretary General Francisco Largo Caballero led a revolt throughout Spain (which succeeded, ephemerally, only in Asturias) through which he sought to establish a Soviet-style regime. In February of 1936, new elections were held, and this time the leftist coalition, the Popular Front, prevailed.[96] This time, however, it was the right wing parties that refused to accept the outcome. The Army rebelled in July, sparking the beginning of the Spanish Civil War.

There emerged, then, in non-democratic Europe two diametrically opposed camps: supporters of communist dictatorships and those who defended the triumph of the totalitarian, National Socialist or fascist models,[97] which collided in the Spanish Civil War (1936–1939), the immediate ideological and military prelude to World War II (1939–1945).[98]

## 17.7.2 *From the Spanish Civil War to World War II*

The tension between communists and fascists swelled throughout Europe and ended up exploding in Spain, whose Civil War served as a brutal stage vividly illustrating the ideological clash in question, and the fierce commitment of the respective sides to their principles. While the democratic nations adopted policies of non-intervention, the totalitarian regimes sent aid to support their ideological

[96] It is important to note that the left-wing coalition was headed up by the Communist Party, as Stalin had given orders to this effect (Ulam 2007, 402). As Communist parties were still insignificant at the beginning of the 1930, the Soviet leader saw these electoral coalitions as an opportunity to expand Communist political influence. It is significant that in the same year, 1936, there formed two Popular Fronts in Spain and France, and in both cases they won the elections. The Spanish Communist Party became the most important political movement under the Spanish Republic during the Spanish Civil War, especially after 1937. Something similar occurred with the French Communist Party in 1942, as following the outbreak of the Civil War in Spain the USSR provided massive aid to the Spanish Popular Front (*republicanos*) by rallying sympathizers and activists throughout Western Europe (Whealey 2005, 20). After Hitler invaded Russia, the USSR ended up passing over to the side of the Allies, and at the war's end the French Communist Party was France's leading leftist political force. Immediately following the war there were even communists serving in the French government under De Gaulle. Communism would grow more isolated in the west after 1947 when Stalin rejected the implementation of the Marshall Plan for Eastern Europe and the Iron Curtain fell.

[97] Even more surprising when one considers that both, in essence, defended a totalitarian model of the state. See Bullock (1993, xxi).

[98] For an overall examination of the confrontation between the totalitarian and communist conceptions of the law and the state, see McDonough (2001).

allies. Stalin defended the Popular Front, or *republicanos* (the Republic disappeared, *de facto*, in July of 1936) while Mussolini and Hitler supported the *España Nacional*, a term employed by those who perpetrated the military coup following the creation of the *Junta de Defensa Nacional* on July 24, 1936, which gave rise to the common term for the insurgent right-wing forces: *nacionales*.[99]

The Spanish Civil War would prove to be only a prologue to a much greater global conflagration, World War II, whose origins may be traced to the imperialist policies through which Mussolini, and especially Hitler, strove to expand their nations' territory, in Germany's case in search of *Lebensraum*, or "vital space".[100]

---

[99] The rebels used the term "*nacional*" to legitimize their revolt, suggesting that they were the true "Spanish nationals" (Aguilera-Barchet 2012, 651–652) rather than their Republican enemies, who they considered to be *rojos* (reds), communists, as evidence pointing to the victory of pro-Soviet parties in the 1936 elections. The idea that the rebels wished to project was that they had been forced to go to war to save the Spanish nation from international Communist revolution.

[100] The term *Lebensraum* referred to the surface area required to support a given population and mode of existence (Barnes and Minca 2013, 673), and was one of the most important topics Hitler mentioned in *Mein Kampf*, specifically in Chap. 14 ("Germany's policy in Eastern Europe"): "*If the National Socialist movement really desires to be consecrated by history to a great mission for our people, it must, penetrated by knowledge of, and filled with suffering for, her real situation on this earth, valiantly and conscious of its goal, take up the fight against the aimlessness and incompetence which have heretofore guided the German people on the course of foreign affairs. It must, then, without regard to 'traditions' and prejudices, find the courage to assemble our people and their might for a march forward on that road which leads out of the present constriction of the domain of life, and hence also permanently liberates from the danger of vanishing off this earth or having to enter the service of others as a slave nation. The National Socialist movement must endeavor to eliminate the discrepancy between our population and our area, the latter viewed not only as a source of nourishment, but also as a point of support for power politics between our historical past and the hopelessness of our impotence today.* [. . .] *Much as we all today recognize the necessity for a reckoning with France, it will remain largely ineffective if our foreign-policy aim is restricted thereto. It has and will retain significance if it provides the rear cover for an enlargement of our national domain of life in Europe. For we will find this question's solution not in colonial acquisitions, but exclusively in the winning of land for settlement which increases the area of the motherland itself, and thereby not only keeps the new settlers in the most intimate community with the land of origin, but insures to the total area those advantages deriving from its united magnitude*" (Hitler 1941, 939–940 and 949–950). We quote the Reynal and Hitchcok edition of 1941 because it is the only English version complete, unabridged, and fully annotated, translated by a committee from the New York's New School for Social Research. It is important to point out that Hitler only accepted as official English version of his work the James Murphy translation of 1939. Nevertheless, as far as historical accuracy is concerned, Murphy's edition is paraphrased. He did not use Hitler's words, though in most places his text is true to the meaning. As the editor points out, it was certainly chosen by the Third Reich authorities because it is a fairly easier read for those who speak/read British English and have a good vocabulary. To understand this, we add the quoted text of the Reynal and Hitchcok edition, the Murphy's version: "*If the historians who are to write our national history at some future date are to give the National Socialist Movement the credit of having devoted itself to a sacred duty in the service of our people, this movement will have to recognize the real truth of our situation in regard to the rest of the world. However painful this recognition may be, the movement must draw courage from it and a sense of practical realities in fighting against the aimlessness and incompetence which has hitherto been shown by our people in the conduct of their foreign policy. Without respect for*

Both dictators had initiated widespread rearmament campaigns during the 1930s, portending the outbreak of a new worldwide conflict. In the final years of the decade Hitler moved audaciously to expand German territory, with the 1938 annexation of Austria (*Anschluss*), and the Sudetenland (a German-speaking region of Czechoslovakia), abided by England and France in the Munich Agreement (September 30, 1938)—a concession which would go down in history as a cowardly and imprudent act of appeasement. His next step was to occupy the Danzig corridor, imposed by the 1919 Versailles Treaty, which had divided Germany in two. Then, on August 23, 1939, Hitler shocked and appalled the world by signing a "Non-aggression Pact" with Stalin[101] through which Germany and Russia effectively

---

*'tradition,' and without any preconceived notions, the movement must find the courage to organize our national forces and set them on the path which will lead them away from that territorial restriction which is the bane of our national life today, and win new territory for them. Thus the movement will save the German people from the danger of perishing or of being slaves in the service of any other people. Our movement must seek to abolish the present disastrous proportion between our population and the area of our national territory, considering national territory as the source of our maintenance or as a basis of political power. And it ought to strive to abolish the contrast between past history and the hopelessly powerless situation in which we are today. [. . .] Today we are all convinced of the necessity of regulating our situation in regard to France; but our success here will be ineffective in its broad results if the general aims of our foreign policy will have to stop at that. It can have significance for us only if it serves to cover our flank in the struggle for that extension of territory which is necessary for the existence of our people in Europe. For colonial acquisitions will not solve that question. It can be solved only by the winning of such territory for the settlement of our people as will extend the area of the motherland and thereby will not only keep the new settlers in the closest communion with the land of their origin, but will guarantee to this territorial ensemble the advantages which arise from the fact that in their expansion over greater territory the people remain united as a political unit*" (Hitler 2012, 525 and 531). The term genocide was coined by Raphael Lemkin in 1943. According to Barrett (2010, 35–54), he uses the word genocide broadly, not only to describe policies of outright extermination against Jews and Gypsies, but for less immediate Nazi goals as well. In Lemkin's analysis, Nazi Germany had undertaken a policy for the demographic restructuring of the European continent. Therefore he also used the word genocide to describe a "coordinated plan of different actions" intended to promote such goals as an increase in the birthrate of the "Aryan" population, the physical destruction of the Slavic population over a period of years, and policies to bring about the destruction of the "culture, language, national feelings, religion" and separate economic existence (but not physical existence) of non-German "Aryan" nations thought to be "linked by blood" to Germany. In the Part III, Lemkin provides English translations of 334 statues, decrees, and laws from the 17 occupied countries and territories. Most of the documents are from the years 1940 and 1941, though the collection spans a five and half year period March 13, 1938 to November 13, 1942. The range of the dates underscores the fact that Axis Rule was a work of analysis of the enemy's public documents written during wartime (and not those captured at the end of the war). These documents were available to Lemkin and others from sources in the neutral countries in Europe. This chapter has become one the most widely quoted (Lemkin 2008, 79–98). See also the book's preface, dated November 15, 1943.

[101] A still highly controversial pact because, as Roberts (2006, 6) points out, on one side some historians argue that Stalin turned his back on an anti-German alliance with Britain and France, and that the price of this miscalculation was not only that he facilitated the takeover of most of continental Europe, but also suffered the devastating blow which began on June 22, 1941: the nearly successful German invasion of the Soviet Union. On the other side are those who maintain

divided up Poland between them, and which, by removing Russia as a potential enemy in the impending conflict, spared Germany the daunting prospect of fighting a two-front war, as was the case in World War I.

On September 1, 1939, Wehrmacht troops crossed the Polish border, thereby igniting World War II, as the Allies declared war two days later.[102] On September 17, it was the Russians' turn to invade Poland, which they did under the pretext of protecting the Ukrainians and Belarusians inhabiting the eastern part of the country.[103]

For 21 months, the *Wehrmacht* seemed invincible—until June 22 when Hitler committed the colossal and fateful blunder of invading Russia (Operation Barbarossa), an offensive that would end in absolute failure, culminating in the Germans' ultimate defeat at Stalingrad (June 1942–February 1943). The surrender of Von Paulus (commanding 90,000 soldiers, surviving from his initial force of 250,000), marked the beginning of the end for Hitler.

The paradox was that Stalinist Russia emerged on the side of the victors, and during the early post-war years the communists touted themselves, and were recognized by many in the west, as heroes and saviors. Celebrations of the Soviets' feat, however, were short-lived as Stalin soon revealed his antagonism to any collaboration with the western democracies and his determination to subject territories gained during the War to the Russian yoke. Rejecting aid from the Marshall Plan (1947) for Eastern Europe, the Soviets occupied and laid claim to the region. The result was the dramatic geographical and ideological division of Europe: in the west capitalist democracies received massive aid from the United States, while in the east the Soviet Union took control over its recently seized satellite republics; what Churchill vividly termed the "Iron Curtain" had fallen with striking suddenness.[104]

---

that the USSR was not ready for war with Germany in 1939, and that Stalin, like Hitler, made strategic decisions that were based on a calculation of their best interests.

[102] Hitler was absolutely shocked when the British and French declared war on Germany, respecting their promise to do so if Poland were invaded. He was thoroughly convinced they would not honor this commitment.

[103] The Allies (France and England, mainly) declared war on Hitler in response to his invasion of Poland. They did not, however, respond in the same way when Stalin's Soviet Union invaded it too, despite the fact that its occupation of Poland was extremely bloody, as demonstrated by the Katyn Massacre in which the Russians executed more than 27,000 Polish officers in cold blood. The act would not be recognized by the Russian government until April 13, 1990, when Soviet President Mikhail Gorbachev publicly acknowledged the Soviet Union's responsibility for the murders. On October 14, 1992, the Soviet Government finally made public the order of March 5, 1940, which authorized the execution of more than 27,000 thousand Polish "nationalists and counterrevolutionaries", including the officers of the Polish Army in the Katyn Forest (Hastings 2013, 21–22). In November of 2010, the Russian Parliament issued a resolution acknowledging that Stalin had ordered the massacre (Lunde 2012, 347). A documented history on the NKVD massacres of Polish prisoners of war at Katyn, Kharkov, and Tvern-subsumed under "Katyn" in Cienciala et al. (2008)

[104] In a celebrated speech, delivered at the request of Westminster College in the U.S. small Missouri town of Fulton (March 5, 1946), officially called "The Sinews of Peace" Speech, and

Soviet Russia would continue to control and support communist dictatorships until the fall of the Berlin Wall in 1989, which brought about the dramatic and unforeseen implosion of the Soviet Union by the end of 1991.[105]

## 17.8 The Triumph of the Welfare State Model

Hitler's defeat halted the spread of the totalitarian model of the state—at least in Western Europe. In contrast and opposition to the communist Soviet model, the United States stood as the primary defender and champion of the liberal state—though America was hardly as liberal as it once been, having clearly accepted enhanced social welfare as a legitimate end of government, and having adopted policies to pursue it. Consequently, following World War II a new model of the state arose according to which democracy and freedom would have to be reconciled with government intervention in the economic and social spheres. This interventionism, however, proved legally problematic both in the U.S., where the New Deal was initially attacked as unconstitutional, and in Western Europe, where the architects of the law and state had to develop a model in which public power could once again be delimited by constitutions.

generally considered as the beginning of Cold War, Winston Churchill declared that "From Stettin in the Baltic to Trieste in the Adriatic, an Iron Curtain has descended upon the Continent" (Churchill 2013, 413–423). A collection of essays on the significance of this speech for the Western democracies in those past 50 years in Muller (1999). On the Russian *intelligentsia* after Stalin, see Zubok (2011).

[105] The Soviet Union, formally created by Lenin in 1922 after his victory in the Russian Civil War, disappeared officially in December of 1991. On December 25, Gorbachev resigned as Soviet president and transferred to Russian Federation President Boris Yeltsin the control mechanism for authorizing the launch of Soviet nuclear weapons (Combs 2008, 188). Proliferation threats arise either from the using of highly enriched uranium (HEU) which has been enriched up to 70 % (and higher) or from the production or separation of plutonium. Hundreds of tons of highly enriched uranium and weapon-grade plutonium derived from the dismantled nuclear weapons found in American and Russian stockpiles are the "deadly legacy" of the Cold War that give rise to so much concern… Apart from deriving from disarmed nuclear warheads, both highly enriched uranium and plutonium can also be produced using the technology currently available in many nuclear energy-producing countries. As soon as uranium becomes more than 20 % enriched, the intentions are evidently for destructive ends; such action in any declared facility is immediately detected by the IAEA. Enrichment facilities are not present in all nuclear energy-producing countries. The threat of nuclear weapon proliferation is extremely relevant given the current state of affairs in the world (Taebi 2012, 295–318).

### *17.8.1 The Welfare State and the Rule of Law*

From the point of view of Western constitutional history, the defeat of Italian fascism and German Nazism was followed by a need to regain a vision of the state based on and bound by the rule of law. This did not, however, involve the restoration of the pure liberal state, as it was understood that political power ought to continue to be exercised to prevent social injustice. This essential transformation had important constitutional consequences. In the United States Roosevelt's New Deal faced opposition in both Congress and the Supreme Court, while in Europe, Hans Kelsen had to revive a constitutional model that made the rule of law compatible with government attention to social concerns.

#### 17.8.1.1 The New Deal and the U.S. Constitution: New Measures Raise New Questions

Once the panic unleashed by the Great Depression had subsided, voices in America's private sector began to criticize the terms of the interventionist legislation that had been introduced to deal with the crisis. Many businessmen declared war on the New Deal, calling it a "socialist" program incompatible with traditional American individualism. Conservative politicians revolted[106] and succeeded in getting the United States Supreme Court to declare some of the laws implemented under the New Deal unconstitutional. The Roosevelt Administration, however, fought hard against the idea of the Supreme Court attacking a democratically elected authority enacting policies allowing the country to overcome economic crisis.[107]

The confrontation between the Democratic president and the Supreme Court was an ongoing affair. The former was committed to establishing a new model of an interventionist government acting to defend the disadvantaged (welfare state), while the latter sought to retain the traditional *laissez faire* conception of the economy and the state. In the end Roosevelt won the clash with the Supreme Court simply because he remained in office for so long, winning re-election in 1936, 1940 and 1944. As a result, judges opposed to the New Deal gradually retired and were replaced by others sympathetic to the welfare state model, that consolidated what has been called the "New Deal Constitutional Revolution" (Purcell 2002, 238–255), which created in the U.S. the bases for the development of Administrative Law (White 2002, 94–128). When Roosevelt died in April 1945, he was succeeded by Vice President Harry S. Truman who, against all odds, was

---

[106] On the conservative reaction in Congress against the New Deal, see Patterson (1981, 211–249), Denton (2012, 154–160) and Phillips-Fein (2010, 3–25).

[107] As Pestritto (2005, 99–132) suggests, this conception was originally conceived during the presidency of Woodrow Wilson. On Roosevelt's failed attempt to reform The Supreme Court, see Shesol (2011)

re-elected in 1948 in an extremely close election.[108] Thus, when Dwight D. Eisenhower became the 34th President in 1953, the Democrats had held the White House for 24 years. By this point, the Republicans were in no position to abolish Roosevelt's historic reforms, which had become entrenched. The principle of the Administrative State had come to be recognized as compatible with the U.S. Constitution[109]

The New Deal did not provide definitive solutions at the economic level, as the United States failed to truly emerge from the crisis until massive rearmament activity began in response to the outbreak of World War II, when the country became what President Roosevelt called "the arsenal of democracy". However, it did radically change the social landscape in the United States, where social inequality was mitigated and unions protecting the rights of workers grew stronger. Though the nation's pronounced commitment to free markets was pared back and tempered, even after these changes, the United States continued and still continues to embrace *laissez faire* much more strongly than does Europe.

Things were and are a little bit different in Europe, where the notion of a strong state, as we have seen, has deeper historical roots. This is why after the end of World War II in European democratic nations, from a constitutional point of view, there appeared an intermediate state model lying somewhere between the liberal and totalitarian alternatives, an interventionist state but one bound by the Rule of Law, a new constitutional pattern whose principles were perhaps best defined by the Austrian jurist Hans Kelsen.

#### 17.8.1.2 The Recovery of the Idea of the Social Pact. Hans Kelsen and the Contemporary Revival of the Rule of Law

After the Nazis' defeat in 1945, eminent western lawyers and legal scholars acted to redefine a model of the state that, without giving up elements of social welfare, would be compatible with the democratic system. The leading figure of this movement was, without any doubt, the founder of the Vienna School of legal theory, Hans Kelsen (1881–1973). The Austrian devised a Pure Theory of Law (*Reine Rechtslehre*) through which he advanced the principle of *Geltungsgrund der Rechtsnormen* ("a foundation of legal validity") aimed at rendering the law independent of political power.

The case of Kelsen is all the more interesting because initially, in his youth, he had been a strong advocate of law's subordination to the state. In fact, in an early stage he had fully linked the two. In his first work, entitled *Main Problems in the*

---

[108] The election was so close that Truman was photographed the day after his victory holding up the front page of the *Chicago Daily Tribune* declaring his opponent, Republican Thomas Dewey, the winner.

[109] On the conflict between the Administrative State and the U.S. Constitution concerning social rights, see Postell (2012, 1–34). A study on the key fields of public administration in Shafritz and Hyde (2011).

*Theory of Public Law* (*Hauptprobleme der Staatsrechtslehre*), first published in 1911 in the Austro-Hungarian Empire, he argued that the foundation of a law should only be sought in the mandate which affords it obligatoriness, by virtue of what he called the principle of "attribution" (*Zurechnung*), according to which a given act (illicit) necessitates a specific reaction (the sanction). According to this doctrinal approach, the law was simply whatever the state decided (Vinx 2008, 15–23)—which makes it easier to understand why the relatively late consolidation of the state in Germany, in the last third of the nineteenth century, led German lawyers to defend the idea of a strong state. Thus, for a young Kelsen the law required no other justification other than its simple recognition by legislators, who in this way became the legal sphere's primary agents, to the manifest detriment of judges, whose function was not to transcend a perfunctory application of the law.

The political events culminating in the rise of Hitler's Third Reich (1933–1945), however, prompted Kelsen (who had fled the Nazi regime, first taking refuge in Switzerland and later the United States) to alter his thinking, calling for a separation of the legal sphere from political power, differentiating legality and legitimacy (Maccormick 1989, 184–193). This was the concept which inspired his works *The Pure Theory of Law—Reine Rechtslehre*—1934—a work revised in 1960 (Kelsen 2005)—and, above all, *General Theory of Law and State*, published in 1941[110] (Kelsen 2007). It was during this second stage of his thought that Kelsen formulated his famous theory of the logical structure which, applied to the general legal system, resulted in the formulation of the principle of a hierarchy of norms. Kelsen structured the legal system as an imaginary pyramid in which legal norms supported each other, constituting a "rising formation" (*Stufenbau*) at the top of which was the "fundamental norm" (*Grundnorm*), characterized by not depending upon on any other (Raz 2009, 122–160) and constituting the ultimate foundation of the legal system's validity (Janzen 1937, 205–226).

From the point of view of legal history, Kelsen's thinking unquestionably marks a return to the idea of the social pact (Leroy 2011, 361–374). The basic norm (*Grundnorm*) is the basis of the legal system's legitimacy because it is the product of said pact, the essential rule by which a social community agrees to abide. The novel development was that in his new approach Kelsen did not focus on the state. Rather, the state occupied a secondary role, eclipsed by and subordinated to the law, to be administrated by a legal system that became the essence of the social pact. According to current legal thinking, the law becomes, then, a separate category, insofar as it justifies itself. It is "pure", to use Kelsen's terminology, because is separated or differentiated from the state (Somek 2006, 753–774) and not at its mercy, as was the case during the era of absolute monarchy, or under the totalitarian regimes of the twentieth century (MacCormick 1993, 1–18).

This does not, however, preclude the "constitutional pact" from including social rights as the basis of the agreement upon which the state rests.[111] That is, the

[110] It was directly published in English in the US.

[111] On this crucial aspect of the compatibility of social rights with legislative constitutionalism, see Sunstein et al. (2009, 36–107).

principle is compatible with greater or less state intervention in the lives of individuals. Thus, a Kelsenian approach is fully compatible with a "welfare state" provided that it is bound by the Rule of Law.

#### 17.8.1.3 The "Constitutionalization" of Public Law in Europe as a Buffer Against the Strengthening of the Executive

Kelsen's doctrine represents a victory of law over power, the primacy of limits imposed by the legal sphere over the political realm (Kalyvas 2007, 122–160). Thanks to him, the trend in Western Europe after WWII was for constitutions to stand above and beyond election campaigns, and the establishment of constitutional courts has become widespread to ensure the protection of the social pact outlined in and guaranteed by state constitutions, thereby protecting minorities from temporary political majorities.[112]

In broad strokes, then, it may be said that Europe is moving towards the American constitutional model, according to which constitutions may be defended by judicial means from attacks upon them by politicians. The law must prevail—at least theoretically—against the "anything goes" spirit of political combat. However, this effort undoubtedly requires the "depoliticization" of the constitutional courts, which is not always easy.[113]

### *17.8.2 The Spread of the Welfare State After 1945*

Prior to World War II, the adoption of social measures in the West did not mean the establishment of universal social welfare systems financed by the state—at least in democratic regimes, though, as we have seen, Hitler and Mussolini did institute sweeping state social welfare systems. After 1945, however, the western democracies which had defeated Hitler and Mussolini would take major steps towards the establishment of welfare states, within democratic and constitutional frameworks, by virtue of social welfare legislation, such as the adoption of the Beveridge System

[112] This has been no easy task, however, and not only in the countries of southern Europe which were under dictatorships until the 1970s—Greece, Portugal, and Spain—but also in stable democracies in which the state is **very** powerful, such as France, where the principle of judicial review was not introduced, as we have already seen, until 2008 when President Sarkozy backed constitutional reform that entailed it.

[113] As Sajó (2004, 127) has pointed out, constitutional courts in and outside of Europe are increasingly depicted as non-partisan entities bound only by the constitution, whose main task is to solve partisan conflicts impartially. It is in this way that constitutional courts contribute significantly to the appearance of neutrality, as parliamentary political conflicts are brought in front of them in such a way that they tend to be discussed and handled in relatively depoliticized terms of legal doctrine.

in the U.K.—the first comprehensive public health system fully funded by the state to appear in Western Europe (Majnoni d'Intignano 1993, 27–30).

The policy of economic interventionism initiated by Roosevelt in the United States had repercussions in Europe, where democratic governments also began to implement interventionist policies in the defense of workers. A quite significant example is that of France, where a provisional government issued an executive order (*ordonnance*) creating a Social Security system in 1945[114]—something that the Third Republic proved incapable of doing, even during the Popular Front (leftist coalition) period.[115] In the second half of the twentieth century, most advanced western countries established universal public health systems financed by taxation, controlled by the legislative branch, and managed by a public body—with the exception of the United States.[116]

### *17.8.3 The United States Stands Alone: From Roosevelt to Obama*

Despite the implementation of the New Deal to fight the consequences of the Great Depression, following World War II America diverged from its European counterparts by never providing for universal, state-provided medical coverage, leaving Americans to continue to depend upon private medical insurance. For decades, many members of the Democratic Party have called and campaigned for the introduction of federally-backed medical coverage for all citizens, with plans and efforts intensifying during the 1960s under President Kennedy and President Johnson, with their "New Frontier", "Great Society" and "War on Poverty" programs. Despite the optimism and idealism which characterized the era, these plans never came to fruition, and support for them withered amidst the turmoil of the late 1960s, the malaise and economic crisis of the 1970s, and the conservative revolt of the 1980s. It would not be until Democratic President Bill Clinton (1992–2000), that another serious presidential campaign for universal coverage was attempted: the Health Care of Act of 1993 faced massive opposition and went down to defeat in Congress.[117]

The establishment of universal medical coverage would not prevail in the U.S. until 2010 and passage under President Barack Obama of the "Patient

[114] "Ordonnances" of February 22, October 4 and 19, 1945. These orders, issued unilaterally by the government without approval by the National Assembly, are still the cornerstone of the French Social Security System (Majnoni d'Intignano 1993, 33).

[115] On the origins of the French Social Security System, see Rosanvalllon (1992, 154–157). Also, Dutton (2005, 184–219) and Smith (2003, 13–50).

[116] On class conflict and the development of the modern Welfare State, see Baldwin (2003, 1–54) and Mares (2003, 4–6).

[117] On the relationship between liberalism and the principles of welfare states from the American perspective, see West and Jeffrey (2004, 50–57).

Protection and Affordable Care Act" (ACA) and the "Health Care and Education Reconciliation Act" (HCERA) more commonly known as "Obamacare".[118] These two pieces of historic legislation were met with cries of protest and opposition, and brought before the Supreme Court for review by those alleging that federal power could not extend global medical coverage throughout the 50 states.[119] In 2012, the nation's high court ruled that both laws were, in fact, constitutional, marking a landmark decision in the history of the welfare state in the U.S.[120]

## 17.9 The Transformation of the Totalitarian Model of State: Communism After 1945

Despite fascism's failure and defeat in World War II, the democratic model of the state did not go on to prevail throughout the world, by any means. One of World War II's great victors was the Soviet Union, which espoused a totalitarian model of the state utterly anathema to a market economy. The paradox is that Stalin, after having been allied with Hitler from 1939–1941, ended up on the side of the triumphant Allies, associated with the United States and the European democracies,

---

[118] The federal medical coverage legislation passed under President Obama ("Obamacare") features, firstly, an "individual mandate" according to which, as of January 1, 2014, every citizen with sufficient financial resources is required to have their own medical insurance. Next, via the federal government's Medicaid program each one of the 50 states must expand (also as of January 1, 2014) the number of people who qualify for assistance, thereby entitling them to government-guaranteed medical care. For an expert view on key topics in health care policy and management of the U.S. Health Care System, see Kominski (2014)

[119] Those who appealed said law before the Supreme Court did so based on two substantive arguments. The law's critics argued that the "individual mandate" increases the power of the federal government over individuals and represents a violation of personal liberty. Although the Bill of Rights contains nothing specific that would preclude *Obamacare*, its opponents contend that it is contrary to the spirit of the Bill of Rights and, consequently, unconstitutional. As the U.S. is a country in which common law prevails, the judges of the Supreme Court have the power to interpret the Constitution to prohibit Obamacare. Secondly, concerning the requirement for the states to expand their medical coverage, Obamacare opponents argued that the Constitution does not grant Congress the right to pass such a law because it does not fall under the purview of the federal government. In other words, the Constitution does not expressly authorize the federal government to obligate states to expand their medical coverage; if the Constitution does not grant this right to the federal government, it is held only by the states. Based on this argument only the states have the right to decide if they wish to provide their citizens with medical coverage. For a constitutional analysis of The Supreme Court's decision in the Health Care Case—Nfib v. Sebelius, see Persily et al. (2013)

[120] The Supreme Court of the United States, in the case *National Federation of Independent Business v. Sebelius*, 132 U.S. 2566 (2012), declared that Congress had the power to enact most provisions of the Patient Protection and Affordable Care Act (ACA) and the Health Care and Education Reconciliation Act (HCERA). See the legislation in Haugen and Musser (2012). For a review of the Affordable Care Act Decision from a range of academic disciplines—law, philosophy, and political science, see Allhoff and Hall (2014)

the United Kingdom and France foremost among them. This coalition would prove short-lived, as the totalitarian model of the state, based on party discipline and central planning, and the liberal system, based on democratic processes and free markets, were, of course, irreconcilable.

### *17.9.1 The Marshall Plan and the Raising of the Iron Curtain*

The fragile alliance between the democratic nations and the totalitarian Soviet Union would end up rupturing after the launch of the Marshall Plan (June 5, 1947), as Stalin refused to accept the reestablishment of democracy and market economies[121] in that portion of Europe which had fallen under his control (Roberts 2006, 317). The confrontation started with the dramatic Berlin Airlift (June 24, 1948–May 12, 1949), the first episode in a process that ended up splitting Europe into two blocks: Western Europe, in which the democratic model of the state was recovered; and Eastern Europe, in which Soviet-style totalitarianism prevailed until 1989 (Roeder 1994, 61–101). The Berlin Wall (*Berliner Mauer*), erected in 1961, would become the most tangible and dramatic symbol of this state of affairs.

In fact, the split affected the whole world after the Korean War (1950–1953) (Fousek 2000, 62–186). This was the Cold War period, defined by the ongoing struggle between the liberal, capitalist West, led by the United States, and the communist East, headed by the Soviet Union (Engerman 2010, I, 20–43). For over four decades (1945–1989), these two political, economic, and ideological juggernauts would remain at loggerheads, generating a perpetual state of international tension and rivalry that at times sparked armed conflicts in which the two superpowers squared off, though by proxy, providing support to their respective allies. During this protracted confrontation the democratic nations of Europe founded NATO for their common defense from the communist threat posed by the Soviet Union, which responded by creating an analogous entity, the Warsaw Pact.[122] The Soviet bloc had begun with bold and ambitious plans for the strengthening of the Soviet state and the spreading of communist revolution around the world, but over time it became evident that the Soviet Union was failing to export its model internationally, and that the country itself was coming apart at the seams because

[121] On the origins of Stalin's confrontation with the West, see Zubok (2007, 1–28) and Zimmerman (2014, 75–101).

[122] Which involved bloody events, such as the crushing of the Hungarian Revolt (Gati 2006).

of its ineffectual economic policies and widespread yearning for greater freedoms amongst its people.[123]

### *17.9.2 The Expansion of Communism After 1945*

The Soviet Union was, however, not the only state in the world that had embraced a totalitarian, communist regime. In 1919, Lenin had founded the *Kommintern* to expand Communism internationally, as a result of which communist regimes would eventually develop in different regions around the globe. The Soviet model spread during the era of decolonization above all in Asia, where in 1945, Ho Chi Minh founded the Democratic Republic of Vietnam (Olsen 2006, 1–12). In 1947, in response to the Marshall Plan, Stalin created a new version of the *Kommintern*, the *Kominform*, for the international expansion of the Soviet model of the state (Mastny 2010, 30–34). The Soviets would go on to provide support to North Korean dictator Kim Il-sung during the Korean War (1950–1953), which left Korea divided into a communist north and democratic south (Gardner 2004, 126–143), and for the ensuing decades, during which the dictator would remain in power.

In China, meanwhile, Mao Tse-tung rose to power (Brown 2009, 179–193) and headed the People's Republic of China from its establishment in 1949,[124] governing the country as Chairman of the Communist Party of China until his death in 1976.[125] Mao transformed China into a thoroughly communist state controlled by one party, with industry nationalized and sweeping communist reforms undertaken to govern every aspect of life. Stalin's death did not mark the end of Communism's expansion, as "revolution" would also cross the Atlantic in Cuba with the triumph of the revolution led by Fidel Castro against dictator Fulgencio Batista (January 1, 1959),[126] while other Latin American revolutionaries, such as Che Guevara, would also seek to spread communist revolts throughout the Americas during the 1960s.[127]

---

[123] For a general examination of the evolution of post-Soviet communist regimes, see Levitsky and Way (2010, 37–84). An overview on contemporary development of the Russian state in Tsygankov (2014).

[124] The People's Republic of China was formally established on October 1, 1949, though it needed 12 years to be consolidated. On this crucial period, see Teiwes (2011, 6–86).

[125] As Brown (2009, 313) points out, after Stalin's death Mao's China went through four decisive periods that saw increasing levels of repression: the "Hundred Flowers" campaign, the "Great Leap Forward", which ended in a disaster; the Sino-Soviet split, a turning point in the history of the international Communist movement; and the "Great Proletarian Cultural Revolution", during Mao's last decade, a movement which inflicted terrible suffering and about which official regrets are harbored.

[126] On the origins of this "Caribbean Communist State", see Brown (2009, 293–312).

[127] Fueled by widespread criticism of America's war in Vietnam in and after 1968, there was an international reaction against capitalism (Marcuse 1989), which sparked major riots and revolts in the U.S. (Berkeley 1969) and France (Paris May '68 Revolution). During this era, Che Guevara

The signs of Communism's erosion became increasingly evident during the 1980s (Eley 2002, 363), though even then the considerable importance which communist parties enjoyed in democratic European states should not be overlooked, as these parties were integrated into the Communist International, and their general secretaries continued to receive instructions from Moscow.[128] All of this, nevertheless, came crashing down like a house of cards after the Soviet Union's demise in 1991, when President Mikhail Gorbachev opted to pursue vital and sweeping economic and political reform (*perestroika*) while at the same time opening up Russia to the international community (*glasnost*) (Brown 2009, 481–502). The stunning result was the total collapse of the Soviet Union, followed by the vanishing of Eastern Europe's communist regimes (Suny 2011, 469–485) in what Cornelius Castoriadis has called the "pulverization of Marxism-Leninism" (Castoriadis 2009, 58–69).

### 17.9.3 The Transformation of the Communist Model of State: The Chinese Example

The collapse of the Berlin Wall (1989) and the Soviet Union (1991) did not, then, do away with communist autocracies, as there still remain Cuba, North Korea, Vietnam, and the People's Republic of China.

It has to be pointed out, however, that some of these countries have adopted—in practice, if not in theory—new models of the state, such as the People's Republic of China. Chinese Communist regime, after suffering the final years of Mao's rule, marked by an extremely violent and convulsive period during the Cultural Revolution (1968–1976)—whose excesses have been officially recognized and condemned-, took a very different direction, when Mao's successor, Deng Xiaoping (1904–1997), decided to undertake massive economic transformation while leaving the country's communist political structures (MacFarquhar 2011, 246–336) intact, during the crucial period of 1978–1992, in what he called "Market Socialism"

was killed by the Bolivian army, in October of 1967. Alberto Korda's 1960 portrait made of him an icon of the revolution and a regular symbol of the 1968 student revolution (Odih 2010, 89). Marcuse held a critical view of Bureaucratic Communism (Kellner 1984, 197–228).

[128] In Spain, communist leaders like Dolores Ibárruri and Santiago Carrillo possessed Soviet nationality, and Julio Anguita even attended Communist Party general secretariat meetings into the early 1980s. Only the Croatian Tito in Yugoslavia, and some "Eurocommunist" leaders, such as Italy's Enrico Berlinguer (Fasanaro 2012, 163–174) and, Santiago Carrillo (Carrillo 1978), that adopted critical attitudes towards Moscow's dictates. Meanwhile, beginning in 1949 Mao-tse Tung's China began to establish itself as an independent communist power. See a synthesis on Marxism and modern European history in Busky (2002). On differing views on the abilities of Marxist thought and politics to create an existing alternative to capitalist society, see Marcuse and Aron (2014, 355–358).

(Dittmer 1993, 3–35), a Socialism with Chinese characteristics (Goodman 2002, 99–101).

While Beijing's regime remains nominally and officially communist, after Mao's death it has not only joined the community of free market economies, but also has, ironically, evolved into the world's premier industrial power. Needless to say, the meaning of the dictatorial state has shifted, as rather than attempting to suppress the market system it has actually ended up fomenting it, creating a state-administrated form of capitalism (Amin 2005, 128–149), coated with economic imperialism, and not devoid of a certain trace of revenge for the colonial era during which China was dominated by the west. Such is the "Chinese model" (Tian 2005, 1–6).[129]

The path taken by China has, without any doubt, yielded dramatic results, as the country has become an economic superpower. Its industrial and financial might has forced the leaders of democratic regimes around the world to express respect for and tolerance of the Chinese regime, even though it is clearly a police state that continues to perpetrate executions of purported criminals and to relentlessly suppress free expression and protest. China and states like it are, in short, autocratic states ruled by isolated elites who adopt euphemistic descriptions of themselves as "socialist", "democratic", and "popular", despite the glaring fact that they are so far none of these things.[130]

[129] As Chen (1995, 4) points out, incorporating capitalist economic thinking into the official economic ideology has created major tensions, as capitalist ideas and methods must be stretched and manipulated to conform, at least theoretically, to the socialist dogma.

[130] Among other reasons, because Beijing's government, through its capitalists, is buying massive amounts of debt issued by western states, which are struggling to maintain spending levels out of line with their economies, damaged by the recent waves of financial crisis. In exchange for investing in the west's debt, citizens from China receive privileges from western states. Thus, for example, a Chinese high school diploma is valid for entrance into Spanish universities, and Chinese citizens who settle in Spain pay no taxes when establishing their first business. In this way, Chinese "capitalism" is imposing its hegemony all over the World, particularly in Africa (Rothberg 2008, 1–18). A similar dynamic was sustained with the now-overthrown Gaddafi (October 2011) who, thanks to his oil wealth, for decades managed to impose a dictatorship that enjoyed the tacit acceptance of western governments. It is not difficult to find an abundance of photos on the Internet of western leaders—such as Obama, Zapatero, Sarkozy, and Merkel—effusively embracing the dictator. The only western state, which ultimately stood up to the tyrant, was Switzerland that, as a result of abuses committed by one of Gadhafi's sons against a woman, expelled him from the Confederation and severed diplomatic relations with Libya. For an analysis of the current relationship between western democracies and dictatorial regimes, see Escribà Folch (2010, 335–359).

## 17.10 The Contemporary Transformation of the State Model in Western Capitalist Countries: A Return to Oligarchy?

### *17.10.1 The "Thirty Glorious Years", or the Contemporary Way of Addressing the Social Question*

The economic recovery following World War II—which in France came to be called the "Thirty Glorious Years" (1945–1975), or the "invisible revolution" (Fourastié 1987, 79)—generated in the west a feeling of general affluence which ended up dampening the political struggle for worker protection and economic equality (Eley 2002, 405–428). As the distinction between the proletariat and the bourgeoisie blurred and faded in the post-War era, particularly through the 1960s, trade union and workers rights initiatives waned, in large measure because working class individuals, rather than striving to seize power, concentrated their efforts on bettering their economic situations and forming part of the expanding and increasingly accessible middle class (Stark 1990, 310–329).

The dwindling cogency of Marxist precepts was described by post-Marxist thinkers such as Cornelius Castoriadis (1922–1997)[131] and Herbert Marcuse (1898–1979) who tried to adapt the leftist approach to advanced industrial societies (Marcuse 2007).[132] Critiques of capitalist society's values and examinations of its paradoxes and contradictions, offered up by thinkers such as Thorstein Veblen (1857–1929), who popularized the concepts of the "leisure class" (Diggins 1999) and "conspicuous consumption", proved more pertinent than the old orthodox Marxist doctrine.[133]

The assumption that unlimited economic growth would allow all to enjoy higher standards of living, that a "rising tide would lift all boats", was called into question by the first oil crisis, in 1974. To prevent an economic standstill western societies increasingly resorted to incurring public and private debt, which paved the way for the "financial economy", which began to play an increasingly pivotal role superseding truly productive sectors and activities. We should not forget that it was excessive debt that gave rise to the financial crisis, which swept the globe in 2007,

---

[131] Essentially, in his most famous work *The Imaginary Institution of Society* (Castoriadis 2005, 359–363). For a general look at Castoriadis, see Williams (2010, 93–109). For an analysis of Castoriadis's work, see Adams (2007, 44–60) and Klooster (2012, 488–504).

[132] Mainly in his capital work *Soviet Marxism: A Critical Analysis* (1958) (Marcuse 2014). For an overview of the relationship between Marcuse and his mentor, Martin Heidegger, see Feenberg (2004) and Wolin (2003, 134–172).

[133] In his pivotal work *The Theory of the Leisure Class: An Economic Study of Institutions* (1899) Veblen (2009). On Veblen as a historical figure, see Edgell (2001) and Meéstroviâc (2003). For an analysis of his thinking, see Brette (2003, 455–477), and Dugger (2006, 651–672). On the political consequences of Veblen's theory, see Plotkin and Tilman (2011). A comprehensive view in Reinert and Viano (2012).

leading to the historic bankruptcy of Lehman Brothers in 2008, and sinking the world in an unprecedented global economic crisis.

### *17.10.2 The Neoliberal Way and John Rawls' Theory of Justice*

From the point of view of legal and constitutional history, the welfare state model was openly criticized and challenged during the 1980s by the conservative administrations of President Ronald Reagan (1981–1989) in the U.S., and Prime Minister Margaret Thatcher in the United Kingdom (1979–1990). Both leaders implemented policies of "deregulation", favoring private initiative and enterprise in the economic sphere while restoring the principle that the role of the state is not to assure the welfare of all, but rather to promote prosperity by allowing free markets to generate maximum levels of wealth.[134] These leaders' economic advisors[135] and allies were also quick to point out that the private sector offers far more effective and efficient management than do public entities.[136]

This resurgence of the liberal model of the state also had consequences in the field of legal theory, particularly in the work of the American legal philosopher John Rawls (1921–2002), who besides redefining the idea of public reason (Rawls 1997, 765–807) and political liberalism (Rawls 2011), in his most acclaimed works *A Theory of Justice* (1971),[137] and *Justice as Fairness: A Restatement* (2001)[138] examined and presented justice as a search for what was fair rather than as a struggle between clashing interests (Päivänsalo 2012), thereby breaking with the abovementioned influential theories advanced by Rudolf von Ihering (Gaus 2003, 177–204).[139]

### *17.10.3 Growing Inequality and Its Constitutional Consequences*

Though the deregulatory policies adopted in the United Kingdom and United States in the 1980s yielded considerable economic prosperity in the short term, in the long term they fostered not only to structural imbalances in the western economies, but

[134] For an overview of what has been called the "Neoliberal Revolution", see Fukuyama (2012, 39–55) and Gaus (2003, 25–54).

[135] On the neoconservative movement see Halper and Clarke (2005, 9–39) and Heilbrunn (2008).

[136] For a contemporary criticism of state interventionism, see Cabrera and del Rey Regullo (2007, 10–15) and Skocpol (1996, 153–310).

[137] Rawls (2005).

[138] Rawls (2003).

[139] For an analysis of Rawls' conception of the law, see Freeman (2007).

also pronounced social inequality as the richest grew richer, the position of the middle class stagnated, and the increase in the numbers of the poor became alarming (Atkinson et al. 2010, 664–692). Between 1980 and 2000, the richest of the rich, the top 1 %,[140] went from controlling 8 % to 16 % of GDP, while the moderately rich, representing 10 % of the world population,[141] did only from 25 % to 27 % (Kempf 2013, 33–34). Nevertheless, despite a considerable increase in inequality in the European Union, this economy remains one of the most egalitarian in the world.[142]

This trend is not unique to the most advanced western countries, as inequality has grown in the developing world as well, where China and India are prime examples (Piketty and Qian 2010, 44–47). In 2012, China already boasted a growing number of millionaires, and a huge gap with its rural population that generally lives in poverty (Sicular et al. 2010, 85–104). India's 100 richest people, meanwhile, have gone from controlling 0.4 % of the nation's wealth in 1998 to 25 % in 2009.[143] This trend is even more significant when one considers that in 2010 the "developing countries" accounted for 50 % of the world's total wealth, according to OECD sources, which raises the question of whether the days of western economic supremacy are numbered.[144] In any case, what is indisputable, according to critics of the current system, is that decreased wealth should be

---

[140] Usually defined as those earning over 57,000 euros/month. Cowell (2011) According to van Praag (2011, 111–127), inequality is traditionally measured using the Gini co-efficient—defined as the relationship of cumulative shares of the population arranged according to the level of equivalized disposable income, to the cumulative share of the equivalized total disposable income received by them. However, this fails to capture in many instances the extraordinary rise in the incomes of the top 1 % or even 0.01 %, so a combination of both Gini and the amounts accruing to different sections of society is needed to fully understand the scope and scale of inequality. The United Nations Department of Economic and Social Affairs (DESA) and Non-governmental Organizations as Oxfam warned that extreme wealth and income is *not only unethical it is also economically inefficient, politically corrosive, socially divisive and environmentally destructive*.

[141] Defined as those earning over 5,000 euros/month.

[142] According to a recent OECD report, inequality has risen over the last three decades, from the mid 1980s to the late 2000s. In the 20 years prior to the current economic crisis, real disposable household incomes in OECD countries increased by an average of 1 % a year, but in most of these countries the incomes of the richest grew faster than those of the poor (except in France, Japan and Spain). In the OECD, the richest 10 % earned nine times as much as the poorest 10 % of the population. In Europe the biggest income disparities between rich and poor, appear in the UK and Italy (Vasconcelos 2012, 75).

[143] According to the *Forbes* list, 2009. See recent trends and data in Ghandi and Walton (2012, 10–14). It is indeed worrisome that social protection models are facing considerable struggles in the developing world, as evidenced by the dramatic inequalities they feature. On the implementation of the welfare state in the developing world, see Rudra (2007, 378–396).

[144] On the end of Western leadership, see Arnason (2003, 323–359). On the supposed beginning of the "Chinese World Order", see Jacques (2012, 585–635). An explanation through the historical legacies that largely define China's present-day trajectory, providing a framework for understanding its meteoric rise in Wasserstrom (2013). On how the diverging interests of Europe and America are weakening western influence in the New World Order, see Kagan (2003).

accepted and expected by western political leaders as they look to the future, as ever-greater prosperity based on perpetual growth is simply not sustainable.[145]

The system, however, is sustained, as observed by Susan George, because the masses are afraid of losing their jobs, and anxious of their own futures, and anxious about their children. In fact, this is the first generation that believes that its offspring will have it worse than they did. In this context the middle classes of the developed world, however, must recognize and bear in mind that they continue to be extremely fortunate, which generates a widespread feeling of TINA (There Is No Alternative).[146]

The feeling that nothing can be changed explains the growing political apathy among the citizens of democratic nations, to the point that, we are witnessing the consolidation of a trend towards chronic abstention (Subileau and Toinet 1993).[147] The shifts in the percentages of those not voting in European elections are illustrative: 38 % in 1979, 41 % in 1984, 41.5 % in 1989, 43.3 % in 1994, 50.5 % in 1999, 54.6 % in 2004, and 56.8 % in 2009—a troubling trend that is also being observed in the United States, in both legislative and presidential elections (Barbour and Wright 2013, 391–392).

### *17.10.4 Towards a New Oligarchic Model of the State?*

The legal and constitutional consequence of these important economic and social transformations is that, from the point of view of constitutional history, the democratic principle runs the risk of being progressively supplanted by oligarchy, as the massive fortunes forged during the 1980s have allied with the political class (Le Goff 2003, 136–137). This situation is far from the "Property-Owning Democracy" advanced by John Rawls and James Meade as the necessary alternative to liberal democratic socialism,[148] and which some call "Post Democracy" (Crouch

[145] For a critique of the current system see Hessel (2011), Kempf (2009) and Lovins and Cohen (2012). For an ecological alternative to what the New Left considers an unsustainable system, see Blühdorn and Welsh (2008), Hawken (2010), Paterson (1997) and Pooley (2010).

[146] After the fall of the Soviet Union, Margaret Thacher proclaimed "There is no Alternative", an expression for which procapitalists coined the acronym TINA. The Anti-globalization activist Susan George (1934) made up her own acronym TATA, meaning "There are Thousands of Alternatives" Kaufman (2012, 33). Susan George has become one of the leading critics of deregulation and its consequences in books as *How the Other Half Dies*: *The Real Reasons for World Hunger* (George 1991) or *Another World is Possible If* (George 2004).

[147] For an analysis of the degradation of our democracies and the rise of "Competitive Authoritarianism" see Levitsky and Way (2002, 51–65 and 2010, 37–84).

[148] In a "property-owning democracy" government is to be engaged in macroeconomic planning, the regulation of economic institutions, establishing market rules, and implementing resource transfers, and has also to be engaged in providing both essential and nonessential public goods. The primary aim in this new approach to public intervention is not to maximize economic growth but rather to ensure that capital is widely distributed and that no group is allowed to dominate

2004, 53–69). This trend is by no means one exclusive to democratic regimes, as even in autocratic, emergent powers, such as the People's Republic of China power is increasingly held by a political/financial oligarchy which, after concentrating in its hands the lion's share of the country's wealth, has proceeded to amass political power in an increasingly clear and uncontested fashion. As scholar Jean-Luc Domenach has explained, the bureaucratic class that has governed the country for over 50 years has partially morphed into a cadre of businessmen constituting a plutocratic oligarchy (Domenach 1984, 23–39).[149]

It should not be overlooked that the return to oligarchic government was already advanced in 1942 by Joseph Schumpeter in his book *Capitalism, Socialism and Democracy*, in which he endorsed returning to government by a ruling class rather than fully embracing egalitarian values and democratic government understood as maximum attentiveness to the dictates of the masses.[150] Democracies' regression to oligarchy was already noted by Robert Michels in 1911 (Michels 2008), a constitutional situation fast evolving from a threat into a patent reality.[151]

The situation seems particularly dangerous when these oligarchies convene at international forums to set global policies, with decisions made by groups of a private nature that seek to conceal the magnitude of their power. Cases in point include the Trilateral Commission created in 1973, the Bilderberg Group, and the Davos Forum, which Susan George calls the "Davos class" (George 2010, 6)—influential pressure groups which play decisive roles in determining government policy around the world. Today it seems that the state has granted itself license to

economic life (O'Neill and Williamson 2012, 4). For an overview of the development of this "constitutional" model, see Jackson (2012, 33–52).

[149] Recently the French newspaper *Le Monde*, associated with the Consortium of Investigative Journalism, has revealed what is already called "Chinaleaks", showing how the relatives of the Chinese financial elite, the "Red Princes", hide colossal fortunes in a series of different tax havens (Le Monde 23, 24 and January 25, 2014).

[150] "Beyond 'direct democracy' lies an infinite wealth of possible forms in which the 'people' may partake in the business of ruling or influence or control those who actually do the ruling. None of these forms [...] has any obvious or exclusive title to being described as 'Government by the People' if these words are to be taken in their natural sense" (Schumpeter 2010, 247). On the relationship between capitalism and democracy, see Rueschemeyer et al. (1992). A historical overview on the links between global capital flows, the policy elites, and national security in Viotti (2014).

[151] This is the contention of popular protest movements, such as Spain's *indignados* (the outraged), and analysts such as French environmentalist thinker Hervé Kempf (1957), according to whom the two illusions which characterize political life in the western countries at the start of the twenty-first century are, on the one hand, believing that we are still living under democratic regimes, when in reality we are clearly closer and closer to oligarchy; and, on the other, considering the economy as the almost exclusive object of politics (Kempf 2013). For an interesting essay on how to strengthen democracy against financial power in our contemporary societies, see Corfe (2013, 29–41). On Michel's theories and the Iron law of oligarchy, see Lipset (1988, 342–356).

intervene in the lives of individuals, with the means justified by the end of optimal resource management, as if it were a kind of businessman.[152] This premise is dangerous, as this kind of intervention could ultimately take precedence over representativeness and, taken to its extreme, over democracy itself[153] and the Rule of Law.[154]

For some critics the state has already become a kind of giant company, with everything determined by what its "managers" decide. According to this view public leaders have become all but businesspeople, with the important caveat that the constitutional pact prevails, and citizens enjoy a constitutional framework through which they may recover their freedom when circumstances make clear—for example, by recurring economic crises—that running the state based on a corporate model has its limitations (Sandel 2012, 6–16). The solution for many lies in a new way of governing, not based on power but on negotiation, with governance replacing government.

## 17.11 The End of the Nation-State Era and the Beginning of Global Constitutional History?

The nation-state, as a western constitutional model, has certainly not disappeared from our contemporary world, and new nation-states are still being created, such as South Sudan, founded in 2011 in response to the War in Darfur (Toïngar 2014, 5–8). Unilateral, nation-based approaches to international relations and conflict resolution have, however, been in crisis ever since World War I, progressively superseded by global approaches that tend to replace mandated and imposed solutions with multilateral, negotiated settlements, i.e., governance rather than government.

### *17.11.1 From the League of Nations to the United Nations*

In the wake and in light of World War I, it became clear that the nation-state model was incapable of successfully addressing the new world order by preventing war and assuring widespread public well-being. U.S. President Woodrow Wilson was

[152] For a criticism of this tendency, see Macloskey (2011).

[153] This is precisely what anti-establishment, anti-globalization protestors have been decrying for years, taking particular exception with international trade agreements (World Trade Organization), which can deprive the citizens of participating nations of their right to democratic representation. For an accurate overview of the interconnections between the new "western nobility" at the international level, see Badie (2011, 135–156).

[154] For an excellent contemporary critique of a process that is corroding the rule of law, see Tamanaha (2006, 215–250).

the first major international figure to conceive and promote a system by which conflicts between states would be resolved globally through the mechanism of a broadly supported international institution granted considerable authorities. Wilson's 14-point plan, taken before the U.S. Congress on January 8, 1918, called for the formation of "a general association of nations" designed to assure the peace.

Unsurprisingly, Wilson became the arbiter of the Versailles Treaty, its first 30 articles and an addendum establishing the Pact of the League of Nations, which entered into effect on January 10, 1920. The League of Nations' primary mission, as set forth in its covenant, was to prevent wars through collective security and disarmament and settle international disputes through negotiation and arbitration. Despite these lofty and admirable aims, it would fail to achieve any of them. 22 years after Versailles, its most obvious failure would be its inability to prevent the outbreak of World War II. It did not help that that the United States, ironically, refused to join the very institution that President Wilson had designed and championed, as the League faced too much opposition in Congress (Cooper 2010, 330–376).

After Hitler's defeat, the same approach was revived and carried out once again with the creation of the United Nations and the founding of a whole series of international organizations designed to prevent international conflicts. In the economic sphere other multilateral accords were reached, such as the Bretton Wood Agreements and the creation of institutions like the World Bank, the International Monetary Fund (IMF), the GATT, and the International Trade Organization and the foundation of the World Trade Organization (WTO) (van den Bossche and Zdouc 2013, 74–81), to cite only a few. The fundamental assumption underlying these different bodies is that international concerns and crises—which grow in number and complexity as the globe becomes increasingly interconnected—should be addressed and solved not by the dominant powers within states, or through unilateral or bilateral agreements, but rather through ongoing negotiations and multilateral agreements supported by alliances of states granted progressively expanded missions and authorities. Government is being replaced by "governance".[155]

[155] As explained by Bertrand Badie, the word "governance" was employed in the 1970s to respond to the world's growing internationalization, as a rejection of the old term "government", the idea being that the era of business-like political management had begun. "Governance" suggested the need, during the making of decisions, to account for the parameters of globalization, in which states would depend upon each other, including the weakest among them, which were to be incorporated as essential actors in the new international order. See Badie (2011, 157). For an analysis of the new global political framework, see Korpi and Palme (2003, 425–446).

### 17.11.2 Governments and Governance: From Authority to Negotiation

The fall of the Berlin Wall and the disappearance of the Soviet Union were viewed by some thinkers as the "end of history", as they concluded that the end of the Cold War left the U.S. as the uncontested leader of the world, and a period would begin relatively devoid of conflicts (Fukuyama 2012, 199–210). This rosy outlook came crashing down on September 11, 2001 with the World Trade Center attacks as the world's gaze turned to the danger posed by a new threat: radical Islam. The ensuing War on Terror, undertaken and waged by the U.S. in collaboration with its allies, is a new type of conflict in which states are required to form broad and tight-knit coalitions to fight an often invisible enemy.

The global economy, meanwhile, is no longer driven principally by the U.S., but rather by the world's fastest growing economies, particularly Brazil, Russia, India, and China (the BRIC countries). The result is the need for increasingly multilateral approaches to international relations (Cutler 2012, 56–70), a development seen by French political scientist Bertrand Badie (1950) as, ironically, the "*beginning* of history" (Badie 2012), because it marks the dawn of a new era in which no state or nation will wield enough power to impose itself at the world level, and government shall be replaced by governance, understood as a collective and negotiated approach to international problems.[156] According to this vision, the changes in the world are of such a magnitude that they can no longer be resolved by any one country, and it shall be necessary to globally administrate the planet, advancing towards a model of international governance (Gaus 2003, 148–176). States around the world shall be called upon to converge,[157] while politics is destined to become a collaborative and multilateral affair.

Governance has become particularly important in Europe since 1945, as after World War II its nations were eclipsed and overshadowed on the world stage by the hegemonic superpowers of the Cold War era: the United States and the Soviet Union. Europeans were forced to react and forge a powerful union if they were to play a major role and exert their influence in the new world order. This was to be no easy task, as for centuries Europeans had been organized into sovereign states, each with their own traditions, institutions and peculiarities, and European governments had been traditionally reluctant to sacrifice their sovereignty, often won only after hard-fought historical struggles. Nevertheless, Europe was compelled to adapt and devise a peculiar way of integration, based essentially on negotiation. These efforts shall be the subject of the next chapter.

---

[156] For a reflection on the role of the state in the global era, see Marinetto (2007, 119–142). On the expansion of US executive power in the wake of 9/11 and the apparent abdication of the other branches in terms of checks and balances, see Fisher (2006, 123–150).

[157] For a general approach to globalization from a legal perspective, see Fischer Lescano and Teubner (2004, 999–1046).

## TIMELINE

1797 May 27. Babeuf is executed after the "Conspiracy of Equals" fails.
1848 February 21. Publication in London of the *Communist Manifesto* by Karl Marx and Friedrich Engels.
1864 Foundation in London of the International Workingmen's Association (IWA), also known as the "First International".
1867 Marx publishes the first volume of *Das Kapital.*
1871 March 18–May 28. Paris Commune.
1872 V Congress of the First International in The Hague. Split between Marx (social democrat) and Bakunin (revolutionary anarchist).
1875 Foundation of the Social Democratic Party of Germany.
1879 Madrid's Pablo Iglesias founds the PSOE. Marxist party of the working, revolutionary socialist class.
1883 Karl Marx dies in London on March 14. Bismarck introduces legislation providing health insurance for workers. The following year an industrial accident insurance law is passed. In 1889, also thanks to an initiative backed by the Iron Chancellor, the German Empire approves Europe's first system of pensions and disability benefits.
1889 July 14–19. Foundation in Paris of the "Second International".
1895 August 5. Death of Friedrich Engels in London.
1902 II Congress of the Russian Social Democratic Labor Party. Lenin, a Bolshevik ("member of the majority") imposes his radical theses upon the Mensheviks ("members of the minority"), led by Julius Martov.
1904 February 8. Outbreak of the Russo-Japanese war. The Russians are ultimately defeated.
1905 January 22. First Russian Revolution. Trotsky creates "soviets" (assemblies of workers and soldiers).
1910 August 29. Japan annexes Korea.
1917 February 5. Promulgation of the Constitution of the United Mexican States.
March 3–15. Revolution of February (Julian Calendar). Abdication of Tsar Nicholas II.
April 3. Lenin publishes his revolutionary program (April Theses).
July 21. Alexander Kerensky, President of Russia's provisional government.
November 7. Triumph of the Soviet Revolution (October Revolution; Julian Calendar).
1918 July 17. The tsar and his family are executed, shot in Yekaterinburg by order of Lenin.
November 9. Abdication of William II and the *Kronprinz*. Proclamation of the Republic (November Revolution). Socialist Friedrich Ebert heads an interim government (Chancellor until February 11, 1919).
November 11. An armistice is signed in the Forest of Compiègne. End of World War I.
1919 January 1–15. Spartacist Revolution (Karl Liebknecht and Rosa Luxemburg).

January 19. Elections to the "Constitutional Assembly" (*Nationalversammlung*) in Germany. The SPD (Social Democratic Party) wins
On February 11, Philip Scheidemann succeeds Ebert as chancellor.
March 2–6. The Communist International's World Congress.
Foundation of the *Kommintern* (Third International).
June 28. Signing of the Treaty of Versailles.
July 31. Promulgation of the Weimar Constitution. The German Reich becomes a parliamentary republic. Friedrich Ebert serves as its first president.

1922 April 3. Stalin is appointed General Secretary of the Central Committee of the Communist Party.
October 28. Mussolini seizes power (March on Rome).
November 16. Mussolini obtains the confidence of the Legislature (316 to 116, with 7 abstentions) and becomes President of the Council of Ministers.

1923 July 21. The Italian Chamber of Deputies approves a new election law ("Acerbo Law") 223 to 123.
September 13. Dictatorship of Primo de Rivera.
November 8–9. Failure of the Beer Hall Putsch. Hitler is incarcerated.

1924 January 21. Death of Lenin. Kamenev and Zinoviev take control of the Party.
June 10. Socialist deputy Giacomo Matteotti, a harsh critic of Mussolini's government, is kidnapped by fascist militia. His body is found on August 16.

1925 February 28. Friedrich Ebert, President of the Weimar Republic, dies in office and is succeeded by Paul von Hindenburg.

1927 December 2–19. XV Congress of the Communist Party. Stalin seizes power.

1929 February. Stalin expels Trotsky from the Soviet Union.
October 24–29 (Thursday–Tuesday). The New York Stock Exchange (Wall Street) collapses.

1931 April 14. Proclamation of the Second Spanish Republic.
September 18. Japan invaded Northeastern China.

1932 March 1. The Kwantung Army established the Japanese puppet state of Manchukuo in Manchuria.
November 8. Franklin Delano Roosevelt is elected, with 57.4 % of the vote and winning 42 States; Herbert Hoover takes 39.7 % of the vote and wins 6 States.

1933 January 30. Hitler is appointed Chancellor (NSDAP: 33 % of the votes).
February 27. The Reichstag Fire.
March 4. Franklin Delano Roosevelt takes office as the 32nd President of the United States (serving until April 12, 1945, being reelected three times).
March 5. Parliamentary elections in Germany (NSDAP: 43 % votes). The detention of socialist and communist representatives gives Hitler the two-thirds majority needed to alter the Constitution.

March 23. Enabling Act (*Emächtigungsgesetz*). The Reichstag grants Hitler full powers. Beginning of the dictatorship.

1934 June 30–July 2. Night of the Long Knives (*Nacht der langen Messer*). Hitler orders the *Geheime Staatspolizei* (secret state police, or *Gestapo*) and the *Schutzstaffel* (SS) to kill the principal leaders of the *Sturmabteilung* (the SA or "brown shirts"). The fascist militias are incorporated into the army.

1936 July 18. Military revolt in Spain against the Republic. Beginning of the Civil War.

August. initiation of the first political trials in Moscow. The "Great Purges" begin. Stalin judges and executes his former political rivals (until March 13, 1938).

1937 July 1. China–Japan War begins.

1938 March 12. Incorporation of Austria into the Third Reich (*Anschluss*).

September 3. Leon Trotsky founds the Fourth International in Paris.

September 30. The Munich Agreement. Chamberlain and Daladier cave in to Hitler on the question of the Sudetenland in an infamous act of appeasement.

1939 April 1. End of the Spanish Civil War, with the absolute victory of General Francisco Franco.

August 23. Ribbentrop and Molotov sign the Non-aggression Pact between the Third Reich and the Soviet Union.

August 31. The Soviet Union and Japan fought a massive tank battle on the Mongolian border. Japan was defeated.

September 1. Germany invades Poland.

September 7. The Soviet Union invades Finland, occupies part of Poland, and takes over Lithuania, Estonia, and Latvia.

1940 April–May. Katyn Massacre (Poland). Soviet troops gun down 22,000 Polish soldiers in cold blood.

August 21. Leon Trotsky is assassinated in Coyoacán (Mexico) by Catalonian Ramón Mercader, at Stalin's behest.

September 23–29. Japanese troops begin to occupy the French colony of Indochina.

September 27. Germany, Italy, and Japan sign the Tripartite Pact, against England and France. The treaty is also seen as a warning to the United States.

1941 June 22. The Germans invade Russia (Operation Barbarossa).

December 7. (December 8 in Japan) Japan attacks Pearl Harbor in Hawaii as well as Guam, Wake Island, the Philippines, Hong Kong, and Malaya. War with the West has begun.

December 8. Japanese troops invade Malaya and Thailand and seize Shanghai. Later in December, Japanese army invades Burma and Hong Kong.

1942 January 20. Wannsee Conference, at which the implementation of Jewish extermination, the "Final Solution" (*Endlösung*), is decided.
February 19. By the Executive Order 9066, the U.S. government forces over 120,000 Japanese-Americans to move from the U.S. West Coast to "relocation" camps in isolated areas.
1943 January 31. Von Paulus surrenders at Stalingrad.
July 24. Mussolini is dismissed by the Grand Council of Fascism and replaced by Marshal Pietro Badoglio.
1944 June 6. Landing of the Allies at Normandy.
1945 April 12. Roosevelt dies and is replaced in office by Harry S. Truman.
April 28. Mussolini is shot, along with Claretta Petacci.
April 30. Hitler commits suicide in his Berlin bunker.
May 7. Unconditional surrender of Germany.
June 20. Okinawa falls to the Allies. In addition to the military casualties, some 120,000 civilians also died.
July 26. The U.S., Great Britain, and China issue the Potsdam Declaration calling for Japan *to immediately and unconditionally surrender or to suffer prompt and utter destruction.*
August 6–9. Atomic bombs are dropped on Hiroshima and Nagasaki.
August 15. Japan surrenders.
September 2. Ho Chi Minh founds the Democratic Republic of Vietnam.
1946 March 5. Churchill popularizes the term "Iron Curtain" in reference to the separation between eastern Europe under Soviet influence and western Europe.
June 2. In a referendum, 54 % of Italians vote against the monarchy. Proclamation of the Italian Republic (Constituted on December 22, 1947).
1947 June 5. George Marshall's speech at Harvard University. Launch of the European Recovery Program (ERP), better known as the Marshall Plan.
1948 June 25. Initiation of the Berlin Airlift (*Luftbrücke*) to rescue western Berlin from the blockade imposed by Stalin.
1949 April 4. Signing in Washington of the North Atlantic Treaty Organization (NATO) agreement, forming a western alliance against Soviet expansionism.
May 23. Enactment of the Basic Law for the Federal Republic of Germany. The Federal Republic of Germany is born.
October 1. Mao Tse-tung proclaims the People's Republic of China at the Gate of Tiananmen Square (Forbidden City).
December 10. Final military victory of Mao over nationalist forces. Chiang Kai-Shek takes refuge in Taiwan.
1950 June 25. Start of the Korean War.
October. China invades Tibet.
1953 March 5. Stalin dies. His legacy: 14 million dead Russians (four million killed in political purges, ten million dead from starvation).
July 17. End of the Korean War. Division between North Korea and South Korea (demilitarized zone). 4 km wide and 238 long.

1954 May 7. A French army surrenders at Dien Bien Phu. Ho Chi Minh is proclaimed President of the Democratic Republic of Vietnam.

1956 February. 20th Congress of the CPSU (Russian Communist Party). Condemnation of Stalinism (Nikita Khrushchev). October 23–November 10. The Hungarian Revolution against the Soviet Union is brutally put down by Soviet tanks.

1959 January 1. Triumph of the Cuban Revolution (Flight of Fulgencio Batista. Fidel Castro seizes power).

1961 April 15–19. Anti-Castro invasion of Cuba ends in disaster at the Bay of Pigs.
August 13. Building of the Berlin Wall (*Berliner Mauer*), which would stand until November 9, 1989.

1962 October. The Cuban Missile Crisis. President Kennedy is on the verge of declaring war on the Soviet Union (under Khrushchev).

1963 November 22. President John F. Kennedy is assassinated in Dallas.

1964 August 2. The Gulf of Tonkin Incident. An American warship is purportedly attacked by a North Vietnamese patrol boat. The U.S. would exploit the incident to justify the Vietnam War.

1965 February 6. President Johnson orders the bombing of North Vietnam. The Vietnam War begins.

1966 August 8. Mao launches the “Cultural Revolution”, which seeks to eradicate traditional Chinese culture. For 10 years, the Revolution implements a series of radical policies.

1967 October 9. Revolutionary leader Che Guevara is executed in La Higuera (Bolivia) by order of Bolivian President Barrientos.

1968 January 5–August 20. Stage of political liberalization in Czechoslovakia (Prague Spring), with Alexander Dubcek emerging as a leader. The invasion of Warsaw Pact troops puts down this attempt at reform.
May. A state of emergency is declared in France in response to student and worker protests (May 1968).

1973 January 27. Signing of the Peace of Paris between the United States and North Vietnam.
March 29. The last U.S. soldiers leave Vietnam.
October 16. The Nobel Peace Prize is awarded to Henry Kissinger.

1975 April 17. The Khmer Rouge conquers Phnom Penh. Pol Pot (Saloth Sar) perpetrates genocide against all non-revolutionaries. Two million Cambodians are killed.
April 30. North Vietnamese troops occupy Saigon.
November 20. Francisco Franco dies in Madrid.

1976 September 9. Death of Mao Tse-tung in Beijing. End of the “Cultural Revolution”. Deng Xiaoping opens up the Chinese economy to capitalism.

1977 June 15. The first democratic elections in Spain since February 1936.

1979 January 7. The Vietnamese Army occupies Phnom Penn. End of the Khmer Rouge regime. Pol Pot, one of history's most prolific killers, dies in prison in 1998.

1982 November 10. Leonid Brezhnev dies in Moscow (in power since October 20, 1964).

1985 March 11. Mikhail Gorbachev comes to power in the Soviet Union (in office until August 24, 1991).

1989 April 15–June 4. Tiananmen Square Revolt. Harshly repressed by the "People's Liberation Army".
November 9. Fall of the Berlin Wall.

1990 August 31. Signing in Berlin of the "Unification Treaty" (*Einigungsvertrag*). Ratified by the *Volkskammer* (GDR) and the *Bundestag* (RFA) on September 20.
September 12. Germany fully recovers its sovereignty as a state. Signing in Moscow of the 2 Plus Four Agreement. Two (Federal Republic of Germany and the German Democratic Republic) plus Four (the powers that defeated the Third Reich in 1945: France, the United Kingdom, the U.S.A., and the Soviet Union).

1991 March 15. The Two Plus Four Agreement enters into force.
December 26. The Supreme Soviet declares the Soviet Union defunct.

2001 September 11. Airplanes hijacked by radical Islamic terrorists fly into and destroy the Twin Towers of the World Trade Center (New York) and part of the Pentagon (Washington, DC).

2005 October 10. Angela Dorothea Merkel becomes the first female chancellor of unified Germany.

2006 July 31. Raúl Castro replaces Fidel Castro as the acting president of Cuba.

2008 February 24. Raúl Castro is elected President of the Council of State in Cuba by members of the National Assembly of People's power. He definitively succeeds his brother Fidel, who announces his resignation two days prior.
August 8–24. Beijing Olympics. The games are held despite worldwide protests against the People's Republic of China's human rights violations.

2012 The U.S. Supreme Court declares President Barack Obama's universal health care legislation constitutional.

## References

Abromeit, J. (2011). *Max Horkheimer and the foundations of the Frankfurt School.* Cambridge, UK: Cambridge University Press.

Adair, G. (1997). *Thomas Alva Edison: Inventing the electric age.* Oxford: Oxford University Press.

Adams, S. (2007). Castoriadis and the permanent riddle of the world: Changing configurations of worldliness and world alienation. *Thesis Eleven: Critical Theory and Historical Sociology, 90* (1), 44–60.

Adams, M. (2012). *Lee de Forest: King of radio, television and film.* New York: Copernicus Books.

Agee, J., & Evans, W. (2000). *Let us Praise famous men: Three tenant families.* Boston: Hoghton Mifflin.

Aguilera-Barchet, B. (2012). De la etapa liberal a la era social: Las transformaciones jurídicas del Estado español entre 1923 y 1939. *Anuario de Historia del Derecho español, 82*, 603–680.

Allhoff, F., & Hall, M. (Eds.). (2014). *The Affordable Care Act decision: Philosophical and legal implications.* New York: Routledge.

Aly, G. (2008). *Hitler's beneficiaries: Plunder, racial war, and the Nazi welfare state.* New York: Metropolitan.

Amin, S. (2005). Theory and practice of the Chinese "market socialism" project: Is "market socialism" and alternative to liberal globalization? In T. Y. Cao (Ed.), *The Chinese model of modern development* (pp. 128–149). London: Routledge.

Andrew, N., & Cleven, N. (1921). Some social aspects of the Mexican constitution of 1917. *The Hispanic American Historical Review, 4*(3), 474–487.

Arnason, J. (2003). Questioning the west: The uses and abuses of anti-Eurocentrism. In *Civilizations in dispute: Historical questions and theoretical traditions* (pp. 323–359). Leiden: Brill.

Aron, R. (2009). *The opium of the intellectuals.* New Brunswick, NJ: Transaction Publishers.

Atkenson, A., & Kehoe, P. J. (2007). Modeling the transition to a new economy: Lessons from two technological revolutions. *American Economic Review, 97*(1), 64–88.

Atkin, N. (2014). *Pétain.* New York: Routledge.

Atkinson, A. B., Piketty, T and Saez E. (2010). Top incomes in the long run of history. In A. B. Atkinson & T. Piketty (Eds.), *Top incomes: A global perspective* (pp. 664–760). Oxford: Oxford University Press.

Aunós, E. (1928). *Las corporaciones del trabajo en el Estado moderno.* Madrid: Ministerio del Trabajo.

Badie, B. (2011). *La diplomatie de connivence: Les dérives oligarchiques du système international.* Paris: La découverte.

Badie, B. (2012). *Quand l'histoire commence.* Paris: Éditions du CNRS.

Baldwin, P. (2003). Introduction: Welfare redistribution and solidarity. In *The politics of social solidarity class bases of the European welfare state, 1875–1975* (pp. 1–54). Cambridge, UK: Cambridge University Press.

Barbour, C., & Wright, G. C. (2013). *Keeping the republic. Power, citizenship in American politics.* Thousand Oaks, CA: Sage Publications.

Barnes, J. J., & Barnes, P. P. (2010). *Nazis in pre-war London, 1930–1939: The fate and role of German party members and British sympathizers.* East Sussex, UK: Sussex Academic Press.

Barnes, T. J., & Minca, C. (2013). Nazi spatial theory: The dark geographies of Carl Schmitt and Walter Christaller. *Annals of the Association of American Geographers, 103*(3), 669–687.

Barr, D. A., & Field, M. G. (1996). The current state of health care in the former Soviet Union: Implications for health care policy and reform. *American Journal of Public Health, 86*(3), 307–312.

Barrett, J. Q. (2010). Raphael Lemkin and 'Genocide' at Nüremberg: 1945–1946. In C. Safferling & E. Conze (Eds.), *The genocide convention sixty years after its adoption* (pp. 35–54). The Hague: T.M.C. Asser Press.

Beall, J., & Fox, S. (2009). Urbanisation and development in historical perspective. In *Cities and development* (pp. 34–66). London: Routledge.

Beatson, J., & Zimmermann, R. (2007). *Jurists uprooted: German-speaking émigré lawyers in twentieth-century Britain.* Oxford: Oxford University Press.

Beauchamp, C. (2014). *Invented by law: Alexander Graham Bell and the patent that changed America.* Cambridge, MA: Harvard University Press.

Beaudrau, B. C. (2005). *The National Industrial Recovery Act Redux: Technology and transitions*. Lincoln, NE: iUniverse.
Berlin, I. (2013). *Karl Marx* (5th ed.). Princeton, NJ: Princeton University Press.
Bernanke, B. S. (2000). *Essays on the great depression*. Princeton, NJ: Princeton University Press.
Bevan, G., & Hood, C. (2006). What's measured is what matters: Targets and gaming in the English public health care system. *Public Administration, 84*(3), 517–538.
Bilstein, R. E. (2001). The awkward years: Early flight to 1918. In *Flight in America: From the wrights to the astronauts* (3rd ed., pp. 3–40). Baltimore, MD: Johns Hopkins University Press.
Birchall, I. (1997). *The spectre of Babeuf*. New York: St. Martin's Press.
Blainey, G. (2008). A tempest of change. In *A short history of the twentieth century* (pp. 31–44). London: Penguin.
Blanc, J. J. L. (1844). Saint-Simon's doctrines. In *The history of ten years: 1830–1840* (pp. 548–573). 1. London: Chapman and Hall.
Blanc, J. J. L. (1982). *Louis Blanc (1811–1882)*. Paris: Les Editions ouvrières.
Blinder, C. (Ed.). (2010). *New critical essays on James Agee and Walker Evans: Perspectives on let us now praise famous men*. New York: Palgrave Macmillan.
Blinkhorn, M. (2006). *Mussolini and Fascist Italy* (3rd ed.). Oxon, UK: Routledge.
Bloom, H. (2007). Introduction. In J. Steinbeck (Ed.), *The grapes of wrath* (pp. 7–9). New York: Chelsea House.
Blühdorn, I., & Welsh, I. (2008). *The politics of unsustainability: Eco-politics in the post-ecologist era*. Abingdon, UK: Routledge.
Boland, F. K. (2009). *The first anesthetic: The story of Crawford Long*. Athens, GA: University of Georgia Press.
Bomhoff, J. (2013). *Balancing constitutional rights. The origins and meanings of postwar legal discourse*. Cambridge, UK: Cambridge University Press.
Boot, M. (2006). *War made new: Technology, warfare, and the course of history, 1500 to today*. New York: Gotham Books.
Boyce, R. W. D. (2012). *The great interwar crisis and the collapse of globalization*. Basingstoke, UK: Palgrave Macmillan.
Boyns, T., & Edwards, J. R. (2013). The second industrial revolution: c. 1870–c. 1918. In *A history of management accounting: The British experience* (pp. 167–203). New York: Routledge.
Branderberger, D. (2002). Popularizing state ideology through mass culture. In *National bolshevism: Stalinist mass culture and the formation of modern Russian national identity, 1931–1956* (pp. 77–94). Cambridge, MA: Harvard University Press.
Brayer, E. (2012). *George Eastman: A biography*. Rochester, NY: University of Rochester Press (Annotated ed.).
Brette, O. (2003). Thorstein Veblen's theory of institutional change: Beyond technological determinism. *The European Journal of the History of Economic Thought, 10*(3), 455–477.
Brown, A. (2009). *The rise and fall of communism*. New York: Random House.
Browning, C. R. (2004). The final solution from conception to implementation. In *The origins of the final solution: The evolution of Nazi Jewish Policy, September 1939–March 1942* (pp. 374–423). Lincoln, NE: University of Nebraska Press.
Bullock, A. (1993). *Hitler and Stalin: Parallel lives*. New York: First Vintage Books.
Bullock, A. (2005). *Hitler: A study in Tyranny*. Harmondsworth, UK: Penguin (Rev. Ed.).
Busky, D. F. (2002). *Communism in history and theory: The European experience*. Westport, CT: Praeger.
Butler, T. (1997). The debate over the middle class. In *Gentrification and the middle classes* (pp. 14–34). Ashgate, UK: Aldershot.
Cabrera, M., & del Rey Regullo, F. (2007). The incompetence of an interventionist state. In *The power of entrepreneurs: Politics and economy in contemporary Spain* (pp. 10–15). New York: Berghahn Books.
Caron, F. (2013). *Dynamics of innovation: The expansion of technology in modern times*. New York: Berghahn Books.

Carrillo, S. (1978). *Eurocommunism and the state*. Westport, CT: L. Hill.
Castoriadis, C. (2005). *The Imaginary Institution of Society*. Cambridge, MA: Polity.
Castoriadis, C. (2009). *World in fragments: Writings on politics, society, psychoanalysis, and the imagination*. Stanford, CA: Stanford University Press.
Chambers, J. W. (2000). *The Tyranny of change: America in the progressive era, 1890–1920*. New Brunswick, NJ: Rutgers University Press.
Chapman, J. (2003). Silent cinema. In *Cinemas of the world: Film and society from 1895 to the present* (pp. 10–15). London: Reaktion.
Chen, F. (1995). *Economic transition and political legitimacy in post-Mao China: Ideology and reform*. Albany, NY: State University of New York Press.
Childers, T. (2014). The middle classes and national socialism. In D. Blackbourn & R. J. Evans (Eds.), *The German Bourgeoisie: Essays on the social history of the German middle class from the late eighteenth to the early twentieth century* (pp. 318–337). Oxon, UK: Routledge (Reprint).
Churchill, W. Sir. (2013). 'An iron curtain has descended' 5 March, 1946, Fulton Missouri. In *Never give in!: The best of Winston Churchill's speeches* (pp. 413–423). London: Bloomsbury.
Cienciala, A. M., Lebedeva, N. S. and Materski. W. (Eds.) (2008) *Katyn a Crime Without Punishment*, New Haven & London: Yale University Press.
Combs, D. (2008). *Inside the Soviet alternate universe: The cold war's end and the Soviet Union's fall reappraised*. University Park, PA: Pennsylvania State University.
Cooper, J. M. (2010). *Breaking the heart of the world: Woodrow Wilson and the fight for the league of nations*. Cambridge, MA: Cambridge University Press.
Cooter, R. (2011). Medicine and modernity. In M. Jackson (Ed.), *The Oxford handbook of the history of medicine* (pp. 100–116). Oxford: Oxford University Press.
Corfe, R. (2013). *The democratic imperative: The reality of power relationships in the nation-state*. Southgate Green, UK: Arena.
Corn, J. J. (2002). *The Winged Gospel: America's romance with aviation, 1900–1950*. Baltimore, MD: Johns Hopkins University Press.
Cowell, F. A. (2011). *Measuring inequality* (3rd ed.). Oxford: Oxford University Press.
Crosby, M. B. (2008). *The making of a German constitution: A slow revolution*. Oxford: Berg.
Crossick, G., & Haupt, H.-G. (2004). *The Petite Bourgeoisie in Europe, 1780–1914: Enterprise, family and independence* (pp. 133–165). Oxon, UK: Routledge.
Crouch, C. (2004). *Post-democracy*. Cambridge, MA: Polity.
Cutler, A. C. (2012). Private transnational governance and the crisis of global leadership. In S. Gill (Ed.), *Global crises and the crisis of global leadership* (pp. 56–70). Cambridge, UK: Cambridge University Press.
Daniels, R. V. (Ed.). (1993). *A documentary history of communism in Russia: From Lenin to Gorbachev*. Hanover, NH: University of Vermont.
Dans, E. (2010). *Todo va a cambiar: tecnología y evolución*. Barcelona: Deusto.
de Bertier de Sauvigny, G. (1970). Liberalism, nationalism and socialism: The birth of three words. *Review of Politics, 32*(2), 147–166.
de la Calle, M. D. (1989). *La Comisión de Reformas Sociales, 1883–1903: Política social y conflicto de intereses en la España de la Restauración*. Madrid: Ministerio de Trabajo y Seguridad Social.
Serna de la Garza, J. M. (2013). *The constitution of Mexico: A contextual analysis*. Oxford: Hart.
De Vries, J. (2006). Proletarianization. In *European urbanization: 1500–1800* (pp. 237–238). Cambridge, MA: Harvard University Press.
Denton, S. (2012). That Jew Cripple in the White House. In *The plots against the president: FDR, a nation in crisis, and the rise of the American right* (pp. 154–160). New York: Bloomsbury.
Diggins, J. P. (1999). *Thorstein Veblen: Theorist of the leisure class* (2nd ed.). Princeton, NJ: Princeton University Press.

Dittmer, L. (1993). Chinese reform socialism under Deng Xiaoping: Theory and practice. In M. Y. M. Kau & S. H. Marsh (Eds.), *China in the era of Deng Xiaoping: A decade of reform* (pp. 3–35). Armonk, NY: M.E. Sharpe.

Domenach, J. -L. (1984, September–November). Le totalitarisme n'arrête pas l'histoire: Communisme et société en Chine. *Esprit*, pp. 23–39.

Duggan, C. (2013). *Fascist voices: An intimate history of Mussolini's Italy*. New York: Oxford University Press.

Dugger, W. M. (2006). Veblen's radical theory of social evolution. *Journal of Economic Issues, 40*(3), 651–672.

Duncan, J. (2011). *Any colour – so long as it's black. Designing the model T Ford: 1906–1908*. Auckland, New Zealand: Exisle Publishing Ltd.

Durkheim, É. (2010). *Socialism and Saint-Simon*. London: Routledge.

Dutton, P. V. (2005). Retrenchment and reform 1939–1947. In *Origins of the French welfare state: The struggle for social reform in France, 1914–1947* (pp. 184–219). Cambridge, UK: Cambridge University Press.

Duverger, M. (1973). *Institutions politiques et droit constitutionnel. 1. Les grands systèmes politiques* (13th ed.). Paris: Presses Universitaires de France.

Edgell, S. (2001). *Veblen in perspective: His life and thought*. Armonk, NY: M.E. Sharpe.

Eley, G. (1976). Social imperialism in Germany: Reformist synthesis or reactionary sleight of hand? In J. Radkau & I. Geiss (Eds.), *Imperialismus im 20. Jahrhundert: Gedenkschrift für George W.F. Hallgarten* (pp. 71–86). München: C. H. Beck.

Eley, G. (1996). *Reshaping the German Right: Radical nationalism and political change after Bismarck*. New Haven, CT: Yale University Press (2nd. print).

Eley, G. (2002). *Forging democracy: The history of the left in Europe, 1850–2000*. Oxford: Oxford University Press.

Elkin, D. C. (2009). Foreword. In F. K. Boland (Ed.), *The first anesthetic: The story of Crawford Long* (p. v). Athens, GA: University of Georgia Press.

Eltscher, L. R. (2013). *Traitors or patriots?: A story of the German anti-Nazi Resistance*. Bloomington, IN: iUniverse.

Enfantin, B. P and Bazard, S. A. (1829). Lettre à un catholique sur la vie et le caractère de Saint-Simon: Exposition de la doctrine de Saint-Simon. In *Doctrine Saint-Simonienne: Exposition* (pp. 1–15). Paris: Au Bureau de L'Organisateur.

Engerman, D. C. (2010). Ideology and the origins of the cold war, 1917–1962. In *The Cambridge history of the cold war* (pp. 20–43). I. Cambridge, UK: Cambridge University Press.

Escribà Folch, A. (2010). Dealing with Tyranny: International sanctions and the survival of authoritarian rulers. *International Studies Quarterly, 54*(2), 335–359.

Evans, E. (2001). The new political economy and the early impact of Laissez-Faire. In *The forging of the modern state: Early industrial Britain, 1783–1870* (3rd ed., pp. 47–55). London: Longman.

Fasanaro, L. (2012). Neither one bloc, nor in the other: Berlinguer's vision at the end of the cold war. In F. Bozo et al. (Eds.), *Visions of the end of the cold war in Europe, 1945–1990* (pp. 163–176). New York: Berghahn Books.

Feenberg, A. (2004). *Heidegger and Marcuse: The catastrophe and redemption of history*. London: Routledge.

Ferro, M. (1996). *L'internationale d'Eugène Pottier et Pierre Degeyter*. Paris: Éditions Noêsis.

Filmer, R. Sir. (1652). *Observations upon Aristotles Politiques, touching forms of government: Together with directions for obedience to governours in dangerous and doubtful times*. London: Printed for R. Royston, at the Angel in Ivie-Lane.

Firsov, F. I., Klehr, H. and Haynes, J. E. (2014). *Secret cables of the Comintern: 1933–1943*. New Haven, CT: Yale University Press.

Fischer Lescano, A., & Teubner, G. (2004). Regime collisions: The vain search for legal unity in the fragmentation of global law. *Michigan Journal of International Law, 25*(4), 999–1046.

Fisher, L. (2006). Constitutional safeguards after 9/11. In T. E. Baker & J. F. Stack (Eds.), *At war with civil rights and civil liberties* (pp. 123–150). Lanham, MD: Rowman & Littlefield.

Fleck, R. K. (2011). The political economy of progress: Lessons for the causes and consequences of the new deal. In P. Rode et al. (Eds.), *Economic evolution and revolution in historical time* (pp. 311–335). Palo Alto, CA: Stanford University Press.
Fleischacker, S. (2009). From Babeuf to Rawls. In *A short history of distributive justice* (pp. 80–124). Cambridge, MA: Harvard University Press.
Forgan, S. (2010). From modern Babylon to White City: Science, technology and urban change in London, 1870–1914. In M. R. Levin et al. (Eds.), *Urban modernity: Cultural innovation in the second industrial revolution* (pp. 75–133). Cambridge, MA: The MIT Press.
Fourastié, J. (1987). *Les Trente Glorieuses: Ou la révolution invisible de 1946 à 1975*. Paris: Fayard.
Fousek, J. (2000). *To lead the free world: American nationalism and the cultural roots of the cold war*. Chapel Hill, NC: University of North Carolina Press.
Frankel, R. E. (2005). The legitimization of right-wing populism and the radicalization of the right during the Wilhelmine crisis period. In *Bismarck's shadow: The cult of leadership and the transformation of the German right, 1898–1945* (pp. 68–86). Oxford: Berg.
Frankenberg, G. (2014). Constellations of law-rule and the state of exception. In *Political technology and the erosion of the rule of law: Normalizing the state of exception* (pp. 51–96). Cheltenham, UK: Edward Elgar.
Freeman, S. (2007). *Justice and the social contract: Essays on Rawlsian political philosophy*. Oxford: Oxford University Press.
Freud, S. (2011). *On Cocaine = Über Coca*. London: Hesperus Press. (With a translation of the original from 1885).
Freymond, J., & Molnár, M. (1966). The rise and fall of the first international. In M. M. Drachkovitch (Ed.), *The revolutionary internationals: 1864–1943*. Stanford, CA: Stanford University Press.
Friedel, R. D., & Israel, P. (2010). *Edison's electric light: The art of invention*. Baltimore, MD: Johns Hopkins University Press.
Frolik, L. A. (2006). The grapes of wrath (1940): Can justice be found on Route 66? In R. Strickland et al. (Eds.), *Screening justice -the cinema of law: Significant films of law, order, and social justice* (pp. 35–50). Buffalo, NY: W.S. Hein.
Fukuyama, F. (2012). *The end of history and the last man*. London: Penguin.
Fulbrook, M. (2009). *A history of Germany 1918–2008: The divided nation* (3rd ed.). Malden, MA: Blackwell.
Galbraith, J. K. (2009). *The great crash: 1929*. New York: Mariner Books.
García Pelayo, M. (2011). Epilogo in Schmitt. In Carl *Teoría de la Constitución* (pp. 489–494). Madrid: Alianza Ed.
Gardner, L. C. (2004). Korean borderlands: Imaginary frontiers of the cold war. In W. Stueck (Ed.), *The Korean war in world history* (pp. 126–143). Lexington, KY: The University Press of Kentucky.
Gati, C. (2006). *Failed illusions: Moscow, Washington, Budapest, and the 1956 Hungarian revolt*. Washington, DC: Stanford University Press.
Gaudreault, A., et al. (Eds.). (2012). *A companion to early cinema*. Malden, MA: Wiley-Blackwell.
Gaus, G. F. (2003). *Contemporary theories of liberalism: Public reason as a post-enlightenment project*. Thousand Oaks, CA: Sage.
Geary, D. (1984). The emergence of organization protest. In *European labour protest: 1848–1939* (pp. 25–89). London: Methuen.
Gentile, E. (2005). *The origins of fascist ideology: 1918–1925*. New York: Enigma Books.
George, S. (1991). *How the other half dies: The real reasons for world hunger*. London: Penguin (Reprint).
George, S. (2004). *Another world is possible if*. London: Verso.
George, S. (2010). *Whose crisis? Whose future?: Towards a greener, fairer, richer world*. Cambridge, UK: Polity.

Gerwarth, R. (2005). Towards the abyss: Bismarck and the dissolution of the Weimar republic. In *The Bismarck myth: Weimar Germany and the legacy of the Iron Chancellor* (pp. 118–145). Oxford: Oxford University Press.

Getzler, I. (2003). *Martov: A political biography of a Russian social democrat*. Cambridge, UK: Cambridge University Press.

Ghandi, A., & Walton, M. (2012). Where do India's billionaires get their wealth? *Economic & Political Weekly, 47*(40), 10–14.

Ghisalberti, C. (2012). *Storia Costituzionale d'Italia 1848–1948* (8ª ed.). Roma: Laterza.

Gillespie, R. (1989). *The Spanish Socialist Party. A history of factionalism*. Oxford: Oxford University Press.

Glass, R. (1964). Introduction: Aspects of change. In *London: Aspects of change* (pp. xiii–xlii). London: MacKibbon and Kee.

Gluckstein, D. (2008). Deciphering the internationale: The Eugène Pottier code. *International Socialism: A Quarterly Journal of Socialist Theory,* (120). http://isj.org.uk/index.php4?id=485&issue=120. Accessed 1 June 2014.

Goldstone, L. (2014). *Birdmen: The Wright Brothers, Glenn Curtiss, and the battle to control the skies*. New York: Random House.

González Cuevas, P. C. (1998). Charles Maurras en Cataluña. *Boletín de la Real Academia de la Historia, 195*(2), 309–362.

Goodman, D. S. G. (2002). *Den Xiaoping and the Chinese revolution. A political biography*. London: Routledge.

Gorky, M. (2004). *Days with Lenin*. Honolulu, HI: University Press of the Pacific.

Gould, R. V. (1995). Class mobilization in the revolution of 1848. In *Insurgence identities: Class, community, and protest in Paris from 1848 to the commune* (pp. 32–64). Chicago, IL: University of Chicago Press.

Gray, C. (2011). *Reluctant Genius: Alexander Graham Bell and the passion for invention*. New York: Skyhorse Publishing.

Gregor, J. A. (2005). *Mussolini's intellectuals: Fascist social and political thought*. Princeton, NJ: Princeton University Press.

Grunberger, R. (2013). *A social history of the third Reich*. London: Weinfeld and Nicolson.

Gustavson, T. (2012). Eureka moments: Niépce, Daguerre, Talbot. In *Camera: A history of photography from daguerreotype to digital* (pp. 2–23). New York: Sterling Publishing (Reprint ed).

Haimsom, L. H. (2005). *Russia's revolutionary experience: 1905–1917*. New York: Columbia University Press.

Haines, M. R., & Steckel, R. H. (2000). *A population history of North America* (pp. 305–370). Cambridge, MA: Cambridge University Press.

Halper, S., & Clarke, J. (2005). The neoconservatives: A new political interest group. In *America alone: The neo-conservatives and the global order* (pp. 9–39). Cambridge, MA: Cambridge University Press.

Hanagan, M. N. (1992). *Nascent proletarians: Class formation in post-revolutionary France*. Oxford: Oxford University Press.

Hardach, G. (1981). *The First World War: 1914–1918*. Los Angeles, CA: University of California Press.

Harris, J. (2002). From poor law to welfare state? A European perspective. In P. O'Brien & D. Winch (Eds.), *The political economy of British historical experience* (pp. 409–438). Oxford: Oxford University Press.

Harris, J. (2013). *The anatomy of terror: Political violence under Stalin*. Oxford: Oxford University Press.

Hastings, M. (2013). *All hell let loose: The world at war, 1939–1945*. London: HarperPress.

Haugen, D., & Musser, S. (Eds.). (2012). *Health care legislation*. Detroit, MI: Greenhaven Press.

Hawken, P. (2010). *The ecology of commerce: A declaration of sustainability*. New York: Harper Business (Revised Ed).

Heilbrunn, J. (2008). *They knew they were right: The rise of the Neocons*. New York: Anchor Books.
Henig, R. (2006). *The Weimar republic: 1919–1933*. London: Routledge.
Herz, J. (1948). The fiasco of denazification in Germany. *Political Science Quarterly, 63*(4), 569–594.
Hessel, S. (2011). *Time for outrage!* New York: Hachette.
Hildermeier, M. (2000). *The Russian Socialist Revolutionary Party before the First World War*. New York: St. Martin's Press.
Hitler, A. (1941). *Mein Kampf. Complete and unabridged. Fully annotated*. New York, NY: Reynal & Hitchcock.
Hitler, A. (2012). Germany's policy in Eastern Europe. In *Mein Kampf = My battle* (pp. 521–541). Charleston, SC: CreateSpace.
Hoffman, P. (2003). *Wings of madness: Alberto Santos Dumont and the invention of flight*. New York: Theia.
Hohenberg, P. M., & Lees, L. H. (1996). Industrialization and the cities. In *The making of urban Europe: 1000–1950* (pp. 179–214). Cambridge, MA: Harvard University Press.
Hunt, T. (2010). *Marx's general: The revolutionary life of Friedrich Engels*. London: Macmillan.
Jackson, J. (1998). Bread: The Blum new deal. In *The popular front in France: Defending democracy, 1934–1938* (pp. 159–187). Cambridge, MA: Cambridge University Press.
Jackson, B. (2005). The conceptual history of social justice. *Political Studies Review*, (3), 356–373.
Jackson, B. (2012). Property-owning democracy: A short history. In M. O'Neill & T. Williamson (Eds.), *Property-owning democracy: Rawls and beyond* (pp. 33–52). Malden, MA: Wiley-Blackwell.
Jacques, M. (2012). *When China rules the world: The end of the western world and the birth of a new global order*. New York: Penguin (Revised ed).
James, H. (1986). *The German slump: Politics and economics, 1924–1936*. Oxford: Clarendon.
James, T. M. (2014). *Mexico's Supreme Court, 1867–1934: Between liberal individual rights and revolutionary social rights, 1867–1934*. Albuquerque, NM: University of New Mexico Press.
Janzen, H. (1937). Kelsen's theory of law. *The American Political Science Review, 31*(2), 205–226.
Jennings, J. (2011). *Revolution and the republic: A history of political thought in France since the eighteenth century*. Oxford: Oxford University Press.
Johnston, W. M. (1983). *The Austrian mind: An intellectual and social history, 1848–1938*. Berkeley, CA: University of California Press.
Kagan, R. (2003). *Of paradise and power: America and Europe in the new world order*. New York: Alfred A. Knopf.
Kahan, A. S. (2010). *Mind vs. money: The war between intellectuals and capitalism*. New Brunswick, NJ: Transaction Publishers.
Kalyvas, A. (2007). The basic norm and democracy in Hans Kelsen's legal and political theory. *Philosophy and Social Criticism, 32*(5), 573–599.
Katznelson, I. (1986). Working class formation: Constructing cases and comparisons. In I. Katznelson & A. R. Zolberg (Eds.), *Working class formation: Nineteenth century patterns in Western Europe and the United States* (pp. 3–44). Princeton, NJ: Princeton University Press.
Kaufman, C. (2012). *Getting past capitalism: History, vision, hope*. Plymouth: Lexington Books.
Kellner, D. (1984). Marcuse's critique of Bureaucratic Communism: Soviet Marxism. In *Herbert Marcuse and the crisis of Marxism* (pp. 197–228). Berkeley, CA: University of California Press.
Kelsen, H. (2005). *Pure theory of law*. Clark, NJ: The Lawbook Exchange.
Kelsen, H. (2007). *General theory of law and state*. Clark, NJ: The Lawbook Exchange.
Kempf, H. (2009). *How the rich are destroying the earth*. Lane Cove, NSW: Finch Publishing.
Kempf, H. (2013). *L'oligarchie ça suffit, vive la démocratie*. Paris: Éditions du Seuil.

Kennedy, E. (2004). *Constitutional failure: Carl Schmitt in Weimar*. Durham, NC: Duke University Press.
Kershaw, I. (2000). *Hitler 1889–1936: Hubris*. New York: W.W. Norton and Company.
Kindleberger, C. P. (2013). *The world in depression: 1929–1939*. Berkeley, CA: University of California Press. (40th Anniversary Ed.)
Kirchheimer, O. (1999). The transformation of the Western European Party System. In J. LaPalombara & M. Weiner (Eds.), *Political parties and political development* (pp. 177–182). Princeton, NJ: Princeton University Press.
Kirk, T. (2014). *Nazi Germany*. London: Routledge.
Klein, H. S. (2012). The creation of an industrial and urban society: 1860–1914. In *A population history of the United States* (pp. 107–144). Cambridge, UK: Cambridge University Press.
Klooster, J. (2012). Plurality and indeterminacy: Revising Castoriadis's overly homogeneous conception of society. *European Journal of Social Theory, 15*(4), 488–504.
Kominski, G. (Ed.). (2014). *Changing the U.S. health care system: Key issues in health services policy and management* (4th ed.). San Francisco, CA: Wiley.
Korpi, W., & Palme, J. (2003). New politics and class politics in the context of austerity and globalization: Welfare state regress in 18 countries, 1975–1995. *American Political Science Review, 97*(3), 425–446.
Lanzoni, R. F. (2002). *French cinema: From its beginnings to the present*. New York, NY: The Continuum International Publishing Group.
Le Goff, J. -P. (2003). *La démocratie post-totalitaire*. Paris: La Découverte.
Lees, A., & Lees, L. H. (2007). The challenge of the big cities. In *Cities and the making of modern Europe: 1750–1914* (pp. 129–168). Cambridge, UK: Cambridge University Press.
Lees, L., Slater, T. and Wyly, E. (2013). *Gentrification*. London: Routledge.
Lemkin, R. (2008). *Axis rule in occupied Europe: Laws of occupation, analysis of government, proposals for redress*. Clark, NJ: The Lawbook Exchange
Leroy, M. (2011). The social contract of interventionist democracy. In *Action publique (Public action)* (pp. 361–374). 7. Bruxelles, Belgium: Peter Lang AG.
Levitsky, S., & Way, L. A. (2002). Elections without democracy: The rise of competitive authoritarianism. *The Journal of Democracy, 13*(2), 51–65.
Levitsky, S., & Way, L. A. (2010). Explaining competitive authoritarian regime trajectories: International linkage and the organizational power of incumbents. In *Competitive authoritarianism: Hybrid regimes after the cold war* (pp. 37–84). Cambridge, UK: Cambridge University Press.
Lewis, P. H. (2002). *Latin Fascist Elites: The Mussolini, Franco and Salazar regimes*. Westport, CT: Greenwood.
Linehan, T. P. (2000). *British fascism, 1918–1939: Parties, ideology and culture*. Manchester, UK: Manchester University Press.
Lipset, S. M. (1988). Democracy and the iron law of oligarchy. In *Revolution and counterrevolution: Change and persistence in social structures* (pp. 342–356). New Brunswick, NJ: Transaction Publisher.
López García, J. A. (1996). La presencia de Carl Schmitt en España. In *Revista de Estudios Políticos*, (91), 139–168.
Loubère, L. A. (2012). *Louis Blanc. His life and his contribution to the rise of French Jacobin Socialism* (no. 1). Evanston, IL: Northwestern University Studies in History.
Lovins, L. H., & Cohen, B. (2012). *The way out: Kick-starting capitalism to save our economic ass*. New York: Hill and Wang.
Luhman, M. (2004). *Law as a social system*. Oxford: Oxford University Press.
Lukacs, J. (2013). "Middle Class" is not "Bourgeois". In *A short history of the twentieth century* (pp. 78–89). Cambridge, MA: Harvard University Press.
Lunde, P. D. (2012). *Roosevelt's war: What really happened during World War II*. Bloomington, IN: iUniverse.
MacCormick, N. (1989). The ethics of legalism. *Ratio Juris, 2*(2), 184–193.
MacCormick, N. (1993). Beyond the sovereign state? *Modern Law Review, 56*(1), 1–18.

MacFarquhar, R. (2011). The succession to Mao and the end of Maoism, 1969–1982. In R. MacFraquhar (Ed.), *The politics of China: Sixty years of the People's Republic of China* (pp. 246–336). Cambridge, UK: Cambridge University Press.
MacLeod, C. (2002). *Inventing the industrial revolution: The English Patent System, 1660–1800*. Cambridge, UK: Cambridge University Press.
MacLoskey, D. N. (2011). *Bourgeois dignity: Why economics can't explain the modern world*. Chicago, IL: University of Chicago Press.
Maier, C. S. (2011). *Recasting bourgeois Europe: Stabilization in France, Germany, and Italy in the decade after World War I*. Princeton, NJ: Princeton University Press (Reprint).
Majnoni d'Intignano, B. (1993). *La Protection sociale*. Paris: Éditions de Fallois.
Manuel, F. E. (1997). *A requiem for Karl Marx*. Cambridge, MA: Harvard University Press.
Marcuse, H. (1989). *Counterrevolution & revolt*. Toronto: Beacon.
Marcuse, H. (2007). *One-dimensional man: Studies in the Ideology of Advanced Industrial Society*. New York: Routledge (Reprint).
Marcuse, H. (2014). *Soviet Marxism: A critical analysis*. Charleston, SC: Nabu Press.
Marcuse, H., & Aron, R. (2014). Marx and Para-Marx on capitalist contradictions: Excerpts from a debate. In *Marxism, revolution and Utopia: Collected papers of Herbert Marcuse* (pp. 355–358). VI. London: Routledge.
Mares, I. (2003). Class conflict and the development of the modern welfare state. In *The politics of social risk: Business and welfare state development* (pp. 4–6). Cambridge, UK: Cambridge University Press.
Marinetto, M. (2007). *Social theory, the state and modern society: The state in contemporary social thought*. New York: Open University Press.
Markel, H. (2012). *An anatomy of addiction: Sigmund Freud, William Halsted, and the Miracle Drug, Cocaine*. New York: Vintage Books (Reprint).
Martín, B. (1992). *Los problemas de la modernización: Movimiento obrero e industrialización en España*. Madrid: Ministerio de Trabajo y Seguridad Social.
Mason, T., & Broadwin, J. (1997). *Social policy in the Third Reich: The working class and the 'National Community', 1918–1939* (3rd ed.). Oxford: Berg.
Mastny, V. (2010). *The cold war and Soviet insecurity: The Stalin years*. Oxford: Oxford University Press (Reprint).
McDonough, F. (2001). *Conflict, communism and fascism: Europe 1890–1945*. Cambridge, MA: Cambridge University Press.
McDonough, F. (2003). The Ideology of Hitler and the Nazi Party. In *Hitler and the rise of the Nazi Party* (pp. 51–66). Harlow, UK: Pearson.
Meade, T. A. (2010). *A history of modern Latin America: 1800 to the present*. Malden, MA: Blackwell.
Meéstroviâc, S. (2003). *Gabriel Thorstein Veblen on culture and society*. Thousand Oaks, CA: Sage Publications.
Mehring, R. (2014). *Carl Schmitt: A biography*. Malden, MA: Polity.
Michels, R. (2008). *Political parties: A sociological study of the oligarchical tendencies of modern democracy*. Montana, Kessinger Publishing. (Translation from the allemande originale ed.: *Zur Sociologie des Parteiwesens in der sodernen demokratie*.)
Mikkelsen, F. (1996). Origin of a European proletariat. In *Working-class formation in Europe: In search of a synthesis* (pp. 8–10). Amsterdam: International Institute of Social History.
Millbrooke, A. M. (2006). *Aviation history*. Englewood, CO: Jeppesen Sanderson.
Moch, L. P. (2003). *Moving Europeans: Migration in Western Europe since 1650* (2nd ed., pp. 147–157). Bloomington, IN: Indiana University Press.
Moggach, D. (2000). The social question and political struggles in 1848: The case of Germany. In D. Moggach & P. L. Browne (Eds.), *The social question and the democratic revolution: Marx and the legacy of 1848* (pp. 21–42). Ottawa: University of Ottawa Press.
Mommsen, W. J. (2011). Liberals, radicals and the revolutions of 1848. In G. S. Jones & G. Claeys (Eds.), *The Cambridge history of nineteenth century political thought* (pp. 416–420). Cambridge, UK: Cambridge University Press.

Morris, C. R. (2005). *The Tycoons: How Andrew Carnegie, John D. Rockefeller, Jay Gould, and J.P. Morgan Invented the American Supereconomy*. New York: Owl Books.
Mosse, G. L. (1989). The mystical origins of national socialism. In M. R. Marrus (Ed.), *The origins of the Holocaust* (pp. 43–58). Westport, CT: Walter de Gruyter.
Muller, J. W. (Ed.). (1999). *Churchill's "Iron Curtain" speech fifty years later*. Columbia, MO: University of Missouri Press.
Murkens, J. E. K. (2013). *From empire to union: Conceptions of German constitutional law since 1871*. Oxford: Oxford University Press.
Murphree, R. B. (2005). Dawes plan. In T. Adam (Ed.), *Germany and the Americas: Culture, politics and history* (pp. 269–272). 1. Santa Barbara, CA: ABC-CLIO.
Mussolini, B. (1935). *Four speeches on the corporate state: With an appendix including the labour charter, the text of laws on syndical and corporate organizations and explanatory notes*. Roma: Laboremus.
Neale, R. S. (1972). Class and class consciousness in early nineteenth century. In *Class and ideology in the 19th century* (pp. 15–40). London: Routledge.
Neumann, F., Marcuse, H. and Kirchheimer, O. (2013). *Secret reports on Nazi Germany: The Frankfurt School contribution to the war effort*. Princeton, NJ: Princeton University Press.
Neville, P. (2004). *Mussolini*. Oxon, UK: Routledge.
Niemeyer, E. V. (1991). *Revolution at Querétaro: The Mexican constitutional convention of 1916–1917*. Austin, TX: University of Texas Press.
Noiret, S. (1990). *Political strategies and electoral reforms: Origins of voting systems in Europe in the 19th and 20th centuries*. Baden-Baden, Germany: Nomos.
Nomad, M. (1966). The anarchist tradition. In M. M. Drachkovitch (Ed.), *The revolutionary internationals: 1864–1943* (pp. 57–94). Stanford, CA: Stanford University Press.
Nord, P. (2010). The French model. In *France's new deal: From the thirties to the postwar era* (pp. 17–24). Princeton, NJ: Princeton University Press.
Nye, M. J. (1986). *Science in the provinces: Scientific communities and provincial leadership in France, 1860–1930*. Berkeley, CA: University of California Press.
O'Neill, R. (2012). *Prodigal genius: The life of Nikola Tesla*. Memphis, TN: Bottom of the Hill.
O'Neill, M., & Williamson, T. (2012). Introduction. In M. O'Neill & T. Williamson (Eds.), *Property-owning democracy: Rawls and beyond* (pp. 1–14). Malden, MA: Wiley-Blackwell.
Odih, P. (2010). *Advertising and cultural politics in global times*. Farnham, UK: Ashgate.
Olsen, M. (2006). *Soviet–Vietnam relations and the role of China, 1949–1964: Changing alliances*. Oxon, UK: Routledge.
Orwell, G. (2013). *1984*. Boston, MA: Houghton Mifflin Harcourt. (Ed. based on Orwell's typescript of November 1948, amended according his proof corrections).
Ott, J. C. (2011). *When Wall Street met Main Street*. Cambridge, MA: Harvard University Press.
Overy, R. (2001). The German economy: 1919–1945. In P. Panayi (Ed.), *Weimar and Nazi Germany: Continuities and discontinuities* (pp. 33–73). Harlow, UK: Pearson Education Limited.
Päivänsalo, V. (2012). *Balancing reasonable justice: John Rawls and crucial steps beyond*. Burlington, VT: Ashgate.
Paterson, M. (1997). *Global warming and global politics*. London: Routledge.
Patterson, J. (1981). Recession politics: 1938. In *Congressional conservatism and the new deal* (pp. 211–249). New York: Praeger.
Paxton, R. O. (2007). Creating fascist movements. In *The anatomy of fascism* (pp. 24–54). London: Palgrave Macmillan.
Pearson, M. (1991). *The sealed train*. Waukegan, IL: Fontana Press.
Persily, N., Metzger, G. E and Morrison, T. W. (Eds). (2013). *The health care case: The Supreme Court's decision and its implications*. Oxford: Oxford University Press.
Pestritto, R. J. (2005). *Woodrow Wilson and the roots of modern liberalism*. Lanham, MD: Rowman & Littlefield.
Pestritto, R. J. (2007). The birth of the administrative state: Where it came from and what it means for limited government. *Special Report on Political Thought*, (16), 1–16.

Phillips-Fein, K. (2010). Paradise lost. In *Invisible hands: The businessmen's crusade against the new deal* (pp. 3–25). New York: W. W. Norton.

Piketty, T., & Qian, N. (2010). Income inequality and progressive income taxation in China and India: 1986–2015. In A. Atkinson & T. Piketty (Eds.), *Top incomes: A global perspective* (pp. 40–75). Oxford: Oxford University Press.

Pilbeam, P. (2006). Political mobilisation: The insurrectionary tradition in France, 1835–1848. In P. H. Wilson (Ed.), *1848: The year of revolutions* (pp. 168–180). Burlington, VT: Ashgate.

Pilbeam, P. (2008). The Bourgeoisie and the state. In S. Berger (Ed.), *A companion to nineteenth-century Europe: 1789–1914* (pp. 88–89). Oxford: Wiley.

Plotkin, S. A. (Ed.). (2011). *History of vaccine development*. New York: Springer.

Plotkin, S., & Tilman, R. (2011). *The political ideas of Thorstein Veblen*. New Haven, CT: Yale University Press.

Pollard, S. (2002). *Peaceful conquest: The industrialization of Europe, 1760–1970*. Oxford: Oxford University Press (Reprint).

Pollard, J. (2005). *The fascist experience in Italy*. London: Routledge.

Pooley, E. (2010). *The climate war: True believers, power brokers, and the fight to save the earth*. New York: Hyperion.

Popple, S., & Kember, J. (2004). *Early cinema: From factory gate to dream factory*. London: Wallflower.

Postell, J. (2012). From administrative state to constitutional government. *Special Report on Political Thought,* (116), 1–34.

Pretzer, W. S. (Ed.). (2002). *Working at inventing: Thomas A. Edison and the Menlo Park experience*. Baltimore, MD: Johns Hopkins University Press.

Pringle, R. W. (2006). *Historical dictionary of Russian and Soviet intelligence*. Oxford: Rowman & Littlefield.

Pugh, M. (2012). The reorientation: The emergence of the interventionist state, 1902–1918. In *State and society: A social and political history of Britain since 1870* (4th ed., pp. 119–178). London: Bloomsbury.

Purcell, E. A. (2002). The new deal "Constitutional Revolution" as a historical problem. *The Virginia Quarterly Review, 78*(2), 238–255.

Rancière, J. (2012). *Proletarian nights: The workers' dream in nineteenth-century France*. New York: Verso Books.

Rawls, J. (1997). The idea of public reason revisited. *The University of Chicago Law Review, 64* (3), 765–807.

Rawls, J. (2003). *Justice as fairness: A restatement*. Cambridge, MA: Belknap Press of Harvard University Press.

Rawls, J. (2005). *A theory of justice*. Cambridge, MA: Belknap Press of Harvard University Press (Reprint from the original ed).

Rawls, J. (2011). *Political liberalism*. New York: Columbia University Press.

Raz, J. (2009). Kelsen's theory of the basic norm. In *The authority of law: Essays on law and morality* (2nd ed., pp. 122–160). Oxford: Oxford University Press.

Rees, J. (2006). Lenin and Trotsky on the socialist revolution and the democratic revolution. In *Imperialism and resistance* (pp. 147–149). New York: Routledge.

Reich, W. (2013). What is class consciousness? In *Sex-pol: Essays, 1929–1934* (pp. 275–358). New York: Verso Books.

Reinert, E. S., & Viano, F. L. (Eds.). (2012). *Thorstein Veblen: Economics for an age of crises*. New York: Anthem Press.

Roberts, G. (2006). *Stalin's wars: From world war to cold war, 1939–1953*. New Haven, CT: Yale University Press.

Rockoff, H. (2005). Until it's over, over there: The US economy in World War I. In S. Broadberry & M. Harrison (Eds.), *The economics of World War I* (pp. 310–342). Cambridge, UK: Cambridge University Press.

Roeder, P. G. (1994). Varieties of post-Soviet authoritarian regimes. *Post-Soviet Affairs,* (10), 61–101.

Rohr, J. A. (1986). Founding the administrative state in deed: The new deal. In *To run a constitution: The legitimacy of the administrative state* (pp. 111–194). Lawrence, KN: University Press of Kansas.

Rosanvalllon, P. (1992). *La crise de l'État-providence.* Paris: Seuil.

Rose, R. B. (1978). *Gracchus Babeuf. The first revolutionary communist.* Palo Alto, CA: Stanford University Press.

Roth, G. (1984). *The social democrats in imperial Germany: A study in working-class isolation and national integration.* Salem, NH: Ayer Co.

Rothbard, M. N. (2008). *America's great depression* (5th ed.). Auburn, AL: Mises Institute.

Rothberg, R. I. (2008). China's quest for resources, opportunities and influence in Africa. In R. I. Rothberg (Ed.), *China into Africa: Trade, aid, and influence* (pp. 1–18). Cambridge, MA: World Peace Foundation.

Rousseau, J. J. (2009). *Discourse on inequality. On origins and basis of inequality among men.* London: The Floating Press.

Rubio Carracedo, J. (1995). From democracy to corporatism: Genealogy of a historical frustration. In M. Troper & M. M. Karlsson (Eds.), *Law, justice and the state II. The nation, the state and democracy* (pp. 69–78). Stuttgart, Germany: Franz Steiner Verlag.

Rudra, N. (2007). Welfare states in developing countries: Unique or universal? *Journal of Politics, 69*(2), 378–396.

Rueschmeyer, D., Stephens, J. D., and Stephens, E. H. (1992). *Capitalist development and democracy.* Cambridge, UK: Polity.

Ruiz Resa, J. D. (2008). Franquismo y trabajo: el nacionalsindicalismo y los derechos de los trabajadores. In F. F. -C. López & A. M. Hespanha (Eds.), *Franquismus und Salazarismus: Legitimation durch Diktatur?* (pp. 235–264). Frankfurt am Main: Vittorio Klostermann.

Russell, C. A. (2000). *Michael Faraday: Physics and faith.* Oxford: Oxford University Press.

Saint-Pierre, D. (2006). *Maurice Laporte: Une Jeunesse Révolutionnaire. Du Communisme à l'Anticommunisme (1916–1945).* Saint-Nicolas, QC: Les Presses de l'Université Laval.

Sajó, A. (2004). Concepts of neutrality and the state. In R. Dworkin et al. (Eds.), *From liberal values to democratic transition.* Budapest: Central European University Press.

Salvatorelli, L. (1999). *Sommario della storia d'Italia* (2nd ed.). Torino: Einaudi.

Sánchez Ron, J. M. (2010). *Descubrimientos, innovación y tecnología: Siglos XX y XXI.* Madrid: Consejo Superior de Investigaciones Científicas.

Sandel, M. J. (2012). *What money can't buy: The moral limits of markets.* New York: Farrar, Straus and Giroux.

Sapega, E. W. (2008). *Consensus and debate in Salazar's Portugal: Visual and literary negotiations of the national text, 1933–1948.* University Park, PA: Pennsylvania State University Press.

Sartori, G. (2009). *Parties and party systems: A framework for analysis.* Colchester: ECPR Press.

Scheuerman, W. E. (2013). The Frankfurt School at war: The Marxists who explained the Nazis to Washington. *Foreign Affairs, 92*(4), 171–176.

Schilperoord, P. (2012). *The extraordinary life of Josef Ganz: The Jewish Engineer behind Hitler's Volkswagen.* New York: RVP Publishers.

Schivelbusch, W. (2007). *Three new deals: Reflections on Roosevelt's America, Mussolini's Italy, and Hitlers Germany 1933–1939.* New York, NY: Picador.

Schlich, T. (2004). The emergence of modern surgery. In D. Brunton (Ed.), *Medicine transformed: Health, disease and society in Europe: 1800–1930* (pp. 61–91). Manchester, UK: Manchester University Press.

Schmitt, C. (2008). *The Leviathan in the state theory of Thomas Hobbes: Meaning and failure of a political symbol.* Chicago, IL: University of Chicago Press.

Schmitt, C. (2012). *Auf der gefahrenvollen Straße des öffentlichen Rechts: Briefwechsel Carl Schmitt-Rudolf Smend 1921–1961. Mit ergänzenden Materialien.* Berlin: Duncker & Humblot.

Schumpeter, J. A. (2010). *Capitalism, socialism and democracy.* London/New York, NY: Routledge/Harper Colophon.

Seligman, M. S., & Mclean, R. R. (2000). Social policy. In *Germany: From Reich to Republic, 1871–1918* (pp. 35–38). London: Palgrave Macmillan.

Semashko, N. (1990). The tasks of public health in Soviet Russia. In W. G. Rosenberg (Ed.), *Bolshevik visions: First phase of the cultural revolution in Soviet Russia* (2nd ed., pp. 130–132). Ann Arbor, MI: University of Michigan.

Service, R. (2008). *Stalin: A biography.* London: Pan Macmillan.

Sewell, W. H. (1997). *Work and revolution in France: The language of labor from the old regime to 1848.* Cambridge, UK: Cambridge University Press.

Shafritz, J. M., & Hyde, A. C. (2011). *Classics of public administration* (7th ed.). Wadsworth: Cengage Learnings.

Shesol, J. (2011). *Supreme power: Franklin Roosevelt vs. the Supreme Court.* New York: W.W. Norton.

Shulman, S. (2009). *The telephone gambit: Chasing Alexander Graham Bell's secret.* New York: W. W. Norton.

Sicular, T., Ximing, Y. Gustafsson, B. and Shi, L. (2010). How large is China's rural–urban income gap? In M. K. Whyte (Ed.), *One country, Two societies: Rural–urban inequality in contemporary China* (pp. 85–104). Cambridge, MA: Harvard University Press.

Silverman, D. P. (1998). *Hitler's economy: Nazi work creation programs, 1933–1936.* Cambridge, MA: Harvard University Press.

Silverman, K. (2008). *Lightning man: The accursed life of Samuel F.B. Morse.* New York: Alfred A. Knopf.

Skocpol, T. (1996). The failure of a paternalist welfare state. In *Protecting soldiers and mothers: The political origins of social policy in the United States* (4th ed., pp. 153–310). Cambridge, MA: Harvard University Press.

Skowronek, S. (2003). State building as reconstitution: 1900–1920. In *Building a new American State: The expansion of national administrative capacities, 1877–1920* (pp. 173–284). Cambridge, MA: Cambridge University Press.

Slater, T. (2013). Gentrification of the city. In G. Bridge & S. Watson (Eds.), *The New Blackwell Companion to the city* (pp. 571–585). Chichester, UK: Wiley-Blackwell.

Smaldone, W. (2014). *European socialism: A concise history with documents.* Plymouth, UK: Rowman & Littlefield.

Smith, T. B. (2003). The French social service: Landscape prior to World War I. Localism vs. centralization. In *Creating the welfare state in France: 1880–1940* (pp. 13–50). Montreal: McGill-Queen's University Press.

Somek, A. (2006). Stateless law: Kelsen's conception and its limits. *Oxford Journal of Legal Studies, 26*(4), 753–774.

Sosa Wagner, F. (2008). *Carl Schmitt y Ernst Forsthoff: Coincidencias y confidencias.* Madrid: Marcial Pons.

Soto Carmona, Á. (2003). *El trabajo en España: de la crisis del sistema gremial a la flexibilización.* Madrid: Entrelíneas Ed.

Sperber, J. (2005). Society and social conflicts during the 1840s. In *The European revolutions: 1848–1851* (2nd ed., pp. 5–55) Cambridge, UK: Cambridge University Press.

Standage, T. (2009). *The Victorian Internet: The remarkable story of the telegraph and the nineteenth century's on-line pioneers.* New York: Bloomsbury.

Stark, D. (1990). Class struggle and the transformation of the labour process: A relational approach. In A. Giddens & D. Held (Eds.), *Classes, power, and conflict: Classical and contemporary debates* (pp. 310–329). London: Macmillan.

Steiner, Z. (2007). The diplomacy of the depression: The triumph of economic nationalism. In *The lights that failed: European international history 1919–1933* (pp. 635–705). Oxford: Oxford University Press.

Steininger, R. (2008). 12 November 1918–12 March 1938: The road to the Anschluß. In R. Steininger et al. (Eds.), *Austria in the twentieth century* (pp. 85–114). New Brunswick, NJ: Transaction Publisher.

Stolleis, M. (1998). *The law under the Svastika: Studies on legal history in Nazi Germany*. Chicago, IL: The University of Chicago Press.

Stolleis, M. (2004). *A history of public law in Germany: 1914–1945*. Oxford: Oxford University Press.

Stolleis, M. (2013). *Origins of the German welfare state: Social policy in Germany to 1945*. Berlin: Springer.

Stolleis, M. (2014). Social policy in the empire: The insurance solution. In *History of social law in Germany*. Berlin: Springer.

Straus, K. M. (1997). State and society revisited in factory and community. In *Stalin's Russia: The making of an industrial working class* (pp. 1–10). Pittsburgh, PA: University of Pittsburgh Press.

Subileau, F., & Toinet, M. F. (1993). *Les chemins de l'abstention. Une comparaison franco-amé ricaine*. Paris: Éditions La Découverte.

Sunstein, C., Michelman, F., Forbath, W., Tushnet, M., West, R., Balkin, J. et al. (2009). Social rights and legislative constitutionalism. In J. M. Balkin & R. B. Siegel (Eds.), *The constitution in 2020* (pp. 36–107). Oxford: Oxford University Press.

Suny, R. G. (2011). *The Soviet experiment: Russia, the USSR, and the successor states*. Oxford: Oxford University Press.

Swain, G. (2014). *Trotsky*. London: Routledge.

Taebi, B. (2012). Intergenerational risks of nuclear energy. In S. Roeser (Ed.), *Handbook of risk theory: Epistemology, decision theory, ethics, and social implications of risk* (pp. 295–318). Berlin: Springer.

Takenaka, H. (2014). *Failed democratization in Prewar Japan: Breakdown of a hybrid regime*. Stanford, CA: Stanford University Press.

Tamames, R. (2008). *Ni Mussolini ni Franco: la dictadura de Primo de Rivera y su tiempo*. Barcelona: Planeta.

Tamanaha, B. Z. (2006). *Law as a means to an end: Threat to the rule of law*. Cambridge, UK: Cambridge University Press.

Tarr, Z. (2011). *The Frankfurt School: The critical theories of Max Horkheimer and Theodor W. Adorno*. New Brunswick, NJ: Transaction Publishers.

Taylor, B. (2004). *Volkswagen military vehicles of the Third Reich: An illustrated history*. Cambridge, MA: Da Capo Press.

Taylor, B. (2010). "The Führer's Roads": Nazi Autobahnen ribbons of concrete, 1933–1945. In *Hitler's engineers: Fritz Todt and Albert Speer* (pp. 24–62). Havertown, PA: Casemate.

Taylor, F. (2014). *The downfall of money: Germany's hyperinflation and the destruction of the middle class*. London: Bloomsbury.

Teiwes, F. C. (2011). The establishment and consolidation of the new regime, 1949–1957. In R. MacFraquhar (Ed.), *The politics of China: Sixty years of the People's Republic of China* (3rd ed., pp. 6–86). Cambridge, UK: Cambridge University Press.

Thurlow, R. C. (2005). The Security Service, The Communist Party of Great Britain and British Fascism. In N. Copsey & D. Renton (Eds.), *British fascism, the labour movement, and the state* (pp. 27–45). New York: Palgrave Macmillan.

Thurston, R. H. (2011). The development of the modern steam engine: James Watt and his contemporaries. In *A history of the growth of the steam engine* (pp. 79–143). Ithaca, NY: Cornell University. (Reprod. of the 4th. ed., 1902).

Tian, Y. C. (2005). Modernization, globalization and the Chinese path. In *The Chinese model of modern development* (pp. 1–6). London: Routledge.

Tilly, C. (1997). Demographic origins of the European proletariat. In *Roads from past to future* (pp. 293–386). Boston, MD: Rowman & Littlefield.

Tocqueville, A. (2009). *Tocqueville on America after 1840: Letters and other writings* (pp. 394–403). Cambridge, UK: Cambridge University Press.

Toïngar, É. B. (2014). Chad, Sudan and Darfur. In *Idriss Deby and the Darfur conflict* (pp. 5–8). Jefferson, NC: McFarland & Company.

Tooze, A. (2008). *The wages of destruction: The making and breaking of the Nazi economy*. New York: Penguin.

Torp, C. (2011). The great transformation: German economy and society, 1850–1914. In H. W. Smith (Ed.), *The Oxford handbook of modern German history* (pp. 336–358). Oxford: Oxford University Press.

Toscano, A. A. (2012). *Marconi's wireless and the rhetoric of a new technology*. Dordrecht, Netherlands: Springer.

Travers, T. (1992). *How the war was won. Command and technology in the British Army on the Western Front, 1917–1918*. New York: Routledge.

Trebilcock, C. (1981). *The industrialization of the continental powers, 1780–1914*. London: Longman.

Trotsky, L. (2014). *The essential Trotsky*. London: Routledge.

Tsygankov, A. P. (2014). *The strong state in Russia: Development and crisis*. Oxford: Oxford University Press.

Ulam, A. B. (2007). *Stalin the man and his era*. London: Tauris.

United States. (2010). *Patient Protection and Affordable Care Act*. Washington, DC: U.S. G.P.O.

van den Bossche, P., & Zdouc, W. (2013). *The law and policy of the World Trade Organization: Text, cases and materials* (3rd ed.). Cambridge: Cambridge University Press.

van Praag, B. M. S. (2011). Well-being, inequality and reference groups: An agenda for new research. *Journal of Economic Inequality*, (9), 111–127.

Vasconcelos, Á. (Ed.). (2012). *Citizens in an interconnected and polycentric world. Global trends 2030*. Paris: Institute for Security Studies.

Veblen, T. (2009). *The theory of the leisure class: An economic study of institutions*. Oxford: Oxford University Press.

Vicens Vives, J. (1988). *Historia general moderna: Del Renacimiento a la crisis del siglo XX* (2nd ed., 2 Vols, 3rd printing). Barcelona: Vicens Vives.

Vidal Manzanares, G. (2009). *La vida y la época del fundador del PSOE y UGT, Pablo Iglesias*. Madrid: Ediciones Nowtilus.

Vijayan, S. K. (2010). Freud and anaesthesia: The historical link. In *History of medicine on line*. http://www.priory.com/anaesthesia/Freud.htm. Accessed 29 May 2014.

Vinx, L. (2008). *Hans Kelsen's pure theory of law: Legality and legitimacy*. Oxford: Oxford University Press.

Viotti, P. R. (2014). *The dollar and national security: The monetary component of hard power*. Stanford, CA: Stanford University Press.

Viroli, M. (2002). *Jean Jacques Rousseau and the 'Well Ordered Society'*. Cambridge, UK: Cambridge University Press.

von Ihering, R. (1964). *Scherz und Ernst in der Jurisprudenz: Eine Weihnachtsgabe für das juristische Publikum*. Darmstadt: Wissenschaftl Buchges. (Reprint of the 13th edition: Leipzig 1924).

von Ihering, R. (1997). *The struggle for law*. Union, NJ: The Lawbook Exchange LTD. (Reprint of 1915 English edition).

von Ihering, R. (1999). *Law as a means to an end*. Union, NJ: The Lawbook Exchange LTD. (Reprint of 1913 English edition).

Wahrman, D. (2003). The pillar of the social and political order. In *Imagining the middle class: The political representation of class in Britain, c. 1780–1840* (pp. 169–183). Cambridge, UK: Cambridge University Press.

Wasserstrom, J. N. (2013). *China in the 21st century: What everyone needs to know* (2nd ed.). Oxford: Oxford University Press.

Watson, R., & Rappaport, H. (2014). *Capturing the light. A true story of genius, rivalry and the birth of photography*. London: PanMacmillan.

Weber, A. F. (2012). *The growth of cities in the nineteenth century: A study in statistics.* Schweinfurt, Germany: Ulan Press (Reprint of the 1899 ed.).
Weichlein, S. (2011). Nation state, conflict resolution and culture war, 1850–1878. In H. W. Smith (Ed.), *The Oxford handbook of modern German history* (pp. 281–306). Oxford: Oxford University Press.
Weisberg, R. H. (2013). *Vichy Law and the Holocaust in France*. London: Routledge.
West, T. G., & Jeffrey, D. A. (2004). Implementing the theories of modern liberalism: The welfare state. In *The rise and fall of constitutional government in America* (pp. 50–57). Claremont, CA: The Claremont Institute.
West, B. A., & Murphy, F. T. (2010). *A brief history of Australia*. New York: Infobase Publishing.
Whealey, R. H. (2005). *Hitler and Spain: The Nazi role in the Spanish civil war*. Lexington, KY: The University Press of Kentucky.
White, G. E. (2002). *The constitution and the new deal*. Cambridge, MA: Harvard University Press.
Wiesen, S. J. (2010). *Creating the Nazi marketplace: Commerce and consumption in the Third Reich*. Cambridge, MA: Cambridge University Press.
Williams, C. (2010). Cornelius Castoriadis: (1922–1997). In J. Simons (Ed.), From *Agamben to Žižek: Contemporary critical theorists* (pp. 93–109). Edinburgh: Edinburgh University Press.
Winston, B. (2002). *Media, technology and society: A history from the telegraph to the internet.* New York: Taylor & Francis.
Wolin, R. (2003). Herbert Marcuse: From existential Marxism to Left Heideggerianism. In *Heidegger's children: Hannah Arendt, Karl Löwith, Hans Jonas, and Herbert Marcuse* (pp. 134–172). Princeton, NJ: Princeton University Press.
Wood, M. (2012). *Film: A very short introduction*. Oxford: Oxford University Press.
World Health Organization. (2013). *Health risk assessment from the nuclear accident after the 2011 Great East Japan earthquake and tsunami, based on a preliminary dose estimation.* Geneva, Switzerland: WHO.
Worley, M. (2009). *The foundations of the British Labour Party: Identities, cultures and perspectives, 1900–1939*. Farnham, UK: Ashgate.
Wright, G. (1970). *The reshaping of French democracy*. New York: H. Fertig.
Wrigley, E. A. (2004). The great commerce of every civilized society: Urban growth in early modern Europe. In *Poverty, progress, and population* (pp. 268–289). Cambridge, UK: Cambridge University Press.
Wuthnow, R. (2009). Bismarck's contribution to German socialism. In *Communities of discourse: Ideology and social structure in the reformation, the enlightenment, and European socialism* (pp. 377–408). Cambridge, MA: Harvard University Press.
Yeadon, G., & Hawkins, J. (2008). *The Nazi Hydra in America: Suppressed history of a century*. Joshua Tree, CA: Progressive Press.
Zimmerman, W. (2014). From narrow selectorate to autocracy. In *Ruling Russia: authoritarianism from the revolution to Putin* (pp. 75–101). Princeton, NJ: Princeton University Press.
Zubok, V. M. (2007). The Soviet people and Stalin between war and peace: 1945. In *The failed empire: The Soviet Union in the cold war from Stalin to Gorbachev* (pp. 1–28). Chapel Hill, NC: University of North Carolina Press.
Zubok, V. M. (2011). *Zhivago's children: The last Russian intelligentsia*. Cambridge, MA: Belknap Press of Harvard University Press.

## *Further Reading*

Adams, S. (2011). *Castoriadis's ontology: Being and creation*. New York: Fordham University Press.

Adebajo, A. (2010). *The curse of Berlin: Africa after the cold war*. New York: Columbia University Press.
Alexander, R. S. (2012). *Europe's uncertain path: 1814–1914: State formation and civil society*. Malden, MA: Wiley.
Amable, B. (2003). *The diversity of modern capitalism*. Oxford: Oxford University Press.
Aolain, N., Fionnuala, D., & Gross, O. (Eds.). (2013). *Guantánamo and beyond: Exceptional courts and military commissions in comparative perspective*. Cambridge, MA: Cambridge University Press.
Arendt, H. (2010). Totalitarianism. In *The origins of totalitarianism* (pp. 305–482). Memphis: General Books.
Arrighi, G. (1994). *The long twentieth century: Money, power, and the origins of our times*. New York: Verso.
Atkenson, A., & Kehoe, P. J. (2001). *The transition to a new economy after the second industrial revolution*. Cambridge, MA: National Bureau of Economic Research.
Avril, E., & Zumello, C. (Eds.). (2013). *New technology, organizational change, and governance*. New York: Palgrave Macmillan.
Bak, R. (2014). *Henry and Edsel: The creation of the Ford Empire*. Hoboken, NJ: Willey.
Ball, C., & Westhorpe, R. N. (2003). Local anaesthesia: Freud, Koller and cocaine. *Anaesthesia and Intensive Care, 31*(3), 249.
Baume, S. (2012). *Hans Kelsen and the case for democracy*. Colchester, UK: ECPR.
Beauchamp, K. (2001). *History of telegraphy*. London: Institution of Engineering and Technology.
Bell, D. S. (2005). *François Mitterrand: A political biography*. Cambridge, UK: Polity.
Bell, J. (2004). *The liberal state on trial: The cold war and American politics in the Truman years*. New York: Columbia University Press.
Belmonte, L. A. (2008). *Selling the American way: U.S. propaganda and the cold war*. Philadelphia, PA: University of Pennsylvania Press.
Binder, D. (2008). The Christian Corporatist State: Austria from 1934 to 1938. In R. Steininger et al. (Eds.), *Austria in the twentieth century* (pp. 72–84). New Brunswick, NJ: Transaction Publisher.
Blanc, J. J. L. (2005). *The organization of labour*. Farmington Hills, MI: Thomson Gale. (Reprod. of original ed. Translation of: *Organisation du travail*. 1839).
Boix, C., & Svoliks, M. W. (2013). The foundations of limited authoritarian government: Institutions, commitment, and power-sharing in dictatorships. *Journal of Politics, 75*(2), 300–1316.
Block, F., & Evans, P. (2005). The state and the economy. In N. J. Smelser & R. Swedberg (Eds.), *The handbook of economic sociology* (2nd ed., pp. 505–521). Princeton, NJ: Princeton University Press.
Bloxham, D. (2008). *Genocide, the world wars and the unweaving of Europe*. Edgware, UK: Vallentine Mitchell.
Bourg, J. (2004). *After the deluge: New perspectives on the intellectual and cultural history of postwar France*. Lanham, MD: Lexington Books.
Bracken, P. J. (2012). *The second nuclear age: Strategy, danger, and the new power politics*. New York: Henry Holt and Co.
Brzezinski, Z. (2012). *Strategic vision: America and the crisis of global power*. New York: Basic Books.
Brooks, C., & Manza, J. (2006). Why do welfare states persist? *The Journal of Politics, 68*(4), 816–827.
Brown, D. (Ed.). (1998). *Thorstein Veblen in the twenty-first century: A commemoration of the theory of the leisure class (1899–1999)*. Cheltenham, UK: Edward Elgar.
Bruneteau, B. (2003). *"L'Europe nouvelle" de Hitler: une illusion des intellectuels de la France de Vichy*. Monaco: Rocher.
Cannadine, D. (2011). Economy: The growth and fluctuations of the industrial revolution. In *Making history now and then: Discoveries, controversies and explorations* (pp. 83–111). Basingstoke, UK: Palgrave Macmillan.

Cartier, E. (2007). The liberation and the institutional question in France. In A. Knapp (Ed.), *The uncertain foundation: France at the liberation, 1944–1947* (pp. 23–40). Basingstoke, UK: Palgrave Macmillan.
Casetti, F. (2008). *Eye of the century: Film, experience, modernity*. New York: Columbia University Press.
Castoriadis, C. (2010). *A society adrift: Interviews and debates, 1974–1997*. New York: Fordham University Press.
Chadwick, O. (2000). The social problem. In *The secularization of the European mind in the nineteenth century* (pp. 21–141). Cambridge, UK: Cambridge University Press (Reprint).
Chiozza, G., & Goemans, H. E. (2011). *Leaders and international conflict*. Cambridge, UK: Cambridge University Press.
Christie, K. (2008). *United States foreign policy and national identity in the 21st century*. London: Routledge.
Clarke, J. L. (Ed.). (2006). *Armies in homeland security: American and European perspectives*. Washington, DC: National Defense University Press.
Coates, K. (Ed.). (2008). *Obama's Afghan dilemma*. Nottingham, UK: Bertrand Russell Peace Foundation.
Cointet, J.-P. (2008). *Expier Vichy: l'épuration en France (1943–1958)*. Paris: Perrin.
comte de Saint-Simon, C. -H. (1976). *The political thought of Saint-Simon*. Oxford: Oxford University Press.
comte de Saint-Simon, C. -H. (1998). *Henri comte de Saint-Simon (1760–1825): Selected writings*. New Delhi, India: Deep & Deep.
Conway, M. (2004). The rise and fall of Western Europe's Democratic Age, 1945–1973. *Contemporary European History, 13*(01), 67–88.
Cooke, J. G., & Morrison, J. S. (2009). *U.S. Africa policy beyond the Bush years: Critical challenges for the Obama administration*. Washington, DC: CSIS Press.
Cruz, J. (2011). Bourgeois culture and modernity. In *The rise of middle-class culture in nineteenth-century Spain* (pp. 1–19). Baton Rouge, LA: Louisiana State University Press.
Dahrendorf, R. (2001). *Class and class conflicts in industrial society*. Stanford, CA; Stanford University Press (Reprint).
Damodaran, H. (2008). *India's new capitalists: Caste, business and industry in a modern nation*. New Delhi, India: Permanent Black.
Darlington, R. (2008). State and revolution. In *Syndicalism and the transition to communism: An international comparative study* (pp. 247–265). Aldershot, UK: Ashgate.
Davies, P., & Lynch, D. J. (2005). *The Routledge companion to fascism and the far right*. London: Routledge.
Davis, A. (2004). Marcuse's legacies. In J. Abromeit & C. Mark (Eds.), *Herbert Marcuse: A critical reader* (pp. 43–50). London: Routledge.
Dean, M. (2010). Authoritarian governmentality. In *Governmentality: Power and rule in modern society* (2nd ed., pp. 155–174). London: Sage.
De Meneses, F. R. (2010). *Salazar: A political biography*. New York: Enigma.
Derrida, J. (2002). Force of law: The "Mystical Foundation of Authority". In G. Anidjar (Ed.), *Acts of religion* (pp. 230–298). New York: Routledge.
Domenach, J.-L. (2012). *China's uncertain future*. New York: Columbia University Press.
Dorrien, G. J. (2012). *The Obama question: A progressive perspective*. Lanham, UK: Rowman & Littlefield.
Engelhardt, T. (2010). *The American way of war: How Bush's wars became Obama's*. Chicago, IL: Haymarket Books.
Epstein, R. A. (2011). Where natural law and utilitarianism diverge. In *Design for liberty: Private property, public administration, and the rule of law* (pp. 55–65). Cambridge, MA: Harvard University Press.
Evans, H. J. S. (2010). "The Path to Freedom"?: Transocean and German Wireless Telegraphy, 1914–1922. *Historical Social Research (Historische Sozialforschung), 35*(1), 209–233.
Finaldi, G. (2013). *Mussolini and Italian fascism*. London: Routledge.

Fisher, L. (2008). *The constitution and 9/11: Recurring threats to America's freedoms*. Lawrence, KS: University Press of Kansas.

Forbes, J. (2001). *Contemporary France: Essays and texts on politics, economics, and society* (2nd ed.). Harlow, UK: Longman.

Freeman, C., & Louça, F. (2002). *As time goes by: From the industrial revolutions to the information revolution*. Oxford, UK: Oxford University Press.

Friedman, T. L. (2010). *The world is flat: A brief history of the twenty-first century*. Bridgewater, NJ: Paw Prints.

Garrick, J. (Ed.). (2012). *Law and policy for China's market socialism*. New York: Routledge.

Gaus, G. F. (2011). *The order of public reason: A theory of freedom and morality in a diverse and bounded world*. Cambridge, MA: Cambridge University Press.

Gay, P. (2002). Fundamentals: Bourgeoisie(s). In *Schnitzler's century: The making of middle-class culture, 1815–1914* (pp. 3–34). London: Allen Lane.

Gellately, R. (2013). *Stalin's curse: Battling for communism in war and cold war*. Oxford: Oxford University Press.

Gerring, J., Bond, P., Barndt, W. T. and Moreno C. (2005). Democracy and economic growth: A historical perspective. *World Politics, 57*(4), 323–364.

Gerson, G. (2004). Liberalism and modernity, and a complex heritage. In *Margins of disorder: New liberalism and the crisis of European consciousness* (pp. 1–7 and 19–24). Albany, NY: State University of New York Press.

Getzler, J. (2004). Law, history, and the social sciences: Intellectual traditions of late nineteenth- and early twentieth-century Europe. In A. Lewis & M. Lobban (Eds.), *Law and history* (pp. 215–265). Oxford: Oxford University Press.

Geyer, M., & Fitzpatrick, S. (Eds.). (2009). *Beyond totalitarianism: Stalinism and Nazism compared*. Cambridge, MA: Cambridge University Press.

Gladstone, D. (1999). *The twentieth century welfare state*. London: St. Martin's Press.

Goldhagen, D. J. (2013). *Hitler's willing executioners: Ordinary Germans and the Holocaust*. New York: Vintage Books.

Gordon, R. I. (2009). *The grapes of wrath: An opera in three acts*. New York: Carl Fischer.

Grachev, A. (2008). *Gorbachev's Gamble: Soviet foreign policy and the end of the cold war*. Malden, MA: Polity.

Griffin, R. (2007). The fascist regime as a modernist state. In *Modernism and fascism: The sense of a beginning under Mussolini and Hitler* (pp. 219–249). London: Palgrave Macmillan.

Grosvenor, E. S., & Wesson, M. (1997). *Alexander Graham Bell: The life and times of the man who invented the telephone*. London: Harry N. Abrams.

Gunn, S., & Bell, R. (2003). Creating a middle-class culture in the late nineteenth century. In *Middle classes: Their rise and sprawl* (pp. 21–57). Phoenix, AZ: Orion Books.

Gunn, S., & Bell, R. (2000). *The public culture of the Victorian middle class: Ritual and authority in the English industrial city, 1840–1914*. Manchester, UK: Manchester University Press.

Habermas, J. (2007). *The structural transformation of the public sphere: An inquiry into a category of Bourgeois society*. Cambridge, UK: Polity.

Halfin, I. (2000). *From darkness to light: Class, consciousness, and salvation in revolutionary Russia*. Pittsburgh, PA: University of Pittsburgh Press.

Hanagan, M., & Stephenson, C. (1986). *Confrontation, class consciousness, and the labor process: Studies in proletarian class formation*. New York: Greenwood.

Hart, C. W. (2010). *Barack Obama*. Oxford: Macmillan.

Headrick, D. (2009). *Technology: A world history*. Oxford: Oxford University Press.

Heavilin, B. A. (2002). *John Steinbeck's the grapes of wrath: A reference guide*. London: Greenwood.

Hermann, W., & Linn, J. F. (Eds.). (2012). *Central Asia and the Caucasus: At the crossroads of Eurasia in the 21st century*. Thousand Oaks, CA: Sage publications.

Hiott, A. (2013). *Thinking small: The long, strange trip of the Volkswagen beetle*. New York: Ballantine Books.

Horowitz, S. (2013). *Friendship and politics in post-revolutionary France*. University Park, PA: Penn State University Press.

Hunt, T. (2010). *The frock-coated communist: The revolutionary life of Friedrich Engels*. London: Penguin.

Iglesias, J. D., et al. (Eds.). (2013). *New nation-states and national minorities*. Colchester, UK: ECPR Press.

Ikenberry, G. J. (2011). *Liberal leviathan: The origins, crisis, and transformation of the American world order*. Princeton, NJ: Princeton University Press.

Inbar, E. (2013). *The Arab spring, democracy and security: Domestic and international ramifications*. London: Routledge.

Jackson, J., et al. (Eds.). (2011). *May 68: Rethinking France's last revolution*. Basingstoke, UK: Palgrave Macmillan.

Jacobson, A. J., & Schlink, B. (Eds.). (2000). *Weimar: A jurisprudence of crisis*. Berkeley, CA: University of California Press.

Judt, T. (2011). *Past imperfect: French intellectuals, 1944–1956*. New York: New York University Press.

Kautsky, K. (2011). *The labour revolution*. London: Routledge.

Kegley, C. W., & Blanton, S. L. (2012). *World politics: Trends and transformations*. Boston, MA: Wadsworth Cengage Learning.

King, D., & Lieberman, R. C. (2009). American state building: The theoretical challenge. In L. Jacobs & D. King (Eds.), *The unsustainable American state* (pp. 299–322). Oxford: Oxford University Press.

Klooster, J. (2009). *Castoriadis: Psyche, society, autonomy*. Leiden: Brill.

Koppelman, A. (2013). *The tough luck constitution and the assault on health care reform*. Oxford: Oxford University Press.

Kuhne, T. (2013). *Belonging and genocide: Hitler's community, 1918–1945*. New Haven, CT: Yale University Press.

Landes, D. (2003). *The unbound prometheus: Technical change and industrial development in Western Europe from 1750 to the present* (2nd ed.). Cambridge, MA: Cambridge University Press.

Lansford, T. (2012). *9/11 and the wars in Afghanistan and Iraq: A chronology and reference guide*. Santa Barbara, CA: ABC-CLIO.

Langewiesche, D. (1993). Liberalism and the middle classes in Europe. In J. Kocka & A. Mitchell (Eds.), *Bourgeois society in nineteenth-century Europe* (pp. 40–69). Providence: Berg.

Laub, T. J. (2010). *After the fall: German policy in occupied France, 1940–1944*. Oxford: Oxford University Press.

Layton, G. (2005). *Weimar and the rise of Nazi Germany: 1918–1933* (3rd ed.). London: Hodder Murray.

Leffler, M. P., & Legro, J. W. (Eds.). (2008). *To lead the world: American strategy after the Bush doctrine*. Oxford: Oxford University Press.

Lindert, P. H. (2007). *Growing public: Social spending and economic growth since the eighteenth century*. Cambridge, UK: Cambridge University Press (Reprint).

Linz, J. J. (2000). *Totalitarian and authoritarian regimes*. Boulder, CO: Lynne Rienner.

Lucassen, J. (2006). Writing global labour history *c.* 1800–1940: A historiography of concepts, periods, and geographical scope. In *Global labour history: A state of art* (pp. 39–90). Berna: Peter Lang.

Luckacs, J. (2005). Misuse and misreading of totalitarianism. In *Democracy and populism: Fear & hatred* (pp. 126–130). New Haven, CT: Yale University Press.

Lundestad, G. (2013). How (not) to study the origins of the cold war. In O. A. Westad (Ed.), *Reviewing the cold war: Approaches, interpretations, theory* (pp. 64–80). Hoboken, NJ: Taylor and Francis.

Lvi-Valensi, J. (Ed.). (2006). *Camus at combat: writing 1944–1947*. Princeton, NJ: Princeton University Press.

MacCormick, N. (2007). *Institutions of law: An essay in legal theory (law, state, and practical reason)*. Oxford: Oxford University Press.
MacDonough, F. (2001). *Conflict, communism and fascism: Europe 1890–1945*. Cambridge, MA: Cambridge University Press.
Macgilvray, E. (2004). *Reconstructing public reason*. Cambridge, MA: Harvard University Press.
Marcuse, H., & Aron, R. (1972). Can communism be liberal? *The New Statesman*, (23), 860–861 (London, 23 June 1972).
Mason, D. S. (2009). *The end of the American century*. Lanham, UK: Rowman & Littlefield.
McCaffrey, J. M. (2009). *Inside the Spanish-American War: A history based on first-person accounts*. London: McFarland & Co.
McCormack, J. (2007). *Collective memory: France and the Algerian war (1954–1962)*. Lanham, MD: Lexington Books.
McPhee, P. (2004). *A social history of France, 1789–1914* (2nd ed.). New York: Palgrave Macmillan.
Melucci, A. (1996). *Challenging codes: Collective action in the information age*. Cambridge, UK: Cambridge University Press.
Miles, M. (2012). *Herbert Marcuse: An aesthetics of liberation*. London: Pluto Press.
Miles, A., & Vincent, D. (1993). *Building European Society: Occupational change and social mobility in Europe, 1840–1940*. Manchester, UK: Manchester University Press.
Moran, R. (2002). *Executioner's current: Thomas Edison, George Westinghouse, and the invention of the electric chair*. New York: Vintage Books.
Morgan, I. W. (2009). *The age of deficits: Presidents and unbalanced budgets from Jimmy Carter to George W. Bush*. Lawrence, KA: University Press of Kansas.
Murphy, C. (2007). *Are we Rome?: The fall of an empire and the fate of America*. Boston, MA: Houghton Mifflin Co.
Murray, D., & Brown, D. (Eds.). (2012). *Multipolarity in the 21st century: A new world order*. New York: Routledge.
Mussolini, B. (2008). *My autobiography*. Whitefish, MO: Kessinger Publishing.
Natella, A. A. (2011). *International relations in the post-industrial era: Rephrasing the third world*. New York: Palgrave Macmillan.
Nester, W. R. (2010). *Globalization; A short history of the modern world*. Basingstoke, UK: Palgrave Macmillan.
Nojeim, M. J., & Kilroy, D. P. (2011). *Days of decision: Turning points in U.S. foreign policy*. Washington, DC: Potomac Books.
Offner, A. A. (2002). *Another such victory: President Truman and the cold war, 1945–1953*. Stanford, CA: Stanford University Press.
Parsons, C. (2003). *A certain idea of Europe*. Ithaca, NY: Cornell University Press.
Patten, C. (2006). *Cousins and strangers: America, Britain, and Europe in a new century*. New York: Times Books.
Pedersen, S. (1993). *Family, dependence, and the origins of the welfare state: Britain and France, 1914–1945*. Cambridge, UK: Cambridge University Press.
Perry, M. (2013). The authoritarian and totalitarian states. In *Western civilization: A brief history* (10th ed., pp. 400–506) Boston, MA: Wadsworth Cengage Learning.
Persson, T., & Tabellini, G. (2006). *The economic effects of constitutions*. Cambridge, UK: The MIT Press.
Pilbeam, P. (1990). *The middle classes in Europe : 1789–1914: France, Germany, Italy and Russia*. Basingstoke, UK: Macmillan Education.
Pinto, A. C. (1996). *Salazar's dictatorship and European fascism: Problems of interpretation*. New York: Columbia University Press.
Potts, L. (1990). *The world labour market: A history of migration*. London: Zed Books.
Powrie, P. (Ed.). (2006). *The cinema of France*. New York: Wallflower.
Prunier, G. (2008). *Darfur: A 21st century genocide* (3rd ed.). Ithaca, NY: Cornell University Press.

Rachman, G. (2011). *Zero-sum future: American power in an age of anxiety*. New York: Simon & Schuster.

Ramsden, J. (1995). *The Age of Churchill and Eden: 1940–1957*. London: Longman.

Rees, G. (2001). *The great slump: Capitalism in crisis 1929–1933*. London: House of Stratus.

Reuter, D., & Yoo, J. (Eds.). (2011). *Confronting terror: 9/11 and the future of American national security*. New York: Encounter Book.

Riding, A. (2010). *And the show went on: Cultural life in Nazi-occupied Paris*. New York: Alfred A. Knopf.

Rosen, W. (2012). *The most powerful idea in the world: A story of steam, industry, and invention*. Chicago, IL: University of Chicago Press.

Ruppert, B. (2010). *The formative debates and arguments sustaining Germany's constitutional supranationalism: A rhetorical history of political and economic ideas*. Lewiston, NY: Edwin Mellen Press.

Santos-Dumont, A. (2002). *My airships: The story of my life*. Honolulu, HI: University Press of the Pacific.

Sarat, A. (Ed.). (2004). *The Blackwell companion to law and society*. Malden, MA: Blackwell.

Sartori, G. (2002). *Comparative constitutional engineering: An inquiry into structures, incentives and outcomes* (2nd ed.). Basingstoke, UK: Palgrave Macmillan.

Savage, C. (2008). The politics of presidential power. In *Takeover: The return of the imperial presidency and the subversion of American democracy* (pp. 308–329). New York: Back Bay Books.

Sawyer, S. W. (2012). Louis Blanc's theory of the liberal democratic state. *The Tocqueville Review (La revue Tocqueville), 33*(2), 141–163.

Schama, S. (2008). *The American future: A history from the founding fathers to Barack Obama*. London: Vintage.

Schmidt, D. E. (2005). *The folly of war: American foreign policy, 1898–2004*. New York: Algora Publishing.

Scott, T. (2014). *Anonymous agencies, backstreet businesses, and covert collectives rethinking organizations in the 21st century*. Stanford, CA: Stanford University Press.

Service, R. (2010). *Comrades!: A history of world communism*. Cambridge, MA: Harvard University Press.

Shields, J. (2007). *The extreme right in France: From Pain to Le Pen*. London: Routledge.

Shorten, R. (2012). *Modernism and totalitarianism: Rethinking the intellectual sources of Nazism and Stalinism, 1945 to the present*. Basingstoke, UK: Palgrave Macmillan.

Silver, B. J. (2003). *Forces of labor: Workers' movements and globalization since 1870*. Cambridge, UK: Cambridge University Press.

Skocpol, T. (1996). *States, social knowledge, and the origins of modern social policies*. Princeton, NJ: Princeton University Press.

Smith, A. D. (2013). *Nationalism: Theory, ideology, history*. Malden, MA: Polity.

Stavrianakis, A., & Selby, J. (Eds.). (2012). *Militarism and international relations: Political economy, security and theory*. New York: Routledge.

Steinweis, A. D., & Rachlin, R. D. (Eds.). (2013). *The law in Nazi Germany: Ideology, opportunism, and the perversion of justice*. New York: Berghahn Books.

Stoetzler, M. (2008). *The state, the nation, & the Jews: Liberalism and the antisemitism dispute in Bismarck's Germany*. Lincoln, NE: University of Nebraska Press.

Sutton, M. (2007). *France and the construction of Europe, 1944–2007: The geopolitical imperative*. New York: Berghahn Book.

Sykes, A. (2005). *The radical right in Britain: Social imperialism to the BNP*. Basingstoke, UK: Palgrave Macmillan.

Szabo, S. F. (2004). *Parting ways: The crisis in German-American relations*. Washington, DC: Brookings Institution Press.

Tarrow, S. (2002). The birth of the modern social movement. In *Power in movement* (2nd ed., pp. 27–29). Cambridge, MA: Cambridge University Press (Reprint).

Thalakada, N. (2012). *Unipolarity and the evolution of America's cold war alliances*. New York: Palgrave Macmillan.

Thompson, E. P. (1995). Class and class struggle. In P. Joyce (Ed.), *Class* (pp. 133–141). Oxford: Oxford University Press.

Tilly, C. (2004). *Contention and democracy in Europe, 1650–2000*. Cambridge, UK: Cambridge University Press.

Tilly, C. (2006). *Social movements: 1768–2004*. London: Paradigm.

Tuck, S. G. N. (2010). *We ain't what we ought to be: The black freedom struggle from emancipation to Obama*. Cambridge, MA: Belknap Press of Harvard University Press.

Turner, R. S. (2011). *Neo-liberal ideology: History, concepts and policies*. Edinburgh, Scotland: Edinburgh University Press.

Veblen, T. (2011). *Essential writings of Thorstein Veblen*. London: Routledge.

Vinen, R. (2010). *A history in fragments: Europe in the twentieth century*. London: Hachette UK.

Vinen, R. (2002). *Bourgeois politics in France, 1945–1951*. Cambridge, UK: Cambridge University Press.

Wakeman, R. (2009). *The heroic city: Paris, 1945–1958*. Chicago, IL: The University of Chicago Press.

Warikoo, K. (2007). *Afghanistan: The challenge*. New Delhi, India: Pentagon Press.

Warren, A. (2013). *The Obama administration's nuclear weapon strategy: The promises of Prague*. New York: Routledge.

Weatherley, R. (2006). *Politics in China since 1949: Legitimizing authoritarian rule*. London: Routledge.

Wieviorka, O. (2012). The work of the provisional government of the French Republic (1944–1946). In *Divided memory: French recollections of World War II from the Liberation to the present* (pp. 10–35). Stanford, CA: Stanford University Press.

Winkler, A. M. (2012). *Home front U.S.A.: America during World War II* (3rd ed.). Wheeling, IL: Harlan Davidson.

Winkler, A. M. (2011). *The cold war: A history in documents* (2nd ed.). New York: Oxford University Press.

Winkler, A. M. (2006). *Franklin D. Roosevelt and the making of modern America*. New York: Pearson/Longman.

Wu, G. (2005). *The anatomy of political power in China*. Singapore: National University of Singapore.

Yu, P. K.-H. (2012). *International governance and regimes: A Chinese perspective*. London: Routledge.

# Part V
# The End of the Nation State?

# Chapter 18
# The Crisis of the Nation-State in the Era of European Integration

For amongst democratic nations *each generation is a new people*—Alexis de Tocqueville (1805–1859)[1]

(. . .) the situation in which Europe finds itself today is similar to that of twenty-six people of a dubious moral and intellectual level who are living in a very small space and armed to the teeth with toxic poisons, bombs, guns and daggers. All of those who have declined are seeking to enrich themselves at the expense of the others. Spurred by hatred and jealousy, the desire for revenge and envy, they engage in conspiracies, crafting weapons, training with them, and insulting each other, in public and in private, in the most offensive manner. For no price are they willing to renounce what they conceive, wrongly, as freedom. Thus, they prefer a system of absolute anarchy to any organization, determined to settle their opposing interests or their differences of opinion by means of duels or struggles before choosing the path of Justice.—Richard N. Coudenhove-Kalergi (1894–1972)[2]

If Europe were once united in the sharing of its common inheritance, there would be no limit to the happiness, to the prosperity and glory which its three or four hundred million people would enjoy [. . .] We must build a kind of United States of Europe.—Winston Churchill (1874–1965)[3]

And we know – God knows we know! – that there is a different conception of a European federation under which, in accord with the dreams of those who have conceived it, the countries would lose their national personality and in which . . . they would be governed by some technocratic, stateless and unaccountable Ares Rock.—Charles de Gaulle (1890–1970)[4]

Above all, we must love Europe; our Europe, sonorous with the roaring laughter of Rabelais, luminous with the smile of Erasmus, sparkling with the wit of Voltaire; in whose

1 Dans les démocraties, chaque génération est un peuple nouveau (de Tocqueville 1982, 152).

2 Coudenhove-Kalergi (1926, 85).

3 Zurich Speech, September 19, 1946 (Churchill 2013a, 427–430).

4 *"Or on sait –Dieu si on le sait!- qu'il y a une conception différente au sujet d'une fédération européenne dans laquelle, suivant les rêves de ceux qui l'ont conçue, les pays perdraient leur personnalité nationale et où [. . .] ils seraient régis par quelque aéropage technocratique, apatride et irresponsable"*. From a press conference at the Élysée Palace, September 9, 1965. (Edward and Lane 2013, 9, n. 19).



B. Aguilera-Barchet, *A History of Western Public Law*,
DOI 10.1007/978-3-319-11803-1_18

mental skies shine the fiery eyes of Dante, the clear eyes of Shakespeare, the serene eyes of Goethe, the tormented eyes of Dostoyevski; this Europe for whom La Gioconda forever smiles, where Moses and David spring to perennial life from Michelangelo's marble, and Bach's genius rises spontaneous to be caught in his intellectual geometry; where Hamlet seeks in thought the mystery of his inaction, and Faust seeks in action comfort for the void in his thought; where Don Juan seeks in women the woman never found, and Don Quixote, spear in hand, gallops to force reality to rise above itself; this Europe where Newton and Leibniz measure the infinitesimal, and whose Cathedrals, as Musset once wrote, pray on their knees in their robes of stone; where rivers, silver threads, link together strings of cities, jewels wrought in the crystal of space by the chisel of time . . . this Europe must be born. And she will, when Spaniards will say "our Chartres", Englishmen "our Krakow", Italians "our Copenhagen;" when Germans say "our Bruges", and step back horrorstricken at the idea of laying murderous hands on it. Then will Europe live, for then it will be that the Spirit that leads History will have uttered the creative words: FIAT EUROPA![5]—Salvador de Madariaga (1886–1978).

## Contents


18.1 The Precedents for European Integration ........ 650
18.1.1 The Survival of the Universal Model ........ 650
18.1.2 "Composite Monarchies" as a Prime Example of Unions of States in Europe 652
18.1.3 Assembly-Based Integration: The Singular Case of the Swiss Confederation ........ 657
18.1.4 Westphalia's Peace and the Triumph of the Europe of States ........ 662
18.1.5 Europe Between Imperialism and Coordination: 1789 to 1914 ........ 663
18.2 The Idea of Europe from 1918 to 1939 ........ 664
18.2.1 Europe Lies in Ruins, at the Mercy of the United States and the Soviet Union ........ 664
18.2.2 The Resurgence of Nationalisms and Disunity in Europe ........ 665
18.2.3 Some Attempts at Integration ........ 667


[5] From the Closing Speech at The Hague Congress (1948) (de Madariaga 1967, 3–4). Text in Spanish: "*Ante todo amemos a Europa, nuestra Europa sonora de las carcajadas de Rabelais, luminosa de la sonrisa de Erasmo, chispeante del ingenio de Voltaire, en cuyos cielos mentales brillan los ojos fogosos de Dante, los claros ojos de Shakespeare, los ojos serenos de Goethe, los ojos atormentados de Dostoievski; esta Europa a la que siempre sonríe la Gioconda, y en la que Moisés y David surgen a la vida perenne del mármol de Miguel Ángel, y el genio de Bach se alza espontáneamente en los aires de la melodía para quedar captado en su geometría intelectual; donde Hamlet busca en el pensamiento el misterio de su inacción y Fausto busca en la acción el consuelo al vació de la mujer que nunca encuentra, y Don Quijote, lanza en ristre, galopa para obligar a la realidad a alzarse sobre sí misma; esta Europa en donde Newton y Leibniz miden lo infinitesimal, y las catedrales como dijo inmortalmente Musset, rezan de rodillas en sus trajes de piedra; donde los ríos, hilos de plata, hacen rosarios de ciudades, joyeles cincelados en el cristal del espacio por el buril del tiempo... Esta Europa tiene que nacer. Y nacerá cuando los españoles digan "nuestro Chartres", y los ingleses "nuestra Cracovia", y los italianos "nuestra Copenhague"; y cuando los alemanes digan "nuestra Brujas" y retrocedan de horror a la mera idea de poner sobre ella manos asesinas. Entonces Europa vivirá, porque entonces, el Espíritu que guía la Historia habrá pronunciado las palabras creadoras. FIAT EUROPA!*" (de Madariaga 2011, 46–47).

18.3 European Integration During World War II ... 672
18.3.1 The Franco-British Union (June 1940) ... 672
18.3.2 Hitlerian Europe ... 673
18.3.3 The "Integrationist" Idea in Anti-Hitlerian Europe ... 674
18.4 European Integration During the Post-War Period (1945–1949) ... 677
18.4.1 Europe in 1945 ... 677
18.4.2 A First, Unsuccessful Attempt at Integration: The Congress of The Hague (1948), and the Failure to Form a Federal Europe ... 681
18.5 Step by Step Integration: The Invention of the "Community Method" (1950) ... 684
18.5.1 The Pioneers: Jean Monnet and Robert Schuman ... 684
18.5.2 The Schuman Declaration of May 9, 1950 ... 687
18.6 From the European Coal and Steel Community to the European Economic Community (1951–1957) ... 689
18.6.1 The 1951 Treaty of Paris and the Creation of the ECSC ... 689
18.6.2 From the Failure of the EDC to the Treaties of Rome (1951–1957) ... 690
18.7 The Extension of the Community Method to Create a Common European Market, and the Institutionalization of European Integration (1957–1965) ... 691
18.7.1 The Court of Justice of the European Communities and the European Parliament ... 691
18.7.2 The European Free Trade Association: A British "Tantrum" ... 692
18.7.3 The Merging of Community Executives ... 692
18.8 A Step Back in the Integration Process: A Return to the Intergovernmental Method (1966–1986) ... 693
18.8.1 The Rejection of Qualified Majority Voting and the Return of Unanimity: The Luxembourg Compromise ... 693
18.8.2 On the Path Towards Expansion ... 693
18.8.3 The Democratization of the Integration Process: An Elective European Parliament ... 694
18.9 Returning to the Community Method: From the Single European Act to the Maastricht Treaty (1986–1992) ... 694
18.9.1 The Schengen Agreement ... 695
18.9.2 The Single European Act ... 695
18.10 Combining the Community and the Intergovernmental Methods: From the Europe of Communities to the European Union (1992–2009) ... 695
18.10.1 The Maastricht Treaty and the Appearance of the Structured Integration Pillar ... 696
18.10.2 Towards an Economic and Monetary Union: The Euro as a Common Currency ... 697
18.10.3 Many New Members ... 698
18.10.4 The Need to Reorganize the EU: From Amsterdam to Lisbon ... 698
18.11 The EU of the Twenty-First Century ... 699
18.11.1 The Lisbon Treaty ... 699
18.11.2 A Legally Complex Integration ... 700
18.12 A Provisional Conclusion for an Unfinished Process: What Kind of Integration Are Europeans Looking For? ... 702
References ... 711

## 18.1 The Precedents for European Integration

We tend to think that Europe has been traditionally characterized by its diversity rather than its unity, and this conception is not entirely false. As we have seen, since the fall of Rome, the barbaric invasions, and the creation of the Germanic kingdoms, Europe has never truly been politically unified. Nevertheless, most of today's European countries have a common past. We should not overlook or underestimate the fact that for long periods of their history Europeans have shared similar ideas and institutions.

In this book thus far, we have seen how over the course of their history European nations and states developed a particular system of public law based upon a common heritage, despite the diversity of the different nation-state models on the Continent. In this chapter, we shall see how prior to the post-War era Europe's nation-states made different attempts at alliance, but with limited success, and only in specific geographical areas. It would not be not until after World War II that, for the first time in their history, European nation-states understood that they had to unite to survive in a global world. The problem was how to do so.

### *18.1.1 The Survival of the Universal Model*

After the fall of the Western Roman Empire, the aspiration for European unity survived, to an extent. As we have seen, despite the formation of "national" kingdoms, following the Germanic invasions, popes, and emperors sought to uphold the idea that all Christendom—in this period essentially limited to modern-day Europe—formed a common community bound together by its faith.

Even if this conception was more theoretical than real because of the pronounced divisions inherent to feudalism, the idea of a universal empire controlled by the pope as head of the Catholic (universal) church and an emperor marked Europe until 1648. While there were a number of different kingdoms, their kings considered the emperor, and especially the Roman pontiff, a kind of spiritual or symbolic leader. Charles V (1519–1558) made the last notable attempt to unify the continent under the symbolic authority of the Holy Roman Empire. This universal idea of Europe had important consequences in the legal field, as from 1100 until 1800 Europeans shared a *ius commune* based on roman, canon and feudal law (Bellomo 1995, xi), a common jurisprudence studied in the different European universities, attended by students and staffed by professors from across the Continent, where instruction was carried out in Latin, the common language of the time.

Lutheran reform dashed the idea of a universal community and split Europe into two, pitting Catholics and Protestants against each other in a series of bloody religious wars, which ended in 1648 with the Peace of Westphalia.[6] From the perspective of constitutional history, the most important consequence of the Westphalia Treaty was that henceforward Europe became a set of competing states seeking to establish their ascendancy (Treasure 2003, 161–192). The ultimate result was that European history was marred by a succession of wars between the different European states. Spain lost the supremacy it gained with Philip II in 1559 through the Pyrenees Treaty (1659), while France's decline began at Utrecht (1713), leading to the United Kingdom's predominance as the leading European power until the end of World War I.

Despite the Westphalia Treaty, the universalist model was not entirely lost, enduring and shaping history as the institution of the state developed, drawing, as we have seen, a more or less continuous line that transformed Western public law, from the territorial monarchies of the Late Middle Ages, through the era of absolute monarchy, both classic and enlightened, until the consolidation of Britain's parliamentary monarchy, the decline of absolutism and the triumph of the nation-state model, the American Revolution and France's assembly-based republic, and the return of strong Executives in the form of the American presidential Republic and Napoleonic monarchy. Moreover, the Holy Roman Empire—German's first Reich—was not officially abolished until the year 1806.

Even after the Holy Roman Empire disappeared, the imperial idea did not.[7] Spain's Philip II (1556–1598), meanwhile, though not elected emperor, came to head a "universal" monarchy claiming possessions all around the world, forming an entity that would be termed the "Spanish Empire", which lasted until 1898. From 1804 to 1815, Napoleon ruled as "Emperor of the French", as did his nephew Louis Napoleon, better known as Napoléon III (1852–1870). Queen Victoria (1837–1901), a symbol of the apogee of the British Empire, was formally the "Empress" of India, and even Bismarck, to avenge the humiliations which Napoleon had inflicted on the Prussians, founded in 1871 the German Empire (*Deutsches Reich*, or II Reich) precisely in the Palace of Versailles, imposing conditions on a defeated and humiliated France.[8]

---

[6] As White (2007, 142–143) points out, the importance of the Treaty of Westphalia lies in the fact that it curtailed and eventually brought to an end the ruling classes' practice of waging a series of wars that were essentially family feuds. Henceforth war had to be justified on behalf of state-based rather than familial interests. The Treaties of 1648 also laid down the foundations of modern international practices such as the establishment of diplomatic ties between states rather than between their royal families, and alliances and rules for war and peace which drew upon many of the ideas advanced by Hugo Grotius with regards to "just war", according to whom justifiable causes of war included "defense, the obtaining of that which belongs to us or is our due, and, finally, the inflicting of punishments" (Grotius 2012, 61–68). Also quoted in van Nifterik (2009, 407) and Blom (2005, 121–147).

[7] For an overview of the difficulties involved in a comparative historiographical approach to imperial polities, see Reynolds (2012, 151–166).

[8] As Howe (2002, 13) points out, the terms "empire" and "imperialism", in their most general use, have been used to refer to any and every type of relationship between a more powerful state or society and a less powerful one.

Half a century later this destructive dynamic of revenge and resentment would spur the French, victorious in World War I, to humiliate the vanquished Germans at the Peace of Versailles, forcing them to sign a treaty in which they had had no say, and to do so (by no means coincidentally) at Versailles once again, in Louis XIV's Hall of Mirrors. The Germans' tragically inevitable revenge, of course, was meted out by Adolf Hitler who, defying the dictates of Versailles, built up the Third Reich in 1933, going on to lead a maniacal quest to crush France and establish a new German-led world order.

Precisely because this imperialist, nation-based model of Europe ended up generating a series of self-destructive wars, by the middle of the twentieth century, the need became clear for a framework that would unite its different nation-states and prevent any state from imposing itself upon all others. Though a united Europe for a long time proved impossible, it is worth noting there were some attempts to integrate different kingdoms into single entities. We have to remember the case of the "composite monarchies": independent European kingdoms that had shared the same sovereign while maintaining their independence, their own laws, and political institutions, such as the United Kingdom, the Crown of Aragon, and the Spanish Catholic Monarchy. Far from being an isolated invention, this was actually quite a common formula of political organization in modern European history (Piña Homs 2007, 335).[9]

Also, worthy of note is the Swiss Confederation, a group of small states (cantons) that were able to retain their independence, remaining outside the Holy Roman Empire by forming a league. Composite monarchies and the Helvetic Confederation are interesting precedents of how independent states in European history were able to maintain their own legal and constitutional peculiarities while acting in concert with other states.

### *18.1.2 "Composite Monarchies" as a Prime Example of Unions of States in Europe*

The transition from the feudal stage to the territorial monarchies of the Late Middle Ages was characterized, as we have seen, by kings' efforts to amass the greatest possible expanses of land for their kingdoms. In some cases (Castile & León, for example), the territories ended up unified into a single political and legal entity. In others, however, each territory maintained its political and legal autonomy despite recognizing and respecting the same sovereign; these were composite monarchies.[10]

[9] The author mentions as other cases the Polish-Lithuanian Federation, the German Hanseatic League, and Scandinavia's Kalmar Union.

[10] For an overview of the history of composite monarchies in European constitutional history, see Elliot (2009, 3–24).

Such was the case with the Crown of Aragon, which annexed the kingdoms of Aragon, Valencia, Mallorca and the Principality of Catalonia, in addition to a series of Mediterranean territories like Sicily, Sardinia, Naples and Athens (Bisson 2002, 2). The same was true of Spain's Catholic Monarchy which, in addition to its Iberian kingdoms, held the Crowns of Aragon and Castile (the latter including Navarre, the Canary Islands, the American colonies and a series of islands in the Pacific), and, as of 1580, Portugal and its entire colonial empire, claiming a number of territories across Europe, such as the Netherlands, the Franche-Comté, Luxembourg, and much of the Italian Peninsula (Naples, Sicily and Lombardy).

#### 18.1.2.1 From the Crown of Aragon to the Spanish Catholic Monarchy

The origin of the "Crown of Aragón" was the 1137 marriage between the Count of Barcelona, Ramon Berenguer IV, and Petronila, the daughter and heiress of Ramiro II of Aragon. This union enabled their son, Alfonso II of Aragon (1164–1196) to become both the King of Aragon and the Count of Barcelona. However, the Crown's definitive structure would be set by Jaime I, who, after reconquering the Kingdom of Valencia in 1238, rather than distributing it between the Aragon and Catalonia, converted it into an independent Kingdom. This paved the way for the subsequent incorporation of the Kingdom of Sicily at the end of the thirteenth century, the Kingdom of Mallorca in the mid-fourteenth century, and the Kingdom of Naples in the first half of the fifteenth century, among other Mediterranean territories.

All these kingdoms conserved their "constitutional" and legal autonomy even while recognizing the same king. In this way, they formed a kind of "confederation of states"[11] according to which the monarch was to respect the traditional privileges of each of the kingdoms and to convoke their respective estate-based assemblies, or *cortes*. The model was decidedly flexible and easily allowed for the incorporation of new states. It was, however, problematic in terms of facilitating effective and efficient government and administration. Montesquieu, for one, criticized the former Crown of Aragon's constitutional practices that, according to him, needlessly wasted energies on "minutiae" and "vain efforts".[12]

[11] Romantic Catalonian historians used the term "confederacy", but as Ferro (1999, 24) indicates, however, this is not an accurate description of their institutional reality.

[12] Specifically, in his Persian Letters (no. 109) he reported that "Great deliberative bodies apply themselves so strongly to minutiae, to formalities, to empty rituals, that only later is thought given to essential matters. For example, in 1610 when the king of Aragon called together representatives of Aragon and Catalonia, the first sessions were given over to deciding in which language the proceedings should be conducted. Only after a compromise was reached according to which questions would be asked in Catalan and replies given in Aragonese could any business be transacted". *("Les grands corps s'attachent toujours si fort aux minuties, aux vains usages, que l'essentiel ne va jamais qu'après. J'ai oui dire qu'un roi d'Aragon ayant assemblé les états d'Aragon et de Catalogne, les premières séances s'employèrent à décider en quelle langue les délibérations seraient conçues; la dispute était vive, et les états se seraient rompu mille fois, si l'on*

Despite this, the model of the Crown of Aragon applied to the Spanish monarchy[13] was created by the Union of the Catholic Kings (1474–1504) Isabella of Castile and Ferdinand of Aragon.[14] Both ruled as monarchs of a whole conglomeration of territories forming a union of states under the "Catholic Monarchy".[15] This composite monarchy was also termed "Hispanic", in reference to the Iberian Peninsula (Roman *Hispania*), the nerve center of all its domains, which Philip II recognized when he moved the royal court to Madrid in 1561, because it was the geographical center of the Peninsula.

By respecting the constitutional structure of the Crown of Aragon, the Catholic Monarchy was able to significantly enlarge its territorial holdings. The government and administration of this patchwork of territories was hindered, however, by its slow and complex institutional apparatus. The king was assisted by a number of councils (*consejos*), and the processes involved were labyrinthine. Affairs were handled even slower under kings like Philip II, who insisted on personally dealing with nearly everything.[16] This system was inefficient, at best. One of the causes of

*n'avait imagine un expedient, qui était que la demande serait faite en langage catalan et la ré ponse en aragonais").* English version in Runyon (2005, 193). French text in Montesquieu (2012, 255).

[13] The Crown of Aragon lacked the power and wealth of the combined Plantagenet domains in Anjou, Normandy, Aquitaine and England, the grandeur of the Hohenstaufen Empire, or the glamorous impudence of Charles of Anjou. It was, moreover, set back by catastrophic defeat in the Albigensian Wars and stripped of Provence in the thirteenth century, which explains why historians have stressed its political and economic failings in the Late Middle Ages. Nevertheless, the Crown of Aragon is memorable as far as constitutional history is concerned because, as Bisson (2002, 2) points out, it "outlasted the dynasty itself to become Ferdinand the Catholic's gift to the patrimony of modern Spain".

[14] The lucid Count-Duke of Olivares, in a secret instruction addressed to Philip IV in 1624, advised the young monarch to: "... consider the most important business of your monarchy to become King of Spain; that is, Sir, not to be content with being the King of Portugal, of Aragon, of Valencia, Count of Barcelona... but work and strive, guided by quiet and discreet advice, to bring these kingdoms that make up Spain into line with the style and laws of Castile, so that there should be no difference between them. Should your Majesty achieve this, he shall be the most powerful prince in all the world". (*Tenga Vuestra Majestad por el negocio más importante de su Monarquía, el hacerse Rey de España: quiero decir, Señor, que no se contente Vuestra Majestad con ser Rey de Portugal, de Aragón, de Valencia, Conde de Barcelona, sino que trabaje y piense, con consejo mudado y secreto, por reducir estas reinos de que se compone España al estilo y leyes de Castilla, sin ninguna diferencia, que si Vuestra Majestad lo alcanza será el Príncipe más poderoso del mundo*) de Guzmán Olivares (2013, 87). The ideas that Olivares conveyed to his sovereign in his grand memorandum on a future union of the kingdoms of Spain have often been regarded as a first attempt at political centralization in modern Spain. An analysis of his arguments in Fernández Albaladejo (2009, 73–81).

[15] Pope Alexander VI conferred the title of "Catholic" upon the Kings of Spain to offset the bestowal of the title of "Most Christian Majesty" on the Kings of France. From Isabella and Ferdinand down to King Don Juan Carlos I, Spanish kings bear the title of "Catholic Majesty" (Hunt 2001, 25–28).

[16] "The King spent more than 40 years engaged in the tasks of government and the handling of paperwork, with such determination and tenacity that it is difficult to find a comparable example in any another monarch of any country or time" (Escudero 2002, 15). There are many parallels

the disaster of the Spanish Armada in 1588, was the slowness with which the massive, sluggish military apparatus of the Catholic Monarchy was put into action, as opposed to an England which, while much smaller, was infinitely more united and boasted a more effective government (Irigoin and Grafe 2008, 173–209).

In fact, the ineffectiveness of the Crown of Aragon's composite model prompted the Catholic Monarchy to opt for a process of "Castillianization", simply because Castile was an absolute state in which the king exercised undisputed power, a system that greatly facilitated decision-making. Thus, Philip V did not hesitate to seize upon the pretext of his victory against the Hispanic territories which had rebelled against him in the War of the Spanish Succession (1704–1714) to quash the "constitutional" singularity of the ancient kingdoms of the Crown of Aragon, subjecting them to a Castilian regime of government, which thereafter became a synonym for "Spanish". In 1712, the king convoked the Assembly of Estates (*Cortes*) for the first time in Spanish history, which represented not only Castile but also all of Bourbon Spain (Kamen 2001, 82). By 1716, only Navarre and the Basque Country continued to enjoy special constitutional arrangements vis-à-vis the Spanish Monarchy, which both would keep until the end of the Carlist Wars, between 1839 and 1876 (Gunther et al. 2004, 45).

Spanish integration was reconsidered and came under attack at the end of the nineteenth century, with the resurgence of regionalist movements—mainly Catalonian and Basque—which took on a separatist dimension in the early twentieth century. During the Second Republic (1931–1936), there emerged the model of an "integral state" (*estado integral*) divided into "autonomous regions". The Civil War gave way to the longstanding Franco dictatorship, which marked an emphatic return to the unitary state. With the "Transition" era and the ratification of the 1978 Constitution, Spain would give rise to a "State of Autonomous Regions", which since 1996 has fomented a dynamic of regionalist separatism, especially in the Catalonian (Guibernau 2006, 216–224) and Basque (Jáuregui 2006, 239–257) territories, on which strains and threatens the country's model of territorial integration, and has spawned unsustainable levels of public spending. Curiously, the European integration process has served as an effective deterrent against territorial disintegration.[17]

between the history of Spain and its component territories and that of Britain in the modern era. Among the most striking is that 1707 saw a turning point in the relationship between the kingdoms of Castile and Aragon in Spain and of England and Scotland in Britain. On the topic, see Arrieta and Elliot (2009).

[17] Among other reasons because any new state would fall, at least initially, outside the EU, and would be required to apply for membership, a daunting and monumental administrative process. It is interesting to note that it was precisely pressure from EU to cut this excessive spending that led to the reform of Article 135 of the Spanish Constitution—published in the Official State Journal (Boletín Oficial del Estado) on September 27, 2011—passed to force the autonomous communities (regional governments) to rein in their spending and balance their budgets. The reform measure was, remarkably, supported by Spain's two major parties, conservative and socialist, overpowering the regionalist parties, who were powerless to halt the severe limitations it placed on their financial autonomy.

However, the Crown of Aragon and the Spanish Catholic Monarchy are not the only examples of composite monarchies in the European constitutional tradition. The English Crown, which brings together the United Kingdom of Great Britain, is yet another.

#### 18.1.2.2 The English Crown and the United Kingdom of Great Britain

In the medieval era, the kings of England became the dominant political force on the island of Great Britain, bringing the territories of Wales and Scotland under their power. Since 1301, the heir to the English throne has, significantly, received the title of "Prince of Wales"—despite the fact that the Welsh actually launched several revolts against English rule, and it was not until Henry VIII that the territory joined the English kingdom (Gower 2012, 147–164).[18] The annexation of the Kingdom of Scotland was even more difficult, requiring numerous military campaigns, which met with fierce resistance by the Scottish.[19] The formal union of the kingdoms of England and Scotland finally came about in 1603, when James VI of Scotland became James I of England after Elizabeth I died without leaving an heir. This union, however, was not legally consolidated until a century later, in 1706, with the signing of the Treaty of Union, ratified by the English and Scottish parliaments.[20] Thus, on May 1, 1707 the Kingdom of Great Britain was born, adopting a flag featuring elements of those of England, Scotland and Wales.

The next step was the incorporation of Ireland, which took place a hundred years later. Although the green isle was conquered by England in 1691, the Kingdom of Ireland did not formally join the British Crown until the year 1800, forming the United Kingdom of Great Britain and Ireland.[21] This union would last a little more than a century, as at the end of World War I, in 1918, the victory in Ireland of the

[18] Henry VIII incorporated the territory into England by introducing the English legal system and his royal administration into Wales, and allowing members representing constituencies in Wales to be elected to the Westminster Parliament through the "Laws in Wales Acts", approved between 1535 and 1542. On the circumstances of this integration, see also Jones (1999, 64–68) and Roberts (2012, 49–70).

[19] Led by leaders such as William Wallace (1270–1305). Though the uprising of 1297–1298 failed, a protracted guerrilla war ensued, which lasted until 1328. Wallace, executed in London in 1305, became a Scottish national hero (Ferguson 1994, 25). See also, Cowan (2012).

[20] On the negotiations of the treaty and the attainment of the Union, see Ferguson (1994, 232–278) and Riley (1969, 498–527). An exploration on the terms in which the Scot s discussed union with England in the century between 1603 and 1707 in Robertson (2009, 125–137). To establish the nature of the union of 1603, in theory—through the tracts—and practice and on the history of the hostile relations between both countries, see Wormald (2009, 109–124). For the Treaty of 1707, Fry (2006). An overview on Britain politics, commerce and culture in this period in Hamilton and Macinnes (2014).

[21] By virtue of the "Acts of Union", approved on July 2 and August 1, 1800, by the Irish and the English Parliaments. One hundred Irish representatives were integrated into the House of Com mons at Westminster. For a constitutional analysis of this union, see Russell (2003, 133–146).

nationalist party Sinn Fein sparked armed conflict with England. This "War of Independence" (1919–1922) ended up dividing the country. After the creation of the Irish Free State in 1922, Northern Ireland remained part of the entity, which became known as "The United Kingdom of Great Britain and Northern Ireland". This split continues to generate considerable tension between Unionist Northern Irish Protestants and independent Catholics, whose paramilitary organization, the Irish Republican Army (IRA), carries on with its struggle to unite the entire island.

Today the United Kingdom[22] is a monarchy with a Parliament in London but with three decentralized administrations headquartered in Edinburgh, Cardiff and Belfast, the respective capitals of Scotland, Wales and Northern Ireland. In 1997, under the "Scottish Devolution Referendum" 75 % of Scots voted in favor of the restoration of their own Parliament, in a demonstration of support that has forced the government in London to rethink the terms of Scottish integration into the United Kingdom. This led to the decentralization of the United Kingdom through the three 1998 Devolution Acts, which restructured the relationships between Scotland, Wales and Northern Ireland and the Union (Wicks 2006, 167–193). In the case of Scotland this led, in addition, to a commitment to hold a referendum on independence.[23]

### 18.1.3 *Assembly-Based Integration: The Singular Case of the Swiss Confederation*

#### 18.1.3.1 *Unus Pro Omnibus, Omnes Pro Uno*

"All for one and one for all" is, in reality, the slogan of one of the unique countries in the world,[24] a "nation" composed of several states that retain, even today, their political autonomy: the Swiss Confederation, better known as Switzerland. The country's name comes from one of its founding cantons, Schwyz, whose flag served

[22] The Channel Islands and the Isle of Man do not form part of the Crown, but are linked by personal union. They are not included in the United Kingdom of Great Britain and Northern Ireland, but for purposes of international relations, they are represented by the British government. To this must be added the former holdings of the once all-powerful British Empire: the 14 overseas territories integrated into the Commonwealth. One ought not to forget that the Queen of England is still the head of state in Canada and Australia, for example (Bradley and Ewing 2011, 38 and 320–327).

[23] In response to Scottish independence, the Shetland and Orkney islands are considering opting out from a separate Scotland. On the history of movements for Scottish independence, see Pittock (2008, 155–183).

[24] Despite the fact that the phrase "all for one and one for all" is commonly associated with Alexandre Dumas and his novel *The Three Musketeers (Les trois mousquetaires)*, published in 1844 (Dumas 2008, 105). An explanation of the *motto* in Mould (2011, 68).

as a model for the Confederation's current one, adopted at the end of the nineteenth century. From the point of view of constitutional history, the Swiss case is perhaps the only example of a political union of autonomous territories (cantons) effectively fused into a functioning confederation.

#### 18.1.3.2 From Its Beginnings to the *Rütlischwur* (The Rutli Oath, 1291)

It is ironic that Switzerland would not have existed had it not been for Roman invaders. If today there are still Swiss it is because Julius Cesar, as he recorded himself in his *Commentaries on the Gallic Wars*, blocked an attempt by the "Helvetians" to abandon their mountainous lands en masse and settle in southern France. In fact, this early people went so far as to burn their own cities and initiate a mass emigration. In response, Caesar defeated them twice and forced them to return to their smoldering homes. The Roman leader, of course, did not act out of altruism, but rather viewed the Helvetians as a valuable buffer between Rome and the barbarian Germanic peoples to the north.[25]

The unique autonomy and independence of the Swiss is largely due to their mountainous terrain, featuring deep valleys, which has historically permitted them to withstand the pressure exerted by the larger states surrounding them, especially that of the Holy Roman Empire. Their national hero is William Tell, a legendary figure who may have lived between 1200 and 1300, and who stands as the symbol of Swiss freedom.[26] It was then when Switzerland, taking advantage of the clashes between popes and emperors, and the fragmentation of feudal Europe, succeeded in forging an autonomy that was initially reflected in the pact signed by the

[25] "He ordered the Helvetii, the Tulingi, and the Latobrigi, to return to their territories from which they had come, and as there was at home nothing whereby they might support their hunger, all the productions of the earth having been destroyed, he commanded the Allobroges to let them have a plentiful supply of corn; and ordered them to rebuild the towns and villages which they had burned. This he did, chiefly, on this account, because he was unwilling that the country, from which the Helvetii had departed, should be untenanted, lest the Germans, who dwell on the other side of the Rhine, should, on account of the excellence of the lands, cross over from their own territories into those of the Helvetii, and become borderers upon the province of Gaul and the Allobroges" (Caesar 2005, 1.28).

[26] According to the tradition, for refusing to bow before the hat symbolizing the power of the evil imperial overlord Gessler, Governor of Altdorf (in the canton of Uri), William was forced to demonstrate his skill with the crossbow by knocking an apple off his son's head. Days later Tell took his revenge by shooting the tyrant through the heart. The legend served as the pretext for outstanding Swiss historian Jean-François Bergier, a disciple of Fernand Braudel, a member of the Annales School and a Professor at the Federal Polytechnic School of Zurich, to turn out a splendid synthesis on the origins of Swiss autonomy in his book simply entitled *William Tell* (Bergier 2001). For a biography in English of the first Swiss national hero, see Dettwiler (1991). On the influence of William Tell as a constitutional symbol, see Head (1995, 527–557). The story of Tell's deeds emerged after 1470, to become a central point of reference for Swiss identity (Church 2013, 43–72).

representatives of the cantons of Uri, Schwyz and Unterwalden in Grutli Meadow, on the shores of Lake Lucerne, on August 1, 1291.

#### 18.1.3.3 The Strengthening of the Swiss Confederation

Since that time the union progressively absorbed other cantons, successively forming the Confederation of Eight Cantons (*Acht Orte*), the 13 cantons' Old Swiss Confederacy (*Eidgenossenschaft*), and the ephemeral parenthesis of the Helvetic Republic (1798–1803) formed after the invasion of the French Revolutionary Army, before finally reaching its current total of 26 cantons (the most recent, the Canton of Jura, was not incorporated until 1979).[27]

In this first confederal phase, each of the cantons was almost totally autonomous, with their own borders, currencies and armies. Despite theoretically forming part of the Holy German Roman Empire, each canton enjoyed de facto independence from it thanks to successive military victories obtained by the Swiss against foreign troops, from that scored at the Battle of Morgarten in 1315 against imperial soldiers, to their victories at Grandson and Morat over Charles the Bold, Duke of Burgundy in 1476 (which put an end to Burgundy's independence), to their defeat of Maximilian, Charles V's grandfather, in 1499. The Swiss, in fact, earned for themselves a reputation as Europe's finest soldiers, spurring the leading European courts to hire them as mercenaries. Thus, for example, they defended Louis XVI and his family with their lives during the assault on the Palace of the Tuileries on August 10, 1792,[28] and even today, the pope's personal guard in the Vatican is Swiss.

The Swiss defeat against the French King François I at the Battle of Marignano (1515) and the success of the Reformation, which sparked religious conflicts between the cantons (Bruening 2005), certainly weakened the strength of the cantons. The Confederation, nevertheless, survived and finally received international recognition at the Peace of Westphalia (1648).[29]

Switzerland was last invaded by Napoleon, in 1798, in the course of his Italian Campaign against Austria. Paradoxically, this was an occupation which served to strengthen the Confederation through the formation of the vassal state (van Caenegem 2009, 241) called the Helvetian Republic, as Bonaparte incorporated

[27] For an overview of Swiss constitutional history, see Fleiner-Gerster et al. (2005, 21–25); also, Kriesi and Techsel (2010, 1–17).

[28] They are buried in the Expiatory Chapel in Paris, just two steps from the Élysée Palace, along with Louis XVI and Marie Antoinette.

[29] For an understanding of the essential period of the Old Swiss Confederation from a constitutional history perspective, see Maissen (2010, 105–120). On the emergence of the national security policies of small, neutral powers like the Netherlands, Belgium, Denmark, Norway and Switzerland in the period 1900–1940, see Amersfoort and Klinkert (2011). For Switzerland's unwillingness to join the EU after the cold war, Morris and White (2011).

into it the cantons of Vaud, Saint Gall, Grisons, Aargau, Thurgau and Ticino. Since this time, Switzerland has suffered no further invasions and has remained an essentially neutral country, avoiding participation in both World War I and World War II. Not even Hitler dared to invade it (Leitz 2000, 13–24).

#### 18.1.3.4 The Stage of the Federal State

The strictly "confederal" stage ended, however, in an especially fateful year in European history: 1848 (Humair 2009). Until then the cantons were completely independent, maintaining only temporary alliances between them. On occasion, these alliances were defensive and other times, offensive, such as that forged by the Canton of Bern in the sixteenth century. Bern's imperialism, which was strongly consolidated in the eighteenth century,[30] however, would end up setting off a revolt by the Catholic cantons in November of 1847, fought for separation from the others in the Sonderbund War (*Sonderbundskrieg*) (Andrey 1991, 263–265). The Protestant cantons prevailed, imposing the federal Constitution of September 12, 1848, which was partially revised in 1866.[31] On May 29, 1874, the Confederation was given a new constitution that, among other innovations, introduced referendums as a standard instrument to provide for direct democracy (Zimmer 2007, 168). This constitution was ultimately replaced by the new Swiss Federal Constitution, adopted by the cantons on April 18, 1999 and which entered into force on January 1, 2000.[32]

#### 18.1.3.5 The Most Democratic Country in the World?

Switzerland is a truly unique country, in many ways. It is one of the few "confederations" that works, consisting of 26 cantons and almost 3,000 municipalities. Since 1848, the Swiss Confederation has been a "federal state". However, unlike the United States of America, for example, it lacks a strong executive power. It is essentially a state controlled by its legislative assembly, in which the most important powers are shared at the three territorial levels: local, canton and federal.[33] There is an executive council consisting of seven federal councilors who take turns

[30] On Bern's hegemony, see Kapossy (2006, 227–247).

[31] On the origins of the Swiss federal state from 1848 to 1871, see Ruffieux (1983, 8–32). Also, Lerner (2012).

[32] For a comparative analysis of the recent evolution in Swiss constitutional law, see Schmitt (2012, 140–163) and Haller (2009). On its basic constitutional principles, see Fleiner-Gerster et al (2012, 53–11).

[33] For a look at how this complex system of government works, see Turku (2013, 809–874).

representing the federal government. The office of president is largely ceremonial, which is why almost no one can name the current Swiss president, a post that changes every year.

Of the three levels of government—local, cantonal and confederal—the least important is probably the latter, as the cantons and municipalities enjoy a great degree of autonomy. Thus, for example, the granting of Swiss nationality is decided by the municipalities rather than by the canton or the federal government.[34] If one is not accepted by his neighbors, he simply cannot become Swiss. Taxes, on the other hand, are paid and distributed across the three levels. Income taxes are earmarked mainly for the municipalities, which have the authority to determine whether an aspiring immigrant is allowed to reside in them or not. The federal state is essentially sustained by customs duties. Although today its revenues have increased thanks to the creation of new taxes, it continues to be the least-funded stage of government. Each level of government features checks and balances. Thus, for example, at the city level there are councilmen who elect the mayor, who is overseen by a Communal Council that verifies and manages the accounts.[35]

Switzerland is also a country featuring a striking degree of "direct democracy". Its eight million inhabitants (For the first quarter 2014, a permanent resident population of 8,160.9:6,208.9 Swiss, 1,952.0 foreigners, according to The Federal Statistical Office) are frequently consulted via referendums on a whole range of topics. Twenty thousand signatures are sufficient for the confederal government to be compelled to hold these votes, such that several are held every year. Participation is not very high (around 30 %) but this does not keep them from yielding decisions on matters of great importance.[36]

Switzerland, however, is also a country of contrasts. Despite its many progressive policies, it was the last European country to grant its women the vote, as they only gained the right to suffrage throughout the entire confederation, via a federal order, in 1971. At the canton level, it took even longer to grant women the vote, among other things because women themselves voted against it (in a 1959 refer-

[34] On the foreign relations of the Swiss cantons in the framework of the latest constitutional reform, see Schmitt (2000).

[35] This is why Switzerland is considered a paragon as far as the republican model of state is concerned. See Würgler (2008, 29–43).

[36] For example, the Swiss people decided directly if a minimum wage of approximately 3,000 euros should be adopted (failed); a proposal to deport foreigners committing crimes (passed); whether the federal state should pay for administrative support for each federal representative (failed); and a ban on the construction of minarets in Swiss territory (passed). For an enlightening analysis of how direct democracy works in Switzerland, especially from the perspective of its relationship to the political elite, see Kriesi and Techsel (2008, 230–232).

endum). Thus, for example, in the Apenzell Canton, the introduction of women's suffrage did not come about until November 27, 1990 because of a ruling by the Federal Court (Charnley et al. 1998). Moreover, in some cantons voting is still carried out by a raise of hands. Switzerland is, without any doubt, a very special country,[37] though it is changing as the result of the pressure exerted upon it by the European Union (Steiner 2001, 137–154).[38]

### 18.1.4 Westphalia's Peace and the Triumph of the Europe of States

Despite the examples of integration offered by the composite monarchies and the Swiss Confederation, in 1648 Europe essentially became a continent made up of independent states beholden to no overarching power. This state of affairs led to a series of military confrontations as Europe's nations vied for supremacy. Spanish hegemony gave way to French power after the Treaty of the Pyrenees (1659), and Louis XIV's France was the premier power until the Treaty of Utrecht (1714). During the eighteenth century, the United Kingdom became the preeminent European power, though its loss in the American War of Independence (1783) came as a blow. The French Revolution, nevertheless, shook all of Europe as France stepped to the fore once again though its aggressive imperialism under the Convention, the Directory, and, of course, Napoleon.

[37] Switzerland, of course, also has its problems. Most German-speaking Swiss do not get along well with their French-speaking compatriots. In 1914, the country almost split because the massive gulf between the German and French speaking communities nearly led to a permanent fissure and national disintegration (McGrathe 2014, 7). The country is making an effort, however, to improve these relations and to strike a balance, such as in the area of political representation (Schmid 2001, 143). Switzerland has traditionally had conservative governments (Church 2004, 60–70), but they have admitted as a counterbalance a certain number of socialist representatives in their different political institutions. These are just some of the Swiss paradoxes. A comparative analysis that explores why woman suffrage came to Switzerland so much later than the United States, with informative statistical analyses of state and cantonal level data in Banaszak (2001).

[38] Especially problematic concerning fiscal issues, as Swiss legislation allows wealthy people to move to Switzerland where they pay less in taxes (up to a maximum of 30 %) if they reach an agreement with the city council of the municipality in which they wish to reside. This is the case, for example, of Ikea owner Ingvar Kamprad (1926), the world's fourth richest man (though he, modestly, continues to drive an 18-year old Volvo in Switzerland). He has escaped Swedish taxes because he negotiated with the small Swiss town where he now lives to pay almost all of the local taxes himself. For an overview of the tricky fiscal issues involved in Switzerland's complex relationship with the EU, see Church et al. (2011, 126–147, specially? 136–138). Also, Trampusch and Mach (2011).

### *18.1.5 Europe Between Imperialism and Coordination: 1789 to 1914*

European politics were hit by a tidal wave in the form of the French Revolution and the Napoleonic era, whose new ideas, propagated through French imperialism, sent all of *Ancien Régime* Europe trembling. Napoleon transformed the map of European nations, creating some new states in old Europe, such as the Italian revolutionary Cisalpine and Ligurine Republics (1797), the Parthenopean Republic (1799), the Helvetic Republic (1798–1803), the Batavian Republic (1802–1806) in the Low Countries, in addition to the complete restructuring of Germany through the Final Recess (*Reichsdeputationshauptschluss*) of 1803 and the creation of the Confederation of the Rhine—*Rheinbund* (1806–1813).[39]

For 25 years, the European balance of power was so heavily altered that Europe's rulers convened at the Congress of Vienna (1814–1815), where they did their utmost to reestablish the *Ancien Régim*e and restore the Continent's old borders. Paradoxically, this effort, headed up by Austrian Chancellor Metternich, obliged European rulers to coordinate their efforts to prevent the possibility of revolution. As we have seen, Europe's leaders, to quash revolutionary activities, resolved to sign alliances and act together, through the Holy Alliance—an effort that some scholars have considered a precedent of European integration (Phillips 2005). For almost 15 years a united Europe was implemented through the Metternich System, a period during which coordination replaced imperialism and the relationships between European nation-states were characterized by their stability (Sofka 2011, 33–80).

Conflicts between European nations flared up again, however, after the 1830 French Revolution. In the middle of the century, from 1853 to 1856, the Crimean War was waged, in which French and British imperial policy clashed with that of the Russian Empire. In 1859, the French and the Sardinian armies defeated the Austrians in Magenta and Solferino, opening up the way for Italian national integration. Then it was time for Bismarck's Prussia, which defeated Austria at Sadowa (1866) and the French in 1870 (Franco-Prussian War). In this era thanks to colonial expansion the different European nation-states were rich enough to maintain powerful armies that enabled them to keep or increase their power at the world level through alliances, such as the Dual (1879) and Triple Alliance (1882) between Austria, the German Empire and the Ottoman Empire, versus the "Entente Cordiale" (1904) and the "Triple Entente" (1907) between France, the UK and Russia. This was, as we know, the "Armed Peace", which led to the apocalyptic First World War.

[39] On this essential aspect of Napoleon's influence on the restructuring of Europe, see Woolf (1991, 238–245) An overall view on the Emperor's European policies, in Grab (2005).

The major European nation-states did not consider uniting when their power was at its peak.[40] As their hegemonic stage came to an abrupt halt in 1918, however, some European leaders began to consider the possibility of a united Europe in which different states would act together instead of against each other.

## 18.2 The Idea of Europe from 1918 to 1939

### *18.2.1 Europe Lies in Ruins, at the Mercy of the United States and the Soviet Union*

World War I was a cataclysm, which left the major European nations devastated. In 1914, the nations of Europe dominated the world, controlling 44 % of industrial production (edging out the U.S., with 38 %). Europe's merchant marine fleet transported 79 % of sea traffic and controlled over 90 % of all capital invested in the world. It was still the golden age of colonialism and European interests prevailed on all the continents. The defeat of Germany, Austria and its allies was, to some extent, a Pyrrhic victory for the Allies, as all Europe, both the winners and the losers, had been laid waste. In 1914, their trade balance had been clearly in favor of the nations of the Continent, with the United States owing the various European states some 3 billion dollars. By 1918 the tables had turned, with the European states owing the U.S. federal government no less than 14 billion dollars. Almost five times more.[41]

Europe emerged not only surpassed by the United States, but also eclipsed by the power of Soviet Russia. Lenin, aware from the very outset that the new Soviet state would not be strong internationally if it could not incorporate its various neighboring states, appointed Comrade Stalin as People's Commissar of Nationalities, thereby creating the Union of Soviet Socialist Republics (USSR) in 1922, the only European force that could rival American power in the twentieth century.

---

[40] On the idea of Europe prior to 1914 see den Boer (1995, 13–82) and Stirk (1996, 1–38). For an overall view of the European and USA society and history of the quarter century that led to World War I, see Tuchman (2014).

[41] For an overview of the economic situation in Europe in 1918, see Broadberry and Harrison (2009, 3–40). According to Smith (2010, 17), in the 20th anniversary of German reunification (October 3, 2010), the country quietly finished paying the last of its debt stemming from reparations imposed by the Versailles Peace Treaty more than 92 years ago. The so-called "guilt clause" of the 1919 Treaty placed full blame for the war on Germany and ordered reparations of 132 billion German marks (roughly $400 billion in today's dollars/337,000 million euros). The debt fed a cycle of hyperinflation that pushed Germany to the brink of financial collapse. On the unsustainable financial and economic settlements of the Treaty, not only to Germany but to prosperity and peace in Europe overall, see Hölscher and Klaes (2014).

### 18.2.2 The Resurgence of Nationalisms and Disunity in Europe

The decline of Europe's nation-states could have been averted had their governments undertaken a policy of convergence. Instead, nationalism grew stronger than ever before and the tension between states was only exacerbated.

American President Woodrow Wilson, the primary architect of the Peace of Versailles (1919), and the author of the agreement's famous Fourteen Points, believed that the new international order ought to be based on a strict respect for nationalities, which meant that, in his opinion, states should coincide with "nations"—in the sense of peoples or ethnic groups. To this end, at Versailles Wilson advanced the principle of "national" self-determination (Keene 2006, 26) to ensure that minorities were able to gain statehood—as in the cases of Ireland, Poland, and Czechoslovakia—or achieve internal autonomy within the framework of a multinational state—as happened with Flanders in Belgium and the reunification of Yugoslavia. The Allies expressed, therefore, their sympathies with the fate of historically oppressed ethnic groups and acted to guarantee the resurgence of the nation-state at a time when this structure was inoperative at the global level, and a union of European states was indispensable for Europe to maintain its clout in the new world yielded by World War I.

The upshot of Wilson's idea was that all those nations that were not independent states in 1914, obtained statehood after the collapse of Germany and the disintegration of Austria–Hungary in 1919. Consequently, the map of Central Europe became considerably more complicated—and volatile. This policy of state creation did not only fail to resolve the problems, but in many cases actually aggravated them. Thus, for example the new Yugoslavia was established favoring the Serb majority, to the detriment of the Croats. Independence, thus, progressively heightened tensions and conflict between Belgrade and Zagreb until the head of the Croatian Peasant Party was assassinated during a session of the central Parliament.[42] The same dynamic was repeated with the government in Prague, which was strongly supported only by the Czechs, who represented just half of the population under the new state, the other half being made up of Slovaks, Germans from the Sudetenland, Ruthenians and Hungarians (Slapnicka 1993, 173–197). Thus, the reorganization of central Europe in the wake of World War I created a precarious and unstable concoction that would lead to deadly strife later in the century.

Another consequence of the implementation of the nationalities principle in Europe was the secession of Ireland from the United Kingdom. In January of

[42] Stjepan Radic (1871–1928) was shot during a regular session of the Yugoslav Parliament by a Serbian deputy from Montenegro in June of 1928, and died 2 months later of his wounds. His assassin was tried and sentenced to 60 years in prison (which was immediately reduced to 20) but was celebrated as a hero throughout much of Serbia (Despalatovic 2000, 86–87). On the situation of the Balkan States categorized as social and economically backward between 1914 and 1939, see Aldcroft (2007, 68–93).

1919, Ireland declared independence from the United Kingdom unilaterally, giving rise to the Irish Republic. After a 2-year war of independence, the Anglo-Irish Treaty was signed on December 6, 1921, and a year later, the entire island became a self-governing British dominion: the Irish Free State, a constitutional monarchy under the British crown.[43] The IFS featured a governor-general, a bicameral parliament, a cabinet called the "Executive Council" and a prime minister called the President of the Executive Council. A portion of the Irish people, led by Eamon de Valera, refused to accept the treaty and began a civil war (1922–1923) against pro-treaty (Free State) forces, led by Michael Collins, which, with British aid, won the war.[44] The Irish Free State, however, ultimately ended when Irish citizens voted via referendum for a new constitution in 1937, which created the new state of Ireland (Eire), virtually independent from the United Kingdom but still theoretically under the authority of the British Crown. This arrangement lasted until the new state seceded from the Commonwealth (Mansergh 1997, 170) through the Republic of Ireland Act of 1948, which came into force on April 18, 1949. The situation had been further complicated by the secession of Northern Ireland from the Irish Free State in 1921, creating a separate territory still technically forming part of the United Kingdom. Through the 1960s the Provisional IRA led a war aimed at overturning British rule in Northern Ireland. The conflict between Nationalists and Unionists did not end until April 10, 1998, with the Belfast Agreement (Aughey 2005, 81–97), which set in motion a process of disarmament culminating in the Provisional IRA's decommissioning of its weapons in July of 2005. Under the Northern Ireland Act (November 19, 1998), Northern Ireland has (since 2007) an elected first minister and a deputy first minister so that power may be shared by the leaders of the two main parties: the Democratic Unionist Party and Sinn Fein (Barnett 2002, 366–367).

With the settlement of the Irish question nationalist movements did not disappear in Europe, as some minorities, even during the present era of European integration, still clamor for the partitioning of their countries and the foundation of new nation-states based on ethnic and cultural affinities and purported rights to political independence, in some cases triggering dreadful civil wars. Fresh in the minds of Europeans are the atrocities of the Bosnian War (1992–1995). Ongoing struggles and demands by certain regions and peoples for autonomy continue to form part of Europe's constitutional history (Keating 2001, 19–43) as is the case in Belgium, with its Wallon and Flemish communities; in Spain, where separatist

[43] After months of difficult negotiations on December 6, 1921, the five delegates representing the Irish Republican Government signed the Anglo-Irish Treaty, which granted Ireland "dominion" status. As the solution reached did not recognize an "isolated Republic" the Irish republican movement was divided, and by the time the agreement was ratified by a narrow margin in January of 1922, Ireland was drifting towards civil war (Nelson 2012, 242). On the historical roots of the conflict, see McEvoy (2008, 21–43).

[44] Michael Collins was assassinated on August 22, 1922, at 31 years of age (Coogan 2000, 410–411). On Michael Collins' roles as a military man and a politic, see Dwyer (2009). A view about the Irish insurgency and the causes of Britain's defeat in Hittle (2011).

movements endure in the Basque Country and Catalonia; and in the United Kingdom, with Scotland.

### *18.2.3 Some Attempts at Integration*

Despite the resurgence of militant nationalism,[45] it must be said that there were also farsighted and commendable attempts to curb these excesses and promote a policy of European integration.

#### 18.2.3.1 The Pan-European Movement of R. Coudenhove-Kalergi (1923)

The first general movement aimed at integrating the nations of Europe was opened by the work of Richard Coudenhove-Kalergi, who in 1923 published a book that made a major impact and was widely circulated, in part because of its striking title: *Pan-Europe* (Coudenhove-Kalergi 1926). In it, he defended a union of European states to prevent the nations of the Continent from succumbing to either Russian Bolshevism or American economic domination. Above all, he argued that union was the only way for Europe to maintain its influence around the world.

It is significant that Coudenhove-Kalergi's proposal omitted Russia and the U.K. In the first case, because the Russian Revolution had marked a break with the European states' democratic system, making the Soviet Union "a Eurasian world power". As for the U.K., Coudenhove held that after World War I the United Kingdom had transformed its internal structure to evolve from a European kingdom with colonies to a "federal intercontinental" regime.

The question of the structure of the United States of Europe, which Coudenhove-Kalergi advocated, was still one to be settled. The author of *Pan-Europe* was aware of the resurgence of nationalism in Europe after 1919 and, therefore, considered it unrealistic to expect all Europe's nation-states, especially its most recent ones, to accept the authority of a federal government. For this reason, he advocated a formula that respected the sovereignty of nation states, in line with that adopted by the Pan-American Union, which at its conference in Santiago (Chile) in 1922 seemed to have managed to reconcile national independence with an effort at regional international cooperation. Coudenhove-Kalergi wished to extrapolate Pan Americanism to Europe and constitute a "Pan-European" authority equipped

[45] Translator's note: the term "nationalism" may be confusing, as it may be used to refer to two very different phenomena: support for a powerful central authority which aspires to represent the nation, often encompassing and ruling over a vast expanse of territory featuring a variety of different regions and cultures; and the rejection of and resistance to precisely this kind of central authority, based on demands by a region or ethnic group for autonomy. In both cases, the crux of the question is the legitimate definition of the nation and the scope of its rightful jurisdiction.

with a Council consisting of delegates from different states, an assembly of delegates from the different parliaments, and a court of justice (Prettenthaler-Ziegerhofer 2012, 89–110). In this way, Pan-Europe was to serve as one of the world's regional organizations, one of the five major spheres on the globe, along with the American, British, Russian and Far Eastern, led by Japan.

Coudenhove-Kalergi knew that after the Great War, when public opinion was charged with strongly nationalist sentiment, his project would not attract the European masses. In fact, the Pan-European idea never took hold with the people—except perhaps in central Europe, particularly in Austria and Germany, where public opinion saw in it a way of overcoming the consequences of defeat. Coudenhove-Kalergi, therefore, decided to make his appeal to the ruling classes: parliamentarians and businessmen.[46]

#### 18.2.3.2 Attempts at Economic Union

The growth of nationalism following the signing of the Peace of Versailles had important economic consequences, as the multiplication of European borders and the brash self-interest with which the new states sought to consolidate their national economies generally spawned a resurgence of aggressively protectionist policies. This trend was all the more regrettable given that the Continent's economy as a whole was in clear decline, and only the union of markets and the abandonment of customs duties and restrictions would have made possible Europe's revival in the international economic arena.

Some of Europe's most dynamic employers, very impressed by the United States' enormous economic power by the beginning of the 1920s, however, began to back the creation of a massive European-wide market as a means of favoring the growth of industrial production and lowering the prices of manufactured goods. Hence, two types of initiatives emerged: the establishment of customs unions, such as that led by Prussia in the mid-nineteenth century (*Zollverein*), and the development of international production agreements.

Among the first mention must be made of the European Customs Union, established in 1926 (Lipgens 1984, 6), initially chaired by economist Charles Gide, and later by Yves Le Trocquer.[47] French fears of Germany's industrial

[46] To achieve this in 1923, he created the Pan-European Union, headquartered in Vienna, and with national divisions in all countries. *Pan-Europe* was a great success because Coudenhove-Kalergi managed to receive support from a significant number of politicians, such as Aristide Briand, Louis Loucheur, Léon Blum, Joseph Caillaux, Charles de Gaulle and Edouard Herriot in France; Eduardo Bénès in Czechoslovakia; the President of the Reichstag; Paul Loebe, Konrad Adenauer and Franz Joseph Strauss in Germany; and Austrian Chancellors Ignaz Seipel and Bruno Kreisky (Prettenthaler-Ziegerhofer 2012, 97–100).

[47] Its purpose was to spread the European idea in the economic sphere, given that reluctance and opposition was too strong in the political arena. The aim was to gradually remove tariffs, thereby encouraging the creation of increasingly larger markets. Thus, a European Customs Union Action

power, however, ended up dashing the project. Efforts were also made to encourage the signing of international agreements between producers, which was a very widespread and common practice. It was during this period when the first major intra-European economic accords were signed, including the industrial agreements that the French and German governments sought to sign between the century's world wars to solve the problem of war reparations.[48]

These ideas were never brought to fruition because of the outbreak of the Great Depression (1929) and Hitler's rise to power in 1933. However, during the 1920s, these concepts and proposals did affect the thinking of an elite group of politicians and senior international officials who supported inter-state dialogue as a means of addressing the problems afflicting Europe. Hence, the Pan-European idea was very well received in intellectual circles and media.

#### 18.2.3.3 Intellectual Pan-Europeanism

In addition to politicians, economists, and businessmen, the Pan-European idea was generally embraced with enthusiasm by a whole series of leading European intellectuals during the interwar period. Coudenhove-Kalergi, for example, was supported by Paul Valéry, Paul Claudel, Rainer María Rilke, Thomas Mann, Salvador de Madariaga and Miguel de Unamuno, among others. Thanks to them, until the mid-1930s, there was an intense intellectual movement in favor of a united Europe, which resulted in the publication of influential books calling for European integration.[49]

Committee (Moravcsik 2005, 145) was created in Paris in which politicians, economists, industrialists, bankers and trade unionists were to defend the progressive disappearance of customs duties between the different European states. Coudenhove-Kalergi himself established a Franco-German intra-European council to encourage an interpenetration of both nations' economics to prevent a new conflict between them. On the actual EU custom laws, see Fabio (2012).

[48] The most resounding success in this field was scored by Luxembourgian industrialist Emile Mayrish, a strong supporter of the Pan-European idea and improving Franco-German relations. Specifically, in 1926 he created a metal cartel made up of iron and steel businessmen from France, Germany, Belgium, Luxembourg and the territory of the Saar (Barthel 2004, 125–144). France's Minister Louis Loucheur aspired to go further than Mayrish, as he advocated the constitution of Franco-German cartels for the production of basic raw materials, and the lifting of customs duties in these cases. These European cartels were to be overseen by a League of Nations to prevent possible harm to consumers. On the League, the Cartel des gauches and the internationalisation of security, see Jackson (2013, 235–275 and 427–521).

[49] As argued in the very interesting essay by Francis Delaisi, in which the author openly criticizes the nation-state as inoperative in the context of increasing globalization (Delaisi 1927), Gaston Riou's *Europe, ma patrie* with a foreword by Raymond Poincaré (Riou 1928) or the work by the Count Carlo Sforza (Liebmann 2008, 129–173), exiled by Mussolini, on the United States of Europe (Sforza 1948). Also Bertrand de Jouvenel: *Towards the United States of Europe* (de Jouvenel 1930) and *The Awakening of Europe* (de Jouvenel 1938), Édouard M. Herriot: *The United States of Europe* (Herriot 1930) and Sir Arthur Salter in his 1933 book *The United States of Europe and Other Papers* (Salter 1933). A reassessment on the life and work of Jouvenel in Mahoney (2005).

Due to the movement set in motion by Coudenhove-Kalergi, the idea of a European union was no longer monopolized by prophets, dreamers, and theorists, as it had been historically, but became a concept enjoying wide support amongst the European ruling classes. Thus, despite not having made major headway in terms of public opinion, European integration advocates came to form interest groups featuring study committees turning out reports with the hope that a government would take the first step towards an alliance.

#### 18.2.3.4 Briand's Proposal for a European Union (1929)

Government initiatives in favor of European unification, however, took time to materialize.[50] The trailblazer in this respect was Aristides Briand, France's Minister of Foreign Affairs as of 1925, and Honorary President of the Pan-European Union as of 1927 (Wright 2005, 31–67). In 1929, he rose to head the French Government, at which time he seized the opportunity to present his proposal for European integration.[51]

Briand soon realized that the League of Nations was an instrument incapable of ensuring the peace, and considered it more pragmatic to back Franco-German political rapprochement within the framework of a united Europe. To this end, after he enjoyed the assistance of his German counterpart Gustav Stresemann, he made public his plans for a united Europe in a speech delivered on September 5, 1929, on the League of Nations' fall meeting (Bellon 2009, 87–104). In it, he defended the advisability of establishing a link between Europe's states that would enable them to deal with serious circumstances together given the need to do so. His proposal was not well-received by European leaders.[52] Nevertheless, the delegates of 26 European nations present at the September meeting of the League of Nations asked Briand to draft a memorandum expanding and fleshing out his ideas. This document was finally published in May of 1930 (Doerr 1998, 115), although it did not enthuse anybody because he stressed political unification rather than economic union—which was understandable, however, given the fact that it was written after the outbreak of the Wall Street Crash in October, leading directly to the Great Depression. In response to the proposal's rejection, he watered down his proposals

[50] The first statesman who spoke openly of a united Europe was Édouard Herriot, a leader of France's radicals, in a speech on January 25, 1925, in the Senate. Herriot had assumed the presidency of the Council of Ministers in 1924 (Jessner 1974). See also Muron (1997).

[51] He was the French Prime Minister twice: from November 28, 1925 to July 17, 1926, and from July 29 to October 22, 1929. On Briand, see also Unger (2006).

[52] The idea failed to convince the French Right, which remained a supporter of the nation-state, nor did it find favor amongst the Left, headed up by Léon Blum, who thought that the proposal did not go far enough. Meanwhile, in Germany pro-European Gustav Stresemann supported Briand, but only backed isolated economic measures such as a monetary Union and the creation of a European postal seal. In England, Labour leader Ramsay MacDonald considered Briand's proposal premature. The untimely death of Stresemann on October 3, 1929 would be fatal for Briand's proposal (Steiner 2005, 413).

in a report dated September 1, 1930, endorsing not the creation of special bodies to achieve political union, but simply the meeting of a Study Commission in the interest of "European union".[53]

Despite all this, it is evident that the initiative was a failure. The governments of the various European states were unwilling to cede one bit of their sovereignty, and most of their leaders were either indifferent or opposed to the idea of European union—in large measure because for each of them European unification meant something different. For the victorious states, integration was to be a means of consolidating the European order arising from the Treaty of Versailles. The defeated countries, on the other hand, were willing to participate in a European unification project only if said treaty was revised. However, the decisive development was the radical political change that occurred in Germany after the death of Gustav Stresemann in October 1929, and the electoral victory of the Nazi Party in 1930.

In any case, the Depression dissolved the European euphoria of 1926 and 1927 and shifted the priorities of most European states, which abandoned any support for a united Europe. In fact, the prevailing trend was just the opposite: over the course of the 1930s, Europe's economic fragmentation tended to accentuate because of increased customs duties, the establishment of exchange controls, and the consolidation of autarchic economies in general. To make matters worse, the League of Nations failed to keep new hostile blocs from arising in Europe. In 1935, a Franco-Soviet Pact was signed to consolidate the strategic alliances established by France with Poland and Czechoslovakia (Jordan 2002, 39). To counter this alliance the Rome–Berlin Axis would emerge in 1936. In the end, the Soviet Union switched sides after the signing of the 1939 German–Soviet Non-Aggression Pact. The resurgence of nationalism would lead to a gradual increase in international tensions, dragging Europe into World War II.

[53] The full original text of Briand's Memorandum, in French and English on opposite pages, was translated by the USA Department of State (France. Ministère des affaires étrangères 1930, 1–33). Also, in Briand (1930, 327–353). Partially reproduced in Salmon and Nicoll (1997, 9–14). The reaction by Europe's different governments to the Briand Memorandum was generally quite unfavorable. Some countries, such as Germany, demanded the revision of the Treaty of 1919 as a precondition for European integration. England was the most reluctant country and that which most effectively opposed the proposal. The English did not want to participate in the project of a European union, but neither did they wish for a European bloc to be formed without them. The smaller states were those most amenable to the project, specifically the Low Countries in Western Europe, and some eastern countries, such as Poland, Czechoslovakia, and Yugoslavia. The United States of America was not, a priori, opposed to Briand's idea, except if it meant tariffs that would hamper the penetration of American products into the European market. The Soviet Union, meanwhile, expressed its clear wariness of any alliance made up of Europe's capitalist states. On Briand's initiative see Navari (1992, 74–104). Also, Görtemaker (2013, 33–48).

## 18.3 European Integration During World War II

The outbreak of World War II did not put an end to attempts at integration, though, because of the conflict, these took other forms.

### *18.3.1 The Franco-British Union (June 1940)*

The beginning of the war almost brought about an unexpected union that would have been inconceivable during a period of peace: the merging of historic rivals France and the United Kingdom into a single state. Initially, the project was only of a theoretical nature, but starting on March 28, 1940, it seemed to be materializing when the French and British governments mutually pledged not to negotiate a separate armistice and to maintain, after the peace, a joint effort aimed at reconstruction. On June 16, 1940, the British government proposed the constitution of a Franco-British union to the French government.[54]

Churchill, with De Gaulle at his side, even phoned French President Paul Reynaud to convey London's proposal to him (Diamond 2007, 100). The call, however, came too late, as Reynaud finally decided to resign and the new President of the Republic, Albert Lebrun, had entrusted the task of forming a government to

---

[54] The great English historian Arnold Toynbee, then director of the Royal Institute of International Affairs at Chatham House, since the outset of Hitler's attacks conceived the possibility of forging a permanent Franco-English union to combat German hegemony and to establish a stable balance of power in Europe. Arnold J. Toynbee, retomó una idea que ya había expuesto también el 11 de marzo de 1939 un senador francés, Jean-Jacques Honorat. On June 16, 1940, the following draft of a joint declaration was issued: "*At this most fateful moment in the history of the modern world, the Governments of the United Kingdom and the French Republic make this declaration of indissoluble union and unyielding resolution to a system which reduces mankind to a life of robots and slaves. The two Governments declare that France and Great Britain shall no longer be two nations, but one Franco-British Union. The constitution of the Union will provide for joint organs of defense, foreign, financial and economic policies. Every citizen of France will enjoy immediately citizenship of Great Britain, every British subject will become a citizen of France. Both countries will share responsibility for the devastation of war, wherever it occurs in their territories, and the resources of both shall be equally, and as one, applied to that purpose. During the war there shall be a single War Cabinet, and all the forces of Britain and France, whether on land, sea, or in the air, will be placed under its direction. It will govern from wherever best it can. The two Parliaments will be formally associated. The nations of the British Empire are already forming new armies. France will keep her available forces in the field, on the sea, and in the air. The Union appeals to the United States to fortify the economic resources of the Allies, and to bring her powerful material aid to the common cause. The Union will concentrate its whole energy against the power of the enemy no matter where the battle may be. And thus we shall conquer*" (Churchill 2013b, 183–184). Also, in Great Britain, Parliament. House of Commons (1940, columns 701–702).

Marshal Pétain, a strong supporter of signing an armistice. The would-be Franco-British union became but a historical curiosity.[55]

### *18.3.2 Hitlerian Europe*

It is well known that Hitler managed to militarily dominate most of the Continent in the early years of World War II. It is less clear, however, whether at any point he seriously considered European unity.

On the one hand, it seems that in *Mein Kampf*, he makes it clear that the only important thing for him was the supremacy of the Aryan race and its need to expand its living space (*Lebensraum*), essentially eastward. Thus, it is not surprising that Hitler originally did not have the creation of a united Europe in mind.[56] It was only as German domination spread throughout Europe, and especially after the start of the war against Russia (June 1941), that he began to conceive the idea of placing the entire Continent under the Third Reich.[57] To bring about this Great Germany Hitler acted to install satellite and puppet regimes in neighboring nations, with governments willing to do Germany's bidding.

The idea of organizing a united Europe according to the fascist or National Socialist model had already been advanced by the likes of Carl Schmitt,[58] whose ideas were taken up by Joseph Goebbels, who saw to it that they were disseminated by his official propaganda apparatus. Goebbels proposed forming a European *Lebensraum* that would encompass "White Russia" and the Ukraine, territories whose occupation he considered indispensable to Europe's provisioning. In total the Third Reich aimed to occupy some 6 million km$^2$, home to 450 million people, aiming at constituting an anti-Bolshevik Europe under what came to be called the "New Order".[59]

The first step was the annexation of Austria (*Anschluss*) in March of 1938. In the absence of any resistance by the Allies, Hitler moved to also annex the Sudetenland

---

[55] For the British vision of Europe during World War II, see Wilson (1996, 39–62).

[56] As Fest (2013, 688) points out, Hitler spoke of Europe's "rubbish heap of small countries" that he intended to clean out, as he saw Germany in the position of Rome overpowering the other city states of Latium as, according to his view, Old Europe had "outlived its usefulness".

[57] After the disaster of Stalingrad (January 31, 1943), Goebbels was given permission by Hitler to develop a "program for Europe". In his diary, he noted on May 8, 1943 that "the Reich will one day rule the whole of Europe" as he considered that "whoever owns Europe will by that fact take leadership of the world" (Müller 2003, 538).

[58] In 1939, the latter had published a pamphlet setting forth a theory of large spaces with state directors (Schmitt 1991). On Carl Schmitt's Interwar perspective on European political unity, see Untea (2012, 155–168).

[59] In successive articles published in the magazine *Das Reich* in 1942 (Salewski 1984, 50). For an overview of Goebbel's ideology and his rising influence in the Nazi regime, see Longerich (2014) and Shirer (2011, 123–129).

region, the northwestern part of Czechoslovakia, where the majority of the population was German-speaking, at which point Europe teetered on the brink of war. The leaders of France (Daladier) and the United Kingdom (Chamberlain), however, met with Hitler and Mussolini in Munich and accepted the situation in September 1938 (Hildebrand 1973, 65–73). War seemed to have been averted (Weinberg 2010, 526–638).

For Nazi leaders the integration of European was to be forged not through the creation of federal institutions, but by way of ensuring that the Continent's different political regimes embraced their peculiar political philosophy.[60] This vision of the Europe of the New Order was shared by collaborationist elements, motivated by their extreme anti-communism, and the governments of German satellite regimes (such as Vichy France, headed by Marshall Pétain), theoretically independent (Chopra 1974, 4–6).[61] In other cases, as in the case of Franco's Spain, for example, support for integration came only in the form of armed divisions sent to fight on the Russian front, such as the Spanish Blue Division, commanded by General Agustín Muñoz Grandes (Payne 2008, 160–161).[62]

Most Europeans, however, wanted nothing to do with this anti-Bolshevik, German, racist and totalitarian "new Europe", organizing, and supporting resistance movements to defy Nazi Germany and its allies.

## *18.3.3 The "Integrationist" Idea in Anti-Hitlerian Europe*

### 18.3.3.1 The Resistance and the "United States of Europe"

The anti-Nazi resistance was from the beginning much more amenable to the idea of a united Europe (Mommsen 2003, 246–259).[63] In June of 1941, a handful of antifascist prisoners on the island of Ventotene, led by Altiero Spinelli and Ernesto Rossi, released a manifesto (the Ventotene Manifesto) in favor of a European federation (Spinelli and Rossi 2006). After Mussolini's fall, the initiative resulted in the creation of the European Federalist Movement.[64]

---

[60] For an overview of Nazi-occupied Europe during World War II, see Baranowski (2011, 223–295).

[61] As Callil (2006, 210) points out, the ambition of Pétain and his head of government Pierre Laval was to situate France alongside Germany in a new world order. This is why first Laval, and then Pétain, met with Hitler at Montoire (October 24, 1940). A history of the Free French movement and Charles de Gaulle's wartime career as the leader of France's resistance in Argyle (2014).

[62] As Stanley Payne observes, Hitler judged Franco to be insufficiently fascist (Payne 2008, 62–63).

[63] For an overview of what resistance to Hitler meant during World War II, see Moore (2000, 1–18).

[64] This same federalist trend appeared, as of 1942, in the clandestine program of the Belgian Socialist Party, and also in Holland, with the ideas of H.D. Salinger (Lipgens 1984, 593–601). In France, aspirations for a united Europe were a recurring theme in the clandestine press.

#### 18.3.3.2 Towards a Federal Europe?

In general, in those countries not occupied by the Nazis there arose movements receptive to European federalism. In Britain, there appeared the "Federal Union" movement, which endorsed a worldwide form of federalism. Also, in 1942 Coudenhove-Kalergi founded a research institute at the University of New York (Prettenthaler-Ziegerhofer 2012, 100) to establish a European federation after the war, and convened a pan-European congress made up of politicians in exile. His activities were widely reported by the American and European press, allowing for the broad dissemination of pan-European ideas.

#### 18.3.3.3 Governments in Exile and European Integration

These movements translated into political action, as most governments in exile, whose countries had been occupied by Hitler, set about laying the foundations for the organization of Europe once a peace had been signed. The Belgians and the Dutch began to negotiate the terms of a future customs union, the Greeks and Yugoslavs managed to sign a cooperation agreement, and the Poles and Czechs founded a "Coordinating Committee". Most importantly, it was during this time and against this backdrop that there emerged the first major proponents of European integration, leading to the first real union of European states: Belgium, the Netherlands, and Luxembourg.[65]

#### 18.3.3.4 The Benelux Is Formed

Negotiations were held with the aim of initiating a process of European integration in the year 1942, but they were discontinued in 1943 because, on the one hand, Soviet authorities were opposed to any incorporation of Central European countries not under Soviet control, and, on the other, the countries of northern Europe

---

Publications such as *Combat* (September 1942) *Résistance,* and *Le Populaire* (1943), called for the establishment of a United States of Europe after the victory (Chopra 1974, 6–8). In June of 1944, a French Committee for the Federation of Europe was founded in Lyon, its mission to establish contacts with various underground resistance networks. On the ideas of the French Resistance on future foreign policy, see Lipgens (1984, 264–361). A historical survey on the main developments of European integration from 1945 to 1963, in Wells (2007).

[65] These leaders included Paul Henry Spaak, Foreign Affairs Minister of the Belgian Government in exile, who pushed for a military, political, and economic union for Belgium, the Netherlands (Holland), and France, which would include the three colonial empires. Former Belgian Prime Minister Paul Van Zeeland, meanwhile, tirelessly argued for a customs and monetary union for Western Europe. General Sikorsky, the Prime Minister of the Polish Government exiled in London, agreed, while representatives of the Czechoslovakian government proposed that Europe pool its coal supplies into a common fund. For the specific vision of Europe developed by De Gaulle, see Warlouzet (2010, 21–31).

rejected any proposal for a union without Great Britain's participation. In the end, the only positive result of all of these attempts was an agreement signed between Belgium, the Netherlands, and Luxembourg to establish a customs and economic union, created on September 5, 1944: the Benelux (Harryvan 2009, 69–98)

#### 18.3.3.5 The Tepid Europeanism of Free France

The French Committee of National Liberation (CFLN) was also concerned about how Europe would be organized after the war. In France, the project of European integration was spearheaded by Jean Monnet who, after having launched the "Victory Program" in the United States to bolster the development of the American arms industry, became the commissioner for the provisioning and armament of the CFLN. Monnet managed for René Mayer, a senior official who worked with him at the CFLN's provisioning service, to send a note to General de Gaulle on September 30, 1944, in which he specifically proposed to the leader of free France the creation of a "Federation of Western Europe". General de Gaulle was willing to study the proposal, but his advisers were not enthusiastic about the prospect of integrating free France into a coherent European Union project. In the end, on March 18, 1944, before the Consultative Assembly of Algiers, De Gaulle presented the CFLN's official position, one of timid support for the integration of Western Europe (Chopra 1974, 8–12; Warlouzet 2011, 419–434).

The initiative would fail, however, because of the strong opposition put up by Soviet authorities to any such western alliance, and because De Gaulle thought he needed Moscow to counterbalance the growing power of the Anglo-Saxon bloc. In fact, the leader of free France traveled to Russia on December 10, 1944, to sign a Franco-Soviet alliance with Stalin (Reynolds 1994, 99).

#### 18.3.3.6 Churchill as an Early Champion of European Unity

In the end, however, France was unable to play a key role in the reconstruction of the world order because it was excluded from the crucial post-war conferences at Tehran, Yalta, and Potsdam, where the only Western European power present was the United Kingdom, represented by Churchill.

The main concerns of Britain's then prime minister were maintaining the cohesion of the Commonwealth and strengthening the tight relations between Great Britain and the United States (Harbutt 2010, 284–288). However, Churchill was sympathetic to the idea of a European alliance because he feared that a political vacuum might be created when American troops left the European continent, ripe for exploitation by the Soviets to expand their sphere of influence.[66]

[66] It is within this context that the speech the British premier delivered at the Pan-European Congress in New York on March 21, 1943 should be understood (Larres 2002, 81–82). In this

At his successive meetings with Roosevelt and Stalin Churchill proposed the creation of three international councils: one for the Americas, one for Europe and a third for Asia. His proposition met with American opposition, however, as Roosevelt believed that the terms of the peace ought to be determined by the two great superpowers of the time: the Soviet Union and the United States. Roosevelt was convinced that a European Council without the United States would encourage American isolationism, and that France's weakness would lead to a Europe dominated by Britain, which would worry the Soviet Union and jeopardize world peace. This is why the ailing U.S. President (who would die just 2 months after the Yalta Conference) acquiesced to Stalin's views on Eastern Europe.[67]

Roosevelt's notion of a world split between two areas of influence would eventually prevail, as Europe was, unfortunately, torn in two, with Western Europe under American influence and Eastern Europe under Soviet power. It is true that at the Yalta Conference (February 4–11, 1945), Roosevelt and Churchill managed to convince Stalin to sign the "Declaration of Liberated Europe", which provided for the establishment of democratic governments by way of free elections for all nations previously under German control (Miscamble 2007, 66). The countries of Western Europe, however, lacked the capacity to ensure respect for the democratic principle in Eastern Europe, which led to the falling of the "Iron Curtain", a figurative barrier which would divide Europe until the fall of the Berlin Wall in 1989 (Muller 1999).

## 18.4 European Integration During the Post-War Period (1945–1949)

### *18.4.1 Europe in 1945*

Hitler was ultimately not defeated by the heart of Europe, but by the two new superpowers lying east and west of it: Russia and the United States, which met to discuss the new international order to be established after the end of World War II. Europe was once again universally ravaged by war: those regimes which had been conquered by the Third Reich, those which had collaborated with it, and those

address, he expressed for the first time the idea of setting up a "Council of Europe" as a high court to settle the differences between the various European states, with sentences enforced by a European army. Churchill viewed such an instrument as a way to keep Germany in check and form a buffer against Soviet influence.

[67] Harbutt (2010, 132–133) speaks of a "bargain" to refer to the unmistakable American support for Stalin's aspirations in Eastern Europe, in return for the Soviet promise to participate in the United Nations. On Stalin's position at the Tehran, Yalta and Potsdam conferences, see Roberts (2007, 6–40). On the agreements reached at Yalta on Liberated Europe, see Plokhy (2010, 263–271). For an overview of Stalin's position with regards to Europe at the end of the War, see Roberts (2006, 228–253).

which struggled to resist it, particularly the United Kingdom, which had tenaciously defended itself. In any case, by 1945 Europe was the great loser, left bankrupt and buried in the devastation of the conflict (Judt 2007, 13–40)—literally, as much of Europe's cities had been reduced to rubble by massive bombing raids. The most disturbing example in England was Coventry, while in Germany it was the city of Dresden, totally destroyed by four consecutive bombing runs carried out between February 13 and 15, 1945, which left over 30,000 dead.[68]

For the formerly all-powerful Europeans the problem was now survival. Italy, which had become a republic, was completely impoverished, and the maps of Germany and Austria were mangled. France had been laid waste, and the United Kingdom, no longer a great power, began to dismantle its empire with the foundation of the "Commonwealth", a community by virtue of which its former colonies became independent states while maintaining a symbolic allegiance to the British Crown[69]—a fact which may explain why in 1946, Churchill supported the creation of a United States of Europe in his aforementioned speech at the University of Zurich.[70]

#### 18.4.1.1 The Dollar Gap

The top priority was reconstruction. This is why the first thing the Americans did after the end of World War II was to provide Europe with material and financial aid. The funds provided, however, quickly evaporated given the dire needs of the devastated Continent. In 1947, the exorbitant amount of 11.5 billion dollars practically disappeared, in what is known as the era of the "dollar gap" (Erhard 2006, 181–182).

#### 18.4.1.2 The Marshall Plan (1947)

President Truman's advisors soon came to the conclusion that a change in strategy was needed. The United States was willing to facilitate Europe's overall reconstruction, but not that of each state individually (Jackson 1979, 1043–1068). This was the gist of a speech given by Secretary of State George Marshall on June 5, 1947, at Harvard University, in which he stated that:

---

[68] The bombing of Dresden remains highly controversial, as in February 1945, it was clear that Germany had lost the war and the city was not a military target (Hansen 2008, 253–254).

[69] On the situation of the European states after World War II see Buchanan (2012, 8–50) and Milward (20100, 21–45).

[70] In Churchill's view these United States of Europe were supposed to function as a regional organization of the United Nations. Churchill's objective was not the federal reconstruction of Europe but rather the creation of a European group that, through political cooperation, would minimize conflicts between rival European states, especially France and Germany. A sort of "coherent national grouping in the new post-war balance of power" (Moschonas 1996, 14–15).

> It is already evident that, before the United States Government can proceed much further in its efforts to alleviate the situation and help start the European world on its way to recovery, there must be some agreement among the countries of Europe as to the requirements of the situation and the part those countries themselves will take in order to give proper effect to whatever action might be undertaken by this Government. It would be neither fitting nor efficacious for this Government to undertake to draw up unilaterally a program designed to place Europe on its feet economically. This is the business of the Europeans. The initiative, I think, must come from Europe. The role of this country should consist of friendly aid in the drafting of a European program and of later support of such a program so far as it may be practical for us to do so. The program should be a joint one, agreed to by a number, if not all European nations.[71]

To channel this aid, two organizations were created: the European Recovery Program (ERP) and the Organization for European Economic Cooperation (OEEC), the former an American agency, and the latter European. Marshall's efforts did not constitute full integration, and by no means did they endorse "supranational" institutions. However, thanks to the OEEC (today's OECD) ministers from different countries ceased to deal with their national problems as something confidential that did not impact their neighboring nations, and progressed in the establishment of priorities through negotiations, as the intention was for aid to be used by the European countries in a coordinated way rather than be allocated individually to specific countries for particular purposes (Milward 2013, 56). The implementation of the Marshall Plan also had the institutional result of creating the "European Payments Union" which imposed a common monetary policy (Bozyk 2006, 154). The most important shift, however, was that public opinion and the positions of the governments of the various European states began to move towards the idea of European cooperation and alliances (Geiger 1999, 23–41).[72]

Another pivotal consequence of the Marshall Plan was that, because it was utterly rejected and opposed by Stalin, it was instrumental in cutting off Eastern Europe, occupied by Soviet troops, from Western Europe.

#### 18.4.1.3 Eastern Europe Splits Off

The Allies originally thought that military cooperation had softened Stalin's communism. Soviet Russia took advantage of the West's naiveté in this regard to extend its tentacles across Eastern Europe, which Stalin was determined to seize for Russia. Truly paradoxical is the fact that Stalinism continued to enjoy good press and favor in European public opinion, a striking circumstance which allowed the communists to enjoy significant electoral success throughout postwar Western Europe. In France the 1945 legislative elections were won by the communists, who obtained 25 % of the

[71] For the whole text, see Marshall (1947, 1159–1160).

[72] On the impact of the Marshall Plan on European integration, see Cini (2001, 13–38), Killick (1997, 134–146) and Spagnolo (2004, 275–298). For the history of the Plan, see Bossuat et al. (2008, 11–68).

votes; in Italy, after the proclamation of the Republic, Christian Democrat Alcide De Gasperi governed in coalition with communists and socialists; in Germany, the first political party authorized by the Allied occupation forces was the Communist Party (KPD); Churchill was defeated by the Labour Party, led by Clement Attlee; and the Communist Party of Great Britain had two members of Parliament. The triumph of leftist parties in post-war Europe seemed certain[73] until George Marshall appeared and announced that he had a plan to rebuild Europe.

Stalin, however, thoroughly opposed the plan (Grogin 2001, 117) while Poland, Czechoslovakia, Hungary, Romania, Bulgaria, Albania and, one by one, the countries of Eastern Europe fell behind the "Iron Curtain". Russia administrated all of them after the replacement of Lenin's old Comintern with the Cominform, an association of various national communist parties led by the CPSU, founded by Stalin in June of 1947. The lone exception was Yugoslavia, where partisan leader and communist Marshall Tito managed for his Balkan Federation, based on the independence and equality of its peoples ("within the framework of the principles stated in the Charter of the United Nations") to evade Soviet domination thanks to the unanimous support of Yugoslavia's Communists (Belgrade Conference).[74]

#### 18.4.1.4 Germany Splits and Spurs European Integration

The quintessential symbol of Europe's prostration to foreign powers after the end of World War II was undoubtedly Germany, a defeated and decimated nation divided (at the Yalta and Potsdam conferences) by the Allies into four zones, controlled by the Russians, Americans, British, and French. This division became twofold when the German territory controlled by the Soviets was transformed into a "popular democracy" to differentiate it from the other three areas controlled by the western Allies, which fully benefitted from the Marshall Plan (Parish 1997, 268–290). Thus, the western Allies decided to merge the three zones—American, English, and French—into one. On June 20, 1948 the Allies, as we know, approved the

[73] As Judt (2007, 88) points out, in the early postwar years the attraction of Communism was very real. Even if the communist parties of Italy, France, Belgium, Finland and Iceland were in governing coalitions, they did a good job of mobilizing popular anger against the failures of their own governments and capitalizing on them through trade union affiliates and popular demonstrations. The path of socialism seemed plausible and seductive. By 1947, 907,000 men and women had joined the French Communist Party. The Italian Communist Party boasted 2.5 million members. Even in Denmark and Norway, one voter in eight was initially attracted to the promise of a communist alternative.

[74] On the 1948 break between Tito and Stalin and how the Yugoslav Party placed itself outside the united communist front, maintaining Yugoslavia's independence and building socialism without the support of the communist parties of other countries, especially without the support of the Soviet Union, see Wilson (1993, 49–59). Also, Haug (2012).

revaluation of the *Deutschmark* that replaced the worthless *Reichsmark* and launched the German Economic Miracle (*Wirtschaftswunder*) (Loedel 1999, 2).[75]

In response, Stalin imposed an "Eastern Deutschmark" throughout Berlin and a blockade of the areas of the capital controlled by western forces. The Allies responded, beginning on June 26, 1948, by organizing the famous "Berlin Airlift" to provision western Berlin (Miller 2000). The Soviet blockade would not cease until May 21, 1949. The border between the two areas would be relatively permeable until the construction of the Berlin Wall which, beginning on August 13, 1961, became the ultimate symbol of the new state of things (Landsman 2005, 173–207) one that would stand for nearly 30 years.[76]

The dismantling of Germany by the Allies after the end of the war resulted in the country's total economic collapse. The Germans struggled just to survive in their wasted land, wallowing amidst the ruins. Epidemics ravaged the population. In 1947 the number of TB patients far surpassed the number of available hospital beds.[77] Under these dire circumstances the Allies faced a dilemma. On the one hand it was unacceptable to abandon Germany to its fate, but, on the other, they had to do their utmost to prevent the resurgence of German nationalism (Lewkowicz 2010, 15–36). The only solution was for Germany to be brought into a process of European integration. The question of German resurgence thus became the main engine and spur for a European alliance.

### 18.4.2 A First, Unsuccessful Attempt at Integration: The Congress of The Hague (1948), and the Failure to Form a Federal Europe

As a preliminary step it was necessary to decide the path to be followed to achieve integration.[78] A portion of the European public opinion, the federalists, wished to

---

[75] On the German economic recovery, see Glossner (2013).

[76] On the history of the relationship between Western and Eastern Germans, see Gehler (2013), Naimark (1995) and Turner (1987).

[77] As Weber (2004, 3–4) points out, by the end of 1945 the most pressing problem in Germany was survival itself. Millions of homes, especially in the towns, had been completely destroyed. Many sought shelter in ruins. Families were torn apart and millions of people displaced. Most Germans were on the edge of starvation, to mention the 1.9 million German women raped at the end of the war by Red Army soldiers (Grossman 2004, 121). For an overview of Germany during the Reconstruction period, see Carlin (1996, 463–467). On German's politics and laws of Amnesty and Integration in that time, see Frei (2013).

[78] Pan-European movements started to emerge in the period from 1946 to 1947, including the reconstituted Pan-European Union, the European Parliamentary Union, and the Union of European Federalists (UEF), which acted as promotional groups for the idea a supranational Europe, starting from a "European constituent assembly". The first meeting of all these groups was organized by the UEF and was the Montreux Congress of August 27–31, 1947. For an overview of the rising idea of European federalism during the early postwar years, see Sidjanski (2000, 13–18).

move directly towards a federal political union, similar to that of the United States of America.[79] Another camp, the statists, preferred a model based on intergovernmental cooperation in which states would retain their independence and autonomy, and decisions would be made by way of negotiations between them.[80]

A European "Congress" met on May 8, 1948 in The Hague (Netherlands). The European federalists, to insure reconciliation and reconstruction, called for the creation of an economic and political union (Moschonas 1996, 15). The problem was that the European Congress was not attended by representatives of Europe's states, but rather a host of members of various federalist movements from all different corners of European society: political (the German delegation was headed by Konrad Adenauer, and were also present notorious figures as Churchill, Schuman or Spaak), social, economic, cultural, intellectual and artistic (Reinfeld 2009, 287–298). None of the 800 participants, however, had the power to actually commit their states to any agreements. It was, essentially, a gathering of representatives from different political parties and other European democratic groups interested in the reemergence of the Old Continent on the international scene (Samaniego Boneu 2009, 52).[81]

Churchill underscored the euphoria of the "atmosphere" which imbued "this historic gathering" and the participants' enthusiasm led to some gushing overstatements by those who defined the Congress as a new "Tennis Court Oath" or the "Saint Bartholomew's Day for national sovereignty" (Larres 2002, 144–145). In reality the Congress of The Hague was a loud yet fruitless forum in which two postures clashed: the federalists wanted to choose a "representative assembly" to establish a federal European state, while the statists, led by the British delegation, were only willing to endorse an assembly of fundamentally autonomous states, such

[79] On the European approach to federalism, see Burgess (2006, 7–26) and Moravcsik (2003, 161–190). For a comparative approach to federalism from the American and European perspectives, see Elazar (2005, 31–53) and Weiler (2001, 54–72).

[80] As Moschonas (1996, 13–14) observes, the statist approach was essentially advanced by the British, because the British government thought that the preservation of its former status as a major world power required three overlapping circles of relationships: with the United States, the Commonwealth, and the European states associated in the traditional intergovernmental form. This approach was reinforced by the British political tradition and its respect for the supremacy of Parliament, perceived as the guardian of national sovereignty. The British position prevailed initially in the organization of the OEEC as an intergovernmental body operating under the control of a ministerial council operating on a unanimous basis.

[81] Among the delegates that attended the European conference from May 7 to 10, 1948 were 12 former presidents of the Council of Ministers, 20 current ministers, and 100 MPs of diverse political affiliations, and famous writers, such as Jules Romain, Raymond Aron, Salvador de Madariaga and Denis de Rougemont. There were also many figures from the academic world, the trade unions, and the churches (Sidjanski 2000, 18). Some Spaniards attended the Congress, but only expatriates who did not represent Franco's regime. From the political realm, socialist Indalecio Prieto was there, as was Salvador de Madariaga, from the cultural sphere.

as the framework of the United States of America under the Articles of Confederation (1777–1787) government.[82]

The attendees sought to reach a compromise. The federalists got their Representative Assembly, while the statists got a Council of Ministers, the embryo of a European executive power. Together the institutions formed the Council of Europe, a body established on May 5, 1949, a year after the opening of the Congress of The Hague (Dedman 2010, 14–29).

An Assembly of 87 deputies was elected, in which large states had more representatives, with seating in alphabetical order. The Assembly, however, was invariably overpowered by the Council of Ministers, which exercised all power because of Britain's emphatic opposition to the Council of Europe serving as anything more than a meeting of representatives from states seeking intergovernmental cooperation.[83]

By early 1950, the federal formula had failed to achieve the objective of European integration. The Council of Europe, however, did not disappear, and ended up establishing itself as a Human Rights Tribunal after the signing of the European Convention for the Protection of Rights and Fundamental Freedoms in Rome on November 4, 1950. This agreement would come into force in 1953, since which time states may be legally reported to the Tribunal of the Council of Europe based in Strasbourg for human rights violations. Its rulings constituted since the beginning a moral reference point in the defense of fundamental freedoms and the consolidation of democracy, and are binding since December 1, 2009. In any case, they have progressively informed the *acquis communautaire* and laws of the member states.[84]

Another result of The Hague Congress was the foundation of the College of Europe, in Bruges (Belgium), an institution dedicated to educating "European elites" which continues to fulfill this mission today.[85]

---

[82] As Sidjanski (2000, 19) explains, a notable feature of the debates was the struggle between unionists (partisans of the statist approach) and federalists. Generally speaking The Hague Congress was not dominated by party or national considerations—with the important exception of the British, Conservative and Labor alike, who unanimously defended "unionism" and rejected the federal model.

[83] On the compromise reached in the Treaty of London of May 5, 1949 that gave rise to the original version of the Council of Europe, see Petaux (2009, 47–50).

[84] On the origins of the European Convention on Human Rights, which was opened for signature in Rome on November 4, 1950, and entered into force on September 3, 1953, and the European Court of Human Rights, see Petaux (2009, 143–161).

[85] The idea originally came from the Spanish diplomat Salvador de Madariaga (1886–1978), a conservative republican who was also a writer, historian and pacifist who presided over the Commission of Culture at The Hague Congress (Samaniego Boneu 2009, 43–56).

## 18.5 Step by Step Integration: The Invention of the "Community Method" (1950)

### *18.5.1 The Pioneers: Jean Monnet and Robert Schuman*

After the failure of the federal formula some "integrationists" sought a solution so that, despite British opposition, the principle of supranationality would prevail, at least in certain areas. The key players behind this partial solution were two Frenchmen: Jean Monnet and Robert Schuman.

#### 18.5.1.1 The Dazzling Career of Jean Monnet

Jean Monnet (1888–1979) never went to college. He was not a theorist, but a pragmatist. His father was a businessman who frequently travelled with his son to London, and especially the United States. As a result he developed an international spirit and extensive experience in business negotiations. However, Monnet would go down in history thanks to his achievements in the field of international politics.

It all started in 1914, at the outbreak of World War I. Monnet was 26 years old and exempted from military service for health reasons. Though he never fought he did participate in the war in a decisive way. His constant travels between France and England allowed him to observe how troops and military material were transported from Britain to the Continent. A lucid Monnet realized that there was a total lack of coordination between the French and British fleets, and conceived the idea for all transport operations to be run jointly. Monnet was bold, not hesitating to request an appointment with the President of the French Republic, Raymond Poincaré, who he managed to convince to create the Inter-Allied Maritime Transport Council, with full powers to organize the transport of troops and supplies (Fransen 2006, 23–27). The initiative was a resounding success, and contributed decisively to tipping the balance in favor of the Allies during the last months of the war. Jean Monnet proved to everyone that organization was the key to victory.

Monnet's success earned him a special prestige in the international arena, which led to him being appointed Deputy Secretary General of the League of Nations (Dûchene 1994, 41). Monnet had little interest in titles and honors, however. When he concluded that the League of Nations was ineffectual because the sovereign states were unwilling to subject themselves to the principle of supranationality, he resigned from his post in 1923 and returned home to take over the family business.[86]

He took an interest in international politics again in 1936 when he realized that Hitler was bent on another war. It was then when he decided to make every effort to

[86] Three years later, however, he found France too small and began to travel the world again. After founding the International Commercial Bank, headquartered in the United States, he spent enough time in Shanghai to help Chiang-Kai-shek modernize China's economy (Ugland 2011, 56).

keep the democratic nations from being defeated by totalitarianism. Statesmen continued to rely on him. In 1938 France's Prime Minister Edouard Daladier asked him to secretly buy warplanes from the United States (Fransen 2006, 68). This was a prickly task because the U.S. government's Neutrality Act prohibited the sale of weapons to any belligerent nation. Monnet, however, convinced Roosevelt not only to allow the sale of the planes, but also to make him part of the president's brain trust, thereby making the Frenchman the most influential European in the United States.

However, Monnet was still worried about his native Europe. In June of 1940, after France's military collapse, he was decisive in convincing Churchill and De Gaulle to create an indissoluble union between the United Kingdom and France, which failed when Marshall Pétain signed an armistice with the Nazis. Churchill then sent him as his representative to the United States to convince the Americans to produce armaments for the Allies. Once again Monnet brought Roosevelt around to his point of view, persuading him that America must become "the arsenal of democracy" (Nathan 1991, 72). The results of this policy were spectacular: 300,000 aircraft, 100,000 tanks, and 124,000 warships were produced by American factories for use in Europe and the Pacific. According to the prestigious English economist John Maynard Keynes, Jean Monnet's efforts reduced the duration of the war by one full year (Ugland 2011, 67).

After Germany's defeat Monnet committed himself to the reconstruction of Europe, beginning with his native France. To do so he dealt with General De Gaulle, but only became effective after being appointed the General Commissioner of the Marshall Plan, a position to which he was appointed by President Truman himself.[87] During his time at this post he came to realize to what extent Europe's resurgence depended upon breaking down its borders. A pragmatist first and foremost, Monnet eschewed grandiose theoretical statements and decided to concentrate his efforts on promoting the principle of "supranationality" in Europe with regards to a specific point. Defeated Germany served as a testing ground and platform for him to put his idea into practice.

The confrontation with the Soviet bloc raised the need to incorporate West Germany into the anti-Communist bloc, prompting the Allies to back the foundation of the Federal Republic of Germany on May 23, 1949. On this basis Jean Monnet had the idea of integrating the regions of the Ruhr and the Saar (Germany) and Alsace and Lorraine (French), bases of European coal and steel production, into a community that would encompass French and German production, although it was to be open to more states (Gillingham 1991, 129–162). Monnet's idea was received with enthusiasm by German President Konrad Adenauer, who saw in it a

[87] At the request of General De Gaulle Jean Monnet had prepared a plan for modernizing and equipping France (France's postwar Reequipment and Modernization Plan) that aimed at restoring France as a major power and the bulwark of democracy on the European Continent. The French Plan, which eventually became the "Monnet Plan", was extremely well received in France (Gimbel 1976, 157) with Monnet serving as the High Commissioner for the French Plan (Bossuat 2004, 127). For disentangling all those complex historical processes, see also, Griffiths (2014).

way to prevent a potential "Versailles Effect" by placing a defeated Germany on an equal footing with France in the constitution of a supranational entity binding upon both states.[88]

Apparently modest in its objective, Monnet's Coal and Steel Community was revolutionary in terms of its method: the freely consented cession of sovereignty in certain and decisive sectors to common and independent institutions (Community Method).

To carry out his plan, however, Jean Monnet needed political support, and Robert Schuman was just the man to give it to him.

#### 18.5.1.2 Robert Schuman, the Most German of Frenchmen

Robert Schuman (1886–1963) was born in Luxembourg but spent his childhood and youth in Germany. He studied in Berlin, Munich, Metz, Bonn, and Strasbourg, a German city since 1871. During World War I, as he did not physically qualify for military service, he served the Second Reich in the War Administration (Bitsch 2010, 19).[89] Living in Metz after the Treaty of Versailles (1919), he became a French citizen,[90] soon entered politics, and managed to be elected to the French National Assembly.[91] Politically he was a conservative but above all a pragmatic realist, with great expertise in financial matters. After World War II[92] he became a

---

[88] Monnet met Adenauer for the first time in the Schaumburg Palace (Bonn) on May 23, 1950. After Monnet explained the basis of his plan, Adenauer rose to his feet and said: "Monsieur Monnet, I regard the implementation of the French proposals as my most important task. If I succeed, I believe my life will not have been wasted" (Williams 2000, 360). About the fundamental foreign policy orientation of the Federal Republic given by Adenauer, see Schwarz (2011, 68–106).

[89] For years Schuman's political enemies, particularly the communists, insinuated that Schuman had been a German officer during the war, though the truth was that he had never worn a uniform (Fimister 2008, 152).

[90] After the Armistice of November 11, 1918, Schuman automatically received French citizenship, like all the inhabitants of the two provinces of Alsace and Lorraine. The "Old Germans"—Germans who immigrated to the Reichsland during the annexation period—were expelled (Bitsch 2010, 20).

[91] The Treaty of Versailles was signed on June 28, 1919, and on November 16, 1919, Schuman was elected deputy of the French National Assembly as part of a departmental list, a system that favored the relatively unknown Schuman, a Christian-Democrat willing to defend Catholicism and Catholic Social teaching (Fimister 2008, 153).

[92] In 1940, he became for the first time part of the government, called upon by French Prime minister Paul Reynaud as the state's undersecretary for refugees (Bitsch 2010, 20). In September 1940, Schuman was arrested by the Gestapo in Metz and held in solitary confinement until 1941, when he was transferred to Germany. Nevertheless, he was given considerable freedom and could go on walks in the surrounding area and enjoy the revenues from his property in Luxembourg. He escaped in August 1942 to Vichy France. After the occupation of the "free zone", he was driven into hiding in a series of different monasteries. After liberation, Schuman was barred from holding public office as he was classified as a Petainist minister. His good name was restored thanks to De Gaulle's personal intervention (Fimister 2008, 163–165).

minister and then Prime Minister under the Fourth French Republic. Under these conditions, a union between France and Germany seemed to him an excellent idea.

If Jean Monnet had the idea, Schuman can be credited with implementing it politically, a task at which he received the support of other European politicians, such as the German Konrad Adenauer (1876–1967), Joseph Bech (1887–1975) of Luxembourg, and the Italian Alcide de Gasperi (1881–1954).

### *18.5.2 The Schuman Declaration of May 9, 1950*

In the spring of 1950, a new government was formed in France in which Robert Schuman was appointed Minister of Foreign Affairs. From his position, he was able to convince the French cabinet of the merits of Monnet's plans, and received permission to hold a press conference on May 9, 1950. The result was the Schuman Declaration, which laid a cornerstone in the construction of a united Europe (Dinan 2014, 37–45).[93]

The Declaration (Schuman 2011, 1–3) first proposed a method for the construction of a common Europe: concrete achievements that first create real solidarity.[94] The first tangible achievement was going to be built on the basis of the Franco-German union (Milward 2013, 126–140)[95] "on one limited but decisive point. . .that Franco-German production of coal and steel as a whole be placed under a common High Authority".

According to the Declaration this concrete action had three main objectives:

The common cause resulting from the joint implementation of coal and steel production was aimed, firstly, at preventing confrontation between regions which had long been dedicated to the manufacturing of weapons, of which they themselves had been the first victims. The objective, essentially, was to demonstrate that the shared production thus created would show that any war between France and Germany was not only unthinkable, but also materially impossible.[96]

---

[93] Since then, Europe Day is celebrated every year on May 9.

[94] Europe will not be made all at once, or according to a single plan. It will be built through concrete achievements which first create a de facto solidarity. (Schuman 2011, 1).

[95] The coming together of the nations of Europe requires the elimination of the age-old opposition of France and Germany. Any action taken must in the first place concern these two countries. (Schuman 2011, 1–2).

[96] "*The pooling of coal and steel production [. . .] will change the destinies of those regions which have long been devoted to the manufacture of munitions of war, of which they have been the most constant victims. The solidarity in production thus established will make it plain that any war between France and Germany becomes not merely unthinkable, but materially impossible*" (Schuman 2011, 2). As Gillingham (2002, 372) points out, the Schuman Plan succeeded in part because it gave the European nations an opportunity to surmount historic antagonisms that were fast becoming irrelevant.

Secondly, the pooling of coal and steel was seen as a tool for economic development, as it ensured the merging of markets and the expansion of production through the modernization of production and the improvement of its quality. The provisioning of coal and steel under conditions identical to the French market and the German markets, and to those of member countries, would assure the development of common exports to other countries, giving equal opportunities and improving living conditions for workers in these industries.[97] This was all to be achieved while respecting free market rules.[98]

Thirdly, the new organization was to be the first stage of a European federation because subjecting the production of coal and steel to a common authority was something open to all other European countries wishing to participate in it:

> The setting up of this powerful productive unit, open to all countries willing to take part and bound ultimately to provide all the member countries with the basic elements of industrial production on the same terms, will lay a true foundation for their economic unification [...] In this way, there will be realized simply and speedily that fusion of interest which is indispensable to the establishment of a common economic system; it may be the leaven from which may grow a wider and deeper community between countries long opposed to one another by sanguinary divisions. By pooling basic production and by instituting a new High Authority, whose decisions will bind France, Germany and other member countries, this proposal will lead to the realization of the first concrete foundation of a European federation indispensable to the preservation of peace.

Finally, the Declaration stipulated how France and Germany were to proceed to submit the production of Coal and Steel to a High Authority independent of their respective governments:

First, it was stipulated that, legally, the concrete transfer of sovereignty was to be incorporated into a treaty as a way to bind the member states.[99] Secondly the "High

---

[97] This production will be offered to the world as a whole without distinction or exception, with the aim of contributing to raising living standards [...] The task with which this common High Authority will be charged will be that of securing in the shortest possible time the modernization of production and the improvement of its quality; the supply of coal and steel on identical terms to the French and German markets, as well as to the markets of other member countries; the development in common of exports to other countries; the equalization and improvement of the living conditions of workers in these industries; the pooling of coal and steel production should immediately provide [...] for economic development.... (Schuman 2011, 2).

[98] The movement of coal and steel between member countries will immediately be freed from all customs duty, and will not be affected by differential transport rates. Conditions will gradually be created which will spontaneously provide for the more rational distribution of production at the highest level of productivity. In contrast to international cartels, which tend to impose restrictive practices on distribution and the exploitation of national markets, and to maintain high profits, the organization will ensure the fusion of markets and the expansion of production. (Schuman 2011, 2–3).

[99] The essential principles and undertakings defined above will be the subject of a treaty signed between the states and submitted for the ratification of their parliaments. (Schuman 2011, 3).

Authority" was to be fully independent from the member states so its decisions would have executive force in the signatory states:

> The common High Authority entrusted with the management of the scheme will be composed of independent persons appointed by the governments, giving equal representation. A chairman will be chosen by common agreement between the governments. The Authority's decisions will be enforceable in France, Germany and other member countries. Appropriate measures will be provided for means of appeal against the decisions of the Authority.

## 18.6 From the European Coal and Steel Community to the European Economic Community (1951–1957)

### *18.6.1 The 1951 Treaty of Paris and the Creation of the ECSC*

The next step was the establishment of a specialized committee to handle the project's technical details, which Monnet chaired himself. Soon representatives from France and Germany joined those from Italy and the three Benelux countries. The negotiations were carried out on new bases, as they were no longer adversaries but "teammates" who, as stated by Schuman, were engaged in a "common search".

The committee worked quickly. On April 18, 1951 the Treaty establishing the European Coal and Steel Community (ECSC) was signed in Paris. This first European Community was essential because it heralded the three basic institutions of the European integration process: an **executive power**, the High Authority—today the Commission—with sovereign powers which was responsible to an **assembly** (the current European Parliament) and whose decisions were monitored a posteriori by a European **Court of Justice** (today the Court of Justice of the European Union in Luxembourg) (Wilson 2003, 133).

The ECSC was dissolved on July 23, 2002, but not before playing an essential and historic role by paving the way for the European communities that succeeded it (Gillingham 2002, 299–363). In fact, the constitution of the ECSC was a great blow to the statist camp, in particular the British, as the United Kingdom was excluded from the process.[100]

[100] On how Foreign Office Secretary Ernest Bevin encouraged Attlee's government to reject British participation in the Schuman Plan (and by doing so relinquished a leading role in fashioning European integration, according to the testimony of one of Bevin's advisers), see Dell (2004).

For the first time the ECSC implemented the "Community Method", aimed at supranationality by assigning the High Authority power[101] that superseded that of the member states.

### 18.6.2 *From the Failure of the EDC to the Treaties of Rome (1951–1957)*

The six signatory states decided to forge ahead with the integration process, despite British resistance. Current events at the time seemed to affect the course taken towards integration, as on June 25, 1950 the Korean War began. The confrontation with the communist bloc, of which Mao's China now formed part (October 1, 1949), made Europeans uneasy, spurring them to request the formation of a military alliance with the United States, which led to the establishment of the North Atlantic Treaty Organization (NATO) on April 4, 1949 (Hanhimäki and Westad 2004, 107).

It is, then, understandable that the next step in European integration was the creation of a European Defense Community (EDC), a new idea of Jean Monnet's endorsed by René Pleven, then France's Minister of Foreign Affairs (Bossuat 1996, 191). The objective was to create an organization of European armed forces, integrating West Germany (FRG) into the European Community. The treaty was signed by the six members of the ECSC on May 27, 1952 and was ratified by five national parliaments. In the end, it failed because the French National Assembly, the parliament of the country that had advanced it, voted against ratification on August 30, 1954 (Sanderson 2003, 336).[102] It would not be until the Amsterdam Treaty of 1999 that Europe considered adopting a common defense policy again.

The failure of the EDC prompted Jean Monnet to resign from the presidency of the High Authority of the ECSC to concentrate his energies on establishing and leading an "Action Committee for the United States of Europe", established in 1955 (Fransen 2006, 125). This was a pressure group comprised of qualified leaders (politicians, trade union representatives and employers) with the authority to make decisions in their respective fields, and charged with promoting European integration (Hayward 2008, 15–27).

[101] The fact that this common institution was going to have sovereign authority over the British Parliament was the most disturbing aspect of the Schuman Plan for the British government (Dell 2004, 171).

[102] France had just lost the war in Indochina, with its defeat at the Battle of Dien Bien Phu (June 1954). Curiously, the conservative Gaullists in this case voted together with the communists and part of the socialists and radicals on the nationalist side against the pro-European government. The result of the vote was 319 against 264, with 43 abstentions.

As in France nationalist politicians had triumphed, the political initiative for European integration fell to the "Benelux" countries, then led by Joseph Bech (Luxembourg), Paul Henri Spaak (Belgium), and Jan Wilem Beyen (Netherlands). Thanks to them the decisive Messina Conference (June 1955) was held,[103] which yielded two new European communities: the European Economic Community (EEC), or Common Market, and the European Atomic Energy Community (EAEC or EURATOM). Their founding treaties were signed on March 25, 1957 in Rome (Gilbert 2012, 51–56).

## 18.7 The Extension of the Community Method to Create a Common European Market, and the Institutionalization of European Integration (1957–1965)

Of the two Rome Treaties the EEC was by far the most important, as it aimed to create a Common European market based on the principle of the free movement of goods, workers, and services, and the full application of competition rules. The exception was agricultural production, which relied upon public subsidies from the EEC. This was a very important exception, as in 1957 European public aid to Agriculture represented 75 % of expenses in the EEC's budget.[104] The Community Method was applied to the framework of the three Communities created between 1951 and 1957, which led to the institutionalization of common institutions and procedures.

### *18.7.1 The Court of Justice of the European Communities and the European Parliament*

With the adoption of the Treaties of Rome, European integration had been "institutionalized". The formal structure of the ECSC was modified. On March 19, 1958 the European Parliamentary Assembly was created in Strasbourg, superseding the

[103] An interesting aspect of the Messina Conference was that the British were invited to attend it, as the governments of the six member states wished to encourage their participation. The British did all they could to boycott the conference (Gifford 2008, 35–37).

[104] Today it is still extremely important, though this amount has been reduced to 50 %. Article 39 of the EEC Treaty defined the objectives of a Common Agricultural Policy (CAP) intended to increase agricultural productivity by promoting technical progress and ensuring the rational development of agricultural production, ensure a fair standard of living for the agricultural community, stabilize markets, and assure the availability of supplies at a reasonable price. The CAP was essential, as without it there would never have been a Common Market (Gilbert 2012. 54).

Common Assembly of ECSC,[105] and the Court of Justice of the European Communities was established in Luxembourg on October 7.[106] On March 30, 1962, the European Parliamentary Assembly changed its name to the European Parliament (EP) (Evans and Silk 2008, 305).

### *18.7.2 The European Free Trade Association: A British "Tantrum"*

The success of the Common Market incited the British, who had stayed out of the treaties, to create their own international trade association. The British government, conscious that they had relinquished European leadership (Dell 2004), reacted to the Schuman plan and the further development of the first three European communities by creating the European Free Trade Association (EFTA), a product of the Stockholm Convention of January 4, 1960. This alliance was initially composed of Austria, Denmark, Great Britain, Norway, Portugal, Sweden, and Switzerland. The EFTA, however, proved a failure, as most of its members, starting with the United Kingdom, dropped out of it, and joined the European Community, the EEC (Denmark, United Kingdom, and Portugal) or the EU (Austria, Finland, and Sweden).[107]

### *18.7.3 The Merging of Community Executives*

The creation of the EFTA did not halt the institutionalization of the European integration process. Despite British pressure, European integration of the six member states of the three communities, implemented according to the Schuman Plan, became an unstoppable movement that moved ahead through the merging of Community executives. As each of the three European communities (ECSC,

[105] The Common Assembly had first met from September 10 to 13, 1952 (Evans and Silk 2008, 305).

[106] For an overview of the history of this crucial institution see Tamm (2013, 9–36) and Wallace (2010, 84–86).

[107] As Blanchet et al. (1994, 1) point out, the EFTA was initially established between those states which did not wish to become members of the EC. This is why they opted for the creation of a free trade zone limited to free trade in industrial goods. From the institutional perspective, the new association was governed by intergovernmental bodies without legislative powers or any supranational element. After Denmark and the UK joined the EC in 1973, the remaining EFTA countries concluded bilateral free trade agreements essentially aimed at guaranteeing the maintenance of free trade with the new EC member states and their ex-EFTA colleagues. The EFTA continues in existence today, but with only four members: Iceland, Liechtenstein, Norway, and Switzerland. See also Fenger (2012).

CVEE, and EAEC) had its executive power, in contrast to the Parliament and the Court, which were common, the six decided to fuse the three executive authorities into one. Thus, on April 8, 1965 the Executive Merger Treaty was signed in Brussels, entering into force on July 1, 1967 (Laursen 2012, 78).

## 18.8 A Step Back in the Integration Process: A Return to the Intergovernmental Method (1966–1986)

De Gaulle rose to power in France during the Algeria crisis in 1958. After overseeing the drafting of a new constitution he consolidated the French presidential system in 1962 by introducing the direct election of the President of the Republic. De Gaulle was a proud nationalist convinced that France had gone too far as European integration was concerned. Thus, he endeavored to bring about a return to the intergovernmental method of integration, returning power to member states and weakening Community institutions (Giauque 2002, 126–157).

### *18.8.1 The Rejection of Qualified Majority Voting and the Return of Unanimity: The Luxembourg Compromise*

Despite the creation of the first three European communities, the governments of the member states were still not willing to subject themselves to the principle of supranationality by mere majority votes. France, then led by De Gaulle, ceased from attending community meetings (the "empty chair" policy) to block the application of the majority vote principle. On January 30, 1966, through the **Luxembourg Compromise**, six Community countries agreed that a *unanimous* vote would be necessary to make decisions on essential issues.[108]

### *18.8.2 On the Path Towards Expansion*

The success of the European Community's integration process became clear when England requested membership, a step delayed by De Gaulle's staunch opposition

[108] As Douglas-Scott (2002, 80) explains, the Luxembourg Compromise was never accepted by the Commission or the European Court of Justice. The latter stated in 1986—the year of the Single European Act—that "the rules regarding the manner in which Community institutions arrive at their decisions are laid down in the treaty and are not at the disposal of the member states or the institutions themselves". Case 68/78 UK vs. Council [1988] ECR 855. Also, Schütze (2012, 21–22).

(Chopra 1974, 148).[109] When he stepped down in 1969, however, the United Kingdom's entry became inevitable. On January 1, 1973, the **United Kingdom**, along with **Ireland** and **Denmark**, carried out the first expansion of the European Community, giving rise to "the Europe of the 9".[110] This configuration lasted until 1981 when **Greece** joined, soon followed by **Spain** and **Portugal** (1986), countries that had emerged from dictatorships.

### *18.8.3 The Democratization of the Integration Process: An Elective European Parliament*

As we have seen, the European Parliament appeared in 1962, since which time its members were appointed by each of the member states' national parliaments, which meant that all MEP's had a dual mandate. All this changed between May 7–10, 1979, 2 months after Jean Monnet's death, when the first EP elections would be held by direct universal suffrage simultaneously in the then nine member states to elect 410 MEPs, with a turnout of 63 %. These elections marked a breakthrough, as for the first time European citizens, previously excluded from the integration process, became direct participants in determining the European authorities who would govern them. Direct elections were intended not only to make the integration process more legitimate but also to consolidate the EP's powers, prestige and influence (Smith 1999, 56) Since then elections have been held every 5 years.[111]

## 18.9 Returning to the Community Method: From the Single European Act to the Maastricht Treaty (1986–1992)

The Luxembourg Compromise imposed by De Gaulle had quite clearly impeded the process of integration. The objective of a common market was far from being achieved as member states continued to feature legislation posing many obstacles to its establishment. Two treaties were drafted to address this problem: the **Schengen Agreement** (1985) and the **Single European Act** (1986).

---

[109] For an overview of the British attitude towards European integration, see Geddes (2013), Kaiser (1996), and Preda and Pasquinucci (2010).

[110] On how the British Prime Minister Edward Heath (1970–1974) fought for the UK's integration into the EC, see Gwoland et al. (2010, 72–76).

[111] In 1984, 1989, 1994, 1999, 2004, 2009 and 2014. See Nugent (2010, 176–206).

### 18.9.1 The Schengen Agreement

The treaty signed on June 14, 1985 by the ten member states of the EEC, near the town of Schengen in Luxembourg, was intended to initiate a process leading to the gradual abolition of impediments at the signatories' borders within a period of 10 years.[112] In 1990 the agreement was complemented by the Schengen Implementation Agreement (Kölliker 2006, 217), which introduced the principle of the abolition of internal borders and a common visa policy. Ireland and the United Kingdom opted out and do not belong to the Schengen Area.

### 18.9.2 The Single European Act

The Single European Act was signed in Luxembourg on February 17, 1986, and at The Hague on February 28. The aim of this treaty was to create a Single Market (Swann 2004, 3–24) in the EEC Community by 1992 by removing barriers to increase harmonization and competitiveness among EEC member states (Allen 2004, 26–52). To achieve this the treaty reformed the legislative procedure, introducing the "cooperation procedure" according to which the European Parliament had a real say in legislating for the first time, cooperating with the Council and extending Qualified Majority Voting to new Areas (the Environment, Regional Policy and Consumer Protection) in the Council.[113]

## 18.10 Combining the Community and the Intergovernmental Methods: From the Europe of Communities to the European Union (1992–2009)

On Thursday, November 9, 1989 the Berlin Wall fell. With the most vivid symbol of the Cold War gone, Germany undertook a process of reunification. On September 12, 1990, the foreign ministers of the United States of America, the Soviet Union, the United Kingdom, and France signed the Two-Plus-Four Treaty, which granted

[112] The ultimate aim of the Treaty was the reinforcement of external border controls, which required the establishment of the Schengen Information System and the implementation of the Schengen rules of asylum. For an overview of the approval and development of the Schengen system, see Kölliker (2006, 211–219).

[113] Under the procedure the Council could, with the support of Parliament and acting on a proposal by the Commission, adopt a legislative proposal by a qualified majority, but the Council could also overrule a rejection of a proposed law by the Parliament by adopting a proposal unanimously. For an overview of the consequences of the Single European Act on this crucial aspect of decision-making in the European integration process, see Dinan (2014, 206–215). Also, Parsons (2010, 706–734).

Germany full sovereignty (Quint 1997, 268–285). On the night of October 2–3, 1990, the German people officially celebrated German Unity. Also, on December 2, 1990, all Germans elected a pan-German parliament for the first time since 1933. The end of the Cold War brought about the dissolution of the Soviet Union on December 21, 1991. The Iron Curtain was lifted and Western Europe discovered that the Eastern European countries were eager to participate in the European integration process (Mazzucelli 1999, 35–56). The European Communities responded by strengthening integration through the signing of the Maastricht Treaty in 1992, which led to a tighter-knit Economic and Monetary Union, and by accepting the addition of new member states.[114] During this crucial 10-year period (1985–1995) Jacques Delors served as president of the European Commission.[115]

### 18.10.1 The Maastricht Treaty and the Appearance of the Structured Integration Pillar

On February 7, 1992, the 12 Member States of the European Communities convened in the Dutch city of Maastricht to sign the Treaty on European Union (TEU), which came into force on November 1, 1993. Through this agreement the "Europe of Communities" (ECSC, EAEC, and EEC) was apparently simplified into a single Community: the European Union. In fact, it was not that simple. What was approved via the Maastricht Treaty was the introduction of the three-pillar structure for the process of European integration, each pillar representing a certain policy area and a specific type of decision-making and institutional structure (Verdun and Stavridis 2002, 56).

The first pillar, called the "Community Pillar" corresponded to the three existing Communities: the European Coal and Steel Community, the European Community and the European Atomic Energy Community. When in 2002 the Treaty of Paris expired, all ECSC activities and resources were absorbed by the European Union, and all the areas encompassed by this pillar[116] were subject to the Community integration method, which meant that the decision-making procedure followed a supranational approach was based essentially on Qualified Majority Voting

[114] For an overview of the historical prelude to Maastricht, see Mazzucelli (19997, 35–55). Also, Krotz and Schild (2013, 114–157).

[115] On Delors, the man who many consider the best president the European Commission has had, and his decisive role in the strengthening of European integration, see Drake (2000) and Ross (1995).

[116] The areas included in the first pillar were: Customs Union and Single Market, Common Agricultural Policy, Common Fisheries Policy, EU Competition Law, Economic and Monetary Union, EU Citizenship, Education and Culture, Trans-European Networks, Consumer Protection, Healthcare, Research, Environmental Law, Social Policy, Asylum Policy, the Schengen Treaty, Immigration Policy, the European Coal and Steel Community (ECSC, until 2002), the Coal and Steel Industry, European Atomic Energy Community (EURATOM), including Nuclear Power.

(QMV).[117] The second pillar dealt with Common Foreign and Security Policy, and the third addressed Police and Judicial Cooperation in Criminal Matters. The integration method concerning these two pillars was intergovernmental, which meant that in these areas[118] the decision-making procedures essentially followed the Unanimity Principle.[119]

Another important aspect introduced by the Maastricht Treaty was the notion of European citizenship, which included rights such as that to vote in European elections; the right to free movement, settlement and employment across the EU; and the right to consular protection from other EU states' embassies when a person's country of citizenship does not maintain an embassy or consulate in the country in which they need protection (Maas 2007, 45–52). Since 1994 it also provides for the right to vote in local elections in a member state of which one is not a citizen.[120]

### *18.10.2 Towards an Economic and Monetary Union: The Euro as a Common Currency*

The Maastricht Treaty was only one more step forming part of the European integration process. Next was the European Economic and Monetary Union (EMU). To achieve integration the TEU included criteria for economic convergence that imposed strict controls on inflation, public debt and public deficit, exchange rate stability, and the convergence of interest rates (Underhill 2002, 31–52).

Thanks to the EMU in 1995 EU authorities invented the euro, which was introduced into the world's financial markets as a currency on January 1, 1999, replacing the former European Currency Unit (ECU), though physical notes and coins were introduced on January 1, 2002 (Cohen 2008, 37–53).[121]

---

[117] The Community Method of Integration is essentially characterized by the Commission's monopoly on the right of initiative; a widespread use of qualified majority voting in the Council; an active role for the European Parliament (opinions, proposals for amendments, etc.); and a uniform interpretation of Community law by the Court of Justice.

[118] The areas of the second pillar are in the domain of Foreign Policy: Human Rights, Democracy, Foreign Aid; and regarding Common Security and Defense Policy: EU battle groups, Helsinki Headline Goal, Force Catalogue and Peacekeeping. The areas included in the Third Pillar (Police and Judicial Cooperation in Criminal Matters) are Drug Trafficking and Weapons Smuggling; Terrorism; Trafficking in Human Beings; Organized Crime; Bribery and Fraud.

[119] The Intergovernmental Method of Integration is characterized essentially by the fact that the Commission's right of initiative is shared with the member states or confined to specific areas of activity; the Council generally acts unanimously; the European Parliament has a purely consultative role; and the Court of Justice plays only a minor role.

[120] Council Directive 94/80/EC of December 19, 1994.

[121] To date, 17 member states have joined the Eurozone. An overview on actual EU citizenship issues in Strumia (2013).

### *18.10.3 Many New Members*

In 1992, when the Treaty of Maastricht, was signed the EU was comprised of 12 member states, though the repercussions of the Cold War's end would soon facilitate the EU's further expansion.

On January 1, 1995, **Austria**, **Finland,** and **Sweden**, hitherto neutral countries during the Cold War period, were able to join the European Communities.[122] As developed and democratic countries, they readily accepted the *acquis communautaire*: the cumulative body of European Community laws, comprising the EC's objectives, substantive rules, policies and, in particular, primary and secondary legislation and case law, all of which form part of the legal order of the European Union (EU).[123]

Next was the integration of Europe's former communist countries (the Easter Enlargement), which was far more difficult, as these countries were not only emerging from dictatorships, and in need of democratization, but also suffered from serious economic underdevelopment. To ensure that they did not fall back into the Russian sphere of influence, on May 1, 2004, the **Czech Republic**, **Estonia**, **Hungary**, **Latvia**, **Lithuania**, **Poland**, **Slovakia**, and **Slovenia**, plus two Mediterranean countries (**Malta** and **Cyprus**), joined the European Union, followed by **Romania** and **Bulgaria** on January 1, 2007. Finally, on July 1, 2013 **Croatia** joined the Union, becoming its 28th member state.[124]

### *18.10.4 The Need to Reorganize the EU: From Amsterdam to Lisbon*

Operating as a single market, the European Union covers 4 million km$^2$ and has a population of 503 million. The EU's economy—measured in terms of the goods and services it produces (GDP)—is now larger than that of the U.S., as in 2012 it boasted a GDP of 15.97 trillion USD, edging out the US, with 15.94. Booming China, meanwhile, came in at 8.22, Japan at 5.96, and Germany at 3.57.

[122] East Germany automatically became part of the European Communities when it was reunified with West Germany on October 3, 1990, so it did not increase the number of states. On the fall of the Berlin Wall, and its consequences, see Hansmann (2011).

[123] The term *acquis communautaire* is most often used in connection with preparations by candidate countries to join the Union. They must adopt, implement, and enforce the entire *acquis* to be allowed to join the EU (Horspool and Humphreys 2006, 12). Often it requires changing national laws as well, which entails setting up or changing the necessary administrative or judicial bodies overseeing legislation.

[124] On the access to democracy and the process of incorporating former communist countries into the European Union, see Haerpfer (2002, 109–140) and Pridham (2008, 1–24). An overview in Wolchik and Curry (2011) and a comparative study between East-Central and Western Europe political systems in Hloušek and Kopeček (2010).

However, dealing with 28 countries and 503 million people makes things difficult in terms of decision-making. European integration is irreversible, but it continues to be a miracle because its legal and institutional foundations are of considerable complexity, based on several overlapping treaties whose texts have been successively amended. The European states have integrated, but *in spite of* rather than *because of* this complex system, which represents a veritable legal morass. The participating governments are aware that there is no turning back now, but have been unable to simplify the Union's foundations. Its legal bases, its treaties, are still a dizzying maze.

This is why the governments of the EU Member States have been trying to restructure it in a manageable way. Following the Treaty of Maastricht came the Treaty of Amsterdam on October 2, 1997, which entered into force on May 1, 1999; and the Treaty of Nice on February 26, 2001, which set the majorities necessary for decision-making after the successive expansions (Felsenthal and Machover 2013, 593–614), entering into force on February 1, 2003 upon the completion of the corresponding ratification procedures.

The truth is that there was an attempt to clarify the EU's organization through the signing of a single treaty in 2004, the deceptively entitled "Treaty of the European Constitution" (as it was not a constitution in the technical sense of the term, but a consolidation of the treaties). On October 29, 2004, in Rome, the heads of state and government and their respective ministers of foreign affairs signed a treaty establishing a Constitution for Europe (Amato 2007). The initiative failed because the agreement was rejected in referendums by the citizens of France and the Netherlands in 2005, rejections which raised the question again about whether the European integration process suffers from a democratic deficit (Weiler 1995, 12). Yo no pondría una referencia aquí anterior a 2005 (Thomassen 2009, 118).

## 18.11 The EU of the Twenty-First Century

### *18.11.1 The Lisbon Treaty*

After this setback to the cause of European Union, another step forward was taken on December 13, 2007, with the signing of the Treaty of Lisbon, which superseded the Constitutional Treaty of 2004. After a long and knotty ratification process, ultimately all 27-member states approved the treaty, which went into force on December 1, 2009. On January 1, 2010, the EU named the first full-time president of the European Council: Belgium's Herman Van Rompuy (b. 1947).

The Treaty of Lisbon abolished the three-pillar structure, and for the first time the European Union became an entity with legal personality, which it means it can establish and enforce international law distinct from that of its member states.[125] It

[125] Prior to the Lisbon Treaty, the EC was accorded legal personality by article 281 of the EEC Treaty. There was no direct equivalent provision in the Maastricht (TEU) Treaty, although its

also reinforces democracy by giving more power to the European Parliament, by approving the right of European citizens to present legislative initiatives upon the gathering of one million signatures, and by enforcing the Charter of Fundamental Rights of the European Union.

However, as far as the integration process is concerned the abolition of the "pillar" structure did not entail the "Communitization" of the Common Foreign and Security Policy at which the intergovernmental method is aimed. Similarly, although the areas of police and judicial cooperation in criminal matters have been integrated into the regime of ordinary law, specific procedures, where member states retain significant powers, continue to be applicable to them (Weber 2012, 311–322).

## *18.11.2 A Legally Complex Integration*

The Treaty of Lisbon has marked a considerable step forward, but it has not ended the integration process. Thus, the European Union, unlike the United States, continues to grope towards real unity.[126] Besides political and economic difficulties, an important part of the problem is that, legally speaking, the integration is extremely complex. Firstly, because the EU still has no supranational constitution, and, secondly, because its legislative basis is extraordinarily complicated.

### 18.11.2.1 The Absence of a Common Supranational Constitution

The legal consequence of the fact that the EU has not followed the Convention Method in a federalist approach (Oberhuber 2006, 90–119), but relies on the Community and Intergovernmental methods, is that the national constitutions of

---

Article 24 specified that international agreements were to be concluded by the EU. The Lisbon Treaty states in Article 47 that the "Union shall have legal personality". For an analysis of the consequences of this important statement in the European integration process, see Gautier (2000, 331–361), Kuijper et al. (2013, 1–22), de Schoutheete and Andoura (2007, 1–9) and Thürer and Marro (2012, 47–70).

[126] Crisis promotes European integration. In this regard, the depreciation of public debt affecting mainly Greece, Ireland, Spain, and Italy led German Chancellor Angela Merkel and French President Nicolas Sarkozy, in the summer of 2011, to propose a single economic government for the Eurozone to reduce the deficit and debt. This approach was soon echoed in Spain, where the two major parties, PP and PSOE, agreed to constitutional reform, changing Article 135 of the 1978 Spanish Constitution (García Andrade Gómez 2012, 31–66) to compel the country's regional governments (*Autonomías*) to respect the Spanish state's fiscal and budgetary policy, in line with the guidelines set by the Franco-German axis. In this way European integration has decisively transformed the functioning of the Spanish state and unilaterally reduced the competencies of its autonomous regions (Bassols Coma 2012, 317–338). Also, Ruiz Almendral (2013, 189–204). On The Treaty on Stability, Coordination and Governance in the Economic and Monetary Union or Fiscal Compact, see Adams et al. (2014).

the 28 member states take legal precedence over the European treaties. This means that every time a step towards integration is taken at the treaty level the procedure for implementing it is long and complex, as every state maintains full constitutional sovereignty over the matter. Ratification procedures become long, complex, and uncertain, as a single member country can halt the whole process, and sometimes it is necessary to provide for opt-out solutions for certain states to reach a final agreement. The result is that decision-making is inefficient, but there is a serious constitutional deficit caused by the disconnect between those who manage EU affairs and the wider public (O'Neill 2009, 8). The result is that the EU's *acquis communautaire* has become extremely complex.

#### 18.11.2.2 The Accretion of Treaties, or the Legislative Labyrinth of the *Acquis Communautaire*

As far as legislation is concerned, the complexity of European Community Law is overwhelming. One only needs to look at the Treaty of Lisbon, whose defining legislative feature is that it cannot be read alone, because it consists of a series of amendments to previous accords. (1) The European Union Treaty (Maastricht 1992) (2) The European Community Treaty—now called Treaty on the Functioning of the European Union (signed in Rome in 1957 and which created the EEC, amended by the Lisbon Treaty) (3) The European Atomic Energy Community Treaty (also signed in Rome in 1957) (4) The Charter of Fundamental Rights of the European Union (signed and promulgated in the year 2000, for the first time becoming binding after the entry into force of the Treaty of Lisbon on December 1, 2009, which is one of the most important innovations of the latter reform).

In summary, in order for one to ascertain the laws to which we citizens of the EU are subject, i.e. to understand the scope of the EU's *acquis communautaire*, one has to examine no less than four treaties: two from 1957, one from 1992, and another from 2000, the amended (consolidated) version coming on December 1, 2009—a truly maddening legislative task. It is especially exasperating when one compares it to the mere nine articles of the 1787 United States Constitution, a model of succinctness.[127]

[127] As an indication of how labyrinthine the Community's *acquis communautaire* is, the following is only the first article of the Lisbon Treaty: "*The Treaty on European Union shall be amended in accordance with the provisions of this Article. PREAMBLE. 1) The preamble shall be amended as follows: (a) The following text shall be inserted as the second recital: 'DRAWING INSPIRATION from the cultural, religious and humanist inheritance of Europe, from which have developed the universal values of the inviolable and inalienable rights of the human person, freedom, democracy, equality and the rule of law'; (b) In the seventh, which shall become the eighth, recital, the words 'of this Treaty' shall be replaced by 'of this Treaty and of the Treaty on the Functioning of the European Union'; (c) In the eleventh, which shall become the twelfth, recital, the words 'of this Treaty' shall be replaced by 'of this Treaty and of the Treaty on the Functioning of the European Union.' GENERAL PROVISIONS. 2) Article 1 shall be amended as follows: (a) the following words shall be inserted at the end of the first paragraph: 'on which the Member States confer*

On this point mention should be made of the essential task of the European Court of Justice in furthering integration through the application of the *acquis communautaire*—which must be considered at least as important as the intervention of the U.S. Supreme Court in consolidating federalism in the American Union, in what has been called the "constitutionalization" of EC Law (Martinico 2013, 3–10).[128]

## 18.12 A Provisional Conclusion for an Unfinished Process: What Kind of Integration Are Europeans Looking For?

As twenty-first-century Europeans most of us do not live in autonomous nation-states, for whether we are Spanish, Slovakian, French, Latvian, German, Czech, British, Finnish, Romanian, Austrian, Italian, Cypriot, Belgian, Estonian, Swedish, Portuguese, Bulgarian, Greek, Slovenian, Hungarian, Lithuanian, Dutch, Irish, Maltese, Luxembourgian, Polish, Croatian or Danish, all citizens of the 28 states of the European Union are subject to legislation most of which (approximately by 60 %, and rising) is not determined by our national political and constitutional systems, but in Brussels.[129]

Another issue is whether we are actually aware of this fact or not. We may have little interest in the elections for the European Parliament and do not really understand how EU institutions function and what they are for. To some extent, this is understandable, as until now European integration has been carried out *sotto voce*, with citizens not closely engaged in the process, as the whole enterprise is one of extreme complexity. This explains why it is the member states, or rather, their governments, which have spearheaded this integration of a series of states which,

*competences to attain objectives they have in common.'; (b) the third paragraph shall be replaced by the following: 'The Union shall be founded on the present Treaty and on the Treaty on the Functioning of the European Union (hereinafter referred to as "the Treaties"). Those two Treaties shall have the same legal value. The Union shall replace and succeed the European Community"* (European Union 2010, 1). A comprehensive analysis of the Lisbon Treaty, its legal and political reforms and changes, and the fiscal crisis as well in Craig (2013).

[128] As Schepel and Blankenburg (2001, 10) point out, one of the tasks of the European Court of Justice is to achieve greater cohesion between the peoples of Europe and to infer from the "lofty objectives" of the treaties the necessity to endow Community law with "direct effect" and "supremacy". This is what EU lawyers call the "constitutionalization" of EC Law. For a historical approach to the ECJ's legal integration work, see Alter (2009, 47–109) and Cohen (2013, 21–43). On the EU as an international legal experiment, see De Witte (2012, 19–56). An insight to the 60 years of case-law of the Court of Justice and its role in the progress of European Integration in Rosas et al. (2013).

[129] On the relationship between European integration and the idea of the state and nation, see Keating (2006, 23–34). Also, Mayall (2013, 537–555). An overview in Danero Iglesias et al. (2013).

for the most part, had been independent for centuries, each with its own languages, histories, particular cultures, and idiosyncrasies. It is easy to understand how managing to reconcile the varying demands of 500 million citizens who have been living in separate nations for centuries is a daunting, if not outright impossible, task. Thus, it is their respective governments that lead the way and make decisions about integration, which we, as citizens, generally find out about after the fact.

One example will serve to illustrate this. The adoption of the far-reaching educational reform package known as the Bologna Process was decided upon at a meeting of education ministers representing the different member states. The "man on the street" in Europe was not asked if he agreed with it or not, if he liked his traditional education system the way it was or wanted to modify it. Instead, a small number of "Eurocrats" decided, on their own, that we should imitate the U.S. educational model (Aguilera-Barchet 2012, 12) disregarding the fact that higher education in Europe has traditionally been essentially not a private but a public service, and, at the same time, overlooking perhaps the best aspect of the American system: the 4 years of liberal arts education at the college level generally required before specializing in a specific professional field. This did not, however, prevent our ministers of education from wiping the slate of our traditional education system clean (which hitherto had not functioned so badly) and from dictating that henceforth our young people ought to study according to their (peculiar) understanding of the American higher education system.[130]

That said, Bologna is a complex issue that may be better addressed elsewhere. I do wish, however, to indicate and underscore here that a significant reform of European higher education, one which has dramatically changed our teaching and research practices, was implemented without even seeking the opinion of the students, professors, and researchers directly involved. Instead, a group of ministers made this decision at a meeting unilaterally.

While the integration process is not necessarily deleterious, hitherto it must be said that so far it has not been very democratic.[131] Rather, it has been the work of

[130] Some may think that the excellent university model conceived by the German Friedrich Wilhelm Heinrich Alexander Freiherr von Humboldt (1769–1859), which advanced the general education of the individual, was in some regards excessively theoretical, but at least it focused on the student's capacity to think and furnished him with a general culture which allowed him to better understand the world in which he lived. Professional specialization came later. The Bologna System, in contrast, is excessively pragmatic, as it focuses on short-term results and not on improving students' ability to think or providing them with cultural understanding (Aguilera-Barchet 2012, 20–21 and 41). Another analysis on The Bologna Process in Crosier and Parveva (2013). A global, comparative study in Streitwieser (2014).

[131] Because, as O'Neill (2009, 8) points out, there is a lack of effective channels for popular participation, and exiguous accountability between decision-makers and citizens. This is why EU governance, its polity and policy procedure are seen by citizens as remote from their everyday concerns. The problem is that to date European integration has been primarily managerial in orientation, driven more by technocrats and insider interests than by citizens. For an overview of this approach to European integration and how it undermines the democratic legitimacy of the whole process, see Schulz-Forberg and Stråth (2010).

governments, while citizens have barely been consulted as to whether we want to integrate or not, essentially because, when the citizens are consulted, there exists the danger that integration will be stymied. In fact, a series of specific referendums in recent history ended up hampering the integration process. On September 28, 2000, for example, the Danes said "no" to the euro; on September 14, 2003 the Swedes voted against the common currency; on May 29, 2005 54 % of the French rejected ratification of the European Constitution Treaty (TCE); on June 2 of the same year 61 % of Dutch voters did the same; and on June 12, 2008 53 % of the Irish people spurned the Lisbon Treaty, making it necessary to hold a second referendum, held on October 3, 2009, when 67 % of the Irish voted in favor of it.[132]

When consulted, then, the people are not always in favor of European integration. This reticence complicates and slows down the process (Markantonatou 2013, 43–60), but that is a risk which democracy entails, and one which must, of course, be taken. The case of France and the 2005 referendum was extremely significant because the referendum submitted by President Chirac gave rise to an intense debate in French society. The pro-treaty and anti-treaty camps fought it out in the press, on television and on the radio.[133] There were numerous rallies and demonstrations centering on the issue. French public opinion regarding integration was taken seriously. The debate stirred up passions and rankled many. As a result of this, the French realized the significance of their vote regarding the treaty signed by their government in Rome in 2004. Basically, the bone of contention was the liberalization of the economy through the progressive privatization of all sectors. That is, the fundamental principles upon which the European Union was based and, prior to 1992, the European Economic Community: free competition, private initiative, minimal market regulation and the prohibition of public subsidies (Steinberg 2006, 340–366). In short, a return to the old principles of the liberal state, which we have already examined, and a rejection of the interventionist state model which appeared after 1917.[134]

Is the implementation of a pure free market system good or bad? The question is tricky. The liberal state promotes economic development, which is good. However, it does not protect the least privileged, which relegates a sector of our affluent societies to living in precarious conditions. This creates social tensions, which is not good. On the other hand, the state may effectively intervene to moderate free market oscillations and to mitigate the crises that follow times of prosperity, which is good. Aiding the weak out of social solidarity is great and, above all, serves to prevent social conflict. When an all-powerful state seeks to regulate everything, however, and to control every aspect of our lives, private initiative is

---

[132] For an overview of voting power in the European Union, see Nurmi and Holler (2013), 500–614).

[133] For the anti-Liberal integrationist approach, see Faye (2011) and Scholl (2013, 127–142). An analysis on the political discourse, specifically on national interest by Tony Blair, Jacques Chirac, and Gerhard Schröder in Milzow (2012).

[134] On the social dimension of European integration, see Krueger (2000, 117–134).

frustrated and freedom is curtailed (de Grazia 2005, 336–376). Also, when politics always takes precedence over the individual, this is the first step towards dictatorship. And that is bad.

Thus, European integration has its positive and negative aspects. However, that is not the real issue. The most important point is that European integration is inevitable. In today's world, populated by six billion people, Europe's nation-states have no choice but to unite to survive. It is a question of economies of scale. How can 46 million Spaniards or 80 million Germans compete with 1.6 billion Chinese, or over 300 million Americans? It is not feasible. 500 million Europeans, on the other hand, *can* have an impact, or at least exert some degree of influence around the world, so that things are not entirely dictated by the president of the United States or the president of the People's Republic of China. The price to be paid, however, is a reduction in our states' levels of autonomy, and complying with the decision of EU-level leaders and officials, or "Eurocrats". It is obvious that solutions that are the product of consensus reached among 28 different states, each one with its own history and peculiarities, are not going to please or favor each state equally.

It is true, and encouraging, however, that although governments have to date been the drivers behind the process, the idea of Europe has already begun to make headway with the public. Hence, the democratization of the process must necessarily be a mid- to long-term process. In fact, a clear explanation of the advantages of "integration" makes it possible for public opinion to get behind it. This is what happened in Ireland from 2008 to 2009, where in just 16 months support for ratification of the Lisbon Treaty shot from 46 to 67 %. This is the way to expand political integration and, above all, to nurture the idea of a shared "civilization": through cultural and educational efforts that may pave the way towards a "European nation" (Shore 2006, 15–39).

To achieve this, some questions remain unanswered: do European states have no choice but to unite to transcend a nation-state model that generated two devastating world wars, put an end to European supremacy, and shattered the optimistic vision of the future harbored at the outset of the century? (Macormick 1995, 259–266) Are Europe's nation-states bound to disappear, or shall nationalism and regionalism end up redefining Europe's map?[135] Shall our idiosyncrasies and cultural peculiarities eventually be lost, swallowed up by a single and homogenized model?[136] The answers should come in the near future in a fascinating and ongoing process that will entirely depend on how we Europeans face the transformations shaping the world in which we live (de Benoist and Champetier 2012).

[135] On the resurgence of nationalism in Europe and the regional issue see Banks and Gingrich (2006, 1–28) and Hettne and Söderbaum (2005, 535–552).

[136] On the debate surrounding Europe's identity, see Díez Medrano (2010, 315–333) and Stråth (2012, 80–96).

## TIMELINE

### European Integration, 1918–1945

1918 11 November. The signing of an armistice puts an end to World War I.

1919 January. The Irish Republic unilaterally declares its independence from the UK.
June 28. Signing of the Treaty of Versailles. The treaty encompasses the foundation of the League of Nations, with headquarters in Geneva.

1920 January 10. Entry into force of the Treaty of Versailles.
March 19. The Congress of the United States rejects ratification of the Treaty of Versailles.

1921 December 6. An Anglo-Irish Treaty puts an end to the Irish War of independence.

1922 October 27–29. March on Rome. Mussolini seizes power.
Fifth Pan-American Conference in Santiago de Chile (the first was held on the initiative of the U.S. between 1889 and 1890; the last, the 10th, in Caracas in 1954).
December 6. Ireland becomes a self-governing British Dominion called the Irish Free State. Beginning of the Irish Civil War (1922–1923).

1923 January 1. France and Belgium begin the military occupation of the Ruhr.
Publication of the Pan-European manifesto of Richard Coudenhove-Kalergi. The origin of the International Pan-European Union.
September 13. Spain. The dictatorship of Primo de Rivera begins.
8–9 November. Germany. Beer Hall Putsch.

1925 January 25. French Prime Minister Édouard Herriot delivers a speech in the Senate in favor of European unification.
August 25. The last French troops abandon the Ruhr.

1926 European Union Customs Union. Gustav Stresemann manages to bring Germany into the League of Nations.

1929 September 5. Aristides Briand delivers a speech in Geneva to the League of Nations laying out his plans for a united Europe.
October. The New York Stock Exchange collapses.

1931 April 14. Founding of the Second Spanish Republic.

1933 January 30. Hitler is appointed Chancellor.
March 23. The Reichstag approves the "Enabling Act" (*Ermächtigungsgesetz*), which grants Hitler dictatorial powers.

1935 Signing of the Franco-Soviet Pact.

1936 July. Outbreak of the Spanish Civil War.
October. Constitution of the Rome–Berlin Axis.

1937 A new Irish constitution creates a new state: Ireland (*Eire*).

1938 March 12. Annexation of Austria into the Third Reich (*Anschluss*).

September 30. Munich Accords. Daladier (France) and Chamberlain (England) accept the German occupation of the Sudetenland (Czechoslovakia).
1939 April 1. End of the Spanish Civil War.
May 22. Signing of the German–Soviet Non-Aggression Pact.
September 1. Germany invades Poland.
September 17. Russia invades Poland.
1940 May. Germany invades France.
June. Franco-British union proposal.
1941 June. Germany invades Russia.
1943 February. Surrender of Von Paulus in Stalingrad.
March 21. At the Pan-European Congress in New York Churchill comes out in favor of the creation of a Council of Europe as a high court to resolve differences between the various European states.
December 1. Tehran Conference. First meeting of Stalin, Churchill, and Roosevelt to reestablish the world order after World War II.
1944 March 18. In Algiers General De Gaulle endorses the integration of the nations of Western Europe.
July 1–22. The Bretton Woods (New Hampshire) Accords set down the new world economic order.
September 5. Creation of the Benelux.

## European Integration Since 1945

1945 February 4–11. Yalta Conference.
June 26. Signing of the United Nations Charter.
July 7–August 2. Potsdam Conference.
October 24. Creation of the United Nations in San Francisco, California
1946 2 June. Constitutional referendum in Italy.
June 18. Proclamation of the Italian Republic.
September 19. Speech by Winston Churchill at the University of Zurich in favor of European integration.
1947 February 21. The British Ambassador in the U.S., Lord Inverchapel, delivers President Truman a memorandum announcing that England can no longer oversee the world order.
March 5. Dunkirk Conference. France and England ally against a possible German resurgence. In 1948, the three Benelux countries join the alliance. The Western Union is born.
June 5. Speech by George Marshall, President Truman's Secretary of State, who at Harvard University presents a general outline of the European Recovery Program (ERP), better known as the Marshall Plan.
September 22–27. Stalin creates the Cominform (replacing the Comintern).
1948 May 7. Opening of the Congress of The Hague.

June 25. The Allies initiate the Berlin Airlift (*Luftbrücke*) to supply West Berlin and break the blockade imposed by Stalin. The blockade is lifted on May 12, 1949.

December 10. The United Nations issues the Universal Declaration of Human Rights.

1949 April 4. Foundation of NATO.

April 18. Ireland becomes a Republic.

May 5. Statute of the Council of Europe (Spain joins on March 1, 1978).

May 12. End of the Soviet blockade of West Berlin.

May 23. Approval of the Basic Law for the Federal Republic of Germany. Establishment of the Federal Republic of Germany.

October 1. Mao Tse-tung founds the People's Republic of China.

1950 May 9. Schuman Declaration. European integration (Community Method) process gets underway. June 25. Outbreak of the Korean War (until July 17, 1953).

November 4. The European Convention for the Protection of Human Rights and Fundamental Freedoms is signed in Rome. It enters into force in 1953. Spain joins in 1979.

1951 April 18. Germany, Belgium, France, Italy, Luxembourg, and the Netherlands sign the Treaty of Paris, which constitutes the European Coal and Steel Community (ECSC), entering into force on July 23, 1952.

1952 May 27. Signing of the European Defense Community (EDC) Treaty.

1953 July 17. End of the Korean War.

1954 August 30. The French National Assembly rejects the European Defense Community Treaty, signed by the six on May 27, 1952.

1957 March 25. The six sign the Treaty of Rome, which constitutes the European Economic Community (EEC) and the European Atomic Energy Community (EURATOM).

1958 January 1. Belgium inaugurates the rotating presidency of the European Community Council.

March 19. Creation of the European Parliamentary Assembly ("European Parliament" since 1962) in Strasbourg, which replaces that of the ECSC.

October 7. Establishment in Luxembourg of the Court of Justice of the European Communities, which replaces that of the ECSC.

1960 January 4. Creation of the EFTA, an initiative of the U.K.

1961 August 13. Construction of the Berlin Wall (*Berliner Mauer*) begins.

1962 February 9. Spain officially requests entry into the EEC.

March 27–30. The European Parliamentary Assembly changes its name to the European Parliament.

1964 June 2. Contacts officially begin to discuss Spain's entry into the EEC. Five of the six countries (France, Germany, and the Benelux) are in favor; only Italy objects, but in the end Spain is forced to cede and wait 22 years to enter.

1965 April. Executive Merger Treaty. Signing in Brussels by the six member states of the three European Communities (ECSC, EEC, and EAEC-EURATOM). By virtue of these agreements, the Communities become subject to just one executive, a single Commission and a single Council. It enters into force on July 1, 1967.

1966 January 30. Luxembourg Compromise. The six agree that unanimous votes (rather than by majority) shall be required to make decisions affecting essential issues.

28 November. France vetoes the United Kingdom's entry into the EEC.

1970 June 29. Spain signs a preferential agreement with the European Economic Community. Spain's Minister of Foreign Affairs, Gregorio López Bravo, signs an accord with this European Community lifting tariff barriers between Spain and the Common Market. This is the first step towards Spain's incorporation into the EEC, though this would not come about for 16 years.

1973 January 1. Three new states join the European Communities: Denmark, Ireland, and the United Kingdom. This is the first expansion, creating the "Europe of the Nine".

January 29. In Brussels, Gregorio López Bravo signs an additional protocol related to the preferential agreement signed between Spain and the EEC.

1977 July 28. Spain presents its application to join the three European Communities (ECSC, EEC, and EURATOM). It would take another 9 years for Spain to be admitted.

16 November. The Congress of Deputies unanimously approves Spain's entry into the Council of Europe. Official entry occurs on November 24 after the ratification by the Minister of Foreign Affairs, Marcelino Oreja, of the Statutes of the Council and the signing of the Convention for the Protection of Human Rights and Fundamental Freedoms.

1978 January 23. Spain joins the Assembly of the Council of Europe as a full member, represented by seven deputies and five senators.

1979 March 1. Entry into force of the European Monetary System (EMS).

May 7–10. First elections to the European Parliament by direct universal suffrage. This first democratic Parliament is constituted on the following July 17.

September 18. In Brussels Spain formally begins negotiations to join the European Communities.

October 4. In Strasbourg Spain ratifies the European Convention for the Protection of Human Rights and Fundamental Freedoms.

1981 January 1. Greece becomes the 10th member state of the European Communities.

1982 March 22. In Brussels Spain concludes 6 of the 16 sessions of its negotiations for entry into the EEC.

1984 June 27. At the European Summit in Fontainebleau January 1, 1986 is scheduled as the date for Spain's entry into the EEC.

1985 June 12. Spain signs the treaty to join the European Communities.
June 14. Signing of the Schengen Agreement on the elimination of borders between EU countries. Spain signs in 1991.

1986 January 1. Integration of Spain and Portugal into the European Communities. The Europe of the 12 is born.
February 17 and 28. The Single European Act is signed in Luxembourg and The Hague, amending the Treaty of Rome. It enters into force on July 1, 1987.

1989 January 1. First 6-month presidency of the European Council by a Spaniard.
November 9. Fall of the Berlin Wall.

1990 September 12. Signing in Moscow of the 2 Plus Four Agreement. England, France, the United States, and the Soviet Union renounce the rights they had vis-à-vis Germany since 1945.
October 3. Reunification of Germany.

1991 December 21. Dissolution of the USSR (Alma-Ata Protocol).

1992 February 7. Signing in Maastricht (Netherlands) of the European Union Treaty. It comes into force, once all ratification procedures are finalized, on November 1, 1993.

1995 January 1. Austria, Finland, and Sweden join the EU. The Europe of the 15 is born.
July 1. Spain assumes the Presidency of the European Council for the second time (the 1st being the first half of 1989).

1997 October 2. The foreign ministers of the 15 sign the Amsterdam Treaty. It enters into force on May 1, 1967.

1999 June 19. Bologna Declaration. European education ministers approve the creation of the European Higher Education Area, to be fully implemented by December 31, 2010.

2000 December 7. Ratification of the Charter of Fundamental Rights of the European Union, adopted on October 2. A version of the Charter is officially promulgated on December 12, 2007 in Strasbourg. After the signing of the Lisbon Treaty, the Charter becomes binding upon all states. except Poland and the United Kingdom.

2001 February 26. The Treaty of Nice is signed, setting the majorities necessary to make decisions after the successive expansions carried out. It comes into force on February 1, 2003 after the ratification procedures are finalized.

2002 January 1. The euro enters into force. On February 28 it becomes the sole, official currency, the day that Spain occupies the presidency of the European Council (previously: 1989, 1995) for the third time.
July 23. The ECSC is dissolved.

2004 May 1. Eleven new members are incorporated into the EU: Poland, the Czech Republic, Cyprus, Estonia, Hungary, Latvia, Lithuania, Malta, the Slovak Republic, and Slovenia.
Rome. The heads of state and government and their respective ministers of foreign affairs sign a treaty establishing a Constitution for Europe.

2005 May 29. In a referendum, the French reject the Constitution Treaty.
June 1. The people of the Netherlands also refuse to ratify the Constitutional Treaty.
2006 Approval of Northern Ireland Act, a preliminary step to the restoration of devolved government in the territory.
2007 January 1. Bulgaria and Romania join the EU. The Europe of the 27 is born.
December 13. Signing of the Treaty of Lisbon, which replaces the Constitutional Treaty from 3 years earlier.
2009 December 1. The Treaty of Lisbon enters into force after the 27 ratification processes are completed.
2010 January 1. Herman Van Rompuy begins his term as the EU's first president.
Spain assumes its fourth presidency of the European Council (1989, 1995, and 2002).
2013 July 1. Croatia joins the EU as its 28th member state.

## References


Adams, M., et al. (Eds.). (2014). *The constitutionalization of European budgetary constraints*. Oxford: Hart.

Aguilera-Barchet, B. (2012). *A higher education for the twenty-first century: European and US approaches*. Brussels: Center for European Studies.

Aldcroft, D. H. (2007). *Europe's third world: The European periphery in the interwar years*. Farnham, UK: Ashgate.

Allen, D. (2004). European Union, the Single European Act and the 1992 programme. In D. Swann (Ed.), *The single European market and beyond: A study of the wider implications of the single European Act* (pp. 26–52). Oxon, UK: Routledge.

Alter, K. (2009). The ECJ during the founding period of legal integration: (1952–1980). In *The European Court's political power: Selected essays* (pp. 47–109). Oxford: Oxford University Press.

Amato, G. (2007). *The European Constitution: Cases and materials in EU and Member States' law*. Cheltenham, UK: Edward Elgar.

Amersfoort, H., & Klinkert, W. (Eds.). (2011). *Small powers in the age of total war: 1900–1940*. Leiden: Brill.

Andrey, G. (1991). La quête d'un État national. In *Nouvelle Histoire de la Suisse et des suisses* (pp. 171–266). Lausanne: Payot.

Argyle, R. (2014). *The Paris Game: Charles de Gaulle, the Liberation of Paris, and the Gamble that Won France*. Toronto: Dundurn.

Arrieta, J., & Elliot, J. H. (Eds.). (2009). *Forms of union: The British and Spanish monarchies in the seventeenth and eighteenth centuries*. Donostia, Spain: Eusko Ikaskuntza.

Aughey, A. (2005). *The politics of Northern Ireland. Beyond the Belfast Agreement*. Oxon, UK: Routledge.

Banaszak, L. A. (2001). *Why movements succeed or fail: Opportunity, culture, and the struggle for woman suffrage*. Princeton, NJ: Princeton University Press.

Banks, M., & Gingrich, A. (2006). Neo-nationalism in Europe and beyond. In A. Gingrich & M. Banks (Eds.), *Neo-nationalism in Europe and beyond: Perspectives from social anthropology* (pp. 1–28). Oxford: Berghahn.

Baranowski, S. (2011). *Nazi Empire: German colonialism and imperialism, from Bismarck to Hitler* (pp. 233–295). Cambridge: Cambridge University Press.

Barnett, H. (2002). *Constitutional and administrative law* (4th ed.). London: Cavendish Publishing.

Barthel, C. (2004). Émile Mayrish et les dirigeants del'Arbed entre la Belgique, la France et l'Allemagne: Rivalités et complicités (1918–1925). In M. Dumoulin (Ed.), *Economic Networks and European Integration* (pp. 125–144). Brussels: P.I.E. Peter Lang.

Bassols Coma, M. (2012). La reforma del artículo 135 CE y la constitucionalización de la estabilidad presupuestaria: el proceso parlamentario de elaboración de la reforma constitucional. In J. Gifreu I Font & L. Casado Casado (Eds.), *Estructuras administrativas y racionalización del gasto público: Actas del VII Congreso de la Asociación Española de Profesores de Derecho Administrativo* (pp. 317–338). Madrid: Instituto Nacional de Administración Pública.

Bellomo, M. (1995). *The common legal past of Europe: 1000–1800*. Washington, DC: The Catholic University of America Press.

Bellon, C. (2009). L'européen "Pèlerin de la paix"; (1918–1932). In *Aristide Briand: l'Européen* (pp. 87–104). Paris: Documentation française.

Bergier, J. F. (2001). *Guillaume Tell*. Paris: Fayard.

Bisson, T. N. (2002). *The Medieval Crown of Aragon: A short history*. Oxford: Clarendon (Reprint).

Bitsch, M. T. (2010). *Robert Schuman: Apôtre de l'Europe (1953–1963)*. Bruxelles: P.I.E. Peter Lang.

Blanchet, T., Pipponen, R. and Wetman-Clément, M. (1994). *The agreement on the European economic area (EEA)*. Oxford: Oxford University Press.

Blom, H. W. (2005). Grotius and socianism. In M. Mulsow & J. Rohls (Eds.), *Socinianism and arminianism: Antitrinitarians, calvinists, and cultural exchange in seventeenth-century Europe* (pp. 121–147). Leiden: Brill.

Bossuat, G. (1996). *L'Europe des Français, 1943–1959: la IVe République aux sources de l'Europe*. Paris: Publications de La Sorbonne.

Bossuat, G. (2004). The Marshall Plan and European Integration: The limits of an ambition. In J. Agnew & J. N. Entrikin (Eds.), *The Marshall Plan today: Model and metaphor* (pp. 127–154). Los Angeles, CA: University of California.

Bossuat, G., Berghahn, V., Geremek, B. and Machado, B. (2008). History, diplomacy, democracy and development. In *The Marshall Plan: Lessons learned for the 21st century* (pp. 11–68). Paris: OECD.

Bozyk, P. (2006). *Globalization and the transformation of Foreign Economic Policy*. Aldershot, UK: Ashgate.

Bradley, A. W., & Ewing, K. D. (2011). *Constitutional and administrative law* (15th ed.). Harlow, UK: Pearson.

Briand, A. (1930). Memorandum on the organization of a regime of European Federal Union addressed to twenty-six governments of Europe. In *International Conciliation: Special Bulletin*, June, pp. 327–353. (By Aristide Aristide Briand, May 17, 1930. Text in French and English).

Broadberry, S., & Harrison, M. (2009). The economics of World War I: An overview. In S. Broadberry & M. Harrison (Eds.), *The economics of World War I* (pp. 3–40). Cambridge, UK: Cambridge University Press.

Bruening, M. (2005). *Wilson Calvinism's first battleground: Conflict and reform in the Pays de Vaud, 1528–1559*. Dordrecht: Springer.

Buchanan, T. (2012). The war and its legacy: Europe between the powers: 1945–1953. In *Europe's troubled peace: 1945 to the present* (pp. 8–50). Malden, MA: Wiley.

Burgess, M. (2006). Federalism and the Federalists. In *Federalism and European Union: Political ideas, influences, and strategies in the European Community 1972–1986* (pp. 7–15). London: Routledge.

Caesar, J. (2005). *Caesar's commentaries on the Gallic War and on the Civil War*. [1.28]. El Paso, TX: Norte Press.
Callil, C. (2006). Vichy France. In *Bad faith: A forgotten history of family and fatherland* (pp. 197–375). London: Vintage.
Carlin, W. (1996). West German growth and institutions, 1945–1990. In N. Crafts & G. Toniolo (Eds.), *Economic growth in Europe since 1945* (pp. 455–496). Cambridge, UK: Cambridge University Press.
Charnley, J., Pender, M. and Wilkin, A. (eds) (1998). *25 years of emancipation?: Women in Switzerland, 1971–1996*. Bern: P.I.E. Peter Lang.
Chopra, H. S. (1974). *De Gaulle and European Unity*. New Delhi, India: Shakti Malik, Abhinav Publications.
Church, C. H. (2004). *The politics and Government of Switzerland*. Basingstoke, UK: Palgrave Macmillan.
Church, C. H. (2013). Creating the Swiss Confederacy: 1386–1520. In *A concise history of Switzerland* (pp. 43–72). Cambridge, UK: Cambridge University Press.
Church, C. H., Severin, C. and Hurni, B. (2011). Sectors, structures and suspicions: Financial and other aspects of Swiss economic relations with the EU. In C. H. Church (Ed.), *Switzerland and the European Union: A close, contradictory and misunderstood relationship* (pp. 126–147). London: Routledge.
Churchill, W. S. Sir. (2013a). A 'United States of Europe', 19 September 1946, Zurich, Switzerland. In *Never give in!: The best of Winston Churchill's speeches* (pp. 427–430). London: Bloomsbury.
Churchill, W. S. Sir. (2013b). The Bordeaux Armistice. In *Their finest hour: The Second World War* (pp. 175–192). London: Bloomsbury.
Cini, M. (2001). From the Marshall Plan to the EEC. In M. Schain (Ed.), *The Marshall Plan: Fifty years after* (pp. 13–38). New York: Palgrave.
Cohen, B. J. (2008). The Euro in a global context: Challenges and capacities. In K. Dyson (Ed.), *The Euro at 10: Europeanization, power and convergence* (pp. 37–53). Oxford: Oxford University Press.
Cohen, A. (2013). Ten majestic figures in long Amaranth Robes: The formation of the Court of Justice of the European Communities. In A. Vauchez & B. de Witte (Eds.), *Lawyering Europe: European law as a transnational social field* (pp. 21–43). Oxford: Hart.
Coogan, T. P. (2000). *Michael Collins: The man who made Ireland*. New York: Palgrave.
Coudenhove-Kalergi, Graf von, R. N. (1926). *Pan-Europe*. New York: Alfred A. Knopf.
Cowan, E. (2012). *The Wallace Book*. Edinburgh: Birlinn.
Craig, P. (2013). *The Lisbon Treaty: Law, politics, and treaty reform*. Oxford: Oxford University Press (Revised ed.).
Crosier, D., & Parveva, T. (2013). *The Bologna process: Its impact on higher education development in Europe and beyond*. Paris: International Institute for Educational Planning (UNESCO).
Danero Iglesias, J., et al. (Eds.). (2013). *New nation-states and national minorities*. Colchester, UK: ECPR Press.
de Benoist, A., & C. Champetier. (2012). *Manifesto for a European renaissance*. London: Arktos.
de Grazia, V. (2005). The consumer-citizen: How Europeans traded rights for goods. In *Irresistible Empire: America's advance through twentieth-century Europe* (pp. 336–376). Cambridge, MA: Harvard University Press.
de Guzmán Olivares, G. (Conde-Duque de). (2013). Documento IV: Gran Memorial (instrucción secreta dada al rey en 1624). In *Memoriales y cartas del Conde Duque de Olivares: Política interior, 1621 a 1627* (pp. 77–124). Madrid: Centro de Estudios Europa Hispánica.
de Jouvenel, B. (1930). *Vers les États-Unis d'Europe*. Paris: Valois.
de Jouvenel, B. (1938). *Le réveil de l'Europe*. Paris: Gallimard.
de Madariaga, S. (1967). Foreword. In *Portrait of Europe* (pp. 1–6). London: Hollis & Carter.
de Madariaga, S. (2011). Prólogo. In *Bosquejo de Europa* (2nd ed., pp. 45–50). Madrid: Encuentro.

de Schoutheete, P. & Andoura, S. (2007). The legal personality of the European Union. *Studia Diplomatica, LX*(1), 1–9.
de Tocqueville, A. (1982). The cultural consequences of democracy. In *Alexis de Tocqueville on democracy, revolution, and society: Selected writings* (pp. 130–162). Chicago, IL: University of Chicago Press.
de Witte, B. (2012). The European Union as an international legal experiment. In G. de Búrca & J. H. H. Weiler (Eds.), *The worlds of European constitutionalism* (pp. 19–56). Cambridge, UK: Cambridge University Press.
Dedman, M. (2010). The impact and significance of the European Federalist movements and the Council of Europe. In *The origins and development of the European Union 1945–2008: A history of European Integration* (2nd ed., pp. 14–29). Oxon, UK: Routledge.
Delaisi, F. (1927). *Les contradictions du monde modern: Political myths and economic realities*. London: N. Douglas.
Dell, E. (2004). *The Schuman Plan and the British abdication of leadership in Europe*. Oxford: Clarendon (Reprint).
den Boer, P. (1995). Europe to 1914: The making of an idea. In K. J. Wilson (Ed.), *The history of the idea of Europe* (pp. 13–82). London: Routledge.
Despalatovic, E., (2000). The roots of the war in Croatia. In J. M. Halpern & D. A. Kideckel (Eds.), *Neighbors at war: Anthropological perspectives on Yugoslav ethnicity, culture and history* (pp. 81–102). University Park, PA: The Pennsylvania State University.
Dettwiler, W. (1991). *William Tell: Portrait of a legend*. Zurich: Swiss National Museum.
Diamond, H. (2007). *Fleeing Hitler: France 1940*. Oxford: Oxford University Press.
Díez Medrano, J. (2010). Europe's political identity: Public sphere and public opinion. In: J. Lacroix & K. Nicolaides (Eds.), *European stories: Intellectual debates on Europe in national contexts* (pp. 315–333). Oxford: Oxford University Press.
Dinan, D. (2014). *Europe recast: A history of European Union* (2nd ed.). Boulder, CO: Lynne Rienners.
Doerr, P. W. (1998). *British foreign policy: 1919–1939*. Manchester, UK: Manchester University Press.
Douglas-Scott, S. (2002). *Constitutional law of the European Union*. Harlow, UK: Pearson Education Limited.
Drake, H. (2000). *Jacques Delors: Perspectives on a European leader*. London: Routledge.
Dûchene, F. (1994). *Jean Monnet: The first statesman of interdependence*. New York: W. W. Norton & Company.
Dumas, A. (2008). *The three musketeers*. London: Penguin.
Dwyer, T. R. (2009). *Michael Collins: The man who won the war*. Cork, Ireland: Mercier Press (Revised ed.).
Edward, D. A. O., & Lane, R. (2013). *On European Union law*. Cheltenham, UK: Edward Elgar.
Elazar, D. J. (2005). The United States and the European Union: Models for their epochs. In *The Federal Vision: Legitimacy and levels of governance in the United States and the European Union* (pp. 31–53). Oxford: Oxford University Press.
Elliot, J. H. (2009). A Europe of composite monarchies. In *Spain, Europe and the Wider World: 1500–1800* (pp. 3–24). New Haven, CT: Yale University Press (Previously published in *Past & Present*, No. 137, 1992, pp. 48–71. Special Issue: The Cultural and Political Construction of Europe).
Erhard, L. (2006). *Germany's comeback in the world market: The German 'Miracle' explained by the Bonn Minister for Economics*. Oxon, UK: Routledge.
Escudero, J. A. (2002). *Felipe II: El rey en el despacho*. Madrid: Universidad Complutense.
European Union. (2010). *Consolidated versions of the treaty on European Union and of the treaty on the functioning of the European Union: Charter of fundamental rights of the European Union*. Luxemburg: Office for Official publications of the European Communities.
Evans, P., & Silk, P. (2008). *The Parliamentary Assembly: Practice and procedure* (10th ed.). Strasbourg: Council of Europe Publishing.

Fabio, M. (2012). *Customs law of the European Union* (4th ed.). Alphen aan den Rijn, The Netherlands: Kluwer International.
Faye, G. (2011). *Why we fight: Manifesto of the European resistance*. London: Arktos.
Felsenthal, D. S., & Machover, M. (2013). The QM rule in the nice and Lisbon Treaties: Future projections. In M. J. Holler & H. Nurmi (Eds.), *Power, voting, and voting power: 30 years after* (pp. 593–611). Berlin: Springer.
Fenger, N. (2012). *European Free Trade Association and the European economic area*. The Hague: Kluwer Law International.
Ferguson, W. (1994). *Scotland's relations with England: A survey to 1707*. Edinburgh: The Saltire Society.
Fernández Albaladejo, P. (2009). Common souls, autonomous bodies: The language of unification under the Catholic Monarchy, 1590–1630. In J. Arrieta & J. H. Elliot (Eds.), *Forms of union: The British and Spanish monarchies in the seventeenth and eighteenth centuries* (pp. 73–81). Donostia, Spain: Eusko Ikaskuntza.
Ferro, V. (1999). *El Dret Public català: Les Institucions a Catalunya fins al Decret de Nova Planta* (2nd ed.). Barcelona: Eumo.
Fest, J. C. (2013). *Hitler*. New York: Houghton Mifflin.
Fimister, A. (2008). *Robert Schuman: Neo scholastic humanism and the reunification of Europe*. Brussels: P.I.E. Peter Lang.
Fleiner-Gerster, T., Misic, A. and Töpperwien, N. (2005). Outline of Swiss constitutional history. In *Swiss constitutional law* (pp. 21–25). The Hague: Kluwer Law International.
Fleiner-Gerster, T., Misic, A. and Töpperwien, N. (2012). Sources of constitutional law and state organization. In *International Encyclopaedia of Constitutional Law. Switzerland* (pp. 53–112). The Hague: Kluwer.
France. Ministère des affaires étrangères. (1930). *Memorandum on the organization of a régime of European federal union*. New York: Carnegie Endowment for International Peace.
Fransen, F. J. (2006). *The supranational politics of Jean Monnet: Ideas and origins of the European Community*. Westport, CT: Greenwood.
Frei, N. (2013). *Adenauer's Germany and the Nazi Past: The politics of Amnesty and Integration*. New York: Columbia University Press (Reprint).
Fry, M. (2006). *The Union: England, Scotland and the Treaty of 1707*. Edinburgh: Birlinn.
García Andrade Gómez, J. (2012). La reforma del artículo 135 de la Constitución española. *Revista de Administración Pública*, (187), 31–66.
Gautier, P. (2000). The reparation for injuries case revisited: The personality of the European Union. In *Max Planck Yearbook of United Nations Law*. 4. (pp. 331–361). Leiden: Martinus Nijhoff.
Geddes, A. (2013). *Britain and the European Union*. Basingstoke, UK: Palgrave Macmillan.
Gehler, M. (2013). *Three Germanies: West Germany, East Germany and the Berlin Republic*. London: Reaktion.
Geiger, T. (1999). Reconstruction and the beginnings of European Integration. In M. -S. Schulze (Ed.), *Western Europe: Economic and social change since 1945* (pp. 23–41). London: Longman.
Giauque, J. G. (2002). De Gaulle and the rise and fall of the Fouchet plan: 1958–1963. In *Grand designs and visions of unity: The Atlantic powers and the reorganization of Western Europe, 1955–1963* (pp. 126–157). Chapel Hill, NC: University of North Carolina Press.
Gifford, C. (2008). *The making of Eurosceptic Britain: Identity and economy in a post-imperial state*. Aldershot, UK: Ashgate.
Gilbert, M. (2012). *European Integration: A concise history*. Plymouth, UK: Rowman & Littlefield.
Gillingham, J. (1991). Jean Monnet and the European Coal and Steel Community: A preliminary appraisal. In D. Brinkley & C. Hackett (Eds.), *Jean Monet: The path to European Unity* (pp. 129–163). New York: St. Martin's Press.

Gillingham, J. (2002). *Coal, steel and the rebirth of Europe: 1945–1955: The Germans and French from Ruhr conflict to economic community*. Cambridge, UK: Cambridge University Press.

Gimbel, J. (1976). *The origins of the Marshall Plan*. Stanford, CA: Stanford University Press.

Glossner, C. L. (2013). *The making of the German post-war economy: Political communication and public reception of the social market economy after World War II*. London: I.B. Tauris.

Görtemaker, M. (2013). The failure of EDC and European Integration. In L. Kühnhardt (Ed.), *Crises in European Integration: Challenges and responses, 1945–2005* (pp. 33–48). New York: Berghahn Books.

Gower, J. (2012). *The story of Wales*. London: Random House.

Gowland, D., Turner, A. and Wright, A. (2010). *Britain and European Integration since 1945: On the sidelines*. Oxon, UK: Routledge.

Grab, A. I. (2005). *Napoleon and the transformation of Europe*. Basingstoke, UK: Palgrave Macmillan.

Great Britain, Parliament. House of Commons. (1940). *Parliamentary debates, House of Commons Official Report Eleventh: Volume of Session 1939–1940* (Fifth Series, Vol. 365, columns 701–702). London: His Majesty's Stationery Office.

Griffiths, R. T. (2014). *'Thank you M. Monnet': Essays on the history of European Integration*. Leiden, Netherlands: Leiden University Press.

Grogin, R. C. (2001). *Natural enemies: The United States and the Soviet Union in the Cold War, 1917–1991*. Lanham, MD: Lexington Books.

Grossman, A. (2004). A question of silence: The rape of German women by occupation soldiers. In N. A. Dombrowski (Ed.), *Women and war in the twentieth century: Enlisted with or without consent* (pp. 120–137). New York: Routledge.

Grotius, H. (2012). Of the causes of war: First, defence of self and property. In *The rights of war and peace, in three books. Wherein are explained, the law of nature and nations... = De jure belli ac pacis libri tres : in quibus ius naturae et gentium, item iuris publici praecipua explicantur, cum annotatis auctoris...* (pp. 61–68). Clark, NJ: The Lawbook Exchange, Ltd.

Guibernau, M. (2006). Nations without states in the EU: The Catalan case. In J. McGarry & M. Keating (Eds.), *European Integration and the Nationalities Question* (pp. 216–224). Oxon, UK: Routledge.

Gunther, R., Montero, J. and Botella, J. (2004). *Democracy in modern Spain*. New Haven, CT: Yale University Press.

Haerpfer, C. W. (2002). *Democracy and enlargement in post-Communist Europe: The democratisation of the general public in Fifteen Central and Eastern European Countries, 1991–1998*. New York: Routledge.

Haller, W. (2009). *The Swiss Constitution in a comparative context*. Zurich: Dike.

Hamilton, D., & Macinnes, A. I. (Eds.). (2014). *Jacobitism, enlightenment and empire, 1680–1820*. London: Pickering & Chatto.

Hanhimäki, J. M., & Westad, O. A. (Eds.). (2004) The Marshall Plan and NATO. In *The cold war: A history in documents and eyewitness accounts* (pp. 105–136). Oxford: Oxford University Press.

Hansen, R. (2008). *Fire and fury: The allied bombing of Germany, 1942–1945*. Toronto: DoubleDay.

Hansmann, M. (2011). *Twenty years since the fall of the Berlin Wall: Transitions, state break-up and democratic politics in Central Europe and Germany*. Berlin: Berliner Wissenschafts-Verlag.

Harbutt, F. J. (2010). *Yalta 1945: Europe and America at the crossroads*. Cambridge, UK: Cambridge University Press.

Harryvan, A. G. (2009). The Netherlands, Benelux and the *Relance Européenne*. In *In pursuit of influence: The Netherland's European Policy during the formative years of the European Union, 1952–1973* (pp. 69–98). Brussels: P.I.E. Peter Lang.

Haug, H. K. (2012). Self-management socialism and Yugoslav Unity 1949–1958. In *Creating a socialist Yugoslavia: Tito, communist leadership and the national question* (pp. 115–132). London: I.B. Tauris.
Hayward, J. (2008). Strategic innovation by insider influence: Monnet to Delors. In J. Hayward (Ed.), *Leaderless Europe* (pp. 15–27). Oxford: Oxford University Press.
Head, R. C. (1995). William Tell and his comrades: Association and fraternity in the propaganda of fifteenth and sixteenth-century Switzerland. *The Journal of Modern History, 67*(3), 527–557.
Herriot, É. (1930). *The United States of Europe*. New York: The Viking Press.
Hettne, B., & Söderbaum, F. (2005). Civilian power or soft imperialism?: The EU as a global actor and the role of interregionalism. *European Foreign Affairs Review,* (10), 535–552.
Hildebrand, K. (1973). *The foreign policy of the Third Reich.* Berkeley, CA: University of California Press.
Hittle, J. B. E. (2011). *Michael Collins and the Anglo-Irish War: Britain's counterinsurgency failure.* Washington, DC: Potomac.
Hloušek, V., & Kopeček, L. (2010). Origin, ideology and transformation of political parties: East-Central and Western Europe compared. Burlington, VT: Ashgate.
Hölscher, J., & Klaes, M. (2014). *Keynes's economic consequences of the peace: A reappraisal.* London: Pickering & Chatto.
Horspool, M., & Humphreys, M. (2006). *European Union Law.* Oxford: Oxford University Press.
Howe, S. (2002). *Empire: A very short introduction.* Oxford: Oxford University Press.
Humair, C. (2009). *1848: Naissance de la Suisse moderne.* Lausanne: Éditions Antipodes.
Hunt, J. (2001). *Spain: 1474–1598.* London: Routledge.
Irigoin, A., & Grafe, R. (2008). Bargaining for absolutism: A Spanish path to nation-state and Empire Building. *Hispanic American Historical Review, 88*(2), 173–209.
Jackson, S. (1979). Prologue to the Marshall Plan: The origins of the American Commitment for a European Recovery Program. *Journal of American History, 65*(4), 1043–1068.
Jackson, P. (2013). Towards a post-war security order: The Eastern settlement, economic security and the League of Nations; The Cartel des gauches and the internationalisation of security. In *Beyond the balance of power: France and the politics of national security in the era of the First World War* (pp. 235–275 and 427–521). Cambridge, UK: Cambridge University Press.
Jáuregui, G. (2006). Basque nationalism: Sovereignty, independence and European integration. In J. McGarry & M. Keating (Eds.), *European Integration and the Nationalities Question* (pp. 239–257). Oxon, UK: Routledge.
Jessner, S. (1974). *Edouard Herriot, patriarch of the Republic.* New York: Haskell House.
Jones, G. E. (1999). *Modern Wales: A concise history* (2nd ed.). Cambridge, UK: Cambridge University Press.
Jordan, N. (2002). *The popular Front and Central Europe: The dilemmas of French Impotence, 1918–1940.* Cambridge, UK: Cambridge University Press.
Judt, T. (2007). *Postwar: A history of Europe since 1945.* London: Pimlico.
Kaiser, W. (1996). *Using Europe, abusing the Europeans: Britain and European Integration, 1945–1963.* Basingstoke, UK: Palgrave Macmillan.
Kamen, H. (2001). *Philip V of Spain: The King who reigned twice.* New Haven, CT: Yale University Press.
Kapossy, B. (2006). Neo-Roman Republicanism and Commercial Society: The example of eighteenth-century Berne. In M. van Gelderen & Q. Skinner (Eds.), *Republicanism: A shared European Heritage* (3rd printing, pp. 227–247). Cambridge, UK: Cambridge University Press.
Keating, M. (2001). Nations without states: The accommodation of nationalism in the new state order. In M. Keating & J. McGarry (Eds.), *Minority nationalism and the changing of international order* (pp. 19–43). Oxford: Oxford University Press.
Keating, M. (2006). Europe, the state and the nation. In J. McGarry & M. Keating (Eds.), *European Integration and the Nationalities Question* (pp. 23–34). Oxon, UK: Routledge.
Keene, J. D. (2006). *World War I.* Westport, CT: Greenwood.

Killick, J. (1997). The Marshall Plan and European Integration. In *The United States and European Reconstruction: 1945–1960* (pp. 134–146). Edinburgh, Scotland: Edinburgh University Press.
Kölliker, A. (2006). *Flexibility and European Unification. The logic of differentiated integration.* Oxford: Rowman & Littlefield.
Kriesi, H., & Techsel, A. H. (2008). *Direct democratic choice: The Swiss experience.* Plymouth, UK: Lexington Books.
Kriesi, H., & Techsel, A. H. (2010). The development of the modern Swiss nation-state. In *The politics of Switzerland: Continuity and change in a consensus democracy* (pp. 1–17). Cambridge, UK: Cambridge University Press (Reprint).
Krotz, U., & Schild, J. (2013). Polity shaping, I and II. In *Shaping Europe: France, Germany, and embedded bilateralism from the Elysée Treaty to twenty-first century politics* (pp. 114–157). Oxford: Oxford University Press.
Krueger, A. B. (2000). From Bismarck to Maastricht: The March to European Union and the labor compact. *Labour Economics, 7*(2), 117–134.
Kuijper, P. H., Wouters, J., Hoffmeister, F. Baere, G. de and Ramopoulos, Th. (2013). Personality and powers of the EU. In *The law of EU external relations: Cases, materials, and commentary on the EU as an International Legal Actor* (pp. 1–22). Oxford: Oxford University Press.
Landsman, M. (2005). Crisis revisited: The main economic task and the building of the Berlin Wall. In *Dictatorship and demand: The politics of consumerism in East Germany* (pp. 173–207). Cambridge, MA: Harvard University Press.
Larres, K. (2002). *Churchill's cold war: The politics of personal diplomacy.* New Haven, CT: Yale University Press.
Laursen, F. (2012). The 1965 Merger Treaty: The first reform of the founding European Community Treaties. In F. Laursen (Ed.), *Designing the European Union: From Paris to Lisbon* (pp. 77–97). Basingstoke, UK: Palgrave Macmillan.
Leitz, C. (2000). *Nazi Germany and neutral Europe during the Second World War.* Manchester, UK: Manchester University Press.
Lerner, M. H. (2012). *A laboratory of liberty: The transformation of political culture in republican Switzerland, 1750–1848.* Leiden: Brill.
Lewkowicz, N. (2010). American structural interests in Western Europe and the revival of Germany. In *The German question and the origins of the cold war* (pp. 15–36). Milano, Italy: IPOC.
Liebmann, G. W. (2008). Count Carlo Sforza. In *Diplomacy between the wars: Five diplomats and the shaping of the modern world* (pp. 129–173). London: I. B. Tauris.
Lipgens, W. (1984). General introduction. In W. Lipgens (Ed.), *Documents on the history of European Integration. 1. Continental plans for European Union. 1939–1945* (pp. 1–36). Berlin: Walter de Gruyter.
Loedel, P. H. (1999). *Deutsche Mark politics: Germany in the European Monetary System.* Boulder, CO: Lynne Rienner.
Longerich, P. (2014). *Goebbels: A biography.* New York: Random House.
Maas, W. (2007). *Creating European citizens.* Plymouth, UK: Rowman & Littlefield.
Macormick, N. (1995). The Maastricht-Urteil: Sovereignty now. *European Law Journal, 1*(3), 259–266.
Mahoney, D. J. (2005). *Bertrand de Jouvenel: The conservative liberal and the illusions of modernity.* Wilmington, DE: ISI Books.
Maissen, T. (2010). Why did the Swiss miss the Machiavellian moment?: History, myth, imperial and constitutional law in the early modern Swiss Confederation. *Republics of Letters: A Journal for the Study of Knowledge, Politics, and the Arts, 2*(1), 105–120.
Mansergh, N. (1997). *Nationalism and independence: Selected Irish Papers.* Cork, Ireland: Cork University Press.
Markantonatou, M. (2013). The post-welfare state and changing forms of political participation. In K. N. Demetriou (Ed.), *Democracy in transition: Political participation in the European Union* (pp. 43–60). Heidelberg: Springer.

Marshall, G. C. (1947). Speech delivered by General George Marshall at Harvard University on June 5, 1947 (Marshall Plan). *Department of State Bulletin, 16*(415), 1159–1160.

Martinico, G. (2013). *The tangled complexity of the EU constitutional process: The frustrating knot of Europe*. Oxon, UK: Routledge.

Mayall, J. (2013). International society, state sovereignty and national self determination. In J. Breuilly (Ed.), *The Oxford handbook of the history of nationalism* (pp. 537–555). Oxford: Oxford University Press.

Mazzucelli, C. (1999). The historical Prelude to Maastricht. In *France and Germany at Maastricht: Politics and negotiations to create the European Union* (pp. 35–56). London, Garland Science Publishing.

McEvoy, J. (2008). Background to the conflict. In *The politics of Northern Ireland* (pp. 21–43). Edinburgh, Scotland: Edinburgh University Press.

McGrathe, A. E. (2014). *Emil Brunner: A reappraisal*. Malden, MA: Wiley.

Miller, R. G. (2000). *To save a city: The Berlin Airlift, 1948–1949*. Texas, TX: A&M University Press.

Milward, A. S. (2010). The post-war nation-state. In *The European rescue of the nation state* (2nd ed., pp. 21–45). London: Routledge.

Milward, A. S. (2013). *The reconstruction of Western Europe: 1945–1951*. Hoboken, NJ: Taylor and Francis.

Milzow, K. (2012). *National interests and European Integration: Discourse and politics of Blair, Chirac and Schröder*. Basingstoke, UK: Palgrave Macmillan.

Miscamble, W. D. (2007). *From Roosevelt to Truman: Postdam, Hiroshima, and the cold war*. Cambridge, UK: Cambridge University Press.

Mommsen, H. (2003). Beyond the nation-state: The German resistance against Hitler, and the future of Europe. In A. McElligott & T. Kirk (Eds.), *Working towards the Führer: Essays in honour of Sir Ian Kershaw* (pp. 246–259). Manchester, UK: Manchester University Press.

Montesquieu, Charles Louis de Secondat, Baron de. (2012). Lettre CIX. In *Oeuvres complètes* (p. 255). Paris: Classiques Garnier.

Moore, B. (2000). Defining resistance. In B. Moore (Ed.), *Resistance in Western Europe* (pp. 1–18). New York: Berg.

Moravcsik, A. (2003). Federalism in the European Union: Rhetoric and reality. In K. Nicolaidis & R. Howse (Eds.), *The Federal Vision: Legitimacy and levels of governance in the United States and the European Union* (pp. 161–190). Oxford: Oxford University Press.

Moravcsik, A. (2005). *The choice for Europe: Social purpose & state power from Messina to Maastricht*. Oxon, UK: Routledge.

Morris, K., & White, T. (2011). Neutrality and the European Union: The case of Switzerland. *Journal of Law and Conflict Resolution, 3*(7), 104–111.

Moschonas, A. (1996). The logic of European Integration. In G. A. Kourvetaris & A. Moschonas (Eds.), *The impact of European Integration: Political, sociological and economic changes* (pp. 9–38). Westport, CT: Greenwood.

Mould, M. (2011). *The Routledge dictionary of cultural references in modern French*. Abingdon, UK: Routledge.

Muller, J. W. (1999). *Churchill's 'Iron Curtain' speech, fifty years later*. Columbia, MO: University of Missouri Press.

Müller, R. -D. (2003). Organization and exploitation of 'Fortress Europe'. In *Germany and the Second World War*. 5–2. (pp. 536–583). Oxford: Oxford University Press.

Muron, L. (1997). *Edouard Herriot: (1872–1957)*. Lyon: Editions lyonnaises d'art et d'histoire.

Naimark, N. M. (1995). *The Russians in Germany: A history of the Soviet Zone of occupation, 1945–1949*. Cambridge, MA: Harvard University Press.

Nathan, R. R. (1991). An unsung hero of World War II. In D. Brinkley & C. Hackett (Eds.), *Jean Monet, the path to European Unity* (pp. 86–113). New York: St. Martin's Press.

Navari, C. (1992). Origins of the Briand Plan. In *Diplomacy and statecraft*. 3. (pp. 74–104). London: F. Cass.

Nelson, B. (2012). *Irish nationalists and the making of the Irish race*. Princeton, NJ: Princeton University Press.

Nugent, N. (2010). The European Parliament. In *The government and politics of the European Union* (7th ed., pp. 179–206). Durham, NC: Duke University Press.

Nurmi, H., and Holler, M. J. (2013). Voting power in the European Union. In M. J. Holler & H. Nurmi (Eds.), *Power, voting, and voting power: 30 years after* (pp. 500–614). Berlin: Springer.

O'Neill, M. (2009). *The struggle for the European Constitution: A past and future history*. Oxon, UK: Taylor and Francis.

Oberhuber, F. (2006). The convention method: An institutional device for consensus-building. In S. P. Riekmann & W. Wessels (Eds.), *The making of a European Constitution: Dynamics and limits of the convention experience* (pp. 90–119). Wiesbaden, Germany: VS Verlag Für Sozialwissenschaften.

Parish, S. (1997). The Marshall Plan, Soviet-American relations, and the division of Europe. In N. Naimark & L. Gibianski (Eds.), *The establishment of Communist regimes in Eastern Europe: 1944–1949* (pp. 268–290). Boulder, CO: Westview.

Parsons, C. (2010). Revisiting the Single European Act (and the common wisdom on globalization). *Comparative Political Studies, 43*(6), 706–734.

Payne, S. G. (2008). *Franco and Hitler: Spain, Germany and World War II*. New Haven, CT: Yale University Press.

Petaux, J. (2009). *Democracy and human rights for Europe: The Council of Europe's contribution*. Strasbourg: Council of Europe Publishing.

Phillips, W. A. (2005). *The Confederation of Europe: A study of the European alliance, 1813–1823, as an experiment in the International Organization of Peace* (2nd ed.). Clark, NJ: The Lawbook Exchange, Ltd (Reprint).

Piña Homs, R. (2007). Los reinos de la Corona de Aragón. In *Obra Dispersa: Corona de Aragón América Hispana* (pp. 333–370). Palma de Mallorca, Spain: Govern de les Illes Balears.

Pittock, M. (2008). *The road to independence: Scotland since the sixties*. Chippenham, UK: Reaktion.

Plokhy, S. M. (2010). *Yalta: The price of peace*. London: Penguin.

Preda, D., & Pasquinucci, D. (2010). *The road Europe travelled along: The evolution of the EEC/EU institutions and policies*. Brussels: P.I.E. Peter Lang.

Prettenthaler-Ziegerhofer, A. (2012). Richard Nicolaus Coudenhove-Kalergi, Founder of the Pan-European Union, and the birth of a 'New Europe'. In M. Hewitson & M. D'Auria (Eds.), *Europe in crisis: Intellectuals and the European Idea. 1917–1957* (pp. 89–110). New York: Berghan Books.

Pridham, G. (2008). Theoretical perspectives on European enlargement and democratisation. In *Designing democracy: EU enlargement and regime change in post-Communist Europe* (pp. 1–24). Basingstoke, UK: Palgrave Macmillan.

Quint, P. E. (1997). *The imperfect Union: Constitutional structures of German unification*. Princeton, NJ: Princeton University Press.

Reinfeld, A. (2009). The Hague "Congress of Europe": A Congress of the Europeans? Elites, the Public and European Unification. In J.- M. Guieu & C. Le Dréau (Eds.), *Le "Congrès de l'Europe" à la Haye: (1948–2008)* (pp. 287–298). Bruxelles: P.I.E. Peter Lang.

Reynolds, D. (1994). *The origins of the cold war in Europe: International perspectives*. New Haven, CT: Yale University Press.

Reynolds, S. (2012). Empires: A problem of comparative history. In *The Middle Ages without Feudalism: Essays in criticism and comparison on the medieval west* (pp. 151–165). Farnham, UK: Ashgate.

Riley, P. J. W. (1969). The Union of 1707 as an episode in English politics. *The English Historical Review, 84*, 498–527.

Riou, G. (1928). *Europe, ma patrie*. Paris: Librairie Valois.

Roberts, G. (2006). *Stalin's wars: From world war to cold war, 1939–1953*. New Haven, CT: Yale University Press.

Roberts, G. (2007). Stalin at the Tehran, Yalta, and Potsdam conferences. *Journal of Cold War Studies, 9*(4), 6–40.

Roberts, P. R. (2012). The Union with England and the identity of Anglican Wales. *Transactions of the Royal Historical Society, 22*, 49–70.

Robertson, J. (2009). The conceptual framework of Anglo-Scottish Union. In J. Arrieta & J. H. Elliot (Eds.), *Forms of union: The British and Spanish monarchies in the seventeenth and eighteenth centuries* (pp. 125–137). Donostia, Spain: Eusko Ikaskuntza.

Rosas, A., Levits, E. and Bot. Y. (2013). *The Court of Justice and the construction of Europe: Analyses and perspectives on sixty years of case-law (La Cour de Justice et la Construction de l'Europe: Analyses et Perspectives de Soixante Ans de Jurisprudence)*. The Hague: T.M.C. Asser Press.

Ross, G. (1995). *Jacques Delors and European Integration*. Oxford: Oxford University Press.

Ruffieux, R. (1983). La Suisse des radicaux: (1848–1914). In *Nouvelle Histoire de la Suisse et des suisses* (pp. 8–87). Lausanne: Payot III.

Ruiz Almendral, V. (2013). The Spanish legal framework for curbing the public debt and the deficit. *European Constitutional Law Review, 9*(2), 189–204.

Runyon, R. P. (2005). *The Art of the Persian Letters: Unlocking Montesquieu's "Secret Chain"*. Cranbury, NJ: Rosemont Publishing.

Russell, C. (2003). Composite monarchies in early modern Europe: The British and Irish example. In A. Grant & K. Stringer (Eds.), *Uniting the Kingdom?: The making of British history* (pp. 133–146). London: Routledge.

Salewski, M. (1984). National socialist ideas on Europe. In W. Lipgens (Ed.), *Documents on the history of European Integration. 1. Continental plans for European Union. 1939–1945* (pp. 37–172). Berlin: Walter de Gruyter.

Salmon, T. C., & Nicoll, W. (Eds.). (1997). *Building European Union: A documentary history and analysis*. Manchester, UK: Manchester University Press.

Salter, A. (1933). *The United States of Europe and other papers*. New York: Reynald and Hitchcok.

Samaniego Boneu, M. (2009). L'Europe de Salvador de Madariaga. In A. Bachoud et al. (Eds.), *Les intellectuels et l 'Europe, de 1945 à nos jours* (pp. 43–56). Paris: L'Harmattan.

Sanderson, C. (2003). *L'impossible alliance ? France, Grande-Bretagne et défense de l'Europe 1945–1958*. Paris: Publications de La Sorbonne.

Schepel, H., & Blankenburg, E. (2001). Mobilizing the European Court of Justice. In G. de Búrca & J. H. H. Weiler (Eds.), *The European Court of Justice* (pp. 9–42). Oxford: Oxford University Press.

Schmid, C. L. (2001). *The politics of language. Conflict, identity, and cultural pluralism in comparative perspective*. Oxford: Oxford University Press.

Schmitt, C. (1991). *Völkerrechtliche Großraumordnung mit Interventionsverbot für raumfremde Mächte. Ein Beitrag zum Reichsbegriff im Völkerrecht* (1941). Berlin: Duncker & Humblot.

Schmitt, N. (2000). *The foreign relations of Swiss Cantons within the framework of the new 1999 Swiss Constitution*. Fribourg: PIFF.

Schmitt, N. (2012). New constitutions for all Swiss Cantons: A contemporary challenge. In M. Burgess & A. G. Tarr (Eds.), *Constitutional dynamics in federal systems. Sub-national perspectives* (pp. 140–163). Montreal: McGill-Queen's University Press.

Scholl, C. (2013). Europe as contagious space: Cross-border diffusion through EuroMayday and climate justice movements. In C. Flesher Fominaya & L. Cox (Eds.), *Understanding European movements: New social movements, global justice struggles, anti-austerity protest* (pp. 127–142). London: Routledge.

Schulz-Forberg, H., & Stråth, B. (2010). *The political history of European Integration: The hypocrisy of democracy-through-market*. London: Routledge.

Schuman, R. (2011). Declaration of 9th May 1950. *European Issue*, (204), 1–3.

Schütze, R. (2012). Constitutional history: From Paris to Lisbon. In *European constitutional law* (pp. 9–46). Cambridge, UK: Cambridge University Press.

Schwarz, H. -P. (2011). Foreign policy. In *The meaning of Adenauer* (pp. 68–106). Wien: Herder.

Sforza, C. (1948). Gli Stati Uniti d'Europa: Le aspirazioni e la realtà (Conferenza 19, febbraio 1930). In *O federazione europea o nuove guerre* (pp. 17–43). Firenze: La Nuova Italia.

Shirer, W. L. (2011). The emergence of Paul Joseph Goebbels. In *The rise and fall of the Third Reich* (pp. 123–129). New York: Simon and Schuster (Reissued ed.).

Shore, C. (2006). Forging a European nation-sate? The European Union and questions of culture. In *Building Europe. The cultural politics of European Integration* (pp. 15–39). Oxon, UK: Routledge.

Sidjanski, D. (2000). *The Federal Future of Europe: From the European Community to the European Union*. Ann Arbor, MI: The University of Michigan Press.

Slapnicka, H. (1993). Majorities and minorities in an inverted position: Czechoslovakia, 1918–1939. In S. Vilfan et al. (Eds.), *Comparative studies on governments and non-dominant ethnic groups in Europe: 1850–1940*. III. *Ethnic groups and language rights* (pp. 173–197). New York: New York University Press.

Smith, J. (1999). *Europe's Elected Parliament*. Sheffield, UK: Sheffield Academic Press.

Smith, P. (2010). World War I end – Again. *New York Times Upfront, 143*(7), 17 (12/13/2010).

Sofka, J. R. (2011). Metternich and the International System: (1): Federalism, Equilibrium, and the Conference System and (2): The Workings of the Conference System and the Collapse of the European Confederation, 1815–1822. In *Metternich, Jefferson and the Enlightenment: Statecraft and Political theory in the early nineteenth century* (pp. 33–80). Madrid: Consejo Superior de Investigaciones Científicas.

Spagnolo, C. (2004). Reinterpreting the Marshall Plan: The impact of the European recovery programme in Britain, France, Western Germany and Italy: 1947–1952. In D. Geppert (Ed.), *The postwar challenge: Cultural, social, and political change in Western Europe, 1945–1958* (pp. 275–298). Oxford: Oxford University Press.

Spinelli, A., & Rossi, E. (2006). *Il manifesto di Ventotene*. Milano, Italy: Oscar Mondadori.

Steinberg, R. H. (2006). The transformation of European trading states. In J. D. Levy (Ed.), *The state after statism: New state activities in the age of liberalization* (pp. 340–366). Cambridge, MA: Harvard University Press.

Steiner, J. (2001). Switzerland and the European Union: A puzzle. In M. Keating & J. McGarry (Eds.), *Minority nationalism and the changing of international order* (pp. 137–154). Oxford: Oxford University Press.

Steiner, Z. S. (2005). *The lights that failed: European international history, 1919–1933*. Oxford: Oxford University Press.

Stirk, P. M. R. (1996). Pre-1914: Origins. In *A history of European Integration since 1914* (pp. 1–38). London: Pinter.

Stråth, B. (2012). The idea of a European identity as an escape forward: A historical perspective on the present Euro crisis. *The Review of International Affairs, LXIII*(1145), 80–96.

Streitwieser, B. (Ed.). (2014). *Internationalisation of higher education and global mobility*. Oxford: Symposium Books.

Strumia, F. (2013). *Supranational citizenship and the challenge of diversity: Immigrants, citizens and Member States in the EU*. Leiden, The Netherlands: Brill.

Swann, D. (2004). The single market and beyond – An overview. In D. Swann (Ed.), *The single European market and beyond: A study of the wider implications of the Single European Act* (pp. 3–25). Oxon, UK: Routledge.

Tamm, D. (2013). The history of the Court of Justice of the European Union since its origin. In A. Rosas et al. (Eds.), *The Court of Justice and the construction of Europe: Analyses and perspectives on sixty years of case-law (La Cour de Justice et la Construction de l'Europe: Analyses et Perspectives de Soixante Ans de Jurisprudence)* (pp. 9–36). Heidelberg: Springer.

Thomassen, J. (2009). *The legitimacy of the European Union after enlargement*. Oxford: Oxford University Press.

Thürer, D., & Marro, P. -Y. (2012). The Union's legal personality: Ideas and questions lying behind the concept. In H. -J. Blanke & S. Mangiameli (Eds.), *The European Union after Lisbon: Constitutional basis, economic order and external action* (pp. 47–70). Heidelberg, Germany: Springer.

Trampusch, C., & Mach, A. (2011). *Switzerland in Europe: Continuity and change in the Swiss political economy*. London: Routledge.

Treasure, G. (2003). Diplomacy and war. In *The making of modern Europe: 1648–1780* (pp. 161–192). New York: Taylor and Francis.

Tuchman, B. W. (2014). *The proud tower: A portrait of the world before the war, 1890–1914*. London: Viking.

Turku, H. (2013). The international system of states' checks and balances on state sovereignty: The case of Switzerland. *The North Carolina Journal of International Law & Commercial Regulation, 38*(3), 809–874.

Turner, H. A. (1987). *The two Germanies since 1945: East and West*. New Heaven, CT: Yale University Press.

Ugland, T. (2011). *Jean Monnet and Canada: Early travels and the European Unity*. Toronto: University of Toronto Press.

Underhill, G. R. D. (2002). Global integration, EMU, and monetary governance in the European Union: The political economy of the 'Stability Culture'. In K. Dyson (Ed.), *European states and the Euro: Europeanization, variation and convergence* (pp. 31–52). Oxford: Oxford University Press.

Unger, G. (2006). *Aristide Briand: le ferme conciliateur*. Paris: Fayard.

Untea, I. (2012). New Middle Ages or new modernity? Carl Schmitt's interwar perspective on political unity in Europe. In M. Hewitson & M. D'Auria (Eds.), *Europe in crisis. Intellectuals and the European idea: 1917–1957* (pp. 155–168). New York: Berghan Books.

van Caenegem, R. (2009). *An historical introduction to western constitutional law*. Cambridge, UK: Cambridge University Press.

van Nifterik, G. P. (2009). Grotius and the origin of the rulers right to punish. In H. W. Blom (Ed.), *Property, piracy and punishment. Hugo Grotius on War and Booty in De Iure Praedae – Concepts and contexts* (pp. 396–416). Leiden: Brill.

Verdun, A., & Stavridis, S. (2002). Democracy in the European Union in Columbus. In H. Frank (Ed.), *European economic and political issues*. 7. (pp. 55–65). New York: Nova Science Publishers.

Wallace, H. (2010). An institutional anatomy and five policy modes. In M. A. Pollack et al. (Eds.), *Policy-making in the European Union* (pp. 49–90). Oxford: Oxford University Press.

Warlouzet, L. (2010). Charles de Gaulle's Idea of Europe : The lasting legacy. *KONTUR*, (19), 21–31.

Warlouzet, L. (2011). De Gaulle as a Father of Europe: The unpredictability of the FTA's failure and the EEC's success (1956–1958). *Contemporary European History*, (20), 419–434.

Weber, A. (2012). The distribution of competences between the Union and the Member States. In H. -J. Blanke & S. Mangiameli (Eds.), *The European Union after Lisbon: Constitutional basis, economic order and external action* (pp. 311–322). Heidelberg, Germany: Springer.

Weber, J. (2004). *Germany 1945–1990: A parallel history*. Budapest: Central European University Press.

Weiler, J. H. H. (1995). After Maastricht: Community legitimacy in post-1992 Europe. In W. J. Adams (Ed.), *Singular Europe: Economy and polity of the European Community after 1992* (pp. 11–41). Ann Arbor, MI: The University of Michigan Press.

Weiler, J. H. H. (2001). Federalism without constitutionalism: Europe's *Sonderweg*. In K. Nicolaidis & R. Howse (Eds.), *The Federal Vision: Legitimacy and levels of governance in the United States and the European Union* (pp. 54–72). Oxford: Oxford University Press.

Weinberg, G. L. (2010). *Hitler's foreign policy 1933-1939: The road to World War II*. New York, NY: Enigma Books.

Wells, S. B. (2007). *Pioneers of European Integration and Peace, 1945–1963: A brief history with documents*. New York: Palgrave Macmillan.
White, G. W. (2007). *Nation state and territory: Origins, evolutions and relationships*. 1. Plymouth, UK: Rowman & Littlefield.
Wicks, E. (2006). *The evolution of a constitution: Eight key moments in British constitutional history*. Portland, OR: Hart.
Williams, C. (2000). *Adenauer: The Father of the New Germany*. Boston, MA: Little Brown & Co.
Wilson, J. (2003). *Globalization and the limits of national merger control laws*. The Hague: Kluwer Law International.
Wilson, P. (1996). The new Europe debate in wartime Britain. In P. Murray & P. B. Rich (Eds.), *Visions of European unity* (pp. 39–62). Montreal: Westview.
Wilson, D. Sir. (1993). *Tito's Yugoslavia*. Cambridge, UK: Cambridge University Press.
Wolchik, S. L., & Curry, J. L. (Eds.). (2011). *Central and East European politics: From communism to democracy* (2nd ed.). Lanham, MD: Rowman & Littlefield.
Woolf, S. J. (1991). *Napoleon's Integration of Europe*. London: Routledge.
Wormald, J. (2009). 'A Union of Heart s and Minds?' The making of the Union between Scotland and England, 1603. In J. Arrieta & J. H. Elliot (Eds.), *Forms of Union: The British and Spanish monarchies in the seventeenth and eighteenth centuries* (pp. 109–124). Donostia, Spain: Eusko Ikaskuntza.
Wright, J. (2005). Social reform state reform, and Aristide Briand's moment of hope in France. *French Historical Studies, 28*(1), 31–67.
Würgler, A. (2008). The league of the discordant Members' or how the old Swiss confederation operated and how it managed to survive for so long. In A. Holestein et al. (Eds.), *The republican alternative: The Netherlands and Switzerland compared* (pp. 29–43). Amsterdam: Amsterdam University Press.
Zimmer, O. (2007). *A contested nation: History, memory and nationalism in Switzerland, 1761–1891* (2nd ed.). Cambridge, UK: Cambridge University Press.

## Further Reading

Abell, J., Condor, S. and Stevenson, C. (2006). "We are an island": Geographical imagery in accounts of citizenship, civil society, and national identity in Scotland and in England. *Political Psychology, 27*(2), 207–226.
Acosta, D. (2011). *The long-term residence status as a subsidiary form of EU citizenship*. Leiden, The Netherlands: Martinus Nijhoff.
Almeida, D. (2012). *The impact of European Integration on political parties: Beyond the permissive consensus*. London: Routledge.
Amtenbrink, F., et al. (Eds.). (2010). *The constitutional integrity of the European Union*. The Hague: T.M.C. Asser Press.
Anslover, N. L. (2014). A new direction in foreign policy: The Truman Doctrine, Marshall Plan and Israel. In *Harry S. Truman: The coming of the cold war* (pp. 49–72). New York: Routledge.
Armitage, D. (2000). *The ideological origins of the British Empire*. Cambridge, UK: Cambridge University Press.
Baranowski, S. (2011). *Nazi Empire: German colonialism and imperialism from Bismarck to Hitler*. Cambridge, UK: Cambridge University Press.
Baun, M., & Marek, D. (Eds.). (2013). *The new Member States and the European Union: Foreign policy and Europeanization*. London: Routledge.
Beach, D. (2005). *The dynamics of European Integration: Why and when EU institutions matter*. Basingstoke, UK: Palgrave Macmillan.

Behrman, G. (2007). *The most Noble adventure: The Marshall Plan and how America helped rebuild Europe*. New York: Free Press.
Beiner, R. (2003). *Liberalism, nationalism, citizenship: Essays on the problem of political community*. Vancouver, BC: University of British Columbia Press.
Berstein, S. (1986). *Bailing out the system: Reformist socialism in Western Europe, 1944–1985*. London: Bookmarks.
Bouquet, J. -J. (2011). *Histoire de la Suisse* (8e éd.). mise à jour. Paris: Presses Universitaires de France.
Brady, S. (2010). *Eisenhower and Adenauer: Alliance maintenance under pressure, 1953–1960*. Lanham, MD: Lexington Books.
Briand, A. (2000). *Aristide Briand: la paix mondiale et l'Union européenne* (2e éd.). Louvain-la-Neuve, Belgium: Academia-Bruylant.
Bruun, N., et al. (Eds.). (2012). *The Lisbon Treaty and social Europe*. London: Hart.
Buonanno, L., & Nugent, N. (2013). *Policies and policy processes of the European Union*. Basingstoke, UK: Palgrave MacMillan.
Carayannis, E. G., & Korres, G. M. (Eds.). (2013). *European socio-economic integration: Challenges, opportunities and lessons learned*. Boston, MA: Springer.
Carayannis, E. G., & Korres, G. M. (Eds.). (2013). *The innovation union in Europe: A socio-economic perspective on EU Integration*. Cheltenham, UK: Edward Elgar.
Carrera, S. (2009). *In search of the perfect citizen? The intersection between integration, immigration and nationality in the EU*. Leiden: Martinus Nijhoff.
Charnock, G., Purcell, T. and Ribera-Fumaz, R. (2014). *The limits to capital in Spain: Crisis and revolt in the European South*. Basingstoke, UK: Palgrave Macmillan.
Chickering, R., & Förster, S. (Eds.). (2009). *The shadows of total war: Europe, East Asia, and the United States, 1919–1939*. Washington, DC: German Historical Institute.
Chryssochoou, D. N. (2008). *Theorizing European Integration*. London: Routledge.
Conti, N. (Ed.). (2014). *Party attitudes towards the EU in the member states: Parties for Europe, parties against Europe*. London: Routledge.
Conti, N., et al. (Eds.). (2012). *Perspectives of national elites on European citizenship: A South European view*. London: Routledge.
Cotta, M., & Best, H. (2007). *Democratic representation in Europe: Diversity, change, and convergence*. Oxford: Oxford University Press.
de Lombaerde, P., & Schulz, M. (Eds.). (2009). *The EU and world regionalism: The Makability of regions in the 21st century*. Burlington, VT: Ashgate.
Dehousse, R., Maurer, A., Nestor, J. Quermonne, J.L. and Schild, J. (2003). *The institutional architecture of the European Union: A third Franco-German way?* Paris: Notre Europe.
Delanty, G. (2012). *Inventing Europe: Idea, identity, reality*. London: Palgrave.
Devine, T. M. (2010). *Scotland and the Union: 1707–2007*. Edinburgh: Edinburgh University Press (Reprint).
Duncan, A. A. M. (2002). *The Kingship of the Scots 842–1292: Succession and independence*. Edinburgh: Edinburgh University Press.
Eichengreen, B. (2007). *The European economy since 1945: Coordinated capitalism and beyond*. Princeton, NJ: Princeton University Press.
El-Agraa, A. M. (2011). *The European Union* (9th ed.). Cambridge, UK: Cambridge University Press.
Ellison, J. (2007). *The United States, Britain and the transatlantic crisis: Rising to the Gaullist challenge, 1963–1968*. Basingstoke: Palgrave Macmillan.
Ellwood, D. (1992). *Rebuilding Europe: Western Europe, America and postwar reconstruction*. London: Longman.
Ellwood, D. (2012). Was the Marshall Plan necessary? In F. Guirao et al. (Eds.), *Alan S. Milward and a century of European change*. New York: Routledge, pp. 240–254.
Elvert, J., & Kaiser, W. (2013). *European Union enlargement: A comparative history*. New York: Taylor & Francis.

European Commission. Directorate-General for Education and Culture. (2013) *Erasmus: facts, figures & trends: The European Union support for student and staff exchanges and university cooperation in 2011–2012*. Luxembourg: Publications Office of the European Union.
Fabbrini, F. (2014). *Fundamental rights in Europe*. Oxford: Oxford University Press.
Fahrni, D. (2003). *An outline history of Switzerland: From the origins to the present day* (8th enl. ed.). Zurich: Pro Helvetia.
Fornäs, J. (2012). Introducing and interpreting the name and the myth of Europe. In *Signifying Europe* (pp. 8–16). Bristol, UK: Intellect.
Geppert, D. (Ed.). (2003). *The postwar challenge: Cultural, social and political change in Western Europe, 1945–1958*. Oxford: Oxford University Press.
Giauque, J. G. (2002). *Grand designs and visions of unity: The Atlantic powers and the reorganization of Western Europe, 1955–1963*. Chapel Hill, NC: University of North Carolina Press.
Gillingham, J. (2003). *European Integration: 1950–2003*. Cambridge, UK: Cambridge University Press.
Ginsberg, R. H. (2010). *Demystifying the European Union: The enduring logic of regional integration* (2nd ed.). Lanham, MD: Rowman & Littlefield.
Govaere, I. (Ed.). (2014). *The European Union in the world: Essays in honour of Professor Marc Maresceau*. Leiden, The Netherlands: Martinus Nijhoff.
Grant, C. (1994). *Delors: Inside the house that Jacques Built*. London: Nicholas Brealey.
Greengrass, M. (1991). *Conquest and coalescence: The shaping of the state in early modern Europe*. New York: E. Arnold.
Griffin, R. (2008). *Modernism and fascism: The sense of a beginning under Mussolini and Hitler*. Basingstoke, UK: Palgrave Macmillan.
Gstöhl, S. (2002). *Reluctant Europeans: Norway, Sweden, and Switzerland in the process of integration*. Boulder, CO: Lynne Rienner.
Guild, C., et al. (Eds.). (2013). *The reconceptualisation of European Union citizenship*. Leiden, The Netherlands: Martinus Nijhoff.
Guillén, A. M., & León, M. (Eds.). (2011). *The Spanish welfare state in European context*. Surrey, UK: Ashgate.
Guisan, C. (2011). *A political theory of identity in European Integration: Memory and policies*. Oxon, UK: Routledge.
Haas, E. B. (2004). *The uniting of Europe*. Notre Dame, IN: Notre Dame University Press.
Halbrook, S. P. (2006). *The Swiss and the Nazis: How the Alpine republic survived in the shadow of the Third Reich*. Stroud, UK: Spellmount.
Hart, P. (2009). *Mick: The real Michael Collins*. New York: Viking.
Harvie, C. (2004). *Scotland nationalism: Scottish society and politics 1707–1977* (4th ed.). London: Routledge.
Hearn, J. (2000). *Claiming Scotland: National identity and liberal culture*. Edinburgh: Edinburgh University Press.
Heisenberg, D. (2005). The institution of "Consensus" in the European Union: Formal versus informal decision making in the Council. *European Journal of Political Research*, *44*(1), 65–90.
Herborn, G. (1995). *European modernity and beyond: The trajectories of European societies 1945–2000*. London: Sage.
Hitchcock, W. I. (2003). *The struggle for Europe: The turbulent history of a divided continent, 1945–2002*. New York: Doubleday.
Hitler, A. (2010). *Hitler's second book: The unpublished sequel to 'Mein Kampf'*. New York: Enigma Books.
Hogan, M. J. (1987). *The Marshall Plan: America, Britain, and the reconstruction of Western Europe, 1947–1952*. Cambridge, UK: Cambridge University Press.
Jackson, C. (1994). The European Community and the challenges of the 1990s: Change and competitiveness. In M. Lützeler (Ed.), *Europe after Maastricht: American and European perspectives* (pp. 41–52). Providence, RI: Berghahn Books

Kaiser, W., et al. (Eds.). (2009). *The history of the European Union: Origins of a trans- and supranational polity, 1950–1972*. London: Routledge.
Kattago, S. (2011). *Memory and representation in contemporary Europe: The persistence of the past*. Burlington, VT: Ashgate.
Keukeleire, S., & Delreux, T. (2014). *The foreign policy of the European Union*. Houndmills, UK: Palgrave McMillan.
Killick, J. (1997). *The United States and European reconstruction. 1945–1960*. Edinburgh: Edinburgh University Press.
Kimmich, C. M. (2013). *German Foreign Policy, 1918–1945: A guide to current research and resources*. Plymouth, UK: Rowman & Littlefield.
Kinkaid, J. (Ed.). (2011). *Federalism: Historical and theoretical foundations of federalism*. I. Los Angeles, CA: Sage.
Klamert, M. (2014). *The principle of loyalty in EU law*. Oxford: Oxford University Press.
Klimke, M., & Scharloth, J. (Eds.). (2008). *1968 in Europe: A history of protest and activism, 1956–1977*. New York: Palgrave Macmillan.
Kochenov, D., & Amtenbrink, F. (Eds.). (2014). *The European Union's shaping of the international legal order*. Cambridge, UK: Cambridge University Press.
Laible, J. (2009). *Separatism and sovereignty in the new Europe: Party politics and the meanings of statehood in a supranational context*. Houndmills, UK: Palgrave McMillan.
Lebow, R. N., et al. (Eds.). (2006). *The politics of memory in postwar Europe*. Durham, NC: Duke University Press.
Leffler, M. P. (2010). *Origins of the cold war: An international history* (2nd ed. repr.). London: Routledge.
Leikam, F. (2009). A strategy that failed: Great Britain, Commonwealth Africa and EEC Association Policy, 1957–1963. In M. Rasmussen & A. C. L. Knudsen (Eds.), *The road to a United Europe: Interpretations of the process of european integration*. Brussels: P.I.E. Peter Lang.
Leonard, M., & Kundnani, H. (2013). Think again: European decline. *Foreign Policy*, (200), 46–50.
Lukacs, J. (2007). *June 1941: Hitler and Stalin*. New Haven, CT: Yale University Press.
Macormick, J. (2013). The evolution of the EU. In *Understanding the European Union: A concise introduction* (pp. 56–83). Basingstoke, UK: Palgrave MacMillan.
Maes, I., & Verdun, A. (2005). Small states and the creation of the EMU: Belgium and the Netherlands pace-setters and gate-keepers. *Journal of Common Market Studies, 43*(2), 327–348.
Maíz Suárez, R. (2012). *The inner frontier: The place of nation in the political theory of democracy and federalism*. Brussels, Belgium: P.I.E. Peter Lang.
Malmborg, M., & Stråth, B. (Eds.). (2002). *The meaning of Europe: Variety and contention within and among nations*. Oxford: Berg.
Marcussen, M., Risse, T., Engelmann-Martin, D., Knopf, H. J. and Roscher, K. (1999). Constructing Europe?: The evolution of French British and German Nation State Identities. *Journal of European Public Policy, 6*(4), 614–633.
Mathijsen, P. S. R. F. (2010), *A guide to European Union law: As amended by the Treaty of Lisbon* (10th ed.). London: Sweet & Maxwell.
Maulucci, T. W. (2012). *Adenauer's foreign office: West German diplomacy in the shadow of the Third Reich*. DeKalb, IL: Northern Illinois University Press.
Milward, A. S. (1993). *The frontier of national sovereignty: History and theory, 1945–1992*. London: Routledge.
Mouritzen, H., & Wivel, A. (2006). *The geopolitics of Euro-Atlantic Integration*. London: Routledge.
Murray, P., & Rich, P. (Eds.). (1996). *Visions of European unity*. London: Westview.
Neumann, I. B., & Gstöhl, S. (2004). *Lilliputians in Gulliver's world: Small states in international relations*. Reykjavik, Iceland: Centre for Small State Studies.

Nicolaidis, K., & Lacroiz, J. (2003). Order and justice beyond the nation state: Europe's competing paradigms. In R. Foot et al. (Eds.), *Order and justice in international relations* (pp. 125–154). Oxford: Oxford University Press.
O'Brenan, J., & Raunio, T. (Eds.). (2007). *National parliaments within the enlarged European Union: From 'Victims' of integration to competitive actors?* London: Routledge.
Oechsli, W. (2013). *History of Switzerland: 1499–1914*. Cambridge, UK: Cambridge University Press.
Papa, E. R. (2007). Gli Stati uniti d'Europa nel pensiero di Carlo Sforza (1919–1946). In G. Monina (Ed.), *1945–1946: le origini della Repubblica* (pp. 119–151). Soveria Mannelli, Italy: Rubbettino.
Persson, H.-Å., & Stråth, B. (Eds.). (2007). *Reflections on Europe. Defining a political order in time and space*. Brussels: P.I.E. Peter Lang.
Phinnemore, D. (2004). Institutions and governance. In N. Nugent (Ed.), *European Union enlargement* (pp. 118–131). Basingstoke, UK: Palgrave.
Pierson, P. (1996). The path to European Integration: A historical institutionalist analysis. *Comparative Political Studies,* (29), 123–163.
Piketty, T. (2014). *Capital in the twenty-first century*. Cambridge, UK: The Belknap Press of Harvard University Press.
Poguntke, T. (Ed.). (2007). *The Europeanization of national political parties: Power and organizational adaptation*. London: Routledge.
Ponjaert, F., & Telò, M. (Eds.). (2013). *The EU's foreign policy: What kind of power and diplomatic action?* Burlington, VT: Ashgate.
Requejo Coll, F. (2005). *Multinational federalism and value pluralism: The Spanish case*. London: Routledge.
Rittberger, B., Gilbert, M., Cowles, M. G., Laursen, F., Vanhoonacker, S. Sbragia, et al. (2012). Treaties of Paris; The Treaties of Rome; The Single European Act; The Treaty of Maastricht; The Treaty of Amsterdam; Treaty of Nice; The Constitutional Treaty and Lisbon". In E. Jones et al. (Eds.), *The Oxford handbook of the European Union* (pp. 79–180). Part II: Treaties. Oxford: Oxford University Press.
Rodriguez-Ruiz, B., & Rubio-Marín, R. (Eds.). (2012). *The struggle for female suffrage in Europe: Voting to become citizens*. Leiden, Netherlands: Brill.
Rosamond, B. (2010). *Theories of European Integration*. Basingstoke, UK: Palgrave Macmillan.
Roselli, A. (2014). *Money and trade wars in interwar Europe*. Basingstoke, UK: Palgrave Macmillan.
Saurugger, S. (2014). *Theoretical approaches to European integration*. Basingstoke, UK: Palgrave Macmillan.
Scales, L., & Zimmer, O. (Eds.), (2006). *Power and the nation in European history*. Cambridge, UK: Cambridge University Press.
Schiek, D. (2012). *Economic and social integration: The challenge for EU constitutional law*. Cheltenham: Edward Elgar.
Schipper, F. (2008). Setting the stage: The dawn of the spirit of Geneva 1898–1921. In *Driving Europe: Building Europe on roads in the twentieth century* (pp. 45–82). Amsterdam University Press.
Schissler, H. (Ed.). (2001). *The miracle years: A cultural history of West Germany, 1949–1968*. Princeton, NJ: Princeton University Press.
Schmitt, H., & Thomassen, J. (Eds.). (1999). *Political representation and legitimacy in the European Union*. Oxford: Oxford University Press.
Schueler, J. (2008). *Materialising identity: The co-construction of the Gotthard Railway and Swiss national identity*. Amsterdam: Aksant.
Schütze, R. (2009). *From dual to cooperative federalism: The changing structure of European law*. Oxford: Oxford University Press.
Schwartz, R. A. (2006). *The cold war reference guide: A general history and annotated chronology, with selected biographies*. Jefferson, NC: McFarland.
Schwarz, H.-P. (2011). *The meaning of Adenauer*. Wien: Herder.
Smith, A. D. (2000). *Nations and nationalism in a global era*. Malden, MA: Blackwell.

Spolaore, E. (2013). *What is European Integration really about? A political guide for economists*. Cambridge, MA: National Bureau of Economic Research.

Stark, R. (2014). *How the west won: The neglected story of the triumph of modernity*. Wilmington, DE: ISI Books.

Stråth, B. (2002). A European identity: To the historical limits of a concept". *European Journal of Social Theory, 5*(4), 387–401.

Sutton, M. (2011). *France and the construction of Europe, 1944–2007: The geopolitical imperative*. New York, NY: Berghahn Books.

Swenden, W. (2006). *Federalism and regionalism in Western Europe: A comparative and thematic analysis*. Basingstoke, UK: Palgrave Macmillan.

Tallberg, J. (2013). *European governance and supranational institutions*. New York: Taylor and Francis.

Tan, C. (2013). *Learning from Shanghai: Lessons on achieving educational success*. Heidelberg, Germany: Springer.

Thacker, T. (2009). *Joseph Goebbels: Life and death*. Basingstoke: Palgrave Macmillan.

Thorhallsson, B., & Wivel, A. (2006). Small states in the European Union: What do we know and what would we like to know? *Cambridge Review of International Affairs, 19*(4), 651–668.

Toye, R. (2013). *The roar of the Lion: The untold story of Churchill's World War II speeches*. Oxford: Oxford University Press.

Trachtenberg, M. (1999). *A constructed peace: The making of the European settlement, 1945–1963*. Princeton, NJ: Princeton University Press.

Tuori, K., & Tuori, K. (2014). *The Eurozone crisis: A constitutional analysis*. Cambridge, UK: Cambridge University Press.

Unkovski-Korica, V. (2014). *The economic struggle for power in Tito's Yugoslavia: From World War II to Non-Alignmen*. London: I.B. Tauris.

Urwin, D. W. (2007). *The community of Europe: A history of European Integration since 1945* (2nd ed., 15th. impr.). London: Longman.

Van Vooren, B. (2012). The Maastricht Treaty: A watershed for EU external relations. In *EU external relations and the European neighbourhood policy: A paradigm for coherence* (pp. 30–43). New York: Routledge.

Van Vooren, B. et al. (Eds.). (2013). *The EU's role in global governance: The legal dimension*. Oxford: Oxford University Press.

Walker, N. (2006). Late sovereignty in the European Union. In *Sovereignty in transition* (pp. 3–32). Oxford: Hart (Reprint).

Walker, W. T. (2014). The Marshall Plan, June 5, 1947. In *America in the cold war* (pp. 189–191). Santa Barbara, CA: ABC-CLIO.

Wall, S. (2009). *A stranger in Europe: Britain and the EU from Thatcher to Blair*. Oxford: Oxford University Press.

Walter, F. (2012). *Histoire de la Suisse* (3e éd., 5 vols). Neuchâtel, Switzerland: Presses Universitaires Suisses.

Warlouzet, L. (2008). France and the Treaty of Rome: Negotiation and implementation (1956–1974). In M. Gehler (Ed.), *From common market to European Union building: 50th anniversary of the Rome Treaties 1957–2007* (pp. 541–555). Weimar: Böhlau.

Warlouzet, L., & Witschke, T. (2012). The difficult path to an economic rule of law: European competition policy, 1950–1991. *Contemporary European History*, (21), 437–455.

Weigall, D., & Stirk, P. (Eds.). (1992). *The origins and development of the European Community*. Leicester, UK: Leicester University Press.

Wessel, R. A., & Blockmans, S. (Eds.). (2013). *Between autonomy and dependence: The EU legal order under the influence of international organisations*. The Hague, The Netherlands: T.M.C. Asser Press.

Whatley, C. A. (2007). *The Scots and the Union*. Edinburgh, Scotland: Edinburgh University Press.

Wiener, A., & Diez, T. (2009). Federalism. In *European Integration theory* (pp. 25–44). Oxford: Oxford University Press.

# Index

**A**
Abderramán I, 169
Abderrammán III, 568
Abolition of inheritances, 568
Aboukir Bay, 405, 475
Absolute monarchy, 54, 200, 211–249, 258, 259, 322, 351, 371–405, 455, 456, 465, 476, 491, 492, 497, 500–502, 504, 527, 537, 557, 600
Absolute royal power, 211
Absolutism, 11, 54–56, 141, 142, 203, 212, 220, 223, 231, 234–244, 257–280, 289, 294–295, 297, 298, 305, 352, 371–405, 491–493, 496, 505, 506, 511, 512, 518, 527, 528, 651
Abyssinia, 532
Academic Palms, Order of, 463
Acadia, 327, 344
Accounts Chamber, 184
Accretion of treaties, 701–702
Accursio, Francesco di, 217
Acerbo Law (1923), 578, 617
Achaeans, 20, 23
*Acquis communautaire*, 2, 683, 698, 701–702
Acropolis, 19, 22, 26
Act(s)
  of Parliament, 225, 240, 301, 343
  of Settlement (1701), 300, 302
  of Supremacy (1534), 215, 246, 295, 309
  of Union (1707), 301
  of Union (1800), 656
*Acte additionnel aux constitutions de l'Empire*, 455
Action Committee for the United States of Europe, 690
Actium, 40, 49, 59
Adams, John Quincy, 334, 428
Adams, Samuel, 347, 421
Adenauer, Konrad, 668, 682, 685–687
Administrative
  jurisdiction, 457–458
  law, 598
  monarchy, 183–185, 188
  reform, 268, 278, 457
  state, 456–458, 587, 599
  tutelage, 457
Adrianople, battle of, 94
Advanced industrial societies, 608
*Aerarium*, 53
Aeropagus, 21
Aeschylus, 26
Aetius, 95, 96, 113
Africa, 56, 59, 96, 98, 114, 214, 276, 300, 484, 530–532, 607
Agee, James, 585
Agricultural
  Adjustment Act, 12 May, 1933, 586
  society, 565
Aircraft, 562, 685
Aix-la-Chapelle
  Congress of, 537
  peace of, 344
Akhenaten IV, 67
Akkadian Empire, 13, 31
Alabama State, 437
Alamanni, 94, 96, 98, 106, 108, 113, 124
Alani, 96, 113
Alaric I, 94, 95, 113
Alaska State, 430, 437, 443
Álava, 237


B. Aguilera-Barchet, *A History of Western Public Law*,
DOI 10.1007/978-3-319-11803-1

Albany, 327
Albertine Statute (1848), 513, 519–521, 538, 578
Alboin, king of the Lombards, 97, 114, 144
Alcalá de Henares, Cortes of, 195, 221, 232
Alcaldes de corte, 184
Alcibiades, 27
Aleksandrovich, Nikolai, 587
Alexander the Great, 14, 27–29, 31–33, 261
Alexander VI, Pope, 186, 654
Alexandrine Bulls (1493), 186, 326
Alfonso IX king of León Alfonso XII, King of Spain, 192, 198, 201
Alfonso VI, king of Castile and León, 170
Alfonso X king of Castile and León, 201
Alfred the Great, king of the Anglo-Saxons, 308
Algeria crisis, 693
Aljubarrota, batlle of, 202
*Allgemeine*, 265, 274
  *Landrecht* (1794), 274
  *Schulordnung*, 265
Alliances of states, 614
Almodis, 166
Almohads, 164
Almoravids, 163, 164, 170
Alodial tenure, 153
Alsace, 111, 188, 380, 399, 470, 532, 685, 686
Alsace-Lorraine, 399
Altamaha river, 340
Alvarado, Pedro de, 329
Alvares Cabral, Pedro, 186, 245, 326
Ambrose of Milan, 79
Amendments, 311, 354, 426–428, 435, 437–439, 441–443, 469, 472, 477, 499, 524, 570, 586, 697, 701
American
  Civil War (*see* War of Secession)
  colonies, 248, 277, 304, 305, 310, 324, 336, 344, 350, 507, 653
  constitutionalism, 334, 417, 467
  constitutional model, 601
  economic system, 585
  Imperialism, 532
  individualism, 598
  legal system, 354
  nation, 334
  polity, 353
  presidential republic, 651
  republic, 350, 371
  Revolution, 38, 199, 322–358, 372, 373, 384, 391, 417, 605, 651
  revolutionary war, 345
  territorial expansion, 432
  troops, 541, 676
Amsterdam Treaty (1999), 710
Amun, 13
Anagni, 141, 146, 185, 202, 217
*Anchorites*, 103
Ancien Régime, 184, 191, 196, 234, 238–240, 261, 269, 271, 324, 377, 381, 382, 394, 396
  et la Révolution, 372
Andes, 508
Andrinopolis, Treaty of (1829), 509
Anesthesia, 562, 563
Angles, 94, 96–98, 108, 113, 122, 308
Anglican Church, 146, 215, 300, 333
Anglicanism, 296, 333
Anglicans, 297
Anglo-Frisians, 292
Anglo-Irish Treaty (1921), 666, 706
Anglos, 292
Anglo-Saxon England, 290
Angoulême, Duke of, 507
Anguita, Julio, 606
Annales School, 658
Annapolis Convention, 420–421, 440
Anne Boleyn, 215, 230, 233, 235, 246, 295, 300
Annexation of Hawaii, 540
Anointment, ceremony of, 107, 374, 376
*Anschluss*, 591, 595, 618, 673, 706
Anthony and Pachomius, 103
Anthropologists, 16, 20
Anti-Bolshevik Europe, 673, 674
Anti-Catholicism, 300
Anti-establishment, 613
Anti-Federalist, 352, 419, 422, 427–429, 437, 438
Anti-globalization protestors, 613
Antilles, 327
*Anti-Machiavel: Essay on the criticism of Machiavelli*, 271
Anti-Nazi resistance, 674
Antisepsis, 562
Antonio Pérez, 240, 243, 247
Apenzell Canton, 662
Apologists, 77, 85
Apostasis, 74
Apostolos, 69
Application of the law, 185, 600
April Theses, 616
Aquinas, Thomas of, 139, 140
Aragon, kingdom of, 170, 196, 200
Arbitration, 46
Archbishops, 291, 466
Argentina, 507, 508, 565

Ariadne, 19
Arianism, 78, 82, 106, 107, 114, 115
Aristocracy, 15, 21–24, 28, 45, 48, 324, 387, 397, 501
Arizona State, 436, 437, 442
Arkansas State, 436
Armed peace, 492, 531–533, 540, 663
Armistice
of Compiègne (November 11, 1918), 616
of Villafranca, 521
Army of Italy, 405, 475
Aron, Raymond, 568
Arrondissements, 457
Arsenal of democracy, 599
Article 48 of the Weimar constitution, 323
Articles of Confederation, 326, 355–358, 417–421, 430, 431, 440
Artisan class, 306
Artisans, 13, 20, 21, 24, 45, 473, 501
Aryan blood, 578
Aryanism, 114
Asepsis, 562
Ashley, Lord, Earl of Shaftesbury, 338
Asia, 39, 96, 326, 330, 530, 592, 605, 677
Asia Minor, 20, 29, 81
Asquith, Herbert Henry, 308
Assemblée consultative provisoire, 471
Assemblée Nationale, 466, 469
Assemblies of Notables, 227
Assembly
of colonists, 332
of estates, 201, 292, 293, 655
of representatives, 342, 394
Assembly-based government, 289–294, 399–405, 450, 456–458, 472
Assignats, 460
Assize
circuits (itinerant justice tribunal), 291
of Clarendon, 291–292, 309
Asturian monarchy, 181
Asturias, 169, 181, 183, 593
Ataulf, 95, 113
Ateneo de Madrid, 501, 567
Athens, 18, 19, 21, 22, 24–28, 32, 39, 48, 75, 260, 653
Atlantic world, 325
Attila, 96, 113
Attlee, Clement, 680
Auctoritas, 100, 182
Audiencias, 184, 231, 328
Aufklärer, 263
Aufklärung, 259, 271, 322
Augustus, 17, 38, 40, 49–53, 55, 57, 60, 61, 73, 84, 127, 130, 139, 180, 182, 183, 199, 289, 291, 374, 376, 455, 468
Aula regia, 99, 101, 191, 290
Aunós, Eduardo, 589
Austerlitz, Battle of, 476
Australia, 536, 566
Austria, 143, 223, 248, 261, 262, 264, 265, 268, 269, 274, 275, 279–281, 392, 405, 492–495, 506, 509, 511–519, 521–524, 526, 532–540, 572, 591, 595, 618, 659, 663–665, 668, 673, 678, 692, 698, 706, 710
Austrian Empire, 263, 268, 379, 515–516, 518
Austro-Hungarian Empire, 533, 534, 600
Authoritarian
regime, 510, 593
stateá, 272, 569, 579
Authority, 20, 21, 40, 51, 53, 56, 57, 71, 73, 75, 78, 81–85, 100, 102–107, 122–125, 130–136, 138–142, 144–146, 154, 157, 158, 161–164, 166–168, 179, 181, 188–190, 193, 197, 198, 200, 212, 213, 215–218, 221, 224, 227, 228, 230–232, 236, 238, 240–242, 258–263, 268, 270, 273, 274, 290, 294–296, 298, 299, 305, 308, 325, 329, 333, 337, 339, 341, 342, 348, 353–357, 374, 376, 382, 383, 385, 386, 388, 420, 422, 429, 438, 440, 442, 443, 452–454, 459, 464, 469, 496–498, 527, 587, 588, 591, 598, 615–621, 650, 661, 666, 667, 687–690
Autobahn, 577
Autocracy, 234–240, 276, 527–530, 574, 579
Autocratic regime, 242, 323, 578, 580
Autonomous
communities, 112, 655
regions, 655, 700
Aviation, 559, 562
Avignon, 141, 146, 185, 188, 202, 399
Ayacucho, battle of, 532, 537
Azaña, Manuel, 498

**B**

Babeuf, François-Noël, 568
Babylon, 14, 31, 33, 68, 84
Baden, 143, 504
Badoglio, Pietro, 619
Bailly, Jean-Sylvain, 389
Bakunin, Mikhail, 469
Balbo, Cesare, 520

Baldus de Ubaldis, 202, 217
Balladur, Édouard, 478
Balthes, lineage of, 94
Baltimore, Lord, 337
Bankers, 164, 214, 223, 352, 418, 468, 492, 496, 669
Bank of England, 585
Bank of France, 459, 460
Bankruptcy of Lehman Brothers (2008), 609
Baptists, 300
Barbarians, 94
Barbarossa, Operation, 596, 618
Barbés, Armand, 467
Barcelona, 111, 158, 159, 165, 166, 169, 179, 183, 192, 199, 200, 228, 562, 653, 654
Barons, 139, 178, 188, 191, 193, 196, 231, 291–294
Barry, Madame du, 379
Bartolo de Sassoferrato, 202
Basic Law for the Federal Republic of Germany, 619, 708
Basic legal framework of colonial life, 343
Basilica, 76, 127
Basilokon Doron (royal gift), 296
Basque
  country, 112, 500, 655, 667
  Provinces, 237, 277
Bastille, 234, 373, 380, 391, 392, 395, 403, 559
Batavian Republic, 663
Batista, Fulgencio, 605, 620
Bavaria, 98, 108, 130, 131, 135, 143, 504, 563
Bayeux
  Speech, 473
  Tapestry, 288
Bayle, Pierre, 241
Beauharnais, Joséphine de, 475
Beaumarchais, Pierre-Augustin de, 371
Beaune, Jacques de, Baron of Semblançay, 234
Bebel, August, 571
Beccaria, Cesare, 275
Bech, Joseph, 687, 691
Beckett, Thomas, 201
Beer Hall Putsch, Munich, 1923, 577
Beetle, 577
Beginning of history, 372
Beijing, 607, 620
  Olympics, 621
Belarusians, 596
Belfast, 657
  Agreement (1998), 666
Belgian
  Constitution of 1831, 510, 537
  gentry, 509
  neutrality, 535
  Socialist Party, 674
  state, 509–510
Belgrade, 665, 680
Benedictine Order, 104, 115, 136
Benedict of Nursia, 104, 115
Benefice, 156, 158
Beneficium, 156
Benelux, 675–676, 689, 707, 708
Benevento, Duchy of, 126
Benz, Karl, 562
Berges, Aristide, 561, 568
Berkeley, Lord, 337, 340, 508
Berlin
  Airlift (Berliner Luftbrücke), 604, 619, 681, 707
  bunker, 619
  rebellion (1848), 517
Berliner Mauer (Berlin Wall), 604, 620, 708
Berlinguer, Enrico, 606
Bernard of Clairvaux, 163
Bern, Canton of, 660
Beveridge Plan (1942), 588
Beveridge, W.H., 572
Bevin, Ernest, 689
Beyen, Jan Wilem, 691
Bèze, de Theodore, 236
Bible, 67, 68, 83, 85, 104, 105, 133, 187, 219, 335, 561, 569
Bicameral structure, 293, 342
Biddle, Nicholas, 428
Bielfeld Baron of, 275
Big Capitalism, 558–564
Bilderberg Group, 612
Bill
  of Rights (1689), 262, 299, 300
  of Rights (1791), 354, 499
Bills of attainder, 230, 231, 234
Biology, 562
Bishops, 73, 74, 76–83, 99, 101, 106, 107, 122, 126, 135–139, 160, 162, 163, 165, 166, 177, 178, 180, 181, 187, 191, 192, 198, 215, 290–293
Bismarck's Sozialpolitik, 571–572
Bismarck, von Otto, 524, 525
Black
  Sea, 47, 94, 275
  Tuesday (29 October 1929), 584
Blackstone, W., 333
Blanc, Louis, 569
Bleeding Kansas, 437
Bloody Week, 555
Blum, André Léon, 588
Bodin, Jean, 218, 219, 247, 499
Boer War (1899-1902), 531, 540
Bohemia, 131, 132, 261, 268, 270, 504, 515, 516

Boletín Oficial del Estado, 655
Boleyn, Anne, 215, 230, 233, 235, 246, 295, 300
Bolingbroke, Viscount of, 417
Bolívar, Simon, 537
Bologna
 Declaration (1999), 710
 Process, 703
 University of, 111, 133, 170, 200
Bolshevik Party, 587
Bolsheviks, 574
Bolshevism, 307, 376, 667
Bonaparte, Napoleon, 143, 402, 435, 450–452, 455, 462, 475, 477, 514, 651
Bonapartism, 449–479
Bonfire Night, 297
Boniface VIII, 140, 185, 193, 197, 202, 213, 217, 376
*Book of the Covenant*, 68
Books of grievances, 387–388
Bosnian War (1992-1995), 666
Boston
 Harbor, 346
 Latin School, 335
 Massacre (1770), 346
 Tea Party (1773), 346, 358
Bourbon(s), 262, 278, 279, 329, 505, 510
 era, 329
 House of, 216, 247, 377
 state, 329
Bourgeoisie, 178, 189, 191, 193, 194, 201, 223–225, 295, 297, 309, 322, 330, 381, 386, 391, 397, 466, 467, 496, 500–502, 509, 511, 557, 568, 570, 586, 608
Bourgeois parties, 572
Boxer Rebellion (1899-1901), 531, 540
Bracton, Henry, 197
Bradford, William, 333
Brahmanism, 103
Brandenburg, 271, 280, 323
Braudel, Fernand, 658
Bravo, Juan, 241
Brazil, 186, 326, 327, 357, 508, 566, 615
Bremen, 190
Brest Litovsk, Treaty of, 541
Bretton Woods Agreements, 614, 707
Brezhnev Constitution of 1977, 580
Brezhnev, Leonid, 621
Briand, Aristides, 670, 706
Bribery, 302, 697
BRIC, 615
Bristol, 331
 Shipo wners, 327
Britain's parliamentary monarchy, 511
British
 colonies, 351, 536
 Commonwealth, 676
 constitutional history, 297
 constitutional system, 354
 Crown, 143, 183, 305, 325, 330–348, 355, 417, 666
 Empire, 350, 532, 535, 539, 651, 657, 672
 feminists, 307
 government, 307, 344, 345, 572, 657, 672, 682, 690, 692
 monarchy, 343
 Parliament, 249, 307, 346, 353, 388, 690
 prime minister, 694
 sovereignty, 340
 subjects, 303, 672
Britons, 98
Brittany, 56, 227, 288, 384
Bronte
 Charlotte, 324
 Emily, 324
Brownie, 560
Bruges, 111, 190, 648, 683
Brüning, Heinrich, 323
Brussels, 246, 515, 693, 702, 708, 709
Budapest, 515
Buddha, 14, 30, 103
Buddhism, 103
Budget Law, 194, 308
Bulgaria, 94, 535, 680, 698, 702, 711
Bundesrat, 524
Bundestag (RFA), 621
Bureaucracy, 13, 15, 19, 45, 154, 269, 270, 582
Bureaucratic state, 15, 298
Bürgerliches Gesetzbuch, 134
Burgoyne, John, English General, 349
Burgundians, 94, 96–98, 106, 108, 113–115, 122
Burgundy, 108, 124, 162, 190, 201, 203, 227, 384, 659
Burschenschaft, 504
Bush, George Walker, 425
Businessmen, 214, 352, 492, 598, 612, 668, 669
Byzantine Empire, 104, 123, 126
Byzantines, 108, 114, 122–123, 125, 144

C
Cabezas de San Juan (Seville), 505, 537
Cabildos, 329
Cabinet, 301, 302, 308, 344, 472, 473, 525, 666, 672, 687
Cabot, John and Sebastian, 327
Caciquismo, 269
Cádiz, 328, 501, 507, 537
Cady Stanton, Elizabeth, 307, 438
Caesaropapism, 78–79
Calas Affair, 234
Calatrava, order of, 164
California State, 436, 437, 442, 559, 707
Calonne, 380, 384, 402
Calvert
- Cecil, 337
- George, First Lord Baltimore, 337
- Leonard, 337

Calvinism, 215
Cambacéres, Jean Jacques Régis, 400, 453, 455, 463
Cambodians, 620
Cambó, Francesc, 589
Cambridge university, 531
Camicie rosse (red shirts), 521
Camillo Benso, 520
Canada, 112, 246, 326, 343, 344, 349, 357, 379, 418, 535, 657
Canary Islands, 245, 331, 653
Canning, Robert, 507
Cannossa, castle of, 138
Canon Law, 82, 124, 184, 214, 216, 217
Canons, 71, 79, 82, 107, 133, 180, 650
Cánovas del Castillo, Antonio, 501, 505
Cantons, 652, 657–662
Cape Cod, 248, 334, 357
Capet Dynasty, 376
Capetian monarchy, 375
Capitalism, 214, 564, 566, 574–576, 589, 590, 605, 607, 612, 620
Capitalist society, 606, 608
Capitani del popolo, 189
Capitularia (capitulary), 158
Capitulary of Quierzy (877), 153, 158, 169
Captains general, 328
Carbonari, 504
Cardiff Castile and León, 170, 181
Caribbean Communist State, 605
Caribbean sea, 331, 605
Carlist Wars, 277, 510, 655
Carlos María Isidro, 510
Carlsbad (Bohemia), 504
Carlton House, 305
Carolina, province of, 339
Carolingian Empire, 123, 128–134, 158, 169
Carranza, Venustiano, 573
Carrillo, Santiago, 606
Cars, 562
Carteret, Sir George, 340
Carthage, 17, 33, 39, 46, 47, 49, 59, 114
Carthusians, 242
Cartier, Jacques, 246, 326, 357, 478, 479, 704
Casa de Contratación, 328
Casos de corte, 184
Castelar, Emilio, 267
Caste system, 12
Castile, 111, 132, 163, 169, 170, 178, 183–189, 192, 195, 196, 199, 201–203, 221, 223, 232, 237, 240, 241, 243, 277–279, 357, 655
Castilians, 17, 111, 178, 184, 186, 195, 200, 202, 227, 228, 231–233, 237, 241, 245, 277, 326, 328, 329, 655
Castilian town governments, 329
Castillianization, 655
Castlá, 159
Castlereagh, Lord, 495, 506
Castoriadis, Cornelius, 606, 608
Castro
- Fidel, 605, 620, 621
- Raúl, 621

Catalaunic Fields, battle of, 96
Catalonia, 111, 112, 159, 165, 179, 188, 189, 192, 196, 199–201, 228, 231, 237, 238, 279, 500, 623, 667
Catherine II the Great, tsarinaáof Russia, 275
Catherine of Aragon, 146, 215, 233, 242, 295, 300
Catholic (s)
- apologetic literature, 77
- Church, 66, 77, 105, 137, 141, 213, 246, 267, 298, 459, 509, 522, 527
- Irish, 300
- Kings, 163, 186, 203, 215, 216, 222, 223, 231, 243, 300, 654
- Majesty, 235, 654
- monarch, 241, 261
- Monarchy, 196, 222, 229, 231, 243, 247, 277, 652–656
- nobility, 337

Caudillo, 590
Cavaignac, Eugéne, 467
Celebration of the Federation, 373, 394, 395, 403
Celibacy, 137, 462
Celtic dialects, 292

Cenobites, 103
Censitary
requirements, 501
suffrage, 306, 310, 432, 435, 492, 500–502, 509, 557, 564, 567, 579
Central
America, 326
planning, 604
Powers, 533, 535
Centralization, 144, 200, 223, 278, 329, 394, 396, 421, 457, 654, 657
Cerularius, Michael (patriarch of Constantinople), 170
Cervantes, Miguel de, 247, 248
Cesar, Julius, 17, 48, 59, 658
Chaeronea, 28
Chamberlain, Neville, 618, 674, 706
Chamberland, Charles, 562
Chamber of Peers, *(Chambre des Pairs)*, 466
Chambre
des députés, 470
Introuvable, 476
Champlain, Samuel de, 326
Champs-Élysées, 559
Chancellery of State (Staatskanzlei), 268
Chancellor, 182, 184, 218, 235, 239, 243, 268, 323, 383, 493, 524, 527, 572, 578, 616, 617, 621, 663, 668, 700, 706
Chancilleréas, 184, 231
Channel islands, 567
Chant de guerre. *See* Marseillaise
Charlemagne, 107, 125–129, 131, 132, 134, 143, 145, 155, 169, 212, 374–375, 462
Charles Martel, 123, 124, 145, 155, 157, 169, 374
Charles the Bald, 129, 145, 153, 158, 162
Charles the Bold, Duke of Burgundy, 659
Charles the Simple, 129, 145, 288
Charles town, 339
Charles V, emperor, 146
Charles VI, Austrian emperor, 280
Charroux, 165
*Charte* of 1814, 538
Charter
of Fundamental Rights of the European Union, 710
of Privileges of Pennsylvannia, 341
of the United Nations, 680
Chartered companies, 336
Chateaubriand, F.R., 371, 507
Châtellenies, 161
Che Guevara, 605, 606, 620
Chemistry, 562
Cheptel sur Epte Treaty, 288
Chesapeake Bay, 331
Chiang Kai-Shek, 684
Chicago, 439, 442, 563, 582, 599
Chief Justice, 240, 247, 421, 425, 429, 438, 440, 441, 504
Chile, 507, 508, 667, 706
Chilean navy, 507
China, 14–15, 31, 48, 530, 538–540, 575, 592, 605–607, 610, 612, 615, 617–619, 690, 698, 705, 708
Chinaleaks, 612
Chin Dynasty, 15
Chinese
model, 607
regime, 607
World Order, 610
Chirac, Jacques, 478, 479, 704
Chotek, Sophie, 534
Christ, 68–70, 72, 76, 77, 79, 106, 139, 337, 523
Christendom, 82, 107, 115, 126, 137, 163, 201, 271, 290, 374, 650
Christian(s), 60, 69–76, 79–81, 84, 85, 103, 105, 122, 327
Majesty, 344, 374, 654
rulers, 260
Universal Empire, 245
universalism, 141, 142, 185–186, 212–216
Christianity, 54, 66–79, 82–85, 94, 103, 105–106, 114, 115, 374, 393, 459
Christianization, 75, 393, 404
Chronic abstention, 611
Church
of England, 146, 246, 297, 333
hierarchy, 333
social doctrines, 77
Churchill, Winston, 572, 596, 597, 707
Cicero, 38, 44, 49, 59, 72
Cid, Rodrigo Diaz de Vivar, 170
Cinema, 560
Cinematographer, 560
Cisalpine Republic, 506
Cisneros, cardinal, 163
Cities/City, 11–13, 16–21, 23–29, 31, 38–43, 45, 47–49, 53, 55–57, 66, 70, 76, 77, 80–83, 95, 111, 138, 157, 178, 181, 184, 187–190, 192–194, 198, 199, 201, 217, 221–223, 226, 227, 233, 241, 265, 266, 269, 275, 288, 292, 293, 306, 309, 327, 329, 335, 337, 339, 341, 344–347, 351, 421, 439, 442, 466, 469, 470, 477, 511,

520, 523, 560, 562–566, 587, 619, 648, 658, 661, 662, 673, 678, 686, 696
Citizens, 2, 5, 21–22, 32, 38, 40, 42–45, 50, 51, 53, 54, 57, 58, 70–72, 94, 101, 109, 140, 182, 189, 190, 192, 193, 198, 262, 266, 271–273, 292, 299–301, 334, 335, 342, 354, 356, 376, 387, 390, 392, 394, 396, 397, 400, 401, 403, 428, 431, 435, 438, 439, 442, 443, 450, 453, 455, 464, 472, 490, 493, 496, 499–503, 516, 557, 569, 570, 572, 576, 587, 602, 603, 607, 611, 613, 666, 672, 686, 694, 697, 699–704
City-state, 19, 21, 23, 24, 26, 27, 39, 42, 43, 47, 48, 222, 673
*Cives romani*, 58
Civil
  constitutional State (bürgerlicher Rechtsstaat), 579
  rights, 23, 230, 300
  servants, 15, 183, 269, 383, 457, 458, 470
  society, 274, 351, 352, 582
  War Amendments, 439
Civitas, 18, 39–43, 47–49, 56, 194, 217, 219, 351
Clarendon, Constitutions of, 200
Classic Absolutism, 220, 258–260, 491
Class struggle, 568, 570, 589
Claudel, Paul, 669
Cleisthenes, 25–26, 32
Clemenceau, Georges, 471
Clement VII, 215, 246
Clement XIV, 262, 329
Clergy, 75, 107, 126, 135–138, 140, 142, 147, 163, 166, 187, 191, 193, 198, 214, 215, 225, 235, 242, 261–263, 275, 288, 293, 294, 300, 340, 376, 381, 384–390, 393, 403, 459, 496, 523, 564
Clientela, 18–19, 156
Clinton, William Jefferson, 602
Cluniac movement, 163
Cluny, 136–139, 163
Cnut II The Great, 309
Coal, 558, 561, 584, 675, 685–691, 696, 708
Cobos, Francisco de los, 243
Cochinchina, 539
Code
  Civil, 460, 464, 465
  Noir, 233
  Savary, 233
Codex Abrogans, 132
Codification, 3, 233, 528, 529, 589
Coercive Acts, 346
*Cognitio extraordinem*, 102
Cohabitation, 21, 474, 478, 479
Coimbra, 186, 202, 266, 590
Coke, 429, 558
Colbert, Jean Baptiste, 223, 378
Cold War, 597, 615, 659, 695, 696, 698
Colegios mayores, 111, 266
Collapse of the Soviet Union, 134, 606
Collective
  bargaining agreements, 588
  security, 111, 614
College of Europe, 683
Colleton, Sir John, 338
Collins, Michael, 666
Colloquium, 292
Colombia, 508
Coloni, 156
Colonial
  America, 336
  charter, 353
  era, 354, 607
  expansion, 330, 343, 530, 532, 533, 540, 573, 663
  explosion, 343–344
  government, 342
  imperialism, 564
  interests, 344, 507
  officials, 328
  proprietary ventures, 336
  regimes, 342
  rule, 342
Colonialism, 3, 502, 530–533, 664
Colonies/Colonists, 20, 26, 32, 40, 233, 246, 305, 325, 326, 328–353, 355, 356, 358, 402, 417, 420, 437, 536, 537, 592, 653, 667, 678
Colorado River Dam, 5887
Colorado State, 436, 437, 442
Columbus, Christopher, 203, 245
Combustion engine, 562
Comes, 12, 17, 71, 100, 114, 182, 202, 246, 260, 310, 402, 477, 509, 540, 581, 621, 707, 710
*Comitatus*, 55, 156
*Comitatus Portucalensis*, 163
*Comitia*
  *curiata*, 41, 42
  *tributa*, 18, 41–43
Commendation, 155, 156
*Commentaries on the Gallic Wars*, 658
Commentators, 79, 133, 216, 217, 380
Commercial
  Congressional authority, 356
  Revolution, 168, 178
Committee for Foreign Plantations, 343

Common
  Agricultural Policy, 691, 696
  Assembly of the European Coal and Steel Community, 689–691
  Council, 340
  European Market, 691–693
  Foreign and Security Policy, 697
  good, 75, 582
  law, 24, 184, 185, 195, 197, 200, 230, 231, 240, 291, 298, 309, 342, 464, 603
Commoners, 294
*Commonwealth*, 18, 214, 218, 219, 337, 338, 351, 657, 666, 676, 678, 682
  *matters*, 225
Communal Council, 661
Commune. *See* Municipality
Communism, 570, 575, 592–593, 603–607, 680
Communist
  China, 606
  dictatorships, 593, 597
  International, 571, 575, 605, 616
  *Manifesto (Manifest der Kommunistischen Partei)*, 568
  parties, 575, 593, 606, 680
  Party of China, 605
  Party of the Soviet Union (CPSU), 580, 680
  regime, 110, 605–606
  revolution, 568, 594, 604
  state, 605
Communities, War of. *See* Comuneros Revolt
Communitization, 700
Community
  method, 684–693
  pillar, 696
*Compagnies d'ordonnance*, 183
Company of Jesus. *See* Jesuits
Competitive Authoritarianism, 611
*Complete Collection of the Laws of the Russian Empire*, 529
Composite monarchies, 183, 652–657, 662
Compromise of 1850, 436
Comptos, 184
Compulsory military service. *See* Conscription
Compurgation, 164
Computer technology, 559
Comuneros Revolt, 221
*Concilia plebis*, 42, 43
*Concilium*, 82, 292
Concord, 180, 219, 257, 347
Concordat of 1801, 459
*Concordia discordantium canonum (decretum)*, 200
Confederacy, 437, 524, 527, 653, 659
Confederates, 531
Confederate States of America, 442
Confederation
  of Eight Cantons *(Acht Orte)*, 659
  of the Rhine *(Rheinbund, Confédération du Rhin)*, 514
  of states, 660
Confucius, 1, 14–15, 31
Congress
  of Italian Workers, 571
  of Panama (1826), 537
  of Vienna, 143, 492–495, 504, 506, 509, 514, 537, 663
*Conjuratio*, 165
Connecticut
  colony of, 338
  river, 430
Conscription, 492, 535
*Conseil*
  *de la République*, 218
  *d'en Haut*, 243, 379
  *des anciens*, 466
  *des Cinq-Cents*, 466
  *des Dépêches*, 379
  *du Roi*, 230
*Conseillers généraux*, 470
*Consejo de Hacienda*, 228
Consejo Real de Castilla, 221
Conservative
  politicians, 598
  revolt of the 80s, 239, 246, 383–385
Consilium, 191
Conspicuous consumption, 608
Conspiracy of the Equals, 616
Constant, Benjamin, 466, 503
Constantine, 55, 61, 73, 74, 76, 78, 82, 85, 123, 126, 144
Constantinople, capture of, 203
Constituent Assembly, 299, 353, 354, 390–393, 396, 399, 400, 403, 457, 467, 472, 478, 509, 555, 681
Constitution
  of Cádiz (1812), 501, 537
  for Germany, 517
  of Peace and Truce, 166
  of the United Mexican States (1917), 573, 616
  of the United States of America, 425
  of the Year VIII (*see* 1799 Constitution)
1799 Constitution, 452, 454
Constitutional
  Convention, 299, 353, 416, 420–423, 429, 441, 450

Constitutional (*cont.*)
council (Conseil constitutionnel), 475
courts, 197, 601
dictatorship, 511
documents, 343
history, 4, 50, 127, 154, 199, 213, 214, 220, 288–289, 297, 301, 325, 341, 372–373, 378, 423, 439, 465–479, 491, 510, 559, 564, 580, 586, 592, 593, 598, 609, 611, 613–621, 651, 652, 654, 658, 659, 666
laws of 1875, 470
Legal Theory (Staatsrechtslehre), 579
model of the state, 423, 492, 494, 502, 519, 573, 581, 598, 601, 612, 613
monarch, 301, 392, 393, 399, 465, 476, 509, 528, 529, 666
order, 355, 497, 498, 592
pact, 352, 399, 600, 613
state, 510, 579
system, 341, 354, 421, 470, 479, 491, 501, 518, 558, 565
*Theory (Verfassungslehre)*, 581
tradition, 218, 299, 353, 354, 390, 425, 576, 666
Constitutionalization
of EC Law, 702
of public law, 601
Constitution de l'An III (1795), 400
Consul for life, 455, 460
Consuls, 42–44, 46, 49, 51, 53, 55, 111, 453, 454
Continental
Army, 349
Congresses, 355
*Contrafueros*, 229
Convention
of 1688, 299
English constituent assembly, 288–289
Method, 700
of Philadelphia 1787, 421
for the Protection of Rights and Fundamental Freedoms (1950), 683, 708
Second French Constituent Assembly, 147, 466, 569
Conventions of the Constitution, 288
Coolidge, Calvin, 584
Corinth, 24, 25, 28
Cornwallis, Charles, British General, 350, 358
Coronation oath, 187
Corporate
promotion, 566, 589
state, 556, 588, 589
Corpus Iuris Civilis. *See* Justinian compilation
*Corregidor*, 221
Corruption, 302
Corsica, 32, 38, 451, 475
*Cortes*
*of Aragon*, 279
*de Toledo of 1480*, 228
*de Toro of 1505*, 228
*of Leon-Castile*, 228
*of Navarra*, 196
Cortés, Hernán, 245
*Corvée*, 380
Costums, 189
Coty, René, 473, 478
Coudenhove-Kalergi, Richard N., 647, 667–670, 675, 706
Council(s)
of Conscience, 261
of elders, 101
of Europe, 677, 683, 707–709
of 500, 18, 25, 466
of Italy, 222
of Ministers, 278, 473, 539, 590, 617, 670, 682, 683
of nobles, 292–293
of Orders, 164
of State (*Conseil d'État*), 453
of Toledo, 101, 102, 106, 107, 162
of Trent, 147, 213, 246
Count
of Barcelona, 158, 159, 165, 166, 179, 200, 653, 654
of Cavour (*see* Camillo Benso)
Counter-Reformation, 213
Counterrevolution/ Counterrevolutionary, 458, 495, 596
Count of Cavour. *See* Camillo Benso
Coup d'état, 107, 276, 393, 401, 405, 450–452, 465, 473, 475, 505, 511, 576
*Cour*
*d'assises*, 291
*des pairs*, 188
Court
Chancellors (Hofkanzler), 268
of Justice of the European Communities, 691–692, 708
Courts of appeal, 457
Coütumes, 237, 463
Coventry, 678
Coyoacán (Mexico), 618
Craftsmen, 566
Crecy, battle of (1346), 293
Crete, 19, 31

Crimean War, 539
Croatia, 698, 711
Croatian Peasant Party, 665
Croats, 534, 665
Cromwellian
  Protectorate, 297
  Revolution, 300
Cromwell, Oliver, 248, 297, 310
Cromwell, Thomas, 230, 243
Crónica Abeldense, 181
Crown
  of Aragon, 181, 183, 189, 192, 196, 199–203, 222, 228, 231, 237, 277, 382, 497, 651–656
  of Castile, 183, 213, 231, 245, 329
  lands, 225
  prince (Kronprinz), 181, 228, 271, 380
  property, 267
Crusader(s), 138–140, 146, 163, 164, 170, 201
Crusades, 140, 163, 164, 201
Cuartelazo, 505
Cuba, 508, 532, 537, 540, 605, 606, 620, 621
Cuban
  Missile Crisis, 620
  Revolution, 620
Cuirassiers, 559
Cultural Revolution, China (1968-1976), 620
Curacao, island of, 327
Curia, 18, 41, 166, 184, 187, 290, 291
Curiae, 41, 42, 192, 193, 201
Curia regia, 178, 291
Cursus honorum, 44, 46, 58
Custom, 17, 74, 101, 105, 107, 112, 157–160, 165, 166, 185, 190, 197, 211, 214, 221, 232, 301, 302, 310, 396, 465, 586, 669
Customs duties, 346, 517, 661, 668, 669, 671
Custoza, battle of, 293
Cyclades, 19, 27
Cyprus, 698, 710
Cypselus, 25
Czechoslovakia, 536, 620, 665, 668, 671, 674, 675, 680, 706
Czech Republic, 698, 710
Czechs, 534, 565, 675

**D**
Daedalus, 19
Daguerre, Louis, 560
D'Aguesseau, Henry François, chancellor, 239
Daladier, Edouard, 618, 674, 685, 706
D' Alembert, Jean le Rond, 259
Dallas, 620
Dans, Enrique, 559
Dante Alighieri, 142, 220, 648
Danton, Georges Jacques, 398
Danzig corridor, 595
Darfur, 613
*Das Kapital*, 568, 616
Daunou, Pierre Claude François, 452
*Dauphin*, 181, 385, 386, 403
Dauphiné, 385, 386
Davis, Jefferson, 382, 437, 442, 515
Davos
  class, 612
  Forum, 612
Dawes Plan (1924), 584
Dead Sea, 68, 69
Death penalty, 68, 69, 75, 276, 400
Debré, Michel, 473
Decembrist Uprising (1825), 528
*Décima* tax, 226
Declaration
  of Independence (July 4, 1776), 348, 352, 355, 358, 440
  of Liberated Europe, 677
  of Rights, 299, 354, 355, 390, 401
  of the Rights of Man and of the Citizen (1789), 401, 403
Decolonization, 605
Decree for the Protection of the German People and the State. *See Verordnung des Reichspräsidenten zum Schutz von Volk und Staat*
Decretalists, 133, 216
Decretals, 83, 133, 201
Decretists, 133, 216
Defense of workers, 602
Defensive alliances, 492, 533
De Gasperi, Alcide, 687
De Gaulle, Charles, 449, 471, 675
Delaware
  colony of, 340
  river, 340
  territory of, 341
Delian League, 27
*Della monarchia rappresentativa en Italia* (1857), 520
Delors, Jacques, 696
De los Ríos, Fernando, 589
Delphi, 28

Demilitarized zone, 619
Democracy, 21, 22, 25–27, 44, 45, 48, 182, 192, 260, 321, 351, 352, 433, 458, 468, 472, 496, 501, 528, 535, 555, 567, 571, 574, 582, 591, 597, 599, 604, 611–613, 660, 661, 680, 683, 685, 697, 698, 700, 701, 704
Democratic
 electoral procedures, 564
 governments, 602, 677
 model of the state, 242, 273, 492, 496, 503, 522, 557, 581, 582, 586, 591, 593, 597, 599, 603–605, 609, 611
 nations, 593, 599, 604, 611, 647, 685
 Party, 433, 438, 602, 616
 processes, 604
 regime, 32, 306, 592, 601, 607, 612
 Republic of Vietnam, 605, 619
 revolution, age of the, 325
 states, 580
 system, 24–25, 599, 667
 Unionist Party, 666
Democratization, 306–308, 310, 398, 433, 511, 694, 698, 705
Demographic
 expansion, 563–564
 growth, 558
 stagnation, 535
Demosthenes, 28
Denmark, 132, 182, 298, 309, 536, 565, 659, 680, 692, 694, 709
*Depatrimonialization*, of the monarchy, 267–270
Depoliticization, 601
Deprez, Marcel, 561
Deregulation, 440, 609, 611
Deregulatory policies, 609
Descartes, René, 248, 258
Despot, 142, 218, 241, 259, 260, 264, 450
Despotism, 235, 259, 260, 276, 277, 329, 352, 397, 452, 468
Deuteronomy, 67
*Deutsch*, 132
*Deutsches Reich,. See* Second Reich (1871)
*Deutschland*, 132
Developed Socialism, 580
Developing countries, 610
Devolution Acts (1988), 657
Dewey, Thomas, 599
Diadochi, 29, 31, 33
*Diakonos*, 80
Diarchy, 51–53
Diaspora, 68, 84
Dictates of the masses, 612
Dictatorship
 of Primo de Rivera, 617, 706
 of the proletariat, 571, 580
*Dictatus papae*, 121, 137, 146
Diderot, Denis, 264
Dien Bien Phu, 690619
Diet, 134, 135, 146, 191, 245, 513, 514, 516, 524
*Digest of the Laws*, 529
Digital revolution, 559
Dioceses, 56, 79–81, 138
Diocletian, 40, 48, 54–56, 61, 85
*Diputación del General*, 196
Direct democracy, 612, 660, 661
Directive, 697
Directorate, 568
Directory, 269, 392, 393, 401, 402, 405, 451–453, 460, 463, 662
Disarmament, 614, 666
*Discourse on the Origin and Basis of Inequality Among Men*, 555
Discovery, 10, 68, 186, 212, 331, 561
 of America, 212
Disraeli, Benjamin, 306
Divine
 legitimacy, 142–145, 232, 235, 494
 Right, 141, 217, 226, 235, 259–263, 279, 295, 296, 374, 376, 388, 399, 417, 451, 465, 504
Doctrinaire liberalism, 504. *See also* Moderate liberalism
*Doctrinaires*, 503, 504
Dollar gap, 678
Dollfuss, Engelbert, 591
Domesday Book, 309
Dominant powers, 614
Dominate, 14, 21, 40, 47, 54–56, 83, 102, 131, 132, 154, 159, 182, 191, 193, 222, 229, 241, 242, 301, 423, 432, 466, 472, 501, 508, 517, 532, 534, 607, 611, 664, 673, 683
Dominion, 13, 47, 48, 78, 135, 142, 170, 305, 328, 337, 340, 666, 706
*Dominus*, 48, 54, 55, 100, 101, 262, 329
 *ac Redemptor*, bull (1733), 262, 329
 *ac Redemptor*, bull *(1733)*, 262, 329
Don Pedro, Emperor of Brazil, 508
Dorian, 20, 22, 23, 32
Dred Scott v Sandford Decision (1857), 438, 442
Dresden, 678
Dreux de Brézé, Marquis of, 390
Dreyfus Affair, 470, 525, 671

Droit
*Administratif*, 458
*de rémontrance*, 382
Dubcek Alexander, 620
Ducos, Roger, 452, 454
Duke of Gerona, 181
Dukes of Burgundy, 190
Duma, 276, 498, 528–530, 657
Dumas, Alexander, 657
Dumium, St. Martin of, 106, 114, 115
Dunant, Henri, 531
Dutch
expeditions, 326–327
Guiana, 327
Republic, 298
settlers, 531
West India Company, 327
Dynamo, 560, 561
Dynastic question, 510

**E**

Earls, 160, 291, 293
Early Middle Ages, 102, 110, 126, 158, 165, 169, 179, 184, 187, 188
Easter Enlargement, 698
Eastern
Deutschmark, 681
Europe, 593, 594, 596, 604, 606, 619, 677, 679–680
Europe's communist regimes, 606
Schism, 136, 145, 170
Eastman, George, 560
Ebert, Friedrich, 576, 616, 617
Ecclesiastical offices, 135, 137
Ecological alternative, 611
Economic
authoritarianism, 568
convergence, 697
crisis of the 70s, 602
elite, 492, 497, 566
equality, 433,
growth, 21, 214, 558, 573, 592, 608, 611
imperialism, 564
and Monetary Union (EMU), 696, 697, 700
prosperity, 557, 584, 609
Ecuador, 508
Ecumenical, 82, 85, 106, 139, 144
Edict
of Milan, 73–75, 78, 85
on religion (1788), 263
of Thessalonica, 75, 76, 85, 114
Edinburgh, 657
Edison, Thomas Alva, 560
Edwardian Reformation, 226
Edward the Confessor, 309
Egmont, count of, 234, 246
Egypt, 11–13, 16, 19, 29–33, 39, 56, 59, 67, 83, 84, 103, 405, 452
Eisenhower, Dwight David, 599
*Ekklesia*, 79
*Election*, 55, 133, 138, 154, 180, 181, 202, 222, 280, 304, 306, 342, 387, 388, 417, 422–429, 432, 437, 440–442, 454, 467, 474, 478, 504, 577–579, 584, 586, 599, 601, 617, 693
Elective succession, 179
Electoral
colleges, 417, 470, 502
districts, 511
fraud, 306
Reform Act of 1832, 511
reforms, 306, 310, 509, 511, 538, 578
systems, 502, 569
Elector of Hanover, 302
Electricity, 561, 587
Electric telegraph, 561
Elío, Francisco Javier de, general, 505
*Émigrées*, 339
Émigrés, 399
Emirate of Córdoba, 169
*Empereur des Français*, 182, 455
Emperor Julian, 74
Empire, 3, 13, 39, 72, 94, 122, 155, 178, 212, 263, 330, 371, 418, 455, 492, 559, 650
Ems Dispatch, 539
Ems Telegram. *See* Ems Dispatch
Enabling Act ("Law to Remedy the Distress of People and Reich" *Gesetz zur Behebung der Not von Volk und Reich-*), 578
Encyclopedia, 258, 264
*Endlösung*, 578, 619
End of history, 615
Engels, Friedrich, 379, 568, 616
*Engla land*, 292
England, 108, 139, 146, 159, 170, 178, 181–185, 188–191, 193–195, 199–203, 214, 215, 219, 220, 223–226, 230, 233, 234, 238, 240–244, 246–250, 262, 269, 279, 288–306, 308–311, 323, 324, 327, 330–335, 337–340, 342–345, 347, 352, 355, 356, 358, 376, 377, 379, 381, 382, 390, 401, 417, 418, 420, 423, 424, 430, 434, 495–497, 499, 501, 503, 504, 506, 507, 509, 511, 531, 532, 535, 536, 538, 540, 561, 563, 564, 567, 585, 588, 592, 595, 596, 618, 655–657, 670, 671, 678, 684, 693, 706, 707, 710

English
Catholics, 337
Civil War, 219, 297, 338
colonies, 305, 330, 332, 336–338, 341
colonists, 328, 336, 343, 344
colonization, 326, 328–343
Crown, 333, 343, 656
educational system, 324
electoral system, 25, 498, 501, 502, 569
expeditions, 330
Justinian (*see* Edward I)
Labour Party, 571
language, 292
nobility, 199, 201, 224
Parliament, 194, 195, 224, 226, 233, 249, 271, 292–205, 309, 656
settlers, 326, 357
working class, 501
Enlightened
Absolutism, 260–262, 264, 270–281, 491, 527–528
monarchs, 268, 270–274
nationalism, 514
Enlightenment, 259, 260, 262–264, 267, 271, 274–281, 303, 322, 353, 373, 379, 499
Ensenada, marquis of, 279
*Entente cordiale*, 533, 540
Epaminondas, 27
Ephors, 23
Epinay Congress (1971), 571
Equal Franchise Act (1928), 307
Equals, 22, 23, 55, 165, 167, 273, 405, 568, 616
*Equidad*, 184
Erechtheion, 26
Erfurt Union, 518, 538
Escobedo, Rafael de, 234
*España Nacional*, 594
Espartero, Baldomero, 538
Espartero's Regency, 538
*Espéculo*, 184
Esquilache
marquis of, 279
Riots, 279
*Essay on the forms of government and the duties of Sovereigns*, 272
Essenes, 68, 69
*Estado Novo*, 591
Estates general *(États généraux)*, 141, 183, 184, 191, 193–197, 202, 213, 226, 227, 239, 294, 341, 376, 377, 381, 382, 384–389, 403, 426, 460
Estatuto Real (1834), 510
Estonia, 618, 698, 702, 710
État français, 471
Ethiopia, 532, 588
Ethnic groups, 578, 665
Étienne Marcel, 190, 202
Eton, 324
*Etymologiae* (St. Isidore of Seville), 107
Eugenic engineering, 578
Euripides, 26
Euro, 332, 697, 704, 710
Eurocommunist leaders, 606
Eurocrats, 703, 705
Europe of Communities, 695–699
European
Atomic Energy Community (EAEC or EURATOM), 691, 696, 701, 708
citizenship, 697
Coal and Steel Community (ECSC), 689–691, 696, 708
Commission, 696
Congress system, 493
constituent assembly, 681
Constitution Treaty (TCE), 2004, 704
Council, 669, 677, 699, 710, 711
Court of Human Rights, 683
Currency Unit (ECU), 697
Customs Union, 668
Defense Community (EDC), 690, 708
democratic nations, 599
Economic Community (EEC), 689–691, 704, 708
elections, 611
Elites, 683
emigration, 565
Federalist Movement, 674
federation, 647, 675, 688
Free Trade Association (EFTA), 692
Integration, 4, 144, 495, 496, 515, 647–710
monarchies, 183, 274, 279, 300, 373, 404, 493
nation(s), 109, 122, 144, 198, 458, 492, 499, 502, 530, 532, 559, 567, 583, 650, 663, 664, 670, 679, 687
nation-states, 122, 198, 492, 502, 532, 559, 567, 650, 663, 664
oligarchies, 576–591
Parliament, 501, 557, 681, 689, 691–692, 694, 695, 697, 700, 702, 708, 709
Parliamentary Assembly, 691, 692, 708
Parliamentary Union, 681
Payments Union, 679
Recovery Program (ERP) (*see* Marshall Plan)
Union, 2, 144, 610, 662, 668, 670, 671, 676, 681, 689, 695, 696, 698–702, 704, 706, 710
universities, 4, 111, 133, 141, 178, 184, 185, 193, 197, 531, 650
European Court of Human Rights, 683

Europeans, 4, 111, 133, 141, 178, 184, 185, 193, 197, 531, 650
Evans, Walker, 585
Exarchate, 122, 123, 125, 126, 145
Exchequer, 184
Excommunication, 124, 125, 138, 140, 166, 186, 199
Executive
 councils of government, 301
 government, 457
 Merger Treaty (1967), 693, 708
 power, 46, 243, 354, 416–417, 423, 450, 453, 467, 472–474, 491, 498, 520, 615, 660, 683, 689, 693
Exodus, 67, 68, 139, 214, 266, 579
Expiatory Chapel, 659
Exploitation of man by man, 568
Extermination, 393, 535, 578, 595, 619

**F**

*Falange*, 590
Family, 13, 15–18, 21, 23, 25, 28, 40, 41, 49, 58, 77, 100–102, 104, 111, 124, 125, 159, 161, 223, 271, 327, 336, 337, 391, 400, 403, 428, 451, 452, 456, 462, 464, 471, 568, 577, 588, 616, 651, 659, 684
Faraday, Michael, 561
Farewell Address, 415, 417
Fascism, 556, 585, 586, 592–593, 598, 603, 619
Fascist
 militia, 617
 model, 593
 *ventenio*, 578
Fathers of the Church, 77
Federal
 courts of justice, 425
 Europe, 675, 681–683
 government, 356, 420–423, 426–429, 437–441, 458, 517, 524, 585, 587, 603, 661, 664
 medical coverage legislation, 603
 power, 422, 426, 428, 438, 603
 Republic of Germany, 619, 621, 685, 708
 Union, 419, 430, 431, 434, 439, 441, 508, 675
 Union movement, 675
Federalism, 419, 428, 675, 681, 682, 702
Federalist
 Papers, 419
 Party, 424, 429
Federation
 of Australia, 536
 of Western Europe, 679
*Féodalité*, 154
Ferdinand and Isabella kings of Castile and Aragon, 146, 188, 203, 216
Ferdinand I, Emperor of Austria, 170, 186, 202, 516
Ferdinand II king of Castile and León, 512
Ferdinand II King of the Two Sicilies, 521
Ferdinand the Catholic, 163, 196, 199, 203, 245, 654
Fernán González, count of Castile, 169
Ferrero, 28
Ferry, Jules, 470
*Fête de la Fédération*. *see* Celebration of the Federation
Feudal
 anarchy, 162, 164, 165
 bond, 160, 161, 179, 375
 court, 168, 191
 law, 134, 158, 650
 pyramid, 375
 revolution, 161–162
 servitude, 380, 564
Feudalism, 14, 154, 156, 158–162, 165, 167–170, 179, 185, 189, 190, 193, 242, 267, 650
Feudalization, 135, 168, 169, 375
*Feudum*, 156
*Fevum*, 156
Fichte, Johann Gottlieb, 514
Fief, 154, 156, 158, 159, 161, 375, 462
Fiefdom, 157–160, 162
*Fiesta del Trabajo*, 590
Fifth Republic, 473, 474, 478, 479
Final
 Recess of February 1803, 513
 Solution (*see Endlösung*)
Financial
 crisis, 585, 607, 608
 economy, 608
Finland, 536, 618, 680, 692, 698, 710
First
 Boer War, 540
 Carlist War, 277, 510, 538, 655
 consul, 38, 43, 453–455, 457, 459, 460, 463, 464
 Continental Congress (1774), 347, 358
 English revolution, 297
 Inaugural Address, 321
 International, 555, 616

First (*cont.*)
oil crisis (1974), 608
Opium War, 538
Reich, 133, 142, 145, 514, 525
Russian Revolution (1905), 540, 616
Spanish Republic, 268, 539
Fiscal policy, 291
*Fiscus*, 53, 155, 267
Fishing monopoly, 344
Flemish, 2, 111, 112, 188, 666
Fleury, 379
Florence, 138, 189, 218, 221, 222, 512, 520, 522
Florida State, 425, 435
Floridablanca, Count of, 279, 350
Foch, Ferdinand marshall, 541
*Foederati*, 94
*Foedus*, 94, 95, 112, 113
Fontenoy, battle of, 129, 145, 378
Ford, Henry, 562
Ford, John, 585
Forest of Compiègne, 616
Fort Orange, 327
Founding Fathers, 352, 424
Fouquet, Nicolas, 234
Fouquier-Tinville, Antoine, 397
Fourier, Charles, 568
Four-stroke gasoline engine, 562
Fourth
Coalition, 514
French Republic, 687
International, 618
Fourth Estate, 303, 564
Frame of Government of Pennsylvania, 341
France, 38, 95, 129, 159, 178, 213, 261, 288, 344, 372, 416, 450, 489, 558, 651
France's assembly-based republic, 651
*Franc germinal*, 460
Franchise requirements, 342
Francis II, Holy Roman Emperor, 131, 142, 143, 514
Franco-British union (June 1940), 672, 707
Franco, Francisco, 2, 618, 620
Franco-German axis, 700
Franco-Prussian War, 470, 523, 525, 526, 539, 663
Franco-Sardinian Alliance, 539
Franco's Fundamental Laws, 498, 590
Franco's New State, 589
Franco-Soviet Pact (1935), 706
Frankfurt Parliament, 517, 538
Franklin, Benjamin, 350, 358, 421
Franks, 94, 96–98, 102, 107, 108, 113, 114, 122 126, 128, 130, 131, 145, 157, 169, 180, 182, 374–376, 499
Franz Ferdinand, 533, 534
Franz Joseph, Emperor of Austria, 515, 516, 668
Frederic II Hohenstauffen, Holy Roman emperor, 212, 232
Frederick I Barbarossa, Holy Roman Emperor, 134, 146, 200
Frederick II of Prussia, 257, 263, 265, 275, 281, 344
Frederick III of Saxony, 213
Frederick the Great. *See* Frederick II of Prussia
Frederick William I, the ôSergeant Kingö, 280
Free
market economies, 607
masons, 504
person, 564
states, 435, 437, 439
Freedom
of the press, 304, 388, 401
French
Canada, 326
Catholic Church, 459
Cavalry, 559
colonists, 344, 358
Committee for the Federation of Europe, 675
Committee of National Liberation (CFLN), 676
Communist Party (PCF), 571, 593, 680
Constitution of 1848, 570
Convention, 299, 373
Empire, 147, 468, 559
flag, 395
imperialism, 493, 663
language, 358, 373
monarchy, 125, 130, 141, 197, 214, 279, 298, 344, 374, 377–379, 399, 454
mutinies (1917), 541
National Day, 395
National Guard, 469
Popular Front, 575, 588, 593, 594, 602
public opinion, 344, 379, 383, 385, 470, 704
Resistance, 675
Revolution, 109, 140, 142, 143, 147, 167, 183, 196, 230, 239, 244, 260, 263, 266, 273, 279, 298, 324–325, 371–405, 425, 426, 456, 460, 464, 469, 491, 493, 496, 498, 499, 510, 569, 662, 663
Revolution of 1830, 510
Second Republic's Constitutional Assembly, 467, 570
Section of the Communist International (SFIC), 571
Section of the Workers' International (SFIO), 571
settlement, 326

settlers, 344
Socialist Party, 571, 575
Social Security System, 602
State (*see* Marshall Pétain)
workers, 555, 588
French and Indian War, 345, 348
Fronde
revolution of, 223, 239
War of the, 248
*Fuero*
*de los Españoles* (1945), 590
*del Trabajo*, (Labor Charter) 1938, 590
*Real*, 184
*Fueros*, 189, 211, 221, 222
Full employment, 587
Fundamental
Constitutions of Carolina (1669), 339
laws, 224, 235, 236, 240, 498, 528, 590
*Laws of the State, On the*, 528
Orders of Connecticut (1639), 338
rights and liberties, 428
*Fundus*, 156
*Fürstenstaat*. *See* State of the prince
Fustel de Coulanges, Numa Denis, 17

G

*Gabelle*, 183, 377
*Gaceta de Madrid*, 567
Gadsden Purchase, 436
Gaeta, 512
Gage, British general, 347
Galla Placidia, 95
Gallicanism, 142, 215, 261
Gallican tradition, 459
Gallipoli (Dardanelles), battle of, 541
Gálvez, Bernardo, 345
Gambetta, Leon, 468
Ganges, 11
García Pelayo, Manuel, 582
Garibaldi, Giuseppe, 513, 521–523, 539
Garros, Roland, 540
Gas warfare, 541
Gates, Bill, 559
GATT, 614
Gattinara, Mercurino, 142
Gaul, 53, 56, 59, 95, 96, 98, 106, 108, 113, 124, 180, 658
*Gefolgschaft*, 100
*Geheime Staatspolizei* (Secret State Police, or Gestapo), 618
*Geltungsgrund der Rechtsnormen* (Foundation of legal validity principle), 599
*Gemeinde*, peasant communes, 265
*Gemót*, 290
Gendarme of Europe. *See* Nicholas I of Russia
General
agent of the clergy, 261
Assembly of the Clergy, 215, 261
Assembly of Virginia, 332
Congress, 325, 493
Court, 335, 421
Directory, 269
elections, 308, 593
Secretary of the Communist Party, 579
Security, Committee of, 396, 400
*Theory of Law and State*, 600
*Generalitat*, 196
*Généralités des pays d'élections*, 385
*General-Landschul-Reglement* (1763), 265
Geneva Conventions, 531
Genoa, 329, 451, 506, 571
Genocide, 393, 595, 620
*Gens*, 17, 18, 41, 94, 96, 100, 111
*Gente de la ordenanza*, 163
Gentiles, 69, 71, 72
*Gentilitas*, 41
Gentry, 215, 223, 224, 269, 295, 306, 324, 381, 432, 492, 502, 509
Geographers, 432
George III's madness, 305
George, Susan, 611, 612
Georgia, Colony of, 340, 341, 344
German
Economic Miracle *(Wirtschaftswunder)*, 681
Empire *(Deutsches Reich)* (*see* Second Reich)
Empire's first constitution (1849), 538
First Reich, 142, 145
Hanseatic League, 652
Historical School of law, 500, 528
lawyers, 600
mercenaries, in US Independence War, 348
middle class, 585
nation, 111, 137, 513, 516, 526, 527, 582
"national" integration, 524
nationalism, 513, 514, 532, 681
National Socialist State, 582
Nazism, 598
people *(Deutsches Volk)*, 94, 516, 524, 576–578, 594, 696
princes, 275, 280
Reich, 144, 147, 323, 617
Royalty, 99–101, 178
satellite regimes, 674
Slump, 585
Social policy, 572
State, 134, 144, 323, 456, 511, 513, 515–518, 525, 527, 577

German (*cont.*)
supremacy, 516
territorial organization, 513
Territories, 504, 509, 513, 516
unification, 134, 523–527, 530, 539
war reparations, 584
Germanic
Confederation *(Deutscher Bund)*, 514, 515, 523
kingdoms, 97–102, 106, 109, 113, 122, 154, 155, 157, 179, 182, 189
Kings, 95, 98, 101, 102, 105–108, 122, 128, 154, 155, 180, 212
nations, 108
Tribes, 93–115, 161, 292
German-led world order, 652
German-Soviet Non-Aggression Pact, 671, 707
German-speaking peoples. *See* Pan-Germanism
Germany, 108, 130–135, 138, 143–145, 189, 190, 229, 272, 279, 323, 456, 477, 499, 504, 515–517, 519, 524–526, 532–536, 561, 563, 571, 574–579, 585, 586, 588, 591, 592, 594–596, 600, 616–619, 621, 663–665, 668–671, 673, 674, 677, 678, 680–681, 685, 698, 706–708, 710
Germany's "national socialism," 586
*Gesta comitum Barcinonensium*, 159
Ghent, 190, 221
Ghibellines, 217
Gibbon, 38
Gibraltar, 344, 350
Girón de Velasco, José Antonio, 590
*Girondins*, 392, 404
Giscard d'Estaing, Valéry, 478
Gladstone's Act (1884), 501
Gladstone, William, 306
Glasgow, 275, 511
*Glasnost*, 606
Global
constitutional history, 613
economy, 584, 615
era, 615
financial crisis, 585
medical coverage, 603
policies, 612
Globalization, 3, 611, 613–615, 669
Glorious Revolution (England 1688), 249, 310
Glorious Revolution (Spain, 1868), 539
*Glossa magna*, 217
Glossators, 133, 200, 202, 216, 217
Godolphin, Sir Sidney, 302
Godspeed, 331
Goebbels, Joseph, 673
Golden age of European colonialism, 530–531
Golden Liberty, 182
Gold standard, 460
Gomez Labrador, Pedro, 493
Gonzalo Fernández de Córdoba, 222
Gorbachev, Mikhail, 606, 621
Gorges, Sir Ferdinando, 338
Gorton, Samuel, 336
Gotha, 571
Governance, 52, 54, 222, 338, 340, 587, 613–15, 700, 703
Government
commissioners, 685
of Cuba, 540
by the People, 612
Governor General, 338, 666
Governors, 14, 47, 48, 56, 74, 222, 224, 229, 328, 342, 346, 565
Gracious Majesty, 325, 330, 507
Grafton, 304
Graham Bell, Alexander, 561
Gramme, Zénobe, 561
*Gran Capitán. See* Gonzalo Fernández de Córdoba
Grand
Alliance (1815), 495
Council of Fascism, 619
Duchy of Finland, 536
*siècle*, 378
*Grandes*
*Écoles*, 463
*Ordonnances*, 233
Grandson, battle of, 132, 134, 249, 338, 375, 659
Granja, Mutiny (1836), 510, 538
*Grapes of Wrath*, 585
Gratian, 75, 133, 200
Great
Britain, 96, 98, 113, 238, 288, 292, 302, 308, 324, 325, 341, 418, 436, 619, 656, 657, 672, 676, 680, 692
Compromise, 423
council *(magnum concilium)*, 292
Depression, 577, 583–586, 598
Elector (of Brandenburg), Frederick William, 270, 280, 466, 478
Germany, 673
Leap Forward, 605
Migration, 335
Proletarian Cultural Revolution, 605
Purges, 618

Schism, 185
Society Program, 602
Terror, 397
War (*see* World War I)
Greece, 16, 19–21, 23, 26, 28, 31–33, 38, 39, 56, 59, 260, 506–509, 537, 601, 694, 700, 709
Greek, 14, 16–29, 32, 38–40, 43, 46, 50, 58, 66, 67, 69, 74, 76, 77, 79–82, 94, 103, 105, 122, 136, 166, 296, 506, 508, 509, 537, 675, 702
Greek independence, 509, 537
Gregorian Reform, 136–138, 163, 170
Gregory I (the Great), pope, 104, 122, 144, 162, 374
Gregory II, pope, 122, 123, 144
Gregory of Tours, 180
Gregory VII, pope, 82, 125, 137–139, 146, 170
Grenville, 304
Grey, Lord, 306, 511, 538
Grimm
Brothers, 500
Jacob, 500
Wilhelm, 500
*Großdeutsche Lösung*, 517
Grotius, Hugo, 248, 651
*Grundnorm* (fundamental norm), 600
Grutli Meadow, 659
Guadalupe Hidalgo Treaty, 436, 442
Guardian of the constitution, 582
Guelphs, 217
Guipuzcoa, 237
Guise, Henry of, 216
Guizot, François, 465, 489
Gulf
of Mexico, 327, 350
of Tonkin Incident, 620
Gunpowder Plot, 296
Guy Fawkes, 296, 297
Gypsies, 578, 595

**H**

Habeas corpus, (1679), 310
Habsburg, peace of, 215
Hadrian, 53, 60, 84
Hague
Congress of 1872, 469, 571
Congress of 1948, 681
Hall of Mirrors (Versailles), 532, 539, 652
Hamilton, Alexander, 350, 415, 418, 419, 421, 423, 424
Hammurabi, Code of, 31, 68
Hancock, John, 347, 421, 504
Hannibal, 47, 560
Hanover Dynasty, 301–311
Harappa, 11, 30
Harold II, 288
Harrow, 324
Harvard
College, 335, 336
University, 678, 707
Harvard, John, 335
Hastings, battle of, 170, 288, 309
Haugwitz, Christian von, Austrian chancellor, 268
*Hauptprobleme der Staatsrechtslehre (Main Problems in the Theory of Public Law)*, 600
Havana, 540
Hawaii State, 430, 437, 443
Health
Care Act of 1993, 440, 603
Care and Education Reconciliation Act (HCERA), 440, 603
Heidegger, Martin, 608
Heidelberg, 516
Hellas, 20, 27
Helvetians, 658
Helvetic Confederation, 652
Helvetic Republic (1798-1803), 659, 663
Henry IV, Holy roman emperor, 143, 214
Henry, Patrick, 421
Henry the Navigator, 203, 328
Hereditary benefits, 158–159
Hereditary nobility, 15, 339
Heresy, 75–77, 134, 213, 240
Hermits, 103
*Herrenhaus*, 518
Herriot, Edouard, 668, 670, 706
Hertz, Heinrich, 561
Hesiod, 24, 32
Hierarchy of norms, principle of, 600
High
Authority, 687–690
bourgeoisie, 391, 496, 502
High-voltage lines, 561
Higuera, la (Bolivia), 620
Hincmar, Arschbishop of Reims, 162
Hindenburg, Paul von, 578, 617
Hipparcus, 25
Hippias, 25
Hispania, 47, 53, 56, 57, 59, 74, 82, 96, 108, 654
Hispano-Suiza, 562

*Historia*
*Francorum*, 180
*Gloriosi regis Ludovici*, 179
History of the welfare state, 603
Hitler, Adolf, 323, 576, 594, 595, 652
Hobbes, Thomas, 219, 248, 556
*Hochabsolutismus*,. *See* Classic absolutism
Ho Chi Minh, 605, 619
Hohenstaufen, 131, 132, 139, 146, 212, 654
Hohenzollern, 143, 280, 515, 525
Holland, 2, 132, 214, 247, 298, 330, 340, 479, 515, 532, 674, 675
Hollande, François, 479
Holy
Alliance, 494, 495, 537, 663
German-Roman Empire, 178, 514
Roman emperor, 134, 143, 214, 215
Roman Empire, 125, 128–136, 142, 143, 145–147, 169, 179, 216, 245, 268, 375, 513, 514, 525, 650, 651, 658
Homer, 20, 21, 32
Homeric kingdoms, 20–21
*Honnête liberté des Français*, 236
Honorius, Roman emperor, 61, 95, 113
Hoover, Dam, 587
Hoover, Herbert Clark, 584
Hoplite reform, 24
Horizontal class-based unions, 590
Horn, count of, 234, 246
Hosius of Corduba, 79
House
of Burgesses, 332
of Commons, 194, 202, 225, 226, 294, 295, 297, 303, 304, 308, 309, 311, 501, 656, 672
of Lords, 194, 195, 294, 308, 309, 466
of Representatives, 423, 424, 429, 518
Householders, 306, 501
Hudson, Henry, 327
Bay, 344
River, 327, 357
Hugh Capet, 130, 145, 169, 375, 376
Hugo
the Great, 129, 145
Victor, 465
Human exploitation, 567
Humboldt, Alexander von, 514
Humboldt, Wilhelm von, 265
Hundred
court, township moot of the, 290
Days' Offensive (1918), 541
Flowers campaign, 605
Thousand Sons of Saint Louis, 537
Years War, 183, 194, 195, 202, 203, 309, 376, 381
Hungarian Revolt, 604
Hungarians, 131, 516, 534, 665
Hungary, 132, 261, 268, 515–517, 528, 533–535, 665, 680, 698, 710
Huns, 94, 96, 113
Hutchinson, Anne, 336
Hydroelectric plants, 561
Hygiene, 558
Hyperinflation, 585, 664

**I**

Ibárruri, Dolores, 606
Iberian Peninsula, 16, 111, 114, 158, 159, 163, 169, 170, 179, 189, 191, 196, 201, 227, 247, 276
Iconoclastic Crisis, 122
Ideological
clash, 593
nationalism, 499
Iglesias, Pablo, 616
Iguala Plan, 508
Ihering, Rudolf Von, 581, 609
Iliad, 20
Iliberis, 82, 85
Illinois, State, 350, 434
Illness Insurance, 590
Immemorial order, 157
Immunities, 375, 439
*Imperator*, 50, 51, 54, 59, 178, 212, 217, 375, 376
Imperial
Catechism, 459
Diet (Reichstag), 134, 513
Prussia, 526
Russia, 527–530
Imperialist policies, 531
*Imperium*, 37–61, 179, 232
Independent States, 141, 214, 325, 353, 355, 356, 652, 662, 678
India, 29, 33, 103, 143, 245, 276, 327, 379, 402, 563, 610, 615, 651
Indiana State, 350, 434
Indians, 327, 329, 331, 332, 346, 357, 431, 433
*Indias*, 243, 278, 326, 328
Indictment, 291
*Indignados* (outraged), 612
Indirect suffrage, 478, 496, 502, 567
Individual rights, 390, 439, 490, 503, 556, 568, 573
Indochina, 536, 618, 690

Indo-European, 16–18, 20, 32, 40, 41, 43, 49, 99
Indus, 11–13, 30, 306
Industrial revolution, 258, 558, 565, 566, 570
Inequality, 555, 568, 573, 599, 609, 610
Inflationary crisis, 577
Innocent III, pope, 139, 146, 163, 177, 199, 201
Innocent IV, pope, 139
Inquisition, 164, 203, 213, 231, 243, 336
Institute of Social Reform *(Instituto de Reformas Sociales)*, 589
Insurance for retired workers *(Retiro Obrero)*, 589
Integral state, 655
Integration, 4, 18, 22, 39, 40, 49, 134, 144, 183, 191, 196, 198, 310, 430, 434, 436, 456, 495, 496, 515, 517–519, 521, 524, 526, 527, 615, 647–711
Intendants, 223, 329, 385, 387, 457
*Intendente* (intendant), 278
Inter-Allied Maritime Transport Council, 684
Interbellum period, 583
Interests of the Crown, 342
Intergovernmental Method of Integration, 693, 697
Intermediate-level officials, 342
Internal combustion engine, 562
International
  conflicts, 614
  disputes, 399, 614
  governance, 615
  Monetary Fund (IMF), 614
  organizations, 614
  relations, 181, 296, 613, 615, 657
  Socialist hymn, 12, 555
  Trade Organization interventionism, 555–621
  Workingmen's Association (IWA) (*see* First International)
Interventionist
  legislation, 598
  measures, 536
  policies, 602
  state, 458–465
Intolerable Acts. *See* Coercive Acts
Invasion of Poland, 596
Inventions, 558, 560
Investiture Contest, 137–138
Invincible Armada, 247, 295
Invisible revolution, 608
Iósiv Dzugashvili, 574
Iowa State, 437
*iPad*, 559
*iPhone*, 559
*iPod*, 559
Ireland (Eire), 666, 706
Irish
  Civil War, 706
  Free State, 657, 666, 706
  independence, 301
  Monks, 103, 104
  Republic, 311, 657, 666, 706
  Republican Army (IRA), 657
Irnerius, 133, 200
Iron
  *Chancellor (Eiserner Kanzler)*, 524, 527, 572, 616
  Curtain, 593, 596, 619, 677, 680, 696
Isabella and Ferdinand kings of Castile and Aragon, 326, 654
Isabella II, queen of Spain, 510, 525, 539
Isidore of Seville, 101, 107
Isle of Man, 657
Italian
  Chamber of Deputies, 617
  Communist Party, 680
  Fascism, 586, 598
  Labor Charter of 21 April, 1927, 588
  Law on Corporations of 5 February, 1934, 588
  nation, 526, 663
  Parliament, 522, 523
  patriots, 513, 521
  Republic, 506, 578, 619, 707
  Socialist Party, 571
  State(s), 147, 506, 512, 522, 523
  unification, 512, 520, 522, 523, 539
  unity, 512, 521, 523, 526, 531
Italy
  kingdom of, 126, 131, 145, 147, 509, 522, 539
Itinerant justice, 185, 291
Iturbide, Juan Manuel, 508
*Iurisdictio*, 167
*Ius*
  *commune*, 184, 216, 217, 240, 650
  *in iure aliena*, 156
  *latii*, 57

## J

Jackson, Andrew, 417, 432
Jacksonian democracy, 433
Jacobin, 273, 372, 391, 393, 395, 401, 403, 405, 452, 472, 475, 504
Jacobinism, 393

James II of England, 327
James I of England, VI of Scotland, 656
Jamestown, 247, 331, 332, 334, 360
Jansenism, 262
Japan, 15, 531, 535, 559, 592, 610, 616–619, 668, 698
Jay, John, 419
Jefferson, Thomas, 321, 345, 348, 351, 417, 429, 452
Jenkinson, Robert, British Prime minister, 507
Jenner, Edward, 562
Jerusalem, 14, 68–70, 81, 83, 84, 164, 170, 200, 201
Jesuits, 146, 213, 216, 262, 263, 265, 266, 275, 277, 296, 329, 462
Jesuit schools, 462
Jesus Christ, 68–70, 106, 337
*Jeu de paume*, 389
Jewish extermination, 619
Jews, of Alsace, 380
Joan of Arc, 202, 203, 376, 377
Jobs, Steve, 559
John Lackland, 188, 199, 201, 291
Johnson, Lyndon Baines, 602, 620
Joseph II Emperor of Austria, 131, 259, 261, 262, 264, 265, 268, 275, 279, 281, 380
Josephism, 262
Jospin, Lionel, 479
Judaism, 67–71, 75, 83, 122
Judges, 23, 101, 102, 163, 184, 185, 231, 235, 238–240, 270, 290, 336, 342, 354, 383, 424, 425, 427, 429, 457, 458, 465, 598, 600, 603, 618
Judicial
  power, 424–425, 428, 520
  procedures, 328
  review, 424, 428, 429, 475, 601
Julian Calendar, 616
Julius Caesar, 17, 48, 50, 59
July
  crisis (1914), 534
  Monarchy, 465–466, 468, 470, 476, 501, 509, 537
  Revolution (1830), 476
*Junkers*, 323, 518
*Junta*
  *Central Suprema*, 278
  *de Defensa Nacional*, 594
  for the Provision of Learning, 266
Jurisprudence of Concepts (Begriffsjurisprudenz), 581
Jury
  trials, 342
  verdicts, 290
Justice as Fairness: A Restatement, 609
*Justice retenue*, 230
Justicia Mayor de Aragón, 240
Justinian, 52, 53, 75, 80, 97, 98, 114, 133, 134, 144, 192, 193, 197, 216, 217, 232, 233, 293
  Code, 192
Justinian compilation, 217

**K**

Kaiser, 517, 526, 539, 540, 694
*Kaiserzeit*, 131
Kalahari, 11
Kamenev, Lev, 579, 617
*Kammerdeputationen*, 269
Kamprad, Ingvar, 662
Kansas-Nebraska Act, 436, 442
Kansas, State, 326, 435–436, 442
Karl August von, 514
Karnak, 13
Katyn Massacre, 596, 618
Kaunitz, Wenzell Anton von, Austrian chancellor, 268
Kelsen, Hans, 598–600
Kempf, Hervé, 610, 612
Kennedy, John Fitzgerald, 297, 371, 582, 620
Kentucky, 350, 430, 431, 434, 437, 441
  State, 350, 434, 437
Kerensky, Alexander, 530, 616
Keynes, John Maynard, 685
Khmer Rouge, 620
Khrushchev, Nikita, 580, 620
Kim Il-sung, 605
King
  of Bourges, 377
  of France, 130, 141, 142, 162, 164, 169, 179, 182, 196, 199, 202, 203, 235, 245, 247, 248, 345, 375–377, 379–381
  of the Franks, 113, 124–126, 130, 131, 141, 145, 169, 182, 376
  of Germany, 130–132, 139, 145
  of Hungary and Bohemia, 261
  of Italy, 127, 128, 131, 132, 522
  of Portugal, 186, 202, 654
  of the Romans *(Rex Romanorum)*, 131, 133
Kingdom
  of Belgium, 509
  of Great Britain, 418, 436, 656, 657
  of Hawaii, 532
  of Israel, 67, 69, 83
  of Italy, 126, 131, 145, 147, 506, 522, 539

of Navarra, 196
of Piedmont-Sardinia, 519, 522, 539
of Prussia, 143, 280, 514, 515, 519, 526, 538
of Sardinia, 512, 521, 522
of the Two Sicilies, 274, 506, 522
King of Aragon
Alfonso II, 200, 653
Jaime I the Conqueror, 201
Peter II, 139
Peter III, 192, 222
Peter IV, 181
Sancho Ramírez, 170
King of Asturias
Alfonso II, 181
King of Castile
Henry III, 211
Henry IV, 188, 241
John II, 186, 188, 196, 223, 232, 326
King of England
Charles I, 249, 337
Charles II, 249, 340
Edward I, 181, 199, 201, 292, 293, 309
Edward II, 181, 194, 195, 202, 293, 309
Edward III, 194, 195, 202, 293, 309
George I, 302, 310
George II, 302, 303, 310, 339, 340
George III, 302–305, 346, 348, 349, 492
George IV, 305
Henry II Plantagenet, 291, 309
Henry III, 188, 199, 211, 292, 294, 309
Henry IV, 188
Henry VII, 195, 203, 225, 294, 327
Henry VIII, 146, 215, 216, 224, 225, 230, 233, 234, 240, 242, 246, 294, 295, 297, 300, 301, 309, 656
James II, 111, 249, 298–301, 310, 327, 340
John I, 139
Richard II, 294
King of France
Charles VI the Mad, 376
Charles VII, 377
Charles VIII, 222
Charles X, 509
Francis I, 131, 221, 227, 233, 234, 245, 246, 326, 357, 377
Henry II, 246, 292
Henry IV, 131, 247
Louis IX, 179, 376
Louis XI, 203, 377
Louis XII, 222
Louis XIII, 223, 241, 247, 377
Louis XV, 279–280, 345
Louis XVI, 191, 279, 280, 384, 460
Louis XVIII, 394, 476, 493, 495, 498, 504
Philip VI, 181
King of Franks
Childeric III, 124, 145, 374
Clovis, 374
King of Germany
Conrad I, 130, 145
King of León
Alfonso V, 198
Garcia I, 169
Ramiro II, 181
Ramiro III, 181
King of Navarre
Charles III, 181, 274, 278–281, 328, 350
King of Portugal
Alfonso I Henriques, 186
Dionis I, 201
John II, 186, 188, 196, 223, 232, 326
Joseph I, 276, 277, 279, 280
King of Prussia, 257, 271, 272, 280, 494, 518, 524–526
Frederick III, 526, 540
Frederick William III, 272, 518
Frederick William IV, 498, 516–518, 523, 524, 538, 539
William II, 534
King of Sardinia
Charles Albert, 512, 513, 520, 538
King of Spain
Alfonso XIII, 540
Charles III, 274, 281
Charles IV, 505
Ferdinand VI, 277, 280, 505
Ferdinand VII, 267, 505, 507, 510, 537
Juan Carlos I, 181, 654
Philip III, 247, 330
Philip V, 249, 262, 274
King of the Franks
Louis VI, 180, 375
Louis VII, 180
King of Visigoths
Euric, 97, 113
King's Bench court, 331
Kingship, 28, 99, 100, 107, 130, 163, 179, 180, 188, 215, 296, 451
Kissinger, Henry, 620
*Kleindeutsche Lösung*, 517
Knights, 156, 160, 163–165, 168, 193, 224, 292–294
Knossos, 19, 31
Knox, Henry, general, 349
Kodak machine, 560

*Kominform*, 605
*Kommintern*, 575, 577, 605, 617
König, 100
Königgrätz-Sadowa, battle of, 524
Korda, Alberto, 606
Korean War, 604, 619, 690, 708
*Kreise*, 268, 269
*Kronprinz*, 616
*Kulturkampf*, 527

**L**

Labour
 Charter, 588
 conflicts, 589
 Party, 311, 571, 573, 592, 616, 680
Labrador, coast of, 327
Lafargue, Paul, 557
Lafayette, Marquis of, 386
Lagasca, Pedro de, 328
Lagash, 13
Laibach, Congress of (1821), 506
Laissez-faire, 497, 501, 522, 557, 568–571, 583, 598, 599
Lake Superior, 350
Lamartine, 467
Lamoignon de Malesherbes, Chrétien Guillaume, 385
Lancaster, House of, 195, 203, 294
Landed aristocratic classes, 501
Land Ordinance
 of 1784, 431
 of 1785, 432, 433, 440, 442
Landowners, 21, 24, 43, 44, 157, 164, 323, 348, 352, 432, 435, 511
*Landrat*, 270
Landtag, 229, 271, 498, 518, 519
*Landtage sind Geldtage*, 271
Lange, Dorothea, 585
Languedoc, 227, 384
Largo Caballero, Francisco, 589, 593
Las salle, Ferdinand, 571
Lateran Accords, 142, 523
Latin, 12, 15–18, 29, 41, 57, 70, 74, 77, 79, 82, 85, 99, 100, 105, 132, 158, 159, 166, 188, 191, 216, 218, 219, 271, 291, 292, 302, 338, 371, 375, 537, 564, 565, 580, 605, 650
Latin American states, 537
Latvia, 618, 698, 702, 710
Laval, Pierre, 674
Law(s)
 of the colony, 342
 of Guarantees (May, 1871), 523
 *as a Means to and End (Der Zweck im Recht)*, 581
 of the Realm, 180
 subordination to the state, 599
 of Supremacy, (1534), 295
 in Wales Acts, 301, 656
Lawful men, 291
League of Nations, 613–614, 669, 670, 684, 706
*Lebensraum*, 594, 673
Lebrun, Albert, 672
Ledru-Rollin, Alexandre, 467
Lefrancais, Gustave, 555
Legal
 framework, 343, 557, 579, 580
 scholars, 288, 579, 599
 system, 42, 105, 134, 189, 195, 200, 216, 228, 229, 240, 272–274, 324, 341, 354, 581, 582, 600, 656
 system's legitimacy, 600
 thinking, 600
Legality, 59, 270, 388, 392, 436, 471, 477, 578, 582, 600
Legion of Honor, 460
Legislative
 assembly, 340, 342, 392, 403, 423, 504, 660
 Body *(Corps Législatif)*, 453
 branch, 402, 416, 417, 423, 424, 453, 602
 commission, 275, 276
 power, 55, 83, 196, 231–233, 325, 341, 353, 401, 453, 466, 467, 473, 692
 sovereignty, theory of, 133
Legislators, 24, 140, 221, 233, 378, 503, 600
*Légistes*, 217
Legists, 179
Legitimacy, 13, 52, 78, 124, 125, 141, 142, 163, 179–182, 186, 215–220, 233, 235, 245, 260–263, 273, 288, 376, 381, 393, 397, 417, 424, 427, 451, 455, 456, 471, 474, 494, 517, 555, 580, 582, 600, 704
Legitimate intervention, principle of, 495
Légitimistes, 469
*Lehnswesen*, 154
Leibniz, Gottfried Wilhelm, 258, 648
Leiden, 333
Leiría, Cortes of, 186
Leisure class, 608
Lenin. *See* Vladimir Illich Ulianov
Lenin's first constitution, 579
Lenoir, Jean J., 562
Leo III, pope, 145, 169
Leon Carta Magna, 201
Leonidas, 23
Leopold I, king of Belgium, 509

Leovigild, King of the Visigoths, 98, 114
Leo XIII, pope, 590
Lepanto, battle of, 222, 246
Lerma, Duke of, 243, 247, 330
*Lettres de cachet*, 230, 234, 235
*Let Us Now Praise Famous Men: Three Tenant Families*, 585
Leuctra, 27, 32
Lev Davidovich Bronstein, 574
Levée en masse. *See* Military service
Leviathan, 219, 220, 248, 428, 490, 556, 582
Lewes, battle of (1264), 292
Lexington, battle of, 347–348
Liberal
  bourgeoisie, 496, 501
  constitutional model, 502, 581
  democratic socialism, 611
  oligarchy, 500–502
  regime, 323, 492, 503, 586
  revolution, 492, 502–512, 527, 528, 609
  state, 198, 351–358, 401, 501–503, 511–519, 530, 533–541, 568–571, 573, 583–587, 597, 598, 704
  state model, 502, 503, 533–541, 583–587
  system, 505, 536, 604
  Triennium, 507, 537
Liberalism, 489–541, 557–558, 566–568, 571, 581, 590, 602, 609
*Liber Iudiciorum (Lex Visigothorum)*, 109
Liberté, Egalité, Fraternité, 471, 588
*Libre albedrío (equidad)*, 184
*Libri Feudorum*, 134, 158
Libya, 532, 588, 607
Liebknecht, Karl, 575, 616
Liebknecht, Wilhelm, 571
Liechtenstein, 536, 692
*Liege homage*, 160
Light bulb, 560
Ligurian Republic, 506
Lili'uokalani, queen of Hawaii, 540
Lincoln, Abraham, 437, 442
*Lingua franca*, 292
Lisbon Treaty, 699–702, 704, 705, 710
*Lit de justice*, 184, 191, 238
Lithuania, 618, 652, 698, 702, 710
Liutprand, king of the Lombards, 123, 145
Liverpool, 306
Lliga, 589
Lloyd George, 572
Local
  administrative systems, 342
  oligarchies, 221, 227, 241, 277, 329
Locke, John, 339, 343, 351
Logical structure, theory of, 600
Loi de séparation des Églises et de l'État, 147, 477
Lois ordinaires, 236
Lombardian kingdom, 126
Lombards, 97, 98, 104–106, 108, 113–115, 122–123, 125, 126, 144, 145, 158, 182, 462, 506, 512, 653
Lombardy, 97, 108, 114, 126, 144, 158, 506, 512, 653
Loménie de Brienne, 373, 380, 385, 386, 402
London
  Company, 331, 334
  Treaty of (1949), 683
Long, Crawford E., 562
Long Knives, Night of the (Nacht der langen Messer), 618
Lords
  Grey, British Prime minister, 306, 511
  North, 304
  protector, 297, 310
  of Trade, 343
Lorentz, Dutch, 561
Lorraine, 131, 132, 156, 399, 532, 685, 686
Lothair, 128, 129, 145
Louisiana Purchase, 435
Louisiana State, 435, 442
Louisiana Territory, 327, 350
Louis IX, Saint Louis, 218
Louis Napoleon Bonaparte. *See* Napoleon III
Louis Philippe I of Orléan, king of French, 465
Louis the Pious, 128, 145, 159
Louis XIV, 142, 187, 212, 214, 223, 227, 233, 239, 241, 243, 249, 261, 276, 280, 297, 298, 358, 372, 373, 377–379, 381, 382, 384, 402, 454, 462, 532, 539
Louppy-le-Châtel, 183
Lower chambers (assemblies), 342
Loyalists, 348, 349
Lübeck, 190
Lucerne, Lake of, 659
Lumière, Auguste and Louis, 560
Luneville, Treaty of, 513
Lutheran
  Church, 263
  Reformation, 213
Luxembourg Compromise (1966), 693, 694, 709
Luxemburg, Rosa, 576, 616
Luxor, 13, 30
Lycées, 267, 461, 462
Lycurgus, 24, 433

## M


Maastricht Treaty. *See* Treaty on European Union (1992)
Macedonia, 27–29, 32, 33, 39, 56
Machiavelli, Niccolo, 218, 245
Machine guns, 474, 540, 559
Madariaga, Salvador de, 648, 669, 682, 683
Madison, James, 417, 419, 421–424, 426
Madrid, 221, 246–248, 266, 268, 279, 350, 438, 501, 538, 567, 569, 579, 616, 620, 654
  Treaty of (1795), 350
Magenta, battle of, 521, 531
Magistracies, 24, 44, 46, 51, 53, 54, 590
Magistrates, 18, 21, 25, 42–46, 49, 51, 52, 57, 58, 189, 216, 230, 239, 273, 336, 342, 452, 454, 468
*Magistratura de Trabajo* (Work Magistracy), 590
Magna Carta, 188, 198, 199, 201, 225, 291–292, 309, 353, 390, 497
Magna Glossa, 197, 201
Magnates, 100, 130, 155, 157, 191, 198, 293, 375
Magyar, 516
Maine
  Province of, 338
  State, 338, 435
  U.S. battleship, 540
Main River, 524
Maire. *See* Mayor
Maldonado, Pedro, 2241
Mallorca, kingdom of, 183, 199, 237, 653
Mallus, 100, 289
Malta, 698, 710
Managers, 450, 613
Manchester, 306, 511
Mandarins, 15
Manhattan, island of, 327
Mann, Thomas, 669
Mansi, 156
Mao Tse-tung, 605, 606, 619, 620, 708
Marbury *vs*. Madison, 425, 429, 438, 441
March on Rome, 576, 592, 617, 706
Marconi, Guglielmo, 561
Marcuse, Herbert, 579, 608
María Cristina, Regent of Spain (1833-1843), 498, 538
Mariana, Juan de, 216
Maria Theresa of Austria, 268, 280
Marignano, battle of, 659
Mark Anthony, 40
Market
  economy, 603, 604, 607
  Socialism, 606
Marne, battle of, 540
Maroto, Rafael, general, 538
Marsala (Sicily), 539
Marseillaise, 395, 396, 403
Marshall
  George, 619, 678, 680, 707
  John, 421, 429
  Plan (1947), 678–679
Marshall Pétain, 588, 674
Marshall Plan, 593, 596, 604–605, 619, 678–680, 685, 707
Marsilius of Padua, 140, 141
Martínez Campos, Arsenio, general, 539
Martov, Julius, 573, 616
Martyrs, 72, 279
Marx and Engels, 565, 568–570
Marxism, 568, 575, 606, 608
Marxist
  doctrine, 608
  orthodoxy, 573
  Socialism, 570
Marx, Karl, 467, 469, 568, 616
Maryland
  Province of, 337
  State, 420
  Toleration Act (1649), 337
Mary, queen of the Scotts, 296
Mary Wollstonecraft, 305
Mason
  Captain John, 338
  George, 354, 419
Masonic lodges, 505, 507
Mass
  culture, 558
  organizations, 581
  parties, 469, 471, 580
  production, 583
Massachusetts
  Bay Company, 335, 336
  charter (1691), 342
  General Court, 421
Massification, 581
Maternity insurance (1923), 589
Matteotti, Giacomo, 617
Matters of state, 191, 225
Maupeou, René Nicolas de, Chancellor of France, 383
Maurras, Charles, 589
Maximilian I, Emperor of Mexico, 508
Maxwell, James Clerk, 561
May 1968, 620
Mayflower, 248, 333–335, 357
  Compact (11 November 1620), 334, 357
Mayor, 111, 123, 124, 193, 197, 211, 223, 240, 457, 661
Mazarin, Jules, cardinal, 111, 243, 379

Mazzini, Giuseppe, 512
Means of production, 398, 563, 564, 568
Mechanization, 563
Mediatization, 513
Medical science, 558, 562
Medici, 227, 246, 247, 520
Médicis, Marie de, 227, 247, 386
Medieval universities, 110, 111
Mediterranean Highway, 588
Megara, 24, 32
Meiji Era (1868-1912), 531
Mein Kampf, 594, 673
*Memory of Solferino (Un souvenir de Solferino)*, 531
Mendès France, Pierre, 473
Menorca, 344, 350
Mensheviks, 573, 616
Mentana, battle of, 523
Mercader, Ramón, 574, 618
Mercantilism, 244
Merchant (nations), 12, 24, 111, 161, 190, 202, 222, 269, 295, 323, 331, 346, 349, 352, 381, 418, 664
Merkel, Angela Dorothea, 621
Merovingians, 38, 102, 113, 123, 124, 145, 155, 161, 374
Mesolithic, 11, 30
Mesolonghi, 537
Mesopotamia, 11, 13–14, 16, 19, 31, 39
Messiah, 69
Messina Conference, 691
Mesta privileges, 278
Metropolitans, 81
Metternich
  Klemenz Wenzell von, 449
  System, 495–496, 506–508, 534, 663
Mexican-American War, 436
Mexican Constitution of 1917, 573
Mexico, 245, 326, 327, 350, 357, 436–438, 442, 508, 573, 574, 618
Michigan State, 350, 434
Microsoft, 559
Middle class, 23, 226, 267, 306, 386, 501, 502, 524, 564–565, 567, 579, 585, 586, 608–611
  revolution, 226
Milan, 55, 73–75, 77–79, 85, 222, 238, 329, 512, 520
Militant nationalism, 667
Military revolution, 229
Military service, 42, 157, 159, 398, 404, 405, 684, 686
Ministers, 81, 107, 242, 243, 263, 268, 271, 278, 279, 302–305, 308, 311, 336, 378–380, 384, 401, 453, 457, 468, 470, 473, 519, 539, 590, 617, 670, 682, 683, 695, 699, 703, 710
  of the Crown Act (1937), 308
Ministries, 144, 268, 278, 458
Minnesota State, 437
Minos, 19
Minotaur, 19
Minuit, Peter, 327
Minute men, 347
Mirabeau, Honoré Gabriel Riquetti Count of, 386, 390
*Missi dominici*, 155
Mission territories, 329
Mississippi
  River, 327, 345, 350
  State, 435
Missouri
  Compromise, 435, 436, 442
  State, 435, 437
Mithras, 72
Mitteleuropa, 144, 532
Mitterrand, François, 473, 478, 479
Mixed negotiation commissions, 589
Mobile warfare, 540
Model T, 562
Modena, duchy of, 512, 521, 539
Moderate liberalism, 503–504
Mohenjo-Daro, 11, 30
Molay, Jacques de, 164
Molotov, Viatcheslav, 618
Monarch, 20, 29, 38, 54, 55, 78, 99, 102, 123, 125, 130, 141, 142, 145, 157, 167, 168, 181, 182, 184, 187, 192, 195, 197, 198, 203, 215–217, 219, 220, 224, 226, 233, 236, 238, 243, 244, 247, 248, 257–281, 292, 294–296, 301, 303, 305, 322, 338, 340, 354, 373, 376, 377, 379, 380, 382, 385, 388–390, 394, 396, 399, 400, 451, 492, 494, 496, 498, 499, 503, 518, 520, 653, 654
Monarchical society, 325
Monarchization, 455
Monarchy, 13, 44, 99, 123, 154, 178, 211, 258, 287, 321, 371, 417, 450, 491, 557, 651
Monastic communities, 68, 103, 104, 136
Monks, 103, 104, 137, 242
Monnet, Jean, 676, 684–687, 690, 694
Monroe, James, 508
Montagnards, 392, 404
Montagne, 400
Montana State, 437
Montcalm, Marquis of (Louis-Joseph de Montcalm-Gozon), 344
Monte Cassino, 104, 115

Montesquieu, Charles Louis de Secondat, baron de la Brède, 280
Montfort, Simon de, 139, 201, 292, 309
Montijo, Eugenia de, Empress of France, 523
Montoire, 674
Montreal, 326, 345
Montreux Congress, 681
Moots, 289
Morat, battle of, 659
Morbus gothicus, 180
More, Thomas, 230, 235
Morgan, 16–18, 346, 430, 434, 436, 437, 469
Morgarten, battle of, 659
Morse, Samuel, 561
Mortimer, George, 293
Morton, William T.G., 562
Mos
 *gallicus*, 217
 italicus, 216
Moscow, 606, 618, 621, 676, 710
 Trials, 579
Moses, 17, 67–69, 83, 648
Most Christian Majesty, 654
Most Serene Republic, 222
Mount Sinai, 67, 69
*Mouvement Républicain Populaire*, 472
Mozart, Wolfgang Amadeus, 280
MPs, 306, 307, 682
Multilateral accords, 614
Munich Agreement (September 30, 1938), 595, 618
Municipality, 457, 586, 662
Municipia, 40
Muñoz Grandes, Agustin, 674
Murderers, 291
Museo del Prado, 267
Muslims, 98, 108, 114, 123, 145, 157, 159, 169, 189, 202, 275, 374, 473
Mussolini
 Benito, 142, 556, 576
 dictatorship, 588
Mutation féodale, 159
Mycenae, 19, 20
My Political Testament, 489

**N**

Nacional, 589, 594
*Nacionales*, 594
Nakaz, 260, 275
Namibia, 532
Nantes, Edict of, 214, 247, 249
Naples, 60, 104, 126, 199, 222, 238, 274, 278, 280, 506, 521, 522, 539, 653
Napoleon
 Bonaparte, 143, 402, 435, 450, 451, 455, 475, 477
 university, 266
Napoleonic
 constitutionalism, 452–453
 monarchy, 143, 651
 State, 454
 wars, 492, 507, 527
Napoleon III, 143, 147, 465, 467–469, 477, 508, 513, 521–523, 525, 539
Narváez, Ramón María, general, 511
National
 anthem, 279, 395, 396, 403
 Assembly (Assemblée nationale), 299, 389, 390, 394, 399, 400, 403, 416, 464, 468–474, 477, 478, 505, 517, 570, 579, 588, 602, 621, 686, 690, 708
 capitalism, 530
 Government, 357, 418, 420, 422, 428, 432, 464
 Guard, 403, 469, 570
 identities, 500
 Industrial Recovery Act of June 16, 1933, 586
 Institute of Social Welfare *(Instituto Nacional de Previsión)* in 1908, 589
 law, 39, 98, 108, 185, 698, 699
 legislature, 355, 578
 monarchies, 244–249
 Movement, 590
 Recovery Administration (NRA), 586
 representation, 557
 Savings Bank *(Caja Nacional)*, 1931, 589
 self-determination, 665
 sentiments, 244, 499, 506, 513, 668
 Socialism, 565, 576–591
 Socialist German Workers Party (*Nationalsozialistische Deutsche Arbeiterpartei*, NSDAP), 577
 Syndicalistic Revolution, 590
 Workshops *(ateliers nationaux)*, 570
 Work Statute (1933), 591
Nationalism, 2, 3, 109, 110, 112, 244, 395, 490, 499, 513, 514, 530–533, 665–668, 671, 681, 705
Nationalist movements, 519, 666
Nationalities, principle of, 110
Nationality, 57–61, 66, 109, 499, 606, 661
*Nationalversammlung*, 617
Nation-state, 3, 122, 143, 198, 489–541, 559, 564, 567, 573–576, 581, 592, 613–621, 647 711
Native Americans, 501

Natural
- borders, 398
- Law, 217, 235–236, 274, 351

Naumann, Friedrich, 532
Navarre, 169, 170, 237, 243, 245, 277, 653, 655
Nazis
- dictatorship, 591
- Germany, 578, 579, 595, 674
- Party, 586, 671
- regime, 579, 600, 673

Nazism, 582, 585, 586, 598
Nebraska State, 437, 442
Nebuchadnezzar, 14, 31, 83
Necker, Jacques, 386
Neoclassicism, 462
Neoconservative movement, 609
Neoliberal, 609
- Revolution, 609

Neolithic Revolution, 11
Netherlands, 132, 191, 214, 234, 238, 246–248, 267, 333, 341, 504, 509, 536, 537, 653, 659, 675, 676, 682, 691, 699, 708, 710
Neutrality Act, 685
Nevada, State, 436, 437, 442, 587
New Amsterdam, 327, 341, 357
Newark
- city of, 340
- on-Trent, Reverend Abraham Pierson of, 340

Newcomen, Thomas, 558
New Deal, 583–591, 597–599, 602
- Constitutional Revolution, 598

Newfoundland, 326
New Frontier Program, 602
New Hampshire
- Province of, 338
- State, 441

New Jersey
- colony of, 339
- Plan, 423
- Royal Province of, 340

New Kingdom, 13, 30, 102, 106, 274
New Left, 611
New Mexico, 326, 436–438, 442
- State, 436

New Order, 137, 144, 496, 557, 673, 674
New Orleans, 345
Newport, 420
New Princes, 581
New State, 49, 110, 226, 295, 353, 354, 417, 420, 428, 430, 431, 433–435, 437, 442, 454, 459–461, 496, 508, 521, 525, 589, 591, 653, 655, 663, 665, 666, 668, 681, 706, 709
Newton, Isaac, 258, 351, 648
New Western
- Empire, 127–128
- nobility, 613

New World, 326, 328, 329, 331, 337, 338, 343, 344, 353, 372, 566, 595, 610, 613, 615, 665, 674, 707
- Order, 610, 613, 615, 674

New York
- Bay, 326, 357
- City, 347
- colony of, 327
- State of, 327, 340, 416, 441
- Stock Exchange, 617, 706

New Zealand, 536
Nice, 521, 560, 699, 710
Nicholas I of Russia, 506
Niépce, Nicéphore, 560
Nile, 11–13
Nivelle Offensive, 541
Nobiles, 100
Nobility, 14, 15, 24, 44, 73, 100, 101, 106, 130, 178, 180, 182, 184, 187–189, 191, 193, 198, 199, 201, 203, 220, 222–224, 241, 242, 265, 266, 269, 271, 275, 291, 292, 294, 295, 324, 337, 339, 371, 376, 381, 384, 386, 388–391, 403, 451, 460, 496, 518, 528, 564, 613
Nobles, 20, 21, 24, 28, 100–102, 111, 124, 130, 132, 138, 154, 156, 162, 163, 167, 178, 187, 188, 190–195, 197–200, 223, 224, 226–228, 241, 242, 291–293, 295, 309, 323, 383–385, 388, 389, 401, 454
- of the Robe *(noblesse de robe)*, 193

Nogaret, Guillaume de, 141, 217
*Nomenclatura*, 580
Non-aggression Pact, 595, 618, 671, 707
Non-Anglican Protestants, 300
Non-intervention, 593
Non-slave states, 567
Normandy, 164, 169, 288, 477, 619, 654
- Landing (*see* Operation Overlord)

Norman invasion, 291
Normans (Norsemen), 288
North America, 246–248, 296, 305, 326, 327, 330–332, 334, 338–341, 343–350, 357, 358, 373, 379, 402, 415–443
North Atlantic Treaty Organisation (NATO), 604, 619, 690, 708
North Briton, newspaper, 304

North Carolina, 331, 339, 426, 441
North Dakota State, 437
Northern Ireland, 288, 301, 311, 657, 666, 711
  Ireland Act (1998), 666
North German Confederation *(Norddeutscher Bund)*, 524
North Korea, 605, 606, 619
North Vietnam, 620
Northwest Ordinance of 1787, 433–434, 436, 441
Northwest Territory, 434
Norway, 182, 309, 536, 659, 680, 692
*Notabiles*, 101
Notables, 4, 23, 106, 224, 227, 268, 290, 372, 374, 378, 384, 421, 427, 453, 454, 466, 469, 650, 683
Novara, battle of, 512
November Revolution, 616
Nueva Planta Decrees, 200, 237, 277
Nutrition, 558

**O**

Obama, Barack Hussein, 440, 602, 621
Obamacare, 603
Oberste Justizstelle, 270
Obligatoriness of the law, 600
Obligatory Old Age and Invalidity Insurance (1947), 590
*Obrigkeitstaat*, 272
Observancias, 197, 240
October Manifesto (Russia, 1905), 540
October Revolution, 574, 579, 587, 616
Odoacer, 61, 94, 97, 98, 113
O'Donnell, Leopoldo, general, 532
*Odyssey*, 20
OECD, 610, 679
OEEC. *See* Organization for European Economic Cooperation (OEEC)
Official records, 292
*Officium Palatinum (Palatium Regis)*, 101
Oglethorpe, James Edward, 339, 340
Ohio
  River region, 350, 430, 431, 434
  State, 350, 434
  Valley, 344
Oidores, 184
Oklahoma, 326, 437
Old
  English, 292
  Order, 279, 322, 325, 373, 399, 456, 496
  Regime (*see* Ancien Régime)
  Swiss Confederacy *(Eidgenossenschaft)*, 659
Oligarchic model of the state, 611–613
Oligarchies, 192, 221, 227, 241, 277, 329, 492, 575–591, 612
Oligarchy, 22, 24, 222, 306, 384, 392, 400, 468, 497, 500–502, 530, 557, 564, 608–613
Olivares, Count Duke of, 243, 248, 654
Olympic Games, 27, 32
Operation Overlord, 477
*Opium of the Intellectuals*, 568
Opium Wars (1839-1842 and 1856-1860), 531, 538, 539
Oporto, 276
  Revolt (1846), 510
Orange, House of, 222
*Ordenamientos*
  *de Alcalá* (1348), 195, 221
  *de leyes*, 232
*Orden de prelación*, 228
Order of the Temple, 164, 200
Ordinary laws, 580, 700
*Ordo clericalis*, 80
*Ordo-liberalism*, 497
*Ordonnances* (executive orders), 519
Oregon
  state, 436
  Territory, 436
Organic
  Articles, 459
  Statute (1832), 538
Organization for European Economic Cooperation (OEEC), 679, 682
Orkney Islands, 657
Orléanistes, 469
*Orléanistes*, 469
Orleans, 162, 183, 202, 239, 345, 376, 382
Orlov, Grigori Grorievitch, 275
Orry, Jean, 278
Orthodox, 69, 76, 77, 82, 83, 103, 136, 137, 145, 213, 263, 275, 428, 538, 573, 580, 608
Orwell, George, 110, 490, 565
*Ostelbien*, 323
Ostracism, 25–27, 46
*Ostraum*, 533
Ostrogoths, 94, 97, 98, 108, 113–114, 122, 144
Otto I, 130–131, 134, 135, 145, 169, 375
Ottoman
  Empire, 212, 500, 506, 508, 509, 533, 535, 537, 663

Turks, 203, 212, 508
Otto, Nikolaus August, 562
Ourique, battle of, 186
Oviedo, 169, 181

**P**

*Paciarii*, 166
Pactism, 168, 196, 199
Padilla, Juan de, 241
Paine, Thomas, 421
Paleolithic, 10, 11
Palermo (Sicily), 512, 538
Pallas Athena, 22
Pamphlets, 268, 304, 339, 346, 386, 419, 451, 462, 565, 673
Panama Congress, 508, 537
Pan-American Union, 667
Panathenaea, 21, 22
Pan-Europe, 667, 668
Pan-European
Congress, 675, 707
movement, 667–668, 681
Union, 668, 670, 681, 706
Pan-Germanism, 516
Panhard and Levassor, 562
Pan-Hellenic league, 28
Pankhurst, Emmeline, 307
Pan-Serbian propaganda, 534
Papacy, 3, 66, 82–85, 104, 105, 122–128, 131, 136, 138–143, 145–147, 157, 170, 178, 185–187, 201, 212, 215, 217, 226, 246, 261, 263, 300, 374–376, 523
Papal
States, 123–126, 142, 145, 147, 169, 399, 513, 521–523, 539
theocracy, 134–142, 146, 163, 213
Papin, Denis, 558
Papist Catholics, 300
Pappas, 82
Paraguay, 277, 329
Paris
Commune, 469, 477, 539, 571, 616
Treaty of (1763), 345, 350, 356, 689–690, 696, 708
Parish, 80, 137, 163, 164, 265, 680
Parker, captain, 347
Parliament(s)
Act (1911), 308, 311
of Besançon, 385
of Bordeaux, 385
of England, 301
of Grenoble, 385
of Paris, 188, 216, 217, 238, 239, 291, 380, 382, 383, 403
of Scotland, 301
of Westminster, 192, 301, 342
Parliamentary
custom of consent, 190
government, 289, 301, 303, 402, 520, 526, 592
immunity, 304
preeminence, 301
regime, 302–311, 465, 474, 496, 503, 511
representatives, 297, 306, 502, 557
system, 190, 273, 289, 303–307, 310, 323, 423, 424, 474, 492, 496, 501, 503, 504, 529, 530, 576
*Parliamentum*, 292
Parma, duchy of, 512
*Paroikois*, 80
Parthenon, 22, 26
Parthenopean Republic, 506, 663
Partidas, Las, 184, 510
Partocracies, 581
Party
discipline, 581, 604
government, 298
Pase region, 215
Pasteur, Louis, 562
Patent of Tolerance, 263
Patient Protection and Affordable Care Act (ACA), 440, 603
Patiño, José, 279
Patriarchs, 69, 81
Patrimonial Absolutism, 243
Patriotism, 44, 110, 225, 394, 398, 417, 490
Patriot King, 417
Patriots, 347, 352, 386–389, 391, 512, 513, 516, 519, 521
Patronage, 24, 163, 168, 261, 269, 302, 306, 558
system, 302
Paul of Tarsus, 70
*Pax Dei*, 165
*Pays*
*conquis*, 237
*d'élection*, 237, 385
*d'états*, 237
Peace
of Paris (1898), 540
and Truce of God, 165, 166
Peasants, 12, 13, 20, 23, 24, 135, 156, 178, 193, 265, 275, 323, 388, 398, 566
Peisistratus, 24, 260
Pelayo, Don, 181

Pelopidas, 27
Peloponnesian Wars, 26, 27, 32
Peninsula War, 114, 505, 507
Penn
charter, (1681), 342
William, 341, 343, 357
Pennsylvania
colony of, 339, 343
General Assembly, 341
Province of, 341
Pentagon, 621
Pentapolis, 123, 125, 126, 145
Pentateuch, 67, 68
People's
Liberation Army, 621
Republic of China, 605, 606, 612, 619, 621, 705, 708
Pepin the Short, 123–124, 126, 141, 145, 157, 162, 169, 374, 375
Pere Albert, Les Commemoracions de, 179
Père Lachaise, 261
Perestroika, 606
Pérez, Antonio, 240, 243, 247
Pericles, 14, 26, 27, 32
*Perieques*, 23
Pernambuco, 327
Persian
Empire, 14, 28, 31, 33
Wars, 23
Peru, 246, 328, 507, 508
Petacci, Claretta, 619
Pètain, Philippe, Marshall, 471, 588
Petit Clamart, 474, 478
Petronilla, queen of Aragon, 159
Peugeot, 562
Pflimlin, Pierre, 473
Phaedra, 19
Phalanx, 24, 27
Pharaoh, 12–13
Pharisees, 68–71
Philadelphia, 341, 347–349, 355, 357, 358, 420–423, 429, 441
Philip II
Armada (*see* Invincible Armada)
Augustus, king of France, 130, 182, 374
king of Spain, 234, 246–248, 300, 651
Philip IV
the Fair, king of France (Philip IV), 140, 141, 146, 164, 198, 202, 217
king of Spain, 248, 249
Philippics, 28
Philippines, 508, 532, 537, 540, 618
Philosopher king, 260, 263
Philosophes (friends of wisdom), 258
Phnom Penh, 620
Phonograph, 560
Photography, 560
Phratry, 18
Piedmont, 507, 512, 513, 519–522, 539
Pilgrims, 80, 164, 200, 333–335, 357
Pippin the Short, king of the Franks, 107
Pitt the Elder, William, 303, 310, 344
Pius IX, pope, 147, 512
Pius XI, pope Pizarro, Gonzalo, 328
Placet. *See* Pase region
Plains of Abraham, Battle of the, 344–345
Plebiscite. *See* Referendum
*Plena potestas*, 292
Plombières Agreement (1858), 521
Plutocratic oligarchy, 612
Plymouth
colony, 335
Company, 331, 338
Pocahontas, 247, 332, 357
Pocket boroughs, 306
Podestá, 217
Poilus, 536
Poincarè, Raymond, 669, 6848
Poland, 132, 191, 268, 275, 509, 528, 536, 538, 596, 618, 665, 671, 680, 698, 707, 710
Poles, 534, 675
Polis, 9–33, 38–40, 43–46, 49, 81, 94
Polish-Lithuanian Federation, 652
Polish revolt (1830), 537
Political
authoritarianism, 570
combat, 601
liberalism, 609
majorities, 601
parties, 297–298, 403, 424, 433, 474, 581, 682
power, 12, 13, 21, 45, 55, 56, 99, 157, 185, 188, 190, 194, 196, 198, 218, 222, 223, 308, 351, 384, 396, 417, 470, 497, 499, 568, 576, 595, 598–600
rights, 23, 472, 489, 492
Pol Pot, (Saloth Sar), 620
Polybius, 38, 46, 57
Pombal, marquis of, Sebastian Carvalho y Mello, 276
Pompidou, Georges, 478
Pontius Pilate, 69, 70
Poor laws, 572
Pope, 66, 76, 79, 82, 83, 104, 105, 107, 115, 121–128, 131, 132, 136–141, 143–147, 162, 163, 169, 170, 185, 186, 188, 192,

193, 199, 201, 202, 213–217, 231, 243, 246, 262, 376, 381, 468, 512, 513, 522, 523, 650, 654
Popery, 300
Popular
assemblies, 21, 25, 42–43, 45, 52, 53, 194, 289, 290
Fronts, 575, 588, 593, 602
revolution, 391, 400, 403
Populist leader, 576, 586
Populus Romanus, 42, 52, 56–58
Porsche, Ferdinand, 577
Portalis, Jean Étienne Marie, 464
Portugal, 163, 186, 201, 202, 229, 238, 243, 247, 262, 265, 274, 276–277, 279, 280, 326, 329, 330, 357, 510, 532, 535, 536, 590, 601, 653, 654, 692, 694, 710
military class, 590
Portuguese
colonization, 328
expansion, 328
Post-Democracy, 611
Postglossators, 133
Post-Marxist thinkers, 608
Post-Soviet communist regimes, 605
Post-War era, 608
Potemkine, Grigori, 275
Potestas, 51, 55, 182, 292
Potomac River, 421
Potsdam, 272, 619, 676, 677, 680, 707
Conference, 677, 680, 707
Pottier, Eugene, 555
Pound sterling, 585
Powers of society, 582
Praetors, 42, 46, 53, 55, 56, 69
Pragmáticas, 200, 228, 233
Pragmatic Sanction, 510, 537
Prague, 248, 515, 620, 665
Spring, 620
Préameneu, Felix Julien Jean Bigot, 464
Prerogative courts, 230
Prerogatives of the Crown, 301
Presbyterians, 296, 300
*Presbyteros*, 80
Presidency, 230, 417, 423, 432, 472, 473, 584, 598, 670, 690, 708, 710, 711
of the European Council, 699, 710, 711
President
of the Reich, 582
of the Republic, 469, 470, 472–475, 478, 479
of the United States, 352, 423, 424, 428, 433, 437, 442, 474, 617
Presidential system, 416–417, 422–425, 430
Press, 303, 304, 339, 346, 388, 401, 525, 560, 582, 607, 647, 674, 675, 679, 687, 704
Pressure groups, 261, 612, 690
Prieto, Indalecio, 589, 682
Primaries, 424
Prime Minister, 223, 227, 302–306, 308–311, 424, 472, 474, 478, 479, 501, 609, 666, 670, 675, 676, 685–687, 694, 706
Primo de Rivera
dictatorship, 589
José Antonio, 590
Miguel, general, 592
*Primum inter pares*, 165
Prince
of Asturias, 181
of Viana, 181
of Wales, 181, 305, 310, 656
Princeps, 38, 40, 50–52, 54, 55, 57, 60, 123, 140, 179, 181, 194, 217, 232
legibus solutus est, 217, 232
Principate, 47, 48, 50, 53, 56, 57, 60, 84, 232, 289, 454, 455
Princip, Gavrilo, 534
Private
colonies, 342
initiative, 276, 330–332, 420, 704
medical insurance, 602, 603
property, 161, 338, 352, 568
sector, 584, 598, 609
Privileged classes, 45, 178, 193, 194, 241, 279, 294, 322, 381, 383, 384, 388, 496, 497, 557, 564
*Privilegios de la Unión*, 199
Privy Council, 230, 243, 290, 305, 340
Progressive liberals, 538
Proletarian revolution, 575
Proletariat. *See* Fourth Estate
Pro-magistrates, 51
Promissio carisiaca, 125, 145
Pronunciamiento, 505
Propaganda, 144, 195, 217, 395, 534, 580, 592, 673
Property
churches *(ecclesia propria or Eigenkirche)*, 135
colonies, 341
owners, 307, 352, 398, 466, 567
Owning Democracy, 611
*Proprietas*, 156
Proprietors of the private colonies, 342
Propylaea, 26

Pro-Russian regime, 538
Prosperity, 21, 168, 190, 222, 242, 278, 415, 505, 557, 576, 583–585, 609, 611, 647, 664, 704
Protection of the social pact, 601
Protestant
  dissident sects, 300
  Reformation, 141, 185, 245
*Protofeudalism*, 102
Proto-Indo-European, 16
Proto-nationalism, 244
Proudhon, Pierre, 569
Provence, 124, 164, 227, 384, 654
Provinces, 40, 46–49, 51, 55, 56, 58, 59, 81, 82, 105, 126, 135, 144, 222, 223, 236, 237, 247, 248, 267, 269, 277, 288, 327, 328, 333, 339, 340, 384, 395, 464, 466, 509, 516, 537, 686
Provincial
  Assemblies, 340
  Estates, 227, 269, 336, 380, 384–385, 387, 403, 457
Provisional
  Consultative Assembly, 471, 477
  Government of the Republic (1944), 477
Provisions of Oxford, 292, 309
Prussian
  aristocracy, 323, 572
  army, 524
  Constitution (1850), 323, 498, 502, 519, 577
  Empire, 273
  hegemony, 524
  monarchy, 471, 518
  protonationalism, 514
  regeneration, 514
  society, 519
  state, 263, 270, 271, 273
Prussia Prussian Constitution (1850), 323, 498, 502, 519, 577
PSOE. *See* Spanish Socialist Workers Party
Ptolemies, 29
Public
  bills, 308
  education, 335
  Health Service, 587
  health system, 587, 602
  housing, 587
  office, 26, 44, 58, 104, 161, 221, 300, 310, 323, 426, 460, 686
  offices venality, 44
  opinion, 242, 303–305, 310, 344, 372, 379, 383, 385, 387, 418, 420, 452, 470, 523, 525, 528, 534, 668, 670, 679, 681, 704, 705
  reason, 609
  Safety, Committee of, 393, 395, 404
  schools, 324, 432, 527
  sector, 584
  works, 24, 570, 576, 587, 588, 591
Puissance réglée, 181
Pulverization of Marxism-Leninism, 606
Punctation of Olmütz (Olmützer Punktation), 518, 523, 524, 538
Purchasing of votes, 306
Puritan inquisition, 336
Puritans, 215, 296, 300, 333, 335–337, 340
Pygmalion, 324
Pyramids, battle of the, 475
Pyrenees Treaty, 651

## Q

*Quadragesimo Anno* (1931), 591
Quadruple Alliance Querétaro, 495
Quaestors, 46, 55
Qualified Majority Voting (QMV), 693, 695–697
Québec, 112, 246, 326, 344, 357, 358
Queen of England
  Anne I, 301, 302
  Caroline, 302
  Elizabeth I, 215, 243, 247, 294, 296, 297, 300, 309, 537, 656
  Elizabeth II, 537, 538
  Henrietta Maria of France, 297
  Mary II, 249, 301
  Mary Tudor, Mary I, 246
Queen of France
  Anne of Austria, 223
  Marie Antoinette, 380, 659
  Marie de Médicis, 227, 247, 386
*Question prioritaire de constitutionalité*, 475
Quierzy-sur-Oise, 125, 158
Quixote, Don, 234, 247, 648
*Quod omnes tangit, ab omnibus approbetur*, 192
Quod principi placuit legis habet vigorem, 53, 232

## R

Radetzky, Joseph, marshall, 512, 513
Radical Islam, 615
Radic, Stjepan, 665
Radio, 560, 561, 704
Railroads, 439, 442, 558
Railways, 558, 588
Raleigh, Sir Walter, 331, 357

Ramon Berenguer I, count of Barcelona, 165, 166
Ramon Berenguer IV, count of Barcelona, 159, 200, 653
Randolph, John, 428
Raspail
  Benjamin, 395
  François Vincent, 525
Rassemblement du Peuple Français, 472
Ratification
  procedures, 356, 699, 701, 710
  of the US constitution, 425–427
Ratio scripta, 217
Ravaillac, François, 216
Rawls, John, 609, 611
Raw materials, 532, 669
Raymond of Penafort, 133
Reading revolution, 303
Reagan, Ronald, 440, 609
Real economy, 584
Rebellion, 84, 124, 144, 190, 192, 202, 214, 222, 226, 227, 241, 246, 248, 305, 325, 328, 345–347, 388–391, 402, 403, 405, 419–420, 440, 505–507, 512, 515–517, 531, 538, 540, 575
  of the Third Estate, 389–391
Reccared, king of the Visigoths, 106, 115
Recht, 273, 581
*Rechtsstaat*, 272, 579
Reconquest, 98, 159, 164, 169, 181, 183, 189, 203
Red Cross, 301, 531
Redistribution Act (1885), 307
Reductions, 4, 294, 329, 422, 513, 514, 566, 588, 591, 705
Referendum, 400, 450, 472–474, 477–479, 498, 521, 578, 619, 657, 666, 704, 707, 710
Reform Act (1832), 302, 306, 501, 511
Reformation
  Parliament, 294, 295
  Statutes, 300
Reformist Legal Movement, *Rechtserneuerungsbewegung*, 581
Regalism, 215, 262
Regency Bill (1811), 305
Regensburg, 513
Regent, 95, 163, 223, 227, 239, 248, 305, 310, 382, 498, 510, 538
Regidores, 221
Regionalist
  sentiments, 500
  separatism, 655
Réglements, 464
Regnum Franciae, 182
Regulations, 2, 15, 68, 73, 157–158, 211, 340, 343, 432, 453, 454, 456, 464, 473, 529, 580, 589, 611, 704
*Reichsdeputation*, 513
*Reichskammergericht*, 134
Reichskirche (Imperial Church), 135
Reichsland, 686
Reichsmark, 681
Reichstag, 134, 513, 524, 526, 527, 572, 578, 618, 668, 706
Reichstag fire, 578, 617
Reims, 106, 141, 162, 202, 377
*Reine Rechtslehre* (Pure Theory of Law), 599, 600
Religious
  colonies, 336, 342, 357
  colonization, 333–336
  dissidents, 333
  orders, 266, 295, 329
  question, 300
  wars, 214, 651
Remontrances, 238, 239, 382
Renaissance, 183, 188, 217, 220, 261, 353, 564
Renaissance civic humanists, 353
Renan, Ernest, 68, 110
Renault FT 17, 559
Reparation payments, 585
Representation of the People Act (1867), 501
Representation of the People Act (1918), 307
Representative
  assemblies, 200, 223, 271, 332, 354, 496, 501, 503, 583, 682
  principle, 192–197
Republic
  government, 57, 424, 469, 666
  of Ireland Act, 666
  monarchy, 578
  principles, 267, 325, 535
  revolution, age of the, 325
  of Venice, 222 (*see also* Most Serene Republic)
Republicanism, 273, 325, 353, 401, 418, 465, 469, 474
Republicanos, 593
Republicans of order, 458
Rerum Novarum (1891), 590
*Residencia, juicios de*, 328
*Res publica*, 37–61, 95, 109, 155, 161
Restoration, 22, 27, 123, 138, 139, 299, 310, 323, 336, 338–341, 385, 402, 404, 455, 465–468, 470, 471, 476, 492–497, 503,

504, 507, 510, 514, 520, 537, 567, 598, 657, 711
Resurgence of state power, 536
Reunification of Germany, 710
Revere, Paul, 347
Revolt of the Nobles, 383
Revolt of the Privileged. *See* Revolt of the Nobles
Revolution
of 1789, 239, 391, 569
of 1830, 510, 511
of 1848, 273, 492, 511–519, 538, 569
after power, 578
Revolutionary
anarchist, 469, 616
calendar, 142, 147, 393, 404
liberalism, 503–505
prosecutors, 457
Sexennium (1868-1874), 567
*Rex*
*est imperator in regno suo*, 178, 376
*Franciae*, 182
*Francorum*, 182, 375
*portugalensium*, 163, 186
*in regno suo est imperator*, 212, 217
Reynaud, Paul, 672, 686
Rhode Island, 336, 419–421, 426, 441
Ribbentrop, Joachim von, 618
Richard the Lionhearted, 291
Richelieu, Armand Jean du Plessis, cardinal of, 223, 241, 243, 248, 377
Riego
Rafael de, 505, 507
uprising, 505
Right
to property, 464, 568
to veto, 51, 340, 342
wing parties, 593
Righteous king *(roi justicier)*, 157
Rights of voters, 304
Rig-Veda, 12, 30
Rilke, Rainer María, 669
Risorgimento, 520
Roanoke island, Lost Colony, 331
Roaring 20s, 584
Robespierre
Augustin, 451
Maximilien, 397
Rocco, Alfredo, 588
Rochambeau, Jean Baptiste Donatien de Vimeur, comte de, 350
Rockefeller, John Davidson, 584
Rockingham, 304
Roederer, Pierre Louis, 453
Roi
de la révolution, 455
justicier, 157, 187, 232, 378
législateur, 187, 232, 378
Très Chrétien, 235
Rois fainéants, 124
Rojos (reds), 594
Rollo, 288
Romain, Jules, 682
Roman
aristocracy, 43–45, 127, 138
conquest, 292
empire, 3, 37, 39, 40, 48, 53, 54, 58, 60, 61, 66, 71–83, 94, 97–99, 101–103, 108, 112, 122, 125, 127–136, 142, 143, 145–147, 155, 156, 169, 178, 179, 197, 200, 216, 245, 268, 374, 375, 499, 513, 514, 525, 650–652, 658, 659
Forum, 588
law, 57, 58, 72, 133, 134, 156, 178, 193, 197, 216, 217, 464
public law, 50, 56, 162
question, 522–523
Republic, 38, 41–46, 454, 455, 513
state, 40, 47–49, 52, 56, 58, 101, 102, 122, 133
Romanesque cloisters, 288
Romania, 534, 680, 698, 702, 711
Romanians, 534, 702
Romanization, 39, 48, 57, 106–107
Romantic
ideal, 499
Socialism, 568–569
Rome, 3, 16, 38, 66, 94, 122, 202, 215, 262, 289, 329, 459, 512, 576, 650
Treaties of (1957), 690–691
Rome-Berlin Axis, 671, 706
Romulus Augustulus, 61, 94, 97, 113
Roosevelt, Franklin Delano, 427, 617
Rotten boroughs. *See* Pocket boroughs
Rouen, 288
Rougemont, Denis de, 682
Rouget de l'Isle, 395
Roundheads, 297
Rousseau, Jean Jacques, 280, 555
Royal
authority, 141, 162–163, 179, 190, 217, 224, 236, 238, 240, 241, 331–332, 334, 335, 382, 383, 498
authorization, 331–332

charter, 211, 337–339, 343, 510
colony, 332
Council of Castile (*see* Consejo Real de Castilla)
court of law, 292
grant, 337, 342
judges, 184, 290
Navy, 339, 344, 348
officials, 156, 161, 221, 269
prerogative, 200, 224, 280, 294, 306, 394, 500, 525
Statute (*see* Estatuto Real (1834))
tribunals, 184, 240
writs, 299
Royalism, 393
Royalists, 179, 342, 372, 393, 399, 451
Royauté contractuelle, 188
Royer-Collard, Pierre Paul, 503
Rudolf of Habsburg, 132
Ruhr, 685, 706
Rule of law, 187–190, 197, 225, 235, 259, 270–274, 430, 470, 528–529, 582, 598–601, 613, 701
Ruling
classes, 46, 107, 168, 295, 323, 324, 356, 492, 497, 501, 524, 527, 531, 557, 568, 576, 612, 651, 668, 670
oligarchy, 557
Rural
areas, 563
county laborers, 501
workers, 306
Russia, 274–276, 280, 281, 476, 493–496, 502, 505, 506, 508, 509, 511, 516, 527–530, 533–535, 537, 538, 540, 541, 579, 587, 592, 593, 595–597, 606, 615, 618, 663, 664, 667, 673, 676, 677, 679, 680, 707
Russian Prussian
codification, 528, 529
constitution (1906), 498, 529, 540
Empire, 259, 273, 535, 536, 539, 663
Federation, 597
Fundamental Law, 529
liberals, 530
Parliament, 526, 530, 596
Revolution of 1905, 496, 529–530
Revolution of February 1917, 616
Revolution of October 1917, 530, 574
Social Democratic Labor Party, 616
Socialist-Revolutionary Party, 571
Russia's provisional government, 616
Russo-Japanese War, 529, 540, 592, 616
Ruthenians, 534, 665
Rutli Oath (Rütlischwur), 1291, 658–659

**S**
Saar, 669, 685
Sachsenspiegel, 158
Sack of Rome, 215, 246
*Sacraria*, 166
Sadducees, 69
Sagasta, Práxedes Mateo, 567
Sagunto, 539
Saigon, 620
Sailors Advocate, 339
Saint Andrew's cross, 301
Saint Bartholomew's Day Massacre, 147, 214, 218, 246
Saint George's cross, 301
Saint Helena, island of, 476, 537
Saint Patrick's flag, 301
Saint Petersburg, 280, 528, 535, 537, 575
Saint Remigius, 106, 115, 374
Saint-Simon, Count of, 568
Salamanca, 111, 178, 201
Salazar, Oliveira, 590
Salem Witch Trials, 336
Sale of offices, 221, 269
Salic Law, 510, 537
Sancho III of Navarre, 170
Sanction, 166, 310, 343, 385, 510, 537, 600
Sanhedrin, 69, 459
San Ildefonso, Treaty of (1800), 345
San Marino, 536
San Martín, José de, 508
San Salvador de Bahia, 327
Sans culottes, 391, 392, 397, 400, 404
Sanskrit, 12, 16, 103
Santiago, order of, 164
Santos Dumont, A., 562
Sarajevo, 533–534, 540
Saratoga, battle of, 349
Sargon, 14
Sarkozy, Nicolas, 474, 475, 479, 601, 607, 700
Sartre, Jean Paul, 307
Savannah River, 340
Savigny, Friedrich Carl von, 500
Savoy, 521, 538
Saxons, 96–98, 113, 122, 130, 131, 158, 292, 308
Scandinavia's Kalmar Union, 652
Scharnhorst, Gerhard Johann David von, general, 514
Scheidemann, Philip, 617
Schengen Agreement (1985), 695, 709
Schliemann, 20
Schmitt, Ánima, 582
Schmitt, Carl, 455, 490, 556, 579, 581–583, 673

Scholars, 3, 10, 14, 16, 68, 71, 74, 111, 112, 133, 141, 197, 213, 215, 261, 288, 332, 334, 500, 517, 579, 599, 663
Schuman, Robert, 684–688
  Declaration, 687–689, 708
  Plan, 687, 689, 690, 692
Schumpeter, Joseph, 612
Schuschnigg, Arthur, 591
*Schutzstaffel* (SS), 618
Schwarzenberg, Prince of, 516
Schwyz, 657, 659
Scientific Socialism, 571, 658–659
Scipio Aemilianus, 46
Scotland, 104, 112, 183, 188, 238, 288, 293, 296, 301, 310, 311, 655–657, 667
Scottish
  Devolution Referendum, 657
  independence, 657
Scutage, 159
Second American Revolution, 439
Second Continental Congress (1775), 355
Second Empire, 466–468, 477, 511, 523, 525, 526
Second French Republic, 466
Second French Republic (1848-1851), 569
Second Industrial Revolution, 558
Second International, 616
Second Opium War, 539
Second Reform Act (1867), 307
Second Reich (1871), 532, 572
Second Spanish Republic, 617, 706
Secret Army Organisation (OAS), 474
Secular autocrats, 226, 295
Sedan, battle of, 525, 539
Seigneurial officers, 168
Seleucids, 29, 39
Self-government, 237, 330, 332, 335, 351
Seminary of the Nobility, 266
Semi-presidential regime, 474
Senate, 38, 41, 43–46, 49–53, 55, 57, 59, 60, 73, 128, 342, 417, 423, 424, 426, 429, 435, 439, 442, 453–456, 466–473, 476, 477, 522, 579, 670, 706
Senators, 50, 51, 55, 72, 73, 423, 426, 433, 435–437, 454, 468, 470, 473, 709
*Senatus*, 101
*Senatus consulta*, 51, 53, 454
*Senatus Populusque Romanus*, 57, 455
Seniors, 45
Separation of powers, 424, 425, 458
September 11, 2001, 615
Septembrists, 510
Serbia, 534, 535, 665
Serbian government, 534
Serbs, 534, 665
*Servicio de millones*, 228, 269
Settlers, 326, 329, 331, 334, 336, 337, 339–342, 344, 347, 348, 357, 431, 432, 437, 531, 594, 595
Seven Weeks' War, 539
Seven Years War. *See* French and Indian War
Seville, 201, 328, 329, 505
Sforza, Carlo, 669
Shared sovereignty, 503
Shaw, Bernard, 13, 324
Shay's Rebellion, 419–420, 440
Shelley, Mary. *See* Mary Wollstonecraft
Shetland Islands, 657
Shipping industry, 562
Sicilian Vespers, rebellion of the, 202
Sicily, 126, 199, 222, 238, 274, 278, 280, 512, 521, 538, 539, 653
Sicyon, 24
Siege of Paris, 468, 539
Siena, 189, 222, 520
Sieyès, E.J. abbot, 386, 452
Silicon Valley, 559
Silos (Burgos, Spain), 288
Simony, 137
*Sindicatos del Movimiento* (Movement Unions), 590
Single European Act (1986), 693, 694
Sinn Fein, 656, 657
*Sippe*, 154
Sixtus IV, pope, 213, 231
Slavery, 58, 68, 276, 279, 339, 396, 433, 435–439, 442
Slave states, 428, 435–437, 439, 442
Slave traders, 329
Slovakia, 698
Slovaks, 534, 665
Slovenes, 534
Slovenia, 698, 710
Small council, concilium, 292
Small property owners, 567
Smith, Adam, 275
Smith, John, 247, 331, 357
Social classes, 12, 13, 23, 44, 178, 186, 387, 497, 571
Social contract theory, 351
Social Democracy, 571, 574
Social Democratic Workers' Party (*Sozialdemokratische Arbeiterpartei*), 571

Social Insurance Code of 1911, 572
Social insurance system, 589
Socialism, 469, 555, 568–571, 606, 612, 680
Socialist Party of Italian Workers (*Partito socialista dei lavoratori italiani*), 571
Socialist, The, 466, 472, 555, 568–572, 576, 598, 607, 690
Socialist Workers' Party of Germany (*Sozialistische Arbeiterpartei Deutschlands; SAPD*), 571
Social justice, 466, 556, 569
Social pact, 325, 381, 599–601
Social policy (*Sozialstaat*), 572
Social protection, 572, 589, 590, 610
  protection laws, 589
Social question, 502, 565–573, 585, 608–609
Social reform, 277, 460–461, 467, 576, 589
Social rights, 467, 570, 571, 573, 599, 600
Social Security Act, August 14, 1935, 586
Social Security system, 577, 587, 590, 591, 602
Social structure, 11–16, 220, 323, 398, 558
Social welfare
  legislation, 566, 572, 601
  system, 586, 589, 601
Society of Jesus (Jesuits), 146, 216, 246, 262, 329, 527
Society of Prosperity, 505
Software, 559
Solferino, battle of, 521, 531, 663
Solomon, 69, 83, 84, 423
Solon, 24, 32, 433
Somalia, 532
Somme, Battle of the, 541
Sonderbund War *(Sonderbundskrieg)*, 660
*Sonderweg*, 272–273
Sophocles, 26
Sorbonne University, 110, 111
South Africa, 214, 531
South America, 326, 329, 565
South Australia, 536
South Carolina State, 339, 437, 442
South Dakota State, 437
Southern German states, 504, 525
South Korea, 619
South Sudan, 613
Southwest Territory, 95
Sovereign, 14, 53, 58, 125, 126, 141, 167, 168, 178, 180, 182, 187, 191, 193, 197, 200, 215, 219, 231, 233, 241, 245, 260, 261, 263, 264, 267, 270, 271, 273, 340, 348, 354, 374–376, 388, 426, 462, 493, 494, 504, 506, 514, 516, 519, 523, 582, 615, 652, 654, 684
Sovereignty, 2, 50, 53, 57, 109, 158, 166, 179, 187, 194, 217–219, 226, 227, 295, 298, 321, 325, 356, 375–376, 381, 389, 394, 397, 399, 418, 422, 428, 431, 435, 436, 451, 457, 494, 499, 504, 513, 519, 521, 523, 534, 557, 569, 615, 621, 667, 671, 682, 686, 688, 696, 701
Soviet
  constitutions, 580
  expansionism, 619
  Marxism, 608
  model, 597, 605
  nuclear weapons, 597
  Revolution, 574–576, 616
  style regime, 593
  Union, 110, 134, 565, 580, 595–597, 603–606, 611, 615, 617, 618, 620, 621, 664, 667, 671, 677, 680, 695, 696, 710
*Sozialstaat*, 572
Spaak, Paul Henry, 675, 682, 691
Spain, 2, 4, 47, 82, 85, 97, 98, 100, 101, 106, 108, 109, 159, 163, 164, 179–183, 186, 189, 192, 193, 196, 198, 200, 203, 213, 216, 220–223, 229, 231, 234, 235, 237, 244–249, 262, 266, 267, 269, 274, 276–279, 281, 288, 300, 328–331, 345, 348–350, 373, 377, 382, 417, 418, 428, 456, 493, 496, 498, 500, 501, 503, 505–511, 513, 528, 532, 536–540, 562, 563, 567, 573, 575, 582, 588–590, 592, 593, 601, 606, 607, 610, 618, 620, 651, 654, 655, 666, 674, 694, 700, 706, 708–711
  labor laws, 589
Spanish
  America, 328, 329, 506–508
  Armada, 225, 655
  Blue Division, 674
  Catholic Monarchy, 196, 231, 243, 652–656
  Civil War (1936-1939), 593–597, 618, 706, 707
  colonials, 329
  colonization, 326, 328–329
  Communist Party (PCE), 575, 593
  constitutional history, 510
  Constitution of 1837, 510
  Constitution of 1876, 510
  Constitution of 1931, 498
  Constitution of 1978, 498
  Crown, 181, 199, 222, 249, 326–328, 330, 434
  Empire, 142, 330, 350, 371, 508, 651
  Florida, 338
  interregnum (1763-1800), 345
  Monarchy, 181, 196, 213, 216, 227–229, 237, 239, 240, 246, 248, 274, 278, 295, 330, 456, 655

Spanish (*cont.*)
Parliament (*see Cortes*)
Popular Front, 593
Revolution (1820), 505–509
Socialist Workers' Party *(Partido Socialista Obrero Español(PSOE))*, 575, 593, 616, 700
Social Reforms Commission, 589
Social Security system, 590
state, 2, 181, 279, 700
Succession War, 143, 277, 280, 378, 655
Work Code of 1926, 589
Spanish-American War, 540
Spanish Socialist Workers Party, 571, 575
Spann, Othmar, 591
Sparta, 22–25, 27, 28, 32, 39
Spartacist Uprising, 575, 577
Special envoys, 328
Speculation, 10, 383
Speech against the right to work. *See* Tocqueville, Alexis de
Speransky, Mijail, 528–529
Spirit of the people. *See Volksgeist*
Spoleto, Duchy of, 123, 126
Springfield, 419
*Staatskanzler*, 268
Stalin. *See* Iósiv Dzugashvili
Stalingrad, battle of, 596, 619, 673, 707
Stalinist
constitution of 1936, 587
Russia, 596
Stamp
Act, 346
Act Congress, 347
Stanhope, J., 302
Star Chamber, 230, 295
State
assemblies, 190–192
attorneys (*see* Government commissioners)
Council (tsarist Russia), 454–456, 458, 459, 461, 529
of Great Britain, 325
intervention, 536, 573, 601
leaders, 102
social welfare systems, 601
society, 26
State-administrated form of capitalism, 607
State-making, 430
State of the prince, 229–233
States General of the United Netherlands, 341
States rights, 419, 428
Statute law, 199, 301
Statute of Proclamations, 225
Statutes of the Italian urban republics, 520
*Statuto fondamentale*, 520
Steam engine, 558
Steinbeck, John, 585
Stein, Karl Sigmund Franz vom, baron of, 514
Stephen II, pope, 109, 125–126, 145
Stilicho, 95
Stock exchange, 585, 617, 706
Stockholm Convention (1960), 692
Stone Age, 10
Strasbourg, 136, 683, 686, 691, 708–710
Stresemann, G., 670, 706
Strong Executives, 356, 400, 416, 423, 450, 453, 467, 478, 491, 651, 660
Structural imbalances, 609
Struggle for Law *(Kampf ums Recht)*, 581
Stuart Mill, J., 109, 307
Stuarts, 224, 230, 240, 249, 269, 296, 297, 300, 310, 338
*Stufenbau* (rising formation), 600
*Sturmabteilung* (the SA, "brown shirts," fascist militias), 618
Stuyvesant, Peter, 327
Sucre, Antonio José de, general, 508
Sudetenland, 595, 618, 665, 673, 706
Suebi, 96, 98, 106, 108, 113–115
Suger, abbot of Saint Denis, 179, 375
Sulla, 40, 49, 52, 59
Sumerian, 13, 31
Sun King. *See* Louis XIV
*Supper at Beaucaire*, 451
Supranationality, principle of, 684, 685, 693
Supremacy
of the executive, 323
of parliament, 301, 682
Supreme
Being, 142, 147, 393, 404
Court, 419, 421, 424, 425, 427, 430, 438–441, 470, 598, 603
Court of the United States, 425, 428, 440–442, 603
Soviet, 621
*Susan Constant*, 331
Suzerain, 135, 167, 179, 375, 462
Suzerainty, 179
Sweden, 182, 536, 692, 698, 710
Swiss Confederation. *See* Helvetic Confederation
Swiss flag, 531
Switzerland, 104, 132, 234, 509, 536, 574, 600, 607, 657–662, 692
Sydenham, T., 339
*Synodos*, 81

Synoecism, 21–22
System
  of agents, 343
  of terror, 592

T
*Taille*, 183, 377
Taiwan, 592, 619
Talleyrand-Périgord, Charles Maurice de, 453, 455
Taney, Roger B., 438
Tanks, 559, 620, 685
Tannenberg, Battle of, 540
Tarquinius Superbus, 44
TATA. *See* There are Thousands of Alternatives (TATA)
Taxation, 2, 161, 183, 194, 229, 243, 271, 332, 443, 570, 576, 602
Tax dispute, 346
Taxes, 48, 155, 159, 183, 196, 197, 226–228, 269, 271, 293, 342, 346, 347, 355, 377, 382, 385, 387, 422, 502, 519, 524, 572, 607, 661, 662
Tax revolt. *See* Tax dispute
Taylorism, 583
Taylor, J., 428
Tea Act (1773), 346
Technical Revolution. *See* Second Industrial Revolution
Tehran Conference, 707
Telegraph, 560, 561
Telephone, 450, 560, 561
Television, 561, 704
Tell, W., 658
Templars, 164, 197
Temple
  of Jerusalem, 69, 200
  Order of, 164, 200
Ten Commandments, 67
Tenement, 156
Tennessee
  River, 587
  State, 350, 434, 441
  Valley Authority Act, May 18, 1933, 587
Tennis Court Oath, 389–390, 394, 403, 682
Terranova, 344
Territorial states, 39, 101, 109
Terror, 392, 393, 397, 401, 404, 464, 580, 587, 592, 615
Teruel, 590
Test Act, 297
*Teutonicorum regnum*, 132
Texas State, 436, 442
Thanksgiving Day, 334
Thatcher, Margaret, 609
Theban, 27, 28
Thebes, 13, 27, 32
Themistocles, 26, 27
Theocracies, 13, 14
Theodoric I, king of the Visigoths, 95, 96
Theodoric, king of the Ostrogoths, 97, 98, 113, 114
Theodosius I, Roman emperor, 61, 75, 79, 94
Theory of corporativism, 588
*Theory of Justice*, 609
Theory of the two-kingdoms, 213
*Theotisca lingua*, 131
There are Thousands of Alternatives (TATA), 611
There Is No Alternative (TINA), 611
*Theresianum*, 265
Thermidorian Reaction, 396, 397, 400, 401, 404, 451, 466, 496
Thermopylae, 23, 31, 32
Theseus, 19, 21
Thiers, A., 469
Thieves, 291
Third Estate, 381, 386–391, 394, 403, 496, 564
Third French Republic, 469, 470, 477
Third Reich, 144, 147, 525, 594, 600, 618, 621, 652, 673, 677, 706
Third Way, 576
Thirty Glorious Years. *See* Invisible revolution
Thirty Years War, 147, 221, 248, 262
Three-pillar structure, 696, 699
Thucydides, 26
Tiananmen Square
  Forbidden City, 619
  Revolt (1989), 621
Tiberius, 51, 60, 69, 84
Tibet, 619
Tilsitt, Treaties of (1807), 514
Times, The London, 304
TINA. *See* There Is No Alternative (TINA)
Titanic, 463, 540
Tito, Josip Broz, 680
Tobacco, 332
Tocqueville, Alexis de, 321, 372, 396, 467, 490, 555, 570, 647
Tomar, Count of, 510
Top officials, 342
Torah, 67, 68
Tordesillas, Treaty of, 186, 326, 357

Tories, 297
Totalitarian
model of state, 577, 593, 597, 603–607
regime, 571, 578, 580, 593, 600
Totalitarianism, 536, 555–621
Total war, 393, 536
Toulouse, Kingdom of, 95, 113
Tours Congress (25-30 December, 1920), 575
Town representatives, 292
Townshend Act (1767), 346
Toynbee, Arnold, 672
Trade union, 573, 608, 680, 682, 690
representation, 588
Trafalgar, battle of, 476
Trans-appalachian territory, 430
Transition, 11, 44, 66, 180, 182, 183, 189, 296, 372, 567, 576, 652, 655
Trastamara dynasty, 196
*Travail, Famille, Patrie*, 588
Treaty
on European Union (TEU), 1992, 696
of Nice (2001), 699
of Tordesillas (1494), 186, 326
of Union (1707), 656
Treaty of Paris, 345, 350, 356, 689–690, 696, 708
Treaty on European Union (1992), 696
*Tregua Domini*, 165
Trenches, 536, 541, 559
Trench warfare, 540
Trial juries, 290
Tribe, 16–19
*Tribunal de Tumultos*, 234
Tribunal of the Council of Europe. *See* European Court of Human Rights
Tribunate (Tribunat), 46, 453, 454, 461
*Tribunicia potestas*, 51
*Tribus*, 41, 43
Triennial Act, 298
Trilateral Commission, 612
Tripartite estate system, 564
Triple Alliance (1882), 663
Triple Entente, 533, 663
Tripolitania (Libya), 532
Trocadero, Fort of (Cádiz), 537
Trochu, General, 468
Tronchet, François Denis, 463
Troppau, Congress of (1820), 506
Trotsky, León. *See* Lev Davidovich Bronstein
Troy, 20, 32
Truce of God, 165–167
*True Law of Free Monarchies*, 296
Truman, Harry S., 598, 619
Trustees for the Establishment of the Colony of Georgia in America, 340
Tsarist Russia, 502
Tsar of Russia
Alexander I, 494, 508, 527
Alexander II, 528
Alexander III, 39, 163, 186, 528
Nicholas I, 518, 528
Nicholas II, 498, 534, 616
Peter III, 280
Peter I the Great, 280
Tudor
dynasty, 203, 294
Revolution, 295
*Tugendbund*, 504
Tuileries Palace, 391, 396, 400, 403, 476
Tuluyas (Tuluges), 166
Turgot, 380, 402
Turin, 513, 522
Turkish soldiers, 541
Turmoil of the late 60s, 602
Tuscany, 68, 264, 512, 513, 521, 539
Twelve tribes of Israel, 68
Twin Towers, 621
Two Floridas, 350
Two Plus Four Agreement, 621, 710
*Two Treatises of Government*, 351
Tycoons, 584
Tyrant, 24, 32, 216, 241, 259, 260, 397, 607, 658

U
Ukraine, 268, 673
Ukrainians, 596
Ulfilas, 105, 106, 114
Unamuno, Miguel de, 669
Unanimity Principle, 697
Unanimous vote, 709
Unicameralism, 466
Unification Treaty *(Einigungsvertrag)*, 621
Unilateral, 138, 228, 389, 496, 613
Union Jack flag, 301
Union of European Federalists (UEF), 681
*Union sacrée*, 471
United Colonies, 325, 355
United Kingdom, 2, 238, 288, 301, 305, 310, 346, 471, 472, 496, 498, 501, 535, 557, 592, 604, 609, 621, 651, 652, 657, 662, 665, 666, 672, 674, 676, 678, 685, 689, 692, 694, 695, 709, 710
United Kingdom of Great Britain and Northern Ireland, 325, 436, 656–657
United Kingdom of the Netherlands, 267, 509, 537
United Nations, 214, 613–614, 677, 678, 707, 708

United Provinces, 222, 247, 248, 509
United States Constitution, 231, 356, 701
United States of America (USA), 199, 325, 350, 402, 416, 418, 423, 425, 427, 430, 440, 450, 456, 493, 561, 579, 586, 660, 664, 671, 683, 695
United States of Europe, 647, 667, 669, 674, 675, 678, 690
United States Supreme Court, 421, 425, 429, 439–443, 473, 598, 603, 621, 702
Universal
  idea of Europe, 650
  medical coverage, 602
  model, 650–652
  Monarchy, 142, 225, 651
  public health systems, 602
  Social Security system, 590
  social welfare, 601
  state, 129, 132, 602
  suffrage, 311, 398, 432, 435, 453, 467, 470, 496, 501, 511, 516, 517, 524, 567–568, 571, 593, 694, 709
  (male) suffrage, 401, 467, 476, 502, 529, 540, 567
University
  of Berlin, 514
  of France, 266, 462
  of Marburg, 500
  nations *(collegia)*, 111
Unterwalden, 659
*Unus pro omnibus, omnes pro uno*, 657–658
Ur, 13, 14
Urban
  areas, 563
  bourgeoisie, 191, 193, 194, 511
  populations, 563–564
  workers, 306
Urbanization, 563
*Urbes*, 40
Uri, 658, 659
*Usatges*, 158
Utah State, 436, 442
Utrecht
  Peace of (1713), 274, 343, 506
  Treaty of, 274, 662

**V**
Vaccines, 562
Valencia, 170, 183, 186, 188, 192, 196, 199–201, 228, 229, 231, 237, 238, 277, 279, 505, 653, 654
Valens, Roman emperor, 75, 94, 112
Valentinian III, Roman emperor, 95
Valera, Eamon de, 666
Valéry, Paul, 669
Valia king of the Visigoths, 95, 113
*Válidos*, 224, 243
Valois, House of, 183, 377
Van Artevelde, captain of Ghent, 190
Vandals, 96, 98, 113
Van Rompuy, Herman, 699, 711
Varennes, Fligh to, 399, 403
Vassal, 139, 154–162, 167–169, 178, 184, 190, 191, 375
  ties, 160, 376
Vassaldom, 135, 155–157, 160
*Vassi dominici*, 156
*Vassus (homo)*, 155
Vatican State, 142, 147, 523
Vaud, Canton of, 660
Vázquez de Coronado, Francisco, 326, 357
Vázquez, Mateo, 243
Veblen, Thorstein, 608
Vedas, 12, 30
Vegas, 587
Venaissin, 399
Vendée, 393, 404
Veneto, 512, 522
Venezuela, 329, 508
Venice, 123, 132, 222, 329, 513, 522
Ventotene Manifesto, 674
Verdun
  battle of (1916), 541
  Treaty of (843), 129, 145, 169
Vergara, Convention of, 538
Vergennes, French Foreign Minister, 349
Vermont state, 430, 434, 437, 441
Verona, Congress of, 537
*Verordnung des Reichspräsidenten zum Schutz von Volk und Staat*, 578
Verrazano, Giovanni da, 326, 357
Versailles
  *Diktat*, 577
  Palace of, 143, 249, 350, 526, 539, 651
  Peace of (1783), 434 (*see also* Treaty of Paris)
  Treaty, 595, 614
Vertical unions, 588, 590
Very Christian Majesty, 374
Veto, 46, 51, 308, 340, 342, 399, 498
Viceroyalties, 328
Viceroys, 224, 328
Vichy
  France, 674, 686
  Syndrome, 471

*Vicomte*, 161
Victor Emmanuel II, king of Italy, 513, 519–522, 538, 539
Victoria I, queen of England and Empress of India, 306
Victorian Age, 306
Victory Program, 676
Vienna, 276, 329, 493, 494, 512, 515, 516, 521, 523, 539, 668
  School of legal theory, 599
Vietnam War, 620
*Vill* (township), 291
*Villae*, 156
Virginia
  Company, 331, 332, 334
  Declaration of Rights (1776), 354
  General Assembly, 421, 431
  militia, 344
  Plan, 423
  state, 420
Visigoths, 94–97, 100, 106, 108, 112–114, 122, 182
Visitors, 54, 328
*Vita Karoli*, 127
Vizcaya, 237
Vizille, Palace of, 385, 386
Vladimir Illich Ulianov, 574
*Volksgeist*, 500
Volkskammer (GDR), 621
Volkswagen, 562, 577
Voltaire, 133, 234, 237, 259, 260, 271, 272, 280, 461, 463, 647, 648
Von Ihering, Rudolf, 581, 609
Von Justi, Johann Heinrich Gottlob, 275
Von Papen, Franz, 578
Von Paulus, Friedrich, 596, 619, 707
Vouillé, battle of, 97, 114, 374

**W**

Wales, 98, 183, 238, 288, 301, 310, 656, 657
Wallace, William, 656
Wallon Amendment, 469, 477
Walloons, 2, 112
Wall Street, 585, 670
  collapse, 585, 617
Walpole, Robert, Earl of Oxford, 302–303, 310
Walshingham, Sir Francis, 331
Wannsee Conference, 619
War
  of extermination, 393, 535
  of Granada, 203
  of Independence, 213, 310, 311, 325–326, 347–350, 355, 430, 492, 662, 666, 706
  on Poverty Program, 602
  of the Roses, 195, 203, 224, 230, 242, 294, 295, 309
  of the Spanish Succession, 143, 277, 280, 378, 655
  on Terror, 615
War of Secession, 437, 439–443
Warrior bishop, 163
Warsaw Pact, 604, 620
Wars of Religion, 147, 216, 218, 227, 241, 247, 381
Washington, George, 38, 344, 348, 349, 415, 420–422, 427, 441, 501, 586
Washington State, 415, 428
Water filter, 562
Waterloo, battle of, 465, 476, 493, 537
Watt, James, 558
Wealthy oligarchy, 564
Wehrmacht, 596
Weimar
  Constitution, 323, 524, 579, 617
  Republic, 273, 525, 527, 572, 576, 579, 617
Welfare state, 569, 570, 572, 577, 588, 591, 598, 601–603, 610
  model, 597–603, 609
Welser, Bartholomew, 329
Western Christian Empire, 137
Western Empire, 61, 94–97, 126–128
Western Europe, 244, 587, 593, 597, 601, 602, 604, 619, 671, 675–677, 679, 696, 698, 707
Western lands, 430–432
Western lawyers, 599
Western Polity, 103, 161
Western powers, 125, 530
Western Roman Empire, 66, 94, 98, 101, 103, 108, 122, 178, 374, 499, 650
Western Schism, 146, 202, 213
West Germany, 690, 698
Westminster
  city of, 194, 292
  Parliament, 192, 195, 225, 226, 291–293, 295, 299, 301, 304, 309, 336, 342, 353, 656
  Treaty of (1667), 340
Westphalia
  peace of, 3, 214, 215, 245, 651, 659
  Treaty, 111, 248, 651
West Virginia State, 350, 437
What is the Third Estate?, 386
Whig party, 302
Whigs, 297, 306
White coal, 561
White House, 371, 586, 599
White male adults, right to vote, 342
White Russia, 673

Wihelmine period, 577
Wilfred the Hairy, count of Barcelona, 159
Wilkes, John, 304
  Affair, 304, 305
William I
  the Conqueror, 309
  king of the Netherlands, 509
  of Prussia, 280, 539
William of Orange, William III king of England, 298, 310
William Pitt the Elder, Lord Chatham, 303
Williams, Reverend Roger, 336
Wilson
  14-points, 614
  Woodrow, 110, 598, 613, 665
Winthrop, John, 335
Wisconsin State, 350, 434, 436, 442
*Wita*, 290
*Witan*, 289, 290
*Witenagemot*, 290
Wolfe, General, 345
Wolsey, Cardinal, 230, 243
Women
  Social and Political Union, 307
  suffrage, 567
  Suffrage Movement, 307
Worcester, battle of (1651), 297
Work Accidents Law *(Ley de protección de los trabajadores accidentados)* of 1900, 589
Worker
  card, 588
  protection, 566, 588, 589, 608
Workers rights initiatives, 608
Working class, 501, 564, 565, 568, 572
Work magistracies, 590
World Bank, 614
World's fastest growing economies, 615
World Trade Center, 615, 621
World Trade Organization (WTO), 613, 614
World War I, 307, 350, 432, 460, 492, 502, 527, 530, 533–536, 540–541, 567, 572–575, 577, 583–585, 596, 613, 616, 651, 652, 656, 660, 664, 665, 667, 684, 686, 706
World War II, 110, 432, 477, 531, 532, 561, 575, 586, 593–597, 599, 602, 603, 608, 614, 650, 671–678, 680, 686, 707
Worms, Concordat of, 138–139, 146, 200
Wright brothers, 562
Writs, 291, 299
Written constitutions, 66, 288, 325, 353, 496, 498
Written language of the law, 292
Württemberg, 143, 504
Wyoming State, 437

**X**
Xiaoping, Deng, 606, 620

**Y**
Yahweh, 67
Yalta Conference, 677, 707
Yangtze, 11
Yekaterinburg, 616
Yeltsin, Boris, 597
York
  Duke of (*see* James II of England)
  House of, 195, 203, 295
Yorktown, battle of, 350, 358
Young Bosnia nationalist group, 534
Young Plan (1930), 584
Ypres, 190
  Second Battle of, 541
Yugoslav
  Parliament, 665
  Party, 680
Yugoslavia, 606, 665, 671, 680

**Z**
Zacharias, pope, 123–124, 145
Zagreb, 665
Zamoyski, Chancellor of Poland, 182
Zinoviev, Grigori, 579, 617
Zollverein, 515, 668
*Zurechnung* (Attribution, principle of), 600
Zurich, University of, 678, 707

MIX
Papier aus verantwortungsvollen Quellen
Paper from responsible sources
FSC® C105338
FSC
www.fsc.org

If you have any concerns about our products,
you can contact us on
**ProductSafety@springernature.com**

In case Publisher is established outside the EU,
the EU authorized representative is:
**Springer Nature Customer Service Center GmbH**
**Europaplatz 3, 69115 Heidelberg, Germany**

Printed by Libri Plureos GmbH
in Hamburg, Germany